The **Roug**

New E

this edition researched and updated by

Ken Derry, Sarah Hull, S.E. Kramer, Emma Lozman, and Todd Obolsky

NEW YORK • LONDON • DELHI

www.roughguides.com

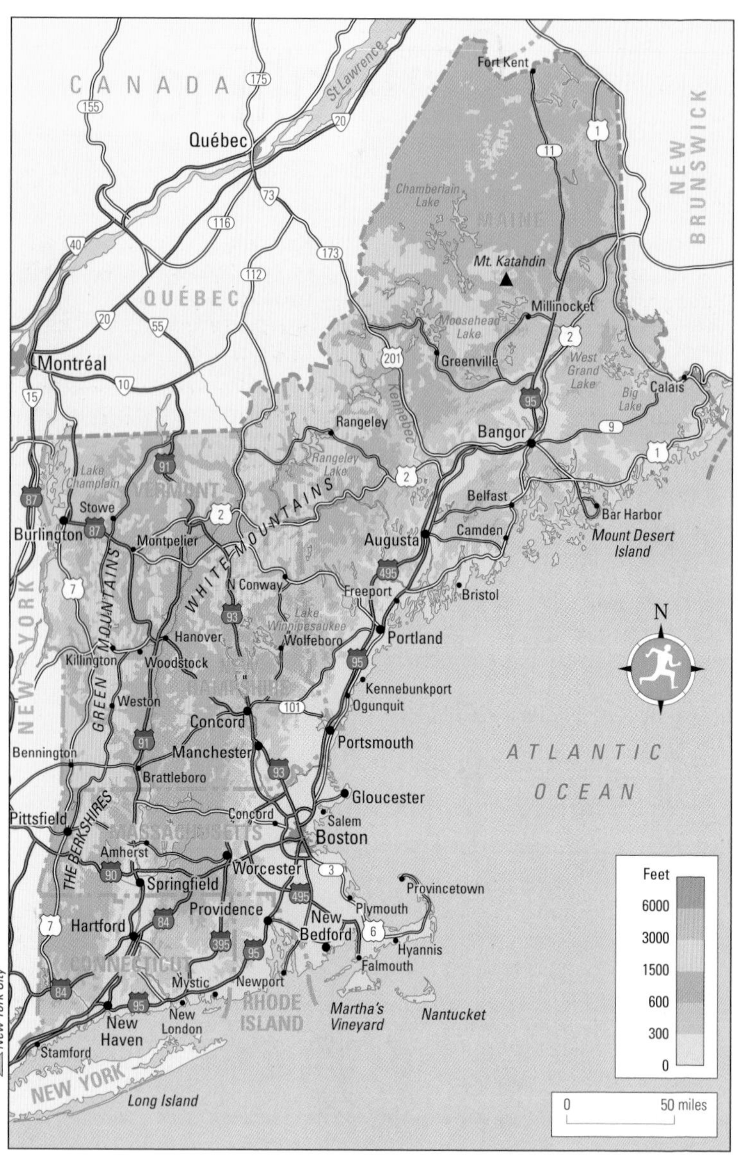
CANADA
Québec
Montréal
QUÉBEC
St Lawrence
NEW BRUNSWICK
Fort Kent
Chamberlain Lake
MAINE
Mt. Katahdin
Millinocket
Moosehead Lake
Greenville
West Grand Lake
Big Lake
Calais
Kennebec
Rangeley
Rangeley Lake
Bangor
Belfast
Bar Harbor
Camden
Mount Desert Island
Augusta
Bristol
Freeport
Portland
Lake Champlain
VERMONT
Stowe
Burlington
Montpelier
WHITE MOUNTAINS
GREEN MOUNTAINS
N Conway
Lake Winnipesaukee
Hanover
Wolfeboro
Killington
Woodstock
NEW HAMPSHIRE
Kennebunkport
Weston
Ogunquit
Concord
Portsmouth
NEW YORK
Bennington
Manchester
Brattleboro
ATLANTIC OCEAN
Gloucester
Pittsfield
THE BERKSHIRES
Concord
Salem
MASSACHUSETTS
Boston
Amherst
Worcester
Springfield
Provincetown
Providence
Plymouth
Hartford
New Bedford
Hyannis
CONNECTICUT
Falmouth
Mystic
Newport
New Haven
New London
RHODE ISLAND
Martha's Vineyard
Nantucket
New York City
Stamford
NEW YORK
Long Island
N
Feet
6000
3000
1500
600
300
0
0
50 miles

Contents

◄◄ Cranberry bog, Carver, Massachusetts

Introduction to

New England

The New England states of Massachusetts, Rhode Island, Connecticut, Vermont, New Hampshire, and Maine often regard themselves as the repository of all that is intrinsically American. In this version of history, the tangled streets of old Boston, the farms of Connecticut, and the villages of Vermont are the cradle of the nation. It's a picture that has some truth to it, however, and, although nostalgia plays a big part in the tourist trade here, and innumerable small towns have been dolled up to recapture a past that can occasionally be wishful thinking, the appeal of New England is undeniable.

It is indeed the most **historic** region of the United States; its towns and villages are often rustic and pretty, with white-spired churches sitting beside tidy greens and colonial churchyards; and its **landscape** is surprisingly diverse – ranging from stark coastlines to green rolling hills and, further inland, even snowy mountains. Like most regions that have a well-developed tourist industry, the trick is to find the unspoiled corners, and to distinguish the artificial from the authentic.

Above all, New England packs an enormous amount of variety into what is by American standards a relatively small area. There are the region's **literary connections** – with well-visited shrines to Emily Dickinson, Mark Twain, and Edith Wharton, to name just a few. There is no shortage of inviting places to **ski**, **hike**, **cycle**, or just watch the leaves change color and drop from the trees – which phenomenal numbers of people come to do each fall. And there are the

◀ Annisquam Lighthouse, Cape Ann, Massachusetts

Fact file

- Boston is the only New England city to rank among the top 100 in population in the US.
- The highest point in the region is New Hamphsire's Mount Washington, 6288ft above sea level.
- Cambridge is home to the oldest college in the US, Harvard, founded in 1636.
- The Thanksgiving holiday is often traced back to a harvest celebration that took place in Plymouth back in 1621, though direct correlations are not certain.
- Vermont produces around seventy million pounds of cheese a year.
- Maine has around 3500 miles of shoreline and, at more than 30,000 square miles, is by far the largest state in the region. Rhode Island, at little more than 1000 square miles, is not only the smallest state in the region, but in the entire country.

▽ Trinity Church reflected in Hancock Tower, Boston

New England packs an enormous amount of variety into what is by American standards a relatively small area.

historic sights, which manage to catalog all manner of New England **architecture** and **design**, not to mention Yankee pride and ingenuity. Boston especially is celebrated as the birthplace of American independence – so many of the seminal events of the Revolutionary War took place here, or just outside, in Lexington or Concord; and, although the genteel seaside towns of Massachusetts and Rhode Island can seem a far cry from the first European settlements in New England, plenty of traces of those early years remain. This is, after all, the stretch of the United States where the **Pilgrims** and other religious sects put down their stakes, their survival aided by groups of **Native Americans** who themselves were eventually displaced, though their legacy remains, too, in place names throughout the region.

Later, as the European foothold on the continent became more secure, the coastline became increasingly prime real estate, lined with grand patrician homes, from the Vanderbilt **mansions** of Newport to the presidential compounds of the Bush and Kennedy families. Inland, the **Ivy League colleges** of Harvard, Yale, Brown, Dartmouth, and others still embody New England's strong sense of its own superiority, and contribute to accusations of provincialism and snobbishness; in fact, the region's traditional role as home to the WASP elite is due more to the vagaries of history and ideology than to economic realities. Its thin soil and harsh climate made it difficult for the first pioneers to sustain an agricultural way of life, while the industrial prosperity of the nineteenth and early twentieth centuries is now but a distant memory. Indeed, New England has pockets, in Vermont and the other more northerly states, that are as poor as anywhere in the US; and the southern states have all the problems that are normally associated with long-established conurbations.

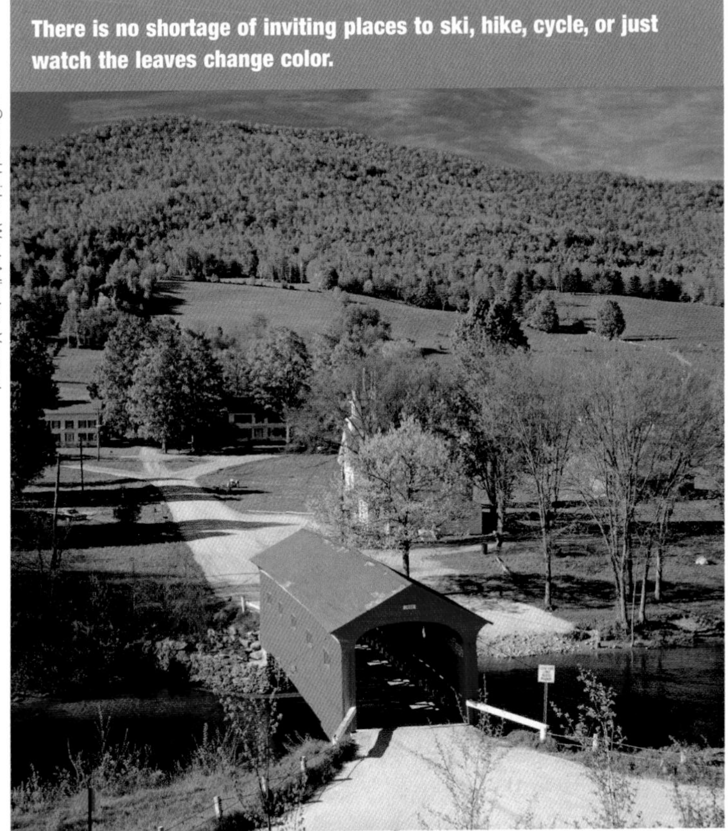

There is no shortage of inviting places to ski, hike, cycle, or just watch the leaves change color.

△ Covered bridge, West Arlington, Vermont

Maritime history

The region's longtime connection with the sea has left its indelible imprint on much of the landscape. The whitewashed houses dotted along the coast make for picture-postcard scenes, complemented by the grand mansions built a bit further from the shore to house the merchants who got rich off the spoils of maritime trade. Both Newport and Marblehead lay claim to the crown of birthplace of the US Navy; Provincetown and Plymouth for where the Pilgrims first alighted from their Mayflower voyage (they landed at the former, settled at the latter). As for vintage lighthouses, you can't throw a stone without hitting one – there are nearly two hundred along the entire coast, and of all shapes and stripes. It's not always a historical legacy either; if the heyday of shipbuilding and whaling, along with much of the canning industry, is long gone, plenty still make their lives hauling in catch up and down the rocky shores. Visit Maine's Mid-Coast or Gloucester in Massachusetts to see the sea's importance in locals' everyday lives.

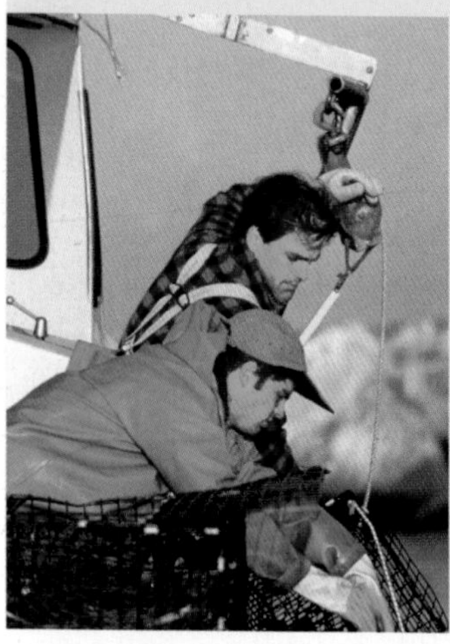

Despite the apparent gulf between its **interior** and **coast** – and, too, its **northern** and **southern halves** – New England is compact and well defined, and quite easy to get around; only Maine, New England's biggest and most rural state by some way, takes any real time and effort to navigate. Most of its states offer the same mix (to differing degrees) of picturesque **small towns** and **villages**, and at times dramatic landscapes, though each has its own distinctive character. The southern states of Connecticut, Massachusetts, and Rhode Island are more urban and historic and, where nature intervenes, it is usually along the spectacular coastline. Here, the tourist facilities are aimed as much at weekenders from the big cities as outsiders

▽ Plymouth Rock

△ Green Mountains, Vermont

– Cape Cod, the Berkshires, and Martha's Vineyard are all convenient (and very popular) targets for moneyed locals. Further north, the lakes and mountains ofVermont, New Hampshire, and particularly Maine offer **wilderness** to rival any in the nation.

Where to go

Boston is the undisputed capital of New England, perhaps America's most historic city, and certainly one of its most elegant, full of enough colonial charm and contemporary culture to satisfy most appetites. Together with its energetic student neighbor, **Cambridge**, Boston has plenty to merit a visit of at least a few days, including a fine array of restaurants, bars, and venues for both high and popular culture. It's as logical place as any to start your wanderings, and also makes a good base for day-trips out to historic Lexington and Concord, the rocky North Shore where the witch sights of Salem probably hold the most interest, and **Cape Cod** – a charming but usually very crowded peninsula, with delightful, quirky Provincetown at its outermost tip. Ferries head from the Cape to the popular summer retreats of **Martha's Vineyard** and **Nantucket**.

West of Boston, there's the collegiate **Pioneer Valley**, which gives way to the **Berkshires**, a scenic if somewhat twee retreat for Boston and New York's cultural elite – much like its Connecticut cousin, the Litchfield Hills, just to the south. Southwest of Boston, along the coast, tiny Rhode Island's

Fall foliage

New England is undoubtedly a year-round destination, with summer resorts dotted along the coast, winter sports destinations in the Green and White mountains, and springtime perhaps the nicest time of all to visit, everything considered. But nothing really compares to how towns and tourist bureaus alike make such hay out of the fall foliage season. In a way it might seem unbelievable that such a thriving industry can be predicated on watching leaves (slowly) turn color, but that's how spectacular the display is in some places. If you plan on heading there during the prime times – much of October, though with some variance depending on where you are – be sure to make reservations long in advance, and be prepared to pay a bit more than normal. Then take a drive into the mountains or along some river valley (preferably in the Berkshires, White Mountains, or most anywhere in Vermont), and admire the fiery reds, yellows, and oranges of the maples, birches, and poplars along the way.

two main attractions are energetic **Providence** and wealthy **Newport**, beyond which you can take in the better parts of the Connecticut coast: the seaport of **Mystic**, and, further on, likeable **New Haven**, home to Yale University.

In the opposite direction from Boston, in the three states to the north, New England is more varied: the weekenders are thinner on the ground, there's a greater sense of space, and a simpler way of life holds sway. In Vermont, outside of the relaxed, pleasant towns of **Brattleboro** and **Burlington**, both worthy of exploration, you're best off just wandering the state's backroads in search of country inns, dairy farms, and some peace and quiet – unless of course you've come to make the pilgrimage to Ben & Jerry's in Waterbury, to see how an ice-cream empire began. If you've come for winter sports, resorts like **Killington** and **Stowe** rank among the best the Northeast has to offer. Over in New Hampshire, the rugged glory of the **White Mountains** is the most dramatic lure, with the highest peaks in the region and countless outdoor opportunities; indeed, if you enjoy camping or hiking you won't want to miss this area. Coastal **Portsmouth** is also as nice a town as you'll find most anywhere in the region.

△ Jack-o'-lanterns, Salem

Finally, there's Maine, in the far northeast of the country, which has perhaps New England's most extreme blend of seaside towns (Portland, Bar Harbor) and untamed interior wilderness, in which you can spot moose outside of **Rangeley**, whitewater raft near **Moosehead Lake**, and do some remote hiking in **Baxter State Park** along the Appalachian Trail, which runs through all three of New England's northern states.

When to go

New England can be a pricey place to visit, especially in late September and October, when visitors flock to see the magnificent **fall** foliage. The region is at its most beautiful during this time, which makes the crowds and prices understandable, if not more bearable. It can get quite cold during the **winter** months, but that's fine if you're thinking of skiing or other winter sports, or a cabin retreat. Bear in mind, though, that whichever resort you choose, you likely won't be alone. **Summers** are warm and dry, but this is New England's prime season and it can get extremely crowded, especially in getaway towns like those on Cape Cod, Martha's Vineyard, the Rhode Island coast, southern Maine, and in the Berkshires – though the upside of coming then is that at least you know everything will be open. On balance, late **spring** is probably the nicest time to come: the temperature is generally agreeable, if a little unpredictable, the crowds are more dispersed, and prices have yet to go up for the tourist season.

Average daytime temperatures and rainfall in New England

	Jan	Feb	Mar	April	May	June	July	Aug	Sept	Oct	Nov	Dec
Bangor, ME												
max F°	27	28	37	52	63	73	79	75	68	57	45	30
max C°	-3	-2	3	11	17	23	26	24	20	14	7	-1
min F°	9	10	21	34	43	52	57	55	48	39	30	16
min C°	-13	-12	-6	1	6	11	14	13	9	4	-1	-9
rain (in)	3.0	2.9	3.2	3.3	3.5	3.3	3.3	3.3	3.4	3.4	4.6	3.9
rain (mm)	76.2	73.7	81.3	83.8	88.9	83.8	83.8	83.8	86.4	86.4	116.8	99.1
Boston, MA												
max F°	36	37	45	57	66	77	82	81	72	63	52	39
max C°	2	3	7	14	19	25	28	27	22	17	11	4
min F°	23	25	32	41	50	59	64	64	57	46	39	27
min C°	-5	-4	0	5	10	15	18	18	14	8	4	-3
rain (in)	3.6	3.6	3.7	3.6	3.3	3.1	2.8	3.2	3.1	3.3	4.2	4.0
rain (mm)	91.4	91.4	94.0	91.4	83.8	78.7	71.1	81.3	78.7	83.8	106.7	101.6
Burlington, VT												
max F°	25	27	37	54	66	75	81	79	70	57	45	30
max C°	-4	-3	3	12	19	24	27	26	21	14	7	-1
min F°	9	9	21	34	45	54	59	57	48	39	30	16
min C°	-13	-13	-6	1	7	12	15	14	9	4	-1	-9
rain (in)	1.8	1.6	2.2	2.8	3.1	3.5	3.6	4.1	3.3	2.9	3.1	2.4
rain (mm)	45.7	40.6	55.9	71.1	78.7	88.9	91.4	104.1	83.8	73.7	78.7	61.0

things not to miss

It's not possible to see everything that New England has to offer in one trip – and we don't suggest you try. What follows is a selective taste of the region's highlights: dramatic scenery, picturesque villages, colonial relics, and unusual festivals. They're arranged in five color-coded categories, which you can browse through to find the very best things to see and experience. All highlights have a page reference to take you straight into the Guide, where you can find out more.

01 Burlington Page **435** • One of New England's most purely enjoyable towns, with an assured sense of vitality, plenty of culture, and a lovely setting on Lake Champlain in Vermont.

02 The houses of Beacon Hill Page **113** • Be on the lookout for purple-tinted windowpanes and bow-fronted townhouses as you stroll Boston's most elegant neighborhood.

03 Newport's mansions Page **305** • Such ostentation was called "conspicuous consumption" in Thorstein Veblen's day; in ours, you don't have to be self-conscious at all to gawk at the folly.

04 Tracing colonial history Pages **96**, **170** & **171** • Very much where America began, New England has all sorts of symbols of its birth, from the sights along Boston's Freedom Trail to the battlegrounds at Lexington and Concord.

05 Provincetown's beaches Page **221** • These might be the nicest strips of sand anywhere in the region, and the town itself the most enjoyable on the Cape.

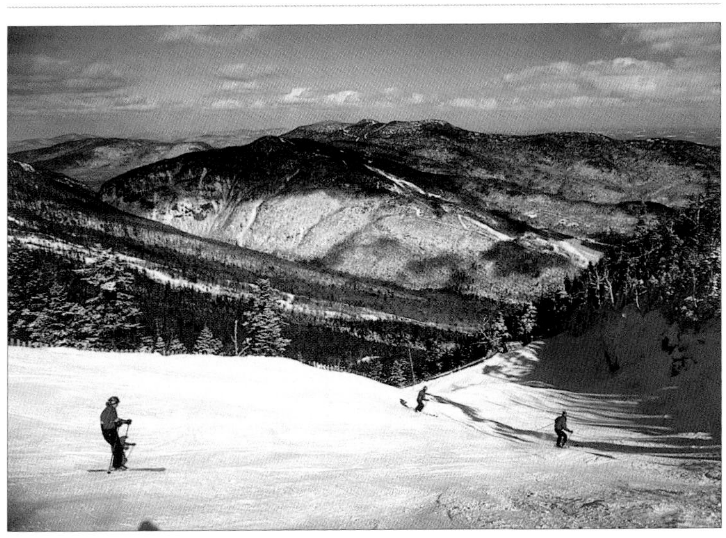

06 Skiing Stowe Page **431** • Steeps abound in Vermont and New Hampshire, but the oldest resort – and one-time home to the real life Von Trapp family – is still one of the best.

07

Canterbury Shaker Village Page **475** • The only thing missing at this perfectly restored Shaker village near Concord, New Hampshire, are the Shakers themselves.

08

Berkshire's summer festivals Page **272** • Tanglewood is the most celebrated outdoor venue of all, but there are plenty of places to take in music, drama, and much more in the Berkshires.

09

Shelburne Museum Page **440** • Outside of Burlington, this collection of Americana is never less than enjoyable, as daily life over the past two centuries is re-created in exacting detail.

10 Naumkeag Page **274** • One of a handful of magnificent private estates around Stockbridge, Naumkeag has much less forced opulence than its Newport mansion counterparts, and stunning gardens to boot.

11 Block Island's inns Page **322** • Watch the sun set from any of a number of grand Victorian inns perched along the island's Old Harbor.

12 Fanueil Hall Page **97** • There's lots of history around Boston, and you get a good sense of it at this vaunted longtime meetingplace, which also abuts the restaurants and shops of Quincy Market.

13
Worcester Art Museum Page **250** • Some excellent works by big names are on display here, in sculpture, painting, photography, and much more.

14 **Whale-watching** Page **184** • Take advantage of the seasonal migration habits aboard a whale-watching cruise, one of the best wildlife-spotting opportunities around.

15 **Eating in Portsmouth** Page **466** • There are a raft of surprisingly upscale restaurants in this seafront New Hampshire town, including some enjoyable ones right on the water.

16 **The hills of Providence** Pages **295** & **298** • College Hill and Federal Hill are two of the town's most delightful neighborhoods, the former full of historic houses and the buildings of Brown University, the latter crammed with cafés and Italian groceries.

17 **Mystic Seaport** Page **333** • So what if it's a bit of a tourist trap? It's still the easiest way to retreat to port life in the late 1800s.

18 **Harvard Square** Page **136** • The epicenter of Cambridge, Harvard Square buzzes with youthful activity day and night.

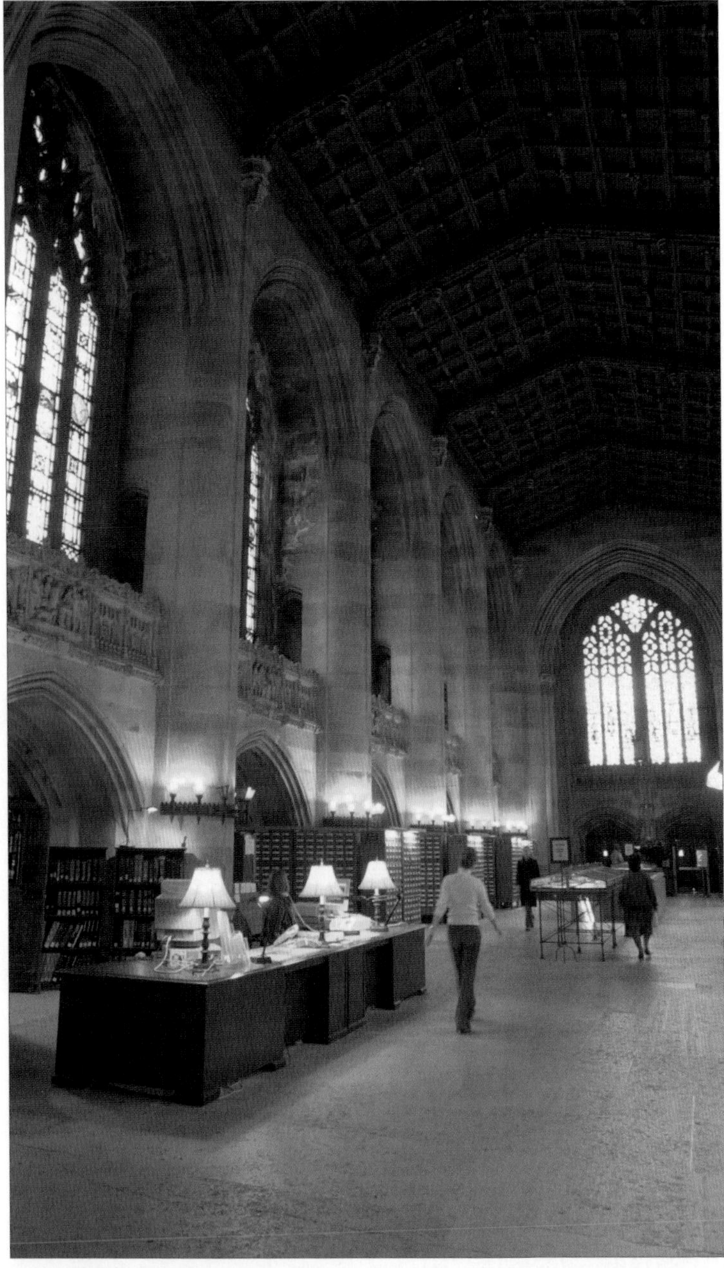

19 Joining the Ivy League Pages **349**, **486** & **140** • Maybe you didn't make it there on academic merit, but the libraries, greens, and stately campuses at Yale, Dartmouth, and Harvard will have you advocating the merits of going back to school.

20 Wild blueberries Page **582** • They grow all over Maine and crop up in all sorts of delectable dishes, from pancakes to pies to sauce for chicken.

21 Mass MoCA Page **285** • The far corner of Western Massachusetts is an unlikely place for a first-class contemporary art museum, but that only adds a special thrill to seeing such strange exhibits.

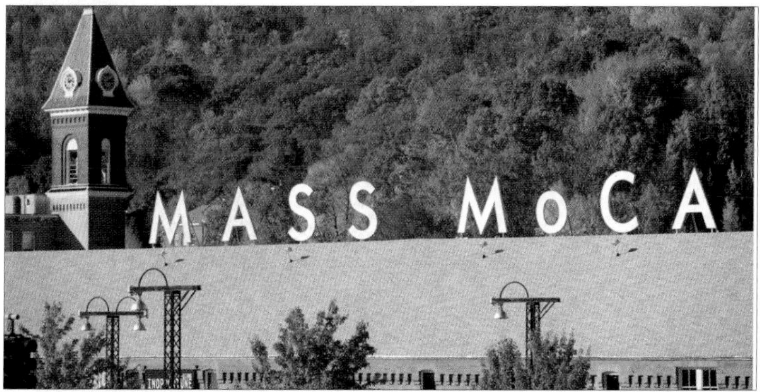

22 Hiking the Long Trail Page **402** • The region is perfect for active nature-lovers, who can catch the northern bit of the Appalachian Trail as it runs through Vermont's mountainous interior.

23 Revolutionary War Festival

Page **468** • In Exeter, New Hampshire, summer means the chance to elaborately re-create the Revolutionary fervor of a few centuries ago.

24 Acadia National Park, ME

Page **578** • Maine holds New England's only national park, and it's a beauty – rugged, varied, and dramatic, even in a relatively small area.

25 A day on Nantucket

Page **235** • Less crowded than the Vineyard, this lovely island is full of wild beauty, accessible beaches, and a few picture-perfect towns.

26 **Ben & Jerry's Factory Tour** Page **428** • Perhaps the little ice-cream company that could has become a bit co-opted by the mainstream, but that doesn't mean they don't still churn out all manner of irresistible flavors.

27 **Monhegan Island** Page **559** • The kind of splendid, low-tech solitude you just may be looking for, right off the Maine coast.

28 **Montpelier** Page **423** • In an area full of cultivated quaintness, Vermont's tiny state capital exudes plenty of natural charm.

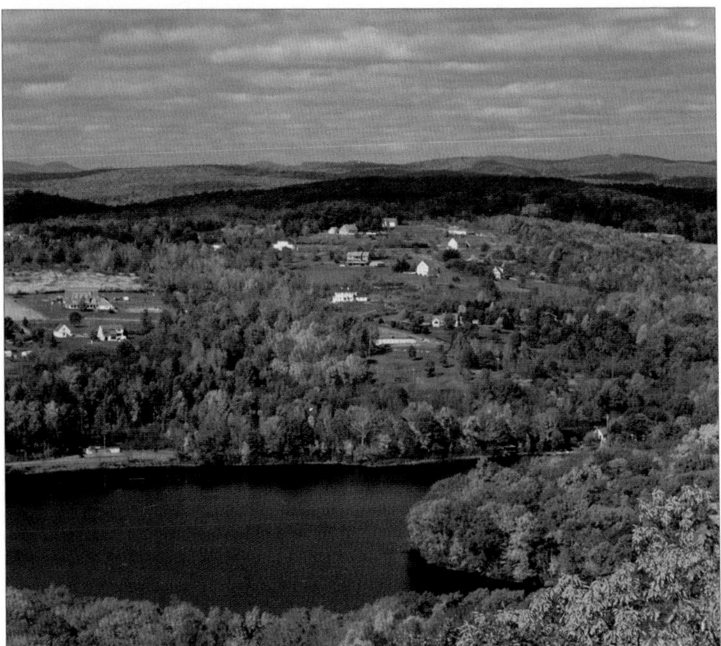

29 Litchfield Hills Page **375** • If you're looking for scenic villages and manicured town squares, amidst some surprisingly rural patches, this Connecticut alternative to the Berkshires should do the trick.

30 The Mount Washington Hotel Page **512** • There was once a time when vacationing in the White Mountains was the preserve of the extremely well-to-do; at this grand resort hotel you'll understand why.

Basics

Basics

Getting there

The primary point of arrival into New England is Boston, Massachusetts, the region's largest city and busiest airline hub. All the major airlines operate daily scheduled flights to Boston's Logan International Airport from the United States, Canada, and Europe – those coming from further afield typically connect with domestic flights on the West Coast. While air travel may be fastest, New England is also easily accessible by road or rail from points throughout North America.

Generally, the most expensive time to fly is **high season**, which in New England stretches from mid-May to early September; note, though, that intraregional flights can continue to stay pricey well into Nov thanks to the popularity of the **fall foliage** season (mid-Sept to mid-Nov), when throngs descend upon the region to gape at the glorious arboreal colors. April to May and September to October are considerably less expensive for flights from abroad, while the rest of the year – with the exception of Thanksgiving, Christmas, and New Year's, when the prices skyrocket again – is considered **low season** and is cheaper still.

If you don't want to fly, or have already arrived from abroad somewhere else in the US or Canada, the **railroad** is a decent second option for getting to major regional cities like Boston, Portland, and Providence, and is particularly useful for visitors traveling along the East Coast, where Amtrak has a reliable (but not cheap) high-speed route between Washington, DC and Boston.

For budget travelers and those without a car, the Greyhound, Peter Pan, and Bonanza **bus** companies are good options, and are especially useful for reaching smaller hinterland towns; they tend to have more flexible departure times and destination ranges than either trains or airplanes. Most are relatively comfortable nowadays, as well.

Probably the best option for getting to New England, though – especially if you're planning on covering a lot of the region during your stay – is **driving** a car.

Online booking agents and general travel sites

The most inexpensive and convenient way to book tickets is on the **Internet**. Individual airline websites have caught up with cheap booking sites, so both can be a good source for affordable tickets (see p.20 for airline website listings). Keep in mind that most of the travel portals like Travelocity, Expedia, and so on do not include tickets on domestic discount airlines like Southwest or Jet Blue (which are often much cheaper than the biggies); these you'll need to seek out on your own. Make sure, too, that you read the small print before buying, as it can be difficult (if not impossible) to claim refunds or change your ticket, especially on last-minute deals.

Ⓦ **www.cheapflights.com** and Ⓦ **www.cheapflights.co.uk** Does a survey of prices on other websites – Travelocity, CheapAir.com, Orbitz, etc. You can't buy a ticket directly through them, but they provide links to the sites themselves.
Ⓦ **www.cheaptickets.com** Searches for and sells tickets from the major US carriers.
Ⓦ **www.ebookers.com** and Ⓦ **www.ebookers.ie** Low fares on an extensive selection of flights from the UK and Ireland.
Ⓦ **www.etn.nl/discount.htm** A hub of consolidator and discount agent Web links. Difficult to navigate, but comprehensive.
Ⓦ **www.expedia.com** Discount airfares, airline search engine, and daily deals.
Ⓦ **www.flyaow.com** Online air travel info and reservations website.
Ⓦ **www.hotwire.com** Bookings from the US only, with last-minute savings of up to forty percent off regular published fares. The downside is that you can't select when your flight will leave, and in fact you don't find the time, or the airline providing the flight, until after you've paid for it.

Ⓦ **www.lastminute.com** Good last-minute holiday package and flight-only deals; UK bookings only.
Ⓦ **www.orbitz.com** Good flight price round-up engine; US bookings only.
Ⓦ **www.priceline.com** and Ⓦ **www.priceline.co.uk** Name-your-own-price website that has deals at around forty percent off standard fares. You can't specify flight times (although you do specify dates).
Ⓦ **www.skyauction.com** Bookings from the US only. Auctions tickets and travel packages using a "second bid" scheme. The best strategy is to bid the maximum you're willing to pay, since if you win you'll pay just enough to beat the runner-up, regardless of your maximum bid.
Ⓦ **www.smilinjack.com/airlines.htm** Has an up-to-date compilation of airline Web addresses.
Ⓦ **www.travel.com.au** and Ⓦ **www.travel.co.nz** Discount fares and destination advice for travelers from Australia and New Zealand.
Ⓦ **travel.yahoo.com** Incorporates a lot of Rough Guides material in its coverage of destination countries and cities across the world, with information about places to eat, sleep, etc. Reader reviews keep it honest.
Ⓦ **www.travelocity.com** and Ⓦ **www.travelocity.co.uk** Destination guides, along with deals for car rental, lodging, and airfares.
Ⓦ **www.travelshop.com.au** Australian website offering discounted flights, packages, insurance, and online bookings.
Ⓦ **www.tripadvisor.com** This is the place to go for consumer reviews of hotels. Contains destination information as well as links to booking sites.

From North America

Getting to New England **from anywhere in North America** is only problematic in the harsh winter months, when roads get icy and airports occasionally close due to inclement weather. All the main airlines operate daily scheduled flights from across the US to Boston, and there are daily scheduled flights from Toronto, Montréal, Vancouver, and Ottawa as well. Though flying remains the best but most expensive way to travel, if you're coming from the mid-Atlantic states driving may make more sense. Trains are comfortable but may not save you much, while bus travel, though the cheapest method, is also the slowest.

By plane

Direct **flights** to Boston's Logan International Airport are available from all the major hubs in North America, though you may find yourself connecting through Chicago, New York, or another large East Coast city. Some of the discount domestic airlines use other New England cities as hubs: Southwest flies to Providence's T.F. Green Airport; JetBlue flies to Burlington in addition to Boston. Smaller airports in Manchester (NH), Portland (ME), Bangor (ME), and Windsor Locks (near Hartford, CT) are serviced less regularly by smaller aircraft, though some have international terminals as well. It's also worth checking flights to New York City, as these are often cheap enough to make taking a bus, train, or rental car the rest of the way to New England worth the inconvenience. The Albany (NY) international airport is also close by and a good bet for reasonable fares.

East Coast visitors have the best access to the region, as frequent **shuttles** originate from New York's LaGuardia Airport (Delta and US Airways) and Washington, DC's Reagan National Airport (US Airways); most of these fly hourly during the week and every couple of hours on the weekend. Southwest also runs a near-hourly shuttle from Baltimore's BWI Airport (near DC) to Providence for just under $100 each way.

Fares are lowest in the heavily trafficked Northeast corridor; a round-trip fare from New York can cost as little as $90–100, although $120–170 is more typical; from Washington, DC and Miami, the range is usually $200–250; from Chicago, $260–300. The price of flights from the West Coast is more likely to fluctuate: round-trip fares from LA, San Francisco, or Seattle typically cost $450–550, though these can go as low as $300. From **Canada**, be prepared to pay around Can$400–500 from Toronto and Montréal, and closer to Can$700, or as high as Can$1200, from Vancouver.

Airlines

Air Canada Ⓣ 1-888/247-2262, Ⓦ www.aircanada.com
AirTran Ⓣ 1-800/247-8726, Ⓦ www.airtran.com
America West Ⓣ 1-800/235-9292, Ⓦ www.americawest.com
American Airlines and **American Eagle** Ⓣ 1-800/433-7300, Ⓦ www.aa.com
American Trans Air Ⓣ 1-800/225-2995, Ⓦ www.ata.com

Airports in New England

Connecticut

Bradley International Airport I-91, Exit 40, Windsor Locks, CT (near Hartford) ⓣ860/292-2000 or 1-888/624/1533, ⓦwww.bradleyairport.com

Maine

Portland International Jetport 1001 Westbrook St, Portland, ME ⓣ207/774-7301, ⓦwww.portlandjetport.org

Massachusetts

Logan International Airport East Boston, MA ⓣ1-800/235-6426, ⓦwww.massport.com

New Hampshire

Manchester Airport Brown Ave, Manchester, NH ⓣ603/624-6556, ⓦwww.flymanchester.com

Pease International Airport 601 Spaulding Turnpike, Portsmouth, NH ⓣ603/433-6088, ⓦwww.peasedev.org

Rhode Island

T.F. Green Airport, 2000 Post Rd, Warwick, RI ⓣ401/737-8222 or 1-888/268-7222, ⓦwww.pvdairport.com

Vermont

Burlington International Airport 1200 Airport Drive, South Burlington, VT ⓣ802/863-1889, ⓦwww.burlingtonintlairport.com

Cape Air ⓣ1-800/352-0714, ⓦwww.flycapeair.com

Continental ⓣ1-800/523-3273, ⓦwww.continental.com

Delta Airlines and **Delta Shuttle** ⓣ1-800/221-1212, ⓦwww.delta.com

Frontier ⓣ1-800/432-1359, ⓦwww.frontierairlines.com

JetBlue ⓣ1-800/538-2583, ⓦwww.jetblue.com

Midwest Airlines ⓣ1-800/452-2022, ⓦwww.midwestairlines.com

Northwest ⓣ1-800/225-2525, ⓦwww.nwa.com

Southwest ⓣ 1-800/435-9792, ⓦwww.southwest.com

United ⓣ1-800/241-6522, ⓦwww.united.com

US Airways, **Shuttle**, and **Express** ⓣ1-800/428-4322, ⓦwww.usairways.com

Travel agents

Airtech ⓣ212/219-7000, ⓦwww.airtech.com. Standby seat broker; also deals in consolidator fares and courier flights.

STA Travel ⓣ1-800/777-0112 or 1-800/781-4040, ⓦwww.statravel.com. Worldwide specialists in student and youth travel; they also do student IDs, travel insurance, car rental, etc.

TFI Tours International ⓣ1-800/745-8000 or 212/736-1140, ⓦwww.lowestairprice.com. Consolidator with flights to Boston from Canadian and US cities.

Travelers Advantage ⓣ1-877/259-2691, ⓦwww.travelersadvantage.com. Discount travel club; annual membership fee required ($1 for a one-month trial, $120/year thereafter).

Travel Cuts Canada ⓣ1-866/832-7564, US ⓣ1-866/592-CUTS, ⓦwww.travelcuts.com. Canadian-run student travel organization, for trips from the US or Canada.

Package tours

Plenty of travel operators offer **package tours** and camping trips covering several New England destinations. A seven-day itinerary typically features a day or two in Boston followed by visits of Revolutionary War or foliage sites. Though these tours are usually a good bit more expensive than the DIY version, they certainly involve less planning.

Tour operators

Backroads ⓣ510/527-1555, 1-800/462-2848, ⓦwww.backroads.com. Tours for active people, including a biking tour of Vermont ($2000) and a walking and hiking trip in Maine ($2500); both are six-day trips.

Collette Vacations ⓣ1-800/340-5158, ⓦwww.collettevacations.com. Runs various New England-themed tours, including "Islands" and "Back Roads," that travel to towns both small and large. Eight days from $1149.

Contiki Holidays ⓣ1-888/CONTIKI, ⓦwww.contiki.com. Trips for the 18–35-year-old crowd; the ten-day "North by Northeast" tour (from $1269, airfare not included) takes in all the New England states with some of Canada and the Midwest thrown in for good measure.

Globus and Cosmos ⓦwww.globusandcosmos.com. Deluxe escorted tours, including stays at expensive hotels and some meals. The "Cape Cod Escape" (eight days, from $1599), "Great Cities of the East" (ten days, from $2299), and "Fall Foliage Getaway" (six days, from $1289) tours all include time in Boston as well as additional outposts.

Trek America ⓣ1-800/221-0596, ⓦwww.trekamerica.com. Trekking company geared to 18–38-year-olds offering one- to two-week day-camping and hiking tours through the eastern US, many with a Canadian leg thrown in (from $500).

By train

If you don't mind taking your time getting there, and hanker after a few more creature comforts (such as dining or bar cars, for instance), then an **Amtrak train** (ⓣ1-800/USA-RAIL, ⓦwww.amtrak.com) may be just the ticket for you. Train travel is most convenient for those traveling to New England from Washington, DC and New York, though it's not much less expensive than air travel. The Amtrak trains that service the Northeast corridor are the fleet's most reliable, which means that they sometimes stick to their official schedules. **Fares** from New York to Boston range from $108 to $224 round-trip – trains that leave late at night are the least expensive, while the Acela express train is the most expensive (but will only shave about fourty minutes off the normal 4.5-hour travel time. From Washington, DC the regular train runs just shy of eight hours ($152 round-trip) while the Acela express takes 6.5 hours ($341 round-trip).

Although train travel is possible long-distance to New England **from the West Coast**, the Midwest, or the South, your trip will be anything but fast – count on three days and up from California nor is it cost-effective, with fares beginning at $370 round-trip. The same applies to visitors approaching the region **from Canada** on Via Rail (ⓣ1-888/842-7245, ⓦwww.viarail.ca); you can only do so by connecting in New York City, and on an indirect itinerary at best. The rail journey can take anywhere from twelve to twenty hours from Toronto and Montréal, and over three days from Vancouver. Fares start at around Can$400 round-trip from the closer points, and go up from there.

Amtrak also offers several **rail passes** for both North American and international travelers that allow unlimited travel within certain time frames in certain areas, which can be good value; see the box on p.47 for details. Amtrak's website also offers special **deals** and weekly rail sales, and can be worth a look. If you want to travel in a bit more **comfort**, Amtrak's fares rise quickly. Sleeping compartments, which include meals, small toilets, and showers, start at around $160 per night for one or two people for short-haul trips, but can go well over $500 for coast-to-coast travel.

By bus

Considering how expensive rail travel is in the US, getting to New England by **bus** can be an appealing – if less comfortable – option, especially as buses quite often get there faster than trains do, given the notorious unreliability and tardiness of rail travel in the States. **Greyhound** (ⓣ1-800/231-2222, ⓦwww.greyhound.com) is the sole long-distance bus operator and has an extensive network of destinations in New England. As with air and train routes, Boston is the best-served destination, especially if you're coming from New York or Washington, DC; barring rush-hour traffic and highway accidents, trips typically take 4.5 hours from New York and 10.5 from DC; round-trip **fares** cost around $70 and $132, respectively. Another way to travel from New York to Boston is via the legendary **Chinatown bus**, which, though noisy and cramped, will get you there very cheaply. The two Chinatown bus companies are Fung Wah (ⓣ212/925-8889, ⓦwww.fungwahbus.com) and Lucky Star (ⓣ1-888/881-0887, ⓦwww.luckystarbus), both of which charge $15 each way and leave on the hour from their pick-up spot in New York's Chinatown. There is also a Chinatown bus that runs from Washington, DC to New York (New Century Travel; $20 each way; ⓣ202/789-8222, ⓦwww.2000coach.com/newyorkdc.html).

Coming **from Canada**, several daily buses from Toronto reach Boston with at least one changeover – usually in Syracuse, New York – contributing to a minimum twelve-hour ride (Can$160 round-trip). Buses from Montréal take around seven hours and have the added benefit of direct service (Can$116 round-trip). In both cases, contact Greyhound (ⓣ1-800/229-9424, ⓦwww.greyhound.ca). For more information on traveling by bus within New England, see "Getting around," p.46.

By car

Renting a car involves the usual steps of phoning the local branch, or checking the website, of one of the major companies (see "Getting around," p.43), of which Thrifty tends to be the cheapest. Most have offices at destination airports, and addresses and phone numbers are comprehensively documented in the *Yellow Pages*. Also worth considering are fly-drive deals, which give cut-rate (and sometimes free) car rental when buying an air ticket. They usually work out cheaper than renting on the spot and are especially good value if you intend to do a lot of driving. A car rented in Canada can normally be driven across the border into the US, but you will pay a much higher fee if you do not return it to its country of origin. Most of the larger companies have offices in Canada. To rent a car you must be **over 21** years old, and drivers under 25 are charged a per-day surcharge of approximately $20.

Drivers planning on hitting Boston during their New England tour should be prepared for interminable **traffic jams** and detours caused by ongoing work to put I-93 underground – aka "the Big Dig" (see the box on p.81 for more). If you insist on driving in the city, stay informed of road closures and reroutings by tuning into 1030 AM on the radio. Aside from the Boston headache, the I-93 is useful for visitors heading seaward from New Hampshire, as it connects the state with southern Rhode Island. Several other **major highways** also transect the region: I-95, which runs along the Atlantic coast south from Canada and circumscribes the Boston area; I-90 (the Massachusetts Turnpike or "Masspike"), which approaches Massachusetts from the west and is popular with those arriving from New York State; and I-91 which heads south from Québec and rims Vermont and New Hampshire before hitting Amherst, Massachusetts, and Hartford, CT.

New England driving times

To Boston

From Chicago 16hr, 30min (982 miles)
From Miami 25hr (1488 miles)
From New York 4hr (216 miles)
From San Francisco 52hr (3100 miles)
From Montréal 6hr (310 miles)
From Toronto 9hr, 30min (552 miles)

From Boston

To Providence just under 1hr (50 miles)
To Hyannis 1hr, 20min (70 miles)
To Provincetown 2hr, 20min (116 miles)
To Portland 1hr, 40min (107 miles)
To New Haven 2hr, 10min (137 miles)
To Hartford 1hr, 35min (101 miles)
To Burlington 3hr, 40min (216 miles)
To Newport 1hr, 15min (71 miles)
To Concord 1hr, 15min (68 miles)
To Northampton 1hr, 35min (103 miles)

From Britain and Ireland

There are plenty of direct flights **from Britain and Ireland** to Boston, fewer to other regional cities. Keep in mind that the first place the plane lands on American soil is your point of entry into the US, which means you'll have to collect your bags and go through customs and immigration formalities there, even if you're continuing on via the same plane to other regional points.

Most flights from Britain and Ireland leave early to mid-afternoon and arrive mid-afternoon or evening. British Airways, Virgin Atlantic, and American Airlines have the most daily non-stop **flights** to Boston from London's Heathrow Airport; travelers from elsewhere in the UK will have to connect in London, or else fly to New York. Aer Lingus operates the only non-stop service to Boston **from Ireland**.

As there's not a lot of price differentiation between the major airlines, you'll have to shop around to get the best **deals**. Your best bet for finding what cut-rate tickets exist is by checking the travel ads in the weekend papers, the holiday pages of ITV's *Teletext*, and, in London, scouring *Time Out* and the *Evening Standard*. Giveaway magazines aimed at young travelers, like *TNT*, are also very helpful.

Fares hover around £250 in low season (Nov to mid-Dec & Jan–March), £350 in spring and fall, and over £400 in high season (May–Sept). Flights from Ireland (Shannon) can ring in at over €700. All fares are subject to a tax of approximately £63, and weekend flights incur additional surcharges. A non-restricted economy fare ticket, allowing the greatest flexibility in departure times, can cost you upwards of £1000.

Airlines

All flights below are to Boston.

Aer Lingus UK ⓣ0845/084 4444, Republic of Ireland ⓣ0818/365 000, ⓦwww.aerlingus.com. Daily flights from Dublin and Shannon.

American Airlines UK ⓣ0845/778 9789, ⓦwww.aa.com. Up to ten direct flights daily from London Heathrow.

British Airways UK ⓣ0845/773 3377, Republic of Ireland ⓣ1800/626 747, ⓦwww.ba.com. Three flights daily from London Heathrow.

Continental UK ⓣ0845/607 6760, Republic of Ireland ⓣ1890/925 252, ⓦwww.flycontinental.com. Operates one daily direct flight from London Heathrow.

United Airlines UK ⓣ0845/844 4777, ⓦwww.ual.com. Daily non-direct flights (usually transferring in Washington, DC).

US Airways UK ⓣ0845/600 3300, Republic of Ireland ⓣ1890/925 065, ⓦwww.usairways.com. Daily non-direct flights from Heathrow.

Virgin Atlantic UK ⓣ0870/380 2007, Republic of Ireland ⓣ01/873 3388, ⓦwww.virgin-atlantic.com. Daily flight from London Heathrow.

Travel agents

In the UK

Dial A Flight ⓣ0870/333 4488, ⓦwww.dialaflight.com. Discounts on airfares, as well as car rental, hotels, and insurance.

Flightbookers ⓣ0870/814 0000, ⓦwww.ebookers.com. Low fares on an extensive selection of scheduled flights.

Flight Centre ⓣ0870/499 0040, ⓦwww.flightcentre.co.uk. Large choice of discounted flights.

Lastminute.com ⓣ0871/222 3423 (10p/min), ⓦwww.lastminute.com. Discount airfares, as well as inclusive packages for US travel.

North South Travel ⓣ01245/608 291, ⓦwww.northsouthtravel.co.uk. Discounted fares worldwide; profits are used to support projects in the developing world, especially the promotion of sustainable tourism.

Quest Worldwide ⓣ0870/442 3542, ⓦwww.questtravel.com. Specialists in round-the-world and discount fares.

STA Travel ⓣ0870/160 6070, ⓦwww.statravel.co.uk. Worldwide specialists in low-cost flights and tours for students and under-26s (other customers welcome); Amtrak passes also available.

Trailfinders ⓣ0845/058 5858, ⓦwww.trailfinders.com. One of the best-informed and most efficient agents for independent travelers; Amtrak passes also available.

Travel Bag ⓣ0800/082 5000, ⓦwww.travelbag.co.uk. Discount flights to the US and round-the-world fares.

In Ireland

Blackpool Travel Cork ⓣ021/439 8742, ⓦwww.blackpooltravel.ie. General flight agent.

CIE Tours International Dublin ⓣ01/703 1888, ⓦwww.cietours.ie. General flight and tour agent.

Joe Walsh Tours Dublin ⓣ01/872 2555 or 241 0800, Cork ⓣ021/427 7959, ⓦwww.joewalshtours.ie. General budget fares agent.

Premier Travel Derry ⓣ028/7126 3333, ⓦwww.premiertravel.uk.com. Discount flight specialists.

Rosetta Travel Belfast ⓣ028/9064 4996, ⓦwww.rosettatravel.com. Flight and holiday agent.

Trailfinders Dublin ⓣ01/677 7888, ⓦwww.trailfinders.ie. One of the best-informed and most efficient agents for independent travelers; Amtrak passes also available.

Twohigs Travel Dublin ⓣ01/648 0800, ⓦwww.twohigs.com. General flight and travel agent.

Usit Now ⓣ01/602 1904, ⓦwww.usitnow.ie. Student and youth travel specialists offering flights and Amtrak passes.

Package tours and fly-drive deals

There are plenty of companies running package deals **from the UK** to New England, and especially to Boston – mostly short city breaks that span three to five days. For a three-day trip, typical rates run around £600 per person in summer, though prices drop to around £450 out of high season, and sometimes less than that. It's usually around £100 more for the five-star or superior-grade hotel package. If you plan to see more of New England, **fly-drive** deals – which include car rental when buying a transatlantic ticket from an airline or tour operator – are always cheaper than renting a car on the spot. Most of the specialist companies offer fly-drive packages, though watch out for hidden extras, such as local taxes, "drop-off" charges, and extra insurance.

Tour operators

American Connections ⓣ01494/473 173, ⓦwww.connectionsworldwide.net. Tailor-made trips, escorted coach tours, and the "Heart of New England" fly-drive package, a thirteen-day holiday starting at £1200.

American Express Vacations ⓣ01273/696 933, ⓦwww.americanexpress.com/travel. Flights, hotels, last-minute specials, city-break packages, and specialty tours.

American Holidays Belfast ⓣ028/9023 8762, Dublin ⓣ01/673 3840, ⓦwww.american-holidays.com. Specialists in travel to the US and Canada with independent travel options and escorted tours; a ten-day tour including Boston, Nantucket, and Martha's Vineyard costs £1675.

Bon Voyage ⓣ0800/316 3012, ⓦwww.bon-voyage.co.uk. Flight-plus-accommodation deals and tours covering Stowe, Boston, Plymouth, and Newport.

British Airways Holidays ⓣ0870/850 9850, ⓦwww.baholidays.co.uk. Using British Airways and other international airlines, quality package and tailor-made New England holidays by phone or online.

Contiki Tours UK ⓣ0208/290 6777, ⓦwww.contiki.com. Trips for the 18–35-year-old crowd; some of their tours include New England states.

Explore Worldwide ⓣ0870/333 4001, ⓦwww.explore.co.uk. Small-group adventure tours; the 16-day "Active New England" option starts at £1299 and includes Salem, Boston, Freeport, Acadia National Park, Mount Washington, and Stowe.

Funway USA ⓣ0870/444 0770, ⓦwww.funwayholidays.co.uk. Boston city breaks, flight-only deals, and car rental.

Globus and Cosmos ⓣ0800/083 9837, ⓦwww.cosmostourama.co.uk. Deluxe escorted tours. The "Autumn Glory" tour (eleven days, from £1195) includes meals, accommodation, and flights from the UK.

Individual Travellers ⓣ0870/780 194, ⓦwww.indiv-travellers.com. Complete self-guided packages, including rental car, flight, and select accommodation in traditional New England clapboard cottages, colonial houses, hunting lodges, and more, usually starting at around £1007 per person.

Kuoni London ⓣ08700/780 195, Manchester ⓣ01306/747 731, ⓦwww.kuoni.co.uk. Multi-center flight-plus-accommodation-plus-car-rental deals, as well as organized fly-drive tours; the twelve-day "Classic New England" option includes Provincetown, Boston, the Berkshires, Newport, and more.

North America Travel Service ⓣ0113/242 6242, ⓦwww.travelshop.com. Tailor-made holidays as well as five pre-planned fly-drive holidays.

Northwest Flydrive ⓣ01424/224 400, ⓦwww.holiday-america.net. Flight-plus-accommodation and fly-drive specials. Boston weekend breaks start from £299.

Premier Holidays ⓣ0870/043 5950, ⓦwww.premierholidays.co.uk. Flight-plus-accommodation deals starting as low as £295.

Thomas Cook ⓣ0870/750 5711, ⓦwww.thomascook.co.uk. Long-established one-stop 24hr travel agency for package holidays, city breaks, and scheduled flights, with *bureaux de change* issuing Thomas Cook travelers' checks, travel insurance, and car rental.

Travelpack ⓣ0870/121 2010, ⓦwww.travelpack.co.uk. Boston city breaks, as well as escorted and self-driven New England tours.

TrekAmerica ⓣ01295/256 777, ⓦwww.trekamerica.com. Youth-oriented (18–38-year-olds) camping tours including Boston as part of larger tours of the region. The one-week "Freedom Trail" tour, departing from New York, costs from £350 (flights, meals, and personal expenses extra).

World Travel Centre Dublin ⓣ01/416 7007, ⓦwww.worldtravel.ie. Irish specialists in flights to the US and Boston.

From Australia and New Zealand

There are no direct flights to Boston **from Australia** or **New Zealand**, and most people reach the eastern United States by way of the West Coast and gateway cities such as Los Angeles and San Francisco. However you do it, it's a pretty long trip, considering that flying time is about fourteen hours to the West Coast and another six to New England.

Fares to LA and San Francisco from eastern **Australian** cities cost the same, while from Perth they're about Aus$400 more. There are daily non-stop flights from Sydney to LA and San Francisco on United Airlines and to LA on Qantas, for around Aus$1800 in low season (Oct–Nov & Jan–March); figure another Aus$1000 to continue on to Boston. There are also several airlines that fly via Asia, which involves either a transfer or stopover in their home cities. The best deal is on JAL (Aus$1600–1900), which includes a night's stopover accommodation in Tokyo or Osaka in the fare. If you don't want to spend the night, Cathay Pacific and Singapore Airlines can get you there, via a transfer in their home cities of Hong Kong and Singapore, for around Aus$1750, while Korean Air (via Seoul) is sometimes a few dollars cheaper.

From **New Zealand**, most flights are out of Auckland (add about NZ$200–250 for Christchurch and Wellington departures). The best deals are on Air New Zealand, to Los Angeles or San Francisco either non-stop or via Honolulu, Fiji, Tonga, or Papeete; or on United Airlines, also non-stop to LA or San Francisco; Air Pacific via Fiji; and Qantas via Sydney (though direct is cheaper). Via Asia, Singapore Airlines offers the best connecting service to LA and San Francisco, while the best value for money is on JAL via either a transfer or stopover in Tokyo. A two-tiered flight (non-stop to the West Coast and non-stop again to Boston) ranges from NZ$3000 to 3500 in high season. You can shave off a few hundred more by making more stops along the route. If you intend to take in New England as part of a world trip, a **round-the-world** (RTW) ticket offers the greatest flexibility. In recent years, many of the major international airlines have aligned themselves with one of two globe-spanning networks: the "Star Alliance," which links Air New Zealand, Ansett Australia, United, Lufthansa, Thai, SAS, Varig, and Air Canada; and "One World," which combines routes run by American, British Airways, Canadian Airlines, Cathay Pacific, LAN Chile, and Qantas. Both offer RTW deals with three stop overs in each continental sector you visit, with the option of adding additional sectors relatively cheaply. Fares depend on the number of sectors required, but a 21-day advance ticket from Australia to Boston, Burlington, Hartford, or Providence usually starts at around Aus$3000 (low season) for a US–Europe–Asia–home itinerary.

Airlines

Air New Zealand Australia ⓣ13 24 76, New Zealand ⓣ0800/737 000, ⓦwww.airnz.com
American Airlines Australia ⓣ1300/650 747, New Zealand ⓣ0800/887 997, ⓦwww.aa.com
British Airways Australia ⓣ02/8904 8800, New Zealand ⓣ09/356 8690, ⓦwww.british-airways.com
Continental Airlines Australia ⓣ61/9244 2242, New Zealand ⓣ09/308 3350, ⓦwww.flycontinental.com
Delta Air Lines Australia ⓣ1-300/302 849, New Zealand ⓣ09/997 2235, ⓦwww.delta.com
Japan Airlines (JAL) Australia ⓣ02/9272 1111, New Zealand ⓣ09/379 9906, ⓦwww.japanair.com
Northwest Airlines/KLM Australia ⓣ1300/303 747, New Zealand ⓣ09/309 1782, ⓦwww.nwa.com
Qantas Australia ⓣ13 13 13, ⓦwww.qantas.com.au, New Zealand ⓣ0800/0014 0014, ⓦwww.qantas.co.nz
United Airlines Australia ⓣ13 17 77, New Zealand ⓣ09/379 3800, ⓦwww.ual.com
Virgin Atlantic Australia ⓣ1300/727 340, ⓦwww.virgin-atlantic.com

Travel agents

Anywhere Travel Australia ⓣ02/9663 0411, ⓦwww.anywheretravel.com.au. General fares agent.
Destinations Unlimited New Zealand ⓣ09/414 1680, ⓦwww.travel-nz.com. General and RTW fares.
Flight Centre Australia ⓣ133 133, New Zealand ⓣ0800/243 544, ⓦwww.flightcentre.com.au. Specialist agent for budget flights, especially RTW.
STA Travel Australia ⓣ1300/733 035 ⓦwww.statravel.com.au, New Zealand ⓣ0508/782 872, ⓦwww.statravel.co.nz. Discount flights, travel passes, and other services for youth/student travelers.
Trailfinders Australia ⓣ1300/780 212, ⓦwww.trailfinders.com.au. One of the best-informed and efficient agents for independent travelers; Amtrak passes also available.

Tour operators

Adventure World Australia ⓣ02/9956 7766, ⓦwww.adventureworld.com.au, New Zealand ⓣ09/524 5118, ⓦwww.adventureworld.co.nz. Boston hotel bookings, car rental, and organized tours.
Canada and America Travel Specialists Australia ⓣ02/9922 4600, ⓦwww.canada-americatravel.com.au. Can arrange flights and accommodation in North America, plus Greyhound and Amtrak passes.

Contiki Holidays Australia ⓣ02/9511 2200, New Zealand ⓣ09/309 8824, ⓦwww.contiki.com. Trips for the 18–35-year-old crowd; some of their tours include New England states.
Creative Holidays Australia ⓣ1300/747 400, ⓦwww.creativeholidays.com.au. Offers package vacations that can be booked through other agents such as STA (see above).
Sydney International Travel Centre ⓣ02/9250 9320, ⓦwww.sydneytravel.com.au. US flights, accommodation, city stays, and car rental.

Red tape and visas

Under the Visa Waiver Program, citizens of the UK, Ireland, Australia, and New Zealand – as well as citizens of many other countries – visiting the US for a period of less than ninety days only need a machine-readable passport and a visa waiver form. The latter will be provided either by your travel agency, by the airline before check-in, or on the plane, and must be presented to immigration upon arrival. The same form covers entry across the borders with Canada and Mexico, whether by land or by air. However, those eligible for the scheme must apply for a visa if they intend to work, study, or stay in the country for more than ninety days.

Prospective visitors from parts of the world not covered by the Visa Waiver Program, and those without machine-readable passports, require a valid passport and a **non-immigrant visa**. How you'll obtain a visa depends on what country you're in and your status when you apply, so telephone the nearest US embassy or consulate (see the list below). You'll need to provide a passport valid for at least six months beyond your intended stay and two passport photos, and will be charged the equivalent of $65. Expect it to take up to three weeks, though it could be substantially quicker. More general information on visas for the US can be found online at ⓦwww.travel.state.gov/visa/temp/temp_1305.html.

US embassies and consulates abroad

Australia

ⓦusembassy-australia.state.gov
Canberra Moonah Place, Yarralumla, ACT 2600 ⓣ02/6214 5600, ⓕ6214 5970
Melbourne 553 St Kilda Rd, PO Box 6722, Vic 3004 ⓣ03/9526 5900, ⓕ9510 4646
Sydney MLC Centre, 59th floor, 19–29 Martin Place, NSW 2000 ⓣ02/9373 9200, ⓕ9373 9125
Perth 16 St George's Terrace, 13th floor, WA 6000 ⓣ08/9202 1224, ⓕ9231 9444

Canada

ⓦwww.usembassycanada.gov
Ottawa 490 Sussex Drive, ON K1N 1G8 ⓣ613/238-5335, ⓕ688-3082
Calgary 615 Macleod Trail SE, room 1000, AB T2G 4T8 ⓣ403/266-8962, ⓕ264-6630
Halifax Purdy's Wharf Tower II, suite 910, 1969 Upper Water St, NS B3J 3R7 ⓣ902/429-2480, ⓕ423-6861
Montréal 1155 St Alexandre St, Québec B 1Z1 ⓣ514/398-9695, ⓕ398-0973
Toronto 360 University Ave, ON M5G 1S4 ⓣ416/595-1700, ⓕ595-0051
Vancouver 1075 W Pender St, BC V6E 2M6 ⓣ604/685-4311, ⓕ685-5285

Ireland

Belfast Queen's House, 14 Queen St BT1 6EQ ⓣ028/9038 6100, ⓕ9068 1301.
Dublin 42 Elgin Rd, Ballsbridge ⓣ01/668 8777, ⓕ668 9946, ⓦ dublin.usembassy.gov

New Zealand

ⓦusembassy.org.nz
Wellington 29 Fitzherbert Terrace, Thorndon ⓣ04/462 6000, ⓕ478 1701
Auckland Citibank Building, 3rd floor, 23 Customs St ⓣ09/303 2724, ⓕ366 0870

South Africa

Pretoria 877 Pretorius St, Pretoria ⓣ012/431 4000, ⓕ342 2299, ⓦusembassy.state.gov/pretoria
Cape Town Monte Carlo Building, 7th floor, Heerengracht, Foreshore ⓣ021/421 4280, ⓕ425 3014
Durban 2901 Durban Bay Building, 333 Smith St ⓣ031/305 7600, ⓕ305 7691
Johannesburg 1 River St, Killarney ⓣ011/644 8000, ⓕ646 6916

UK

ⓦwww.usembassy.org.uk
London 24 Grosvenor Square, W1A 1AE ⓣ020/7894 0925, visa hotline (£1.30/min) ⓣ09055/444 546
Edinburgh 3 Regent Terrace, EH7 5BW ⓣ0131/556 8315, ⓕ557 6023

Embassies and consulates in New England

All of the following, with the exception of New Zealand, are located in Boston.

Australia 22 Thomson Place ⓣ617/261-5555
Canada 3 Copley Place, suite 500 ⓣ617/262-3760
Ireland 535 Boylston St ⓣ617/267-9330
New Zealand 57 North Main St, PO Box 1318, Concord, NH ⓣ603/225-8228
UK 600 Atlantic Ave ⓣ617/245-4500

Immigration controls

The standard immigration regulations apply to all visitors, whether or not they are using the Visa Waiver Program. During the flight, you'll be handed an **immigration form** (and a customs declaration; see below), which must be presented at immigration control once you land. The form requires that you cite your proposed length of stay and to list an address where you'll be staying, at least for your first night. Previously, "touring" was a satisfactory entry here, but since 9/11 controls have become more stringent and a verifiable address is now required. If you have no accommodation arranged for your first night, pick a plausible-sounding hotel from the appropriate section of this *Guide* and list that.

You probably won't be asked unless you look disreputable in the eyes of the official on duty, but you should be able to prove that you have a **return air ticket** (if flying in) and enough money to support yourself while in the US; anyone revealing the slightest intention of working while in the country is likely to be refused admission. Around $300–400 a week is usually considered sufficient to support yourself – waving a credit card or two may do the trick. You may also experience difficulties if you admit to being HIV-positive or having AIDS or TB. Part of the immigration form will be attached to your passport, where it must stay until you leave, when an immigration or airline official will detach it.

Customs

Upon arrival in the States, **customs** officers will take your customs declaration and check to see if you're carrying any banned items, such as animals, plants, fresh foods, and so on. You'll also be asked if you've visited a farm in the last month – if you have, you may well have your shoes taken away for inspection. The **duty-free** allowance if you're over 17 is 200 cigarettes and 50 cigars, a liter of spirits (if you're over 21), and $400 worth of gifts. As well as foods and anything agricultural, it's prohibited to carry into the country any articles from Afghanistan, Cuba, Iran, Libya, North Korea, Serbia, and Sudan, or obscene publications, drug paraphernalia, lottery tickets, and switchblades. Prescription drugs should be labeled and accompanied

Canadian citizens are in a particularly privileged position when it comes to crossing the border into the US. Though it is possible to enter the States without your passport, you should really have it with you on any trip that brings you to New England. Only if you plan to stay for more than ninety days do you need a visa. Bear in mind that if you cross into the US by car, trunks and passenger compartments are subject to searches by customs personnel. Remember too, that without the proper paperwork, Canadians are legally barred from seeking employment in the US.

by a prescription or doctor's note explaining that the drug is for use under his or her direction.

Extending your stay

The date stamped on your passport is the latest you're legally allowed to stay. Leaving a few days later may not matter, especially if you're heading home, but more than a week or so can result in a protracted, rather unpleasant interrogation from officials, which may cause you to miss your flight and be denied entry to the US in the future.

To get an **extension** before your time is up, apply as early as possible to the US Immigration and Naturalization Service Center at 75 Lower Welden St, St Albans, VT (Ⓦuscis.gov/graphics/howdoi/extendstay.htm, Ⓣ1-800/375-5283). Do not go to the local INS office; the Vermont Service Center handles all New England states. You must provide evidence of ample finances, and you'll also have to explain why you didn't plan for the extra time initially. The application fee is $195, and the INS must receive your application for extension by the day your authorized stay expires.

Information, websites, and maps

Advance information for a trip to New England can be obtained by calling the appropriate state's information center (see below). A publicly funded firm called Discover New England (Ⓣ802/253-2500, Ⓦwww.discovernewengland.org) also exists to provide advance information on all six New England states.

Once you've arrived, you'll find most towns have **visitors' centers** of some kind – often called the Convention and Visitors Bureau (CVB) or the Chamber of Commerce: many are listed within the *Guide*. The essential difference between the two types of visitors' centers is that the former deals exclusively with tourism-related businesses, while the latter represents all types of commerce. Either one will give out detailed information on the local area, however, and can often help with finding accommodation. Additionally, free newspapers in most places carry news of events and entertainment. Of the several **publications** with travel information specific to New England, check out the range of magazines published by Yankee Publishing (Ⓦwww.yankeemagazine.com). *Yankee Magazine* is published ten times a year, and contains travel features and coverage of the latest New England living trends. Their annual *Yankee Magazine Travel Guide to New England* also contains travel features, accompanied by plenty of useful practical information. The *Yankee Magazine's Bed & Breakfast and Inn Directory*, meanwhile, features more than six hundred places to stay in New England. Lastly, *Boston* magazine (Ⓦwww.bostonmagazine.com) is a fine monthly publication which has feature articles on its title town as well as the rest of New England.

New England state information centers

Connecticut 505 Hudson St, Hartford, CT 06106 Ⓣ860/270-8080 or 1-800/282-6863, Ⓦwww.ctbound.org

Maine 9 State House Station, Augusta, ME 04333 Ⓣ1-888/624-6345, Ⓦwww.visitmaine.com

Massachusetts 10 Park Plaza, suite 4510, Boston, MA 02116 Ⓣ617/973-8500 or 1-800/227-MASS, Ⓦwww.massvacation.com

New Hampshire 172 Pembroke Rd, Concord, NH 03302 Ⓣ603/271-2665 or 1-800/FUN-IN-NH, Ⓦwww.visitnh.com

Rhode Island 1 West Exchange St, Providence, RI 02903 Ⓣ1-800/556-2484, Ⓦwww.visitrhodeisland.com

Vermont 6 Baldwin St, Montpelier, VT 05633 Ⓣ802/828-3236 or 1-800/VERMONT, Ⓦwww.vermontvacation.com

Websites

Though we've listed relevant **websites** for accommodation, organizations, major sights, and so on throughout this guide, the following might help you pursue a few special areas of interest in preparation for your visit.

AlpineZone ⓦwww.alpinezone.com. Check up on ski and hiking trail reports in the northeast, as well as accommodation on all the mountains.
Boston Online ⓦwww.boston-online.com. General info on the city, including a dictionary of Bostonian English and a guide to public bathrooms.
New England History ⓦwww.newenglandhistory.info. Well-organized site for limited historical background on each state, plus some good old images and notable quotes.
New England Lighthouses ⓦwww.lighthouse.cc. Organized by state, with photos, history, and pretty much everything you might need to find out about your favorite lighthouse.
New England Rail Photography Archive ⓦroadphotos.nerail.org. If you have an unhealthy interest in seeing shots of every imaginable railroad and railroad car in New England, check out this archive – and follow the links that lead to sites on the history of railroads in the region.
New England for Visitors ⓦ gonewengland.about.com. Links to all sorts of fairly mainstream info, including tour operators, major ski resorts, and the like.

Maps

Most of the tourist offices we've mentioned here or throughout the *Guide* can supply you with good **maps**, either free or for a small charge, and, supplemented with the ones in this book, these should be enough for general sightseeing and touring. If you need more specific detail, pick up our full-size, tear-proof *Rough Guide New England Map*, available for $9.99 from most bookstores or from ⓦwww.roughguides.com. For driving or cycling through **rural** areas, Maine-based Delorme (ⓦwww.delorme.com) publishes its valuable *Atlas & Gazetteer* for each of the New England states ($19.95 each), with marked campgrounds and reams of national park and forest information. For detailed **hiking** maps, check with ranger stations in parks and wilderness areas or with camping stores.

Insurance

Getting travel insurance is highly recommended, especially if you're coming from abroad and are at all concerned about your health – prices for medical attention in the US can be exorbitant. A secondary benefit is that most policies also cover against theft and loss, which can be useful if you're toting around an expensive camera or any high-tech gear. Before paying for a new policy, though, check to see if you're already covered: some home insurance policies may cover your possessions while overseas, and many private medical schemes include cover when abroad.

In Canada, provincial health plans usually provide partial cover for medical mishaps outside of the country, while holders of official student/teacher/youth cards are entitled to meager accident coverage and hospital inpatient benefits. Students will often find that their student health coverage extends during the vacations and for one term beyond the date of their last enrollment.

After exhausting these possibilities, you might want to contact a specialist travel insurance company, or consider the **Rough Guides travel insurance** deal (see box opposite). A typical travel insurance policy usually provides cover for the loss of baggage, tickets, and – up to a certain limit – cash or checks, as well as cancellation or curtailment of your journey. Most policies

Rough Guides travel insurance

Rough Guides has teamed up with Columbus Direct to offer you **travel insurance** that can be tailored to suit your needs.

Readers can choose from many different travel insurance products, including a low-cost backpacker option for long stays; a short-break option for city getaways; a typical holiday package option; and many others. There are also annual multi-trip policies for those who travel regularly, with variable levels of cover available. Different sports and activities (trekking, skiing, etc) can be covered if required on most policies.

Rough Guides travel insurance is available to the residents of 36 different countries with different language options to choose from via our **website** – Ⓦwww.roughguidesinsurance.com – where you can also purchase the insurance.

Alternatively, US residents should **call** Ⓣ1-800/749-4922; UK residents Ⓣ0800/083 9507; and Australians Ⓣ1300/669 999. All other nationalities should dial their international access code followed by Ⓣ44 870/890 2843.

exclude so-called **high-risk activities**, such as skiing, snowboarding, and rockclimbing, unless an extra premium is paid; be sure to check on this before you buy. Keep in mind, too, that many policies can be chopped and changed to exclude coverage you don't need – sickness and accident benefits, for example, can often be excluded or included at will. If you do take medical coverage, ascertain whether benefits will be paid as treatment proceeds or only after return home, and whether there is a 24hr medical emergency number. When securing **baggage cover**, make sure that the per-article limit – typically under $500 – will cover your most valuable possession. If you need to make a claim, you should keep receipts for medicines and medical treatment, and in the event you have anything stolen, you must obtain an official statement from the police.

Health

Visitors from Europe, Australia, New Zealand, and Canada don't require any vaccinations to enter the US. All travelers will be comforted to know that if you have a serious accident while you're in New England, emergency services will get to you sooner and charge you later. For emergencies, dial toll-free Ⓣ911 from any phone. If you have medical or dental problems that don't require an ambulance, most hospitals will have a walk-in emergency room: for the nearest hospital, check with your hotel or dial information at Ⓣ411.

Should you need to see a **doctor**, lists can be found in the *Yellow Pages* under "Clinics" or "Physicians and Surgeons." Be aware that even simple consultations are costly, usually around $75–100 each visit, which is payable in advance. Keep receipts for any part of your medical treatment, including prescriptions, so that you can claim against your insurance once you're home. (See "Insurance" above for more).

For minor ailments such as headache or the common cold, stop by a local **pharmacy**; some are open 24 hours, especially in the larger cities. Foreign visitors should note that many medicines available over the counter at home – codeine-based painkillers, for one – are available by prescription only in the US.

Costs, money, and banks

To help with planning your New England vacation, this book contains detailed price information for accommodation, eating, and various activities. Unless otherwise stated, the hotel price codes (explained on p.49) are for the average cost of the least expensive double room typically available, exclusive of any local taxes, while any meal prices quoted include food only and not drinks or tip. For museums and similar attractions, the prices we quote are generally for adults; you can assume that children, students, and seniors get in at a discount. Naturally, costs will increase slightly overall during the life of this edition, but the relative comparisons should remain valid.

Costs

Accommodation is likely to be your biggest single expense in New England. Few hotel, motel, or B&B rooms cost under $50 a night, you're likely to pay more than $80 for anything halfway decent in a city, and rates in rural areas are not much cheaper. In Boston, it may well be difficult to find anything at all for less than $150 a night. On the plus side, these prices are almost invariably for a double room, so you will save money if you can split the cost with a travel companion. Hostels offering dorm beds – usually for $20–25 a night – are available, but they are by no means everywhere, and save little money for two or more people traveling together. Camping, of course, is cheap (anywhere from free to $25 per night), but rarely practical in the big cities.

As for **food**, $20 a day is enough for an adequate life-support diet – strictly self-catering, mind – while for a daily total of around $30 you'll be able to afford a bagel or muffin for breakfast, a sandwich for lunch, and dinner at an inexpensive restaurant or café. From there, of course, the sky's the limit: restaurants in the larger cities (Boston especially) can break the bank of all but the most well-off, and even in the country you'll often come across pricey, storied establishments. Beyond this, everything hinges on how much sightseeing, taxi-cabbing, and drinking you do. Much of any of these – especially in the cities – and you're likely to be going through upwards of $50 a day (not including accommodation, of course).

The rates for **getting around** New England, especially on buses, and to a lesser extent on trains and planes, may look inexpensive on paper, but the distances involved mean that costs soon mount up. For a group of two or more, renting a car can be a very good investment (see "Getting around," p.43), not least because it enables you to stay in the ubiquitous budget motels along the interstate highways instead of relying on expensive downtown hotels.

Remember that a **sales tax** of between five and seven percent is added to virtually everything you buy in stores except for groceries, but will not be included as part of the marked price. Exceptions to this rule are that there is no sales tax in New Hampshire, and clothing is exempt in Massachusetts and Rhode Island. Finally, many accommodations apply a **hotel tax**, which can add as much as fourteen percent to the total bill.

Money and banks

Cash and an **ATM** or **debit card** are the best way to carry and obtain money while in New England, for both American and foreign visitors. You'll find ATMs on nearly every corner in the big cities, and they shouldn't be too difficult to locate in rural areas, either. Any ATM or debit card issued in the US should work in all ATMs, while travelers from abroad should make sure their card is part of the Cirrus or Plus network; look on the machine you're about to use and, if it bears one of these logos, withdraw away. Keep in mind that you'll usually be charged $1–2 every time you make a withdrawal from an

Money: a note for foreign travelers

US currency comes in **bills** of $1, $5, $10, $20, $50, and $100. All are roughly the same size and color, making it necessary to check each bill carefully. The dollar is made up of 100 cents with **coins** of 1 cent (known as a penny), 5 cents (a nickel), 10 cents (a dime – smaller than the nickel), and 25 cents (a quarter). Inconveniently enough, none of the coins has a number on it telling you how much it's worth: look for the small print that reads five or ten cents. New gold-colored dollar coins were recently introduced in the US, though you'll only really find them when receiving change from vending machines. Occasionally you might find JFK half-dollars (50¢), Susan B. Anthony dollar coins, or a two-dollar bill. Change (quarters are the most useful, pennies are almost never accepted) is needed for buses, vending machines, parking meters, and telephones, so it's a good idea always to have some on hand.

ATM not owned and operated by your home bank.

If you'd rather not carry around a lot of cash, you might want to supplement your dollars with **travelers' checks**, which offer the security of knowing that lost or stolen checks will be replaced. Don't forget to keep the receipt and a record of the serial numbers safe and separate from the checks themselves; in the event that checks are lost or stolen, the issuing company will expect you to report the loss forthwith (see below for phone numbers), and will require these serial numbers. Travelers' checks can be used same as cash in virtually all shops, restaurants, and gas stations – though in the hinterlands they might provoke a moment of head-scratching and manager-consulting before being accepted.

It's a good idea to carry a **credit card** or two in case of emergency; the major companies (MasterCard, Visa, and American Express) will work anywhere in America, no matter where the card was issued. A compromise between plastic and travelers' checks is **Visa TravelMoney**, a disposable pre-paid debit card with a PIN which works in all ATMs that accept Visa cards. You load up your account with funds before leaving home, and when they run out, you simply throw the card away. The card is available in most countries from branches of Thomas Cook and Citicorp. For more information, check the Visa TravelMoney website at Ⓦ www.usa.visa.com/personal/cards/index.html.

Banks are generally open from 9am until 5pm Monday to Thursday, and 9am to 6pm on Friday. Some have limited hours on Saturdays, and ATMs are usually accessible 24 hours a day. Most major banks change foreign travelers' checks and currency as well. **Exchange bureaus**, found at airports, tend to charge less commission than banks: Thomas Cook and American Express are the biggest names. If your traveler's checks and/or credit cards are stolen or if you need to find the nearest bank that sells a particular brand of travelers' check, or to buy checks by phone, call one of the following numbers: American Express (Ⓣ1-800/221-7282), Travelers' Check Customer Service (Ⓣ1-800/645-6556), MasterCard International/Thomas Cook (Ⓣ1-800/223-7373), or Visa (Ⓣ1-800/227-6811).

Wiring money

Having money **wired** from home is never convenient or cheap (sending $200, for example, will cost you around $20), and should be considered a last resort. The two largest money-wiring companies in the

ATMs

Automatic Teller Machines (aka **ATMs**) are everywhere in New England, and many are open 24 hours. Unlike in Europe, most American ATMs charge a fee of $1–2 for customers who are not affiliated with the bank that runs the machine. Washington Mutual, a Seattle-based bank, is one of the few exceptions to this rule, and is expanding as a banking chain in New England.

US are MoneyGram (Ⓣ1-800/926-3947, Ⓦwww.moneygram.com) and Western Union (Ⓣ1-800/325-6000, Ⓦwww.westernunion.com); call or visit either company's website to find the location nearest you.

It's also possible to have money wired directly from a bank in your home country to a bank in the US, although this is somewhat less reliable because it involves two separate institutions. If you do go this route, your home bank will need the address of the branch bank where you want to pick up the money and the address and routing number of that bank's state head office, which will act as the clearing house; money wired this way normally takes two working days to arrive, and costs around $40 per transaction.

Youth and student discounts

Once obtained, various official and quasi-official **youth/student ID cards** soon pay for themselves in savings. Full-time students are eligible for the International Student ID Card (ISIC; Ⓦwww.isiccard.com), which entitles the bearer to special air, rail, and bus fares, as well as discounts at museums, theaters, and other attractions. For Americans there's also a health benefit, providing up to $3000 in emergency medical coverage and $100 a day for sixty days in the hospital, plus a 24-hour hotline to call in the event of a medical, legal, or financial emergency. The card costs $22 for Americans; Can$16 for Canadians; Aus$16.50 for Australians; NZ$21 for New Zealanders; and £6 in the UK.

You only have to be 26 or younger to qualify for the **International Youth Travel Card**, which costs US$22/£7 and carries the same benefits. Teachers qualify for the **International Teacher Card**, offering similar discounts and costing US$22, Can$16, Aus$16.50, and NZ$21. All of these cards are available from student-oriented travel agents in North America, Europe, Australia, and New Zealand. Several other travel organizations and accommodation groups also sell their own cards, good for various discounts. A university photo ID might open some doors, but they are not as easily recognizable as are ISIC cards. Keep in mind that the latter are often not accepted as valid proof of age, for example in bars or liquor stores.

Getting around

Although rural areas can be nearly impossible to access if you don't have a car, getting from one large city to the next is seldom much of a problem on public transportation in New England. Good bus links and reasonable, though limited, train services are nearly always available. If you want to visit every small town, though, or be able to travel without being tied to a bus or train schedule, renting your own car is highly recommended.

By car

Driving is by far the best way to get around New England. Keep in mind, though, that things get confusing within the larger cities such as Boston, where complicated freeway networks intertwine with narrow one-way city streets that were originally designed for horse-drawn carriages. Away from the cities, many places are almost impossible to reach without your own transportation; most national and state parks and forests are only served by infrequent public transportation as far as the main visitors' center, if that. What's more, if you are planning on doing a fair amount of camping, renting a car can save you money by allowing access to less expensive out-of-the-way campgrounds, not to mention easing the burden of carting your equipment around.

Drivers wishing to **rent cars** are supposed to have held their licenses for at least one year (though this is rarely checked); people **under 25 years old** but older than 21 will have to pay higher rates, while those under 21 are generally not allowed to rent cars. Car rental companies (see below) will also expect you to have a credit card; if you don't, they may let you leave a hefty deposit (at least $200), but don't count on it. The likeliest tactic for getting a good deal is to phone the major firms' toll-free numbers and ask for their best rate – most will try to beat the offers of their competitors, so it's worth haggling.

In general the **lowest rates** are available at the airport branches – $200 a week for a subcompact is a fairly standard base rate – although many airports now add "Airport Accessibility" fees, calculated as a percentage, which serve to increase your total fairly quickly. Always be sure to get free **unlimited mileage**, and be aware that returning the car in a different city from the one in which you rented it can incur a drop-off charge. However, many companies do not charge drop-off fees to certain cities, so check before you book if you plan a one-way drive. Also, don't automatically go for the cheapest rate, as there's some difference in the quality of cars from company to company; industry leaders like Hertz and Avis tend to have newer, lower-mileage cars, and they also may have fewer hidden add-on charges than firms that initially seem less expensive.

Alternatively, various local companies rent out new – and not so new (try Rent-a-Heap or Rent-a-Wreck) – vehicles. They are certainly cheaper than the big chains if you just want to spin around a city for a day, but you have to drop them back where you picked them up, and free mileage is seldom included. Addresses and phone numbers are listed in the *Yellow Pages*.

When you rent a car, read the small print carefully for details on **Collision Damage Waiver** (CDW), sometimes called Liability Damage Waiver (LDW); this is a form of insurance which often isn't included in the initial rental charge but is well worth considering. It specifically covers the car that you are driving yourself, as you are in any case insured for damage to other vehicles. At $9–13 a day, it can add substantially to the total cost, but without it you're liable for every scratch to the car – even those that aren't your fault. Some credit-card companies offer automatic CDW coverage to anyone using their card; read the fine print beforehand in any case.

You should also check your **third-party liability**. The standard policy often only covers you for the first $15,000 of the third party's claim against you, a paltry sum in litigation-conscious America. Companies strongly advise taking out third-party insurance, which costs a further $10–12 a day but indemnifies the driver for up to $2,000,000.

If you **break down** in a rented car, there'll be an emergency number pinned to the dashboard, tucked away in the glove compartment, or printed on your rental contract. You can summon the highway patrol on one of the emergency phones stationed along freeways (usually at half-mile intervals) and many other remote highways (mostly every two miles) – although as the highway patrol and state police cruise by regularly, you can just sit tight and wait. Raising your car hood and switching on your hazard lights is recognized as a call for assistance, although women traveling alone should be wary of doing this.

Another tip, for women especially, is to rent a **mobile telephone** from the car rental agency – you often only have to pay a nominal amount until you actually use it, and in larger cities they increasingly come built into the car. Having a phone can be reassuring at least, and a potential lifesaver should something go terribly wrong.

Major car rental agencies

In North America

Alamo US ⓣ1-800/522-9696, ⓦwww.alamo.com
Avis US ⓣ1-800/331-1084, Canada ⓣ1-800/272-5871, ⓦwww.avis.com
Budget US ⓣ1-800/527-0700, ⓦwww.budgetrentacar.com
Dollar US ⓣ1-800/800-4000, ⓦwww.dollar.com
Enterprise Rent-a-Car US ⓣ1-800/325-8007, ⓦwww.enterprise.com
Hertz US ⓣ1-800/654-3131, Canada ⓣ1-800/263-0600, ⓦwww.hertz.com
National US ⓣ1-800/227-7368, ⓦwww.nationalcar.com
Thrifty US ⓣ1-800/367-2277, ⓦwww.thrifty.com

In the UK

Avis ⓣ0870/606 0100, ⓦwww.avis.co.uk
Budget ⓣ08701/539 170, ⓦwww.budget.co.uk
National ⓣ0870/5365 365, ⓦwww.nationalcar.com
Hertz ⓣ0870/844 8844, ⓦwww.hertz.co.uk
Holiday Autos ⓣ0870/400 00 99, ⓦwww.holidayautos.co.uk
Suncars ⓣ0870/500 5566, ⓦwww.suncars.com
Thrifty ⓣ01494/751 600, ⓦwww.thrifty.co.uk

In Ireland

Argus Republic of Ireland ⓣ01/490 4444, ⓦwww.argus-rentacar.com
Avis Northern Ireland ⓣ028/9024 0404, Republic of Ireland ⓣ01/605 7500, ⓦwww.avis.co.uk
Budget Republic of Ireland ⓣ0/9066 27711, ⓦwww.budgetcarrental.ie
Hertz Republic of Ireland ⓣ01/660 2255, ⓦwww.hertz.ie
Holiday Autos Republic of Ireland ⓣ01/872 9366, ⓦwww.holidayautos.ie
Thrifty Northern Ireland ⓣ028/9445 2565, Republic of Ireland ⓣ01/844 1944 ⓦwww.thrifty.co.uk

In Australia

Avis ⓣ13 63 33, ⓦwww.avis.com.au
Budget ⓣ1300/362 848, ⓦwww.budget.com.au
Dollar ⓣ02/9223 1444, ⓦwww.dollarcar.com.au
Hertz ⓣ13 30 39, ⓦwww.hertz.com.au
Thrifty ⓣ1300/367 227, ⓦwww.thrifty.com.au

In New Zealand

Avis ⓣ09/526 2847, ⓦwww.avis.co.nz
Budget ⓣ0800/283 438, ⓦwww.budget.co.nz
Hertz ⓣ0800/654 321, ⓦwww.hertz.co.nz
National ⓣ0800/800 115 or 03/366 5574, ⓦwww.nationalcar.co.nz
Thrifty ⓣ09/309 0111, ⓦwww.thrifty.co.nz

Renting an RV

Besides cars, recreational vehicles or **RVs** (camper vans) can be rented from around $470 a week (usually with no or limited free mileage), although outlets are surprisingly rare. The Recreational Vehicle Rental Association (ⓣ703/591-7130 or 1-800/336-0355, ⓦwww.rvra.org), publishes a directory of rental firms in the US and Canada ($10, $15 outside North America) or you can get details of their many members online. Two of the larger companies offering RV rentals are Cruise America (ⓣ1-800/327-7799, ⓦwww.cruiseamerica.com) and Moturis (ⓣ1-800/890-2909, ⓦwww.moturis.com).

On top of the rental fees, take into account the cost of gas (some RVs do twelve miles to the gallon or less) and any drop-off charges, in case you plan to do a one-way trip across the country. Also, it is rarely legal simply to pull up in an RV and spend the night at the roadside – you are expected to stay in designated parks that cost $20 or more per night.

Motoring organizations

In North America

American Automobile Association ⓣ1-800/222-4357, ⓦwww.aaa.com. Each state has its own club – check the phone book for local address and phone number.
Canadian Automobile Association ⓣ613/247-0117, ⓦwww.caa.ca. Each region has its own club – check the phone book for local address and phone number.

In the UK and Ireland

AA UK ⓣ0870/600 0731, ⓦwww.theaa.co.uk
AA Ireland ⓣ01/617 9999, ⓦwww.aaireland.ie
RAC UK ⓣ0800/55 00 55, ⓦwww.rac.co.uk

In Australia and New Zealand

Australian Automobile Association Australia ⓣ02/6247 7311, ⓦwww.aaa.asn.au
New Zealand Automobile Association New Zealand ⓣ0800/500 444, ⓦwww.aa.co.nz

Roads

There are several types of roads in New England. The best for covering long distances quickly are the wide, straight, and fast **interstate highways**, usually at least six lanes and always prefixed by "I" (eg I-95); these are marked on maps by a red, white, and blue shield bearing the number. Even-numbered interstates run east–west and those with odd numbers run north–south. Though most roads are free, some of the more traveled highways, known as **turnpikes**, charge anywhere from 50¢ to several dollars to cruise down their broad lanes. You'll be warned in advance that a toll booth is coming. If you're severely strapped for cash, you can usually get to the same destination on smaller – and

Foreign drivers

UK, Canadian, Australian, and New Zealand citizens can all drive in the US provided they have a regular driver's license; International Driving Permits are not required. If in any doubt about your driving status in the US, check with your local motoring association (see opposite).

Some foreign travelers have trouble at first adjusting to **driving on the right**. In terms of technical skills, it's actually pretty easy to make the switch; a more common problem is that people simply forget and set out on the left – try taping a reminder to the steering wheel.

Note that rules and regulations aren't always nationally fixed. Some standard rules: no making a U-turn on an interstate or anywhere where a single unbroken line runs along the middle of the road; no parking on a highway; and front-seat passengers must ride with a fastened seat belt. At junctions, one rule is crucially different from the UK: you can **turn right on a red light** if there is no prohibiting sign, and no traffic approaching from the left; otherwise red means stop. Stopping is also compulsory (on both sides of the road) when you come upon a school bus disgorging passengers with its lights flashing. A blinking red light should be treated as a stop sign; for a blinking yellow one, you should cross the intersection with caution, but do not need to come to a complete stop.

considerably slower – roads, but the extra effort is usually not worth it.

A grade down, and broadly similar to British dual carriageways and main roads, are the **state highways** (eg Hwy-1) and the **US highways** (eg US-395). Some major roads in cities are technically state highways but are better known by their local names. Hwy-1 in Brunswick, Maine, for instance, is better known as Mill Street. In rural areas, you'll also find much smaller **county roads**, which are known as routes (eg Rte-11).

Rules of the road

Although the law says that drivers must keep up with the flow of traffic, which is often hurtling along at 75 miles per hour (mph), the **maximum speed limit** in New England is 65mph, with lower posted limits – usually around 25–35mph – in built-up areas. The default speed limit in most cites is 25mph, so if you don't see a sign, you'd probably do well to adhere to this limit. If given a ticket for speeding, your case will come to court and the size of the fine will be at the discretion of the judge; $100 is a rough minimum.

If the police do flag you down, don't get out of the car, and don't reach into the glove compartment as the cops may think you have a gun. Simply sit still with your hands on the wheel; when questioned, be polite and don't attempt to make jokes. If you are signaled to pull over at night on a deserted stretch of road that makes you uneasy, know that it's within your rights to proceed to the next well-lit area before pulling over; you should put your right turn signal on (indicating you intend to pull over) and drive slowly until you feel comfortable about a place to stop.

As for other possible violations, US law requires that any alcohol be carried unopened in the trunk (boot) of the car, and it can't be stressed enough that **driving while intoxicated** (DWI) or driving under the influence (DUI) is a very serious offense. If a police officer smells alcohol on your breath or has reason to believe that you are under the influence, he or she is entitled to administer a breath, saliva, or urine test. If you fail, you'll be locked up with other inebriates in the drunk tank of the nearest jail until you sober up. Your case will later be heard by a judge, who can revoke your license, fine you as much as $1000, or in extreme (or repeat) cases, imprison you for thirty days.

By plane

New England is small enough that traveling around by **plane** is generally unnecessary. It can be useful for long trips – from Providence, RI to Burlington, VT, for example

Hitchhiking

The usual advice given to **hitchhikers** is that they should use their common sense; in fact, of course, common sense should tell anyone that hitchhiking in the US is a **bad idea**. We do not recommend it under any circumstances.

– but in those cases the routes are usually not well traveled so the tickets can be quite expensive. At off-peak times, flights between Boston and Portland, ME, cost around $140 round-trip, but may require at least two weeks advance booking.

By train

Amtrak's four main routes in New England provide decent, though limited, **rail** connections between the few major cities in western New England, as well as some of the minor ones. Probably the prettiest route is the *Vermonter*, which winds from Washington, DC through New York City and then western Connecticut, western Massachusetts, and all the way through Vermont to St Albans in the north. Beautiful vistas whisk by your window at all times of the year. The other major north–south Amtrak routes in and around New England, the *Ethan Allen* (Washington, DC to Rutland, VT), the *Twilight Shoreliner* (Boston, MA to Newport News, VA), and the *Acela Regional* (Washington, DC to Boston, MA), are almost as scenic, as is the *Downeaster* (Boston, MA to Portland, ME). There's also a route called the *Lakeshore Limited* that travels the length of Massachusetts (from Chicago, IL), ending up in Boston.

International travelers can cut fares greatly by using one of several Amtrak **rail passes**, which give unlimited travel within certain time periods (see box opposite). Look out also for special deals and weekly sales for all comers, advertised on Ⓦwww.amtrak.com. There is also the Visit USA scheme, available only to non-US or Canadian residents, which entitles the buyer to a 30 percent discount on any full-priced domestic fare, provided you buy the ticket before leaving home. It is certainly worth asking your travel agent, but in many cases there are discount fares available which undercut the Visit USA fare.

For all information on **Amtrak** fares and schedules in the US, use the toll-free number Ⓣ1-800/USA-RAIL (1-800/872-7245) or visit the official Amtrak website: Ⓦwww.amtrak.com. Do not phone individual stations.

By bus

If you're traveling on your own, and making a lot of stops, **buses** are by far the cheapest way to get around. There are several main bus companies which link the major cities and many smaller towns in New England (see box opposite). Out in the country, buses are fairly scarce, sometimes appearing only once a day, and here you'll need to plot your route with care. But along the main highways, buses run around the clock to a fairly full timetable, stopping only for meal breaks and driver changeovers.

To avoid possible hassle, lone female travelers in particular should take care to sit as near to the driver as possible, and to arrive during **daylight hours**, as many bus stations are in fairly unsafe areas. It used to be that any sizeable community would have a bus station; in some places, now, the post office, a convenience store, or a gas station doubles as the bus stop and ticket office, and in many others the bus service has been canceled altogether. Buses do not generally take reservations, so plan to arrive early if you're traveling on the weekend.

As for **fares**, buses are consistently less than taking a train or flying – Providence to Boston, for example, is $8, while via train it's $38. Additionally, Greyhound's **Discovery Passes** are good for unlimited travel nationwide within certain time frames – not necessarily a great deal in New England, but an essential purchase for a cross-country bus trip; see the box opposite for rates.

Bus companies that specialize in New England all publish comprehensive timetables. Most tourist offices are well supplied

Greyhound's nationwide toll-free information service and website (ⓣ1-800/231-2222, ⓦwww.greyhound.com) can give you routes and times, plus phone numbers and addresses of local terminals.

with route information and schedules, particularly at Boston's Logan Airport.

New England bus companies

Bonanza One Bonanza Way, Providence, RI ⓣ401/751-8800 or 1-888/751-8800, ⓦwww.bonanzabus.com. Non-stop service between New York and Providence. Also covers Cape Cod, southern Massachusetts (including Boston), Connecticut, eastern New York, and Bennington, VT.
C&J Trailways Sumner Drive, Dover, NH ⓣ1-800/258-7111 or 603/430-1100, ⓦwww.cjtrailways.com. Service from Logan Airport and Boston's South Station through northern MA to southern NH.
Concord Trailways Trailways Transportation Center, 7 Langdon St, Concord, NH (ⓣ1-800/639-3317, ⓦwww.concordtrailways.com. Good coverage of New Hampshire and Maine, with connecting service to Logan Airport.
Peter Pan Trailways 1776 Main St, Springfield, MA ⓣ1-800/237-8747, ⓦwww.peterpanbus.com. Relatively frequent and extensive service between Boston and New York, via Springfield and Hartford.
Plymouth and Brockton Peter Pan Terminal, South Station, Boston ⓣ508/746-0378, ⓦwww.p-b.com. Comprehensive service to Cape Cod from Boston.
Vermont Transit Lines 345 Pine St, Burlington, VT ⓣ1-800/552-8737, ⓦwww.vermonttransit.com. Service throughout most of New England, plus lines to New York, Toronto, and Montréal. Direct connections with Greyhound.

Cycling

If you have the stamina for it, **cycling** is one of the best ways to see New England. Some of the larger cities have cycle lanes and local buses equipped to carry bikes (strapped to the outside), and even the bustle of Boston can be easily escaped in half an hour by bicycle. Although the terrain is often hilly, there's nothing insurmountable to an experienced cyclist. One is rarely more than an hour's ride from a town or village, and the countryside in between is frequently idyllic, worth taking in at a leisurely pace on two wheels.

Rail and bus passes

Amtrak rail passes

International travelers can take advantage of two regional **rail passes** that may save money and allow you to see more of the region at the same time: the **Northeast Rail Pass** enables you to jump on and off the train anywhere between Virginia and Montréal ($149–247) in five- to thirty-day increments, while the **Eastern Rail Pass**, between Boston, Florida, Chicago, and New Orleans, allows the same flexibility over 15 or 30 days ($260–405). You may purchase the pass in your home country through a travel agent or in the United States with an international passport. Unfortunately there are no rail pass options for Americans or Canadians.

Greyhound bus passes

Foreign visitors and US and Canadian nationals can all buy a **Greyhound Discovery Pass**, offering unlimited travel within a set time limit: most travel agents can oblige or you can order online at ⓦwww.discoverypass.com. They come in several durations – a seven-day pass costs $229, ten days go for $279, fifteen days for $329, thirty days for $439, forty-five days for $499, and the longest, a sixty-day pass, is $609 (fares are slightly higher in the summer). The first time you use your pass, it will be dated by the ticket clerk (which becomes the commencement date of the ticket), and your destination is written on a page that the driver will tear out and keep as you board the bus. Repeat this procedure for every subsequent journey. Also, make sure to check timetables other than Greyhound's – the pass is valid on some participating New England bus lines like Peter Pan and Bonanza.

Bikes can be **rented** for less than $25 a day, or $90–100 a week, from most bike stores; the local visitors' center will have details (we've listed rental options where applicable throughout the *Guide*). For long-distance cycling you'll need a good-quality multispeed bike (but don't immediately splurge on a mountain bike, unless you are planning a lot of off-road use – good road conditions and trail restrictions in national parks make a touring bike an equally good or better choice), maps, spare tires, tools, panniers, and a helmet (not a legal necessity for adults, but a very good idea). A route avoiding the interstates (on which cycling is illegal) is essential, and it's also wise to cycle **north to south**, as the wind blows this way in the summer and can make all the difference between a pleasant trip and acute leg-ache. The main problem you'll encounter is **traffic**: wide, cumbersome RVs spew unpleasant exhaust in your face and, in northern Maine, and in Vermont close to the Canadian border, enormous logging trucks have slipstreams that will pull you towards the middle of the road. Be particularly careful if you're planning to cycle along Hwy-1 on the Maine coast, since besides heavy traffic it also has narrow shoulders; again, you're much better off on the quiet country roads that New England is known for.

When asking for **directions**, stick to other cyclists or bike shops; others will give you directions along the most direct, and therefore the busiest and least scenic, route. Many states also have **rail trails**, old railway routes that have been paved and turned into bike paths. These are great choices for bikers because they are scenic and tend to take steep hills gradually. A good source for cycling **information** in New England, including trail and bike store locations, is the New England Mountain Bike Association (ⓣ1-800/576-3622, ⓦwww.nemba.org). Meanwhile, the Adventure Cycling Association (ⓣ406/721-1776 or 1-800/755-2453, ⓦwww.adv-cycling.org) sells detailed biking maps of routes that travel along smaller roads and bike paths. They also include information on camping along the route.

For more information, the following **books** are easy to find online and in bookstores around New England: *Best Bike Rides in New England*, by Paul Thomas; *Best Bike Paths of New England: Safe, Scenic, and Traffic-Free Bicycling*, by Wendy Williams; and *The Official Rails-to-Trails Conservancy Guidebook to New England*, by Cynthia Mascott.

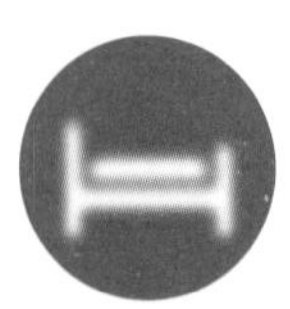

Accommodation

Accommodation standards in New England – as in the rest of the US – are high, and costs inevitably form a significant proportion of the expenses for any trip to the area. It is possible to haggle, however, especially in the chain motels, and if you're on your own, you can possibly pare down costs by sleeping in dormitory-style hostels, where a bed will usually cost $20–25 a night. However, groups of two or more will find it only a little more expensive to stay in the far more plentiful budget motels and hotels, where basic rooms away from the major cities typically cost around $40 per night. Many hotels will set up a third single bed for around $5–10 on top of the regular price, reducing costs for three people sharing. By contrast, the lone traveler will have a hard time of it: "singles" are usually double rooms at an only slightly reduced rate. Prices quoted by hotels and motels are almost always for the whole room rather than for each person using it.

Accommodation price codes

Throughout this book, accommodation has been price-coded according to the average cost of the least expensive **double room** typically available. Note that there can be a great deal of fluctuation with room rates, especially in areas like the Berkshires during the popular fall foliage season, when prices can rise drastically; as well, many establishments charge more on Friday and Saturday nights, while big-city business hotels often slash their prices on weekends. We've listed specific prices rather than codes for hostels, apartments, and campsites. As the high and low seasons for tourists vary across the region, astute planning can save a lot of money. Watch out also for local events, which can raise rates far above normal. Only where we explicitly say so do the price codes include local taxes, which range from seven to thirteen percent.

- ❶ up to $30
- ❷ $30–45
- ❸ $45–60
- ❹ $60–80
- ❺ $80–100
- ❻ $100–130
- ❼ $130–175
- ❽ $175–250
- ❾ $250+

Most hotels will require a credit card number to take a reservation, though this does not mean that you'll have to pay by card. Since cheap accommodation in the cities and on the popular sections of the coast is snapped up fast, **book ahead** whenever possible. **Reservations** are only held until 5pm or 6pm unless you've told the hotel that you'll be arriving late. Hotel and motel rooms in New England in general adhere to a uniform standard of comfort – double beds with bathroom, TV, and phone – and you don't get a much better deal by paying, say, $70 instead of $50. Over $70, the room and its fittings simply get bigger and more aesthetically pleasing; there may even be a swimming pool which guests can use for free. Paying over $150 or so may allow you to have a suite-type room, or a room which includes a minibar or other extras.

A growing number of New England hotels provide a **complimentary breakfast**. Generally, this will be no more than a cup of coffee and a doughnut, but in cities and business hotels it is increasingly a sit-down affair likely to comprise fruit, cereals, muffins, and toast, even made-to-order entrees in the pricier spots. In most places you'll be able to find cheap hotels and motels simply by keeping your eyes open – they're usually advertised by enormous roadside signs. Alternatively, there are a number of budget-priced chains whose rooms start at $50–70, such as *Econolodge*, *Motel 6*, and *Travelodge*. Mid-priced options include *Best Western*, *Howard Johnson*, and *Ramada* – though if you can afford to pay this much ($70–120) there's normally somewhere nicer and more personal to stay. When it's worth splurging on somewhere really atmospheric we've said as much in the *Guide*. Bear in mind that the most upscale establishments have all manner of services which may appear to be free but for which you'll be expected to tip in a style commensurate with the hotel's status.

Discounts and reservations

During off-peak periods many motels and hotels struggle to fill their rooms and it's worth haggling to get a few dollars off the asking price. Staying in the same place for more than one night may bring further reductions. Read the small print, though: what appears to be an amazingly cheap room rate sometimes turns out to be limited to midweek. During the off season hotels may make their rooms available to online booking consolidators like hotels.com, where the rate can be much lower than even the hotel is allowed to offer. Taking advantage of these deals might require some advance planning, and may lead to lower-quality rooms with non-refundable rates – read the fine print and make sure to print out your confirmation number and a written description of what you're getting in exchange for what you've paid. For motels in particular, note also that you might be able to get a **discount** by presenting a membership card from a motoring organization like AAA (see p.44). In addition, look out for discount coupon booklets at information centers.

Bed and breakfasts

Bed and breakfasts are everywhere in New England – nearly every town with any tourist traffic at all will have one – though some are nothing more than a converted room in the back of someone's home. Typically, the bed-and-breakfast inns, or "**B&Bs**", as they're usually known, are restored old buildings with fewer than ten rooms and plenty of antique furnishings. Television is refreshingly absent from most, as are in-room phones. Abundant flowers, stuffed cushions, and a contrived homely atmosphere are commonplace. Then, of course, there's the breakfast, often an extravagant feast, served around a common dining table (anywhere between 7–9am); it can be fun if you're a "morning person," but a nightmare if you'd rather down your poached pears in peace.

B&B **prices** vary greatly: anywhere from $60 to $300 depending on location, season, and facilities. Most fall between $80 and $130 per night for a double, a little less for solo travelers. Bear in mind, too, that they are often booked well in advance, and even if they're not full, the cheaper rooms may already be taken.

New England B&B contacts

B&B Cape Cod ⓣ1-800/541-6226, ⓦwww.bedandbreakfastcapecod.com. A good resource, but does not allow you to contact B&Bs directly.

B&B Online ⓦwww.bbreserve.com. B&Bs throughout the country advertise here – a good selection of New England lodging is organized geographically.

Boston Area B&B Reservations ⓣ617/964-1606 or 1-800/832-2632, ⓦwww.bbreserve.com. Apart from Boston, also includes limited listings from Maine, New Hampshire, and Vermont.

New England Innkeepers Association ⓣ603/964-6689, ⓦwww.newenglandinns.com. Represents properties all over New England.

Nutmeg B&B ⓣ203/263-4479, ⓦwww.nutmegbb.com. Connecticut only.

Passport to New England ⓦwww.passporttonewengland.com. A partnership of upscale inns throughout New England.

Hostels

At an average of $20–25 per night per person, **hostels** are the cheapest accommodation option in New England other than camping. There are three main kinds of hostel-type accommodation in the US: YMCA/YWCA (known as "Ys"), offering accommodation for both sexes or, in a few cases, women only; official HI-AYH; and the growing AAIH (American Association of Independent Hostels) organization. There is a fairly good concentration of hostels in New England, at least compared with the rest of the US. HI-AYH are the most prevalent, though there are many unaffiliated hostels as well. For a complete listing of the hostels in the region, check out ⓦwww.hostels.com.

Prices in **YMCAs** range from around $20 for a dormitory bed to $35 for a single or double room. Some Ys are basically health clubs and do not offer accommodation. As well, in recent years, many YMCAs have become exclusively long-term residential; indeed, the only Ys currently available lie in Connecticut and Massachusetts.

You'll find **HI-AYH** hostels (the prefix is usually shortened to HI in listings) in major cities and popular hiking areas, including national and state parks, mostly in Vermont and Massachusetts. Most urban hostels have 24hr access, while rural ones may have a curfew and limited daytime hours. Rates at HI hostels range from $8 to $28 for HI members; non-members generally pay an additional $3 per night. If you plan on staying in several hostels, it obviously makes sense to join – membership is only $25 a year. Each location will have registration information.

The **independent hostels** in the AAIH group are usually a little less expensive than their HI counterparts, and have fewer rules. The quality is not as consistent; some can be quite poor, while others are absolutely wonderful. There is often no curfew and, at some, a party atmosphere is encouraged at barbecues and keg parties. Their independent status may be due to a failure to come up to the HI's (fairly rigid) criteria, but often it's simply because the owners prefer not to be tied down by HI regulations.

One good New England **hosteling information service** is the Eastern New England Council in Boston (ⓣ617/718-7990, ⓦwww.usahostels.org), which can tell you which hostel you're nearest, whether it's open or booked, and also sell you a membership card. *USA Hostel Directory,* the HI guide to hostels in the US and Canada, is available free of charge to any overnight guest at HI-AYH hostels or direct for $3 from the HI National Office, 733 15th St NW, suite 840, Washington, DC 20005 (ⓣ202/783-6161, ⓦwww.hiusa.org).

Worldwide youth hostel information

In the US and Canada

Hosteling International–American Youth Hostels ⓣ202/783-6161, ⓦwww.hiayh.org. Annual membership is $28 for adults (ages 18–55), $18 for seniors (55 and over), and free for under-18s and groups of ten or more. Lifetime memberships are $250.

Hostelling International Canada ⓣ1-800/663-5777 or 613/237-7884, ⓦwww.hostellingintl.ca. Rather than sell the traditional one- or two-year memberships, the association now sells one individual adult membership with a 16- to 28-month term. The length of the term depends on when the membership is sold, but a member can receive up to 28 months of membership for just $35. Membership is free for under-18s and you can become a lifetime member for $175.

In the UK and Ireland

Hostelling International Northern Ireland ⓣ028/9032 4733, ⓦwww.hini.org.uk. Adult membership £13; under-18s £6; family £25; lifetime £75.

Irish Youth Hostel Association ⓣ01/830 4555, ⓦwww.irelandyha.org. Annual membership €20; under-18s €10; family €40; lifetime €100.

Scottish Youth Hostel Association ⓣ0870/155 3255, ⓦwww.syha.org.uk. Annual membership £6, for under-18s £2.50.

Youth Hostel Association (YHA) England and Wales ⓣ0870/770 8868, ⓦwww.yha.org.uk and www.iyhf.org. Annual membership £15.50; under-26s £10; lifetime £200 (or five annual payments of £45).

In Australia and New Zealand

Australia Youth Hostels Association ⓣ02/9261 1111, ⓦwww.yha.com.au. Adult membership rate Aus$52 (under-18s Aus$19) for the first twelve months and then Aus$37 each year after.

Youth Hostelling Association New Zealand ⓣ0800/278 299 or 03/379 9970, ⓦwww.yha.co.nz. Adult membership NZ$40 for one year, NZ$60 for two, and NZ$80 for three; under-18s free; lifetime NZ$300.

Camping

New England **campgrounds** range from the primitive (a flat piece of ground that may or may not have a water tap) to places more like open-air hotels, with shops, pools, game rooms, restaurants, and washing facilities. Naturally enough, **prices** vary accordingly, from nothing for the most basic plots to $35 a night for something comparatively luxurious. There are plenty of campgrounds but often plenty of people intending to use them as well. Call ahead for **reservations** at the bigger parks, or anywhere at all during national holidays or the summer, when many grounds will be either full or very crowded. Many save a number of sites for same-day arrivals, but to claim one of these you should plan on arriving early in the day – before 9am to be safe. Keep in mind that vacancies often exist in the grounds outside the parks – where the facilities are usually marginally better – and some of the more basic campgrounds in isolated areas will often be empty whatever time of the year you're there. If there's any charge at all you'll need to pay by leaving the money in the bin provided.

Much of the backcountry **forest land** in New England is owned by paper and logging companies, though many cooperate with campers (and hikers) who are hoping to make use of their pristine but soon to be destroyed lands. Contact the local chamber of commerce for information on land usage and **wilderness camping**. In other designated public lands you can camp rough pretty much anywhere you want provided you first obtain a wilderness permit (either free or about $5) and, usually, a campfire permit; these can be procured from the nearest park ranger's office. You should also take the proper precautions: carry sufficient food and drink to cover emergencies, inform the park ranger of your travel plans, and watch out for bears and the effect your presence can have on their environment; see "Backcountry camping and wildlife" on p.63. For more information on these undeveloped regions – which are often protected within either "national parks" or "national forests" – contact the **US Forest Service** (ⓣ202/205-1706, ⓦwww.fs.fed.us).

Reserving a campground

Kampgrounds of America (KOA; ⓣ406/248-7444, ⓦwww.koakampgrounds.com) privately oversees a multitude of **campgrounds** all over New England; although these are largely for RVs, there are one-room "Kabins" available at almost all their sites. More tent-friendly (and aesthetically pleasing) sites can be found in the state parks and public lands. These can be booked ahead (for a fee) through a centralized system in each state (except for Rhode Island, where all reservations must be made directly through the campsite). To reserve a site at public campgrounds, contact the individual state's division of parks and recreation: CT (ⓣ860/424-3200), MA (ⓣ1-877/422-6762), ME (ⓣ207/287-3821), NH (ⓣ603/271-3556), and VT (ⓣ802/879-6565). The Appalachian Mountain Club (AMC) also has some very well-maintained camping areas and mountain huts; call their headquarters in Boston for reservation information (ⓣ617/523-0636, ⓦwww.outdoors.org).

Food and drink

Food in New England is difficult to categorize, though there is certainly a tradition of hearty Yankee cooking which permeates the landscape. And as with elsewhere in the US, you'll find a mess of typical all-American family restaurants with lots of basic meat, seafood, and pasta dishes, and little to say in the way of ambience.

New England **seafood** is excellent and well loved – lobster is almost worshiped – and, especially along the coast, a multitude of "lobster pounds" and low-key seafood joints will try to tempt you with "wicked good" homemade clam chowder ("chowdah"), oysters, clams, fish, and of course fresh lobsters. Any of these ocean creatures can be part of a traditional New England **clambake**, a delicious way of enjoying the fruits of the sea. Signature Boston baked beans, a once-popular salty stewed mix of pork, onions, and beans, are still found on more nostalgic New England menus. Good attempts at more refined American and international food are available in touristed areas and the larger urban centers, where New England's version of **California cuisine** – using fresh, locally grown ingredients – has caught on with the well-heeled crowds. Country inns and bed and breakfasts that serve dinner are good bets for high-quality food in a romantic setting; many have professional chefs on staff. And, of course, there's an abundance of pizza, hamburger, and fast-food places that have become the unfortunate (and not always accurate) symbol of American cuisine.

For more on New England **food and drink**, see the color section in the middle of this book.

The region produces its own range of nutritious **produce**: corn, apples, pears, strawberries, blueberries, peaches, plums, and cranberries are all grown locally. **Maple syrup** is a big product in New England, and every state produces at least some amount of the sweet sticky liquid. Vermont is probably the most culinarily distinct of the states, and is well known for its quality **dairy** products: cow, sheep, and goat's cheese, milk, and yogurt – not to mention Ben and Jerry's ice cream (see p.428).

Meals

For the price, on average $5–8, **breakfast** is the best-value and most filling meal of the day. Diners, cafés, and coffeeshops all serve breakfast until at least 11am, with some diners serving it all day. Between 11am and 3pm look for excellent-value **lunchtime set menus** – Chinese, Indian, and Thai restaurants frequently have help-yourself buffets for $5–8, and many Japanese restaurants give you a chance to eat sushi much more cheaply ($8–12) than usual. Most diners are decently priced all the time: you can get a good-sized lunch for $5–10. Along the coast, many seafood restaurants and shacks sell all manner of breaded and fried fish, clams, and various shellfish, not to mention the prized lobster roll – lobster meat mixed with a bit of mayonnaise and lemon, and served on a hot-dog bun. Look, too, for New England **clam chowder**, a thick, creamy shellfish soup served almost everywhere for $4–5, sometimes using a hollowed-out sourdough cottage loaf as a bowl.

For quick snacks or eating on the run, you'll find many **delis** do a range of sandwiches to go, which can be meals in themselves. In the larger cities you might find street stands selling hot dogs, burgers, or a slice of pizza for around $2, while most shopping malls have stalls with ethnic fast food that is usually edible and filling. And of course the burger chains are as ubiquitous here as anywhere in the US: *Wendy's*, *Burger King,* and *McDonald's* are the most familiar.

Besides sodas, available everywhere in any number of varieties, a wide stock of **juices** is also available at most casual restaurants: Snapple is a favorite, as are locally produced Nantucket Nectars. Each has at least a dozen different flavors, though when you read the fine print you'll be sorry to learn that both have no more than fifteen percent real fruit juice – and plenty of sweeteners. You're better off with a cold jug of **bottled water**, which is also available everywhere, despite the fact that New England tap water is clean and perfectly drinkable.

Restaurants

Traditional American cooking – juicy burgers, steaks, fries, salads (served before the main dish), and baked potatoes – is found in restaurants all over New England. **Seafood** is particularly abundant along the coast, where it is served in both upscale expensive gourmet restaurants and no-nonsense harborside shacks where you'll sit at an outdoor bench with other hungry tourists (and often seafood-loving locals as well). Ethnic cuisines are plentiful too. Many fishing towns in New England have large **Portuguese** and growing Brazilian communities – Portuguese restaurants in these areas are on the whole authentic and inexpensive. Chinese food can be found even in the most rural towns, while Japanese cooking is more expensive and somewhat fashionable, though sushi is not worshiped here the way it is in, say, New York or California. Italian food is very popular, but can be expensive once you leave the simple pizzas and pastas to explore the specialist Italian regional cooking that's fast catching on. French food, rarely found outside the larger cities, can be quite expensive. Thai, Korean, Vietnamese, Indian, and Indonesian foods are similarly city-based, though usually cheaper.

Drinking

Typical bars and cocktail lounges are prevalent across New England, and in college-dominated Boston the bars are particularly lively, with plenty of young, often extremely drunken revelers. Similarly, younger and more tourist-driven towns like Portland, ME, Portsmouth, NH, Burlington, VT, and Providence, RI, hold most of New England's worthwhile pubs and microbreweries.

To **buy and consume alcohol** in the US you need to be 21, and in puritan New England you will be asked for ID even if you look much older. Alcohol laws vary from state to state – for example bars everywhere are open on Sunday, but in Massachusetts liquor stores are not. Bars and nightclubs are likely to be fully licensed, while restaurants may only have half-licenses allowing them to serve beer and wine but no hard liquor. It is sometimes permitted to take your own bottled wine into a restaurant, where the corkage fee will be $5–10. You can buy beer, wine, or spirits more cheaply and easily in supermarkets, delis, and liquor stores. Most towns and cities have open-container laws as well, which make it a misdemeanor to carry an open container of alcohol in a public place, including parks and riversides. You'll probably get away with a warning to take it home, but you could get a fine.

American **beers** fall into two diametrically opposite categories: wonderful and tasteless. The latter includes light, fizzy brands such as Budweiser, Miller Lite, and Michelob. The alternative is a fabulous range of "**micro-brewed**" beers, the product of a wave of backyard and in-house operations that has matured to the point that many pump out over 150,000 barrels a year and are classified as "regional breweries." Head for one of these brewpubs and you'll find handcrafted beers such as crisp pilsners, wheat beers, and stouts on tap, at prices only marginally above those of the national brews.

Alternatively, you can always find a selection of **imported beers** from most anywhere. Expect to fork out $3–5 for a glass of draft beer, about the same for a bottle of imported beer. In all but the most high-end bars, several people can save money by buying a pitcher of beer for $6–10. Six-packs from a supermarket should run $6–11 for domestic and imported brews.

If you're partial to **wine**, you might choose to try lesser-known wines found in the region, for example from Connecticut's Wine Trail. Otherwise, you'll find a wide variety available most everywhere, hailing from both the US and abroad. A decent glass of wine in a bar or restaurant costs about $5, a bottle $18–30 (though of course a particularly accliamed vintage can set you back much more). Buying from a supermarket or liquor store is cheaper – a quality bottle can be purchased for as little as $7.

Cocktails are extremely popular, especially during happy hours (usually any time between 5pm and 7pm) when drinks are discounted, sometimes half-price, sometimes two-for-one, and there's occasionally free food laid on as well. Cocktail varieties are innumerable, sometimes specific to a single bar or cocktail lounge, and they cost anywhere between $3 and $10.

An alternative to drinking dens, **coffee-shops** play a vibrant part in New England's social scene, and are havens of high-quality coffee far removed from the stuff served in diners and convenience stores. It's worth looking beyond the ubiquitous *Starbucks* to smaller, local joints, where the ambience will be more enjoyable and the coffee most likely much better. In larger towns and cities, cafés will boast of the quality of the roast, and offer specialties such as espresso with lemon peel as well as a full array of cappuccinos, lattes, and the like, served straight, iced, organic, or flavored with syrups. Herbal teas and light snacks are often on the menu, too.

Communications

Staying in touch with friends and family back home won't be a problem in New England. Virtually every hotel room comes equipped with a phone (though these can be expensive to use), public pay phones are widespread, and public libraries will allow you to check your email for free. You can buy stamps at multiple regional post offices, and mailboxes are easy to find.

Mail

Post offices are usually open Monday through Friday from about 9am to 5pm, and in some cases on Saturday from 9am to noon; there are also **blue mailboxes** on many street corners, into which you can deposit already-stamped mail – just be sure you apply the right amount of postage, or your letter will be returned to you.

Ordinary mail within the US costs 37¢ for

New England state abbreviations

Connecticut: CT
Maine: ME
Massachusetts: MA
New Hampshire: NH
Rhode Island: RI
Vermont: VT

a letter weighing up to an ounce; addresses must include the zip code (postal code), and a return address should be written on the upper left corner of the envelope; postcards cost 23¢ to mail. **Air mail** between New England and Europe generally takes about a week to arrive. Aerograms and international postcards cost 70¢, while letters weighing up to one ounce cost 80¢.

Letters can be sent **c/o General Delivery** (what's known elsewhere as *poste restante*) to any post office in each state, but must include that post office's zip code and will only be held for thirty days before being returned to sender – so make sure there's a return address on the envelope. If you're receiving mail at someone else's address, it should include "c/o" and the regular occupant's name, or it is likely to be returned.

Note that if you want to send any **parcels** out of the country, you'll need a green customs declaration form, available from post offices.

Telephones

New England has several telephone area codes (see overleaf); simply dial 1 + area code + seven-digit number to reach a specific town or city from elsewhere in the US or Canada; from abroad, dial your country's international access code, then 1 + area code and the seven-digit number.

Local calls range from 25¢ to 75¢ in coin-operated public phones, which accept denominations of 5¢, 10¢, and 25¢; when making a local call in eastern Massachusetts cities, dial all ten digits, including the area code. Operator assistance (Ⓣ0) and directory information (Ⓣ411) are toll-free from public telephones, though not from in-room hotel phones.

Phoning home

With respect to calling abroad from the US, you've got several options, the most convenient of which is using your **credit card** – most pay phones now accept them. A cheaper option is using a **prepaid phone card**, sold at many convenience stores in denominations of $5 and $10. You'll find a phone number and special PIN number on the back – just dial the number, enter the PIN, and compose the number you're trying to reach (see below).

More expensive is using a **telephone charge card** from your phone company back home that will charge the call to your home account. Since most major charge cards are free to obtain, it's certainly worth getting one at least for emergencies, but bear in mind that rates aren't necessarily cheaper than calling from a public phone with a calling card; in fact, they may well be more expensive.

If all else fails, you can call **collect** by dialing Ⓣ0, and then the number you wish to reach; the operator will take it from there. Otherwise, Ⓣ1-800/COLLECT and Ⓣ1-800/CALL-ATT both claim (vehemently) to have the cheapest collect calling options.

Mobile phones

If you're from overseas and you want to use your **mobile phone** in New England, you'll need to check with your phone provider whether it will work abroad, and what the call charges are. Only phones with SIM cards are likely to work in the US, through the T-Mobile network (Ⓦwww.tmobile.com).

In the UK, for all but the very top-of-the-range packages, you'll have to inform your phone provider before going abroad to get international access switched on. You may get charged extra for this, depending on your existing package and where you are traveling. You're also likely to be charged extra for incoming calls when abroad, as the people calling you will be paying the usual rate. If you want to retrieve messages while you're away, you'll have to ask your provider for a new access code, as your home one is unlikely to work abroad. For further information about using your phone abroad, check out Ⓦwww.telecomsadvice.org.uk/features/using_your_mobile_abroad.htm.

Useful phone numbers and codes

Emergencies and information

Emergencies ⓣ911; ask for the appropriate emergency service: fire, police, or ambulance.
Directory information ⓣ411
Directory inquiries for toll-free numbers ⓣ1-800/555-1212
Long-distance directory information ⓣ1-(area code)/555-1212
Operator ⓣ0

New England area codes

Connecticut northern Connecticut t860/959; southern Connecticut ⓣ203
Maine ⓣ207
Massachusetts Boston ⓣ617/857; suburban Boston ⓣ781/339; Cape Cod ⓣ508/774; northern MA ⓣ978/351; western MA ⓣ413
New Hampshire ⓣ603
Rhode Island ⓣ401
Vermont ⓣ802

International calling codes

Calling TO New England from abroad your country's international access code + 1 + area code + seven-digit number
Calling FROM New England
To Australia ⓣ011 + 61 + city code
To Canada ⓣ1 + area code
To New Zealand ⓣ011 + 64 + city code
To the Republic of Ireland ⓣ011 + 353 + city code
To the UK and Northern Ireland ⓣ011 + 44 + city code (minus the initial zero)

Email

Public Internet access in New England is still mostly the reserve of public libraries and universities – there are very few designated Internet cafés, since most people have service at home. That said, every major city will have one or two Internet cafés, as well as a 24-hour Kinkos copy shop, which usually provides Internet access for around 30¢ a minute. While libraries and universities have more limited hours (usually Mon–Fri 9am–5pm, Sat 10am–noon, closed Sun) and time constraints (around 15min per person), their major advantage is that the service is free to everyone.

The media

Despite its legacy as the birthplace of America's first newspaper, *Publick Occurences*, which was published in Boston in 1690, New England hardly ranks among the country's most media-savvy regions today. You'll find local listings in slew of leftist weeklies, while the local paper of record is the *New York Times*-owned *Boston Globe* (ⓦwww.boston.com/globe).

Newspapers

Boston's oldest **newspaper**, the *Boston Globe* (50¢) remains the region's best general daily; its fat Sunday edition ($2) includes substantial sections on art, culture, and lifestyle. The *Boston Herald* (50¢; ⓦwww.bostonherald.com) is the *Globe*'s conservative tabloid competitor and is best for getting your gossip and local sports coverage fix. The two stalwarts are complemented by smaller papers like the *Hartford Courant* (ⓦwww.courant.com), the *Bangor Daily News* (ⓦwww.bangornews.com), and the *Providence Journal* (ⓦwww.projo.com), which tend to excel at local coverage, but typically rely on agencies such as the Associated Press (AP) for foreign and even national news stories.

Every community of any size also has at least a few **free newspapers**, found in distribution bins, cafés, bars, or just lying around in piles. It's a good idea to pick up a full assortment: some simply cover local goings-on, while others provide specialist coverage of interests ranging from long-distance cycling to getting ahead in business – and the classified and personal ads can provide hours of entertainment. Many of them are also excellent sources of **listings** information; we've mentioned the most useful titles where relevant throughout this guide.

Overall, New England's news coverage is parochial at best; you can get your international fix by stopping by a larger newsstand or library, where you'll find the *New York Times* and magazines like *The Economist*.

TV and radio

New England **TV** is pretty much the standard network barrage of sitcoms, newscasts, and talk shows found all over the US, though PBS, the national public television station, broadcasts a steady stream of interesting documentaries, informative (if slightly dry) news programs, and educational children's television. **Cable television** is ubiquitous, and with an ever-increasing number of channels, there's bound to be something on of at least marginal interest. That said, the major networks will likely carry everything you need or want to see: you'll be able to catch regular **news**, as well as keep abreast of your favorite dramas and sitcoms from the comfort of your hotel room.

Radio stations are also abundant, and run up and down both the FM and AM dials; the latter is strong on news and talk, while the former carries some of the region's best stations, including National Public Radio (NPR) and college broadcasts of jazz, classical, world music, and other genres neglected by mainstream radio; all of these can be found between 88 and 92 FM.

Public holidays, festivals, and opening hours

Someone, somewhere is always celebrating something in New England, although, apart from national holidays, few festivities are shared throughout the entire region. Instead, there is a disparate multitude of local events: arts-and-crafts shows, county fairs, ethnic celebrations, music festivals, parades, and many others of every hue and shade. New England tourist offices can provide full lists, or you can just phone ahead to the visitors' center in a particular region to ask what's coming up. The calendar below provides a good overview of unusual or particularly worthwhile area festivals.

Public holidays

The biggest and most all-American of the national holidays is **Independence Day** on July 4, when the entire country grinds to a standstill as people get drunk, salute the flag, and take part in fireworks displays, parades, beauty pageants, and more, all in commemoration of the signing of the Declaration of Independence in 1776. **Halloween** (October 31) lacks any such patriotic overtones, and is not a public holiday despite being one of the most popular yearly flings. Traditionally, costumed kids run around the streets banging on doors demanding "trick or treat," and receiving pieces of candy. These days that sort of activity is mostly confined to rural and suburban areas, while in bigger cities Halloween has grown into a massive drunken celebration of the macabre. More sedate is **Thanksgiving Day**, on the fourth Thursday in November, essentially a domestic affair, when relatives return to the familial nest to stuff themselves with roast turkey, and (supposedly) fondly recall the first harvest of the Pilgrims in Massachusetts – though in fact Thanksgiving was already a national holiday before anyone thought to make that connection.

On the national, or federal, **public holidays** listed below, banks and offices (and many shops) are liable to be **closed** all day. Many states also have their own additional holidays, and in some places Good Friday is a half-day holiday. The traditional summer season for tourism runs from Memorial Day to Labor Day, and some tourist attractions are only open during that period.

Jan 1 New Year's Day
Third Mon in Jan Martin Luther King Jr's Birthday
Third Mon in Feb Presidents' Day
Late March/April (varies) Good Friday
Last Mon in May Memorial Day
July 4 Independence Day
First Mon in Sept Labor Day
Second Mon in Oct Columbus Day
Nov 11 Veterans' Day
Fourth Thurs in Nov Thanksgiving Day
Dec 25 Christmas Day

Opening hours

Shops and services are generally open Monday to Saturday from 8 or 9am until 5 or 6pm. Many stores are also open on Sundays, and larger towns and cities will invariably have 24-hour supermarkets and pharmacies. For banking and post office hours, see pp.41 and 54 respectively.

Festivals and events

January

Stowe Winter Carnival Stowe, VT, third week; ⓣ1-800/247-8693, ⓦwww.stowecarnival.com. Hard-partying celebration of all things winter – also includes movie nights, church dinners, and a snow volleyball tournament.

February

Railroad Show West Springfield, MA, first weekend (or last weekend in Jan); ⓣ413/436-0242, ⓦ www.amherstrail.org/show. An extravaganza of trains, both model and real.

Winter Festival Newport, RI, second week; ⓣ401/847-9000, ⓦwww.newportevents.com. Discounts at area shops and restaurants with the purchase of a festival button, plus hayrides and ice sculpting.

February–March

Winter Carnival Jackson, NH, last week in Feb and first week in March; ⓦwww.mwvevents.com. Ice sculptures, sleigh rides, and Nordic skiing.

Mardi Gras Bretton Woods, NH, weekend before Ash Wednesday; ⓣ1-800/258-0330. A masquerade ball held in the historic *Mount Washington Hotel* (see p.512) is the apex of this traditional celebration including beads, bands, and a King Cake.

Saints and Spirits Celebration Rockport/ Camden, ME, mid-March; ⓣ207/236-4404). St Patrick's Day parties and Irish singalongs meant to dispel the "mud season blues."

April

Boston Marathon Boston, MA, third Mon; ⓣ617/236-1652, ⓦwww.bostonmarathon.org. Perhaps the premier running event in the US.

Vermont Maple Festival St Albans, VT, last full weekend; ⓣ802/524-5800, ⓦwww.vtmaplefestival.org. Maple exhibits/demonstrations, food contests, and, of course, pancake breakfasts.

May

Moose Mainea Greenville, ME, mid-May to mid-June; ⓣ207/695-2702. Moose-watching, boat and bike races, and family activities.

Open Studios VT (statewide), last weekend; ⓣ802/223-3380. Artists open their homes and studios to the public.

June

Ethan Allen Days Sunderland, VT, mid-month; ⓣ802/375-2800. Revolutionary battle enactments along Vermont's Ethan Allen Highway (Rte-7A).

Revels North Norwich, VT, late June; ⓦwww.revelsnorth.org/summer.html. Music, food, and puppets from 5pm until dark on the Sat closest to the longest day of the year.

July

Fourth of July Celebration Boston, MA ⓣ1-888/484-7677, ⓦwww.july4th.org. Boston holds the largest Fourth of July celebration in the country. The main attraction is a concert by the Boston Pops at the Hatch Shell that is accompanied by an impressive fireworks display. People arrive early in the morning, or even the night before to get prime seats for the concert, while others line up in boats along the Charles River. The Pops perform an identical program (minus the fireworks and the 1812 Overture) on the evening of July 3.

Fourth of July Celebration Bristol, RI ⓦwww.july4thbristolri.com. The small seaside town of Bristol operates the oldest Fourth of July festival in the country, including an impressive parade, fireworks, and weeks of events leading up to the occasion. Crowds here, though large, are nothing compared to those in Boston.

Moxie Festival Lisbon Falls, ME, mid-month; ⓣ207/783-2249, ⓦwww.moxiefestival.com. Activities and entertainment in celebration of an odd-tasting soda in a bright orange can.

Revolutionary War Festival Exeter, NH, mid-month; ⓦwww.independencemuseum.org. Mock battles (by local militia buffs) are waged, while costumed locals wander the town.

Folk Festival Lowell, MA, last weekend; ⓦwww.lowellfolkfestival.org. Traditional music and dance on six outdoor stages, plus food, parades, and crafts.

August

Maine Lobster Festival Rockland, ME, first weekend; ⓣ207/596-0376, ⓦwww.mainelobsterfestival.com. Features eight tons of boiled lobster.

Newport Folk Festival Newport, RI, early Aug; ⓦwww.newportfolk.com. This three-day festival has been drawing big names since 1959 – it's where Bob Dylan first caused an outrage by going electric. Get tickets in advance, as it's a summer staple for many music lovers around the country.

Narragansett Powwow Charlestown, RI, second weekend; ⓣ401/364-1100. Native American dancing, music, crafts, and food festival.

Crane Beach Sand Blast Ipswich, MA, late Aug; ⓣ978/356-4351. Sandcastle-building contest.

Union Fair and Blueberry Festival Union, ME, mid-month; ⓦwww.union-fair.com. One of the oldest traditional fairs in the state, with music, rides, barnyard animals, and blueberry pies.

September

Windjammer Weekend Camden, ME, first weekend; ⓣ207/236-4404, ⓦwww.windjammerweekend.com. Maine's largest windjammer gathering, with boat parade, fireworks, contests, and concerts, set in Camden's beautiful harbor.

Oyster Festival Norwalk, CT, second weekend; ⓣ203/838-9444. Seaport Association extravaganza, featuring tall ships, a juried craft show, and oysters every which way.

World's Fair Tunbridge, VT, second weekend; ⓣ802/889-5555, ⓦwww.tunbridgefair.com. Agricultural fair with butter-churning, cheesemaking, sheepshearing, and the like.

October

Renaissance Faire Woodstock, CT, last weekend in Sept and first two weekends in Oct, including Columbus Day; ⓣ860/928-0600, ⓦwww.ctfair.com. King Arthur comes to Connecticut, with a small realm of archers, merchants, elves, and court entertainers.

Cranberry Harvest Celebration Wareham, MA, first weekend; wwww.cranberries.org. A free harvest festival that includes helicopter rides over the flooded red fields of berries ($25), harvest tours, and cooking demonstrations.

Head of the Charles Regatta Cambridge, MA, mid-month; ⓣ617/868-6200, ⓦwww.hocr.org. One of the largest racing shell events in the world, with over six hundred teams participating.

Haunted Happenings Salem, MA, late Oct; ⓦwww.hauntedhappenings.org. Learn to cast spells and visit haunted houses in the days leading up to Halloween.

Wellfleet OysterFest Wellfleet, MA, second weekend; ⓦwww.wellfleetoysterfest.org. Run by SPAT, the Cape Cod -ased Shellfish Promotion and Tasting organization, this weekend includes concerts, art fairs, shellfish education and tasting, and – strangely enough – a spelling bee.

November

Antiquarian Book Fair Boston, MA, mid-month; ⓦwww.bostonbookfair.com. Tons of old books on display and for sale, plus author panels and signings.

Victorian Holiday Portland, ME, weekend after Thanksgiving; ⓣ207/772-6828. Horse-drawn carriages and Victorian garb abound.

December

Christmas Town Festival Bethlehem, CT, first weekend; ⓣ203/266-5557. Caroling, crafts, and the lighting of the town tree by Santa himself.

Christmas in Newport Bethlehem, RI, month-long; ⓣ401/849-6454, ⓦwww.christmasinnewport.org. Events all over town including concerts, make-your-own-gifts workshops, "The Nutcracker," and the Santa Train.

First Night various cities, Dec 31. In order to stave off drunkenness and hysteria in the streets, many New England cities host First Night festivals on New Year's Eve, lasting generally all day and into the night. A button will grant you admission into venues throughout the town that will have concerts and activities that provide a more cultured alternative to the local pub. Check local papers or call city councils for details.

Sports and outdoor activities

Boston is the only city in New England with major professional sports teams; excepting football, they have one team in each of the primary sports – baseball, hockey, and basketball. The region's only professional football team is based slightly afield, in Foxboro, MA. Until a few years ago New England residents could do very little but complain about their local teams – the New England Patriots (football) had never won a Super Bowl, and their beloved Boston Red Sox (baseball) had not won a World Series since 1918. All that has changed now – the Sox won their first Series in 86 years in 2004, while the Patriots have seemed nearly unstoppable, winning the 2002, 2004, and 2005 Super Bowls. There's not a lot of happy news for New England's two other professional teams, however – the Boston Celtics (basketball) and the Boston Bruins (hockey). As for outdoor pursuits, there's plenty to keep you out of breath: the most popular activities include skiing and snowboarding, hiking, and fishing and hunting.

Football

Football in America attracts the most obsessive and devoted fans of any sport, perhaps because there are fewer games played – only sixteen per team in a season, which lasts through the fall and into midwinter. With many quick skirmishes and military-like movements up and down the field, the game is ideal for television, and nowhere is this more apparent than during the televised games, which are a feature of many bars on Monday nights – though most games are played on Sundays.

The game lasts for four fifteen-minute quarters, with a fifteen-minute break at half-time. But since time is only counted when play is in progress, matches can take up to three hours to complete, mainly due to interruptions for TV advertising. Commentators will discuss the game throughout to help your comprehension, though they use such a barrage of statistics to illustrate their remarks that you may feel hopelessly confused. Not that it matters – the spectacle of American football is fun to experience even if you haven't a clue what's going on. The best players (or the flashiest, most obnoxious ones) become nationally known celebrities, raking in (on top of astronomical salaries) millions of dollars in fees for product endorsements.

Teams and tickets

All major teams play in the **National Football League** (NFL), the sport's governing body, which divides the teams into two conferences of equal stature, the National Football Conference (NFC) and the American Football Conference (AFC). The football season begins in late summer and lasts through the end of January. **Tickets** for New England's only team, the Patriots, who play at Gillette Stadium in Foxboro, MA (ⓣ1-800/543-1776, ⓦwww.gillettestadium.com), cost $20–80, but it is nearly impossible to get one: home games have been sold out for years, and are already pre-sold for years to come. When they are available, ticket sales are handled by Ticketmaster (ⓣ617/931-2000, ⓦwww.ticketmaster.com); for more current **information**, call or visit the Patriots' website (ⓣ508/543-1776, ⓦwww.patriots.com). If you're desperate to see a live game, you can always try to buy tickets from a scalper outside of the stadium on game day – though be aware that you're sure to pay very inflated prices, and that buying tickets from a scalper is technically illegal.

Baseball

Baseball, much like cricket in its relaxed, summertime pace and seemingly Byzantine rules, is often called "America's pastime," though its image has been tarnished by numerous bitter strikes by players – one of which shortened the 1994 season and saw the unthinkable canceling of the World Series. Games are played, 162 each full season, all over the US almost every day from April to September, with the league championships and the World Series, the final best-of-seven playoff, lasting through October. Watching a game, even if you don't understand what's going on, can be at the least a pleasant day out, drinking beer and eating hot dogs; in the unshaded bleachers beyond the outfield, tickets are comparatively cheap ($18–20) and the crowds usually friendly and sociable.

Teams and tickets

All Major League baseball teams play in either the **National League** or the **American League**, each split into three divisions, East, Central, and West. For the end-of-season playoffs and the World Series, the best team in each of the six divisions, plus a second-place wildcard from each league, fight it out for the title. New England's Major League team is the **Boston Red Sox**. The Sox's two "farm teams" – minor league clubs that are training grounds for future baseball stars – are also located in New England. The Pawtucket Red Sox (known as the Pawsox) play just minutes from Providence, RI, while the Portland Sea Dogs are based out of Maine. Tickets to farm team games are almost never sold out, and are much cheaper than Major League games, around $15 or so, leaving more money to spend on beer. **Tickets** to see the Red Sox (ⓣ617/267-9440, ⓦwww.redsox.com) cost $20–75 per seat but are often sold out, especially when playing their hated rivals the New York Yankees. Scalped tickets are usually readily available outside the stadium, though you'll pay through the nose.

Basketball

Basketball is one of the few professional sports that is also actually played by many ordinary Americans, since all you need is a ball and a hoop. The professional game is played by athletes of phenomenal agility, seven-foot-tall giants who float through the air over a wall of equally tall defenders, seeming to change direction in mid-flight before slam-dunking the ball to score two points. Games last for an exhausting 48 minutes of play time, around two hours total from start to finish.

Teams and tickets

New England's basketball team, the **Boston Celtics** (ⓣ617/523-6050, ⓦwww.nba.com/celtics), have been struggling ever since their domination ended in the late 1980s, when Larry Bird and company parted ways. Call Ticketmaster (ⓣ617/931-2000, ⓦwww.ticketmaster.com) for available seating and pricing ($10–85). On the college level, the University of Connecticut, the University of Massachusetts, and Providence University all field perpetually competitive teams. Additionally, in recent years quite a lot of buzz has been generated around the University of Connecticut **women's basketball** team, the Huskies, who were the 2000, 2002, and 2004 NCAA (National Collegiate Athletic Association) champions. **Tickets** cost $5–25 for college games. Call each school's athletic department for game and ticket info: UConn ⓣ1-877/288-2666; UMass ⓣ413/545-0810; Providence ⓣ401/865-4672.

Ice hockey

Ice hockey is popular in New England, not least because the cold winter weather is so conducive to the sport. Many children grow up playing it and go on to compete at the area's highly competitive colleges and universities; a very small percentage go on to play in the professional **National Hockey League** (NHL) team, the **Boston Bruins**. Though hockey enjoys some popularity in New England, it is a much less popular, and therefore profitable, sport throughout the country than other professional sports. None of this was helped when the 2004 season was scrapped entirely due to stalled salary negotiations. The two sides eventually reached an agreement and got back on the ice for the 2005–2006 season, though it remains to be seen whether or not national professional hockey will ever fully recover in the US.

Teams and tickets

New England has one NHL team, the **Boston Bruins** (ⓦwww.bostonbruins.com), which manages to draw a considerable crowd, and games are fun to watch if only for the possibility that a fight will break out on the ice. **Tickets** start at about $25. Call Ticketmaster (☎617/931-2000) for more information.

Skiing and snowboarding

Skiing and **snowboarding** are the biggest mass-market participant sports, with downhill resorts all over northeastern New England, where it snows heavily most winters. In fact, the mountains that cap the northern ends of Maine, New Hampshire, and Vermont offer the best skiing in the eastern US. Bigger resorts are more expensive, but they also have the best snow-making facilities, making skiing possible even in cold but dry winters. In **Maine,** Sugarloaf and Sunday River are good spots, while **Vermont**'s best are Killington, Mount Snow, Stowe, Stratton, and Okemo. Though **New Hampshire**'s mountains are less tall and steep, you can still get a good day of skiing in at Waterville Valley or Attitash. Smaller mountains can be great learning spots, and are often less crowded. You can **rent** equipment for about $50 a weekend, and lift tickets for the best locations top out at around $60 a day.

The Internet is a great source for additional **information**: each state detailed above has its own website with links to mountains and weather reports (Ⓦwww.skimaine.com, Ⓦwww.skivermont.com, and Ⓦwww.skinh.com). A number of companies run all-inclusive ski trips (including transportation, lift tickets, equipment, and accommodation) from the larger cities. In addition to convenience, these outfits usually offer good deals. The best way to find out about these if you're already in a southerly city like Boston or Providence is to visit a ski equipment store. Hotels also offer all-in vacations, sometimes including lessons as well.

A cheaper alternative to downhill is **cross-country skiing**, or ski-touring. A number of backcountry ski lodges offer a range of rustic accommodation, equipment rental, and lessons, from as little as $20 a day for skis, boots, and poles, up to about $200 for an all-inclusive weekend tour. For additional information, consult Ⓦwww.nensa.net, an exhaustive reference pertaining to the sport in New England, with information on resorts, trail conditions, equipment, and ski shops.

Hiking

Hiking is huge, especially in the northern areas of New England, although you'll find good places to get out into nature just about anywhere outside of the main cities. Most state and federally operated parks maintain good networks of trails, not least the famous **Appalachian Trail**, which originates in Georgia and winds through the beautiful backcountry of New England before traversing New Hampshire's White Mountains and terminating in desolate northern Maine.

Wilderness areas start close to the main areas of national parks. There is normally no problem entering the wilderness for day walks, but overnight trips require **wilderness permits**. In peak periods, a quota system operates for the most popular paths, so if there's a hike you specifically want to do, obtain your permit well ahead of time (at least two weeks in advance, or more for popular hikes). When completing the form for your permit, be sure to ask a park ranger for weather conditions and general information about the hike you're undertaking.

The **Appalachian Mountain Club** (AMC; ☎617/523-0655, Ⓦwww.outdoors.org) offers a range of backcountry hikes into otherwise barely accessible parts of the wilderness, with food and guide provided. The hikes take place at all times of the year, cost anywhere from $50 to $800, last from a day to two weeks, and are heavily subscribed, making it essential to book well in advance. Club members pay around $20 less, though you'll also have to pay $50 to join. AMC also has some very well-maintained camping areas and mountain huts; call their headquarters in Boston (see number above) for information on how to make reservations.

Hikes covered in the *Guide* are given with length and estimated walking time for a healthy but not especially fit adult. State parks have many graded trails designed for people who drive to the corner store, so anyone used to walking and with a moderate degree of fitness will find these ratings very conservative.

Hunting and fishing

Hunting and **fishing** are two of the most popular outdoor pursuits in New England, although the more physically challenging hiking, mountain-biking, and kayaking all fall right behind. Duck, deer, and sometimes even the mighty moose are all popular targets, though hunting laws are strict and you'll need a **permit** (ask the local chamber of commerce how you can get one) before you start dropping victims in the forest. Streams, lakes, ponds, and rivers fill up with fishermen (and women) in season, though, as with hunting, permits are required and laws are strict. Trout and salmon are found in most bodies of fresh water.

Backcountry camping and wildlife

New England has some fabulous backcountry and wilderness areas, coated by dense forests, splashed with sparkling lakes, and capped by monumental mountains. Unfortunately, while still immensely rewarding – and it's one of the compelling reasons for coming to New England – it isn't all as wild as it once was, thanks to the thousands who tramp through each year. If you're intending to do the same, you can help preserve the special qualities of the environment by observing a few simple rules. For practical information on traveling through the forest, see the box overleaf.

The protected backcountry areas in the US fall into a number of potentially confusing categories. Most numerous are **state parks**, owned and operated by the individual states. They include state beaches, state historic parks, and state recreational areas, often around sites of geological or historical importance and not necessarily in rural areas. Daily **fees** are usually less than $5, though beaches in high season can charge as much as $20 per carload; a $40–75 annual pass gives free access to most sites for a year.

Acadia National Park in Maine (Ⓦwww.nps.gov/acad/home.htm; see p.578), a large, preserved area of great natural beauty, is the only national park in New England; entry is $5 for one person on bicycle or motorbike, or $20 for up to four in a car. Excellent free ranger programs – such as guided walks or slide shows – are held throughout the year. The federal government also operates national recreation areas. Campgrounds and equipment-rental outlets are available, though not always in adequate numbers.

Essential camping equipment

Many campgrounds are on rock with only a thin covering of soil, so driving pegs in can be a problem; freestanding dome-style tents are therefore preferable. Go for one with a large area of mosquito netting and a removable fly sheet: tents designed for harsh European winters can get horribly sweaty once the sun rises, unless, of course, you're camping in the winter.

Most developed campgrounds are equipped with fire rings with some form of grill for cooking, but many people prefer a Coleman stove, powered by white gas, a kind of super-clean gasoline. Both stoves and white gas are widely available in camping stores. Other camping stoves are less common. Equipment using butane and propane – Camping Gaz and, to a lesser extent, EPI gas, Scorpion, and Optimus – is on the rise, though outside of major camping areas you'll be pushed to find supplies, so stock up when you can.

Backcountry dangers and wildlife

You're likely to meet many kinds of **wildlife** and come upon unexpected **hazards** if you head into the wilderness, but with due care, many potential difficulties can be avoided.

Bugs and pests

Hiking in the foothills should not be problematic but you should check your clothes frequently for **ticks** – pesky, blood-sucking, burrowing insects which are known to carry **Lyme disease**, a health hazard especially in southern New England (it's named after a town in Connecticut). One early sign of Lyme disease is a bull's-eye rash that forms around a bite – if you develop one of these, seek treatment immediately. Less harmful but more prevalent are **mosquitoes**; bring along insect repellent to keep them at bay. **Black flies** also come out in force in the warm summer months, and, with a tenacious appetite for human heads, ears, and faces, and a perpetual buzz, can be tremendously annoying; again, carry insect repellent.

Bears

You're highly unlikely to encounter a **bear** in New England, though the American black bear is native to the region, and prevalent in the northern wilderness areas. To reduce whatever likelihood there is of running into one, make noise (carrying bells in your pack isn't a bad idea) as you walk. If you do come across a bear, keep calm, and make sure it is aware of your presence by clapping, talking, or making other sounds. Black bears may **charge** with no intention of attacking when attempting to steal food or if they feel threatened. If you are so unlucky, don't run, just slowly back away.

If a bear visits your camp, it will be after your food, which should be stored in airtight containers. Some campgrounds are equipped with bear-proof lockers, which you are obliged to use to store food when not preparing or eating it. Elsewhere, you should hang both food and garbage from a high branch some distance from your camp. **Never feed a bear**: it will make the bear dependent on humans for food and increase the risk of attacks on humans in the future. Bears within state and national parks are protected, but if they spend too much time around people the park rangers are, depressingly, left with no option but to shoot them.

New England's two **national forests**, the Green Mountain National Forest in Vermont (see p.401) and the White Mountain National Forest in New Hampshire (see p.501), are huge, covering fifty percent of all public land in Vermont and an area larger than the state of Rhode Island in New Hampshire. They are federally administered by the US Forest Service (www.fs.fed.us), but with much less protection than national parks. More roads run through national forests, and often there is some limited logging and other land-based industry operated on a sustainable basis.

All the above forms of protected land can contain **wilderness areas**, which aim to protect natural resources in their most native state. In practice this means there's no commercial activity at all; buildings, motorized vehicles, and bicycles are not permitted, nor are firearms and pets. Overnight camping is allowed, but wilderness permits (free to $5) must be obtained in advance from the land management agency responsible. In New England, the White and Green mountains both have large wilderness areas, with only the regions near roads, visitors' centers, and buildings designated as less stringently regulated "front country."

When camping rough, check that **fires** are permitted before you start one; if they are, use a stove in preference to local materials – in some places firewood is scarce, although you may be allowed to use deadwood. No open fires are allowed in wilderness areas, where you should also try to camp on previously used sites. Where there are no toilets, bury human waste at least four inches into the ground and a hundred feet from the nearest water supply and camp. Always carry away your **trash**.

Moose

Moose, which live in the lush, unpopulated regions near the Canadian border, seldom attack unless provoked. The largest member of the deer family, they can be up to nine feet tall and weigh as much as 1200 pounds, and look like badly drawn horses. They are mostly active at night, but can also be seen at dusk and dawn, when they may gather to feed near lakes and streams. Though they may seem slow, tame, and passive at first, moose can be unpredictable, especially during the mating season in September and October. If you happen upon one in the forest, move slowly, avoid making any loud noises, and keep your distance. The best place to view a moose is from your automobile, though you should be careful when driving along northern country roads – collisions are often fatal for the driver and car, if not the moose.

Poison ivy

Poison ivy is one thing that isn't going to come and get you, though you may come up against it, especially in the spring. Recognizable by its configuration of three leaves to a stem, poison ivy can be matte or shiny, green or, in the fall yellow and red. Plants can be low-growing or can climb as vines to surround trees, and both forms are found in open woods or along stream banks throughout much of New England. It's highly allergenic, so avoid touching it. If you do, washing with strong soap, taking frequent dips in the sea, and applying cortisone cream usually helps to relieve the symptoms; in extreme cases, see a doctor.

Avalanches and meltwaters

In the mountains, your biggest dangers have nothing to do with the flora or fauna. **Spring snows** are common, giving rise to the possibility of **avalanches** and **meltwaters**, which make otherwise simple stream-crossings hazardous. Drowning in fast-flowing meltwater rivers is one of the biggest causes of death in New England wilderness areas. The riverbanks are often strewn with large, slippery boulders, so keep clear unless you are there for river activities. Sudden changes in the weather are also common in mountainous regions, when temperatures can fluctuate wildly and high winds and storms appear out of nowhere; be sure to have warm clothing with you at all times, and check with park rangers before long backcountry treks.

One potential problem while camping is **giardia**, a water-borne protozoan causing an intestinal disease, symptoms of which are chronic diarrhea, abdominal cramps, fatigue, and loss of weight; if you contract it, you will require treatment. To avoid catching it, **never drink** from rivers and streams, however clear and inviting they may look (you never know what unspeakable acts people – or animals – further upstream have performed in them). Water that isn't from taps should be boiled for at least five minutes, or cleansed with an iodine-based purifier (such as Potable Aqua) or a giardia-rated filter, available from camping or sports stores. Finally, don't use ordinary **soaps** or detergents in lakes and streams; you can buy special ecological soap for washing needs.

Crime and personal safety

New England is one of the safest regions in the US, and you're unlikely to incur great risks traveling in any one of its six states. While it pays to be cautious, especially in big cities such as Boston or Hartford, or on lonely country roads, the region is pretty unmenacing. Driving during the harsh winter months in the northern and mountain areas is perhaps the biggest threat to your personal safety, and extreme care should be taken if you'll be making such trips.

Avoiding crime

All over New England, **crime** has been on the decline since the early 1990s. Even in built-up urban centers where theft and assaults do occur on a somewhat regular basis (namely Boston and the region's other larger cities), tourists are seldom involved or targeted.

In the more risky areas, common sense and a certain degree of caution should be enough to avoid most problems. For instance, seek local advice before exploring unfamiliar and run-down parts of a city, avoid walking along deserted streets at night, leave valuables in hotel safes, don't leave luggage clearly visible in cars (especially rental cars), don't resist violent theft, and beware of various tourist scams. One such scam, by no means restricted to tourists (and, for that matter, by no means restricted to New England) is known as "bump and rob." The thief bumps his (usually stolen) car into the back of another, and when the victim gets out to inspect the damage and swap insurance details, the thief drives away in the unoccupied car. Therefore, if you are bumped from behind, indicate to the other driver to follow you to a well-lit, public place before thinking about leaving your vehicle.

The **emergency number** for police is ⓣ911; phone numbers for lost or stolen credit cards, travelers' checks, and the like can be found on p.41.

Winter driving

Driving in the **winter** is actually less perilous than some may expect. The northerly states that get the most snow – New Hampshire, Vermont, and Maine – have truly excellent road care. They've learned to take care of their roads efficiently so that residents can drive to work and school all winter long. As long as you don't drive *during* a snowstorm and take care in the mountains, there's not a lot to worry about. Massachusetts, Connecticut, and Rhode Island, however, are another matter. Although these states receive far less snow, they are also less equipped to handle it. Be prepared for ice on the roads and highways, poorly ploughed back streets, and parking bans in cities when there's snow.

In general, during New England winters it's smart to check road and weather conditions before setting out and keep your gas tank two-thirds full to prevent the vehicle's fuel line from freezing. Automobiles that run on **diesel fuel** are especially testy in cold weather – most gas stations will sell single-use bottles of diesel fuel treatment to add to a full tank to make the car start up more easily. It's also a good idea to bring along a **mobile phone** in case of emergency, though you shouldn't be over-dependent on it: consider carrying an **emergency car-care kit** on trips in difficult weather conditions. Such a kit typically contains antifreeze, windshield washer fluid, shovel, ice scraper, jumper cables, flares or reflectors, blankets, non-perishable food, and a first-aid kit. Lastly, there are **emergency phones** stationed along freeways at regular intervals, though you won't find these on quieter roads.

Travelers with disabilities

Travelers with mobility problems or other physical disabilities are likely to find New England – as with the US in general – to be much more in tune with their needs than anywhere else in the world, thanks in part to the 1990 Americans with Disabilities Act (ADA). All public buildings must be wheelchair-accessible and have suitable toilets; most city street corners have dropped curbs; subways have elevators; and most city buses are able to kneel to make access easier and are built with space and handgrips for wheelchair users. Most hotels, restaurants, and theaters (certainly any built in the last ten years or so) also generally have excellent wheelchair access. The golden rule when traveling with a disability is to plan well in advance. Most obstacles can usually be overcome – or avoided altogether – if you call 48 hours or so before your arrival at a bus or train station, airport, hotel, restaurant, park, or other such facility.

Contacts for disabled travelers

In the US and Canada

Access-Able Ⓦwww.access-able.com. Online resource for travelers with disabilities.
Mobility International USA Ⓣ541/343-1284, Ⓦwww.miusa.org. Information and referral services, access guides, tours, and exchange programs. Annual membership $35 (includes quarterly newsletter).
Society for the Accessible Travel and Hospitality (SATH) Ⓣ212/447-7284, Ⓦwww.sath.org. Non-profit educational organization which has actively represented travelers with disabilities since 1976.
Twin Peaks Press PO Box 129, Vancouver, WA 98666 Ⓣ1-800/637-2256. Publishes *Travel for the Disabled, Wheelchair Vagabond*, and *Directory of Travel Agencies* for the Disabled.
Wheels Up! Ⓣ1-888/389-4335, Ⓦwww.wheelsup.com. Provides discounted airfare, tour, and cruise prices for disabled travelers; also publishes a free monthly newsletter and has a comprehensive website.

In the UK and Ireland

Disability Action Group Belfast Ⓣ028/9029 7880, Ⓦwww.disabilityaction.org.
Irish Wheelchair Association Dublin Ⓣ01/818 6400, Ⓦwww.iwa.ie. Useful information provided about traveling abroad with a wheelchair.
Tripscope Bristol Ⓣ08457/585 641, Ⓦwww.tripscope.org.uk. National telephone information service offering free advice on transport and travel (helpline open Mon–Fri 9am–5pm). They provide information for the government-sponsored travel guide for disabled people, *Door to Door*, which can be accessed online at Ⓦwww.dptac.gov.uk/door-to-door.
Tourism for All Andover Ⓣ0845/124 9971, Ⓦwww.holidaycare.org.uk or Ⓦwww.tourismforall.info. Provides information on all aspects of travel for the disabled and elderly.

In Australia and New Zealand

ACROD (Australian Council for Rehabilitation of the Disabled) Ⓣ02/6283 3200, Ⓦwww.acrod.org.au. Lists of travel agencies and tour operators.
Disabled Persons Assembly Ⓣ04/801 9100, Ⓦwww.dpa.org.nz. New Zealand resource center with lists of travel agencies and tour operators for people with disabilities.

Getting there and around

Most **airlines**, transatlantic and within the US, do whatever they can to ease your journey, and will usually let attendants of people with serious disabilities accompany them at no extra charge. US carriers are not covered by the ADA, although the Air Carriers Access Act does contain a number of requirements pertaining to air travel for handicapped passengers. The Aviation Consumer Protection Division runs a hotline (Ⓣ1-800/778-4838) that is open for calls from 7am–11pm seven days a week to advise consumers of their rights and help with complaints, while their website (Ⓦairconsumer.ost.dot.gov) has a manual for air travelers with disabilities.

Almost every Amtrak **train** includes one or more coaches with accommodation for disabled passengers using wheelchairs. Guide dogs travel free, and Amtrak will provide wheelchair assistance at its train stations, adapted seating on board, and a fifteen percent discount on the regular fare, all provided 24 hours' notice is given.

Traveling by Greyhound or regional **buses** is more difficult for those with disabilities. Only occasionally are Greyhound buses equipped with lifts for wheelchairs, although every effort will be made to assist travelers with disabilities, especially if such assistance is requested 48 hours prior to departure. Contact the Greyhound Customers with Disabilities Travel Assistance Line on ⓣ1-800/752-4841 to mention specific travel needs. Under the PCA (Personal Care Attendant) Program, those traveling with disabled passengers in order to help them through their journey may be allowed to travel free of charge.

The major **car rental** firms can, given sufficient notice, provide vehicles with hand controls (though these are usually only available on the more expensive models). The American Automobile Association produces the *Disabled Driver's Mobility Guide* for drivers with disabilities, available free from the Highway Safety Division Manager, AAA, 815 Farmington Ave, West Hartford, CT 06119 (ⓣ860/236-3261).

As in other parts of the world, the rise of the **self-service gas station** is unwelcome for many disabled drivers. The states of New England have addressed this by changing its laws so that most service stations are required to provide full service to disabled drivers at self-service prices.

Local information

The state information centers (see p.37) all have **information** on handicapped facilities at places of accommodation and attractions. They should also be able to provide lists of wheelchair-accessible properties – hotels, motels, apartments, B&Bs, hostels, RV parks – in the cities and surrounding countryside, while some of the free tourist guides include accessibility ratings for accommodation. Even so, it's always a good idea to call the property in question to confirm details.

Accommodation

The big motel and hotel chains are often the best bet for **accessible accommodation**; there are plenty of excellent local alternatives, of course, but with a chain at least you'll know what to expect. The ADA obligated all hotels, motels, inns, and other places of lodging designed or constructed after 1993 to be usable by persons with disabilities, be they ambulatory handicaps or other disabilities such as blindness and deafness. This means that, theoretically at least, the newer accommodation should have features such as raised letter signs and cane-detectable warnings of safety hazards, easy-to-use heating, air-conditioning, and faucet controls, as well as ways of moving about the property without having to use steps or stairs. Even if a lodging is described as "accessible" in a brochure, however, always ask about the special facilities on offer before completing a reservation. Where large chains are involved, avoid calling the central reservations number; instead contact the property at which you intend to stay for the most accurate and detailed information about its accessibility.

The great outdoors

Most of the **handicapped sports associations** in New England are based around skiing, for the simple reason that skiing is adaptable to many types of disabilities. The New England Handicapped Sports Association is based at the Mount Sunapee ski area in New Hampshire (ⓣ1-800/628-4484, ⓦwww.nehsa.org) and has a few summer programs, as does Maine Handicapped Skiing (ⓣ207/824-2440, ⓦwww.skimhs.org). In addition to skiing, Vermont Adaptive Ski and Sports (ⓣ802/786-4991, ⓦwww.vermontadaptive.org) helps those with special needs participate in outdoor programs like hiking, sailing, horseback-riding, and canoeing. It runs individual and group programs at very reasonable prices.

Citizens or permanent residents of the US who have been "medically determined to be blind or permanently disabled" can obtain the **Golden Access Passport**. Each state also offers Disabled Discount Passes, which give similar concessions for state-run parks, beaches, and historic sites. Reduced rates are available for permanently disabled people who apply by mail ($3.50 once-only payment) to the relevant state's Department of Parks and Recreation Disabled Discount Pass Program.

Packages

Many US **tour operators** cater to disabled travelers or specialize in organizing disabled group tours. State tourist departments should be able to provide lists of such companies; failing that, ask the National Tour Association (Ⓣ1-800/682-8886, Ⓦwww.ntaonline.com), who can put you in touch with operators whose tours match your needs. Empress Travel and Cruises (Ⓣ1-800/533-5343, Ⓦwww.empressusa.com) specializes in bookings for people with disabilities, while The Guided Tour (Ⓣ215/782-1370 or 1-800/783-5841, Ⓦwww.guided-tour.com), places the emphasis on serving travelers with mental or developmental disabilities.

Senior travelers

For many senior citizens, retirement brings the opportunity to explore the world in a style and at a pace that is the envy of younger travelers. As well as the obvious advantages of being free to travel for longer periods during the quieter – and less expensive – seasons, anyone over the age of 62 (with suitable ID) can enjoy a tremendous variety of discounts. Amtrak, Greyhound, local buses, and many US airlines offer (smallish) percentage reductions on fares to older passengers. In addition, museums, art galleries, and even hotels offer small discounts, and since the definition of "senior" can drop to as low as 55, it is always worth asking.

In addition, any US citizen or permanent resident aged 62 or over is entitled to free admission to all national parks, monuments, and historic sites using a **Golden Age Passport**, for which a once-only fee of $10 is charged; it must be issued in person at any such site, and proof of age is required. This free entry also applies to any accompanying car passengers or, for those hiking or cycling, the passport-holder's spouse and children. It also gives a fifty percent reduction on fees for camping, parking, and boat launching. The individual states also offer senior citizen **discounts** on admission to state-run parks, beaches, and historic sites; these give $1 off parking and $2 off family camping in state-operated parks, except where the fee is less than $2. Finally, several states offer special senior citizen general discount passes – contact the relevant state's tourist information center for details (see p.37).

The **American Association of Retired Persons** (AARP; Ⓣ202/434-2277 or 1-800/424-3410, Ⓦwww.aarp.org), organizes group travel for senior citizens and can provide discounts on accommodation, car rental, air travel, and vacations with selected tour operators. Annual membership (which includes a subscription to their excellent *Modern Maturity* magazine for both North American and international members) is available to anyone over 50, costing $12.50 ($29.50 for three years) for US residents, $17 for Canadians, and $28 for those living in other countries.

There are a number of Boston-based **tour operators** specializing in vacations for seniors. Elderhostel, 11 Ave de Lafayette (Ⓣ1/877-426-8056, Ⓦwww.elderhostel.org), runs an extensive worldwide network of educational and activity programs for people over 55 (companions may be younger). Trips range anywhere from their Boston "Day of Discovery" ($89) to those that last a week or more, and costs are on the whole in line with those of commercial tours. There are numerous programs offered in New England, with themes ranging from brush painting in Massachusetts to sea-kayaking off the Maine coast. In the UK, Saga Holidays (Ⓣ0130/377 1111 or 0800/096 0078, Ⓦwww.saga.co.uk/travel) is the country's biggest and most established specialist in vacations aimed at older people. New England tours include most of the major sights, and are conducted during the popular "fall foliage" season.

Kids' New England

New England is a great place to bring the kids, as so many of the region's historical sights – ships, lighthouses, recreated colonial villages with character actors – are actually *more* fun with a wide-eyed youngster to show around. In addition, there are several zoos, aquariums, and children's museums in the area.

Check the *Yellow Pages* and you'll find that in addition to commercial attractions catering to children – mini-golf, water slides, arcades, and the like – many states also have apple **orchards** for picking in the fall and farms with strawberries and raspberries for picking in the spring and summer. All destination **ski areas** in New England have reputable and licensed ski schools for children that include lessons, lift tickets, and meals. Most restaurants offer children's menus and booster chairs, and all but the nicest boutique hotels are child-equipped and friendly.

In **Boston**, the Children's Museum (p.100), the Museum of Science (p.117), and the Aquarium (p.99) are all world-class sights geared towards children. In nearby Acton, the Discovery Museums (Ⓣ978/264-4200), Ⓦwww.discoverymuseums.org) are well worth a trip out of the way for a day with younger kids. In Connecticut the Mystic Seaport and Aquarium (p.33) and Dinosaur State Park (p.371) outstrip the area's museums in excitement for kids. One good resource is the Association for Children's Museums website (Ⓦwww.childrensmuseums.org), which has a state-by-state breakdown of museums for the kiddies.

Amusement parks in New England are not destination sights the way they are in Florida. The area does have a smattering of small-town carnivals, though these can be pretty seedy affairs; if the kids are clamoring for a roller-coaster, consider Six Flags New England (Ⓦwww.sixsflags.com), StoryLand in New Hampshire (p.516), or Funtown/Splashtown USA in Maine (Ⓦwww.funtownsplashtownusa.com) – though note that a day out at any of these parks can be fairly pricey.

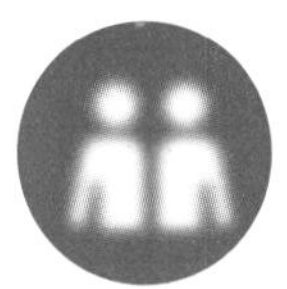

Gay and lesbian New England

Go to the right places, and New England can be a very enjoyable destination for gay and lesbian visitors. The region possesses some firm favorites on the gay North American travel circuit, and gay-friendly accommodations can be found dotted all over the region. However, go to the wrong places – mainly rural areas – and you will find that the narrow-minded attitudes of "small town America" are still alive and well. Be cautious, then, with open displays of affection and the like. As difficult and frustrating as this may be, it's usually the most effective way to keep the bigots at bay.

There are sizeable predominantly gay areas in almost all of the New England states. The **South End** of Boston is what Greenwich Village is to New York and the Marais is to Paris. Other "gay" cities in Massachusetts include **Provincetown**, one of the world's premier gay beach resorts, and **Northampton**, well known for its large lesbian community. Elsewhere, the Rhode Island city of **Providence**, although somewhat overshadowed by Boston, has a vibrant gay scene, while **Ogunquit** is the quieter, Maine-version of Provincetown. Indeed in **Maine**, where you would expect there to be a backcountry-fueled opposition to anything different, locals are so obsessed with living life their own way that gays and lesbians are enjoying more public acceptance. **Vermont** is notoriously liberal, while even traditionally conservative **New Hampshire** has recently joined other New England states in passing anti-discrimination laws. The latest show of acceptance was by the venerable *Boston Globe*, which started to include same-sex commitment ceremonies in the "Announcements" section of the paper a few years back.

Contact the International Gay & Lesbian Travel Association (ⓣ954/776-2626 or 1-800/448-8550, ⓦwww.iglta.org), for a list of gay- and lesbian-owned or -friendly **tour operators**. Meanwhile, gaytravel.com (ⓣ1-800/429-8728, ⓦwww.gaytravel.com) is a good online travel agency where you can make bookings and get help with travel planning.

Getting married

In July of 2000, **Vermont**, the state with the second-largest per capita lesbian population in the US, became the first state in the Union to legally recognize **civil unions** for same-sex couples. This groundbreaking move has made Vermont, always one of the country's more gay-friendly states, a prime destination for gay and lesbian couples looking to get married. Hotels, inns, and B&Bs have caught on to the trend, and have begun to offer their premises for civil wedding ceremonies. For more information on how to enter into a civil union in Vermont with your partner, call the Secretary of State's office on ⓣ1-802/828-2363; another good resource is ⓦwww.vermontgaytravel.com/guidelines.

A step further was taken in **Massachusetts**, when in May of 2004 it became the first state to recognize **gay marriages** (which differ from civil unions). Opponents of gay marriage in Massachusetts are trying to pass an amendment to the state constitution that would ban gay marriage, so keep an eye on developments. For more information see ⓦwww.boston.com/news/specials/gay_marriage.

Publications

There are a number of **publications** covering New England's various gay scenes. *Bay Windows* (ⓣ617/266-0393, ⓦwww.baywindows.com) is the region's largest gay and lesbian weekly, with cultural listings for all of the region's six states. *Out in the Mountains* (ⓣ802/861-6486, ⓦwww.mountainpridemedia.org) is Vermont's monthly gay newsletter, while the bimonthly *Metroline Magazine* (ⓣ860/231-8845, ⓦwww.metroline-online.com) has information on the gay scene in Connecticut, with additional news pertaining to greater New England. Some tourist information centers stock the free *Pink Pages* (Ⓣ617/423-1515, Ⓦwww.linkpink.com) a complete listing of gay- and lesbian-friendly businesses and community organizations in the New England states – although about half of the book is devoted to Boston.

For additional research try one of many **online publications**, such as gay and lesbian travel resources like Ⓦwww.qtmagazine.com, or something more specific to New England, such as Ⓦwww.vermontgaytravel.com and Ⓦwww.gayinmaine.com. Lastly, Now Voyager (Ⓣ1-800/255-6951, Ⓦwww.nowvoyager.com) is a gay and lesbian travel consolidator with Boston-based packaged tours.

Directory

Addresses Though initially confusing for overseas visitors, American addresses are masterpieces of logical thinking. Generally speaking, roads in major cities are laid out to a grid system, creating "blocks" of buildings: addresses of buildings refer to the block, which will be numbered in sequence, from a central point usually downtown; for example, 620 South Cedar will be six blocks south of downtown. In some larger cities, "streets" and "avenues" often run north–south and east–west respectively.

Airport tax All airport, customs, and security taxes are included in the price of your ticket.

Cigarettes and smoking Smoking is as much frowned upon in New England as in the rest of the US (excepting the fanatic West Coast, perhaps). Cinemas are nonsmoking, smoking is prohibited on public transportation and flights, and all New England states except New Hampshire and Vermont have banned smoking in restaurants and bars. Throughout New England, however, you'll find dive bars that flout the smoking ban late at night. Cigarettes are sold in almost any food shop, convenience store, drugstore, or bar. A pack of twenty costs upwards of $6.

Drugs Possession of under an ounce of marijuana is a misdemeanor in every New England state except Maine, and will result from a fine that varies from $200 to $400 in Maine to a whopping $2000 in New England's most conservative state, New Hampshire. Being caught with more than an ounce, however, means facing a criminal charge for dealing, and a possible prison sentence – stiffer if caught anywhere near a school. Other drugs are, of course, completely illegal, and it's a much more serious offense if you're caught with any.

Electricity 110V AC. Laptops will need plug adaptors only, but all other foreign electronics from 220V AC systems will probably require an expensive converter as well.

ID Should be carried at all times. Two pieces will satisfy any inquiry, one of which should have a photo: a driving license, passport, and credit card(s) are your best bets. Not having your license with you while driving is an arrestable offense.

Measurements and sizes Measurements are in inches, feet, yards, and miles; weight is in ounces, pounds, and tons. American pints and gallons are about four-fifths of imperial ones. Clothing sizes are two figures less than what they would be in Britain – a British women's size 12 is a US size 10 – while British shoe sizes are 1.5 sizes below American ones for women, and one size below for men.

Tax Added on to your bill will invariably be some sort of surcharge, be it a food tax (5–7 percent), hotel tax (7–13 percent), or sales tax (5–7 percent). New Hampshire, however, has no sales tax, and Vermont has none for hotels. Car rentals are notorious for loading on taxes for a variety of reasons, which may add up to 30 percent to your final bill.

Temperatures Always given in Fahrenheit.

Time New England runs on Eastern Standard Time (EST), five hours behind GMT in winter and three hours ahead of the US West Coast. East Coast daylight savings time (4 hours behind GMT) runs from the first Sunday in April to the last Sunday in October.

Tipping You are expected to tip pretty much all service-related help, from waitstaff (15–20 percent) to bartenders (10–15 percent) to cab drivers (15–20 percent), as well as anyone who carries your bags in a hotel (figure a dollar per bag).

Guide

Guide

1 Boston

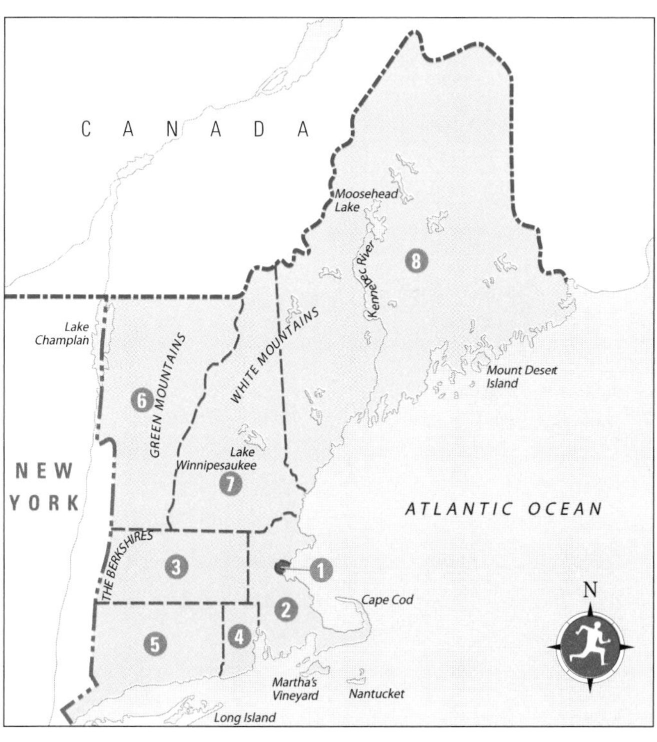

CANADA
Moosehead Lake
Kennebec River
8
Lake Champlain
GREEN MOUNTAINS
WHITE MOUNTAINS
Mount Desert Island
6
Lake Winnipesaukee
7
NEW YORK
ATLANTIC OCEAN
THE BERKSHIRES
3
1
Cape Cod
N
2
5
4
Martha's Vineyard
Nantucket
Long Island

CHAPTER ONE

Highlights

* **North End** You'll find some of Boston's most famed sights, plus its best *cannoli*, in its most authentic Italian neighborhood. See p.104

* **Beacon Hill** Long the neighborhood of choice for the city's elite, with stately red-brick Federalist townhouses and gaslights lining the narrow, cobblestoned streets. See p.112

* **Newbury Street** This swanky promenade of designer boutiques and cafés will tempt you to break the bank. See p.122

* **A Red Sox game at Fenway** Watch one of baseball's most storied teams play in one of the country's classic stadiums. See p.128

* **Isabella Stewart Gardner Museum** Styled after a fifteenth-century Venetian palace, this delightful museum boasts an eclectic collection and a sublime central courtyard. See p.131

* **Arnold Arboretum** The crown jewel of Boston's Emerald Necklace is a botanist's delight and one of the finest arbore-tums in North America. See p.134

* **Harvard Square** Cambridge's buzzing heart is steps from the ivy-covered walls of Harvard University and close to the colonial mansions of Brattle Street. See p.136

△Fenway Park

1

Boston

Boston might be as close to the Old World as the New World gets, an American city that proudly trades on its colonial past, having served a crucial role in the country's development from a few wayward pilgrims right through the Revolutionary War. It occasionally takes this a bit too far – what's a faded relic anywhere else becomes a plaque-covered tourist sight here – but none of it detracts from the city's overriding historic charm, nor from its present-day energy. Indeed, there are plenty of tall skyscrapers, thriving business concerns, and cultural outposts that are part and parcel of modern urban America, not to mention excellent mergers of past and present, such as the redeveloped – and bustling – Quincy Market, a paradigm for successful urban renewal. True, nowhere else will you get a better feel for the events and the personae behind the birth of a nation, all played out in Boston's wealth of emblematic and evocative colonial-era sights. But the city's cafés and shops, its attractive public spaces, and the diversity of its neighborhoods – student hives, ethnic enclaves, and stately districts of preserved townhouses – are similarly alluring, and go some way to answering the twin accusations of elitism and provincialism to which Boston is perennially subjected.

As the undisputed commercial and cultural center of New England, Boston is the highlight of any trip to the region, truly unmissable because almost every road in the area leads to it (indeed Boston was, until the late 1700s, America's most populous and culturally important city). It's also the center of the American university system – more than sixty colleges call the area home, including Harvard, in the neighboring city of Cambridge – and it enjoys a youthful buzz that again belies any reputation for stuffiness it might have. This academic connection has also played a key part in the city's left-leaning political tradition, the kind that spawned a line of ethnic mayors and, most famous of all, the Kennedy clan.

Today, Boston's relatively small size – both physically and in terms of population (eighteenth among US cities) – and its provincial feel are actually to the city's great advantage. Though it has expanded since it was first settled in 1630 through landfills and annexation, it has never lost its center, a tangle of streets clustered around Boston Common which can really only be explored on foot. Steeped in Puritan roots, the residents of these areas often display a slightly anachronistic Yankee pride, but it's one that has served to protect the city's identity, while groups of Irish and Italian descent have carved out authentically and often equally unchanged communities in areas like the North End, Charlestown, and South Boston. Indeed, the districts around the Common exude an almost small-town atmosphere and, until recently at least, were relatively unmarred by chain stores and fast-food joints. Even as Boston has evolved from busy port to blighted city to the rejuvenated place it is today, it has remained, fundamentally, a city on a human scale.

Some history

Boston's first permanent settlement was started by **William Blackstone**, who in 1630 split off from a settler's camp in Weymouth for more isolated territory. He was rapidly joined by Puritan settlers, to whom he sold most of the land he had staked out; then called the Shawmut Peninsula, it was soon renamed by the Puritans after their hometown in England: Boston.

Early Bostonians enjoyed almost total political autonomy, but with the restoration of the British monarchy in 1660, the Crown began appointing governors to oversee the Massachusetts Bay Colony. The colonists clashed frequently with these appointees, their resentment growing with a series of acts over the next ninety or so years that restricted various civil and commercial liberties. This culminated in such skirmishes as the Boston Massacre and the Boston Tea Party, events that went a long way towards igniting the **Revolutionary War**, which effectively started just outside Boston, in Lexington.

Post-Revolution, Boston emerged as a leading port city, eventually moving on to prominence in textiles and other industries. Its success in these fields brought wave after wave of nineteenth-century immigrants, notably Irish and Italian, ethnicities that still largely populate the city and have made great inroads into local and regional politics. Chinese immigrants, too, had by the turn of the nineteenth century established a budding Chinatown upon former mudflats south of downtown. But despite a strong history of progressive thought in abolitionism, the city was less successful in integrating African-Americans into the fold, and **racial tensions** flared up frequently in the twentieth century, most notoriously with the advent of public school busing – a result of court-ordered desegregation – in the 1970s. Race relations have been somewhat healed of late, assisted by community revitalization efforts that have strengthened the business centers of African-American neighborhoods. In addition, the financial doldrums that plagued the city for the latter half of the last century have been mostly forgotten, and a renewed sense of confidence – so emblematic of Boston's storied past – has taken hold.

Arrival, information, and city transit

Boston is the unchallenged travel hub of New England, and if it's not the only place in the region you'll visit, it almost certainly will be the first. Conveniently, all **points of arrival** are located inside the city boundaries, none more than a few miles away from downtown, and all are well connected to public transport.

By air

Busy **Logan International Airport** (ⓣ1-800/23-LOGAN, ⓦwww.massport.com/logan), servicing both domestic and international flights, has five terminals lettered A through E that are connected by a series of courtesy buses. You'll find car rental and currency exchange in terminals A, B, C, and E (daily 10am–7pm), plus information booths and ATMs in all five.

After arriving at Logan, the most convenient way downtown is by **subway**, or, as it's more commonly known in Boston, the **T**. The Airport subway stop is a short ride away on courtesy buses #22 and #33, which you can catch outside

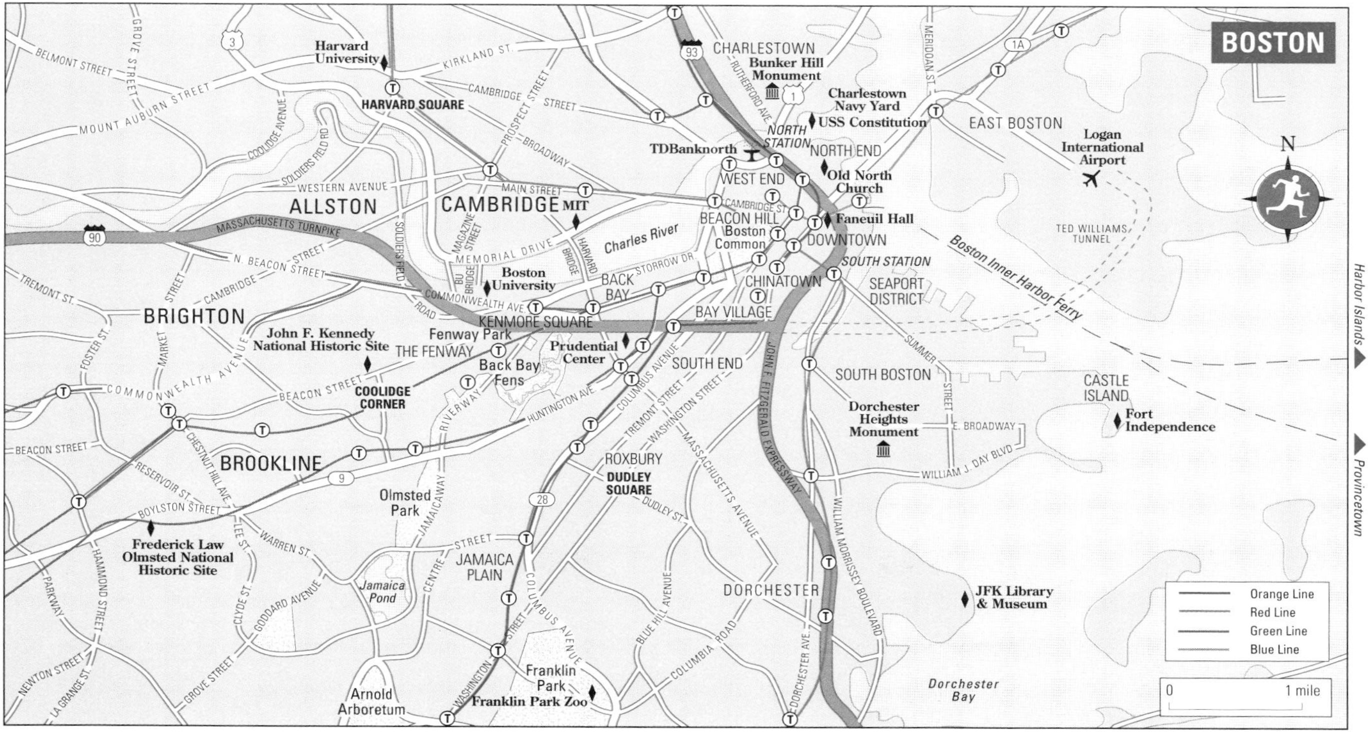

BOSTON

N

Harbor Islands
Provincetown

CHARLESTOWN
Bunker Hill Monument
Charlestown Navy Yard
USS Constitution
NORTH STATION
TDBanknorth
NORTH END
Old North Church
WEST END
Faneuil Hall
BEACON HILL
Boston Common
DOWNTOWN
SOUTH STATION
CHINATOWN
SEAPORT DISTRICT
BAY VILLAGE
EAST BOSTON
Logan International Airport
TED WILLIAMS TUNNEL
Boston Inner Harbor Ferry
CASTLE ISLAND
Fort Independence
SOUTH BOSTON
Dorchester Heights Monument
SOUTH END
ROXBURY
DUDLEY SQUARE
DORCHESTER
JFK Library & Museum
Dorchester Bay
JAMAICA PLAIN
Jamaica Pond
Olmsted Park
Franklin Park
Franklin Park Zoo
Arnold Arboretum
BROOKLINE
Frederick Law Olmsted National Historic Site
COOLIDGE CORNER
John F. Kennedy National Historic Site
BRIGHTON
ALLSTON
CAMBRIDGE
MIT
Harvard University
HARVARD SQUARE
Charles River
Boston University
KENMORE SQUARE
Fenway Park
THE FENWAY
Back Bay Fens
Prudential Center
BACK BAY

BELMONT STREET
GROVE STREET
MOUNT AUBURN STREET
COOLIDGE AVENUE
SOLDIERS FIELD RD
WESTERN AVENUE
KIRKLAND ST.
CAMBRIDGE STREET
PROSPECT STREET
BROADWAY
MAIN STREET
CAMBRIDGE ST
MAGAZINE STREET
MEMORIAL DRIVE
HARVARD BRIDGE
BU BRIDGE
STORROW DR.
SOLDIERS FIELD ROAD
MASSACHUSETTS TURNPIKE
N. BEACON STREET
CAMBRIDGE STREET
TREMONT ST.
FOSTER ST.
MARKET STREET
COMMONWEALTH AVENUE
COMMONWEALTH AVE.
BEACON STREET
RIVERWAY
HUNTINGTON AVE.
COLUMBUS AVENUE
TREMONT STREET
WASHINGTON STREET
MASSACHUSETTS AVENUE
JOHN F. FITZGERALD EXPRESSWAY
WILLIAM MORRISSEY BOULEVARD
WILLIAM J. DAY BLVD
E. BROADWAY
STREET
SUMMER
MERIDOAN ST.
RUTHERFORD AVE.
CHESTNUT HILL AVE.
RESERVOIR ST.
BOYLSTON STREET
LEE ST.
WARREN ST.
JAMAICAWAY
CENTRE STREET
DUDLEY ST.
BLUE HILL AVENUE
COLUMBIA ROAD
DORCHESTER AVE.
COLUMBUS AVENUE
WASHINGTON STREET
GODDARD AVENUE
CLYDE ST.
GROVE STREET
HAMMOND STREET
PARKWAY
NEWTON STREET
LA GRANGE ST.

Orange Line
Red Line
Green Line
Blue Line

0 1 mile

on the arrival level of all five Logan terminals. From there, you can take the Blue Line to State or Government Center stations in the heart of downtown, and transfer to the Red, Orange, and Green lines to reach other points; the ride to downtown lasts about fifteen minutes ($1.25).

Just as quick, and a lot more fun, is the **water taxi** (ⓣ617/422-0392, ⓦwww.citywatertaxi.com), which whisks you across the harbor to numerous points around Boston. Water taxis don't run in the winter, nor do they run on a set schedule; if there isn't a boat waiting in the harbor, contact them via the checkerboard call box at the Logan dock (April–Nov Mon–Sat 7am–10pm, Sun 7am–8pm; $10). From the airport, courtesy bus #66 will take you to the pier.

By comparison, taking a **taxi** is expensive – from the airport to a downtown destination will cost $20–25, plus an extra $6 or so in tolls – and time-consuming, given Boston's notorious traffic jams. Save yourself the trouble and avoid them. If you insist on taking a car into the city, ride in style with Boston Town Car, which costs the same (ⓣ1-888/765-5466, ⓦwww.bostontowncar.com).

By bus or train

The main terminus for both **buses** and **trains** to Boston is **South Station**, in the southeast corner of downtown at Summer Street and Atlantic Avenue. Amtrak trains arrive at one end, in a station with an information booth, newsstands, a food court, and several ATMs (but no currency exchange), while bus carriers arrive at the clean and modern terminal next door, from where it's a bit of a trek to reach the subway (the Red Line), which is through the Amtrak station and down a level. Those with sizeable baggage will find the walk particularly awkward, as there are no porters or handcarts. Despite its modernity, the bus terminal's departure and arrival screens are anything but up-to-date – confirm your gate with an agent to be sure. Trains also make a second stop at **Back Bay Station**, 145 Dartmouth St, on the **T**'s Orange Line – this station has two ATMs and a *Dunkin' Donuts*, but little else in the way of amenities.

By car

Driving into Boston is the absolute worst way to get there, and is sure to put a damper on your trip if you're a first-time visitor. Boston drivers are notorious for their aggressive, impatient style of driving, and the learning curve for navigating the city by car is so steep that ability to do so has become a source of pride and cultural identity for local residents. To make use of public transportation after you get here, see p.163 for parking information.

Two highways provide direct access to the city: **I-90**, known locally as the MassPike or The Pike, and **I-93**, known as the Central Artery. The latter cuts north–south through the heart of Boston and provides the most majestic entrance to the city, courtesy of the newly opened Zakim Bridge. Even with Big Dig improvements (see box opposite), this portion of highway has historically been the most congested part of town – don't be surprised if you get stuck in traffic for a while, especially if you arrive during rush hour (generally from 7.30–9am and 4.30–7pm). If you're coming from western Massachusetts, I-90 is the most direct route to Boston; from points north of the city utilize I-93. Once you reach Boston, **Storrow Drive** is the main local drag, running alongside the Charles River and providing access to the core of the city. A third highway, **I-95**, circumnavigates the greater Boston area, affording entry points for its many suburbs.

The Big Dig

Whether you arrive in Boston by air, rail, or highway, you're likely to notice a downtown in seeming disarray. This mess has been created by the **Big Dig**, a grand attempt – and one that has been dogged by political controversy and logistical setbacks – to bury the city's central traffic artery (I-93) underground.

The project, which is currently in its final, clean-up stages of completion, began in 1991 as an attempt to alleviate central Boston's heinous traffic – roads were often gridlocked for ten hours a day – by relocating some seven and a half miles of highway underground, a move that would free up an estimated 27 acres of land for use as a downtown park, recently christened the Rose Kennedy Greenway. The project has succeeded in unclogging Boston's major arteries: an expanded I-93 has been buried underneath downtown Boston and access to Logan Airport has been dramatically improved via linkage to the MassPike (I-90). The Big Dig has also boosted Boston's aesthetics: courtesy of the new, tongue-twisting "Leonard P. Zakim Bunker Hill Memorial Bridge," portions of I-93 have been elegantly, and more efficiently, rerouted. The surface areas of the former expressway are also currently being transformed into the aforementioned Greenway. Not all is smooth roads and parkland, however: the budget, originally estimated at $2.6 billion, is now expected to reach $15 billion since an inquiry discovered that city planners had hidden over $2 billion of their project's cost overruns from the public. Perhaps most embarrassing, however, are the leaks that plague the Big Dig tunnels. In September 2004 water flooded the northbound tunnel, backing up rush-hour traffic for miles. Inspectors have since located 169 leaky defects in the tunnels, expected to cost $38 million in repairs. If this civic headache interests you, visit the Museum of Science's permanent **Big Dig exhibit**, or go online to Ⓦwww.masspike.com/bigdig, where you can learn, among other impressive figures, that by the time the dig is finished, "more earth will [have been] moved than during the construction of the Great Pyramids."

Information and media

Boston's main public tourist office is the **Boston Visitor Information Pavilion** on Boston Common, near the Park Street **T** stop (daily 9am–5pm). You'll find loads of maps and brochures, plus information on historical sights, cultural events, accommodation, restaurants, and bus trips. Across the street from the Old State House, at 15 State St, is a **visitor center** maintained by the Boston National Historical Park (daily 9am–5pm); it too has plenty of free brochures, plus a bookstore. In Back Bay, there is a visitor **kiosk** in the Prudential Center, 800 Boylston St (daily 9am–5pm). Visitors to **Cambridge** can get all the information they need from the Cambridge Office of Tourism (Ⓣ617/441-2884 or 1-800/862-5678, Ⓦwww.cambridge-usa.org), which maintains a well-stocked kiosk in Harvard Square (Mon–Sat 9am–5pm). For advance information, the best source is the Greater Boston Convention & Visitors Bureau (GBCVB) website, Ⓦwww.bostonusa.com.

The city's oldest **newspaper**, *The Globe* (50¢; Ⓦwww.boston.com/globe), is Boston's finest general daily; its hefty Sunday edition ($2) includes meaty sections on art, culture, and lifestyle. The *Boston Herald* (50¢; Ⓦwww.bostonherald.com) is the *Globe*'s tabloid competitor and is best for local gossip and sports coverage. The rest of the city's print media are primarily listings-oriented and **free weeklies**. To know what's on, the *Boston Phoenix* (free; Ⓦwww.bostonphoenix.com), available at sidewalk newspaper stands around town, is essential, offering extensive entertainment **listings** as well as good feature articles. Other freebies like *Boston's Weekly Dig* (Ⓦwww.weeklydig.com) and *The Improper Bostonian* (Ⓦwww.improper.com), have good listings of new and noteworthy goings-on about town. *Bay Windows* (Ⓦwww.baywindows.com), a small weekly catering to the **gay and lesbian** population, is available free in the South End (the city's primary gay neighborhood) and around. The lone monthly publication, *Boston Magazine* ($4.99; Ⓦ www.bostonmagazine.com), is a glossy lifestyle **magazine** with good restaurant reviews and a yearly "Best of Boston" roundup.

The **Boston CityPass** (available online or at the attractions that accept it; $39; Ⓦ citypass.net) is a ticket booklet that covers admission to the Prudential Skywalk Observatory, the John F. Kennedy Library and Museum, the Museum of Fine Arts, the New England Aquarium, the Harvard Museum of Natural History, and the Museum of Science; if you plan to visit all or most of these sights, you'd do well to pick one up, as it will save you about $33.

Guided tours of Boston

Perhaps the best way to orient yourself in Boston, aside from walking, is by taking a **trolley tour**, on small open-air buslike vehicles painted to look like streetcars. Most of the trolleys let you hop on and off at various locations and they make pick-ups at major hotels; full tours usually last about two hours, and there is little difference from tour to tour in what historical sights you'll actually see.

Narrated trolley tours

Beantown Trolley Ⓣ 1-800/343-1328 or 781/986-6100, Ⓦ www.beantowntrolley.com. One of the oldest and most popular history tours, covering the gamut from waterfront wharfs to Beacon Hill Brahmins and Fenway area museums, with multiple pick-up and drop-off points around town. $27.

Discover Boston Multilingual Trolley Tours Ⓣ 617/742-1469, Ⓦ www.discoverbostontours.com. Tours in English; audio devices available in French, German, Italian, Japanese, and Spanish. $28.

Old Town Trolley Tours Ⓣ 617/269-7010, Ⓦ www.trolleytours.com. Another hop-on, hop-off tour, this one on ubiquitous orange-and-green trolleys with thematic routes like "Sons and Daughters of Liberty" and "Ghosts and Gravestones." $29.

Other city tours

Boston by Foot Ⓣ 617/367-2345, Ⓦ www.bostonbyfoot.com. Informative 90min walking tours that focus on the architecture and history of different Boston neighborhoods such as Beacon Hill, the North End, and Victorian Back Bay. Also has "Boston by Little Feet" tours, geared towards the Freedom Trail's smaller pedestrians. $8–10.

Boston Duck Tours Ⓣ 617/267-DUCK, Ⓦ www.bostonducktours.com. Excellent tours that take to the streets and the Charles River in restored World War II amphibious landing vehicles; kids get to skipper the bus/boat in the water. Tours depart every half-hour from the Prudential Center at 101 Huntington Ave and the Museum of Science at Science Park; reservations advised in summer. $25.

Boston National Historical Park Visitor Center Freedom Trail Tours Ⓣ 617/242-5642. Led by park rangers and taking in a third of the Freedom Trail sights, these 90min tours begin at the Visitor Center (15 State St) and run at 2pm Mon–Fri, and at 10am, 11am, and 2pm Sat–Sun. Free.

Brush Hill Grayline Tours Ⓣ 1-800/343-1328 or 781/986-6100, Ⓦ www.brushhilltours.com. Day-long bus tours to surrounding towns such as Concord, Lexington, Plymouth, and Salem. Late March to Nov, some tours summer only. $26–49.

Literary Trail of Greater Boston Ⓣ 617/621-4020, Ⓦ www.literarytrailofgreaterboston.org. Three walking tours that take in all the local literary hotspots of Boston, Cambridge, and Concord. $25.50–65.

North End Market Tours Ⓣ 617/523-6032, Ⓦ www.cucinare.com. Award-winning walking and tasting tours of the North End's Italian *salumerias*, *pasticcerias*, and *enotecas*. Often booked up, so reserve well in advance. Wed & Sat 10am & 2pm, Fri 10am & 3pm. $48.

City transport

Much of the pleasure of visiting Boston comes from being in a city built long before cars were invented. Walking around the narrow, winding streets can be a joy; conversely, driving around them is a nightmare. Be particularly cautious in traffic circles known as "rotaries": when entering, always yield the right of way. If you have a car, better park it for the duration of your trip (see p.163) and get around either by **foot** or **public transit** – a system of subway lines, buses, and ferries run by the Massachusetts Bay Transportation Authority (MBTA, known as the **T**; ⓣ1-800/392-6100, ⓦwww.mbta.com).

Subway (the T)

While not the most modern system, Boston's subway is cheap, efficient, and charmingly antiquated – its Green Line was America's first underground train, built in the late nineteenth century, and riding it today is akin to riding a tram – albeit underground.

Four **subway** lines transect Boston and continue out into some of its more proximate neighbors. Each line is color-coded and passes through downtown before continuing on to other districts. The **Red Line**, which serves Harvard, is the most frequent, intersecting South Boston and Dorchester to the south and Cambridge to the north. The **Green Line** hits Back Bay, Kenmore Square, the Fenway, and Brookline. The **Blue Line** heads into East Boston and is most useful for its stop at Logan Airport. The less frequent **Orange Line** traverses the South End and continues down to Roxbury and Jamaica Plain.

All trains travel either **inbound** (towards the quadrant made up of State, Downtown Crossing, Park Street, and Government Center stops) or **outbound** (away from the quadrant). If you're confused about whether you're going in or out, the train's terminus is also designated on the train itself; for instance, trains to Harvard from South Station will be on the "Inbound" platform and heading towards "Alewife."

The four lines are supplemented by a bus rapid transit (BRT) route, the **Silver Line**, which runs above ground along Washington Street from Downtown Crossing **T**. More of a fast bus than a subway, the line cuts through the heart of South End.

The **fare** is $1.25, payable by a token purchased at the station or by exact change; when boarding a subway at a station with no token-seller, you can squeeze your dollar bill into the slot at the bottom left of the conductor's till. If you're planning to use public transit a lot, it's a good idea to buy a **visitor's pass** for one ($7.50), three ($18), or seven days ($35) of unlimited subway, bus, and harbor ferry use. A cheaper option may be the weekly combo commuter passes ($16.50), which are good from Sunday to Saturday, and are sold from Sunday until Wednesday of the week they're valid for. Buy them at the Harvard, Kenmore, or Park Street **T** stations.

The biggest drawback to the **T** is its **hours** (Mon–Sat 5.15am–12.30am, Sun 6am–12.30am); the 12.30am closing time means you'll be stuck taking a taxi home after last call at the bar. Free transit **maps** are available at any station.

Buses

The MBTA also manages a whopping 170 **bus routes** both in and around Boston. The buses run less frequently than the subway and are harder to navigate, but they bear two main advantages: they're cheaper (90¢, exact change only) and they provide service to many more points. It's a service used primarily by natives who've grown familiar with the Byzantine system of routes. If you're

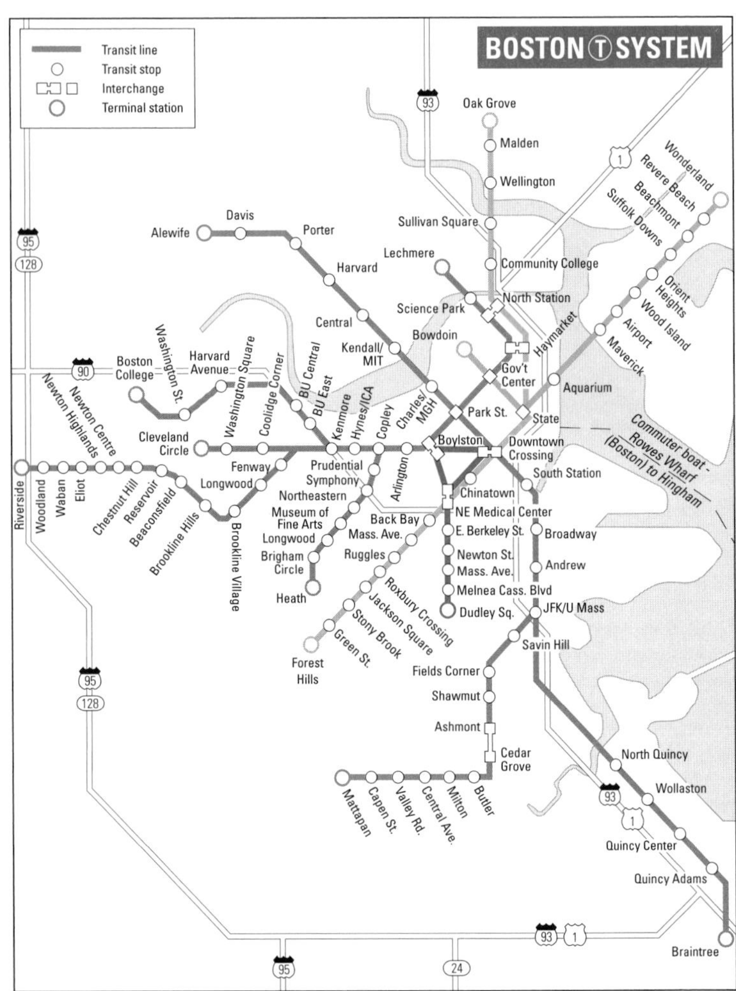

transferring from the **T**, you'll have to pay the full fare; transferring between buses is free, however, as long as you have a transfer from your original bus. Note that the **T**'s visitor pass (see overleaf) includes unlimited bus access over one, three, or seven days, depending on the package you've purchased. Be sure to arm yourself with the *Official Public Transport Map*, available at all subway stations, before heading out. Most buses run from 5.30am to 1am.

Ferries

Of all the MBTA transportation options, the Inner Harbor **ferry** is by far the most scenic: $1.50 gets you a 10min boat ride with excellent views of downtown Boston. The boats, covered 100-seaters with exposed upper decks, navigate several waterfront routes by day, though the one most useful to visitors is that connecting Long Wharf with the Charlestown Navy Yard (Mon–Fri 6.30am–8pm, every 15min; Sat & Sun 10am–6pm, every 30min).

Bikes

In and around Boston are some eighty miles of **bike trails**, making it an excellent city to explore on two wheels. The usual precautions – wearing a helmet and carrying a whistle – are advised. You can rent a bike starting at about $25 per day from Community Bicycle Supply, 496 Tremont St (ⓣ617/542-8623, ⓦwww.communitybicycle.com); Ace Wheelworks, 145 Elm St, Somerville (ⓣ617/776-2100); or Back Bay Bicycles, 366 Commonwealth Ave (ⓣ617/247-2336, ⓦwww.backbaybicycles.com). Wheelworks and Back Bay bicycles also do **repairs**. A copy of *Boston's Bike Map* ($5.25) is available at any decent bike store and will help you find all the trails and bike-friendly roads in the area.

Taxis

Given Boston's small scale and the efficiency of its public transport, **taxis** aren't as necessary – or as prevalent – as in bigger cities such as New York or London. You can generally hail one along the streets of downtown or Back Bay, though competition gets pretty stiff after 1am, when the subway has stopped running and bars and clubs begin to close; in this case, go to a hotel, where cabs cluster, or call the cab company directly. In Cambridge, taxis mostly congregate around Harvard Square. Boston Cab (ⓣ617/536-5010) and Metro Cab (ⓣ617/782-5500) have 24 hour service and accept major credit cards. In Cambridge, call Yellow Cab (ⓣ617/547-3000) or Ambassador Cabs (ⓣ617/492-1100). As a general rule, the rate starts at $1.75 and goes up by 30¢ per 1/8 mile.

Accommodation

For such a popular travel destination, Boston has a surprisingly limited range of well-priced **accommodation**. Though there are still bargains to be found, prices at many formerly moderate **hotels** have inched into the expense-account range. Your best bet is to visit in the off season, around November through April (excepting holidays), when many hotels not only have more vacancies but offer special discounts too. At any other time of year, be sure to make reservations well in advance. September (start of the school year) and June (graduation) are particularly busy months, due to the large student population. Even if Boston's hotels are not suited to every traveler's budget, they do cater to most tastes, and range from the usual assortment of **chains** to some excellent independently run hotels, the best of which, not to mention the highest concentration, are in Back Bay. Most of the business hotels are located in or around the Financial District.

A surprising number of **bed and breakfasts** are tucked into renovated brownstones in Back Bay, Beacon Hill, and the South End, or outside the city in Cambridge and Brookline. The industry is thriving, largely because it is so difficult to find accommodation at a hotel for under $100 a night – and many B&Bs offer just that. You can make reservations directly with the places we've listed; there are also numerous B&B **agencies** that can do the booking for you.

Short-term **furnished apartments**, spread throughout the city, are another option, though most have two-week minimums. There are also a handful of decent **hostels** if you're looking for real budget accommodation, though definitely book ahead, especially in summer. Hotels and B&Bs are listed below by neighborhood, with hostels listed separately.

Downtown

Boston Marriott Long Wharf 296 State St ⓣ617/227-0800 or 1-888/236-2427, ⓦwww.marriott.com; Aquarium **T**. Many of the rooms here boast harbor views, but the stunning, vaulted lobby is what really makes this *Marriott* stand out. 7–9

Courtyard Boston Tremont Hotel 275 Tremont St ⓣ617/426-1400 or 617/228-9390, ⓦwww.marriott.com; NE Medical Center **T**. The opulent lobby of this 1925 hotel, the former national headquarters of the Elks Lodge, somewhat compensates for its smallish rooms; and, if you want to be in the thick of the Theater District you can't do better. 8

Harborside Inn 185 State St ⓣ617/723-7500, ⓦwww.hagopianhotels.com; State **T**. This small hotel is housed in a renovated 1890s mercantile warehouse across from Quincy Market; the rooms – with exposed brick, hardwood floors, and cherry furniture – are a welcome surprise for this part of town. 7

Langham 250 Franklin St ⓣ617/451-1900 or 1-800/543-4300, ⓦwww.langhamhotels.com; State **T**. Located in the heart of the Financial District, this stern granite building is the former Federal Reserve Bank of Boston. The rooms are spacious and modern, but the overall atmosphere is a bit stiff. 7–8

Marriott's Customs House 3 McKinley Square ⓣ617/310-6300 or 1-888/236-2427, ⓦwww.marriott.com; Aquarium **T**. All the rooms at this downtown landmark-turned-hotel are high-end, one-bedroom suites with spectacular Boston Harbor and city views. 9

Millenium Bostonian Hotel 26 North St, Faneuil Hall Marketplace ⓣ617/523-3600 or 1-866/866-8086, ⓦwww.milleniumhotels.com; Government Center **T**. Formerly known as the *Regal Bostonian*, this hotel has splendid quarters, some with fireplaces and en-suite balconies, and is located in the heart of downtown. The rooms and lobby are festooned with portraits of famous Colonials. 8–9

Milner 78 Charles St S ⓣ617/426-6220 or 1-877/MILNERS, ⓦwww.milner-hotels.com; Boylston **T**. Uninspiring but affordable digs convenient for Bay Village, the Public Garden, and the Theater District. All room rates include a continental breakfast, served in a European-style nook in the lobby. 6–7

Nine Zero 90 Tremont St ⓣ617/772-5800, ⓦwww.ninezero.com; Park St **T**. Probably Boston's trendiest accommodation, with hip, modern furnishings, a fancy cheese plate to welcome you, and beds so lovely they had to start selling them retail. 7–9

Omni Parker House 60 School St ⓣ617/227-8600 or 1-800/843-6664, ⓦwww.omniparkerhouse.com; Park **T**. No one can compete with the *Omni Parker House* in the history department: it's the oldest continuously operating hotel in the US. Though the present building only dates from 1927, the lobby, decorated in dark oak with carved gilt moldings, recalls the splendor of the original nineteenth-century building that once housed it. Though the rooms are small, they have been recently renovated. 7–8

XV Beacon 15 Beacon St ⓣ617/670-1500 or 1-877/XVB-EACON, ⓦwww.xvbeacon.com; Park St **T**. Luxurious boutique hotel across from the Boston Athenaeum, with 61 spectacular rooms equipped with marble bathrooms, in-room fax, high-speed Internet connection, Kiehl's toiletries, CD player, decadent upholstery, and working gas fireplaces. Room rates include use of a chauffeured Mercedes. 9

Charlestown

Bed & Breakfast Afloat 28 Constitution Rd ⓣ617/241-9640, ⓦwww.bedandbreakfastafloat.com; Community College **T**. Guests at this original B&B hole up on a houseboat, sailboat, or yacht, right in Boston Harbor; the fancier vessels come with DVD players and deck-top Jacuzzis. All come with continental breakfast and access to the marina pool. 6–9

Constitution Inn 150 Third Ave ⓣ617/241-8400 or 1-800/495-9622, ⓦwww.constitutioninn.com; North Station **T**. This inn, from which downtown is but a ferry ride away, has 150 private rooms equipped with cable TV, a/c, and private baths, in addition to an on-site weight-room, sauna, and pool. Though predominantly servicing military personnel, civilians are more than welcome, though they pay significantly more. 7

Beacon Hill and the West End

Beacon Hill Bed & Breakfast 27 Brimmer St ⓣ617/523-7376; Charles **T**. Two spacious rooms with fireplaces in a well-situated brick townhouse, built in 1869. Sumptuous full breakfasts are served in the morning; two-night minimum stay, three on holiday weekends. 8

Beacon Hill Hotel 25 Charles St ⓣ617/723-7575 or 1-888/959-BHHB, ⓦwww.beaconhillhotel.com; Charles **T**. A luxurious boutique hotel set in two mid-1800s brownstones; the thirteen sleek chambers come with flat-screen televisions and balconies. ❽

Charles Street Inn 94 Charles St ⓣ617/314-8900, ⓦwww.charlesstreetinn.com; Charles T. Intimate inn with rooms styled after the (presumed) tastes of various Boston luminaries; the Isabella Stewart Gardner room features a rococo chandelier, while Oliver Wendell Holmes's staid digs boast a king-sized sleigh bed. All rooms come with working fireplaces. ❽–❾

The John Jeffries House 14 David G. Mugar Way ⓣ617/367-1866, ⓦwww.johnjeffrieshouse.com; Charles T. Mid-scale hotel at the foot of Beacon Hill, with a cozy lounge and Victorian-style rooms featuring cable TV and a/c; single-occupancy studios include kitchenettes. And, though it's wedged in between a busy highway and the local T stop, it's not too noisy. ❺–❻

The Shawmut Inn 281 Friend St ⓣ617/720-5544 or 1-800/350-7784, ⓦwww.shawmutinn.com; North Station T. Located in the old West End near the TDBanknorth Garden, the *Shawmut* has 66 comfortable, modern rooms, all of which have kitchenettes. ❻

Back Bay and the South End

82 Chandler Street 82 Chandler St ⓣ617/482-0408 or 1-888/482-0408; Back Bay T. Basic rooms with minimal service in a restored, 1863 brownstone that sits on an up-and-coming street in the South End. ❻–❼

463 Beacon Street Guest House 463 Beacon St ⓣ617/536-1302, ⓦwww.463beacon.com; Hynes T. The good-sized rooms in this renovated brownstone, located in the heart of Back Bay, are available by the night, week, or month, and come equipped with kitchenettes, cable TV, and various hotel amenities (though no maid service); some have a/c, hardwood floors, and ornamental fireplaces. There are some less expensive rooms with shared baths. Ask for the top-floor room. ❹–❼

Boston Park Plaza Hotel & Towers 64 Arlington St ⓣ617/426-2000 or 1-800/225-2008, ⓦwww.bostonparkplaza.com; Arlington T. The *Plaza's* old-school elegance and hospitality – plus its central location – make it stand out; the high-ceilinged rooms are quite comfortable, too. ❽

Charlesmark Hotel 655 Boylston St ⓣ617/247-1212, ⓦwww.thecharlesmark.com; Copley T. New, 33-room European-style hotel; while the rooms are on the small side, they compensate with cozy beechwood furnishings and modern accoutrements like in-room CD players, VCRs, and wireless Internet. ❻–❼

The Colonnade 120 Huntington Ave ⓣ617/424-7000 or 1-800/962-3030, ⓦwww.colonnadehotel.com; Prudential T. With its beige poured-concrete shell, the *Colonnade* looks weirdly like a parking garage. Still, there are spacious rooms and, in summer, a rooftop pool – the only one in Boston. ❺–❾

Copley Inn 19 Garrison St ⓣ617/236-0300 or 1-800/232-0306, ⓦwww.copleyinn.com; Prudential T. Comfortable rooms with full kitchens, friendly staff, and a great location make this a fine option in the Back Bay. If you stay six days, the seventh night is free. ❻–❼

Copley Square Hotel 47 Huntington Ave ⓣ617/536-9000 or 1-800/225-7062, ⓦwww.copleysquarehotel.com; Copley T. Situated on the eastern fringe of Copley Square, this family-run, low-key hotel is popular with a European crowd; the rooms won't win any style awards, but they're spacious enough and equipped with wireless Internet, cable TV, coffeemakers, and the like. ❻–❼

Eliot 370 Commonwealth Ave ⓣ267-1607 or 1-800/442-5468, ⓦwww.eliothotel.com; Hynes T. West Back Bay's answer to the *Ritz*, this calm, plush, nine-floor suite hotel has rooms with luxurious Italian marble baths. ❽–❾

Fairmont Copley Plaza 138 St James Ave ⓣ617/267-5300 or 1-800/795-3906, ⓦwww.fairmont.com; Copley T. Built in 1912 and it shows, from the somewhat severe facade facing Copley Square to the old-fashioned rooms. It does boast Boston's most elegant lobby, and even if you don't stay here, you should at least have a martini in the fabulous *Oak Bar* (see p.151). ❼–❾

Four Seasons 200 Boylston St ⓣ617/338-4400 or 1-800/332-3442, ⓦwww.fourseasons.com; Arlington T. The tops in city accommodation, with 288 rooms offering quiet, contemporary comfort. It's also home to the tempting *Aujourd'hui* restaurant (see p.148). ❾

The Lenox 710 Boylston St ⓣ617/536-5300 or 1-800/225-7676, ⓦwww.lenoxhotel.com; Copley T. Billed as Boston's version of the *Waldorf-Astoria* when its doors first opened in 1900, *The Lenox* is a far cry from that now, though it's still one of the most comfortably upscale hotels in the city. ❽–❾

Newbury Guest House 261 Newbury St ⓣ617/437-7666, ⓦwww.newburyguesthouse.com; Copley T. Big Victorian brownstone with 32 rooms that run the gamut from cramped chambers with overstuffed chairs to spacious bay-windowed quarters with hardwood floors and sleigh beds. Continental breakfast included. ❸–❺

Ritz-Carlton 15 Arlington St ⓣ617/536-5700 or 1-800/241-3333, ⓦwww.ritzcarlton.com; Arlington T. This is the *Ritz-Carlton* flagship, and even if the rooms are a bit cramped, the hotel retains a certain air of refinement, aided by a view overlooking the Public Garden. ❾

Kenmore Square, The Fenway, and Brookline

Beacon Inn 1087 and 1750 Beacon St ⓣ617/566-0088 or 1-888/575-0088, ⓦwww.beaconinn.com; Hawes **T**. Fireplaces in the lobbies and original woodwork contribute to the relaxed atmosphere in these two nineteenth-century brownstones, part of the same guesthouse. ❼

Brookline Manor Inn 32 Centre St ⓣ617/232-0003, ⓦwww.brooklinemanorinn.com; Coolidge Corner **T**. This small guesthouse, with private and shared baths, is located on a pleasant stretch off Beacon Street; it's just a short subway ride from Kenmore Square. They also have monthly rates. ❺–❼

The Buckminster 645 Beacon St ⓣ617/236-7050 or 1-800/727-2825, ⓦwww.bostonhotel-buckminster.com; Kenmore **T**. Though renovated not so long ago, the 1897 *Buckminster* retains the feel of an old Boston hotel with its antique furnishings. Breakfast included. ❺

Gryphon House 9 Bay State Rd ⓣ617/375-9003 or 1-877/375-9003, ⓦgryphonhouseboston.com; Kenmore **T**. This hotel-cum-B&B around the corner from Fenway has eight wonderfully appointed suites equipped with working gas fireplaces, cable TV, VCR, CD player, and high-speed Internet connection. Free parking. ❼–❽

Oasis Guest House 22 Edgerly Rd ⓣ617/267-2262, ⓦwww.oasisgh.com; Symphony **T**. Sixteen comfortable, affordable rooms, some with shared baths, in a renovated brownstone near Symphony Hall. ❹–❼

Cambridge

A Cambridge House 1657 Cambridge St ⓣ617/868-7082 or 1-877/994-0844, ⓦwww.cambridgebnb.com; Harvard **T**. This cozy Colonial Revival house has three pleasant rooms outfitted with canopy beds, and a common room furnished with overstuffed chairs and plenty of lace. Shared bath. Free parking. ❻–❾

Charles Hotel 1 Bennett St ⓣ617/864-1200 or 1-800/882-1818, ⓦwww.charleshotel.com; Harvard **T**. Clean, bright rooms – some overlooking the Charles – that have a good array of amenities: cable TV, three phones, minibar, Shaker furniture, and access to the adjacent Well-Bridge Health Spa. There's also an excellent jazz club, *Regattabar*, an iconic restaurant, *Henrietta's Table*, and a sultry bar, *Noir*, on the premises – see pp.155, 159, and 152, respectively, for reviews. ❼–❾

A Friendly Inn 1673 Cambridge St ⓣ617/547-7851, ⓦwww.afinow.com/afi; Harvard **T**. Just a few minutes', walk from Harvard Square, the rooms here are nothing special and the service doesn't exactly live up to the name, but there are private baths, cable TV, and laundry service. ❻–❼

Harding House 288 Harvard St ⓣ617/876-2888, ⓦwww.irvinghouse.com; Harvard **T**. This cozy Victorian home has 14 bright rooms with hardwood floors, throw rugs, TVs, and a/c; includes breakfast. Shared or private bath. Free parking. ❻–❼

Harvard Square Hotel 110 Mt Auburn St ⓣ617/864-5200 or 1-800/458-5886, ⓦwww.harvardsquarehotel.com; Harvard **T**. The rooms here are only adequate, but the Harvard Square location is just right. ❼–❾

Hotel @ MIT 20 Sidney St ⓣ617/577-0200 or 1-800/458-5886, ⓦwww.hotelatmit.com; Kendall Square **T**. Contemporary hotel anchoring an office tower near MIT, with a lobby festooned with AI robots created by the university's tech-savvy students; the sleek, modern rooms come with high-speed Internet access. ❼–❾

Inn at Harvard 1201 Massachusetts Ave ⓣ617/491-2222 or 1-800/458-5886, ⓦwww.theinnatharvard.com; Harvard **T**. This carefully constructed hotel is designed to give the impression of old-school grandeur; plus it's so close to Harvard you can smell the ivy. ❽–❾

Irving House 24 Irving St ⓣ617/547-4600, ⓦwww.irvinghouse.com; Harvard **T**. Excellent option near Harvard Square sharing the same management as the *Harding House* (see above), with laundry facilities and breakfast included; both shared and private baths. ❻–❼

Mary Prentiss Inn 6 Prentiss St ⓣ617/661-2929, ⓦwww.maryprentissinn.com; Porter **T**. Eighteen clean, comfortable rooms in a mid-nineteenth-century Greek Revival building. Full breakfast and snacks are served in the living room, or, weather permitting, on a pleasant outdoor deck. ❼

Hostels

There are fairly limited **hostel** accommodations in Boston, and if you want to get in on them, you should definitely book ahead, especially in the summertime.

Beantown Hostel 222 Friend St ⓣ617/723-0800, ⓦwww.hostelz.com; North Station **T**. Boston's only independent youth hostel is above the *Hooters* in the West End, and not far from Faneuil Hall. The place can be noisy, but prices include free admission to *McGann's* pub gigs on most nights, and free barbecues on Tues and Sun. Curfew 2.15 am.

B&B agencies and short-term accommodation

Bed & Breakfast Agency of Boston 47 Commercial Wharf ⓣ617/720-3540 or 1-800/248-9262, UK ⓣ0800/895 128, ⓦwww.boston-bnbagency.com; Aquarium **T**. Can book you a room in a brownstone, a waterfront loft, or even on a yacht. Nightly, weekly, or monthly options.
Bed & Breakfast Associates Bay Colony ⓣ781/449-5302 or 1-888/486-6018, ⓦwww.bnbboston.com. Features some real finds in Back Bay and the South End.
Bed & Breakfast Reservations ⓣ617/964-1606 or 1-800/832-2632, ⓦwww.bbreserve.com. Lists B&Bs in Greater Boston, North Shore, and Cape Cod.
Boston Reservations/Boston Bed & Breakfast ⓣ617/332-4199, ⓦwww.bostonreservations.com. Competitive rates at B&Bs as well as at leading hotels.

$22.50/dorm bed if booked online, $30/dorm bed walk-in.
Berkeley Residence YWCA 40 Berkeley St ⓣ617/375-2524, ⓦwww.ywcaboston.org; Back Bay **T**. Clean and simple rooms next door to a police station. All rates include breakfast; dinner is an additional $7.50. Singles are $60, doubles $90, and triples $105, plus a $2 membership fee. Longer-term accommodation only available to women.
Greater Boston YMCA 316 Huntington Ave ⓣ617/927-8040, ⓦwww.ymcaboston.org; Northeastern **T**. Good budget rooms, and access to the Y's health facilities (pool, weight room, etc). Singles are $46–66, but you can get a four-person room for $96. Co-ed facilities are available from late June until early Sept; the rest of the year it's men only. Ten days' maximum stay.
HI–Boston 12 Hemenway St ⓣ617/536-1027, ⓦwww.bostonhostel.org; Hynes **T**. Around the Back Bay–Fenway border, standard dorm accommodation with up to six beds per room. Members $35, nonmembers $38.
HI–Boston at Fenway 575 Commonwealth Ave ⓣ617/536-9455, ⓦwww.bostonhostel.org; Kenmore **T**. A summer-only hostel (June 1–Aug 18) that functions as a BU dorm in winter months, it's perhaps the best hostel in Boston. Spacious rooms and a great location within walking distance of nightclubs and Fenway Park. Members $35, nonmembers $38.

Neighborhoods and orientation

Boston is small for an American city, and its tangle of old streets makes it far easier to get around on foot than by car, especially in the city center. Boston's **downtown** area is situated on a peninsula that juts into Boston Harbor; most of the other neighborhoods branch out south and west from here mainly along the thoroughfares of Washington, Tremont, and Beacon streets.

Downtown really begins with Boston Common, a large public green that holds either on or near its grounds many of the city's major historical sights, including the State House, Old Granary Burying Ground, and Old South Meeting House. Nothing, however, captures the spirit of the city better than downtown's Faneuil (pronounced like "Daniel") Hall, the so-called "Cradle of Liberty," and the always animated Quincy Market, adjacent to the hall. On the other side of Surface Street (formerly I-93) from the marketplace is the **North End**, which occupies the northeast corner of the peninsula; aside from being the city's Little Italy, it's home to Old North Church and the Paul Revere House. Just across Boston's Inner Harbor is **Charlestown**, the quiet home of the world's oldest commissioned warship, the USS *Constitution*.

North of the Common are the vintage gaslights and red-brick Federalist townhouses that line the streets of **Beacon Hill**, the city's most exclusive residential neighborhood. Charles Street runs south along the base of the hill and separates Boston Common from the Public Garden, which marks the beginning of **Back Bay**. This similarly well-heeled neighborhood holds opulent row houses alongside modern landmarks like the John Hancock Tower, New England's tallest skyscraper; while appended south of Back Bay is the gay enclave of the **South End**, known for its hip restaurants and residents. The student domains of **Kenmore Square** and **Fenway** are west of Back Bay: the former has some of the area's best nightlife, while the latter is home to the Museum of Fine Arts, the Isabella Stewart Gardner Museum, and hallowed Fenway Park, where the Red Sox play. South of all these neighborhoods are Boston's vast **southern districts**, which don't hold too much of interest other than some links in Frederick Law Olmsted's series of parks known as the "Emerald Necklace," such as the dazzling Arnold Arboretum and Franklin Park, home to the city zoo. Across the Charles River from Boston lies **Cambridge**, a must for its excellent bookstore-and-funky-café scene and, above all, the ivy-covered walls of Harvard University.

Downtown Boston

Boston's compact **downtown** encompasses both the colonial heart and contemporary core of the city, an assemblage of red-brick buildings and modern office towers that, if not rivaling the glamour of other American big-city centers, still holds a number of the best reasons for visiting. Quite lively by day, when commuters and tourists create a constant buzz, the streets thin out come nightfall, with a few exceptions: the touristy **Quincy Market** area, which has a decent, if somewhat downmarket, bar scene; **Chinatown**, with its ever-popular restaurants; and the **Theater District**, particularly animated on weekends.

King's Chapel, on Tremont, and the nearby **Old State House** mark the periphery of Boston's earliest town center, where the first church, market, newspaper, and prison were all clustered. **Spring Lane**, a tiny pedestrian passage off Washington Street, recalls the location of one of the bigger springs that lured the earliest settlers over to the Shawmut Peninsula from Charlestown. The most evocative streets, however, are those whose character has been less diluted over the years – **School Street**, **State Street**, and the eighteenth-century enclave known as **Blackstone Block**, near Faneuil Hall.

You can get the flavor of Boston Harbor, once the world's third busiest, along the **waterfront**, now somewhat isolated on account of the endless Big Dig construction clean-up that converges in this area. The **Freedom Trail**, a self-guided walking tour that connects an assortment of historic sights by a line of red bricks embedded in the pavement and/or paint, begins in **Boston Common**, a king-sized version of the tidy green space at the core of innumerable New England villages. One of the many historic places the trail passes is the ever-popular meeting-place **Faneuil Hall**, a 15min walk from the Common. South is the **Financial District**, its short streets still following the tangled patterns of colonial village lanes; west of it is the small but vibrant Chinatown and adjacent Theater District.

Boston Common and around

Boston's premier open space is **Boston Common**, a fifty-acre chunk of green, neither meticulously manicured nor especially attractive, which effectively separates downtown from its posh neighbors, the Beacon Hill and Back Bay districts. It's the first thing you'll see when emerging from the **Park Street T station**, the central transfer point of America's first subway and, unfortunately, a magnet for panhandlers. Established in 1634 as "a trayning field" and "for the feeding of cattell" – so a slate tablet opposite the station recalls – the Common is still primarily utilitarian, used both by pedestrian commuters on their way to downtown's office towers and by tourists seeking the **Boston Visitor Information Pavilion** (see p.73), down Tremont Street from the Park Street **T** and the official starting-point of the Freedom Trail. Along the northern side of the Common, the lovely **Beacon Street** runs from the gold-domed State House to Charles Street, opposite the Public Garden.

Even before John Winthrop and his fellow Puritan colonists earmarked Boston Common for public use, it served as pasture land for the Reverend William Blackstone, Boston's first white settler. Soon after, it disintegrated into little more than a gallows for pirates, alleged witches, and various religious heretics; a commoner by the name of Rachell Whall was once hanged here for steal-

△ Boston Common

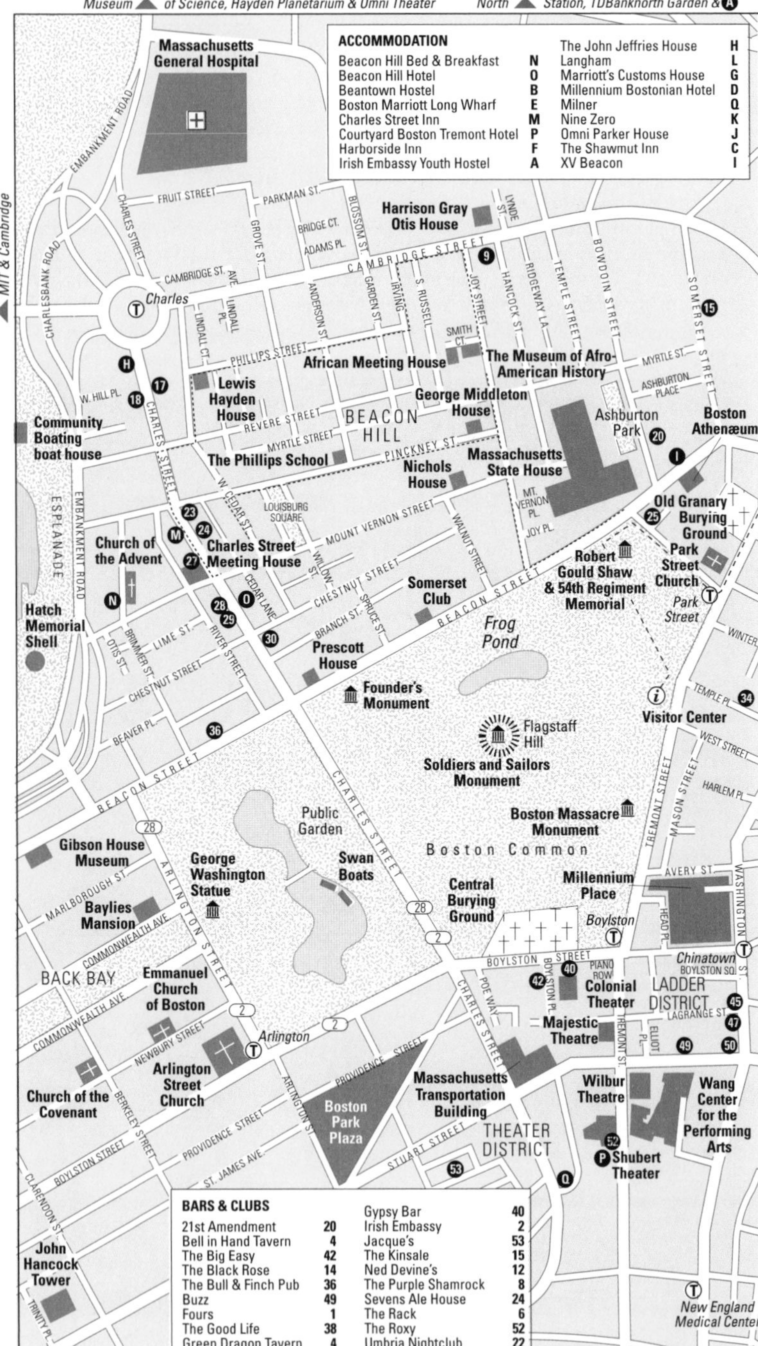
Museum of Science, Hayden Planetarium & Omni Theater
North Station, TDBanknorth Garden & A
MIT & Cambridge
South End
ACCOMMODATION
Beacon Hill Bed & Breakfast N
Beacon Hill Hotel O
Beantown Hostel B
Boston Marriott Long Wharf E
Charles Street Inn M
Courtyard Boston Tremont Hotel P
Harborside Inn F
Irish Embassy Youth Hostel A
The John Jeffries House H
Langham L
Marriott's Customs House G
Millennium Bostonian Hotel D
Milner Q
Nine Zero K
Omni Parker House J
The Shawmut Inn C
XV Beacon I
BARS & CLUBS
21st Amendment 20
Bell in Hand Tavern 4
The Big Easy 42
The Black Rose 14
The Bull & Finch Pub 36
Buzz 49
Fours 1
The Good Life 38
Green Dragon Tavern 4
Gypsy Bar 40
Irish Embassy 2
Jacque's 53
The Kinsale 15
Ned Devine's 12
The Purple Shamrock 8
Sevens Ale House 24
The Rack 6
The Roxy 52
Umbria Nightclub 22
Massachusetts General Hospital
Harrison Gray Otis House
African Meeting House
The Museum of Afro-American History
Lewis Hayden House
George Middleton House
BEACON HILL
Ashburton Park
Boston Athenæum
Community Boating boat house
The Phillips School
Nichols House
Massachusetts State House
Old Granary Burying Ground
Park Street Church
Church of the Advent
Charles Street Meeting House
Robert Gould Shaw & 54th Regiment Memorial
Somerset Club
Hatch Memorial Shell
Frog Pond
Prescott House
Founder's Monument
Visitor Center
Flagstaff Hill
Soldiers and Sailors Monument
Public Garden
Boston Massacre Monument
Boston Common
Gibson House Museum
George Washington Statue
Swan Boats
Central Burying Ground
Millennium Place
Baylies Mansion
BACK BAY
Emmanuel Church of Boston
Colonial Theater
LADDER DISTRICT
Majestic Theatre
Arlington Street Church
Massachusetts Transportation Building
Wilbur Theatre
Wang Center for the Performing Arts
Church of the Covenant
Boston Park Plaza
THEATER DISTRICT
Shubert Theater
John Hancock Tower
Charles
Park Street
Boylston
Chinatown
Arlington
New England Medical Center
CAMBRIDGE STREET
BEACON STREET
CHARLES STREET
ARLINGTON STREET
BOYLSTON STREET
TREMONT STREET
WASHINGTON ST.
ESPLANADE
EMBANKMENT ROAD
CHARLESBANK ROAD
MOUNT VERNON STREET
CHESTNUT STREET
PINCKNEY ST.
REVERE STREET
MYRTLE STREET
PHILLIPS STREET
JOY STREET
BOWDOIN STREET
SOMERSET STREET
COMMONWEALTH AVE.
MARLBOROUGH ST.
NEWBURY STREET
PROVIDENCE STREET
STUART STREET
ST. JAMES AVE.
BERKELEY STREET
CLARENDON ST.
TRINITY PL.

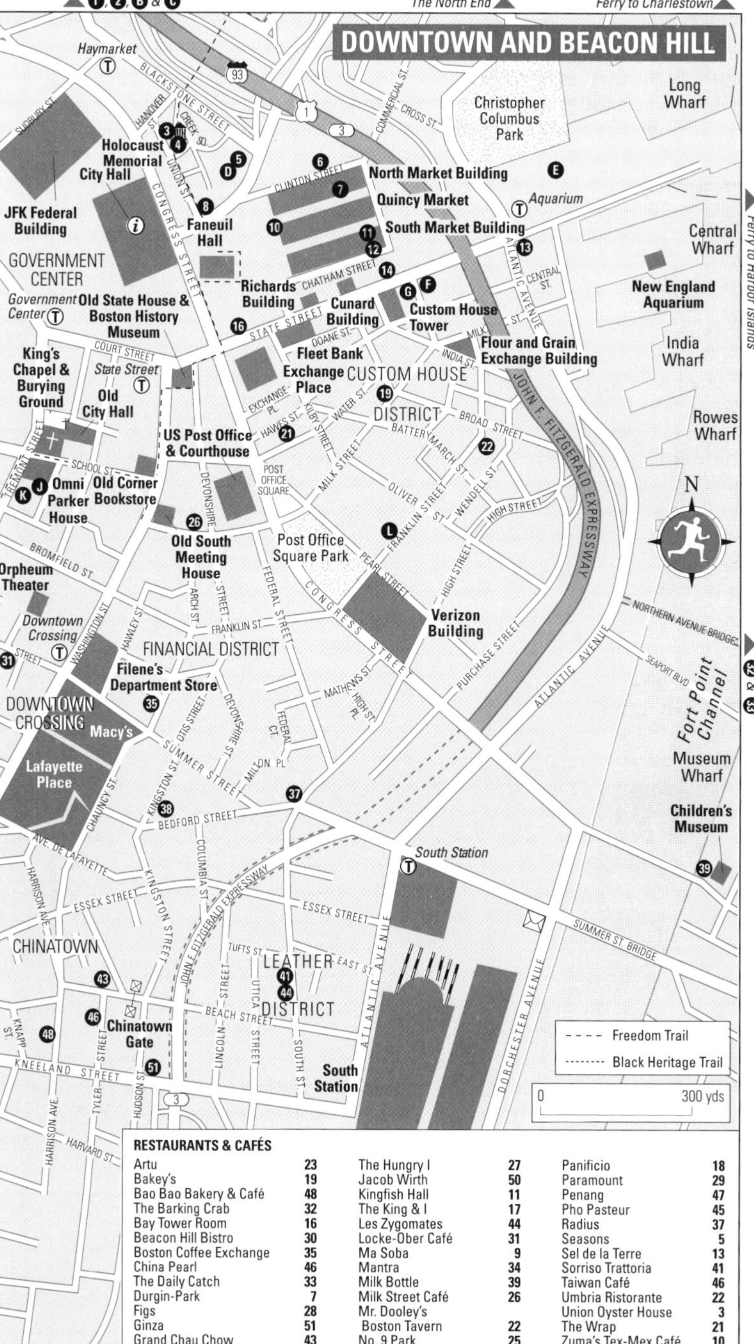

RESTAURANTS & CAFÉS

Artu	23	The Hungry I	27	Panificio	18
Bakey's	19	Jacob Wirth	50	Paramount	29
Bao Bao Bakery & Café	48	Kingfish Hall	11	Penang	47
The Barking Crab	32	The King & I	17	Pho Pasteur	45
Bay Tower Room	16	Les Zygomates	44	Radius	37
Beacon Hill Bistro	30	Locke-Ober Café	31	Seasons	5
Boston Coffee Exchange	35	Ma Soba	9	Sel de la Terre	13
China Pearl	46	Mantra	34	Sorriso Trattoria	41
The Daily Catch	33	Milk Bottle	39	Taiwan Café	46
Durgin-Park	7	Milk Street Café	26	Umbria Ristorante	22
Figs	28	Mr. Dooley's		Union Oyster House	3
Ginza	51	Boston Tavern	22	The Wrap	21
Grand Chau Chow	43	No. 9 Park	25	Zuma's Tex-Mex Café	10

ing a bonnet worth 75¢. Newly elected president George Washington made a much celebrated appearance on the Common in 1789, as did his aide-de-camp, the Marquis de Lafayette, several years later. Ornate nineteenth-century iron fencing encircled the entire park until World War II, when the majority of it was taken down for use as scrap metal: it is now said to grace the bottom of Boston Harbor.

One of the few actual sights here is the **Central Burying Ground**, which has occupied the southeast corner of the Common, near the intersection of Boylston and Tremont streets, since 1754. Artist Gilbert Stuart, best known for his portraits of George Washington – the most famous of which is replicated on the dollar bill – died penniless and was interred in Tomb 61. Among the other notables are members of the largest family to take part in the Boston Tea Party, various soldiers of the Revolutionary Army, and Redcoats killed in the Battle of Bunker Hill.

From the Burying Ground it's a short walk to **Flagstaff Hill**, the highest point on the Common, crowned with the granite-pillared Civil War **Soldiers and Sailors Monument**, which is topped by a bronze statue of Lady Liberty and encircled by four plaques displaying scenes of cap-wearing sailors and bayonet-toting foot soldiers. A former repository of colonial gunpowder, the hill overlooks the **Frog Pond**, once home to legions of unusually large amphibians and site of the first water pumped into the city. These days, it's nothing more than a kidney-shaped pool, used for wading in summer and ice-skating in winter. From here, a path east of the pond leads to the elegant, two-tiered **Brewer Fountain**, an 1868 bronze replica of one from the Paris Exposition of 1855; the scantily clad gods and goddesses at its base are watched over by cherubs from above.

Park Street Church to the Old Granary Burying Ground

The 1809 **Park Street Church**, on the northeast corner of Park and Tremont streets just across from Boston Common (mid-June to Aug daily 8.30am–3pm, rest of year by appointment; free; ⓣ617/523-3383; Park Street T), is an oversized and rather uninteresting mass of bricks and mortar, though its ornate 217-foot-tall white telescoping **steeple** is undeniably impressive. To get an idea of the immensity of the building, including the spire, walk to tiny Hamilton Place, across Tremont Street. The church's reputation rests not on size but on events that took place inside: this is where William Lloyd Garrison delivered his first public address calling for the nationwide abolition of slavery (Massachusetts did away with the practice in 1783), and where the patriotic song *America* ("My country 'tis of thee . . .") was first sung, on July 4, 1831.

Park Street itself slopes upward from the church along the edge of Boston Common toward the State House (see p.114). It was once known as **Bulfinch Row**, for its many brick townhouses designed by the architect Charles Bulfinch, but today only one remains, the imposing bay-windowed **Amory-Ticknor House** at no. 9, built in 1804 for George Ticknor, the first publisher of *The Atlantic Monthly*; it's now home to the first-rate restaurant *No. 9 Park* (see p.146).

Adjacent to the church is one of the more peaceful stops on the always busy Freedom Trail, the **Old Granary Burying Ground** (daily 9am–5pm; free), final resting place for numerous leaders of the American Revolution. The entrance, an Egyptian Revival arch, fronts Tremont Street, and it's from the Tremont sidewalk that some of the most famous gravesites can be best appreciated: the boulder and plaque commemorating revolutionary James Otis; Samuel Adams' tomb; and the group grave of the five people killed in the **Boston Massacre** of 1770. From any angle you can see the stocky **obelisk** at dead center that marks the grave of Benjamin Franklin's parents. Further inside are the graves of Peter Faneuil, **Paul Revere**, and **John Hancock**, although, as the rangers will tell you, "the stones and the bones may not match up."

The Boston Athenaeum and King's Chapel

Around the block from the Old Granary Burying Ground, the venerable **Boston Athenaeum**, at 10 1/2 Beacon St (Mon 8.30am–8pm, Tue–Fri 8.30am–5.30pm, Sat 9am–4pm; free; ⓣ617/227-0270, ⓦwww.bostonathenaeum.org; Park Street T), was established in 1807, and is one of the oldest and most ornate independent research libraries in the country. In naming their library, the founders demonstrated not only their high-minded classicism but marketing sensibility too, as its growing stature was a potent enough force to endow Boston with a lofty sobriquet – the "Athens of America" – that has stuck. During the nineteenth century, the Athenaeum's art collection was the most significant in New England, and its holdings were used as the underpinnings of the original Museum of Fine Arts. Best known today are its special collections, including the original holdings of the library of King's Chapel, which included the 1666 edition of Sir Walter Raleigh's *History of the World*, and its prominent artworks: an impressive array of sculptures, coupled with paintings by the likes of Sargent and Stuart, contribute to the atmosphere of studious refinement. However, unless you're going to go to the trouble of becoming a member, you'll be confined to the first floor of the library – not a bad spot to hunker down with a newspaper.

Just a block or so east from the Athenaeum is Boston's oldest cemetery, the atmospheric **King's Chapel Burying Ground**, 58 Tremont St (daily: June–Oct 9.30am–4pm, Nov–May 10am–4pm; hours may fluctuate; free; Park Street T), not to mention its accompanying church, both well worth a tour despite the din of nearby traffic. One of the chief pleasures of walking amongst the graves is to examine the many beautifully etched ancient tombstones, with their winged skulls and contemplative seraphim, such as that of one Joseph Tapping, near the Tremont Street side. King's Chapel Burying Ground was one of the favorite Boston haunts of author **Nathaniel Hawthorne**, who drew inspiration from the grave of a certain Elizabeth Pain to create the famously adulterous character of Hester Prynne for his novel *The Scarlet Letter*. (Hawthorne himself is buried in Concord's Sleepy Hollow Cemetery; see p.171).

The most conspicuous thing about the gray, foreboding **chapel** that stands on the grounds (June–Sept Mon–Sat 10am–4.30pm, Sun 1.30pm–4pm; free; Park Street T) is its absence of a steeple (there were plans for one, just not enough money). A wooden chapel was built on the site first, amid some controversy. In 1686, King James II revoked the Massachusetts Bay Colony's charter and installed Sir Edmund Andros as governor, giving him orders to found an Anglican parish, a move that for obvious reasons didn't sit too well with Boston's Puritan population. The present chapel was completed in 1754, with the pillar-fronted portico added in 1789, and the belfry boasts the biggest bell ever cast by Paul Revere. Most visitors never go past the entrance, but it is well worth a look inside, ideally during one of the weekly chamber music concerts (Tues 12.15–12.45pm; $3 suggested donation). While hardly ostentatious, the elegant Georgian interior, done up with wooden Corinthian columns and lit by chandeliers, provides a marked contrast to the minimalist adornments of Boston's other old churches. It also features America's oldest pulpit, dating from 1717, and many of its original pews.

The Freedom Trail

Boston's history is so visible that the city often stands accused of living in its past, and tourist-friendly contrivances like the **Freedom Trail** only serve to perpetuate the notion. The Freedom Trail originated when, like many American cities, Boston experienced an economic slump in the postwar years as people migrated to the suburbs; in response, resident William Schofield came up with the idea of a trail highlighting historic Boston sights to lure visitors – and their money – back into town.

Delineated by a 2.5-mile-long red-brick (or paint) stripe in (or on) the sidewalk, the trail stretches from Boston Common to Charlestown, linking sixteen points "significant in their contribution to this country's struggle for freedom." It's a somewhat vague qualifier that allows for the inclusion of several sights that have little to do with Boston's place in the American Revolution. In the relevant column, there's the Revolutionary-era **Old North Church**, whose lanterns warned of the British arrival (see p.107); **Faneuil Hall**, where opposition to the Brits' proposed tea tax was voiced (see opposite); the **Old South Meeting House**, wherein word came that said tax would be imposed (see p.101); the **Old State House**, which served as the Boston seat of British government (see p.108); and the site of the **Boston Massacre** (see p.91). Other stops on the trail, however, have nothing whatsoever to do with the struggle for independence, like the **USS Constitution** (see p.109), built fully two decades after the Declaration of Independence (but which failed, notably, to sink under British cannon fire, earning her the nickname "Old Ironsides"); the **Park Street Church** (see p.94), built another fifteen years after that; and the **Old Corner Bookstore** (see p.101), a publishing house for American (and some British) writers. You'll also find two instances of British dominion along the trail: the **Bunker Hill Monument** (see p.104), an obelisk commemorating, ironically, a British victory, albeit in the guise of a moral one for America, and **King's Chapel** (see p.95), built to serve the King's men stationed in Boston. Finally, you can check out the gilt-domed **Massachusetts State House** (see p.114) after visiting the gravesites of the Boston luminaries who fought for it – they lie interred in three separate **cemeteries** (see pp.94 and108).

Unfortunately, some of the touches intended to accentuate the attractions' appeal move closer to tarnishing it. The people in period costume stationed outside some of the sights can't help but grate a little, and the artificially enhanced atmosphere is exaggerated by the bright-red brick trail and pseudo-old signage that connects the sights. Still, the Freedom Trail remains the easiest way to orient yourself downtown, and is especially useful if you'll only be in Boston for a short time, as it does take in many "must-see" sights. For more info and an interactive timeline of Boston's history, visit ⓦwww.thefreedomtrail.org. You can also pick up a detailed National Park Service **map** of the trail from the visitor center at 15 State St.

Government Center

Most visitors pass through **Government Center**, due north of King's Chapel Burying Ground and west of Faneuil Hall, during their time in Boston, as it's an essential travel hub located in the midst of the city center. That said, passing through is just about all there is to do in this sea of towering gray government buildings which stands on the former site of **Scollay Square**, once Boston's most notorious den of porn halls and tattoo parlors. Scollay was razed in the early 1960s, eliminating all traces of its salacious past and lively character; indeed, the only thing that remains from the Square's steamier days is the Oriental Tea Company's 227-gallon Steaming Kettle advertisement. The area is now overlaid with concrete, thanks to an ambitious plan developed by I.M. Pei, and towered over by two monolithic edifices: Boston City Hall, at the east side of the plaza, and the John F. Kennedy Federal Building, on the north.

Faneuil Hall, Quincy Market, and around

Located between the Financial District and the North End, the **Faneuil Hall Marketplace** is the kind of active, bustling, public gathering ground that's none too common in Boston, popular with locals and tourists alike. Built as a market during colonial times to house the city's growing mercantile industry, it declined during the nineteenth century and, like the area around it, was pretty much defunct until the 1960s, when it was successfully redeveloped as a restaurant and shopping mall.

The much-hyped **Faneuil Hall** (May–Sept Mon–Sat 10am–8pm, Sun noon–6pm; Oct–April 10am–6pm, Sun noon–6pm; ⓣ617/523-1300, ⓦwww.faneuilhallmarketplace.com; State Street **T**) itself doesn't appear particularly majestic from the outside; it's simply a small, four-story brick building topped with a golden grasshopper weathervane, hardly the grandiose auditorium one might imagine would have housed the Revolutionary War meetings that earned it its "Cradle of Liberty" sobriquet. Nevertheless, this was where revolutionary firebrands such as Samuel Adams and James Otis whipped up popular support for independence by protesting British tax legislation on the second-floor meeting space. The first floor now houses a panoply of tourist shops which make for a less than dignified memorial; you'll also find an information desk, a post office, and a BosTix kiosk (see p.157). The second floor is more impressive: the auditorium has been preserved to reflect modifications made by Charles Bulfinch in 1805. Its focal point is a massive – and rather preposterous – canvas depicting an embellished version of "The Great Debate," during which Daniel Webster argued for the concept of the United States as one nation against South Carolina Senator Robert Hayne. While the debate was an actual event, the painting contains a number of nineteenth-century luminaries who certainly weren't in attendance – the artist simply thought this would help him sell his painting.

The three oblong markets just behind Faneuil Hall were built in the early eighteenth century to contain the trade that had quickly outgrown its space in

△ Faneuil Hall

the hall. The center building, known as **Quincy Market** (Mon–Sat 10am–9pm, Sun noon–6pm; ⓣ523-1300, ⓦwww.faneuilhallmarketplace.com; State Street **T**), holds a super-extended corridor lined with stands vending a variety of decent though pricey takeout treats – it's the mother of mall food courts. To either side of Quincy Market are the **North and South markets**, which hold restaurants and popular chain clothing stores, as well as specialized curiosity shops (one sells only purple objects, another nothing but vests). There's not much to distinguish it from any other shopping complex, save a few good restaurants and some surrounding bars, but sitting on a bench in the carnivalesque heart of it all on a summer day, eating scrod while the mobs of locals and tourists mill about, is a quintessential (if slightly absurd) Boston experience.

On the other side of Faneuil Hall from Quincy Market is **Dock Square**, so named for its original location directly on Boston's waterfront; carvings in the pavement indicate the shoreline in 1630. The square's center is dominated by a statue of **Samuel Adams**, interesting mostly for its over-the-top caption: "A Statesman, incorruptible and fearless." A dim, narrow corridor known as Scott's Alley heads north of the market to reach Creek Square, where you enter **Blackstone Street**, the eastern edge of a tiny warren of streets bounded to the west by Union. Its uneven cobblestoned streets and low brick buildings have remained largely untouched since the 1750s; many of them, especially those along Union Street, now house restaurants and pubs.

The corner of Union and North marks the location of the former home of **William Dawes**, one of the (forgotten) riders who joined Paul Revere on his midnight ride. Unlike Revere, his house has not been favorably preserved – it's now a *McDonald's* – but you can view a plaque commemorating the site. One touch of modernity (besides the Golden Arches) is just north on Union, where you'll see six tall hollow glass pillars erected as a **memorial** to victims of the **Holocaust**. Built to resemble smokestacks, the columns are etched with six million numbers recalling the tattoos the Nazis gave the Jews and other victims. Steam rises from grates beneath each of the pillars to accentuate their symbolism, an effect that's particularly striking at night.

Old State House

That the graceful three-tiered window tower of the red-brick **Old State House**, at the corner of Washington and State streets (daily 9am–5pm; $5; ⓣ617/720-1713, ⓦwww.bostonhistory.org; State Street **T**), is dwarfed by skyscrapers amplifies, rather than diminishes, its colonial-era dignity. For years this three-story structure was the seat of the Massachusetts Bay Colony, and consequently the center of British authority in New England. Later it served as Boston's city hall, and in 1880 it was nearly demolished so that State Street traffic might flow more freely.

An impassioned speech in the second-floor Council Chamber by James Otis, a Crown appointee who resigned to take up the colonial cause, sparked the quest for independence from Britain fifteen years before it was declared. The **balcony** overlooking State Street was the place from which the Declaration of Independence was first read publicly in Boston, on July 18, 1776. Two hundred years later, Queen Elizabeth II – the first British monarch to set foot in Boston – performed the same feat from the balcony as part of the American Bicentennial activities. Inside, a **museum** tracks, through images and artifacts of varying interest, the events that led up to the establishment of the Commonwealth of Massachusetts (though not, curiously, the US), along with Boston's role in the Revolutionary War. Upstairs are rotating exhibits on city history as well as a somewhat low-rent sound-and-light display re-enacting the Boston Massacre.

The Boston Massacre

Directly in front of the Devonshire Street side of the Old State House, a circle of cobblestones embedded in a small traffic island marks the site of the **Boston Massacre**, the tragic outcome of escalating tensions between Bostonians and the British Redcoats that occupied the city. This riot of March 5, 1770, began when a young wigmaker's apprentice began heckling an army officer over a barber's bill. The officer sought refuge in the Custom House, which stood opposite the Old State House at the time, but by this time, a throng of people had gathered, including more soldiers, at whom the mob flung rocks and snowballs. When someone threw a club that knocked a Redcoat onto the ice, he rose and fired. Five Bostonians were killed in the ensuing fracas. Two other patriots, John Adams and Josiah Quincy, actually defended the offending eight soldiers in court; six were acquitted, and the two guilty were branded on their thumbs.

The waterfront

Stretching from the North End to the South Station **T**, Boston's **waterfront** is still a fairly active area, although it's no longer the city's focal point, as it was up until the mid-1800s. Today, the waterfront thrives on tourism, with stands concentrated around **Long Wharf** hawking everything from tacky T-shirts to furry lobsters. Nevertheless, strolling the atmospheric **Harborwalk** that edges the water affords unbeatable views of Boston, and is a pleasant respite from the masses that can clog Faneuil Hall and the Common. You'll also find plenty of diversion, if you've got little ones in tow, as the **Children's Museum** and **Aquarium** are both found here. Otherwise, you can do some waterborne exploring on a number of boat tours, or even escape the city altogether by heading out to the **Harbor Islands**.

Long Wharf, the New England Aquarium, and around

The best place to head when hitting the waterfront is **Long Wharf**, which was built in 1710 and is still the area's hub of activity. As you might expect, summer is its most active season, when the wharf comes alive with vendors selling tacky souvenirs and surprisingly good ice cream. This is also the main point of departure for **harbor cruises**, whale-watching trips, and ferries to Cape Cod. Walk out to the end of the wharf for an excellent vantage point on **Boston Harbor**. It's perhaps most enjoyable – and still relatively safe – at night, when even the freighters appear graceful against the moonlit water.

Next door to Long Wharf is the waterfront's main draw, the **New England Aquarium** (July–Aug Mon–Thurs 9am–6pm, Fri–Sun 9am–7pm; Sept–June Mon–Fri 9am–5pm, Sat & Sun 9am–6pm; $16, kids $9; CityPass accepted; ⓣ617/973-5200, ⓦwww.neaq.org; Aquarium **T**). Especially fun for kids, the aquarium has plenty of good exhibits, like the penguins on the bottom floor – be sure to play with the device that maneuvers a fish-shaped point of light around the bottom of their pool; the guileless waterfowl mistake the light for a potential meal and follow it around hopefully. In the center of the aquarium's spiral walkway is an impressive collection of marine life: a three-story, 200,000-gallon cylindrical tank packed with giant sea turtles, moray eels, sharks, stingrays, and a range of other ocean exotica that swim by in unsettling proximity. The Aquarium also runs **whale-watching** trips (April–Oct; 3.5–5hr, call for times; $29, kids $20; ⓣ617/973-5281) and is home to a **3D IMAX theater** (daily 9.30am–10.30pm; $9.50, kids $7.50), which, at more than six stories high, has the largest screen in New England.

The Seaport District and the Children's Museum

It's hard to miss the larger-than-life 1930s-era **Hood Milk Bottle** across the Congress Street bridge in the **Seaport District**, though the only dairy product the 40ft structure serves is ice cream. In fact, most of its trade is in hot dogs and bagel sandwiches. Behind it, the engaging **Children's Museum**, 300 Congress St (Mon–Thurs, Sat & Sun 10am–5pm, Fri 10am–9pm; $9, kids $7, Fri 5–9pm $1; ⓣ617/426-8855, ⓦwww.bostonkids.org; South Station **T**), comprises four floors of educational exhibits, craftily designed to trick kids into learning about a huge array of topics, from musicology to Latin American *supermercados*. Before you leave, be sure to check out the Recycle Shop where industrial leftovers are transformed into appealing craft-fodder.

The Harbor Islands

Extending across Massachusetts Bay from Salem to Portsmouth, the 34 islands that comprise the bucolic **Harbor Islands** originally served as strategic defense points during the American Revolution and Civil War. It took congressional assent to turn them into a national park, in 1996, with the result that five are now easily accessible by ferry from Long Wharf (see overleaf). The most popular and best serviced of the lot, the skipping-stone-shaped **George's Island,** saw heavy use during the Civil War era, as evidenced by the remains of **Fort Warren** (May to mid-Oct, daily dawn–dusk; free), a mid-nineteenth-century battle station covering most of the island. Constructed from hand-hewn granite, and mostly used as a prison for captured Confederate soldiers, its musty barracks and extensive fortress walls have an eerie feel, although the parapets offer some stunning downtown views. You'll get more out of a visit by taking a park ranger tour (free).

The remaining Harbor Islands needn't rank high on your must-see list. The densely wooded and sand-duned **Lovell** is probably your best bet after George's, as it hosts the islands' only life-guarded sand beach. The largest of all, the 134-acre **Peddocks**, is laced with hiking trails connecting the remains of Fort Andrews, a harbor defense outpost used from 1904 to 1945 (closed to the public), with a freshwater pond and wildlife sanctuary. **Bumpkin** and **Grape** islands round out the list of accessible stops, though there's not much to see on either.

Island-bound

To visit the Harbor Islands, take the 25min ferry ride connecting Long Wharf with central **George's Island** (May to mid-Oct daily on the hour 9am–4pm; call to confirm times; $10, kids $7; ⓣ617/222-6999, ⓦwww.harborexpress.com; Aquarium **T**), the hub from which water taxis (free) shuttle visitors to four of the other thirty islands. You would do well to pack a picnic lunch (best arranged through nearby *Sel de la Terre*, see review p.146), though if you've come without, you can make do on beachfare from George's **snack bar**. None of the islands has a freshwater source, so be sure to bring bottled water with you. Note, too, that in the interest of preserving the islands' fragile environment, no bicycles or in-line skates are allowed. You can **camp**, however, for a nominal fee, on four of the islands (May to mid-Oct; Lovell and Peddocks ⓣ617/727-7676; Bumpkin and Grape ⓣ1-877/422-6762); you'll need to bring your own supplies. In all cases, good walking shoes are a must, as most of the pathways consist of dirt roads. The Harbor Islands **information** kiosk, at the foot of Long Wharf, keeps a detailed shuttle **schedule** and stocks excellent **maps**.

Washington Street shopping district

The **Washington Street shopping district** takes up much of downtown proper, and it holds some of the city's most historic sights – the Old Corner Bookstore, Old South Meeting House, and Old State House – but it tends to shut down after business hours. The stops can be seen in half a day, though you'll need to allow more time if shopping is on your agenda.

Across School Street from King's Chapel is the legendary **Omni Parker House**. It was in this hotel that Boston cream pie – really a layered cake with custard filling and chocolate glaze on top – was concocted in 1855, and the hotel reportedly still bakes 25 of them a day. On a more bizarre note, both Ho Chi Minh and Malcolm X used to work here, the former in the kitchen and the latter as a busboy.

Only one block long, School Street offers up some of the best of Boston charm, beginning with the antique gaslights that flank the severe western wall of King's Chapel. Just beyond is a grand French Second Empire building that served as **Boston City Hall** from 1865 to 1969. A few doors down on the left, the gambrel-roofed, red-brick former **Old Corner Bookstore** anchors the southern end of School as it joins Washington. The stretch of Washington from here to Old South Meeting House was nineteenth-century Boston's version of London's Fleet Street, with a convergence of booksellers, publishers, and newspaper headquarters; the bookstore itself – as home to the publishing house of Ticknor & Fields – was the hottest literary salon Boston ever had, with the likes of Emerson, Longfellow, and even Dickens and Thackeray, all of whom Ticknor & Fields published.

At the corner of School and Washington is the **Irish Famine Memorial**, commemorating the Irish refugees who immigrated to Boston as a result of the fungal potato crop that claimed one million lives. Its focus is an unsettling pair of statues, one depicting an Irish family holding their hands out for food, the other, a (presumably) Bostonian family that chooses to ignore them.

Old South Meeting House

Washington Street's big architectural landmark is the **Old South Meeting House**, at no. 310 (daily: April–Oct 9.30am–5pm, Nov–March 10am–4pm; $5, kids $1; ⓣ617/482-6439, ⓦwww.oldsouthmeetinghouse.org; Downtown Crossing **T**), a charming brick church recognizable by its tower, a separate, but attached, structure that tapers into an octagonal spire. An earlier cedarwood structure on the spot burned down in 1711, clearing the way for what is now the second oldest church building in Boston, after Old North Church in the North End. The spacious venue soon saw its share of anti-imperial rhetoric. The day after the Boston Massacre, outraged Bostonians assembled here to demand the removal of the troops that were ostensibly guarding the town. Even more telling was the meeting on December 16, 1773, when nearly five thousand locals came to await word on whether the Crown would permit the withdrawal of three ships in Boston Harbor containing sixty tons of taxed tea or repeal the reviled tax. When a message was received that neither ships nor tax would be removed, Samuel Adams rose and announced, "This meeting can do nothing more to save the country" – the signal that triggered the Boston box on Tea Party (see box on p.103).

Before becoming the **museum** it is today, the Meeting House served as a stable, a British riding-school, and even a bar. One of the things lost in the transition was the famous original high pulpit, which the British tore out during the Revolution and used as firewood; the ornate one standing today is a replica from 1808. There's not much to see other than the building itself – take note of the exterior **clock**, the same one installed in 1770, which you can still set your watch by – but if you take the audio tour, included in the admission price, you will hear campy re-enactments of a Puritan church service and the Boston Tea Party debates, among other more prosaic sound effects.

South of the meeting house, pedestrian-friendly **Downtown Crossing**, centered on the intersection of Washington and Summer streets, brims with department stores and smaller shops that mostly cater to lower-income shoppers. Its nucleus is Filene's Basement, home to the legendary "Running of the Brides" event where frenzied brides-to-be feverishly claw their way to marked-down gowns. The everyday shopping experience is more calm, and caters to bargain hunters of all socioeconomic stripes.

The Financial District and around

Boston's **Financial District** hardly conjures the same image as those of New York or London, but it continues to wield influence in key areas (such as with mutual funds, invented here in 1925) and is not entirely devoid of historic interest – though this is generally more manifest in plaques rather than actual buildings. Like most of America's business districts, it beats to an office-hours-only schedule, and many of its little eateries and Irish pubs are closed on weekends – though some brave new restaurants are beginning to make inroads. The generally immaculate streets follow the same short, winding paths as they did three hundred years ago, only now, thirty- and forty-story skyscrapers have replaced the wooden houses and churches that used to clutter the area.

The most dramatic approach is east from Washington via Milk Street. A bust of **Benjamin Franklin** surveys the scene from a recessed Gothic niche above the doorway at 1 Milk St, across from the Old South Meeting House. The site marks Franklin's birthplace, although the building itself only dates from 1874. A prime Art Deco specimen is nearby at 185 Franklin St, the head office of telephone company **Verizon**. The step-top building was a 1947 design; more recently the phone booths outside were given a Deco makeover. **Exchange Place**, at 53 State St, is a mirrored-glass tower rising from the facade of the old Boston Stock Exchange; the *Bunch of Grapes* tavern, watering hole of choice for many of Boston's revolutionary rabble-rousers, once stood here. Behind it is tiny **Liberty Square**, once the heart of Tory Boston and now home to an *Aspirations for Liberty* sculpture honoring the Hungarian anti-Communist uprising of 1956. The statue is an elegant depiction of rebels rising to hold up a (presumably rebellious) baby.

Downtown vistas

Whether from in or out of town, people can't seem to get enough of Boston's skyline – its pastiche of brownstone churches and glass-paneled skyscrapers framing Massachusetts Bay ranks among the country's finest. You can check out Boston from every angle by ascending the **Marriott Customs House** (see p.86), the **Prudential Tower** (see p.124), and the **Bunker Hill Monument** (see p.112). The best lay of the land, though, is had from the water – board the **Charlestown ferry** (see p.109) or visit the **Harbor Islands** (see p.100) and watch the city recede.

The Boston Tea Party

The first major act of rebellion preceding the Revolutionary War, the **Boston Tea Party**, was far greater in significance than it was in duration. On December 16, 1773, a long-standing dispute between the British government and its colonial subjects, involving a tea tax, came to a dramatic head. At nightfall, a group of five thousand waited at Old South Meeting House to hear the governor's pronouncement regarding three ships full of tea moored in Boston Harbor. After receiving word that the Crown would not lift the tax, the civil throng converged on Griffin's Wharf. Around one hundred of them, most dressed in Indian garb, boarded the brigs and threw their cargo of tea overboard. The partiers disposed of 342 chests of tea each weighing 360 pounds – enough to make 24 million cups, and worth more than one million dollars by today's standards. While it had the semblance of spontaneity, the event was in fact planned beforehand, and the mob was careful not to damage anything but the offending cargo. In any case, the Boston Tea Party transformed protest into revolution. The ensuing British sanctions, colloquially referred to as the "Intolerable Acts," and the colonists' continued resistance, further inflamed the tension between the Crown and its colonies, which eventually exploded at Lexington and Concord several months later.

The Custom House District

The wedge of downtown between State and Broad streets and Atlantic Avenue is the unfairly overlooked **Custom House District**, dotted with some excellent architectural draws, chief among which is the **Custom House Tower**, surrounded by 32 huge Doric columns; 1847, the thirty-story Greek Revival tower itself was added in 1915. Not surprisingly, it is no longer the tallest skyscraper in New England (a status it held for forty-nine years), but it still has plenty of character and terrific views – you can check them out from the 360-degree observation deck free of charge (tours Mon–Thurs at 10am & 4pm, Fri & Sat 4pm only; ⓣ617/310-6300).

State Street originally extended into the Boston harbor, and the area still retains glimpses of its maritime past. Get a look at the elaborate cast-iron facade of the **Richards Building** at no. 114 – a clipper ship company's office in the 1850s – and the **Cunard Building** at no. 126, its ornamental anchors recalling Boston's status as the North American terminus of the first transatlantic steamship mail service. Another landmark, just a block south from the Custom House Tower, is the **Flour and Grain Exchange Building**, 177 Milk St, a fortress-like construction with a turreted, conical roof that recalls the Romanesque Revival style of prominent local architect H.H. Richardson.

Chinatown, the Ladder District, and the Leather District

Colorful and authentic, Boston's **Chinatown** lies wedged into just a few square blocks between the Financial and Theater districts, but it makes up in activity what it lacks in size. Lean against a pagoda-topped pay phone on the corner of **Beach and Tyler streets** any time and watch the way life here revolves around the food trade. By day, merchants barter in Mandarin and Cantonese over the going price of produce; by night, Bostonians arrive in droves to nosh in Chinatown's restaurants. Walk down either of those streets – the neighborhood's two liveliest thoroughfares – and you'll pass most of the restaurants, bakeries, and markets, in whose windows you'll see the usual complement of roast ducks hanging from hooks and aquariums filled with future seafood dinners. There's not much else to actually see, though the impressive **Chinatown Gate**, a three-story red-and-gilt monolith guarded by four Fu dogs, overlooks the intersection of Hudson and Beach streets. Chinatown is at its most vibrant during various festivals, none more so than the **Chinese New Year** in late January (sometimes early Feb); at the **Festival of the August Moon**, not surprisingly held in August, there's a bustling street fair. Call the Chinese Merchants Association for more information (Ⓣ617/482-3972).

The tenor around Washington Street, between Essex and Kneeland, was until recently relatively dodgy. Designated as an "adult entertainment zone" in the 1960s, when it replaced Scollay Square as the city's red-light district, and known enigmatically as the Combat Zone, the **Ladder District** was home to a few X-rated theaters and bookshops until trendy restaurants and nightclubs pushed the smut peddlers out. PR hacks successfully renamed the area after its ladder-like layout (Tremont and Washington form the rails, Winter and Avery streets the top and bottom rungs), but failed to alter its daylight character. Today, it's little more than Downtown Crossing run-off, home to a few nail salons and chain restaurants.

Just east of Chinatown are six square blocks, bounded by Kneeland, Atlantic, Essex, and Lincoln streets, that designate the **Leather District**, which takes its name from the days when the shoe industry was a mainstay of the New England economy, and the leather needed to make the shoes was shipped through the warehouses here. Since then, the Financial District – with which it is frequently lumped – has horned in, and the leather industry has pretty much dried up. The distinction between the two areas is actually quite sharp, most evident where High Street transitions into South Street: gleaming modern skyscrapers are replaced by stout brick warehouses, and the place of suited bankers is taken by a melange of merchants and gallery owners, who have taken advantage of the abundance of cheap warehouse space. Some of the edifices still have their leather warehouse signs on them, like the Boston Hide & Leather Co, at 15 East St. The nearby **South Street Station** is Boston's main train and bus terminus.

The Theater District

Just south of Boston Common is the slightly seedy **Theater District**, the chief attractions of which are the flamboyant buildings that lend the area its title, such as the Wilbur, Colonial, and Majestic theaters. Not surprisingly, you'll have to purchase tickets in order to inspect their grand old interiors (see p.157), but it's well worth a quick walk along Tremont Street to admire the facades. The **Wang Center for the Performing Arts** – still the grande dame of Boston theater – is just around the corner from **Piano Row**, a section of Boylston St between Charles and Tremont that was the center of American piano manufacturing and music publishing in the nineteenth and early twentieth centuries. There are still a few piano shops around, but the hip restaurants and clubs in the immediate vicinity are of greater interest; many, like *Mistral* (see p.149), are tucked between Charles and Stuart streets around the mammoth **Massachusetts Transportation Building** and cater to the theatergoing crowd.

The North End

The **North End** is a small yet densely populated neighborhood whose narrow streets are chock-a-block with Italian bakeries and restaurants, and also hold some of Boston's most storied sights. Bordered by Boston Harbor and cut off from downtown by what's left of I-93, it may seem an inaccessible district at first, but you can avoid the hassle – and get a much better sense of the area's attractiveness – by entering from the waterfront Christopher Columbus Park, then taking Richmond Street past quiet North Square to Hanover Street, the North End's main drag, from where you can explore the must-sees fairly quickly.

The North End's detached quality goes back to colonial times, when it was actually an island, later to be joined by short bridges to the main part of town. Though landfill eventually ended the district's physical isolation, the North End remained very much a place apart. Irish immigrants poured in after the potato famine of 1845–48, but were just the first of several immigrant groups to settle

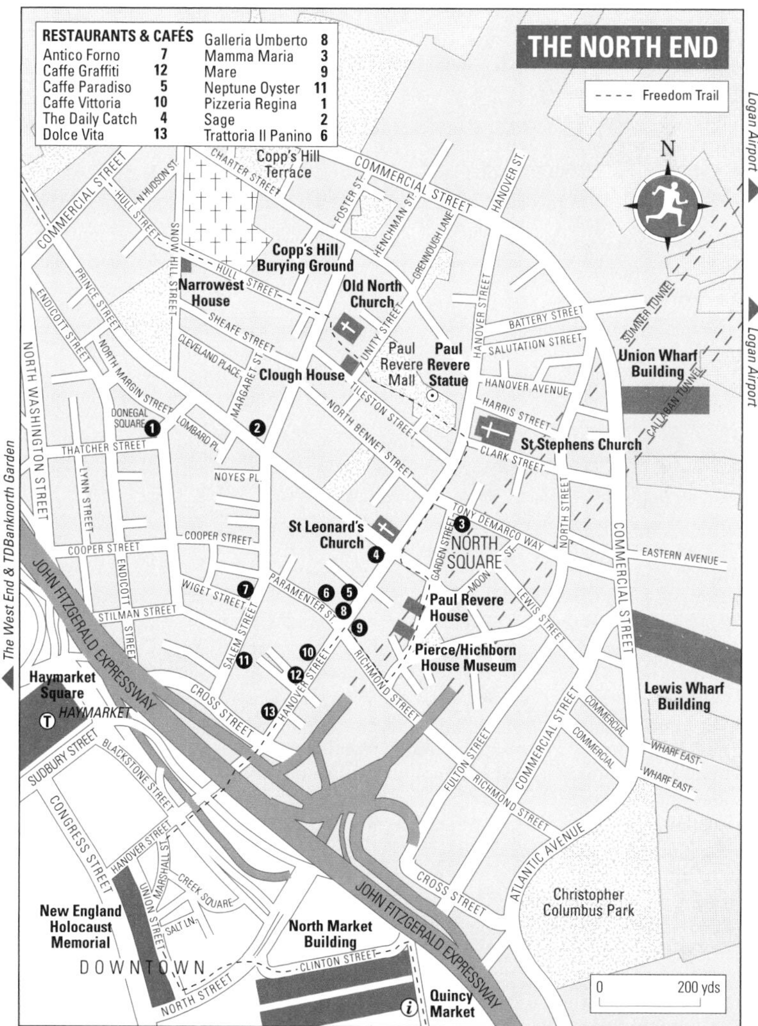

here, followed by Eastern European Jews in the 1850s and southern Italians in the early twentieth century. The latter have for the most part stayed put, and the North End is still Boston's most authentically Italian neighborhood, with its proliferation of bakeries and produce and meat markets. In recent years, however, yuppies have begun to overtake the area's waterfront side and are now making inroads into rehabilitated tenements. Though you can still see laundry dangling from upper-story windows and grandmothers chattering in Italian in front of their apartment buildings, it's perhaps only a matter of time before gentrification wins out, particularly since the city is bent on using the area that fronts the North End (formerly I-93) as a park to improve the neighborhood's accessibility.

Hanover Street and North Square

Hanover Street has long been the main connection between the North End and the rest of Boston, and it is along here – and the small side streets like Parmenter and Richmond (actually a continuation of each other on either side of Hanover) – that many of the area's *trattorias*, cafés, and bakeries are located. It's also where you'll find, in its first few blocks, perhaps Boston's most authentically European flavor: although there are a handful of chain stores in the neighborhood, the majority of businesses remain refreshingly independent.

The little triangular wedge of cobblestones and gaslights known as **North Square**, one block east of Hanover between Prince and Richmond, is among the most historic and attractive pockets of Boston, although its actual center is cordoned off by a heavy chain. Here the eateries recede in deference to the **Paul Revere House**, the oldest residential address in the city, at 19 North Square (mid-April to Oct daily 9.30am–5.15pm, Nov to mid-April Tues–Sun 9.30am–4.15pm; $3; Ⓣ617/523-2338, Ⓦwww.paulreverehouse.org). The three-story post-and-beam structure, which dates from about 1680, stands on the former site of the considerably grander home of Puritan heavyweight Increase Mather, which burned down in the Great Fire of 1676. The building, in which Revere lived from 1770 to 1800, was restored in 1908 to reflect its seventeenth-century appearance; prior to that it served variously as a grocery store, tenement, and cigar factory. Though the house is more impressive for its longevity than its appearance, from the outside the third-story overhang and leaded windows provide quite a contrast to the red-brick buildings around it. Examples of Revere's self-made silverware upstairs merit a look, as does a small but evocative exhibit about the mythologizing of Revere's famed horseback ride.

A small courtyard, the focus of which is a glass-encased 900-pound bell that Revere cast, separates the Paul Revere House from the **Pierce/Hichborn House** (tours by appointment only; $3; Ⓣ617/523-2338), a simple Georgian-style house built in 1710, making it the oldest surviving brick house in Boston. Moses Pierce, a glazier, built the house; it later belonged to Paul Revere's shipbuilding cousin, Nathaniel Hichborn. Although you won't be dazzled by its interior, the house does hold some noteworthy architectural details: it retains its original staircase as well as two painted fireplaces, all dating to the early 1700s.

At Hanover's intersection with Clark Street is **St Stephen's Church**, the only still-standing church in Boston built by Charles Bulfinch and one with a striking three-story recessed brick arch entrance. Originally called New North Meeting House, it received its present-day name in 1862, in order to keep up with the increasingly Catholic population of the North End. Though it seems firmly planted today, the whole building was actually moved back sixteen feet when Hanover Street was widened in 1870.

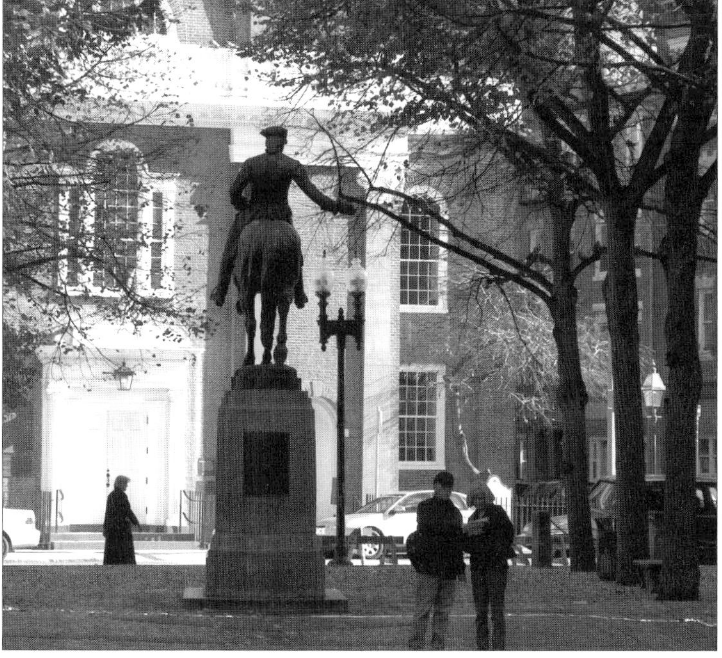

△ Statue of Paul Revere

Just across Hanover, the famous bronze **statue** of Paul Revere astride his borrowed horse marks the edge of the **Paul Revere Mall**. The cobblestoned park they inhabit (also known as the Prado) was carved out of a chunk of apartment blocks in 1933 and runs back to tiny Unity Street. At 21 Unity you can find the small 1712 red-brick **Clough House**, a private residence built by the mason who helped lay the brick of the nearby Old North Church.

Old North Church

Few places in Boston have as emblematic a quality as the simple yet noble **Old North Church**, 193 Salem St (daily: June–Oct 9am–6pm, Nov–May 9am–5pm; free; ⓣ617/523-6676, ⓦwww.oldnorth.com), rising unobstructed above the uniform blocks of red-brick apartments around it. Built in 1723, it's the oldest structure in Boston, and easily recognized by its gleaming 191-foot **steeple** – actually a replica as hurricanes toppled both the original in 1804 and its first replacement in 1954 (the weather vane, however, is the original). What secured its place in history were the two lanterns that church sexton Robert Newman is said to have hung inside it on the night of April 18, 1775, to signal the movement of British forces "by sea" from Boston Common, which then bordered the Charles River. That steeple is clearly visible from Charlestown across the water and even from the other side of I-93's remnants, lending a certain credence to its reputation as a watch and signal tower. Still, some historians speculate that the lanterns were actually hung from another church, called North Meeting House, which occupied the North Square spot where the **Sacred Heart Italian Church** now stands, at no. 12; that irate Tories burned that one for firewood in 1776 adds fuel to the theory. In any case, the spotlessly white interior contains the oldest clock still ticking in an American public building, made in 1726. The timber on which the high box pews rest is supported by 37 basement-level bricks crypts. One of the 1100 bodies encased therein is that of John Pitcairn, the British major killed in the Battle of Bunker Hill. His remains were tagged for Westminster Abbey, but didn't quite make it.

Some of Old North's greatest charms are actually outside the church itself, notably the diminutive **Washington Memorial Garden**, the brick walls of which are bedecked with commemorative plaques honoring past church members, and the inviting **Bigelow Garden**, cultivated with floral varieties that were popular in the eighteenth century.

Copp's Hill Burying Ground

Up Hull Street from Old North Church, atmospheric **Copp's Hill Burying Ground** (daily dawn–dusk), with its eerily tilting slate tombstones and stunning harbor views, holds the highest ground in the North End. Among the ten thousand interred are nearly a thousand men who had lived in the "New Guinea Community," a long-vanished colonial enclave of free blacks at the foot of the hill. The most famous gravesite here is that of the Mather family, just inside the wrought-iron gates on the Charter Street side. Increase Mather and son Cotton – the latter a Salem Witch Trial witness for the prosecution – were dominant clerics in Boston's congregational meeting houses, a fact not at all reflected in the rather diminutive, if appropriately plain, brick vault tomb. You'll notice that many gravestones have chunks missing, the consequence of British soldiers using them for target practice during the 1775 Siege of Boston; the grave of one Captain Daniel Malcolm, in the third row of gravestones (starting at the left), bears particularly strong evidence of this.

The granite **Copp's Hill Terrace**, a plateau separated from the burial ground by Charter Street, was the place from which British cannons bombarded Charlestown during the Battle of Bunker Hill. In 1919, a 2.3-million-gallon tank of molasses exploded nearby, creating a syrupy tidal wave thirty feet high that engulfed entire buildings and drowned 21 people along with a score of horses. Old North Enders claim you can still catch a whiff of the stuff on an exceptionally hot day. Lastly, across the street from Copp's Hill is Boston's **narrowest house**, at 44 Hull St. It really *is* narrow – 9 1/2 feet wide – and that's about it, as it's a private residence and you can't go in.

Salem and Prince streets

While the Old North Church is **Salem Street**'s star attraction, in the lower blocks between Prince and Cross streets, Salem is arguably the North End's most colorful thoroughfare. The actual street – whose name is a bastardization of "Shalom Street," as it was known to the earlier European Jewish settlers – is so narrow that the red-brick buildings seem to lean into one another, and light traffic makes it a common practice to walk right down the middle of the road. Along here you'll find an agreeable assemblage of Italian grocers, aromatic *pasticcerias*, and cafés.

Meanwhile, serpentine **Prince Street** cuts through the heart of the North End on an east–west axis, linking Salem and Hanover streets. Like most in the neighborhood, this appealing artery also has its share of restaurants, but it tends to be more social – locals typically pass the day along the pavement here on folding chairs brought from home. At the corner of Hanover Street, **St Leonard's Church**, 14 N Bennet St (Mon–Fri 9am–1pm; ⓣ617/523-2110), was supposedly the first Italian Catholic church in New England. The ornate interior is a marked contrast to Boston's stark Protestant churches, while the so-called "Peace Garden" in front, with its prosaic plantings and tacky statuary, is – in a sense – vintage North End.

Charlestown

Charlestown, across Boston Harbor via Charlestown Bridge from the North End, is a largely Irish working-class neighborhood that's quite isolated from the city, despite its annexation more than a century ago. Most visitors only make it over this way for the historic frigate the **USS Constitution**, Charlestown's number-one draw. There's not much in the way of atmosphere, as the area's core of quiet streets and elegant rowhouses is all but surrounded by elevated highways and construction, though you won't have to worry much about the inelegant environs if you arrive on one of the trolley tours – or even better, by the short $1.50 ferry trip (Ⓣ617/227-4321) from Long Wharf to the Charlestown Navy Yard.

The earliest Puritan settlers had high hopes for developing Charlestown when they arrived in 1629, but an unsuitable water supply pushed them over to the Shawmut Peninsula, which they promptly renamed Boston. Charlestown grew slowly after that, and had to be completely rebuilt after the British burned it down in 1775. The mid-1800s witnessed the arrival of the so-called "lace-curtain Irish," somewhat better off than their East Boston brethren, and the district remains Irish at heart. The longtime locals, known as "townies," have acquired a reputation for being standoffish, due to episodes such as their resistance to school desegregation in the 1970s. Recent years have seen urban professionals practically take over the Federal- and Colonial-style town homes south of the **Bunker Hill Monument** – Charlestown's other big sight – much to the chagrin of the townies. The rest of the neighborhood is fairly nondescript and even somewhat dodgy in parts.

The USS Constitution ("Old Ironsides")

The sprawling **Charlestown Navy Yard** was one of the first and busiest US naval shipyards – riveting together an astounding 46 destroyer escorts in 1943 alone – though it owes most of its present-day liveliness to the **USS Constitution**, at Constitution Wharf (April to late Oct Tues–Sun 10am–5.50pm, Nov–March Thurs–Sun 10am–3.50pm; free; Ⓣ617/242-5671, Ⓦwww.uss-constitution.navy.mil). In 1974 the Yard became part of the Boston National Historical Park after President Nixon decommissioned it, and since then it has been ambitiously repurposed as marinas, upscale condos, and offices. But its focal point remains the USS *Constitution*, the oldest commissioned warship afloat in the world. Launched two centuries ago to safeguard American merchant vessels from Barbary pirates and the French and British navies, she earned her nickname during the War of 1812, when cannonballs fired from the British HMS *Guerrière* bounced off the hull (the "iron sides" were actually hewn from live oak, a particularly sturdy wood from the southeastern US), leading to the first and most dramatic naval conquest of that war. The ship went on to win 33 battles – never losing one – before it was retired from service in 1830.

Authentic enough in appearance, the *Constitution* has certainly taken its hits – roughly ninety percent of the ship has been reconstructed. Even after extensive renovations, though, Old Ironsides is still too frail to support sails for extended periods of time, and the only regular voyages it makes are annual

△ USS *Constitution*

Fourth of July turnarounds in Boston Harbor. There's often a line to visit the ship – especially in the summer – but it's worth the wait to get a close-up view of the elaborate rigging that can support some three dozen sails totaling almost an acre in area. After ambling about the main deck, scuttle down to the lower deck, where you'll find an impressive array of cannons. Though most are replicas, two functional models face downtown from the bow from where they mark mast-raising and -lowering daily. Were they to fire the 24-pound balls for which they were originally outfitted, they'd topple the Custom House Tower across the bay in downtown Boston.

The rest of Charlestown Navy Yard

Housed in a substantial granite building a short walk from Old Ironsides and across from Pier 1, the **USS Constitution Museum** (daily: April to late Oct 9am–6pm; Nov–March 10am–5pm; free; ⓣ617/426-1812, ⓦwww.ussconstitutionmuseum.org) is worth visiting before boarding the ship. The downstairs covers the history of the ship, including the story of how, in the 1920s, US schoolchildren contributed $154,000 in pennies toward its preservation. Upstairs is perhaps more fun, with hands-on exhibits putting you in the role of a sailor: determine whether your comrades have scurvy or gout, attempt to balance yourself on a shifting footrope, and ponder whether you would be willing to eat a biscuit "as hard as a brick."

Berthed in between Old Ironsides and the ferry to Long Wharf is the hulking gray mass of the World War II destroyer **USS Cassin Young** (same hours as the *Constitution*; free). You can stride about the expansive main deck and check out some of the cramped chambers below, but it's mostly of interest to World War II history buffs. At the northern perimeter of the Navy Yard is the **Ropewalk Building**. Between 1830 and 1970 "ropewalkers" made every single strand of rope for the US Navy in this narrow, quarter-mile-long granite building, the only one of its kind still standing in the country; unfortunately it's not open to the public.

City Square to Bunker Hill Monument

Toward Charlestown's center, there's a wealth of eighteenth- and nineteenth-century townhouses, many of which you'll pass on your way from the Navy Yard to the Bunker Hill Monument. John Harvard, the young English minister whose library and funds launched Harvard University after his death, lived in

The Battle of Bunker Hill

The Revolutionary War was at its bloodiest on the hot June day when British and colonial forces clashed in Charlestown. In the wake of the battles at Lexington and Concord two months before, the British had assumed full control of Boston, while the patriots had the upper hand in the surrounding countryside. The British, under the command of generals Thomas Gage, William Howe, and "Gentleman Johnny" Burgoyne, intended to sweep the area clean of "rebellious rascals." Americans intercepted the plans and moved to fortify **Bunker Hill**, the dominant hill in Charlestown. However, when Colonel William Prescott arrived on the scene, he chose to occupy **Breed's Hill** instead, either due to confusion – the two hills were often confused on colonial-era maps – or tactical foresight, based on the proximity of Breed's Hill to the harbor. Whatever the motivation, more than a thousand citizen-soldiers arrived during the night of June 16, 1775, and fortified the hill with a 160-foot-long earthen redoubt by morning.

Spotting the Yankee fort, the Redcoats, each carrying 125 pounds of food and supplies on their backs, rowed across the harbor to take the rebel-held town. On the patriots' side, Colonel Prescott had issued his celebrated order to his troops that they not fire "'til you see the whites of their eyes," such was their limited store of gunpowder. When the enemy's approach was deemed near enough, the patriots opened fire; though vastly outnumbered, they successfully repelled two full-fledged assaults. Some British units lost more than ninety percent of their men, and what few officers survived had to push their men forward with their swords to make them fight on. By the third British assault, the Redcoats had shed their gear, reinforcements had arrived, and the Americans' supply of gunpowder was dwindling – as were their chances of clinching victory. The rebels continued to fight with stones and musket butts; meanwhile, British cannonfire from Copp's Hill in the North End was turning Charlestown into an inferno. Despite the eventual American loss, the patriots were invigorated by their strong showing, and the British, who had lost nearly half of their men who fought in the battle, became convinced that victory over the determined rebels would only be possible with a much larger army.

Charlestown and left a legacy of street names here: directly behind **City Square** – a traffic circle anchored by one of Boston's most popular restaurants, *Olives* (see p.147) – Harvard Street curves through the small **Town Hill** district, site of Charlestown's first settled community. You'll also find Harvard Mall and adjacent Harvard Square (not to be confused with the one in Cambridge), both lined with well-preserved houses.

At the corner of Main and Warren streets is the atmospheric **Warren Tavern**, a small three-story wooden structure built after the British burned Charlestown in the Battle of Bunker Hill, and named for Dr Joseph Warren, who was killed in combat. From the tavern, crooked Devens Street to the south and Cordis Street to the north are packed with historic, private houses; the most imposing is the Greek Revival mansion at **33 Cordis Street**. West on Main Street, at Thompson Square, the landmark **Five Cents Savings Bank Building**, with its steep mansard roof and Victorian Gothic ornamentation, looms above the street-level convenience stores. Further west is the **Phipps Street Burying Ground**, which dates from 1630. While many Revolutionary soldiers are buried here, it's not part of the Freedom Trail – perhaps even more of a reason to make the detour.

Double back and head up Monument Avenue, toward the Bunker Hill Monument. The red-brick townhouses that you'll pass are some of the most eagerly sought residences in town. Nearby is **Winthrop Square**, Charlestown's unofficial common, just south of the monument. The prim rowhouses overlooking it form another upscale enclave.

Bunker Hill Monument

Commemorating the Battle of Bunker Hill is the **Bunker Hill Monument** (daily 9am–4.30pm; free), a gray, dagger-like obelisk that's visible from just about anywhere in Charlestown, thanks to its position atop a butte confusingly known as Breed's Hill (see box overleaf). It was here that the New England militia built a fort on the night of June 16, 1775, to wage what was ultimately a losing battle – despite its recasting by US historians as a great moral victory in the fight for independence. The tower is centrally positioned in **Monument Square** and fronted by a statue of Colonel William Prescott, who commanded the Americans; at its base is a lodge that houses some decent dioramas of the battle. Inside, 294 steps wind up the 221-foot granite shaft to the top; hardy climbers will be rewarded with sweeping views of Boston, the harbor, and surrounding towns – and, to the northwest, the stone spire of the **St Francis de Sales Church**, which stands atop the real Bunker Hill.

Beacon Hill and the West End

No visit to Boston would be complete without an afternoon spent strolling around delightful **Beacon Hill**, a dignified stack of red brick rising over the north side of Boston Common. This is the Boston of wealth and privilege, one-time home to numerous historical and literary figures – including John Hancock, John Quincy Adams, Louisa May Alcott, and Oliver Wendell Holmes – and still the address of choice for the city's elite. Its narrow, hilly byways are lit with gaslights and lined with quaint, nineteenth-century-style townhouses, all part of an enforced preservation that prohibits modern buildings, architectural innovations, or anything else to disturb the carefully cultivated atmosphere of urban gentility.

It was not always this way. In colonial times, Beacon Hill was the most prominent of three peaks known as the Trimountain which formed Boston's geological backbone. The sunny south slope was developed into prime real estate and quickly settled by the city's political and economic powers, while the north slope was closer in spirit to the **West End**, a tumbledown port district populated by free blacks and immigrants; indeed, the north slope was home to so much salacious activity that outraged Brahmins termed it "Mount Whoredom." By the end of the twentieth century, this social divide was almost entirely eradicated, though today it can still be seen in the somewhat shabbier homes north of Pinckney Street and in the tendency of members of polite society to refer to the south slope as "the good side." Still, both sides have much to offer, if of very different character: on the south slope, there's the grandiose **Massachusetts State House**, attractive boulevards like **Charles Street** and the **Beacon Street Promenade**, in addition to the residences of past and present luminaries. More down to earth are the north slope's **Black Heritage Trail** sights, such as the **African Meeting House**, and some vestiges of the old West End.

Beacon Street

Running along the south slope of Beacon Hill above the Common, **Beacon Street** was described as Boston's "sunny street for the sifted few" by Oliver Wendell Holmes in the late nineteenth century. This lofty character remains today: the row of stately brick townhouses, fronted by ornate iron grillwork, presides regally over the area. The story behind the **purple panes** in some of their windows – most visible at nos. 63 and 64 – evinces the street's long association with Boston wealth and privilege. When the panes were installed in some of the first Beacon Street mansions, they turned purple upon exposure to the sun, due to an excess of manganese in the glass. At first, their owners perceived the purple panes as nothing more than an irritating accident, but due to their prevalence in the windows of Boston's most prestigious houses, they eventually came to be perceived as the definitive Beacon Hill status symbol by subsequent generations – in fact, some residents have gone so far as to shade their windows purple in imitation.

While it lacks the purple-tinted panes, the elegant bowfronted 1808 **Prescott House**, at no. 55 (May–Oct Wed, Thurs & Sat noon–4pm, tours every 30min; $4; ⓣ617/742-3190, ⓦwww.nscda.org/ma; Park St Ⓣ), is still worthy of a visit. Designed by an understudy of Charles Bulfinch, the house's most distinguished inhabitant was Spanish historian William Hickling Prescott, whose family occupied its five floors from 1845 to 1859. Hung above the pastiche of Federalist and Victorian furniture inside are a photograph of two crossed swords that once belonged to Colonel William Prescott and British Captain John Linzee – the historian and his wife's respective grandfathers. The men fought against each other at Bunker Hill (see box on p.111), and the sight of their munitions here inspired William Thackeray, a frequent house visitor, to write his novel, *The Virginians*.

Across the street, the **Founder's Monument** commemorates Boston's first European settler, William Blackstone, a Cambridge-educated loner who moved from England with his entire library to a piece of wilderness he acquired for next to nothing from the Shawmut Indians – the site of present-day Boston. A stone bas-relief depicts the apocryphal moment in 1629 when Blackstone sold most of his acreage to a group of Puritans from Charlestown.

Back on the north side of Beacon Street, and a few steps past Spruce Court, is the last of a trio of **Charles Bulfinch** houses (see box overleaf) commissioned by lawyer and future Boston mayor Harrison Gray Otis over a ten-year period;

The architecture of Charles Bulfinch

America's foremost architect of the late eighteenth and early nineteenth centuries, **Charles Bulfinch** developed a distinctive style somewhere between Federal and Classical that remains Boston's most recognizable architectural motif. Mixing Neoclassical training with New England practicality, Bulfinch built residences characterized by their rectilinear brick structure and pillared porticoes – examples remain throughout Beacon Hill, most notably at 87 Mount Vernon St and 45 Beacon St. Although most of his work was residential, Bulfinch, in fact, made his name with the design of various government buildings, such as the 1805 renovation of **Faneuil Hall** and, more significantly, the **Massachusetts State House**, whose dome influenced the design of state capital buildings nationwide. His talents extended to urban planning as well, including the layout of Boston's **South End**, and an area known as Tontine Crescent, a half-ellipse planned around a small park that won Bulfinch praise but ruined him financially; what vestiges remain are found around the Financial District's Franklin and Arch streets.

the four-story Classical house has been home to the American Meteorological Society since 1958. Just east of here, it's hard to miss the twin-swelled granite building at no. 42–43, built for Colonel David Sears' family by Alexander Parris, of Quincy Market fame. Its stern Greek Revival facade has welcomed members of the exclusive **Somerset Club** since 1872, a club so elitist that when a fire broke out in the kitchen, the firemen who arrived were ordered to come in via the cumbersome servants' entrance, a heavy iron-studded portal.

Farther up the street, on the edge of the Commons facing the Massachusetts State House, is the majestic monument honoring **Robert Gould Shaw and the 54th Massachusetts Regiment**. The memorial commemorates America's first all-black company to fight in the Civil War, a group led by Shaw, scion of a moneyed Boston Brahmin clan. Isolated from the rest of the Union army, given the worst of the military's resources, and saddled with menial or terribly dangerous assignments, the regiment performed its service bravely; most of its members, including Shaw, were killed in a failed attempt to take Fort Wagner from the Confederates. Augustus Saint-Gaudens' 1897 high-relief bronze sculpture depicts the regiment's farewell march down Beacon Street, and the names of the soldiers who died in action are listed on its reverse side (though these were only belatedly added in 1982). Robert Lowell won a Pulitzer Prize for his poem, *For the Union Dead*, which took its inspiration from the monument; the regiment's story was also depicted in the 1989 film *Glory*, starring Matthew Broderick as Shaw.

Massachusetts State House

Across from the memorial rises the large gilt dome of the Charles Bulfinch-designed **Massachusetts State House** (Mon–Fri 10am–4pm, last tour at 3.30pm; free; Park Street T), the scale and grandeur of which recall the heady spirit of the then newly independent America in which it was built. Though only three stories high, it seems taller, sitting at the confluence of the steep grade of Park and Beacon streets. Of the current structure, only the central section was part of Bulfinch's original design; the huge wings jutting out toward the street on either side and the section extending up Bowdoin Street behind the State House were all added much later. An all-star team of Revolution-era luminaries contributed to its construction: built on land purchased from John Hancock's estate, its cornerstone was laid by Samuel Adams, and the copper for its dome was rolled in Paul Revere's foundry (though it was covered over with gold leaf in the 1870s).

Once inside the labyrinthine interior, make your way up one flight and proceed to the central hallway, the only section of any real interest to visitors and the easiest to navigate. The best section is the sober and impressive **Memorial Hall**, a circular room surrounded by tall columns of Siena marble, displaying transparencies of the original flags carried by Massachusetts soldiers into battle and lit by a vaulted stained-glass window bearing the state seal. On the third floor, the carved wooden fish known as the **Sacred Cod** hangs above the public gallery in the House of Representatives. The politicos take this symbol of maritime prosperity so seriously that when it was stolen by Harvard pranksters in the 1930s, the House didn't reconvene until it was recovered.

Behind the State House, on Bowdoin Street, lies pleasant, grassy **Ashburton Park**, centered on a pillar that is a replica of a 1789 Bulfinch work. The column indicates the hill's original summit, which was sixty feet higher and topped by a 65 foot post with the makeshift warning light – constructed from an iron pot filled with combustibles – that gave Beacon Hill its name.

Nichols House

The only Beacon Hill residence open year-round to the public is the **Nichols House**: it's to the left of the State House, up the slope of Joy Street, and a few steps eastward along Mount Vernon Street, at no. 55 (May–Oct Tues–Sat noon–4pm; Nov–April Thurs–Sat noon–4pm, tours start 15min past the hour; $5; ⓣ617/227-6993, ⓦwww.nicholshousemuseum.org; Park Street **T**). It's yet another Bulfinch design, and was most recently the home of landscape designer and pacifist Rose Standish Nichols, the favorite niece of sculptor Augustus Saint-Gaudens. She lived in the house until her death in 1960 and left it to the public as a museum rather than bequeathing it to her greedy relatives. Crowded with a patchwork of pieces from the seventeenth to the twentieth centuries, the interior isn't too gripping unless you have an abiding interest in antique furnishings; best go to get some perspective on the interior life of overstuffed leisure led by Beacon Hill's moneyed elite.

Louisburg Square and around

Farther down the street, between Mount Vernon and Pinckney streets, **Louisburg Square** forms the gilded geographic heart of Beacon Hill. The central lawn, surrounded by wrought-iron fencing and flanked by statues of Columbus and Aristides the Just, is owned by local residents, making it the city's only private square. On either side of this oblong green space are rows of stately brick townhouses, though the square's distinction is due less to its architectural character than to its long history of illustrious residents and the sense of elite civic parochialism that has made this Boston's most coveted address. Among those to call the area home were novelist Louisa May Alcott and members of the illustrious Vanderbilt family; it's currently home to former presidential candidate Senator John Kerry and his wife, ketchup heiress Teresa Heinz.

Just below Louisburg Square, between Willow and West Cedar streets, narrow **Acorn Street** still has its original early nineteenth-century cobblestones. Barely wide enough for a car to pass through, it was originally built as a minor byway to be lined with servants' residences. Locals have always clung to it as the epitome of Beacon Hill quaint; in the 1960s, residents permitted the city to tear up the street to install sewer pipes only after exacting the promise that every cobblestone would be replaced in its original location. One more block down, **Chestnut Street** features some of the most intricate facades in Boston, particularly Bulfinch's **Swan Houses**, at nos. 13, 15, and 17, with their recessed arches and touches like scrolled door-knockers and wrought-iron-lace balconies.

The Black Heritage Trail

In 1783, Massachusetts became the first state to declare slavery illegal, partly as a result of black participation in the Revolutionary War. Not long after, a large community of free blacks and escaped slaves sprang up in the North End and Beacon Hill. Very few blacks live in either place today, but the **Black Heritage Trail** traces Beacon Hill's key role in local and national black history – and is the most important historical site in America devoted to pre-Civil War African-American history and culture. Starting from the **Robert Gould Shaw Memorial** (see p.114), the 1.6-mile loop takes in fourteen historical sights, detailed in a useful **guide** available at the **Museum of Afro-American History** and at the Boston National Historical Park **visitor center** at 15 State St. The best way to experience the trail is by taking a National Park Service **walking tour** (Mon–Sat 10am, noon & 2pm; call to reserve; free; ⓣ617/742-5415, ⓦwww.nps.gov/boaf; Park Street Ⓣ).

Smith Court and the African Meeting House

The north side of the slope intersects with tiny **Smith Court**, once the center of Boston's substantial pre-Civil War black community when the north slope was still a low-rent district, and now home to a few stops on Boston's Black Heritage Trail (see box above). The **African Meeting House**, at no. 8 (Mon–Sat 10am–4pm; donations welcomed; ⓣ617/725-0022, ⓦwww.afroam-museum.org; Park Street Ⓣ), is the oldest black church in the country, and in its heyday served as the spiritual and political center for Boston's black community. It is also the birthplace of abolitionism: in 1832, William Lloyd Garrison founded the New England Anti-Slavery Society here, the first group of its kind to call for the immediate abolition of slavery. The place is currently being remodeled to look as it did in 1854, and plans to reopen in December of 2006, in time to celebrate its 200th birthday.

At the end of Smith Court, you can walk along part of the old Underground Railroad used to protect escaped slaves, who once ducked into the doors along narrow **Holmes Alley** that were left open by sympathizers to the abolitionist cause. Built in 1843, the **Abiel Smith School**, at 46 Joy St, was the first public building in the country established for the purpose of educating black children. Today, it houses the **Museum of Afro-American History** (Mon–Sat 10am–4pm; donations welcomed; ⓣ617/725-0022, ⓦwww.afroammuseum.org; Park Street Ⓣ) and rotates a number of well-tailored exhibits centered on abolitionism and African-American history.

Charles Street and the Esplanade

Back towards the river, **Charles Street** is the commercial center of Beacon Hill, lined with scores of restaurants, antique shops, and pricey specialty boutiques. A jaunt just off Charles down **Mount Vernon Street** brings you past some of Beacon Hill's most beautiful buildings – none of which you can enter, unfortunately – including the Federal-style **Charles Street Meeting House**, at the corner of the two streets, now repurposed as an office building, and the vegetation-enshrouded Victorian Gothic **Church of the Advent**, at Mount Vernon's intersection with Brimmer Street.

Connected to Charles Street at its north end by a footbridge and spanning nine miles along the Charles River, the **Esplanade** is yet another of Boston's well-manicured public spaces, with the requisite playgrounds, landscaped hills, lakes, and bridges. The stretch alongside Beacon Hill is the nicest, providing a picturesque way to appreciate the Hill from a distance as well as a popular spot for jogging and rollerblading on summer days. Just below the Longfellow Bridge (which connects to Cambridge) is the Community Boating Center, the point of departure for sailing, kayaking, and windsurfing outings on the Charles (April–Oct Mon–Fri 1pm–sunset, Sat & Sun 9am–sunset; two-day visitor's pass $100; must be able to prove sailing abilities; ⓣ617/523-1038, ⓦwww.community-boating.org; Charles T). The white half-dome rising from the riverbank along the Esplanade is the **Hatch Memorial Shell**, a public performance space best known for its Fourth of July celebration, which features a free concert by the Boston Pops, a pared-down, snappy version of the Boston Symphony Orchestra. Free movies and jazz concerts occur almost nightly in summer; call ⓣ617/227-0627 or visit ⓦwww.hatchshell.com for a schedule of events.

The West End

North of Cambridge Street, the tidy rows of townhouses give way to a more urban spread of office buildings and old brick structures, signaling the start of the **West End**. Once Boston's main port of entry for immigrants and transient sailors, this area has seen its lively character pretty much disappear. A vestige of the old West End manages to remain in the small tangle of byways behind the high-rise buildings of **Massachusetts General Hospital**, where you'll see urban warehouses interspersed with Irish bars, some of which swell to a fever pitch after Celtics basketball and Bruins hockey games. Those games take place nearby at the **TDBanknorth Garden**, 150 Causeway St, the corporate home to both the former Boston Garden and the FleetCenter.

Back along Cambridge Street, at no. 141, the brick **Harrison Gray Otis House** (Wed–Sun 11am–4.30pm, tours every half-hour; $8; ⓣ617/227-3956, ⓦwww.historicnewengland.org; Charles T), originally built for the wealthy Otis family in 1796, sits incongruously among mini-malls and office buildings. Its first two floors have been painstakingly restored – from the bright wallpaper right down to the silverware sets – in the often loud hues of the Federal style.

Situated on a bridge over the Charles, Boston's beloved **Museum of Science** (July to early Sept Mon–Thurs, Sat & Sun 9am–7pm, Fri 9am–9pm; Sept–June Mon–Thurs, Sat & Sun 9am–5pm, Fri 9am–9pm; $15, kids $12; CityPass accepted; ⓣ617/723-2500, ⓦwww.mos.org; Science Park T) consists of several floors of interactive, though often well-worn, exhibits illustrating basic principles of natural and physical science. The best exhibit is the Theater of Electricity in the Blue Wing, a darkened room full of optical illusions and glowing displays on the presence of electricity in everyday life. Containing the world's largest Van de Graaff generator (which utilizes 2.5 million volts of electricity), the theater puts on daily shows in which simulated lightning bolts flash and crackle around the space. The museum also houses a five-story IMAX theater as well as the Charles Hayden Planetarium (call for showtimes; $9, kids $7; ⓣ617/723-2500, ⓦwww.mos.org); along with its standard starry productions, the latter also features a number of semi-rocking laser shows, including the infamous "Laser Floyd: Dark Side of the Moon."

Back Bay and the South End

Back Bay, a meticulously planned neighborhood where elegant, angular, tree-lined streets form a pedestrian-friendly area that looks much as it did in the nineteenth century, right down to the original gaslights and brick sidewalks, is Boston at its most cosmopolitan. It's also the city's chief gay and lesbian district,

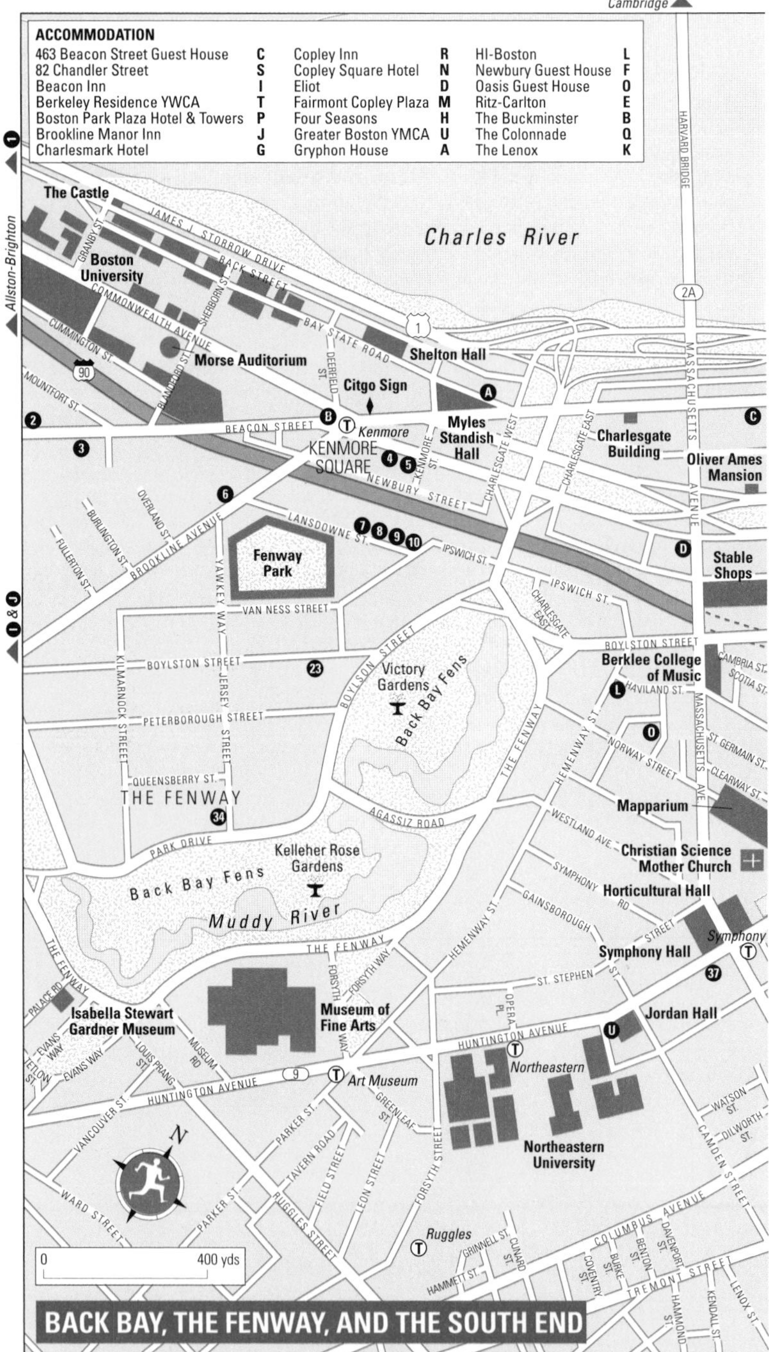
ACCOMMODATION
463 Beacon Street Guest House C
82 Chandler Street S
Beacon Inn I
Berkeley Residence YWCA T
Boston Park Plaza Hotel & Towers P
Brookline Manor Inn J
Charlesmark Hotel G
Copley Inn R
Copley Square Hotel N
Eliot D
Fairmont Copley Plaza M
Four Seasons H
Greater Boston YMCA U
Gryphon House A
HI-Boston L
Newbury Guest House F
Oasis Guest House O
Ritz-Carlton E
The Buckminster B
The Colonnade Q
The Lenox K
Cambridge
Allston-Brighton
I & J
Charles River
The Castle
Boston University
James J. Storrow Drive
Back Street
Bay State Road
Commonwealth Avenue
Cummington St.
Mountfort St.
Granby St.
Sherborn St.
Blandford St.
Deerfield St.
Morse Auditorium
Shelton Hall
Citgo Sign
Beacon Street
Kenmore
Kenmore Square
Kenmore St.
Myles Standish Hall
Charlesgate West
Charlesgate East
Charlesgate Building
Harvard Bridge
Massachusetts Avenue
Oliver Ames Mansion
Newbury Street
Lansdowne St.
Ipswich St.
Stable Shops
Overland St.
Burlington St.
Fullerton St.
Brookline Avenue
Fenway Park
Yawkey Way
Van Ness Street
Boylston Street
Kilmarnock Street
Jersey Street
Peterborough Street
Queensberry St.
The Fenway
Victory Gardens
Back Bay Fens
Berklee College of Music
Haviland St.
Cambria St.
Scotia St.
Hemenway St.
Norway Street
St. Germain St.
Clearway St.
Mapparium
Westland Ave.
Christian Science Mother Church
Symphony Rd
Horticultural Hall
Gainsborough Street
Symphony
Symphony Hall
Agassiz Road
Park Drive
Kelleher Rose Gardens
Muddy River
Forsyth Way
St. Stephen St.
Opera Pl.
Jordan Hall
Isabella Stewart Gardner Museum
Palace Rd
Museum of Fine Arts
Museum Rd
Evans Way
Tetlow St.
Louis Prang St.
Huntington Avenue
Art Museum
Northeastern
Northeastern University
Vancouver St.
Greenleaf St.
Parker St.
Tavern Road
Field Street
Leon Street
Forsyth Street
Ward Street
Ruggles Street
Ruggles
Grinnell St.
Cunard St.
Hammett St.
Columbus Avenue
Coventry St.
Burke St.
Benton St.
Davenport St.
Tremont Street
Hammond St.
Kendall St.
Lenox St.
Watson St.
Dilworth St.
Camden Street
N
0 400 yds
BACK BAY, THE FENWAY, AND THE SOUTH END

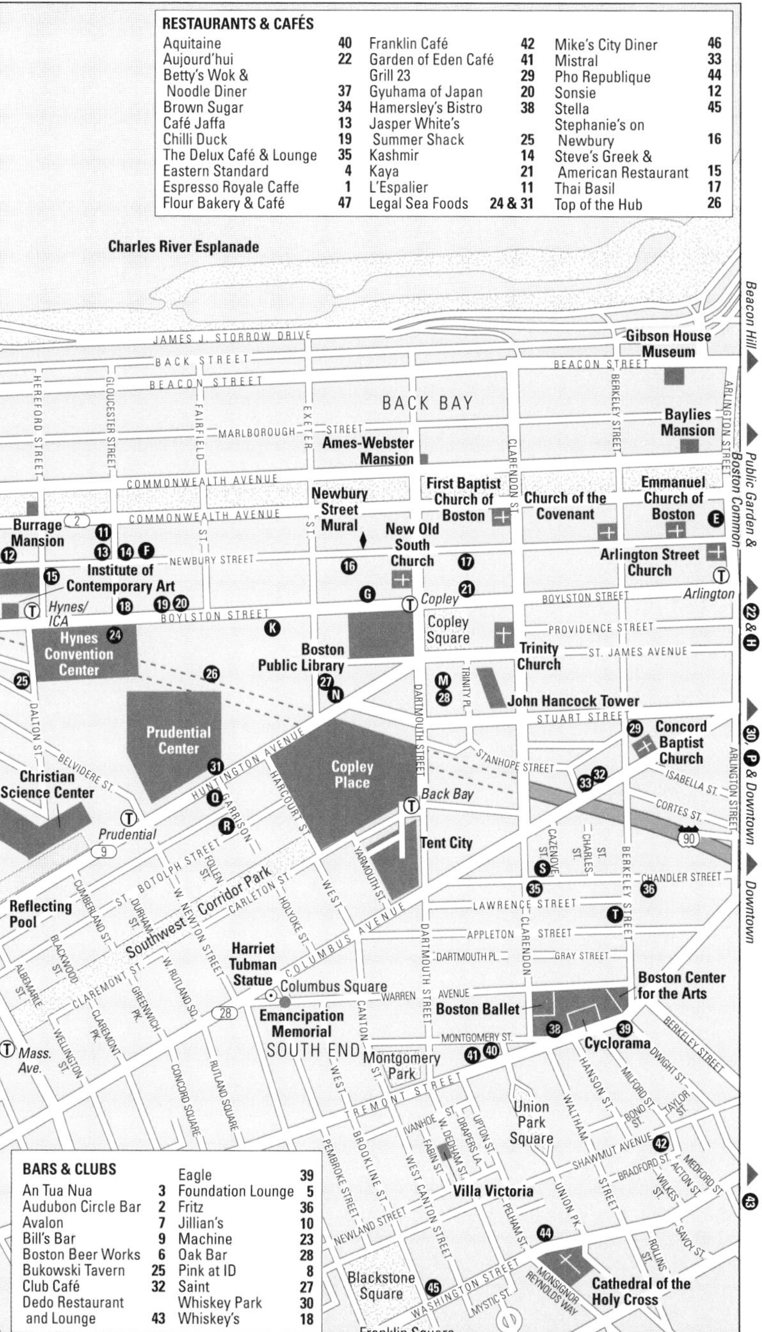
RESTAURANTS & CAFÉS
Aquitaine 40
Aujourd'hui 22
Betty's Wok & Noodle Diner 37
Brown Sugar 34
Café Jaffa 13
Chilli Duck 19
The Delux Café & Lounge 35
Eastern Standard 4
Espresso Royale Caffe 1
Flour Bakery & Café 47
Franklin Café 42
Garden of Eden Café 41
Grill 23 29
Gyuhama of Japan 20
Hamersley's Bistro 38
Jasper White's Summer Shack 25
Kashmir 14
Kaya 21
L'Espalier 11
Legal Sea Foods 24 & 31
Mike's City Diner 46
Mistral 33
Pho Republique 44
Sonsie 12
Stella 45
Stephanie's on Newbury 16
Steve's Greek & American Restaurant 15
Thai Basil 17
Top of the Hub 26
BARS & CLUBS
An Tua Nua 3
Audubon Circle Bar 2
Avalon 7
Bill's Bar 9
Boston Beer Works 6
Bukowski Tavern 25
Club Café 32
Dedo Restaurant and Lounge 43
Eagle 39
Foundation Lounge 5
Fritz 36
Jillian's 10
Machine 23
Oak Bar 28
Pink at ID 8
Saint 27
Whiskey Park 30
Whiskey's 18
Charles River Esplanade
BACK BAY
SOUTH END
Gibson House Museum
Baylies Mansion
Ames-Webster Mansion
Burrage Mansion
Institute of Contemporary Art
Newbury Street Mural
First Baptist Church of Boston
Church of the Covenant
Emmanuel Church of Boston
New Old South Church
Arlington Street Church
Hynes Convention Center
Boston Public Library
Copley Square
Trinity Church
John Hancock Tower
Prudential Center
Copley Place
Concord Baptist Church
Christian Science Center
Tent City
Reflecting Pool
Southwest Corridor Park
Harriet Tubman Statue
Columbus Square
Emancipation Memorial
Boston Center for the Arts
Boston Ballet
Cyclorama
Montgomery Park
Union Park Square
Villa Victoria
Blackstone Square
Franklin Square
Cathedral of the Holy Cross
Hynes/ICA
Copley
Arlington
Back Bay
Prudential
Mass. Ave.
Beacon Hill
Public Garden & Boston Common
22 & H
30, P & Downtown
Downtown
43
46, 47 & Roxbury

From swamp to swank: the building of Back Bay

The fashioning of **Back Bay** occurred in response to a shortage of living space in Boston. An increasingly cramped Beacon Hill prompted developers to revisit a failed dam project on the Charles River, which had made a swamp of much of the area. **Arthur Gilman** manned the huge landfill project, which began in 1857. Taking his cue from the grand boulevards of Paris, Gilman decided on an orderly street pattern extending east to west from the Public Garden, itself sculpted from swampland two decades before. By 1890, the cramped peninsula of old Boston was flanked by 450 new acres, on which stood a range of churches, townhouses, and schools. You'll notice that, with a few exceptions, the brownstones get fancier the farther from the Garden you go, a result of architects and those who employed them trying to one-up each other. The exteriors of most of the buildings remain unaltered, although visually that's as far as you'll usually get, unless the place has been converted into a shop, salon, or gourmet eatery; in that case, step inside and hang onto your wallet.

where a hip population helps offset stodginess and keeps the place, which begins at the **Public Garden**, buzzing with chic eateries, trendy shops, and an aura of affluence. Its other main draw is its trove of Gilded Age rowhouses, specifically their exquisite architectural details; there really is no end to the fanciful bay windows and ornamental turrets. On its southern border, the sprawl of the **South End** offers another impressive, if less opulent, collection of Victorian architecture, alongside some of Boston's more inventive restaurants.

Starting with the side closest to the Charles River, the east–west thoroughfares of Back Bay are **Beacon** and **Marlborough** streets, **Commonwealth Avenue**, and **Newbury** and **Boylston** streets. These are transected by eight shorter streets, so fastidiously laid out that not only are their names in alphabetical order, but trisyllables are deliberately intercut by disyllables: Arlington, Berkeley, Clarendon, Dartmouth, Exeter, Fairfield, Gloucester, and Hereford, until you get to Massachusetts Avenue. Generally, the grandest townhouses are found on Beacon Street and Commonwealth Avenue, though Marlborough, in between the two, is more atmospheric; Boylston and Newbury are the main commercial drags. In the middle of it all is a small greenspace, **Copley Square**, surrounded by the area's main sights: **Trinity Church**, the imposing **Boston Public Library**, and the city's classic skyscraper, the **John Hancock Tower**.

The Public Garden

The value of property in Boston typically goes up the closer its proximity to the lovingly maintained **Public Garden**, a 24-acre park first earmarked for public use in 1859. Of the garden's 125 types of trees, many identified by little brass placards, most impressive are the weeping willows which ring the picturesque man-made **lagoon**, around which you can take a fifteen-minute ride in one of six **swan boats** (April to late June daily 10am–4pm; late June to early Sept daily 10am–5pm; early to mid-Sept Mon–Fri noon–4pm, Sat & Sun 10am–4pm; $2.50; ⓣ617/522-1966, ⓦwww.swanboats.com; Arlington T). There's often a line to hop on board – instead of waiting, you can get just as good a perspective on the park from the tiny suspension bridge that crosses the lagoon. The park's other big family draw is the cluster of bronze bird sculptures collectively called **Mrs Mallard and Her Eight Ducklings**, installed to commemorate Robert McCloskey's 1941 children's tale *Make Way for Ducklings*, which was set in the Public Garden. Of the many statues and monuments throughout the park, the oldest and oddest is the 30-foot-tall **Good Samaritan** monument, a granite and red-marble column that is a tribute to, of all things, the anesthetic qualities of ether; controversy as to which of two Boston men invented the wonder drug led Oliver Wendell Holmes to dub it the "Either Monument." Finally, a dignified equestrian statue of **George Washington**, installed in 1869 and the first of the general astride a horse, watches over the Garden's Commonwealth Avenue entrance.

Commonwealth Avenue

The garden leads into the tree-lined median of **Commonwealth Avenue**, the 220-foot-wide showcase street of Back Bay. The mall here forms the first link in Frederick Law Olmsted's so-called **Emerald Necklace**, which begins at Boston Common and extends all the way to the Arnold Arboretum in Jamaica Plain. "Comm Ave," as locals ignobly call it, is at its prettiest in early May, when the magnolia and dogwood trees are in full bloom.

On the street proper, the **Gamble Mansion**, at no. 5, now houses the Boston Center for Adult Education, but feel free to slip inside for a look at the opulent ballroom built expressly for his daughter's coming-out (in the old-fashioned sense) party. You'll have to be content to see the **Ames-Webster House**, a few blocks down at 306 Dartmouth St, from the outside. Built in 1872 for railroad tycoon, Massachusetts governor, and US congressman Frederick Ames, it features a two-story conservatory, central tower, and imposing chimney. Farther down Commonwealth, at no. 314, is the **Burrage House**, a fanciful synthesis of Vanderbilt-style mansion and the French chateau of Chenonceaux. The exterior of this 1899 urban palace is a riot of gargoyles and carved cherubim; inside it's less riotous – it serves as a retirement home.

Rising above the avenue, at no. 110, is the landmark belfry of the **First Baptist Church of Boston** (Mon–Fri 11am–3pm), designed by architect H.H. Richardson in 1872 for a Unitarian congregation, though at bill-paying time

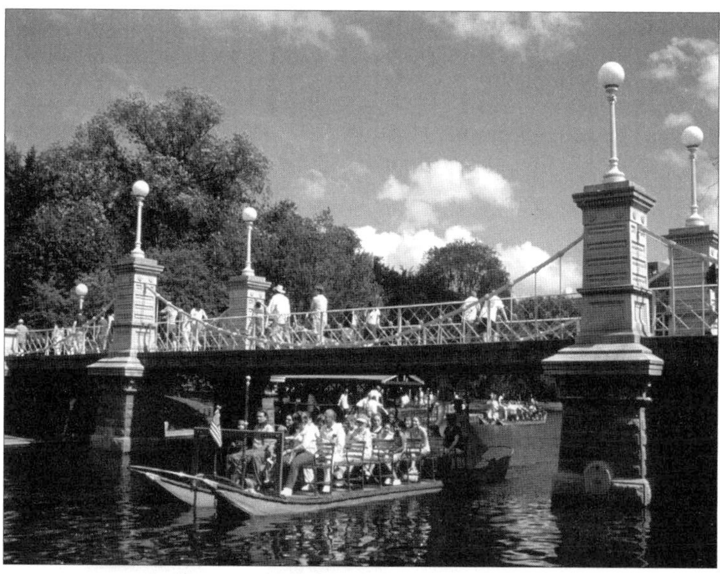

△ The Public Garden

only a Baptist congregation was able to pony up the necessary funds. The puddingstone exterior is topped off by a 176-foot **bell tower**, which is covered by four gorgeous friezes by Frederic-Auguste Bartholdi, of Statue of Liberty fame, a product of his friendship with Richardson that developed at the Ecole des Beaux Arts in Paris. Richardson's lofty plans for the interior never materialized, again for lack of money, but its high ceiling, exposed timbers, and Norman-style rose windows are still worth a peek if you happen by when someone's in the church office.

Newbury, Boylston, Beacon, and Marlborough streets

Newbury Street takes in eight blocks of alternately traditional and eclectic boutiques, art galleries, and designer spas, all tucked into Victorian-era brownstones. Despite the encroachment of big chain stores and the occasional nod to pretentiousness in some of its swankier spaces, it remains an atmospheric and surprisingly inviting place to wander round. And not all is shopping: Newbury and neighboring **Boylston** are home to most of the old schools and churches built in the Back Bay area.

Right on the corner of Boylston and Arlington streets is Back Bay's first building, the squat **Arlington Street Church** (Mon–Fri 10am–5pm, Sun 10am–3pm), a minor Italianesque masterpiece designed in 1859 by Arthur Gilman; its host of Tiffany stained-glass windows (believed to be the largest assemblage of Tiffany windows unified under one church) were added from 1898 to 1933. A block down is the prison-like **New England Mutual Life Building**, at 501 Boylston, now bearing the corporate moniker "The Newbry"; it's worth nipping inside to have a look at the **murals**, which depict such historic local events as Paul Revere sounding his famous alarm.

Back on the first block of Newbury Street itself, at no. 67, the full-blown Gothic Revival **Church of the Covenant** boasts a soaring steeple and 30-foot-high stained-glass windows, also by Tiffany. The church's chapel houses one of Boston's biggest contemporary art spaces in the form of the Gallery NAGA (Tues–Sat 10am–5.30pm; ⓣ617/267-9060, ⓦwww.gallerynaga.com). Designed as an architect's house, the medieval flight-of-fancy at **109 Newbury St** is more arresting for its two donjon towers than the Cole-Haan footwear inside. A block down, **271 Dartmouth** houses a *Papa Razzi* restaurant, but again the burnt sienna-colored building with mock battlements hunkered over it steals the show: originally the *Hotel Victoria* in 1886, it looks like a combination Venetian–Moorish castle. A block west, on the exposed side of no. 159, is the **Newbury Street Mural**, a fanciful tribute to a hodgepodge of notables from Sam Adams to Sammy Davis, Jr. A key to who's who is affixed to the fence on Newbury Street, directly in front of the parking lot. Housed in a Romanesque-style police and fire station built in 1886, half of which Back Bay's firefighters still call home, the **Institute of Contemporary Art**, 955 Boylston St (Tues, Wed & Fri noon–5pm, Thurs noon–9pm, Sat & Sun 11am–5pm; $7, free Thurs 5–9pm; ⓣ617/266-5152, ⓦwww.icaboston.org; Hynes T), is Boston's main venue for contemporary art, with no permanent collections.

As a continuation of Beacon Hill's stately main thoroughfare, **Beacon Street** was long the province of blueblood Bostonians. It is the Back Bay street closest to the Charles River, yet its buildings turn their back to it, principally because in the nineteenth century the river was a stinking mess. On the first block of the Back Bay portion of Beacon, at no. 137, is the only house museum in the neighborhood, the **Gibson House Museum** (Wed–Sun 1–3pm, tours hourly;

$7; ⓣ617/267-6338, ⓦwww.thegibsonhouse.org). Built in 1859, this standard-issue Back Bay row house has an ornate, more or less preserved interior, and still boasts an almost complete lack of sunlight as well as a host of Victoriana: gold-embossed wallpaper, antique clocks, and gilt-framed photos of relatives of the long-gone Bostonian Catherine Hammond Gibson.

Sandwiched between Beacon Street and Commonwealth Avenue is quiet **Marlborough Street**, which with its brick sidewalks and vintage gaslights is one of the most prized residential locales in Boston, after Louisburg Square in Beacon Hill and the first few blocks of Commonwealth Avenue. Even though the townhouses here tend to be smaller than elsewhere in Back Bay, they display a surprising range of stylistic variation, especially on the blocks between Clarendon and Fairfield streets. The final block, which links Massachusetts Avenue to Charlesgate East, is the only street in Back Bay proper that curves.

Copley Square and around

Bounded by Boylston, Clarendon, Dartmouth, and St James streets, **Copley Square** is the busy commercial center of Back Bay. The square itself is a relatively nondescript grassy expanse, but its periphery holds quite a bit of interest. On the northeast corner is its star, **Trinity Church**, 206 Clarendon St (daily 9am–5pm; $5, includes guided tour, call for times; ⓣ617/536-0944, ⓦwww.trinityboston.org; Copley Ⓣ), whose original interior design concept was to create the experience of "walking into a living painting." The result is H.H. Richardson's 1877 Romanesque masterpiece, a breathtaking display of polychromatic eye candy fashioned by legendary artist John La Farge. The majestic central tower reaches an eye-opening ten stories, and is situated between sweeping arches and a glamorous golden chancel. While it's all quite lovely, Trinity's finest feature is La Farge's aquamarine *Christ in Majesty* triptych, a bold, multidimensional stained-glass window. Aim to make your visit while the sun is setting and the stained glass is at its most brilliant, or during one of the free organ recitals (Fridays at 12.15pm).

A decidedly secular building anchors the end of Copley Square opposite Trinity Church, in the form of the **Boston Public Library** (Mon–Thurs 9am–9pm, Fri & Sat 9am–5pm; ⓣ617/536-5400, ⓦwww.bpl.org). It's the largest public research library in New England, and the first one in America that permitted the borrowing of books. Architects McKim, Mead & White built the Italian Renaissance Revival structure in 1895; the massive inner bronze doors were designed by Daniel Chester French (sculptor of the Lincoln Memorial in Washington, DC). Inside, check out the imposing **Bates Reading Room**, with its barrel-vaulted ceiling and dark oak panelling. The library's most remarkable facet is tucked away on the top floor, however, where the darkly lit **Sargent Hall** is covered with more than fifteen astonishing murals painted by John Singer Sargent between 1890 and 1919. Entitled the *Triumph of Religion*, the multidimensional panels range from the brazen *Pagan Gods* to the serene, harp-strumming scenes of *Heaven*. After viewing, you can take a breather in the library's open-air central **courtyard**, modeled after that of the Palazzo della Chancelleria in Rome.

Opposite the Boston Public Library is one of Boston's most attractive buildings, the **New Old South Church** (Mon–Fri 9am–5pm), a name to which there is actually some logic: the congregation in residence at downtown's Old South Meeting House (and church) outgrew it and decamped here in 1875 – hence, the "New" Old South Church. The names of former Old South members reads like a who's who of Boston historical figures: Benjamin Franklin,

Phyllis Wheatley, Samuel Adams, and even Mother Goose all congregated here. You need not be a student of architecture to be won over by the Italian Gothic design, most pronounced in the ornate, 220-foot bell tower, its copper roof lantern replete with metallic dragons. Its interior is an alluring assemblage of dark woods set against a rose-colored backdrop, coupled with fifteenth-century -English-style stained-glass windows.

At 62 stories, the **John Hancock Tower**, 200 Clarendon St, is the tallest building in America north of New York City, and in a way Boston's signature skyscraper – first loathed, now loved, and taking on startlingly different appearances, depending on your vantage point. In Back Bay, the characteristically angular edifice is often barely perceptible, due to designer I.M. Pei's deft understatement in deference to adjacent Trinity Church and the old brownstones nearby. From Beacon Hill, it appears broad-shouldered and stocky; from the South End, taller than it really is; from across the Charles River, like a crisp metallic wafer. You'd never guess from any angle that soon after its construction, dozens of windowpanes popped out, showering Copley Square with glass. Though the building serves as an office tower, visitors were, until recently, allowed to ascend to its sixtieth-floor **observatory** for some of the most stunning views around – but security concerns have prompted its closure; now, you'll have to head instead to the Prudential Skywalk (see below) for Boston vistas. Next door to the tower is the *old* Hancock Tower, which cuts a distinguished profile in the skyline with its truncated step-top pyramid roof.

Nothing can cloak the ugliness of the **Prudential Tower**, at 800 Boylston St, just west of Copley Square. This 52-story gray intruder in the Back Bay skyline is one of the more unfortunate by-products of the urban renewal craze that gripped Boston and most other American cities in the 1960s – though it did succeed in replacing the Boston & Albany rail yards, a blighted border between Back Bay and the South End. The running joke about the "Pru Tower" is that it offers the best view of Boston – because it's the only view where you don't have to actually look at the Pru Tower. That said, the fiftieth-floor **Skywalk** (daily 10am–10pm; $9.50; CityPass accepted; ⓣ617/859-0648, ⓦwww.prudentialcenter.com; Prudential Ⓣ) does offer a stunning 360-degree aerial view of Boston. If you're hungry (or just thirsty) you can avoid the admission charge by ascending two more floors to the *Top of the Hub* restaurant (see p.148); your bill may well equal the money you just saved, but during most daytime hours it's fairly relaxed, and you can linger over coffee or a drink.

Christian Science buildings

People gazing down from the top of the Prudential Tower are often surprised to see a 224-foot-tall Renaissance Revival basilica vying for attention amidst the urban outcroppings lapping at its base. This rather artificial-looking structure is the central feature of the sprawling world headquarters of the **First Church of Christ, Scientist**, at 75 Huntington Ave (Mon–Sat 10am–4pm; free; ⓦwww.tfccs.com; Hynes Ⓣ), which dwarfs the earlier, prettier Romanesque **Christian Science Mother Church** just behind it, built in 1894. There may be no better place in Boston to contemplate the excesses of religion than around the center's 670-foot-long red granite-trimmed reflecting pool.

The highlights of a visit here, though, are on the ground floor of the **Mary Baker Eddy Library**, in the Christian Science Publishing building at 200 Massachusetts Ave (Tues–Sun 10am–4pm; $6; ⓣ1-888/222-3711, ⓦwww.marybakereddylibrary.org; Hynes Ⓣ). The library's original Art Deco lobby has been transformed into the grandly named Hall of Ideas, home to a trippy glass and bronze fountain that appears to cascade with words rather than water; the sayings – a diverse collection of inspiring tidbits – are projected from the ceiling for an effect that verges on holographic. Tucked behind the Hall of Ideas is the equally marvelous **Mapparium**, a curious stained-glass globe whose thirty-foot diameter you can cross on a glass bridge. The technicolor hues of the six hundred-plus glass panels, illuminated from behind, reveal the geopolitical reality of the world in 1935, when the globe was constructed, as evidenced by country names such as Siam, Baluchistan, and Transjordan. Intended to symbolize the worldwide reach of journalism, the Mapparium has a more immediate payoff: thanks to the spherical glass surface, which absorbs no sound, you can whisper, say, "What's Tanganyika called today?" at one end of the bridge and someone on the opposite end will hear it clear as a bell – and perhaps proffer the answer (Tanzania).

Bay Village

Back near the Public Garden, one of the oldest sections of Boston, **Bay Village**, bounded by Arlington, Church, Fayette, and Stuart streets, functions now as a small atmospheric satellite of Back Bay. This warren of gaslights and tiny brick houses has managed to escape the trolley tours that can make other parts of the city feel like a theme park; of course, that's in part because there's not all that much to see. The area is, however, popular with Boston's **gay community**, who colonized it over a decade ago, before nearby South End came into favor.

The area's overall resemblance to Beacon Hill is no accident; many of the artisans who pieced that district together built their own, smaller houses here throughout the 1820s and 1830s. A few decades later, water displaced from the filling in of Back Bay threatened to turn the district back into a swamp, but Yankee practicality led to the lifting of hundreds of houses and shops onto wooden pilings fully eighteen feet above the water level. Backyards were raised only twelve feet, and when the water receded many building owners designed sunken gardens. You can still see some of these in the alleys behind slender Melrose and Fayette streets. A more unusual remnant from the past is the **fortress** at the intersection of Arlington and Stuart streets and Columbus Ave, complete with drawbridge and fake moat, that was built as an armory for the **First Corps of Cadets**, a private military organization.

Bay Village's proximity to the theater district made it a prime location for **speakeasies** in the 1920s, not to mention a natural spot for actors and impresarios to take up residence; indeed, the building at **48–50 Melrose Street** originally housed a movie studio. Around the corner is the site of the Coconut Grove Fire of 1942, in which 490 people perished in a nightclub because the exit doors were locked. There's little else to see here by day; Bay Village wakes up after the sun sets, when its clubs get going.

The South End

Trendy **South End**, a predominantly residential neighborhood extending below Back Bay from Huntington Street to I-93, and loosely cut off from downtown by I-90, is almost always modified by the term "quaint" – though for once, the tag fits. The term truly hits home in the heart of the neighborhood, an area loosely shaped like a triangle and bounded by Tremont Street, Dartmouth Street, and Columbus Avenue. The tony enclave, nicknamed the "Golden Triangle" by South End realtors, boasts a spectacular concentration of **Victorian architecture** which, when taken together with the examples found in the rest of the neighborhood, is surely unmatched anywhere in the US. The sheer number of such houses here earned the South End a National Landmark

District designation in 1983, making the 500-acre area the largest historical neighborhood of its kind in the country. The South End is also known for its well-preserved **ironwork**; a French botanical motif known as Rinceau adorns many of the houses' stairways and windows. Details like these have made the area quite popular with upwardly mobile Bostonians, who have been moving in and gentrifying the neighborhood over the past decade. The result is some of the most upbeat and happening **street life** in town – most clustered on Tremont and on pockets of Washington, a few blocks below the Back Bay **T**, the neighborhood's only **T** stop.

Dartmouth Street to Columbus Avenue

Dartmouth Street, anchored by Copley Place on the far side of the road, gets tonier the closer it gets to Tremont Street, a few blocks southeast. Immediately below Copley Place, at 130 Tremont, is the street's most important tenant, **Tent City**, a mixed-income housing co-op that owes its name to the 1968 sit-in protest – tents included – staged on the formerly vacant lot by residents concerned about the neighborhood's dwindling low-income housing. Their activism thwarted plans for a parking garage, and the result is a fine example of environmental architecture planning.

The northern edge of the Golden Triangle, **Columbus Avenue**, is lined with handsome Victorian houses, though the main interest is a tiny wedge of parkland known as **Columbus Square**, four blocks southwest of Dartmouth, between Pembroke and West Newton streets. The space is the repository of two outstanding bronze relief sculptures commemorating Boston's role as part of the Underground Railroad. The nine-foot-tall **Harriet Tubman "Step on Board" Memorial** depicts the strident abolitionist leading several weary slaves to safety, while the nearby 1913 **Emancipation** statue is a more harrowing portrait of slaves' plight: the three figures here are achingly thin and barely clothed.

Appleton and Chandler streets

Cobblestoned **Appleton Street** and quiet **Chandler Street**, which jut off to the northeast from Dartmouth below Columbus Avenue, are the most sought-after South End addresses. The tree-lined streets are graced with refurbished flat- and bow-fronted rowhouses that would easily be at home in London's Mayfair. In addition, unlike many of their neighbors, the houses here have an extra, fourth story, and are capped off by mansard roofs. If you're here in October, you can catch the annual South End Historical Society's **house tour** for a better perspective on the area. Call ⓣ617/536-4445 or visit ⓦwww.southendhistoricalsociety.org for more information.

The Cyclorama and the Stanford Calderwood Pavilion

The heart of the South End is at the intersection of Clarendon and Tremont streets, where some of the trendiest restaurants operate. That said, the area's only real sights are a collection of performance spaces, chief among which is the domed **Cyclorama** rotunda, at 539 Tremont, which was built in 1884 to house an enormous, 360-degree painting of the Battle of Gettysburg (since moved to Gettysburg itself). Later used as a carousel space and even a boxing ring, the repurposing continued until 1972, when its current tenants, the **Boston Center for the Arts** (ⓣ617/426-7700, ⓦwww.bcaonline.org), moved in, providing a home for more than a dozen low-budget theater troupes. Right next door to the Cyclorama is the celebrated, newly opened **Stanford Calderwood Pavilion** (ⓣ617/266-0800, ⓦwww.huntingtontheatre.org), home to two brand-new theater spaces – the first new theaters to be built in Boston in over seventy-five years. These vary widely in their design: the Wimberly is a luxurious proscenium theater favored for contemporary productions, while the Roberts Studio employs a black-box, flexible stage set-up and is generally used for smaller theater company productions. Call or visit the website for current productions.

Kenmore Square, The Fenway, and Brookline

At the western edge of Back Bay, the decorous brownstones and smart shops fade into the more casual **Kenmore Square** and **Fenway** districts, both removed from the tourist circuit but good fun nonetheless, with a studenty vibe and home to some of the city's more notable cultural institutions, such as the **Museum of Fine Arts** and the **Isabella Stewart Gardner Museum**. Farther west and more residential is the town of **Brookline**, which feels like just another sleepy part of the city, though one in which you're unlikely to find yourself spending much time.

Kenmore Square and Boston University

Kenmore Square, at the junction of Commonwealth Avenue and Beacon Street, is the primary point of entry to Boston University and the unofficial playground for its students. Back Bay's Commonwealth Avenue Mall leads right into this lively stretch of youth-oriented bars, record stores, and casual restaurants that cater to the late-night cravings of local students – as such the square is considerably more alive when school's in session. Many of the buildings on its north side have been snapped up by BU, such as the bustling six-story Barnes & Noble mall, 660 Beacon St, on top of which is perched the monumental **Citgo Sign**, Kenmore's most noticeable landmark. This 60-square-foot neon advertisement, a pulsing red-orange triangle that is the oil company's logo, has been a popular symbol of Boston since it was placed here in 1965.

Boston University, one of the country's largest private schools, has its main campus alongside the Charles River, on the narrow stretch of land between Commonwealth Avenue and Storrow Drive. The school has made inventive reuse of old buildings, such as the dormitory **Myles Standish Hall**, at 610 Beacon St, a scaled-down version of New York's Flatiron Building that was once a hotel where notables like baseball legend Babe Ruth camped out. **Shelton Hall**, behind Standish on Bay State Road, is another hostelry-turned-dorm where playwright Eugene O'Neill undramatically made his long day's journey into night. **Bay State Road** was the westernmost extension of Back Bay, evidenced by its wealth of turn-of-the-century brownstones, most of which now house BU graduate institutes and smaller residence halls. An ornate High Georgian Revival mansion at no. 149 houses the office of the university president. The street ends at **The Castle**, an ivy-covered Tudor mansion now used for university functions and housing a BU-only pub. Continuing the theme back on Commonwealth is the domed **Morse Auditorium**, formerly a synagogue. One long block down is the closest thing the BU campus has to a center, **Marsh Plaza**, with its Gothic Revival chapel and memorial to Martin Luther King, Jr., who graduated from the school.

The Curse: Reversed!

In 1903, the **Boston Pilgrims** (as they were then called) became the first team to represent the American League in baseball's World Series, upsetting the heavily favored Pittsburgh Pirates to claim the championship; their continued financial success allowed them to build a new stadium, **Fenway Park**, in 1912. During their first year there, Boston won the Series again, and repeated the feat in 1915, 1916, and 1918, led in the latter years by the young pitcher **George Herman "Babe" Ruth**, who also demonstrated an eye-opening penchant for hitting home runs.

The team was poised to become a dynasty when its owner, Harry Frazee, began a fire sale of the team to finance a Broadway play that was to star his ingenue girlfriend. Most of the players went for bargain prices, including Ruth, who was sold to the New York Yankees, who went on to become the most successful professional sports franchise ever, with the Babe and all his home runs at the forefront. Indeed, Yankee Stadium is often referred to as "The House that Ruth Built."

After the departure of Ruth, the Red Sox embarked upon a long period in the **wilderness**, with 86 demoralizing years at bat without a World Series win. This drought began, over the years, to be blamed on "**the Curse of the Bambino**" (aka Babe Ruth) – punishment meted out by the baseball gods for selling off one of the game's greatest players. After coming maddeningly close to the title many times – most notably in 1986, when the Sox were one strike away from clinching the Series before a ground ball rolled through the legs of first baseman Bill Buckner – the team finally broke the curse in 2004: after losing the first three games of a best of seven series to the Yankees, the Red Sox won four in a row, then went on to sweep the St Louis Cardinals for the **World Series** crown. As you might expect, there's no longer much talk of the curse – unless you count the emphatic "The Curse: Reversed!" bumper stickers found all over Boston.

The Fenway

The Fenway spreads out beneath Kenmore Square like an elongated kite, taking in sights disparate enough to please most any visitor. Lansdowne Street marks the northern edge of the district, and it is here that you'll find a concentration of many of Boston's nightclubs. Just around the corner from the clubs, the district starts in earnest with **Fenway Park**, the venerable baseball stadium where the resurgent Boston Red Sox play. This is quite removed, however, from the highbrow spaces of Fenway's eastern perimeter, dotted with some of Boston's finest cultural institutions: **Symphony Hall**, the **Museum of Fine Arts**, and the **Isabella Stewart Gardner Museum**. Running down the neighborhood's spine is the **Back Bay Fens**, a huge green space banking the Muddy River and designed by Frederick Law Olmsted, urban landscaper extraordinaire.

Fenway Park

Baseball is treated with reverence in Boston, so it's appropriate that it is played here in what may be the country's most storied stadium, the unique **Fenway Park**, at 24 Yawkey Way (daily 9am–4pm, tours every hour on the hour; $12 adults, $10 children; ⓣ617/226-6666, ⓦwww.redsox.com; Kenmore or Fenway T), whose giant 37-foot-tall left-field wall, aka the **Green Monster**, is an enduring symbol of the quirks of early ballparks. Fenway Park was constructed in 1912 in a tiny, asymmetrical space just off Brookline Avenue, resulting in its famously awkward dimensions, which also include an abnormally short right-field line (302ft) and a fence that doesn't at all approximate the smooth arc of most outfields. That the left-field wall was built so high makes up for some of the short distances in the park and also gives Red Sox leftfielders a distinct advantage over their counterparts – it takes some time before one gets accustomed to the crazy caroms a ball hit off the wall might take. You can go on tours of the stadium, where greats like Ted Williams, Carl Yazstremski, and even Babe Ruth roamed about, but your best bet is to come see a game, really a must for any baseball fan and still a reasonable draw for anyone remotely curious. The season runs from April to October, and **ticket** prices are fairly reasonable, though often very hard to come by: since clinching the 2004 World Series title, Red Sox hysteria has surpassed even its own mind-boggling standards for fan devotion. Call ⓣ617/267-1700 or visit ⓦwww.redsox.com for ticket info.

The Back Bay Fens

The Fenway's defining element is the **Back Bay Fens** (daily 7.30am–dusk; ⓦwww.emeraldnecklace.org/fenway.htm), a snakelike segment of Frederick Law Olmsted's Emerald Necklace that rather uninspiringly takes over where the prim Commonwealth Avenue Mall leaves off. The Fens were fashioned from marsh and mud in 1879, a fact reflected in the name of the waterway that still runs through them today – the **Muddy River**. In the northern portion of the park, local residents maintain small garden plots in the wonderfully unmanicured **Victory Garden**, the oldest community garden in the US. Nearby, below Agassiz Road, the more formally laid out **Kelleher Rose Garden** boasts colorful hybrid species bearing exotic names like Marmalade Skies, Glowing Peace, and Climbing White Iceberg. Though pretty, the Fens get a bit dodgy as night falls, and it would behoove you to leave before it gets dark.

Not far from the Fens' northern tip, the renowned **Berklee College of Music** makes its home on the busy stretch of Massachusetts Avenue south of Boylston Street. A few short blocks south, **Symphony Hall**, home to the Boston Symphony Orchestra, anchors the corner of Massachusetts and Huntington avenues. The inside of the 1900 McKim, Mead & White design resembles an oversized cube, apparently just the right shape to provide the hall with perfect acoustics (call ⓣ1-888/266-1200 or visit ⓦwww.bso.org for ticket info). The modern campus of **Northeastern University** spreads out on both sides of Huntington farther south, though it lacks the collegiate atmosphere and charm of other Boston schools.

Frederick Law Olmsted and the Emerald Necklace

The string of urban parks that stretches through Boston's southern districts, known as the **Emerald Necklace**, grew out of a project conceived in the 1870s, when landscape architect **Frederick Law Olmsted** was commissioned to create for Boston a series of urban parks like those he had done in New York and Chicago. A Romantic naturalist in the tradition of Rousseau and Wordsworth, Olmsted conceived of nature as a way to escape the ills wrought by society, and considered his urban parks a means for city-dwellers to escape the clamor of their everyday lives. He converted much of Boston's remaining open space, which was often disease-breeding marshland, into a series of fabulous, manicured parks beginning with the Back Bay Fens, including the Riverway along the Boston–Brookline border, and proceeding through Jamaica Pond and the Arnold Arboretum to Roxbury's Franklin Park (see "Boston's southern districts," p.132). While Olmsted's original skein of parks was limited to these, further development linked the Fens, via the Commonwealth Avenue Mall, to the Public Garden and Boston Common, all of which now function as part of the Necklace. This makes it all the more impressive in scale, though the Necklace's sense of pristine natural wonder has slipped in the century since their creation – the more southerly links in the chain, starting with the Fens, have grown shaggy and are unsafe at night. The **Boston Park Rangers** (9am–5pm; ⓣ617/635-7383) organize free walking tours covering each of the Necklace's segments from Boston Common to Franklin Park.

Museum of Fine Arts

Rather inconveniently located in south Fenway – but well worth the trip – the **Museum of Fine Arts**, at 465 Huntington Ave (Mon & Tues 10am–4.45pm, Wed–Fri 10am–9.45pm, Sat & Sun 10am–4.45pm; Thurs–Fri West Wing and select galleries only after 4.45pm; $15, additional charge for Gund Gallery exhibits, by donation Wed after 4pm; CityPass accepted; ⓣ617/267-9300, ⓦwww.mfa.org; Museum T), is New England's premier art space. Founded in 1870, the MFA boasts one of the most distinctive art collections in the country, though it continues to be a privately supported and administered institution. In 1909, the museum was moved from its original location in Copley Square to its permanent, Neoclassical home on Huntington Avenue. It is currently undergoing an ambitious renovation that will include a new wing and a glass pavilion for the central courtyard.

Art of the Americas collection

On the first floor of the MFA, a marvelously rich **American collection** features Gilbert Stuart's nationalistic *Washington at Dorchester Heights* and a number of John Singleton Copley portraits of revolutionary figures, plus his gruesome narrative *Watson and the Shark*. Romantic naturalist landscapes from the first half of the nineteenth century – such as Albert Bierstadt's quietly majestic *Buffalo Crossing* – dominate several rooms; and from the latter half of the century there are several seascapes by Winslow Homer; Whistler's morose *Nocturne in Blue and Silver: the Lagoon*; and works from the Boston school, notably Childe Hassan's gauzy *Boston Common at Twilight* and John Singer Sargent's spare *The Daughters of Edward Darley Boit*. Early twentieth-century American work finds Edward Hopper's dour *Drugstore* hanging beside his uncharacteristically upbeat *Room in Brooklyn*. The standout of early to mid-twentieth-century American works is Jackson Pollock's tense, semi-abstracted *Troubled Queen*, which pre-dates his famous drip painting style; it hangs near Georgia O'Keeffe's majestically antlered *Deer's Skull with Pedernal* and Charles Sheeler's ironically titled *View of New York* – which you'll have to see for yourself to appreciate the joke.

While the collection is quite strong in North American works, finding any non-anthropological **Latin American** pieces is a bit of a hunt, and there is a surprising lack of them on display. Highlights of what you can see are Fernando Botero's voluptuous *Venus*, bold sentinel of the West Wing lobby, and Claudio Bravo's introspective *In the Gallery* and *Interior with Landscape Painter*, both unfairly hidden in the upstairs *Bravo* restaurant.

European collection

The second-floor **European wing** begins with Dutch paintings from the Northern Renaissance, featuring two outstanding Rembrandts, *Artist in his Studio* and *Old Man in Prayer*, and follows with several rooms of grandiose Rococo and Romantic work from the eighteenth and early nineteenth centuries. The culmination of the wing is the late nineteenth-century collection, which begins with works by the Realist Jean-François Millet, whose *Man Turning over the Soil* and *The Sower* exhibit the stark use of color and interest in common subjects that characterized later French artists. The subsequent **Impressionist** room contains Monet's heavily abstracted *Grainstack (Snow Effect)* and *Rouen Cathedral (Morning Effect)*, although the real show-stopper, his tongue-in-cheek *La Japonaise* – a riff on Parisian fashion trends – is around the corner in the Rosenburg gallery. Degas figures prominently with his agitated *Pagans and Degas' Father* and a bronze cast of the famous *14-Year Old Dancer*, as does Renoir, whose renowned *Dance at Bourgival* looks onto *Psyche*, a delicate Rodin marble.

The room's highlight, however, is its selection of Post-Impressionist art, best of which are Picasso's coldly cubist *Portrait of a Woman*, Van Gogh's richly hued *Enclosed Field with Ploughman*, and Gauguin's sumptuous display of existential angst *Where Do We Come From? What Are We? Where Are We Going?*.

Ancient art and other galleries

A series of MFA-sponsored digs at Giza has made its **Egyptian collection** the standout of a fine collection of **ancient art**. Pieces range from prehistoric pots to artifacts from the Roman period. While rather modest by comparison, the Nubian collection is nevertheless the largest of its kind outside Africa. Most of the pieces are funerary and actually quite similar to their Egyptian contemporaries. Not nearly as well represented, the Classical section is worth a glance mostly for its numerous Grecian urns, a fine Cycladic *Female Figure*, and several Etruscan sarcophagi with elaborately wrought narrative bas-reliefs.

Between the second-floor Egyptian and Asian galleries is the outstanding **Shapiro Rotunda**, its dome and en-suite colonnade inset with multiple murals and bas-reliefs by John Singer Sargent, who undertook the commission following his work in the Boston Public Library (see p.123). Operating under the belief that mural painting – not portraiture – was the key to "artistic immortality," this installation certainly guaranteed the artist a lasting place in the MFA, and some attending controversy to boot: when the ten-year project was completed shortly before Sargent's death in 1925, his Classical theme was falling out of vogue and his efforts were considered the "frivolous works of a failing master." The rotunda leads off to the **Koch Gallery**, which ranks among the museum's more spectacular showings. Designed to resemble a European palace hallway, its wood-inlaid ceilings cap walls hung two-high with dozens of portraits and landscapes of varying sizes, including three religious pieces by El Greco.

For those in the know, the MFA's **Asian galleries** are a highlight. The Chinese, Indian, Southeast Asian, and Islamic collections are excellent, but the standout is the museum's **Japanese collection**, quite simply one of the best in the world, in part because of the MFA's partnership with the Foundation for the Arts, Nagoya. One room is filled with striking displays of intricately decorated samurai swords, lacquer boxes, and kimonos, while another has temple guardian and Buddha statues arranged in a setting designed like the great hall of a temple. There's also an astounding collection of hanging scrolls and *ukiyo-e* woodblock prints.

The Isabella Stewart Gardner Museum

Less broad in its collection, but more distinctive and idiosyncratic than the MFA, is the nearby **Isabella Stewart Gardner Museum**, at 280 The Fenway (Tues–Sun 11am–5pm; $10, $11 on weekends, free admission for those named "Isabella"; ⓣ617/566-1401, ⓦwww.gardnermuseum.org; Museum T). Eccentric Boston socialite Gardner collected and arranged more than 2500 objects in the four-story Fenway Court building she designed herself, making this the only major museum in the country that is entirely the creation of a single individual. It's a hodgepodge of works from around the globe, presented without much attention to period or style; Gardner's goal was to foster the love of art rather than its study, and she wanted the setting of her pieces to "fire the imagination." Your imagination does get quite a workout – there's art everywhere you look, with many of the objects unlabeled, placed in corners or above doorways, for an effect that is occasionally chaotic, but always striking. To get the most out of a visit, aim to join the hour-long **tour** (Tues–Fri 2.30pm; free), but get there early as only fifteen people are allowed on a first-come-first-served basis.

Alternatively, the **gift shop** sells a worthwhile **guide** ($6) detailing the location and ownership history of every piece on display.

The Gardner is best known for its spectacular central **courtyard**, styled after a fifteenth-century Venetian palace, where flowering plants and trees bloom year-round amid statuary and fountains. However, the museum's greatest success is the **Spanish Cloister**, a long, narrow corridor which perfectly frames John Singer Sargent's ecstatic representation of flamenco dance, *El Jaleo*, and also contains fine seventeenth-century Mexican tiles and Roman statuary and sarcophagi. The **Gothic Room** on the third floor holds another Sargent show-stopper – a stunning portrait of Isabella herself. Although quite mild by today's standards, the Gardners feared its near-erotic quality was too scandalous for public consumption, and the painting was not exhibited publicly until after her death (when, indeed, it did cause a stir). The painting hangs amidst sixteenth-century Italian choir stalls and stained glass from Milan and Soissons cathedrals, as well as Paul-Cesar Helleu's moody representation of the *Interior of the Abbey Church of Saint-Denis*.

The **Titian**, **Veronese**, and **Raphael rooms** comprise a strong showing of Italian Renaissance and Baroque work, including Titian's famous *Europa*, Botticelli's *Tragedy of Lucretia*, and Crivelli's mannerist *St George and the Dragon*. What was once a first-rate array of seventeenth-century Northern European works was debilitated in 1990 by the biggest art heist in history: three Rembrandts and a Vermeer were among thirteen artworks stolen. Fortunately, the majority of works in the **Dutch Room** remain, with an early *Self-Portrait* by Rembrandt and Rubens' austere *Thomas Howard, Earl of Arundel.*

Brookline

The leafy, affluent town of **BROOKLINE**, south of Boston University and west of The Fenway, appears as if it's just another well-maintained Boston neighborhood, though in fact it's a distinct municipality. It holds a couple of vaguely diverting attractions, and is centered around bustling **Coolidge Corner**, at the intersection of Beacon and Harvard streets. Close by is the **John F. Kennedy National Historic Site**, at 83 Beals St (Wed–Sun 10am–4.30pm; $3; ⓣ617/566-1689), the outwardly unremarkable house where JFK was born on May 29, 1917. The inside is rather plain, too, though a narrated voiceover by the late president's mother, Rose, adds some spice to the roped-off rooms. Along Brookline's southern fringe is the **Frederick Law Olmsted National Historic Site**, 99 Warren St (Fri–Sun 10am–4.30pm; free; ⓣ617/566-1689, ⓦwww.nps.gov/frla), which doubled as Olmsted's family home and office; it's currently closed for renovations until 2007. To reach Brookline, take the Green Line's C branch to Coolidge Corner.

Boston's southern districts

The parts of Boston that most visitors see – downtown, Beacon Hill, Back Bay, the North End – actually only cover a small proportion of the city's geography. To the south lies a vast spread of residential neighborhoods known collectively as the **southern districts**, including largely Irish **South Boston**, historical **Dorchester**, blighted **Roxbury**, and pleasant, trendy **Jamaica Plain**, which count just a handful of sites among them, most notably Jamaica Plain's **Arnold Arboretum** and Dorchester's **John F. Kennedy Library and Museum**. None of these areas, though fairly easily accessible on the **T** from downtown (although not always safe to walk around, especially after dark), will keep your attention for too long, with perhaps the exception of Jamaica Plain (popularly known as "JP"), whose Centre Street has boomed into one of the hippest eating and junk shopping strips in the city – somewhat to the distress of local residents, who have seen their rents more than double in the past few years.

Castle Island and Fort Independence

South Boston narrows to an end in Boston Harbor on a strip of land called **Castle Island**, off the end of William J. Day Boulevard, a favorite leisure spot for Southie residents. The island, reachable by bus #9 or #11 from the Broadway **T**, is covered by parks and beaches, though swimming's inadvisable: the waters here, while cleaner than in years past, are far from non-toxic – and they're freezing to boot. At the tip of the island is **Fort Independence** (guided tours Sat & Sun noon–3.30pm; free), a stout granite edifice that was one of the earliest redoubts in the Americas, originally established in 1634, though it has been rebuilt several times since; what you see today is actually a thicker rendition of the 1801 version. Its granite-gray walls aren't much to look at from the outside, although supposedly a gruesome incident that happened inside served as inspiration for Edgar Allan Poe's story "The Cask of Amontillado."

John F. Kennedy Library and Museum

There's not much to see in Dorchester besides the **John F. Kennedy Library and Museum** (daily 9am–5pm; $10; CityPass accepted; ⓣ617/514-1600, ⓦwww.jfklibrary.org; JFK/UMass **T**; free shuttle every 20min), at Columbia Point, spectacularly situated in an I.M. Pei-designed building overlooking Boston Harbor. The museum's presentation opens with a well-done 18min film covering Kennedy's political career through the 1960 Democratic National Convention. The remaining displays cover the presidential campaign of 1960 and the highlights of the brief Kennedy administration. The campaign exhibits are most interesting for their television and radio ads, which illustrate the squeaky-clean self-image America possessed at that time. The section on the Kennedy administration is more serious, highlighted by a 22min film on the Cuban Missile Crisis that well evokes the tension of the event, if exaggerating Kennedy's heroics. The final section of the museum is perhaps the best: a spacious glass pavilion overlooking the harbor, with modestly presented excerpts from Kennedy's *Profiles on Courage* – affecting enough to move even the most jaded JFK critic. Oddly enough, the museum is also the repository for Ernest Hemingway's original manuscripts. Call to make an appointment to see them (ⓣ617/514-1530).

Dorchester Heights Monument

Back at the convergence of South Boston and Dorchester rises the incline of **Dorchester Heights**, whose northernmost point, Thomas Park, is crowned by a stone **tower** commemorating George Washington's bloodless purge of the Brits from Boston. After the Continental Army had held the British under siege in the city for just over a year, Washington wanted to put an end to the whole thing. On March 4, 1776, he amassed all the artillery he could get his hands on and placed it on the towering peak of Dorchester Heights, so the tired Redcoats could get a good look at the patriots' firepower. Intimidated, they swiftly left Boston – for good. The park is generally empty, pristinely kept, and still commands the same sweeping views of Boston and its southern communities that it did during the Revolutionary War. The best vista is from the top of the tower itself, though it's only open by appointment (free; ⓣ617/242-5642). Next to the park is South Boston High School, the location of nationally televised racial turmoil during the busing riots of the 1970s.

Franklin Park

Roxbury's **Franklin Park Zoo**, at 1 Franklin Park Rd in Franklin Park (April–Sept Mon–Fri 10am–5pm, Sat & Sun 10am–6pm; Oct–March daily 10am–4pm; $9.50, kids $5.50; ⓣ617/541-LION, ⓦwww.zoonewengland.com; Forest Hills **T**), the southernmost link in the Emerald Necklace, has little besides its backdrop to distinguish it from any other zoo, and is perhaps only an essential stop if you're traveling with kids. It does boast the impressively re-created African Tropical Forest, the largest indoor open-space zoo design in North America, housing bats, warthogs, and gorillas. Check out Bird's World, too, a charming relic from the days of Edwardian zoo design: a huge, ornate, wrought-iron cage you can walk through while birds fly overhead.

Franklin Park itself was one of Olmsted's proudest accomplishments when it was completed, due to the sheer size of the place, and its scale is indeed astounding – 527 acres of greenspace, with countless trails for hikers, bikers, and walkers leading through the hills and thickly forested areas. That's about all that's still particularly impressive, as much of the park is overgrown from years of half-hearted upkeep and it borders some of Boston's more dangerous areas.

Jamaica Plain and the Arnold Arboretum

Diminutive **Jamaica Plain** is one of Boston's more successfully integrated neighborhoods, with a good mix of students, immigrants, and working-class families. Located between Roxbury and the section of the Emerald Necklace known as the Muddy River Improvement, the area's activity centers around, appropriately, **Centre Street**, which holds some inexpensive cafés and restaurants.

Jamaica Plain's star attraction – and really the only must-see sight in all the southern districts – is the 265-acre **Arnold Arboretum**, at 125 Arborway (daily: March–Oct dawn–dusk, Nov–Feb Mon–Fri dawn–dusk, Sat & Sun 10am–2pm; $1 donation; ⓣ617/524-1718, ⓦwww.arboretum.harvard.edu; Forest Hills **T**), the most spectacular link in the Emerald Necklace. Its collection of flowering trees, vines, and shrubs has benefited from more than one hundred years of both careful grooming and ample funding, and is now one of the finest in North America. The plants are arranged along a series of paths populated by runners and dog-walkers as well as serious botanists, though it certainly doesn't require any expert knowledge to enjoy the grounds. The array of Asian species – the best in the world outside of Asia – is highlighted by the **Larz Anderson Bonsai Collection** and is brilliantly concentrated along the Chinese Path, a walkway near the center of the park. It's best to visit during spring, when magnolias, crab apples, and lilacs complement the greenery with dazzling chromatic schemes. "**Lilac Sunday**," a celebration held on the third Sunday in May, sees the Arboretum at its most vibrant (and busiest), when its collection of lilacs – the second largest in the US – is in full bloom.

Cambridge

A walk down most any street in **CAMBRIDGE** – just across the Charles River from Boston, but a world apart in atmosphere and attitude – takes you past plaques and monuments honoring literati and revolutionaries who lived and

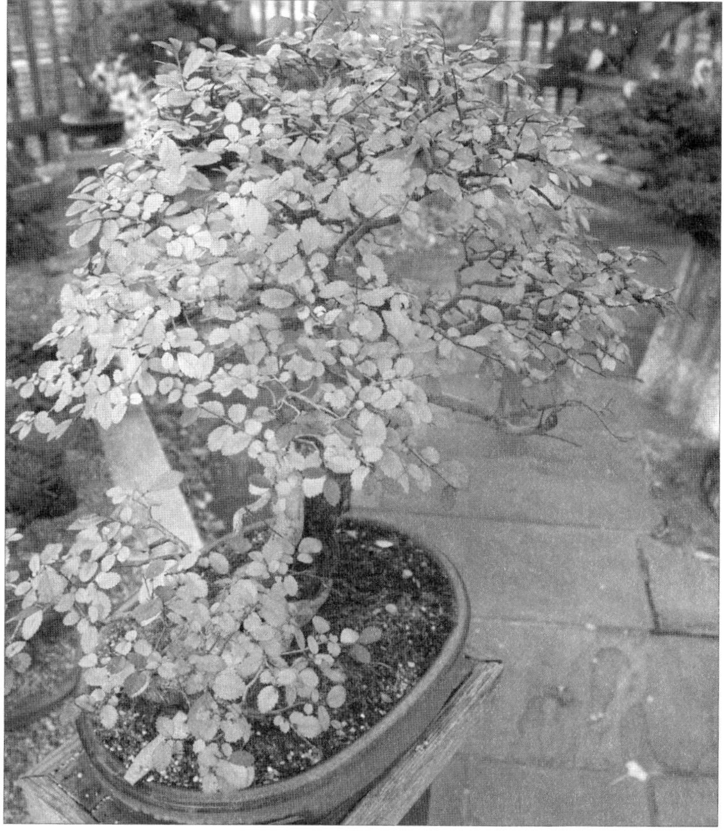

△ Arnold Arboretum

worked in the area as early as the seventeenth century. But along its Colonial-period brick sidewalks and narrow, crooked roads, Cambridge vibrates with a vital present: starched businesspeople bustle past disaffected punks; clean-cut college students coexist with a growing homeless population; and busloads of tourists look on as street people purvey goods and perform music. It's all enough to make Cambridge an essential stopover on your trip.

The city is loosely organized around a series of squares – confluences of streets that are the focus of each area's commercial activity. By far the most important of these is **Harvard Square**, center of the eponymous university, and the top draw for Cambridge's visitors. The area around it is home to the city's main sights, particularly the stretch of Colonial mansions in **Old Cambridge**. The squares of **Central** and **East Cambridge** are more down-to-earth. Blue-collar **Central Square** is less touristy but no less urban than its collegiate counterpart: here you can eat at *McDonald's* (a rarity in Cambridge) and enjoy the city's best blues bars and rock music shows. Farther east along the Charles is **Kendall Square**, home to a cluster of tech companies and also the beginning of East Cambridge, a mostly Hispanic working-class district. The only part of this area that really warrants a visit is the **Massachusetts Institute of Technology** (MIT), one of the world's premier science and research institutions and home to some peculiar architecture and an excellent museum.

Harvard Square and the University

Harvard Square – a public space in the shadow of Harvard Yard with a buzz generated by outdoor cafés, street performers, and a steady stream of browsers who descend on the square's main tenant, Out of Town News – radiates out from the **T** stop along Massachusetts Avenue, JFK Street, and Brattle Street. A small **tourism kiosk** run by the Cambridge Tourism Office (daily 9am–5pm; ⓣ617/441-2884 or 1-800/862-5678, ⓦwww.cambridge-usa.org) faces the station exit, but more of the action is in the adjacent sunken area known as **The Pit**, a triage center for fashion victims of alternative culture. Moody students spend entire days sitting here admiring each other's green hair and body piercings while homeless locals hustle for change and other handouts. This is also the focal point of the **street music scene**, at its most frenetic and fascinating on Friday and Saturday nights and Sunday afternoons, when all the elements converge: crowds mill about; evangelical demonstrators engage in shouting

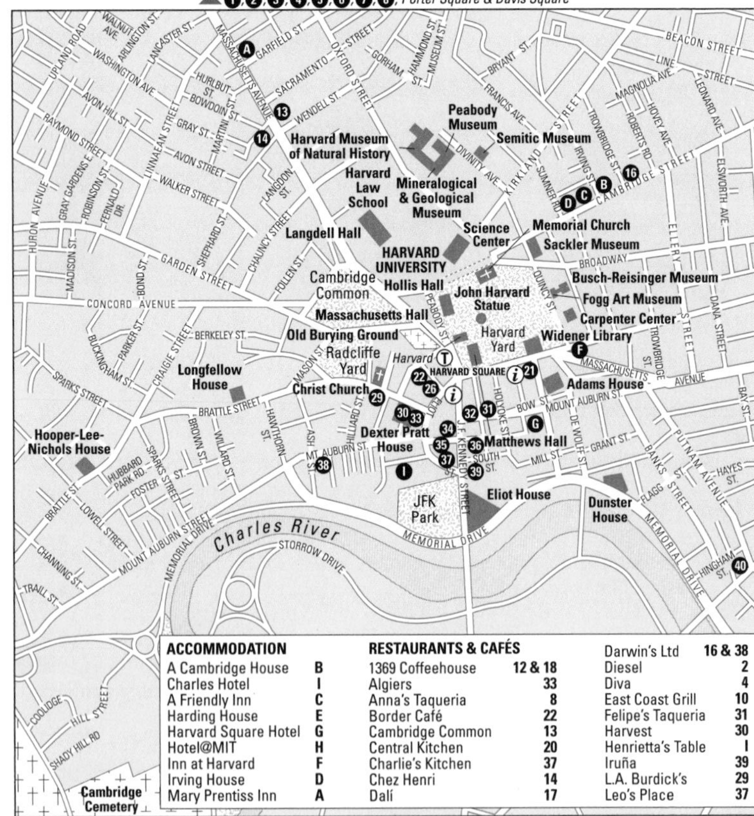

matches with angry youths; and magicians, acrobats, and bands perform on every corner.

North of Harvard Square along Massachusetts Avenue lies one of Cambridge's first cemeteries, the **Old Burying-Ground**, whose style and grounds have scarcely changed since the seventeenth century. The stone grave markers are adorned in a style somewhere between Puritan austerity and medieval superstition: inscriptions praise the simple piety of the staunchly Christian deceased, but are surrounded by death's-heads carved to ward off evil spirits. You're supposed to apply to the sexton of Christ Church for entry, but if the gate at the path behind the church is open (as it frequently is), you can enter – just be respectful of the grounds.

A triangular wedge of concrete squeezed into the intersection of Massachusetts Avenue and Garden Street, **Dawes Park** is named for the other patriot who rode to alert residents that the British were marching on Lexington and Concord on April 19, 1775. While Longfellow chose to commemorate Revere's midnight ride instead, as have all history classes, the Cambridge citizens must have appreciated poor Dawes' contribution just as much. Actually, there was a third rider, Dr. Samuel Prescott, who's generally credited as the only one to complete the ride. Bronze hoofmarks in the sidewalk mark the event, and

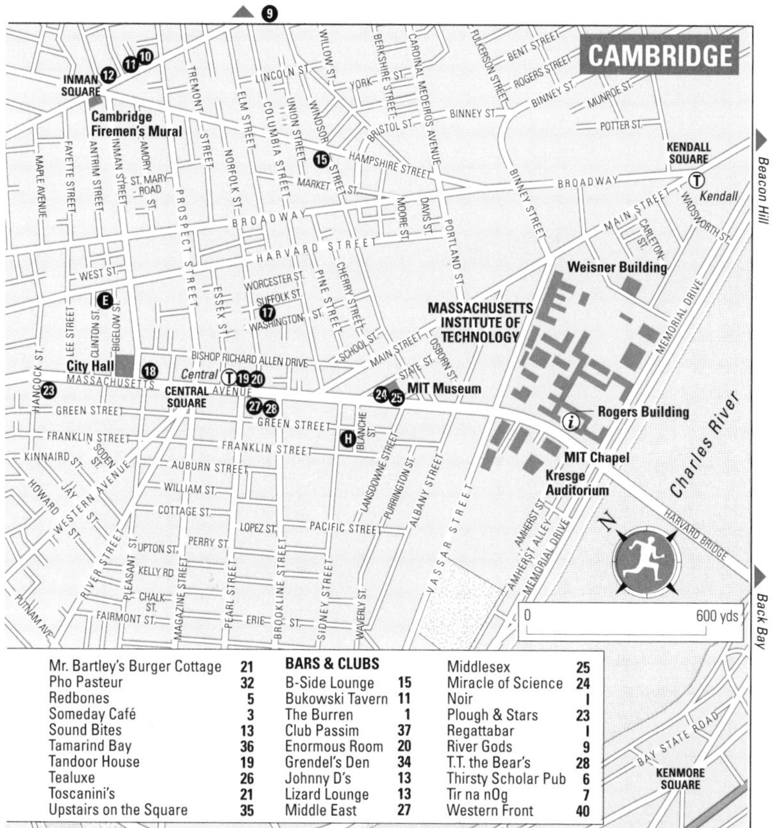

A brief history of Cambridge

Cambridge began inauspiciously in 1630, when a group of English immigrants from Charlestown founded **New Towne** village on the narrow, swampy banks of the Charles River. These Puritans hoped New Towne would become an ideal religious community; to that end, they founded a college in 1636 for the purpose of training clergy. Two years later, the college took its name in honor of a local minister, **John Harvard**, who bequeathed his library and half his estate to the nascent institution. New Towne was eventually renamed Cambridge for the English university where many of its figureheads were educated, and became an enormous publishing center after the importation of the printing press in the seventeenth century. Its printing industry and university established Cambridge as a bastion of intellectual activity and political thought. This status became entrenched over the course of the United States' turbulent early history, particularly during the late eighteenth century, when the Cambridge population became sharply divided between the numerous artisans and farmers who sympathized with the Revolution and the minority of moneyed Tories. When fighting began, the Tories were driven from their mansions on modern-day Brattle Street (then called "Tory Row"), their place taken by Cambridge intelligentsia and prominent Revolutionaries.

In 1846, the Massachusetts Legislature granted a city charter linking Old Cambridge (the Harvard Square area) and industrial East Cambridge as a single municipality. Initially, there was friction between these two very different sections; in 1855, citizens from each area unsuccessfully petitioned for the regions to be granted separate civic status. Though relations improved, the distinctive characters remain. A large immigrant population was drawn to opportunity in the industrial and commercial sectors of East Cambridge, while academics increasingly sought out Harvard, whose reputation had continued to swell, and the Massachusetts Institute of Technology, which moved here from Boston in 1916. The district's political leanings are less liberal today than in the 1960s, when Cambridge earned the name "Moscow on the Charles" due to its unabashedly Red character, but the fact that nearly half of its 90,000-plus residents are university affiliates ensures that it will remain one of America's most opinionated cities.

placards behind the pathway provide information on the history of the Harvard Square/Old Cambridge area.

Cambridge Common

In **Cambridge Common**, a roughly square patch of greenspace between Massachusetts Avenue, Garden Street, and Waterhouse Street, you can retrace the old **Charlestown–Watertown path**, along which Redcoats beat a sheepish retreat during the Revolutionary War, and which still transects the park from east to west. The most prominent feature on the Common is, however, the revered **Washington Elm**, under which it's claimed George Washington took command of the Continental Army. The elm, at the southern side of the park near the intersection of Garden Street and Appian Way, is accompanied by a predictable wealth of commemorative objects: three cannons captured from the British when they evacuated Boston, a statue of Washington, and monuments to two Polish army captains hired to lead Revolutionary forces. What the memorials don't tell you is that the city of Cambridge cut down the original elm in 1946 when it began to obstruct traffic; it stood at the Common's southwest corner, near the intersection of Mason and Garden streets. The present tree is only the offspring of that tree, raised from one of its branches. To further confuse the issue, the Daughters of the American Revolution erected a monument

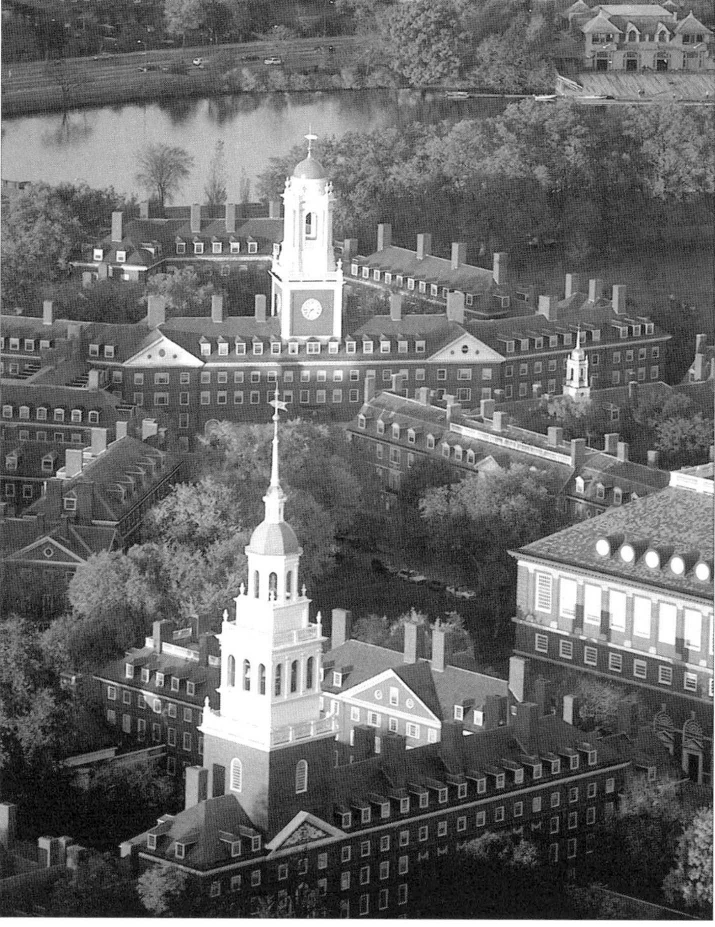

△ Harvard University

commemorating the south*east* corner of the park as the spot where Washington did his historic thing. And recently, historians have suggested that Washington never commissioned the troops on the Common at all, but rather in Wadsworth House at Harvard Yard.

JFK Street and the Harvard Houses

The stretch of JFK Street below Harvard Square holds more of the city's many public spaces, certainly the least of which is **Winthrop Square**, site of the original New Towne marketplace and since converted into a tiny, well-shaded park. **John F. Kennedy Park**, where JFK Street meets Memorial Drive, was only finished in the late 1980s, making it an infant among Harvard Square's venerable spaces, though certainly not the first pious shrine to the university's favorite modern son. The unusual **memorial** to Kennedy in its center is worth a look: a low granite pyramid inscribed with Kennedy platitudes, covered constantly but imperceptibly by a thin film of flowing water.

Harvard's fancy upperclassmen's residences, most of which are nested in the area east of JFK Street and south of Harvard Yard, are a visible remnant of the university's elite past. Just south of **Adams House**, once a hotbed of counterculturalism, juts the graceful, blue-topped bell tower of **Lowell House**, at 2 Holyoke Place, which boasts one of Harvard's most beautiful courtyards. Further west on the banks of the Charles rises the purple spire of **Eliot House**, at 101 Dunster St, formerly a blueblood bastion of social privilege. To the east, at 945 Memorial Drive, lies **Dunster House**, whose red Georgian top is a favorite of Cambridge's tourist brochures.

Harvard Yard

The transition from Harvard Square to **Harvard Yard** – the proper center of the university – is brief and dramatic: in a matter of only several feet, the buzz of car traffic and urban life gives way to grassy lawns and towering oaks pervaded by an aura of Ivy League intellectualism. The atmosphere is more mythological than real, however, as the Yard's narrow, haphazard footpaths are constantly plied by preoccupied students and as many camera-clicking tour groups, who often make the place seem more like an amusement park than a staid university campus. You can join the hullabaloo by taking a free one-hour guided tour from the **Holyoke Center**, 1350 Massachusetts Ave (June–Aug Mon–Sat 10am, 11.15am, 2pm & 3.15pm; Sept–May Mon–Fri 10am & 2pm, Sat 2pm; ⓣ617/495-1573). The Center also provides limited free Internet use, as well as **maps** and brochures detailing everything Harvard-related.

The most common entrance is the one directly across from Harvard Square proper, which leads to the **Old Yard**, a large, rectangular area enclosed by freshman dormitories that has been around since 1636. In front of stark, symmetrical, marble-hued University Hall is the Yard's trademark icon, the **John Harvard statue**, around which chipper student guides inform tour groups of the oft-told story of the statue's three lies (it misdates the college's founding; erroneously identifies John Harvard as the college's founder; and isn't really a likeness of John Harvard at all). While it's a popular spot for visitors to take pictures, male students at the college covet the statue as a site of public urination; it's a badge of honor around here – as a result, there are surveillance cameras trained on the statue.

Situated in front of the statue, the architectural contrast between modest **Hollis Hall**, which dates from 1762, and its grandiose southern neighbor, **Matthews Hall**, built around a hundred years later, mirrors Harvard's transition from a quiet training ground for ministers to a wealthy, cosmopolitan university. The indentations in Hollis's front steps also hold some historical interest: students used to warm their rooms by heating cannonballs, and, when it came time to leave their quarters for the summer, they would dispose of them by dropping them from their windows rather than having to carry them down the stairs.

To the east of the Old Yard lie the grander buildings of the **New Yard**, where a vast set of steps leads up to the enormous pillars of **Widener Library**. Named after Harvard grad and *Titanic* victim Harry Elkins Widener, whose mother paid for the project, it's the center of the largest private library collection in the US, boasting 65 miles of bookshelves. At the opposite side of the New Yard is **Memorial Church**, whose narrow, white spire strikes a balancing note to the heavy pillared front of Widener.

North lies the main quad of the famed **Harvard Law School**, focusing on the stern gray pillars of **Langdell Hall**, the imposing edifice on its western border. Above Langdell's entrance is a Latin inscription encapsulating the Western ideal of the rule of law, tinctured with an unusual degree of religiosity: *"Non sub homine, sed sub deo et lege"* ("Not under man, but under God and law"). Inside is the renovated **Harvard Law Library**, where you can practically smell the stress in the air.

It's hard to miss the conspicuously modern **Carpenter Center** as you walk past down Quincy Street, a slab of granite-gray amidst Harvard's ever-present brick motif. Completed in 1963 as a center for the study of visual art at Harvard, the Carpenter Center is the only building in America designed by the French architect Le Corbusier. Be sure to traverse its trademark feature, a walkway that leads through the center of the building, meant to reflect the path worn by students on the lot on which the center was constructed. The basement of the building houses the **Sert Gallery** (free; ⓣ617/495–9400), curated jointly by the university art museums and visual arts students.

Harvard University museums

Harvard's three **art museums** have benefited from years of scholarly attention and donors' financial generosity – the collections are easily some of the finest in New England. A ticket to one buys you entry to the other two (all museums Mon–Sat 10am–5pm, Sun 1–5pm; $7.50, free Sat 10am–noon; ⓣ617/495-9400, ⓦwww.artmuseums.harvard.edu).

Fogg Art, Busch-Reisinger, and Sackler museums

Housed on two floors which surround a lovely mock sixteenth-century Italian courtyard, the collections of the **Fogg Art Museum**, at 32 Quincy St, show-case the highlights of Harvard's substantial collection of Western art. Much of the first floor is devoted to medieval and Renaissance material, mainly religious art with the usual complement of suffering Christs. This part of the collection is best for a series of capitals salvaged from the French cathedral of Moutiers-Saint-Jean, which combine a Romanesque predilection for classical design with medieval didactic narrative. Additional first-floor chambers are devoted to portraiture of the seventeenth and eighteenth centuries, featuring two Rubens, a Rembrandt, and three Poussins, whose startling *Hannibal Crossing the Alps* depicts the great Carthaginian instructing his troops from atop a massive tusked elephant.

The museum's permanent holdings are strongest in **Impressionism** and **modernism**, especially the late-nineteenth-century French contingent of Degas, Monet, Manet, Pissarro, and Cezanne. But it's the focus on American counterparts to European late-nineteenth- and early twentieth-century art-ists that truly distinguishes the collection, from the fine range of John Singer Sargent portraits, his solitary *The Breakfast Table* among them, to an ethereal Whistler *Nocturne* in blue and silver tints. Modernism is represented by, among others, Pollock's narrow beige-and-black *No. 2*, and Sheeler's outstanding *Upper Deck*, a representation of technology that ingeniously combines realism with abstraction.

Secreted away at the rear of the Fogg's second floor is the entrance to Werner Otto Hall, home of the **Busch-Reisinger Museum**, which focuses exclusively on the culture of German-speaking countries. Despite its small size, it's one of the finest collections of German and Bauhaus works in the world. Its six rooms include Renaissance sculpture as well as fin de siècle works, such as Klimt's *Pear Tree*, a dappled meditation on the natural environment, and several Bauhaus standouts like Feininger's angular *Bird Cloud* and Moholy-Nagy's *Light-Space Modulator* – a quirky sculpture-machine set in motion for ten minutes just once a week (Wed 1.45pm) due to its fragility. The gallery is strongest, however, in Expressionist portraiture, notably Kirchner's sardonic *Self-Portrait with a Cat* and Beckmann's garish *The Actors*, a narcissistic triptych.

Right out of the Fogg and dead ahead is the five-floor Arthur M. Sackler Building, 485 Broadway, the first, second, and fourth floors of which comprise the **Sackler Museum**, dedicated to the art of classical, Asian, and Islamic cultures. The museum's holdings far outstrip its available space, which is why the first floor is devoted to rotating exhibits. Islamic and Asian art are the themes of the second floor, featuring illustrations from Islamic texts and Chinese landscapes from the past several centuries. The fourth floor is best for its excellent array of sensuous Buddhist sculptures from ancient China, India, and Southeast Asia.

Museum of Natural History, Peabody Museum, and Semitic Museum

North past the Sackler Museum is the **Harvard Museum of Natural History**, at 26 Oxford St (daily 9am–5pm; $7.50, includes entry to the Peabody Museum, free Sun 9am–noon; CityPass accepted; ⓣ617/495-3045, ⓦwww.hmnh.harvard.edu), the public museum front for Harvard University's three natural history institutions. If you don't know much about geology, the **mineralogical galleries** probably won't do too much for you, though most of the gems are aesthetically pleasing. The adjacent gallery houses the museum's *pièce de resistance*, the stunning **Ware Collection of Glass Models of Plants**. This project began in 1886 and terminated almost fifty years later in 1936, leaving the museum with an absolutely unique and visually awesome collection of flower models constructed to the last detail, entirely from glass; it's really not to be missed. Down the hall, the stellar **zoological galleries** are home to some freakishly huge dinosaur fossils, including a 42 foot-long prehistoric marine reptile, the *Kronosaurus*. Around the corner is the *Glyptodont*, which looks like a heavily inflated armadillo.

The Museum of Natural History is connected to the **Peabody Museum**, at 11 Divinity Ave (same hours and cost as above; ⓣ617/496-1027, ⓦwww.peabody.harvard.edu), which displays archeological and ethnographic mate-rials, many culled from Harvard University expeditions. The Peabody also features interesting exhibits on North American Native Americans, though the strength of the museum lies in its collection of pieces from Mesoamerica. Best are the enormous, carved Copan stelae on which practical information such as birth, death, and historic deeds are all recorded in ancient Mayan.

Facing the Peabody is the **Harvard Semitic Museum**, at 6 Divinity Ave (Mon–Fri 10am–4pm, Sun 1–4pm; free; ⓦwww.fas.harvard.edu/~semitic), which lacks the magnetism of its neighbors but holds some Near Eastern archeological artifacts that are worth a look. The museum currently exhibits a full-scale replica of an Iron Age village house, circa 700 BC, and an Egyptian exhibit focusing on death and the afterlife.

Old Cambridge

After the outbreak of the American Revolution, Cambridge's patriot dissidents ran the Tories out of town, leaving their sumptuous houses to be used as barracks for the Continental Army. What was then called Tory Row is modern-day **Brattle Street**, the main drag of the **Old Cambridge** district. The area has remained a tree-lined neighborhood of stately mansions, although only two of the houses are open to the public; the rest you'll have to view from across their expansive, impeccably kept lawns.

Just off Harvard Square is the **Brattle House**, at 42 Brattle St, which fails to reflect the unabashedly extravagant lifestyle of its former resident, William Brattle. The house doesn't appear nearly as grand as it once did, dwarfed as it is by surrounding office buildings and currently housing the Cambridge Center for Adult Education; they don't mind if you pop in for a look. A marker on the corner of Brattle and Story streets commemorates the site of a tree which once stood near the **Dexter Pratt House**, home of the blacksmith celebrated by Longfellow in the popular poem *The Village Blacksmith*.

Longfellow House

One house you can visit for more than just a look is the recently renovated **Longfellow House**, 105 Brattle St (June–Oct Wed–Sun 10am–4.30pm, tours hourly 10.30–11.30am & 1–4pm; $3; Ⓣ617/876-4491, Ⓦwww.nps.gov/long; Harvard **T**), the best-known and most popular of the Brattle Street mansions, where the poet Henry Wadsworth Longfellow lived while serving as a professor at Harvard. It was erected for Loyalist John Vassall in 1759, who promptly vacated it on the eve of the Revolutionary War. During the war, it was used by George Washington as his headquarters during the siege of Boston, and it wasn't until 1837 that it became home to Longfellow, who moved in as a boarder; when he married the wealthy Fanny Appleton, her father purchased the house for them as a wedding gift. Longfellow lived here until his death in 1882, and the house is preserved in an attempt to portray it as it was during his residence. The halls and walls are festooned with Longfellow's furniture and art collection: most surprising is the wealth of nineteenth-century pieces from the Far East, amassed by Longfellow's adventurous son Charlie on his world travels; four of his Japanese screens are included, the best of which, a two-panel example depicting geishas in spring and winter costumes, is in an upstairs bedroom.

Hooper-Lee-Nichols House

The second of the Brattle Street mansions open to the public, half a mile west of the Longfellow House and well worth the trip if you've got the stamina, is the bluewashed **Hooper-Lee-Nichols House**, at no. 159 (Tues & Thurs 2–5pm, tours at 2, 3 & 4pm; $5; Ⓣ617/547-4252, Ⓦwww.cambridgehistory.org), one of the oldest residences in Cambridge and the best example of the character of housing design during Cambridge's colonial period. The house began as a stout, post-medieval farmhouse, and underwent various renovations until it became the Georgian mansion it is today. Knowledgeable tour guides open secret panels to reveal centuries-old wallpaper and original foundations; otherwise, you'll see rooms predictably restored with period writing tables, canopy beds, and rag dolls.

At the terminus of Brattle Street is the **Mount Auburn Cemetery**, an unexpected treasure. Laid out in 1831 as America's first "garden cemetery," its 175 acres of stunningly landscaped grounds, with ponds and fountains, provide a gorgeous contrast with the many spare "burying grounds" scattered all over Cambridge and Boston. Resting here are a medley of famous names such as the painter Winslow Homer and art patron Isabella Stewart Gardner, among others. Pick up a **map** at the visitors' center at the entrance to find out who's where and get a sense of its scope by ascending the **tower** that lies smack in its center – from here, you can see not only the entire grounds but all the way to downtown Boston.

Central and Inman Squares

Working-class **Central Square**, as you might expect, is located roughly in the geographical center of Cambridge, and is appropriately the city's civic center, home to its most important government buildings. There's nothing much to see, but it's a good place to shop and eat, and is home to some of the best nightlife in Cambridge.

Overshadowed by Cambridge's busier districts, **Inman Square** marks a quiet stretch directly north of Central Square, centered around the confluence of Cambridge, Beacon, and Prospect streets. The area is essentially a pleasant, mostly residential neighborhood where much of Cambridge's Portuguese-speaking population resides, though Inman has become more cosmopolitan of late, and there are some good shopping and eating opportunities to be had here. The lone landmark here is the charmingly inexpert **Cambridge Firemen's Mural**, at the corner of Cambridge and Hampshire streets, a work of public art commissioned to honor the local men in red.

Massachusetts Institute of Technology

Eastern Cambridge is mostly taken over by the **Massachusetts Institute of Technology** (MIT), which occupies over 150 acres alongside the Charles and provides an intellectual counterweight to the otherwise working-class character of the area. Originally established in Back Bay in 1861, MIT moved to this more auspicious campus across the river in 1916 and has since risen to international prominence as a major center for theoretical and practical research in the sciences.

The campus buildings and geography reflect the quirky, nerdy character of the institute, emphasizing function and peppering it with a peculiar notion of form. Everything is obsessively numbered and coded: you can, for example, go to 1-290 (the Pierce Laboratory) for a lecture in 1.050 (Engineering Mechanics 1), which gets you closer to a minor in 1 (Civil and Environmental Engineering).

Behind the massive pillars that guard the entrance of the aforementioned **Pierce Laboratory**, at 77 Massachusetts Ave, you'll find a labyrinth of corridors through which students can traverse the entire east campus without ever going outside – known to Techies as the **Infinite Corridor**. Just inside Pierce's entrance you'll find the **MIT Information Center** (Mon–Fri 9am–5pm, campus tours at 10.45am & 2.45pm; ⓣ617/253-4795), while atop the nearby McLaurin Building is MIT's best-known architectural icon, a massive gilt hemisphere called the **Great Dome**.

MIT has drawn the attention of some of the major architects of the twentieth century, who have used the university's progressiveness as a testing ground for some of their more experimental works. Two of these are located in the courtyard across Massachusetts Avenue from the Rogers Building. The **Kresge Auditorium**, designed by Finnish architect Eero Saarinen, resembles a large tent, though its real claim to fame is that it puzzlingly rests on three, rather than four, corners; the architect allegedly designed it over breakfast by cutting into his grapefruit. In the same courtyard is the red-brick **MIT Chapel**, also the work of Saarinen, and shaped like a stocky cylinder with an abstract sculpture crafted from paper-thin metals serving as a rather unconventional spire; inside, a delicate metal screen scatters light patterns across the floor. The I.M. Pei-designed Weisner Building is home to the **List Visual Art Center** (Tues–Thurs, Sat & Sun noon–6pm; free), which displays contemporary artworks that utilize a wide range of media. Of perhaps more interest, down Massachusetts Avenue at no. 265, the **MIT Museum** (Tues–Fri 10am–5pm, Sat & Sun noon–5pm; $5;

Ⓣ617/253-4444, Ⓦweb.mit.edu/museum) has two main permanent displays, the Hologram Museum and the Hall of Hacks, the latter of which provides a retrospective on the various pranks ("hacks") pulled by Techies, and details how the madcap funsters once wreaked havoc at the annual Harvard–Yale football game by inflating a massive weather balloon in the middle of the gridiron.

Eating

There is no shortage of places to **eat** in Boston. The city is loaded with bars and pubs that double as restaurants, cafés that serve full meals, and plenty of higher-end dinner-only options. There's a new level of dining adventurousness these days, too, partly in response to the traditional New England-type fare that is still the area's hallmark: hearty standbys like broiled scrod, clam chowder, and Yankee pot roast, all of which owe a bit of debt to the cold-winter mentality in Boston. Most of this has shown up in the explosion of restaurants, particularly in Back Bay and the South End, serving modern, eclectic food that unfortunately doesn't always quite hit the mark.

At **lunchtime**, many places offer meals at about half the cost of dinner, a plus if you want to sample some of the food at the city's pricier and more exclusive restaurants. Pubs and taverns are also a good bet, serving sandwiches and old-fashioned grub that won't let you go hungry. **Dinner**, usually from 5pm on, is a much more exciting deal, with a wide array of **restaurants** that range from Boston's own local cuisine to ethnic foods of every stripe. You'll probably want to book ahead if you're planning to show up at a popular place (say, a bistro in the South End or on Newbury Street) after 6pm; places are generally open until 10 or 11pm, though in Chinatown there are numerous **late-night** spots. Also, some restaurants are closed on Sundays and/or Mondays, so call ahead for either of those nights, too.

As far as Boston's culinary landscape goes, there are ever-popular **Italian** restaurants, both traditional Southern and more trendy Northern, that cluster in the **North End**, mainly on Hanover and Salem streets. The city's tiny **Chinatown** packs in all types of Asian fare. **Dim sum**, where you choose selections from carts wheeled past your table, is especially big here, and you can find it any time, though mostly at lunch – the best places are always packed on weekends, with lines down the streets. Boston's trendiest restaurants, usually of the **New American** variety, tend to cluster in **Back Bay** and the **South End**.

Cambridge dining life centers around Harvard, Inman, and Central squares, and is perhaps best distinguished for its **Indian** restaurants, forever competing against each other to offer lower prices – resulting in some of the best food values in the city.

In most places, save certain areas of downtown, you won't have a problem finding somewhere to grab a **quick bite,** whether it's a diner, deli, or some other kind of snack joint. In addition to all the spots listed below, see the bars and cafés starting on p.150, many of which offer food all day long.

Downtown, Chinatown, and the waterfront

Bakey's 45 Broad St Ⓣ617/426-1710; State **T**. Easily recognized by its decorative sign depicting a man slumped over an ironing board, *Bakey's* serves inexpensive, reliable pub grub and New York-style deli sandwiches.

The Barking Crab 88 Sleeper St, at the Northern Avenue Bridge Ⓣ617/426-CRAB; South Station **T**. This endearing seafood shack aims to please with its comfortable atmosphere and unpretentious, inexpensive menu, centered around anything they can pull from the ocean. Excellent city skyline views – plus it's right on the harbor.

China Pearl 9 Tyler St ⓣ617/426-4338; Chinatown **T**. Boston's best spot for dim sum. Authentic dishes like shrimp shumai and barbecued pork buns are offered alongside more adventurous fare like chicken feet. Expect a long wait for Sunday brunch.

Durgin-Park 340 Faneuil Hall Marketplace ⓣ617/227-2038; Government Center **T**. A Boston landmark in operation since 1827, *Durgin-Park* has a no-frills Yankee atmosphere and a waitstaff known for their surly charm. It's a good place to go for iconic New England foods like roast beef, baked beans, and warm Indian pudding. The downstairs bar is cheaper and livelier.

Ginza 16 Hudson St ⓣ617/338-2261; Chinatown **T**. Open until 4am on weekends, *Ginza* is a popular after-hours spot serving some of the best sushi in the city. Additional location in Brookline at 1002 Beacon St (ⓣ617/566-9688; St Marys **T**).

Grand Chau Chow 41–45 Beach St ⓣ617/292-5166; Chinatown **T**. One of the first Chinatown restaurants to specialize in seafood, and still one of the best. The setting is stripped-down so there's nothing to distract you from delicious salt-and-pepper shrimp or, if you're in a more adventurous mood, sea cucumber.

Jacob Wirth 31 Stuart St ⓣ617/338-8586; Boylston **T**. A German-themed Boston landmark, around since 1868; even if you don't like bratwurst washed down with a hearty lager, something is sure to please. There are sing-alongs on Fridays. A Boston must-visit.

Kingfish Hall Faneuil Hall Marketplace ⓣ617/523-8862; Government Center **T**. Beautifully displayed, tastefully done seafood, all best enjoyed in the outdoor dining area. Try the Dancing Fish – the fish of the day, grilled just right.

Les Zygomates 129 South St ⓣ617/542-5108; South Station **T**. Busy French bistro with good wine selections and gourmet *frites* a few blocks away from South Station. Try the duck confit for dinner, and for dessert indulge in wine with chocolate fondue.

Locke-Ober Café 3 Winter Place ⓣ617/542-1340; Park **T**. Don't be fooled by the name: *Locke-Ober Café* is very much a restaurant, and one of the most blueblooded in Boston. The fare consists of stuff like steak tartare and oysters on the half shell, while the setting is dark, ornate, and stuffy. There's an archaic dress code, too – jacket and tie for men.

Milk Bottle 300 Congress St ⓣ617/426-8855; South Station **T**. This Boston landmark in front of the Children's Museum dishes out bagels and cream cheese, salads, and coffee from its tiny kiosk window; patrons lounge contentedly at nearby picnic tables.

Milk Street Café 50 Milk St ⓣ617/542-3663; State **T**; Post Office Square Park ⓣ617/350-7273; Downtown Crossing **T**. Kosher and quick are the key words at these two downtown eateries, popular with suits and vegetarians for the large designer sandwiches and salads. No credit cards.

Mr. Dooley's Boston Tavern 77 Broad St ⓣ617/338-5656; State **T**. One of the many Irish pubs downtown, though with a quieter and more atmospheric interior than the rest. Also known for its live music acts and Traditional Irish Breakfast Sundays – nice, especially since finding anything open around here on Sunday is a challenge.

No. 9 Park 9 Park St ⓣ617/742-9991; Park St **T**. Highly recommended restaurant with sedate green walls and plates busy with Southern French and Italian entrees. A seven-course tasting menu ($85; with wine $135) allows you to try almost everything.

Pho Pasteur 682 Washington St ⓣ617/482-7467; Chinatown **T**. Very popular Vietnamese restaurant offering a multitude of tasty variations on *pho* noodle soup.

Radius 8 High St ⓣ617/426-1234; South Station **T**. Housed in a former bank, this ultramodern French restaurant injects a dose of minimalist industrial chic to the cautious Financial District with über-cool decor and an innovative menu. The tasty nouvelle cuisine is complemented by an extensive wine list.

Sel de la Terre 255 State St ⓣ617/720-1300; Aquarium **T**. The less-expensive sister to upscale *L'Espalier* (see review, p.148) *Sel de la Terre* honors its name ("Salt of the Earth") with rustic Provençale fare like hearty bouillabaisse, roasted lamb and eggplant, and perhaps the best french fries in Boston. Conveniently, you can acquire the fixings for a waterfront picnic here, too, by calling ahead to order ($11/person) and picking it up on your way to the ferry.

Sorriso Trattoria 107 North St ⓣ617/259-1560; South Station **T**. Dine on fancypants brick-oven pizzas and rustic Italian fare such as portabella *carpaccio,* all while relaxing in roomy chocolate-colored booths. Reservations recommended.

Taiwan Café 34 Oxford St ⓣ617/426-8181; Chinatown **T**. Locals swoon over this busy, authentic Taiwanese eatery which serves up mustard greens with edamame, clams with spicy black bean sauce, and steamed pork buns done just right. Open until midnight. Credit cards not accepted.

Umbria Ristorante 295 Franklin St ⓣ617/338-1000; State **T**. Very swish financial district spot serving beautifully prepared, succulent Italian cuisine such as the fantastic *bufala mozzarella* with truffle dressing or the handmade lobster ravioli.

Union Oyster House 41 Union St ☎617/227-2750; Government Center or State **T**. The oldest continuously operating restaurant in America has two big claims to fame: French king Louis-Philippe lived over the tavern during his youth, and, perhaps apocryphally, the toothpick was first used here. The food is pretty good too: fresh, well-prepared seafood, although a bit overpriced.
The Wrap 82 Water St ☎617/357-9013; State **T**. Fresh fixings wrapped in warm tortillas, vitality-infused fruit smoothies, and other lunchtime treats, all quick, easy, and cheap at this ubiquitous Boston chain.

The North End and Charlestown

The Daily Catch 323 Hanover St ☎617/523-8567; Haymarket **T**; 2 Northern Ave ☎617/772-4400; South Station **T**. Ocean-fresh seafood, notably calamari and shellfish – Sicilian-style, with megadoses of garlic – draws big lines to this tiny storefront restaurant. The downtown location offers a solid alternative to the touristy Yankee scrod-and-chips thing.
Dolce Vita 221 Hanover St ☎617/720-0422; Haymarket **T**. Relax in the airy, alfresco dining room in this longstanding North End spot to savor their famous *ravioli rosso*, in a tomato cream sauce. Don't come here if you're in a hurry, though – ser-vice can be slow.
Galleria Umberto 289 Hanover St ☎617/227-5709; Haymarket **T**. North End nirvana. There are fewer than a dozen items on the menu, but the lines are consistently to the door for Umberto's perfect pizza slices and savory *arancini*. Lunch only, and get there early – they always sell out.
Mamma Maria 3 North Square ☎617/523-0077; Haymarket **T**. A favorite special-occasion restaurant; its location, on historic North Square, is as good a reason as any to come. The Northern Italian fare is of consistently impeccable quality. Dinner only.
Mare 135 Richmond St ☎617/723-6273; Haymarket **T**. *Mare* features first-rate seasonal seafood dishes amidst trippy decor: flat-screen TVs mysteriously broadcast images of swimming fish, presumably so you can ponder the life of your food before you eat it.
Neptune Oyster 63 Salem St ☎617/742-3474; Haymarket **T**. Snazzy little raw bar filled with devoted fans who swoon over the fantastic shucked shellfish. Closed Mon and Tues.
Olives 10 City Square ☎617/242-1999; Community College **T**. *Olives* is consistently rated among Boston's best restaurants, and justifiably so. Chef Todd English turns out New Mediterranean food of unforgettable flavor in sizeable portions. Reservations recommended; very expensive. Closed Sun.
Pizzeria Regina 11 1/2 Thacher St ☎617/227-0765; Haymarket **T**. Visit *Regina* for tasty, cheap pizza, served in a neighborhood feed station where the wooden booths haven't budged since the 1940s. Vintage North End. Don't be fooled by chains bearing the *Regina* label in other parts of town – this is the original, vastly superior location.
Sage 69 Prince St ☎617/248-8814; Haymarket **T**. Diminutive Italian restaurant that doesn't scrimp on flavor; the refreshing seasonal menu is strong on dishes like savory lemon and asparagus risotto and vegetable casserole – perfect fodder for an intimate tête-à-tête.
Sorelle Bakery and Café 1 Monument Ave ☎617/242-2125; Community College **T**. Phenomenal muffins and cookies, plus pasta salads and other lunch fare which you can enjoy on a delightful hidden patio.

Beacon Hill

Artu 89 Charles St ☎617/227-9023; Charles **T**. Squeezed into a tiny storefront on Charles Street, *Artu* keeps things fresh, flavorful, and affordable. Authentic Italian country cooking focused on roast meats, risotto, and a dreamy *melanzane parmigiana*.
Beacon Hill Bistro in the *Beacon Street Hotel*, 25 Charles St ☎617/723-1133; Charles **T**. Sleek New American and French bistro with an upscale neighborhood feel. Short ribs with prunes share counter space with cod with capers and tomatoes; breakfast is traditional American. They also have a gorgeous stained-glass and mahogany bar – go for the blood-orange martinis and killer mojitos.
Figs 42 Charles St ☎617/642-3447; Charles **T**. This noisy, popular offshoot of *Olives* (see above) has excellent thin-crust pizzas, topped with such savory items as figs and prosciutto or caramelized onions and arugula.
The King & I 145 Charles St ☎617/727-3320; Charles **T**. Excellent, inventive Thai with bold, but not overbearing, flavors. The "Shrimp in Love" is almost worth trying for its name alone.
Ma Soba 156 Cambridge St ☎617/973-6680; Charles **T**. Dazzling, nearly unbelievable displays of what is possibly Boston's best sushi. It's not overpriced, either.
Paramount 44 Charles St ☎617/720-1152; Charles **T**. The Hill's neighborhood diner serves Belgian waffles and *frittatas* to the brunch regulars by day, and decent American standards like hamburgers and meatloaf by night.

Back Bay

Aujourd'hui in the *Four Seasons*, 200 Boylston St ⓣ617/351-2037 or 1-800/332-3442; Arlington **T**. One of Boston's best, this is a good place to splurge. Dine on roasted Maine lobster – accompanied by crabmeat wontons, pineapple compote, and fenugreek broth – from antique china while enjoying the view out over the Public Garden.

Café Jaffa 48 Gloucester St ⓣ617/536-0230; Hynes **T**. One of Back Bay's best inexpensive dining options, with great Middle Eastern fare served up in an inviting space. They're known for their falafel and locally-famous lamb chops, but you can't really go wrong here.

Chilli Duck 829 Boylston St ⓣ617/236-5208; Hynes **T**. Good, cheap Thai classics (chicken satay, drunken noodles, pad Thai) amidst a bright pink interior.

Grill 23 161 Berkeley St ⓣ617/542-2255; Arlington **T**. This carnivore-fest is as clubby as Boston gets: the steaks are aged in-house, the fish is from exotic locales, and it's all accompanied by a myriad of wines. Be prepared to drop some serious dough.

Gyuhama of Japan 827 Boylston St ⓣ617/437-0188; Hynes **T**. Noisy basement-level "rock 'n' roll" sushi bar, favored by students for late-night Japanese snacks (open till 2am).

Jasper White's Summer Shack 50 Dalton St ⓣ617/867-9955; Hynes **T**. Spacious seafood locale with kitschy maritime decor and lots of seating. The raw bar is tops, and the grilled fish fare is also quite good. Plus they have corn dogs. Good spot for families.

Kashmir 279 Newbury St ⓣ617/536-1695; Hynes **T**. The food and decor are equally inviting at Newbury Street's only Indian restaurant, and one of Boston's best. The lunch buffet is life-changing.

Kaya 581 Boylston St ⓣ617/236-5858; Copley **T**. This is the place to go when the craving for Japanese-Korean food – like hot and authentic *kimchi* stew with tofu – kicks in. Open till 2am.

Legal Sea Foods in the *Park Plaza Hotel*, 26 Park Plaza ⓣ617/426-4444; Arlington **T**; 100 Huntington Ave, level two, Copley Place ⓣ617/266-7775; Copley **T**; 800 Boylston St, Prudential Center ⓣ617/266-6800; Prudential **T**; 5 Cambridge Center ⓣ617/864-3400; Kendall **T**. Truly the *Starbucks* of the sea: it seems you can't turn a corner in Boston without encountering one of these ubiquitous, pricey chains. If you must go, get the fried fish; it's the only thing that's still great at this formerly charming establishment.

L'Espalier 30 Gloucester St ⓣ617/262-3023; Hynes **T**. A ravishing French restaurant in a Back Bay brownstone. The food is first-rate, but the lofty prices suggest that ambience is factored into your bill.

Sonsie 327 Newbury St ⓣ617/351-2500; Hynes **T**. This Newbury Street staple is good for contemporary bistro fare, particularly the swanky sandwiches, pastries, and chocolate bread pudding. In the summertime, aim for their Sunday brunch – the restaurant opens onto the street, jazz filters lazily through the air, and of course the food is fabulous.

Stephanie's on Newbury 190 Newbury St ⓣ617/236-0990; Copley **T**. Though they pride themselves on their yellowfin tuna salad, what sets *Stephanie's* apart is the sidewalk dining in the prime people-watching territory of Newbury Street. Open until midnight.

Steve's Greek & American Restaurant 316 Newbury St ⓣ617/267-1817; Hynes **T**. Excellent Greek food and large portions make this one of Boston's classic cheap eats.

Top of the Hub 800 Boylston St ⓣ617/536-1775; Prudential **T**. Inventive New England fare on the 52nd floor of the Prudential Tower. Nice date spot – although you have to go through an unromantic security check first.

South End

Aquitaine 569 Tremont St ⓣ617/424-8577; Back Bay **T**. This swanky French brasserie is *the* place to be and be seen; settle into a marvelous leather banquette, gape at the astonishing array of wine, and feast on the best *steak frites* and bouillabaisse in town.

The Delux Café & Lounge 100 Chandler St ⓣ617/338-5258; Back Bay **T**. This retro hideaway has all the fixings of a great dive spot: fantastic kitschy decor, constant cartoon viewing, and a Christmas-lit Elvis shrine. The menu is funky American fusion blended with old standbys like grilled-cheese sandwiches and split-pea soup. No credit cards.

Franklin Café 278 Shawmut Ave ⓣ617/426-0862; Back Bay **T**. New American cuisine at very reasonable prices, enjoyed by a hip, unpretentious clientele. There are only eleven tables – be prepared to wait at the bar for at least two martinis.

Hamersley's Bistro 553 Tremont St ⓣ617/423-2700; Back Bay **T**. *Hamersley's* is widely regarded as one of the best restaurants in Boston, and with good cause. Every night star chef (and owner) Gordon Hamersley dons a baseball cap and takes to the open kitchen, where he dishes out unusual – and unforgettable – French-American fare that changes with the seasons.

Mike's City Diner 1714 Washington St ⓣ617/267-9393; Back Bay **T**. Classic diner breakfasts and lunches in this beloved, out-of-the way eatery.

Mistral 223 Columbus Ave ☎617/867-9300; Arlington T. Still one of *the* places to go in Boston, *Mistral* serves pricey modern Provençal food in a bright, airy space above the Turnpike. Despite the raves, the food doesn't live up to the cost. Dinner only.

Pho Republique 1415 Washington St ☎617/262-0005; Back Bay T. Hip Indochine restaurant that attracts a young, stylish clientele who dine on hearty servings of *pho* and sip divine lemongrass martinis under ambience-diffusing seashell chandeliers.

Stella 1525 Washington St ☎617/247-7747; Back Bay T. Fantastic, fancypants Italian fare in a beautiful white interior. Nice outdoor seating in the summer. Open late.

Kenmore Square, The Fenway, and Brookline

Anna's Taqueria 1412 Beacon St, Brookline ☎617/739-7300; Coolidge Corner T. Exceptional tacos, burritos, and quesadillas are the only things on the menu at this bright and extremely cheap Mexican eatery – but they're so good branches had to be opened around the corner at 446 Harvard St (Coolidge Corner T) and in Cambridge at 822 Somerville Ave (Porter T) to accommodate its legions of devotees.

Brown Sugar 129 Jersey St ☎617/266-2928; Kenmore T. Charming neighborhood restaurant near the Museum of Fine Arts, serving some of Boston's best Thai food. Everything here is wonderfully fresh, and some selections, like the basil chicken, are superbly spicy. There are ample vegetarian options, too.

Eastern Standard 528 Commonwealth Ave ☎617/532-9100; Kenmore T. Loosely French bistro serving up fairly fancy, pre-Red Sox game fare. The menu can be a bit hit or miss – go for the spaghetti carbonara and veal schnitzel (or just to watch the game in their atmospheric bar).

Matt Murphy's 14 Harvard St, Brookline ☎617/232-0188; Brookline Village T. Authentic Irish comfort food such as warm potato and leek soup with brown bread and shepherd's pie with a crispy potato crust. The place is tiny, and you may have to wait, but it's well worth it. They also have occasional live music. No credit cards.

Washington Square Tavern 714 Washington St, Brookline ☎617/232-8989; Washington Square T. Cozy, off-the-beaten-path restaurant/bar with an eclectic seasonal menu that turns out inventive meals like pork tenderloin with fig glaze and sweet potatoes.

Southern districts

Bob's Southern Bistro 604 Columbus Ave, Roxbury ☎617/536-6204; Mass Ave T. The best soul food in New England, with good chitlins, black-eyed peas, and collard greens; don't miss the "glori-fried chicken," the house specialty. There's also a wonderful, waist-expanding Sunday brunch buffet, accompanied by live jazz.

Centre Street Café 669A Centre St, Jamaica Plain ☎617/524-9217; Green St T. At weekend brunchtime, the line stretches down the street in front of this lovely, laidback, local institution. Lunch is less of a big deal and is just as good.

Cambridge

Border Café 32 Church St ☎617/864-6100; Harvard T. Cambridge's most popular Tex-Mex place is pretty good, though not nearly enough to justify the massive crowds that form on weekend nights. The margaritas are salty and strong, and the moderately-priced food is so pungent that you'll carry its aroma with you for hours afterward.

Central Kitchen 567 Massachusetts Ave ☎617/491-5599; Central T. Hip Central Square bistro with a delightful chalkboard menu offering European classics (*moules frites*) and contemporary American twists (mushroom ragout with ricotta dumplings) in an intimate, stylish setting.

Charlie's Kitchen 10 Eliot St ☎617/492-9646; Harvard T. Marvelously atmospheric local hangout in the heart of Harvard Square, with red vinyl booths, sassy waitresses with hipster hairdos, and greasy diner food. Try the cheap yet filling Double Cheeseburger Special. There is also an equally cool bar upstairs.

Chez Henri 1 Shepard St ☎617/354-8980; Harvard or Porter T. If you can get a table (no reservations, and the weekend wait tops one hour even late at night), you'll enjoy what may well be Cambridge's finest cuisine. Chef Paul O'Connell's experiment in fusion brings Modern French together with Cuban influences, best sampled in the light salads and excellent Cuban crabcake appetizers. If you're looking to spend less cash, head to the adjacent bar for the Cuban pressed sandwich – amazing.

Darwin's Ltd 148 Mt Auburn St ☎617/354-5233; 1629 Cambridge St ☎617/491-2999; both Harvard T. Two locations, both housing fantastic delis with wonderfully inventive combinations such as roast beef, sprouts, and apple slices, served on freshly baked bread. No credit cards.

East Coast Grill 1271 Cambridge St ☎617/491-6568; Harvard or Central Square T. A festive and funky atmosphere – think shades of *Miami Vice* –

in which to enjoy fresh seafood (there is a raw bar tucked into one corner) and Caribbean side dishes such as grilled avocado, pineapple salsa, and fried plantains. The Sunday serve-yourself Bloody Mary bar is reason enough to visit.

Felipe's Taqueria 83 Mt Auburn St ☎617/354-9944; Harvard **T**. There are only a handful of things on the menu, but the place is always packed with regulars hankering after their super burritos, quesadillas, and good-looking guacamole.

Harvest 44 Brattle St ☎617/868-2255; Harvard **T**. Upscale, white-tableclothed Harvard Square institution with an oft-changing menu of rich New American cuisine; the smashing outdoor courtyard is another fine feature.

Henrietta's Table in the *Charles Hotel*, 1 Bennett St ☎617/761-5005; Harvard **T**. One of the only restaurants in Cambridge that serves classic New England fare. Some might say, however, that a trip to *Henrietta's* is wasted if it's not for their famous brunch, served Sundays from noon to 3pm; it costs $39 per person but allows unlimited access to a cornucopia of farm-fresh treats from around New England.

Mr. Bartley's Burger Cottage 1246 Massachusetts Ave ☎617/354-6559; Harvard **T**. A Cambridge must-visit. The walls here are decorated with references to political humor and pop culture, while the names of the dishes on the menu poke fun at celebrities of the hour. The food itself is artery-clogging joy, in the form of a juicy burger and "frappe" (milkshake). Good veggie burgers, too.

Tamarind Bay 75 Winthrop St ☎617/491-4552; Harvard **T**. This basement eatery (with a bright-yellow interior) serves up what is probably the best Indian food in the city (and, yes, that also includes Boston). The banana dumplings, *lallal mussal dal* (black lentils simmered in spices), and *murg-ki-chaat* (tandoori chicken in a *chaat-masala* dressing) will make you stand up and cheer.

Tandoor House 569 Massachusetts Ave ☎617/661-9001; Central **T**. Consistently at the top of the list of Cambridge's many fine Indian restaurants, *Tandoor* has excellent chicken *saag* and a great mushroom *bhaji*.

Upstairs on the Square 91 Winthrop St ☎617/864-1933; Harvard **T**. Amidst a whimsical decor of animal-striped carpet patterns, glorious green walls, and winged light bulbs, *Upstairs on the Square* serves equally inventive food, falling somewhere between New American and Old Colonial. They also have a carved pink bar where they mix up fanciful cocktails accented with gummi sharks. Reservations essential.

Drinking

Despite – or perhaps because of – the lingering Puritan anti-fun ethic that pervades Boston, people here seem to **drink** more than in most other American cities. The most prevalent place to nurse a pint is the **Irish pub**, of which there are high concentrations in the **West End** and downtown around **Quincy Market**. More upscale are the bars and lounges of **Back Bay**, along Newbury and Boylston streets, which offer attitude as much as anything else. The rest of the city's neighborhood bars, pick-up joints, and yuppie hotspots are differentiated by their crowds: **Beacon Hill** tends to be older and a bit stuffy; **downtown**, mainly around Quincy Market and the Theater District, draws a healthy mix of tourists and locals; while **Kenmore Square** and **Cambridge** are fairly student-oriented. The **café** scene is not quite as diverse, but still offers a decent range of places to hang out. The fanciest spots are again those that line Back Bay's **Newbury Street**, where you pay as much for the fancy environs as for the quality of the coffee. Value is much better in the **North End**, but the most lively cafés are across the river in **Cambridge**, and cater, unsurprisingly, to the large student population.

Bars

Bars stop serving at 2am (at the latest), and most strictly enforce the drinking-age minimum of 21; be prepared to show either a driver's license or passport.

The one potential for after-hours drinking is **Chinatown**, where some restaurants will bring you a beer if you ask for the "cold tea."

Downtown

Bell in Hand Tavern 45 Union St ⓣ617/227-2098; State or Government Center T. The oldest continuously operating tavern in Boston draws a fairly exuberant mix of tourists and young professionals.

The Black Rose (Roisin Dubh) 160 State St ⓣ617/742-2286; State T. Down-home Irish pub specializing in imported beers from the Emerald Isle.

The Good Life 28 Kingston St ⓣ617/451-2622; Downtown Crossing T. This dive bar (and restaurant) generates quite a buzz, due as much to its potent martinis as its 1970s decor, which features wicked groovy orange vinyl walls.

Green Dragon Tavern 11 Marshall St ⓣ617/367-0055; Government Center T. Another tavern that dates to the Colonial era. There's a standard selection of tap beers, a raw bar, and a full menu rife with twee historical humor ("One if by land, two if by seafood"). Less of a meat market than some of the other bars in the area.

The Kinsale 2 Center Plaza ⓣ617/742-5577; Government Center T. Shipped brick by brick from Ireland to its current location in the shadow of Government Plaza, this outrageously popular Irish pub is as authentic as it gets; the menu even lists beer-battered fish and hot pastrami on a "bulkie" (Boston slang for a sandwich bun).

The Purple Shamrock 1 Union St ⓣ617/327-2060; State or Government Center T. A lively watering hole that draws a broad cross-section of folks, the *Shamrock* has one of Boston's better straight singles scenes, including a fun dance floor. It gets very crowded on weekends.

The Rack 24 Clinton St ⓣ617/725-1051; Government Center T. Well-dressed twenty- and thirtysomethings convene at this pool hall to dine, drink a bewildering variety of cocktails, and, of course, shoot a rack or two.

Charlestown

Tavern on the Water 1 Pier 6, 8th St ⓣ617/242-8040; Community College T. Located right on the water (the USS *Constitution* is anchored nearby), the *Tavern* sports what is possibly Boston's best skyline view. The food is forgettable; stick with whatever's on tap.

Warren Tavern 2 Pleasant St ⓣ617/241-8142; Community College T. An atmospheric place to enjoy a drink, and the oldest standing structure in Charlestown. The *Warren* also has a generous menu of good tavern food.

Beacon Hill and the West End

21st Amendment 148 Bowdoin St ⓣ617/227-7100; Bowdoin T. This dimly lit, down-home watering hole, which gets its name from the amendment that repealed Prohibition, is a favorite haunt of legislators from the adjacent State House and students from nearby Suffolk University.

The Bull & Finch Pub 84 Beacon St ⓣ227-9605; Arlington T. If you don't already know, and if the conspicuous banners outside don't tip you off, this is the bar that served as the inspiration for the TV show *Cheers*. If you've gotta go, be warned – it's packed with camera-toting tourists, the inside bears little resemblance to the NBC set, and the food, though cutely named (eNORMous burgers), is pricey and mediocre. Plus, it's almost certain that nobody will know your name.

Fours 166 Canal St ⓣ617/720-4455; North Station T. The classiest of the West End's sports bars, with an army of TVs to broadcast games from around the globe, as well as paraphernalia from the Red Sox, the Bruins, and other local teams.

Irish Embassy 234 Friend St ⓣ617/742-6618; North Station T. Up in the West End, this is one of the city's most authentic Irish (rather than Irish-American) pubs, with the crowd to match. Live Irish entertainment most nights, plus broadcasts of Irish soccer matches.

The Sevens 77 Charles St ⓣ617/523-9074; Charles T. While the tourists pack into the *Bull & Finch*, you can drop by this cozy wood-paneled joint to watch the game or shoot darts in an authentic Boston neighborhood bar.

Back Bay and the South End

Bukowski Tavern 50 Dalton St ⓣ617/437-9999; Hynes T. Arguably Boston's best hipster bar, this parking garage watering hole has views over the MassPike and such a vast beer selection that a homemade "wheel of indecision" is spun by waitstaff when patrons can't decide. There's a smaller, equally cool location at 1281 Cambridge St in Inman Square (ⓣ617/497-7077; #69 bus).

Oak Bar in the *Fairmont Copley Plaza*, 138 St James Ave ⓣ617/267-5300; Copley T. Rich wood paneling, high ceilings, and excellent martinis make this one of the more genteel Back Bay spots to drink.

Whiskey Park in the *Park Plaza*, 64 Arlington St ⓣ617/542-1482; Arlington T. Owned by Randy

Gerber (aka Mr.Cindy Crawford), this lounge's chic chocolate-brown leather chair design was conceived by Michael Czysz, the guy behind Lenny Kravitz's swinging Miami pad. The prices match the celebrity name-dropping, but there's hardly a better place in town to grab a cocktail.

Whiskey's 885 Boylston St ☎617/262-5551; Hynes T. A real-life beer commercial: young guys wearing baseball caps, sports on TV, and a pervasive smell of booze. Still, it's not a bad place to watch a Sox game.

Kenmore Square, The Fenway, and Brookline

Audubon Circle Bar 838 Beacon St ☎617/421-1910; Kenmore T. Sleek bar where a well-dressed crowd gathers for cocktails and fancy, tasty bar food before and after games at nearby Fenway Park.

Cask 'n Flagon 62 Brookline Ave ☎617/536-4840; Kenmore T. An iconic neighborhood bar located right by Fenway Park, the *Cask 'n Flagon* is a popular place for the Red Sox faithful to warm up before games and celebrate after.

Foundation Lounge 500 Commonwealth Ave ☎617/859-9900; Kenmore T. Spacious, upscale marble bar amidst a hip (but not hipper-than-thou) clientele. A more discreet Red Sox-viewing ambience.

Southern districts

Brendan Behan 378 Centre St, Jamaica Plain ☎617/522-5386; Green St T. The godfather of Boston's Irish pubs, this dimly lit institution has the usual friendly staff all week long and live music available on most weekends.

James's Gate 5–11 McBride St, Jamaica Plain ☎617/983-2000; Forest Hills T. Beat Boston's harsh winter by sipping Guinness by the blazing fireplace in this cozy pub, or by trying the hearty fare in the excellent restaurant out back.

Cambridge

B-Side Lounge 92 Hampshire St ☎617/354-0766; Kendall T. It's a hipster bar, but not in an alienating way – preppy patrons will not feel scorned. Lots of live tunes, a great drinks menu, and surprisingly tasty and creative bar food.

Enormous Room 577 Massachusetts Ave ☎617/491-5550; Central T. Walking into this comfy, tiny lounge tucked above *Central Kitchen* (see review, p.149) is tantamount to entering a swanky slumber party. The clientele lounges, sans shoes (these are discreetly placed in cubbies), along myriad plush couches. DJs nightly.

Grendel's Den 89 Winthrop St ☎617/491-1160; Harvard T. A favorite spot of locals and grad students for drinking ale; these dark, conspiratorial environs have a fantastic happy-hour special, with big plates of appetizers for just $1.50 each.

Middlesex 315 Massachusetts Ave ☎617/868-6739; Central T. A slightly hipper-than-thou vibe, but with good reason – the gorgeous space (high ceilings, exposed brick, and pretty wood paneling) makes you want to dress to impress. Lush lounge chairs on wheels and minimalist tables you can move around to design your own drinking environs.

Miracle of Science 321 Massachusetts Ave ☎617/868-ATOM; Central T or #1 bus. Surprisingly hip despite its status as an MIT hangout. There's noir decor and a laidback, unpretentious crowd, though the place can get quite crowded on weekend nights. The bar stools will conjure up memories of high school chemistry class.

Noir in the *Charles Hotel*, 1 Bennett St ☎617/661-8010; Harvard T. With its sultry red lighting and tall black leather booths, *Noir* seems the perfect setting to carry on a discreet affair. Most patrons just come for the decadent martinis, however.

Plough & Stars 912 Massachusetts Ave ☎617/441-3455; Central or Harvard T. Off-the-beaten-path neighborhood hideaway that's very much worth the trek, whether for its animated cribbage games, live UK and European soccer broadcasts, quality pub grub, or nightly live music.

River Gods 125 Cambridge St ☎617/576-1881; Central T. Though a bit of an underground spot, it's worth the trip. An Irish bar with a twist, they serve good cocktails alongside Guinness on tap, fantastic food, and DJs spinning good tunes; patrons lounge in throne-like chairs and ogle the suits of armor.

Cafés

Although the *Starbucks* invasion has done some real damage to the eclectic **café** scene in Boston and Cambridge, there are still any number of independent places where you can relax with a book and a hot drink. At many cafés, you can just as easily get an excellent full meal as you can a cup of coffee. Below are the best choices for casual hanging out; there are also plenty of cafés more suited for meals listed under "Eating" (see p.145).

Downtown

Boston Coffee Exchange 101 Arch St, entrance on 32 Summer St ⓣ617/737-3199; Downtown Crossing **T**. Cramped coffeeshop with a good selection of pastries and sweets to nosh while imbibing some of the best java in town.

North End

Caffe Graffiti 307 Hanover St ⓣ617/367-3016; Haymarket **T**. A continuous stream of Rai Uno soccer matches is broadcast from the ceiling-mounted TVs, making for an agreeable din amongst a very local crowd. Beer, wine, espresso, and sambuca.

Caffe Paradiso 255 Hanover St ⓣ617/742-1768; Haymarket **T**. Not much on atmosphere, but the pastries are, hands-down, the best in the North End, and their superb gelato is the only homemade stuff around.

Caffe Vittoria 296 Hanover St ⓣ227-7606; Haymarket **T**. A Boston institution, the *Vittoria*'s atmospheric original section, with its dark wood paneling, pressed-tin ceilings, murals of the Old Country, and Sinatra-blaring Wurlitzer, is vintage North End. It's only open at night, though a street-level addition next door is open by day for excellent cappuccinos.

Beacon Hill

Panificio 144 Charles St ⓣ617/227-4340; Charles **T**. Fine cups o' joe, fresh tasty pastries (*biscotti* is the standout), and some of the best home-baked bread in the city.

Back Bay

29 Newbury 29 Newbury St ⓣ617/536-0290; Arlington **T**. A small upscale café/bar and eatery with good, if pricey, salads and the like. Don't miss the 29 Smooch, their signature dessert made with brownies and *dolce de leche* ice cream. Open until 1.30am.

Armani Café 214 Newbury St ⓣ617/437-0909; Copley **T**. People-watching is the *mot du jour* at this fashionista hotspot, though the good contemporary Italian fare shouldn't be overlooked.

The Other Side Cosmic Café 407 Newbury St ⓣ617/536-9477; Hynes **T**. This ultracasual hipster hangout on "the other side" of Newbury Street offers gourmet sandwiches, tasty salads, and fresh juices. They also have pitchers of good beer. Open late.

Trident Booksellers & Café 338 Newbury St ⓣ617/267-8688; Hynes **T**. Great little bookstore café (see bookstore review, p.160), featuring a "perpetual breakfast" and tasty, organic-ish lunch and dinners.

The South End

Flour Bakery + Café 1595 Washington St ⓣ617/267-4300; Back Bay **T**. Quite possibly the best café in town, this stylish South End spot has a drool-worthy array of *brioche au chocolat*, old-fashioned sour cream coffee cake, gooey caramel nut tarts, rich cakes, savory sandwiches, homemade breads, and thirst-quenching drinks. Choosing just one can be torture.

Garden of Eden Café 571 Tremont St ⓣ617/247-8377; Back Bay **T**. The doyenne of the South End café scene has a prime streetside terrace, perfect espressos, and delectable morsels like orange-and-pistachio-encrusted paté de canard and chocolate and raspberry mousse cakes.

Kenmore Square and The Fenway

Espresso Royale Caffe 736 Commonwealth Ave ⓣ617/277-8737; BU Central **T**. Although it's part of a burgeoning chain, this funky little coffeeshop serves traditional cups of java alongside original blends like a zesty orange cappuccino; the cheerful decor is enhanced by abstract wall paintings and cozy seating.

Cambridge

1369 Coffeehouse 757 Massachusetts Ave ⓣ617/576-4600; Central **T**. The *1369* mixes earnest thirtysomething leftists with youthful hipsters in a relaxed environment; your best bets are the standard array of caffeinated beverages and particularly exquisite desserts. Its original location is at 1369 Cambridge St (ⓣ617/576-1369; #69 bus).

Algiers 40 Brattle St ⓣ617/492-1557; Harvard **T**. North African café popular with the artsy set; there are few more atmospheric spots in which to sip first-rate coffee.

L.A. Burdick's 52D Brattle St ⓣ617/491-4340; Harvard **T**. Simply breathing in the aromas at this fabulous *chocolaterie* is an exercise in indulgence: iced chocolate, chocolate mousse cake, and little chocolate mice and penguins, all waiting to be consumed.

Tealuxe 0 Brattle St ⓣ617/441-0077; Harvard **T**. Now a chain, this is the original, and still a great spot. The place is smaller than a teacup, but they manage to stock over a hundred varieties of tea including crème de la Earl Grey, reported to taste like birthday cake.

Toscanini's 1310 Massachusetts Ave ⓣ617/354-9350; Harvard **T**. Inventive, ever-changing ice-cream list that includes original flavors like chocolate sluggo, which mixes up light & dark chocolate ice cream, ganache, chocolate chips, almonds, and Hydrox cookies.

Nightlife

In recent years the city's **nightlife** has received something of a wake-up call, with stylish new **clubs** springing up in places such as Downtown Crossing that were once ghost towns at night. Though Boston is by no means a 24-hour city, these spots have given a bit of fresh air to a scene that lived in the shadow of the city's so-called high culture. Most of the clubs, however, tend to be geared toward – or at least chiefly attract – either moneyed students, suburbanites, or the secretarial set.

The **live music** scene plays perhaps a bigger part in the city's nightlife. Many of the bars and clubs, especially around Kenmore Square and Harvard Square, are just as likely, if not more, to have a scruffy garage band playing for only a nominal cover as they are to have a slick DJ spinning house tunes. And Boston has spawned its share of enormous **rock** acts, from the ever-enduring Aerosmith to a smattering of indie rock favorites such as the Pixies and Sebadoh. There is a bit less in the way of **jazz** and **blues**, but you can usually find something cheap and to your liking most days of the week. For **club and music listings**, check Thursday's *Boston Globe* "Calendar," the *Boston Phoenix*, or *Boston's Weekly Dig*; the two best websites are Ⓦwww.boston.com and Ⓦwww.stuffatnight.com.

Nightclubs

Boston's **nightclubs** are mostly clustered in downtown's Theater District and around Kenmore Square, with a few prominent ones in Back Bay and the South End. Many of the Back Bay and South End venues are **gay clubs**, often the most happening in town. For a listing of these, see "Gay and lesbian Boston," p.159. Otherwise, a number of the clubs below have special gay nights. **Cover charges** are generally in the $5–10 range, though sometimes there's no cover at all.

An Tua Nua 835 Beacon St, Kenmore Square Ⓣ617/262-2121; Kenmore **T**. Despite its Gaelic name ("the new beginning"), this popular neighborhood hangout is just as much dance bar as it is Irish pub. Thursday's hip-hop nights get especially crowded with BU and Northeastern undergrads. Wednesdays are salsa nights.

Avalon 15 Lansdowne St, Kenmore Square Ⓣ617/262-2424, Ⓦwww.avalonboston.com; Kenmore **T**. The biggest dance club in Boston, and any weekend night the place is positively jamming, usually to music spun by top international DJs. Sunday is gay night.

The Big Easy 1 Boylston Place, Back Bay Ⓣ617/351-7000, Ⓦwww.bigeasyboston.com; Boylston **T**. Known locally as the "Big Sleazy," this bumping, New Orleans-themed lust magnet has a hopping bar and dance floor; for the best people-watching go on a weeknight.

Gypsy Bar 116 Boylston St, downtown Ⓣ617/417-1333; Boylston **T**. Very posh lounge popular with the European set; you can watch the jellyfish pulsing peacefully behind the bar while ordering an *Indulgence* cocktail.

Jillian's 145 Ipswich St, Kenmore Square Ⓣ617/437-0300; Kenmore **T**. Massive entertainment club complex housing an arcade, a raucous, spacious dance club, and a Lucky Strike bowling alley.

Milky Way 405 Centre Street, Jamaica Plain Ⓣ617/524-3740; Green Street **T**. "Lanes and lounge" – that's right, bowling alley-cum-nightclub, in the heart of Boston's hippest neighborhood.

Ned Devine's Fanueil Hall Marketplace, Quincy Market building, downtown Ⓣ617/248-9900; Government Center **T**. Irish pub and rowdy nightclub, populated by fun-loving tourists and dancing oglers.

The Roxy 279 Tremont St, downtown Ⓣ617/338-7699, Ⓦwww.roxyboston.com; Boylston **T**. Cavernous singles' scene nightclub in an old-fashioned dance hall.

Saint 90 Exeter St, Back Bay Ⓣ617/236-1134; Copley **T**. Upscale lounge and club with lush decor and chi-chi drinks – the tables tend to be occupied by people more famous or well-off than you, however.

Umbria Nightclub 295 Franklin St, downtown Ⓣ617/338-1000,Ⓦwww.umbriaristorante.com; State **T**. Downstairs is a swanky *trattoria*; upstairs is a three-story disco, one of the hottest in town.

Live music

The strength of Boston's **live music** is its diversity, and the city serves as both a stop on the world tours of superstar performers and a hotbed of small, experimental acts. Two of the biggest venues are out of town: the Tweeter Center, south of the city in Mansfield (ⓣ508/339-2333), and the DCU Center, an hour or so west in Worcester (ⓣ508/755-6800). There are still, however, plenty of places in town to see either name bands or more obscure acts.

Rock and pop

Bill's Bar 5½ Lansdowne St, Kenmore Square ⓣ617/421-9678; Kenmore **T**. Relaxed and comfortable spot, with lots of beer, lots of TV, and occasional live music – in which case expect a cover charge of $5.

FleetBoston Pavilion Fan Pier, 290 Northern Ave, downtown ⓣ617/728-1600, ⓦwww.fleetboston-pavilion.com; South Station **T**. Formerly the Harborlights Pavilion; during the summer, concerts by well-known performers are held here under a huge white tent at Boston Harbor's edge.

Lizard Lounge 1667 Massachusetts Ave, Cambridge ⓣ617/547-0759; Harvard or Porter **T**. This, the downstairs portion of the restaurant *Cambridge Common*, has rock and jazz acts pretty much nightly, for a fairly nominal cover charge.

Middle East 472 Massachusetts Ave, Cambridge ⓣ617/354-8238, ⓦwww.mideastclub.com; Central **T**. Local and regional progressive rock acts regularly stop in at this Cambridge institution. Downstairs hosts bigger bands; smaller ones ply their stuff in a tiny upstairs space. They also have *ZuZu*, a tasty little lounge.

Orpheum Theater 1 Hamilton Place, downtown ⓣ617/931-2000; Park or Downtown Crossing **T**. Once an old-school movie house, it's now a vintage venue for big-name bands. The small space means you're closer to the action, but it sells out quickly and the cramped seating discourages dancing.

Paradise Rock Club 967–969 Commonwealth Ave, Brookline ⓣ617/562-8800; Pleasant Street **T**. One of Boston's classic rocking venues. Lots of greats have played here – Blondie, Elvis Costello, and Tom Waits, to name a few. It's still as happening as it was 25 years ago, only now it also has a restaurant-cum-rock lounge next door.

TDBanknorth Garden 50 Causeway St, West End ⓣ617/624-1750, tickets ⓣ617/931-2000, ⓦwww.tdbanknorthgarden.com; North Station **T**. This arena, in the West End, attracts a decent number of the big-name acts – when the Celtics or Bruins aren't playing, that is.

T.T. the Bear's 10 Brookline St, Cambridge ⓣ617/492-2327, ⓦwww.ttthebears.com; Central **T**. A downmarket version of *Middle East*: lesser-known bands, but in a space with a grittiness and intimacy its neighbor lacks. Mostly punk, rock, and electronica.

Jazz, blues, and folk

Cantab Lounge 738 Massachusetts Ave, Cambridge ⓣ617/354-2685; Central **T**. Although from the outside it looks like the kind of sleazy place your mother wouldn't want you to set foot in, it's actually one of the few truly bohemian spots in town, with hopping live jazz and blues.

Club Passim 47 Palmer St, Cambridge ⓣ617/492-7679, ⓦwww.clubpassim.org; Harvard **T**. Folkie hangout where Joan Baez and Suzanne Vega got their starts. There's also world music and spoken word performances.

Regattabar in the *Charles Hotel*, 1 Bennett St, Cambridge ⓣ617/661-5000, ⓦwww.regattabar-jazz.com; Harvard **T**. The *Regattabar* draws top national jazz acts, although, as its location in the swish *Charles Hotel* might suggest, the atmosphere – and clientele – is decidedly sedate. Dress nicely and prepare to pay at least $10 cover.

Wally's Cafe 427 Massachusetts Ave, Roxbury ⓣ617/828-1754, ⓦwww.wallyscafe.com; Massachusetts Avenue **T**. Founded in 1947, this is one of the oldest jazz clubs around. Refreshingly unhewn, they host lively jazz and blues shows that draw a vibrant crowd. No cover.

Western Front 343 Western Ave, Cambridge ⓣ617/492-7772; Central **T**. The *Front* puts on rollicking jazz, blues, hip-hop, and reggae shows for a dance-crazy audience. Drinks are cheap, and the Jamaican food served on weekends is delectably authentic.

Performing arts and film

Boston's **cultural scene** is famously vibrant, and many of the city's artistic institutions are second to none. Foremost among them is the **Boston Symphony Orchestra**, which gave its first concert on October 22, 1881; in fact, Boston is arguably at its best in the **classical music** department, and there are many smaller but internationally known chamber and choral music groups, from the Boston Symphony Chamber Players to the Handel & Haydn Society, to shore up that reputation. The **Boston Ballet** is also considered world-class, though it's probably best known in Boston itself for its annual holiday production of *The Nutcracker*.

The **theater** here is quite active too, even if it is, in a way, a shadow of its 1920s heyday. Boston remains a try-out city for Broadway productions in New York City, and smaller companies have increasingly high visibility. It's a real treat to see a play or musical at one of the opulent old theaters such as the **Wang Center** or the **Cutler Majestic**. For current productions, check the listings in the *Boston Globe*'s Thursday "Calendar" section or the *Boston Phoenix*.

The **film** scene is dominated by the Sony/Loews conglomerate, which runs several multiplexes featuring major first-run Hollywood movies. For foreign, independent, classic, or cult cinema, you'll have to look to other municipalities – Cambridge is best, though Brookline has some arthouse movie theaters as well.

Classical music

Boston prides itself on being a sophisticated city of high culture, and nowhere does that show up more than in its proliferation of **orchestras** and **choral groups** – and the venues to house them. This is helped in no small part by the presence of three of the foremost music academies in the nation: the Peabody and New England conservatories, and the Berklee College of Music.

Chamber music ensembles

Alea III ⓣ617/353-3340 and **Boston Musica Viva** ⓣ617/354-6910, ⓦwww.bmv.org. Two regulars at BU's Tsai Performance Center (see review opposite).

Boston Baroque ⓣ617/484-9200, ⓦwww.bostonbaroque.org. The country's first permanent baroque orchestra is now a resident ensemble at Jordan Hall and the Sanders Theater at Harvard.

Boston Camerata ⓣ617/262-2092, ⓦwww.bostoncamerata.com. Regular performances of choral and chamber concerts, from medieval to early American, at various locations in and around Boston.

Boston Chamber Music Society ⓣ617/349-0086, ⓦwww.bostonchambermusic.org. This society has soloists of international renown who perform in Jordan Hall (Fridays) and the Sanders Theater (Sundays).

Boston Symphony Chamber Players ⓣ1-888/266-1200, ⓦwww.bso.org. The only permanent chamber group sponsored by a major symphony orchestra and made up of its members; they perform at Jordan Hall as well as other venues around Boston.

The Cantata Singers & Ensemble ⓣ617/868-5885, ⓦwww.cantatasingers.org. Boston's premier choral group, which also performs at Jordan Hall.

Handel & Haydn Society ⓣ617/266-3605, ⓦwww.handelandhaydn.org. Performing chamber and choral music since 1815, these distinguished artists can be heard at Symphony Hall, Jordan Hall, and at the Cutler Majestic.

Pro Arte Chamber Orchestra ⓣ617/661-7067, ⓦwww.proarte.org. Cooperatively run chamber orchestra in which musicians have full control. They have frequent performances at Harvard's Sanders Theater.

Dance

The city's longest-running **dance** company is the **Boston Ballet** (ⓣ617/695-6950 or 1-800/447-7400, ⓦwww.bostonballet.org), with an unparalleled reputation in America and beyond; their biggest blockbuster, the yearly performance of *The Nutcracker*, boasts annual attendance of more than 140,000.

Venues

Berklee Performance Center 136 Massachusetts Ave ⓣ617/747-2261 for scheduling information or 931-2000 for tickets, ⓦwww.berkleebpc.com; Symphony T. Berklee College of Music's main performance center, known for its quality contemporary repertoire.

Isabella Stewart Gardner Museum 280 The Fenway ⓣ617/278-5156, ⓦwww.gardnermuseum.org; Museum T. Chamber and classical concerts, including many debuts, are held regularly at 1.30pm on Sundays (Sept–May) in the museum's decadent Tapestry Room. The $20 ticket price includes museum admission.

Jordan Hall 30 Gainsborough St ⓣ617/585-1260, ⓦwww.newenglandconservatory.edu; Symphony T. The impressive concert hall of the New England Conservatory, just one block west from Symphony Hall, is the venue for many chamber music performances as well as those by the Boston Philharmonic (ⓣ617/236-0999).

Museum of Fine Arts 465 Huntington Ave ⓣ617/369-3300 or 267-9300 ⓦwww.mfa.org; Museum T. During the summer, the MFA's jazz, folk, and world music "Concerts in the Courtyard" take place each Wednesday at 7.30pm; a variety of indoor performances are also scheduled for the rest of the year.

Symphony Hall 301 Massachusetts Ave ⓣ617/266-1492 for concert information or 1-888/266-1200 for tickets, ⓦwww.bso.org; Symphony T. This is the regal, acoustically perfect venue for the Boston Symphony Orchestra; the famous Boston Pops concerts happen in May and June; in July and August, the BSO retreats to Tanglewood, in the Berkshires (see p.272).

Tsai Performance Center 685 Commonwealth Ave ⓣ617/353-TSAI for event information or 353-8725 for box office, ⓦwww.bu.edu/tsai; Boston University T. Improbably tucked into Boston University's School of Management, this mid-sized hall is a frequent venue for chamber music performances, prominent lecturers, and plays; events are often affiliated with BU and thus can be very inexpensive.

Theater

It's quite possible to pay dearly for a night at the **theater**. Tickets to the bigger shows range from $25 to $100 depending on the seat, and there is, of course, the potential of a pre- or post-theater meal (see p.146 for restaurants in the Theater District). Your best option is to pay a visit to **BosTix**, a half-price, day-of-show ticket booth with two outlets: in Copley Square at the corner of Dartmouth and Boylston streets, and in Faneuil Hall Marketplace, by Abercrombie & Fitch (both Mon–Sat 10am–6pm, Sun 11am–4pm; ⓣ617/482-2849, ⓦwww.artsboston.org); tickets go on sale at 11am, and only cash is accepted. Full-price tickets can be had through **Ticketmaster** (ⓣ617/931-2000, ⓦwww.ticketmaster.com) or by contacting the individual theater directly. If you have a valid school ID or ISIC card, a number of theaters offer vastly cheaper **student rush** tickets on sale the day of the performance; call the venue in question for more information. The **smaller venues** tend to showcase more offbeat and affordable productions, and shows can cost under $10 – though you shouldn't bank on that.

Major venues

American Repertory Theatre at the Loeb Drama Center, 64 Brattle St ⓣ617/547-8300, ⓦwww.amrep.org; Harvard T. Excellent, eccentric, fairly avant-garde theater near Harvard Square known for staging plays by the likes of Shaw, Wilde, Ionesco, and Stoppard. They also have a flexible performance space, Zero Arrow, at the corner of Mass Ave and Arrow St in Harvard Square.

Boston University Theatre 264 Huntington Ave ⓣ617/266-0800, ⓦwww.huntingtontheatre.org; Symphony T. The largest non-touring playhouse in Boston, known for their phenomenal sets. Productions here range from the classic to the contemporary and can be hit or miss.

Charles Playhouse 74 Warrenton St ⓣ617/426-6912, ⓦwww.broadwayinboston.com; Boylston **T**. The Charles is more or less the permanent home of *Shear Madness* (ⓦwww.shearmadness.com; $38), a participatory, comic murder mystery, and *Blue Man Group* (ⓦwww.bluemangroup.org; $65), an eye-opening, edgy multimedia show performed by three bald and blue-painted men. They also host a select number of other big-name performances.

Colonial Theatre 106 Boylston St ⓣ617/426-9366, ⓦwww.broadwayinboston.com; Boylston **T**. Built in 1900 and since refurbished, this is the grande dame of Boston theaters, known primarily for its Broadway-scale productions.

Cutler Majestic Theatre 219 Tremont St ⓣ1-800/233-3123, ⓦwww.maj.org; Boylston **T**. This lavish venue, with soaring Rococo ceiling and Neoclassical friezes, has recently completed extensive renovations; it hosts productions of the Emerson Stage company and the Boston Lyric Opera.

The Opera House 539 Washington St ⓣ617/259-3400, ⓦwww.broadwayinboston.com; Downtown Crossing **T**. Built in 1928, this opulent vaudeville theater recently reopened after a multi-million dollar restoration. It hosts large-scale traveling company productions (such as *Wicked*), as well as the Boston Ballet's Christmastime production of *The Nutcracker*.

Shubert Theatre 265 Tremont St ⓣ617/482-9393 or 1-800/447-7400, ⓦwww.wangcenter.org; Boylston **T**. Stars from Sir Laurence Olivier to Kathleen Turner have played the city's "Little Princess" at some point in their careers. Recent renovations have restored the 1680-seat theater to its prettier early 1900s appearance, with white walls and gold leaf accents replacing the previous gaudy brown tones.

Wang Center for the Performing Arts 270 Tremont St ⓣ617/482-9393 or 1-800/447-7400, ⓦwww.wangcenter.org; Boylston **T**. The biggest performance center in Boston opened in 1925 as the Metropolitan Theater, a movie house of palatial proportions – its original Italian marble, gold leaf ornamentation, crystal chandeliers, and 3800 seats all remain. The Boston Ballet (see p.157) has residency here (although the legendary Christmas *Nutcracker* has moved to The Opera House); when their season ends, Broadway musicals often take center stage.

Wilbur Theatre 246 Tremont St ⓣ617/423-4008, ⓦwww.broadwayinboston.com; Boylston **T**. *A Streetcar Named Desire*, starring Marlon Brando and Jessica Tandy, debuted in this small Colonial Revival theater before going to Broadway, and the Wilbur has been trying to live up to that production ever since.

Small venues

Boston Center for the Arts 539 Tremont St ⓣ617/426-2787, ⓦwww.bcaonline.org; Back Bay **T**. Several theater troupes, many experimental, stage productions at the BCA, which incorporates a series of small venues on a single South End property. These include the Cyclorama and the Stanford Calderwood Pavilion (see p.126).

Hasty Pudding Theatre 12 Holyoke St ⓣ617/495-5205, ⓦwww.hastypudding.org; Harvard **T**. Harvard University's Hasty Pudding Theatricals troupe, one of the country's oldest, mounts one show per year (usually a musical comedy; Feb & March) at this theater, then hits the road, after which the Cambridge Theatre Company moves in.

Institute of Contemporary Art 955 Boylston St ⓣ617/927-6620, ⓦwww.icaboston.org; Hynes **T**. Boston's leading venue for all things cutting-edge.

Lyric Stage 140 Clarendon St ⓣ617/437-7172, ⓦwww.lyricstage.com; Copley **T**. Both premieres and modern adaptations of classic and lesser-known American plays take place at this intimate theater within the renovated YWCA building.

Film

In Boston, as in any other large American metropolis, it's easy enough to catch general release **films** – the usual listings sources carry all the details you'll need. If you're looking for out-of-the-ordinary fare, however, you'll have to venture out a bit from the center. Whatever you're going to see, admission will cost you between $7 and $9, though matinees before 6pm can be cheaper. You can call ⓣ617/333-FILM for automated listings.

Brattle Theater 40 Brattle St ⓣ617/876-6837, ⓦwww.brattlefilm.org; Harvard **T**. A historic basement indie cinema that pleasantly looks its age. They have thematic film series plus occasional author appearances and readings.

Coolidge Corner Moviehouse 290 Harvard St, Brookline ⓣ617/734-2500, ⓦwww.coolidge.org; Coolidge Corner **T**. Film buffs flock to this classic theater for foreign and independent movies. The interior has balconies and is adorned with Art Deco murals.

Harvard Film Archive Carpenter Center, 24 Quincy St ⓣ617/495-4700, ⓦwww.harvardfilmarchive.org; Harvard T. A mixed bag of artsy, foreign, and experimental films.

Kendall Square Cinema 1 Kendall Square, Cambridge ⓣ617/499-1996, ⓦwww.landmarktheatres.com/market/boston; Kendall T. All the neon decoration, cramped seating, and small screens of your average multiplex, but this one has the area's widest selection of first-rate foreign and independent films. It's actually located on Binney St near Cardinal Medieros Ave.

Museum of Fine Arts Theater 465 Huntington Ave ⓣ617/267-9300, ⓦwww.mfa.org/film; Museum T. Offbeat art films and documentaries, mostly by locals, and often accompanied by lectures from the filmmaker, in addition to hosting several showcases like the Jewish Film and the French Film festivals.

Gay and lesbian Boston

Boston is a fairly gay-friendly city and has a decent number of establishments that cater to a gay crowd. The center of the **gay scene** is the South End, a largely residential neighborhood whose businesses, mostly restaurants and cafés, are concentrated on a short stretch of Tremont Street above Union Park. Adjacent to the South End, on the other side of Arlington Street, is tiny **Bay Village**, which has several gay bars and clubs. The **lesbian scene** is pretty well mixed in with the gay scene, and there are very few exclusively lesbian bars or clubs.

Boston's two free **gay newspapers** are *in newsweekly* (ⓦwww.innewsweekly.com) and *Bay Windows* (ⓦwww.baywindows.com). The latter is one of two good sources of **club information**, the other being the gay-friendly alternative paper *The Boston Phoenix*. All can be found in various venues and bookstores, notably Calamus Bookstore, 92B State St (ⓣ617/338-1931), and New Words, 186 Hampshire St, Cambridge (ⓣ617/876-5130). Both vestibules have gay and lesbian community bulletin boards, with postings for apartment rentals, club happenings, and so forth.

Bars and clubs

Boston has a great variety of gay **bars** and **clubs**, ranging from the sophisticated (*Dedo*) to the low-key (*Fritz*) – and of course a number of bumping dance clubs (*Buzz*, *Pink at ID*). For night owls who haven't gotten their fill of dancing after the clubs close, ask around for an invite to Boston's on the down-low after-hours private party, "Rise," at 306 Stuart St (ⓣ617/423-7473); this members-only stomping ground for gays and straights only gets going at 2am.

Buzz 67 Stuart St ⓣ617/267-8969, ⓦwww.buzzboston.com; New England Medical T. Resident DJs Michael Sheehan and MaryAlice lay down dance and house tracks at this two-floor dance club where the drinks are poured by pumped and shirtless bartenders. Cover $10–15.

Club Café 209 Columbus Ave ⓣ617/536-0966, ⓦwww.clubcafe.com; Back Bay T. This combination restaurant/video bar popular among South End yuppies has a back lounge, *Moonshine*, showing the latest videos. They make a wide selection of martinis with fey names like Pouty Princess and Dirty Birdie.

Club Felt 533 Washington St ⓣ617/350-5555, ⓦwww.feltclubboston.com; Downtown Crossing T. A fun hip-hop/Top 40 lesbian dance club converges in the penthouse here on Thurs nights. Cover $5.

Dedo Restaurant and Lounge 69 Church St ⓣ617/338-9999; Arlington T. Fine dining downstairs, sophisticated, inviting gay bar and lounge upstairs. There are piano sing-alongs on Tues, Wed & Sat.

Eagle 520 Tremont St ⓣ617/542-4494; Back Bay T. Generally tends to be the last stop of the night, with a cruise-y, dive-y flavor and long lines at the boys' bathroom. Prepare for salty bar service.

Fritz 26 Chandler St ⓣ617/482-4428; Back Bay T. South End sports bar likened to the gay version of *Cheers* because of its friendly staff and mix of casually attired locals and visitors.

Jacque's 79 Broadway ⓣ617/426-8902; Arlington T. *Priscilla, Queen of the Desert* invades New England at this drag dream where past-it divas lip-synch *I Love the Nightlife*. There's a nice melting pot of patrons; it's quite popular for bachelorette parties. Showtime is 10.30pm Tues–Sun. Cover $5–10.

Machine 1254 Boylston St ⓣ617/536-1950; Kenmore **T**. A favorite with the gay crowd on Fridays and Saturdays when the club's large dance floor and top-notch music has the place pumping. The adjacent pool tables and bar let you take a breather from dancing while you soak up the scene. Cover $6–8.

Midway Café 3496 Washington St, Jamaica Plain ⓣ617/524-9038 ⓦwww.dykenight.com; Green Street **T**. Neighborhood hangout with a popular Thursday karaoke dyke night. You get to choose from their box of costume finery before you rock out in front of your friends; it usually dissolves into a dance party.

Pink at ID 13 Lansdowne St ⓣ617/262-2437; Kenmore **T**. A dancing lesbian lovefest rocks out here on Saturday nights. Cover $10.

Shopping

Boston is an extremely pleasant place to **shop**, with attractive stores clustered on atmospheric streets like Charles in Beacon Hill, and Newbury in Back Bay. Harvard Square is another excellent place for a window-shopping wander, with especially good **bookstores** in the vicinity. Otherwise, most of the action takes place downtown, first and foremost at the **Faneuil Hall Marketplace**. Though the area has become more commercialized over the years, there's still enough homespun boutiques, plus the many food stalls of **Quincy Market**, to make a trip worthwhile. There's also the somewhat downmarket Downtown Crossing, at Washington and Summer streets, centered on Filene's Basement, a bargain-hunter's delight.

Books

Boston has a history as a literary city, enhanced by its numerous universities and the authors and publishing houses that once called it home. This is well reflected in the quality and diversity of **bookstores** to be found both in Boston and neighboring Cambridge.

Barnes & Noble Downtown Crossing ⓣ617/426-5502; Downtown Crossing **T**; 660 Beacon St ⓣ617/267-8484; Kenmore **T**. Two large outposts of the national bookstore chain. The one on Beacon Street is capped by the neon Citgo sign (see p.127).

Brattle Book Shop 9 West St ⓣ617/542-0210; Park St **T**. One of the oldest antiquarian bookstores in the country. You can buy a book for $1 outside, or find one for $10,000 inside (they recently sold a first-edition *Walden* for a few grand).

Brookline Booksmith 279 Harvard St ⓣ617/566-6660; Coolidge Corner **T**. This cozy shop doesn't seem to have a particular specialty, but its friendly staff makes it perfect for browsing.

Bryn Mawr Book 373 Huron Ave ⓣ617/661-1770; Porter **T**. This neighborhood bookstore vends used titles in a relaxed Cambridge setting. Weather permitting, there are sidewalk displays for pedestrian browsers.

Calamus Bookstore 92B South St ⓣ617/338-1931; South Station **T**. Boston's only gay bookstore, with a good selection of reasonably priced books and cards, plus a vast community bulletin board at the entrance.

Grolier Poetry Bookstore 6 Plympton St ⓣ617/547-4648; Harvard **T**. With 14,000 volumes of verse, this tiny shop has gained an international following among poets and their fans. Frequent readings.

Harvard Book Store 1256 Massachusetts Ave ⓣ617/661-1515; Harvard **T**. Three huge rooms of new books upstairs, a basement for used volumes, and its award-winning remainder department downstairs. Academic and critical work in the humanities and social sciences dominate, with a healthy dose of fiction thrown in.

Trident Booksellers & Café 338 Newbury St ⓣ617/267-8688; Hynes **T**. One of the last great independent bookstores in Boston. Has a bit of an alternative vibe; buy an obscure magazine and pretend to read it over coffee in the café (see review p.153).

Food and drink

Eating out in Boston may prevail, but should you choose to cook your own **food**, or get provisions for a picnic, you won't do so badly either. There are also some excellent spots to pick up pastries, pies, and other dessert-oriented items.

Formaggio Kitchen 244 Huron Ave ⓣ617/354-4750; Harvard Square T; 268 Shawmut Ave, ⓣ617/350-6996; Back Bay T. Although regarded as one of the best cheese shops in Boston, the gourmet meats, salads, sandwiches, and baked goods here are also worth sampling.

Mike's Pastry 300 Hanover St ⓣ617/742-3050; Haymarket T. The famed North End bakery is one part Italian and two parts American, meaning in addition to *cannoli* and tiramisu, you'll find counters full of brownies and cookies. The homemade ice cream is not to be missed, but expect to wait in line for it.

Modern Pastry 257 Hanover St ⓣ617/523-3783; Haymarket T. You can't miss Modern's glorious vintage sign out front, nor would you want to – inside is fresh *torrone*, *cannoli*, little marzipan fruits and some of the North End's best pastries. Family-owned for seventy years.

Salumeria Italiana 151 Richmond St ⓣ617/523-8743; Haymarket T. Arguably the best Italian grocer this side of Roma, this shop stocks only the finest cheeses, meats, and more.

Savenor's 160 Charles St ⓣ617/723-6328; Charles T. Known for its meats, this small gourmet food shop in Beacon Hill also has a produce selection, in addition to prepared foods – ideal for taking to the nearby Charles River Esplanade for an impromptu picnic.

Malls and department stores

Boston's **malls** are widely scattered about, and are good places to visit if you need to pick up a number of diverse items on the same shopping trip. They often contain the city's biggest **department stores**, though a few unattached ones stand out, mostly around Downtown Crossing.

CambridgeSide Galleria 100 Cambridgeside Place ⓣ617/621-8666; Kendall T. Not too different from any other large American shopping mall. The haze of neon and packs of hairsprayed teens can be exhausting, but there's no similarly dense and convenient conglomeration of shops in Cambridge.

Copley Place 100 Huntington Ave ⓣ617/369-5000; Copley T. This ambitious, upscale office-retail-residential complex features more than a hundred stores and an eleven-screen multiplex.

Faneuil Hall Marketplace Faneuil Hall ⓣ617/523-1300; Government Center T. The city's most famous market, with a hundred or so shops, plus Quincy Market next door. It's a bit tourist-oriented, but still worth a trip.

Filene's Basement 426 Washington St ⓣ617/542-2011; Downtown Crossing T. Discounted merchandise from Macy's upstairs and other big-name department stores, plus a few Boston boutiques.

The Harvard Coop 1400 Massachusetts Ave ⓣ617/499-2000; Harvard T. Harvard's local department store, with a wide selection of fairly expensive insignia clothing and the like.

The Heritage on the Garden 300 Boylston St ⓣ617/426-9500; Arlington T. Not so much a mall as a very upscale mixed-use complex across from the Public Garden that consists of condos, restaurants, and boutiques.

Louis Boston 234 Berkeley St ⓣ617/262-6100; Arlington T. The place to go if you want to drop some serious dough on designer threads. A Boston landmark.

Neiman Marcus 5 Copley Place ⓣ617/536-3660; Copley T. Another luxurious department store, with prices to match.

The Shops at Prudential Center 800 Boylston St ⓣ617/236-3060; Prudential T. This is a fairly new conglomeration of a hundred or so mid-market shops, heavily patronized by local residents and conventioneers who seem genuinely to enjoy buying commemorative T-shirts and ties.

Music

The best places for new and used **music** in Boston are on Newbury Street in Back Bay, around Massachusetts Avenue near Kenmore Square, and up in Harvard Square – as you might expect, basically all the places students can be found hanging about.

In Your Ear Records 957 Commonwealth Ave ⓣ617/787-9755; Pleasant Street **T**. Indulge in their massive collection of used CDs, records, and other agreeable esoterica to sate your vintage music cravings. It's worth the trek out.
Looney Tunes 1106 Boylston Street ⓣ617/876-5624; Symphony **T**. The way a record store should be – walls bedecked with sultry vintage jazz records, a great selection of CDs and vinyl, and a hip staff that's not snooty.
Newbury Comics 332 Newbury St ⓣ617/236-4930; Hynes **T**. Boston's biggest alternative record store carries lots of independent labels you won't find at the national chains along with a substantial array of vinyl, posters, zines, and kitschy T-shirts. It's also a good place to pick up flyers on local club happenings. There's a branch in Cambridge at the Garage mall, 36 JFK St (ⓣ617/491-0337; Harvard **T**).
Nuggets 486 Commonwealth Ave ⓣ617/536-0679; Kenmore **T**. American jazz, rock, and R&B are the strong suits at this venerable new and used record store.
Planet Records 54B JFK St ⓣ617/492-0693; Harvard **T**. Unpretentious and well priced with a good selection of used CDs. It doesn't get more rock 'n' roll than the charred guitar they have hanging by the register – a remnant from the fire that decimated their former location.
Skippy White's 538 Massachusetts Ave ⓣ617/491-3345; Central **T**. Excellent collection of jazz, blues, R&B, gospel, funk (all manners), and hip-hop. Hum a few bars and the salesfolk will guide you to the right section.
Underground Hip Hop 234 Huntington Ave ⓣ2617/262-0200; Symphony **T**. One of the best selections of hip-hop here or anywhere. It's well-organized too – sit on a comfy stool, listen all you want to the tunes on their extensive website (ⓦwww.undergroundhiphop.com), and then they'll grab what you want from the back.

Specialty shops

Fresh 121 Newbury St ⓣ617/421-1212; Arlington **T**. More than three hundred varieties of French-milled soaps, lotions, oils, and makeup, packaged so exquisitely you won't want to open them.
Leavitt and Pierce 1316 Massachusetts Ave ⓣ617/547-0576; Harvard **T**. Old-school tobacconists with an outstanding selection of cigars, imported cigarettes, and smoking paraphernalia, plus an upstairs chess parlor right out of the carefree past.
The London Harness Company 60 Franklin St ⓣ617/542-9234; Downtown Crossing **T**. Chiefly known for its high-quality luggage goods, this atmospheric shop reeks of traditional Boston – indeed, Ben Franklin used to shop here. They also vend a wide array of items like chess sets, clocks, candlesticks, and inlaid decorative boxes.
Shake the Tree Gallery 95 Salem St ⓣ617/742-0484; Haymarket **T**. A good spot for a little retail therapy – bright, chunky gemstone necklaces, funky sock monkeys, yuppie candles, and other modern, pretty *objets* that you will never need but must have.

Listings

Banks and currency exchange Bank of America is Boston's largest, with branches and ATMs throughout the city. Bureaux de change are not very prevalent. You can find locations at Logan Airport Terminal E (International); Thomas Cook, 224 Tremont St; and many Bank of America branches.
Consulates Canada, 3 Copley Place, suite 400 (ⓣ617/262-3760, ⓦwww.dfait-maeci.gc.ca); UK, 1 Memorial Drive, Cambridge (ⓣ617/245-4500, ⓦwww.britainusa.com/boston); Ireland, 535 Boylston St (ⓣ617/267-9330); Australia, 55 Thomson Place (ⓣ617/261-5555, ⓦwww.australiannyc.org).
Hospitals Massachusetts General Hospital, 55 Fruit St (ⓣ617/726-2000, ⓦwww.mgh.harvard.edu; Charles/MGH **T**); Beth Israel Deaconess Medical Center, 330 Brookline Ave (ⓣ617/667-7000, ⓦwww.bidmc.harvard.edu; Longwood **T**); New England Medical Center, 750 Washington St (ⓣ617/636-5000, ⓦwww.nemc.org; NE Medical **T**); Brigham & Women's Hospital, 75 Francis St (ⓣ617/732-5500 or 1-800/BWH-9999, ⓦwww.bwh.partners.org; Longwood or Brigham Circle **T**); Children's Hospital, 300 Longwood Ave (ⓣ617/355-6000, ⓦwww.tch.harvard.edu; Longwood **T**).
Internet Pop into a local university and use one of their free public computers. Harvard's Holyoke Center, at 1350 Massachusetts Ave in Cambridge, has a couple of stations with 10min access maximum. The same goes for MIT's Rogers Building, at 77 Massachusetts Ave (also in Cambridge).

Boston's main public library, at 700 Boylston St, has free 15min Internet access on the ground floor of the Johnson building. Cybercafés are limited to the *Adrenaline Zone*, on the lower level at 40 Brattle St (ⓣ617/876-1314; Harvard **T**). There is also the ubiquitous Kinko's; try the 24hr location at 187 Dartmouth St (ⓣ617/262-6188; Copley **T**).

Laundry Back Bay Laundry Emporium, 409A Marlborough St (daily 7.30am–11pm, last wash at 9pm), is a good, clean bet; drop-off service is 90¢ per pound of clothing.

Parking A nightmare. The best parking secret is the Parcel 7 garage, at 136 Blackstone St, across from Martignetti's Liquors (ⓣ617/973-6954). The posted rates won't mention it, but if you get your ticket validated at a North End business the rates are only $1 an hour for the first three hours (after that it goes way up). Another good spot is after 4pm or on weekends at the Garage at Post Office Square ($7 per weekday night, $7 per weekend day; ⓣ617/423-1500). You can also park and ride at the safe and cheap Alewife **T** stop in Cambridge (at the intersection of US-2 and Cambridge Park Drive; $5 a day; ⓣ1-800/392-6100) or try for a metered spot in Back Bay. The parking limit at non-metered spots is two hours, whether posted or not.

Pharmacies The CVS drugstore chain has locations all over the city, though not all have pharmacies. For those, try the branches at 155–157 Charles St, in Beacon Hill (open 24hr; ⓣ617/227-0437, pharmacy ⓣ617/523-1028), and 35 White St, in Cambridge's Porter Square (ⓣ617/876-4037, pharmacy ⓣ617/876-5519).

Police In case of emergency, get to a phone and dial ⓣ911. For non-emergency situations, contact the Boston Police, headquartered at 1 Shroeder Plaza (ⓣ617/343-4200; Ruggles **T**).

Post office The most central post office downtown is at 31 Milk St in Post Office Square (Mon–Fri 7.30am–5pm); Cambridge's central branch is at 770 Massachusetts Ave, in Central Square (Mon–Fri 7.30am–6pm, Sat 7.30am–2pm); and the General Post Office, 25 Dorchester Ave, behind South Sta -tion, is open 24hr.

Sports Baseball: Red Sox (ⓣ617/482-4SOX, ⓦwww.redsox.com) play at Fenway Park, seats $12–120. Basketball: Celtics (ⓣ1-800/4NBATIX, ⓦwww.nba.com/celtics) play at the TDBanknorth Garden, 150 Causeway St, in the West End, seats $10–$700. Hockey: Bruins (ⓣ617/624-6327, ⓦwww.bostonbruins.com), also at the TDBanknorth Garden, seats $10–99.

Travel agents STA Travel, 65 Mt Auburn St, Harvard Square, Cambridge (ⓣ617/497-1497), specializes in student and youth travel; American Express Travel, 170 Federal St (ⓣ617/439-4400),

2

Eastern Massachusetts

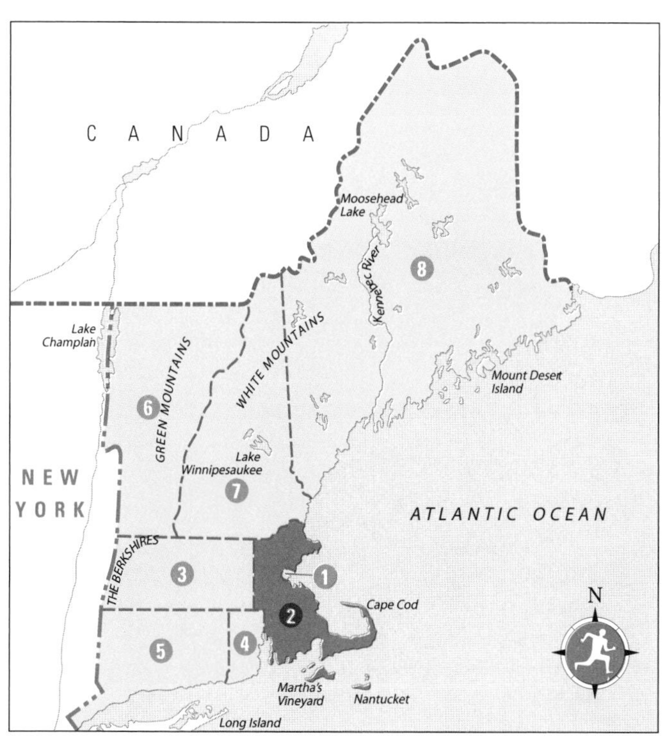

CHAPTER TWO

Highlights

* **Walden Pond** Think transcendentalist thoughts, or just take a relaxing walk and swim at this historically significant and physically beautiful spot. See p.173

* **Salem** The witch-related spots get all the hype, but the maritime legacy here impresses just as much. See p.175

* **Hammond Castle Museum, Gloucester** See how bizarrely some New Englanders lived, at this eccentric cliffside house. See p.184

* **Cape Cod biking** The Rail Trail is great for touring, while the Province Lands bike path takes a more scenic route through the dunes. See pp.208 & 221

* **Provincetown** Perhaps the lone must-see on the Cape, a lively town with great beaches, tasty seafood, and an anything-goes mentality. See p.216

* **Hit the beach** The region's bountiful beaches make a fine excuse to laze about. See pp.212, 232 & 240.

* **House-hunting in Nantucket** Leaf through Melville's *Moby Dick* while admiring the digs of one-time whaleboat captains in Nantucket Town, the *Pequod's* port of call. See p.238

△ Cape Cod lobster shack

2

Eastern Massachusetts

The vast majority of Massachusetts' six million residents live within a few miles of its eastern coast, many of them direct descendants of successive waves of Europeans, going all the way back to the Mayflower Pilgrims, who arrived here, miles off course, in 1620. They were heading, in fact, for Jamestown, Virginia, though after the initial disappointment wore off they must have been impressed by what they had found: natural harbors to facilitate trade and commerce, waters teeming with fish, virgin forests providing endless supplies of wood, even creeks and salt marshes that reminded them of their native England. Heartened by their initially friendly contact with indigenous Native Americans who were willing to share their agricultural knowledge of the terrain, the Pilgrims stayed put. The rest, as they say, is history.

That's apt, considering that **Eastern Massachusetts** has quite a bit to offer in the way of history, cradle as it is of much early American development. Just inland from Boston, and easily done as a day-trip, are the towns of **Lexington** and **Concord**, major players during the Revolutionary War. Otherwise, Massachusetts' long coast can be divided into four sections, all linked by the major highways which radiate from Boston: the **North Shore**, which stretches from Boston's bland northern suburbs to the New Hampshire border, including the famous witch trial town of **Salem** and the rocky **Cape Ann** peninsula with the old fishing ports of **Gloucester** and **Rockport**; the **South Shore**, extending from the southern outskirts of Boston towards **Plymouth**, with its Pilgrim-related sights, all the way to the Rhode Island border, passing the partially restored whaling port of **New Bedford**, among more dreary outposts, in its course; the outstretched arm of **Cape Cod**, a vast glacial deposit reaching more than seventy miles into the Atlantic, and dotted with a range of popular resorts, none better than bohemian **Provincetown**; and the relaxed, upmarket holiday islands of **Martha's Vineyard** and **Nantucket**, playgrounds of the rich and famous. Though Massachusetts' coastline may not be as spectacular as that of California, or even of nearby Maine, swimmable beaches are abundant, as are clam shacks and fun neighborhood dive bars. The sights won't take more than a few days to tour, and the most relaxing way to vacation here is to pick a beach town on the Cape or the islands, and plant yourself for a week of summer activities.

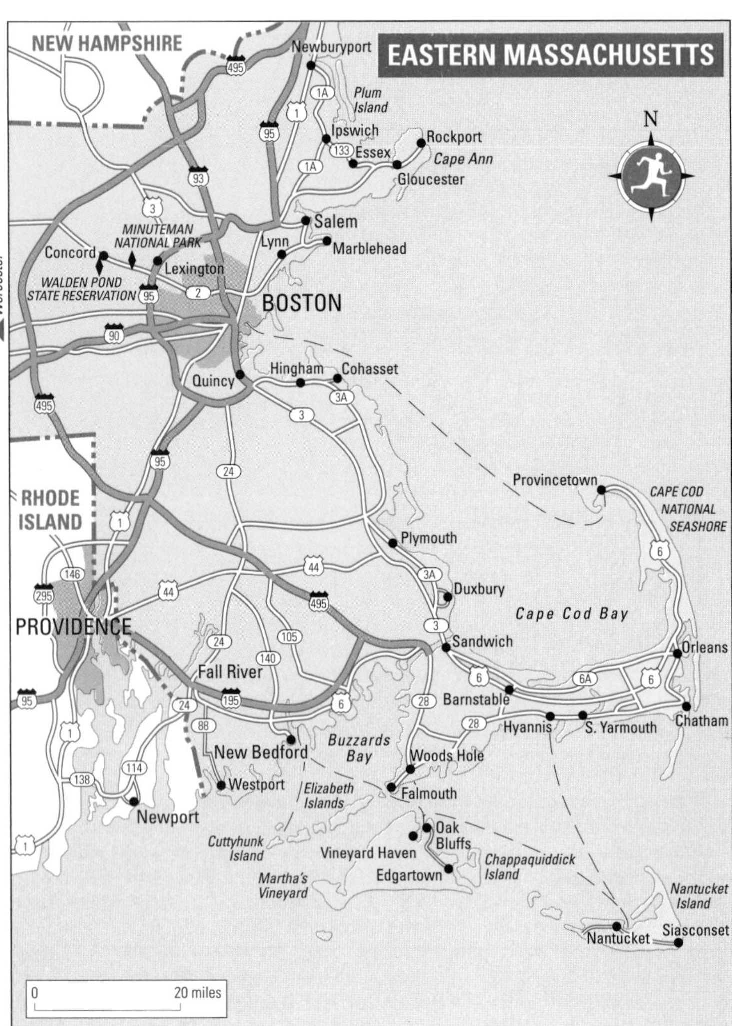

Lexington and Concord

The quiet towns of **Lexington** and **Concord**, almost always mentioned in the same breath, cash in on their fame as the locations of the Americans' first armed confrontations with the British. Lexington is mostly suburban today, while Concord, five miles east, still has the flavor of a genteel country town. Most

Getting to Lexington and Concord

Despite their rural setting, Concord and Lexington are only about a dozen miles from downtown Boston, and therefore readily accessible from the city. The MBTA (☎617/222-3200, www.mbta.com) operates **trains** to Concord from North Station ($5 one-way) and also runs **buses** to Lexington from Cambridge's Alewife Station. Journey time ranges from 40min to 1hr. If you are coming from Boston by **car**, take Rte-2 (Mass Ave) out of the city to Arlington Center, then follow the signs to Lexington. If you're in shape and the weather permits, the beautiful and not overly hilly **Minuteman bike path** goes from Cambridge to Lexington Green. The easiest places to pick up the path are behind Davis or Alewife T stations on the red line.

of the area's historical sights have been incorporated into the **Minute Man National Park**, which takes in the Lexington Battle Green, the North Bridge area in Concord, and much of Battle Road, the route the British followed on their retreat from Concord to Boston. The battles of Lexington and Concord are explained throughout, with visitors' centers full of scale models and remnant musketry, and old colonial houses boasting the odd preserved bullet hole, though only a few of these spots are worth more than a quick look. The whole affair tends to be overly structured – in many instances you must take hour-long tours of tiny houses you could walk through in two minutes. The area also includes many literary sights – houses of great New England writers, and **Walden Pond**, an entire estuary whose seasonal changes were memorialized by Henry David Thoreau.

Some history

On April 19, 1775, the first battle of the American Revolution began here when British troops marched to Concord to seize American munitions. The British plans to attack were hardly a secret; the American "Minute Men" were so called because they were prepared to fight at a moment's notice. When the British set out from Boston Common, Paul Revere and William Dawes rode off on separate routes to sound the alarm. Within minutes, church bells were clanging and cannons roaring throughout the countryside, signaling the rebels to head for Lexington Green; hundreds more converged around the North Bridge area of Concord. Revere, who was questioned at gunpoint en route to Lexington but managed to escape, gave the final alarm to John Hancock and Samuel Adams (who were in town to attend a provincial congress) at the Hancock-Clarke House.

John Parker, the colonial captain, was down the street at the Buckman Tavern, when he received word that the British were closing in on the Green. "Don't fire unless fired upon," he ordered the men, "but if they mean to have a war, let it begin here." With only 77 Americans pitted against seven hundred British regulars, it was more a show of resolve than a hope for victory. Who fired the first shot remains a mystery, but in the fracas that followed, eight Americans were killed, including Parker. The British suffered no casualties, and marched three miles west to Concord.

By the time they arrived, it was already after sunrise on April 19, and hundreds more Minute Men had massed on a farm behind North Bridge near where the lion's share of the munitions was stored. When a British officer accidentally set fire to a building, the Americans believed that the town was going up in smoke. They fired on the British guarding the other side of the bridge – the "shots heard round the world," as history books have it. The British were now outnumbered four to one, and suffered heavily in the ensuing battle, which continued all the way back to Boston.

Lexington

The main attraction in **LEXINGTON** itself is the grassy, meticulously manicured **Battle Green**, where, appropriately enough, the American flag is flown 24 hours a day. The land serves as Lexington's town common and is fronted by Henry Kitson's diminutive but dignified statue *The Minute Man*. Though this musket-bearing figure of **Captain John Parker** was not dedicated until 1900, it stands on boulders dislodged from the stone walls behind which the colonial militia fired at British troops on April 19, 1775. The **Lexington Visitor Center**, 1875 Massachusetts Ave, on the eastern periphery of the Green (April–Oct Mon–Sat 9am–5pm, Nov–March daily 9am–4pm; free; ⓣ781/862-2480, ⓦwww.nps.gov/mima), has a diorama that shows the detail of the battle, while in the **Buckman Tavern**, facing the Green at 1 Bedford St (mid-March to Dec Mon–Sat 10am–5pm, Sun 1–5pm; 30–45min guided tour; $5; ⓣ781/862-5598), a bullet hole from a British rifle has been preserved in an inner door near the restored first-floor tap room. A couple of blocks north, at 36 Hancock St, a plaque affixed to the brown, two-story **Hancock-Clarke House** (same hours, price, and tour info as above; ⓣ781/862-1703) solemnly reminds us that this is where "Samuel Adams and John Hancock were sleeping when aroused by Paul Revere"; the latter was the grandson of Reverend John Hancock, the man for whom the house was built in 1698. Exhibits on the free-admission first floor include the drum on which William Diamond beat the signal for the Minute Men to converge and the pistols that British major John Pitcairn lost on the retreat from Concord. Less interesting is the small, wooden **Munroe Tavern**, somewhat removed from the town center at 1332 Massachusetts Ave (same hours, price, and tour info as above; ⓣ781/862-2016), which served as a field hospital for British soldiers, though only for a mere hour and a half. If you intend to visit all three sights, you'll save a bit by getting a combination ticket ($10), available at each site. Just outside of Lexington town, a contemporary brick-and-glass

△ *The Minute Man* statue

building houses the **National Heritage Museum**, 33 Marrett Rd (Mon–Sat 10am–5pm, Sun noon–5pm; free; Ⓦwww.monh.org), which tries to be just that, with rotating displays on all facets of American history, daily life, and culture, plus a permanent exhibit on the battle events of Lexington.

Practicalities

It's best not to **stay** in Lexington, which is more of a day-trip from Boston or a side-trip from Concord than a destination in itself. The B&Bs here, far from being charming, are homes where guests are just as likely to feel like impositions than welcome patrons. If you must spend the night, your best bet is a chain hotel – either the *Sheraton*, 727 Marrett Rd (Ⓣ781/862-8700, Ⓦwww.starwoodhotels.com; ⑥) or the *Holiday Inn Express*, 440 Bedford St (Ⓣ781/861-0850, Ⓦwww.hiexpress.com; ⑤). For a **meal**, try *Via Lago*, 1845 Massachusetts Ave (Ⓣ781/861-6174), a casual counter-service spot serving fresh, tasty pastas, sandwiches, and salads, or head to *Vinny T's*, 20 Waltham St (Ⓣ781/860-5200), for heaping portions of reliable Italian fare like fennel sausage lasagna and spaghetti bolognese.

Concord and around

CONCORD was one of the few sizeable inland towns of New England at the time of the Revolution, but it hasn't grown much since, which means there are lots of greenspaces, and that it seems a serene place, even in the height of tourist season. It's a good spot to explore by bike; the countryside around town is some of the most pristine in this part of the state, filled with bucolic fields and historic colonial houses. The business district hugs **Main Street**, which intersects Monument Street right by the historic **Colonial Inn**, where many of the wounded from the battles of Lexington and Concord were tended to; today it is an atmospheric place to stay or just to eat a tavern lunch of fish cakes and chips. Main Street crosses Lexington Road at the **Hill Burying Ground**, from the top of which you can survey much of Concord. A few blocks behind the grounds, off Rte-62, lies **Sleepy Hollow Cemetery**, where Concord literati Ralph Waldo Emerson, Nathaniel Hawthorne, Henry David Thoreau, and Louisa May Alcott are interred atop "Authors' Ridge," a centrally located crest.

The most vaunted spot in Concord is the **North Bridge Area**, slightly removed from the town center and site of the first effective armed resistance to British rule in America. If you approach from Monument Street, as most tourists do, you'll be following the route the British took, as a plaque on a group grave of some British regulars reminds: "They came 3000 miles and died to keep the past upon its throne." The focal point, of course, is the bridge, which, though photogenic enough, looks a bit too groomed to provoke much patriotic sentiment – indeed, it's a 1954 replica of an earlier replacement. On the far side of the bridge is another Minute Man statue, this one sculpted by Daniel Chester French, of Lincoln Memorial fame. A short walk from here takes you to a **visitors' center**, 2 Heywood St (May–Oct daily 9.30am–4.30pm), where a diorama of the battle is displayed along with assorted military regalia.

Literally a stone's throw from North Bridge is the **Old Manse** (mid-April to Oct Mon–Sat 10am–5pm, Sun noon–5pm; $7; Ⓣ978/369-3909), a gray clapboard house built for Ralph Waldo Emerson's grandfather, the Reverend William Emerson, who witnessed the nearby hostilities from his window. Of the numerous rooms in the house, all with period furnishings intact, the most interesting is the small upstairs study, which is where Nathaniel Hawthorne, who rented the house in the early 1840s, wrote *Mosses from an Old Manse*, a rather obscure book that endowed the place with its name; it's also here that his wife, following a miscarriage, used her diamond wedding ring to etch the words "Man's accidents are God's purposes" into a window. On the first floor, a framed swath of original English wallpaper features the British "paper" stamp-tax mark on the reverse side.

Another literary landmark is the seventeenth-century **Wayside**, 455 Lexington Rd (tours May–Oct Tues & Wed 2pm & 4pm, Thu–Sun 11am, 1.30, 3 & 4.30pm; $4; ⓣ978/369-6993), where Louisa May Alcott's girlhood memories were made. By the time she was writing and living at the Orchard House (see below), Hawthorne had moved in, making this a good place to visit for those who believe in literary karma. Among the many antique furnishings in this over 300-year-old house, the most evocative is in the fourth-floor "tower" that Hawthorne had added on: the slanted writing desk at which the author toiled, standing up.

Alcott penned *Little Women* at the brown-clapboard **Orchard House**, next door from Wayside at no. 399 (April–Oct Mon–Sat 10am–4.30pm, Sun 1–4.30pm; Nov–March Mon–Fri 11am–3pm, Sat 10am–4.30pm, Sun 1–4.30pm; closed Jan 1–15; $7; ⓣ978/369-4118, ⓦwww.louisamayalcott.org), where she and her family lived from 1858 to 1877. The video and guided tour is well worth your time; although it focuses heavily on the differences between Alcott's life and her most famous book, it is also the best way to get a good impression of Concord's strong literary, intellectual, and liberal activist community in the nineteenth century. Also next door to Wayside is the **Grapevine Cottage**, where in 1849 Ephraim Bull developed the Concord grape, one of only three fruits native to North America (the others are the cranberry and blueberry). You can see the vines that stemmed from the first successful fruit, but that's about it – it's a private home and not open to the public.

Just past the Orchard House, at the intersection of the Cambridge Turnpike and Lexington Road, is what has become known as the **Ralph Waldo Emerson House**, 28 Cambridge Turnpike (mid-April to Oct Thurs–Sat 10am–4.30pm, Sun 2–4.30pm; $7; ⓣ978/369-2236), where the essayist and poet lived from 1835 until his death in 1882. Emerson's study has been reconstructed across the street at the excellent **Concord Museum**, 200 Lexington Rd (Jan–March Mon–Sat 11am–4pm, Sun 1–4pm; April–Dec Mon–Sat 9am–5pm, Sun noon–5pm; $7; ⓦwww.concordmuseum.org), where his apple orchard once stood. The museum has more than a dozen galleries which display period furnishings from eighteenth- and nineteenth-century Concord, including a sizeable collection of Thoreau's personal effects, such as the simple bed from his hut at Walden Pond. More interesting, however, are the Revolutionary War artifacts, including one of the signal lanterns hung from the Old North Church in Boston.

Practicalities

The Chamber of Commerce, 15 Walden St (ⓣ978/369-3120, ⓦwww.concordchamberofcommerce.org), offers guided **walking tours** for $18 (mid-March to Nov Mon & Fri at 11am, Sat & Sun 11am & 1pm). There is also a central **visitor's center** at 58 Main St (April–Oct daily 10am–4pm; no phone). For somewhere to **stay**, the upscale *Colonial Inn*, 48 Monument Square (ⓣ1-800/370-9200 or 978/369-9200, ⓦwww.concordscolonialinn.com; ❼), is a 56-room hotel that still manages to feel like a B&B, while *Amerscot House B&B*, nine miles west in Stow, 61 W Acton Rd (ⓣ978/897-0666, ⓦwww.amerscot.com; ❼), offers attentive hospitality in a restored 1734 farmhouse. The

Concord and transcendentalism

A half-century after the social tumult that precipitated independence, Concord became the center of a revolution in American thinking known as **transcendentalism**, a cerebral mix of religion, philosophy, mysticism, and ethics. Heavily influenced by Unitarianism and the teachings of **Reverend Ellery Channing**, the transcendentalists, many of them Harvard-educated Unitarian ministers unhappy with their church's conservatism, denied the existence of miracles and stressed the conviction that insight and intuitive knowledge were the ways to enhance the relationship between man, nature, and the "over-soul." These beliefs, originating in the Platonic belief of a higher reality not validated by sense, experience, or pure reason, were born of a passion for rural life, liberty, and intellectual freedom. Indeed, the free thinking that transcendentalism unleashed put area writers at the vanguard of American literary expression.

In 1834, **Ralph Waldo Emerson** moved into the Old Manse (see p.171), the house his grandfather had built near the North Bridge; there, in 1836, he wrote the book that would signal the birth of the movement, *Nature*, in which he argued for the organicism of all life, and the function of nature as a visible manifestation of invisible spiritual truths. His stature as an intensely pensive, learned scribe drew other intellectuals to Concord, notably Thoreau, Hawthorne, and the Alcotts, and in 1840 he co-founded *The Dial*, the literary magazine which became the movement's semi-official journal, with Margaret Fuller. These Concord authors formed a close-knit group. Nathaniel Hawthorne, a native of Salem, rented the Old Manse for three happy years, returned to his hometown, then moved back to Concord permanently in 1852. Meanwhile, Emerson financed Thoreau's Walden Pond sojourn and the Alcotts lived in Orchard House, on Lexington Rd. It was a largely wholesome literary movement, and the short-lived utopian farming communities it spawned – Hawthorne's Brook Farm and Bronson Alcott's Fruitlands (see overleaf) – seem almost quaint in retrospect. Its effect was longer lasting than these communities, however, as its proponents were to play an important role in supporting educational innovation, abolition, and the feminist movement.

inexpensive *Concordian Motel*, a few miles west of downtown Concord on Rte-2 at Hosmer St in Acton (☎978/263-7765; ❹), has 52 comfortable air-conditioned rooms. If you're looking for a bite to **eat**, try the *Cheese Shop*, 29 Walden St (☎978/369-5778), a great place to stop for deluxe picnic fixings from paté and sandwiches to, of course, all manner of cheeses. For a sit-down meal, head to *Walden Grille*, 24 Walden St (☎978/371-2233), for crabmeat and avocado salad and grilled duck sausage in a refurbished nineteenth-century firehouse.

Walden Pond State Reservation

The tranquility which Thoreau sought and savored at **Walden Pond**, just south of Concord proper off Rte-126 (daily dawn to dusk; parking $5; ☎978/369-3254), is for the most part gone, thanks mainly to the masses of tourists who pour in to retrace his footsteps. The place itself, however, has remained much the same since the author's famed exercise in independence from 1845 to 1847. Thoreau described this experiment in his 1854 book *Walden*, where he concluded, "A man is rich in proportion to the number of things which he can afford to let alone." Of his life in the simple log cabin, he wrote, "I did not feel crowded or confined in the least." A reconstructed single-room hut, complete with a journal open on its rustic desk, is situated near the parking lot, while the site of the original cabin, closer to the shores of the pond, is marked out with stones. The pond, which gets filled up with swimmers on hot summer days, was

The Acton Discovery Museums

Near Concord is the suburb of **ACTON**, worth visiting (if you're traveling with kids) only for its impressive **Discovery Museums**, 177 Main St/Rte-27 (call ahead, as hours vary; both museums $12, single $8; ⓣ978/264-0030, ⓦwww.discoverymuseums.org). Housed in a small Victorian home, the **Children's Discovery Museum** is aimed at small children, with each room a different theme – one is decorated like a ship, another to simulate a jungle safari. Next door, in a larger concrete building, the **Science Discovery Museum** is geared toward slightly older kids and is full of hands-on activities, including a woodshop.

spared from development by a band of celebrities led, improbably, by ex-Eagle Don Henley. If you take the footpath that meanders around the pond you'll find smaller trails to the water that are rarely crowded and are good spots for quiet contemplation. The best time to visit is dawn, when the pond still "throws off its nightly clothing of mist."

DeCordova Museum, Codman House, and Fruitlands

Though technically a part of the town of Lincoln, the **DeCordova Museum and Sculpture Park**, 51 Sandy Pond Rd (Tues–Sun 11am–5pm; $9, sculpture park free when museum is closed; ⓣ781/259-8355, ⓦwww.decordova.org), is only a few miles south of downtown Concord and very much worth a visit. All manner of contemporary sculpture peppers the museum's expansive grounds, but most fascinating are the bigger works, like John Buck's *Dream World* and Paul Matisse's *Musical Fence*, which look like they've burst through the walls of a museum and tumbled into their present positions; Matisse's piece is interactive – tap it with a wooden stick like you would a xylophone. Most of the sculptures are by American (and in particular New England) artists, and are sufficiently impressive to make the **garden** overshadow the small on-site museum, whose rotating special exhibits are often just as eye-catching, with an emphasis on contemporary multimedia art.

Also in Lincoln, the three-story, gray-shingled **Codman House**, on Codman Road (June to mid-Oct Wed–Sun 11am–5pm; tours on the hour; $10; ⓣ781/259-8843), dates from 1735 and was home to five generations of the Codman family. It contains eclectic architectural features from every period, from Georgian paneling through to a Victorian dining room, while the grounds resemble those of an English country estate and include a hidden Italianate garden with its own reflecting pool. Another interesting Lincoln property is the **Gropius House**, 68 Baker Ridge Rd (June to mid-Oct Wed–Sun 11am–5pm, mid-Oct to May Sat & Sun 11am–5pm; tours on the hour; $10; ⓣ781/259-8098), a twentieth-century Bauhaus home that seems to have accurately predicted the architecture of 1970s office buildings. Constructed in 1937 by Walter Gropius, a teacher at the Harvard School of Design, the house's boxy, unattractive exterior belies the more pleasant, if utilitarian, interior.

Twenty miles west of Lincoln, the small town of **HARVARD** is home to the collection of museums known as **Fruitlands**, 102 Prospect Hill Rd (mid-May to Oct Mon–Fri 11am–3pm, Sat & Sun 10am–5pm; $10; ⓣ978/456-3924, ⓦwww.fruitlands.org), which tell the story of the daily life, art, and beliefs of a high-minded group, headed by **Bronson Alcott**, that aimed to create a "New Eden." Alcott started the idealistic but short-lived commune here with his English friend Charles Lane in 1843, espousing vegetarianism, freedom of expression, and celibacy (the latter after siring four daughters, including Louisa May), but talk of living off the "fruits of the land" proved much easier than actually doing it. True to Alcott's pastoral proclivities, today there are two hundred acres of woodlands and meadows on the site, which you can explore on four well-marked nature trails. The original farmhouse now houses a **museum** with exhibits on the transcendentalist movement, including letters and memorabilia of Alcott, Emerson, and Thoreau. The **Shaker Museum** has displays of furniture, crafts, and artifacts retrieved from a Shaker community that once existed here; the **Picture Gallery** features a collection of American art, including New England landscape paintings by Hudson River School artists Thomas Cole and Frederick Edwin Church; and an **Indian Museum** highlights Native American handicrafts and design, including richly decorated clothing, headdresses, pottery, dolls, and carved wood.

The North Shore

The mainly rocky **North Shore**, which extends north of Boston to the New Hampshire border, takes in some of Massachusetts' most disparate geography and culture. Outside Boston a series of glum working-class suburbs – Revere, Saugus, and Lynn – gradually yield to such bedroom communities as Swampscott and Beverly Farms, then to the charming waterfront towns of **Salem** and **Marblehead**, the first real places of any interest, and the former synonymous with the infamous witch trials. Just north juts the promontory of scenic **Cape Ann**, the so-called "other Cape"; with its lighthouses, seafood shanties, and rocky shores pummeled by the cold Atlantic, it's a scaled-down version of the Maine coast. Highlights include the fishing port of **Gloucester** and the laid-back oceanfront village of **Rockport**. Further up the coast, the land becomes flatter, with acres of salt marshes and white sands, some of the finest in New England, particularly on **Plum Island** and near the sleepy villages of **Essex** and **Ipswich**. Closer to the New Hampshire border, the elegant old fishing burg **Newburyport** is of some historical interest, with scores of Federal mansions and a red-brick commercial district built in the early 1800s. Any of these North Shore towns can be reached in an easy day-trip from Boston, and none should take more than a day to explore.

The quickest route north from Boston is **Rte-1**, but the more scenic (and closer to the coast) is **Rte-1A**, which also traverses the bucolic horse country of Hamilton and Ipswich between Salem and Newburyport. From Rte-1, **Rte-127** branches off to loop around Cape Ann.

Salem

The witch trials of 1692 put **SALEM** on the map for all the wrong reasons, but this unpretentious coastal town sixteen miles north of Boston has done little since to distance itself from such macabre associations; indeed, most of its attractions focus on witch-related activity. It's all a bit misleading, considering

Salem was the site where the **Massachusetts Bay Colony** was first established – with the most elevated of intentions – and also for years an immensely prosperous port. In fact, Salem had such a maritime empire that at one time many Asian merchants were under the impression that the town was the capital of the United States.

A deep, well-protected harbor lured a handful of English settlers from Cape Ann to the spot they first called **Naumkeag**, and the Massachusetts Bay Colony was born. By 1683, Salem was one of the few lawful ports of entry for foreign cargoes in British America, and by the time the Revolutionary War broke out, good fortune on the high seas had turned Salem into an unrivaled commercial dynamo. **Elias Derby**, said to be America's first millionaire, built his fortune by running privateers from Salem during the war; afterwards, when British ports barred American vessels, he sailed his ships farther afield, trading in China and the East Indies.

Of the many goods on the outbound ships of Salem traders, the most lucrative by far was **cod**, which found a huge market in Catholic Europe. Salem's "merchant princes" brought back everything from spices to olive oil to fine china, for a while fairly monopolizing the luxury goods trade in America. But the California Gold Rush, the Civil War, and the silting up of the harbor all conspired to rob Salem of its generations of prosperity. Today the harbor is still home to hundreds of boats, though most are pleasure craft. Ironically, Salem's witch heritage – see the box opposite – has proved to be its ultimate salvation: were it not for the spruced-up town center that capitalizes on the trials, this once-proud port might look as unsightly as many of its North Shore neighbor towns.

Arrival, information, and getting around

MBTA commuter **trains** run hourly (every 2hr on weekends; $3.75 one-way) between Salem and Boston's **North Station**, and there's a regular **bus** service, also operated by MBTA, from Haymarket Square in Boston. If you are traveling

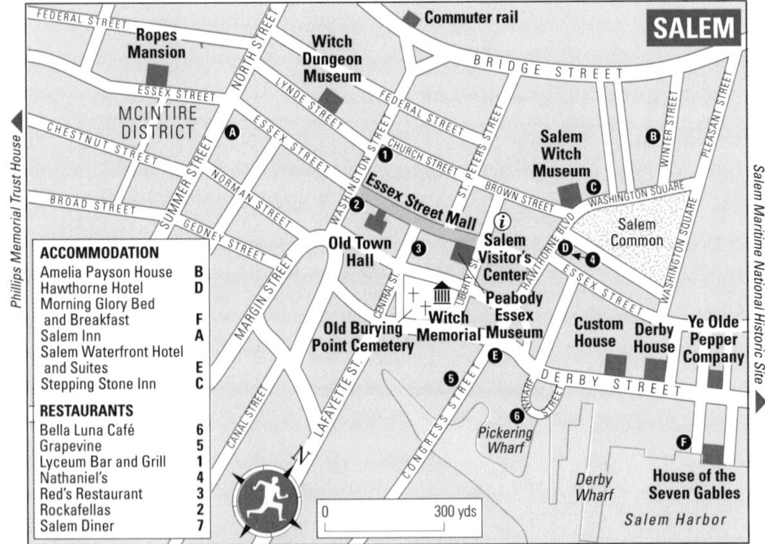

The Salem witch trials

By their quantity alone, Salem's witch memorials and "attractions" speak of the magnitude of the hysteria that gripped the town for much of 1692 and 1693. Bostonians had overthrown the Massachusetts Bay Colony's first Crown-appointed governor, Sir Edmund Andros, in 1689, plunging the region, already under constant threat of French and Indian attack, into political instability. That same year, Boston minister and eventual witch trial judge **Cotton Mather** published his popular book *The Wonders of the Invisible World*, a sort of Rough Guide to the supernatural that would help feed the imagination of the town's gullible inhabitants later on. And Salem itself was experiencing identity trouble: Salem Village, slightly inland, was a struggling community of farmers mired in property disputes and personality clashes, while Salem Town was an increasingly affluent port. Those caught up in the intrigue lived in Salem Village (which separated to form the town of Danvers in 1752), while the actual trials took place in Salem Town, which is known today simply as Salem.

The first casualties of the villagers' Calvinist lifestyle were their young and supremely bored teenage daughters, who reported as truth fireside tales of the occult as told by **Tituba**, a West Indian slave woman. The children ate up the stories and washed them down with hard cider and various potions, also proffered by Tituba. The fun and games took a sinister turn when the daughter and niece of a new clergyman, Samuel Parris, both experienced convulsive fits and started barking. Whether it was epilepsy or the adverse effects of eating mold-contaminated bread, other girls began to copy them, and when the village doctor failed to diagnose the problem, the accusations of witchcraft began to be taken seriously.

The trials that ensued pitted neighbor against neighbor, even husband against wife. Confessing to witchcraft spared you the gallows but meant castigation and the confiscation of your land. Mary Lacy of Andover, for instance, "confessed" that "me and Martha Carrier did both ride on a stick when we went to a witch meeting in Salem Village." Another accused, Giles Cory, first testified that his wife was a witch, then refused to agree that the court had the right to try him. To coerce him into acknowledging the court's authority, he was staked on ground under planks while heavy stones were pressed on top of him. He lasted two days, and died without confessing.

The trials were also marked by the girls' crazed ravings: in a scene re-enacted at the Witch Dungeon Museum (see p.179), Ann Putnam claimed that Sarah Good, a pipe-smoking beggar woman, was biting her, right in front of the judge. Such "**spectral evidence**" was accepted as fact, and the trials soon degenerated into the definitive case study of guilt by association. More than 150 villagers were accused and imprisoned (this in a village of 500), nineteen were hanged and four died in jail. Tituba, who readily confessed to sorcery, was not among them. Two dogs were even hanged after some girls claimed they had given them "the evil eye."

The most grisly day in Salem's history came on **September 22, 1692**, when, on the final day of execution, eight villagers were hanged on **Gallows' Hill**, the precise location of which is not known. Though the hysteria continued for a while unabated, with another 21 people tried in January 1693, the court's legitimacy, shaky from the start, was starting to wear thin. One of the judges, Jonathan Corwin, and his family, stood to gain heavily from the proceedings; indeed, much purloined land fell into the hands of his son George. The new royal governor, **William Phipps**, appalled by the sordid state of affairs, finally intervened after his wife was accused. He responded by forbidding the use of spectral evidence as proof, and all of the accused were acquitted that May, with families of the victims eventually awarded damages.

by **car** from Boston, you can choose between Rte-1A, which reaches Salem via the Dalton Pkwy, or the faster Rte-128, which heads to town from exit 25A. Once you've arrived, downtown Salem is so compact you're unlikely to need anything more than your feet to get around. The **Salem Heritage Trail**, a painted red line on Salem's sidewalks, links some of the key sights, as does the **Salem Trolley** (March & Nov Sat & Sun 10am–4pm, April–Oct daily 10am–5pm; $10; ⓣ978/744-5469, ⓦwww.salemtrolley.com); tickets are valid for a whole day, so you can jump on and off as you please. The town's **information center**, 2 New Liberty St (daily 9am–5pm; ⓣ978/740-1650 or 1-877/SALEM-MA, ⓦwww.salem.org), serves as the Heritage Trail's unofficial starting point.

Accommodation

Salem is full of small **B&Bs** – some with no more than three rooms – in old historic houses with steep staircases. It is perhaps the only town in America where **hotels** are booked for Halloween months in advance; if you plan on coming any time in October, beware of high prices and full houses.

Amelia Payson House 16 Winter St ⓣ978/744-8304, ⓦwww.ameliapaysonhouse.com. Small, friendly B&B in a restored 1845 Greek Revival home. Each room is furnished with period antiques. ❻

Hawthorne Hotel 18 Washington Square W ⓣ978/744-4080 or 1-800/729-7829, ⓦwww.hawthornehotel.com. Right in the heart of things, this full-service hotel is a Salem landmark with surprisingly reasonable prices and a respectable restaurant and pub. The owners also run the *Suzannah Flint House*, a former independent B&B on Essex St with three beautifully renovated rooms. ❻

Morning Glory Bed and Breakfast 22 Hardy St ⓣ978/741-1703, ⓦwww.morningglorybb.com. This three-room B&B down by the water (and the House of the Seven Gables) has a friendly owner and a roof deck and porch with water views. ❻

The Salem Inn 7 Summer St ⓣ978/741-0680 or 1-800/446-2995, ⓦwww.saleminnma.com. Located on the south side of the McIntire District, this historic inn comprises 41 well-maintained rooms in the Captain West House, the main central building, and the Curwen and Peabody houses, smaller ones on either side of the Captain West. Many rooms have working fireplaces. ❻

Salem Waterfront Hotel and Suites 225 Derby St ⓣ978/740-8788, ⓦwww.salemwaterfronthotel.com. This brand-new Best Western branch adds 86 much-needed rooms to the center of town near the water. It's standard large hotel fare – minimalist design, heated indoor pool, and prices to match. ❼

The Stepping Stone Inn 19 Washington Square N ⓣ978/741-8900 or 1-800/338-3022, ⓦwww.thesteppingstoneinn.com. An unassuming B&B in an 1846 building across from Salem Common and next to the Witch Museum. ❻

The Town

You're never very far from the Puritans' woeful legacy in Salem, with its plethora of witch museums, exhibits, and memorials – most child-oriented and some very tacky. Don't waste money on the storefront "museums" that line the streets; they're nothing more than glorified waxworks with spooky lighting and gift shops. There's no shortage of witches hanging around offering tours or, for the open-minded, lessons in communicating with the dead. Haunted tours and scavenger hunts can be fun if you're in the mood, and they'll give you a better sense of what the town has to offer apart from the so-called museums.

Essex Street Mall

The **Essex Street Mall** is the closest thing Salem has to a main drag, a car-free, boutique-filled stretch of Essex Street that is convenient to many of the city's best sights. At its northern end, the hokey **Salem Witch Museum**, 19 1/2 Washington Square (daily: July–Aug 10am–7pm, Sept–June 10am–5pm; $6.50; ⓣ978/744-1692, ⓦwww.salemwitchmuseum.com), provides some entertaining, if kitschy, orientation on the witch trials. Really just a sound-and-light show that makes ample use of wax figures to depict the events of 1692, it's still better and more official than the other "witch museums" in town. In front of the house is the imposing statue of **Roger Conant**, founder of Salem's first Puritan settlement. Even cheesier is the **Witch Dungeon Museum**, on the west side of town at 16 Lynde St (April–Nov daily 10am–5pm; $6; ⓣ978/741-3570, ⓦwww.witchdungeon.com), occupying a nineteenth-century clapboard church situated on the site of the prison where the accused witches were locked up. Inside you're again treated to reconstructions of key events, though this time by real people. Afterwards the actors escort you to a re-created "dungeon," where you see that some of the prison cells were no bigger than a telephone booth. If all this feels a bit too theatrical, head to the simple and moving **Witch Trials Memorial**, at Charter and Liberty streets, a series of stone blocks etched with the names of the hanged. The memorial is wedged into a corner of the **Old Burying Point Cemetery**, where one witch judge, **John Hathorne**, forebear of Salem's most famous son, Nathaniel Hawthorne, is buried. The author of *The Scarlet Letter* added a "w" to his name in an attempt to exorcise the shame.

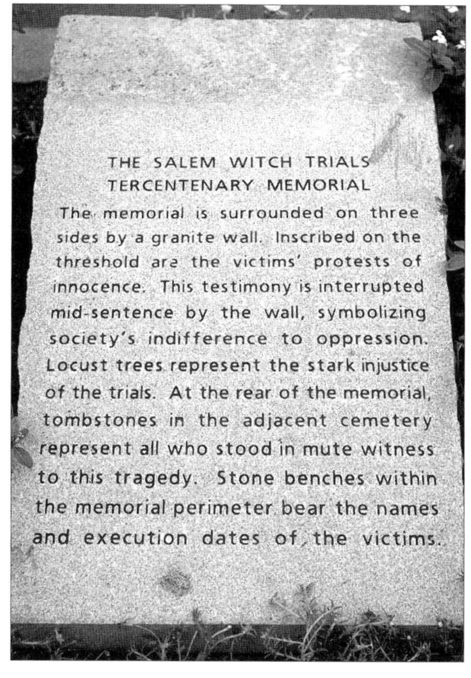

△ Witch Trials memorial

Peabody Essex Museum

The best thing going in Salem is the newly renovated **Peabody Essex Museum**, at East India Square (daily 10am–5pm; $13; ⓣ978/745-9500, ⓦwww.pem.org), the oldest continuously operating museum in the US. The museum's vast, modern space incorporates more than thirty galleries displaying art and artifacts from around the world that illustrate Salem's past importance as a major point of interaction and trade between the East and West. Founded by ship captains in 1799 to exhibit their exotic items obtained while overseas, the museum also boasts the biggest collection of nautical paintings in the world. Other galleries hold Chinese and Japanese export art, Asian, Oceanic, and African ethnological artifacts, American decorative arts, and, in a preserved house that the museum administers, court documents from the witch trials. A creatively curated whaling exhibit features not only the requisite scrimshaw but also Ambrose Garneray's famous 1835 painting, *Attacking the Right Whale*, as well as the gaping lower jaw of a sperm whale. Upstairs highlights include a cavernous central gallery with the fanciful figureheads from now-demolished Salem ships, and the reconstructed salon from America's first yacht, *Cleopatra's Barge*, which took to the seas in 1816. The museum's prize possession, however, is **Yin Yu Tang**, a sixteen-room Qing dynasty house that the museum purchased, dismantled, and brought to Salem to foster awareness and appreciation of Chinese culture. Though the house has been open to the public since 2003, it's still a hot ticket: admission is included with a museum ticket, but you still must reserve a time at the front desk to see it. Only visitors who arrive before noon are guaranteed a time slot.

Salem Harbor

Little of Salem's original waterfront remains, although the two-thousand-foot-long **Derby Wharf** is still standing, fronted by the imposing Federalist-style **Custom House** at its head. These two, and ten other mainly residential buildings once belonging to sea captains and craftsmen, help comprise the **Salem Maritime National Historic Site**, which maintains a **visitors' center** at 174 Derby St (daily 9am–5pm; tours of four houses including the Custom House $5; ⓣ978/740-1650, ⓦwww.nps.gov/sama). The Custom House is where Nathaniel Hawthorne worked as chief executive officer for three years, a stint which he later described as "slavery." The office-like interior is rather bland, as is the warehouse in the rear, with displays of tea chests and such. Park rangers give free tours of the adjacent **Derby House** (daily 9am–5pm), whose millionaire owner, Elias Derby, received it as a wedding gift from his father; it overlooked the harbor to better allow him to monitor his shipping empire. Next door, the **West India Goods Store** emulates a nineteenth-century supply shop by peddling nautical accoutrements like fishhooks and ropes, as well as supplies like molasses candy and "gunpowder tea," a tightly rolled, high-grade Chinese green tea.

The most famous sight in the waterfront area is undoubtedly the **House of the Seven Gables**, at 54 Turner St (daily: July–Oct 10am–7pm, Nov–June 10am–5pm, closed first half of Jan; $12; ⓣ978/744-0991, ⓦwww.7gables.org), a rambling old mansion by the sea that served as inspiration for Hawthorne's eponymous novel. Forever the "rusty wooden house with seven acutely peaked gables" that Hawthorne described, this 1688 three-story house is also notable for its bricked-off "Secret Stairway" that leads to a small room. Standard tours cover the building's history and architecture, but during the Halloween season evening tours called "Spirits of the Gables" and "The Gables by Lantern Light" are also offered for those who prefer to hear ghost stories. The author's birthplace, the **Nathaniel Hawthorne House**, a small, nondescript pre-1750 structure, has also been moved to the grounds.

The McIntire District

The witch attractions pick up again at the so-called **Witch House**, west of the Essex Mall at 310 Essex St (daily: mid-March to June 10am–4.30pm, July–Aug 10am–6pm, Sept–Nov 10am–4.30pm; $6; ⓣ978/744-0180), the well-preserved former home of Judge Jonathan Corwin where the preliminary examinations of the accused took place. For those itching for another witch museum, this one offers more history than most, with real artifacts combined with reconstructed ones. It's also a good point of departure for exploring the **McIntire District**, a square mile of sea captains' homes west of downtown between Federal and Broad streets. The most picturesque stretch of these mansions, built after the Revolutionary War for old salts who wanted to escape the congested waterfront, is along **Chestnut Street**. Of these, the **Stephen Phillips Memorial Trust House**, at no. 34 (mid-May to Oct Mon–Sat 10am–4.30pm; free; ⓣ978/744-0440, ⓦwww

.phillipsmuseum.org), is the only one open to the public. It's a good break from the supernatural, and worth seeing for its trove of bric-a-brac from around the world, including Chinese porcelain, oriental rugs, and Fijian throwing clubs.

Eating and drinking

Though Salem has a decent range of places to **eat** and **drink**, there's nothing too out of the ordinary – unsurprising in a town this tourist-oriented. Most of the top seafood spots are situated near the harbor.

Bella Luna Café 62 Wharf St ⓣ978/744-5555. A bistro-style restaurant where you'll find blackened seafood, pastas with sun-dried tomatoes, and other trendy fare at reasonable prices.

Grapevine 26 Congress St ⓣ978/745-9335. Top-notch, expensive restaurant with exotic dishes like Romesco mussels, roasted red snapper with Thai sauce, and good vegetarian options.

Lyceum Bar and Grill 43 Church St ⓣ978/745-7665. Affordable Yankee cooking with modern updates at this popular eatery. Try their grilled pork tenderloin with goat cheese polenta.

Nathaniel's at the *Hawthorne Hotel*, 18 Washington Square ⓣ978/825-4311. One of two restaurants in the hotel, and the fancier by far, creating moderately priced concoctions like rope-grown mussels steamed in ale with roasted shallots.

Red's Restaurant 15 Central St ⓣ978/745-3527. Downright cheap and hearty breakfast and lunch fare served in a stone house built in 1700; the hamburger special costs a mere $3.

Rockafellas 231 Essex St ⓣ978/745-2411. Standard, reasonably priced American menu including pizza, ribs, large salads, and prize-winning clam chowder. The bar serves creative cocktails, and there's live music nearly every night.

Salem Diner 70 Loring Ave ⓣ978/741-7918. Your basic coffeeshop offerings in an original 1941 Sterling Streamliner diner car, one of only four remaining in the US. Breakfast and lunch only.

Marblehead

Just a few miles on from Salem, **MARBLEHEAD** sits on a peninsula thrusting out into Massachusetts Bay, its rocky shoreline cliffs overlooking a wide natural harbor – which has helped to make it one of the East Coast's biggest yachting centers. Thanks to its occupants' affluence, though, and, strangely, a severe shortage of parking, Marblehead has managed to escape the ravages of rampant commercialism typical of such playpens.

Founded by hardy fishermen from Devon and the English West Country in 1629, Marblehead prides itself on being the birthplace of the US Navy. Originally part of Salem, whose harbor it sits opposite, Marblehead gained its **independence** in 1648 and was incorporated as a town the following year. It became a thriving **fishing** and **trading port**, especially in the years leading up to the Revolution, and by 1760 was the sixth largest town in the colonies, with a population in excess of five thousand. Any aspirations to become one of the nation's great cities were soon dashed, however, after Marblehead sent a regiment to fight in the war that successfully repelled 4000 British in Pelham, New York. Their prowess was recognized by George Washington, who commissioned the local schooner *Hannah*, and four subsequent made-in-Marblehead vessels for use in what became the US Navy. Ironically, his nod to their efforts effectively wiped out the town's prospering commercial fishing trade. Though fishing made a brief comeback, followed by shoemaking, it's boating that the town has become known for. In fact, Marblehead is at its most animated during the annual **Race Week** (the last week of July).

Winding streets lined with old clapboard houses trail down to the waterfront in testimony to the thriving early colonial community, most of them quite modest, their tiny gardens witness to the fact that only fishermen, not farmers, lived downtown. A bit further back from the oceanfront, along **Washington Street**, are the much larger and more sumptuous homes of the wealthy merchants who prospered during the pre-Revolutionary period. Among them is the 1768 **Jeremiah Lee Mansion** (June–Oct Tues–Sat 10am–4pm, Sun 1–4pm; $5; ⓣ781/631-1069), the Georgian home of the eponymous shipping magnate, who imported the decorative materials, including English wallpaper and South American mahogany, for his magnificent home. In fact, Lee's wallpaper is the only eighteenth-century hand-painted paper in existence today. Nearby, at the early eighteenth-century **King Hooper Mansion**, 8 Hooper St (Tues–Sat noon–4pm, Sun 1–5pm; free; ⓣ781/631-2608, ⓦwww.marbleheadarts.org), you can contrast the slave quarters with a lavish third-floor ballroom, and check out local art as well. While you're in the area, stop by **Abbot Hall** on Washington Square (July–Oct weekdays at least 8am–5pm, weekends at least 11am–5pm; call for off-season hours; ⓣ781/631-0000), Marblehead's red-brick town hall, which houses Archibald Willard's famous patriotic painting *The Spirit of '76*.

To get a sweeping view of the port, head to **Fort Sewall**, at the end of Front Street, the remnants of fortifications the British built in 1644 and then enlarged one hundred years later to protect the harbor from French cruisers; these defenses later shielded the USS *Constitution* in the War of 1812. Closer to the center of town, but with similar panoramic views, is **Old Burial Hill**, Orne Street, which holds the graves of more than six hundred Revolutionary War soldiers.

Practicalities

The Chamber of Commerce maintains an **information booth** at the corner of Pleasant and Essex streets (late May to early Sept Mon–Fri 2–6pm, Sat 11am–6pm, Sun 11am–5pm; ⓣ781/639-8469) and an **office** at 62 Pleasant St (Mon–Fri 9am–5pm; ⓣ781/631-2868, ⓦwww.visitmarblehead.com). Of the posh places to **stay** in Marblehead, most of which are B&Bs, best is the central *Harbor Light Inn*, 58 Washington St (ⓣ781/631-2186, ⓦwww.harborlightinn.com; ❼); it's elegant, if a little stuffy, and has a heated outdoor pool in summer. A more casual option is the *Pheasant Hill B&B*, 71 Bubier Rd (ⓣ781/639-4799, ⓦwww.pheasanthill.com; ❻), whose three private rooms with water views are set back from town a bit. Given Marblehead's waterfront location, it's not surprising that seafood headlines the town's **dining** options. For a snack, try *Flynnie's at the Beach*, on Devereaux Beach (ⓣ781/639-3035; summer only), for inexpensive fish and chips. Alternatively, *The Landing*, 81 Front St, serves pricier fresh seafood in a room overlooking the harbor. You can also tuck into a reasonably priced steak at *The Barnacle*, 141 Front St (ⓣ781/631-4246), while sitting on an outdoor waterfront terrace.

Cape Ann

Gloucester and **Rockport** are the two principal, but quite different, towns on low-key **Cape Ann**, which reaches into the Atlantic some forty miles north of Boston. The area draws plenty of visitors mainly on account of its salty air and seafood restaurants, but there aren't many sights per se. In fact the best thing about the place is its unspoiled scenery, the kind of setting that inspired T.S. Eliot, who came here for his family holidays – "The Dry Salvages" in the third of his *Four Quartets* refers to a group of offshore rocks. Rocky headlands,

△ The Dry Salvages

lighthouses, and sea spray define Cape Ann more than the little towns and villages do, and it's quite easy to feel very far from civilization here, if only for an afternoon. From I-95, Rte-128 East will take you all the way to Gloucester, then it's either Rte-127 or scenic Rte-127A to Rockport.

Gloucester

Founded in 1623, gritty **GLOUCESTER** is the oldest fishing port in Massachusetts, though years of over-fishing the once cod-rich waters have robbed the town of any aura of affluence, and federal regulations threaten to reduce the current fleet of fishing boats still further. The town has long had an artistic identity, initially established by the painter **Winslow Homer**, who summered out in the harbor on Ten Pound Island in 1880. Homer was followed by a bevy of other artists who set up a colony on **Rocky Neck**, just east of downtown, where they converted fishermen's shacks into studios. The now run-down district, whose modern galleries are salt-box shacks selling the kinds of tacky nautical prints that end up in motel bathrooms, was once the temporary home of Rudyard Kipling, whose 1897 novel *Captains Courageous* involved a Gloucester ship. At the **visitors' center**, located down by the harbor at Stage Fort Park, Rte-127 (June to mid-Oct daily 9am–5pm; ⓣ978/281-8865), can give you a map detailing area beaches. Though each is small and without many waves, the beaches here are often less crowded than those in nearby Rockport.

The Town

Coming into town you'll likely be drawn toward one of Gloucester's sources of pride, the 1923 bronze *Man at the Wheel*, right on the waterfront near the drawbridge, an overhyped statue of a fisherman at the wheel of a ship. To learn a bit more about the port's fishing past, head to the excellent **Cape Ann Historical Museum**, near the docks at 27 Pleasant St (Tues–Sat 10am–5pm; $6.50; ⓣ978/283-0455, ⓦwww.capeannhistoricalmuseum.org), where the history of Gloucester and Cape Ann is well documented through old photographs, fishing and quarrying implements, and paintings of mostly local scenes by a variety of

Whale-watching and sailing on Cape Ann

One of the most popular and exhilarating activities along this stretch of coast is **whale-watching**; trips depart from Gloucester, Salem, and Newburyport to the important whale feeding grounds of Stellwagen Bank and Jeffreys Ledge, where an abundance of plankton and small fish provide sufficient calories (around one million a day) to keep a fifty-foot, 25-ton humpback happy. Ongoing narration throughout the trips from a marine scientist interprets the sightings and behavior of all whales and marine life encountered, and researchers are available to answer questions on the return journey. Several of the companies rely on reports from deep-sea fishing boats which radio back the location of the feeding whales, so the whale-watch boats know where to go before they even leave the docks. Most claim a 99 percent or higher sighting record, though this does not necessarily mean that you're going to see a whale performing a photogenic pirouette just a few feet away – sometimes you may catch no more than a glimpse of a tail. Most companies also have a guarantee that if you don't see a whale you'll get a free pass to come back anytime.

The best place to begin is Gloucester Harbor, home to the **Whale Center of New England**, with a small **museum** (Mon–Sat 9am–5pm; free; ⓣ978/281-6351) featuring pieces of whale skeleton and an enormous baleen, used by the great beasts to filter their food. Whale-watching companies include the Yankee Fleet, 75 Essex Ave (ⓣ978/283-0313 or 1-800/WHALING, ⓦwww.yankeefleet.com); Captain Bill's (ⓣ978/283-6995 or 1-800/339-4253, ⓦwww.captainbillswhalewatch.com), next to *Captain Carlo's* restaurant, in the Whale Center building; and Cape Ann Whale Watch, at Rose's Wharf (ⓣ1-800/877-5110, ⓦwww.caww.com). During the summer each offers two daily four-hour trips (around $38), with one a day in the spring and early fall. An alternative is a **schooner trip** aboard the *Thomas E. Lannon*. Modeled after a 1903 sword-fishing schooner, the 65ft vessel takes up to 49 passengers on two-hour sailing tours of the Gloucester coast, with up to four sailings daily from Seven Seas Wharf at the *Gloucester House Restaurant* (July & Aug 10am–8pm, early Sept–Oct 15 weekends once daily; $33; ⓣ978/281-6634, ⓦwww.schooner.org).

artists including Homer, Milton Avery, Augustus Buhler, and Gloucester-born marine artist Fitz Hugh Lane. The museum also has a good whaling and fishing section, including three wooden boats.

Over in East Gloucester, at Eastern Point off Rte-127A, **Beauport** (tours hourly: mid-May to mid-Sept Mon–Fri 10am–4pm, mid-Sept to mid-Oct Mon–Sat 10am–4pm; $10; ⓣ978/283-0800), is a 45-room mansion perched on the rocks overlooking Gloucester Harbor. Started in 1907 as a simple summer retreat for the collector and interior designer Henry Davis Sleeper, the house evolved over the following 27 years into a gabled, turreted villa filled with vast collections of European, American, and Asian objects. Sleeper wasn't interested in the historical integrity of his aggregation so much as the aesthetic balance, and the house is an intriguing mixture of styles and themes, each room strikingly different from the next, with cozy, dark Colonial rooms leading directly into bright, open Mediterranean-style rooms with jaw-dropping ocean views. The tour, which meanders through the structure, provides a fascinating view of the lifestyles of the early twentieth-century rich and famous.

More unusual is the **Hammond Castle Museum**, 80 Hesperus Ave, on the harbor's southwestern corner (June–Aug daily 10am–5pm, Sept–May weekends only 10am–3pm; $12; ⓣ978/283-7673, ⓦwww.hammondcastle.org). This was once the home of the eccentric financier and inventor John Hays Hammond, Jr – he made some advances in guided missile and radio communications technology – who desired to bring medieval European relics back to the US. And he succeeded: the austere fortress, which overlooks the ocean and site of the spot that inspired Longfellow's poem *The Wreck of the Hesperus*, is brimming with them, from armor and tapestries to the elaborately carved wooden facade of a fifteenth-century French baker – not to mention the partially crushed skull of one of Columbus's shipmates. Also inside the castle, a murky 30,000-gallon pool can, at the switch of a lever, change from fresh to sea water; it's said that Hammond himself liked to swan dive into it from his balcony.

Practicalities

Gloucester is just over an hour by **commuter rail** from Boston's North Station ($6 one-way; Ⓣ617/222-3200, Ⓦwww.mbta.com); trains arrive about half a mile from the harbor. To get the most out of the town's spread-out sights and the area in general, though, you should probably get around via either a car or a bike. **Accommodation** – which is less expensive than on either Cape Cod or Martha's Vineyard – includes B&Bs like *Julietta House*, 84 Prospect St (Ⓣ978/281-2300, Ⓦwww.juliettahouse.com; ❻), and *The Harborview Inn*, 71 Western Ave (Ⓣ978/283-2277 or 1-800/299-6696, Ⓦwww.harborviewinn.com; ❻), both of which are quiet, friendly, and minutes from all of Gloucester's attractions. A handful of motels also serve the area, several of which with impressive water views, such as the *Cape Ann Motor Inn*, 33 Rockport Rd (Ⓣ978/281-2900 or 1-800/464-VIEW, Ⓦwww.capeannmotorinn.com; ❼), a place right on Long Beach with balconies and kitchenettes.

Many of the city's **restaurants** specialize in fresh seafood, including *Captain Carlo's* at Harbor Loop (Ⓣ978/283-6342); *The Studio*, 51 Rocky Neck Ave (Ⓣ978/283-4123; closed winters), which, though a little touristy and pricey, has deck seating right on the water; and the more creative *Madfish Bar & Grill*, just down the road at 77 Rocky Neck Ave (Ⓣ978/281-4554; closed winters). If you're not the mood for seafood, *Alchemy*, 3 Duncan St (Ⓣ978/281-3997), is open year-round serving Asian-American fusion. For a little **nightlife**, the best places to start are bars like *The Crows Nest*, 334 Main St (Ⓣ978/281-2965), long a fisherman's hangout, and the *Blackburn Tavern*, 2 Main St (Ⓣ978/282-1919), a cozy neighborhood pub with live music.

Rockport

ROCKPORT, about five miles north of Gloucester, is the more scenically situated of the two, and also the more lively and social, with children filling the many ice-cream shops and young couples crowding the bars and clamshacks. Like Gloucester, Rockport began as a fishing village before transforming into an important granite-quarrying center, a business that fizzled out during the 1920s and 1930s and hasn't found much of a replacement since. The drive between the towns, along Rte-127A, is particularly beautiful: it's along this road, just to the south of Rockport, that you'll be able to spot Eliot's "Dry Salvages."

From early on, Rockport attracted summer vacationers and artists, drawn by the picturesque harbor and surrounding shingled shacks, and has some renown as a one-time artists' colony: a red lobster shed near the harbor's edge has been christened "Motif #1" because it's been painted so many times. Works by contemporary local artists, some of them terribly kitsch, can be seen at the **Rockport Art Association**, 12 Main St (mid-May to mid-Oct Mon–Sat 10am–5pm, Sun noon–5pm; Oct–Dec & March to mid-May Tues–Fri 10am–4pm, Sat 10am–5pm, Sun noon–5pm; free; Ⓣ978/546-6604, Ⓦwww.rockportartassn.org), and at a number of small shops and galleries throughout town. The main drag is a thin peninsula called **Bearskin Neck**, lined with old saltbox fishermen's cottages that have been transformed into art galleries and restaurants. The neck rises as it reaches the sea, and there's a nice view of the rocky harbor from its end. Though there's not much else to do along this strip, it's a fine place to hang out and grab a bite to eat.

Just outside of Rockport in Pigeon Cove, everything inside the aptly named **Paper House**, on Pigeon Hill St (daily April–Oct 10am–5pm; free), is made of shellacked paper, from chairs and a piano (keys excepted) to a desk fashioned from copies of the *Christian Science Monitor*. It's the end result of a twenty-year project undertaken in 1922 by a local mechanical engineer who "always resented the daily waste of newspaper."

Practicalities

Rockport is the **last stop** on the Rockport Line from Boston's North Station ($6 one-way; ⓣ617/222-3200, ⓦwww.mbta.com). The town has plenty of **accommodation**, mostly in inns and B&Bs situated near the center; among these, the *Pleasant Street Inn*, at no. 17 (ⓣ978/546-3916 or 1-800/541-3915, ⓦwww.pleasantstreetinn.net; ⑤), is a gracious eight-room Victorian inn perched on a knoll overlooking the village; a separate carriage house contains a two-bedroom apartment. There's also the delightful *Addison Choate Inn*, 49 Broadway (ⓣ978/546-7543 or 1-800/245-7543, ⓦwww.addisonchoateinn.com; ⑦), a Greek Revival house with a lovely shaded porch, homey wallpapered rooms, and a complimentary breakfast buffet. At the *Bearskin Neck Motor Lodge*, at the end of the spit with most of the town's shops and restaurants (ⓣ1-877/507-6272, ⓦwww.rockportusa.com/bearskin; ⑦), every one of the simple rooms has a water view.

Like Gloucester, Rockport's **restaurants** serve moderately priced fresh seafood; the added bonus of a waterfront view is often the only distinction between them. The most spare is *Roy Moore Lobster Company*, on Bearskin Neck (ⓣ978/546-6696), with lobster by the pound and a nice back porch; the *Greenery Restaurant*, 15 Dock Square (ⓣ978/546-9593), has a pleasant atmosphere with a light seafood and vegetarian menu, but no seaside view. Farther down Bearskin Neck is the more-upscale *My Place by the Sea* (ⓣ978/546-9667), with a stupendous waterfront setting to compliment the delicate entrees.

Ipswich and Essex

Little **IPSWICH**, a few miles northwest of Gloucester along Rte-133, doesn't really have a town center – it's just houses and scenery, with a lovely beach to match. Even if you're staying in more active Gloucester or Rockport, it's worth the drive to visit **Crane's Beach** for the day over the smaller beaches closer to town. Crane's is part of the Crane Memorial Reservations, Argilla Road (daily 8am–sunset), four miles of beautiful sand lining Ipswich Bay. There's a large parking lot that fills up on summer weekends, despite a $20-per-car parking fee; weekday visitors get charged $10. Ipswich's other claim to fame is that it has more pre-1725

Rte-127's coastal trail

Rte-127A ends shortly after Rockport, after which you can catch 127 South back inland, or continue along Scenic 127 North to **Halibut Point State Park**, a beautiful stretch of rocky, wooded coast with **hiking trails** to the northernmost tip of Cape Ann. From there, 127 turns back in toward Gloucester and Essex, but stays close to the coast all the way, yielding majestic vistas of ocean and coves. It's one of the most **scenic drives** you'll find along the Massachusetts coast.

houses than any other community in the country. Built in 1640, the double-gabled **John Whipple House**, 1 South Village Green (May to mid-Oct Wed–Sat 10am–4pm, Sun 1–4pm; $7; ⓣ978/356-2811), was one of the nation's first homes to be restored – in 1898 – and is filled with a variety of antiques and Arthur Wesley Dow paintings; an outdoor herb garden contains some fifty varieties of medicinal plants. Admission includes entry to the nearby **John Heard House**, 54 S Main St (same hours as Whipple), a 1795 sea captain's home built in the Federal style, with Chinese and early American furnishings and a collection of carriages.

Ascend Castle Hill for a good view of the oceanside and to see the **Great House**, 290 Argilla Rd (tours late May to mid-Oct Wed & Thurs 10am–4pm, grounds open year-round; tour $10, grounds $8 per vehicle on the weekend, $5 weekdays, $3 off-season; ⓣ978/356-4351), a reproduction 59-room English-style mansion built by plumbing tycoon Richard Crane in the 1920s; you might recognize it as the setting for the movie *The Witches of Eastwick*. It's often rented out for private events, so call ahead.

To best soak up the pristine tidal flats, take a boat out to the **Crane Wildlife Refuge** (daily 8am–4pm; $7; ⓣ978/356-4351), a spectacular 650-acre expanse of dunes, woodlands, and five islands, all maintained by the Trustees of Reservations, a historical conservation group that runs seasonal twice-a-day (10am & 2pm) tours of the refuge aboard the *Osprey*, a 22-seater pontoon. The trip includes a stop at **Hog Island**, where the film *The Crucible* was filmed; you can hike up to the top of the island for great tri-state views.

The former shipbuilding town of **ESSEX**, off Rte-1A, though somewhat notable as an antiques center, should be visited primarily for the splendid **Essex Shipbuilding Museum**, right in the center of the village at 66 Main St (June–Sept Wed–Mon 10am–5pm, Oct–May Sat & Sun 10am–5pm; $7; ⓣ978/768-7541, ⓦwww.essexshipbuildingmuseum.org), where more than four thousand ships have been constructed over the years, including schooners, steamers, and yachts. The museum traces their history through models, tools, and old photographs. At the **Shipyard**, also part of the museum, you can see the *Evelina M. Goulart*, one of five surviving Essex-built schooners, drydocked near the spot where she was first launched in 1927.

Practicalities

Among the few places to **stay** in these parts is the *George Fuller House*, in Essex at 148 Main St (ⓣ978/768-7766 or 1-800/477-0148, ⓦwww.cape-ann.com/fuller-house; ❻), a rambling old Federal home with attractive, air-conditioned rooms, some featuring views over the marshes, and a full breakfast. Cheaper is the *Whittier Motel*, 120 County Rd, Ipswich (ⓣ978/356-5205 or 1-877/418-0622, ⓦwww.whittiermotel.com; ❺; open June–Oct), an unattractive roadside inn, but close to the local attractions. For a treat, a beautiful house on the Crane Estate has been transformed into a boutique B&B, the *Inn at Castle Hill* (ⓣ978/412-2555, ⓦinnatcastlehill.thetrustees.org; ❽), with ten spotless and TV-less rooms, each with its own character and some with water views.

Most of the best area **restaurants** are in Essex. *Woodman's*, 121 Main St (ⓣ978/768-6057), lays claim to being the first restaurant to serve fried clams; less famous, but certainly no less good, is *J.T. Farnham's Seafood and Grill*, Rte-133 (ⓣ978/768-6643; closed Dec–Mar). Over in Ipswich, try the *Choate Bridge Pub* on Market Square (ⓣ978/356-2931) for standard pub fare like steak sandwiches, burgers, and pizza, or for a more upscale meal head to *1640 Hart House* – named for the building's age – at 51 Linebrook St (ⓣ978/356-1640), serving chicken, pasta, and steak.

Newburyport and around

Just south of the New Hampshire border, **NEWBURYPORT** is Massachusetts' smallest city and one of its most appealing, a pleasant and unsullied mix of upscale boutiques and historic homes that still functions as a fishing port. Its location at the mouth of the Merrimack River proved convenient to the English fishermen who settled here as early as 1635, and to shipbuilders in the two centuries that followed, resulting in the accumulation of an enormous amount of shipbuilding wealth, attested to by the imposing mansions on **High Street**, on the northern rim of town. Today Newburyport exudes a real flavor of the past, but the **Market Square Historic District**, with its bricked sidewalks, old lampposts, and upscale shops and eateries, is not quite as historic as you'd think – a fire destroyed the area in 1811, and everything had to be rebuilt.

Your best bet is simply to stroll the city-center streets, especially **State**, sample some incredibly fresh seafood, and watch the boats from the Waterfront Park and Promenade, which faces the Merrimack River as it spills into the ocean. Near the waterfront, the **Custom House Maritime Museum**, 25 Water St, isn't worth visiting for its exhibits, though it also serves as a **visitors' center** for the area. On the other side of downtown, the handsome 22-room Federal-style **Cushing House**, 98 High St (May–Oct Tues–Fri 10am–4pm, Sat noon–4pm; $5; ⓣ978/462-2681, ⓦwww.newburyhist.com), once home to Caleb Cushing, the nation's first ambassador to China, has among its rather musty antique furnishings a lovely hand-painted Dutch baby cradle in the canopy bedroom. All told, you're better off skipping the museums in favor of milling about the eerie **Old Hill Burying Ground**, adjacent to the beautiful Bartlett Mall on High Street, where many Revolutionary War veterans and prominent sea captains are interred.

Plum Island

Plum Island, an eleven-mile barrier beach just south of Newburyport on Rte-1A, is mostly occupied by the remote **Parker River National Wildlife Refuge** (daily dawn–dusk; $5 per car, $2 walk-in; ⓦwww.plum-island.com), a bird-watching sanctuary located on the migratory route of a vast number of different species. In summer the refuge is populated by great blue herons, glossy ibises, and snowy egrets, though there's a less impressive array year-round. The beach itself here gets better, and less developed, the further south you go. Outside of the refuge, the beach is free save for a $10 parking fee.

Practicalities

If you don't have your own transport, Newburyport is accessible by commuter **rail** from Boston's North Station. When you arrive at the train station, it's less than a mile walk to the center of town. Though the town is really best for spending an afternoon or stopping over for dinner, there are a couple of good places to **stay**. Dating from 1803, the *Clark Currier Inn*, 45 Green St (ⓣ978/465-8363 or 1-800/360-6582, ⓦwww.clarkcurrierinn.com; ❺), has plenty of common areas in which to relax, including an outdoor garden with gazebo and pond, while *The Essex Street Inn*, at 7 Essex St (ⓣ978/465-3148, ⓦwww.essexstreetinn.com; ❺), is an attractive Colonial-style house right off the main drag, State Street, with beautiful large rooms and private baths.

Two of the more reliable spots in town for a meal that won't break the bank are *Glenn's*, 44 Merrimac St (ⓣ978/465-3811), where you can savor big portions of grilled seafood, and *Agavé*, 50 State St (ⓣ978/499-0428), an excellent Mexican bistro with both traditional and seafood-oriented dishes (not to mention tequila). On Plum Island try the *Plum Island Grille* on Sunset Boulevard (☎978/463-2290), which serves upscale food and a delicious Sunday brunch.

The South Shore

The **South Shore** makes a clean sweep of the Massachusetts coast from suburban Quincy, just south of Boston, to the former whaling port of New Bedford, west of Cape Cod. **Plymouth** is the only really tourist-driven place along this stretch, on account of the **pilgrim** associations; if you're not interested in reliving the coming of the *Mayflower*, the town, while pleasant enough, will probably not merit more than a few hours' exploration. **New Bedford** has fewer sights, one of which is a well-conceived whaling museum, but its historic associations feel a bit more authentic than those of Plymouth. Still, the South Shore's biggest draw may be its unclogged seaside **villages** and miles of coastal scenery that in other parts of the country would doubtless have already succumbed to strip-mall mania; likely the only reason this hasn't happened is because everybody is too geared up for Cape Cod and the islands beyond to stop off. You won't be able to stop yourself, however, without your own wheels: while Plymouth and Quincy are easily accessible by commuter rail from Boston, the rest of the towns aren't.

Route 3A: Quincy to Duxbury

Although Rte-3 is the most direct route from Boston to Cape Cod, you'll hardly catch a glimpse of the coast from it. A better alternative is to take **Rte-3A**, which splits off from I-93 just south of Boston. Although not by any means a "scenic drive," the road does go through some pretty residential neighborhoods and affords occasional harbor and beach views. The first town you hit on this route is **QUINCY**, not much more than part of the urban sprawl of metropolitan Boston, but which bills itself rather imperiously as the "City of Presidents" – it was the birthplace of John Adams and his son John Quincy Adams, the second and sixth presidents of the United States. This grasp at heritage is preserved at the **Adams National Historic Site**, 1250 Hancock St (mid-April to Nov daily 9am–5pm, grounds open year-round; trolley tours $2; ☎617/770-1175, Ⓦwww.nps.gov/adam). It's highlighted by the Adams Mansion, residence of the family for four generations and boasting, out in the garden, the magnificent cathedral-ceilinged **Stone Library**, which houses presidential books and manuscripts. Just a short walk away in the grounds stands the modest 1681 saltbox where the elder Adams entered the world, and adjacent to that, the 1663 house where his son was born.

Quincy can be reached on the **T** red line from Boston (☎617/222-3200, Ⓦwww.mbta.com). There's nowhere really to **stay** here besides a few large chain hotels and motels which straddle the expressway to Boston and the surrounding roads. There are, however, some decent places for a bite to **eat**: *Tullio's*,

150 Hancock St (Ⓣ617/471-3400), does delectable pastas, while lighter fare, including good wraps and burritos, is available at *Blackboard Café*, 1515 Hancock St (Ⓣ617/847-1605).

Hingham

After a few twists and turns through heavy industrial areas, Rte-3A opens up to picturesque **HINGHAM**. Founded in 1635, it's the kind of affluent place you would more expect to find on Cape Cod, though considerably quieter and less visited. **Main Street** is lined with small, black-shuttered eighteenth- and nineteenth-century houses, none of which is open to the public; in fact, the only house in Hingham you can visit is the **Old Ordinary**, 21 Lincoln St (mid-June to early Sept Tues–Sat 1.30–4.30pm; $3; Ⓦwww.hinghamhistorical.org), its name a reference to "ordinary" meals at fixed prices that used to be served at this former stagecoach stop. Today it's the house museum of the Hingham Historical Society, with a tap room set up as it would have been when the house was a tavern, and a dining room with various Hepplewhite and Chippendale furnishings. Back on Main Street, at no. 107, the **Old Ship Church**, whose roof resembles an inverted ship's hull (it was built by ship carpenters), claims to be the oldest building in continuous ecclesiastical service in the United States – since 1681. Behind the church an attractive garden-style cemetery offers good views of the harbor. If you want to get a bit closer to the water, head to the peninsula of parkland known as **World's End** (daily 9am–5pm; parking $4.50); the five-mile spit isn't quite the end of the world, but it's a sufficiently nice place for a walk or picnic, with impressive views of the distant Boston skyline.

Cohasset and Duxbury

Farther south is the quiet, moneyed town of **COHASSET**, where according to maritime historian Samuel Eliot, "the granite skeleton of Massachusetts protrudes for the last time." Captain John Smith, who in 1607 had helped establish the first permanent English colony in North America at Jamestown, Virginia, disembarked briefly here in 1614 in his initial exploration of New England. Make your detour at the enclave of **Cohasset Village**, slightly east of Rte-3A, a pristine blink-and-miss-it town featuring a wide town green perhaps recognizable from the movie *The Witches of Eastwick*. From here, a drive along **Jerusalem Road** reveals stunning views of the coast and rambling (private) mansions.

Another fifteen miles down 3A is affluent **DUXBURY**, settled in 1627 by Myles Standish and other Plymouth Pilgrims who needed more land for their cows. It has a beautiful five-mile barrier **beach** on Rte-139, access to which is nearly impossible due to residents-only parking. You can, however, get to isolated smaller beaches by parking along the residential streets. The only real sight of note is the **John Alden House**, 105 Alden St (mid-May to mid-Oct Mon–Sat noon–4pm; $5; Ⓦwww.alden.org), originally built in 1653 for John and Priscilla Alden, passengers on the *Mayflower*, and having undergone only minimal structural change since. Check out the East Chamber, or master bedroom, with its post-and-beam construction clearly visible and canopy bed with trundle bed underneath, and the Great Room (living room), centered on an eighteenth-century gate-leg table. South of town, the **Myles Standish State Forest**, 14,000 hilly acres of mostly pine woodlands and meadows, is a good place to stretch out, traversed by hiking trails and bicycle paths and dotted with fifteen ponds. A 116-foot granite shaft at its center, the **Myles Standish Memorial**, is capped by a statue of the strident Plymouth colony captain; if it's open, head up the 125 steps inside for stunning South Shore views.

You probably won't have much need to linger in Duxbury, especially with Plymouth just down the road, but if you're looking for a place to **eat** *and* **stay**, the *Windsor House Inn*, 390 Washington St (Ⓣ781/934-0991; ❼), is an 1803 inn with two guestrooms and two suites done out with reproduction antique furniture. The restaurant specializes in moderately priced seafood (especially lobster) and meat dishes. Stop for a pastry and coffee at *French Memories*, 459 Washington St (Ⓣ781-934-9020); the cookies and the waterfront are equally delightful.

Plymouth

PLYMOUTH, dubbed "America's hometown," is one of the largest towns in area in the United States, about the same size as Boston, though its population is largely clustered around the waterfront area where the Pilgrims landed in December 1620 (they had arrived prior to this near Provincetown, on Cape Cod). Much of the town is given over to commemorating, in various degrees of taste, this event: apart from the expected crop of Pilgrim-related monuments and museums, there is little to distinguish Plymouth's concentration of fast-food restaurants, gas stations, and mini-malls from any of America's other hometowns.

The Town

The most famous – though not the most engaging – attraction in town is **Plymouth Rock**, housed in a pseudo-Greek temple by the sea where the Pilgrims are said to have first touched land. As is typical with most sites of this ilk, it is of symbolic importance only: the Pilgrims had in fact already spent several weeks on Cape Cod before landing here. Also unconvincing is the **Pilgrim Hall Museum**, 75 Court St (Feb–Dec daily 9.30am–4.30pm; $6; Ⓣ508/746-1620, Ⓦwww.pilgrimhall.org), where you enter a room filled with furniture which may or may not have come over on the *Mayflower*. Better is the **Spooner House**, 27 North St (June to early Oct Thurs–Sat 10am–4pm, tours hourly; $5; Ⓣ508/747-1240), which was home to five generations of Spooners, a noted mercantile family, and is decorated with their family heirlooms. The most interesting feature is the secret garden out back, though the tours are pretty tight affairs and you can't simply stroll the gardens at your leisure.

Since "how old is it?" is a question that seems to thread itself throughout a tour of Plymouth, it is worth stopping by two of the town's oldest structures. The **1749 Court House**

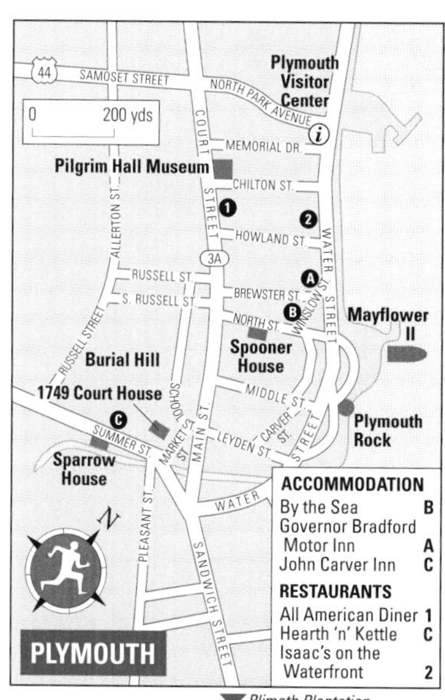

and Museum, 12 Market St (June–Oct Mon–Fri 11am–5pm, Sat–Sun noon-5pm; free; ⓣ508/830-4075), is distinguishable as America's oldest wooden courthouse. The structure nearly went the way of every other wooden courthouse in the country in the early 1950s when it was slated for demolition, but was saved as a historical site. The attached museum is little more than a collection of tools, housewares, and the usual assorted artifacts, but it's fun anyway. Just a little further south on Market Street is the **Sparrow House**, 42 Summer St (daily except Wed 10am–5pm; donation requested; ⓣ508/747-1240). It's the oldest house in Plymouth, built in 1640 by one of the *Mayflower's* brave passengers. The ground-floor gallery contains local pottery and crafts while the upper rooms are decorated in the threadbare style of early settlers.

Mayflower II and Plimoth Plantation

The best way to spend your time in Plymouth is at the newly restored replica of the *Mayflower*, called the **Mayflower II**, at the State Pier in Plymouth Harbor (April–Nov daily 9am–5pm; $8; ⓣ508/746-1622, ⓦwww.plimoth.org). Built in Britain by English craftsmen following the detailed and historically accurate plans of an American naval architect at MIT, the *Mayflower II* was ceremoniously docked in Plymouth in 1957 and given to America as a gesture of goodwill. This version meticulously reproduces the buff brown hull and red strapwork ornamentation that are typical of a seventeenth-century merchant vessel – which is what the original *Mayflower* was, before being outfitted for passengers prior to its horrendous 66-day journey across the Atlantic. Notice the hawthorn, or English mayflower, carved into the stern; whether the original ship was so adorned is unclear. On board, role-playing "interpreters" in period garb, meant to be representatives of the 102 Pilgrim passengers, field visitors' questions. Below the main deck, you can have a look at the "tween decks" area, where the Pilgrims' cramped cabins would have been.

Similar in approach and authenticity is the **Plimoth Plantation**, three miles south of town off Rte-3 (April–Nov daily 9am–5pm; $21; ⓣ508/746-1622, ⓦwww.plimoth.org). The charade in which visitors are expected to participate – pretending to have stepped back into the seventeenth century – can be a little tiresome, but the sheer depth of detail ultimately wins you over. Everything you see, such as the Pilgrim Village of 1627 and the Wampanoag Indian Settlement, has been created using traditional techniques; even the farm animals were "backbred" to more closely resemble their seventeenth-century counterparts. Again, actors dressed in period garb try to bring you back in time – ask one of the pseudo-farmers what crop he's planting, or his wife what she's cooking, and you'll get an answer in an English dialect appropriate to the era and the individual's place of origin. The only portion that makes concessions to the modern age is the crafts center, where interpreters not only weave baskets, which is historically accurate, but also make pottery and ceramics, which is not (the Pilgrims had to import that stuff from England). Even the name, "Plimoth," is spelled thusly in deference to an antique map and to distinguish the Plantation from modern-day Plymouth. Depending on your level of resistance, the whole affair can be quite enjoyable. If you intend to see both the Plantation and the *Mayflower II*, you can purchase a combo ticket ($24, saving you $5) from either admissions counter.

Practicalities

Plymouth's **visitors' center**, 170 Water St (daily 9am–5pm; ⓣ508/747-7525, ⓦwww.visit-plymouth.com), stocks information on local attractions, dining, and accommodations. Plymouth & Brockton **buses** (ⓣ508/746-0378, ⓦwww.p-b.com) run back and forth to Boston, stopping at various points in downtown Plymouth. The best **accommodation** is the *John Carver Inn*, 25 Summer St (ⓣ508/746-7100 or 1-800/274-1620, ⓦwww.johncarverinn.com; ❻), a modern 79-room inn with indoor pool close to the waterfront and all the downtown attractions. Less expensive options include *By the Sea*, 22 Winslow St (ⓣ508/830-9643 or 1-800/593-9688, ⓦwww.bytheseabedandbreakfast.com; ❺; closed in winter), a harborview B&B with two spacious suites with private bath; and the *Governor Bradford*, 98 Water St (ⓣ508/746-6200, ⓦwww.governorbradford.com; ❺), another modern hotel overlooking the water.

America's hometown isn't much of a **restaurant** center, but the casual *Hearth 'n' Kettle*, in the *John Carver Inn*, is a safe bet for well-priced New England specialties, as is *Isaac's on the Waterfront*, 114 Water St (ⓣ508/830-0001), a favorite with locals who also come for the ocean views. For standard breakfast fare, drop by the *All American Diner*, 60 Court St (ⓣ508/747-4763), before 2pm any day of the week.

New Bedford and around

Though **NEW BEDFORD** is still firmly a working-class city – the whaling port, 45 miles south of Boston, remains home to one of the nation's largest fishing fleets – recent efforts at preservation and restoration, with an eye to the town's whaling heritage, have heightened the place's aesthetic appeal. The old mercantile buildings, nineteenth-century houses, and cobblestone streets in the city center now more clearly conjure up the atmosphere that inspired Herman Melville to set the beginning of *Moby Dick* here.

The **downtown** area is now called the New Bedford Whaling National Historic Park, a collection of old buildings, art galleries, and antique stores, the centerpiece of which is the remarkable **New Bedford Whaling Museum**, 18 Johnny Cake Hill (daily 9am–5pm, Thurs in summer to 9pm; $10; ⓦwww.whalingmuseum.org). Housed in a former church, the museum features the

△ New Bedford fishing boats

world's largest ship model and a half-scale version of the whaling vessel *Lagoda*, as well as scrimshaw, harpoons, artifacts retrieved by whalers from the Arctic and the Pacific, and a full-size replica of a ship's forecastle. A smaller section of the museum has the roster of the whaling ship *Acushnet*, which shows Melville as one of its crew. Here you'll also see "tally pages" from the whalemen's logbooks, with rubber stamps depicting sperm whales to indicate the ones killed (a vertical stamp meant the whale was harpooned but lost to the sea). There's also a modern building that houses the 66-foot skeleton of a blue whale named Kobo, King of the Blue Ocean, that washed up on the South Shore in 1998, and a sperm whale skeleton, which washed ashore in Nantucket in 2002.

Immediately opposite the museum stands the **Seamen's Bethel**, the famous "Whaleman's Chapel" built in 1832 and described in *Moby Dick* (May–Oct daily 10am–4pm, mid-Oct to April Mon–Fri 11am–1pm, Sat 10am–5pm, Sun 1–5pm; call ahead, though, as often closed on weekends and for private events; donation requested; ⓣ508/992 3295). The chapel features a rather small replica of the ship-shaped pulpit described in Melville's book. More evocative are the memorials to those who died at sea that line the walls; new ones continue to be added to this day. The park **visitor center**, 33 Williams St (daily 9am–5pm; ⓣ508/996-4095), has interesting guides to local history – the Underground Railroad went through here – as well as maps of the park, waterfront, and nearby **mansions**, remnants of the town's whale-derived wealth. Chief among these are the old Federalist and Victorian houses around **County Street**, of which Melville commented:

> **Had it not been for us whalemen, that tract of land would this day perhaps have been in as howling condition as the coast of Labrador . . . all these brave houses and flowery gardens came up from the Atlantic, Pacific, and Indian oceans. One and all, they were harpooned and dragged hither from the bottom of the sea.**

Generally speaking, the mansions did not belong to working ship captains, but rather to those who had turned to international trade and investment in the whaling industry. The Greek Revival **Rotch-Jones-Duff House & Garden Museum**, 396 County St (Mon–Sat 10am–4pm, Sun noon–4pm; $4; ⓦwww.rjdmuseum.org), built by a Quaker whaling captain in 1834, retains many of its original decorations and furnishings and is festooned with decadent marble fireplace mantles and oriental rugs. The formal gardens, laid out in their original style, with boxwood hedges, roses, and wildflowers, occupy an entire city block. Neighboring **Madison**, **Maple**, and **Orchard streets** also contain a number of fanciful, brightly repainted mansions. It's worth driving by – about all you can do, as they're all private – before heading out of town.

Practicalities

If you want to **stay** in New Bedford, the *Orchard Street Manor* is an atmospheric B&B at 139 Orchard St (ⓣ508/984-3475, ⓦwww.the-orchard-street-manor.com; ❻), but in reality a couple hours' wandering about town should be enough before moving on. Across the street from the visitor center, *Freestone's*, 41 Williams St (ⓣ508/993-7477), serves excellent chowder and microbrews in a restored 1877 bank, or for local flavor try the authentic Portuguese dishes at *Antonio's*, 267 Coggeshall St (ⓣ508/990-3636).

Westport

On either side of New Bedford, fronting Buzzards Bay and Rhode Island Sound, run a series of coastal villages usually consisting of little more than a post office and a general store. By far the most attractive is **WESTPORT**, on the Rhode Island state line, where the Westport River spills into the ocean, forming a natural harbor. Positioned here is **Horseneck Beach**, a two-mile-long stretch of sand that is a favorite with students from the nearby University of Massachusetts at Dartmouth, but never overcrowded because of its vast size. There's ample parking, which costs $10 per car on summer weekends ($8 during the week). For a much starker seascape, head east along Rte-88 to **East Beach**, a half-mile of pebbly shoreline once the site of dozens of homes until the hurricane of 1938 (and the subsequent hurricane of 1954) swept them away. What's left are dozens of telephone and power poles and lines, but no residences to attach themselves to.

In an area that was just far enough away from the ocean to survive the devastation is **Westport Point**, just off Rte-88, a village built on a neck of land leading down to a quay, its main street lined with the white-clapboard eighteenth- and nineteenth-century homes of sea captains. At the foot of the street, nearest the water, the charming *Paquachuck Inn*, 2056 Main Rd (Ⓣ508/636-4398, Ⓦwww.paquachuck.com; ❼), occupies an 1827 building with lovely harbor views. Nearby is a stellar seafood **restaurant** right on the water, *The Back Eddy*, 1 Bridge Rd (Ⓣ508/8636-6500); it's not cheap, but the clam and roasted corn chowder alone is worth the visit.

Fall River

The fate of **FALL RIVER**, a glum-looking town about fifteen miles west of New Bedford, will forever be linked to the sensational trial of **Lizzie Borden**, a spinster Sunday school teacher accused of the ax murders of her wealthy father and stepmother in August 1892; in many ways, the town plays up the associations. Borden was at home when the murders took place, but the prevailing notion that such brutal crimes were beyond a woman's capability bolstered her case. Her lawyer even made her wear antiquated Victorian dresses to the thirteen-day trial to help conceal her sizeable wrists. It must have worked – she was acquitted, though perhaps not in the public's opinion: as the popular rhyme goes, "Lizzie Borden took an ax and gave her mother forty whacks/When she saw what she had done, she gave her father forty-one." The **Fall River Historical Society**, 451 Rock St (April to mid-Nov Tues–Fri 9am–4.30pm, summer weekends also 1–5pm, tours on the hour; $5; Ⓦwww.lizzieborden.org), contains the inevitable exhibits of the affair, including some vintage photographs of Lizzie and her family, as well as more general information about the city, particularly its industrial heritage. There's also a **museum** at the **Lizzie Borden B&B**, 92 Second St (tours daily on the hour 11am–3pm; $8; Ⓣ508/675-7333, Ⓦwww.lizzie-borden.com), where the awful deeds were done; see also "Practicalities" below for lodging details.

More impressive than the remnants of an old murder trial is **Battleship Cove**, accessible from I-195 exit 5 at the Braga Bridge (April–June 9am–5pm, July–Aug 9am–5.30pm, Sept–Oct 9am–5pm, Oct-April 9am–4.30pm; $12; Ⓦwww.battleshipcove.org), the site of an impressive assemblage of World War II naval craft. The USS *Massachusetts*, or "Big Mammie," as she was known to the troops, is enormous, with bunks under the deck stacking five high. Visitors are really given the run of the ship, too: a welcome change from stilted tours of historic houses, and most fun for children. Of the other boats on hand, the submarine USS *Lionfish* is also worth seeing.

Practicalities

Fall River's Chamber of Commerce provides **tourist information** at its office at 200 Pocasset St (Mon–Fri 10am–4pm; Ⓣ508/676-8226, Ⓦwww

.fallriverchamber.com), but a safer bet (if you're driving) might be the **Bristol County Visitors' Bureau** (daily 9am–5pm in winter, 8am–8pm in summer; Ⓣ1-800/268-6263, Ⓦwww.bristol-county.org), located between exits 2 and 3 on I-195 eastbound in neighboring Swansea.

One of the few places to **stay** in Fall River is the campily spooky *Lizzie Borden B&B*, 92 Second St (Ⓣ508/675-7333; ❻). Macabre as it may sound, you can stay in the rooms where Lizzie's parents were found, savor the same kind of breakfast enjoyed by the family on the day of the murders, and load up on Lizzie memorabilia in the gift shop. More mundane is the *Best Western*, 360 Airport Rd (Ⓣ508/672-0011; ❺), just up the hill from Battleship Cove. Fall River supports a large Portuguese population, a fact reflected in its proliferation of Portuguese **restaurants**. The best of these is *Sagres*, 181 Columbia St (Ⓣ508/675-7018), a casual, well-priced restaurant with a good wine list and live Fado music on Friday and Saturday nights at 8pm. The International Institute of Culinary Arts is in town as well, and good upscale food can be found at their restaurant *Giorgio's The Steak House*, 30 Third St (Ⓣ508/672-8242; closed Sun & Mon).

Cuttyhunk Island

If you're really desperate to get away from the crowds, take a one-hour boat trip from Pier 3 in New Bedford out to minuscule **CUTTYHUNK ISLAND**, an entirely uncommercialized chunk of land with unpaved roads and beaches lined with glorious wildflowers throughout the summer months. Two of the best are **Channel Beach**, just a short walk from the ferry dock, and **Church's Beach**, on the other side of the island, ideal for swimming or a peaceful stroll. The outermost of the **Elizabeth Islands**, which stretch for sixteen miles from Buzzards Bay, and one of the few not privately owned, Cuttyhunk was the site of the first English settlement in the Bay State: a short, 22-day sojourn which resulted in the building of a stockade and the planting of a medicinal garden. A small stone tower on an island in **Gosnold Pond**, at Cuttyhunk's western end, honors the event.

Get here via a Cuttyhunk Boat Lines **ferry**, which run to the island and back at least once daily (call for exact times; same-day round-trip $22, plus $1 per unit of baggage; Ⓣ508/992-1432, Ⓦwww.cuttyhunk.com). The ride can be an experience in its own right: it's the only means of transporting goods back and forth, meaning you may find yourself squeezed into a corner surrounded by towers of six-packs – or blocked in by a car.

Bicycles – which you can rent in New Bedford at Yesteryear Cyclery, 330 Hathaway Rd ($10–15/day; Ⓣ508/993-2525), and take over on the ferry – are the best way to get around this tiny island, which has a year-round population of just 26. There are only a couple of **restaurants** here, so you're best off bringing your own lunch. A few commercial establishments are located at **Four Corners**, the island's hub, such as gift shops and markets. If you want to **stay** the night, the *Cuttyhunk Fishing Club*, close to where the ferry lets off (Ⓣ508/992-5585, Ⓦwww.cuttyhunkfishingclub.com; ❻; closed in winter), is an inn with clean and comfortable rooms in an idyllic setting; you can also rent cottages by the week or month through the island website (Ⓦwww.cuttyhunk.com).

Cape Cod

CAPE COD, one of the most celebrated slices of real estate in America, boasts a consistently stunning quality of light which shines over some of the best beaches in New England. The slender, crooked Cape gives Massachusetts an extra three hundred miles of coastline, access to much of which is hampered by shore-hugging upper-middle-class homes. Those parts of the Cape that haven't fallen prey to suburban overdevelopment have been preserved as the snug villages they were a hundred or more years ago, replete with town green, white steepled church, and the odd lighthouse. Only **Provincetown**, at the very tip, manages successfully to mesh the past with the present; its unique art galleries, shops, and restaurants make it far and away the destination of choice here. It's also perched on the best stretch of the extensive **Cape Cod National Seashore**, so there's no overwhelming need to go elsewhere, though tiny upscale towns like **Sandwich**, **Brewster**, and **Chatham** make for scenic stops along the way. In recent years local chambers of commerce have been trying to lure tourists in the off season by touting the region's "historical attractions," but the reality is that for most the beach reigns supreme.

Some history

In all the hype about Plymouth and its associations with the Pilgrims, it's often forgotten that they first set foot on North American soil at Provincetown, where there's an enormous monument commemorating the event. The Cape got its name a bit earlier, though, when the area was visited in 1602 by explorer **Bartholomew Gosnold**, the first European to visit southeastern New England since Leif Erikson's brother in 1004; Gosnold dubbed it "Cape Cod" on account of the profusion of cod in the local waters. Immigration to the Cape up to 1700 was almost exclusively made up of homesick Englishmen who crossed the Atlantic to take advantage of the burgeoning markets of the New World, and who named the places after towns back home, such as Sandwich, Falmouth, and Barnstable. Indeed, during the Revolutionary War many Cape Codders sided with the Crown; how much of this was genuine affection for British rule and how much was prompted by their vulnerability to British naval strength is debatable. By the early 1800s, **whaling** had become the Cape's primary industry, the ports of Provincetown, Barnstable, Wellfleet, and Truro doing particularly well, while other Cape Codders were employed in the fishing and agricultural industries, including the harvesting of **cranberries**. By the time of the Civil War, with the whaling industry in serious decline, Cape Cod inhabitants began to look to the burgeoning railroads for salvation.

Cape Cod's rise as a **tourist destination** is mainly attributable to the development of the motor car and the railroad. Wealthy Bostonians and New Yorkers were, for the first time, able to get to the Cape with relative ease, many purchasing land to build summer homes and returning to live on the Cape permanently upon retirement. Today, the year-round population more than doubles in the summer, when more than 80,000 cars a day cross the **Cape Cod Canal**.

But nature is the real arbiter of the Cape's fate. After the last Ice Age, glaciers deposited huge amounts of debris as they began to melt and retreat, forming Cape Cod, the islands of Martha's Vineyard and Nantucket, and Long Island in the process. Because it lacks the solidity of other sections of the New England coast, and due to rising sea levels, Cape Cod is particularly vulnerable to **erosion**. Between

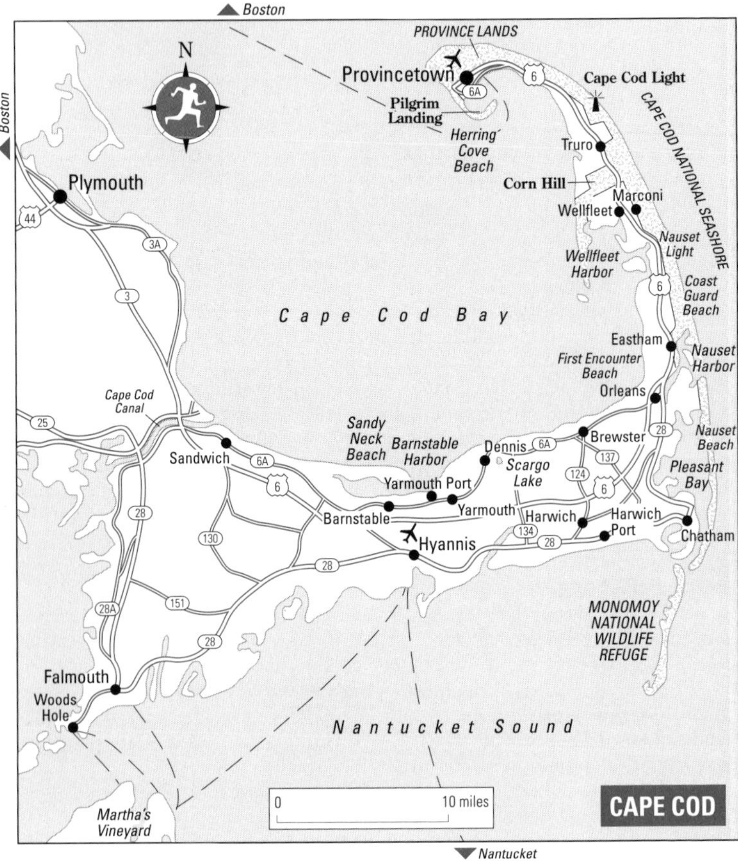

Wellfleet and Provincetown the land is scarcely one mile wide, and narrowing all the time. The one benefit of the adverse environmental situation is that it keeps development in check, especially in the vicinity of the protected **National Seashore**. Even highly developed areas are interspersed with pockets of meadowland and seagrass, lending the Cape at least the illusion of wide-open spaces.

The shape of the Cape

The Cape is shaped like a **flexed arm**, with Sandwich at the shoulder, Chatham at the elbow, and Provincetown the clenched fist at the very end. According to local parlance, the "Upper Cape" is the area you come to after crossing the Sagamore or Bourne bridges from the mainland, the "Lower Cape" is the forearm that stretches approximately from Orleans to Provincetown, and the "Mid-Cape" is everything in between, including the main commercial center of Hyannis. From a traveler's perspective, however, things make more sense in terms of the **north coast** of the Cape from Sandwich to Brewster, the **south coast** from Falmouth to Chatham, and the **outer Cape**. The best plan of attack is Rte-6A, the Old King's Highway, from Sandwich to Brewster. At Orleans, just past Brewster, Rte-6A joins Rte-6, the Mid-Cape Highway, an exceedingly dull road that does little else than get you to Provincetown in a hurry. With a very

The Cape Cod Canal

Between 1909 and 1914 a **canal** was dug across the westernmost portion of Cape Cod, effectively making the Cape an island. It was an old idea – the Pilgrims who landed on the Cape some three hundred years earlier had talked about building a canal as a means of avoiding the shipwreck-prone 135-mile trip around the Cape, thus facilitating trade between the Plymouth colony and the Dutch colony of New Amsterdam (New York), but they lacked the manpower to get the work done. Later on, George Washington, contemplating the advantages a canal would have in protecting naval ships and commercial vessels during war, resurrected the idea, but it was not until 1880 that work finally began. The Cape Cod Canal Company employed more than five hundred immigrant workers to begin the laborious process – they used hand shovels and carted debris away in wheelbarrows. In 1899 wealthy New York businessman Augustus Belmont took over the project; ten years later, state-of-the-art earthmoving equipment was introduced, and the canal was completed in 1914, though at the time it was too shallow and narrow to allow anything but one-way traffic. In 1928 the federal government purchased the canal, and during the Great Depression employed 1400 men to complete it. By 1940 the finished canal was the widest in the world. Hundreds of boats now use the canal every day, many of them leisure craft that have to contend with dramatic shifts in water currents and tides. You can join them on a **boat trip** with Hy-Line Cruises ($10–15; ⓣ508/295-3883, ⓦwww.hy-linecruises.com), which runs a variety of trips ranging from straightforward tours to three-hour jazz outings from Onset Bay Town Pier off routes 6 and 28. Still, you don't have to be on the water to enjoy it; the view of the canal and its verdant shores from the Sagamore and Bourne bridges is one of the most dramatic on the East Coast. There is also a **bike trail** on either side of the canal.

few exceptions, Rte-28, the main thoroughfare on the south coast, wends past baleful outcroppings of suburbia – even Cape Codders will tell you that it's a byway best avoided in favor of its scenic northern cousin.

Arrival, information, and getting around

The main way of reaching the Cape is by **car**, though if you're heading there on a summer weekend, you may well regret this choice. On a fairly quiet day it takes under two hours to get from downtown Boston to the Sagamore Bridge, but expect this to double on summer weekends and holidays. Bonanza (one-way $13.50 to Bourne, slightly more to elsewhere; ⓣ1-800/556-3815, ⓦwww.bonanzabus.com) operates a **bus** service from Boston to Bourne, Woods Hole, Falmouth, and Hyannis, while Plymouth & Brockton (one-way Boston to Hyannis $17, to Provincetown $27; ⓣ508/746-0378, ⓦwww.p-b.com) has a more complete set of Cape destinations. You can also take a **ferry** from Boston to Provincetown: Bay State Cruise Company (ⓣ617/748-1428, ⓦwww.baystatecruisecompany.com) runs two boats daily in the summer from Boston's Commonwealth Pier (90min express round-trip $64, 3hr standard ferry round-trip $29), while Boston Harbor Cruises (ⓣ617/227-4320, ⓦwww.bostonboats.com), does two express services a day from Long Wharf to Provincetown (90min; $59). A Plymouth to Provincetown ferry is run by Captain John's Boats (90min round-trip $32; ⓣ508/746-2400 or 1-800/242-2469, ⓦwww.provincetownferry.com). Finally, a number of **airlines** fly direct to Cape Cod – perhaps the best way to dodge traffic – including US Airways (ⓣ1-800/428-4322, ⓦwww.usairways.com), which goes to Hyannis from Boston, and Cape Air (ⓣ1-800/352-0714, ⓦwww.capeair.com), which heads to Hyannis and Provincetown from Boston several times a day, even in winter.

Once on the Cape, the best way to get around is by **car**. Rentals are available through Thrifty, in Orleans (Ⓣ508/255-2234), or Enterprise, 332 Iyannough Rd, Hyannis (Ⓣ508/778-8293). Alternatively, the Cape Cod Regional Transit Authority (Ⓣ1-800/352-7155, Ⓦwww.thebreeze.info) runs frequent public buses (6.30am–7pm) along routes 28 and 132 connecting the Cape's outlying towns; simply flag them down on the side of the road and cough up $1.50–3.50. The Cape also has plentiful and scenic **bike** paths; you can rent at *Bike Zone* ($15/day; Ⓣ508/775-3299), which has locations in Hyannis, East Falmouth, Mashpee, and South Yarmouth. A more touristy option, from Hyannis anyway, is the **Cape Cod Scenic Railroad** (late May to Oct; $17; Ⓣ508/771-3800, Ⓦwww.capetrain.com) which runs once a day from Center Street along a meandering two-hour circuit west through cranberry bogs to the Cape Cod Canal and Sandwich.

The main Cape Cod **visitors' center**, situated at the junction of routes 6 and 132 in Hyannis (Mon–Fri 8.30am–5pm, summer weekends also 10am–4pm; Ⓣ1-888-332-2732), has information about all the towns on the Cape. You can also research the area and make reservations online before you go at the Cape Cod Chamber of Commerce's website, Ⓦwww.capecodchamber.org.

Cape Cod's south coast

Route 28, which hugs the Nantucket Sound coast of the Cape until it merges with routes 6 and 6A at Orleans, is certainly not the most attractive or scenic route on the Cape; much of it is lined with motels and commercial buildings, and it can get seriously clogged with traffic during the summer. Nonetheless, it runs through a number of important hubs along the south coast, notably **Falmouth** and **Hyannis**. At its end are the two best reasons for hitting this path, the quiet town of **Chatham** and the even quieter **Monomoy National Wildlife Refuge**.

Falmouth and Woods Hole

FALMOUTH boasts more coastline than any other Cape Cod town and no fewer than fourteen harbors among its eight villages, at the center of which is **Falmouth Village**, with its prim, picket-fence-encircled central green surrounded by Colonial, Federal, and Greek Revival homes. Typical of New England, a number of these old sea captains' houses are now B&Bs, and are complemented by a touristy mixture of clothing shops, ice-cream parlors, and real estate agents. The 1794 **Conant House**, at 55–65 Palmer Ave (mid-June to mid-Sept Mon–Fri 10am–4pm, Sat 10am–1pm; $5; Ⓣ508/548-4857, Ⓦwww.falmouthhistoricalsociety.org), run by the Falmouth Historical Society, contains scrimshaw, rare glass and china, and sailors' memorabilia. There's also a room dedicated to local girl **Katherine Lee Bates**, who composed the song **America the Beautiful**; she was born in 1859 down the road at 16 Main St. The Historical Society also maintains the **Julia Wood House**, next door to the Conant House (same hours and price), an early nineteenth-century doctor's home, one room of which is set up as a clinic, with a horrifying display of primitive dental utensils – doctors doubled up as dentists in those days.

The salty drop of a town that is **WOODS HOLE** owes its name to the water passage, or "hole," between Penzance Point and Nonamesset Island, linking Vineyard Sound and Buzzards Bay. It's little more than a clump of casual restaurants and convenience stores clustered around the harbor and the **Woods**

Hole Oceanographic Institute, 15 School St (late May to early Sept Mon–Sat 10am–4.30pm, Sun noon–4.30pm; early Sept to Oct Tues–Sat 10am–4.30pm, Sun noon–4.30pm; Nov–Dec Tues–Fri 10am–4.30pm; April Fri & Sat 10am–4.30pm, Sun noon–4.30pm; closed Jan–March; $2; ⓣ508/457-2034, ⓦwww.whoi.edu), which houses an exhibit on the rediscovery of the *Titanic* in 1986, a project the institute spearheaded, and some neat submarine capsules that children will enjoy, but little else besides. During the summer the Institute offers **tours** once a day (reserve in advance) where you get to walk through some of their otherwise off-limits labs, where scientists study lobsters. Also worthwhile are the informative, hands-on cruises run from the harbor by **OceanQuest**: lobster and scallop traps are pulled up for inspection and those on board are encouraged to handle the sealife (July–Aug Mon–Fri 10am, noon, 2pm & 4pm, more sporadically on summer weekends and in September; $20; ⓣ1-800-37-OCEAN, ⓦwww.oceanquestonline.org).

Back on land, much of the sealife that lurks off the Cape's shores is kept behind glass at the National Marine Fisheries Service, at the corner of Albatross and Water streets (mid-June to early Sept daily 10am–4pm, early Sept to mid-June Mon–Fri 10am–4pm; free; ⓣ508/495-2001, ⓦwww.nefsc.noaa.gov), which maintains America's oldest **aquarium**. With a mission to preserve local marine life, its displays are mostly limited to the likes of codfish, lobster, and other piscine creatures that are more appealing on a plate; the exception, the institute's pet seals, Coco and Sandy, give visitors a thrill at feeding time (daily 11am & 4pm).

Accommodation

Despite having little in the way of in-town diversions, Falmouth has some lovely **accommodation** options that make a good base for exploring the Cape and catching the **ferry** from Woods Hole to Martha's Vineyard.

Mostly Hall 27 Main St, Falmouth ⓣ508/548-3786 or 1-800/682-0565, ⓦwww.mostlyhall.com. An amiably run 1849 mansion with queen-sized canopy beds in each of the six rooms. Closed Jan to mid-Feb. ❼

Scallop Shell Inn 16 Massachusetts Ave, Falmouth ⓣ508/495-4900 or 1-800/249-4587, ⓦwww.scallopshellinn.com. The best in-town spot: a deluxe seven-room inn with views of Nantucket and Martha's Vineyard, and several rooms outfitted with fireplaces and whirlpool tubs. ❽

Woods Hole Passage 186 Woods Hole Rd ⓣ508/548-9575, ⓦwww.woodsholepassage.com. Brightly painted chambers in a refurbished red-shingled carriage house set in spacious grounds. This is the place to go to save some money in the area. ❻

Eating and drinking

Betsy's Diner 457 Main St, Falmouth ⓣ508/540-0060. Worth stopping for – an authentic 1950s diner serving no-nonsense fare and beckoning you to "Eat Heavy."

Chapaquiot Grill 410 Rte-28A, West Falmouth ⓣ508/540-7794. Popular roadside restaurant serving wood-oven-fired pizzas and grilled fish.

The Clam Shack 227 Clinton Ave, Falmouth ⓣ508/540-7758. A local institution which serves up heaping plates of fried seafood (and obviously clams) on outside picnic tables and a smashing rooftop deck with prime waterfront views.

Fishmonger's Cafe 56 Water St, Woods Hole ⓣ508/540-5376. Laidback natural-foods eatery with a surprising number of vegetarian dishes in addition to seafood standards; try the fine fisherman's stew loaded with shrimps, scallops, and mussels ($20).

Hyannis

HYANNIS is primarily a transportation and commercial hub – it's home to the Cape's largest airport, as well as the main ferry service to Nantucket – and while traveling through it may be necessary, it's not a great destination. Much of the city has an industrial feel, with plenty of warehouses and malls, though there are some pleasant public beaches and quaint B&Bs for those who need to stay. What little glamor is associated with Hyannis derives from the **Kennedy Compound**, the family's best-known summer home, located in **Hyannisport**, a private, upscale residential section of town a couple of miles southwest of Hyannis proper. Visitors who come here expecting to take a guided tour will be disappointed: this group of houses is concealed by tall fences, and it's best glimpsed, if you must, from the water: Hy-Line Cruises, at the Ocean Street Docks, runs hour-long cruises that peek in on the compound (mid-April to late Oct; $12; ⓣ1-800/492-8082, ⓦwww.hy-linecruises.com).

If it's Kennedy-ana you've come to see, probably the best place to start is the **John F. Kennedy Hyannis Museum**, 397 Main St (mid-May to Oct Mon–Sat 10am–5pm, Sun noon–5pm; Nov to mid-Dec Wed–Sat 10am–4pm; $5; ⓣ508/790-3077), which displays the expected nostalgia, mainly in the form of old black-and-white photographs. It's not a comprehensive history, and instead focuses on Kennedy's relationship with Cape Cod. For a welcome non-presidential diversion, you might take a free tour of the **Cape Cod Potato Chip Factory**, on Breed's Hill Rd near the Cape Cod Mall (Mon–Fri 9am–5pm; free; ⓣ508/775-7253, ⓦwww.capecodchips.com). The tasty chips, once a local phenomenon but now to be found almost everywhere, are made with natural ingredients hand-cooked in kettles; it's hard to resist the free samples, in any case.

Practicalities

The local Chamber of Commerce maintains an **information center** at 1481 Rte-132 (Mon–Sat 9am–5pm, summer also Sun 9am–5pm; ⓣ1-877-HYANNIS, ⓦwww.hyannis.com), not to be confused with the Cape Cod Visitor Center just up the road. If you have a boat to catch and need to **stay** in Hyannis, options include the family-oriented *Sea Beach Inn*, 388 Sea St (ⓣ508/775-4612, ⓦcapecodtravel.com/seabeach; ❺), with small, neat, affordable rooms, and the wood-shingled *Sea Breeze Inn*, 270 Ocean Ave (ⓣ508/771-7213, ⓦwww.seabreezeinn.com; ❻), which has ten frilly queen-bedded rooms, some with

△ Cape Cod potato chips

shared bath. Both are a short walk from the beach. The *Simmons Homestead Inn*, 288 Scudder Ave (508/778-4999 or 1-800/637-1649, www.simmonshomesteadinn.com; 8), is the only B&B in Hyannisport, a pet-friendly spot with thirteen creatively themed rooms in an 1820 sea captain's home.

Many of Hyannis's **restaurants** are on Main Street, which is unfortunately not all that near the hotels – and so, as public transport stops at 7pm, it's helpful to have a car. Reasonably priced options are *Alberto's*, 360 Main St (508/778-1770), for northern Italian dishes; *Cooke's Seafood*, 1120 Iyanough Rd/Rte-132 (508/775-0450), where it's hard to go wrong with the fresh broiled and fried seafood – especially the clams; *The Egg & I*, 521 Main St (508/771-1596), a great spot for big breakfasts; *Sam Diego's*, 950 Rte-132 (508/771-8816), a dependable, casual restaurant serving Mexican, Southwestern, and barbecue fare; and *Harry's*, 700 Main St (508/778-4188), a Cajun spot serving up spicy jambalaya, barbecued ribs, and live music.

Chatham

The next town worth visiting on the South Shore is genteel **CHATHAM**, a long 21 miles east on Rte-28, whose quiet and posh small-town atmosphere is largely attributable to some strictly enforced zoning laws, which have prevented the kind of indiscriminate attract-tourists-at-all-costs mentality evident in so many other Cape communities. The focal point here is **Chatham Village**, whose **Main Street** is home to a variety of upscale boutiques, provisions stores, and some sophisticated restaurants and charming inns. Just off Main Street is one of the town's best historical attractions, the gambrel-roofed **Atwood House and Museum**, 347 Stage Harbor Rd (early June to Sept Tues–Sat 1–4pm, rainy days 10am–4pm; $3; www.chathamhistoricalsociety.org), built in 1752 as a sea captain's home, and with a variety of seafaring artifacts, antique dolls, seashells, toys, and a herb garden. The adjacent Mural Barn houses the rather gaudy *Stallknecht Murals*, a triptych painted in 1931 by Alice Stallknecht Wight that depicts Chatham townsfolk listening in awe to a contemporarily dressed Christ. Farther north along Stage Harbor Road you come to the Gothic **Railroad Museum**, 153 Depot Rd (mid-June to mid-Sept Tues–Sat 10am–4pm; free; no phone), topped by a tapered turret; the highlight of the railroad-related gear inside is a 75-year-old walk-in refurbished caboose, complete with bells and whistles. Tour **maps** of Chatham are available from the **information booth** at 533 Main St (May–Oct Mon–Fri 9am–5pm; 508/945-5199, www.chathamcapecod.org).

A few minutes' drive outside the village, the 1877 **Chatham Light** stands guard over a windswept bluff beyond which many a ship met its doom on the "Chatham Bars," a series of sandbars that served to protect the town from the worst of the Atlantic storms – until in January 1987, when a fierce Nor'easter broke through the barrier beach to form the **Chatham Break**, leaving Chatham exposed to the vagaries of the ocean. Right below the lighthouse is a nice beach, but with parking limited to half an hour you're better off biking there from town. A mile north on Rte-28, the **Fish Pier** on Shore Road provides a spot to wait for the fleet to come in mid-afternoon. From here you can also take a water taxi to Monomoy Island, a 7600-acre wildlife refuge (see box overleaf).

Accommodation

Chatham is well endowed with tasteful **accommodation**, and the **B&Bs** here are a bit more upscale than those found elsewhere on the Cape. Despite the ample selection, reservations are strongly advised, even outside of high season.

Monomoy National Wildlife Refuge

Stretching out to sea for nine miles south of Chatham, desolate **Monomoy National Wildlife Refuge** is a fragile barrier beach that was attached to the mainland until breached by a storm in 1958. A subsequent storm in 1978 divided the island in half, and today the islands are accessible only by boat – when weather conditions permit. The refuge spreads across 7600 acres of sand and dunes, tidal flats and marshes, with no roads, no electricity, and, best of all, no human residents, though a small fishing community once existed here. Indeed, the only man-made buildings on the islands are the South Monomoy Lighthouse and lightkeeper's house.

It's a perfect stopover point along the North Atlantic Flyway for almost three hundred species of shorebirds and migratory **waterfowl**, including many varieties of gull and the endangered piping plovers, for whose protection several sections of the refuge have been fenced off. In addition, the islands are home to white-tailed deer, and harbor and gray seals are frequent visitors in winter. Several organizations conduct island **tours**, among them the Cape Cod Museum of Natural History (ⓣ508/349-2615, ⓦwww.ccmnh.org) and private carriers like the Monomoy Island Ferry, a small boat run by Keith Lincoln (ⓣ508/945-5450, ⓦwww.monomoyislandferry.com); prices vary, depending, among other things, on the number of people in your group. In any case, if there are six or more of you, you'll need to get a special **permit** from the headquarters of the Wildlife Refuge, located on Morris Island (ⓣ508/945-0594), which also has a **visitors' center** offering leaflets on Monomoy. Morris Island is accessible from Morris Island Road, south of the Chatham Light (see overleaf).

The Captain's House Inn 369–371 Old Harbor Rd ⓣ508/945-0127 or 1-800/315-0728, ⓦwww.captainshouseinn.com. Easy elegance prevails at this sumptuously renovated 1839 Greek Revival whaling captain's home; most rooms have fireplaces, and prices include delicious breakfasts and afternoon tea with freshly baked scones. ❽

The Carriage House Inn 407 Old Harbor Rd ⓣ508/945-4688, ⓦwww.thecarriagehouseinn.com. A newish year-round B&B with young, friendly owners provides seven modern but welcoming rooms and slightly lower prices than the surrounding inns. ❼

Chatham Bars Inn 297 Shore Rd ⓣ508/945-0096 or 1-800/527-4884, ⓦwww.chathambarsinn.com. The grande dame of Cape Cod's seaside resorts, the 205 rooms and cottages spread out over a 22-acre oceanfront property are decorated in country-chic style. Even for this, though, the prices are high; you're paying for the fantastic setting more than anything else. ❾

Chatham Tides Waterfront Motel 394 Pleasant St, South Chatham ⓣ508/432-0379, ⓦwww.chathamtides.com. Choose between standard hotel rooms or self-catering townhouse suites at this relative bargain directly on Nantucket Sound. Closed Oct–May. ❽

Chatham Wayside Inn 512 Main St ⓣ508/945-5550 or 1-800/391-5734, ⓦwww.waysideinn.com. This 56-room refurbished 1860 sea captain's home is one of the finer inns in the area. Great food, too. ❽

Eating

Not surprisingly, given its status as one of the more sophisticated destinations on Cape Cod, Chatham abounds in upmarket **restaurants**, as well as the more casual eateries typical in these parts.

Carmine's Pizza 595 Main St ⓣ508/945-5300. Casual checked-tablecloth joint serving inexpensive and tasty pizzas with an accent on spice – the Pizza from Hell combines garlic, red pepper, jalapeños, and pineapple slices.

Chatham Bars Inn 297 Shore Rd ⓣ508/945-0096 or 1-800/527-4884. The hostelry's formal dining room offers expensive New England cuisine with wonderful ocean views.

Chatham Squire 487 Main St ⓣ508/945-0945. This informal and affordable spot has a raw bar, an eclectic menu that sometimes incorporates elements of Mexican and Asian cuisine, and often live acoustic bands at night.

Christian's 443 Main St ⓣ508/945-3362. The movie posters upstairs are fitting, considering that the menu items are named after films; hard to go wrong with the well-priced Roman Holiday (Caesar salad) followed by A Fish Called Wanda (salmon sautéed with mushrooms).

The Impudent Oyster 15 Chatham Bars Ave ⓣ508/945-3545. Popular upscale bistro with generous portions of inventively prepared fresh seafood.

Marion's Pie Shop 2022 Rte-28 ⓣ508/432-9439. Popular with locals and tourists alike for delicious sweet apple pies, savory chicken pies, and chewy breakfast cinnamon rolls.

Vining's Bistro 595 Main St ⓣ508/945-5033. Imaginative offerings at this appealing dinner spot range from Thai Street Vendor's Beef Salad to a warm lobster taco.

Cape Cod's north coast

The meandering stretch of highway that parallels the Cape Cod Bay shoreline between Sandwich and Orleans is among the most scenic in New England, affording glimpses of the Cape Cod of popular imagination: salt marshes, crystal-clear ponds, ocean views, and tiny villages. What began as a Native American pathway from Plymouth to Provincetown became the Cape's main road in the seventeenth and eighteenth centuries. There are hundreds of historic buildings along the 34-mile stretch, a large number of which have been turned into antiques shops or B&Bs. The towns that hold these are pleasant enough, though **Sandwich** and **Brewster** have the highest concentration of well-preserved historic homes. Even if you're traveling by car, it's worth it temporarily to ditch the wheels in favor of a bike to take the **Cape Cod Rail Trail**, a totally flat but popular bike path on the site of the former Old Colony Railroad track, running from **Dennis**, about fifteen miles past Sandwich, through Brewster to **Wellfleet**, a distance of twenty miles up the Cape.

Sandwich

Overlooked **SANDWICH** kicks off Rte-6A with little of the crass commercialization common to so many Cape towns, thanks in part to its position so close to the mainland. The first permanent settlement on Cape Cod, Sandwich traces its roots to Pilgrim traders in the late 1620s who appreciated its proximity to the **Manomet Trading Post**, where they could barter goods and knowledge with the local Native Americans. The salt marshes in the area also provided an abundant supply of hay for their animals. Unsurprisingly, agriculture was Sandwich's main industry until the 1820s, when Bostonian Deming Jarves established a glassmaking factory here. Though the dense woodlands supplied plenty of fuel for the furnaces, by the 1880s the Sandwich factory was no longer able to compete with the coal-fired glassworks of the Midwest.

A stroll around Sandwich's old **village center** gives you a good taste of things to come along Rte-6A: a little village green, white steepled church, a smattering of bed-and-breakfasts, antiques shops, and a general store. Near Main and River streets, the **Shawme Duck Pond** and adjacent **Dexter Grist Mill**, a replica of one built in 1654, make for a pleasant, peaceful stop, especially if you want to hear about (and maybe even see it in progress) the milling process (mid-June to mid-Sept daily 10am–4pm; $3; no phone). Close to the shore, at 129 Main St, the **Sandwich Glass Museum** (Feb–March Wed–Sun 9.30am–4pm, April–Dec daily 9.30am–5pm; closed Jan; $4.50; ⓣ508/888-0251, ⓦwww.sandwichglassmuseum.org) contains fourteen galleries that house artifacts from the Boston & Sandwich Glass Company, which set up shop here in 1825. Besides thousands of functional and decorative pieces, the museum has a working glassblowing studio, with presentations every hour.

The other museums around town are only really recommended for those with an abiding passion for Americana, primarily the **Heritage Plantation of Sandwich** at Grove and Pine streets (mid-May to Nov daily 9am–6pm, Nov–April Wed–Sun 10am–4pm; $12; Ⓦwww.heritageplantation.org), which features a mega-attic of Currier and Ives prints, old firearms, a working 1912 carousel, replicas of US flags, and a collection of polished old cars. The seventy-plus-acre **gardens** on the grounds are beautiful in season, especially July when the rhododendrons are in bloom. Sandwich's attractions also include several miles of **beach** on Cape Cod Bay. The water here (like all the Cape's bayside beaches) is several degrees cooler than over on the Nantucket Sound side. It will cost you $10 to park at **Town Neck Beach**, on Town Neck Road off Rte-6A.

Practicalities

The place to **stay** in Sandwich is the *Dan'l Webster Inn*, 149 Main St (Ⓣ508/888-3622 or 1-800/444-3566, Ⓦwww.danlwebsterinn.com; ❽), a rambling Colonial-style hostelry modeled on an earlier building that was a haunt of Revolutionary patriots, with commercial hotel-style rooms and charming courtyards. The hotel also does some of the best **meals** in town: top-notch, classic American dishes are served, for a price, every evening, but it's worth it for the compelling opportunity to nibble edible flowers (among other things) from the inn's aquafarm; they also serve breakfast and lunch in a sunlit conservatory.

Barnstable

BARNSTABLE, ten miles east of Sandwich on Rte-6A, was, after Sandwich, the second town to be founded on Cape Cod, in 1639. Early prosperity was attained thanks to its trade in whale products, and Barnstable's harbor was the busiest port on the Cape until it silted up last century. Wayward cetaceans would frequently wash ashore at **Sandy Neck**, a beautiful eight-mile barrier beach that protects Barnstable's harbor. No longer used as a site for burning blubber, the beach is probably your main reason for checking out the town – follow Sandy Neck Road just over the Sandwich line to get here.

Evidence of Barnstable's earlier prosperity can be seen in several imposing domestic and civic buildings in the leafy village center, among them the impressive granite mass of the **Barnstable County Superior Courthouse**, 3195 Rte-6A. Nearby, the dignified red-brick **Donald G. Trayser Memorial Museum**, 3353 Rte-6A (July & Aug Tues–Sat 1.30–4.30pm; donation requested; Ⓣ508/362-2092), was built in 1855 as the town's customs house. Nowadays, it contains an eclectic array of Americana, from vintage clothes to Sandwich glass and, on the grounds, an eighteenth-century jail cell which, according to Henry David Thoreau, was often shut up during the 1850s as, "when the court [came] together at Barnstable, they [had] not a single criminal to try."

Many former residences of Barnstable's hundreds of sea captains survive to this day, including that which belonged to William Sturgis, who set out to sea at the age of fifteen after the death of his father and returned four years later as a captain. Sturgis, uneducated but an avid reader, bequeathed his house to the town for use as a library; the resultant **Sturgis Library**, 3090 Rte-6A (Mon, Wed, Thurs & Fri 10am–5pm, Tues 1–8pm, Sat 10am–4pm; Ⓣ508/362-6636, Ⓦwww.sturgislibrary.org), contains genealogical records dating back to the area's first European settlers, an original 1605 Lothrop Bible, and an extensive collection of maritime maps, charts, and archival material. A few miles away, in West Barnstable, the majestic 1717 Neoclassical **West Parish Meetinghouse**,

Rte-149 at Meetinghouse Way, is the oldest surviving Congregationalist building in the US, and its bell tower contains a bell cast by Paul Revere.

Practicalities

For something to **eat**, try the *Barnstable Tavern*, 3176 Main St (Ⓣ508/362-2355), offering casual American food with an unusual Lebanese touch and a good list of wines by the glass. Waterfront views and classic seafood can be had at the more expensive *Mattakeese Wharf*, 271 Mill Way (Ⓣ508/362-4511; open May–Oct). If you want to **stay** overnight, *Beechwood*, 2839 Rte-6A (Ⓣ508/362-6618, Ⓦwww.beechwoodinn.com; ❽), an 1853 Queen Anne-style house, has six romantic rooms decorated in Victorian style. Another lovely option is the *Honeysuckle Hill Bed & Breakfast*, 591 Old King's Hwy/Rte-6A (Ⓣ508/362-8418, Ⓦwww.honeysucklehill.com; ❼), with four rooms and one suite in a quintessential Cape Cod 1810 home. In addition to the full breakfast, you can enjoy sitting by the fireplace in the living room, perhaps accompanied by the owners' friendly black Labrador.

Yarmouth Port

The only part of Yarmouth, the closest thing the Cape has to an urban sprawl, that's worth visiting is **YARMOUTH PORT**, a delightful hamlet eastward on Rte-6A, marked by a series of old sea captains' houses that have been converted into bed-and-breakfasts. Indeed, along one two-mile stretch, no building was constructed later than the turn of last century, creating something of a time-warp effect, augmented all the more by a visit to **Hallet's**, 139 Rte-6A, a general store that started out as a pharmacy in 1889 – later serving as a post office and town meeting hall – and still boasts its original oak counter and an old-fashioned soda fountain. Nearby, on the town green off Rte-6A at 11 Strawberry Lane, the **Captain Bangs Hallet House** (June to mid-Oct Thurs–Sun 1–3pm, tours hourly; $3; Ⓦwww.hsoy.org) is a 1740 Greek Revival mansion built by one of the town's founders, though its name comes from the successful sea captain who lived here in the late 1800s; it's the only such residence on the Cape that's open to the public. Tours take in the original kitchen, complete with beehive oven, and fine views from the back of the house, enhanced by a glorious weeping beech tree.

In decent weather, you might walk amongst the 53 acres of the **Botanic Trails of Yarmouth**, entered right behind the post office on Rte-6A (trails open year-round during daylight hours; suggested donation $1). This peaceful park contains oak and pine woods and a wealth of flora, including rhododendrons, blueberries, hollies, and lady's slippers. An extension of the trail leads to **Kelley's Chapel**, a seaman's bethel built in 1873 by a father for his daughter who was grieving the death of her son; Kelley is not a surname but the first name of the daughter.

Practicalities

There's no good reason to **stay** here in Yarmouth Port, except to get a dose of good old-fashioned seafaring days. If this sounds appealing, the *Liberty Hill Inn*, 77 Main St (Ⓣ508/362-3976, Ⓦwww.libertyhillinn.com; ❻), offers quintessential country inn ambience in six rooms with canopy beds and fireplaces. You can **eat** Italian fare at *abbicci*, 43 Main St/Rte-6A (Ⓣ508/362-3501), which serves excellent and pricey seafood as well as more traditional meat and pasta dishes. Yarmouth Port is also home to one of the Cape's best Japanese restaurants, *Inaho*, for those looking for a break from fried seafood (Ⓣ508/362-5522). For a great milkshake, hit up *Hallet's*, 139 Rte-6A (☎508/362-3362; closed Dec–March), the 1889 drugstore with an original marble soda fountain (see overleaf).

Dennis

In **DENNIS**, just down the road from Yarmouth, detour onto Old Bass River Road to pristine **Scargo Lake** for sweeping views from a thirty-foot **stone observation tower** built on a bluff overlooking the water. The town itself, named after its founder, the Reverend Josiah Dennis, retains much of its colonial feel, notably in places like the clergyman's home, the **Josiah Dennis Manse** at 77 Nobscusset Rd (July–Aug Tues & Thurs 2–4pm; small donation requested), a saltbox built in 1736 and set up to reflect life in the Reverend's day, filled with antique toys and furniture, china and pewter, plus the inevitable portraits of sea captains. There's also an attic containing spinning and weaving equipment, and, in the grounds, a one-room schoolhouse dating from 1770.

One of the most famous summer theaters in the US, the **Cape Playhouse**, Rte-6A between Nobscusset and Corporation roads (late June to early Sept daily except Sun; for ticket info call ☎508/385-3911 or visit Ⓦwww.capeplayhouse.com), was a Unitarian meeting house until its purchase in 1927 by Raymond Moore, a Californian who had intended to start a theater company in Provincetown but found it too remote. Famous names who have trod the boards here include Basil Rathbone (who starred in the first performance, *The Guardsman*), Lana Turner, Gregory Peck, Humphrey Bogart, and Bette Davis, who also worked here as an usherette. The complex also contains an art cinema, 35 Hope Lane (tickets $8.50; ☎508/385-2503, Ⓦwww.capecinema.com), that's modeled after a Congregational church. On the ceiling is a 6400-square-foot romantic astrological mural designed by Rockwell Kent and Jo Mielziner; look for entwined couples making their way through the Milky Way. Also on-site, the **Cape Museum of Fine Arts** (mid-May to mid-Oct Mon–Sat 10am–5pm, Sun 1–5pm; mid-Oct to April Tues–Sat 10am–5pm, Sun 1–5pm; $7; Ⓦwww.cmfa.org) showcases more than one thousand works of local artists, many of whom have a penchant for seascapes and sealife portraits, though the gallery often has good contemporary fare as well.

For cycling enthusiasts, the **Cape Cod Rail Trail**, a tarred bicycle path that was formerly the Old Colony Railroad track, extends 26 miles from Dennis to Wellfleet (beginning in South Dennis on Rte-134 south of Rte-6). Barbara's Bike & Sports, at 430 Rte-134 in South Dennis (☎508/760-4723), rents bikes for about $15 a day and stocks copies of the free *Cape Cod Bike Guide* (Ⓦwww.capecodbikeguide.com), which details this and a few other island trails.

Practicalities

If you're looking to **stay** in Dennis, the *Isaiah Hall B&B Inn*, 152 Whig St (☎508/385-9928 or 1-800/736-0160, Ⓦwww.isaiahhallinn.com; ❻; closed Nov–May), is an 1857 Greek Revival farmhouse with nine attractive rooms equipped with VCRs, all within walking distance of village and beach. For more resort-like accommodation, check into the *Lighthouse Inn*, 1 Lighthouse Inn Rd (☎508/398-2244, Ⓦwww.lighthouseinn.com; ❾), an expansive compound with private beach, mini-golf, tennis, and shuffleboard on-site. You can **eat** generous portions of tried-and-true New England staples at the inexpensive *Captain Frosty's Fish & Chips*, 219 Rte-6A, Dennis (☎508/385-8548), or go Italian at *Gina's by the Sea*, 134 Taunton Ave (☎508/385-3213; closed Dec–March), and dive into moderately priced fare like shrimp scampi and mozzarella-stuffed ravioli.

Brewster

BREWSTER is yet another agreeable, if anodyne, Cape Cod town, known as a leading antiques center and popular with young couples who choose to tie the knot here, usually in one of the many bed-and-breakfasts that line Rte-6A. The town, as ever, traces its affluence to the sea captains who settled here – even though Brewster doesn't have a harbor. The **cemetery** in which many of these seamen are buried is adjacent to the 1834 **First Parish Church**, at 1969 Rte-6A; it has one of New England's more fascinating legends attached to (or buried in) it. One of the gravestones bears the names of two men lost at sea: Captain David Nickerson and his adopted son, Captain René Rousseau. Nickerson was in Paris during the French Revolution when a veiled woman handed him the infant René; longtime locals maintain he was the son of Louis XVI and Marie Antoinette. More picturesque is the town's last remaining windmill, the 1795 **Higgins Farm Windmill**, 785 Rte-6A (July–Aug Tues–Fri 1–4pm; June & Sept Sat & Sun 1–4pm; free; ⓣ508/896-9521), with its roof resembling a capsized dory, and the still-functioning waterwheel at the **Stony Brook Mill and Museum**, just off Rte-6A at 830 Stony Brook Rd (July & Aug Sat & Sun 2–5pm, call for off-season hours; ⓣ508/896-9521; free), built on the site of an earlier mill that churned out cloth, boots, and ironwork for over a century; the second-story museum displays local bric-a-brac including some recently recovered arrowheads.

Brewster also boasts the **New England Fire & History Museum**, 1439 Rte-6A (late May to early Sept Mon, Wed, & Sat 10am–4pm, Sun noon–4pm; early Sept to mid-Oct Sat & Sun noon–4pm; $7; ⓣ508/896-5711), which lures visitors with the tantalizing invitation to "see the fire-fighting apparatus of yesteryear." That includes more than thirty buffed and polished fire engines, one of which is a one-and-only 1929 Mercedes-Benz Nurburg 460. There is also an extensive collection of fire helmets and a sizeable diorama of the Chicago Fire of 1871. Farther down the road, at 869 Rte-6A, the **Cape Cod Museum of Natural History** (Mon–Sat 9.30am–4.30pm, Sun 11am–4.30pm; $8, trails free; ⓣ508/896-3867, ⓦwww.ccmnh.org) makes for a somewhat more enlightening alternative – especially for kids – with its exhibits on the fragile Cape environment, whales, other sealife, and short but beautiful nature trails that straddle cranberry bogs and salt marshes before continuing on to the bay. The museum organizes several **nature tours**, the most popular of which is a two-hour seal cruise, where you get to view gray seals flopping around on the shores of Monomoy National Wildlife Refuge; the institution also arranges overnight stays at the Refuge (see box on p.204)

Practicalities

The best place to **stay** – and **eat** – in Brewster is the *Bramble Inn*, 2019 Main St (ⓣ508/896-7644, ⓦwww.brambleinn.com; ❼; closed Nov–April), a lovely old place that takes in two rustic homes, with upscale country-style fittings. Its restaurant, one of the Cape's finest, does pricey seafood such as lobster in an open shell filled with scallops, shrimp, and cod covered in toasted almonds and coconut. Another good lodging option is *Brewster by the Sea*, 716 Main St/Rte-6A (ⓣ508/896-3910, ⓦwww.brewsterbythesea.com; ❽), an old eight-room Cape B&B turned upscale, now offering spa services and the like, as well as a delicious breakfast and an outdoor pool in the summer. For contemporary French cuisine, *Chillingsworth*, 2449 Rte-6A (ⓣ508/896-3640), boasts a sumptuous setting and superb food; if you're going to splurge, their five-course *table d'hôte* menu (about $60) can't be beat. *Sprakfish*, 2671 Main St (ⓣ508/896-1067), does good wood-grilled seafood dishes.

Cape Cod National Seashore

The protected **Cape Cod National Seashore**, which President Kennedy saved from development because of his fondness for it, extends along much of the Cape's Atlantic side, stretching forty miles from Chatham north to Provincetown. It's a fragile environment: three feet of the lower Cape is washed away each year, and much of it ends up as extra sand on the beach before the sea takes that away, too. Environmentalists are hoping that an extensive program of grass-planting will help prevent further erosion.

It was on these shifting sands of the outer Cape that the **Pilgrims** made their first home in the New World. They obtained their water from Pilgrim Spring near Truro, and at Corn Hill Beach they uncovered a cache of corn buried by the Wampanoag Indians who had been living on the Cape for centuries – a discovery which kept them alive their first winter, before moving on to Plymouth.

Displays and films at the **Salt Pond Visitor Center**, on Rte-6 just north of Eastham (daily 9am–4.30pm; ⓣ508/255-3421, ⓦwww.nps.gov/caco), trace the geology and history of the Cape. A pretty road and hiking/cycling trail head east to the sands of **Coast Guard Beach** and **Nauset Light Beach**, both of which offer excellent swimming. You can also catch a free shuttle ride there from the visitor center in summer. Another fine beach is **Head of the Meadow**, halfway between Truro and Provincetown. In several areas parking is restricted to residents only, but you can often park by the road and strike off across the dunes to the shore.

The Outer Cape: Orleans to Truro

ORLEANS, at the southernmost portion of the Outer Cape, was named after Louis-Philippe de Bourbon, duc d'Orleans, who is said to have visited the area at the time of his exile from France in the 1790s. Such grasps at royalty are long forgotten, as modern Orleans is basically a series of strip malls on either side of Rte-6A, a place to stock up on snacks for a trip to the beach or to fuel up for the ride onward to Provincetown. In the "town," which is a generous designation, the **Bird Watcher's General Store**, 36 Rte-6A (ⓣ1-800/562-1512), is worth a stop, if only to partake in the store tradition of telling the cashier a joke. If he likes it, he'll ring a little bell and reward you with a gift. On Rte-6A at Town Cove Park, the well-traveled **Jonathan Young Windmill** (July & Aug daily 11am–4pm; free) began life in the 1720s in East Orleans, was subsequently moved to the center of town, then to Hyannisport, and finally, in 1983, moved back to Orleans. Although no longer in operation, this gristmill does have its machinery intact, and there's a resident miller who will explain how it all works. A much better diversion is a visit to atmospheric **Rock Harbor**, at the end of Rock Harbor Road off Main Street, a former landing place for packet ships until it silted up, and now a small fishing port and departure point for charter **fishing trips**; you can book one with Captain Cook Sport Fishing (ⓣ508/255-2065 or 1-888/772-9695). Over in East Orleans is one of the Cape's best beaches, the nine-mile-long oceanside **Nauset Beach**, off Beach Road ($15 parking fee); don't miss the onion rings at the snack bar – they're legendary. You can also hook up with the **Cape Cod Rail Trail** just past the Mid-Cape Home Center; bikes are available for rent in town at Orleans Cycle, 26 Main St (ⓣ508/255-9115).

Orleans has a few surprisingly good **restaurants**. Among the high-end choices, *Captain Linnell House*, 137 Skaket Beach Rd (ⓣ508/255-3400), serves

New England fare in a candelit 1840 clipper captain's mansion; budget-minded travelers can hit *Land Ho!*, 38 Main St (Ⓣ508/255-5165), for generous portions of burgers and fried seafood; and mid-range prices are the norm at *Mahoney's Atlantic Bar & Grill*, 28 Main St (Ⓣ508/255-5505), a hopping place serving pasta and seafood. **Accommodation** in Orleans is plentiful, with a combination of modestly priced motels along Rte-28 and close to Nauset Beach, and several comfortable inns. The *Parsonage Inn*, 202 Main St, East Orleans (Ⓣ508/255-8217 or 1-888/422-8217, Ⓦwww.parsonageinn.com; ❻), is an eighteenth-century house with eight antique-furnished rooms, while the nearby *Ship's Knees Inn*, 186 Beach Rd (Ⓣ508/255-1312, Ⓦwww.shipskneesinn.com; ❼), has similar accommodation with the added bonus of a tennis court (some rooms have shared bath). Both are within walking distance of the beach.

Eastham

Largely undiscovered **EASTHAM**, up Rte-6 past Orleans as the Cape begins to curve toward Provincetown, is home to fewer than five thousand residents, most of whom are quite content to sit and watch the summer traffic pass by on its way north. Though the sum of Eastham's commercial facilities is little more than a small strip of shopping malls and gas stations along Rte-6, if you veer off the highway in either direction you will capture some authentic Cape flavor.

The first detour is the **Fort Hill** area, part of the Cape Cod National Seashore, with a scenic overlook for sweeping views of **Nauset Marsh**, a former bay that became a marsh when **Coast Guard Beach** was formed ($15 parking; free shuttle buses to the beach). North of Coast Guard, at the corner of Ocean View Drive and Cable Road, is the red-and-white **Nauset Light**, originally located in Chatham, but installed here in 1923 and moved back 350 feet a decade ago when it was in danger of crumbling into the sea. In 1838, this spot was home to no fewer than three brick lighthouses, known as the "Three Sisters," built 150ft apart. In 1892, serious erosion necessitated their replacement by three wooden towers; two were eventually moved away in 1918 and the third five years later. Having been acquired by the National Park service, they now stand in the woods well away from today's coastline.

On Eastham's bayside, **First Encounter Beach**, off Samoset Road, refers to the first meeting of Pilgrims and Native Americans in 1620. It was hardly a cordial rendezvous; with the *Mayflower* anchored in Provincetown, an exploration party led by Myles Standish came ashore only to meet a barrage of arrows. Things settled down after a few gunshots were returned, and since then the beach has been utterly tranquil. A plaque set back in the dunes describes the encounter in detail.

Practicalities

The place to **stay** in Eastham is the *Whalewalk Inn*, 220 Bridge Rd (Ⓣ508/255-0617 or 1-800/440-1281, Ⓦwww.whalewalkinn.com; ❽), where immaculate guestrooms and tasty breakfasts are the big draws; the cottages are more spacious than the rooms in the main inn building. There's also a **hostel**, *Mid-Cape American Youth Hostel*, 75 Goody Hallet Drive (Ⓣ508/255-2785, Ⓔmidcape@usahostels.org; $27 non-members; open mid-May to mid-Sept), in a collection of woodsy cabins. For something to **eat**, *Arnold's Lobster & Clam Bar*, 3580 Rte-6 (Ⓣ508/255-2575), provides generous portions of fried New England seafood, while *Box Lunch*, 4205 Rte-6 (Ⓣ508/255-0799), as its name suggests, is the place to go for packed pita sandwiches to take to the beach.

Cape Cod beaches

With over three hundred miles of coastline, Cape Cod certainly doesn't lack **sand**. What it does lack is parking and facilities at its beachfront locations; the few that have the full gamut of services (restrooms, lifeguards, and snack bars) are, not surprisingly, usually busiest. The island's southern stretches, facing Nantucket Sound, tend to be calmer and warmer than its northern options, making this coast more family-oriented than its Atlantic side, where the water tends to be chillier and rougher, but also great fun and good for riding waves on boogie boards. **Parking** across the Cape is a bit of a crapshoot: some counties allow daily non-permit beach parking (usually between $8 and $15/day), whereas others limit beach parking to residents. Your best bet, if you're planning on hitting the beach a good deal during your stay, is to visit the local town hall and inquire about non-resident parking permits (which can range from $30 for three days to $60/week). These town beaches are most often bay or pond, whereas the best ocean beaches are pay as you go – so don't rush to buy a pass until you have an idea of where you'd like to swim.

Around Hyannis

Craigville Beach off Craigville Beach Road in Centerville, just west of Hyannis. Well-oiled and toned sun-worshipers flock to this broad expanse of sand nicknamed "Muscle Beach."

Kalmus Beach off Gosnold Street in central Hyannis. A big windsurfing destination at the mouth of the busy harbor, with full facilities but an urban feel.

Brewster

Breakwater Beach off Breakwater Road. Shallow-water beach close to town and with restrooms.

Paines Creek Beach off Paines Creek Road. One-and-a-half-mile bay beach with great body surfing when the tide comes in.

Dennis

Corporation Beach off Rte-6A. One of the best-maintained beaches on the Cape, it has wheelchair-accessible boardwalks, a children's play area, lifeguards, and full facilities.

Mayflower Beach off Rte-6A. Popular family spot thanks to naturally formed tidal pools.

West Dennis Beach off Rte-28. Well-equipped and narrow 1.5-mile beach with a kite-flying area to boot.

Eastham

Coast Guard Beach off Ocean View Drive. Pristine and picturesque Cape Cod National Seashore beach with views for miles, as well as lifeguards and restrooms; you can catch a shuttle bus from Salt Pond or the Eastham High School.

Nauset Light off Ocean View Drive. Scenic Atlantic-facing beach connected to Coast Guard Beach by shuttle bus and also part of the Cape Cod National Seashore; serviced by lifeguards and with restrooms.

Falmouth

Old-Silver Beach off Rte 28-A in North Falmouth. Popular, calm beach with great sunsets; college kids and young families gather here, the latter drawn to its natural

Wellfleet

WELLFLEET, with a year-round population of just 2500, is, like Eastham eight miles to the south, one of the least developed towns on the Cape. Once wading pool.

Surf Drive Beach off Shore Street. Another family favorite; a shallow tidal pool between jetties is known as "the kiddie pool."

Orleans

Nauset Beach East Orleans. Arguably the Cape's biggest beach scene, this ten-mile-long barrier beach has terrific facilities (and regular sunset concerts), plus prime windsurfing and boogie-boarding conditions.

Skaket Beach off Skaket Beach Road. Calm bay beach ideal for families; when the tide goes out, kids take to the pools left behind.

Provincetown

Long Point Beach A blissfully quiet beach at the end of a trail lined with scented wild roses and beach plums; you can get there on foot (it's a *long* walk on the jetty) or by frequent shuttle from MacMillan Wharf (see p.220).

Herring Cove Beach off Rte-6. Easily reached by bike or through the dunes, and famous for sunset-watching, this beach is actually more crowded than those nearer town, though never unbearably so.

Province Lands off Race Point Road. Beautiful vast, sweeping moors and bushy dunes are buffeted by crashing surf; the site has seen some three thousand known shipwrecks.

Race Point Beach off Race Point Road. Abutting Province Lands, this wide swath of white sand is backed by beautiful, tall dunes – the archetypal Cape Cod beach.

Sandwich

Sandy Neck Beach off Sandy Neck Road, East Sandwich. Six-mile-long barrier beach loaded with low dunes favored by off-roaders; the paths are shut down in summer to encourage the local bird population's hatching season.

Town Neck Beach off Town Neck Road. Narrow and rocky beach 1.5 miles out of town with pretty views of passing ships and decent facilities.

Wakeby Pond Ryder Conservation Area, John Ewer Road. The Cape's largest fresh-water pond has a life-guarded beach and full facilities.

Truro

Head of the Meadow off Head of the Meadow Rd. Remote National Seashore beach with great surfing conditions and restrooms; easily accessed by boardwalk from the parking lot.

Wellfleet

Cahoon Hollow Beach off Ocean View Drive. Good surfing and full facilities make this town-run beach popular with the thirty-something set. Don't miss the famous *Beachcomber* shack for delicious oysters (see box overleaf).

Marconi Beach off Marconi Beach Road. Dramatic cliff-framed beach best hit in the morning before the sun falls behind the bluffs. Good facilities.

White Crest off Ocean View Drive. The main distinction between White Crest and neighboring Cahoon is the clientele – here, it's a predominantly young college crowd.

the focus of a thriving oyster-fishing industry, today it is a favorite haunt of writers and artists who come to seek inspiration from the unsullied landscapes and the heaving ocean. Despite the fact that a number of art galleries have surfaced – most of them along **Main** or **Commercial streets** – the town remains

Oyster shucking

No visit to Wellfleet would be complete without a taste of the town's famous oysters. In fact, the little molluscs are so abundant here that the French explorer Samuel de Champlain named the town "Port aux Huitres" (or Oyster Port) when he disembarked in 1606. The current name of Wellfleet, given by the English in 1763, also has an oyster heritage – it's a nod to England's own Wellfleet oyster beds. One of the best places to dive into a plate of the raw variety is the rowdy *Beachcomber*, on Cahoon Hollow Beach (ⓣ508/349-6055), a fun beach shack with awesome waterfront views. You can also attend the Wellfleet **Oyster Weekend** (every mid to late October; ⓦwww.wellfleetoysterfest.org), complete with raw bars and shucking contests.

a remarkably unpretentious place, with many of the galleries themselves resembling fishing shacks and selling highly distinctive original work aimed at the serious collector, alongside mass-market souvenirs. The Art Gallery Association produces a guide to the galleries which can be picked up at the **information booth** at the corner of Rte-6 and LeCount Hollow Road (ⓣ508/349-2510). The **Wellfleet Historical Society Museum**, 266 Main St (late June to early Sept Tues & Fri 10am–4pm, Wed, Thurs & Sat 1–4pm; free; ⓦwww.wellfleethistoricalsociety.com), has an interesting collection of furniture, items salvaged from shipwrecks, nautical artifacts, and photographs, as well as exhibits on the local oyster industry.

The most scenic part of town is actually outside the center, at the bluff-lined **Marconi Beach**, east off Rte-6 in South Wellfleet, where Guglielmo Marconi issued the first transatlantic radio signal on January 18, 1903, and announced greetings from President Roosevelt to King Edward VII. Nothing remains of the tall radio towers built for this purpose, but there are some scale models beneath a gazebo-type structure overlooking the ocean. A short trail up the cliffside leads to a vantage point from which you can see horizontally across the entire Cape – just a mile wide at this point. Marconi is a good spot for a beach day, too: there are lifeguards, public restrooms and showers, and parking ($15) that rarely fills to capacity.

Practicalities

If you want to **stay** the night in Wellfleet, try the laid-back *Holden Inn*, 140 Commercial St (ⓣ508/349-3450, ⓦwww.theholdeninn.com; ❺; open May–Oct), a farmhouse-style structure with 27 rooms, some with shared baths, or the charming *Inn at Duck Creeke*, 70 Main St (ⓣ508/349-9333, ⓦwww.innatduckcreeke.com; ❺; open May–Oct), a cozy country inn with shared and private baths situated on five woodland acres. Tiny though Wellfleet is, there are a number of casual seafood **restaurants** worth checking out, such as the *Bayside Lobster Hutt*, 91 Commercial St (ⓣ508/349-6333), an old oyster shack, and *Moby Dick's*, on Rte-6 across from Gull Pond Road (ⓣ508/349-9795), which offers family seafood dining. *Finely JP's*, 554 Rte-6 (ⓣ508/349-7500), is a deceptively plain roadside shack that serves downright tasty oysters and other delicious dishes at a good price; try the oysters Bienville, a baked extravaganza of mushrooms, parmesan, cream, and white wine.

Truro

Most of **TRURO**, a sprawling town that continues on Rte-6 right up to Provincetown, falls within the boundaries of the Cape Cod National Seashore, allowing it to keep preserved the kind of natural beauty that has attracted artists, writers, even politicians – Edward Hopper built a summer house here which he used from 1930 to 1967, and Al Gore and his family have vacationed here. Although at over 43 square miles it's one of the largest towns on the Cape, it's the smallest in population – no surprise, then, that downtown is little more than a strip mall with just a few shops.

It was in windswept Truro that Pilgrim leader **Myles Standish** and his companions from the *Mayflower* found the cache of Indian corn that helped them survive their first New England winter in 1620; a plaque at **Corn Hill** marks the exact spot. It wasn't until 1697, however, that the first permanent settlement was established. Originally called Pamet, after the Native American tribe that once lived here, it was changed in 1705 to Dangerfield due to the particularly treacherous offshore currents, and finally to Truro, after the town in England. In its early days, Truro depended on the sea for its economic well-being, even becoming the site of Cape Cod's first lighthouse in 1797, powered by whale oil. Today a golf course unappealingly sidles up to the lighthouse's 1857 replacement, the **Cape Cod Light** on Lighthouse Road. Also known as the Highland Light, it was automated as recently as 1986, and even more recently moved back 450ft from the eroding shoreline where it was in danger of collapsing into the ocean. Thoreau stayed at the old lighthouse during his travels around the Outer Cape, a place where he said he could "put all America behind him." You can visit it, and the nearby **Highland House Museum**, Lighthouse Road (June–Sept daily 10am–4.30pm; $3, $5 with lighthouse; ⓣ508/487-3397, ⓦwww.trurohistorical.org), a 1907 hotel that's now home to some rather prosaic remnants of yesteryear such as fishing and whaling equipment, old photographs, and seventeenth-century firearms; better are the objects obtained from the many shipwrecks that have occurred offshore, as well as the second-floor rooms done up in Victorian style – they emulate the chambers this former hotel's guests occupied in the early 1900s.

Practicalities

Other than privately owned summer homes, which can be rented by the week from Duarte/Downey Real Estate, 12 Truro Center Rd (ⓣ508/349-7588, ⓦwww.ddre.com), places to **stay** in Truro are mainly confined to a strip of sandy terrain which hugs the bay shoreline west of Shore Road (Rte-6A) in North Truro. Due to Truro's windswept nature, all of the following (except for the *Blacksmith Shop*, which closes only from Jan to mid-Feb) are open only in **summer**. *Kalmar Village* (ⓣ508/487-0585, ⓦwww.kalmarvillage.com; ❻) consists of 45 spacious and well-kept one- and two-bedroom cottages in an oceanfront community. In July and August, these can only be rented by the week; at other times, nightly rentals are possible. The *Top Mast*, 209 Shore Rd (Rte-6A), North Truro (ⓣ508/487-1189, ⓦwww.topmastresort.com; ❺), looks like three adjacent motels right on the beach; its rooms are unattractive but the price and location are right. Truro is also home to one of the Cape's two HI **hostels** at 111 North Pamet Rd (ⓣ508/349-3889, ⓔtruro@usahostels.org, from $24/person). The hostel is a former Coast Guard station near the beach with co-ed and private rooms; additionally, like much of Truro, it's just a 10min drive from Provincetown. For something to **eat**, *Adrian's*, 535 Rte-6, North Truro (ⓣ508/487-4360), serves affordable breakfasts and dinners with an Italian touch, while the *Blacksmith Shop*, Truro Center Rd off Rte-6A (ⓣ508/349-6554), is a local institution for its hefty portions of moderately priced prime rib and shrimp.

Provincetown

Far from being out of the way, Provincetown is directly in the way of the navigator... It is situated on one of the highways of commerce, and men from all parts of the globe touch there in the course of a year.

from *Cape Cod* by Henry David Thoreau

The brash fishing burg of **PROVINCETOWN**, at the very tip of Cape Cod, is a popular summer destination for bohemians, artists, and fun-seekers lured by the excellent beaches, art galleries, and welcoming atmosphere. It is known most famously as a **gay** resort destination, complete with frequent festivals and

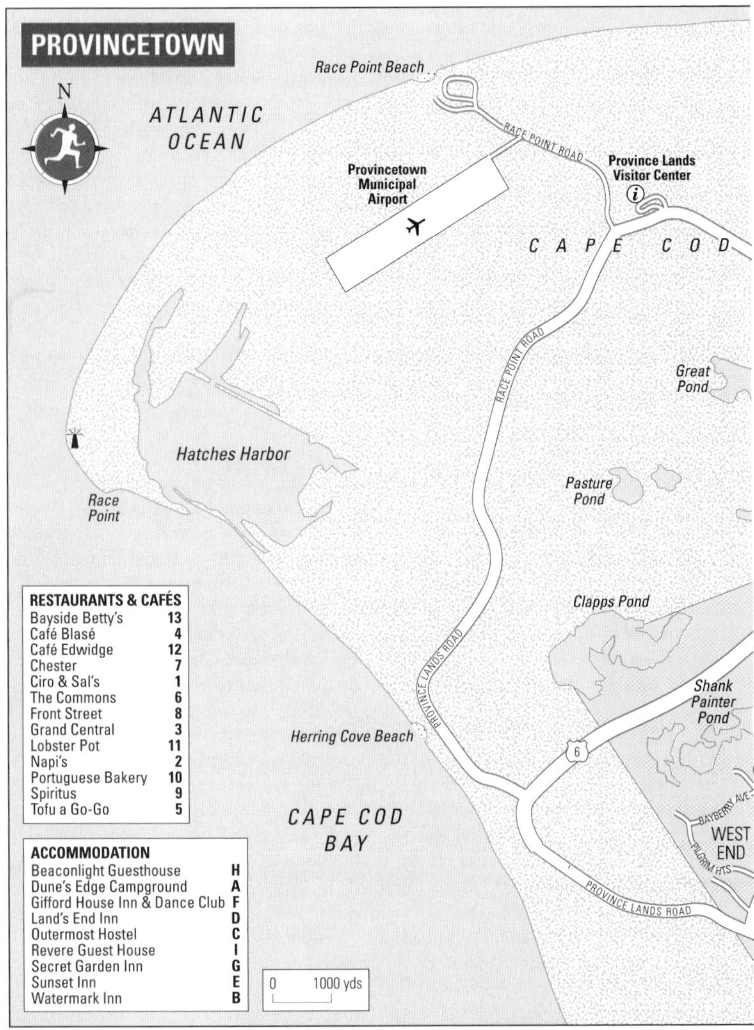

theme weekends. Now that same-sex marriage is legal in Massachusetts, the town sells itself as a home for destination weddings. P-town – as this coastal community of five thousand year-round inhabitants is commonly known – also has a drop of **Portuguese** culture to embellish it, after a smallish population of fishermen began settling here, starting in the mid-1800s; their legacy is now celebrated in an annual June festival complete with music and Portuguese soup-tasting competitions. Throughout the summer, P-town's population swells into the tens of thousands, and there's often a carnival atmosphere in the bustling streets. The appealing hamlet should not be missed by anyone, especially as it's just an hour-and-a-half ferry ride from Boston.

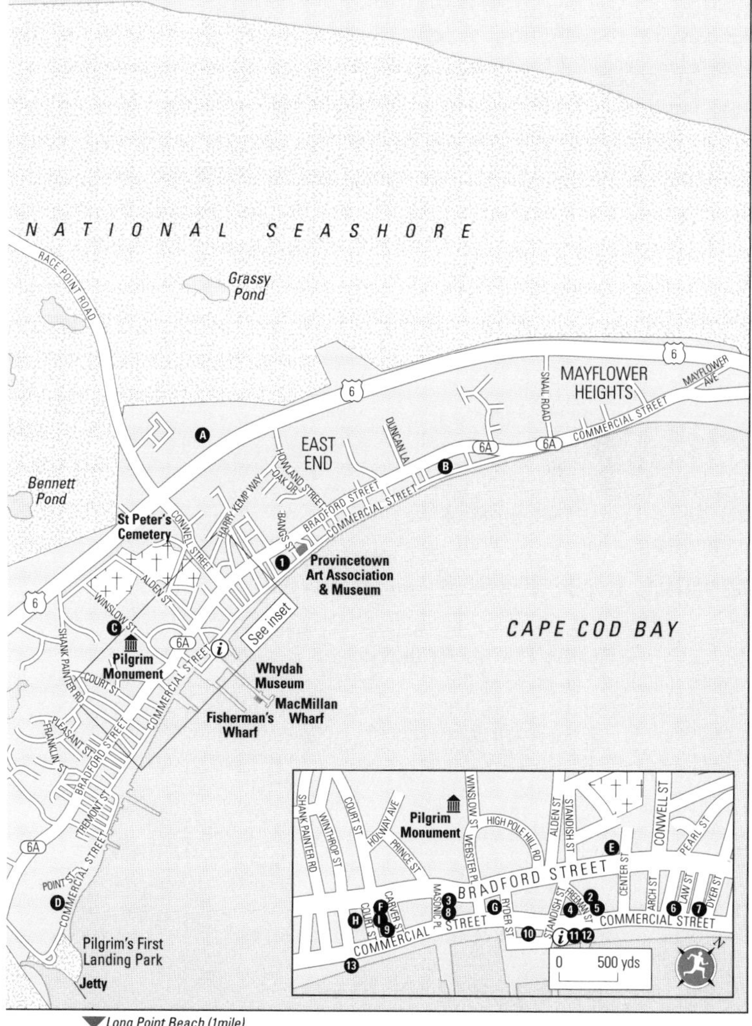

Long Point Beach (1mile)

Some history

Provincetown has a number of **Pilgrim**-related monuments – after all, they landed here before heading to Plymouth – but they were not the first European visitors to arrive at Provincetown. Way back in 1004, Leif Erikson's brother, **Thorvald**, disembarked here to repair the broken keel of his ship and named the place "Cape of the Keel"; it was later dubbed Cape Cod by Bartholomew Gosnold in 1602. The Pilgrims came ashore here and stayed for five weeks in 1620, signing the **Mayflower Compact**, one long and rather vaguely worded sentence espousing a democratic form of self-government, before sailing across Cape Cod Bay.

Provincetown was incorporated in 1727, and soon became a thriving fishing, salt-processing, and whaling port; indeed, by 1880, the town was the richest per capita in Massachusetts. Fishing retains its importance here, but the town's destiny to become one of the East Coast's leading **art colonies** was assured in 1899, when painter Charles W. Hawthorne founded the **Cape Cod School of Art**, which encouraged artists to explore the outdoors and exploit the Mediterranean-like quality of the light. So many of his friends came to investigate the place that it became known as the "Greenwich Village of the North." By the early 1900s, many painters had begun to ply their trade in abandoned "dune shacks" by the sea, and by 1916 there were no fewer than six art schools here. The natural beauty and laidback atmosphere also began to seduce rebellious young writers like Mary Heaton Vorse, who established the **Provincetown Players** theater group in 1915. **Eugene O'Neill** joined the company in 1916, premiering his *Bound East for Cardiff* in a waterfront fish house done up as a theater, and **Tennessee Williams** was another frequent visitor.

As much of an impact as its colorful residents have had, equally important in Provincetown's history has been its **geography**. The entire Cape is a glacial deposit on a crooked sliver of bedrock, but due to its position at the very tip, Provincetown is particularly susceptible to the vagaries of wind and water, the fragile environment lending a certain legitimacy to the strict **zoning laws** that have kept major development at bay and, consequently, continue to preserve the flavor of the old town. There's also evidence that the shifting dunes of this part of the Cape Cod National Seashore, including the barren but beautiful **Province Lands**, were once covered with topsoil and trees that were cut for fuel, thus hastening the process of erosion – a further example of the need for conservation.

Arrival, information, and getting around

Two companies make the ninety-minute trip across Massachusetts Bay to Provincetown: **Boston Harbor Cruises** departs from **Long Wharf** (daily late May to mid-June leaving 9am, returning 4pm; late June to early Oct Mon–Wed leaving 9am, returning 4pm, Thurs leaving 9am & 6.30pm, returning 4pm & 8.30pm, Fri–Sun leaving 9am, 2pm & 6.30pm, returning 11am, 4pm & 8.30pm; $59 round-trip; Ⓣ617/227-4321, Ⓦwww.bostonharborcruises.com), while **Bay State Cruises** leaves, somewhat inconveniently, from the **Commonwealth Pier** by Boston's World Trade Center (daily late May to early June leaving 8am & 5.30pm, returning 10am & 7.30pm; daily late June to early Oct leaving 8am, 1pm & 5.30pm, returning 10am, 3pm & 7.30pm; $64 round-trip; Ⓣ617/748-1428, Ⓦwww.boston-ptown.com). The latter has an excellent **excursion fare** for weekend day-tripping, too: $29 round-trip will get you to P-town and back with a three-hour window to tool around in – but keep in mind that these slower boats take three hours each way (late May to early Sept Fri–Sun leaving 9.30am, returning 3.30pm).

Provincetown is at the end of **Rte-6**, the Cape's main highway, and **buses** regularly trawl this stretch from Boston and all the major Cape towns; Bonanza Bus Lines (Ⓣ401/751-8800 or 1-888/751-8800, Ⓦwww.bonanzabus.com) and Plymouth & Brockton buses (Ⓣ508/746-0378, Ⓦwww.p-b.com) are the ones to call. Buses stop right in the middle of town near MacMillan Wharf. There is a **visitors' center** right by the bus stop, 307 Commercial St (Ⓣ508/487-3424), where you can pick up all sorts of information. You can get online information before you go at Ⓦwww.provincetown.com; gays and lesbians may also want to check Ⓦwww.gayprovincetown.com.

Transit and tours

Provincetown is a very **walkable** place; **bicycles** can come in handy, though, especially if you want to venture a bit further afield. For rentals, Arnold's, 329 Commercial St (Ⓣ508/487-0844), right in the center of town, is open from mid-April to mid-October, as is Nelson's Bike Shop, 43 Race Point Rd (Ⓣ508/487-8849), located close to the **bike trails** that meander through the Province Lands. Bikes at both places go for about $20 per day. Provincetown also claims the title of first **whale-watching** spot on the East Coast; the best company is the Dolphin Fleet (June–Oct; $30; Ⓣ508/349-1900 or 1-800/826-9300, Ⓦwww.whalewatch.com), with cruises leaving frequently from MacMillan Wharf.

If you want to take a **boat ride**, Provincetown Harbor Cruises, MacMillan Wharf (Ⓣ508/487-4330), run forty-minute trips round the bay hourly from 11am to 7pm in season ($7), while Flyer's Boat Rentals, 131A Commercial St (Ⓣ508/487-0898 or 1-800/750-0898, Ⓦwww.flyersrentals.com), provides a range of rental boats, from kayaks to powerboats. Alternatively, take their **shuttle** across Cape Cod Bay to Long Point Beach (mid-June to mid-Sept; $8 one-way, $12 round-trip). You can also opt to ramble about the dunes in a four-wheel-drive vehicle with **Art's Dune Tours**, at Commercial and Standish streets (April–Oct 10am–dusk; $19; Ⓣ508/487-1950, Ⓦwww.artsdunetours.com), or fly over them in a four-seat Cessna ($90, reservations required; Ⓣ508/428-8732). The twenty-minute flights take off from the Cape Cod Airport, near the intersection of Race Lane and Rte-149.

Accommodation

Many of the most picturesque cottages in town are **guesthouses**, some with spectacular views over Cape Cod Bay. The best place to be is the quiet West End, though anything on Bradford Street will also be removed from the summertime racket. Prices are generally very reasonable until mid-June, and off-season you can find real bargains. In addition, there are a few **motels**, mostly confined to the outskirts of town, towards the Truro line. Provincetown Reservations (Ⓣ508/487-2400 or 1-800/648-0364) and the gay-oriented Intown Reservations (Ⓣ508/487-1883 or 1-800/67P-TOWN) can usually rustle up lodging at busy times. The welcoming Dune's Edge Campground, on Rte-6 just east of the central stoplights (Ⓣ508/487-9815, Ⓦwww.dunes-edge.com), charges $22 for use of one of its wooded sites.

Beaconlight Guesthouse 12 Winthrop St Ⓣ1-800/696 9603, Ⓦwww.beaconlightguesthouse.com. Stylish ten-unit guesthouse with individually appointed rooms, equipped with a/c, TV, and VCR. ❼

Gifford House Inn & Dance Club 9–11 Carver St Ⓣ1-800/434-0130, Ⓦwww.giffordhouse.com. Popular gay resort with lobby piano bar, restaurant, and dance floor; continental breakfast included. ❺

Land's End Inn 22 Commercial St Ⓣ1-800/276-7088 or 508/487-0706, Ⓦwww.landsendinn.com. Meticulously decorated rooms and suites, many with sweeping ocean views, in a fanciful turreted house; continental breakfast and daily wine and cheese tasting included. ⑨

Outermost Hostel 28 Winslow St ⓣ508/487-4378. Hostel with thirty $25 beds in five cramped dorm cabins; includes kitchen access and parking.

Revere Guest House 14 Court St ⓣ508/487-2292 or 1-800/487-2292, ⓦwww.reverehouse.com. This pleasant B&B has a garden patio and antiques-accented rooms, one with shared bath. ⑦

Secret Garden Inn 300a Commercial St ⓣ1-866/786-9646 or 508/487-9027, ⓦwww.secret-gardenptown.com. Seven quaint rooms in a house with a verandah, done up in country furnishings, and with modern touches like TVs and air-conditioning; country breakfast included. ⑥

Sunset Inn 142 Bradford St ⓣ508/487-9810, ⓦwww.sunsetinnptown.com. Clean, quiet rooms in an 1850 captain's house with double or queen beds and private or shared bath. ⑦

Watermark Inn 603 Commercial St ⓣ508/487-0165, ⓦwww.watermark-inn.com. Ten immaculate and contemporary suites, several of which come with private decks and ocean views, right on the water. Several are rented by the week in summer ($1050–2175). ⑦

The Town and around

The town center is essentially two three-mile-long streets, **Commercial** and **Bradford**, connected by about forty tiny lanes of no more than two short blocks each. Though much diluted by tourism, the beatnik spirit is still in evidence, most pronounced in regular Friday-night expositions in the many art galleries along Commercial Street. On summer evenings the narrow street fills with hordes of sightseers, locals, and, amazingly, cars, even though they can do little more than crawl along. **Fisherman's Wharf**, and the more touristy **MacMillan Wharf**, busy with whale-watching boats, yachts, and colorful old Portuguese fishing vessels, split the town in half. MacMillan Wharf also houses the **Whydah Museum**, 16 MacMillan Wharf (April–May & Sept–Oct daily 10am–4pm, June–Aug daily 10am–7pm; $8; ⓣ508/487-8899, ⓦwww.whydah.com), which displays some of the bounty from a famous pirate shipwreck off the coast of Wellfleet in 1717. The lifelong quest of native Cape Codder Barry Clifford to recover the treasure from the one-time slave ship *Whydah* – repository of loot from more than fifty ships when it sank – paid off royally with his discovery of the ship in the summer of 1983. Thousands of coins, gold bars, pieces of jewelry, and weapons were retrieved, ranging from odds and ends like silver shoe buckles and flintlock pistols to rare African gold jewelry attributed to West Africa's Akan people. The most evocative display in the museum, glimmering gold coins notwithstanding, is the ship's **bell**, a little rusty but not so corroded that you can't read "The Whydah Galley – 1716" clear as day.

Two blocks north of the piers, atop aptly named Town Hill, is the 252-foot granite tower of the **Pilgrim Monument** (daily: May–June & Sept–Nov 9am–4.15pm, July–Aug 9am–6.15pm; $7; ⓣ508/487-1310, ⓦwww.pilgrim-monument.org), modeled on a bell tower in Siena, Italy. It commemorates the Pilgrims' landing and their signing of the Mayflower Compact. From the observation deck you can see all the way to Boston on a clear day. At the bottom of the hill on **Bradford Street** is another bas-relief monument to the Mayflower Compact. Back on the main drag, the delightful **Provincetown Art Association and Museum**, 460 Commercial St (April to mid-May Sat & Sun noon–5pm; mid-May to June & Sept daily noon–5pm, Sat & Sun noon–5pm & 8–10pm; July–Aug daily noon–5pm & 8–10pm; Oct–April Sat & Sun noon–4pm; $5; ⓣ508/487-1750, ⓦwww.paam.org), rotates works from its two-thousand-strong collection, with equal prominence given to local and established artists. Friday night is best, when openings by new artists frequently take place.

On the other side of the wharves is the quieter and slightly less cramped **West End**, where many of the weathered clapboard houses are cheerfully decorated with colored blinds, white picket fences, and wildflowers spilling out of every

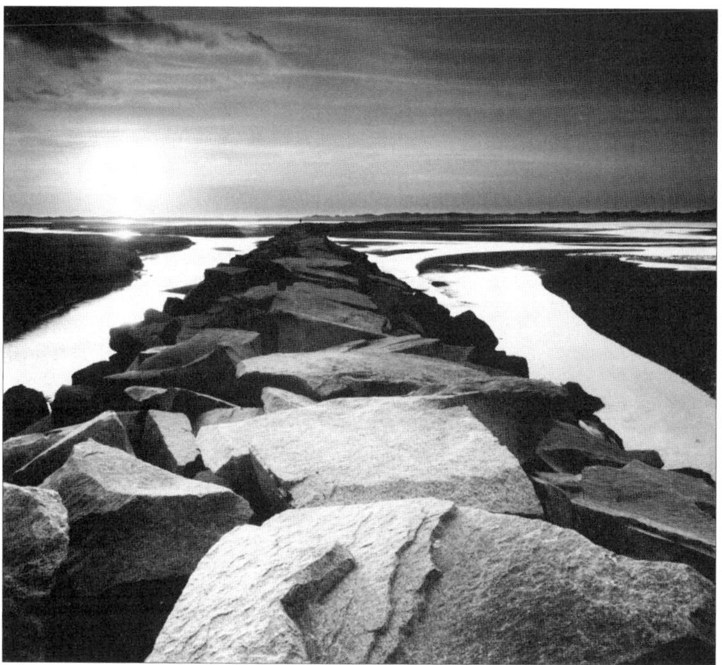

△ Jetty to Long Point Beach

possible orifice. At Commercial Street's western end, the Pilgrim **landing place** is marked by a modest bronze plaque on a boulder. Nearby, just past the *Provincetown Inn*, is the **Breakwater Trail**, a mile-long **jetty** leading to Long Point Beach, a great place to watch the sun set.

A little way beyond the town's narrow strip of sand, a string of **undeveloped beaches** is marked only by dunes and a few shabby huts. The Province Lands **visitors' center**, in the middle of the dunes off Race Point Road (late May to early Sept daily 9am–5pm; early Sept to late Oct & April to late May daily 9am–4.30pm; ⓣ508/487-1256), has an observation deck from which you might spot a whale – or even, when the tide is right, the ruins of the **HMS Somerset**, a sunken British battleship from the Revolutionary War. Province Lands is also home to the best **bike path** on Cape Cod, roaming through the dunes and without a building in sight.

Eating

Food in Provincetown can be expensive: the snack bars around MacMillan Wharf are generally extortionate, and the eclectic cuisine in the sometimes precious restaurants can hit $10 for a salad and a coffee. Still, there are some real discoveries to be made, and they need not break your budget – look out in particular for the **Portuguese** restaurants that can be found throughout town. Whenever possible, especially in the few restaurants where it's possible to eat al fresco (mosquitoes can be a big problem), arrive early or call ahead to make a reservation; many restaurants are packed in season. Most eateries **close** in the winter, though some remain open on weekends only.

Bayside Betty's 177 Commercial St ⓣ508/487-6566. Funky waterfront eatery with hearty breakfasts and seafood dinners that's also a popular martini bar.

Café Blasé 328 Commercial St ⓣ508/487-9465. Touristy pastel café, one of the few places with outdoor seating for great people-watching. Pricey for pasta and steak dinners, but moderate for delicious fresh fruit and waffle breakfasts, and pre-dinner cocktails.

Café Edwidge 333 Commercial St ⓣ508/487-2008. Breakfast's the thing at this popular second-floor spot; try the homemade Danish pastries and fresh fruit pancakes. Creative bistro fare at dinnertime.

Chester 404 Commercial St ⓣ508/487-8200. Preciously chic spot with an award-winning wine list. The menu changes weekly, emphasizing fresh ingredients, unusual combinations like sea scallops with apples and sage, and high prices.

Ciro & Sal's 4 Kiley Court ⓣ508/487-6444. Traditional Northern Italian cooking with plenty of veal and seafood; a bit on the pricey side, but worth it.

The Commons 386 Commercial St ⓣ508/487-7800. French bistro food and tasty pizzas from a wood-fired oven make this a popular spot.

Front Street 230 Commercial St ⓣ508/487-9715. Popular Italian and Continental restaurant located in a Victorian house; menu changes weekly, but you might find dishes like crab-stuffed filet mignon.

Grand Central 5 Masonic Place ⓣ508/487-7599. Directly across from the *Atlantic House* bar (see below), a romantic, eclectically decorated bistro with mid-range prices.

Lobster Pot 321 Commercial St ⓣ508/487-0842. Its landmark neon sign is like a welcome mat for those who come from far and wide for the ultra-fresh crustaceans. Affordable and family-oriented.

Napi's 7 Freeman St ⓣ508/487-1145. Popular dishes at this art-strewn spot include pastas and seafood items, notably a thick Portuguese fish stew. They have a less expensive menu on week nights.

Portuguese Bakery 299 Commercial St ⓣ508/487-1803. This old standby is the place to come for cheap baked goods, particularly the tasty fried *rabanada*, akin to portable French toast.

Spiritus 190 Commercial St ⓣ508/487-2808. Combination pizza place and coffee bar with an especially lively after-hours scene.

Tofu a Go-Go 336 Commercial St ⓣ508/487-6237. Casual upstairs eatery serving exclusively vegetarian fare, like delicious tofu salad.

Nightlife and entertainment

Each in-season weekend, boatloads of revelers seek out P-town's notoriously wild **nightlife**. Heavily geared towards a **gay** clientele, resulting in ubiquitous tea dances, drag shows, and video bars, some establishments have terrific waterfront locations and terraces to match, making them ideal spots to sit out with a drink at sunset. Any cover charge you may come across will fall somewhere in the $5–10 range. You'll also find that many of Provincetown's restaurants have a lively bar scene, too.

The Alibi 291 Commercial St ⓣ508/487-2890. Campy bar with four daily drag shows. Cover.

Atlantic House 6 Masonic Place, behind Commercial St ⓣ508/487-3821. The "A-House" – a dark drinking hole that was a favorite of Tennessee Williams and Eugene O'Neill – is now a trendy (and still dark) gay dance club and bar.

Boatslip 161 Commercial St ⓣ508/487-1669, ⓦwww.boatslipresort.com. The Sunday tea dances at this resort are legendary; you can either dance away on a long wooden deck overlooking the water, or cruise inside under a disco ball and flashing lights.

Club Euro 258 Commercial St ⓣ508/487-2505. Music videos, world-beat sounds, and a good buzz in an 1843 former Congregational church with a 3D mermaid emerging from the wall. Occasional drag nights.

Crown and Anchor 247 Commercial St ⓣ508/487-1430, ⓦwww.onlyatthecrown.com. A massive complex housing several bars, including *The Vault*, P-town's only leather bar, *Wave*, a video-karaoke bar, and *Paramount*, a cabaret with nightly acts.

Pied Piper 193 Commercial St ⓣ508/487-1527. Though largely a lesbian club (it's the oldest in the country), the outdoor deck and inside dance floor at this trendy waterfront space attract a good dose of men, too, for their longstanding After Tea T-Dance (Sun 6.30–9pm).

Martha's Vineyard and Nantucket

Just six miles south of Cape Cod, the sedate, forested island of **Martha's Vineyard** has long been one of the most popular and prestigious vacation destinations in the US, a status that has only grown in recent years, as a gaggle of celebrities have come for its mannerly New England towns, untouched beaches, and, above all, peace and quiet. Like its slightly further afield cousin, **Nantucket**, it mingles an easygoing cosmopolitan atmosphere, assured by some of the best restaurants and B&Bs on the East Coast, with a taste of remoteness, even though Boston and New York are just short flights away. Neither island boasts much in the way of traditional sights, and almost all locals are more than happy to keep it that way.

Martha's Vineyard

The largest offshore island in New England, twenty-mile-long **MARTHA'S VINEYARD** encompasses more physical variety than Nantucket, with hills and pasturelands providing scenic counterpoints to the beaches and wild, windswept moors on the separate island of **Chappaquiddick**. Roads throughout the Vineyard are framed by knotty oak trees, which lend a romantic aura to an already pretty landscape. The most genteel town on the island is **Edgartown**, all prim and proper with its freshly painted, white-clapboard Colonial homes and manicured gardens. The other main town, **Vineyard Haven**, has a more commercial atmosphere, not surprising considering that it is one of the main places where the ferries come in. **Oak Bluffs**, in between the two (and the other docking point for ferries), has an array of wooden gingerbread cottages and inviting eateries. Regardless of where you visit, watch out for the terminology: heading "Up-Island" takes you, improbably, southwest to the cliffs at **Aquinnah** (formerly known as Gay Head); conversely, "Down-Island" refers to the triumvirate of easterly towns mentioned above.

Some history

Martha's Vineyard was named by the British explorer who discovered it in 1602, **Bartholomew Gosnold**, for his daughter, Martha. The "Vineyard" part was for its fertile store of vines – back then the triangular-shaped island was virtually covered with wild grapes, many of which still remain along the sides of the roads. While Gosnold spent only three days on the island, **Wampanoag Indians** had been calling it home for at least ten thousand years, and a small community of around three hundred remains at **Aquinnah**, near the multicolored limestone cliffs of Gay Head. They claimed that in order to separate his tribe from enemies on the mainland, the Indian chief **Moshup** placed his cape on the ground and created Vineyard Sound, though geological records put that event as happening about 50,000 years ago.

For a few decades after Gosnold's departure the island was once again the exclusive province of the natives, but in 1642 one **Thomas Mayhew** bought

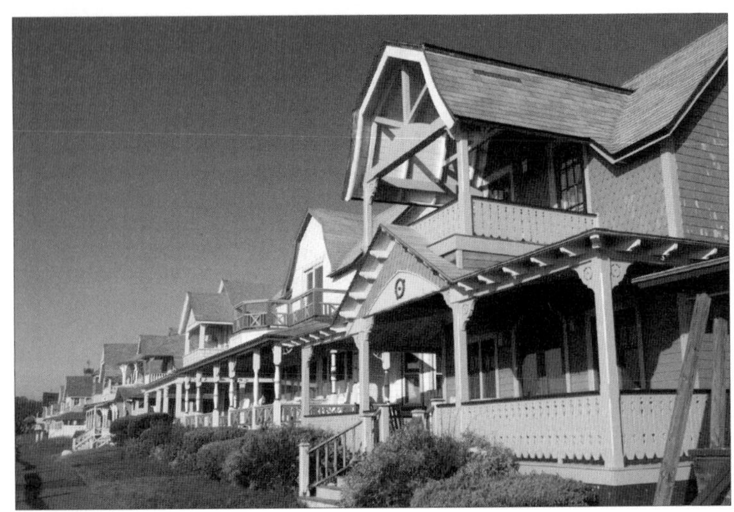

△ Gingerbread houses in Oak Bluffs

it from the earl of Stirling for forty pounds and a beaver hat, paving the way for other English Puritan farmers to settle here. They learned tricks of the whaling industry from the natives, and the economy flourished: while Martha's Vineyard never ousted Nantucket or New Bedford as whaling capital of the East, many of its captains did very nicely from the industry, evidenced by the gracious sea captains' houses that remain in Edgartown and Vineyard Haven. By the time of the Civil War in the 1860s, however, whaling was in serious decline, and had it not been for the **Methodist camp meetings** that started here in 1835, the island's tourist industry might never have taken root. Dozens of Methodist families from churches all over the nation started gathering in tents at sparsely populated **Oak Bluffs** for two weeks of vigorous preaching and recreation; they were looking for an isolated location far away from the temptations of the flesh. As the movement grew, so did the desire of many families to return, some building permanent platforms arranged around the preachers' tent, and later constructing small cottages with extraordinarily fancy facades, now familiar as "**gingerbread**" style – more than half of which remain clustered round the village green. In 1867, recognizing the island's potential as a resort, developers constructed a separate secular community next to the original campground, and large hotels were soon built around the harbor.

Though tourism has never abated, today strictly enforced **zoning** laws ensure that major development is kept to a minimum: billboards, neon signs, and even parking meters are outlawed. Though there can be heavy traffic during summer on the island, there is only one stoplight, and residents have been successful in keeping it that way despite numerous accidents at major intersections.

Arrival, information, and getting around

Most people come to Martha's Vineyard by **ferry**, arriving at either Oak Bluffs or Vineyard Haven, usually from Woods Hole (see box on p.226 for schedules and fares). You can also **fly** via Cape Air (Ⓣ508/771-6944 or 1-800/352-0714, Ⓦwww.flycapeair.com) from Boston (from which there's an hourly shuttle in the summer), Hyannis, Nantucket, or New Bedford. The Vineyard's **airport**

(ⓣ508/693-7022) is in West Tisbury. **Taxis** greet all arriving ferries and flights; all companies use the same fare sheets, and some share phone numbers. Try Martha's Vineyard Taxi (ⓣ508/693-8660), All Island (ⓣ508/693-3705), or Accurate (ⓣ508/627-9798).

The island has an increasingly frequent and reliable **bus** system that connects the main towns, from around 7am to 12.45am daily (ⓣ508/639-9440, ⓦwww.vineyardtransit.com); tickets cost $1 per town, including the town of origin, or $6 per day. Getting a day pass and a map is the best way to get around without a car, but there are also three-hour narrated **tours** run by Martha's Vineyard Sightseeing ($19; ⓣ508/627-TOUR, ⓦwww.mvtour.com); the trolleys run from spring to fall from all ferry arrival points. Another option is to **bike** – in Vineyard Haven you can rent from Martha's Bike Rentals at the Five Corners, just a block from the ferry (ⓣ1-800/559-0312, ⓦwww.marthasvineyardbikes.com), in Oak Bluffs from Anderson Bike Rentals on Circuit Avenue (ⓣ508/693-9346), or in Edgartown from R.W. Cutler Bikes at 1 Main St (ⓣ1-800/627-2763, ⓦwww.edgartownbikerentals.com). A basic mountain bike generally starts at $20/day, no matter the company.

Bringing a **car** over on the ferry is an expensive option, and often impossible on summer weekends without reserving months in advance. If you just can't do without a car, you can rent one from Budget, in Vineyard Haven, Oak Bluffs, Edgartown, or the airport (ⓣ508/693-1911 or 1-800/527-0700, ⓦwww.budget.com), or Adventure Rentals/Thrifty in Vineyard Haven and at the airport (ⓣ508/696-0909 or 508/693-1959, ⓦwww.adventurerentalsmv.com). Tourist **information** is available at the Chamber of Commerce in Vineyard Haven or at the post office in Edgartown, both of which stock the requisite pamphlets and island maps.

Accommodation

There's a tremendous variety of **accommodation** on the island, ranging from resort hotels with every conceivable creature comfort, to old sea captains'

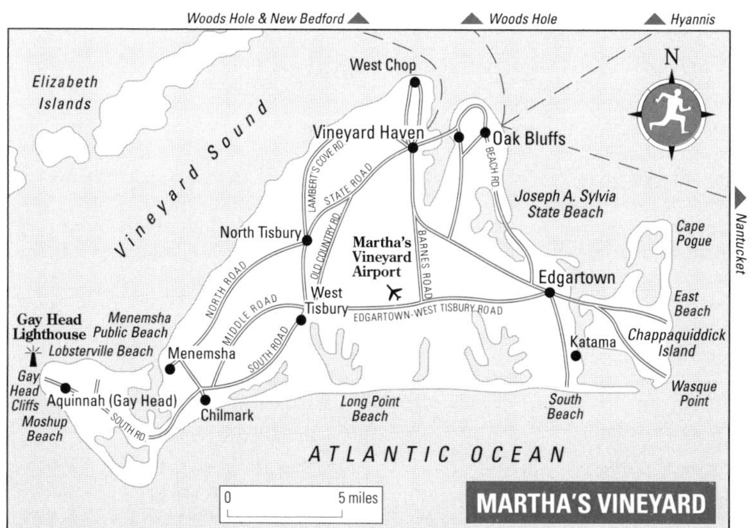

Ferries to Martha's Vineyard

The most frequent ferries – and the only ones that can take cars – run year-round from **Woods Hole**. In addition, the Woods Hole ferry is one of the few reliable ways to get to the island in the **winter**, when ferries run solely to Vineyard Haven. In the summer, however, leaving from somewhere else can be more convenient. **Falmouth** and **Hyannis** have day-boats, though only the Hyannis boats runs in the winter. In order to avoid weekend Cape Cod traffic, the ferries from **New Bedford** and **Quanset Point** in Rhode Island have become popular options. They're more expensive, but for many it's well worth it for the time saved. Unless otherwise specified, the ferries listed below run several times daily in the peak mid-June to mid-September holiday periods. Most have fewer services from mid-May to mid-June and from mid-September to October. **Parking** at the ferries is usually $10 per day, and most charge extra for bikes (up to $6). **Prices** listed below are for a roundtrip.

From Cape Cod

Falmouth to Oak Bluffs (about 35min). Passengers only. The *Island Queen* ($12; ⓣ508/548-4800, ⓦwww.islandqueen.com).
Falmouth to Edgartown (1hr). Passengers only. A small boat, so call ahead for reservations Fri–Sun. Falmouth Ferry Service ($30; ⓣ508/548-9400, ⓦwww.falmouthferry.com).
Woods Hole to both Vineyard Haven and Oak Bluffs (45min). Car ferry, year-round. Reservations required to bring a car on summer weekends and holidays – you can bring a car standby all other times, though the wait can be long. Steamship Authority ($120 high season or $70 low season per car, not including passengers, who must pay $5.50 each way; ⓣ508/477-8600, ⓦwww.steamshipauthority.com).
Hyannis to Oak Bluffs (about 1hr 40min). Passengers only. Hy-Line ($31; ⓣ508/778-2600 or 1-888/778-1132, ⓦwww.hy-linecruises.com).

From elsewhere in Massachusetts and Rhode Island

New Bedford to Vineyard Haven or Oak Bluffs (1hr). Passengers only. A great way to avoid Cape traffic if coming from Rhode Island or New York ($50; ⓣ1-866/453-6800, ⓦwww.nefastferry.com).
Quanset Point, Rhode Island, to Oak Bluffs (1hr 30min). Passengers only. Good for those traveling from Connecticut or New York; Quonset is south of Providence and Warwick. Be forewarned that the ride can get rough on windy days – ask ahead – the staff is honest about what sea conditions are like. Viking Ferry ($58; ⓣ401/295-4040, ⓦwww.vineyardfastferry.com).

homes oozing with charm and personality, as well as rental cottages, usually booked on a weekly basis. Keep in mind that whatever type of lodging you decide on, summer accommodation in Martha's Vineyard gets booked up very early, so reserve well in advance. If you do get stuck with nowhere to stay, the main Chamber of Commerce office will always do their best to help. Remember too that in-season and off-season prices can vary dramatically, making fall and spring a good time to call for discounted rates – though even then the weekends may be booked for weddings. Unless otherwise noted, these hotels close in the dead of winter (Jan & Feb). If you want (or need) to save money, check out the Martha's Vineyard Family **Campground** in Edgartown, 569 Edgartown Rd (ⓣ508/693-3772, ⓦwww.campmvfc.com; $42 for two).

Oak Bluffs

Admiral Benbow Inn 520 New York Ave ⓣ508/693-6825, ⓦwww.admiral-benbow-inn.com. Seven pleasant rooms in a newly restored landmark inn uphill from the harbor. It's on a busy road near a gas station but away from the commercial ruckus of Oak Bluffs. ⑦

Attleboro House 11 Lake Ave ⓣ508/693-4346, ⓦwww.rentalsmv.com/attleborohouse. This old-fashioned Victorian guesthouse is a good budget option – it may have no private bathrooms and sloping ceilings, but the rooms are cozy and neat with access to a harbor-view front porch. Open May–Sept. ⑤

Nashua House B&B 30 Kennebec Ave ⓣ508/693-0043, ⓦwww.nashuahouse.com. Small rooms, some with shared baths, but this very central hotel is an easy walk from the ferry. It can get loud at night, but with rates starting from $99 in high season, one of the less expensive choices for a friendly inn. ⑤

Pequot Hotel 19 Pequot Ave ⓣ1-800/947-8704, ⓦwww.pequothotel.com. Friendly, mid-sized hotel in the gingerbread cottage neighborhood with rocking chairs on the porch and a quick walk to town. ⑦

Wesley Hotel 1 Lake Ave ⓣ508/693-6611 or 1-800/638-9027, ⓦwww.wesleyhotel.com. The last of Oak Bluff's grand hotels, though it's quite commercial now, with small, dimly lit rooms. Overpriced in high season, but with 95 rooms it may have availability when others don't. ⑧

Edgartown

Colonial Inn 38 N Water St ⓣ508/627-4711 or 1-800/627-4701, ⓦwww.colonialinnmvy.com. Very central white-clapboard inn with well-appointed, airy rooms, some off-season bargains, and high midsummer rates. Breakfast included. ⑧

Edgartown Inn 56 N Water St ⓣ508/627-4794, ⓦwww.edgartowninn.com. This eighteenth-century home is a quintessential New England inn with colorful rooms that try to evoke another era. To that end, none of them has a TV. The Garden House and Barn out back have the least expensive rooms. ⑥

Harborside Inn 3 S Water St ⓣ508/627-4321 or 1-800/627-4009, ⓦwww.theharborsideinn.com. Comfortable rooms on the harbor – both centrally located and set away from the noise of town – with heated pool and sauna. ⑨

Shiretown Inn 21 N Water St ⓣ508/627-3353 or 1-800/541-0090, ⓦwww.shiretowninn.com. Variety of differently styled B&B rooms in two old whaling houses and some adjoining cottages in the center of town. The least expensive accommodations are in the non-luxury "Coach Rooms." ⑦

Winnetu Inn & Resort South Beach ⓣ508/627-4747, ⓦwww.winnetu.com. This resort hotel is just a short walk from a private stretch of South Beach. Rooms come with kitchenettes, and it's not all that much more expensive than the in-town options. In high season expect two to three-night minimum stays. ⑧

Elsewhere on the island

HI-Martha's Vineyard Edgartown–West Tisbury Rd ⓣ508/693-2665 or 1-800/901-2087, ⓦwww.usahostels.org. A nice setting and a very neat (both clean and funky) place to stay, but a bit off the beaten track, with 78 beds in dormitory accommodation, with shared bath and a full kitchen. They try to make it easy for people to stay here with bike rental deals and free bike delivery. April to mid-Nov only; non-members $27/night.

Lambert's Cove Country Inn Lambert's Cove Rd, West Tisbury ⓣ508/693-2298, ⓦwww.lambertscoveinn.com. Quiet, secluded country inn on idyllic grounds that include access to a private beach. Very hard to access without a car. ⑧

Menemsha Inn & Cottages and Beach Plum Inn North Rd, Menemsha ⓣ508/645-2521 and 508/645-9454, ⓦwww.menemshainn.com and ⓦwww.beachpluminn.com. These adjacent properties are both beautifully maintained and managed. Within walking distance of the Menemsha beach, they also include access to private town beaches on the south shore. The *Beach Plum* inn is better for young adults, while the cottages at *Menemsha* are better for families. Open May–Nov; book early. ⑧

The island

The Vineyard is basically divided into two sections, the far busier of which is "**Down-Island**," which includes the ferry terminals of **Vineyard Haven** and **Oak Bluffs**, and smart **Edgartown**. The largely undeveloped western half of the island, known as "**Up-Island**," comprises woods, agricultural land, ponds, and nature reserves, with a smattering of tiny villages thrown in, including **West Tisbury**, **Chilmark**, and **Aquinnah** (Gay Head). Although there are plenty of trails to explore, much of the land belongs to private estates and as such is out of bounds to the public.

Vineyard Haven

Most visitors by boat arrive at **VINEYARD HAVEN** (officially named **Tisbury**), at the northern tip of the island. Founded by islanders from Edgartown disillusioned with the iron-fist Puritan rule of the Mayhew family, Vineyard Haven supplanted Edgartown as the island's main commercial center in the mid-1800s, because ferries preferred the shorter run to the mainland; today, the town, which may well be the least attractive on the island, retains its distinctively business-like ambience, its late-Victorian main street lined with a mix of shops, banks, law and real estate offices, and ice-cream parlors.

The brand-new **bus terminal**, visible as you get off the ferry, is also home to a small **visitors' kiosk**, but for more detailed information and help in finding accommodation, walk up Beach Road to the **Chamber of Commerce**, 24 Beach Rd (late May to early Sept daily 9am–5pm, early Sept to late May Mon–Fri 9am–5pm; ⓣ508/693-0085, ⓦwww.mvy.com). Along the way you'll pass the legendary **Black Dog Tavern**, as famous for its souvenirs as for its food and drink; see a review on p.233.

There's no great reason to stay and see the town's sights, as they're more rainy-day curiosities than actual island activities. The **Seamen's Bethel Museum**, 15 Beach Rd (hours vary; free; ⓣ508/693-9317), is set in a wayfarer's synagogue and is chock-full of maritime tidbits given in thanks by homecoming seamen. In addition to the expected carved whale teeth and model schooners, there's a lifebelt from the *Titanic* in the motley collection. From here, it's just a few yards up to **Main Street**, many of whose original buildings were destroyed in the Great Fire of 1883, though it's rebuilt and thriving now. One that escaped the blaze is the 1829 **Mayhew Schoolhouse**, at no. 110, the town's first school (and now a private business); the **liberty pole** out front honors three young island girls who crept out of their homes and risked their lives one night in 1776 to blow up the town's captured liberty pole rather than allow the British sea captain who had seized it to keep it. The 1844 Association Hall at 51 Spring St houses both the **Tisbury Town Hall** and the **Katharine Cornell Theatre**, the latter partly created with funds donated by the famous actress, a longtime summer resident, in her will.

Oak Bluffs

OAK BLUFFS, just across Lagoon Pond from Vineyard Haven, is the newest of the island's six towns, a quiet farming community until the Methodists established their campground, known as "Wesleyan Grove," here in the 1850s. This section of Oak Bluffs remains a relatively tranquil haven filled with the brightly colored "carpenter Gothic" or "**gingerbread**" cottages they built. During the summer, family-oriented events, Sunday-morning church services, and secular Saturday evening concerts are still held in the iron-and-wood-constructed **tabernacle** during summer. The best-known event that takes place here is **Illumination Night** (third Wed in Aug; free), when all the cottages put up Japanese lanterns that they've collected over the years, accompanied by band music at the tabernacle. At one end of the circle, the sweet 1867 **Cottage Museum**, 1 Trinity Park (mid-June to Sept Mon–Sat 10am–4pm; $2 donation) offers a charming collection of photographs, old Bibles, and other artifacts from the campground's history.

In a frenzy of post-Civil War construction, speculators built up the area near the waterfront with dance halls, a skating rink, a railroad linking "Cottage City" to Edgartown, and resort hotels, of which only the 1879 **Wesley Hotel**, on Lake Avenue, survives. Most of the current action focuses on **Circuit Avenue**, where the shops and bars attract a predominantly young crowd. The restored

Flying Horses Carousel, at Circuit and Lake avenues (mid-April to mid-Oct daily 10am–10pm; $2 per ride), is the oldest operating carousel in the country; hand-carved in 1876, the 22 horses on parade here have bona fide horsehair manes.

Oak Bluffs also has a few beaches worth checking out, though the **town beach**, on Sea View Avenue, can get very noisy and crowded in season. Farther south, the **Joseph A. Sylvia State Beach**, a sandy six-mile stretch of shore, is more appealing, and it parallels an undemanding pedestrian/cycle path that leads all the way to Edgartown, with pleasant views to accompany you.

Edgartown

Six miles southeast of Oak Bluffs, **EDGARTOWN**, originally known as Great Harbor, is the oldest and swankiest settlement on the island, and has been extravagantly dolled up for visitors, its elegant Colonial residences glistening white and surrounded by exquisitely maintained gardens and trimmed hedges. It doesn't end there, of course: downtown brims with upmarket boutiques, smart restaurants, and artsy galleries.

Once you've got your bearings at the seasonal **Visitors' Center** on Church St (late May to early Sept daily 9am–5pm), which is basically just public restrooms, a bus stop, and a place to pick up brochures, it's a short walk to the **Vineyard Museum**, at the corner of Cooke and School streets (mid-June to mid-Oct Tues–Sat 10am–5pm; rest of year Wed–Fri 1–4pm, Sat 10am–4pm; $7; Ⓣ508/627-4441, Ⓦwww.marthasvineyardhistory.org), a complex of buildings maintained by the Martha's Vineyard Historical Society. One of them, the 1845 **Captain Frances Pease House**, is full of whaling relics and native arrowheads and, best of all, an Oral History Center, which traces the history of the island through more than 250 recorded narratives of older locals; another, the pre-Revolutionary **Thomas Cooke House**, is decorated in the Colonial style befitting the means of the island's one-time customs officer, while the **Carriage Shed** serves as a hodgepodge storeroom for, among other things, a peddler's cart and a whaleboat.

A couple of blocks to the east, on Main Street, the massive **Old Whaling Church**, whose 92 foot-high clock tower is visible for miles around, started life in 1843 as a Methodist church and is now used as a performing arts center, among other things. Its impressive six-column portico leads into a simple, elegant interior, where the original box pews are still in place. Just behind the church, the 1672 **Vincent House Museum** (May to mid-Oct daily 10.30am–3pm; $5, $8 combo admission includes Whaling Church) is the oldest house on the island, and has the furniture to prove it. A short walk along North Water Street leads past more charming sea captains' homes to the white cast-iron **Edgartown Lighthouse** – it's a replacement of the 1828 original, destroyed in the hurricane of 1938. Take the bus from the visitor's center to **South Beach** in Katama, three miles south of town, for some of the best public access to the Atlantic Ocean on-island.

Chappaquiddick

Chappaquiddick (aka "Chappy") is a strikingly beautiful and sparsely populated little island, just yards away from Edgartown's shores. Unfortunately, it's name will always be associated with scandal: Edward (Ted) Kennedy ruined his chances for the presidency in the summer of 1969 when 28-year-old Mary Jo Kopechne drowned in his car at **Dike Bridge**, under circumstances that conspiracy theorists still debate. The island is an easy five-minute jaunt from Edgartown via the *On Time* ferry (so called because it has no regular schedule and is thus always "on time"; $3 per person, $10 for a car and one driver; ⓣ508/627-9427), which departs frequently from a ramp at the corner of Dock and Daggett streets. There are no stores, restaurants or hotels on Chappy, just private residences and hundreds of acres of dunes, salt marshes, ponds, scrubland, and barrier beach. The island is easy to get around on a bike, though too large to walk comfortably. The Trustees of Reservations' small Japanese garden **Mytoi**, on Dike Road (open dawn-dusk; free), is worth stopping by for a few minutes – it's unusual to see the typical rounded bridges and groomed trees in a pine forest. The Trustees are also the caretakers of **Wasque**, a windswept stretch of beach that is a continuation of South Beach in Edgartown, but much less crowded. In fact, you can walk between Edgartown and Chappy along this stretch of beach. On Chappy's far east side you'll find the five-hundred acre **Cape Pogue Wildlife Refuge**, an important habitat and migration stopover for thousands of birds. Half the state's scallops are harvested here, too. The best way to see it is to take one of the three-hour **natural history tours** that involve walking and kayaking (late May to mid-Oct; $30; ⓣ508/627-3599).

West Tisbury

WEST TISBURY, the largest of the up-island communities, also has some of the best culture on the island. In July of 1999, West Tisbury joined Chappaquiddick in the lore of the Kennedy curse, when **John Kennedy, Jr's** plane crashed in the water less than twenty miles from the landing field. A relatively inexperienced pilot, Kennedy apparently became disoriented and put himself into a fatal dive, killing himself, his wife, and his sister-in-law. Most of West Tisbury's history has been considerably more peaceful. The town was founded in the 1670s by settlers from Edgartown, who happened upon a fast-flowing stream here. As the community developed, sheep farming became the main industry; and although few are left today, West Tisbury residents dote on their town's rural atmosphere, and there are several flourishing horse and agricultural produce farms, some of which you can see if you drive or bike down the scenic **Middle Road**. West Tisbury is also home to the only operating vineyard on the island, **Chicama Vineyards**, on Stoney Hill Road off of State Road (Jan–April Sat 1–4pm, mid-May to Oct Mon–Sat 11am–5pm, Sun 1–5pm, early May and Oct–Dec Mon-Sat 1–4pm; ⓣ508/693-0309, ⓦwww.chicamavineyards.com) which has been producing Massachusetts quality (read: sub-par) wines since 1971. It's a pretty spot, and the tasting is free – you may learn something about wine-making in the process.

The **Farmers' Market**, held at the 1859 **Old Agricultural Hall** on South Road every Saturday morning (and sometimes Wed mornings in the summer), attracts visitors from all over the island for its colorful displays of locally grown produce. Recently an additional Agricultural Hall was built, to be used as a setting for shows, dances, pot-luck suppers, and an annual **agricultural fair** that takes place for three days at the end of August. Across the street from the old hall is the **Field Gallery**, 1050 State Rd (ⓣ508/693-5595), locally famous for Tom Maley's larger-than-life sculptures of ladies dancing on the grass. Also on State Road next to the Old Ag Hall is **Alley's General Store** (ⓣ508/693-0088), an island institution since 1858, selling everything from cans of baked beans to mini *ouija* boards, and with a wide front porch where locals often meet for a chat. There's a place behind the store, appropriately enough named *Back Alley's*, to get good sandwiches. Nearby, at 636 Old County Rd, is the picturesque **Granary Gallery** (open dawn-dusk; free), featuring Ella Tulin's sculpture of a woman with a small torso and seven-foot-high thighs sitting in front, and a variety of notable Vineyard and New England artists' work within.

North of West Tisbury, tiny **Mayhew Chapel**, on Christiantown Road off Indian Hill Road, was dedicated to Reverend Thomas Mayhew, Jr., who converted members of the Wampanoag tribe to Christianity in the mid-1600s. These "Praying Indians," as they became known, established a community here called Christiantown; many of them are buried in the neighboring **Burial Ground**. West Tisbury has a bountiful supply of conservation areas, including the 216-acre **Cedar Tree Neck Wildlife Sanctuary**, Indian Hill Rd (daily sunrise–sunset; free), in which bayberry bushes, swamp azaleas, tupelos, and pygmy beech trees can be spotted. Three main trails lead to a pretty but stony beach and a bluff with views to Gay Head and the Elizabeth Islands. Meanwhile, the **Sepiessa Point Reservation**, on New Lane off West Tisbury Road (daily dawn–dusk; free), surrounds West Tisbury Pond with trails ideal for bird-watching.

Chilmark

Five miles west of Tisbury, unspoiled **CHILMARK**, with just over eight hundred year-round residents, is the land that time almost forgot, full of pastures separated by stone walls, dense woodlands, and rugged roads. That's not to say that the twenty-first century hasn't arrived: **Beetlebung Corner**, where Middle, State, South, and Menemsha Cross roads meet, and which is named for the wooden mallets (aka "beetles") and stoppers ("bungs") once made from the nearby tupelo trees, is the village's center, heralded by a small grocery-deli, a boutique, and some other modern commercial concerns, though there's also an old schoolhouse, the last one-room version on the island.

On South Road the tranquil **Chilmark Cemetery** is the final resting place of writer Lillian Hellman and funnyman John Belushi, who claimed that the island was the only place in the world where he could get a good night's sleep. Near the entrance, a boulder engraved with the comedian's name, a decoy to prevent fans from finding his actual unmarked grave, is where legions leave their rather unceremonious "offerings," like beer cans and condoms. Nearby, a dirt track leads to **Lucy Vincent Beach**, named after the town's prim and proper librarian, who saw it as her mission to protect Chilmark residents from corruption by cutting out from her library books all pictures she deemed to be immoral. Rather ironically, the beach, which is open only to residents and their guests in the summer, today doubles as a **nudist** spot in its less crowded areas. Off North Road, pick up a map at the trailhead of **Waskosim's Rock Reservation** for a fascinating three-mile hike through a variety of habitats including wetlands and black gum and oak woods.

In the northern part of Chilmark, another tiny village, **Menemsha**, is a picturesque but hodgepodge collection of gray-shingled fishing shacks with a man-made harbor used for location shots in the making of *Jaws*. The harbor also serves as an important commercial and sports-fishing port, much of the catch ending up at restaurants all over the island. Stroll past the fish markets of **Dutcher's Dock** for a real sense of the island's maritime heritage, or bring an early-evening picnic to pebbly **Menemsha Beach** to enjoy the spectacular sunsets. The **Menemsha Hills Reservation**, off North Road a couple of miles toward West Tisbury, is also well worth a visit, its mile-long rocky shoreline and sand bluffs along Vineyard Sound peaking at **Prospect Hill**, the highest point on the Vineyard, with wonderful views of the Elizabeth Islands.

Aquinnah (Gay Head)

In 1997, the people of **Aquinnah** voted to revert the town's name back to its original Wampanoag Indian name from its more familiar title – Gay Head – the culmination of a ten-year-plus court battle in which the Wampanoags

Martha's Vineyard beaches

The island's **beaches** vary from calm, shallow waters, predominantly on the northern and eastern sides, to long stretches of pounding surf on the southern side, where the water also tends to be a bit warmer. Unfortunately, many of the best beaches are private, or are only open in the summer to residents, but there are some notable exceptions. All of the beaches listed below have lifeguards in at least some areas during summer days.

Aquinnah (Gay Head)

Lobsterville Beach Lobsterville Road. Two miles of prime Vineyard Sound beach backed by dunes. Parking on Lobsterville Road is prohibited, so bike or get here by taking the ferry from Menemsha.

Moshup Beach (Gay Head Public Beach) State Road/Moshup Drive. Gorgeous setting at the foot of Gay Head Cliffs, best reached by bicycle, shuttle bus, or taxi. Parking costs $15 a day in season.

Chappaquidick

Cape Pogue Wildlife Refuge at the end of Dike Road. This sandy beach is less crowded than Wasque at the far east end of the island. $3 per person for non-members.

Wasque at the end of Wasque Road south of School Road. Wide-open South Shore beach. $3 per person and $3 per vehicle.

Chilmark

Lucy Vincent Beach off South Road. Sandy beach with access to some of the island's clay cliffs (note that bathing in the clay puddles is restricted) through the end of September to residents and visitors with passes.

Menemsha Public Beach next to Menemsha Harbor. The only Chilmark beach open to the public, with sparkling waters and a picturesque setting. It becomes *very* crowded around sunset, since it is one of the few places to see the sun go down over a beach on the East Coast (the north shore of Cape Cod bay is another exception).

Squibnocket off State Road at the end of Squibnocket Road. This narrow, rocky beach is less attractive than the other Chilmark beaches, but the waves break farther

won guardianship of 420 acres of land, to be held in perpetuity by the federal government and known as the **Gay Head Native American Reservation**. Most people come to this part of the island (its westernmost point), to see the multicolored clay **Gay Head Cliffs**, whose brilliant hues are the result of millions of years of geological work. When the oceans were high, and the Vineyard underwater, small creatures died and left their shells behind to form the white layers. At other times, the area was a rainforest and vegetation compressed to form the darker colors. The weight of the glaciers thrust the many layers of stone up at an angle to create the cliffs, dubbed "Gay Head" by passing English sailors in the seventeenth century on account of their bright colors. The clay was once the main source of paint for the island's houses, but now anyone removing any (unless you're a Wampanoag Indian) faces a substantial fine; in any case, the cliffs are eroding so fast that it's not safe to approach them too closely.

A short path lined with seafood shacks and craft stalls leads the way from the parking lot to the **overlook**, which affords stunning views to the Elizabeth Islands, and, on a clear day, as far as the entrance to Rhode Island's Narragansett Bay. The imposing red-brick **Gay Head Lighthouse** (mid-June to mid-Sept Fri–Sun evenings; $3), built in 1854 to replace a wooden structure that dated from 1799, is well situated for sunset views. Below the lighthouse, though not accessible offshore, making it the best island spot for **surfing**. It's a town beach, which means it's off-limits during summer days, but anyone can show up after 5pm and in September – one of the best times to catch the waves.

Vineyard Haven

Lake Tashmoo Town Beach Herring Creek Road. Swim in the warm, brackish water of the lake, or in the cooler Vineyard Sound.

Owen Park Beach off Main Street. A harbor beach close to the center of town. Not much of a swimming hole, or a beach, but it's a walkable distance from downtown.

Oak Bluffs

Joseph A. Sylvia State Beach along Beach Road between Oak Bluffs and Edgartown. A narrow six-mile strand of sandy beach with clear, gentle waters and plenty of roadside parking.

Oak Bluffs Town Beach between the Steamship Authority Dock and the State Beach. Narrow sliver of beach on Vineyard Sound that gets very crowded in season.

Edgartown

Bend-in-the-Road Beach Beach Road. Really an extension of the Joseph A. Sylvia State Beach, with similar facilities and access.

Katama Beach (South Beach) end of Katama Road. Beautiful barrier beach backed by protected salt pond. Strong surf and currents.

Lighthouse Beach Starbuck's Neck, off North Water Street. Close to town, this harbor beach can get a bit too mucked with seaweed.

West Tisbury

Lambert's Cove Beach Lambert's Cove Road. One of the island's prettiest, but open only to residents during high season.

Long Point Wildlife Refuge Beach off South Road. The perfect Vineyard beach: long and wide, with a freshwater pond just behind. Get there early for a parking space, on the south side of the street near the airport.

from it, a **public beach** provides an equally impressive view of the cliffs from a different angle. To reach it, take the wooden boardwalk from the **Moshup Beach** parking lot to the shore, then walk round towards the lighthouse.

Eating and drinking

It's easy enough to find something to **eat** on Martha's Vineyard; the ports in particular have rows of places to tempt tourists who've just disembarked the ferries. Four of the island's six towns are **dry**, meaning you can only purchase alcohol in Oak Bluffs and Edgartown. Note, though, that you can bring wine or beer purchased there to restaurants in the other towns.

Vineyard Haven

The Black Dog Bakery and Tavern Water St ☎508/693-4786. Though you'll see these T-shirts all over the island and the mainland (never a good sign), the original restaurant and bakery serve fare as tasty as the spot is touristy. The (dry) tavern serves full and "light" (less expensive) seafood dinners, while you can stock up on muffins or bagels at the next-door bakery for the return ferry ride.

Café Moxie 70 Main St ☎508/693-1484. A tiny, trendy neighborhood seafood and pasta joint, priced, sadly, to compensate for the lack of liquor license, but tasty nonetheless.

Oak Bluffs

Giordano's 107 Circuit Ave ⓣ508/693-0184. Popular and fairly priced Italian family restaurant. Their chicken cacciatore is particularly good, while the adjoining clam shack has the best fried clams on-island.

Jimmy Seas Pan Pasta 32 Kennebec Ave ⓣ508/696-8550. Huge portions of tasty pasta in this small, casual eatery favored by locals. Not especially inexpensive, but on the whole worth the price.

Zapotec 10 Kennebec Ave ⓣ508/693-6800. Moderately priced seafood variations on Mexican cuisine, like swordfish fajitas, served in a cute and colorful house behind Oak Bluff's main drag.

Edgartown

Atria 137 Main St ⓣ508/627-5850. Of the fancy restaurants on the island this one's your best bet for a great meal – expect your fish to be miso-encrusted and your entrees to be over $20.

The Newes from America 23 Kelley St ⓣ508/627-4397. Swill five hundred beers in this atmospheric pub (not necessarily all in the same night) and they'll name a stool after you. Decent and filling affordable pub grub, too.

The Wharf Lower Main St ⓣ508/627-9966. Fried clams and "chowdah" to go – eat it on the dock overlooking the Chappy ferry.

Elsewhere on the island

Homeport North Rd, Menemsha ⓣ508/645-2679. Unpretentious place serving lobster, swordfish, and steaks, with lovely views of Menemsha Creek.

Humphrey's Bakery 535 State Rd, West Tisbury ⓣ508/693-1079. Fresh sandwiches on fresh bread are great to bring to the beach – also try their homemade cookies and doughnuts.

Lambert's Cove Inn Lambert's Cove Rd, West Tisbury ⓣ508/693-2298. The reasonably priced restaurant at this hideaway inn – surrounded by forest and apple orchards – is a gem; try the delectable soups.

Nightlife and entertainment

Much of the Vineyard's evening **entertainment** comes in the form of private dinner parties, but that doesn't mean there's nothing to do if you're not invited to one. First-run **movies** can be seen at Capawok, an Art Deco theater on Main Street in Vineyard Haven (ⓣ508/696-9200), or in Edgartown at Entertainment Cinemas, 65 Main St (ⓣ508/627-8008). Also in Edgartown, the Old Whaling Church, 85 Main St (ⓣ508/627-4442), hosts regular performances, readings, lectures, and other intellectual pursuits. Weekend **cabaret** and **musical productions** are staged at the Vineyard Playhouse, 24 Church St, Vineyard Haven (ⓣ508/693-6450, ⓦwww.vineyardplayhouse.org), housed in a former Masonic lodge dating from 1833. In Chilmark, The Yard, off Middle Road near Beetlebung Corner (ⓣ508/645-9662, ⓦwww.dancetheyard.org), hosts **modern dance** performances by a resident choreography troupe. Oak Bluffs has some of the most happening **nightlife** around, with a fun bar scene, regular live acts, and boisterous streetlife. Charges for venues listed below range from free to $15.

For current **listings** information, check the *Vineyard Gazette* (ⓦwww.mvgazette.com), good for cultural events, and the weekly *Martha's Vineyard Times* (ⓦwww.mvtimes.com), better for nightlife listings.

Oak Bluffs

Atlantic Connection 124 Circuit Ave ⓣ508/693-7129. A catch-all space that always has something going on, whether it be live music, comedy, or karaoke; everyone from preppy college kids to stars like Spike Lee tend to descend on it at least once during their stay.

Lola's Southern Seafood at the *Island Inn*, Beach Rd ⓣ508/693-5007, ⓦwww.lolassouthernseafood.com. Trendy thirty-something disco with a Top-40 dance floor and nightly live acts during the summer; weekends only rest of the year.

Offshore Ale Company 30 Kennebec Ave ⓣ508/693-2626. Friendly local brewpub with wooden booths, toss-on-the-floor peanuts, and live shows almost nightly in season. They also have great entrees and pizzas.

Ritz Café 1 Circuit Ave ⓣ508/693-9851. This cupboard-sized bar is anything but ritzy, but its pool tables and live music acts (nightly in summer; weekends only rest of the year) make a nice escape from the scene.

Elsewhere on the island

David Ryan's 11 N Water St, Edgartown ⓣ508/627-4100. Loud two-story bar with a chi-chi martini lounge upstairs and raucous dancing to rock 'n' roll downstairs – usually on the tables.

Hot Tin Roof Airport Rd, Edgartown ⓣ508/693-1137, ⓦwww.mvhottinroof.com. The biggest nightclub and live music venue on the Vineyard, this Carly Simon-owned venture blends Top-40 and reggae hits on the dance floor with almost nightly live entertainment during the summer; several murals by local artist Margot Datz bring Vineyard vistas indoors.

Nantucket

The thirty-mile, two-hour sea crossing to **NANTUCKET** from Cape Cod may not be an oceangoing odyssey, but it does set the "Little Gray Lady" apart from her larger, shore-hugging sister, Martha. Just halfway out from Hyannis, neither mainland nor island is in sight, and you realize why the Native Americans dubbed it "distant land." Once you've landed, you can avert your eyes from the smart-money double-deck cruisers with names like *Pier Pressure* and *Loan Star* and let the place remind you that it hasn't always been a rich folks' playground. Indeed, despite the formidable prowess of its seamen, survival for settlers on the island's barren soil was always a struggle. The tiny, cobbled carriageways of **Nantucket Town** itself, once one of the largest cities in Massachusetts, were frozen in time by economic decline 150 years ago. Today, this area of delightful old restored houses is very much the center of activity, while seven flat, easily cyclable miles to the east the rose-covered cottages of **Siasconset** (always abbreviated to 'Sconset) give another glimpse of days gone by. However appealing the island's man-made attractions are, it's Nantucket's gentle natural beauty that's the real draw, with heaths and moorlands, mile after mile of fabulous beaches, and a network of bicycle paths that connect the many spots maintained by conservation trusts.

Some history

European settlement on Nantucket dates from 1659, when **Thomas Mayhew**, who had originally purchased the island sight unseen, sold it on the cheap to a group of nine shareholders from Massachusetts who were eager to escape the repressive policies of the Massachusetts Bay Colony. Those nine then sold half-shares to people whose skills they thought would be needed to expand the new settlement. Even this wasn't enough; the settlers, who landed at **Madaket**, were only able to survive their first winter thanks to assistance from the Wampanoag natives. In time, the number of settlers began to rival that of the natives, who were decimated by disease, and **whaling** became the business of the day. Though Nantucketers had learned to spear whales from the shore, they began to sail the neighboring ocean to pursue their prey. It paid off in 1712, when one of the ships was blown far out to sea and managed to harpoon a sperm whale, whose highly sought-after oil would fetch very high prices.

For the next 150 years, the trade flourished, as did the island; the population grew to more than 10,000, and Nantucket became synonymous with whaling – at its peak, the harbor was base to some one hundred whaling boats. The beginning of the end came when larger ships were needed to cater for the longer (up to five-year) periods at sea. These ships were unable to cross the shallows, and much of Nantucket's whaling activity transferred to the deep-water harbors at New Bedford and Edgartown. Then, a major **fire** in 1846, which started in a hat shop on Main Street, spread to the harbor, where it set light to barrels of whale oil. The harbor was almost completely destroyed, along with a third of Nantucket Town. The final blow to Nantucket's whaling business was whale oil's replacement as the fuel of choice by the much cheaper kerosene.

Nantucket floundered for the next century, until a local entrepreneur revamped the **waterfront** in the 1950s; suddenly people began work to preserve the old buildings and salt-encrusted cottages that still stood. Now the population jumps from 10,000 in winter to 56,000 in the summer, and the property is much more valuable than in the shore towns of Massachusetts like New Bedford and Hyannis.

Arrival, information, and getting around

Most likely you'll arrive in Nantucket by **ferry**. Both the Steamship Authority (ⓣ508/447-8600, ⓦwww.islandferry.com) and Hy-Line (ⓣ508/778-2600 or 1-800/492-8082, ⓦwww.hy-linecruises.com) run year-round passenger services to the island from Hyannis, but only the Steamship Authority's boats take cars. Both have fast ferries that charge from $28 to $36 each way for passengers; the Steamship Authority's car ferry (mid-May to mid-Oct, $175 per vehicle) allows passengers only at $14. Island-hoppers can take Hy-Line's inter-island ferry ($16 one-way), which runs thrice daily June–Sept between Martha's Vineyard's Oak Bluffs and Nantucket. A much quicker way to get to the island is by **air**: Island Airlines (ⓣ1-800/248-7779, ⓦwww.nantucket.net/trans/islandair) and Cape Air (ⓣ1-800/352-0714, ⓦwww.flycapeair.com) run year-round daily services from Hyannis to Nantucket; Cape Air also offers daily services to and from Boston, Providence, and Martha's Vineyard. The **airport** (ⓣ508/325-5300, ⓦwww.nantucketairport.com) is about three miles southeast of Nantucket Town.

Once you've arrived, **getting around** should pose no problem. From the moment you get off the ferry you're besieged by **bike** rental places and tour

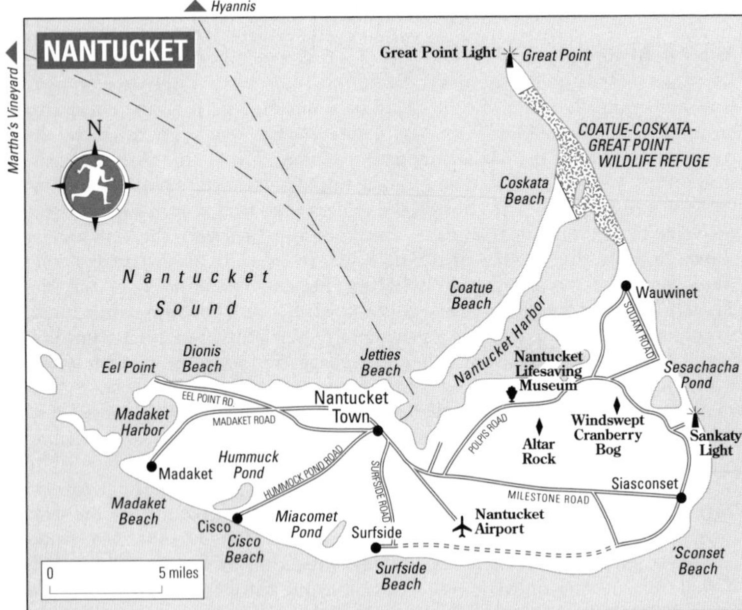

The whalers of Nantucket

The **whalers of Nantucket** drew the attention of many with their skill and resultant domination of such a treacherous trade. The early chronicler Crèvecoeur provided an extensive account of Nantucket as it was in 1782 in his *Letters from an American Farmer*. Although perturbed by the islanders' universal habit of taking a dose of opium every morning, he held them up as a model of diligence and good self-government. Whaling was a disciplined profession, unmarred by the stereotyped debauchery of sailors elsewhere, and to feed themselves and equip their ships the islanders kept up a shrewd and extensive trade with the mainland. The whalemen were not paid; instead each had a share (a "lay") of the final proceeds of the voyage. Crèvecoeur was impressed by the Nantucketers' ambition: "Would you believe that they have already gone to the Falkland Islands and I have heard several of them talk of going to the South Sea." They did indeed reach the Pacific, though Nantucket will always be the locale most closely associated with the whaling industry. Read about the whalers in Herman Melville's *Moby Dick*, a valediction of sorts since by the time it was published in 1851, Nantucket's fortunes had gone into an abrupt decline. As a magazine article of 1873 reported, "Let no traveler visit Nantucket with the expectation of witnessing the marks of a flourishing trade ... of the great fleet of ships which dotted every sea, scarcely a vestige remains."

companies. Try Young's Bicycle Shop (Ⓣ508/228-1151, Ⓦwww.youngsbicycleshop.com), conveniently located on Steamboat Wharf; it should cost $25 per day for a standard mountain bike. Driving a **car** makes little sense here, especially in peak season, when island arteries can easily get clogged, and it won't endear you to the locals. If you didn't bring one with you on the ferry, there is an expensive and limited on-island supply available from Windmill (Ⓣ508/228-1227 or 1-800/228-1227, Ⓦwww.nantucketautorental.com) and two airport outlets, Budget (Ⓣ508/228-5666, Ⓦwww.budget.com) and Hertz (Ⓣ508/228-9421, Ⓦwww.hertz.com). A better way to get around is by **bus**: five shuttle routes round the island are operated between May and September by the Nantucket Regional Transit Authority (7.30am–11.30pm; Ⓣ508/228-7025 Ⓦwww.shuttlenantucket.com), with fares starting at 50¢ per journey for in-town travel; you can get unlimited travel for three days ($10), a week ($15), or a month ($30). Barrett's Tours (Ⓣ508/228-0174 or 1-800/773-0174) runs ninety-minute narrated bus tours ($15) around the island, stopping in 'Sconset, the historic windmill, beaches, and a cranberry bog. You probably won't need the aid of **taxis** while here, but they are usually available at the airport or by the ferry terminal; A-1 (Ⓣ508/228-3330) and All Point (Ⓣ508/228-5779) are both reliable.

Visitor information is available from the **Chamber of Commerce**, 48 Main St (Mon–Fri 9am–5pm; Ⓣ508/228-1700, Ⓦwww.nantucketchamber.org), or from the helpful **Nantucket Information Bureau**, 25 Federal St (April–Dec 9am–6pm; rest of year Mon–Sat 9am–5.30pm; Ⓣ508/228-0925, Ⓦwww.nantucket.net). The **Nantucket Historical Association**, 15 Broad St (Mon–Fri 9am–5pm; Ⓣ508/228-1894, Ⓦwww.nha.org), which maintains twenty historical properties on the island, offers a $18 **combination ticket** for entrance to all its buildings ($6 individually). The sights are generally open daily from late May to mid-October 10am–5pm; from mid-October to early November daily 11am–4pm; and closed the rest of the year.

Accommodation

There's a wide range of **accommodation** in Nantucket Town, from resorts with pools, health clubs, and sophisticated restaurants to cozy inns and B&Bs; further afield, you can rent private homes by the week. One thing you won't find, however, is price diversity – it's not easy to find a room for under $175 in high season, and most doubles cost over $200. For free, easy booking contact **Martha's Vineyard and Nantucket Reservations** (ⓣ508/693-7200 or 1-800/649-5671). If you're stuck at the last minute with nowhere to stay, try the **Nantucket Visitors Service and Information Bureau** (see overleaf) (ⓣ508/228-0925), which maintains a list of vacancies during the season. Unless otherwise indicated, all of the places listed below are in **Nantucket Town**.

Anchor Inn 66 Centre St ⓣ508/228-0072, ⓦwww.anchor-inn.net. Rooms with period-style furnishings and queen-sized canopy beds in the heart of the historic residential district. ⑧

Century House 10 Cliff Rd ⓣ508/228-0530, ⓦwww.centuryhouse.com. Elegant rooms with private baths and country-house ambience in this 1833 late-Federal home. ⑧

Cliff Lodge 9 Cliff Rd ⓣ508/228-9480, ⓦwww.clifflodgenantucket.com. Quiet B&B in a residential area with some low-priced singles in the off-season. ⑧

Hawthorn House 2 Chestnut St ⓣ508/228-1468, ⓦwww.hawthornhouse.com. Central, well-appointed guesthouse with handsome rooms outfitted with tapestries, quilts, and antique furnishings. ⑧

HI-Nantucket Surfside Beach ⓣ508/228-0433, ⓦwww.usahostels.org. Dorm beds a stone's throw from Surfside Beach, just over three miles south of Nantucket Town. $16–27 per night. Lockout 10am–5pm, curfew 11pm. Open only mid-May–Sept.

Martin House Inn 61 Centre St ⓣ508/228-0678 ⓦwww.martinhouseinn.com. Thirteen lovely rooms offer good value in this 1803 seaman's house. ⑦

The Nesbitt Inn 21 Broad St ⓣ508/228-0156. The central location, friendly innkeepers, and affordable rooms, most with antique furniture, compensate for the shared baths (three for thirteen rooms) in this 1872 Victorian inn. ⑤

Ship's Inn 13 Fair St ⓣ508/228-0040 or 1-800/564-2760, ⓦ www.shipsinnnantucket.com. Three-story whaling captain's home with eleven biggish rooms, all with private bath. ⑧

The Wauwinet Wauwinet Rd, Wauwinet ⓣ508/228-0145 or 1-800/426-8718, ⓦwww.wauwinet.com. For the super-rich, *the* place to stay on the island. A bit out from the main town, this luxury historic resort hotel offers a full range of leisure facilities, beautifully appointed rooms, excellent dining, and great views. ⑨

Nantucket Town

Very much the center of activity on the island, the cobbled walkways of **NANTUCKET TOWN** boast a delightful array of eighteenth- and nineteenth-century homes, most of them concentrated around **Main Street**. Before you hit there, though, you can get the salty feel of the half-dozen wharves around Nantucket's harbor when arriving on the ferry, which docks at **Steamboat Wharf**. A number of private summer homes are perched on Old North Wharf just south of that, while lively **Straight Wharf**, which dates to 1723, contains souvenir shops, restaurants, and the restored red-brick building of the **Museum of Nantucket History** (hours vary; free; ⓣ508/228-1700), originally a warehouse for whaling supplies. Exhibits include early firefighting apparatus, old photographs, and a diorama depicting the waterfront's busy goings-on before the fire. Straight Wharf leads directly onto Main Street, where, at its junction with South Water Street, the **Pacific Club**, a three-story Georgian edifice built as a country house for William Rotch, owner of two of the three ships involved in the Boston Tea Party, once served as a customs house, but has been used since 1861 as an elite private club (meaning you can't go in) for retired whaling captains. A short walk north along Federal Street leads to the **Athenaeum**, 1

Lower India St (hours vary; ⓣ508/228-1110, ⓦwww.nantucketatheneum.org), the town library, cultural center, and repository for various antiques, scrimshaw, and old island newspapers.

Continue up Federal Street to Broad Street, where the **Nantucket Whaling Museum** (late May to mid-Oct Mon–Sat 10am–5pm, Thurs until 9pm, Sun noon–5pm; $18) is housed in an old candlemaking factory built just before the big fire. The museum underwent a $14 million renovation in 2004, which may explain the exorbitant ticket price. Among its intriguing collection of exhibits, look out especially for such scrimshaw artifacts as a set of 21 whale types carved from whales' teeth, the astonishing harpoon corkscrewed in the "flurry" or last struggle of a dying whale, and a gigantic sperm whale skeleton.

Back on Main Street, at nos. 75 and 78, the **Henry Coffin House** and the **Charles Coffin House** belonged to two brothers who inherited a fortune from their father's candlemaking business. Their houses were built opposite each other, employing the same carpenters and masons, but in completely different

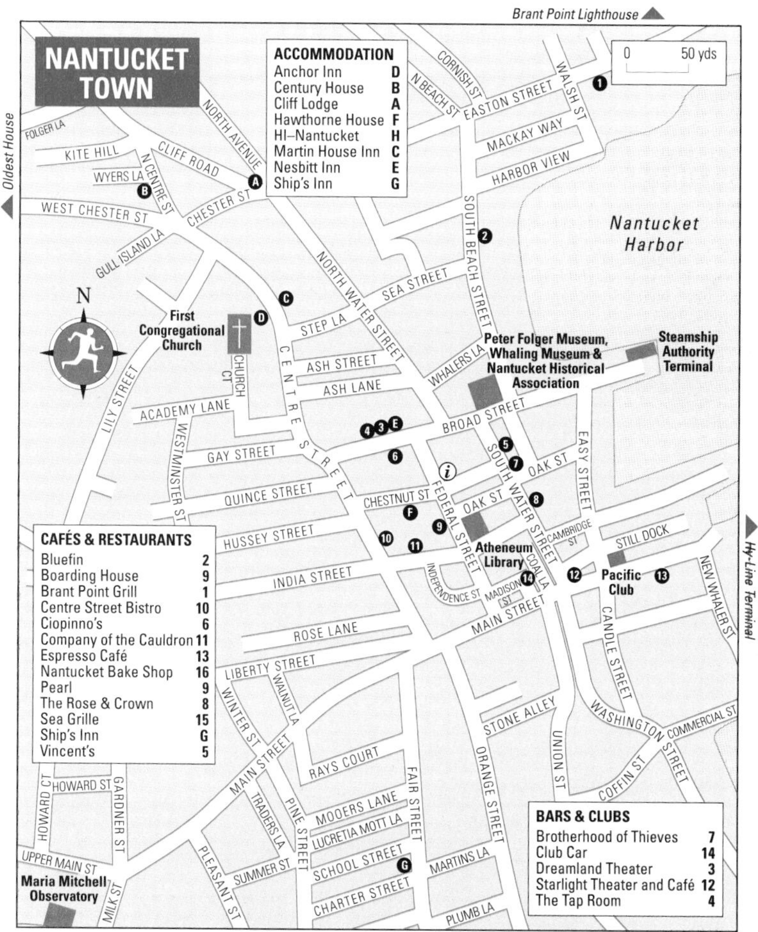

styles: Charles's house a simple yet dignified Greek Revival, Henry's a late Federal-style home with ornate marble tower and cupola. Though you can't visit their interiors, you can stop by another grand house nearby, the Greek Revival **Hadwen House**, 96 Main St (daily: late May to mid-Oct 10am–5pm, mid-Oct to early Dec 11am–4pm, closed the rest of the year; $6; ⓣ508/228-1894, ⓦwww.nha.org), which contains gas chandeliers, colossal pilasters, and silver doorknobs, with a lovely period garden out back.

Built in 1834, the **First Congregational Church**, 62 Centre St (mid-June to Sept Mon–Sat 10am–4pm; $1.50 donation to climb tower; ⓣ508/228-0950), is famous for its 120-foot steeple, from which you can get a spectacular bird's-eye view of the island. The inside is worth a peek, too, for its restored *trompe l'oeil* ceiling, six-hundred-pound brass chandelier, and rows of old box pews. Follow Center Street and West Chester Street past Lily Pond Park to the aptly named **Oldest House** (aka the Jethro Coffin House), on Sunset Hill Road (daily: late May to mid-Oct 10am–5pm, mid-Oct to early Nov 11am–4pm, closed the rest of the year; $6; ⓣ508/228-1894, ⓦwww.nha.org), though there's not much to see other than the central brick chimney; the house is sparsely decorated, with an antique loom serving as the most prominent feature inside.

Nantucket beaches

With fifty miles of **beaches**, most of which are open to the public, Nantucket is more accessible than Martha's Vineyard for ocean enthusiasts. The island's southern and eastern flanks, where the water tends to have rougher surf, is ideal for surfers, while the more sheltered northern beaches are good for swimming. With extremely limited, albeit free, **parking**, it makes sense to walk or cycle to all but the most far-flung of the strands. You can rent **watersports equipment** (kayaks, windsurfers, and the like, for $15–30) from Nantucket Community Sailing, on Jetties Beach (ⓣ508/228-5358, ⓦwww.nantucketsailing.com).

Nantucket Town

Brant Point off Easton Street. Strong currents at the harbor entrance mean this beach is better for tanning and watching the comings and goings of boats in the harbor, rather than swimming.

Children's Beach off South Beach Street. Just minutes from Steamboat Wharf, this calm harbor beach is perfect for children, and has a full range of facilities.

Dionis Beach Eel Point Road. A quiet beach with high dunes and calm waters.

Jetties Beach off Bathing Beach Road. Catch the shuttle bus that runs along North Water and South Beach streets in the centre of town, or leg it to this popular beach whose facilities include lifeguards, changing rooms, and a snack bar.

East of Town

'Sconset Beach (known also as Codfish Park) off Polpis Road. Sandy beach with moderate surf and a full range of facilities. Just a short walk to several eating places.

South Shore

Cisco Beach Hummock Point Road. Long, sandy beach with lifeguards and restrooms; again, ideal for surfing.

Madaket Beach at the end of the Madaket Bike Path. Another long beach with strong surf and gorgeous sunsets over the water. Portable restrooms (not for the squeamish), lifeguards, and shuttle bus (leaves from Broad Street in Nantucket Town).

Surfside Beach off Surfside Road. Wide sands attract a youthful crowd of surfers; there's a large parking lot, but you'd do better to take the shuttle bus from town.

Polpis Road

Polpis Road, an indirect and arcing track from Nantucket Town to 'Sconset, holds a number of natural attractions both on and off its main course, though your first stop off should be the less wild **Nantucket Life Saving Museum**, off the northern side of the road at no. 158 (mid-June to mid-Oct daily 9.30am–4pm; $5; Ⓦwww.nantucketlifesavingmuseum.com), filled with two lifesaving surfboats, buoys, rescue equipment, photographs, artifacts from the *Andrea Doria*, which sunk off Nantucket forty years ago, and a horse-drawn carriage from the Henry Ford Museum. Further on, an unmarked track leads south to **Altar Rock**, the island's highest point, where you'll want to walk around for views of the surrounding bogs. One of these, the two-hundred-acre **Windswept Cranberry Bog**, east on Polpis Road, is a feast of color at most times of the year, especially so in mid-October, when the ripened berries, loosened from the plants by machines, float to the top of the water.

Siasconset, Great Point, and Coatue

Seven flat miles east of Nantucket Town, the village of **SIASCONSET**, or 'Sconset as it's universally known, is filled with venerable cottages literally encrusted with salt and covered over with roses. Once solely a fishing village, it began to attract visitors eager to get away from the foul smells of Nantucket Town's whale-oil refineries, and in the late 1800s, enough writers and actors came from big cities to give 'Sconset some modicum of artistic renown.

There's not too much to see, other than the houses themselves along Broadway and Center streets – certainly picturesque enough – and the year-round population of 150 only supports a few commercial establishments, all close to one another in the center of town. A few miles north, the red-and-white striped **Sankaty Light**, an 1849 lighthouse, stands on a ninety-foot bluff, though it seems only a matter of time until it falls victim to the crashing waves below. North of here, and also accessible heading east on Polpis Road from Nantucket Town, **Wauwinet** is largely notable for holding the inn of choice on the island, simply titled *The Wauwinet* (see p.238 for review and overleaf for details on its restaurant, *Toppers*).

Further north still, **Coatue-Coskata-Great Point**, a five-mile-long, razor-thin slice of sand, takes in three separate wildlife refuges, and is accessible by four-wheel-drive (for which you'll need a special $40 permit; Ⓣ508/228-0006, Ⓦwww.thetrustees.org) or on foot. If you don't feel like walking (the sand is very soft and taxing on the feet), you could take one of the tours offered by Ara's Tours, 25 Federal St (90min; $18; Ⓣ508/221-6852, Ⓦwww.arastours.com). In the Coskata section, the wider beaches are backed by salt marshes and some trees: with binoculars, you may catch sight of plovers, egrets, oystercatchers, terns, and even osprey. The beach narrows again as you approach the **Great Point Light**, at the end of the spit, put up in 1986 after an earlier light was destroyed during a 1984 storm; the new one is solar-powered, and is said to be able to withstand 240mph winds and twenty-foot waves. Unsurprisingly, this is not the safest place to swim, even on a calm day. Coatue, the last leg of the journey, is the narrow stretch that separates Nantucket Harbor from the ocean; so narrow, in fact, that stormy seas frequently crash over it, turning Great Point into an island.

Madaket and the South Shore

At the western tip of Nantucket, rural **MADAKET** is the small settlement located on the spot where Thomas Macy landed in 1659. There's little in the way of visitor attractions, but the area's peacefulness and natural beauty make up for that. Unspoiled **Eel Point**, a couple of miles north, sits on a spit of sand covered with all manner of wild plants and flowers, including wild roses and bayberries, which attract an array of birds, including the graceful egrets which can be seen in late spring and summer stalking the shallow offshore sandbars. **Maps** and **self-guided tours** are available for $4 from the Nantucket Conservation Foundation, 118 Cliff Rd (ⓣ508/228-2884, ⓦwww.nantucketconservation.com). East of Madaket, and only about three miles from Nantucket Town, **Cisco**'s windswept beach faces water popular with surfers, though erosion due to windy blasts here has resulted in several houses being lost. Two miles east of Cisco, freshwater **Miacomet Pond**, surrounded by reeds and grasses, and a favorite haunt of swans and ducks, is a prime spot for a picnic.

Eating and drinking

The early chronicler Crèvecoeur, in an extensive account on Nantucket published in 1782, stated that on Nantucket "music, singing and dancing are holden in equal detestation." Thankfully, eating is not: the island abounds in first-rate **restaurants**, most of them located in Nantucket Town and specializing in seafood. Be prepared, however, for the shock of the bill: it's often Manhattan prices, and then some. As far as **drinking** goes, many of the restaurants have bars attached to them, though there are also a few pubby places to get boozed up. All of the establishments below, unless otherwise indicated, are in **Nantucket Town**.

Bluefin 15 S Beach St ⓣ508/228-2033. Casual Japanese-influenced restaurant with innovative dishes like sake-marinated halibut and a shrimp tempura martini, as well as sushi and steak.

Boarding House 12 Federal St ⓣ508/228-9622. Romantic downstairs dining room serves a range of contemporary Euro-Asian-style meats and fish; lively bar upstairs offers lighter, cheaper bistro fare.

Centre Street Bistro 29 Centre St ⓣ508/228-8470. Intimate (seven tables) café specializing in light seafood fare – the seared salmon with lemon aioli is gorgeously fresh – with wonderful homemade desserts to top it off. Serves a mean weekend brunch, too.

Cioppino's 20 Broad St ⓣ508/228-4622. Stylish Mediterranean and New American cuisine in the center of town. Try their grilled lobster tails and fresh shrimp on a bed of pesto pasta.

Company of the Cauldron 5 India St ⓣ508/228-4016. A romantic, vine-covered, candlelit haven with live harp music thrice weekly. Both seatings of a shifting prix fixe menu ($52) sell out quickly, so make reservations.

Espresso Cafe 40 Main St ⓣ508/228-6930. Inexpensive, mostly healthy sandwich and salad lunches, including some vegetarian dishes, and the finest coffee on the island.

Pearl 12 Federal St ⓣ508/228-9701. Very chic restaurant upstairs from the *Boarding House* (see above), with a stand-out menu featuring the likes of oyster shooters, scallop ceviche, and tempura of Maryland soft-shell crabs with lemongrass risotto.

Rose & Crown 23 S Water St ⓣ508/228-2595. Traditional pub-style saloon that offers affordable sandwiches, chicken wings, and the like. Music and comedy in the evenings.

Sea Grille 45 Sparks Ave ⓣ508/325-5700. Just outside of town; relatively bland decor, but one of the best places for seafood, whether grilled, blackened, steamed, or fried; award-winning wine list too.

Ships Inn 13 Fair St ⓣ508/228-0040. Choose from artfully presented California-French style dishes, such as sauteed halibut, served in an intimate underground space.

Topper's 120 Wauwinet Rd, Wauwinet ⓣ508/228-8768. Pricey (menu prix fixe $78) but outstanding New American cuisine in this quiet, upscale restaurant at the *Wauwinet* hotel and resort a few miles outside Nantucket Town. Dress code enforced.

Vincent's 21 S Water St ⓣ508/228-0189. Moderately priced Italian dishes in a casual, relaxed atmosphere.

Nightlife and entertainment

There are two **movie theaters** on Nantucket; the Dreamland Theater, 19 S Water St (ⓣ508/228-5356), which shows first-run movies from June to September, and the Starlight Theater and Café, 1 N Union St (ⓣ508/228-4435), for more arty flicks year-round. Also in Nantucket Town, the Theater Workshop of Nantucket puts on **plays** and musicals at Bennett Hall, next to the First Congregational Church at 62 Centre St (ⓣ508/228-4305, ⓦwww.theatreworkshop.com), while Actors Theater of Nantucket (ⓣ508/228-6325, ⓦwww.nantuckettheatre.com) produces Broadway-type plays, comedy nights, and children's matinees at the Methodist Church, 2 Centre St. Additionally, the Nantucket Musical Arts Society stages **classical concerts** with renowned musicians through July and August, also in the First Congregational Church.

In terms of tried-and-true **nightlife**, Nantucket is quieter than the Vineyard, but Nantucket Town still has some good options to keep you out until after midnight (though not much later). There's certainly no shortage of live music, especially jazz and folk, to help you kick up your heels, but if you're after a big-city nightclub, you won't find it here. Current **listings** can be found in the weekly *Yesterday's Island* (ⓦwww.yesterdaysisland.com) and the daily *Inquirer and Mirror* (ⓦwww.ack.net).

Brotherhood of Thieves 23 Broad St ⓣ508/228-2551. This basement bar is a Nantucket institution and the place to go for live folk music, year-round.

Club Car 1 Main St ⓣ508/228-1101. Piano bar doubling as a big singles scene.

The Muse 44 Surfside Rd ⓣ508/228-6873. A mix of rock, reggae, and just about anything else you can dance to, as well as a few pool tables, keep this venue popular.

Tap Room 29 Broad St ⓣ508/228-2400. This rollicking pub has live jazz Wednesday through Saturday in the basement of the Jared Coffin House – but only during the season.

3

Central and Western Massachusetts

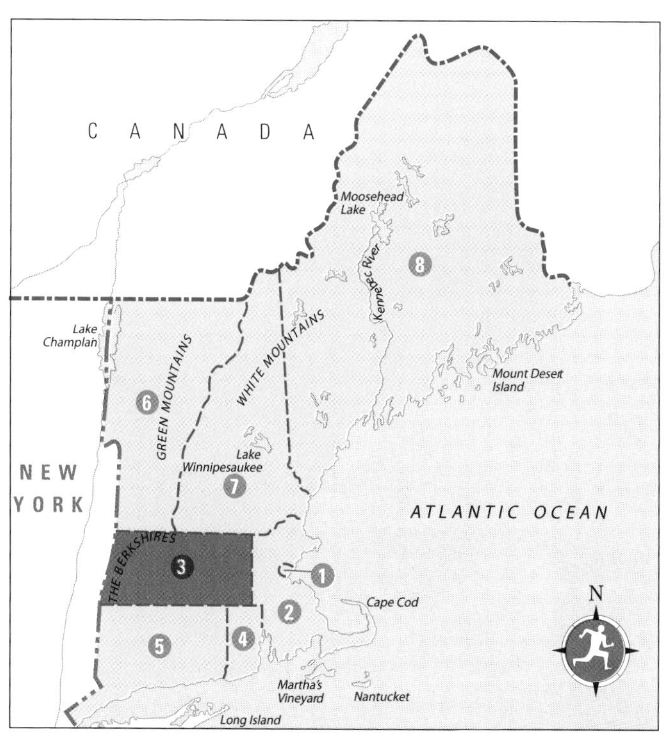

CHAPTER THREE Highlights

* **Worcester Art Museum** One of the largest art collections in New England, featuring an impressive photography collection and dazzling mosaics from Antioch. See p.250

* **Basketball Hall of Fame** A real treat for hoops fans, the Hall of Fame resides in Springfield, the birthplace of the sport. See p.252

* **Five College Consortium** The college towns of Northampton, Amherst, and South Hadley offer plenty in the way of arts, culture, and entertainment. See pp.256–265

* **Berkshires festivals** Music, dance, and drama junkies can get their summertime fix in the Berkshires, with many performances taking place at open-air venues in the countryside. See p.272

* **Naumkeag** Boasting the best of the Newport-style summer "cottages" to be found in the area. See p.274

* **North Adams** A fine contemporary art museum is the centerpiece of a town that has been transformed from a post-industrial eyesore to the hippest place in the Berkshires. See p.284

△ Round stone barn, Hancock Shaker Village

3

Central and Western Massachusetts

Moving west from the coast, Massachusetts' well-preserved and cultivated charm quickly dissolves amid the strip malls, franchises, and faded storefronts of the area loosely known as **Central Massachusetts**. Comprised mostly of semi-industrial towns still struggling to redefine their identities in the shadow of labor migrations, recessions, and Boston's thriving tourist industry, this area is not going to be the focal point of your itinerary, and it will likely not detain you for too long. But it does have a few things worth checking out. Worcester, the first town you reach traveling west from Boston, has one of the state's best collections of art, and Springfield, a bit farther west, is home to the Basketball Hall of Fame, where the game was invented. Springfield is also the most sensible jumping-off point for the **Pioneer Valley**, which stretches north from here, where small-town charisma and New England gentility begin to reassert themselves. Home to four separate colleges and a major university, the "Valley" supports a year-round population of down-to-earth academics, artists, and community activists who, in turn, patronize a bevy of restaurants, cafés, and bookstores – giving the area a continuous, if low-key, buzz. You can base yourself in any one of three or four locations to explore this region, but **Northampton** is probably the liveliest, with a good range of places to stay and most of the area's nightlife. **Amherst**, Northampton's eastern, also-lively neighbor, is home to a museum honoring **Emily Dickinson**, who lived and died here.

From the Pioneer Valley, most roads lead west to the **Berkshires**, as the smattering of tiny towns nestled in among the Berkshire Mountains, dividing Massachusetts from New York state, are collectively known. This area holds some of the Northeast's most desirable vacation spots for local city-dwellers, and is the adopted summer stage of many Boston and New York dance companies, orchestras, and theater troupes. With its spas, pricey inns, and sophisticated cultural happenings, it's a lovely spot for a weekend break if you can afford it. Even if you can't, the region's simpler pleasures – such as camping, hiking, and biking – are all available in abundance. Base yourself in the slightly precious small towns of **Lenox** or **Stockbridge** in the southern Berkshires, or **Williamstown** in the north, which has a good selection of museums and galleries to explore. There's also the outstanding Massachusetts Museum of Contemporary Art (MASS MoCA) in nearby **North Adams**. Williamstown and North Adams

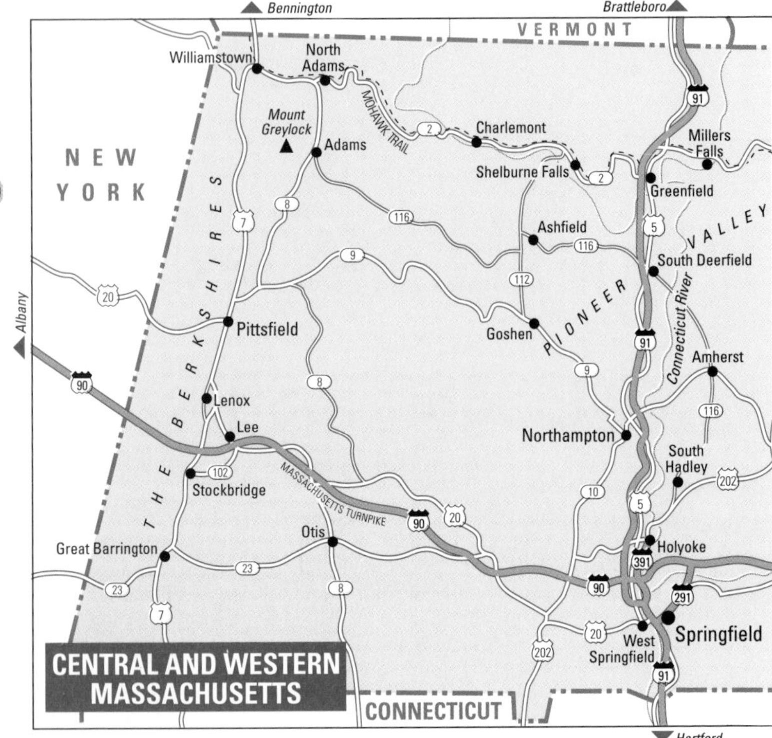

are the first two towns of any note along the 63-mile **Mohawk Trail**, which stretches from the Massachusetts–New York border to the town of Millers Falls on the Connecticut River, and offers perhaps the best scenic driving opportunities in this part of the state.

Central Massachusetts

Central Massachusetts is hardly the state's highlight, and most will probably experience it only from a car or bus window as they travel to the Berkshires or the Pioneer Valley (which, though technically in the middle of Massachusetts, isn't really considered part of "Central Mass"). Nevertheless, the towns in this area are close enough to Boston to be visited in a day-trip, and the region does have a handful of spots worth exploring, most notably Worcester's Art Museum and Springfield's Basketball Hall of Fame.

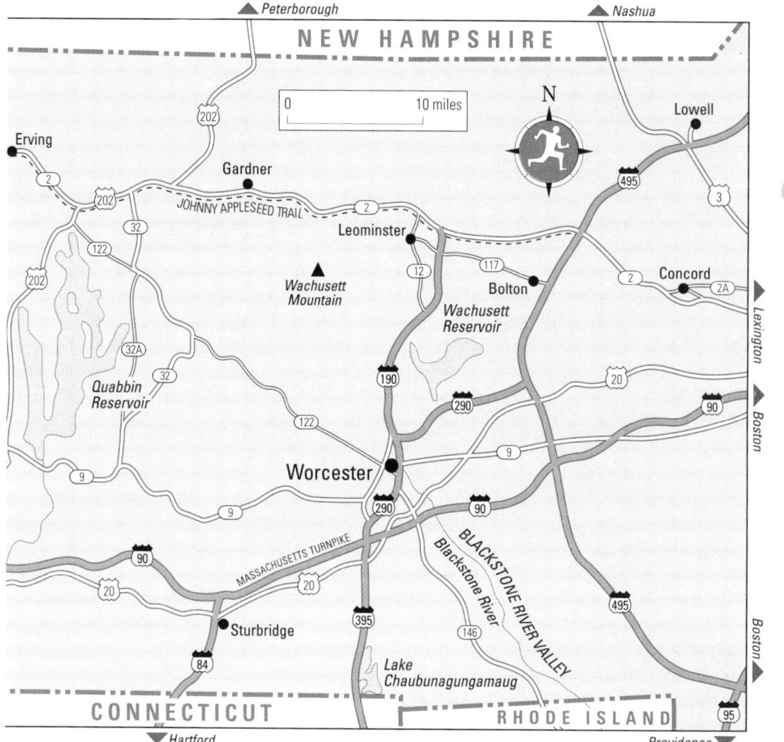

Worcester

Roughly forty miles west of Boston on I-90, **WORCESTER** is Massachusetts' second largest city (the third largest in New England behind Providence, RI) and the only major industrial city in the US beside neither sea, lake, nor river. Incorporated in 1722, Worcester enjoyed a century and a half of unbridled prosperity and was a thriving multi-ethnic town of Greek, Yiddish, and Italian bakeries, textile mills, and close-knit immigrant communities before lapsing into recession during the 1970s and 1980s. Notable (sort of) for birthing a mixed bag of American icons – including Abbie Hoffman and the Valentine's Day card – the town is only beginning to pick itself up, so for the moment its downtown doesn't have much to offer beyond an excellent art museum, a natural history museum, and a reasonable selection of restaurants.

Arrival and information

There are two **train stations** in Worcester: Amtrak and MBTA; if you're coming from Boston, the latter is less than a third of the Amtrak fare, but either way, once you arrive you'll have to navigate across four lanes of traffic, with nary a crossing signal or sidewalk in sight to get into town. It's not deadly, just annoying. The Peter Pan Trailways Terminal, 75 Madison St (ⓣ508/753-1515), is a short walk from downtown, and is served by regular **buses** from Boston and Springfield. A comprehensive **local bus** service is provided by the RTA

(Ⓣ508/791-9782). The friendly and well-equipped **Central Massachusetts Convention and Visitors Bureau**, downtown at 30 Worcester Center Blvd (Mon–Fri 8.30am–5pm; Ⓣ508/755-7400 or 1-800/231-7557, Ⓦwww.worcester.org), has information on Worcester and the rest of Central Massachusetts.

Accommodation

Worcester works best as a day-trip from Boston or Northampton, though if you want to stay the night you'll find plenty of reliable **hotel** chains in and around the city.

Beechwood Hotel 363 Plantation St Ⓣ508/754-5789 or 1-800/344-2589, Ⓦwww.beechwoodhotel.com. Even the smallest rooms at this glitzy hotel are spacious. HBO and Internet are in every room, with complimentary newspaper and continental breakfast to start your day, as well as free transportation anywhere within five miles of the hotel. ❼

Crowne Plaza 10 Lincoln Square Ⓣ508/791-1600, Ⓦwww.cpworcester.com. Designed for the business traveler, these 243 rooms are comfortable, though the staff is a bit stiff around the collar. ❼

Hampton Inn 110 Summer St Ⓣ508/757-0400 or 1-800/426-7866, Ⓦwww.hamptoninn.com. Centrally located with complimentary high-speed wireless Internet and a decent complimentary continental breakfast. ❺

The Town

Worcester's charm rests on its preservation of the past. The **Worcester Art Museum**, 55 Salisbury St (Wed, Fri & Sun 11am–5pm, Thurs 11am–8pm, Sat 10am–5pm; $8, free Sat 10am–noon; Ⓣ508/799-4406, Ⓦwww.worcesterart.org), located in a leafy part of town dominated by brick terraces about two miles north of downtown, is the city's major attraction – and is an absolute gem. Its vast holdings include a Romanesque chapter house from the twelfth century, shipped from Europe and reassembled in Worcester, a permanent gallery of American portrait miniatures, and an impressive collection of mosaics from Antioch. In addition, there are lesser-known paintings by Braque, Cézanne, Gainsborough, Gauguin, Goya, Kandinsky, Matisse, Turner, and Renoir, and the museum is blessed with an extensive photography collection, with works from the Civil War to the present day, including recognizable images from Cartier-Bresson, Stieglitz, and Weston. The museum also stages frequent exhibitions that draw from its holdings of over two thousand prints.

More centrally located is the **Worcester Historical Museum**, 30 Elm St (Tues, Wed, Fri & Sat 10am–4pm, Thurs 10am–8.30pm; $5; Ⓣ508/753-8278, Ⓦwww.worcesterhistory.org), where more is revealed about the city than simply being the coincidental birthplace of, among other things, the space suit, the monkey wrench, barbed wire, the birth control pill, and, least notably, the yellow "smiley face," designed by Harvey Ball, that never ceases to insist we "have a nice day."

Two-and-a-half miles east of the Historical Museum is the **EcoTarium**, 222 Harrington Way (Tues–Sat 10am–5pm, Sun noon–5pm; $8; Ⓣ508/929-2703, Ⓦwww.ecotarium.org). This museum has been inspiring environmental exploration since 1825, and is the second oldest natural history society in the US. It's geared toward families with young ones: children can get their hands dirty with numerous interactive exhibits, outdoor nature walks, and train rides past animals, all in an environment that reminds adults that they were kids once, too.

To visit the remarkable castle-like **Higgins Armory Museum**, 100 Barber Ave (Tues–Sat 10am–4pm, Sun noon–4pm; $8; Ⓣ508/853-6015, Ⓦwww.higgins.org), follow I-290 toward Shrewsbury and take exit 20. The museum is testament to years of careful collecting in post-World War I Europe by John Woodman Higgins, the founder of the Worcester Pressed Steel Company, and is chock-full of armor, swords, knives, chain mail, and helmets from ancient Greece and Rome, medieval and Renaissance Europe, and feudal Japan.

Eating and drinking

Anthony's 172 Shrewsbury St ⓣ508/757-6864. The appetizer of choice at this good Italian spot is the "172 ravioli," a single gargantuan pasta shell enfolding a center of artichoke and roasted garlic.

El-Basha 424 Belmont St ⓣ508/797-0884. A popular Lebanese spot near the UMass Medical Center, where nothing on the menu will set you back more than $10 or so.

Maxwell Silverman's Toolhouse 25 Union St ⓣ508/755-1200. One of the more atmospheric places for surf and turf: the spacious dining room is a restored factory building.

 **The Salem Cross Inn** on Rte-9 in West Brookfield ⓣ508/867-2345. About twenty miles west of Worcester, but worth the detour, this rambling restaurant in a restored 1705 farmhouse on six-hundred rolling acres serves consistently high-quality Yankee cooking.

Sano Café 232 Chandler St ⓣ508/754-3663. Munch on bison and ostrich burgers at this friendly health-food store with an attached café – a welcome oasis in an otherwise impersonal area.

Sole Proprietor 118 Highland St ⓣ508/798-3474. Reliable seafood restaurant that's not especially cheap but is well worth the price. The inflatable lobster on the roof belies the joint's sophisticated atmosphere.

On from Worcester: Sturbridge

Nearly fifteen miles southwest of Worcester, on US-20 near the junction of I-90 and I-84, the small town of **STURBRIDGE** holds but one spot of interest, the restored and reconstructed **Old Sturbridge Village** (daily: winter 9.30am–4pm, summer 9.30am–5pm; $20; ⓣ508/347-3362 or 1-800/SEE-1830, ⓦwww.osv.org). Located a little west of the town center, the village is made up of preserved buildings brought from all over the region to present a somewhat idealized but engaging portrait of a small New England town of the 1830s. It's the usual heritage hokum, with lots of costumed interpreters acting out roles – working in blacksmiths' shops, planting and harvesting vegetables, tending cows, and the like – but they pull it off with some style. The two hundred-acre site, with mature trees, ponds, and dirt footpaths, is also very pretty, making for a pleasant place to while away half a day or so. There is an **information center** just opposite the entrance to Old Sturbridge Village at 380 Main St (ⓣ508/347-7594 or 1-800/628-8379, ⓦwww.sturbridge.org), should you need brochures and more detailed information. Nearby, the *Old Sturbridge Village Lodges*, 371 Main St (ⓣ508/347-3327; ⑤), is a reasonable place to **stay**, while the *Sturbridge Host Hotel*, at no. 366 (ⓣ508/347-7993; ⑤), is another fine option, situated on nine groomed acres with an indoor heated swimming pool and access to beautiful Cedar Lake. For something to **eat**, try *Annie's Country Kitchen*, 140 Main St (ⓣ508/347-2320), known for their skillet breakfasts with home fries and apple-walnut French toast. They do good lunches and dinners as well.

Springfield

SPRINGFIELD, at the southern end of the Pioneer Valley, sprang up along the banks of the Connecticut River in the early 1600s, and went on to become the industrial hub of Central Massachusetts. America's first frozen foods were

The Nashoba Valley Winery

The Nashoba Valley Winery, on Wattaquadoc Hill Road (daily 11am–5pm, tours on weekends 11.00am–4pm; $3; ⓣ978/779-5521, ⓦwww.nashobawinery.com), is located on a pastoral hillside in the town of **BOLTON**, approximately seventeen miles northeast of Worcester. Activities range from picking seasonal peaches, plums, apples, and berries in their 55-acre orchard to sampling their award-winning wines and microbrews. Complete the experience with lunch, dinner, or Sunday brunch at their in-house café, *J's at Nashoba Valley* (closed Mon, dinner not served Tues & Sun, reservations recommended; ⓣ978/779-9816). From Worcester, take Rte-290 east to I-495, exit 27 to Rte-117.

made here, and it was the home of the Springfield rifle and the late children's author **Dr Seuss**, né Theodor Geisel. But, like so many places in this part of the state, the city was hit by recession and became rapidly depopulated. Today, blessed with a central location and the optimistic nickname "The Comeback City of America," the town is slowly restoring its fortunes. Most importantly, Springfield is where **basketball** was invented, and therein lies the main reason for any visit.

Arrival and information

Amtrak **trains** stop regularly at Springfield's downtown station at 66 Lyman St, about a mile from The Quadrangle. Peter Pan Trailways, which provides a daily **bus** service to and from Boston and New York, the Pioneer Valley, and the Berkshires, operates out of the nearby bus station at 1776 Main St (ⓣ413/781-3320). The **Greater Springfield Convention & Visitors Bureau** (ⓦwww.valleyvisitor.com) has two information centers: one opposite Tower Square at 1441 Main St (Mon–Fri 9am–5pm; ⓣ413/787-1548 or 1-800/723-1548) and the other by the river next to the Basketball Hall of Fame, at 1200 W Columbus Ave (daily 8am–8pm, late May to mid-Oct weekends 8am–10pm; ⓣ413/750-2980).

Accommodation

You needn't **stay** the night in Springfield, but if you choose to, there are several options, mostly geared to the convention-goers.

The Red Roof Inn 1254 Riverdale St ⓣ413/731-1010, ⓦwww.redroof.com. Across the river in West Springfield, it's simple and clean here, exactly what you might expect from a chain. ❹

Sheraton Springfield 1 Monarch Place ⓣ413/781-1010, ⓦwww.sheraton-springfield.com. Over three hundred spacious rooms in an atrium setting. Sixteen suites come with in-room Jacuzzis, while a fitness center, indoor pool, and racquetball courts are available to everyone. ❼

Springfield Marriott 2 Boland Way ⓣ413/781-7111, ⓦwww.marriott.com. Smack in the middle of town, with easy access to I-91. On the pricey side, but comfortable and convenient. ❼

Super 8 Motel 1500 Riverdale St ⓣ413/736-8080, ⓦwww.super8.com. An affordable option in nearby West Springfield, within striking distance of all the city's attractions. ❹

The Town

Springfield's unwieldy and unattractive city center is split by the wide Connecticut River. There's not much to see here beyond a handful of museums, and most signs point you in the direction of the **Basketball Hall of Fame**, at 1000 W Columbus Ave next to the river just south of Memorial Bridge (Mon–Sat

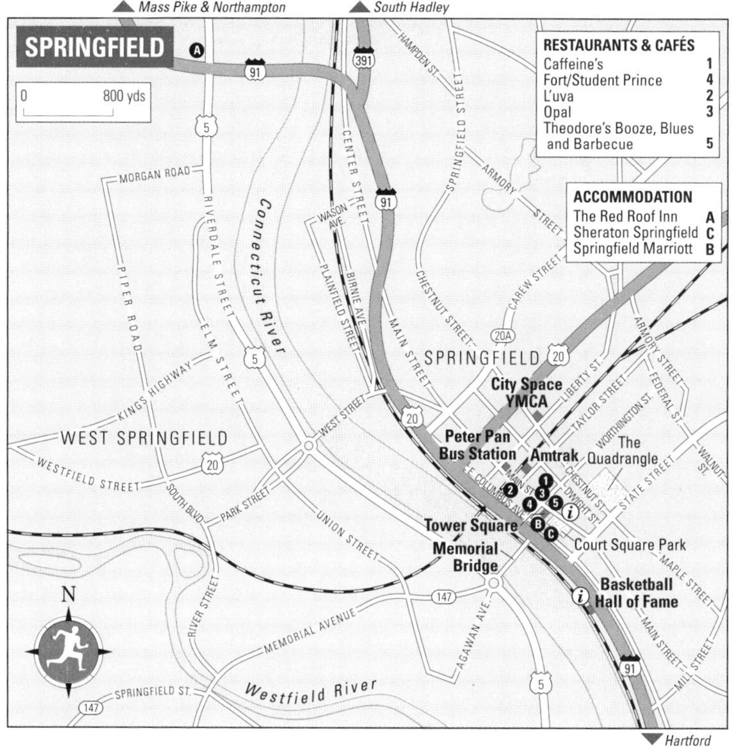

9am–6pm, Sun 10am–5pm; $17; ⓣ413/781-6500 or 1-877/4HOOPLA, ⓦwww.hoophall.com), which commemorates the 1890s invention of Dr James Naismith. Designed as a means of exercise during the harsh New England winters for athletes at the School for Christian Workers, the game's popularity spread with amazing rapidity. After Naismith took a trip to the Berlin Olympics in 1936, the National Association of Basketball Coaches started to discuss the idea of establishing a museum, finally realized in 1959. With the growth of the game, the hall has become a major attraction for anyone who's dreamed of stepping into Michael Jordan's shoes. In the summer of 2002, a revamped hall nearly twice the size of its predecessor opened for business. The renovated hall includes movies, videos, memorabilia, statistical databases, and some high-tech interactive gadgets such as the "Electronic Coach Telestrator," "You Call the Play," and "You Are the Sports Anchor," where you can test your skills as a coach, referee, and basketball commentator. The centerpiece, visible from all three floors, is a full-sized basketball court complete with suspended arena scoreboard.

Back in the center of town, Springfield's other museums are all located at **The Quadrangle**, a tree-lined square at the corner of State and Chestnut streets (all museums Wed–Fri noon–4pm, weekends 11am–4pm, call for additional summer opening hours; $10; ⓣ413/263-6800, ⓦwww.quadrangle.org). The **George Walter Vincent Smith Art Museum**, housed in an airy Italian palazzo-styled building blessed with Tiffany stained-glass windows, displays the eclectic collection of the museum's namesake and Belle Smith (both local art hounds). The holdings focus on Asian decorative arts, including the largest

△ The Basketball Hall of Fame

collection of Chinese cloisonné pottery outside of Asia, though it also takes in nineteenth-century American painting and rugs from the Middle East. **The Museum of Fine Arts** is slightly more coherent, proudly displaying Winslow Homer's *The New Novel* and Frederic Church's *New England Scenery* alongside lesser-known pieces by Monet, Picasso, Calder, and Georgia O'Keeffe. Also of local interest, the **Connecticut Valley Historical Museum** has an interactive exhibit (aka, playroom) on "The World of Doctor Seuss" to keep the kids busy while you check out furniture, toys, paintings, games, and artifacts that were once the possessions of settlers in the region. This museum houses a **Genealogy and Local History Library** with its database, Project Shamrock, which allows descendants of Irish immigrants to search for relatives who may have been living in Massachusetts between 1636 and the present day. Finally, the **Springfield Science Museum** has a crowd-pleasing life-sized replica of a *Tyrannosaurus rex*, exhibits on animal life in the Connecticut River, and a new

Outdoor activities in Central Massachusetts

Not all the fun in Central Massachusetts is targeted toward museum hounds – if you're looking to get your heart rate up, there's plenty of action on offer. The northern strip of Central Massachusetts is good scenic driving country, with the **Johnny Appleseed Trail** taking over from the Mohawk Trail (see p.283) as Rte-2 passes the Quabbin Reservoir and heads east towards Concord, Massachusetts. This was Johnny Appleseed's neck of the woods, who was actually John Chapman, born in 1774 in Leominster, MA; he dedicated his life to planting apple trees and spreading the word of God. Great for running, hiking, or biking, the trail passes 25 towns, numerous orchards, wineries, rolling hills, and **Wachusett Mountain** (ⓣ978/464-2300 or 1-800/SKI-1234, ⓦwww.wachusett.com), a popular spot for skiing and snowboarding. For more hiking, as well as cross-country skiing and snowshoeing, head deeper into the **Leominster State Forest** (ⓣ978/874-2303), part of the Wachusett Mountain State Reservation (ⓣ978/464-2987), where such trails abound. South of Worcester, the **Blackstone River Valley** stretches all the way to Providence, RI. The 46-mile Blackstone River brought great prosperity to the region at the time of America's Industrial Revolution in the late eighteenth century, although today the waterway sees more canoeing and kayaking than commercial activity. There is also a bicycle path that follows the course of the river and the long-since defunct Blackstone Canal. Contact the Blackstone River Valley National Heritage Corridor (ⓣ401/762-0250) for more **information** on the activities available in the area.

astronomy hall and planetarium with daily shows (extra charge). In the middle of The Quadrangle, the **Dr Seuss National Memorial Sculpture Garden** (daily 9am–8pm) contains metallic sculptures of various characters and scenes created and inspired by the Springfield-born children's writer and illustrator, Theodor Geisel.

Eating and drinking

Caffeine's 1338 Memorial Ave, West Springfield ⓣ413/731-5282. Serves a range of entrees, from barbecued chicken pizza to soy burgers and focaccia.

Fort/Student Prince 8 Fort St ⓣ413/734-7475. For over sixty years, this establishment has been a local favorite for German wiener schnitzel, goulash, and sauerbraten.

Gus & Paul's 1500 Main St, at Tower Square ⓣ413/781-2253; also 1209 Sumner Ave ⓣ413/782-5710. The Main St branch has an urban bistro feel, while the Sumner Ave location leans more toward old world-style deli. Either way, the food at both is fresh and tasty. Main St branch closed Sun.

L'uva 1676 Main St ⓣ413/734-1010. The menu at this eatery changes every three months, though the delicious maple-crusted scallops are a staple. Has 325 wines by the bottle and 65 by the glass.

Opal 272 Worthington St ⓣ413/731-0667. Young and trendy atmosphere, serving great (though pricey) filets mignon and vegetarian ratatouille, among other treats.

Theodore's Booze, Blues and Barbecue 201 Worthington St ⓣ413/736-6000. Straight-ahead offerings of barbecued ribs, chicken, and salmon, with a solid beer selection and live blues most nights.

The Pioneer Valley

The Pioneer Valley, a verdant corridor shaped by the Connecticut River and centuries of glacial activity, is the epicenter of recreational and cultural activity in Central Massachusetts. The towns of **Northampton**, **South Hadley**, and **Amherst** share between them no fewer than five colleges: Smith (in Northampton), Mount Holyoke (in South Hadley), and Amherst, Hampshire, and the University of Massachusetts (all in Amherst) – schools that have formalized their relationship through the creation of the cooperative "Five College Consortium," which links the communities academically, economically, and culturally. Just one and a half hours from Boston, the Valley is a good, less expensive, and much less popular alternative to Cape Cod or the Berkshires – an excellent choice for those who like to hike, bike, hang out in cafés, browse bookstores, and pretend, if only for a weekend, that they actually live in this idyllic little spot.

Northampton

In 1654, the Puritans purchased some of the most fertile farmland in the densely wooded hills of Central Massachusetts from the Nonotuck Indians for ten coats, several trinkets, and 100 fathoms of wampum and christened it **NORTHAMPTON**. These vast holdings became a liability after the Revolutionary War, however, when depressed and indebted farmers were in danger of losing their property to creditors looking to recover the war debt. Rising to meet this injustice in 1786 was farmer Daniel Shays, who rustled up hundreds of his compatriots and marched to the county courthouse in Northampton, and soon after attacked the federal arsenal in Springfield in what would later come to be known as **Shays' Rebellion.**

Valley information and transportation

The **Pioneer Valley Transit Authority** (PVTA; ⓣ413/586-5806 or 1-877/779-PVTA) runs shuttle buses between Northampton, Amherst, and South Hadley. Financed and operated by the area colleges and driven by UMass students, the PVTA is free to all. Generally, buses begin circulating at 6am and head home at around midnight (later on Thurs, Fri & Sat), passing each stop every 30min or so. Schedules are available on each bus and posted at the sidewalk stops. If you'd rather get around the area under your own power, the paved **Norwottuck Trail Bike Path** weaves its way for around eight miles between Northampton and Amherst in the track of a former railroad bed. Used for biking, walking, and rollerblading, the path, though crowded in nice weather, offers an attractive alternative to driving the very developed Rte-9.

Bookstores in Northampton and Amherst are a significant source of local maps and advice. *The Valley Advocate*, a free weekly newspaper available in any café, prints a complete listing of area happenings, movie listings, and restaurant reviews. Look out for their "Best of the Valley" Readers' Poll, which gives restaurants, bars, and cafés awards for excellence in a variety of categories. For outdoor activity suggestions and listings of hiking trails and recreation areas, contact the **Conservation Commissions** of Northampton (ⓣ413/586-6950) or Amherst (ⓣ413/256-4045), which between them oversee the maintenance of 37 distinctly different nature preserves.

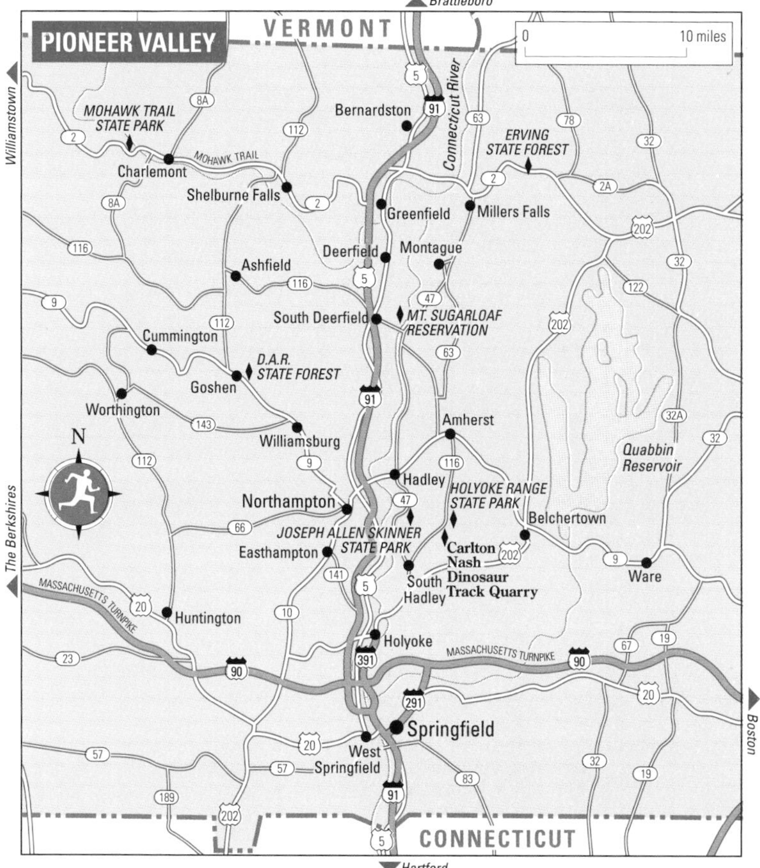

Northampton's canal connection to New Haven, CT, and the Atlantic Ocean was completed in 1835, only to be overshadowed by the 1845 arrival of the railroad. Transportation, in turn, encouraged the development of industry, which by the early to mid-twentieth century was undermined by the rush to use cheaper Southern and international labor. In retrospect, Northampton's saving grace has been its investment in education and the intellectual environment it has fostered. Smith College, founded in 1871 by Sophia Smith and financed with her personal inheritance, survives as a prestigious women's college.

Today, liberal, progressive, and content to march to a different drummer, Northampton (population 30,000 or so), fondly nicknamed "NoHo," has settled into its role as a tolerant town of artists, writers, students, teachers, and activists. Oddly enough, it was cited in *Parents' Magazine* as one of the best small towns in America to raise a family and in *Newsweek* as the "lesbian capital of the Northeast" – both distinctions it accepted with pride.

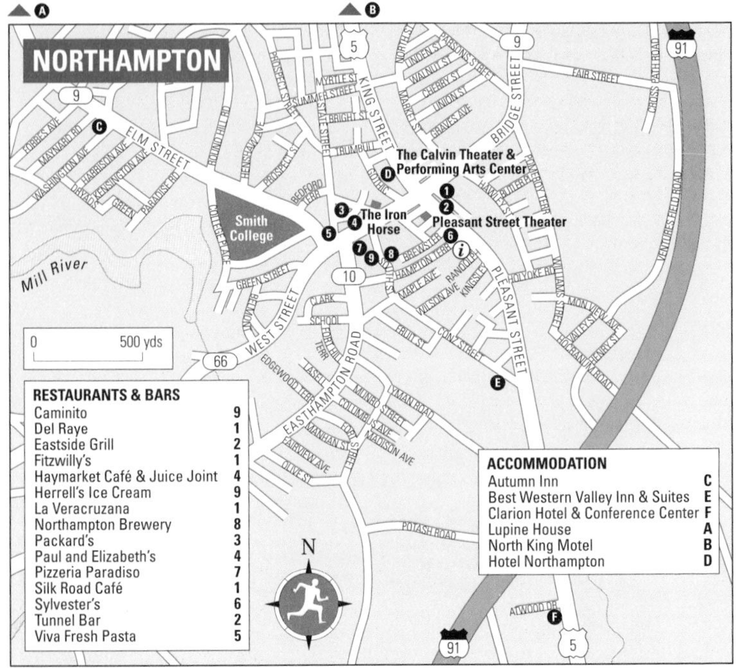

Arrival and information

By **car**, Northampton is off of I-91 approximately fifteen miles north of the Massachusetts Turnpike (I-90); all exits marked "Northampton" lead to the center of town. Peter Pan Trailways **buses** pull in at 1 Roundhouse Plaza (ⓣ413/586-1030), while the closest commercial **airport** to Northampton (and in fact Amherst and South Hadley as well) is Bradley International (ⓣ1-860/292-2000), in Windsor Locks, CT, roughly 45min south of town on I-91. If you need help getting started, the **Greater Northampton Chamber of Commerce**, 99 Pleasant St (Mon–Fri 9am–5pm, May–Oct also weekends 10am–2pm; ⓣ413/584-1900, ⓦwww.northamptonuncommon.com), offers an array of maps and advice, as well as copies of the *Pink Pages* for gay and lesbian travelers.

Accommodation

You shouldn't have a hard time finding somewhere reasonable to **stay** in Northampton, though many places tend to be of the stylish inn variety.

Autumn Inn 259 Elm St ⓣ413/584-7660, ⓦwww.hampshirehospitality.com. A Colonial-style inn boasting an attractive outdoor swimming pool and barbecue area surrounded by trees. Clean, comfortable, and close to the action. Reservations required. ⑤

Best Western Valley Inn & Suites 117 Conz St ⓣ413/586-1500 or 1-800/941-3066, ⓦwww.bestwestern.com. A comfortable and reliable chain that's within walking distance of everything in town. Complimentary continental breakfasts, Internet, indoor pool, exercise facility, and friendly service in a recently renovated hotel. ⑤

Clarion Hotel and Conference Center 1 Atwood Drive ⓣ413/586-1211, ⓦwww.hampshirehospitality.com. Formerly the *Inn at Northampton*, this place is now part of a local chain of hotels. Wood paneling and a roaring fireplace in the lobby set the tone, while an indoor pool topped with a glass dome completes the scene. The smallest bed is a queen-size. Friendly staff. 6

Lupine House 185 N Main St, Florence ⓣ413/586-9766 or 1-800/890-9766. Three antique-furnished rooms with private baths in a lovely Colonial house three miles from downtown Northampton. Continental breakfast included. 4

North King Motel 504 N King St ⓣ413/584-8847. Eighteen clean and basic rooms in a well-worn Fifties-style roadside motel. The chatty owners give this otherwise dreary place a comfortable, lived-in feel. 3

Hotel Northampton 36 King St ⓣ413/584-3100, 1-800/547-3529, ⓦwww.hotelnorthhampton.com. Copious flower arrangements in the entryway of this over-sized historic 1927 hotel give an immediate sense of its inflated – though entirely deserved – self-importance. The attention to detail and charm make up for the smallish rooms. 7

The Town

Although Northampton doesn't have much in the way of tourist attractions per se, the town has a well-earned reputation as one of the most liveable places in the US. Judging by the wealth of shops, restaurants, cafés, and the diversity of the population along Main Street, you could be in a major city, rather than a small college town. The traffic, however, remains relatively light (except for the snail's pace rush-hour commutes to and from Amherst), and the streets clean and safe.

The main thing to see is in the grounds of the institution that most defines the town, Smith, whose **Smith College Museum of Art** (Tues–Sat 10am–4pm, Sun noon–4pm; $5; ⓣ413/585-2760) is superb. Don't miss the bathrooms, which local artists helped overhaul: it's worth taking a peek into both the men's and women's sides – just be sure to knock and announce your presence first. The collection focuses on nineteenth- and twentieth-century art, with works by Monet (*Field of Poppies*), Georgia O'Keeffe (the nearly translucent *Squash Flowers, #1*), Jean Arp (a languid *Torso*), and Frank Stella, who is represented by the enormous *Damascus Gate (Variation III)*. The museum also boasts an eight-thousand-strong print collection, which contains a large number of prints and engravings by Daumier, Delacroix, Dürer, Munch, Picasso, and Toulouse-Lautrec. There are also more than a few off-beat items sprinkled throughout the museum, such as an exquisite Luba ceremonial ax from Zaire.

You may want to call in at other areas on the attractive campus, such as the **botanic garden**; tours can be made from the admissions office, pretty much on the hour during weekday mornings and early afternoons.

Eating and drinking

Northampton is the top place in the Pioneer Valley for **eating**, and establishments are typically a lot less precious here than they are over in the Berkshires. As for **nightlife**, Northampton boasts the Valley's best – though as this is college country, if you look a day under 60 be prepared to have your ID checked every time you enter a place.

Caminito 7 Old South St ⓣ413/387-6387. The menu combines flavors from Italy, France, and Spain, defining the signature influences of this Argentinean hot spot. Good for carnivores and vegetarians alike.

Del Raye 1 Bridge St ⓣ413/586-2664. A sophisticated urban-style bistro serving French-inspired steaks and seafood. Chic and rather pricey (entrees around $30).

Eastside Grill 19 Strong Ave ⓣ413/586-3347. A well-established steakhouse serving steaks, chicken, and seafood with a Cajun bite. Extensive menu and attentive service, but often crowded.

FitzWilly's 23 Main St ⓣ413/584-8666. Smack in the middle of it all, this established local bar is a relaxing place to knock a few back and soak up the atmosphere.

Haymarket Café & Juice Joint 185 Main St ⓣ413/586-9969. Popular hangout for people looking for a cheap fix of the healthy variety. Soups, salads, and sandwiches for around $5. Drinks served in the street-level café, food in the dimly lit basement. Free WiFi.

Herrell's Ice Cream 8 Old South St ⓣ413/586-9700. Home base for a small but illustrious chain of ice-cream stores; owner Steve Herrell was apparently the first to grind up candy bars and add them to his concoctions, though there are plenty more delicious innovations to choose from.

La Veracruzana 31 Main St ⓣ413/586-7181. Bright, cheerful, and informal, the folks at *La Veracruzana* are credited with bringing the take-out burrito to the Valley. There's another branch in Amherst.

Northampton Brewery 11 Brewster Court, behind Thorne's Marketplace ⓣ413/584-9903. With a solid selection of high-quality microbrews on tap, an extensive munchies menu, and a relaxing outdoor patio, this is a great place to while away a summertime happy hour or a snowy winter night.

Packards's 14 Masonic St ⓣ413/584-5957. The plush billiards tables on the third floor give the place a rather gentleman's club-type atmosphere, in stark contrast to the video games and televised football downstairs. Featuring the usual selection of beers and bar food.

Paul and Elizabeth's 150 Main St, in Thorne's Marketplace ⓣ413/584-4832. Vegetarian and seafood entrees, homemade breads, and desserts served in a serenely airy dining room.

Pizzeria Paradiso 12 Crafts Ave ⓣ413/586-1468. A cozy pizza place kept warm with wood-fired ovens imported from Italy. The extensive choice of toppings, drinks, and desserts make this much more than just another pizza joint.

Sylvester's 111 Pleasant St ⓣ413/586-1418. Housed in the former home of Sylvester Graham, the inventor of the graham cracker, *Sylvester's* serves up tasty fare, including delightful breakfast treats such as banana-bread French toast. Very child-friendly staff.

Viva Fresh Pasta 249 Main St ⓣ413/586-5875. They make their own pasta here, and the combinations, such as salmon Rockefeller, shrimp scampi, and meatball ravioli, are mouth-watering. Portions are big but reasonably priced, and the desserts are sweet.

Performing arts and film

Due to its relatively close proximity to New York and Boston, as well as the efforts of energetic local promoters such as "The Iron Horse Entertainment Group," Northampton manages to attracts some of the biggest names in most branches of the **performing arts**. You can reserve tickets for many shows playing in town at the **Northampton Box Office**, 150 Main St, on the second floor of Thorne's Marketplace (ⓣ413/586-8686 or 1-800/THE-TICK, ⓦwww.iheg.com).

The Calvin Theater and Performing Arts Center 19 King St ⓣ413/584-1444. The folks responsible for *The Iron Horse* (see below) have lovingly transformed this 75-year-old movie house into a beacon of the performing arts. Live theater, music, and dance performance for all ages and tastes.

The Iron Horse 20 Center St ⓣ413/585-0479. An institution in the world of folk music, this small, coffeehouse-style venue has been cheering on emerging artists for twenty years and still has a knack for booking the big names of folk, bluegrass, jazz, and blues.

Pleasant Street Theater 27 Pleasant St ⓣ413/586-0935. Independent, classic, and foreign films are screened in this intimate movie theater – a worthy leftover from the pre-multiplex era. Check out the "Forgotten Film at Five" for 5pm screenings of films which, especially in the case of non-English-language productions, never got the chance to be remembered in the first place.

Silk Road Café 29 Main St ⓣ413/587-7900. A restaurant with small bar that caters to the Valley's bold and beautiful. Music is upbeat and jazzy, as is the global fusion menu, with selections like lacquered pork belly. You don't need to hit the dry-cleaners before coming here, but at least plug in the iron.

Tunnel Bar beneath *Union Station Restaurant*, 125A Pleasant St, where Pearl St meets Strong Ave ⓣ413/586-5366. This old underground pedestrian walkway has been renovated into a dark martini bar – a good spot for the sophisticated urbanite, or those who want to feign as such.

Amherst

Settled in 1727, incorporated in 1759, and named for General Jeffrey Amherst, **AMHERST** developed for the most part like its neighbor, Northampton, as a college town. In 1821, the citizens of Amherst financed and opened the Collegiate Charitable Institution to educate the town's young men, and in just four years this had become Amherst College. Forty years later, the Massachusetts Agricultural College opened to teach military, agricultural, and technical skills, and today, as the renamed University of Massachusetts at Amherst, it is the main cog in the Massachusetts public university system. Meanwhile, Hampshire College, just outside of town on the road to South Hadley, was founded in the 1970s by the presidents of four local colleges as an experiment in true liberal arts study, one that emphasized the individual and interdisciplinary nature of education. Today, the town as a whole maintains the feel of a small, bookish community, a bit larger but in fact less hurried than Northampton, with a healthy mix of college students, hippies, young families, and professionals – all in all a good place to kick back for a day or two and explore the surrounding countryside.

Arrival and information

Like Northampton, Amherst is accessible by **car** off I-91, roughly 25 miles north of I-90. During the fall foliage season, those coming from Boston should consider taking the less-traveled and more scenic Rte-2 from Concord, west to

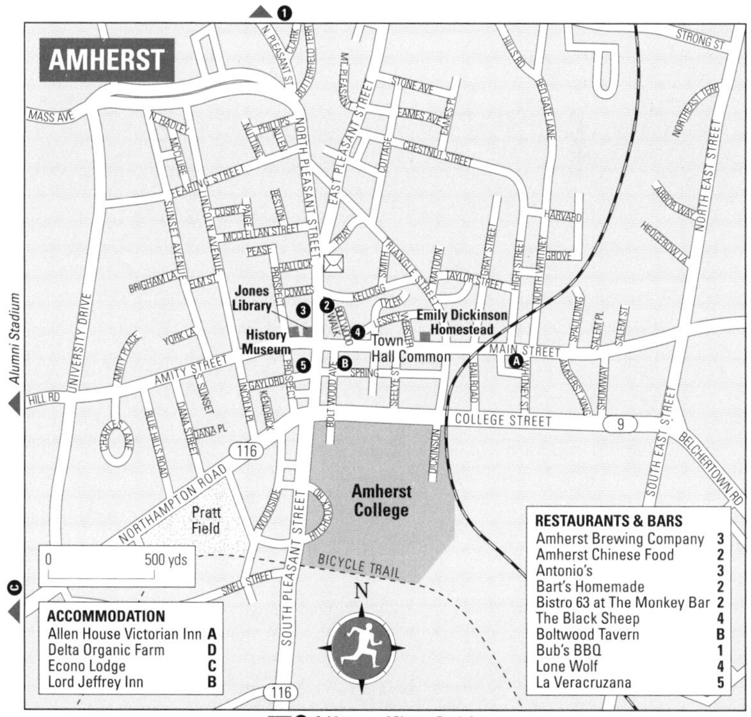

Rte-202 through the woods skirting the Quabbin Reservoir, and picking up Rte-9 into Amherst. Amtrak's Vermonter **train** service between Montréal, New York, and Washington, DC pulls into town at 13 Railroad St, while Peter Pan Trailways **buses** let off at 79 S Pleasant St (ⓣ413/256-0431). For further information, the **Amherst Area Chamber of Commerce**, 409 Main St (Mon–Fri 8am–5pm; ⓣ413/253-0770, ⓦwww.amherstarea.com) will point you in the right direction, arming you with all the necessary maps and brochures.

Accommodation

Amherst's **accommodation** options range from expensive inns and intimate B&Bs with an ecological bent to predictable branches of the national chains. The best bet for inexpensive lodging is to drive the length of Rte-9 and check out some of the smaller, slightly rumpled-looking motels along the way. Many of them are safe and clean, if visually unappealing. Remember, wherever you stay, you can expect to pay more during the fall foliage season.

Allen House Victorian Inn 599 Main St ⓣ413/253-5000, ⓦwww.allenhouse.com. A charming, award-winning Victorian B&B just past the Emily Dickinson Homestead. The *Amherst Inn*, directly opposite the Homestead on a quiet, leafy part of Main Street, is the *Allen House's* sister inn. ❼

Delta Organic Farm 352 E Hadley Rd ⓣ413/253-1893, ⓦwww.deltaorganicfarm.com. An organic nirvana for health-conscious travelers, with special needs and requests welcomed by the concerned and accommodating owners. Organic breakfast. ❺

Econo Lodge 329 Russell St (Rte-9), Hadley ⓣ413/582-7077, ⓦwww.choicehotels.com. A stone's throw from the Hampshire Mall, between Amherst and Northampton, this chain motel is clean, comfortable, and friendly, with a pool and high-speed Internet available. ❻

Lord Jeffrey Inn 30 Boltwood Ave ⓣ413/253-2576 or 1-800/742-0358, ⓦwww.lordjeffreyinn.com. Situated on Amherst Common, this is a quintessential rambling and richly decorated New England inn – so much so that it is often used for weddings. The rooms are a luxurious treat. ❹–❽

The Town

Just about everybody who comes to Amherst visits the **Emily Dickinson Homestead**, 280 Main St (guided tours March & Nov to mid-Dec, Wed & Sat 1–5pm on the hour; April–May & Sept–Oct Wed–Sat 1–5pm on the hour; June–Aug Wed–Sat 10am–5pm, Sun 1–5pm on every half-hour; $8, reservations advised; ⓣ413/542-8161), where the celebrated American poet Emily Dickinson lived all her life. Born in Amherst in 1830, Emily Dickinson attended nearby Mount Holyoke College, but loneliness drove her back home without finishing her studies, and she shortly afterwards began a life of self-imposed exile in the family home here on Main Street. Emily Dickinson read voraciously, wrote incessantly, corresponded with friends, and over the course of her life penned some 1800 poems, most of which mirrored her lifelong struggle between isolation and an intense search for inspiration. Despite this literary hyperactivity, she published fewer than a dozen poems during her life, and was a completely unknown woman, much less poet, when she died in 1886. Her work was collected and published four years later by her sister, and she has since been recognized as influential in giving American poetry its own resounding voice.

The world Dickinson wrote of from her house no longer exists, but her room here is frozen in time, with an array of personal effects, such as the desk where Dickinson's poems were found after her death. It's a pretty low-key display on the whole, but for most visitors – especially those who also visit **Dickinson's grave** in the nearby West Cemetery, off Triangle Street – this seems to be just

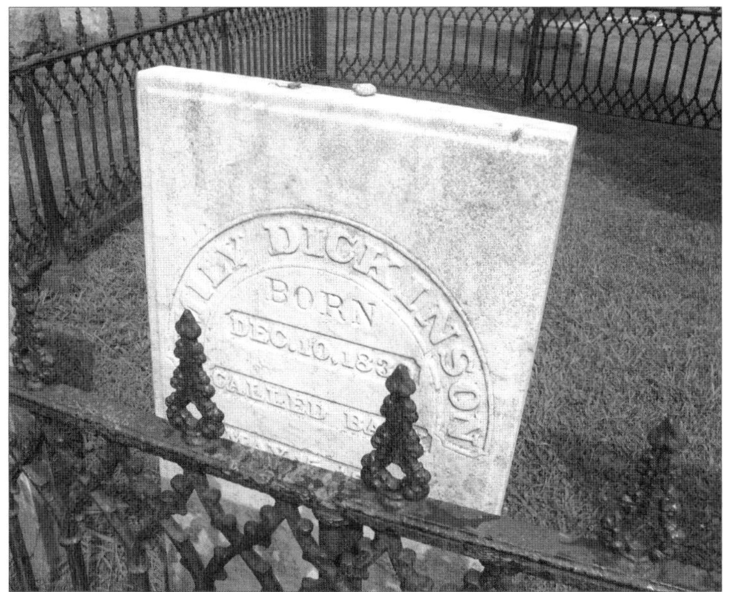

△Emily Dickinson's grave

enough. Also of notable literary interest, the original copy of *Stopping by Woods on a Snowy Evening*, written by the American poet Robert Frost, who was a professor at Amherst College for thirty years, sits under glass in the Special Collections Room at **Jones Library** on Amity Street.

There's further cultural interest in the **Mead Art Museum**, on the lovely campus of **Amherst College** (academic year Tues–Sun 10am–4.30pm, Thurs 10am–9pm; summer Tues–Sun 1–4pm; free), where works by Frederic Church, Thomas Cole, John Singleton Copley, Thomas Eakins, and Winslow Homer dominate a collection strong on early twentieth-century American art. There's also a sprinkling of Renaissance European works, notably a seductive *Salome* by Robert Henri and a gory *Still Life with Dead Game* by Frans Snyders. After visiting the Mead, check out the **Eric Carle Museum of Picture Book Art**, 125 West Bay Rd (Tues–Sat 10am–4pm, Sun noon–4pm; $7; ⓣ413/658-1100), the first museum in America devoted to children's book art. You will kick yourself for not having kept your own elementary school art projects, as some exhibits appear to have been collected from nearby refrigerators. Farther down the road is the **National Yiddish Book Center**, 121 West St (Sun–Fri 10am–3.30pm; closed on Jewish holidays; free; ⓣ413/256-4900), which houses one of the world's largest collections of Yiddish books – many culled from New York City dumpsters – in a sprawling building designed to emulate an Eastern European *shtetl*.

Eating and drinking

Though Amherst doesn't have as many **restaurants** as Northampton, you surely won't go hungry. The high student population has led to a large percentage of sandwich places, pizza joints, chain coffeeshops, and casual eateries. A stroll along either Main Street or North Pleasant Street pretty much sums up the choices.

Amherst Brewing Company 24–36 N Pleasant St ⓣ413/253-4400. The brass bar and exposed brick add a touch of upscale yearning to this prime drinking spot. Live music – mostly jazz – and a street terrace are added attractions.

Amherst Chinese Food 62 Main St ⓣ413/253-7835. The owners of this restaurant grow the organic vegetables they use in their dishes and add nothing artificial as they pick, steam, saute, fry, and deliver them piping hot to your table. Unsurprisingly popular with a health-conscious crowd.

Antonio's 31 N Pleasant St ⓣ413/253-0808. Just a few benches and stools to eat at, but this is *the* pizza place in town, where the slices are always just out of the oven and good.

Bart's Homemade 103 N Pleasant St ⓣ413/253-9371. The street terrace is as inviting as the sundaes, smoothies, and ice creams on warm days.

Bistro 63 at The Monkey Bar 63 N Pleasant St ⓣ413/259-1600. Their lobster corn chowder, seafood Portuguese, and steak *mignonette* are so good that they even offer classes on how to make them.

The Black Sheep 79 Main St ⓣ413/253-3442. Stacked sandwiches, pastries, coffee, and desserts served in a down-to-earth café. Open late for coffee and occasional music, including open-mic nights. Highly recommended.

Boltwood Tavern 30 Boltwood Ave ⓣ413/253-2576. Part of the *Lord Jeffrey Inn*, this is a popular spot for good beers and pub grub. Upstairs is the *Windowed Hearth*, a more expensive and upscale counterpart where you're likely to find professors rather than students.

Bub's BBQ Rte-116, Sunderland ⓣ413/548-9630. Despite the address, this is only minutes by car from Amherst. From Rte-9, take Rte-116 North and look for the fluorescent pink porker on the right inviting you to "Pig out in style," on smokin' barbecue and homestyle sides.

La Veracruzana 63 S Pleasant St ⓣ413/253-6900. Burrito joint that's the sister restaurant of the Northampton place of the same name.

Lone Wolf 63 Main St ⓣ413/256-4643. Open seven days a week until 2pm, they're known for their breakfasts, with dishes like challah French toast, lox and eggs, and vegan omelettes with coconut milk.

South Hadley

Located at the intersection of routes 116 and 47, **SOUTH HADLEY**, the home of bucolic Mount Holyoke College, completes the circle of towns in the Five College Consortium. Founded in 1836 by education pioneer Mary Lyon, Mount Holyoke is the oldest college for women in America and, like its neighbor Smith, is considered to be one of the most prestigious of the "Seven Sisters," a group of seven originally women-only colleges in the Northeast.

The Town

Though the smallest of the area's towns, South Hadley adds an exclamation point to the Pioneer Valley, mainly due to the presence of the **Mount Holyoke College Art Museum**, adjacent to the greenhouse on Lower Lake Road (Tues–Fri 11am–5pm, Sat–Sun 1–5pm; free), which has an impressive permanent collection of Asian, Egyptian, and Mediterranean paintings, drawings, and sculpture, and regularly mounts high-quality special exhibitions. The museum has acquired a *Head of Faustina the Elder*, a marble Roman sculpture of the second-century Empress Faustina, whose likeness was reproduced on coins and statues of the period, and whose elaborate braided hairstyle is a feat of both the art of sculpting and hairdressing.

There's also the **Joseph Allen Skinner Museum**, 35 Woodbridge St/Rte-116 (May–Oct Wed & Sun afternoons; free), which has fantastic exhibits of period glassware, musical instruments, housewares, antique furniture, and weaponry. The museum, a Congregational church built in 1846 and moved to this site from its original resting place – now under the placid waters of the nearby Quabbin Reservoir – houses the eclectic collection of Mr. Skinner a wealthy mill-owner and world traveler.

Food and drink

In the popular perception, **New England cuisine** equals pot roast, baked beans, and boiled dinner (corned beef and cabbage, to be precise) – in essence, comfort food to get you through the cold nights of winter. These hearty meals in truth take a backseat to healthier, though still proudly regional, fare. **Seafood** is the real staple of the day – or catch, if you will – appearing in everything from creamy clam chowder to messy fried platters to the ultimate, if utterly simple, meal of boiled lobster. The region's distinctive **produce**, most vibrant during the colder seasons, includes tart cranberries, rich maple syrup, and crunchy apples.

Lobster

Lobster and other seafood

New England **lobsters** are not only a first-rate meal, they're a source of economic sustenance and a basis of community pride. Once so plentiful that they simply washed ashore, their abundance led Native Americans to use them as fish bait and crop fertilizer. During colonial times, settlers – who thought the animal to be low-class food not fit for consumption by dignified people – fed them to indentured servants and prisoners. These days, however, lobster is a hot commodity. In Maine, where lobster pride is most evident – Rockland's yearly **Lobster Fest** draws around 100,000 fans – fishermen caught 70 million pounds of the critter in 2004, worth a total of $285 million. This translates to about $4 per pound, or on average $25 for a lobster dinner – a pretty major upgrade from what was once prison food.

Locals generally eat lobster two ways: as a simple but delicious **lobster roll** and as a boiled (sometimes grilled or steamed) entrée. Lobster rolls are prepared by mixing together lobster meat, mayonnaise, salt, and pepper; the filling is then stuffed inside a buttered and toasted hot dog bun. **Boiled lobster**, found at

Clambakes

"**Clambake**" is not just the title of a particularly bad Elvis Presley movie, it's a local tradition older than New England itself. Long before the first white settlers arrived, Native Americans had perfected the ritual of cooking plentiful amounts of clams by what now seems a rather unconventional method. A deep pit is dug into a beach's sand, then lined with smooth rocks. Wood is added and ignited; its ashes are eventually swept away, with the rocks left hot enough to cook on. Before the cooking begins, seaweed is piled on these rocks, followed by layers of **potatoes**, **onions**, **corn**, **clams**, and/or lobsters. Then comes another layer of seaweed, and finally a wet canvas covering everything to trap the steam. The result is an unforgettable, and messy, meal, usually eaten with bare hands.

Clambakes are usually organized by churches and similar groups that hold fundraisers; also, a few commercial organizations arrange clambakes in late summer and fall when the fresh corn is at its finest. Your best bet if you want to participate in a clambake is to search out **local papers** for advertisements; towns along the southern coast of **Rhode Island** are the likeliest sites. In any case, don't think of just staging one on your own unless you want trouble from the authorities.

upscale eateries as well as ragged seafood shacks and lobster pounds, is a fun, albeit laborious, eating experience: the claws must be pulled off and cracked open, the hard-shelled body and tail snapped apart, and the tender flesh dug out with fingers or tiny forks. It's worth it, though: fresh boiled lobster dipped in a bit of melted butter is sublime.

Clams are another staple, and can be quite distinctive if you're used to the thin, rubbery strips served up in many places. Here you'll frequently encounter the belly or soft clam, which is plump and tender; it's generally breaded and fried at roadside joints, or simply steamed and eaten from the shell (and called a **steamer**, in that case). Many clams are also reserved for use in New England **clam chowder** – a hearty cream-based stew with chunks of clam, potato, and pork. Other shellfish specialties include **scallops**, baked with a butter-crumb topping, and raw **oysters**, splayed on the half-shell and served on a bed of ice with lemon juice, horseradish, and hot sauce. Though raw bars rotate their varieties, keep an eye out for Damariscotta and Cuttyhunk, two New England classics; Wellfleet and Pemaquid are also popular types.

As for fish, **cod** was a cornerstone of the regional economy during the eighteenth and nineteenth centuries; as a testament to cod-fishing's importance, a wooden "Sacred Cod" still hangs in the Massachusetts State House. Lean, white cod and **scrod** (the name for young cod and haddock) can be found at nearly any seafood restaurant, traditionally broiled with butter and spices.

Oyster shucking

Clam chowder

Produce

Thanks to its unique four-season climate, New England features a wide variety of excellent **produce**. The most unusual, if not exactly a crop in the classic sense, is **maple syrup**: sap drawn from maple trees that is boiled down until it reaches a sweet, thick consistency. Post-production, the syrup is taste-tested and color-graded (darker equals stronger) and then sold principally as a topping for pancakes and waffles. The industry is centered in Vermont, where up to 5.5 million pounds of the stuff are made annually. To see how syrup's made (and to have a taste), seek out one of the hundreds of **sugarhouses** across the state.

Fruit includes the indigenous **cranberry**, a distinctive New England crop mainly because its tricky growing conditions (sandy, acidic bogs) make it difficult to transplant elsewhere.

Maple syrup

Cranberries

While their intensely sour flavor prevents them from being eaten raw, cranberries are frequently found in baked goods or as a relish for meats. Although **blueberries** don't require such an exacting environment (any sunny, rocky soil will do), still 90 percent of the nation's crop comes from northern Maine – an industry immortalized in Robert McCloskey's popular children's book *Blueberries for Sal*. Apples are of course easy to find most anywhere, but **apple-picking** in the fall – when the cider is hot and the leaves ablaze with color – is a memorable New England experience. Western Massachusetts and New Hampshire's ten-mile "Apple Way" are both great orchard areas.

Blueberries

Fresh, sweet **corn** is another treat, found in summer at farm stands throughout the region and served alongside lobster and barbecued meats. Native Americans introduced the Pilgrims to the benefits of planting corn, and it is believed that knowledge of this crop is what preserved them through their first harsh New England winters. In celebration of their survival, the Pilgrims held the first **Thanksgiving** dinner, with corn as a cornerstone of the meal.

Microbreweries

New England is credited with jump-starting the **microbrew** industry (whereby beer is crafted and sold on a small scale) in the US. Boston-based **Sam Adams**, the self-proclaimed original microbrewery, began in 1985, when fifth-generation brewer Jim Koch deemed the nation ready for "better beer." His instincts proved to be astute: the label is currently the largest of the regional beers and is well known throughout the country. Better yet, the success of Sam Adams served as a catalyst for other small-time New England brewers, and the region now boasts a wide variety of tasty beers. While only a select number of these (such as **Harpoon** and **Portsmouth**) are consistently available throughout the region, excellent smaller-time options can be found at any decent New England bar. Most notable are Vermont-brewed **Magic Hat**, Otter Creek, and Rock Art; **Smuttynose** of New Hampshire; Shipyard and Geary's in Maine; and Connecticut's **Ten Penny Ale**. Each of these produces a changing line of beers, all of which are much more lively and flavorful than your standard Budweiser or Miller product. In the fall, keep an eye out for the spicy, complex **Oktoberfest** varieties.

Just outside of town, the **Carlton Nash Dinosaur Track Quarry**, Amherst Road/Rte-116, is one of the more surreal local sights (late May to early Sept Mon–Sat 10am–4pm, Sun noon–4pm; $2.50; ☎413/467-9566), a roadside collection of locally excavated dinosaur bones and footprints. In its previous incarnation as Nash Dinosaur Land, it was something of a roadside legend, as its elderly proprietor would not only show you the dinosaur bones but also spin animated tales about the property to all who would listen. Carlton has since passed away, and the place is a bit more low-key.

Practicalities

By car, Rte-116 runs south about ten miles from Amherst to South Hadley. If you're coming by **bus**, Peter Pan Trailways stops at Redfern Travel Connection, 29 College St (☎413/534-1190). The town doesn't have much in the way of lodging, so you're really better off staying in Amherst or Northampton. For **something to eat**, your only sure choice for several miles is in the shopping area across the street from Mount Holyoke. The best bet here is *Tailgate* (☎413/532-7597), which has a large selection of bagels, sandwiches, pasta salads, and gourmet treats, though the *Main Moon Chinese Restaurant* (☎413/533-8839) and *Fedora's Tavern* (☎413/534-8222) are also good. If you need a snack before heading to one of the nearby parks, be sure to stop at one of these spots first, as you won't pass any other options en route.

Around South Hadley

Farther along Rte-116 between South Hadley and Amherst, The Notch, an impasse between Bare Mountain and Mount Norwottuck, is the location of the entrance and visitors' center of the **Holyoke Range State Park** (for information, call the Joseph Allen Skinner State Park – see below), which consists of 2936 acres spread out over nine miles and rising to heights of over a thousand feet, with marked hiking trails throughout. On Rte-47, about halfway between South Hadley and Northampton, is the entrance to the **Joseph Allen Skinner State Park** (☎413/586-0350), which sits proudly perched atop Mount Holyoke. Head up to the aptly named Summit House (late May to mid-Oct weekends), where the park's visitors' center has wide and stunning views of the river valley, particularly the bend referred to as the "Ox Bow" – immortalized in Thomas Cole's painting of the same name.

The Upper Pioneer Valley

If you have a car and the desire to hit the back roads, exploring the area known as the **Upper Pioneer Valley** can offer many pleasant surprises. In sharp contrast to the relative economic and cultural stability of the college towns of Northampton and Amherst, the smaller rural towns surrounding them embrace an entirely different lifestyle. With the harsh weather, instability of the family farm, and the loss of industrial dollars, life in these hills can be grueling – and the picturesque scenery sometimes masks a rural poverty uncharacteristic of this part of New England. Yet the hills in these parts yield simple pleasures: the odd roadside vegetable stand, good local diners, disarming vistas, eclectic yard sales, maple syrup farms, and, especially in the summer, numerous festivals ranging from the Riverfest in Shelburne Falls (June) to the Turn of the Century Ice Cream Social in Deerfield (July).

The only two towns in the Upper Pioneer Valley accessible by **bus** are Greenfield and Deerfield, with Peter Pan Trailways stopping in front of the Town Hall in Greenfield and at Savage Market, 470 Greenfield Rd, in Deerfield.

Quabbin Reservoir, Mount Sugarloaf, and beyond

Leaving the Five College area, the Pioneer Valley becomes quite rural quite quickly. The beauty of **Quabbin Reservoir** (entrance on Rte-9 between Ware and Belchertown) belies its origins: in 1939, in a bureaucratic decision designed to benefit the eastern part of the state, the Swift River was dammed and the towns of Dana, Greenwich, Enfield, and Prescott were evacuated and flooded with some 39 square miles of water. Since this time, the metropolitan Boston area has had to give little thought to the source and availability of its water. While you cannot swim, camp, or barbecue at Quabbin, its 81,000 acres of protected wildlife reservation land provides a fair degree of serenity for hiking.

Just outside **South Deerfield** (see below), the **Mount Sugarloaf Reservation** (Rte-116) consists of North and South Sugarloaf mountains, the latter of which has a paved road allowing cars to climb to the summit. Scenic views and good picnicking make this a popular spot, and there are opportunities for camping, too – though reservations are advised (call ⓣ1-877/I-CAMP-MA). On the other side of Deerfield, the **Daughters of the American Revolution State Forest**, Rte-112, Goshen (ⓣ413/268-7098), is also a good place for camping, with tent and RV sites available from late May to early Sept ($12). The **Mohawk Trail State Forest**, Rte-2, Charlemont (ⓣ413/339-5504), offers 56 campsites and six cabins (tent sites available mid-April to mid-Oct, cabins year-round), while the **Erving State Forest**, Wendell Depot Road, off Rte-2A at Erving Center (late May to early Sept; ⓣ978/544-3939), is a bit more rough and ready, with no showers or flush toilets – though the place makes up for this lack by allowing almost every outdoor activity you could think of, from snowshoeing to fishing.

South Deerfield

Despite the sedate appearance of present-day **SOUTH DEERFIELD**, its history is punctuated by violent episodes of unusual intensity, even for America. The town was first settled in 1669 as a frontier outpost of British North America. Its position in the woods far away from established colonial centers on the

Maple syrup

Though the raw, muddy, unpredictable, and seemingly endless weeks of March in New England have few virtues, one is the proximity of spring and the other is **maple syrup**. The sugar shacks of the Upper Pioneer Valley are responsible for producing most of the maple syrup made in Massachusetts. Surrounded by ancient maples and using time-honored methods, these tiny, often family-owned and -run sugarhouses welcome visitors, give tours, and even offer weekend brunches where the maple syrup flows generously. The season usually begins the first weekend of March and continues for six weekends afterward. Calling ahead is wise and arriving early is even wiser, as the farms are quite popular. Try **South Face Farm**, Watson-Spruce Corner Road, off Rte-116 in Ashfield (March to mid-April Sat–Sun 8.30am–3.30pm; ⓣ413/628-3268), where they make pancakes, waffles, and fried corn fritters, daring you to top them with both syrup and ice cream.

coast left it vulnerable to attack, which local Indians did on September 18, 1675. One of the bloodiest clashes of King Philip's War (see p.604), the attack culminated in the death of 64 men at "Bloody Brook" in South Deerfield. But it was in February 1704, in a colonial extension of Queen Anne's War, that Deerfield earned its notoriety. In a raid that began at dawn and lasted five hours, some 350 Indians – led by the French – killed 49 settlers and set fire to the town. More than a hundred prisoners were promptly marched three hundred miles to Canada; one-fifth of this number perished en route. Deerfield was abandoned afterward, though it eventually became a prosperous farming town. Today South Deerfield, along routes 5 and 10 (exit 24 off I-91), is home to both Historic Deerfield and the Yankee Candle Company.

Accommodation

Charlemont Inn Rte-2, Charlemont ⓣ413/339-5796, ⓦwww.charlemontinn.com. Travelers from Benedict Arnold to Mark Twain have homed in on this Mohawk Trail inn since 1787. Full of character and comfort, it drips with New England charm. The cheapest rooms come with shared bath. ❹

Deerfield Inn 81 Old Main St (The Street) ⓣ413/774-5587 or 1-800/926-3865, ⓦwww.deerfieldinn.com. The one and only place to stay in Historic Deerfield itself, this commodious and expensive country inn has good dining, too. ❼

Red Roof Inn Rte-5, South Deerfield ⓣ413/665-7161. Completely lacking in rustic charm, but offering clean rooms, friendly service, and reasonable rates. Located in a conifer grove off of I-91 at exit 24. ❹

The Town

Historic Deerfield, with dutifully preserved old houses girdled by one thousand acres of lush meadows and farmland, is a destination frozen in time. The town touts itself as the home of the preservation movement in New England, and is also one of the first to milk the appeal of Olde New England. Restoration began here as early as the 1890s, when Alice Baker purchased the **Frary House**, restored it, and opened the doors to the public. This was something of a first back then, and today, of the 65 or so eighteenth- and nineteenth-century structures on either side of **The Street** (the main drag), fourteen house museums are open for guided tours. These small-scale studies in simple elegance are filled with over 20,000 objects, from furniture and fabrics to silver and glass, either made or used in America between 1650 and 1850. If you don't have the patience for guided tours – and unless you have an overriding interest in antique home decor – you probably need not go on more than one or two. The best are the **Sheldon House**, a self-guided tour illustrating the life and times of a middle-class farming family; the excellent **Memorial Hall Museum**, which exhibits local decorative arts and Native American gems; and the **Henry N. Flynt Silver & Metalware Collection**, which displays both English and American pewter- and silverware, some crafted by **Paul Revere.**

The best way to orient yourself is to check in at the **Hall Tavern Information Center**, across from the *Deerfield Inn*; if you want to go on house tours you have to purchase tickets here anyway (daily 9.30am–4.30pm; $7 single house, $14 unlimited good for two consecutive days; ⓣ413/774-5581, ⓦwww.historic-deerfield.org). Here you'll be able to see which of the fourteen historic houses are open for touring on the day you happen to be there. There's not much to the rest of Deerfield, although the **Yankee Candle Company**, on routes 5 and 10 (daily 9.30am–6pm; ⓣ1-877/636-7707), and the shopping complex it shares with the tourist-targeted, awfully named Bavarian Christmas Village and Kringle Market, is worth a brief stop for its regular demonstrations of traditional candlemaking techniques using 200-year-old equipment.

Eating and drinking

As you exit I-91 and turn north onto routes 5 and 10 (which are, at this point, one road), you will pass the Sugarloaf Shoppes and the *Red Roof Inn* before arriving at a stoplight. Take a right from here onto Elm St, cross the railroad tracks, and the small business district you see represents the extent of the South Deerfield area's **eating** and **drinking** options. Neighboring Greenfield, ten minutes to the north on Rte-5, has a bit more going on.

The People's Pint 24 Federal St, Greenfield ⓣ413/773-0333. Local brewpub even makes its own sodas, as well as serving well-prepared dishes using local and organic ingredients.

Sienna 6 Elm St ⓣ413/665-0215. It may be the fact that it is only open for dinner or possibly that its storefront, when not lit, has the look of an abandoned dime store, but it is easy to miss *Sienna*. Whatever the reason, its unassuming nature undoubtedly contributes to its status as one of the area's best-kept secrets. With a warm terra-cotta-colored, candle-lit interior, and dishes ranging from Chilean swordfish with goat cheese ravioli to jumbo scallops and crabmeat mashed potato, this is a dining experience you will not quickly forget. Entrees in the $21–26 range, desserts and appetizers $7–11. Closed Mon & Tues.

Wolfie's 52 S Main St ⓣ413/665-7068. Cheap lunch and dinner specials, homemade meals, soups, and pies – with free popcorn to boot.

Shelburne Falls

Nestled in the Berkshire foothills and straddling the Deerfield River approximately two miles from Rte-2 is the tiny town of **SHELBURNE FALLS**, a community whose buzz of artistic activity and scenic surroundings give a taste of modern New England small-town life. You wouldn't make a special trip to Shelburne Falls, but the scenic drive you have to make to get here – and its eminently strollable Main Street, dotted with antique shops and glass-blowing galleries – make it a pleasant, if low-key, spot. Note that the town of Shelburne Falls is actually two towns, Shelburne Falls and Buckland, each on its own side of the river – this is momentarily confusing when you drive into what you expect to be Shelburne Falls and are greeted by the Buckland Town Hall.

The Town

The most prominent thing to see in Shelburne Falls is the **Bridge of Flowers**, an old trolley bridge which is festooned with foliage each spring through late fall by the Shelburne Falls Women's Club. Although the event is celebrated by the local authorities as "internationally known," it's basically a well-executed show of civic pride rather than a botanical wonder. That said, all the hype doesn't detract from the bridge's appeal. The town's other attraction is a naturally occurring one, a series of geologically bizarre **glacial potholes**, east of Bridge Street at Salmon Falls, formed by several hundred million years of erosion and pitted by the splashing from the waterfalls upstream. Worth a quick look, they resemble an enormous solid mass of once-molten stone that has now been whittled into a svelte sculpture along the riverbed.

Practicalities

Shelburne Falls is located approximately two miles south of Rte-2 and ten miles west of the intersection of Rte-2 and I-91 at Greenfield. Antique shops, two grocery stores, and restaurants line State Street in Buckland and Bridge Street in Shelburne Falls. In the latter town, you'll also find the **Village Information Center**, 75 Bridge St (May–Oct daily 10am–4pm; ⓣ413/625-2544).

Accommodation options are spread out, but the *Bear Haven Bed & Breakfast*, 22 Mechanic St (ⓣ413/625-9281, ⓦwww.bearhaven.com; ⑤), is centrally located, home to a large collection of teddy bears, and a nice resting-place for

The Book Mill

Lovers of books will feel right at home at the **Book Mill**, 440 Greenfield Rd, off Rte-63 in Montague (daily 10am–6pm; ⓣ413/367-9206, ⓦwww.montaguebookmill.com), which accurately bills itself as offering "books you don't need in a place you can't find." With 40,000 used and discount books, well-seasoned armchairs, and large windows overlooking the river, the Book Mill is a pleasant place to spend a couple of lazy hours. There is also an on-site **café** with reasonable coffee and tables with reading lights. For something more substantial, consider having a meal (Sun brunch is particularly good) next door at the *Blue Heron* (closed Mon; ⓣ413/665-2102).

humans as well. You can't miss its rambling blue and lavender exterior. There are other good options, though these tend to fill up quickly, especially during the summer. If that's the case, *The Huckle Hill Guest Suites* is a bit out-of-the-way in Bernardston (ⓣ413/648-9290, ⓦwww.hucklehill.com; ⑥), but the solitude and friendly innkeeper are welcome changes of pace.

It is hard to go wrong stopping for a **bite to eat** in Shelburne Falls; the town's culinary offerings are packed into the little commercial center and the quality is surprisingly good for a place this small. *Café Martin*, 24 Bridge St (ⓣ413/625-2795), serves international dishes with trendy ingredients, wooing their patrons with homemade soups and lunchtime sandwhiches. Another option, *Mother's*, at 43 Bridge St (ⓣ413/625-6300), offers sandwiches galore plus hearty breakfasts, in a welcoming environment. Finally, *A Bottle of Bread Café and Pub*, 18 Water St (ⓣ413/625-6502), grills organic pub fare to match local beers and wine.

The Berkshires

A rich cultural history, world-class summer arts festivals, and a bucolic landscape of forests and verdant hills – reminiscent of the English Lake District – make the **Berkshires**, at the extreme western edge of Massachusetts, an unusually civilized region. Since the mid-nineteenth century, the beauty and tranquility of this region have attracted a moneyed crowd, the most visible manifestations of which are sumptuous Newport-style summer "cottages" hidden in the woods around the sedate villages of **Stockbridge** and **Lenox**. The latter is also home to **Tanglewood**, summer quarters of the Boston Symphony Orchestra and symbol of putative East Coast cultural superiority. But venture beyond these bastions of gentility and the more typical aspects of New England quickly re-emerge, from the economically battered old mill town of **Pittsfield** to dignified **Williamstown**, along with time-warp hill towns as remote as any in Vermont or New Hampshire.

More so than in other parts of New England, tourism in the Berkshires is **seasonal**. Traveling here in the off-season has its rewards, but you'll miss out on virtually all of the big cultural festivals and find most of the museums either closed or on skeleton winter schedules. On the other hand, in the summer you're competing with East Coasters who have been coming here for years,

Berkshires transportation

Getting around the Berkshires is not difficult, as long as you have a car and a good map – road signage is decidedly geared to residents, not visitors. The main highway, **Rte-7**, runs the length of the region (and the state) from north to south, following the cleft between the Taconic Mountains on the New York border and the Hoosic ranges to the east. Because the Berkshires are at the end of the end of the state, the biggest decision you have to make in terms of driving – assuming you are coming from points east – may well be how you want to arrive. The **Massachusetts Turnpike** takes you from Boston to West Stockbridge in a stupendously dull three hours; a more appealing option might be to pick up I-91 south from Rte-2, sampling the Pioneer Valley before striking off west on pristine Rte-9, which takes you past tourist-free villages such as Williamsburg and Cummington and into Pittsfield, which is very close to Lenox. In the fall, you might opt to take scenic secondary routes that branch west off of Rte-9 itself, notably routes 112 and 143. Alternatively, you can take Rte-2 all the way to Williamstown – the stretch from Miller's Falls (just east of I-91) to the New York border follows the very picturesque **Mohawk Trail** (see p.283); in fact, if you don't take this route into the Berkshires, you'd be remiss not to take it on the way out.

Your options by **public transportation** are predictably limited. Peter Pan Trailways and Bonanza **buses** stop in Lee (at H.A. Johansson's, 50 Main St), Lenox (at the Village Pharmacy, 5 Walker St), Pittsfield (at the Pittsfield Bus Terminal, 57 S Church St), and Williamstown (at the *Williams Inn*, junction of routes 2 and 7) on their way to and from Boston. Hopping from one Berkshire town to another, however, is simplest using the local buses run by the **Berkshire Regional Transit Authority** (maximum fare $4.40; ⓣ413/499-2782 or 1-800/292-BRTA), which cover a surprisingly large number of towns and villages between Great Barrington in the south and Williamstown in the north of the region.

which makes planning far in advance to secure accommodations and/or tickets less a good idea than a requirement. Perhaps the best times to visit are late May – spring is delightful in the Berkshires – or September, when the leaves are changing but the October "leaf peepers" have yet to arrive in force. Note that there is often a three-night minimum stay when booking a room during the summer season.

Stockbridge

Strolling the spotless main street of **STOCKBRIDGE** either entices or unsettles, depending on whether you see it as the picture-postcard New England village it claims to be or as the essence of prefab quaint. Accordingly, you can either credit or curse **Norman Rockwell**, who lived and painted here for 25 years, for your reaction to the place. His Stockbridge paintings, like all the rest, capture a small-town American charm that may have only ever existed on the surface; regardless, his illustrations pass for great art in these parts (especially at his eponymous museum), and buying into the illusion of all-pervasive gaiety – the legacy of his work – for the length of your visit will at least increase your enjoyment. The social reality of Stockbridge is not quite Rockwell: the majority of the residences in town are summer homes for wealthy New Yorkers. Ironically, Stockbridge's other, less celebrated, claim to fame is at quite the other end of the socio-cultural spectrum: it's the setting for Arlo Guthrie's classic anti-draft song/monologue *Alice's Restaurant*. White-clapboard schmaltz aside, there's actually quite a bit to see and

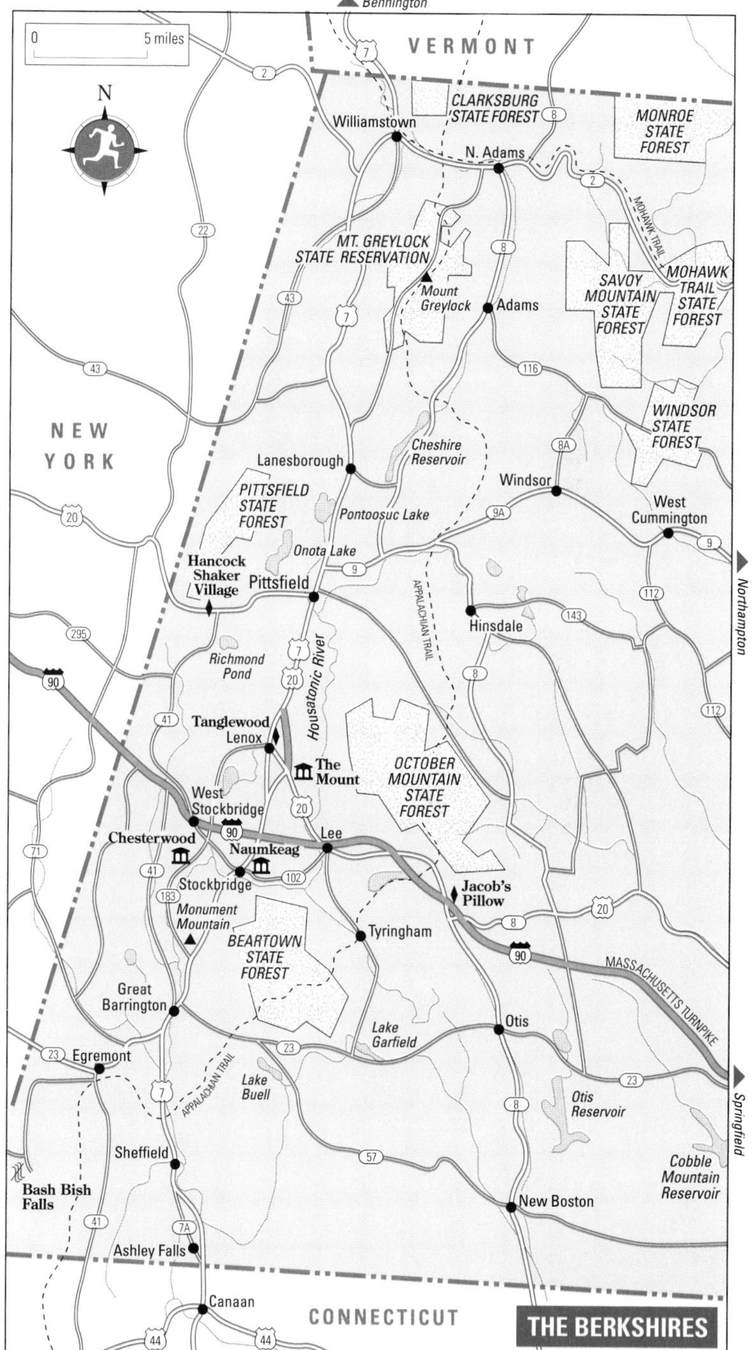

Bennington
VERMONT
0 5 miles
N
CLARKSBURG STATE FOREST
MONROE STATE FOREST
Williamstown
N. Adams
MOHAWK TRAIL
MT. GREYLOCK STATE RESERVATION
Mount Greylock
Adams
SAVOY MOUNTAIN STATE FOREST
MOHAWK TRAIL STATE FOREST
WINDSOR STATE FOREST
NEW YORK
Lanesborough
Cheshire Reservoir
Windsor
West Cummington
PITTSFIELD STATE FOREST
Pontoosuc Lake
Onota Lake
Hancock Shaker Village
Pittsfield
APPALACHIAN TRAIL
Hinsdale
Northampton
Richmond Pond
Housatonic River
Tanglewood
Lenox
The Mount
OCTOBER MOUNTAIN STATE FOREST
West Stockbridge
Chesterwood
Naumkeag
Lee
Stockbridge
Jacob's Pillow
Monument Mountain
Tyringham
BEARTOWN STATE FOREST
MASSACHUSETTS TURNPIKE
Great Barrington
Otis
Lake Garfield
Egremont
Lake Buell
APPALACHIAN TRAIL
Otis Reservoir
Springfield
Sheffield
Bash Bish Falls
Cobble Mountain Reservoir
New Boston
Ashley Falls
Canaan
CONNECTICUT
THE BERKSHIRES

do in and around town, from the Rockwell Museum and the Berkshire Botanic Garden to the sprawling estates of Naumkeag and Chesterwood.

Stockbridge boasts the bulk of weighty **historical associations** in a region that has relatively few, especially compared to Eastern Massachusetts. When in 1722 pioneers wrested a chunk of land along the Housatonic River from local Indians, they set aside a bit as "Indian Town," where they attempted to "English" them – with limited success. Indian Town was soon renamed Stockbridge, and, in the days before it attracted a wealthy summer population, owed its sustained existence to farming and its location on the stagecoach route between Boston and Albany, NY. Later, in the winter of 1786, Daniel Shays organized a band of angry farmers to protest British taxation and oppression. Stockbridge was the designated HQ for what became known as Shays' Rebellion, and the *Red Lion Inn* (see "Accommodation," opposite) was where they holed up during the conflict.

Culture in the Berkshires

There are several **summer cultural festivals** in the Berkshires, but none so prominent as the big three of Tanglewood, Jacob's Pillow, and the Williamstown Theatre Festival. Virtually every concert and performance at the more established festivals is well attended, and tickets for the more popular events sell out far in advance, so plan accordingly. For a current calendar that includes all of the festivals, contact the **Berkshire Visitors' Bureau** (Ⓣ413/743-4500 or 1-800/237-5747, Ⓦwww.berkshires.org).

Aston Magna Festival St James Church, Rte-7 and Taconic Ave, Great Barrington (every Sat from July to early Aug; Ⓣ413/528-3595 or 1-800/875-7156). The country's oldest annual summer festival, devoted to performances of Baroque music played on period instruments.

Berkshire Theatre Festival Main St, Stockbridge (late June to Aug Mon–Sat; Ⓣ413/298-5576). Best known for its four summer productions at the Berkshire Playhouse Mainstage, but also noteworthy for Unicorn Theatre readings of plays in progress.

Jacob's Pillow Rte-20 between Becket and Lee (late June to Aug Tues–Sat; Ⓣ413/243-0745). Perhaps the most famous contemporary dance festival in the country, improbably located in the middle of (an admittedly lovely) nowhere. Artists-in-residence give free performances of works in progress before the main programs.

Shakespeare & Company The Mount, 70 Kemble St, Lenox (May–Nov; Ⓣ413/637-3353). One of the country's biggest Shakespeare festivals uses The Mount, former summer estate of Edith Wharton, as its venue. Productions are not limited to Shakespeare, and include new plays, dance, and dramatizations of stories by Wharton, Henry James, and the like.

Tanglewood West St/Rte-183, Lenox (July to late Aug; for tickets in advance from Sept through May, call Ⓣ617/266-1492; otherwise Ⓣ413/637-1600, Ⓦwww.bso.org). The Boston Symphony Orchestra gives concerts here, perhaps the most celebrated outdoor cultural venue in the country. Full orchestral concerts take place weekends at the Shed, while the newer Ozawa Hall is used on other days, mainly for chamber music concerts. Further musical options include open rehearsals for the BSO on Sat mornings, plus jazz and pop performances. Tickets for the Shed and Ozawa Hall run anywhere from $28 to $108; it's cheaper (general admission $17) and arguably more enjoyable to sit on the grass – though if you do, bring a towel or lawn chair.

Williamstown Theatre Festival 84 Spring St, Williamstown (mid-June to late Aug Tues–Sun; Ⓣ413/597-3400). Every summer some of the most accomplished actors from American stage and screen converge on this stately college town for a series of nearly a dozen productions, both time-tested and experimental.

Accommodation

Meadowlark Chesterwood ⓣ413/298-5545. The second, smaller studio built by Daniel Chester French on his large estate is rented out in season; staying in this unusual spot grants you free admission to the rest of Chesterwood (see overleaf). Make reservations through the *Red Lion Inn* (see below). ❾

One Main Street Bed and Breakfast 1 Main St ⓣ413/298-5299, ⓦwww.onemainbnb.com. Although not on the stretch of Main Street immortalized by Norman Rockwell, still a central – and quiet – location. Three comfortable rooms with private bath and mountain views in an 1825 Colonial-style home. Hearty breakfast included. ❻

Red Lion Inn 30 Main St ⓣ413/298-1690, ⓦwww.redlioninn.com. This grandmotherly inn is for many the quintessential New England hostelry, and therefore popular with tour groups; for others it's a case study in quaintness run amok. The gift shop is called The Pink Kitty. Draw your own conclusions. ❹

Stockbridge Country Inn 26 Glendale Rd/Rte-183 ⓣ413/298-4015, ⓦwww.stockbridgecountryinn.com. Set in an 1856 country house on four acres of private land, this seven-room B&B is close to the Rockwell Museum and offers queen-sized four-poster canopy beds, a heated pool, attractive gardens, and porches from which to view them. Full country breakfast included. ❼

The Town and around

The actual town of Stockbridge is tiny, basically consisting of a few nineteenth-century buildings on Main Street and those around the corner on Elm Street. Unless they're staying at the **Red Lion Inn**, most people tend to park their car near it and wander from there, either having iced tea on the inn's venerable front porch, or else stocking up on provisions at one of the numerous good country markets such as Williams and Sons.

There are few specific sights in the town center. The Historical Room of the **Stockbridge Library**, at the corner of Main and Elm streets (Mon–Fri 9am–5pm, Sat 9am–4pm), contains artifacts from the Mahican Indians, who first lived in the area. The small **Mission House**, at the corner of Main and Sergeant streets (late May to mid-Oct daily 10am–5pm; $6), is where the Reverend John Sergeant planned his missionary work, under the auspices of the London Society for the Propagation of the Gospel in Foreign Lands. Though built in 1739, it was relocated here from a nearby site in 1928. The exterior has a pretty, arched Connecticut River Valley-style doorway, while the inside is noteworthy mainly for the eighteenth-century chairs on which Sergeant is said to have sat. Opposite the Mission House, the **Merwin House** is another period residence (tours by appointment June–Oct; ⓣ1-860/928-4047). The elegant Federal-style building exemplifies gracious Stockbridge living in the early part of the nineteenth century, and is stocked with an interesting selection of paintings and antiques.

Most people skip all this, however, in favor of the **Norman Rockwell Museum** (May–Oct daily 10am–5pm; Nov–April Mon–Fri 10am–4pm, Sat & Sun 10am–5pm; $12.50), just outside the town center off Rte-183. Two floors of Rockwell originals and reproductions are well displayed in a $10 million facility, built in part with a donation from Steven Spielberg. Even the biggest fan of his work may have the limits of their admiration tested by the gallery of Rockwell's advertising endorsements, for everything from cereal to cars, which make it seem like he would have given his name to just about anything. Take the tourists out of the scene, and the facility and grounds – which include the little red building that was Rockwell's own studio – are rather tranquil, though you'd be forgiven for mistaking it for a nursing home.

Beyond the Rockwell Museum, the **Berkshire Botanical Garden**, at the junction of routes 102 and 183 (May–Oct daily 10am–5pm; $7), is home to around fifteen acres of landscaped gardens, with wildflowers on display in spring and roses during summer. You can also make a fragrant loop through the woods.

Norman Rockwell

Love him or hate him, if you spend any time in western New England, it's hard to avoid the work of **Norman Rockwell**. The man dubbed "America's best-loved artist" lived and painted in Arlington, VT, and, more famously, in Stockbridge, MA, and there are no fewer than three museums in his honor. For more than half a century, Rockwell was a fixture on the landscape of American popular culture, known as much for his product endorsements as for his *Saturday Evening Post* covers. Of American artists, perhaps only Warhol, in many ways his spiritual opposite, is so easily recognizable. Born in 1894 in New York City, Rockwell dropped out of high school to attend classes at the National Academy of Design, and at the age of 22 sold his first painting to the *Saturday Evening Post*; in the forty years that followed, he contributed more than three hundred paintings to that publication alone. His work presented, in the artist's own words, "life as it should be": children playing, adults relaxing, doctors examining healthy patients, family struggles that seemed certain to have a happy ending. His work stands in dramatic contrast to the "serious artists" of the twentieth century – the Surrealists, Dadaists, Cubists, and Abstract Expressionists – much as his idyllic images stand in contrast to the often turbulent times in which he lived.

Many have questioned the veracity of these images, yet it seems doubtful that Rockwell saw much in the way of war, riots, or lynchings during his placid small-town life. However, later in his career, working for *Look* magazine, Rockwell did take on such issues as integration of schools and neighborhoods, and did so with the same gentle dignity that he had devoted to more insular concerns.

There's another, rather overrated, attraction just down the road in the form of **Chesterwood**, at 4 Williamsville Rd (May–Oct daily 10am–5pm; $10), the former summer home of sculptor Daniel Chester French, best known for his oversized rendition of President Lincoln that sits in his eponymous memorial in Washington, DC. The humdrum plaster models in the artist's studio perhaps betray the fact that he had no formal training. His 130-acre estate is idyllic, though, as he averred, "I live here six months of the year – in heaven. The other six months I live, well – in New York."

With its spectacular views of the Stockbridge hills, distinctive gardens and aesthetically balanced interiors, the Gilded Age estate of **Naumkeag**, on Prospect Hill Road (late May to mid-Oct daily 10am–5pm; $10, gardens only $8), nestled among several other sumptuous private estates, is like a Newport mansion without the forced opulence. It was built by Stanford White in 1886 as a family home for the prosperous attorney Joseph Hodges Choate, later made ambassador to the Court of St James (the estate's name, pronounced "Nómkeg," derives from the Native American word for Salem, Choate's birthplace). The touches of a master architect are evident everywhere, from the synthesis of American elements such as a shingle roof with European-style brick and stone towers to understated flourishes throughout the 26 rooms of the house, including a combination of cherry, oak, and mahogany paneling and a three-story handcarved oak staircase. Original furnishings and domestic accoutrements, from European tapestries to Asian ceramics, give the impression that the Choates have just slipped out for a ride in the country; indeed, there are even coats left hanging in the closet. Although only guided tours of the inside are available, this is one of the few country "cottages" in the Berkshires where taking one is truly worthwhile.

As impressive as the house is, the real attraction is the eight acres of meticulously planned and tended **gardens**, subtly studded with contemporary sculpture. The first greenspace of note, more like an adjunct to the house, is the

Afternoon Garden, a 1928 addition remarkable for its vividly painted Venetian-style oak posts. The Perugino View, named for a sixteenth-century landscape painter, adjoins the Top Lawn and affords intoxicating views over the grounds and across to Monument Mountain. From here it's a short walk to the Blue Steps, named for a succession of blue-colored fountains flanked by stairs that lead to yet more gardens. The atmospheric Linden Walk ends with a statue of the Roman goddess Diana.

Eating and drinking

An American Craftsman Café Rte-7 and Maple St ⓣ413/298-0250. Linked to the crafts gallery of the same name, this creative eatery concocts everything from an open-faced rabbit tart with mushrooms and truffle cream to a duck pastrami rueben. Weekend brunch is popular.

Glendale River Grille Rte-183 ⓣ413/298-4711. Elegant, spacious grill and tavern, about five miles south of the Rockwell Museum. Some adventurous entrees – such as roast duckling Cantonese with hoisin sauce – in addition to standard grill treats like steaks and swordfish.

Lion's Den at the *Red Lion Inn*, Main Street ⓣ413/298-1654. Repair to the old inn's atmospheric cellar tavern to get down with the rest of the town. Live music most nights, plus standard pub fare.

Main Street Café 40 Main St ⓣ413/298-3060. Said to be the best breakfast in town, served by a staff that could use a few extra hours of sleep.

Michael's Restaurant and Pub 5 Elm St ⓣ413/298-3530. Surf, turf, and pasta with a late-night menu and suds to suit every taste. Great place to watch the game or rack 'em at the pool table. Friday is karaoke night.

Once Upon a Table 36 Main St ⓣ413/298-3870. Quietly tucked in the Mews off Main St, the decor is romantic with a worldly menu. Popular among locals.

Lenox

From Stockbridge, a slight detour off Rte-7 takes you to Rte-7A and the genteel village of **LENOX**, the cultural nucleus of the Berkshires by virtue of its proximity to Tanglewood, the summer home of the Boston Symphony Orchestra. It's a quiet place for most of the year, but on summer weekends during the music festival, traffic jams are not uncommon. Summering in Lenox has been a New York (rather than Boston) tradition since the mid-nineteenth century, and, not surprisingly, although the number of shops and restaurants is necessarily limited by the town's small size, in terms of both price and attitude their atmosphere is more Manhattan than New England.

Accommodation

The **Lenox Chamber of Commerce**, 5 Walker St (ⓣ413/637-3646, ⓦwww.lenox.org), will help you to find a place to stay, although don't expect to stroll into town and find a room while Tanglewood is in session.

Blantyre Blantyre Rd ⓣ413/637-3556, ⓦwww.blantyre.com. A roomy Scottish Tudor mansion with Gothic flourishes – a former summer "cottage" – that has been purposed as one of the country's most luxurious resorts, and as such is almost a destination in itself. 9

Brook Farm Inn 15 Hawthorne St ⓣ413/637-3013 or 1-800/285-POET, ⓦwww.brookfarm.com. The innkeepers at this twelve-room 1870 Victorian B&B are poetry aficionados, so in summer you can borrow a tape recorder and listen to the bard of your choice, on the porch or by the pool, and in winter curl up with a book of verse in front of a fireplace, either in the common area or in your room. 6

The Village Inn 16 Church St ⓣ413/637-0020 or 1-800/253-0917, ⓦwww.villageinn-lenox.com. A country inn-style hotel – with 32 rooms with antiques, bountiful breakfasts, and afternoon English tea – in the center of Lenox. Good-value rooms if you visit during spring. ④

Walker House 64 Walker St ⓣ413/637-1271, ⓦwww.walkerhouse.com. This informal eight-room B&B is pet-friendly – the innkeepers have five cats which roam the jungle-like gardens surrounding the house. ⑥

Wheatleigh Hawthorne Rd ⓣ413/637-0610, ⓦwww.wheatleigh.com. Built by a New York financier in 1893 as a wedding present for his daughter, who married a Spanish count, today this Florentine palazzo-style estate-cum-resort combines antique and contemporary decor to sumptuous, successful effect. The lush grounds were landscaped by Frederick Law Olmsted, designer of Boston's Emerald Necklace, and to stay any closer to Tanglewood you'd have to camp on its lawn. ⑨

Whistler's Inn 5 Greenwood St ⓣ866/637-0975, ⓦwww.whistlersinnlenox.com. Three of the fourteen rooms at this 1820 English Tudor country manor are said to be haunted, which both attracts and repels guests. Rooms vary in decor, from low, angled ceilings above a queen bed in the Artist's Loft to the romantic space of the African Suite.

The Town and around

Even if you're visiting after late August, it's well worth making a stop off West Street (Rte-183), about a mile outside town, to walk around **Tanglewood**. Though its lush grounds were formerly part of the estate of a wealthy Boston banker, it was Nathaniel Hawthorne who coined the name – today musicians practice in a reconstruction of the little red farmhouse where he lived with his wife Sophia in 1850 and 1851, penning *The House of the Seven Gables* on the premises. On summer weekends, concerts are given in the aptly named "Shed," a bare-bones, indoor/outdoor hall, as well as the newer Ozawa Hall (see box on p.272 for more). From the edge of the sprawling lawn there is a good view of the mile-wide Stockbridge Bowl pond, a view which is even better from the more elevated Kripalu Center for Yoga and Health, across the street from Tanglewood's main entrance (just drive through the parking lot and pretend to be in meditation if questioned). Another way to appreciate the countryside around here is on horseback; **Undermountain Farm** (ⓣ413/637-3365) offers guided trail rides.

Fans of Edith Wharton will want to visit **The Mount**, at the corner of Plunkett Street and Rte-7 (early June to early Nov house 9am–5pm, grounds 9am–6pm; $16; ⓣ413/637-1899), the novelist's summer home from 1902 until 1911. Though restorations are ongoing, the grounds now more closely resemble what Wharton intended when she designed the home at the turn of the century. The guided tour is attractive in that it illustrates how the order, scale, and harmony of the place are a reflection of the principles Wharton promoted in her first successful book, *The Decoration of Houses*, published a few years before she moved in. One of her precepts was to ease the transition from outdoors to inside – an example of which is the indoor wrought-iron stair rails, a material typically associated with exterior ornamentation. Though Wharton's years at The Mount were productive – among other things, she wrote *Ethan Frome* here – they were not entirely happy; boredom with her husband and unapologetic disgust for the turpitude of American culture sent her packing for France, where she lived out her final years. These days The Mount is another performance space, with four stages, the main one of which is open-air; adaptations of stories by Wharton and her soul mate, Henry James, also take place in season in the drawing room.

Eating and drinking

Bistro Zinc 56 Church St ⓣ413/637-8800. Power-lunch spot filled with diners on cell phones gobbling up flavorful French fare at reasonable prices – dinner is considerably more expensive.

Café Lucia 90 Church St ⓣ413/637-2640. It may

△ The Mount

not be on the menu, but you're likely to get a serving of attitude along with your pricey, if tasty, Italian entrees at this popular, bustling spot where a Manhattan ambience prevails. Closed Mon.

Church Street Café 69 Church St ⓣ413/637-2745. Tasty New England fare, from sauteed Maine crab cakes to maple- and cider-glazed pork chops, wins accolades for this eatery – more restaurant than café – in the center of Lenox.

Firefly 71 Church St ⓣ413/637-2700. Ask the locals where they go for a night out, and they'll tell you about *Firefly*: the tavern, tapas, and dinner menus have something for every hour, like chili con carne, edamame, and grilled sirloin, while the intimate bar makes it easy to chat it up with strangers.

Wheatleigh Hawthorne Rd ⓣ413/637-0610. Very highly priced, but you get what you pay for – outstanding flavors of contemporary continental cuisine, including low-fat and vegetarian menus, artfully prepared desserts, and impeccable service. The decor, from crystal chandeliers to Italianate paintings, is undeniably soothing.

Lee and Tyringham

During the busy summer cultural season, many last-minute travelers who think they'll find a room in Lenox end up staying in nearby **LEE**, which is just as well, for there is a genuine aspect to the place altogether lacking in its ritzier neighbor. Plus, there are many small inns and B&Bs, all of which have the advantage of being near the thick of things yet removed from the commotion. Like other Berkshire towns, Lee was once a papermaking center, but it was better known for its unusually strong marble – which found its way to the US Capitol, the Empire State Building, St Patrick's Cathedral, and other East Coast landmarks. It's also in evidence in Lee itself, for example in certain buildings along the archetypal Main Street.

One of the better-kept secrets in Massachusetts is the incredibly scenic Tyringham Valley (see overleaf), practically hidden between routes 102 and 23.

TYRINGHAM itself, which basically consists of a post office and a church, was settled as a hinterland community in the eighteenth century and hasn't perceivably changed since. The only tangible sight is an unusual dwelling named **Santarella**, at 75 Main Rd (late May–Oct daily 10am–5pm; free), designed and built by Englishman Sir Henry Hudson Kitson – the sculptor of the *Minute Man* in Lexington – as his sculpture studio in the 1930s. Its signature feature is the eighty-ton roof, a sculpted simulation of thatching that succeeds in conveying the image of undulating Berkshire Hills in autumn. More alluring, however, is the serene garden that surrounds a lily pond behind the house; it can be magical in the afternoon, when the day's glare goes away and the colors come to life.

Just south of Santarella, Tyringham Road opens onto the **Tyringham Valley**, which is more reminiscent of an unsullied Irish glade than any part of New England proper. The highest spot, on the right, is the **Tyringham Cobble**, a forest-covered outcropping of limestone and quartzite that rises 400 feet over the valley: to hike it, make a right on Jerusalem Road after the village and proceed for a quarter of a mile. The reward for your two-mile endeavor will be views that are breathtaking, and on a clear spring or fall day, positively immobilizing. A right turn on Art School Road, the next street down, takes you to the highly regarded **Joyous Spring Pottery** (summer daily 10am–5pm; ⓣ413/528-4115), where you can view pottery made using Japanese techniques and fired in a *nobori gama* (a kiln that can hold up to fifteen hundred pieces).

Accommodation

Applegate 279 W Park St, Lee ⓣ413/243-4451 or 1-800/691-9012, ⓦwww.applegateinn.com. A calm, shipshape B&B in a Southern-style Georgian colonial home, whose six guestrooms have old-fashioned character but a contemporary feel; fresh baked goods contribute to great breakfasts. ❼

Chambéry Inn 199 Main St, Lee ⓣ413/243-2221 or 1-800/537-4321, ⓦwww.chamberyinn.com. This 1885 French country house, built as the country's first parochial school, has nine meticulously refurbished suites with high ceilings, big windows, and modern touches such as in-room phones and cable TV (there are also two standard double rooms). ❼

Historic Merrell Inn 1565 Pleasant St/Rte-102, South Lee ⓣ413/243-1794 or 1-800/243-1794, ⓦwww.merrell-inn.com. Just south of town, between Stockbridge and Lee, this atmospheric old tenroom inn has some interesting relics from its days as a stagecoach stop, such as a vintage birdcage bar in the Tavern Room, where breakfast is served. Ask for a room overlooking the meandering Housatonic River. ❻

Sunset Farm Bed & Breakfast 74 Tyringham Rd, Tyringham ⓣ413/243-3229, ⓦwww.sunsetfarminn.com. Old New England lives on at this blissfully isolated farmhouse on a hillock in the gorgeous Tyringham Valley. Four rooms, of which three have private baths, are a bit frayed at the edges, but the feel is very authentic without being twee. The owners are warm, the food good, and there's a nice place to hike out back. ❺

Eating

Cakewalk Bakery and Café 56 Main St, Lee ⓣ413/243-2806. Offers an affordable menu of soups, sandwiches, salads, quiches, and, oh yes, pastries.

Joe's Diner 85 Center St, South Lee ⓣ413/243-9756. The best place to eat in Lee, whether you want a weighty corned-beef sandwich, tuna salad on rye, or scrambled eggs and waffles. Very low prices and extremely popular.

Salmon Run Fish House 78 Main St, Lee ⓣ413/243-3900. Boasts reasonable prices and an informal atmosphere in which to eat a variety of seafood and pasta dishes.

Great Barrington

South of Stockbridge, the landscape takes on a more rustic flavor, one that colors the only town of any size, **GREAT BARRINGTON**. It was the site of the last attempt of the British to hold court in America: Shays' Rebellion ended with five casualties here on February 27, 1787, when the Sheffield militia confronted one hundred anti-government insurgents and the hostages they had taken from Stockbridge. Another claim to fame is **Monument Mountain**, on US-7, five miles north of the town center, a picturesque peak known in literary lore as the place where Nathaniel Hawthorne and Herman Melville met during an afternoon hike in August 1850. In a thunderstorm-induced interlude, they and some other climbers drank champagne and recited poetry; the two authors became fast friends. Yet Great Barrington is perhaps most notable as the unlikely birthplace of one of the greatest civil rights leaders in US history, Dr W.E.B. Dubois, a well-regarded writer and one of the founders of the **National Association for the Advancement of Colored People (NAACP).**

Today Great Barrington is still a modest country town, though one with alternately hip and hippie touches. What buzz there is centers on Main Street near Railroad and Castle streets, where upmarket home decor shops bestride a number of good eateries. The old-fashioned **Mahaiwe Theater**, on Castle St (ⓣ413/528-0100), was bought by the Berkshire Opera Company, and is the place to go for classical music concerts. If it's the season (mid-Aug to mid-Oct), you may want to pick apples at Windy Hill Farm, 686 Stockbridge Rd (ⓣ413/298-3217), or pumpkins at Taft Farms, Rte-183 (ⓣ413/528-1515 or 1-800/528-1015).

Practicalities

The Great Barrington **Chamber of Commerce** can arrange for accommodation via their lodging hotline (ⓣ413/528-4006 or 1-800/269-4825). If you're looking for a **place to stay**, the *Wainwright Inn*, 518 S Main St (ⓣ413/528-2062, ⓦwww.wainwrightinn.com; ❻), occupies a huge 1766 mansion right outside the center of town, while the *Windflower Inn*, 684 South Egremont Rd/Rte-23 (ⓣ413/528-2720 or 1-800/992-1993, ⓦwww.windflowerinn.com; ❻), is a relaxed country inn with thirteen guest rooms, most with fireplaces – the biggest of which is in room 12. Sitting quietly five minutes outside of town, the *Manor Lane B&B*, 145 Hurlburt Rd (ⓣ413/528-8222; ❻), offers all the amenities you could ask for. Make sure to reserve one of the three large rooms ahead of time, and be sure to take advantage of the outside pool, tennis courts, and walking trails. For something to eat, *20 Railroad Street*, on the stretch of Main St described above (ⓣ413/528-9345), has good casual American **food**, while *Babalouie's*, at no. 289 (ⓣ413/528-8100), does excellent wood-fired sourdough pizzas made with local organic produce. If it's sushi you crave, visit *Bizen*, 17 Railroad St (ⓣ413/528-4343), which has Japanese chefs and an energetic atmosphere.

South of Great Barrington

Rte-23 southwest from Great Barrington takes you to tiny **SOUTH EGREMONT**, near which are the **Bash Bish Falls**, named for the Indian girl whose amorous woes prompted her to plunge fifty feet to her demise in a rock-bottomed pool. Water tumbling through a series of gorges and finally dropping eighty feet into a sparkling pool make this one of the more dramatic waterfalls in the state. Alternatively, heading east on Rte-23 from Great Barrington takes you on a more serene trajectory to Monterey, from where you can head back to Tyringham and Lee.

There's little need to proceed much farther south on Rte-7 unless you want to go antique shopping or hiking. **SHEFFIELD**, the next town down from Great Barrington, is the antique capital of the region. There's not much of a town center, however; if you see an antiques store that grabs your fancy, just pull over by the side of the road and check out the merchandise. **ASHLEY FALLS**, practically straddling the Connecticut border, is the site of **Bartholomew's Cobble**, a mineral outcropping that rises above the placid Housatonic River. A contiguous **nature reserve**, known for its abundant ferns, has a series of easy walking trails that are heavily trodden in summer and fall. Very nearby, on Cooper Hill Road, is the white-clapboard **Ashley House**, a rather unremarkable colonial abode. Built in 1735, this is said to be the oldest house in Berkshire County, but is more interesting for its historical associations than anything inside. In 1773, townsmen here drafted the "Sheffield Declaration," a statement of grievances against English rule; in 1781 Ashley's slave, Mum Bet, sued for freedom – which she won two years later.

One of the more quirky **places to stay** in the Berkshires, largely by virtue of its chintz-free feel, is the *Race Brook Lodge*, 864 S Undermountain Rd (Rte-41), Sheffield (Ⓣ413/229-2916 or 1-888/RB-LODGE, Ⓦwww.rblodge.com; ⑥), which has thirty rooms in a cluster of restored nineteenth-century farm buildings, with cheaper, quite basic cabins also available. For **eating**, *John Andrew's*, Rte-23, South Egremont (Ⓣ413/528-3469), has been roundly praised for its contemporary American fare, excellent wine list, and tasteful decor – a triple surprise for what appears from the outside to be just another building at the edge of a forest. Less upscale, *The Old Mill*, Rte-23, South Egremont (Ⓣ413/528-1421), serves reliably good-tasting New England fare, and sizeable portions of it, in a cozy riverside building that – you guessed it – used to be an old mill.

Pittsfield

PITTSFIELD, once a prosperous center for paper milling and the home of GE's plastics division, is – at least for the moment – attempting to reinvent itself as the **birthplace of baseball**, an honor previously held by Cooperstown, NY, where Abner Doubleday is said to have written the rules of the game. In 2004, baseball historians John Thorn and Jim Bouton went public with a controversial discovery: the two had happened upon a 1791 Pittsfield town ordinance that outlawed baseball nearly half a century before Doubleday's date. The original document is stored at City Hall, and if you ask nicely, they may let you see it. Otherwise, a copy is on display at the public library, the **Berkshire Athenaeum**, 1 Wendall Ave (Mon–Thurs 9am–9pm, Fri 9am–5pm, Sat 10am–5pm; Ⓣ413/499-9480). The only other sight that might keep you in Pittsfield is **Arrowhead**, just south of the town center on Holmes Road (late May to Oct daily 9.30am–5pm; $10), the eighteenth-century farmhouse where Herman Melville lived for thirteen years and wrote *Moby Dick*.

The most obvious **place to stay** in Pittsfield is the *Crowne Plaza*, 1 West St (Ⓣ413/499-2000, Ⓦwww.berkshirecrowne.com; ⑥), which dominates downtown and has comfortable rooms. If you're looking for a much more personal experience, however, head about three miles out of town along Barker Road to *Hollyhock House* (Ⓣ413/443-6901, Ⓦwww.hollyhockbb.com; ❺), a friendly, intimate, and spotlessly clean B&B with three renovated rooms which are good value for money. For something to **eat**, *Dakota*, 1035 South St/Rte-7 (Ⓣ413/499-7900), is a capacious place with updated hunting lodge decor, a bit of a relief from the faux hipness of so many Berkshire restaurants. Big portions of American staples such as Maine lobster and mesquite-grilled chicken are the draws, as is the large salad bar. Meanwhile, the *Court Square Breakfast & Deli*, 95 East St (Ⓣ413/442-9896), across from the courthouse, is one of the brighter, more pleasant places in town to eat straightforward breakfasts and lunches.

Hancock Shaker Village

Our tools are kind and gentle words, our shop is in the heart, and here we manufacture peace, that we may such impart.

from a Shaker song

From 1790 until 1960, the **Hancock Shaker Village**, at the junction of routes 20 and 41, five miles west of Pittsfield (daily: late May to late Oct 9.30am–5pm, rest of year 10am–3pm; summer and fall $15, rest of year $12.50; Ⓣ413/443-0188 or 1-800/817-1137, Ⓦwww.hancockshakervillage.org), was an active community of the famous offshoot of the Quakers from Manchester, England, so named for their convulsive fits of glee experienced when worshiping. The pacifist cult, which was renowned for its vegetable seeds and simply but elegantly crafted furniture, all but disappeared, partly due to its members' vows of celibacy, although one community shakes on at Sabbathday Lake in Maine. Hancock was the third Shaker village established, and retains one of the biggest collections of Shaker furniture and objects. Its twenty preserved buildings, located in fairly close proximity amid 1200 acres, are well worth poking about. The most interesting, and most photographed, is the **Round Stone Barn**, built in 1826 and the only one of its kind. Its circular shape allowed a single man to feed 54 cows at the same time from the center. In another unsung instance of Shaker ingenuity, manure was dropped through trap doors to the barn's cellar, where it was stored until needed as fertilizer. Other structures include a schoolhouse, meeting house, privies, and a two-car garage added in 1914.

Much of the fun to be had at the Hancock Shaker Village is of the pastoral variety. In the Barn Complex you can try your hand at a spinning wheel or quill pen, or model a range of Shaker fashions. You can also milk a plastic cow – if the teats seem spent, ask a guide to turn the heifer on – or chat with a guide tending one of the gardens, where heirloom vegetables are raised. A new, one-mile farm and forest trail circumnavigates the village, passing through fields and woodlands where you can learn the Shaker way of wetlands management and natural history. Other activities and demonstrations vary from day to day, but could include anything from a plowing match to sheep shearing. The highlight of a visit, however, may well be lunch or a snack in the on-site *Village Café*, which serves inexpensive and surprisingly tasty Shaker-inspired dishes, such as ham baked in cider and devilishly savory baked goods. During fall and winter, Shaker dinners are held on certain dates only.

Mount Greylock

To Americans from the western states it will never be more than a sizeable hill, but those from Massachusetts take no small amount of pride in **Mount Greylock**, the tallest peak in the state. Though somewhat short of spectacular,

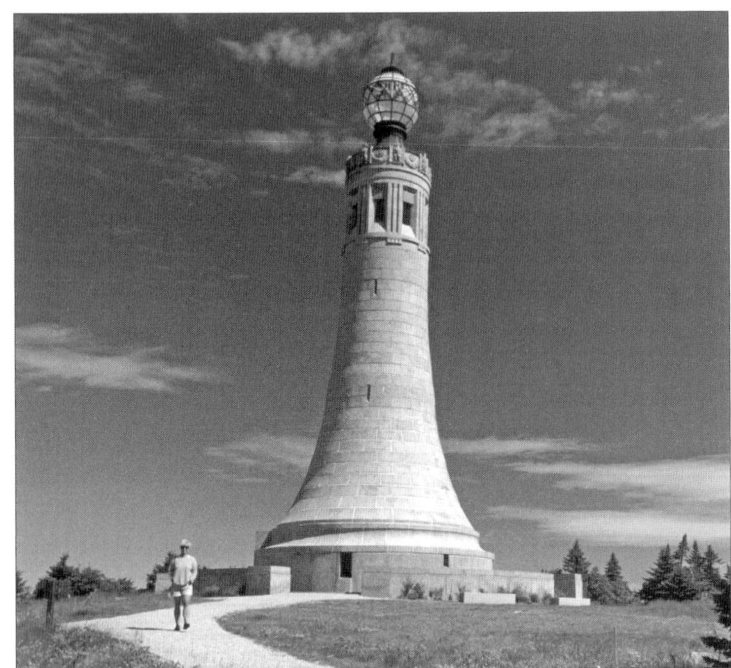

△ War Memorial Tower

it does make for a scenic hike, drive, or bike ride, especially in the fall. From the peak, at 3491 feet, you can sometimes see five states, though admittedly they all look the same from here. The ninety-foot-tall **War Memorial Tower**, erected to honor the Massachusetts casualties of all wars, stands near the top. Access to Mount Greylock is easy enough: from Rte-7 one mile north of Lanesborough, turn right (east) onto Rockwell Rd, where after two miles you'll find a **visitors' center** (①413/499-4262) with trail maps and the like; the summit is eight miles farther. Note that the summit is accessible by vehicle only from May through October; otherwise, strap on your snowshoes or put rugged tires on your bike. If you want to **eat** a cheap, bountiful diner-style breakfast or lunch before or after your hike up Mount Greylock, *Bob's Country Kitchen* (closed Wed; ①413/499-3934) in not unlovely Lanesborough is a good place to stop.

Williamstown

Pretty **WILLIAMSTOWN**, at the northwesternmost corner of the state, may seem a bit remote to be one of the region's premier art destinations, but the presence of the **Clark Institute**, with its excellent Impressionist collections, and the **Williams College Museum of Art** has put it on the map. These two, plus the beautiful campus of Williams College and the town's prime location at the terminus of the Mohawk Trail, make Williamstown a choice spot to spend a few days. Most of the action, of which there is actually little, save for during the summertime **Williamstown Theatre Festival** (see box p.272) – centers on block-long Spring Street, with the requisite range of shops and restaurants, most infused with an unmistakable upscale collegiate atmosphere.

Accommodation

The 1896 House Cold Spring Rd/Rte-7 ⓣ413/458-1896 or 1-888/999-1896, ⓦwww.1896house.com. Close to the center of Williamstown, this easily found hostelry proffers spotless "brookside," "pondside," and "barnside" accommodations and a good restaurant. ❺

Bed & Breakfast at Field Farm Guest House 554 Sloan Rd ⓣ413/458-3135. Five bedrooms, each with private bath, in a 1948 country estate surrounded by more than three hundred acres of meadows and woodlands. ❼

Maple Terrace Motel 555 Main St/Rte-2 ⓣ413/458-9677, ⓦwww.mapleterrace.com. Reliable motel set off from the street, within easy walking distance of the Williamstown Theatre Festival. ❺

The Orchards 222 Adams Rd ⓣ413/458-9611 or 1-800/225-1517, ⓦwww.orchardshotel.com. Modern hotel with a country-inn theme, English antiques, afternoon tea, and several rooms with fireplaces. The spacious rooms were designed for indulgence. ❼–❽

Steep Acres Farm B&B 520 White Oaks Rd ⓣ413/458-3774. Four rooms with shared baths in a 1900 cottage on fifty very scenic acres with an orchard and spring-fed pond; the breakfast is as filling as the environs are relaxing. ❹

The Williams Inn at the junction of routes 7 and 2 ⓣ413/458-9371. Located on-campus at Williams College, two blocks from the center of town, 125 Colonial-style rooms with modern amenities, along with enormous portions of delicious food and large bar. ❼

The Town

What makes Williamstown an essential ingredient of any Berkshires tour is not the college itself – attractive as it is – but rather two superb museums, one

The Mohawk Trail

The best-known scenic route in the Berkshires is the **Mohawk Trail**, otherwise known as Rte-2, from the Massachusetts–New York border to the town of Millers Falls on the Connecticut River. Originally, the 63-mile Mohawk Trail was used by Native Americans of the Five Nations to travel between the Hudson and Connecticut river valleys. During the French and Indian War, they put it to use as an invasion route. Today, the main appeal of the trail – especially during fall foliage season – is simply taking in the bucolic vistas it affords. Tourist facilities in the form of country inns, B&Bs, gift shops, and private and public campgrounds are in plentiful supply along the way, and the attractions are many and varied. Working from west to east, there are the culturally rich towns of **Williamstown** and **North Adams** (see overleaf), with their museums and festivals, as well as Massachusetts' highest peak, **Mount Greylock**, which lies just south of the road, roughly halfway between the two towns. In North Adams, New England's only **natural bridge**, a white marble arch formed by melting glaciers, is worth a visit. Just before Charlemont, you'll pass the **"Hail to the Sunrise" monument**, a huge statue of a Native American with outstretched arms, the trail's symbol. Here, you can access the **Mohawk Trail State Forest** (ⓣ413-339-5504), a scenic woodland with many tall pine trees, hiking trails, and a 56-place campsite (mid-April to mid-Oct; $12 per site). Straddling the Deerfield River, the **Bridge of Flowers** is another highlight, especially if you happen to be passing through in spring when it's adorned with colorful foliage. Just downstream, check out the bizarre glacial potholes on the riverbed at **Salmon Falls**. Turn south at the town of Greenfield and travel a short way down Rte-10 to **Historic Deerfield**, a profusion of well-preserved historic homes which are the main thing to see in the Upper Pioneer Valley. For more info on the trail, contact the **Mohawk Trail Association** in North Adams (ⓣ413/743-8127 or 1-866/743-8127, ⓦwww.mohawktrail.com).

of which, the **Sterling and Francine Clark Art Institute**, 225 South St (Tues–Sun 10am–5pm; $10 June–Oct, free Nov–May), is known for its extensive collection of French Impressionist paintings, including thirty by Renoir. The highlight is *At the Concert*, which established Renoir's niche of beautiful women in fashionable clothing; this 1880 painting is considered by many to be one of his finest. There are also paintings by Fragonard, Géricault, Rembrandt, and Alma-Tadema, as well as a sizeable collection of American works by Homer, Sargent, and Remington, whose *The Scout: Friends or Foes* details the anxiety and loneliness of looking into the future. Allow two hours or so to take it all in, longer if you have a snack or light lunch at the excellent museum café.

Meanwhile, on the Williams campus itself, the **Williams College Museum of Art**, 15 Lawrence Hall Drive (Tues–Sat 10am–5pm, Sun 1–5pm; free) is ravishing on two counts: its facility and its collections. Part of the museum is housed in an 1846 two-story brick octagon, capped by a Neoclassical rotunda; a three-story entrance atrium connects it to a contemporary addition, and from the polished floors to the lighting and crisply painted walls, the place could not be more immaculately maintained. The thrust of the exceedingly well-curated collection is American visual art from the late eighteenth century to the present day, and some of the best exhibits are those by contemporary artists. The non-Western collections include Asian art and a small but stunning selection of Mesopotamian and Greek antiquities.

Music junkies will want to stop at the **Toonerville Trolley**, 131 Water St (⊕413/458-5229), one of the best record stores in the region. There's a cheap selection of used vinyl in the back, an excellent selection of jazz, rock, blues, and world music, as well as a staggering, if pricey, selection of concert recordings. A must for serious collectors.

Eating and drinking

Chopsticks Chinese Restaurant 412 Main St ⊕413/458-5750. This minimal Chinese place probably won't win any awards, but can be a welcome find in an area with very few non-American restaurants.

Cold Spring Coffee Roasters 46 Spring St ⊕413/458-5010. Spacious coffeehouse with a delicious assortment of piping hot teas, pastries, and bagels.

Hobson's Choice 159 Water St ⊕413/458-9101. This country manor with beamed ceilings is a local favorite, known for steaks, prime rib, various chicken dishes, Cajun shrimp, blackened Norwegian salmon, and Alaskan king crab. Dinner only.

Mezze 16 Water St ⊕413/458-0123. Urban contemporary meets rural gentility here, where Mediterranean, Moroccan, and American flavors jump off the menu, like lamb with thyme, salmon in porcini mushroom broth, and seared duck.

Pappa Charlie's Deli & Juice/Tea Bar 28 Spring St ⊕413/458-5969. From chicken cordon bleu to the "Bo Derek" – a sandwich with peppers, onions, mushrooms, melted provolone, sprouts, and tomatoes – they do hot, cold, and vegetarian light fare with flare.

Thai Garden 27 Spring St ⊕413/458-0004. The beige and green ambience makes for a Zen eating experience, with exotic choices like steamed ginger salmon or the fiery seafood *gra prow*.

The Water Street Grill 123 Water St ⊕413/458-2175. From blackened catfish to the grilled sirloin, this is a safe choice for American dining. Nothing too stand-out, but done well.

North Adams

Settled in the 1730s and, during the nineteenth century, a fairly prosperous mill town, **NORTH ADAMS**, five miles east of Williamstown on the Mohawk Trail, might have been just another post-industrial eyesore if it weren't for the

Massachusetts Museum of Contemporary Art, 87 Marshall St (aka MASS MoCA; July–Sept daily 10am–6pm, Nov–May Mon & Wed–Sun 11am–5pm; $10; ⓣ413/662-2111, ⓦwww.massmoca.org). This huge arts center is housed in a resurrected old mill site, and mounts an extensive range of exhibits in its 27 refurbished red-brick buildings, linked by a web of bridges, passageways, viaducts, and courtyards. Most of the work inside is installation-oriented, and although much of the content may provoke even the most open-minded to wonder aloud, "Can you really call this *art*?" there's an undeniable neo-funhouse pleasure in wandering through the configurations of materials, collages, video monitors, found objects, oversized photographs, and flashing lights. The space also hosts modern dance performances, concerts, and a film series; check the website for details of what's on and when.

Practicalities

The opening of MASS MoCA in 1999 spawned a renaissance in North Adams, with trendy restaurants, boutiques, lounges, and cafés now inhabiting many of the town's previously empty factory buildings – and most avoiding the quaintness quotient so prevalent in other Berkshire towns. Just across the street from MASS MoCA, for example, *The Porches Inn*, 231 River St (ⓣ413/664-0400, ⓦwww.porches.com; ❼), is an ultra-modern **hotel** with DVD players, high-speed Internet connections, and not an antique in sight, occupying a row of houses formerly lived in by mill-workers' families. A more affordable option is the *Holiday Inn*, just minutes from the action at 40 Main St (ⓣ1-800/664-9491, ⓦwww.holiday-inn.com; ❺).

As for a **meal**, you can dine at the festive *Latino*, in Building 11 at MASS MoCA (ⓣ413/662-2004), on delectable citrus-braised pork shoulder or salmon with pineapple-rum salsa, or sip *caipirinhas* while facing the ultra-hip backlit bar. A similarly fun – but not as chic – vibe can be found at *Gideon's Luncheon and Nightery*, 23 Eagle St (ⓣ413/664-0404), the town's late-night **drinking** spot, which specializes in great live music. If you'd prefer something more low-key, head a few miles south on Rte-8 to the town of **ADAMS**, where the *Miss Adams Diner*, 53 Park St (ⓣ413/743-5303), has been serving homemade cream pies and classic diner fare long before North Adams had even heard of pineapple-rum salsa.

Rhode Island

CANADA
Moosehead Lake
Kennebec River
8
Lake Champlain
GREEN MOUNTAINS
WHITE MOUNTAINS
Mount Desert Island
6
Lake Winnipesaukee
7
NEW YORK
ATLANTIC OCEAN
THE BERKSHIRES
3
1
Cape Cod
2
4
5
Martha's Vineyard
Nantucket
Long Island
N

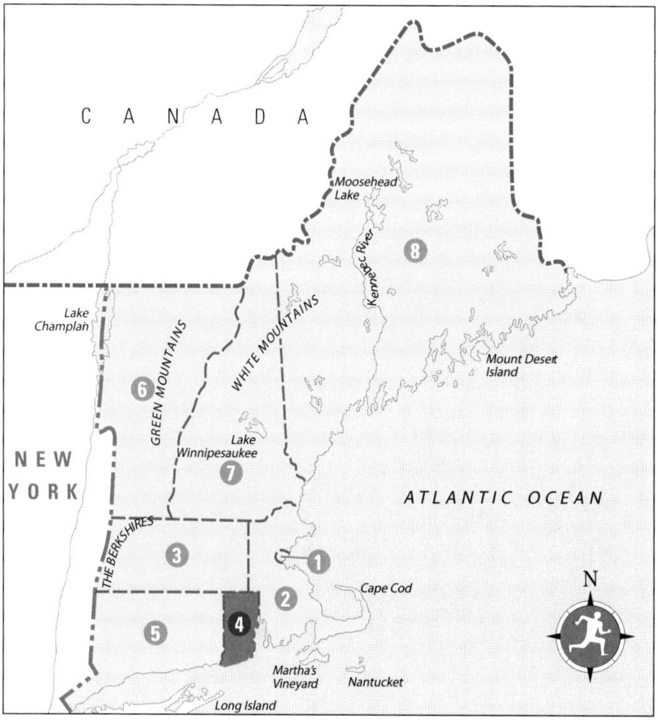

CHAPTER FOUR

Highlights

* **Federal Hill, Providence** This firmly established Italian community west of the Providence River has (almost) as much charm as Naples itself. See p.298

* **Blithewold Mansion and Gardens** In the midst of Bristol's patriotic passion, Blithewold is an oasis of blooming gardens, exotic trees, and giant sequoias. See p.301

* **Blackstone Riverboat Tour** Get off the road and experience Rhode Island as the early settlers did: slowly, along the Blackstone River. See p.301

* **Newport** With its phenomenal mansions, fine beaches, fancy yachts, and world-class summer music concerts, this coastal town has real appeal. See p.301

* **South County** Native American tribal gatherings, green parks, historical sites, and attractive beaches jockey for your attention in this overlooked corner of the state. See p.314

* **Mohegan Bluffs, Block Island** Experience pure desolation at 200 feet up, peering down on the charming tourist community of Block Island below. See p.323

△ WaterFire, Providence River

4

Rhode Island

Just 48 miles north-to-south by 37 miles east-to-west, tiny **Rhode Island** is easily the smallest state in the Union, barely even noticeable on a map of the country. For that reason alone, it often tends to be overlooked as a tourist destination, even if it is home to more than twenty percent of the nation's registered historical landmarks. Indeed, locals take great satisfaction in pointing out the state's disproportionately large influence on national life: it enacted the first law against slavery in North America on May 18, 1652, and was the first of the thirteen original colonies to declare independence from Great Britain. Rhode Island also claims the city of Providence as the birthplace of the US Navy (though Marblehead, MA, among other New England towns, has a rival claim), and the Blackstone River Valley, which runs northwest from Providence, as the cradle of the Industrial Revolution, a process that followed the 1793 construction of America's first water-powered cotton mill in Pawtucket.

Though tiny, Rhode Island has more than four hundred miles of impressive, sometimes spectacular, coastline with more than one hundred public and private beaches, not to mention thousands of acres of pristine woodlands within a surprisingly diverse geography. Most of this coastline is hacked out of the state's most conspicuous feature, **Narragansett Bay**, a vast expanse of water that has long been a determining factor in Rhode Island's economic development and strategic military importance. In fact, more than thirty tiny islands make up the state, including Hope, Despair, and the bay's largest island, Rhode Island, which gives the state its name – though it's more often referred to by its Native American name, "Aquidneck."

Rhode Island's size and compactness is, ultimately, one of its most endearing features, and means that you are rarely more than an hour's drive or bus ride away from any other point in the state. The prime destinations are the colonial college town of **Providence**, right on I-95, the main highway that runs through the state (and indeed, the East Coast), and well-heeled **Newport**, yachting capital of the world, with good beaches and outrageously extravagant mansions. More scenic than I-95, US-1 hugs the coast of Narragansett Bay – which presents endless opportunities for swimming, boating, and other water-related leisure activities – and parallels the Atlantic Coast through **South County** into Connecticut. Along the coast are plenty of sleepy small towns and ports worth a look, most notably **Watch Hill** and **Galilee**. The latter also happens to be the main point of departure for ferries to **Block Island**, a popular excursion for visitors seeking a pleasant stretch of sand.

In a state this small traveling by **car** is your best bet, though getting to and around Rhode Island using public transport is also an option. **RIPTA**, or the

Rhode Island Public Transit Authority (Ⓣ401/781-9400, Ⓦwww.ripta.com), is the means for traveling within state borders, while **T.F. Green Airport** offers a $9 shuttle to downtown Providence hotels and to the train station. Amtrak makes stops at Westerly, Kingston, and Providence; the trains are clean and reliable and make for easy connections if you're traveling between here and Massachusetts or Connecticut.

Some history

The first European to explore the shores of Rhode Island may have been Portuguese navigator **Miguel de Cortereal**, who sailed along the coast in 1511, but

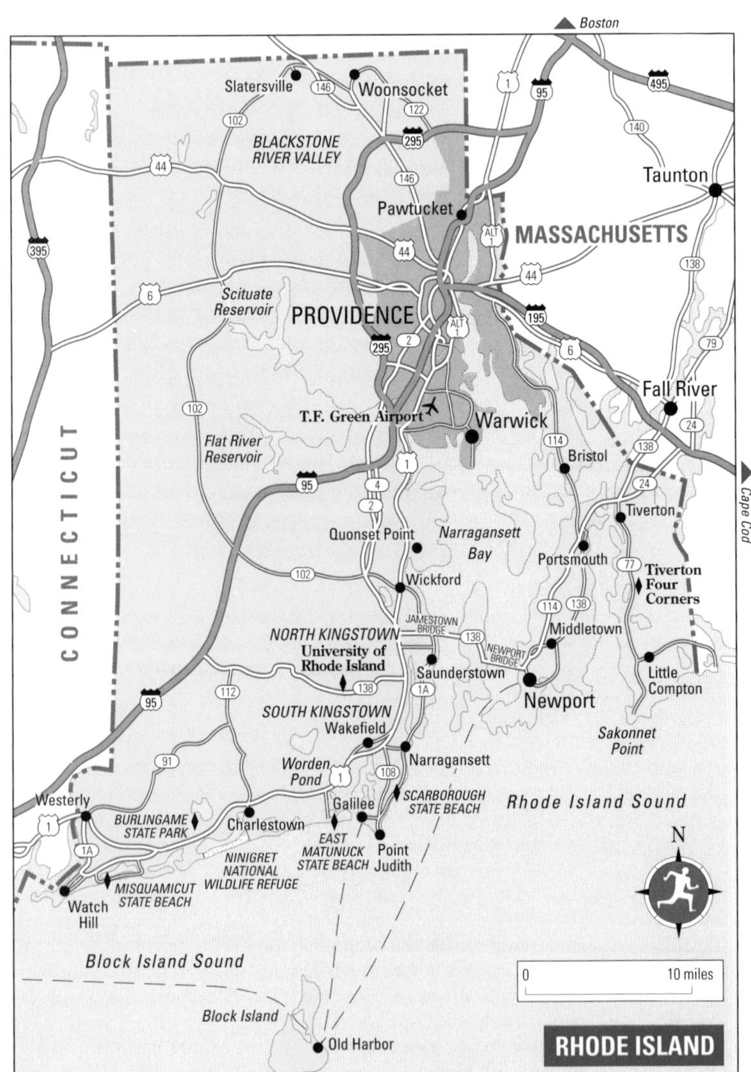

it was **Giovanni da Verrazano**, an Italian explorer working for France, who arrived in 1524 and remarked on its striking resemblance to the Greek island of Rhodes. One can only surmise either that the weather was foggy, or that the summer heat (and a bottle or two of rum) had gone to his head. Others claim that the name is associated with Dutch explorer **Adrian Block**, who in 1614 named an island in Narragansett Bay Roodt Eylandt (Red Island) because of its prominent red clay and rocks.

In 1636, dissent among the ranks of the colonists in Plymouth prompted the **Reverend Roger Williams** to establish a new colony as a "lively experiment" in religious freedom. Williams did not leave fully of his own accord, though – his revolutionary ideas (including notions of Indians' rights and the total separation of church and state) had incurred the wrath of the Puritan zealots, and they covertly arranged to ship the radical cleric back to England. He got word of the plan and managed to escape to present-day Providence, safely out of the jurisdiction of the Massachusetts authorities, where he declared the place a refuge for the oppressed and sent word to his freethinking colleagues in Massachusetts to join him. However, Rhode Island's tolerant basis did not ensure peace: relations with local Native Americans soured in 1675, when Wampanoag chief King Philip (Metacomet) attacked colonists to protect tribal lands, resulting in what became known as **King Philip's War**, one of the bloodiest in the country's history. A series of gory battles over two years in Massachusetts, Connecticut, and Rhode Island resulted in the near annihilation of the Narragansett, Wampanoag, Podunk, and Nipmuck tribes.

Despite the war, Rhode Island prospered economically, and by 1680 the first wharf was built, encouraging maritime trade and commerce, especially whaling; a good deal of smuggling occurred, too, helping earn the state the unflattering nickname of "Rogues' Island." Bolstered by economic power and prosperity, self-assured Rhode Islanders were at the forefront of Revolutionary sentiment, resenting the stringent economic pressures placed on them from England and declaring independence from the Old Country before the other twelve colonies. However, no Revolutionary battles were ever fought on Rhode Island soil, and the state, apprehensive at the prospect of yielding power to a federal government, was the last to ratify the Constitution.

Between the Revolution and the Civil War, the economic focus shifted from maritime trade to manufacturing, and Rhode Island became the birthplace of the American **Industrial Revolution** when, in 1793, Pawtucket became the site of the nation's first water-powered **textile mill**, the brainchild of local entrepreneur Samuel Slater. The textile industry lured thousands of immigrant workers, including Russians, French-Canadians, and British, into Rhode Island, resulting in the ethnic mix that exists today. Manufacturing still plays an important role in the life of the state, though not in the places that people come to see: Providence and Newport both originated as port cities.

In recent years, Rhode Island's economic fortunes have fluctuated, but confidence took a major nosedive in 1990, in a disastrous **banking crisis** which closed many of the state's credit unions and resulted in the loss of millions of dollars from the savings accounts of thousands of ordinary Rhode Islanders. A tightening of regulations has helped put the state on a more secure financial footing, prompting improvements to the state's infrastructure – including repairs to its crumbling roads – along with some decent urban renewal programs and modernization of the state's main airport, T.F. Green, at Warwick. Meanwhile the vastly improved east coast rail link to Boston and New York has made the state more easily accessible; perhaps as a result, travel and tourism receipts have topped $3.25 billion since 1997, and tourism is now the state's second-largest industry.

Providence

Stretching across seven hills on the Providence and Seekonk rivers, **PROVIDENCE** was Rhode Island's first settlement, established "in commemoration of God's Providence" on land given to **Roger Williams** by the Narragansett Indians. The city flourished as one of the most important ports of call in the notorious "**triangle trade**," where New England rum was exchanged for African slaves to be exchanged in turn for West Indian molasses. Many lavish homes were constructed during this period, some of which can still be seen in the Benefit Street district. Among those who prospered was **James Brown**, who opened a lucrative distillery and slaughterhouse, while also entering the shipping trade. His four sons found success, too: Joseph, an architect responsible for many of the city's most elegant buildings; John, a somewhat ruthless merchant; Nicholas, whose son's donation of $5000 to his alma mater sparked its taking the Brown family name; and Moses, who helped Samuel Slater introduce the nation's first water-powered cotton mill in nearby Pawtucket, ensuring that the textile industry was to become a mainstay of the local economy.

Rhode Island's **capital** since 1901, Providence is today one of the three largest cities in New England (Boston is on top, obviously, and Worcester and Bridgeport are up there as well). Until the past decade or so, though, the millions who whizzed towards New York or Boston in either direction on I-95 had little incentive to stop here. Put off by the towering chimneys of the elephantine Narragansett Power Station, drab office buildings, and ugly oil tanks and empty shop-fronts along once-prosperous Westminster Street, few took the time to notice that the city center holds more intact Colonial and early Federal buildings than any other place in the nation. After an aggressive urban renewal program throughout the late 1990s, however, the city has emerged with a new sense of pride and vigor; locals are quick to wax lyrical about their town's vibrant art scene, excellent restaurants, and ethnic and lifestyle diversity. Among other improvements, entire sections of the Providence River, once covered by pavement, have been opened up and moved, encouraging the creation of the new Waterplace Park, a four-acre public space south of the State Capitol, that inspires the popular summer art installation, WaterFire (see p.300).

Nevertheless, to the visitor, Providence doesn't yet feel like it's come into its own. The Providence River and interstates 95 and 195 block off the town's neighborhoods from one another, meaning that the various city sections, while individually easily explored on foot, are rather disconnected. The downtown area, known to locals as **Downcity**, is dominated by the sparkling Providence Place Shopping Mall and beams with new office buildings, but people seem to rattle around in the wide, near-empty streets. The city's highlights center around its older districts: west of I-95 and Downcity is the large Italian community on Federal Hill, while east of the river is the oldest and most attractive section of town, along North and South Main streets as well as Benefit Street, where founder Roger Williams and his followers first settled. Known as the **East Side**, it's crowned by **College Hill**, a showcase of architectural preservation, and home to the Ivy League's **Brown University** and the **Rhode Island School of Design** (RISD or "Rizdee"), both of which give the place a certain cultural verve, at least in their immediate vicinities.

Arrival, information, and getting around

T.F. Green Airport (ⓣ1-888/268-7222) is on Post Road, at the end of exit 13 just off I-95 in Warwick, nine miles south of downtown Providence. The

Amtrak **train station**, 100 Gaspee St (Ⓣ1-800/USA-RAIL), is housed in a domed structure a short walk southeast of the capitol building. Greyhound and Bonanza **buses** stop downtown at the city's transportation center, Kennedy Plaza; Bonanza's main terminus is considerably further out at 1 Bonanza Way, off I-95 (Ⓣ1-888/751-8800).

The well-stocked **Visitors' Center**, in the rotunda lobby of the Rhode Island Convention Center, 1 Sabin St (Mon–Sat 9am–5pm; Ⓣ 1-800/233-1636), provides maps and brochures, as does a small **kiosk** in the concourse of the Providence Place Mall, 1 Providence Place (Mon–Sat 11am–4pm), and another **information center** in the Roger Williams National Memorial Park, 282 N Main St (daily 9am–4.30pm; Ⓣ401/521-7266). Self-guided historic tour info can be had at the **Providence Preservation Society**, 21 Meeting St, in the 1772 Shakespeare's Head (Mon–Fri 8.30am–5pm; Ⓣ401/831-7440, Ⓦwww.ppsri.org), a wood-frame dwelling which once housed the family and printing press of John Carter, a prominent local worthy and publisher of the *Providence Gazette*. Extensive pamphlets on Benefit Street, Downcity, the Waterfront, and other neighborhoods are $3, or for $25 you can purchase the Society's 320-page *Guide to Providence Architecture* and become an expert on the city.

Local **bus transportation** is provided by RIPTA, with most city and statewide services operating from Kennedy Plaza (city buses every 15min; ticket window Mon–Fri 7am–6pm, Sat 9am–noon & 1–5pm; $1.50/trip; ⓣ401/781-9400). Particularly useful for getting around town are RIPTA's Gold Line, which runs north–south across the central area, and its Green Line, running east–west. You don't really need a car to explore, but just in case, **taxis**, which aren't always readily available on the street, can be arranged by calling Providence Taxis (ⓣ401/521-4200) or Yellow Cab (ⓣ401/941-1122). All the major **car rental** outfits are represented at the airport, including Hertz (ⓣ401/738-3550) and Budget (ⓣ401/739-8986); Enterprise has a location downtown at 90 Weybosset St (ⓣ401/861-4408).

Accommodation

Providence is not exactly brimming with **places to stay**, though the city's recent redevelopment included the building of the *Westin* (soon to expand) and the *Hotel Providence* (see below for both); the hopes are – among city officials at least – that an additional two hundred rooms will be added by 2007. There are fairly few **budget rooms** available around town, and no **hostels**, although **B&Bs** are a viable option. Motorists can take advantage of the swath of mid-priced **motels** along I-95 towards Pawtucket, north of the city, and to the south near the airport in Warwick. **Camping** is not much of an option, with the closest sites fifteen miles away in Coventry.

Annie Brownell House B&B 400 Angell St ⓣ401/454-2934, ⓦwww.anniebrownell-house.com. Lovely, spacious Colonial Revival house built in 1899, a few blocks east of the lively Thayer Street neighborhood. The newly refurbished guestrooms are bright, airy, and decorated in period style, all with private bath; the full hot breakfasts are tasty and satisfying. Friendly owner, too. Two-night minimum stay on weekends. ❻

C.C. Ledbetter Bed & Breakfast 326 Benefit St ⓣ401/351-4699. A handful of clean rooms in a compact, 200-year-old house on historic Benefit Street, perhaps once the carriage house for the neighboring John Brown House. Homey breakfast of coffee cake, warm rolls, and fruit, along with excellent New Orleans coffee. Convenient location to Brown, RISD, and Downcity. ❻

The Cady House 127 Power St ⓣ401/273-5398, ⓦwww.cadyhouse.com. An elegant, Classical Revival house set on College Hill, adorned with antiques and folk art. All rooms have private bath and TV; breakfast is continental. Close to Brown and the Thayer and Wickenden shops and restaurants. ❻

Comfort Inn 1940 Post Rd, Warwick ⓣ401/732-0470, ⓦwww.choicehotels.com. Adequate lodging in this chain motel, located right by the airport. Also a branch at 2 George St, in nearby Pawtucket (see p.300; ⓣ401/723-6700). ❻

Courtyard Providence Downtown 32 Exchange Terrace, at Memorial Blvd ⓣ401/272-1191 or 1-888/887-7955, ⓦwww.marriott.com. Located in the heart of Downcity, this large, pricey Marriott relation, with an indoor pool and fitness center, boasts a striking facade designed to match the adjacent historic Union Station building. ❽

Dolce Villa 63 DePasquale Square ⓣ401/383-7031, ⓦwww.dolcevillari.com. Decorated entirely in white, the fourteen suites of this boutique hotel seem either chic or institutional, depending on your state of mind. A classic Italian one-bedroom villa is also available, much more in keeping with the old world charm of the Federal Hill neighborhood. Suites ❼, villa ❾

Fairfield Inn 36 Jefferson Blvd, Warwick ⓣ401/941-6600 or 1-800/228-2800, ⓦwww.marriott.com. Comfortable rooms in Marriott's less expensive chain. Outside the city, but still close to I-95 for easy access. ❻

Hotel Providence 311 Westminster St ⓣ401-861-8000 or 1-800/861-8990, ⓦwww.thehotelprovidence.com. Opened in 2005, Providence's newest hotel has eighty plush and colorful rooms and is already known for its comfort and charm, as well as its excellent Italian restaurant, *L'Epicureo*. Request to stay in the Lederer wing, which has the most character. Note that rooms have only showers, while suites have baths. ❽

The Old Court 144 Benefit St ⓣ401/751-2002, ⓦwww.oldcourt.com. Charming B&B in an old red-brick rectory near RISD, featuring ten rooms done the Victorian way, all with private bath and TV. ❻

The Providence Biltmore 11 Dorrance St ⓣ401/421-0700 or 1-800/294-7709, ⓦwww.providencebiltmore.com. A Providence landmark since 1922, the *Biltmore* may be the prime place to stay here, if you can afford it: it's got elegant city-view rooms and a new Elizabeth Arden Spa in a convenient Downcity location. ❽

State House Inn 43 Jewett St ⓣ401/351-6111, ⓦwww.providence-inn.com. Pleasant, central B&B in a restored former tenement near the State Capitol; rooms have TV and private bath and are outfitted with antique furnishings. If full, ask the friendly proprietors about their other inns nearby. ❻

The Westin 1 W Exchange St ⓣ401/598-8000 or 1-800/937-8461, ⓦwww.westin.com. In the heart of Downcity, deluxe modern accommodations (reflected by the price) in this multistory hotel. ❾

The City

Providence's downtown, or **Downcity**, centers on **Kennedy Plaza**, a large public square that houses the city's transportation center. At the southwestern corner of the plaza, **City Hall** was completed in 1878, designed in the Second Empire style of the Louvre and the Tuileries palaces in Paris; although you'll find nothing to compare with the *Mona Lisa* here, the building's striking mansard roof and grand interior staircase were certainly worth saving from the wrecking ball which threatened them in the 1950s. Another fine example of this kind of historic restoration is the nearby Beaux Arts **Union Station**, built as a rail terminal in 1898 but employed today to house offices and restaurants. To the south of the Plaza, in Westminster Mall, is the 1828 **Arcade**, the sole survivor of many such "temples of trade" built in America during the Greek Revival period and America's oldest indoor shopping mall. It's still a marketplace, though a fairly subdued one, with plenty of places to eat and drink, and small specialty shops to explore.

The state's only National Park Service property, the **Roger Williams National Memorial**, at the corner of North Main and Smith streets, was the site of the original settlement of Providence in 1636, and is now a four-acre greenspace; its small visitors' center (daily 9am–4.30pm; ⓣ401/521-7266) includes replicas of Williams' compass, an Indian Bible, and papers documenting Williams' efforts. West from here, at the top of Constitution Hill, the white-marble **State Capitol** (Mon–Fri 8.30am–4.30pm; guided tours at 9, 10 & 11am, appointment requested; free; ⓣ401/222-2357) dominates the city skyline with a vast dome, supposedly the fourth-largest self-supported marble dome in the world. Inside, you can view the original Rhode Island Charter of 1663 and, in the Reception Room, a portrait of George Washington by Rhode Island artist Gilbert Stuart.

Benefit Street and around

Most of Providence's historic legacy can be found across the river from Downcity in the **College Hill** area, an attractive tree-lined district of Colonial buildings, museums, and **Brown University** facilities. Part of Roger Williams' religious experiment was the establishment of a Baptist church, the first in America, in 1638: the white-clapboard **First Baptist Meeting House**, at 75 N Main St, is the third such church building on the site, built in 1775 and topped by a tall steeple inspired by St Martin-in-the-Fields in London. North Main logically leads into **South Main Street**, once bustling with waterfront activity and now home to a number of new upmarket restaurants, though the neighborhood's real draw is a block up the hill, on **Benefit Street**. This is Providence's "mile of

△ Providence's Union Station

history," the most impressive collection of original Colonial and Federal homes in America. Lined with the beautifully restored, colored-clapboard residences of Providence's merchants and sea captains, it was once just a dirt track leading to graveyards until it was improved in the eighteenth century "for the benefit of the people of Providence" – hence its name. Although most of the buildings here remain private residences and are not open to the public, the history of more than two dozen of them is detailed in the Providence Preservation Society's self-guided tour (see p.293). In addition, the Rhode Island Historical Society leads ninety-minute **walking tours** of the area through the summer (mid-June to mid-Oct Tues, Wed, Fri & Sat 11am and 1pm, Thurs 11am; adults $12, children 12 and under $6; ⓣ401/331-8575, ⓦwww.rihs.org).

The Historical Society also maintains one of the few buildings you can explore, the elegant **John Brown House**, 52 Power St, at Benefit (April–Dec Tues–Sat 10.30am–4.30pm; Jan–March Fri & Sat only, same hours; $7; ⓣ401/273-7507). A three-story residence constructed in 1786, it was home to one of the city's most aggressive merchants (uncle to Nicholas, for whom the University was named), who made his money trading in slaves and building commercial links with China. Designed by his architect brother Joseph, the house has a lovely central hall flanked by large formal rooms used by Brown to entertain his illustrious guests; it also retains much original furnishing, silverware, and china, and holds displays on the formidable Brown family and Rhode Island history in general.

Farther up the street, the small but excellent collection of the **RISD Museum**, 224 Benefit St (Tues–Sun 10am–5pm; $8, free Sun mornings & last Sat of the month; ⓣ401/454-6500, ⓦwww.risd.edu/museum.cfm), Rhode Island's leading museum of fine and decorative arts, is worthy of its association with one of the foremost art schools in the country. The antiquities section contains a Ptolemaic Egyptian mummy, Roman frescoes, and a fabulous array of Greek coins, while the Asian art collection includes more than six hundred Japanese bird-and-flower woodblock prints and a Heian Buddha – the largest historic

Japanese wooden sculpture in the US. Other wings are devoted to textiles and costumes, paintings and prints, and multimedia contemporary art, and a new six-story exhibition space, café, shop, and auditorium is due for construction in 2006 and opening in 2008. Across the road, the Greek Revival **Providence Athenaeum**, at no. 251 (Mon–Thurs 9am–7pm, Fri & Sat 9am–5pm, Sun 1–5pm; closed Sat afternoon & Sun in summer; free; ⓣ401/421-6970, ⓦwww.providenceathenaeum.org), is one of America's oldest libraries, and was where Edgar Allan Poe and Sarah Helen Whitman carried on their courtship among the stacks; portraits of the two poets hang here in the Art Room. The library is small and welcoming, and the cozy reading nooks give it the feel of someone's living room.

A few blocks north is the plain but dignified 1762 **Old State House**, at no. 150 (Mon–Fri 8.30am–4.30pm; free; ⓣ410/222-2678). Although today it mostly houses offices for the Rhode Island Historical Preservation and Heritage Commission, of particular interest here is the courtroom where the Rhode Island General Assembly renounced allegiance to King George III on May 4, 1776, two months before the Declaration of Independence.

Brown University and around

The extensive campus of **Brown University**, a short walk up Waterman Street from RISD, occupies 133 acres of College Hill, giving the whole neighborhood a relaxed, intellectual feel. The third oldest college in New England, and seventh oldest in the nation, it was founded in 1764 in Warren as Rhode Island College before it moved six years later to Providence, where it was renamed after Nicholas Brown, Jr, who donated substantial funds and extensive land. The center wrought-iron **Van Wickle Gates** on Prospect Street are opened only twice a year – for incoming students upon arrival and for graduates on commencement day – though various side entrances lead onto the historic core of the university, pleasant **College Green**, skirted by a collection of primarily Colonial and Greek Revival buildings. Among them stands the 1904 Beaux Arts **John Carter Brown Library** (Mon–Fri 8.30am–5pm, Sat 9am–noon; free; ⓣ401/863-2725, ⓦwww.jcbl.org), which boasts a rich trove of rare Americana, though its collections are mostly closed to the general public except for rotating exhibits. Nearby, the school's oldest building, **University Hall,** was built in 1770 and stood alone on College Hill for its first fifty years; it was used as a barracks for the Revolutionary troops and their French allies.

Of the other two hundred or so buildings that constitute the university, don't miss the **John Hay Library** (Mon–Fri 9am–5pm; free; ⓣ401/863-2146), across the street from University Hall and home to outstanding special collections that are accessible to the general public on request. In addition to rare books in the stacks (such as George Orwell's handwritten manuscript for *1984*), there are also changing and permanent exhibits on display, including a vast collection of miniature soldiers representing armies from ancient Egypt to modern Europe. For **free tours** or self-guided maps of the Brown University campus, contact the admissions office, 45 Prospect St (Mon–Fri 8am–4pm; ⓣ401/863-2378, ⓦwww.brown.edu) – tour schedules vary so it's best to call ahead.

Behind College Hill, happening **Thayer Street** and neighboring lanes are home to typical college-town spots like bookstores, tattoo parlors, and funky thrift stores, while at the eastern end of the hill, **Wickenden Street** buzzes with an assortment of cafés, galleries, and restaurants. Farther towards Gano Street lies the increasingly gentrified **Fox Point** district, once Providence's main Portuguese neighborhood, with many pastel-shaded dwellings and bakeries selling Portuguese delicacies.

The rest of the city

Back west of Downcity, **Federal Hill** – informally considered Providence's **Little Italy** – can be entered through a large arch topped with a bronze pinecone, the Italian symbol for hospitality, at Atwells Avenue. Long a powerful Mafia stronghold, this area is one of the safest and friendliest in the city, where you can savor the nuances of Italian culture and cuisine in dozens of restaurants, bakeries, and grocery stores. If it's just a drink you want, head to the bars and cafés around lively **DePasquale Square**, where there's even a large Italianate fountain, reminiscent of the piazzas found in Naples.

Just south of Downcity in the Jewelry District is the excellent **Providence Children's Museum**, at 100 South St (April–Aug daily 9am–6pm, Sept–March Tues–Sun 9am–6pm; $6.50, free select Fridays during extended evening hours; ⓣ401/273-KIDS, ⓦwww.childrenmuseum.org), where the range of interactive displays includes a fun look at teeth in a giant mouth, a walk-in kaleidoscope, a time-traveling adventure through Rhode Island's history, and a chance to dress up like a veterinarian and give a toy pet a checkup.

A wealth of food history, including ancient utensils, recipes, and menus, can be found at the **Culinary Archives & Museum**, three miles south of the Children's Museum at 315 Harborside Blvd (Tues–Sun 10am–5pm; $7, children and teens 5–18 $2; ⓣ401/598-2805, ⓦwww.culinary.org). Situated on the satellite campus of Johnson & Wales University, one of the country's premier culinary colleges, the exhibits here range from restaurant development and mini kitchen replicas to historical biographies of significant "food people" like Earle MacAusland (founder of *Gourmet* magazine), culinary writer Clementine Paddleford, and Julia Child.

About a mile west of the museum, the 430-acre **Roger Williams Park** spills with serpentine paths, rolling hills, and peaceful ponds. In addition to a carousel and a **Museum of Natural History**, there's the **Roger Williams Zoo**, with nearly a thousand animals, including giraffes, cheetahs, and zebras in a "Plains of Africa" area, a tropical rainforest, an exhibit of endangered Madagascar lemurs, an Australasian section with an open-air aviary, and a snow leopard exhibit. Even if zoos aren't normally your thing, you can't help but admire the imaginative way this one has been laid out, with its close attention to culture and history alongside zoology (daily: spring & summer 9am–5pm, rest of year 9am–4pm; $10, children 3–12 $6; ⓣ401/785-3510, ⓦwww.rogerwilliamsparkzoo.org).

Eating

As the hometown of Johnson & Wales, it's no surprise that Providence has more accredited chefs per capita than any other city in the US. This fact, along with the city's ethnic diversity, means that it's never difficult to find something good to eat. **Thayer Street** is lined with inexpensive eateries, almost all of which stay open until late; nearby **Wickenden Street** is slightly more mature but still eclectic; the family-run Italian restaurants on **Federal Hill** offer great value in a lively atmosphere; and **Downcity** is home to a burgeoning group of up-and-coming establishments.

Al Forno 577 S Main St ⓣ401/273-9760. Wood-grilled pizzas, pasta, and interesting twists on steak and seafood at what has been called one of the five best restaurants in America. Dinner only, closed Sun & Mon.

Angelo's 141 Atwells Ave ⓣ401/621-8171. Despite the unremarkable food, *Angelo's* has been a staple in Federal Hill since it opened in 1924 for its homey, no-frills, family-friendly atmosphere and affordable Italian standards. Cash only.

Café Nuovo 1 Citizens Plaza ⓣ401/421-2525. Excellent and expensive American and continental cuisine with an Asian influence in a large, bright contemporary space. Dine on the outdoor patio during WaterFire (see overleaf) for a great view of the twinkling river. Dinner only Sat, closed Sun.

Caffe Dolce Vita 59 DePasquale Square ☎401/331-8240. Although the interior decor is uninspired, its setting on the lively piazza makes it a nice spot for a drink or traditional Italian dessert (*gelato, panna cotta, frutta di bosco*) on the patio. Paninis, bruschetta, and salads also available.

CAV Restaurant 14 Imperial Place ☎401/751-9164. A contemporary mid-priced menu in an atmospheric historic loft, with live jazz after 8.45pm on Fri and 9.30pm on Sat ($6 cover if you're not dining). Cocktails, antiques, and victuals are all the thing here: as you're enjoying the excellent braised lamb shank in a red wine raisin sauce, consider taking home one of the tribal pieces or handmade oil lamps that decorate the space – they're all for sale.

Coffee Exchange 207 Wickenden St ☎401/273-1198. Feel good about getting your caffeine fix at this popular meeting-place for would-be intellectuals: *Coffee Exchange* serves Fair Trade, shade-grown, mostly organic coffees and sponsors a nonprofit that works to improve living conditions for coffee workers worldwide.

Haruki East 172 Wayland Ave ☎401/223-0332. Known by locals as the best Japanese restaurant in town for its hospitality, presentation, and unique dishes like the Japanese-style crabmeat chili relleno. A separate "cooked" section on the sushi menu is perfect for the less adventurous. Jazz on Sun evenings.

Haven Brothers When you're craving late-night munchies, this diner-on-wheels is the place to go for some good old-fashioned greasy hot dogs, chili, and fries. It parks outside City Hall every night 4.30pm–5am and always draws a crowd; sit at the tiny counter inside or just grab a spot on the curb.

Hemenway's 121 S Main St ☎401/351-8570. Pricey, first-rate classic New England seafood like clam chowder, Narragansett Bay oysters, and fried Maine clams, served in an attractive glass setting.

Kabob 'n' Curry 261 Thayer St ☎401/273-8844. Above-average Indian meals on lively Thayer St; lunch specials with rice or nan bread are around $6, while dinners are around $10. Fun twists like "nanwiches" and "naninis" also on offer for $6–8.

Mediteraneo 134 Atwells Ave ☎401/331-7760. Excellent Italian restaurant that's the place to see and be seen, with prices to match. The nightclub upstairs is pumping on Fri & Sat.

Mill's Tavern 101 N Main St ☎401/272-3331. Contemporary American dining in a large upscale tavern with an open kitchen. An emphasis on wood-fired cooking begets scrumptious dishes like eight-hour braised beef short-ribs and buttermilk and rosemary marinated chicken. Dinner only.

Pot au Feu 44 Custom House St ☎401/273-8953. Expensive salon dining upstairs, moderately priced bistro downstairs, and a cozy, romantic atmosphere and excellent French dishes in both. Try the bouillabaisse, or the namesake dish resembling a soupier beef stew, with the meat and vegetables hugging the sides of the pot and the broth pooled in the center. Salon open Thurs–Sat for dinner, bistro open all week except for Sat lunch and Sun.

Z Bar and Grille 244 Wickenden St ☎401/831-1566. Boxing matches once took place in this spot, the former *Ringside Café*. Today it retains that boisterous environment while serving up decent salads, burgers, steaks, and the like, all made from organic ingredients.

Drinking and nightlife

Providence's **nightlife**, concentrated mainly in the city's commercial core off Kennedy Plaza, is largely student-generated, which means things can get a bit quiet during the vacations, though **Thayer Street** is always throbbing.

AS220 115 Empire St ☎401/831-9327. Unabashedly artsy café/bar hangout for locals and students, exhibiting eclectic works by Rhode Island artists in four galleries (Mon–Fri 11am–6pm; free) and hosting nightly performances featuring everything from mellow jazz to circus acts (cover $2–10).

Finnegan's Wake 397 Westminster St ☎401/751-0290. Despite the name, this spot is more sports bar (thirty TVs, including individual flatscreens in the booths) than Irish pub – though you can still get a pint of Guinness alongside your nachos or cheeseburger. DJs spin Top 40 and hip-hop Tues, Wed, Sat & Sun; cover $3 and up.

The Hi-Hat 3 Davol Square ☎401/453-6500. Trendy nightclub that draws a more mature crowd and features live music – jazz, blues, swing, rock, and R&B. Cover $5 and up most nights.

Lili Marlene's 422 Atwells Ave ☎401/751-4996. Small, dark, low-key bar tucked out of the way in Federal Hill with red-leather booths and a pool table; this locals' haunt draws its crowd by word of mouth. From 6pm to midnight the kitchen serves $3.50 hamburgers and $3 heaping baskets of fries.

Lupo's Heartbreak Hotel 79 Washington St ⓣ401/272-5876. This is *the* spot in town to see nationally recognized bands rock out. Tickets generally $15 or $20 in advance, $20 or $25 day of show.
Mirabar 35 Richmond St ⓣ401/331-6761. Lively gay men's bar and club attracting a somewhat mixed crowd with DJs six nights a week and karaoke on Mondays. Cover $2 on College Night Tuesdays.
Trinity Brewhouse 186 Fountain St ⓣ401/453-2337. Hang out here after a Providence Bruins (minor league hockey) or Friars (college basketball) game to quaff in either celebration or despair. Everything on tap is brewed in-house.

Performing arts and film

Providence has a rich and varied **performing arts** and **film** scene. The Cable Car Cinema, 204 S Main St (ⓣ401/272-3970), and the Avon Rep Cinema, 260 Thayer St (ⓣ401/421-3315), show good independent and art **films**, while the Tony Award-winning Trinity Rep, 201 Washington St (ⓣ401/351-4242, ⓦwww.trinityrep.com), one of America's foremost regional theaters, puts on innovative productions of contemporary and classic **plays** in two different theater spaces from September through June. The Providence Performing Arts Center, 220 Weybosset St (ⓣ401/421-2787, ⓦwww.ppacri.org), hosts **musicals** and other lavish productions in a grand old (recently restored) Art Deco movie house. On Gallery Night (April–Nov, third Thurs of the month, 5–9pm; ⓣ401/751-2628, ⓦwww.gallerynight.info), free Art Buses stop at most of the city's museums and galleries, where admission is also free for the evening. Finally, throughout the summer months the unusual event known as **WaterFire** (several times a month May–Oct; ⓦwww.waterfire.org) enthralls visitors and locals alike with over one hundred small bonfires set at sunset along the center of the Providence River starting at Waterplace Park, tended by gondoliers and accompanied by rousing music. Complete entertainment **listings** can be found in the free weekly *Providence Phoenix* and the *Providence Journal*'s Thursday edition.

Around Providence: Pawtucket, Woonsocket, and Bristol

Northwest of Providence, the **Blackstone River Valley** has been given special status by the Department of the Interior for its role in America's development as the world's leading industrial power. It's a gritty strip, really, with not much of a future, but clearly plenty of past, beginning with **PAWTUCKET**, just a few short miles north on I-95 from downtown Providence. Here you can start your explorations back through time at the **Slater Mill Historic Site**, 67 Roosevelt Ave (March & April Sat & Sun 11am–3pm, May–June & Oct Tues–Sat 10am–3pm, July–Sept Tues–Sat 10am–5pm; $9; ⓣ401/725-8638, ⓦwww.slatermill.org), where the **Old Slater Mill** was built to house the innovative machinery Samuel Slater developed (see box opposite). Today, the mill contains a copy of an original carding engine, a spinning frame and mule, and some very rare textile machines that date from 1838 up to the 1960s, all conspiring to illustrate the process of transforming raw cotton into yarn. Also included in the site is the 1810 **Wilkinson Mill**, where a nineteenth-century machine shop, complete with belt-driven machine tools, still operates, and the 1758 **Sylvanus Brown House**, an early skilled worker's home furnished as it was in the early 1800s. If you're inspired by the Americana, consider heading next to **McCoy Stadium**, also in Pawtucket, to enjoy America's favorite pastime, baseball. The **PawSox**, Boston's minor league affiliate, play here; games are held April–Sept and tickets are only $6 (ⓦwww.pawsox.com).

Another major manufacturing center, **WOONSOCKET**, is situated about fifteen miles northwest of Pawtucket, off Rte-146. Here, at 42 S Main St, you'll find the fascinating **Museum of Work and Culture** (Mon–Fri 9.30am–4pm,

Sat 10am–5pm, Sun 1–4pm; $6; ⓣ401/769-WORK), which traces the story of mill-workers who came from the farms of Québec in the early nineteenth century to work in the shoe and textile factories of New England. A self-guided journey through the workaday world of Woonsocket's residents and immigrant arrivals takes you from the shop floor of a textile mill to the porch of a three-story tenement house and lets you out on today's city streets.

In the other direction, fifteen miles southeast of Providence on Ferry Road (Rte-114), the town of **BRISTOL** holds, unexpectedly, the oldest and perhaps most enthusiastic **Fourth of July** celebration in the nation, a parade and fireworks spectacular that attracts hundreds of thousands of spectators. The town patriotism is highlighted by the red, white, and blue center stripe down Hope Street that remains year-round to mark the parade route. In addition to the growing group of restaurants and shops around town, the main site of interest here is the **Blithewold Mansion, Gardens & Arboretum**, 101 Ferry Rd (grounds open year-round daily 10am–5pm, mansion open mid-April to mid-Oct Wed–Sun 10am–4pm; $10 adults, children 16 and under free; $5 gardens only when house is closed; ⓣ401/253-2707, ⓦwww.blithewold.org). This is the one-time summer residence of Pennsylvania coal magnate Augustus Van Wickle and his wife Bessie, who filled the 45-room manor house with knick-knacks from her globetrotting adventures. The arboretum merits a wander too; seek out the hundred-foot-tall giant sequoia, an anomaly in these parts, for a good photo opportunity.

Newport

NEWPORT, nicknamed "America's First Resort," is probably best known for its summer "cottages" – more like huge palaces – which were built by

The birthplace of the Industrial Revolution

The Blackstone River, which cuts through the northeastern portion of Rhode Island, is not much of a landmark in and of itself – but it was largely along these riverbanks that the seeds of the Industrial Revolution began to grow in America. Dubbed the **Blackstone River National Heritage Corridor**, and stretching from Providence to Worcester, MA, it encompasses two dozen of the original manufacturing communities where thousands of Americans and immigrants came to work and live, at least until the valley's demise.

The area was a desolate wilderness when its first white settler, **Reverend William Blackstone**, arrived here in 1635 after fleeing the intolerant Puritan regime in Boston. More settlers came, of whom one Joseph Jencks, Jr, a blacksmith by trade, realized that the vast forests of **Pawtucket** would provide a virtually inexhaustible supply of timber to fire a forge. His new smithy boomed, and soon other blacksmiths began to settle here, setting the stage for future development.

The industrial expansion received a huge boost in 1790, when **Samuel Slater**, a manufacturer's apprentice originally hailing from Derbyshire, England – with the help of entrepreneur Moses Brown, of the wealthy Providence family – used new technology surreptitiously imported from his native land to produce cotton yarn. The resultant success fueled another century of high prosperity, but, as you'll find touring the preserved mills, much of the machinery has not been spinning for some time, most companies having relocated to the South, where overheads and labor were much cheaper.

For an unusual perspective of the Blackstone River Valley's history and environment, a 45-minute narrated **riverboat tour** run by the Blackstone Valley Tourism Council departs from various locations on Sundays in June through October ($7; ⓣ401/724-2200 or 1-800/454-BVTC, ⓦwww.rivertourblackstone.com).

nineteenth-century industrial magnates and business tycoons each trying to outdo one another. These monuments to opulence and greed, like **Rosecliff** and **Beechwood** on Bellevue Avenue, give a glimpse into the ostentatious lives behind such names as the **Astors** and **Vanderbilts**. Even before these families arrived on the scene, though, Newport had already established itself as a major port, rivaling New York and Boston in size and importance.

Today the city is unashamedly geared to the tourist, as a stroll around the somewhat garish harbor area will testify. Nonetheless, the rough old port still manages to linger, with beer and R&B clubs as evident as cocktails and cruises, making this an essential urban stop, especially during the **summer festival season**. Additionally, Newport is a good base for exploring the more peaceful neighboring town of **Portsmouth** and, across the bay, the appealing villages of **Tiverton Four Corners** and **Little Compton**, full of stone-walled country lanes, rocky shorelines, and idyllic beaches.

Some history

First settled in 1639 by refugees from neighboring Massachusetts seeking **religious freedom**, the area was soon recognized for its excellent **trade location** and quickly developed into a bustling seaport. Although the city became renowned for its liberal approach in matters of religion, which brought an influx of Jews, Quakers, and Baptists, such charity did not extend to the **slave trade**; in the eighteenth century, the local fleet was heavily involved in trading African slaves for West Indian sugar and molasses, and the city was a haven for privateers, often barely distinguishable from pirates.

The prosperity that international trade had brought suffered a severe setback when British and Hessian troops occupied Newport in 1776, blockading the harbor and forcing residents to use the city's timber wharves as firewood during the brutally cold winter. During the next three years, many locals fled, buildings were either destroyed or left to decay, and the city floundered. By the end of the war, the city was so impoverished that townsfolk wanting to expand their properties could not even afford to tear down their own homes, let alone rebuild. This is largely the reason for the wealth of fine **Colonial buildings** still seen today.

In the 1850s, the town became fashionable again as a resort for wealthy Southern merchants, and very soon nouveau riche industrialists such as the Astors, Belmonts, and Vanderbilts were building the mansions along the coastline for which the city has become known. Despite an end to the decadence, the city remained a major naval town, home to the **United States Naval War College**, and is a prime playpen for the yachting set. From 1930 until 1983 the America's Cup Race was held off Newport, and every summer the harbor still becomes lined with majestic sailboats, pleasure boats, and touring vessels.

Arrival, information, and getting around

Newport and Portsmouth are both located on **Aquidneck**, also known formally as Rhode Island, after which the state was named. The island is connected to the mainland from I-95 and the west by Rte-138, which crosses the impressive Newport Bridge ($2 toll). The nearest **Amtrak** station is on Rte-138 at Kingston, some nineteen miles away; you can pick up RIPTA buses (Ⓣ401/781-9400) here, which will take you the rest of the way. The nicest way to arrive, though, is the Providence–Newport **ferry**, which runs daily during the summer from Point Street Landing to Perrotti Park (1hr; $8 each way; Ⓣ401/453-6800, Ⓦwww.nefastferry.com).

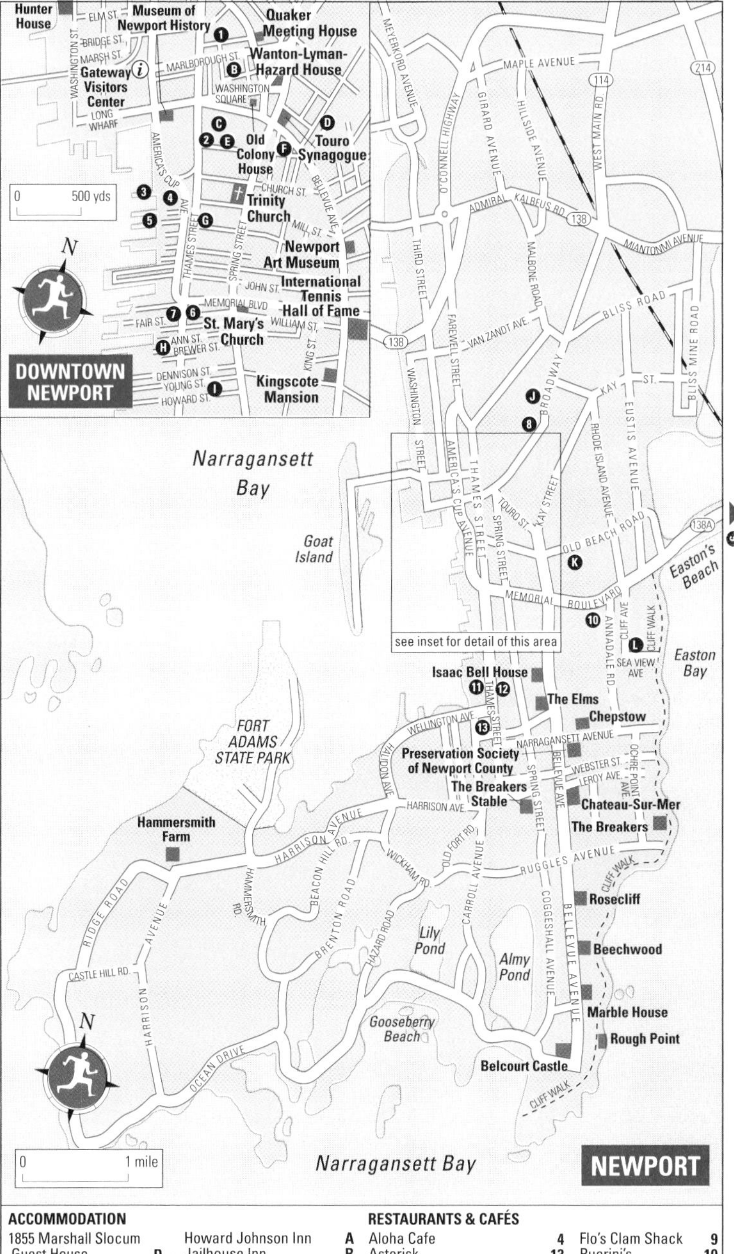

ACCOMMODATION

1855 Marshall Slocum Guest House	D	Howard Johnson Inn	A
Admiral Fitzroy Inn	H	Jailhouse Inn	B
The Almondy	G	Melville House	C
The Clarkeston	E	The Old Beach Inn	K
Cliffside Inn	L	Hotel Viking	F
Commodore Perry Inn	J	William Gyles Guesthouse	I

RESTAURANTS & CAFÉS

Aloha Cafe	4	Flo's Clam Shack	9
Asterisk	13	Puerini's	10
The Black Pearl	3	The Red Parrot	6
Brick Alley Pub & Restaurant	2	Salvation Café	8
Café Zelda	12	Scales & Shells	11
Christie's	7	Smokehouse Café	5
Firehouse Pizza	13	White Horse Tavern	1

Newport itself, spanning only ten miles, is eminently walkable. **Thames** (pronounced *Thaymz*) **Street** is the main drag; its northern end is separated from the shops and restaurants of the harbor district by America's Cup Avenue, a wide, ugly road that's often choked with traffic. It's here, at no. 23, that you will find the **Gateway Visitor Center**, a vast, glitzy operation with plenty of maps, brochures, and advice to keep you busy (daily 9am–5pm; ⓣ401/845-9123 or 1-800/976-5122, ⓦwww.gonewport.com). Parking in the adjacent parking lot is free for the first half-hour with validation.

The Gateway Center is also the terminal for **Bonanza** (ⓣ401/846-1820 or 1-888/751-8800) and **RIPTA** buses, which connect downtown, the mansions, and the beaches for $1.50 a ride; on the summer trolleys, $6 a person ($18 for a group of four) will get you an all-day ticket that allows you to hop on and off at will. Also located here are Viking Tours, whose bus, trolley, and harbor excursions can be combined with admission to one or more mansions ($12–47; ⓣ401/847-6921, ⓦwww.vikingtoursnewport.com). Rental **bikes** are a good way to get around, especially if you're heading to one of the beaches; it's $5 per hour ($25/day, $75/week) from Ten Speed Spokes, 18 Elm St (ⓣ401/847-5609).

The Newport Historical Society, 82 Touro St (Tues–Fri 9.30am–4.30pm, Sat 9.30am–noon; ⓣ401/846-0813, ⓦwww.newporthistorical.org), organizes **walking tours** through Colonial Newport (summer Thurs, Fri & Sat 10am; $7). Other walking tours of the historic district are offered by **Newport on Foot** (April–Oct, schedule varies, call for details; $10, kids under 12 free; ⓣ401/846-5391); they leave from the Gateway Center and cover a little more than a mile in about an hour and a half. Easily the best and most relaxing way of getting a good overview of the mansions and town is on a **boat tour**: you can take the beautiful 72-foot schooner *Madeleine*, which departs four times a day in the summer from Bannister's Wharf for a ninety-minute tour ($25), or the motor yacht *Rum Runner* for a 75-minute tour ($17), both of which are organized by Classic Cruises of Newport (ⓣ401/847-0298).

Accommodation

Newport has plenty of reasonably priced **guesthouses**, though it's always a good idea to **book ahead**, especially on summer weekends when prices can skyrocket. Due in part to the abundance of Victorian mansions, the most common form of accommodation here is the **B&B**. Large rooms – often with fireplaces and ocean views – can be expected, though prices can be steep. To find someplace more stripped down and inexpensive, contact Newport Reservations (ⓣ401/842-0102 or 1-800/842-0102), which can find rooms from around $125 in season, or Bed & Breakfast Newport (ⓣ401/846-5408 or 1-800/800-8765, ⓦwww.bbnewport.com), which specializes in smaller B&Bs you might otherwise find difficult to locate. Note that smaller places are sometimes reluctant to accommodate young children, and that Saturday night-only stays are often not allowed, especially in high season – be sure to call ahead and confirm individual policies.

1855 Marshall Slocum Guest House 29 Kay St ⓣ401/841-5120 or 1-800/372-5120, ⓦwww.marshallslocuminn.com. An unpretentious B&B, well run by a friendly couple and just a short walk from Bellevue Ave. Each of the five rooms is unique, and yours might feature a mahogany sleigh bed, a wood-burning stove, or a Jacuzzi tub. A backyard garden, gourmet breakfasts, and evening baked goods are extra treats. ❼

Admiral Fitzroy Inn 398 Thames St ⓣ401/848-8000 or 1-866/848-8780, ⓦwww.admiralfitzroy.com. Cheerfully decorated B&B in the heart of town, with seventeen hand-stenciled rooms and a roof deck overlooking the harbor. ❼

The Almondy 25 Pelham St ⓣ401/848-7202 or 1-800/478-6155, ⓦwww.almondyinn.com. Across from Bannister's Wharf, most rooms at this 1890s B&B have views of the harbor. Antique furniture and Jacuzzi baths in spacious rooms, with gourmet breakfasts and afternoon tea to boot. ❽

The Clarkeston 28 Clarke St ⓣ401/849-7397 or 1-800/524-1386, ⓦwww.innsofnewport.com. Sumptuous circa-1705 colonial inn with working fireplaces, Jacuzzi tubs, and canopy and feather beds. ❼

Cliffside Inn 2 Seaview Ave ⓣ401/847-1811 or 1-800/845-1811, ⓦwww.cliffsideinn.com. Gorgeous 1880 Victorian manor house, once the summer home of eccentric local artist Beatrice Turner and today decorated with more than one hundred of her works. Guests are pampered here: all rooms have fireplaces (some have two or three) and most have whirlpool baths. Twice-daily maid service, sumptuous full breakfast, and spectacular afternoon tea are included. ❾

Commodore Perry Inn 8 Equality Park West ⓣ401/846-5603, ⓦwww.eatinri.com/perrybb. Two clean and comfortable rooms in a quiet area just a half-mile from downtown. Continental breakfast included unless you request not, in which case rates are slightly reduced. ❻

Hotel Viking 1 Bellevue Ave ⓣ401/847-3300, ⓦwww.hotelviking.com. A Newport institution, the 222-room *Hotel Viking* was built in 1926 to host guests of the wealthy Bellevue homeowners; it still lures jet-setters with Egyptian cotton duvets, antique furnishings, and coddling at Spa Terre. ❼

Jailhouse Inn 13 Marlborough St ⓣ401/847-4638 or 1-800/427-9444. Spacious modern rooms with jailhouse trimmings in this restored 1772 clink, right in the center of town. ❻

Melville House 39 Clarke St ⓣ401/847-0640 or 1-800/711-7184, ⓦwww.melvillehouse.com. Colonial B&B in a tranquil location two blocks from the harbor run. The seven rooms are small, but pleasant; private and shared baths are available. ❻

The Old Beach Inn 19 Old Beach Rd ⓣ401/849-3479 or 1-888/303-5033, ⓦwww.oldbeachinn.com. A handsome seven-room B&B, each decorated in a different floral theme; all with private bath and a/c, some with fireplaces and color TV. Generous continental breakfasts and private parking. ❻

William Gyles Guesthouse 16 Howard St ⓣ401/369-0243, ⓦwww.newporthostel.com. Merrilee Zellner started Newport's only hostel with the explicit aim of opening the town to budget backpackers, who would otherwise be put off by the high prices. Her enthusiasm, passion for travel, and talent at creating a comfortable, welcoming environment make you wish every town had a Merrilee. In summer weekends $59/night, weekdays $35, in winter $16/night and up.

The Town

Newport's main attractions are certainly its **mansions**, but there is nothing to be gained by touring them all. Although the ever-growing profusion of souvenir shops is somewhat off-putting, strolling around the predominantly Colonial **downtown** is a nice way to spend an afternoon. Otherwise, if you don't fancy beautiful-people-spotting on the harbor, you'll do better following the crowds to one of Newport's fine **beaches**.

The mansions

When horrified sociologist Thorstein Veblen visited Newport at the turn of the twentieth century and coined the phrase "conspicuous consumption," he was criticizing the desperate need felt by some of the entrepreneurial millionaires of the time to define their fragile identities by flaunting their newly acquired wealth. More than just a summer resort, Newport became an arena in which families competed, with increasing mania, to outdo each other – though the "season" of wild and decadent parties lasted only a few weeks, and many of the multi-million-dollar homes, described as "white elephants" by author Henry James, remained empty for months, even years, at a time. It's difficult to take in the sheer wealth involved by merely gawking at the impressive facades, but after being herded in and rushed through more than a couple of these famous mansions, the opulence rapidly begins to pall.

To get a peek at the mansions on the cheap, you can take the invigorating **Cliff Walk**, which begins on Memorial Boulevard where it meets First (Easton) Beach. This three-and-a-half-mile oceanside path alternates from pretty sections meandering among jasmine and wild roses to concrete underpasses and dangerous stretches across perilous rocks.

Marble House, Kingscote, and The Breakers

The **Preservation Society of Newport County**, 424 Bellevue Ave (Ⓣ401/847-1000, Ⓦwww.newportmansions.org), manages the bulk of the mansions open for public viewing. Their properties, all of which are on or near Bellevue Avenue, are open daily in July and August from 9 or 10am until 5pm, while during the rest of the year the schedule varies. **Admission** to The Breakers is $15, Hunter House $25, and all others $10. A combination ticket to five Society mansions is $31, with significant discounts for children. Note that some house tours are self-guided, often with accompanying headsets, while others are docent-led.

Southernmost of the Preservation Society holdings is **Marble House**, the most over-the-top example of Gilded Age excess, with a golden ballroom and a Chinese teahouse in the grounds; both this and nearby **Rosecliff**, with its colorful rose garden and heart-shaped staircase, were used as sets during the filming of *The Great Gatsby*. **Kingscote**, at the northern end of the avenue, is a quirky Gothic Revival cottage, built in 1841 and expanded in 1876 by the firm of McKim, Mead & White; its lovely interior features mahogany paneling and a Tiffany glass wall in the dining room.

The biggest and best of the lot, however, is Cornelius Vanderbilt's four-story **The Breakers**, on Ochre Point Avenue, an extravagant Italian Renaissance palace built for the president and chairman of the New York Central Railroad, Cornelius Vanderbilt II, by renowned architect Richard Morris Hunt. Located on a thirteen-acre oceanfront estate – the waves crashing on the rocks below lend the house its name – this imposing "cottage," completed in 1895, includes a 45-foot-high central Great Hall and seventy additional rooms, many of which were constructed overseas by European craftsmen and then shipped to Newport.

The Society has five other homes open for public viewing, from **Chateau-Sur-Mer**, the first of the truly lavish mansions, and the Italian country house **Chepstow**, on Narragansett Avenue, to the ornate French *maison* **The Elms** and the simpler **Hunter** and **Isaac Bell houses**. Unless you're a mansion nut, though, none of these is really essential viewing.

Beechwood

Privately owned, the Astors' **Beechwood**, 580 Bellevue Ave (Feb to mid-May Fri–Sun 10am–4pm, mid-May to Dec daily 10am–4pm, closed Jan; $15; Ⓣ401/846-3772, Ⓦwww.astors-beechwood.com), is an entertaining antidote to the drier historical drills given on other tours. Inside the stucco house, costumed actors welcome visitors as houseguests who have arrived for a party to be given by Mrs Caroline Astor, the self-proclaimed queen of American society, known for her attempts to stave off the advances of "new money" families into society's inner circles. Anecdotes, snarky asides, and a constant stream of activity make it all great fun. On summer Thursdays you can join an evening interactive Murder Mystery Tour ($25; reservations recommended) or on Tuesdays spend the night twirling in the ballroom on the Speakeasy Tour, with hors d'oeuvres and a cash bar ($30).

Belcourt Castle, Rough Point, and Hammersmith Farm

Unusual in that it is still inhabited by its owners, **Belcourt Castle**, 657 Bellevue Ave (July–Aug Wed–Mon noon–5pm, other months days and times vary; $10; Ⓣ401/846-0669, Ⓦwww.belcourtcastle.com), was built to echo owner Oliver

Belmont's love for equines and armor; his horses, in fact, slept in white linen sheets in a specially designed stable – yet another example of Newport excess. Evening candlelight or ghost tours are also available (call for times; $15).

At the southernmost end of Bellevue Avenue stands **Rough Point** (mid-April to mid-May Thurs–Sat 10am–1.45pm, mid-May to Oct Tues–Sat 9am–3.45pm; $25; ⓣ401/845-9130, ⓦwww.newportrestoration.org), the former home of Doris Duke, the only child of James B. Duke, tobacco magnate and benefactor of Duke University. Of particular note are the mansion's textiles (including Flemish tapestries dating to 1510), ornate eighteenth-century French furniture, and a fine collection of brilliant blue Ming vases. Like The Breakers, it's just steps away from the sea cliff, leading to a rock-strewn beach and an empty horizon. In an effort to preserve the property there is no parking available; visitors must reserve and take a shuttle van from the Visitor Center (see p.304).

Where the Cliff Walk ends, Ocean Drive continues on from Bellevue, eventually running past the shingle-sided **Hammersmith Farm**, John and Jackie Kennedy's 28-room summer home. Though not open to the public, Camelot-junkies may still want a glimpse at the outside: the Kennedys' wedding reception was held here in 1953, and the couple were such frequent visitors that it came to be known as the "summer White House."

Downtown Newport

Colonial Newport's political and commercial center, **Washington Square**, starts just southeast of the Gateway Center, where Thames Street meets the **Brick Market**. The 1762 market, off **Long Wharf** (the most important of Newport's colonial wharves), has been reconstructed to include a mixture of galleries and pricey souvenir shops. Among them, the **Museum of Newport History** (Mon & Wed–Sat 10am–5pm, Sun 1–5pm; free; ⓣ401/841-8770, ⓦwww.newporthistorical.org) gives a good overview of Newport's past through interactive exhibits, photographs, and pithy oral histories. Across the square stands the **Old Colony House**, one of Rhode Island's few pre-Revolutionary brick buildings and the state's seat of government from 1739 to 1900. It's one of the oldest capitol buildings in the US, and it was here, in May of 1776, that Rhode Island became the first state to declare its independence from Britain.

Just up from Washington Square, at 17 Broadway, the **Wanton-Lyman-Hazard House** (mid-June to early Sept Thurs–Sun 1–5pm; $3) appears uncomfortably hemmed in by the surrounding commercial buildings, and for good reason: it's one of the oldest dwellings in Newport, built sometime between 1650 and 1700. The central chimney and pitched roof are typical of the early settlers' homes, while inside, the surviving original plasterwork is made from ground shells and molasses. To the north, the **Easton's Point** district, between Washington Square and Spring Street, is lined with the eighteenth-century homes of ship captains. Of these, the carefully restored 1748 **Hunter House**, 54 Washington St (June 25 to Sept 25 daily 10am–5pm; $25), is the only one open to the public.

The oldest religious building in town is the 1699 **Quaker Friends Meeting House**, at the corner of Farewell and Marlborough streets (free tours by appointment; ⓣ401/846-0813), restored to its nineteenth-century state and completely free of adornment. The Quakers, like other religious sects, received a warm welcome in Rhode Island; indeed, the state's penchant for religious tolerance is echoed by the presence of the elegant **Touro Synagogue**, at 85 Touro St, the oldest house of Jewish worship in America. Built in 1763 and modeled on Sephardic Jewish temples in Portugal and Holland, the synagogue displays a copy of a letter to the Newport Jewish community written by George Washington himself, advocating religious freedom, and has just undergone extensive restorations (call for hours; free; ⓣ401/847-4794, ⓦwww.tourosynagogue.org).

Rhode Island's tolerance even extended to the much-despised Anglicans, who were the main reason for the Puritan exodus from England. Their 1726 **Trinity Church** on Queen Anne Square (mid-June to July 4 Mon–Fri 10am–4pm, July 4 to early Sept daily 10am–4pm, rest of year daily 10am–1pm; $2 donation; ⓣ401/846-0660) was based on the Old North Church in Boston and the designs of Sir Christopher Wren, with a bleach-white 150-foot tower which acts as a beacon for ships as well as worshipers. Inside, the only triple-decked, free-standing pulpit left in America stands in its original position in front of the altar, evidence of the emphasis at that time on preaching rather than Communion. The Roman Catholic **St Mary's Church**, Spring Street and Memorial Boulevard (Mon–Fri 7–11am; free; ⓣ401/847-0475), completed in 1852, witnessed the union of Jacqueline Bouvier and John Kennedy on September 12, 1953.

△Touro Synagogue

Bellevue Avenue, the street of Newport's mansions and green-awninged shops, is also home to two noteworthy museums. The **Newport Art Museum**, at no. 76 (late May to mid-Oct Mon–Sat 10am–5pm, Sun noon–5pm; rest of year Tues–Sat 10am–4pm, Sun noon–4pm; $6; ⓣ401/848-8200, ⓦwww.newportartmuseum.com), exhibits New England art from the last two centuries in the 1864 mock-medieval Griswold House. The grand **Newport Casino**, at no. 194, was an early country club which held the nation's first tennis championships in 1881 – the tournament now known as the US Open. The casino currently houses the **International Tennis Hall of Fame** (daily 9.30am–5pm; $8; ⓣ401/849-3990 or 1-800/457-1144, ⓦwww.tennisfame.com), and still keeps its grass courts open to the public for play (mid-May to Sept; $60 per hour per person; indoor and clay outdoor courts also available; ⓣ401/846.0642). Exhibits at the museum include the original patent for the game granted by Queen Victoria in 1874, as well as displays on tennis fashion, tennis-themed artifacts, a portrait of Chris Evert by Andy Warhol, and a theater where you can watch classic matches.

The beaches

The indubitable attraction of Newport's shoreline, with its rocky coves and gently sloping sandy beaches, is slightly marred by the fact that several stretches are strictly private; still, some of the best strands remain within the public domain. The calm waters of **Gooseberry Beach**, nestled among the rocks in an attractive inlet off Ocean Avenue, appeals to families but charges a high parking fee (weekdays $10, Fri $15, weekends $20); biking here is free. The town beach, also known as **First** or **Easton's Beach**, is a wide stretch at the east end of Memorial Boulevard that gets very busy; parking here is $8 ($10–15 on weekends). Amenities are plentiful, including outdoor showers, equipment rental, picnic tables, and volleyball nets, along with various nearby restaurants and shops.

The most attractive of all the Aquidneck Island beaches is farther east in neighboring Middletown: pleasant **Second (Sachuest) Beach**, with a mile and a half of soft gray sand and good surf (weekdays $10, weekends $15). You can combine a few hours on the beach with a visit to the nearby **Norman Bird Sanctuary**, 583 Third Beach Rd (daily 9am–5pm; $4; ⓣ401/846-2577, ⓦwww.normanbirdsanctuary.org), home to nearly ten miles of trails and a nature museum. A half mile farther on, peaceful **Third Beach** is on the inner side of Narragansett Bay, making the calmer waters and tidal pools a good bet for children (same prices as Second Beach).

Eating

Many of Newport's **restaurants** are geared to tourists and overpriced, but with a little hunting you'll find there are some notable exceptions. In general, the seafood here is worth the blowout if you can handle the cost.

Aloha Cafe 18 Market Square ⓣ401/846-7038. Basic sandwiches (like grilled cheese), salads, and baked goods eaten at a counter inside the Seamen's Institute, a refuge for mariners; inexpensive and in the thick of things but off the beaten tourist track. Daily 7.30am–2.30pm.

Asterisk 599 Thames St ⓣ401/841-8833. Happening eatery in a former garage with abstract paintings on the walls. Entrees ($21–36) are eclectic, with Asian flourishes and an emphasis on seafood. Live jazz Sundays 7–11pm. Dinner daily.

The Black Pearl Bannister's Wharf ⓣ401/846-5264. This Newport institution is famed for its chunky clam chowder and harborside location. An outside patio overlooking Bowen's Wharf is hopping in the summer; inside, opt for more formal dining (*escargots bourguignon*) in the Commodore Room or less expensive fare (*escargots* with garlic butter) in the tavern.

Brick Alley Pub & Restaurant 140 Thames St ⓣ401/849-6334. Attracts a good mix of locals and tourists for lunch, dinner, and cocktails; Sunday brunch is especially popular. The cheap to moderately priced offerings are extensive but fairly straightforward: burgers, some seafood options, and the like, along with a soup and salad bar.

Café Zelda 528 Thames St ⓣ401/849-4002. This attractive corner restaurant with a friendly face features dressed-up standards like nori-wrapped tuna and grilled lamb chops with minted white bean salad. Entrees $20–28. Dinner daily year-round, lunch Fri–Sun also in summer.

Christie's 351 Thames St ⓣ401/847-5400. Very popular – and expensive – waterfront seafood restaurant, established in 1945. Try their scrumptious house specialty, Narragansett seafood pie, or one of the awesome lobsters. Live music either on the dock or in the lounge regularly year-round.

Firehouse Pizza 595 Thames St ⓣ401/846-1199. Twelve-inch pan pizzas (thin crust on request if things aren't too busy) starting at $6.50, as well as subs and salads, eaten at kooky hand-painted booths in an old firehouse. Open until 2am on summer weekends.

Flo's Clam Shack 4 Wave Ave ⓣ401/847-8141. If you're on a budget but don't want to miss out on the local seafood, head to this casual joint across from First Beach. It may not be gourmet, but at $4.25 for a cup of clam chowder, three clam cakes, and a beer, you can't go wrong. Closed Jan & Feb.

Puerini's 24 Memorial Blvd W ⓣ401/847-5506. Classic Italian fare at reasonable prices make this a firm favorite with locals and visitors alike. Dinner daily; closed winter Mondays and the month of January.

The Red Parrot 348 Thames St ⓣ401/847-3800. A 22-page menu offering seafood, chicken, and steaks with a Caribbean flare. The specialty frozen and hot drinks like the "butterscotch belly warmer," hot chocolate with butterscotch schnapps and chocolate liqueur, are a must.

Salvation Café 140 Broadway ⓣ401/847-2620. This fun, funky spot off the main drag is something different from the touristy harbor restaurants, serving unique dishes with an Asian focus, like miso steak frites or lo-mein noodles with sesame-seared tofu, at reasonable prices. Dinner daily.

Scales & Shells 527 Thames St ⓣ401/846-FISH. Casual "only fish" restaurant with high-quality seafare and a sense of humor. Dinner daily.

Smokehouse Café America's Cup Ave ⓣ401/848-9800. An oddity in Newport's world of seafood, the *Smokehouse* has great barbecue for under $20 and a lively crowd. Open late May to late Oct Mon–Sat lunch & dinner.

White Horse Tavern Marlborough and Farewell sts ⓣ401/849-3600. First opened in 1687, this very atmospheric restaurant serves up hearty American fare like beef tenderloin, New England lobster stew, and baked Atlantic salmon. Expensive, but more affordable at lunchtime. Dinner daily, lunch Wed–Sun.

Nightlife and entertainment

Newport has a reputation for being a lively party town, with fairly unrefined **nightlife**, which irks many of its residents – to the point that the town council has tried to tone things down through various regulations and restrictions. Most, but by no means all, of the noisiest **bars** and **clubs** are found in the waterfront area.

Atlantic Beach Club 55 Purgatory Rd ⓣ401/847-2750. A relaxed beach bar with volleyball nets and live entertainment throughout the summer.

The Boom-Boom Room downstairs at the *Clarke Cooke House*, Bannister's Wharf ⓣ401/849-2900. One of the most popular discos in town, the *Boom-Boom Room* attracts a fairly mixed crowd with standards, oldies, and Top-40. Thurs–Sun in summer (cover $5–10), Fri & Sat in winter (no cover).

Newport Blues Café 286 Thames St ⓣ401/841-5510. Live blues and jazz from 9.45pm in an old bank building overlooking the harbor. Summer daily, fall & spring Thurs–Sat, closed Jan to mid-March. Cover some nights up to $10.

One Pelham East Thames and Pelham sts ⓣ401/847-9460. Long-established and still popular venue that's hosted live bands for over twenty years. Open daily till 1am. Thurs–Sat cover $5–10, other nights no cover.

Pop 162 Broadway ⓣ401/846-8456. Trendy and urban, *Pop* feels more New York and less Newport. A DJ spins Wed, Fri & Sat; Tues is karaoke. The kitchen (open till midnight) serves excellent tapas-style dishes.

The Rhino Bar & Grille 337 Thames St ⓣ401/846-0707. Original live bands (in the bar) and the best area DJs (playing dance, hip-hop, and techno in the Mamba Room) keep this safari-themed place hopping. Fri & Sat cover $5–10.

The Wharf Pub & Restaurant 37 Bowen's Wharf ⓣ401/846-9233. The least expensive spot in the lively Bowen's Wharf area, serving more than fifty microbrews (no hard liquor). Live bands on summer weekends; no cover.

Newport's music festivals

Newport is nearly world-famous for the plethora of prominent annual music festivals that take place here in the summer months, the two most popular of which are the **Newport Folk Festival** (Ⓦwww.newportfolk.com), in late July or early August, followed by the **JVC Jazz Festival** (Ⓦwww.festivalproductions.net), in the middle of August. Both feature big-name performers in their respective fields; call Ⓣ401/847-3700 for details. Over Labor Day weekend in early September, the **Waterfront Irish Festival** is held at the Newport Yachting Center (Ⓣ401/846-1600, Ⓦwww.newportfestivals.com); it includes several music stages and exhibits of Irish and Celtic literature, art, and step-dancing. The lesser-known two-week **Newport Music Festival** (Ⓣ401/846-1133, Ⓦwww.newportmusic.org) emphasizes classical music and takes place during July in a number of Newport's mansions. The program features world-class artists performing everything from chamber and orchestral music to sea shanties.

Around Newport

There are some worthwhile detours near Newport, including the town of **Portsmouth**, also on Aquidneck Island, and a few communities on the **Sakonnet Peninsula**, a remote area that was once part of Massachusetts and bears little of the development characteristic of other coastal sections of the state. There is virtually no public transport on Sakonnet; to get here from Newport you'll need to drive north to Rte-24 and connect to Rte-77, which runs south the length of the peninsula.

Portsmouth

Founded in 1638 by Anne Hutchinson, another refugee from Massachusetts, **PORTSMOUTH**, about ten miles north of Newport on Rte-114, was until recently a small rural community; now it's little more than a bedroom suburb of Newport. Based in the Christian Union Church at 870 E Main Rd, the **Portsmouth Historical Society** (late May to mid-Oct Sun 2–4pm; free; Ⓣ401/683-9178) comprises several interesting buildings, including what may be the oldest one-room schoolhouse in the country, completed in 1725, as well as the original Portsmouth Town Hall and the church itself, once home to a nineteenth-century religious sect with connections to the abolitionist movement. Displays change yearly and feature local artifacts like photographs and attendance records from early Portsmouth school days. For something a little different, the Preservation Society of Newport administers the **Green Animals Topiary Garden**, on Cory's Lane off Rte-114 (mid-April to mid-Nov daily 9am–5pm; $10; Ⓣ401/847-1000, Ⓦwww.newportmansions.org), which has more than eighty sculpted trees and animal-shaped shrubs set on an idyllic lawn that slopes down to Narragansett Bay. There are espaliered fruit trees, a gourd arbor, and formal flower beds; also on the property is a white clapboard summer house that houses an antique toy exhibit.

Those who choose to **stay** in Portsmouth – not a bad option, as it's little more than a twenty-minute drive from downtown Newport – typically do so at the adequate *Founder's Brook Motel*, 314 Boyd Lane (Ⓣ401/683-1244 or 1-800/334-8765, Ⓦwww.foundersbrookmotelandsuites.com; ❺), where most units include kitchenettes and Jacuzzis. **Eating** revolves around Portsmouth's star contender, the *Sea Fare Inn*, 3352 E Main Rd, (Ⓣ401/683-0577), an

△Green Animals Topiary Garden

excellent place that's consistently voted one of the top ten seafood restaurants in the US.

The Sakonnet Peninsula: Tiverton and Little Compton

The rather nondescript and tatty northern section of **TIVERTON** that you immediately encounter soon after reaching the Sakonnet Peninsula is redeemed only by some delightful views of the **Sakonnet River**, which parallels Rte-77 the length of the peninsula. Heading south, the first spot of interest is **Fort Barton**, on Highland Street, an original redoubt built during the American Revolution and named after Colonel William Barton, who captured Newport's British commander during the war. A climb of the observation tower affords a spectacular view of neighboring Aquidneck Island. Two miles south, Seapowet Avenue leads to the **Ruecker Wildlife Refuge**, fifty acres of shallow marshes and upland woodlots donated to the Rhode Island Audubon Society in 1965. Trails are well marked, and all kinds of birdlife can be seen, including ospreys, egrets, catbirds, and cardinals (daily dawn to dusk; free; ⓣ401/624-2759).

Farther south, **Tiverton Four Corners** is a motley collection of specialty stores, art galleries, and historic homes, several of which date from the eighteenth century, among them the 1730 gambrel-roofed **Chase Cory House**, 3980 Main Rd (June–Sept Sun 2–4.30pm; free; ⓣ401/625-5174 624-2096). Now the base for the Tiverton Historical Society, the house retains many features indigenous to colonial village farms, such as an eight-foot-tall kitchen fireplace with beaded chimney. A mile south of Four Corners, **Fogland Road**, a pretty country lane bordered by lush hedges and rugged stone walls, traverses gentle farmland to reach **Fogland Beach** (parking $5 weekdays, $10 weekends), Tiverton's shingly but safe town beach that skirts the southern edge of a comma-shaped peninsula jutting out into the Sakonnet River. There are splendid views down the river, with the Sakonnet Lighthouse and the various elephantine rocks that surround it looming in the distance.

Little Compton

The 4500 year-round residents of tiny but wealthy **LITTLE COMPTON**, ten miles from Tiverton, owe their place on the map to a bird – the Rhode Island Red chicken was developed here for its shape, color, and egg production, and even has a small granite monument honoring it in the Adamsville section of town. Fowl history notwithstanding, residents are ultra-protective of their environment, as evidenced by car stickers that bluntly demand "Keep Little Compton Little," and the conspicuous absence of places to stay. Rumor has it that its classic village center, **Little Compton Commons** on Meetinghouse Lane, was the favored location for the film *The Witches of Eastwick* (eventually shot in Cohasset, MA), but the residents turned down the opportunity for fear it would put the town rather too firmly on the tourist trail.

Today the square is dominated by the lofty, brilliant-white spire of the 1832 **Congregational Church**, with an adjacent burial ground that predates the building by 150 years. It contains the grave of one Benjamin Church, an Indian-fighter who took part in the execution of King Philip back in the 1600s. Opposite the church, the meandering maze of rooms that is **Wilbur's Store**, established more than two hundred years ago, is Little Compton's own Lilliputian department store, selling everything from food to hardware. Perhaps the biggest draw to these parts, though, is the **Sakonnet Vineyards**, 162 W Main Rd (daily: late May to Sept 10am–6pm, Oct to late May 11am–5pm; ⓣ1-800/91-WINES, ⓦwww.sakonnetwine.com), where you can take a free tour or sample a half-dozen wines for just $5. Continuing along W Main, the **Wilbor House**, no. 548 (June–Sept Thurs–Sun 1–5pm; Sept to mid-Oct Sat & Sun 1–5pm; $5; ⓣ401/635-4035), spans the four centuries that eight generations of the Wilbor family lived here, and includes excellent examples of Colonial, Georgian, and Victorian furnishings.

Main Road struggles south toward the Atlantic to **Sakonnet Point**, where a broad, sweeping vista of an often angry seascape is framed on one side by a newly restored **lighthouse** and on the other by the rocky crags and promontories of Newport and Middletown. In between, the graceful mock English Gothic tower of St George's School punctuates the horizon. With all the watercraft around, it's far too dangerous to swim at the nearby harbor; instead, park at **South Shore Beach**, at the end of South Shore Road (weekdays $7, weekends $12), and walk on to pretty **Goosewing Beach**, which is sandier and quieter than South Shore.

Tiverton and Little Compton practicalities

Should you desire a break on your way to or from Newport, it is possible to **spend the night** hereabouts with a little advance planning. In Little Compton there's the *Stone House Club*, 122 Sakonnet Point Rd (ⓣ401/635-2222; ❺), a rugged three-story granite building overlooking the Atlantic. Though technically a private club, you can book a room here if you pay the $25 membership fee; there's also a cellar bar and a decent restaurant (open to the public) serving basic American entrees like crispy roast duck. The lovely B&B *Arrowhead Farm*, in Tiverton at 630 Punkateest Nest Rd (ⓣ401/624-3630, ⓦwww.arrowhead-farm.info; ❻), is another good option, with three cozy rooms and shared bath.

Places to eat are few and far between as well. The Provender, 3883 Main Rd, Tiverton Four Corners (ⓣ401/624-8096; closed Jan & Feb) is a delightful gourmet food store where you can choose from an exotic array of sandwiches and desserts, while local legend **Walker's Farm Stand**, 261 W Main Rd (ⓣ401/635-4719; open daily June–Nov), is a veritable kaleidoscope of colorful produce, especially in the late summer and fall, when bright orange pumpkins and freshly picked apples bask in the golden autumnal glow.

South County: Rhode Island's southern coast

South County is the unofficial name given to Rhode Island's southernmost towns along a coastal stretch that begins with **North Kingstown**, twenty miles south of Providence, and runs past gently rolling hills, quaint villages, and gray sandy beaches to **Westerly,** just this side of the Connecticut border. Further inland the geography is a bit more diverse, full of dense woodlands, wildlife reserves, and oversize ponds, but somewhat lacking in must-see sights that would make you stray very far off the coastal highway of US-1, actually once the main connecting route between New York and New England.

The area is alive with reminders of its colonial and Native American heritage, the latter attested to by such place names as Misquamicut and Quoquonset. Points of interest include **Smith's Castle**, America's oldest plantation house, and the birthplace of portraitist **Gilbert Stuart**, whose painting of George Washington is seen on all US one-dollar bills. On the coast, **Watch Hill** and **Narragansett** are – albeit on a less grand scale than Newport – known for their massive summer "cottages" and resort facilities, while **Galilee** is the point of departure for ferries to unspoilt **Block Island**, as well as one of the busiest fishing ports in New England, a great place to enjoy a seafood meal while watching the boats come in.

North Kingstown

NORTH KINGSTOWN, known as "plantation country" for its many long-standing farms, is less a town than a collection of rural communities straddling Rte-1A on the eastern shore of Narragansett Bay. The best known of these is the harborside village of **Wickford**, full of shady tree-lined lanes and handsomely preserved eighteenth- and nineteenth-century homes. Wickford is also home to the oldest Episcopal (Anglican) church north of Virginia, the 1707 **Old Narragansett Church**, on Church Lane (July–Aug Thurs–Mon 11am–4pm, other times by appointment; free; ⓣ401/294-4357), which was built in the square "preaching box" style, making it look like a congregational meeting house from the outside. Among its treasures are a Queen Anne Communion set and reputedly the oldest church organ in America, dating back to 1680; austere box pews and a slave gallery are reminders of a grim and turbulent past. The **Wickford Town Dock**, at the end of Main Street, was a bustling waterfront for years, especially when trading with the West Indies; today it's a peaceful, relaxing place where quahog skiffs rub shoulders with posh yachts and the only bustle of any kind comes when the annual Arts Festival is held here in July.

Just north of town is **Smith's Castle**, 55 Richard Smith Drive (May & Sept–Oct Fri–Sun noon–4pm, June–Aug Thurs–Mon noon–4pm, other times by appointment; free for gardens, $5 for house tour; ⓣ401/294-3521,

Getting around South County

Southern Rhode Island has much to offer in terms of attractions, but woefully little as far as public transportation goes. **Amtrak's** South County stops straddle the region in Westerly and Kingston, while RIPTA **buses** connect North and South Kingstown with Providence (bus #66) and Newport (#64) – though most people travel between the sights and beaches by **car**. US-1 is the main thoroughfare; its offshoot Rte-1A is best for getting to Narragansett or the Watch Hill area.

Ⓦwww.smithscastle.org), a white-clapboard plantation house that dates back to 1678, and was the site of much of Roger Williams' preaching. Recently restored, the castle replaced an earlier trading post that was destroyed by Native Americans, having been used to plan the attack against King Philip of the Wampanoags. A few miles east, the only brick hangar on the East Coast houses the **Quonset Air Museum**, 488 Eccleston Ave, Quonset Naval Air Base (daily 10am–4pm; $7; Ⓣ401/294-9540, Ⓦwww.qam-ri.com), which displays vintage aircraft such as a Russian MIG-17 and an A-4 Skyhawk.

Most of North Kingstown's other points of interest are farther south, in and around **Saunderstown**, including the three-hundred-acre **Casey Farm**, 2325 Boston Neck Rd, also known as Rte-1A (June to mid-Oct Sat 11am–5pm; $4; Ⓣ401/295-1030). In business since 1702, this is one of the oldest working farms in the US, and was originally the center of a plantation that produced food for local and foreign markets; today, resident farmers raise organically grown vegetables, herbs, and flowers for subscribing households in a community-supported agriculture program. The farmhouse contains original furniture and family memorabilia, while in the parlor door, a musket hole bears witness to a British attack on the property when it was used as a garrison by American military during the Revolutionary War. Two miles away, the **Gilbert Stuart Birthplace and Museum**, 815 Gilbert Stuart Rd (April–Oct Thurs–Mon 11am–4pm; $5; Ⓣ401/294-3001, Ⓦwww.gilbertstuartmuseum.com), childhood home of the celebrated eighteenth-century portraitist, disappoints in that it only contains one reproduction of the 111 portraits of George Washington that Stuart painted during his lifetime.

Few people choose to **stay** or **eat** in North Kingstown, electing to find such practicalities in more tourist-friendly **Narragansett** and **Galilee**, described below.

Narragansett

Eleven miles along Rte-1A, **NARRAGANSETT** (meaning "little spit of land") occupies a narrow patch snaking out into the Atlantic, its long coastline of rocks interspersed by broad expanses of sand – a major attraction for swimmers, surfers, bird-watchers, and fishermen. The town center, known as **Narragansett Pier**, had its heyday during the Victorian era, when the town competed with Newport as a major resort destination. To some extent it succeeded, luring visitors particularly with the **Narragansett Casino Resort**, designed by the architectural firm of McKim, Mead & White in 1884. Hopes of lasting fame and prosperity came to an abrupt end in 1900, however, when fire swept through the casino complex, destroying all but its turreted towers, which today remain the most striking feature of the town center, and which house the **visitor information center**, 35 Ocean Rd (Mon–Sat 9am–5pm; Ⓣ401/783-7121). For additional explication of Narragansett's role over the years, visit the **South County Museum**, Rte-1A at Canonchet Farm, opposite the Narragansett Beach Pavilion (May–June & Sept–Oct Fri–Sat 10am–4pm, Sun noon–4pm; July–Aug Wed–Sat 10am–4pm, Sun noon–4pm; $5; Ⓣ401/783-5400, Ⓦwww.southcountymuseum.org), which holds thousands of local artifacts, a replicated print shop, smithy, and general store, and a farm exhibit with Rhode Island Red chickens.

Narragansett's long coastline boasts several outstanding **beaches** (see box on overleaf) and the charmingly chaotic fishing port of **Galilee**, four miles south of the town center. The port's potholed main drag, where the fishy smell can at times be overwhelming, is home to a large commercial fishing fleet, half a dozen fish markets, two or three fish-processing works, beach accessory stores, and the **Block Island ferry** (see p.320 for details). If you want to go on a guided **whale-watch**, the boats of Francis Fleet (late May to early Sept daily 1pm; $35, under-12s $25; ⓣ401/783-4988 or 1-800/662-2824) depart for 4.5-hour trips from a point just behind *Finback's* restaurant at 33 State St. A mile east, the **Point Judith Lighthouse**, at the end of Ocean Road, has been warning ships off the rocky coast since the early 1800s. The present lighthouse, built in 1857, is closed to the public, but the view from the car park is breathtaking, especially on a stormy day.

Practicalities

Accommodation isn't hard to come by in Narragansett, except at the height of the season, when it's advisable to book well in advance. In Galilee, opposite the Block Island ferry, the *Lighthouse Inn* (ⓣ401/789-9341 or 1-800/336-6662; ❻) is a recently renovated hundred-room motel near all the beach and boating activities. More atmospheric digs are available in the Narragansett Pier area, where, at 59 Kingstown Rd, the *1900 House* (ⓣ401/789-7971, ⓦwww.1900houseri.com; ❻) is a remnant of Narragansett's glory days. If you prefer to rent a cottage, Durkin Cottage Realty (ⓣ401/789-6659, ⓦwww.durkincottages.com) has the largest selection in the area, starting as low as $600 a week.

The Narragansett Pier area boasts several upmarket **restaurants**, including the *Coast Guard House*, 40 Ocean Rd (ⓣ401/789-0700), where the view, if not the food, is spectacular; *Basil's*, on the pier at 22 Kingstown Rd (ⓣ401/789-3743), has established a strong local following for its fine French cuisine. Galilee

South County beaches

Many of Rhode Island's best **saltwater beaches** can be found in South County, and are generally open to the public, although access to some is virtually impossible without a car, and there is usually a hefty parking fee in summer, especially on weekends. Off-season, parking is often free and the beaches, on weekdays at least, are deserted. Ocean temperatures peak at a refreshing 70–75 degrees during the dog days of August. Fees listed below are per car.

Charlestown Town Beach Charlestown Beach Road, Charlestown. This beach should be in California: lots of volleyball players, surfers, and bronzed bodies. $10 daily.

East Beach Ninigret Conservation Area, off E Beach Road, Charlestown. An almost Caribbean-like beach, with sugar-fine sand and aquamarine waters. Weekdays $12, weekends $14.

East Matunuck State Beach Succotash Road, South Kingstown. Popular with teens, this beach has a gradual drop-off that's good for sand-fishing. Same prices as above.

Misquamicut State Beach Atlantic Avenue, Westerly. Rhode Island's largest state beach at seven miles, but very crowded. Amusements and fast food are close at hand. Same prices as above.

Napatree Point Watch Hill. A complete contrast to Misquamicut; limited access only to this pretty, ecologically fragile beach. No parking.

Narragansett Town Beach Rte-1A, Narragansett. A half-mile-long beach popular with families and known for good surf. Parking $6, plus $5 per person.

Roger Wheeler Beach Cove Wood Drive, Narragansett. A quarter-mile of gray sand with excellent facilities and expansive parking. Weekdays $12, weekends $14.

Scarborough State Beach Ocean Drive, Narragansett. Popular with students from nearby University of Rhode Island. Same prices as above.

South Kingstown Town Beach South Kingstown. Beautiful beach backed by dunes. $15 daily.

is home to a number of excellent seafood spots, the most popular of which are *George's*, 250 Sand Hill Cove Rd (Ⓣ401/783-2306), and *Champlin's*, 256 Great Island Rd (Ⓣ401/783-3152), which has nice views of the fishing boats from an upstairs covered deck. Not far away, *Aunt Carrie's*, 1240 Ocean Rd (Ⓣ401/783-7930; summer only), is a Rhode Island institution, the place for traditional shore dinners in an unpretentious, relaxed atmosphere, while *Spain*, 1144 Ocean Rd (Ⓣ401/783-9770), serves a variety of Spanish, American, and seafood dishes in a contemporary setting.

South Kingstown

Rhode Island's largest town by area, **SOUTH KINGSTOWN** takes in fourteen separate villages covering both sides of Rte-1, quite different in nature depending on whether you're traveling on the inland or coastal side of the highway. Inland, dense woods hide well-preserved colonial villages, potato farms, and wildlife refuges; the most logical first stop here is **Kingston**, which was founded in 1674 and a seat of Rhode Island government until it was centralized in Providence. Many well-preserved examples of Federal-style architecture can still be seen, including the **Kingston Free Library**, 2605 Kingstown Rd, originally the Washington County Courthouse, where the state's General Assembly, Supreme Court, and local town council all held sessions. Nearby, in the **Old Washington County Jail**, 2636 Kingstown Rd (Tues, Thurs & Sat 1–4pm; donation requested; Ⓣ401/783-1328), you can see old jail cells which have been around since 1858, along with a decent museum that contains changing exhibits on South County life over the past three hundred years. Rural Kingston is also the unlikely location of the **University of Rhode Island**, on Rte-138 W, whose leafy 1200-acre campus once centered on a small farmhouse – fitting, as this was begun as an agricultural school. Rte-108 leads south from here to the village of **Wakefield**, whose Main Street holds a pleasant mix of antique shops, restaurants, and historic buildings, though nothing of particular interest.

To the south of Rte-1, a succession of laidback coastal communities are separated by a series of saltwater ponds protected by fragile barrier beaches. Seaside villages worth stopping by include **Jerusalem** and **Snug Harbor**, with their clutch of summer cottages and stately homes. Otherwise, the main reason for coming down here is to join the crowds at the **beaches**, namely Green Hill and East Matunuck, a favorite with university students.

Practicalities

South Kingston's sheer size means a wide variety of accommodation and dining choices are available; you can find simple motels and cozy B&Bs, plain diners, and elegantly prepared meals. **Places to stay** include the *Admiral Dewey Inn*, 668 Matunuck Beach Rd, Matunuck (Ⓣ401/783-2090 or 1-800/457-2090, Ⓦwww.admiraldeweyinn.com; ❻), a traditional beach lodging house where you can relax and unwind on the wraparound porch. In Wakefield, the 175-year-old family-run *Larchwood Inn*, 521 Main St (Ⓣ401/783-5454; shared bath ❹, private bath ❻), offers eighteen cozy rooms, a nice complement to the elegant on-site **restaurant**, which serves well-priced American fare with a Scottish twist. For generous portions of seafood, hit up *Cap'n Jack's* in Jerusalem, 706 Succotash Rd (Ⓣ401/789-4556; closed Mon).

Charlestown

Laidback **CHARLESTOWN**, South Kingstown's western neighbor, is one of the fastest-growing communities in the state, its recent arrivals having been seduced by an attractive coastline – miles of barrier beach backed by pristine salt ponds. First settled by the Narragansett Indians, Charlestown received its charter from King Charles II in 1663, and was thus named for him. The Narragansetts, however, still own plenty of land in town, and maintain a significant cultural impact, best observed during their **Annual Pow-Wow**, held the second weekend of August on tribal lands just off Rte-2 and featuring Native American dancing, crafts, food, and storytelling (☎401/364-1100 ext 203 for details). The oldest such event in the country, this "Gathering of the Green Corn," as it's also known, has been held for more than 330 years. Also located on these lands is the **Narragansett Indian Church**, a reconstruction of an 1859 granite Greek Revival building. The church is not generally open to the public, though you can join the non-denominational Sunday services.

One of a number of recreational areas that surround Ninigret Pond, the **Ninigret National Wildlife Refuge**, 3679 Old Post Rd (8am–dusk; ☎401/364-9124), highlights Charlestown's protected coastline and consists of nine hundred acres of diverse upland and wetland habitats, as well as three miles of trails good for bird-watching or a bit of exercise. Inland, off Rte-1, a number of tiny communities provide a glimpse into rural Rhode Island life, especially **Shannock**, a disarmingly pretty New England mill village of white-clapboard houses near the Pawcatuck River. Once virtually abandoned, the village was purchased and restored by a local developer, with the express intention of turning on upwardly mobile young couples to the charms of country living.

Practicalities

Much of Charlestown's **accommodations**, a mix of motor courts and intimate inns, lines US-1, including the *General Stanton Inn*, 4115 Old Post Rd (☎401/364-8888 or 1-800/364-8011, Ⓦwww.generalstantoninn.com; ❻), which has been a resting-place for travelers on the Providence–New London route since Revolutionary times. An adjacent flea market keeps guests busy at weekends. Just off the main drag, the *Surfside Motel*, 334 Narrow Lane (☎401/364-1010, Ⓦwww.thesurfsidemotel.com; ❺), has fifteen clean rooms, most with kitchenettes. **Camping** is available at nearly seven hundred sites in Burlingame State Park (☎401/322-7994; sites $20; closed in winter), along with canoeing and bird-watching on the thousand-acre Watchaug Pond. The bulk of the Charlestown's **restaurants** specialize in moderately priced seafood, like the casual *Wilcox Tavern*, at 5153 Old Post Rd (☎401/322-1829; Tues–Sun dinner).

Westerly and Watch Hill

WESTERLY, as its name implies, occupies the westernmost point of Rhode Island, eleven miles on from Charlestown and sharing the Pawcatuck River with the town of Pawcatuck, CT. Once a prosperous textiles and granite manufacturer, its downtown area holds few reminders of those days. The most impressive specimen left is the **Babcock-Smith House**, 124 Granite St (June–Oct Sat 2–5pm, July–Aug also Fri 2–5pm; $5; ☎401/596-5704, Ⓦwww.babcock-smithhouse.com), built in 1734 for Dr Joshua Babcock, Westerly's first physician, who moonlighted as the town's postmaster, the state's chief justice, and a major-general in the Revolutionary army. The handsome two-story gambrel-roofed building contains much of its original trimmings, including the wooden paneling, the open fireplace in the kitchen, and, above the dining room mantelpiece, an engraving depicting Babcock engaged in diplomacy at the French court.

Most visitors, however, forsake Westerly's downtown in lieu of the **Watch Hill** area a few miles south, which, after Newport, is Rhode Island's most select resort, with salty seaside shops and 1900s-era **cottages** overlooking the Atlantic. One holdover from its birth as a resort is the **Flying Horse Carousel** at the end of Bay Street, which, like several others in New England, is claimed to be the nation's oldest. The twenty horses are not attached to the floor but instead suspended from a central frame, swinging out or "flying" when in motion; rides are $1 and for children only. The other town highlight, an old granite **lighthouse** on Lighthouse Road (July & Aug Tues & Thurs 1–3pm; free), houses a small **museum** containing the usual bits on lighthouse history. To the west, accessible from Watch Hill Beach, the half-mile-long barrier beach of **Napatree Point** once supported a number of homes before they were destroyed by a devastating hurricane in 1938. Today it's a peaceful conservation area filled with myriad bird species and affording stunning ocean views.

Practicalities

Perhaps the most tourist-friendly of the South County towns, Westerly has upward of thirty hotels, motels, and B&Bs, some of which have more of a resort feel than those of any Rhode Island town except Newport. Try the *Shelter Harbor Inn*, 10 Wagner Rd (Ⓣ401/322-8883, Ⓦwww.shelterharborinn.com; ❽), a 24-room country inn done up with early American fittings, with a rooftop hot tub, a sundeck, and an excellent restaurant. Alternatively the *Winnepaug Inn*, 169 Shore Rd (Ⓣ401/348-8350 or 1-800/288-9906; ❼), is a nondescript three-story motel set on nicely maintained grounds overlooking a golf course.

Of the best places to **eat**, the spacious *My Mary's Restaurant*, 336 Post Rd (Ⓣ401/322-0444; dinner daily), offers pricey surf-and-turf, while next door *Anna McCarthy's Pub* (Ⓣ401/322-7000; daily lunch & dinner) has similarly hearty food at more moderate prices. Closer to downtown, *W.B. Cody's*, 265 Post Rd (Ⓣ401/322-4070), is a good alternative to the local fish fare, serving BBQ and steaks at respectable prices. Down in Watch Hill, *St Clair Annex*, 141 Bay St (Ⓣ401/348-8407; May–Oct daily breakfast & lunch, also dinner in July & Aug), run by the same family for over 100 years, serves wonderful breakfasts and homemade ice cream. For something more substantial, the *Olympia Tea Room*, 74 Bay St (Ⓣ401/348-8211; May–Oct), serves a variety of seafood dishes and mouth-watering desserts.

Entertainment in Westerly centers on theater: the Granite Theatre, 1 Granite St (March–Dec Thurs–Sat, Sun matinees; $17; Ⓣ401/596-2341, Ⓦwww.granitetheatre.com), presents drama, comedy, and, every summer, a classic American musical. There's also the Colonial Theatre's free Shakespeare in the Park productions in July in Wilcox Park (Ⓣ401/596-7909), which is also the venue for the renowned **Westerly Chorus**'s Summer Pops concert. Throughout the rest of the year the ensemble puts on classical concerts at the **Westerly Performance Hall**, 119 High St (Ⓣ401/596-8663, Ⓦwww.chorusofwesterly.org), a former church blessed with excellent acoustics; it's one of the Northeast's best small concert halls.

Block Island

It may not be the "Bermuda of the North" or "one of the last great places on earth," as it is sometimes described, but **BLOCK ISLAND**, twelve miles off Rhode Island's southern coast, has managed to preserve its melancholy, seductive charm even in the face of growing hordes of visitors and the rampant construction of summer homes in the 1970s and 1980s, which threatened to disfigure the landscape's simple beauty as well as destroy its unique natural environment. Inhabited by eight hundred year-round residents, who scatter themselves around the gently rolling hills and broad expanses of moorland, Block Island still exudes an air of desolation, a mood exacerbated off-season when the island ferries are suspended due to bad weather. There's not much to see once you get over, just lovely coves and sandy beaches, but, like its Massachusetts cousins Martha's Vineyard and Nantucket, the island gets chock-a-block between July 4 and early September, when tourists, part-time residents, and day-trippers all seem to take to the small island's scant network of roads at once.

Some history

Native Americans, who called it "Manisses" or "Island of the Little God," inhabited Block Island for centuries before Giovanni de Verrazano spotted it in 1524. With the prospect of a substantial bonus in sight, he cannily named it **Claudia**, after the mother of the French king, Francis I, who had hired him. Later on, in 1614, the intrepid Dutch explorer Adrian Block stopped for a time on the island and gave it the name "**Adrian's Eyelandt**" which eventually became **Block Island**.

A group of English settlers seeking religious freedom arrived here nearly fifty years later and established a small farming and fishing community that still exists today. A relatively quiet couple of hundred years followed until 1842, when the island's first rooming house opened and visitors began to recognize Block Island's many charms; thirty years later a new breakwater was built, meaning that larger ships could dock – bringing even more travelers. Things took a turn for the worse with the 1938 hurricane that devastated much of the New England coast: it destroyed nearly all of Block Island's fishing fleet and caused considerable structural damage to the hotels and other buildings around Old Harbor, the island's commercial center.

There's little remnant of those hard times today. Block Island has become very fashionable, a highly sought-after real estate destination with many properties surpassing the million-dollar mark. In reaction to this, residents of **New Shoreham** (the island's official title) have in recent years passed a number of measures – including a camping ban – designed to preserve the relative tranquility and natural environment they had so expensively become privy to.

Arrival, information, and getting around

Most people arrive on Block Island by **ferry**. From the Galilee State Pier in Narragansett (commonly referred to as Point Judith), the Interstate Navigation Co. (ⓣ401/783-4613 or 1-866/783-7340, ⓦwww.blockislandferry.com) runs at least five ferries a day during the summer months and one to three a day during the winter. High fuel costs have made the price for the one-hour trip rise to $11.05 one-way or $18.85 for same-day return. Passengers taking **cars** ($40.75 each way) must make reservations in advance; foot passengers just need to arrive 45 minutes early. Note that parking lots at the Galilee State Pier generally charge $10 per day. The same company runs daily ferries (no cars) from Newport's Fort Adams State Park from July 1 to early September at 9.15am ($8.50 one-way, $12.50 for same-day return). If you'd rather fly, New England Airlines (ⓣ1-800/243-2460) provides hourly **flights** from Westerly all year for $48 one-way, $84 round-trip.

The **Block Island Chamber of Commerce** (summer daily 9am–5pm, winter Mon–Fri 10am–3pm; ⓣ401/466-2982 or 1-800/383-BIRI, ⓦwww.blockislandchamber.com) operates an **information center** right where you

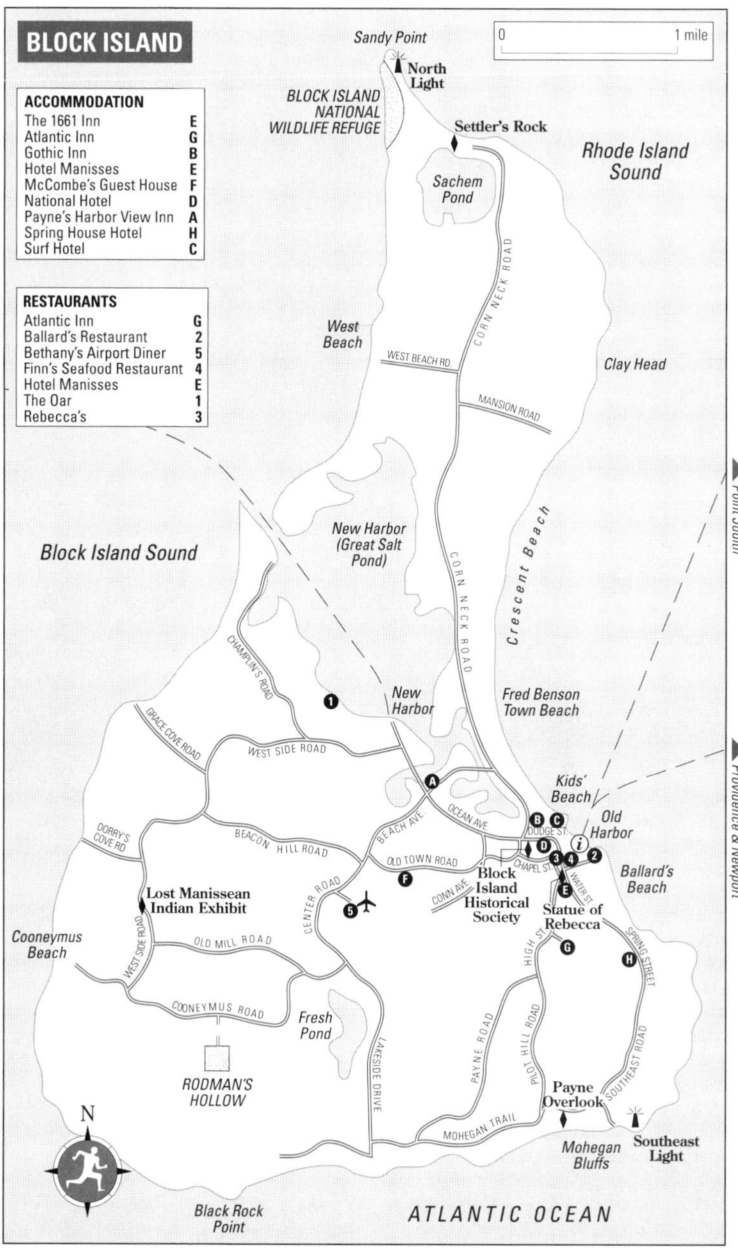

BLOCK ISLAND
ACCOMMODATION
The 1661 Inn E
Atlantic Inn G
Gothic Inn B
Hotel Manisses E
McCombe's Guest House F
National Hotel D
Payne's Harbor View Inn A
Spring House Hotel H
Surf Hotel C
RESTAURANTS
Atlantic Inn G
Ballard's Restaurant 2
Bethany's Airport Diner 5
Finn's Seafood Restaurant 4
Hotel Manisses E
The Oar 1
Rebecca's 3
0
1 mile
Sandy Point
North Light
BLOCK ISLAND NATIONAL WILDLIFE REFUGE
Settler's Rock
Rhode Island Sound
Sachem Pond
CORN NECK ROAD
West Beach
WEST BEACH RD.
Clay Head
MANSION ROAD
New London, CT
Point Judith
Providence & Newport
Block Island Sound
New Harbor (Great Salt Pond)
Crescent Beach
CHAMPLIN'S ROAD
New Harbor
Fred Benson Town Beach
GRACE COVE ROAD
WEST SIDE ROAD
Kids' Beach
OCEAN AVE.
Old Harbor
DORRY'S COVE RD
BEACON HILL ROAD
BEACH AVE.
DODGE ST.
OLD TOWN ROAD
CHAPEL ST.
Ballard's Beach
CENTER ROAD
CONN AVE.
Block Island Historical Society
WATER ST.
Lost Manissean Indian Exhibit
Statue of Rebecca
Cooneymus Beach
OLD MILL ROAD
HIGH ST.
SPRING STREET
WEST SIDE ROAD
COONEYMUS ROAD
Fresh Pond
LAKESIDE DRIVE
PAYNE ROAD
PILOT HILL ROAD
SOUTHEAST ROAD
RODMAN'S HOLLOW
Payne Overlook
N
MOHEGAN TRAIL
Mohegan Bluffs
Southeast Light
Black Rock Point
ATLANTIC OCEAN

get off the ferry. The other thing you'll see as you disembark is a bewildering array of **bike**, **moped**, and **car rental** agencies, with still more lurking behind the shops. Prices vary, so you might want to shop around, but in the height of the season, expect to pay around $80 for a four-hour moped rental, or $40 for one hour; bikes are around $20 per day. Two good options are the dockside Old Harbor Bike Shop (Ⓣ401/466-2029) and Island Moped & Bikes on Chapel Street (Ⓣ401/466-2700). Keep in mind that rental mopeds can only be used between 9am and 8pm, and are not allowed on dirt roads, which means bicycles may be a better option if you want to do some extensive exploring.

There are plenty of **taxis** lined up too, at least on summer days, useful if you're weighted down with luggage or if your accommodation is located at some far-flung corner of the island. Some of the cabs provide narrated (and fairly pithy) **island tours**, at $40 for two people and a further $10 for each additional person; in the absence of tour buses, this can be a good way to get oriented. Mary D's Nightingale Taxi (Ⓣ401/474-Ⓣ6377) is one of the best. You'll mostly want to get around **on foot**, though: there are some 25 miles of walking trails maintained by the Nature Conservancy (Ⓣ401/466-2129), which puts on nature walks during the summer; maps are available for $2 from their High Street office or from the Chamber of Commerce.

Accommodation

If you want to stay on Block Island during the summer, it's advisable to book well in advance; even with more than seventy hotels, inns, B&Bs, and studio rentals, **accommodation** fills up rapidly, especially at weekends. Expect to pay anything from $80 to $450 per night for a room, and $750 a week up to a whopping $7000 for a cottage rental. Because the island is so small, numbers are rarely, if ever, used in addresses; fortunately, it's virtually impossible to get lost, and most hotels are located in any case in **Old Harbor**. The Chamber of Commerce (see contact info p.320) keeps tabs on rooms available for a given night around the island, so they're a great contact if you're having trouble. Note that only a handful of hotels remain open year-round, the *1661 Inn* being the only one listed below.

The 1661 Inn Spring St, Old Harbor Ⓣ401/466-2421, Ⓦwww.blockislandresorts.com. Set on a hill overlooking the sea, nine quietly luxurious rooms opposite the *Hotel Manisses.* ❼

Atlantic Inn High St, Old Harbor Ⓣ401/466-5883 or 1-800/224-7422, Ⓦwww.atlanticinn.com. Laden with mainly Victorian antiques and set on six acres, the *Atlantic* has superior rooms, many with superb views. Guests who feel so inclined can enjoy a game of tennis at the *Inn*'s two courts, or a game of croquet on the lawn. Good restaurant, too – see p.325. ❼

The Gothic Inn Dodge St, Old Harbor Ⓣ401/466-2918 or 1-800/944-8991, Ⓦwww.thegothicinn.com. Perched high above Crescent Beach and just three minutes from the ferry, this family-run Victorian inn has oodles of character; the unusually steep gables come complete with gingerbread trimmings and a wide, relaxing porch above Dodge St. ❼

Hotel Manisses Spring St, Old Harbor Ⓣ401/466-2421 or 1-800/MANISSES, Ⓦwww.blockislandresorts.com. Seventeen comfortable antique-filled rooms, some affording views of the ocean, each named after local shipwrecks. A backyard farm has llamas, black swans, and emus, for a touch of the exotic. ❽

McCombe's Guest House Old Town Rd Ⓣ401/466-2684. Of the two dozen or so small guesthouses on the island, *McCombe's* is an excellent bet, with two beautifully decorated guestrooms, each with private entrance and all modern amenities, in a quiet spot a 15min walk from town. Friendly and helpful owners, too. ❼

National Hotel Water St, Old Harbor Ⓣ401/466-2901 or 1-800/225-2449, Ⓦwww.blockislandhotels.com. This vast Victorian pile dominates everything else on Water St, and its restaurant, serving meals on the expansive wraparound porch, makes it a popular gathering spot. All rooms have cable TV and private bath. Fills up fast, so book early. ❽

Payne's Harbor View Inn Beach Ave, New Harbor Ⓣ401/466-5758, Ⓦwww.paynesharborviewinn

.com. *Payne's* is the newest inn on the island, which means you get all modern amenities, including large and luxurious rooms, new furnishings, whirlpool baths, and even an elevator, but with old-world touches like a wraparound porch and sweeping harbor views. ❽

Spring House Hotel Spring St, Old Harbor ⓣ401/466-5844 or 1-800/234-9263, ⓦwww.springhousehotel.com. Built in 1852, and as such the oldest hotel on the island, the distinctive *Spring House* has hosted notables such as Ulysses S. Grant, Mark Twain, and a Kennedy or two. Rooms, studios, and suites available, many with ocean views. A sprawling lawn and wraparound porch are perfect for whiling away a quiet afternoon; retire to the expensive and well-regarded dining room for an elegant evening meal. ❽

The Surf Hotel Dodge St, Old Harbor ⓣ401/466-2241. Although stuck in a time warp with kitschy furnishings, the *Surf Hotel* is of note for having the least expensive rooms on offer in high season, as well as a convenient location in Old Harbor, steps away from Crescent Beach. Most rooms have shared bath. ❺

The island

Most visitors' first – and last – picture of Block Island is **Old Harbor**, the island's only village, which developed after 1870 when the federal government built the two breakwaters. Huge Victorian hotels were built along **Water Street** to encourage the fledgling tourist industry, many boasting cupolas, porches, and flamboyant gingerbread architecture redolent of Oak Bluffs on Martha's Vineyard. Some of these grand structures still stand, albeit amidst a touristy mix of shops, boutiques, restaurants, and smaller, less atmospheric B&Bs. At the southern end of Water Street, smack in the middle of the road, stands the **Statue of Rebecca**, an 1896 recasting of a biblical allegory erected by the Women's Christian Temperance Movement to remind folks of the dangers of alcohol. Ironically, recent restoration work uncovered that "Rebecca" is in fact more likely "Hebe", cupbearer to the gods. Toward the northern end of town, the **Block Island Historical Society**, Old Town Road at Ocean Avenue (July & Aug daily 10am–4pm; off-season by appointment; donation requested; ⓣ401/466-2481), has a number of exhibits describing the island's farming and maritime past. This structure, once an inn, is furnished with antiques and worth a poke around, though it's mostly useful to get your bearings.

New Harbor, about a mile northwest of Old Harbor along Ocean Avenue, boasts the only other would-be commercial area on the island: a handful of waterfront restaurants and shacks, some facilities for sailing enthusiasts, and, perched on the hill overlooking the Great Salt Pond, *Payne's Harbor View Inn*, one of several here. The pond was totally enclosed by land until a channel from the ocean was dredged to allow boats entry into the newly fashioned harbor. There's not much to see, but the place comes to life on summer weekends with myriad sailboat races, fishing tournaments, and watersports activities.

Continuing north, **Settler's Rock** is not much more than a quick stopping-off point – fitting for a place that commemorates where the settlers first landed – before the half-mile walk up to **North Light**, at Block Island's isolated northern tip. The current incarnation is the fourth go-round for this lighthouse, a grim reminder of the power of nature, since the previous three were destroyed by the elements. A museum traces the island's maritime history and displays old life-saving equipment (July & Aug daily 10am–4pm; $2; ⓣ401/466-2481).

Back from Old Harbor, Spring Street trails to the southernmost tip of the island, where **Mohegan Bluffs**, the spectacular 150-foot cliffs named for an Indian battle that occurred at their base, tower over the Atlantic. Positioned atop is the red-brick **Southeast Light**, built in 1873 but not moved to its present position until 1993 after erosion threatened its survival. Laying claim to being the highest lighthouse in New England, the attraction here is the trip up the sixty-odd steps of the tower for the stunning **ocean views** ($10, kids $5).

△ Southeast Light, Block Island

For a different perspective, head west to Payne Overlook; though the viewing platform is closed due to erosion, a 144-step staircase down the cliffside to the beach begins here.

Farther west, a dirt track (Black Rock Road) leads from Cooneymus Road to the preserved sanctuary of **Rodman's Hollow**, a deep glacial depression offering more panoramic views of the Atlantic. Farther along on the loop back towards Old Harbor, at 1173 West Side Rd, you can head out on a tranquil horse ride along the beaches or through the nature preserves from **Rustic Rides Farm** (summer daily 9am–7pm, winter by appointment only; $45 and up; ⓣ1-401/466-5060). Also at the farm, local eccentric Tim McCabe maintains the **Lost Manissean Indian Exhibit**; among the arrowheads, ax heads, and knives he's collected over the years from digging around the island, he also claims to have ancient mortars and pestles made by the natives and inscribed with intricate hieroglyphics – after his elaborate explanation you may just believe him (summer daily 9am–6pm; $1 with trail ride, $5 requested donation otherwise).

Block Island's beaches

Block Island has some fine **beaches** (all of which are blessedly free of charge), and, with seventeen miles of them, even in the peak of the summer season it's possible to get far from the madding crowd and find the bliss of solitude. The main "family" beach is **Fred Benson Town Beach**, a two-mile-long swath of sand with showers and lockers, chairs, umbrellas, and kayaks to rent, and lifeguards to keep an eye on things. There's ample free parking, extensive bicycle racks, and hot food and drinks at *Rebecca's on the Beach*. At its sheltered southern tip, known as **Kid Beach**, children can play in relatively shallow water, and look for small crabs, mussels, and the like. **Ballard's Beach**, just south of Old Harbor, is the island's only other lifeguard-staffed beach; as it's directly in front of the rowdy restaurant (see opposite), it's not well suited to anyone seeking peace and quiet. **West Beach** on the northwestern coast would be a better bet for some seclusion, bordered by a bird sanctuary to the south and dunes of nesting seagulls to the north. Lastly, a venture to beautiful **Black Rock Point**, on the island's southern shore, rewards not with swimming opportunities (the water is rather dangerous due to strong surf) but with a dramatic seascape in which many ships have met their untimely end.

Eating

For such a small island, there is a remarkable variety of good **places to eat**. Not surprisingly, **fresh seafood** tops the bill at many establishments, with lobster a firm favorite. Note that all of these places reduce their hours drastically for the spring and fall and all but one or two close for the entire winter. Summer weekends, on the other hand, can be very crowded, and not all restaurants take reservations.

Atlantic Inn High St, Old Harbor ⓣ401/466-5883. Contemporary American cuisine like delicious braised short ribs with black truffle risotto is complemented by fantastic ocean views, best enjoyed accompanied by a cocktail or two on the verandah. For a special night out, come here for the excellent $46 four-course prix-fixe dinner.

Ballard's Restaurant Water St, Old Harbor ⓣ401/466-2231. Overlooking the beach, this casual standby offers seafood classics like fish and chips, clam cakes, and fried clams.

Bethany's Airport Diner State Airport, Center Rd ⓣ401/466-3100. You might wonder why anyone would choose to eat at the airport on vacation, but this cozy, atmospheric diner really is worth a stop for homecooked specials like meatloaf and London broil served at an old-fashioned counter with prices to match. Especially fun for kids who will like watching the turboprops take off. Daily breakfast and lunch.

Finn's Seafood Restaurant Water St, Old Harbor ⓣ401/466-2473. Fresh-caught fish and shellfish from the market next door, plus hamburgers and other options, served overlooking the harbor.

Hotel Manisses Spring St, Old Harbor ⓣ401/466-2421. Elegant evening dining in a Victorian inn featuring an innovative menu with tasty twists on local seafood. For $325, have a romantic dinner for two prepared by the chef tableside in your room or on the beach.

The Oar West Side Rd, New Harbor ⓣ401/466-8820. Island landmark famous for the scores of painted oars that hang from the ceiling. The seafood bar's got cheap chowder, peel-and-eat shrimp, fried scallops, and the like; you can take your food outside and enjoy superb views of the Great Salt Pond from the porch.

Rebecca's Water St, Old Harbor ⓣ401/466-5411. Affordable and tasty sandwich wraps, burgers, clam cakes, and chowder at this island favorite, conveniently open 7am to 2am in season.

Nightlife and entertainment

Although Block Island is so quiet for most of the year that you can hear the grass grow, on summer nights the **nightlife** picks up, mostly centering on the ample selection of **bars**. Some of these are staid and courtly, while others are renowned for their boisterous weekend parties. In recent years, the **Spring House Summer Concert Series** has even brought full-blown rock concerts to the island (several each summer, call the *Spring House Hotel* for details; see p.323). More laidback entertainment is provided by two **cinemas**: the Empire Theater on Water St (ⓣ401/466-2555) and the Oceanwest Theater in New Harbor (ⓣ401/466-2971), both of which offer first-run movies; the latter also has occasional children's matinees. Pick up a copy of the local paper, the *Block Island Times*, for current listings and special events. Note that bars close by 1am.

Albion Pub Ocean Ave, Old Harbor ⓣ401/466-9990. Comfortable, dark, and smoky pub on the main strip.

Captain Nick's Ocean Ave, Old Harbor ⓣ401/466-5670. The island's biggest nightclub, featuring live music throughout the summer that ranges from national headliners to locals eager to strut their stuff. Disco Night Mondays are an especially big hit.

Club Soda Connecticut Ave ⓣ401/466-5397. Drinks and music amidst strange, sort of kitsch, decor, as well as pool tables, video games, and a jukebox. Open mic night on Wednesdays.

McGovern's Yellow Kittens Tavern Corn Neck Rd, Old Harbor ⓣ401/466-5855. This island institution has no shortage of activities in which to engage – pool, foosball, video games, pinball – while imbibing. Live music from rock to reggae on weekends, too ($3–5 cover).

Mohegan Café & Brewery 213 Water St, Old Harbor ⓣ401/466-5911. Good microbrews direct from an in-house brewery; open only until 9pm.

Mohogany Shoals Payne's Dock, New Harbor ⓣ401/466-5572. Dockside bar featuring an Irish folk guitarist Wed–Sun during the summer.

Connecticut

CANADA
Moosehead Lake
Kennebec River
8
Lake Champlain
GREEN MOUNTAINS
WHITE MOUNTAINS
Mount Desert Island
6
Lake Winnipesaukee
NEW YORK
7
ATLANTIC OCEAN
THE BERKSHIRES
3
1
Cape Cod
N
2
5
4
Martha's Vineyard
Nantucket
Long Island

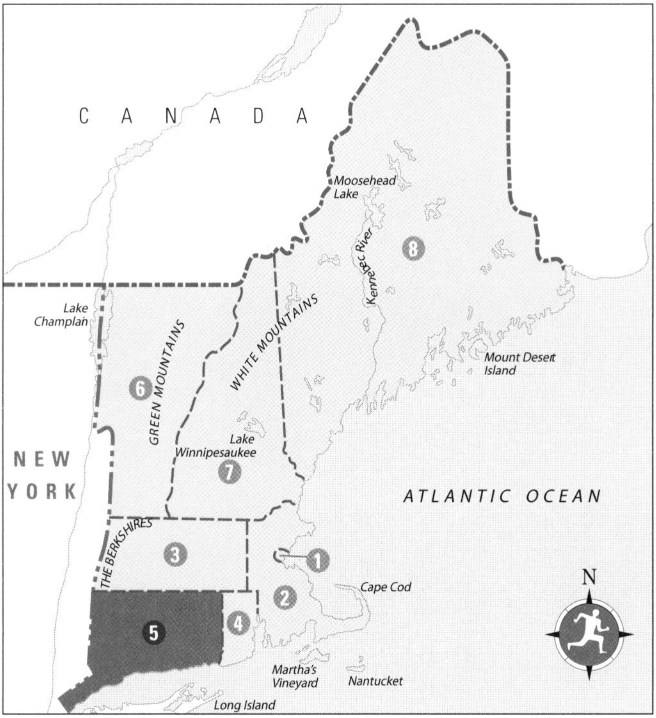

CHAPTER FIVE

Highlights

* **Mystic** Though the seaport can verge on tacky, you'll still be able to trace the authentic maritime history here. See p.333
* **Clinton–Madison–Guilford** This trinity of Connecticut's prettiest small towns offers pristine lawns, historic homes, and an old-fashioned sense of community. See pp.341, 342 & 343
* **Yale University, New Haven** This Ivy League school's green lawns, Classical and Gothic buildings, and erudite but unpretentious vibe make for a welcome oasis. See p.349
* **Maritime Aquarium, Norwalk** One of the best maritime collections to be found anywhere. See p.357
* **Bruce Museum, Greenwich** A broad collection of fine art pieces, anthropological artifacts, and natural science exhibits makes this one of the state's top draws. See p.360
* **Mark Twain House, Hartford** The esteemed Samuel Clemens' eccentric hideaway, befitting the imaginative author. See p.367
* **Litchfield Hills** The stark ruralness of parts of this area makes looking for local wines or antique bargains something of a treasure hunt. See p.375

△ Covered bridge, Cornwall

5

Connecticut

New England's southernmost state, **CONNECTICUT**, a rectangle about ninety miles long by 55 miles wide, was named *Quinnehtukqut* ("great tidal river") by the Native Americans after the river that bisects it and spills into Long Island Sound. The state's first white settlers came in the 1630s when **English** refugees from Massachusetts seeking political and religious freedom arrived at the town of Windsor. Settlements followed in Wethersfield and Hartford, and in 1636 the three united to form the **Connecticut Colony**, adopting the "**Fundamental Orders**," a charter which was later used as a model for the American Constitution; indeed, Connecticut is still sometimes referred to as the "**Constitution State**."

Connecticut soon became known for "**Yankee ingenuity**," principally the invention and marketing (often by notorious and not always honorable peddlers) of many a useful household object. Meanwhile, on the coast, locals were turning to the sea for their livelihood; shipbuilding and whaling were both big business. The Puritan infatuation with education resulted in the establishment of **Yale University**, founded in 1701 as the Collegiate School in Killingsworth before moving to Saybrook, and eventually to New Haven in 1716. Although the colony was hit hard by English raids during the Revolutionary War, its role in providing the war effort with crucial supplies earned it the nickname of the "**Provisions State**." This period also produced one of Connecticut's great folk heroes, **Nathan Hale**, hanged by the British for spying.

Connecticut prospered during the late eighteenth and nineteenth centuries, with steady industrialization helped along by **Eli Whitney**, developer of efficient machine tools, and entrepreneurs like Hartford's **Samuel Colt**, inventor of the repeating pistol. While it was producing some of the nation's great businessmen, the state was also having a cultural impact – during a long sojourn in Hartford, **Mark Twain** wrote *The Adventures of Tom Sawyer* and *Huckleberry Finn*, while **John Brown**, perhaps the nation's greatest abolitionist, was a native of Torrington.

Today, many of Connecticut's traditional industries, like the iron, copper, and brass production facilities that once prospered in areas like the **Litchfield Hills**, have faded away, but the mark of previous generations is still evident in the scores of historic homes and buildings open for tours throughout the state. Connecticut's proximity to New York, Boston, and Philadelphia makes it a popular destination for day-trippers and weekenders, who often fall in love with the calmer pace and end up moving or retiring here. The steady influx of this cosmopolitan crowd has helped ensure Connecticut has retained its position as a cultural center, evident in the many fine restaurants, boutiques, art galleries,

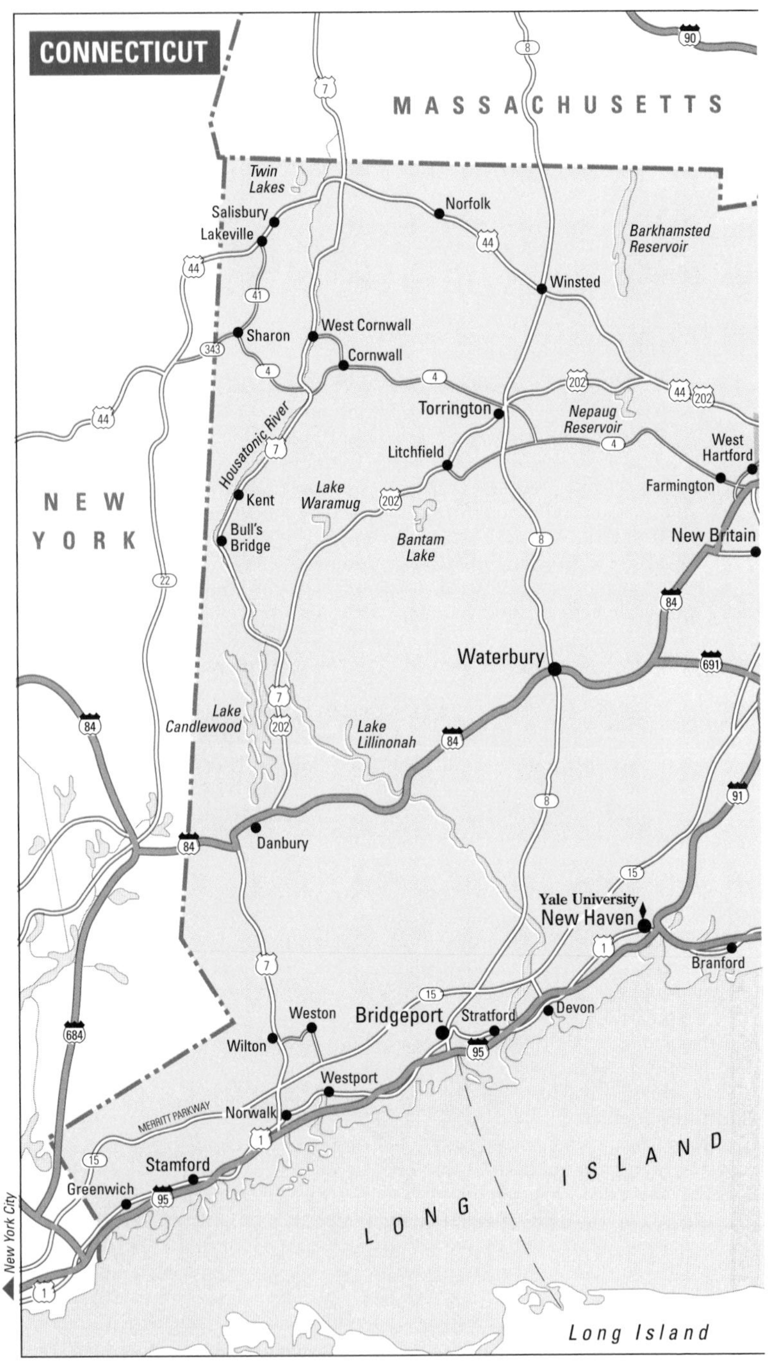
CONNECTICUT
MASSACHUSETTS
NEW YORK
Twin Lakes
Salisbury
Lakeville
Norfolk
Barkhamsted Reservoir
Winsted
Sharon
West Cornwall
Cornwall
Torrington
Nepaug Reservoir
Housatonic River
Litchfield
West Hartford
Farmington
Kent
Lake Waramug
Bull's Bridge
Bantam Lake
New Britain
Waterbury
Lake Candlewood
Lake Lillinonah
Danbury
Yale University
New Haven
Branford
Weston
Bridgeport
Stratford
Devon
Wilton
Westport
MERRITT PARKWAY
Norwalk
Stamford
Greenwich
New York City
LONG ISLAND
Long Island

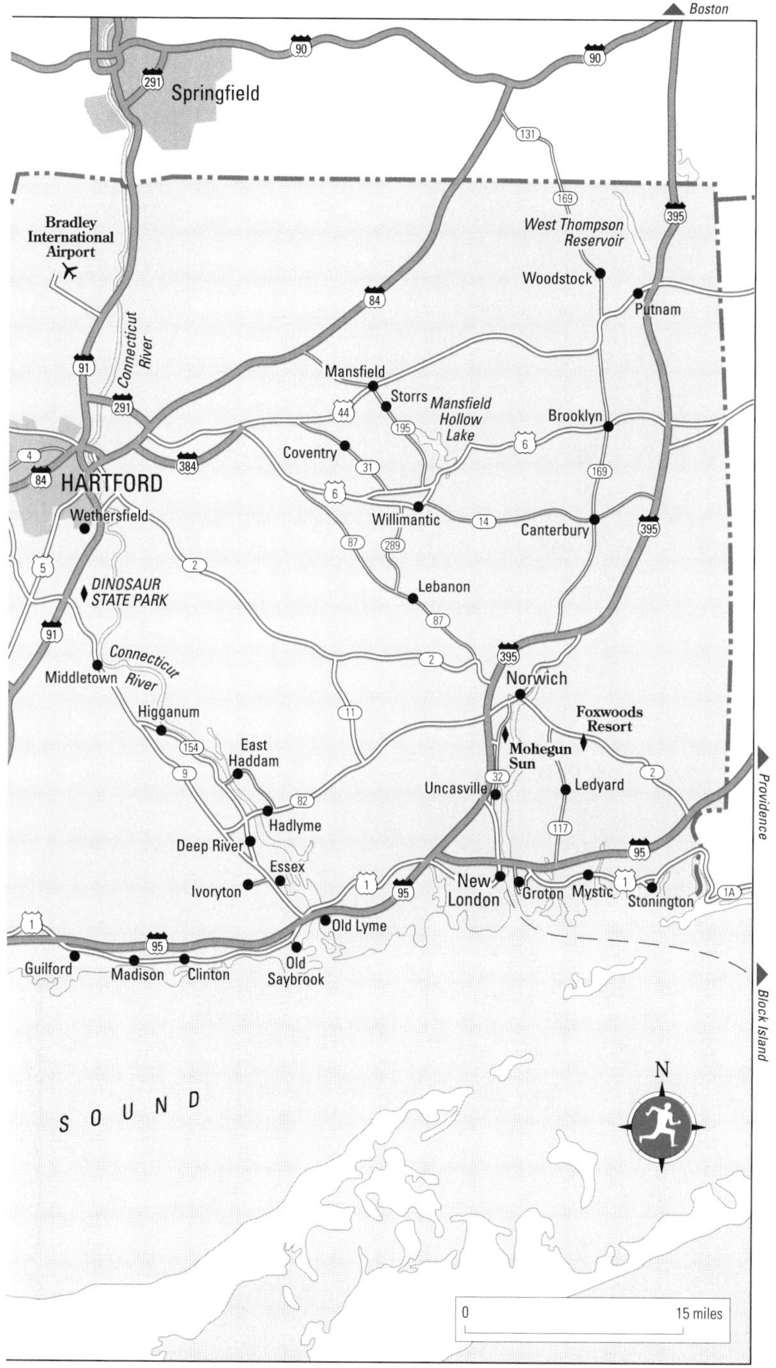

5 CONNECTICUT

and theaters throughout the state, even in the smallest of towns; visitors will find no shortage of rainy-day activities alongside the ample opportunities for hiking, boating, and just admiring the scenery. The **northeast**, or "**quiet**" **corner**, and the Litchfield Hills in the northwest, are particularly known for their large areas of green countryside and vast tracts of verdant forest, while **southeastern** Connecticut, a series of rocky surf-washed outcrops along Long Island Sound, also makes for a scenic trek.

Although the state is predominantly rural, it's also densely populated in parts: the vast majority of residents live in the coastal cities, in and around the capital **Hartford**, or in the **southwestern** corner of the state, which is little more than a conservative, high-rent suburb of New York City where commuters can earn Big Apple salaries while avoiding its high income taxes. The current linchpins of the economy – insurance, medical research, and military bases – hardly make for pleasing aesthetics in the larger cities, as evidenced in the high-rise corporate buildings of Hartford and the submarine fleet in Groton, though they do provide Connecticut's citizens with the highest average annual income in the country. More industrial-based cities like **New Haven**, also home to Yale University, and **Bridgeport**, in particular, have faced problems not usually associated with New England, like drug wars, homelessness, and violent crime, but aggressive development efforts in the last decade have helped ease these concerns.

Though Connecticut is easy enough to **get around** and well served by major roads – I-95 runs parallel to the coast of Long Island Sound from New York to Rhode Island (beware that it's jammed with traffic during rush hour); I-91 runs from New Haven up along the Connecticut River Valley to Vermont; and I-84 cuts a diagonal from the southwest to the northeast – it's more fun to get off the highways and onto the side roads, where you'll have more time to appreciate the attractive rural scenery and pretty colonial villages. Even getting lost can be fun; distances are so small that you'll find your way back sooner rather than later. Public transportation, on Amtrak trains or any of the major bus lines, covers both the coast and the more sizeable inland towns.

Some Connecticut firsts

1639 Connecticut produces the first **written constitution** in the colonies, *The Fundamental Orders*.

1656 The nation's first **public library** is opened in New Haven.

1775 The world's first **submarine** is launched by David Bushnell of Saybrook.

1784 The nation's first **law school** is established in Litchfield by Tapping Reeve.

1794 The first **cotton gin** is manufactured by Yale graduate Eli Whitney.

1796 The first **American cookbook** is published in Hartford, written by Amelia Simmons.

1806 The first **American English dictionary** is published in West Hartford by Noah Webster.

1846 The nation's first **amusement park** is opened in Bristol.

1877 The first **pay telephone** is introduced, followed the next year by the first **telephone exchange** in New Haven with 21 subscribers.

1881 The first **three-ring circus** is staged by Connecticut native P.T. Barnum.

1920 The **Frisbee** is invented in Bridgeport.

1934 The first **Polaroid camera** is produced in Bridgeport.

1975 Ella Grasso becomes the nation's first **elected woman governor**.

2000 Joseph Lieberman, from New Haven, is the first **Jewish candidate** on a presidential ticket.

Southeastern Connecticut

The much-visited **southeastern coast** of Connecticut stretches fifty miles from Stonington in the east to Branford in the west, bisected by the Thames (pronounced *Thaymz*) River. A succession of picturesque colonial communities, old whaling towns, and unattractive industrial cities characterize this section of Long Island Sound. No longer are they the iniquitous and rumbustious ports that so inspired Melville, but they're still keen to preserve – with varying degrees of success – a sense of their history. Among the highlights is **Mystic Seaport**, a reconstructed nineteenth-century maritime village with a fine collection of restored ships; the salty old whaling city of **New London**, which is beginning to bounce back from economic decline brought about by defense cutbacks at neighboring **Groton**, with a cluster of halfway decent galleries and museums as well as some fine old sea captains' houses; farther west, the prosperous towns of **Old Lyme** and **Old Saybrook** are home to a number of beguiling art galleries and museums; while **Guilford** has one of the largest collections of seventeenth- and eighteenth-century homes in the Northeast, several of which are open to the public. A bit inland, the massive casinos opened by local Native Americans at **Foxwoods** and **Mohegan Sun** attract millions of visitors annually; if you're looking to get well away from such bustle, there's no better place than off the coast of **Branford**, where you'll encounter a series of rocky outcrops (some inhabited, some not) known as the **Thimble Islands**.

Mystic

As purists will tell you, the town of **MYSTIC**, right on I-95, does not really exist; it's an area governed partly by Groton and partly by Stonington. Nonetheless, the old whaling port and shipbuilding center does have a small, well-kept, and rather touristy **downtown**, lined with typical New England-quaint clapboard galleries and antique shops. Before going on to see Mystic's main attractions in and around the seaport, you might first want to take a look at the **Mystic Arts Center**, 9 Water St (daily 11am–5pm; $2 donation; ⓣ860/536-7601, ⓦwww.mystic-art.org), with changing exhibits and a section devoted to local artists from the late eighteenth century to present day, including a recommended walking tour that will take you through Mystic village past the artists' homes (self-guided or by appointment). Not far away, the **Portersville Academy**, 76 High St, contains a restored classroom where you can enjoy the thrill of sitting at a school desk more than a hundred years old. The Mystic River Historical Society next door (Tues 9am–noon, Wed & Thurs 1pm–4pm; ⓣ860/536-4779, ⓦwww.mystichistory.org) manages the site; stop by their offices if you'd like to visit. The old drawbridge across the **Mystic River**, which divides the town down the middle, is still raised hourly. Along the western bank of the river is River Road, a four-mile stretch ideal for walking or cycling, which passes **Downes Marsh**, a sanctuary where you may catch a glimpse of ospreys and cranes.

Mystic Seaport and around

What tourists come to Mystic to see is on the other side of the bridge, the meticulously constructed waterfront village of **Mystic Seaport**, also known

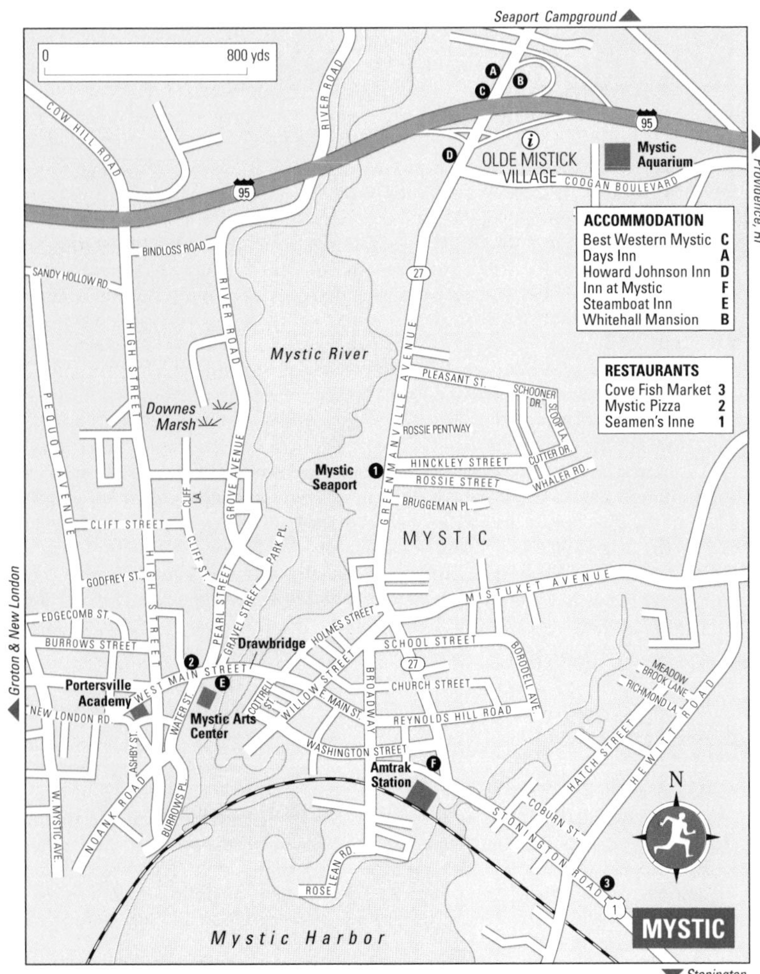

as the Museum of America & the Sea (daily: April–Oct 9am–5pm, rest of year 10am–4pm; $17, children $9; ⓣ860/572-5315, ⓦwww.mysticseaport.org), where more than sixty weathered buildings house old-style workshops and stores, including an apothecary and a printing press. The **Stillman Building** contains beautifully carved scrimshaw, ornate figureheads, and vast numbers of objects made from whales' wax-like spermaceti, as well as disturbing video footage of a bloody whale hunt. Demonstrations of sea-shanty singing, fish-splitting, sail-setting, and knot-tying vie with storytelling and theater, and state-of-the-art interactive computers enable visitors to track hurricanes and encourage children to become sailors. In the **Henry Dupont Preservation Shipyard**, you can watch the building, restoration, and maintenance of a vast collection of wooden ships, among them the *Joseph Conrad*, an 1882 training ship, the *L.A. Dunton*, a 1921 fishing schooner, and the restored *Charles W. Morgan*, a three-masted wooden Yankee **whaling ship** built in 1841, and the last of its kind. Done up as if ready to embark on a two-year voyage, the ship is filled with whaling memorabilia; below deck, accessed by perilously narrow stairs, the blubber room is crowded with huge iron try-pots for melting down the stinking stuff. The Seaport also boasts the nation's most extensive maritime bookstore and the **Mystic Maritime Gallery**, a center for contemporary marine art with a display of model ships.

About a mile north of the Seaport, adjacent to I-95, the **Mystic Aquarium** is the town's other major draw (Jan & Feb Mon–Fri 10am–5pm, Sat & Sun 9am–6pm, March–Dec daily 9am–6pm; adults $19.75, children 3–17 $14.25; ⓣ860/572-5955, ⓦwww.mysticaquarium.org), where more than nine thousand weird and wonderful marine specimens glug about. Just beyond the entrance pavilion, visitors are confronted with an 800,000-gallon saltwater tank that holds the only beluga whales in New England, with views above and below the water line. With an advance reservation (ⓣ860/572-5955 ext 520) and $145 you can even get in the water with the 1500-pound animals. Fun for kids are the sea lion theater and the ray touch pool.

Nearby, at the intersection of I-95 and Rte-27, nearly sixty not-so-quaint craft and gift shops in mock-Colonial buildings occupy the overdone **Olde Mistick Village** (late June to early Sept Mon–Sat 10am–8pm, Sun 11am–6pm, rest of year Mon–Sat 10am–6pm, Sun noon–5pm; ⓣ860/536-4941, ⓦwww.oldemistickvillage.com).

Practicalities

There's a **train station** in Mystic where Amtrak calls in on its Boston-to-Washington route (schedule information ⓣ1-800/872-7245), and South East Area Transit provides a regular **bus** service to Mistick Village (ⓣ860/886-2631). Mystic's **information office**, which has accomodation information, is in the Olde Mistick Village Shopping Mall (Mon–Sat 9am–6pm, Sun 10am–5pm; ⓣ860/536-1641). It may be useful to take advantage of their help, as it's very difficult to find a place to stay in the town in the peak summer months; you should definitely reserve your room well in advance if your visit is in July or August. The Mystic Country Convention and Visitors' Bureau (ⓣ1-800/TOENJOY or ⓦwww.mysticcountry.com) can also provide information.

Lodging options include the *Whitehall Mansion*, 42 Whitehall Ave (ⓣ860/572-7280 or 1-800/572-3993; ❼), a painstakingly restored 1771 mansion with five

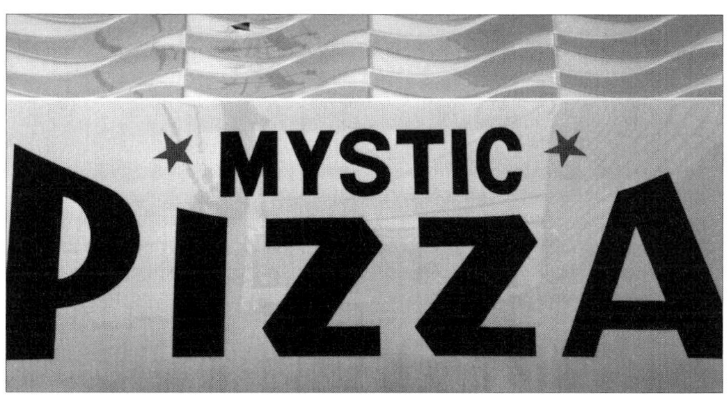

△ *Mystic Pizza* sign

guestrooms furnished with antiques, queen-sized canopy beds, and working fireplaces, and the *Steamboat Inn,* 73 Steamboat Wharf (Ⓣ860-536-8300, Ⓦwww.steamboatinnmystic.com; ❼), with ten elegant rooms with whirlpool baths; they also have five luxurious staterooms on their 97-foot yacht *Valiant* (Ⓦwww.valiantcharters.com; ❽). For a larger but still intimate spot, try the *Inn at Mystic,* at the intersection of routes 1 and 27 (Ⓣ860/536-9604 or 1-800/237-2415, Ⓦwww.innatmystic.com; ❺), which has 67 lovely rooms on a landscaped hillside overlooking the sound; Humphrey Bogart and Lauren Bacall honeymooned here in 1945. The Seaport **campground**, off Rte-184 in Old Mystic (Ⓣ860/536-4044, Ⓦwww.seaportcampground.com; $40), has 130 sites and a swimming pool.

Much the best-known **restaurant** in town, *Mystic Pizza*, 56 W Main St (Ⓣ860/536-3700), is a small, family-run place that for $10–15 serves huge pies; it remains relatively unruffled by its status as pilgrimage site for movie fanatics (see "Films," p.616). In the heart of the seaport, the *Seamen's Inne*, 105 Greenmanville Rd (Ⓣ860/572-5303), serves a hearty seafood pot pie of scallops, lobster, and shrimps for $23; other entrees start at $12. Or for under $5, you can try some award-winning clam chowder (800 gallons sold a month) at an outdoor picnic table at *Cove Fish Market*, 20 Old Stonington Rd (Ⓣ860/536-0061).

Around Mystic

Not far from Mystic are a few hard-working towns, especially charming **Stonington**, which may lack obvious attractions, but certainly make for a more complete picture of the area, and are worth a poke around if you've got more than a short afternoon to spend here. If you're interested in a bit of glitz, just inland are Connecticut's **gambling** facilities, on Native American land.

Stonington

STONINGTON, just south of I-95 near the state's eastern border, is a disarmingly pretty old fishing village, originally settled in 1649 and still very much New England with its attractive whitewashed cottages, white picket fences, colorful gardens, and peaceful waterfront. Its main road, **Water Street**, is brimming with antique shops and upmarket thrift stores, packed with well-to-do bargain hunters on weekends. At no. 7, the **Old Lighthouse Museum** (May–Nov daily 10am–5pm; $5; Ⓣ860-535-1440), moved back a bit from its original position due to the dangers of erosion, dates from 1823 and has six small rooms of exhibits about life in a seventeenth-century coastal town, including whaling and fishing gear. You can climb the stone steps and iron ladder for views over Long Island Sound; on a clear day you can see Rhode Island and New York. Museum admission also allows you access to the Italianate **Captain Nathaniel B. Palmer House**, 40 Palmer St (May–Nov Tues–Sun 10am–4pm; $5; Ⓣ860-535-8445), at the north end of town. The mansion celebrates the life of Palmer, whose main claim to fame was the discovery of the Antarctic Peninsula in 1820, and is topped by an octagonal cupola from which Palmer and his family could identify ships arriving from far-off ports.

A few miles out of the village center, at exit 91 off I-95, follow the "Wine Trail" signs to the **Stonington Vineyards**, 523 Taugwonk Rd (daily 11am–5pm, free tour at 2pm; Ⓣ860-535-1222), for a look around a local wine producer and free tastings of their concoctions like Seaport White and Seaport Blush (for more on the Wine Trail, see box on p.378).

Practicalities

If you'd like to **stay** in Stonington, the *Orchard Street Inn*, 41 Orchard St (ⓣ860/535-2681, ⓦwww.orchardstreetinn.com; ❼), offers three newly renovated and beautifully decorated rooms in a secluded cottage with a quiet patio. Alternatively, try the *Cove Ledge Inn & Marina*, Whewell Circle (ⓣ860/599-4130, ⓦwww.coveledgeinn.com; ❺), with simple, uncluttered rooms close to the water. Two seafood **restaurants**, *Water St Café* and *Skipper's Dock*, are within a hop and a skip of one another. The former, at 143 Water St (ⓣ860/535-2122, lunch Thurs–Mon, dinner daily), has fancy food in a casual spot, while the latter, at no. 66 (ⓣ860/535-0111; closed all of Jan and Tues in winter), is pricey but lively and rowdy, with a Sunday jazz brunch and a deck offering fantastic ocean views. Nearby, *Noah's*, 113 Water St (ⓣ860/535-3925; closed Mon), has an eclectic homestyle menu including Chinese noodles, chili con queso, and homemade fettucine.

Groton

Seven miles west of Mystic Seaport, **GROTON** is a suitably unpleasant name for the home town of the hideous **US Naval Submarine Base**, off Rte-12 on Crystal Lake Road, headquarters for the North Atlantic Fleet. The base has been a crucial fixture in the local economy since 1916 but at the time of writing was facing an uncertain future; nationwide military budget cuts may force its closure. Remaining open, however, is the **Submarine Force Museum** next door (mid-May to Oct Wed–Mon 9am–5pm, Tues 1–5pm; Nov to mid-May Wed–Mon 9am–4pm; free; ⓣ800/343-0079), which traces the history of submersibles from Bushnell's *American Turtle*, used in the Revolutionary War, to the powerful *Trident*. The main hall features a re-created World War II attack center, where you can look through one of three periscopes and take aim on cars in the parking lot. Or to get a little closer to the action, you can tour the **USS Nautilus**, America's first nuclear-powered submarine, which was built at the base and is now docked at the museum: you'll wind your way through narrow, claustrophobic passages past the wardroom and officers' berthing area and the attack center, down a short, steep staircase to the control room, the radio room, and the crew's quarters, with bunks stacked three and four high, complete with pin-ups of Marilyn Monroe.

For an above-ground perspective, **Project Oceanology** runs **boat tours** from the University of Connecticut's Avery Point Campus. The ship *Enviro-Lab* makes 2.5-hour summer excursions up and down the Thames, gathering plankton, water, sand, and oceanographic information with the help of paying customers (daily mid-June–Aug; $19, children 6–12 $16; ⓣ860/445-9007, ⓦwww.oceanology.org). They also do afternoon tours of the Ledge Lighthouse (mid-June–Aug Tues, Thurs & Sat, Sept Sat only), stuck out in the middle of the river in New London, a mansard-roofed, square red-brick structure with a rich history, and, supposedly, a resident ghostly presence. Reservations for either tour strongly recommended.

New London

On the opposite bank of the Thames from Groton, **NEW LONDON**, with 26,000 residents, is the most populated city along this stretch of the coast, though it's hardly a metropolis and spreads over but six square miles. It was a wealthy whaling port in the nineteenth century, and by the 1850s was second only to New Bedford, Massachusetts, for the size of its whaling fleet. After relying for most of the twentieth century on military-base revenue, New London struggled in the

1990s due to spending cuts, though efforts to liven up the downtown area – as well as the construction of pharmaceutical giant Pfizer's R&D HQ – have made great progress in recent years; trendy boutiques, galleries, and restaurants have been rapidly popping up around town. This progress has not come without controversy, however: in June 2005, New London became the focus of national attention for a case brought by the city to the Supreme Court, **Kelo v. City of New London**. The Court ruled that eminent domain, which has traditionally allowed government seizure of private property (with compensation) for the public good, extends to private developers as well. As a result, at the time of writing, a handful of private homes in the town's Fort Trumbull district were to be seized and demolished for the development of a waterfront office and housing complex – though not without protest from defenders of private property.

The Town

One of New London's highlights, the **US Coast Guard Academy**, off I-95 at 15 Mohegan Ave (daily 9am–5pm; free), spreads out on an attractive sloping campus overlooking the Thames. Visitors are welcome to meander around the grounds; maps and guides are available at the visitors' center (May–Oct Wed–Sun 9am–5pm; ⓣ860/444-8611) and at the **US Coast Guard Museum** (open daily, call for hours; free; ⓣ1-860/444-8595), which explores two centuries of coast guard history. The museum houses the figurehead from the USS *Eagle*, the only tall ship on active duty, now used as a training vessel and often docked in town either at the Academy or at the City Pier in New London; in either case, it is open for afternoon tours.

Gambling on Connecticut's Native American reservations

Until the late 1980s, the $400 billion-a-year **gambling** business was confined to just two states, Nevada and New Jersey, but a lobbying push from Native American tribes, eager for greater self-determination to manage their own affairs, moved Congress to pass the Indian Gambling Regulatory Act in 1988. This reform recognized the rights of Native American tribes in the US to establish gambling and gaming facilities on their reservations, so long as the states in which they are located have some form of legalized gambling, and, indeed, today gambling is only wholly illegal in Hawaii and Utah.

Connecticut has since become home to two major Native American casinos, over objections from environmentalists, anti-gambling agencies, and residents. The massive **Foxwoods Resort and Casino**, Rte-2, Ledyard (ⓣ1-800/FOXWOODS, ⓦwww.foxwoods.com), rises dramatically above the virgin pine forests north of New London and draws millions of visitors annually. Built by the Mashantucket-Pequot Indians, the casino's visitors have three huge hotels to accommodate them, as well as all manner of slots, gaming tables, and bingo to entertain. Not content with already being the largest resort casino in the world, Foxwoods has begun a $700 million expansion, including an additional eight hundred rooms, that's slated to open in 2008. Just a few miles away, the **Mohegan Sun Casino**, Rte-2A, Uncasville (ⓣ1-888/226-7711, ⓦwww.mohegansun.com), opened its doors in 1996 as Foxwood's much smaller and quieter competitor. But after a $1 billion expansion which concluded in 2002 with the introduction of a new 1200-room hotel and the largest ballroom in the Northeast, the Sun has become more of a commercial draw, while managing to retain some of the traditional Indian reverence for nature – there's even a fifty-page guide to the cultural significance of the architecture and artwork throughout the casino, including the planetarium ceiling and the sixty-foot-high crystal mountain that encases a dance floor. Most, though, are too busy minding their chips to take notice.

Just opposite the Academy entrance, at the southern end of the **Connecticut College** campus, the **Lyman Allyn Art Museum**, 625 Williams St (Tues–Sat 10am–5pm, Sun 1–5pm; $5; ⓣ860/443-2545), contains all varieties of American fine arts and crafts, including a silver tankard made by Paul Revere, along with rotating exhibits of American and European art from the eighteenth century to today. On a clear day, Connecticut College itself sports a stunning view of Long Island Sound about a five-minute walk from the museum, in front of the Humanities Center.

Information is available at the **Trolley Station**, on Eugene O'Neill Drive (May & Oct Fri–Sun 10am–4pm, June to Sept daily 10am–4pm; ⓣ860/444-7264), and the **Mystic Country CVB**, 32 Huntington St (Mon–Fri 8.30am–4.30pm; ⓣ860/444-2206). Both provide maps for a self-guided downtown walking tour, which takes you past **Whale Oil Row**, a short line of private 1830s Greek Revival homes once owned by leaders in the whale-oil business; **State Street**, New London's main thoroughfare, lined with a variety of shops and restaurants; and the **Nathan Hale Schoolhouse**, on Eugene O'Neill Drive (May–Oct Wed–Sun 11am–4pm; $2; ⓣ860-873-3399). The schoolhouse is where where Nathan Hale, the Revolutionary War hero famed for his last words, "I only regret that I have but one life to lose for my country," taught for sixteen months in 1774–75 before beginning his military service.

A bit south, the **Shaw-Perkins Mansion**, 11 Blinman St (Wed–Fri 1–4pm, Sat 10am–4pm; $5; ⓣ860/443-1209), a stone house built in 1756 for wealthy ship-owner and trader Nathaniel Shaw, has unusual paneled-cement fireplace walls and some period furnishings and portraits. Meanwhile, New London's oldest home, the 1678 **Joshua Hempsted House**, 11 Hempstead St (mid-May to mid-Oct Thurs–Sun noon–4pm; $5; ⓣ860-443-7949), is said to have been used as a safe haven on the Underground Railroad, though you'll find nothing too special to mark it as such. Admission also gets you into the **Nathaniel Hempsted House** – Nathaniel was Joshua's grandson – across the lawn, which stands out for its two-foot-thick stone walls and outdoor stone beehive oven.

New London is renowned as the birthplace of boozy playwright **Eugene O'Neill**, whose childhood home, the **Monte Cristo Cottage**, 325 Pequout Ave (mid-June to mid-Sept Tues–Sat 10am–5pm, Sun and rest of year by appointment; $5; ⓣ860/443-0051), can be toured complete with juicy details of his trauma-ridden early life – though they may already be familiar to you from his *Long Day's Journey into Night*. The influence of the only American Nobel-winning playwright is felt further at the **Eugene O'Neill Theater Center**, at 305 Great Neck Rd in nearby Waterford, an acclaimed testing-ground for playwrights and actors where audiences can watch new, often experimental shows in rehearsal (performances held sporadically June–Aug; ⓣ860-443-1238, ⓦwww.oneilltheatercenter.org). Just beyond the Cristo Cottage, **Ocean Beach Park**, 1225 Ocean Ave (summer Mon–Fri 9am–late, Sat & Sun 8am–late; $10–14 parking includes admission for all occupants, or $5 walk-in; ⓣ860-447-3031) is packed with summer fun, including a "sugar sand" beach, wooden boardwalk and arcade, mini-golf course, waterslide, and massive outdoor pool.

Groton and New London practicalities

Given Groton and New London's proximity to I-95, most, but not all, visitors arrive by road. Other options include a **car ferry** from Orient Point on Long Island (Cross Sound Ferry; ⓣ860/443-5281) and a regular Amtrak **train** from New York, Boston, and other points along the main East Coast line. Greyhound **buses** serve the city, and there's a **local bus** network, SEAT (South East Area

Transit; ⓣ860/886-2631); the #2 and #3 lines can take you around the two towns, but they don't run on Sundays.

It's generally less expensive to **stay** here than touristy Mystic, ten miles away, with several reasonably priced motels along I-95, including the *Holiday Inn*, 269 N Frontage Rd (ⓣ860/442-0631; ❻), and a *Super 8*, 173 Rte-12 (ⓣ860/448-2818; ❹). New London also has the upscale *Lighthouse Inn Resort*, 6 Guthrie Place (ⓣ860/443-8411 or 1-800/443-8411; ⓦwww.lighthouseinn-ct.com; ❼), with 52 spacious rooms furnished with local antiques, as well as an outdoor pool, spa, and beach access.

There are a few good **restaurants** worth stopping into, including *Timothy's* at the *Lighthouse Inn* (see above), where, from your vantage point on the Long Island Sound, you can sample Long Island duckling. On the cheaper side is the *Recovery Room*, 445 Ocean Ave (ⓣ860/443-2619), where the pizzas are one-size-fits-all at twelve inches. For a $1.50 draft, head to the perfect dive bar, *Dutch Tavern*, 23 Green St (ⓣ860/442-3453), complete with the very same 100-year-old tables at which O'Neill once sat. Over the water in Groton, *Abbot's Lobster in the Rough*, 117 Pearl St (ⓣ860/536-7719), serves the delicious creatures daily during the summer and on weekends in the early spring and fall; bring your own alcohol. Neighboring *Costello's Clam Shack*, 145 Pearl St (ⓣ860-572-2779), serves clams and oysters in summer, and has live music on Wednesday evenings.

West to New Haven

Fifteen miles west of New London, at the mouth of the Connecticut River, sits **OLD LYME**, the site of an Impressionist art colony dating from the end of the nineteenth century. It was started in 1899 when an unmarried middle-aged woman faced with a high mortgage opened her home to boarders and began to attract and befriend a regular clientele of artists. The eleven-acre property of the **Florence Griswold Museum**, 96 Lyme St (Tues–Sat 10am–5pm, Sun 1–5pm; $7, kids 6–12 $4; ⓣ860/434-5542, ⓦwww.flogris.org), showcases the Lyme Art Colony and the life of Griswold, with a 10,000 square-foot changing exhibit space next door to the very boarding house "Miss Florence" managed. The house itself was recently restored to its 1910 appearance and includes more than forty original panels painted directly onto the walls by the various artists who stayed here, including Willard Metcalfe, Childe Hassam, and William Chadwick, whose studio is also on-site and set up just as it was during his lifetime. On Sundays from April to December, admission includes a canvas, paints, and a smock so you can paint the same scene of the Lieutenant River that kept the artists returning for more than thirty years. A few doors away, the **Lyme Academy College of Fine Arts**, 84 Lyme St (Mon–Sat 10am–4pm; donation requested; ⓣ860-434-5232), founded in 1976, has two galleries – one housed in a Federal-style house dating from 1817 – that feature drawings, paintings, and sculpture by contemporary artists.

Old Saybrook

The former shipbuilding center of **OLD SAYBROOK**, opposite Old Lyme on the western bank of the Connecticut River, is the oldest town on Connecticut's coast and claims a few historic houses along its main road. Though there's little else to draw your attention, it's a good, centrally located base for a more complete exploration of Connecticut's southeastern coast. Puritan settlers arrived in 1635 and soon erected a fort to guard the river entrance to the town, an act remembered in **Fort Saybrook Monument Park** at the stronghold's former site, though nothing of the fort remains today. In 1707 the town became the home of the **Collegiate School** – later to move to New Haven and rename itself **Yale University**.

Commercial activity centers on Boston Post Road, while the unusually wide **Main Street** becomes progressively more interesting the farther south you get toward Saybrook Point, showcasing architectural styles from seventeenth-century saltboxes to nineteenth-century Federal buildings. Of these, the 1767 **General William Hart House**, 350 Main St (July & Aug Sat & Sun 1pm–4pm; $5; ⓣ860-388-2622), once the residence of a prosperous merchant who owned a fleet of sailing ships and served in the Revolutionary War, has been restored to its original elegance. It contains eight corner fireplaces, one decorated with Sadler and Green transfer print tiles illustrating scenes from Aesop's fables; there's also a reference library and a new gallery of rotating historical exhibits onsite.

Practicalities

Local **bus** services are provided by the Estuary Transit District (ⓣ860/510-0429), and some Amtrak **trains** stop at Old Saybrook (ⓣ1-800/872-7245), with a local commuter service between New Haven and New London provided by Shore Line East (ⓣ1-800/255-7433). The **Old Saybrook Chamber of Commerce** (ⓦwww.oldsaybrookct.com) maintains an office at 146 Main St (Mon–Fri 9am–5pm; ⓣ860/388-3266). They'll have info about the wide variety of **accommodation** in the area, ranging from historic B&Bs like the 1746 *Deacon Timothy Pratt House B&B*, 325 Main St, Old Saybrook (ⓣ860/395-1229, ⓦwww.pratthouse.net; ❻), with rooms furnished in period style, working fireplaces, and four-poster beds, and the luxurious *Saybrook Point Inn & Spa*, 2 Bridge St, Old Saybrook (ⓣ860/395-2000 or 1-800/243-0212, ⓦwww.saybrook.com; ❽), where many of the eighty rooms have water views and functional fireplaces, to a number of motels and inns all located along Boston Post Road (Rte-1). These include the friendly, 45-room *Knights Inn*, at no. 1750 (ⓣ860/399-7973 or 1-800/843-5644, ⓦwww.knightsinn.com; ❹), and the smaller but equally comfortable *Heritage Motor Inn*, at no. 1500 (ⓣ860/388-3743; ❹). In neighboring **Westbrook**, the sprawling *Water's Edge Resort & Spa*, at no. 1525 (ⓣ860/399-5901, ⓦwww.watersedgeresortandspa.com; ❽), offers caviar facials at its posh spa and is the only Connecticut resort on its own private beach.

Many of Old Saybrook's **restaurants** are also to be found on Boston Post Road: the moderately priced *Old Saybrook Diner*, a town fixture at no. 809 (ⓣ860/395-1079), serves great spinach pie, while *Cuckoo's Nest*, no. 1712 (ⓣ860/399-9060), offers tasty and plentiful Mexican, Southwestern, and Cajun dishes for $11–20. Dating from 1896, the *James Gallery & Soda Fountain*, 2 Pennywise Lane, at Main Street (ⓣ860/395-1222), serves two dozen ice cream flavors and was once favored by local Katherine Hepburn. Away from Boston Post, *Dock & Dine*, on College Street, Saybrook Point (ⓣ860/388-4665), has lovely views over the Connecticut River to go with classic American steak and seafood dishes – though you'll pay for it.

Clinton

CLINTON, eight miles west of Old Saybrook, pushes itself as one of the most visited leisure ports on Long Island Sound, thanks to an abundance of well-equipped marinas. Its historic district includes the **Adam Stanton House**, 63

E Main St (by appointment only; donation requested; ⓣ860-669-2132), built around 1790 and where the Marquis de Lafayette stayed in 1824; the bed in which he slept is still displayed in its original surroundings. The house served as a general store for many years, supplying goods and services to the sailors whose boats docked nearby; on display are items that were sold back in those days, together with a collection of antique American and Staffordshire dinnerware. Today Clinton is better known for its **Clinton Crossing Premium Outlets**, just off I-95 exit 63 (July & Aug Mon–Sat 10am–9pm, Sun 10am–8pm, rest of year Mon–Sat 10am–9pm, Sun 10am–6pm), with more than seventy upmarket stores offering savings on designer goods. You're unlikely to **stay** in town, though it is pleasant enough; if you do, consider *A Victorian Village – Marina Cottages*, 345 East Main St (ⓣ860/669-3009 or 1-800/895-9588, ⓦwww.avictorianvillage.com; $400/week), a cluster of comfortable, antique-filled cottages set around a landscaped garden.

Madison

Just a few miles west on Rte-1, posh **MADISON** sits on the waterfront with an attractive shady green overlooked by a white-spired church and a broad main street lined with upmarket boutiques and trendy cafés. There's not much to distinguish it from nearby Clinton, though it does contain two historic buildings of note. Built in 1685, the **Deacon John Grave House**, 581 Boston Post Rd (summer Thurs–Sat 1–4pm, call for rest of year; $2; ⓣ203/245-4798), is Madison's oldest residence, used over the years as a school, a wartime infirmary and weapons depot, an inn, a tavern, and a courtroom, all while remaining under the auspices of the Grave family through the 1980s. Indeed, there's even a surviving ledger of their household expenditures from 1678 to 1895. Farther down Boston Post, the white-clapboard saltbox **Allis-Bushnell House**, at no. 853 (late-May to mid-Oct Wed, Fri & Sat 1–4pm; donation; ⓣ203/245-4567), dates from 1785 and contains original paneling and unusual corner fireplaces. One room has been restored as a turn-of-the-twentieth-century doctor's office in memory of Dr Milo Rindye, a popular physician who lived and worked in the house. There's also an interesting collection of artifacts and the like, from costumes and kitchenware to a Victorian hearing aid and working looms.

About two miles east of downtown Madison, off Rte-1, **Hammonasset Beach State Park** (daily 8am–sunset; parking in summer $10 weekdays, $14 weekends; ⓣ203/245-2785) maintains two miles of prime sandy beach, backed by dunes and a salt marsh. If you don't fancy a swim, there's a **nature center** in the park that contains exhibits about the wildlife and history of the area, and you can **camp** here in the summer for $15/night.

Practicalities

Good **accommodation** choices are *The Inn at Lafayette*, 725 Boston Post Rd (ⓣ203/245-7773 or 1-866/623-7498, ⓦwww.allegrecafe.com/innatlafayette.htm; ❼), a smart downtown establishment with five rooms housed in what was once a church; the *Dolly Madison Inn*, just two minutes from the water at 73 West Wharf Rd (ⓣ203/245-7377; ❹), with cozy rooms and access to one of the town beaches; and the *Tidewater Inn*, 949 Boston Post Rd, a pleasant woodsy retreat (ⓣ203/245-8457, ⓦwww.thetidewater.com; ❻). Places to **eat** include the casual *Perfect Parties*, 885 Boston Post Rd (ⓣ203/245-0250; closed Mon & Tues), with offerings ranging from good inexpensive salads, soups, and sandwiches to gourmet dinners for eat-in or take-out, and *The Wharf*, 94 West

Wharf Rd at the *Madison Beach Hotel* (ⓣ203/245-0005; open April–Nov), where moderately priced, good-value seafood – baked, broiled, fried, or sauteed – is their thing.

Guilford

First settled by English vicar Reverend Henry Whitfield in 1639, **GUILFORD** has one of the largest collections of seventeenth- and eighteenth-century houses in New England, of which only a handful are open to the public. Among them, and dating to 1639, Whitfield's own home at 248 Old Whitfield St, the oldest surviving stone house in New England, has been transformed into the **Henry Whitfield State Museum** (April to mid-Dec Wed–Sun 10am–4.30pm; $4 adults, $2.50 children; ⓣ203/453-2457). The fortress-like dwelling also served as a meeting-place for the village community, and currently contains a collection of antique furniture, weaving and textile equipment, and the first tower clock made in the colonies, dating from 1726; today it's also the home of the **Guilford Tourism Office** (same hours as above; ⓣ203/453-2457, ⓦwww.guilfordct.com). Nearby, at 84 Boston St, the **Hyland House** (June to early Sept Tues–Sat 10am–4.30pm, Sun noon–4.30pm; early Sept to mid-Oct Sat & Sun 10am–4.30pm; donation requested), a saltbox built in the late seventeenth century, belonged to esteemed clockmaker Ebenezer Parmelee (who made the clock now at the Whitfield). Little refurbishment has gone on since; the house is held together by the same old nails and bolts, and has its original casement window and hand-hewn floorboards. The last of the three houses open to the public is a short walk away at 171 Boston St, the **Thomas Griswold House** (June–Sept Tues–Sun 11am–4pm, Oct Sat & Sun 11am–4pm, Nov–May by appointment; $2), another saltbox, built in 1774, and full of period furniture and clothing, photographs, and changing local history exhibits. Outside, there's a working blacksmith's shop and Colonial-style garden. Guilford's spacious **village green** – purported to be the largest in New England – is the attractive location for summer concerts and recitals, lined on two sides with boutiques and restaurants.

Practicalities

For **accommodation** in Guilford, the *Guilford Suites Hotel*, 2300 Boston Post Rd (ⓣ203/453-0123; ❻), has well-equipped rooms; a little more charm can be found at the ★ *B&B at Bartlett Farm*, 564 Great Hill Rd (ⓣ203/457-1657, ⓦwww.thebartlettfarm.com; ❻; two-night minimum stay), fifteen minutes outside of town, offering three rooms on a working farm built in 1784, complete with goats, sheep, and even a buffalo. There's no shortage of excellent **restaurants** along this stretch of the coast. A good stop is *Guilford Mooring*, 505 Whitfield St (ⓣ203/458-2921), where the focus is on moderate to expensive seafood. For a far more casual, and less costly, dining experience, *The Place*, 891 Boston Post Rd (ⓣ203/453-9276; open late April to Oct), does grilled seafood on a huge outdoor wood fire – diners sit on logs and toss their shells onto the gravel.

Branford and the Thimble Islands

You'll have little reason to stop in **BRANFORD**, despite its surprisingly good collection of restaurants, other than perhaps its proximity to the **Thimble Islands**. If you do find yourself with an extra couple of hours to kill, however, stop by the **Harrison House**, 124 Main St (June–Oct Fri & Sat 2–5pm; donation; ⓣ203/488-4828), built in 1724 and restored to its original condition in 1938, and containing an interesting display of farm implements in its barn.

△ The Thimble Islands

Branford's main attraction is the **THIMBLE ISLANDS**, a group of 365 tiny islands off the nearby village of **Stony Creek**, best accessed by exit 56 off I-95. The so-called chain of islands is in reality a cluster of granite rocks within a three-mile radius of shore, ranging in size from one large enough to support a small community of 24 homes (mostly Victorian), to some that actually disappear at high tide. Years ago, they provided a perfect hiding place for pirate ships waiting to attack passing boats in Long Island Sound; one of the individuals who purportedly used these waters to this end was **Captain Kidd**, who is said to have hidden treasure here (he could hardly have buried it) when being chased by the British. You can hear the colorful narratives spun about the islands by taking a **tour** on either the *Islander* ($9; ⓣ203/397-3921) or the *Volsunga IV* ($9; ⓣ203/481-3345), two boats that offer daily 45-minute trips from mid-May until mid-October, departing from the Town Dock at the end of Thimble Island Road. For a little more adventure, you can also **kayak** around the islands on two- to five-hour trips with *Stony Creek Kayak,* 327 Leetes Island Rd ($60–120; ⓣ203-481-6401, ⓦwww.stonycreekkayak.com).

Practicalities

Branford's many fine **restaurants** are primarily located around the Branford Green, like *Assaggio*, 168 Montowese St (ⓣ203/483-5426), with moderately priced contemporary Italian dishes and a nice wine list, and ✱ *Le Petit Café*, 225 Montowese St (ⓣ203/483-9791; dinner only, closed Mon & Tues), one of the best restaurants around serving prix-fixe-only French bistro cuisine – reservations necessary. Much more casual is *Lenny's*, 205 S Montowese St (ⓣ203/488-1500), a moderately priced seafood shack teeming with noisy kids and their parents. Near the dock in Stony Creek, the *Stony Creek Market*, 178 Thimble Island Rd (ⓣ203/488-0145), sports a combined restaurant, bakery, deli, and (in the evenings) pizzeria, with stunning views of the Thimbles from its deck. Branford's absence of inns and B&Bs is compensated for by the abundance of inexpensive and generally basic **hotels** and **motels**, most of which are located on East Main Street, such as the *Motel 6*, no. 320 (ⓣ203/483-5828; ❸), and the *Branford Motel*, no. 470 (ⓣ203/488-5442; ❹).

New Haven and southwestern Connecticut

An essential stop on any tour of Connecticut, **New Haven** is one of the state's more bearable bigger cities, given life by its intriguing mix of downbeat industrial center and college town. It practically divides the shoreline in half, and can really be visited in conjunction with the coastal stretch on either side, or even Hartford, its urban rival just over thirty miles away. Still, it's most similar in character to the built-up coast in the **southwestern** portion of the state, which leads all the way to the outskirts of New York City. Indeed, the southwest is by far the most developed part of Connecticut, and the former hub of its manufacturing base. Although nicknamed the "gold coast" for its exceedingly wealthy towns like **Greenwich** and **Westport**, it's an unattractive region on the whole, a result of the decline in industry, alleviated only in parts by the odd historic building and the grassy sights on the **Merritt Parkway**, also known as **Rte-15**, a good alternative to the parallel – and much busier – I-95, which runs directly along the coast throughout the region. The state's largest city, **Bridgeport**, despite valiant attempts to reverse its urban decline, is still a depressing place to visit, while **Stamford**, marginally less ugly, has been quite successful in managing to entice leading business corporations away from New York City. **Norwalk** is another city which had fallen on bad times and is now working hard to improve itself, while inland, predominantly residential **Danbury**, the city once known as the nation's "hat capital," sits in the **Housatonic Valley**, a pleasant, hilly landscape dotted with rivers and lakes.

New Haven

Don't be put off by the grubby initial impression you get when you arrive in **NEW HAVEN** via I-95 or by train: tucked away among the grimy factories, tall chimneys, and architecturally nondescript office blocks are some of the best restaurants, most exciting nightspots, and diverting cultural activities in all of New England – not to mention, of course, the idyllic, leafy Ivy League campus of **Yale University**. The tensions between these two very different facets once made New Haven a somewhat uneasy place, though since the early 1990s, which saw the Yale presidency of Richard Levin, an active symbiosis has thrived. Residents are encouraged to take advantage of the university's cultural and public offerings, and over half of the student body, eager to contribute to their "home" community, volunteers in some sort of local outreach program.

New Haven is certainly less WASPish and smug than many other Ivy League towns, and aside from the usual city problems like drugs and homelessness, ethnic and racial groups coexist ambivalently in a way unseen in the rest of New England. Even the students themselves seem to be a less snooty breed than their counterparts at Princeton or Harvard. Not only has Yale's influence strongly contributed to the town's revitalization, but also, at the time of writing, the city was planning a **downtown development** to make use of spaces that have been vacant for years in the vicinity of the former Coliseum on George Street. New residential, hotel, and conference spaces are in the works, and both the Long Wharf Theatre and the Gateway Community College are expected to relocate downtown, with construction beginning in phases between 2006 and 2008.

Some history

Founded in 1638 by a group of wealthy **Puritans** on a large natural harbor at the mouth of the Quinnipiac River, New Haven began life as an independent colony, the early settlers living in relative harmony with the native Quinnipiac Indians. Very early on, the town was laid out in nine "**squares**" that can still be seen today in the downtown area's grid pattern. The efforts of the community's

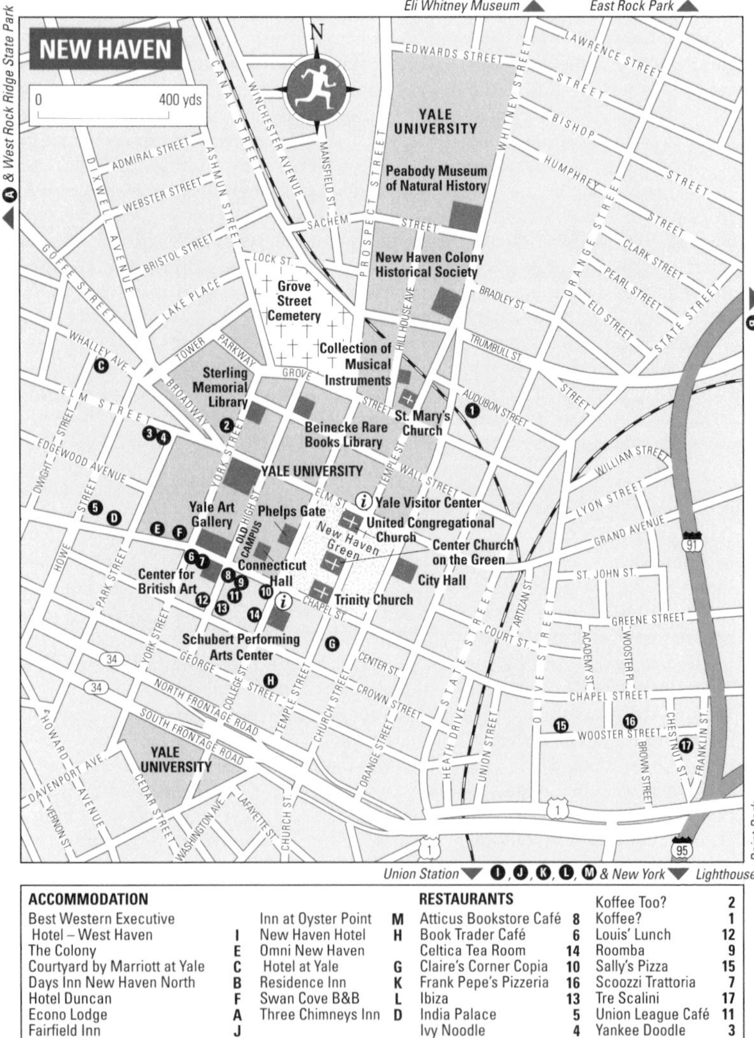

leaders to create a prosperous economy foundered, however, and in 1664 New Haven formally became part of the Connecticut Colony, based in Hartford. In 1701 Connecticut's first university, the Collegiate School, was founded, and classes met in a variety of towns, until, in 1716, the school established a permanent home in New Haven, eventually becoming Yale University as a sign of respect to **Elihu Yale**, a wealthy Anglican who made generous donations. Meanwhile, the town's shipping industry was finally beginning to flourish, the result of a fine deepwater harbor.

Still, it was manufacturing that would lead the city forward. During the Revolutionary War, the city produced gunpowder and cannonballs, and towards the end of the eighteenth century, Yale-educated **Eli Whitney** started manufacturing mass-produced firearms, the result of using standardized parts as the basis of the assembly line in his factory outside of town, dubbed Whitneyville. New Haven also churned out Winchester rifles, musical instruments, tools, carriages, and corsets. Local entrepreneurs, realizing that the city could do better still if it had access to interior New England, decided to build an eighty-mile canal which would extend as far as Northampton, Massachusetts in the late 1820s. The canal, however, was a financial flop with the advent of the railroad a decade later.

Nevertheless, New Haven continued to progress until the middle of the **twentieth century**, when the problems of unplanned urban growth and increasing economic competition from the suburbs began to take their toll. Millions of federal dollars were pumped into the city for urban renewal, but unemployment continued to grow and, today, with little manufacturing activity left, New Haven trades primarily on its Ivy League cachet.

Arrival, information, and city transit

New Haven lies at the fork of I-91 and I-95. Street **parking** downtown is atrocious, but parking lots are located conveniently around town – rates vary so you may want to shop around. New Haven is on the main **train** line between Washington, New York, and Boston; Amtrak's main terminal is in the colossal **Union Station**, on Union Avenue six blocks southeast of the Yale campus downtown. You can also get to Union Station from New York via Greyhound **bus** or on the Metro North Commuter Railroad (Ⓣ1-800/METRO-INFO), which also runs to the station at State Street. Whether you're arriving by train or bus, it may make sense to grab a **cab** to your hotel, as the stations are in potentially unsafe areas. Metro Taxi (Ⓣ203/777-7777) has a good reputation.

Local public transit within New Haven and its outlying areas is provided by Connecticut Transit, 470 James St (Ⓣ203/624-0151), but on some routes the service deteriorates rapidly after 6pm. There are two conveniently located **INFO New Haven** offices, one just off the Green at 1000 Chapel St (Mon–Thurs 10am–9pm, Fri & Sat 10am–10pm, Sun noon–5pm; Ⓣ203/773-9494, Ⓦwww.infonewhaven.com) and the other off I-95 exit 46 (May–Sept Mon–Fri 11am–6pm, Sat & Sun 10am–6pm; Ⓣ203/776-0203). The **Greater New Haven CVB**, 59 Elm St (Mon–Fri 8.30am–5pm; Ⓣ1-800/332-7829, Ⓦwww.newhavencvb.org), also has a helpful staff and publishes a comprehensive **visitors guide**.

Accommodation

New Haven has surprisingly few **hotels** for a city of its size – not even expensive ones for parents visiting their Yalie offspring. The downtown hotels, though somewhat overpriced, are worth it for their proximity to the main sights and for the comparative safety of the location. Because of the shortage of rooms, make sure to book well in advance if you're intending to visit during graduation in early June, or Parents' Weekend in October, always the busiest times of the year.

Downtown

The Colony 1157 Chapel St ⓣ203/776-1234 or 1-800/458-8810, ⓦwww.colonyatyale.com. Intimate full-service hotel with colonial trimmings. ❻

Courtyard by Marriott at Yale 30 Whalley Ave ⓣ203/777-6221 or 1-888/522-1186, ⓦwww.courtyard.com. Recently renovated rooms in a good central location. ❼

Hotel Duncan 1151 Chapel St ⓣ203/787-1273. Good-value, spacious, and comfortable rooms in an old-fashioned hotel built in 1894, on one of New Haven's main thoroughfares. ❸

New Haven Hotel 229 George St ⓣ203/498-3100 or 1-800/NH-HOTEL, ⓦwww.newhavenhotel.com. Small, quiet hotel with 92 better-than-adequate rooms, a lap pool and hot tub, and free entry to the Health and Racquet Club next door. ❼

Omni New Haven Hotel at Yale 155 Temple St ⓣ203/772-6664 or 1-800/THE-OMNI, ⓦwww.omnihotels.com. New Haven's plushest hotel has 306 luxury rooms, health club (also available at the front desk are "get-fit" kits, with dumbbells and a mat for in-room use), and a superb (though expensive) restaurant with spectacular city views. ❽

Three Chimneys Inn 1201 Chapel St ⓣ203/789-1201 or 1-800/443-1554., ⓦwww.threechimneysinn.com. Rooms at this elegant Victorian B&B have king or queen four-poster beds. Formal parlor with complimentary port, sherry, teas, and snacks, and a porch overlooking a landscaped courtyard. ❽

Around town

Best Western Executive Hotel – West Haven 490 Saw Mill Rd, West Haven ⓣ203/933-0344 or 1-866/530-1684, ⓦwww.bestwestern.com. Standard rooms not far from downtown at I-95 exit 42. Hotel features include an indoor pool and fitness center, and a free hot breakfast buffet. ❻

Days Inn New Haven North 270 Foxon Blvd ⓣ203/469-0343, ⓦwww.daysinn.com. Inexpensive but comfortable motel located just off I-91 exit 8 north of town. ❺

Econo Lodge 100 Pond Lily Ave, exit 59 off Rte-15 ⓣ203/387-6651, ⓦwww.choicehotels.com. Good-value standard rooms, all with recently remodeled bathrooms and new carpeting; there's also an indoor pool, Jacuzzi, and sauna. ❹

Fairfield Inn 400 Sargent Drive ⓣ203/562-1111, ⓦwww.fairfieldinn.com. Good-value *Marriott* relation with 152 rooms overlooking the harbor, as well as a pool and fitness room. ❻

Inn at Oyster Point 104 Howard Ave ⓣ203/773-3334 or 1-860/978-3778, ⓦwww.oysterpointinn.com. Six beautifully decorated theme rooms evoking worldwide locales, in an extremely comfortable gay-friendly establishment near the harbor. ❼, shared bath ❺

Residence Inn 3 Long Wharf Drive ⓣ203/777-5337 or 1-800/331-3131, ⓦwww.residenceinn.com. Well-equipped all-suites hotel that's part of the *Marriott* empire. Complimentary shuttle within six miles and grocery-shopping service. ❻

Swan Cove B&B 115 Sea St, exit 44N off I-95 ⓣ203/776-240, ⓦwww.swancove.com. Three homey suites and one queen room in a pleasant and quiet 1890s historic district house. Within walking distance from a marina with a waterfront restaurant, but otherwise a car is advisable. ❻

The City

A succession of remarkably ugly buildings put up during the 1950s rather blighted New Haven, but its **downtown**, centered on the **Green**, remains both attractive and walkable, thanks in part to some sensitive restoration. The Green, laid out in 1638 and originally called "**The Marketplace**," was the site of the city's original settlement, and also functioned as a meeting area and burial ground. Around it are three churches, a grand library, and a number of stately government buildings, and it borders the student-filled College and Chapel Street district.

The Green

Standing in the middle of the Green, and flanked by two other churches, the **Center Church on the Green** (tours April–Oct Thurs & Sat 11am–1pm or

The Amistad

In the spring of 1839, more than five hundred Mendi tribesmen were kidnapped from their Sierra Leone homes and brought to Havana, Cuba. Fifty-three of them were placed on a smaller ship, the **Amistad**, for delivery to another Cuban port. Three days after setting sail, the Africans, led by Joseph Cinque, revolted and took control of the ship with the intent to return home, killing several crew members in the process. After 63 days the ship arrived off Long Island, where it was intercepted by the US Navy. The Africans were taken into custody and charged as pirates and murderers, despite the protests of abolitionists. A series of trials in both Hartford and New Haven followed; after two years of legal wrangling, the case went all the way to the US Supreme Court. Having received the powerful backing by that time of none other than former president John Quincy Adams, the tribesmen were eventually acquitted and released. In 1842, the 35 survivors were able to return home, though slavery was not to be abolished for another twenty years. Steven Spielberg dramatized the affair in the 1997 film *Amistad*. The non-profit organization Amistad America (ⓣ203/495-1839, ⓦwww.amistadamerica.org) sails a replica of the *Amistad* schooner around the globe as a goodwill ambassador and a monument to the lives lost in the slave trade; its home port is Long Wharf Pier in New Haven.

by appointment; donation; ⓣ203/787-0121), built in 1812, is the successor to New Haven's first religious building, the First Church of Christ. Though it once held nearly a dozen Tiffany windows, all but one were given away during a renovation in the 1960s (of which one can be viewed at the Southern Connecticut State University library, 501 Crescent St); the remaining window sits in a place of honor over the pulpit, and depicts John Davenport, the church's first minister, preaching the first service in New Haven colony. Below the church, a fascinating **crypt** holds tombs from as far back as 1687. Close by, fronting Temple Street, the 1816 Gothic Revival **Trinity Episcopal Church** holds more Tiffany windows; and the **United Church**, originally known as **North Church** when it was built in 1813, is based on a design copied from a French book on English architecture. At the northeast corner of the Green is the recently restored 1861 high-Victorian **City Hall**, although the Courthouse next door looks far more like a traditional City Hall building. City Hall overlooks the 1992 **Amistad Memorial** (see box, above), a three-sided bronze-relief monument on the site of the former New Haven jail.

Following Court Street east, you'll hit New Haven's close-knit **Italian District**, featuring the well-kept brownstones and colorful window boxes of **Wooster Street** and Wooster Square, where the city's original Italian immigrants settled when they came to work on the railway. There's little to see here in the way of attractions, but there are some incredibly popular restaurants, and it's well worth stopping by when there's a festival on.

Yale University and around

At the opposite end of the Green, Yale University's **Connecticut Hall**, built in 1750 and based on Harvard's Massachusetts Hall, is notable for being the oldest surviving building in New Haven and the only remaining structure from Yale's Old Brick Row. Just outside of Connecticut Hall stands a statue of Revolutionary War hero **Nathan Hale**, a Yale graduate. A short way down College Street, the 1895 **Phelps Gate**, known as "Yale's front door," allows access to the Old Campus of **Yale University**, New Haven's prime attraction. You can wander at will, though free hour-long student-led **tours** set off daily from the **Yale**

Visitor Information Center at 149 Elm St, on the north side of the Green (Mon–Fri 9am–4.30pm, Sat & Sun 11am–4pm; ⓣ203/432-2300, ⓦwww.yale.edu/visitor); the center also provides free maps and pamphlets ($1) for self-guided tours, and the staff can tell you about campus events. Whatever you decide, expect a good deal of trooping to and fro, as the university's buildings are strewn out over several blocks.

It makes sense to start with the cobbled courtyards of the Old Campus (mostly built in the 1930s but constructed in Gothic Revival style, and painstakingly manicured to look suitably ancient) and ending up at the remarkable **Sterling Memorial Library**, 120 High St (school year: Mon–Thurs 8.30am–midnight, Fri 8.30am–5pm, Sat 10am–5pm, Sun 1–midnight; summer: limited hours and closed Sun; free). Designed by alum James Gamble Rogers in modern Gothic style, and with fifteen butresses, it has the symbolic appearance – inside and out – of a cathedral, albeit one to the power of knowledge and the written word. Inside, leaded glass windows illustrate the history of the Library, Yale, New Haven, and books and printing. At the would-be altar (the Circulation Desk), the Alma Mater receives gifts from Light, Truth, Science, Labor, Music, Fine Arts, Divinity, and Literature in a fifteenth-century-Italian-style mural that's highly expressive. Directly in front of the Library is the **Women's Table**, an ovate granite fountain commemorating the enrollment of women at Yale. It was designed by alum Maya Lin, who also designed the Vietnam Veterans' Memorial in Washington, DC.

Nearby, at 121 Wall St, is the **Beinecke Rare Book and Manuscript Library** (Mon–Fri 8.30am–5pm, Sat 10am–5pm; free), where priceless ancient manuscripts and hand-printed books are viewed with the aid of natural light seeping through the translucent Vermont marble walls. The marble also blocks out harmful solar radiation that would otherwise cause the manuscripts to deteriorate, while providing stunning interior artwork as the sun rises and falls. The collection boasts a 1300-page Gutenberg Bible (the first major book to be printed using moveable type, in 1455), along with some original Audubon prints. Other buildings of interest include the modernist, Louis Kahn-designed **Yale Center for British Art**, 1080 Chapel St (Tues–Sat 10am–5pm, Sun noon–5pm; free), which prides itself on having the most comprehensive collection of British art outside of the UK. The collection traces the development of British art, beginning with paintings from the sixteenth and seventeenth centuries,

△ Nathan Hale statue

highlighting the period from William Hogarth in the early eighteenth century to J.M.W. Turner in the mid-nineteenth, and moving through to the twentieth century via works by Walter Sickert and the Bloomsbury Group, with a special emphasis on Alfred Munnings and Ben Nicholson – favorites of the center's founder, Paul Mellon. The Center's large collection of portraits contains full-lengths by Van Dyck, Gainsborough, and Reynolds and some fine landscapes including Turner's *Dort and Staffa* and John Constable's *Hadleigh Castle*.

The modern building opposite the Center for British Art houses the **Yale University Art Gallery**, 1111 Chapel St (Tues–Sat 10am–5pm, Sun 1–6pm; free), the nation's most venerable university art collection. Founded in 1832 with John Trumbull's original donation of a hundred paintings, the collection now has more than 100,000 objects from around the world, dating from ancient Egyptian times to the present, and featuring American decorative arts, Etruscan vases, regional design and furniture, as well as African and pre-Columbian works. Among the highlights are Vincent Van Gogh's famous 1888 composition *Night Café*, which the artist complained was "one of the ugliest pictures I have done," and works by Manet, Monet, Picasso, and Homer. The surrounding five blocks are a genuinely lively area in which to hang out, filled with bookstores, cafés, clubs, and hip clothing shops. There are some rough pockets, but generally speaking, New Haven is reasonably safe to wander around, especially during term-time, when the streets are brimming with students.

A short walk two blocks east of the Green, **Hillhouse Avenue**, designed by James Hillhouse in the 1790s and completed by his son in 1837, is one of New Haven's most attractive thoroughfares – so attractive that when Charles Dickens visited he proclaimed it to be the most beautiful street in America. Once the domain of New Haven's rich and famous, much of it is now taken up with Yale University's administrative offices. A quirky, eight-hundred-strong **Collection of Musical Instruments**, some dating back as far as the sixteenth century, can be seen at no. 15 (Tues–Thurs 1–4pm; closed summer; donation), while steps away the Gothic **St Mary's Roman Catholic Church**, the first such parish in New Haven, is where Friar Michael McGivney founded the Knights of Columbus in 1882.

Whitney Avenue

Whitney Avenue leads north from the Green, with several worthy stops along the way. Yale's **Peabody Museum of Natural History**, 170 Whitney Ave (Mon–Sat 10am–5pm, Sun noon–5pm; $7; ⓣ203/432-5050, ⓦwww.peabody.yale.edu), one of the largest museums in New England, is easily recognizable by the two-story bronze statue of a *Torosaurus latus* out front, named by Yale's first professor of paleontology. The museum hosts exhibits of dinosaur skeletons, including a 67-foot brontosaurus and a 75-million-year-old turtle, along with a vast section on America's ancient civilizations, in particular the Native Americans of Connecticut. On the same street, the **New Haven Colony Historical Society**, at no. 114 (Tues–Fri 10am–5pm, Sat noon–5pm; $4; ⓣ203/562-4183), housed in a handsome 1930s Colonial Revival building, traces three hundred years of New Haven's history through a series of fine art displays, industrial artifacts, maps, and genealogical records. One of the galleries is dedicated to the *Amistad* story and includes the original iron keys to the Church Street jail as well as the much-reproduced 1840 Nathaniel Jocelyn portrait of the leader of the slaves, Cinque; you can also see Eli Whitney's original cotton gin and Charles Goodyear's rubber inkwell.

More Whitney-related exhibits can be seen at the **Eli Whitney Museum**, two miles out at no. 915 (Wed–Fri & Sun noon–5pm, Sat 10am–3pm; $3; ⓣ203/777-1833, ⓦwww.eliwhitney.org), located in the original gun factory where mass production originated. The museum includes an 1816 barn that was part of Whitney's factory town and a glut of hands-on experiments, mostly designed for children ($5–8 per project).

The city outskirts

When you've had enough traipsing around museums and galleries, head for **East Rock Park**, at the corner of Orange and Cold Springs streets (daily sunrise–sunset, summit drive open April–Nov daily 8am–sunset, Nov–March Fri–Sun 8am–4pm; free; ⓣ203/946-6086), named for the huge outcrop of reddish rock that dominates the skyline for miles around. From the rock's 350-foot summit there are spectacular views of New Haven, Long Island Sound, and beyond.

At the extreme southeastern tip of the city, follow Lighthouse Road at exit 50 off I-95 to **Lighthouse Point Park** (daily 7am–sunset; parking in summer $10; ⓣ203/946-8790), an eighty-acre park with a sandy public beach, nature trails, and a restored antique carousel (50¢ per ride, summer only); it's a stopover point for hawks, eagles, and falcons on their winter migration. Nearby, at the end of Woodward Avenue, are **Fort Nathan Hale** and **Black Rock Fort** (summer daily 10am–4pm; free), the remains of two forts from the Revolutionary and Civil wars, both offering spectacular views of New Haven Harbor, though there's not enough left of either to warrant anything more than a quick poke around.

Eating

Don't leave town without trying the **pizza**, available at all the family Italian **restaurants** in Wooster Square. There are plenty of other ethnic foods to savor as well; for a city of its size, New Haven offers great quality and diversity in cuisine. Many of the best places are located around the Green and on Chapel and College streets. Unsurprisingly for a long-time college town, New Haven also has many fine **cafés**, great for either a quick caffeine fix and a snack or a lazy afternoon of Proust and madelines.

Cafés

Atticus Bookstore Café 1082 Chapel St, next to the Yale Center for British Art ⓣ203/776-4040. Salads, soups, sandwiches, scones, and great coffee in a relaxed bookstore open until midnight.

Book Trader Café 1140 Chapel St ⓣ203/787-6147. Salads, smoothies, and literary-inspired sandwiches like the Tempesto and Vonnegut's Veggie in a gently used bookstore with an outdoor courtyard.

Celtica Tea Room 260 College St ⓣ203/785-8034. Comforting tearoom set back in a gift shop also offering all things Irish. High tea (with a pot of Bewley's) $10 per person; sandwiches and salads also available. Closes at 4.30pm.

Koffee? 104 Audubon St ⓣ203/562-5454. Casual, bright, whimsical all-day hangout, with a wide selection of coffees, teas, and snacks like yummy espresso brownies.

Yankee Doodle 260 Elm St ⓣ203/865-1074. Yalies' favorite low-cost café – once a favored haunt of George W. Bush and Bill Clinton as undergrads – with original 1950s fittings. Opens early, closes in the afternoon.

Restaurants

Claire's Corner Copia 1000 Chapel St ⓣ203/562-3888. Corny name, but excellent Mexican and Middle Eastern food at moderate prices. The local vegetarian for thirty years.

Frank Pepe's Pizzeria 157 Wooster St ⓣ203/865-5762. Most popular of the Wooster Street establishments, and allegedly where the first pizza in the US was served in 1925. Plain, functional, and friendly, after eighty years it's still drawing crowds with its delicious coal-fired pies, like white clam for $23.

Ibiza 39 High St ⓣ203/865-1933. Superb Spanish restaurant serving traditional specialties like Catalan noodles paella with codfish, and braised boneless short ribs; a tasting menu is available for $55. Dinner only except for Thurs.

India Palace 65 Howe St ⓣ203/776-9010. Serviceable North Indian restaurant, most noteworthy for its $8 buffet lunch.

Ivy Noodle 316 Elm St ⓣ203/562-8800. Quick, decent, and cheap Chinese noodles, almost everything under $6.

Louis' Lunch 261–263 Crown St ☎203/562-5507. Small, dark, and ancient burger institution which claims to have served the first hamburger sandwich in the US in 1900. The meat, cooked in an upright broiler which reduces the fat, is presented between two slices of toast, and it's perfect in every way. Very cheap and popular, so expect lines, and don't ask for ketchup, either – it's only accompanied by onions, tomato, and/or cheese. Lunch only.
Roomba 1044 Chapel St, Sherman's Alley ☎203/562-7666. Innovative Nuevo Latino cuisine in a stylish room. Trendy, loud, and popular for its mojitos.
Sally's Pizza 237 Wooster St ☎203/624-5271. Another top-notch Wooster Street pizzeria, and a good alternative to *Pepe's* (above). Dinner only, closed Mon.
Scoozzi Trattoria 1104 Chapel St ☎203/776-8268. Northern Italian restaurant (with a summer outdoor courtyard) with pizzas for $10 and pastas for $20. Popular as a pre-theater spot, or come for the Sunday jazz brunch.
Tre Scalini 100 Wooster St ☎203/777-3373. Upmarket Italian in an elegant setting, with pastas for around $15 and other mains like veal medallions with prosciutto, mozzarella, and sage in a sherry demi-glaze. Lunch and dinner weekdays, weekends dinner only.
Union League Café 1032 Chapel St ☎203/562-4299. Expensive, very French bistro known as one of the finest restaurants in the city, serving entrees like roast Long Island duck breast with fresh corn coquettes, roasted figs, and a carmelized fig sauce. Weekdays lunch and dinner, Sat dinner only.

Nightlife and entertainment

New Haven has an undeniably rich **cultural scene**, especially strong on **theater**. The Yale Rep, 1120 Chapel St (☎203/432-1234, Ⓦwww.yalerep.org), which boasts among its past members Jodie Foster and Meryl Streep, turns out consistently good shows during term-time. The Long Wharf Theater, 222 Sargent Drive, just off I-95 exit 46 (☎203/787-4282), has a nationwide reputation for quality performances, as does the refurbished Shubert Performing Arts Center, 247 College St (☎203/562-5666).

As you'd expect with such a large student population, there are plenty of excellent **bars** and **clubs**, mostly concentrated around Chapel and College streets. The *New Haven Advocate*, a free weekly news and arts paper, has detailed **listings** of what's on in and around the city.

168 York Street Café 168 York St ☎203/789-1915. New Haven's oldest gay joint has two downstairs bars, and a quieter upstairs with lots of TV screens. Busy, especially at weekends. No cover.
Anchor 272 College St ☎203/865-1512. One of the best spots in town (it was Jodie's favorite while an undergrad), this authentic 1950s bar has snug plastic booths, dim orange lighting, and frosted windows.
Backroom @ Bottega Temple St Plaza ☎203/562-5566. Stylish club with a flower-strewn patio, loft lounge, and dance floor. Wed is Latin Night, Thurs has live bands, and DJs spin on weekends. Rustic Italian tapas-like dishes also on offer for around $10, along with an excellent wine list. Open Wed–Sat, $5 cover Fri & Sat after 10pm.
Bar 254 Crown St ☎203/495-8924. A simple name for a not-so-simple spot that's a combination pizzeria, brewery, bar, and nightclub. Live bands Fri & Sun, DJs Thurs–Sat and also on Tues, when the gay community comes to let its collective hair down. Cover $5 Tues after 9pm, Fri & Sat $6 after 10pm.
Cafe Nine 250 State St ☎203/789-8281. Intimate club with live music seven nights a week; Sat is a jazz jam and Sun is a blues jam, also poetry readings Mon nights. Covers vary from $3 to $10.
Gotham Citi 130 Crown St ☎203/498-2484. Large, steamy club where those in the know head for a late night of drinking, dancing, and simply looking good. Open Wed–Sun.
The Playwright 144 Temple St ☎203/752-0450. Four bars, ranging from rowdy pub to dance club, in a massive space with an interior constructed from various churches bought in Ireland, dismantled, and reassembled here; the DJ spins from the pulpit. An unusual must-stop. Live music Fri, DJs Fri & Sat ($5 cover).
Rudy's 372 Elm St ☎203/865-1242. A dive bar with the best jukebox in town, $1.50 pool games, and $2 drafts. Live bands (cover $1–5) Tues, Thurs & Sat, and a DJ on Wed. The Belgian frites – cheap and plentiful, with more than two dozen inventive sauces – are ideal for late-night munchies.
Toad's Place 300 York St ☎203/624-8623, Ⓦwww.toadsplace.com. Mid-sized nationally

renowned live-music venue, where Bruce Springsteen and the Stones used to "pop in" occasionally to play impromptu gigs. Tickets $8.50–30; some shows 21 and over.

Bridgeport and around

Long the state's leading industrial center, **BRIDGEPORT**, not quite twenty miles southwest from New Haven, suffered greatly during the economic decline of the 1960s and 1970s, when dozens of factories and businesses closed down, giving rise to some serious social and environmental problems. Now littered with abandoned factories, boarded-up stores, and run-down neighborhoods, the city is gloomy at best, though it does contain some diverting attractions, especially if you're traveling with kids. The **Beardsley Zoo** is the only zoo in the state, while the entertaining, hands-on **Discovery Museum** is one of the better children's museums on the East Coast. On top of that, the city has close ties to showman **P.T. Barnum**, a one-time mayor of Bridgeport; there's a downtown museum in his honor.

The City

Bridgeport's most endearing attraction is the **Barnum Museum**, 820 Main St (Tues–Sat 10am–4.30pm, Sun noon–4.30pm; $5 adults, kids aged 4–18 $3; ⓣ203/331-1104, ⓦwww.barnum-museum.org), which displays various props and memorabilia from Barnum's circus days, including exhibits on General Tom Thumb and Jenny Lind, the "Swedish Nightingale." Barnum's life and the city's industrial history are showcased as well, both in a permanent collection and in a gallery of changing exhibits. Most impressive of all is a complete scale model of a five-ring circus comprising of nearly four thousand hand-carved pieces. A block away in the Housatonic Community College, the **Housatonic Museum of Art**, 900 Lafayette Blvd (year-round Mon–Fri 8.30am–5.30pm; Sept–May also Sat 9am–3pm, Sun noon–4pm; free; ⓣ203/332-5203), focuses on contemporary art from the 1960s, with works by Picasso, Matisse, and Warhol, plus African ethnographic collections and decent local pieces.

A little way out of the city center, the **Discovery Museum**, 4450 Park Ave (Tues–Sat 10am–5pm, Sun noon–5pm; adults $8.50, children $7; ⓣ203/372-3521, ⓦwww.discoverymuseum.org), is an interactive science and technology museum with a planetarium and more than a hundred engaging exhibits on topics like electricity, nuclear energy, and the science of color. Best of all, perhaps, is the Challenger Learning Center, honoring the memory of the ill-fated *Challenger* space shuttle crew. Another top-drawer destination for kids, the 52-acre **Beardsley Zoological Gardens**, 1875 Noble Ave (daily 9am–4pm; adults $8, children 3–11 $6; ⓦwww.beardsleyzoo.org), has exhibits ranging from North American mammals like the Canadian lynx and bison to exotic animals from South American rainforests. There's also a farmyard-like children's zoo and a splendid working carousel (open seasonally) on the grounds.

Around Bridgeport

Adjacent to Bridgeport, **STRATFORD**, named after its English counterpart Stratford-upon-Avon, shares a connection with that city's most famous son as the longtime home to the prestigious **American Shakespeare Theatre**. It has been closed since 1982, but the Chamber of Commerce is currently involved in a developer bidding process to renovate it. Also in town and open

P.T. Barnum

Phineas Taylor Barnum, the world's greatest showman (and huckster), was born in Bethel, Connecticut, in July 1810, and worked as a lottery ticket salesman before he ventured into the world of show business – and forever altered history – in 1835. With an eye for the bizarre, he purchased a frail hymn-warbling old black woman, and exhibited her as George Washington's 161-year-old nurse. Further "success" followed with the "Feejee mermaid," in reality the upper half of a monkey sewn to the body of a fish. Barnum made his fortune out of the midget Tom Thumb – a native of Bridgeport – and the Swedish singer Jenny Lind, both of whom drew massive crowds thanks to Barnum's publicity efforts. Barnum plowed much of the profits from these efforts into the American Museum in New York City, which he acquired in 1841 and where dozens of curiosities, both of the human and animal variety, were put on show. Part of the complex, a large, well-equipped theater known as the "lecture room," became the venue for a variety of popular dramatic productions and one of New York's most popular places of entertainment. Buoyed by this venture, in 1871 Barnum fulfilled a personal dream by launching a huge traveling **circus** and museum. Attracting vast crowds wherever it performed, it eventually merged with James A. Bailey's London Circus and became known as the Barnum & Bailey Circus, until it was bought out by the Ringling Brothers. Throughout his life, Barnum maintained strong links with his home city and state, serving in the Connecticut state legislature and as one of Bridgeport's most popular mayors. Today, a statue commemorating Barnum's contribution to the city stares out to Long Island Sound from a plinth in Bridgeport's Seaside Park, which he himself gave to the city. For obvious reasons (besides the fact that he didn't say it), the quote most often attributed to Barnum – "There's a sucker born every minute" – does not adorn the statue.

for tours, the **Judson House**, 967 Academy Hill (June–Oct Wed, Sat & Sun 11am–4pm, last tour 3pm; $5; ⓣ203/378-0630, ⓦwww.stratfordhistoricalsociety.com), is a 1750 Georgian home furnished with Stratford antiques; the adjacent **Catharine B. Mitchell Museum** has displays on local American Indian and African-American history. At 400 Honeyspot Rd, the **Stratford Antique Center** (daily 10am–5pm; ⓣ203/378-7754) is a group of over two hundred dealers in collectible furniture, copper, glassware, and artwork.

One of New England's most bizarre museums can be found in northern Stratford, known as **Putney**. The **Boothe Memorial Park & Museum**, on Main St Putney (park open daily 9am–5pm; tours June–Oct Tues–Fri 11am–1pm, Sat & Sun 1–4pm; free; ⓣ203/381-2046), for almost three hundred years the estate of the wealthy Boothe family, comprises an assortment of some fifteen buildings bequeathed to the community by the last surviving family members – two eccentric, globetrotting brothers. Among the highlights are a 44-sided blacksmith's shop (on weekends you can watch tools being forged), a pagoda-like building made from California redwood, a miniature lighthouse and windmill, an Americana Museum focusing on nineteenth-century farming techniques and domestic life, and an extensive collection of odds and ends gathered by the brothers on their travels.

Bridgeport area practicalities

Bridgeport area **accommodation** is rather minimal. The *Holiday Inn*, in Bridgeport at 1070 Main St (ⓣ203/334-1234; ❻) is the only major downtown hotel, while the *Ramada Inn* in Stratford, 225 Lordship Blvd (ⓣ203-375-8866; ❺), has an indoor pool. Since most of their clientele are business travelers, rates will be much lower at weekends. If you're stuck, the Coastal Fairfield County CVB (ⓣ203/853-7770 or 1-800/866-7925, ⓦwww.coastalct.com) can provide listings for the surrounding towns.

There's no shortage of **places to eat** in the area: in downtown Bridgeport, *Ralph 'n' Rich's*, 121 Wall St (ⓣ203/366-3597; closed Sun), has excellent pasta, while the *King & I*, 545 Broadbridge Rd (ⓣ203/374-2081), serves good-value Thai. Over in Stratford, try the prime rib at the pricey *Blue Goose*, 326 Ferry Blvd (ⓣ203/375-9130; closed Mon), or the seafood at the more relaxed *Off the Wall*, 14 Beach Drive (ⓣ203/375-7805; closed Tues lunch), in a pleasant setting overlooking Long Island Sound.

Westport and around

Artsy **WESTPORT**, fifteen miles down the road from Stratford, spent the last century shedding its industrial image, and in place of its mills and tannery now sit the designer boutiques and upmarket galleries of a chic downtown. Residents include Martha Stewart as well as Paul Newman and his wife Joanne Woodward, who served for five years as artistic director of the prestigious **Westport Country Playhouse**, 25 Powers Court (ⓣ203/227-4177, ⓦwww.westportplayhouse.org), one of the oldest repertory theaters in the country. When stars like Henry Fonda, Gene Kelly, and Liza Minnelli first strutted their stuff here, the playhouse was little more than a rural barn with a few seats, but in 2005 it reopened after a $17.8 million renovation and is now more than comfortable while still retaining its rustic charm.

One of the few proper sights in Westport, the 1795 **Wheeler House**, 25 Avery Place (Mon–Fri 10am–4pm, Sat noon–3pm; donation requested; ⓣ203/222-1424), sports beautifully restored Victorian rooms and, viewable by request, a Victorian costume and textile collection. The adjacent Bradley-Wheeler Barn, the only octagonal cobblestone barn in the state, contains a five-square-foot handmade diorama of Westport in 1900, along with local historical archives and genealogical information. Connecticut's first state park, the **Sherwood Island State Park**, Sherwood Connector Rd, I-95 exit 18 (8am–sunset; May–Sept $7 weekdays, $14 weekends; rest of year free; ⓣ203/226-6983), also has one of the state's best beaches, with miles of sandy shoreline and a small nature center with hiking trails.

Practicalities

If you fancy a splurge, there's nowhere better in the area to **stay** than *The Inn at National Hall*, 2 Post Rd W (ⓣ203/221-1351 or 1-800/NAT-HALL, ⓦwww.innatnationalhall.com; ❾), a lavish but intimate Relais & Chataeux hotel with eighteen-foot-high ceilings and individually decorated rooms and suites, some with sweeping river views. By contrast, the simple *Westport Inn*, 1595 Post Rd E (ⓣ203/259-5236 or 1-800/446-8997, ⓦwww.westportinn.com; ❼), offers 115 reasonably priced units, with a smart lounge, fitness center, and indoor pool. There are some fine **restaurants** in downtown Westport, among them *Sakura*, 680 Post Rd E (ⓣ203/222-0802), for relatively inexpensive sushi and traditional and hibachi Japanese dishes – especially fun for families – and the upscale Mediterranean restaurant ✱ *Acqua*, 43 Main St (ⓣ203/222-8899), where seafood is the specialty and the soufflés are superb.

Around Westport: Weston and Wilton

A few miles inland from Westport, in the town of **WESTON**, the nearly 1800-acre **Devil's Den Preserve**, 33 Pent Rd (dawn–dusk; free; ⓣ203/226-4991), is so named for the strange hoof-like rock formations which charcoal-makers who once worked here believed were the footprints of the Devil. Several rare plant species can be found in this nature conservancy, including the hog peanut and Indian cucumber root.

In nearby **WILTON**, don't miss the **Weir Farm National Historic Site**, 735 Nod Hill Rd (grounds open daily dawn–dusk; visitors' center May–Oct Wed–Sun 8.30am–5pm, Nov–April Thurs–Sun 9.30am–4pm; free; ⓣ203/834-1896, ⓦwww.nps.gov/wefa), Connecticut's only national park, which once served as the summer home and studio of prominent Impressionist **J. Alden Weir**, who acquired the 153-acre site in 1882 in exchange for a painting (not one of his own) and a measly $6. Its proximity to New York City enticed a group of artists including John Twachtman and Childe Hassam to visit and subsequently form an informal art colony that became known as the "Ten American Painters." The Weir House remains a private artists' residence, and is not generally open to the public, but a visitors' center in the **Burlingham House** contains historical background, contemporary art exhibits, and a handful of canvases by the three generations of original owners; studio tours are also available. You can combine a visit to Weir Farm with a tour around the enchanting **Wilton Heritage Museum**, 224 Danbury Rd (Mon–Thurs and some Sundays 10am–4pm; $5; ⓣ203/762-7257), encompassing two eighteenth-century center-chimney farmhouses with a collection of dolls and dollhouses, as well as a mid-nineteenth-century barn and blacksmith's shop housing more than six hundred tools.

Norwalk

It was in 1651 that **NORWALK** was first settled by Europeans, soon becoming the largest population along this stretch of the coast, thanks to the economic prosperity brought about by a thriving oyster-fishing industry, and, later, by the prolific output of the Silvermine River mills, which produced, among other things, shoes, boots, hats, earthenware, candles, and ships. The arrival of the railway in 1840 provided another major boost to the city, but many of the factories closed down in the 1960s and 1970s. Today the area is thriving, due to the numerous large companies headquartered here, and to the vision of city officials and private individuals who initiated a massive renovation of **South Norwalk**, affectionately known as "**SoNo**," full of restaurants, clubs, and galleries.

The Town

South Norwalk is anchored by the fabulous **Maritime Aquarium**, 10 N Water St (daily: July & Aug 10am–6pm, Sept–June 10am–5pm; $10.50; ⓣ203/852-0700, ⓦwww.maritimeaquarium.org), which presents a methodical look at the marine life and culture of Long Island Sound, taking you from the creatures at the surface level of salt marshes down through to those of the deep – culminating in a 110,000-gallon tank filled with sharks. Also on display are seals, jellyfish, river otters, and more than a hundred other species of indigenous marine life; you can even take a 2.5-hour boat study **cruise** ($20) out into the Sound to get a firsthand look at the catch of the day and see how lobsters are tagged. A boat ride of a different sort is available from the adjacent Seaport Dock out to the 1868 **Sheffield Island Lighthouse**, whose function until 1902 was to prevent boats from running aground on the Norwalk Islands, a chain of twenty-three islets across the mouth of the Norwalk River. Visitors can take a brief tour of the ten-room lighthouse – from which, on a clear day, the New York City skyline is visible – and then spend a bit of time on the island, depending on ferry times (June to early Sept; $16; call for schedule ⓣ203/838-9444).

Back on the mainland, head to the Second Empire-style **Lockwood-Mathews Mansion Museum**, 295 West Ave (mid-March to Dec Wed–Sun noon–4pm; adults $8; ⓣ203/838-9799, ⓦwww.lockwoodmathewsmansion.org), built in 1864 as the summer home of Norwalk resident LeGrand Lockwood, who made his immense fortune in the insurance and railway industries. Nicknamed "America's first chateau," it would seem more at home among Newport, Rhode Island's grand palaces. Of the mansion's 62 rooms, best is the drawing room, in the rear, where above all the stenciling and grand inlaid woodwork, the ceiling boasts a spectacular gilt chandelier and an oil painting, *Venus at Play with her Cupids*, by Pierre-Victor Galland. About a half-mile away is the **Norwalk Museum**, 41 N Main St (Wed–Sun 1–5pm; free; ⓣ203/866-0202), where the city's retail and manufacturing history is presented via rotating exhibits and a series of mock storefronts, including a hardware store. **Norwalk City Hall**, 125 East Ave (Mon–Fri 8.30am–4.30pm), contains part of a rare collection of brightly colored and sharply detailed WPA murals commissioned during the Great Depression in the mid-1930s, notably *Steamboat Days on the Mississippi*, from the Mark Twain series. Other rescued murals can be seen at the public library, the Norwalk Transit District, and the aquarium.

Practicalities

Pleasant Norwalk **accommodation**, of a refined Yankee sort, is available at the *Silvermine Tavern*, 194 Perry Ave (ⓣ203/847-4558 or 1-888/693-9967, ⓦwww.silverminetavern.com; ❻), which boasts ten delightful rooms and one suite (no TVs or phones) in a nineteenth-century Colonial-style building next to a waterfall, along with a restaurant famous for its Sunday brunch buffet and honey buns. Budget options abound on Westport Ave, where the *Round Tree Inn*, no. 469 (ⓣ203/847-5827 or 1-800/275-2290; ❹), the *Garden Park Motel*, no. 351 (ⓣ203/847-7303; ❹), and the *Norwalk-Westport Motel*, no. 344 (ⓣ203/847-0665; ❹), all provide perfectly adequate accommodation. Or you can **camp** on two of the Norwalk Islands, accessible by kayak or canoe – the Norwalk Recreation & Parks Department (ⓣ203/854-7806) can provide more information.

The city's best **restaurants** are found in SoNo. There, *Papaya Thai*, 24 Marshall St (ⓣ203/866-THAI), has excellent traditional Thai curries along with an unusual BBQ bar; *The Brewhouse*, 18 Marshall St (ⓣ203/853-9110), offers standard American fare of sandwiches and burgers alongside more than fifty beers, plus jazz and blues on Thursday and Friday evenings; the *Rattlesnake Bar and Grill*, 15 N Main St (ⓣ203/852-1716), tastes like the Southwest; and *Habana*, 70 N Main St (ⓣ203/852-9790; dinner only), offers unique Cuban dishes with decor and laid-back attitude to match. Norwalk is also home to one of three Stew Leonard's, 100 Westport Ave (ⓣ203/847-7213, ⓦwww.stewleonards.com), a marvel of a supermarket which strives to entertain its shoppers; in addition to the fresh food (and free samples), there are animatronic displays throughout and a petting zoo.

For **nightlife**, again explore the trendy SoNo district, full of upscale bars and clubs, some of which, like *The Loft*, 97 Washington St (ⓣ203/838-6555), offer live music. For more options, you can always check the listings in the free *Fairfield County Weekly* (Ⓦwww.fairfieldweekly.com).

Stamford

While **STAMFORD** had benefited for many years from its proximity to New York, it's only in the last few decades that businesses have moved to make it their home, attracted by the lower taxes. The results have not been entirely welcome for the city: the upswing in the local economy has been accompanied by the kinds of modern corporate office buildings and chain hotels that taint its downtown area. Still, Stamford does have a few spots worth a visitor's time: check out the 1958 **First Presbyterian Church**, 1101 Bedford St (Mon–Fri 9am–5pm; free; Ⓣ203/324-9522), a unique fish-shaped building (a symbolic reference to Christianity) designed by architect Wallace K. Harrison, that contains the largest mechanical pipe organ in Connecticut. North of downtown, off Rte-15, the **Stamford Historical Society Museum**, 1508 High Ridge Rd (Tues–Sat noon–4pm; $2 donation; Ⓣ203/329-1183), gives a good insight into local history with rotating exhibits and is worth a quick visit, mostly for the admission it provides to the 1699 **Hoyt-Barnum House**, a restored blacksmith's home at 713 Bedford St. Nearby, the **Stamford Museum & Nature Center**, 39 Scofieldtown Rd (Mon–Sat 9am–5pm, Sun 11am–5pm; $3; Ⓣ203/322-1646, Ⓦwww.stamfordmuseum.org), a 118-acre working farm and country store, was once the home of prosperous New York clothier Henri Bendel. Now it houses a slew of family-oriented exhibits and displays of farm tools, Americana, and fine art, as well as an observatory with a 22-inch research telescope, open to the public on Friday evenings (additional $3). At the northern end of the museum property is another good place for nature-lovers, the **Bartlett Arboretum & Gardens**, 151 Brookdale Rd (daily 8.30am–sunset; free; Ⓣ203/322-6971, Ⓦwww.bartlettarboretum.org), which contains 64 acres of woodlands, wetlands, and gardens, with a greenhouse, nature trails, and a special collection of large trees among its assets.

Practicalities

Geared primarily to business travelers, many of Stamford's large chain **hotels** are located downtown; the *Stamford Marriott*, 2 Stamford Forum (Ⓣ203/357-9555 or 1-800/732-9689; ❻), and the *Sheraton Stamford*, 2710 Summer St (Ⓣ203/359-1300; ❻), are particularly good places to take advantage of weekend deals; they also offer nicer than average rooms.

There's no shortage of **restaurants** in Stamford, one of the few benefits of its development as a business center. For generous portions of fairly pricey steaks and seafood try *Giovanni's Steakhouse*, 1297 Long Ridge Rd (Ⓣ203/322-8870), while $15 pastas and other Italian standards can be had at the classy *Il Falco*, 59 Broad St (Ⓣ203/327-0002). If it's pub fare you want, the *Temple Bar*, 120 Bedford St (Ⓣ203/708-9000) will suit you fine, even serving a traditional Irish beef and Guinness stew. *The Sandwich Maestro*, 90 Atlantic St (Ⓣ203/325-0802), offers gourmet sandwiches for about $6.

After dark, check out what's on at the two **theaters** maintained by the Stamford Center for the Arts (Ⓣ203/325-4466, Ⓦwww.onlyatsca.com): the Rich Forum, 307 Atlantic St, has mainly plays, while the Palace Theatre, 61 Atlantic St, puts on musicals in a wonderfully restored music hall.

Greenwich

GREENWICH, nearly as populated as Stamford, has a much more well-heeled feel, with a main thoroughfare, **Greenwich Avenue**, that's eminently walkable and lined with fine shops, boutiques, and restaurants. It was originally a sleepy farming community, but the arrival of the railroad in the 1840s benefited the town by facilitating its development as both an industrial power and a choice resort for New Yorkers. Today it's the second wealthiest town in the country with a population of 20,000 or more, and home to a host of media celebrities as well as the CEOs of several multinational corporations – its private beaches are backed by luxurious homes and fronted by marinas stocked with lavish yachts.

The Town

Although perhaps best known for its affluence, Greenwich also has its share of cultural attractions. The **Bruce Museum**, 1 Museum Drive (Tues–Sat 10am–5pm, Sun 1–5pm; $7, Tues free; ⓣ203/869-0376, ⓦwww.brucemuseum.org), began in a private home that looks like something out of Hitchcock, and has now developed into a major museum with collections on American cultural history and the environmental sciences. Exhibits include a small collection of nineteenth- and early twentieth-century paintings by the Cos Cob School of American Impressionism, and a science and environment wing that features a mine shaft, woodland habitat, minerals, fossils, and a marine touch-tank.

Also worth a visit here is the **Bush-Holley Historic Site**, 39 Strickland Rd (Jan & Feb Sat & Sun noon–4pm, March–Dec Tues–Sun noon–4pm; $6; ⓣ203/869-6899, ⓦwww.hstg.org), a two-story ivory-clapboard building turned into a boarding house by the Holley family in the late 1800s, open today for tours. Like the Griswold home in Old Lyme, the Holley residence began to attract artists eager to escape the summer heat and humidity of the big city – among them Childe Hassam, John Henry Twachtman, and J. Alden Weir, some of whose original works hang today in the house. There's also the fine late-eighteenth-century Connecticut furniture and ornate woodwork of the house itself, not to mention the studio of Elmer Livingston McRae, the artist husband of a subsequent owner, which has been left virtually intact.

The scalloped, shingle-sided **Putnam Cottage**, 243 E Putnam Ave (Jan–March by appointment only, April–Dec Sun 1–4pm and by appointment; $6; ⓣ203/869-9697, ⓦwww.putnamcottage.org), built in 1690 and licensed as the *Knapp Tavern* from 1732, has a bit of romantic history to it: legend has it that one day in 1779, local patriot General Israel Putnam, a regular here, was busy shaving when he noticed advancing British troops in his mirror. Forced to flee, he jumped on a horse and managed to escape down a steep cliff, returning later with reinforcements to rout the enemy. The cottage contains original fieldstone fireplaces and antique furniture.

Practicalities

Accommodation in Greenwich tends to be of the B&B variety. Of these, the Relais & Chateaux *Homestead Inn*, 420 Field Point Rd (ⓣ203/869-7500, ⓦwww.homesteadinn.com; ❾), has eighteen elegant rooms in a 1799 mansion perched on a hill in a peaceful residential area, while the *Harbor House Inn*, 165 Shore Rd (ⓣ203/637-0145, ⓦwww.hhinn.com; ❻), is close to the water in Old Greenwich. The *Cos Cob Inn*, 50 River Rd (ⓣ203/661-5845, ⓦwww.coscobinn.com; ❻) is also on the water but with a view somewhat dominated by the I-95 bridge over the Mianus River; nonetheless, the 1870s Federal-style mansion's fourteen guestrooms have tons of "olde worlde" charm, and the co-owned Greenwich Water Club's pool and fitness center are steps away.

You're spoiled for choice in Greenwich as far as **eating** is concerned – though, not surprisingly in such an affluent place, restaurants can be pricey. If you're up for a splurge, try *Gaia*, 253 Greenwich Ave (Ⓣ203/66-3443), for unique dishes slow-cooked in sealed glass mason jars – the macaroni and truffles with *pave d'affinois* cheese is outstanding – along with a superior wine list, or *Thomas Henkelmann* at the *Homestead Inn*, 420 Field Point Rd (Ⓣ203/869-7500; closed Sun), for top-notch French food. At *L'Escale*, 500 Steamboat Rd, in the luxury hotel *Delamar Greenwich Harbor* (Ⓣ203/661-9800; ⑨), you can dine in style while gazing at the posh yachts in Greenwich Harbor. Less expensive options include *Thataway*, 409 Greenwich Ave (Ⓣ203/622-0947), with its pubby atmosphere and outdoor patio, and *Boxcar Cantina*, 44 Old Field Point Rd (Ⓣ203/661-4774), known for fresh New Mexican treats like quesadillas with roasted vegetables and brie.

Danbury and the Housatonic Valley

The company town of **DANBURY**, 25 miles north of Norwalk on Rte-7, became famous as the "hat capital" of America; the ten-gallon Stetson was first fashioned here, and at one point, there were more than three dozen factories engaged in hatmaking. When that industry declined in the 1960s and 1970s, Danbury's savior became **Union Carbide**, whose headquarters are still located here. There's little of interest in the drab downtown area, where Danbury Green is the focus of an ambitious series of festivals and concerts. Nearby, the **Danbury Museum & Historical Society**, 43 Main St (Wed–Fri 1–4pm and by appointment; $6; Ⓣ203/743-5200, Ⓦwww.danburyhistorical.org), housed in the 1785 John and Mary Rider House, is mostly of note for its nostalgic exhibits relating to the city's hat industry, while the **Military Museum of Southern New England**, 125 Park Ave, I-84 exit 3 (Tues–Sat 10am–5pm, Sun noon–5pm; $4; Ⓣ203/790-9277, Ⓦwww.usmilitarymuseum.org), contains enough life-size dioramas of World War II scenes to sate most any military buff. There's also a 1917 Renault, the first tank ever made in the US, and one of the original self-propelled howitzers. Danbury's other main visitor attraction is the **Railway Museum**, 120 White St (Jan–March Wed–Sat 10am–4pm, Sun noon–4pm; April–Oct Tues–Sat 10am–5pm, Sun noon–5pm; Nov–Dec Tues–Fri 10am–4pm, Sat 10am–5pm, Sun noon–5pm; $6; Ⓣ203/778-8337), with a station and its railroad yard.

About ten miles south of Danbury, picturesque **RIDGEFIELD** nearly seems an extension of the Litchfield Hills, its early buildings having escaped the rampant development so typical in Connecticut. If you make it here, check out the **Keeler Tavern Museum**, 132 Main St (Feb–Dec Wed, Sat & Sun 1–4pm; $5; Ⓣ203/438-5485), which was a popular watering hole even before the Revolutionary War, but a hotbed of patriotic fervor during, especially after it was hit by British artillery. The offending cannonball is still embedded in the building. Down the street, the **Aldrich Contemporary Art Museum**, 258 Main St (Tues–Sun noon–5pm; $7, free Tues; Ⓣ203/438-4519, Ⓦwww.aldrichart.org), was one of the first museums in America devoted solely to contemporary art, originally opened in 1964, and recently reopened after a year-long expansion project. The museum has no permanent collection, but rather its twelve galleries (including an unusual "sound" gallery) feature a series of rotating exhibitions; there's also a lovely two-acre sculpture garden out back.

Apart from Danbury and Ridgefield, the **Housatonic Valley** offers a few natural attractions, with much of its landscape set aside as nature reserves and sanctuaries. Just north of Danbury, Candlewood Lake is the state's largest fresh-water lake, with opportunities for swimming, boating, and fishing. Farther south, Saugatuck Reservoir, near Redding, is so peaceful and undeveloped you'd swear you were in northern Maine, while Huntington State Park is a great place for mountain-biking. For avid hikers, east of Danbury, in Newtown, you can walk along the banks of the Housatonic River in the Paugussett State Forest.

Practicalities

Danbury's *Ethan Allen Hotel*, exit 4 off I-84 (ⓣ203/744-1776 or 1-800/742-1776, ⓦwww.ethanallenhotel.com; ❻), is a large, modern hotel, though rooms are stocked with authentic Ethan Allen furniture. Quieter Ridgefield's *Stonehenge Inn*, Rte-7, Stonehenge Road (ⓣ203/438-6511, ⓦwww.stonehengeinn-ct.com; ❻), is an 1827 Colonial inn set in an idyllic garden next to a duck pond. Also in Ridgefield, the peaceful *West Lane Inn*, 22 West Lane (ⓣ203/438-7323, ⓦwww.westlaneinn.com; ❼), contains twenty antique-stuffed rooms.

For something to **eat**, try *Ondine*, 69 Pembroke Rd, Danbury (ⓣ203/746-4900; Wed–Sun dinner, Sun brunch), for contemporary French cuisine, though it's a bit pricey; by contrast, *Rosy Tomorrows*, also in Danbury at 15 Old Mill Plain Rd (ⓣ203/743-5845), is the place for American staples – barbecued ribs, huge sandwiches, burgers, onion rings, and so on, at moderate prices – with boisterous character. In Ridgefield, the *Stonehenge Inn* (see above; dinner only) serves classic, expensive French meals, like veal medallions in a madeira cream sauce.

Hartford and the Connecticut River Valley

The **Connecticut River**, New England's largest, rises in the mountains of New Hampshire close to the Canadian border and runs all the way down to Long Island Sound. Growing up along either side of it, at least in Connecticut, has been a stretch of relatively peaceful towns, unable to make much industrial use of the river due to its shallowness. The one exception to these slow-paced communities is **Hartford**, the state capital, an unattractive and largely dull city of some importance as a stronghold of the state's economy. A mile west of the city, Nook Farm was home in the late nineteenth century to some of the greatest literary figures of the age, including Mark Twain and Harriet Beecher Stowe, while **West Hartford** is where Noah Webster published his *American Dictionary* in 1828. Farther west, gentle countryside leads to the pleasant town of **Farmington** and the less attractive but stimulating industrial city of **New Britain**, one of the nation's main producers of hardware.

South of Hartford, the Connecticut River wends its way past **Wethersfield**, where Washington planned the final stages of the Revolutionary War; **Rocky Hill**, whose 185-million-year-old dinosaur tracks can be seen in Dinosaur State Park; and **East Haddam**, site of the Goodspeed Opera House and the unusual hilltop Gillette Castle, one of the state's leading peculiarities. **Ivoryton**, famed for its summer theater, and **Essex**, with the excellent Connecticut River Museum, complete the picture as the river widens and nears the sea.

Hartford

The town that Mark Twain once described as "the best built and handsomest ... I have ever seen" is today hardly recognizable as such: rather, it's a hodgepodge of ugly office buildings, multistory parking garages, factories, and sprawling suburbs. Indeed, the modern capital of Connecticut, **HARTFORD**, is best known as the insurance center of the United States, and will probably not take more than a day or so of your time to explore – though the longer you stay, the more unexpected charms you are likely to find. Highlights include the 1878 **State Capitol** with its golden dome and verdant grounds, the superb **Wadsworth Atheneum**, the nation's oldest continuously operating public museum, and the whimsical mansion built by the father of Huck Finn and Tom Sawyer.

Some history

Originally known by the Indian name of *Suckiaug* ("black earth"), Hartford was dubbed "House of Good Hope" by Dutch merchants who established a trading post here in 1633. When a group of Puritans from Massachusetts arrived two years later, they named the place "Newtown," after their Massachusetts home, then renamed it Hartford after the town of Hertford, England. From its earliest days, it was an important center for government: Connecticut's governor John Winthrop, Jr, set out from here in 1661 on a mission to seek from King Charles II a **charter** guaranteeing the colony certain rights. Charles's more authoritarian successor, James II, attempted to rescind those rights and establish his own authority over the colony by dispatching his emissary to the city in 1687. The charter was whisked away by stealth and hidden in the hollow bark of an oak tree on land belonging to Samuel Wyllys. The "Charter Oak" was destroyed during a violent storm in 1856, but the legend lives on in the names Charter Oak Avenue and Charter Oak Place, at which corner the tree stood.

Leading the **manufacturing** charge, the Hartford Woolen Company became the first in the country to devote itself to producing woolen cloth; other goods manufactured locally included Colt revolvers, Sharps rifles, and the Pope motor car; the pioneering city was also the first in the nation to be lit by **electricity**. Hartford's greatest claim to fame, though, has been its position as the nation's **insurance** capital, a status begun with the formation of the Hartford Fire Insurance Company in 1810. By the middle of the twentieth century, there were up to fifty insurance companies based in the city, providing twenty percent of the nation's coverage on certain types of policies. Today, though downtown's Travelers Tower still dominates for miles around, with the headquarters of Phoenix Home Life, Aetna, and a host of other insurers nearby, the twenty-first century – especially post-9/11 – has seen a downturn, and the city is struggling to revitalize. Major developments have been set in motion, however, including the new half-a-million-square-foot **Connecticut Convention Center** and multimillion-dollar expansions and renovations of the Public Library and the Wadsworth Atheneum.

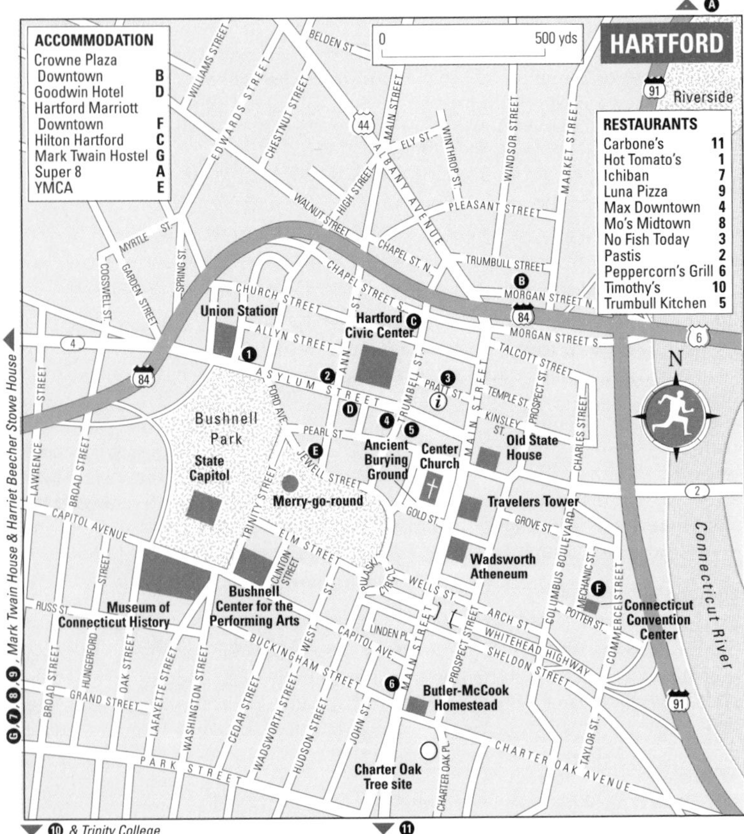

Arrival, information, and city transit

Hartford lies at the junction of the north–south highway I-91 and east–west I-84, so the city is easily accessible by **car**. It's also well served by long-distance **buses** like Greyhound and Peter Pan, which – along with Amtrak **trains** – all pull in to the Union Station terminal. The **local bus** system is operated by Connecticut Transit (Ⓣ860/525-9181, Ⓦwww.cttransit.com), which maintains an information bureau at State House Square and Market St (Mon–Fri 7am–6pm, Sat 9am–3pm). Connecticut's main **airport**, Bradley International, is just twelve miles north of town. Several reliable **taxi** companies serve the city, among them Yellow Cabs (Ⓣ860/666-6666) and Valley Cab Service (Ⓣ860/673-4250). Hartford's downtown is "patrolled" by the **Hartford Guides** (Ⓣ860/522-0855), who can help with directions and information. The knowledgeable staff at the **Greater Hartford Welcome Center**, 45 Pratt St (Mon–Fri 9am–5pm; Ⓣ860/244-0253, Ⓦwww.hartford.com), can help you find accommodation and provide information on attractions and current events.

Accommodation

Hartford has a limited range of **accommodation** options, from a few budget motels and a couple of hostels to three or four large, usually pricey downtown hotels which cater mainly to business travelers and where, consequently, big reductions can be had at weekends.

Crowne Plaza Downtown 50 Morgan St ⓣ860/549-2400, ⓦwww.ichotelsgroup.com. Large 350-room hotel in the center of town with well-lit, oversized rooms, as well as a fitness center and outdoor pool. ❼

Goodwin Hotel Goodwin Square, 1 Haynes St ⓣ860/246-7500 or 1-800/922-5006, ⓦwww.goodwinhotel.com. Elaborately restored luxury hotel opposite downtown's Civic Center, with a full range of facilities, including an excellent restaurant. ❻

Hartford Marriott Downtown 200 Columbus Blvd ⓣ860/249-8000 or 1-800/228-9290, ⓦwww.marriott.com. Opened in the fall of 2005 and connected to the new Convention Center, with 409 rooms in 22 stories, as well as an indoor pool, fitness center, and a Starbucks onsite. ❻

Hilton Hartford 315 Trumbull St ⓣ860/728-5151 or 1-800/HILTONS, ⓦwww.hilton.com. A swanky spot after a multimillion-dollar renovation completed in March 2005, connected to the Civic Center in the heart of downtown. There's a health club, indoor pool and sauna, and a trendy restaurant – *Morty & Ming's* – serving a unique menu of Chinese and Jewish deli food. ❼

Mark Twain Hostel 131 Tremont St ⓣ860/523-7255. Worn but clean, about two miles from downtown. Beds in the dorm-style rooms are $24 a night; private rooms also available ($48–58/night for two), but all are shared bath. Reservations advisable, as the place can get full. HI member hostel.

Super 8 I-91 exit 33 ⓣ860/246-8888 or 1-800/800-8000, ⓦwww.super8.com. Budget motel offering basic, inexpensive accommodation, a half-mile from downtown and close to the Meadows Music Theatre. ❸

YMCA 160 Jewell St ⓣ860/522-9622, ⓦwww.ghymca.org. Has 125 economy single-occupancy rooms; rates with shared bath start are $21, with private bath, TV, and phone $26. Includes use of the fitness room and pool. ID required; must be eighteen or over. Check-in Mon–Fri 7.30am–10pm, Sat & Sun 7.30am–2.30pm.

The City

Bleak insurance towers dominate downtown Hartford's skyline, but despite that it's a surprisingly open city, with wide streets and plenty of greenery to break up the concrete and steel. The broad lawns and plantings of **Bushnell Park**, designed in 1861 by Swiss-born architect Jacob Weidenmann, surround the golden-domed **State Capitol** (free tours hourly Mon–Fri 9.15am–1.15pm, July & Aug additional tour at 2.15pm; also April–Oct Sat 10.15am–2.15pm), an 1878 mixture of Gothic, Classical, and Second Empire styles. Its ornate exterior, with niches containing statues of Connecticut political worthies, looks more like a church; inside, massive granite columns, stained-glass windows, and lofty ceilings continue the ecclesiastical ambience. The Hall of Flags contains some fascinating relics of the state's history, including bullet-ridden flags and the camp bed Lafayette slept on when he visited the city. After you've traipsed round the Capitol you can take a ride on the 1914 **merry-go-round** in the park, which gives jangling rides for a mere fifty cents (mid-May to Oct, closed Mon). Across the road in the Connecticut State Library, 231 Capitol Ave, the **Museum of Connecticut History** (Mon–Fri 9am–4pm, Sat 9am–3pm; free; ⓣ860/757-6535), holds an impressive collection of Colt rifles and revolvers, an extensive collection of American coins from as early as the 1660s, and the original 1662 Connecticut Royal Charter.

Main Street

Many of Hartford's most important buildings are located on **Main Street**, starting (from south to north) with the yellow-clapboard **Butler-McCook Homestead**, no. 396 (Wed–Sat 10am–4pm, Sun 1–4pm; $5; ⓣ860/522-1806), one of the city's few surviving historic homes. Owned by the same family for nearly two hundred years, it contains a collection of armor from Japan and some antique toys and furniture; a small gallery documents life on Main Street for the family from 1750 on, and house tours take about 45 minutes. Behind the house, an always-open 1860s formal garden designed by Jacob Weidenmann is one of the oldest domestic gardens in the US.

Hartford's pride and joy is the Greek Revival **Wadsworth Atheneum Museum of Art**, 600 Main St (Wed–Fri 11am–5pm, Sat & Sun 10am–5pm; $10; ⓣ860/278-2670, ⓦwww.wadsworthatheneum.org), founded by Daniel Wadsworth in 1842 and the nation's oldest continuously operating public art museum. The collection, spanning over five thousand years, includes ancient Egyptian, Greek, and Roman bronzes; Renaissance and Baroque paintings; an extensive collection of seventeenth- and eighteenth-century American furniture and decorative arts; and the "*Amistad*" collection, documenting the development of African-American culture from the slave period to the present. In a bid to increase its display capacity (currently the museum can only show two thousand of its 45,000 items), the museum recently purchased the old *Hartford Times* building just behind it, though specific plans for the new space haven't yet been finalized.

A few hundred yards north, on the corner of Main and Gold streets at 1 Tower Square, the lofty 527-foot-high **Travelers Tower** can be ascended for spectacular views of the city and beyond from an open-air **observation deck**; it'll take some effort, though – after the 24-floor elevator ride, you'll need to climb seventy steps up a spiral staircase. The half-hour tours are free, though reservations are requested (May–Sept; ⓣ860/277-4208). Across the street at 675 Main, the elegant **Center Church** was established by Thomas Hooker, the leader of the band of dissenters from Newtown, Massachusetts. Modeled, like so many others, on London's St Martin-in-the-Fields in Trafalgar Square, the church holds no fewer than five Tiffany windows and a barrel-vaulted ceiling. It overlooks the tranquil 1640 **Ancient Burying Ground** (May–Oct Mon–Sat 10am–4pm, Sun 9am–1pm, otherwise by appointment; free; ⓣ860/561-2585), the final resting-place for many of the city's first settlers.

At 800 Main, the red-brick **Old State House** (Mon–Sat 10am–4pm; free; ⓣ860/522-6766, ⓦwww.ctosh.org), a 1796 Federal-style building designed by Boston architect Charles Bulfinch – his first public commission – provides a dignified contrast to the drab modern office buildings that surround it, especially since its renovation in 1996, when the early nineteenth-century ornamental iron fencing and gaslights were restored. Inside, the Court Room, which witnessed, among others, the *Amistad* trials, has been restored to its 1920 appearance; on the second floor, the **Museum of Natural and Other Curiosities** has a collection of exotic and bizarre items on display, including a two-headed calf.

Trinity College

South of downtown, at 300 Summit St, the beautiful and compact campus of **Trinity College** is located on a hundred acres at the highest point in the city and is a pleasant place to spend an hour or two. Founded in 1823, it hosts an array of stunning architecture, particularly on the main square, known as the Long Walk, notable for its three very impressive brownstone Victorian Gothic buildings. Also striking is the college **chapel**, claimed by some to be the best example of Victorian Gothic in the nation. Organ and chamber concerts are held here regularly while across the green the college's Cinestudio (ⓣ860/297-CINE) hosts independent and classic movies nightly, and is open to the public.

The campus is also home to the excellent Gallows Hill Bookstore (closed Sun; ⓣ860/297-5231), which presents occasional readings with visiting authors. For details on current events at the College, call ⓣ860/297-2001.

The Mark Twain and Harriet Beecher Stowe houses

About a mile west of downtown on Rte-4, a hilltop community known as Nook Farm was home in the 1880s to next-door neighbors **Mark Twain** and **Harriet Beecher Stowe**. Today their Victorian homes, furnished much as they were then, are open for guided tours. The bizarre **Mark Twain House and Museum**, 351 Farmington Ave (May–Dec Mon–Sat 9.30am–5.30pm, Sun noon–5.30pm; rest of year same hours but closed Tues; $12; ⓣ860/247-0998, ⓦwww.marktwainhouse.org), which the author built in 1874 and lived in with his family until 1891, saw him write many of his classic works, such as *The Adventures of Huckleberry Finn*. Looking at the newly restored home, it's easy to see where the author spent the publishing royalties from those books: designed by Edward Tuckerman Potter, the place is outrageously ornate, with black-and-orange brickwork, elaborate woodwork, and the only remaining domestic interior by Louis Comfort Tiffany that's open to the public. In addition to the house tour, a new kitchen tour ($2 with house, $5 stand-alone) takes you into the kitchen and butler's pantry for the servants' perspective.

The much less flamboyant **Harriet Beecher Stowe House**, 77 Forest St (summer and Dec Mon–Sat 9.30am–4.30pm, Sun noon–4.30pm; rest of year same hours but closed Mon; $8; ⓣ860/522-9258, ⓦwww.harrietbeecher-stowecenter.org), celebrates the life of the author of *Uncle Tom's Cabin*, one of the most important American literary works of the nineteenth century – and which, by speaking out against slavery, fueled the fire for the Civil War. The house, built just three years before Twain's, is a fine example of a nineteenth-century "cottage," with a hint of the romantic villas made popular by Andrew Jackson Downing and Calvert Vaux. Inside you can see Stowe's writing table and some of her paintings. Garden tours are also offered in the summer (Wed & Sat; $8).

△ Mark Twain House

Hartford's defining resident

Noah Webster was born in West Hartford on October 16, 1758. A lexicographer and author, he wrote educational textbooks before eventually compiling the **first dictionary** to distinguish American usage of the English language from British usage. His spelling book – informally known as *The Blue-backed Speller* (1783) for its blue binding – helped standardize American spelling and greatly contributed to the country's growing national identity. Encouraged by the enormous success of the first book, he compiled and edited a series of dictionaries culminating in the extensive, two-volume *American Dictionary of the English Language* (1828), which went on to become the nation's most trusted and best-known dictionary. A graduate of Yale, Webster later co-founded Amherst College in Massachusetts, and today *Webster's Dictionary* keeps his name synonymous with the development of the English language in America.

West Hartford

Farmington Avenue, a long strip with a mix of cheap diners, fast-food joints, and a few quaint gourmet shops and bookstores, continues out of the capital to **WEST HARTFORD**, home to a few scattered highlights, in particular the **Noah Webster House**, 227 S Main St (Thurs–Mon 1–4pm; $6; ⓣ860/521-5362), an eighteenth-century farmhouse that was home to the compiler of the pioneering *American Dictionary,* first published in 1828 (see box above).

Back closer to town, north of Farmington Ave at Prospect and Asylum aves, **Elizabeth Park** (daily dawn–dusk; free; ⓦwww.elizabethpark.org) was the first municipal rose garden in the nation. June is the best time to visit to see the more than eight hundred varieties of roses, including rarities such as Earth Song and Grenada, but in addition there are rock gardens, greenhouses (Mon–Fri 8am–3pm), and miles of tranquil walking paths.

Eating

To take advantage of the surprisingly good **eating** options Hartford has to offer, you'll probably end up touring a few different neighborhoods. For home-cooking, head to Farmington Avenue, which offers the city's top diners and cafés. Many of downtown Hartford's choice Italian eateries can be found along Franklin Avenue, the heart of the city's Italian district, while more sophisticated and expensive French and American restaurants operate along the axis of downtown's Main and Asylum streets.

Carbone's 588 Franklin Ave ⓣ860/296-9646. Excellent and expensive Italian restaurant opened in 1938 and still family-owned. Leave room for dessert and try the bocci balls, chocolate-coated vanilla ice cream in Italian liquors, flambeed tableside.

Hot Tomato's 1 Union Place ⓣ860/249-5100. A relaxed, energetic Italian spot, popular for its huge garlicky portions and fair bill.

Ichiban 530 Farmington Ave ⓣ860/236-5599. Tasty sushi, but check out the Korean menu, too, where tofu *bibimbap*, fish stews, and fried meat dishes offer a welcome alternative for those who can't cope with raw fish.

Luna Pizza 999 Farmington Ave, West Hartford ⓣ860/233-1625. Brick-oven thin-crust pizza with a somewhat unusual variety of yummy toppings, such as eggplant and salmon, as well as a lactose-free "cheese" option made from brown rice.

Max Downtown 185 Asylum St ⓣ860/522-2530. Considered Hartford's best restaurant, this dynamic spot, brimming with creative flair, prepares impeccable American-nouveau dishes at a considerable (but worthwhile) cost.

Mo's Midtown 25 Whitney St ⓣ860/236-7741. You get the greatest breakfast to cure all hangovers at this friendly and hugely popular diner right off Farmington Ave. Recommended is the "Papa Mo" breakfast – a classic "fry-up" – and for those with smaller stomachs, the "Momma Mo" and "Baby Mo" still get the job done. Beware of daunting lines on weekends; however, they move along fairly fast.

No Fish Today 80 Pratt St ⓣ860/244-2100. Despite its name (a callback to the days of prohibition when sneaky signs suggested whether or not alcohol was available), Italian-style seafood is the thing in this relaxed, moderately priced downtown restaurant.

Pastis 201 Ann St ⓣ860/278-8852. The closest to a Paris bistro you'll find in the city, with the likes of seared duck breast and steak frites for around $20. Live jazz at the bar Fri & Sat, no cover.

Peppercorn's Grill 357 Main St ⓣ860/547-1714. One of the better eateries in Hartford, rivaling *Max Downtown*, is this minimalist Italian trattoria standout, serving homemade pasta dishes like lobster and scallop ravioli in a lobster cream sauce.

Timothy's 243 Zion St ⓣ860/728-9822. Super little inexpensive restaurant serving an assorted menu (meatloaf, chicken fajitas) using local and organic produce. Burgers and some vegetarian dishes available as well.

Trumbull Kitchen 150 Trumbull St ⓣ860/493-7417. Popular, trendy eatery with an eclectic menu featuring a bit of everything, from dim sum and tapas to pizza (duck and mango sausage, brie, and arugula pesto) and meatloaf, with a caramel chocolate fondue for dessert. Not very pricey, either.

Nightlife and entertainment

There's no shortage of **nightlife** in Hartford, whether you want to see a play, listen to a symphony concert, or bop till the wee hours in a nightclub. Among the main music venues are the **Bushnell Center for the Performing Arts**, 166 Capitol Ave (ⓣ860/987-5900, ⓦwww.bushnell.org), home to the Hartford Symphony Orchestra, the Hartford Ballet, and the Connecticut Opera; the **New England Dodge Music Center**, 61 Savitt Way (ⓣ860/548-7370, ⓦwww.dodgemusiccenter.com), venue for rock, pop, country, blues, and jazz; and the **Hartford Civic Center Coliseum**, Trumbull and Asylum streets (ⓣ860/727-8010), home of the American Hockey League (minor league NHL) Wolfpack hockey team and host to a variety of sports competitions and rock and pop concerts. The award-winning **Hartford Stage Company**, 50 Church St (ⓣ860/527-5151), stages classic plays and bold experimental productions, while **TheaterWorks**, 233 Pearl St (ⓣ860/527-7838), is a local professional company presenting contemporary pieces.

Hartford's **bars** and **nightclubs** are mainly confined to the downtown area. For current listings, check out the free arts and entertainment weekly the *Hartford Advocate* or the city's daily newspaper, the *Courant*.

Black-eyed Sally's 350 Asylum St ⓣ860/278-7427. Live blues bands Thurs–Sat ($5–15 cover) and hearty Cajun cooking in this atmospheric restaurant/club. Wed is open-mic night. Closed Sun.

The Brickyard 113 Allyn St ⓣ860/249-2112. Multi-level hangout with a casual sports bar (with pool tables, air hockey, and ping-pong), a lounge with a patio, and a dance floor, along with live bands and DJs. Thurs $5, Fri & Sat $7.

Coach's 187 Allyn St ⓣ860/522-6224. Part-owned by local legend and UCONN men's basketball coach Jim Calhoun, this bar/restaurant has a sports theme, with the typical memorabilia to show for it. No cover. Closed summer Sun.

Room 960 960 Main St ⓣ860/522-9960. For the uber-trendy, Hartford's answer to the VIP Manhattan club scene.

Standing Stone 111 Allyn St ⓣ860/246-4400. Irish whiskey and beer line the walls of this pub which features 24 beers on tap and live bands; no cover. Open Tues–Sat.

Around Hartford

A cluster of towns within ten miles to the **south** and **west of Hartford** have managed to retain much of their traditional New England atmosphere, even in the face of Hartford's growing suburban sprawl. None exactly overwhelm with things to do, but they make a decent alternative if you tire of spending time in the city. While they're best accessed by car, Connecticut Transit (Ⓣ860/525-9181, Ⓦwww.cttransit.com) has extensive routes in the Greater Hartford area.

Farmington

Lush **FARMINGTON** had its heyday in the 1830s and 1840s, when the Farmington Canal operated between New Haven and Northampton, Massachusetts. Though today a more mundane suburb, it still merits a visit in order to see the **Hill-Stead Museum**, 35 Mountain Rd (May–Oct Tues–Sun 10am–5pm; rest of year Tues–Sun 11am–4pm; $9; Ⓣ860/677-4787, Ⓦwww.hillstead.org), an impressive turn-of-last-century Colonial Revival house that belonged to industrial magnate Alfred A. Pope. Designed by his daughter, Theodate – one of the nation's first female architects, whose illustrious career nearly ended while aboard the ill-fated *Lusitania* (she survived by hanging onto an oar) – it now holds an outstanding assortment of American and European furniture and a collection of Impressionist paintings, including works by Monet, Manet, Degas, and Whistler. Guided tours run just under an hour. Also in Farmington, the **Stanley-Whitman House**, 37 High St (May–Oct Wed–Sun noon–4pm, Nov–April Sat & Sun noon–4pm; $5; Ⓣ860/677-9222, Ⓦwww.stanleywhitman.org), is a Colonial homestead dating from 1720, with some interesting architectural features, such as its narrow casement windows with small diamond panes.

Practicalities

If you prefer to **stay** here rather than in downtown Hartford, options include the *Farmington Inn*, 827 Farmington Ave (Ⓣ860/677-2821 or 1-800/648-9804, Ⓦwww.farmingtoninn.com; ❼), a large, luxury facility whose comfortable rooms and suites contain paintings by local artists, while the *Hartford Marriott*, 15 Farm Springs Rd (Ⓣ860/678-1000; ❻), has a fitness center along with both an indoor and an outdoor pool – also big weekend bargains. For something to **eat**, *Apricots*, 1593 Farmington Ave (Ⓣ860/673-5405), is a true gem with an English-style pub downstairs (typical entrees $10–14) and two formal (and expensive) dining rooms offering Continental cuisine upstairs. The *Connecticut Culinary Institute*, 230 Farmington Ave (Ⓣ860/677-7869; lunch Mon–Fri, dinner Thurs–Sat), is a training school for future chefs, with a varied, good-value menu.

New Britain

Industrial **NEW BRITAIN**, once one of the country's leading producers of locks, tools, ball bearings, and other hardware items, is the unlikely location for one of the Northeast's best collections of American art, with galleries displaying exhibits of the museum's more than five thousand works, including oils, watercolors, drawings, and sculpture spanning 250 years. The **New Britain Museum of American Art**, 56 Lexington St (Tues, Thurs, Fri & Sun noon–5pm, Wed noon–7pm, Sat 10am–5pm; $6, free Sat 10am–noon; Ⓣ860/229-0257, Ⓦwww.nbmaa.org), boasts representative works by Whistler, Copley, Sargent, and Church, plus murals by Thomas Hart Benton, all housed in an attractive nineteenth-century mansion. At the time of writing, an additional 43,000-square-foot space was under construction; renovations are expected to be complete in the spring of 2006. The town's manufacturing past and present are the focus of the **New Britain Industrial Museum**, 185 Main St (Mon–Fri 2–5pm, Wed noon–5pm; free; Ⓣ860/832-8654, Ⓦwww.nbim.org), with exhibits devoted to the large manufacturing companies, such as Stanley Tools and Fafnir Bearings, that brought the city prosperity. Items on display include everything from tools to Art Deco kitchenware.

Wethersfield and around

Situated on the Connecticut River, **WETHERSFIELD** had its own harbor until a major flood in 1692 rerouted the water and so stripped much of the town's wealth; indeed, by the late 1700s, farming had overtaken trade as the main economic activity. Today, a few well-preserved homes lend the place a certain picturesque quality. Much of the town's historical interest focuses on the **Webb-Deane-Stevens Museum**, made up of three eighteenth-century houses at 211 Main St (May–Oct Wed–Mon 10am–4pm, Nov–April Sat & Sun 10am–4pm; $8 for three-house tour, $3 for one-house tour; ⓣ860/529-0612, ⓦwww.webb-deane-stevens.org). The **Webb House**, built in 1752 by a prosperous merchant named Joseph Webb, Sr, and notable for its wide central hall and well-proportioned rooms, contains period furnishings and decorative arts in its rooms, one of which was a bedroom especially designed for the arrival of George Washington, who came here to plan the Yorktown campaign with Jean-Baptiste Rochambeau. The 1766 **Silas Deane House** was home to a lawyer-diplomat who played an important role in the First Continental Congress and traveled to Paris to seek French assistance for the forces of the Revolution. Deane allegedly became involved in some dubious business deals while abroad and was accused of treason; although never found guilty, he spent much of the rest of his life in an unsuccessful attempt to clear his name. The more modest **Stevens House** was built in 1788 by a local leatherworker for his bride, its simple decor and lack of embellishments proving that not everyone here was a member of the aristocracy. Admission to these three houses includes entrance to the charming 1720 **Buttolph-Williams House**, down the road at 249 Broad St (May–Oct Wed–Mon 10am–4pm), one of the oldest surviving homes in town, with characteristic dark clapboards and small windows. A massive fireplace dominates the main living room, and the whole place is filled with period furniture.

Back on Main, at no. 150, **The Old Academy** (Tues–Fri 9am–4pm) is a handsome brick building which has served as a town hall, library, women's seminary, and now the Wethersfield Historical Society's unexciting HQ. At its north end, Main Street dead-ends at Wethersfield Cove, where stands the flood's lone survivor – the **Historic Cove Warehouse** (mid-May to mid-Oct Sat 10am–4pm, Sun 1–4pm; $1; ⓣ860/529-7656).

Dinosaur State Park

In 1966, the discovery of thousands of dinosaur tracks at **Rocky Hill**, south of Wethersfield, led to the foundation of the **Dinosaur State Park**, a mile east of exit 23 off I-91 (park open daily 9am–4.30pm, exhibition center open Tues–Sun 9am–4.30pm; $5; ⓣ860/529-8423, ⓦwww.dinosaurstatepark.org), where you can see hundreds of the prints on display (the rest have been reburied for protection) and explore nature trails, which take you through a variety of natural environments, including a prehistoric swamp. You can even make your own dinosaur print cast to take with you; you just need ten pounds of plaster of Paris, a quarter cup of cooking oil, and a five-gallon plastic bucket. If you don't happen to have these items upon your person at the time, the museum will point you in the direction of local stores that can provide them.

△ Dinosaur tracks, Dinosaur State Park

Practicalities

There isn't too much to choose from regarding **restaurants** in Wethersfield, mainly diners, delis, and pizza joints. An exception to the rule, *Carmen Anthony Fishhouse*, 1770 Berlin Turnpike (Ⓣ860/529-7557), serves a wide variety of Italian-style seafood entrees, as well as award-winning clam chowder and crab cakes. In the event that you want to **stay** in Wethersfield, the *Chester Bulkley House*, right in the center of things at 184 Main St (Ⓣ860/563-4236, Ⓦwww.chesterbulkleyhouse.com; ❺), has five homey and fairly inexpensive rooms in an 1830 Greek Revival home.

The Connecticut River Valley

The suburbs end and the valley starts in earnest again with **MIDDLETOWN**, once the busiest port on the Connecticut River, which retains a number of gracious nineteenth-century merchants' homes, to be found on the attractive campus of prestigious **Wesleyan University**. Of these, the most prominent is the brick Federal-style **General Mansfield House**, 151 Main St (Sun 2–4.30pm, Mon 1–4pm; $5; Ⓣ860/346-0746, Ⓦwww.middlesexhistory.org), constructed in 1810 and home to the Middlesex County Historical Society. Rotating exhibits showcase county history, and there's also a permanent display on Civil War soldiers including photographs, gear, and diary entries. Also on campus, the **Zilkha Gallery**, Washington Terrace/Wyllys Ave (Tues–Sun noon–4pm; free; Ⓣ860/685-2695), showcases a rotating display of modern works in various media.

South on Rte-154, **HIGGANUM** contains little save the yellow-clapboard **Thankful Arnold House**, corner of Hayden Hill and Walkley Hill roads (Wed 9am–3pm, Thurs 2–8pm, Fri noon–3pm; also late May to early Oct Sun 1–4pm; $4; Ⓣ860/345-2400, Ⓦwww.haddamhistory.org), a three-story gambrel-roofed home built around the turn of the nineteenth century, with entrances on two levels and a magnificent **herb and vegetable garden**, carefully researched to reflect period plantings. Another nearby horticultural treat, the **Sundial Herb Garden**, Brault Hill Rd Extension (mid-May to mid-Oct Sat & Sun 10am–5pm; $2; ⓣ860/345-4290, ⓦwww.sundialgardens.com), contains a series of interrelated formal gardens based on seventeenth- and eighteenth-century principles, with topiary, avenues, knots, statuary, and sundials. A tea and gift shop (weekends year-round 10am–5pm) specializes in rare and exotic teas from around the world.

East Haddam

About seven miles south, on the opposite side of the river, the village of **EAST HADDAM** is the unlikely location for the amazing **Goodspeed Opera House**, 6 Main St off Rte-82 (tours June–Oct Sat 11am–1.30pm; $5; performances April–Dec; ⓣ860/873-8668), which rises above the Connecticut River like a giant wedding cake. Built in 1876 by shipping and banking magnate William Goodspeed to provide a venue for his love of theater, the Opera House later served as a military base and as a storage depot for the Connecticut Highway Department, until, in the late 1950s, restoration work on the rundown structure was initiated by a group of local preservationists. East Haddam's other notable feature is the **Nathan Hale Schoolhouse**, behind St Stephen's Church at 29 Main St (summer Sat & Sun noon–4pm; $2; ⓣ860/873-3399), where Hale taught in 1773–74 before moving on to New London. The one-room schoolhouse has a small collection of his possessions as well as items of local historical interest.

A further four miles south, also on the east bank of the river, is the **Gillette Castle**, 67 River Rd (grounds daily 8am–sunset, castle late May to early Oct daily 10am–5pm; grounds free, castle $5; ⓣ860/526-2336), the centerpiece of **Gillette Castle State Park**, a prime hiking and picnicking area. This 24-room granite castle-at-the-top-of-a-hill was built between 1914 and 1919 by actor/playwright William Hooker Gillette, known for his portrayal of cool, unruffled men of action in plays like *Held by the Enemy* and *Secret Service*, and, more famously, in the title role of *Sherlock Holmes*, first produced in New York in 1899; he played the detective until five years before his death in 1937. The actor parlayed his fortune into this mansion, with such incredible features as a dining table on tracks; a grand hall with balconies on three sides and a mirror which allowed Mr Gillette to seize the best moment for his grand entrance; and a replica of the sitting room at 221B Baker St, complete with violin, chemistry set, and pipe.

Practicalities

Among the **places to stay** in East Haddam are *Gelston House*, adjacent to the Opera House at 8 Main St (ⓣ860/873-1411, ⓦwww.gelstonhouse.com; ❻; closed Mon & Tues), providing two rooms and two suites, all luxurious and spacious, and the *Bishopsgate Inn*, Rte-82 (ⓣ860/873-1677, ⓦwww.bishopsgate.com; ❻), a charming 1818 Colonial house with six cozy rooms, four of which have working fireplaces. *Gelston House* is the best stop for **food**, with three restaurants that vary from casual patio dining to moderate tavern fare to formal American and French.

Ivoryton and Essex

Back across the river on Rte-9 is the village of **IVORYTON**, formerly known as Centerbrook until it became a hub – along with the nearby towns of Chester,

Deep River, and Essex – for the production of ivory. Beginning in 1789, when Phineas Pratt first manufactured ivory combs here, the industry grew to include piano keys, crochet needles, brushes, and organ stops. It is estimated that more than three-quarters of all the ivory exported from Zanzibar in 1884 found its way to Ivoryton and Deep River. However, these days the hamlet is best known for its theater, the **Ivoryton Playhouse**, 103 Main St (Ⓣ860/767-7318, Ⓦwww.ivorytonplayhouse.com). Many a showbiz career has been launched from this fairly insignificant-looking dark-brown wooden structure, including that of local girl Katharine Hepburn. For more pomp and circumstance, head to the **Museum of Fife and Drum**, 62 N Main St (July–Sept Sat & Sun 1–5pm; $3; Ⓣ860/767-2237, Ⓦwww.companyoffifeanddrum.org), where the history of military music is traced through costumes, photographs, sheet music, and instruments from early colonial days through the Revolutionary period to the present. The museum sponsors occasional concerts in the summer.

The river begins widening noticeably as you head further south towards tiny **ESSEX**, everyone's idea of how a quaint New England town should look, with some lovely Colonial homes, a main street brimming with inviting stores and boutiques, and a riverfront marina lined with posh boats. At the end of Main Street, in an 1878 waterfront dockhouse, the **Connecticut River Museum** (Tues–Sun 10am–4pm; $6; Ⓣ860/77-8269, Ⓦwww.ctrivermuseum.org) traces local history through paintings, photographs, models, and artifacts. The chief item of interest is a full-sized reproduction of the *American Turtle*, the world's first submarine, powered by hand cranks. Meanwhile, the **waterfront park** outside is a great place to watch the boats coming and going; Connecticut River Expeditions offers **cruises** that leave from the dock outside the museum (summer daily, spring and fall weekends; $15; Ⓣ860/662-0577, Ⓦwww.ctriv-erexpeditions.org).

Just south of downtown, the 1701 **Pratt House**, 19 West Ave (June–Sept Sat & Sun 1–4pm, other times by appointment; donation; Ⓣ860/767-1191), is one of the oldest houses in the area, once belonging to the town founders. Besides the usual period furnishings, there's ironwork created by the former Pratt smithy, and a reproduction post-and-beam barn at the back, containing exhibits on Essex's agricultural and domestic history. For something completely different, the restored steam trains of the **Valley Railroad**, 1 Railroad Ave (summer daily; fall, spring, and Dec weekends; train only $16, kids $8; train and boat $24, $12 kids; Ⓣ860/767-0103, Ⓦwww.valleyrr.com), chug slowly about an hour upriver; you can return by either boat or rail.

Practicalities

Accommodation options in Ivoryton and Essex include the *Griswold Inn*, 36 Main St, Essex (Ⓣ860/767-1776, Ⓦwww.griswoldinn.com; ❻), open as an inn since 1776, with some luxurious suites complete with four-poster beds and wood-burning stoves, and the *Copper Beech Inn*, 46 Main St, Ivoryton (Ⓣ860/767-0330 or 1-888/809-2056; ❼), a restored carriage house with spacious, well-appointed guestrooms and a fine French **restaurant** spread out over three elegant rooms. If it's just a snack you want, try *Crow's Nest*, 35 Pratt St, Essex (Ⓣ860/767-3288), for fresh-baked breakfast treats, excellent coffee, and lunchtime soups and sandwiches.

The Litchfield Hills

The rolling, tree-clad **LITCHFIELD HILLS**, tucked away in Connecticut's tranquil northwestern corner, provide a vivid contrast to the hustle and bustle of the state's coastal stretch, not to mention the industrial centers of New Haven and Hartford. Lakes, rivers, clear rushing brooks, and dense pine-scented forests permeate the area, interrupted by picturesque villages. Right at the center, the small town of **Litchfield** is prototypical New England: a wide, maple-dotted green surrounded by elegant clapboard homes, all overlooked by a dazzling white church steeple.

Around Litchfield are the luxurious inns and excellent restaurants of **Washington** and **New Preston**, along with antique-laden **Woodbury**. Due west is **Kent**, virtually unheard of until it was "discovered" by artists, craftspeople, and designers from New York in the 1980s, and nearby **Cornwall** and **West Cornwall**, with its famous covered bridge. In the far northwestern corner, **Salisbury** and **Lakeville** are close to Connecticut's tallest peaks, Bear Mountain and Bald Peak, as well as pretty **Norfolk**, home of the Yale Summer School of Music. All these places abound with traditional country inns, some surprisingly inexpensive. The area's commercial centers, **Torrington** and **Waterbury**, are relatively insignificant for visitors, save for a handful of industrial museums and some interesting architecture.

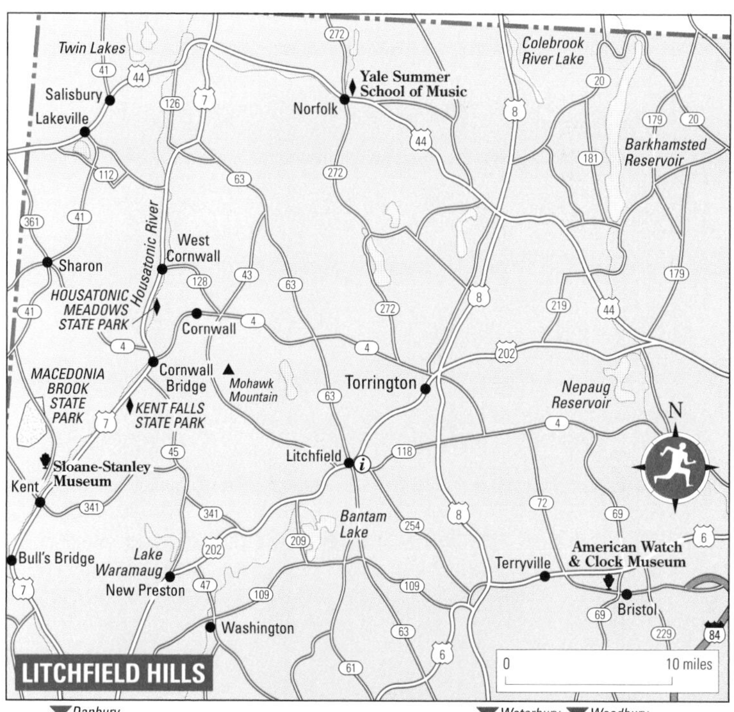

A good source of **information** for the area is the *Unwind* guide, published yearly by the Northwest Connecticut CVB (Ⓣ860/567-4506, Ⓦwww.northwestct.com), which gives extensive information on area attractions, lodging, dining, and more, and is available at various businesses throughout the region. The Litchfield **visitors' kiosk**, right on the **Litchfield Green** (May–Oct, daily 11am–4pm), has brochures and maps, as well as the CVB's excellent *Touring* guide, which describes driving, hiking, boating, and biking tours in the area.

Litchfield

LITCHFIELD, first settled in 1720 by families from Hartford, Windsor, and Farmington, spreads out around an exceptionally long and pretty village green from which radiate quaint streets lined with centuries-old churches and private houses. During and immediately after the Revolutionary War, the town was a hive of activity: thanks to the abundance of iron ore in the hills, Litchfield became a major center for the manufacture of supplies for George Washington's war effort, even producing one of the Revolution's great heroes, Ethan Allen, born here in 1738. After the war, the town achieved fame as the home of **Tapping Reeve's Litchfield Law School**, the first in the nation, and the highly esteemed finishing school for girls, the **Litchfield Female Academy**, one of whose students was Harriet Beecher Stowe. Since then, a new kind of notoriety has developed from its popularity with day-trippers and short-break visitors from New York.

The Town

Much of Litchfield's interest focuses on **North Street**, with its stately white-clapboard mansions, many dating from the eighteenth century and designed by the popular architect William Spratt. The best way to explore is by picking up a walking map from the visitors' kiosk (see above), but unless you strike lucky and arrive here on the one day in July each year when these private homes open – to raise money for a local children's charity – you'll have to be content simply to view them from the outside. Look out anyway for the 1760 **Sheldon Tavern**, North St, a graceful mansion with entrance portico and Palladian window that were added some time after the building had ceased to function as a public house. Nearby, the most striking feature of the Green is the graceful 1828 **Congregational Church**, restored a century later after being used as an armory, dance hall, and movie theater. One of the early pastors here was Reverend Lyman Beecher, father of locals Henry Ward Beecher and Harriet Beecher Stowe. Home to the Litchfield Historical Society, the **Litchfield History Museum**, also on the Green at the corner of East and South streets (mid-April to Nov Tues–Sat 11am–5pm, Sun 1–5pm; $5; Ⓣ860/567-4501, Ⓦwww.litchfieldhistoricalsociety.org), traces the development of northwestern Connecticut with special emphasis on the so-called "golden age" of the late 1700s and early 1800s.

The Historical Society also maintains the **Tapping Reeve House & Law School** (same hours as History Museum; $5 entry good for both), former home of the College of New Jersey (now Princeton) graduate who began practicing law in Litchfield in 1773 and opened the law school in 1774, the first such school in the United States. Among many of his notable achievements was his instigation of the movement to allow married women to control their own property. Under his guidance, later students of the school were Aaron Burr, John C. Calhoun, and Horace Mann. As the size of the student body grew, Reeve required more room and eventually built the adjacent one-room schoolhouse, which now contains exhibits on the life and work of Reeve, his influence on legal education in America, and the achievements of some of his students after graduation.

About two miles southwest of the Green, on Rte-202 West, the **White Memorial Foundation** (daily dawn–dusk; free; ⓣ860/567-0857, ⓦwww.whitememorialcc.org), at four thousand acres the largest wildlife sanctuary in the state, has miles of trails for hiking and horseback riding; there are also plenty of bird-watching, fishing, and picnicking opportunities. For a complete contrast, the **Lourdes in Litchfield Shrine**, east of Litchfield Green on Rte-118, liberally re-creates the famous shrine of Our Lady of Lourdes, France, by means of a grotto built with local fieldstone, where services are held regularly. Even if you don't subscribe to the faith, it's a fine place for a bit of quiet reflection.

Practicalities

There are plenty of charming **places to stay** in Litchfield, starting with the *Abel Darling B&B*, 102 West St (ⓣ860/567-0384; ❺), a 1782 Colonial building close to Litchfield's main attractions. West of the Green, *The Litchfield Inn*, Rte-202 (ⓣ860/567-4503 or 1-800/499-3444, ⓦwww.litchfieldinnct.com; ❼), is a modern hotel built in the Colonial style, with spacious, elegant rooms, and many extras, while the eighteenth-century *Tollgate Hill Inn*, Rte-202 (ⓣ860/567-1233 or 1-800/567-1233, ⓦwww.tollgatehill.com; ❻), has twenty gracious rooms containing antique reproduction furniture.

Many of Litchfield's **restaurants** line the Green along West Street; reservations are recommended on the weekends. Casual *Aspen Garden*, at no. 51 (ⓣ860/567-9477), has a large outdoor patio and Mediterranean-influenced dishes. Close by, you can choose from a small but fabulous international menu at *West Street Grill* (ⓣ860/567-3885). For a cheaper alternative, *The Village*, at no. 25 (ⓣ860/567-8307), offers homestyle cooking, while slightly further afield, *The Bistro East*, inside the *Litchfield Inn* (see above), does contemporary American cuisine in a relaxed, torch-lit bistro setting.

New Preston, Washington, and Woodbury

About ten miles southwest of Litchfield on Rte-202 lies tiny **NEW PRESTON**, home to a handful of pricey boutiques, but best known for its picturesque Lake Waramaug, the second-largest natural lake in Connecticut, and its attendant **State Park** (daily 8am–sunset; weekday parking free, summer weekends $10; campsites $13; park office ⓣ860/927-3238 or reservations 1-877/668-2267). You're welcome to launch canoes and kayaks from here, and there's a small beach with a roped-off swimming area. If you plan to camp here, right alongside the lake, be sure if you're coming on the weekend to reserve a spot well in advance.

Neighboring **WASHINGTON** is purportedly the first town in the nation to have been named for the country's first president, who traveled through the area several times while strategizing for the Revolutionary War. Built in 1908, the **Gunn Memorial Library**, 5 Wykeham Rd (daily except Wed & Sun; ⓦwww.gunnlibrary.org), is notable for its intricate ceiling mural painted by Henry Siddons Mowbray in 1914, and for a Connecticut Room devoted to reference materials on Connecticut history and local genealogical information. Meanwhile, just off Rte-199, **The Institute for American Indian Studies**, 38 Curtis Rd (Mon–Sat 10am–5pm, Sun noon–5pm; $4; ⓣ860/868-0518, ⓦwww.birdstone.org) opened in 1975 as the premier archeological research center on New England Woodlands native people. Today, in addition to its research, the institute houses three galleries of changing exhibits, a recreated longhouse room, and a replica of a traditional Algonkian village; visitors can also participate in numerous workshops and even join a dig.

Farther south on Rte-47 is **WOODBURY**, touted as the antiques capital of New England, with a two-mile-long main street lined by eighteenth- and nineteenth-century houses that have nearly all been converted into shops. Of particular note is **Mill House Antiques**, which has an extensive array of French and English furniture and collectibles in fifteen showrooms. Also of note is the **Glebe House Museum & Gertrude Jekyll Garden**, 49 Hollow Rd (May–Oct Wed–Sun 1–4pm, Nov Sat & Sun 1–4pm, other times by appointment; $5; ⓣ203/263-2855, ⓦwww.theglebehouse.org), where the nation's first Episcopal bishop was elected in 1783. It opened as a historic house museum in 1925, at which point a garden was commissioned – but it wasn't until the plans were rediscovered in the 1970s that planting of the English-style garden began.

Practicalities

Lodging in these parts is luxurious, with prices to match. Warm and charming, the *Boulders Inn*, East Shore Road, New Preston (ⓣ860/868-0541 or 1-800/455-1565, ⓦwww.bouldersinn.com; ❾), has stunning views of Lake Waramaug; in addition to the rooms in the main lodge, there are four cottages with private decks and fireplaces. The *Mayflower Inn*, Rte-47, Washington (ⓣ860/868-9466, ⓦwww.mayflowerinn.com; ❾) is an elegant Relais & Chateaux property with 25 individually decorated rooms and suites, manicured gardens, and an elaborate spa. On the less expensive side, Woodbury lays claim to the oldest inn in the state, the *Curtis House*, 506 Main St S (ⓣ203/263-2101, ⓦwww.thecurtishouse.com; shared bath ❸, private ❹), which retains simple old-world charm.

Dining options include *Doc's*, Rte-45, Lake Waramaug (ⓣ860/868-9415), a cozy and reasonably priced upscale pizzeria; *Oliva*, E Shore Road, New Preston (ⓣ860/868-1787; closed Mon & Tues, reservations essential), an outstanding Mediterranean eatery where the chef has a loyal following; and *Good News Café* in Woodbury, 694 Main St S (ⓣ203/266-4663; closed Tues), a vibrant spot with unusual dishes like pecan-crusted oysters with tomatillo salsa and chili aioli.

Connecticut's Wine Trail

Contrary to popular belief, it *is* possible to create quality wines away from the West Coast's ideal climes. In Connecticut, wineries flanking the state borders and a few others scattered around comprise what is known as Connecticut's **Wine Trail**. The Farm Winery Act, passed in 1978 by the State House, opened up the soil to such establishments, and **Haight Vineyard** was soon growing Chardonnay and Riesling grapes behind its handsome English Tudor building in Litchfield. **Hopkins Vineyard**, on land in New Preston settled by the original Hopkins family in 1787, conducts tastings in a huge, renovated, bright-red 1800s barn; furthermore, it's the only Connecticut grape farm to benefit from a microclimate (yielding a longer season) due to its location on Lake Waramaug. Some interesting choices are produced by the folks at **DiGrazia Vineyards** in Brookfield, who add honey (eliminating the need for sulfites), blueberries, or pears to their formula. Across the state, picturesque Rte-169 leads to **Heritage Trail Vineyard** in Lisbon, established in 1996 by a transplanted Californian on the site of an eighteenth-century farmstead. **Tastings** are available at these and other Wine Trail vineyards; opening times, driving directions, and other information can be found at ⓦwww.ctwine.com or by calling ⓣ860/267-1399.

The scenic northwest corner

Connecticut's **northwest corner** boasts perhaps the most striking scenery the state has to offer: verdant hills abound with weathered barns, sleeping cows, and grazing horses; farms are lined with beautifully maintained split-rail wooden fences; fields burst with corn in the summer and glisten with snow in the winter. The area has become a hotspot for New Yorkers looking for a quiet retreat away from the glitz of Connecticut's gold coast or the Hamptons on Long Island, and as a result the small country towns which dot the greenery – including **Kent**, the two **Cornwalls**, and **Norfolk** – offer pricey galleries and superb restaurants (not to mention pricey but posh accommodation) beside local coffeeshops and fruit stands.

Kent

It's hard to imagine the scene witnessed by early English traveler Benjamin Wadsworth when he described **KENT**, nestled on a flat alluvial plain among the hills which border the Housatonic Valley, as a "howling wilderness" in 1694. The wilds have certainly been tamed, and Kent has evolved into a refined country town, with perhaps the most on offer in the vicinity. The opening of Jacques Kaplan's contemporary art gallery **Paris-New York-Kent** in 1984 is largely responsible for the influx of boutiques and galleries that line Kent's Main Street today. Although small, Paris-New York-Kent has received prominent coverage in the *International Herald Tribune* and *The New York Times* and features artists who have exhibited everywhere from the Louvre to the Whitney. With its increased cachet, Kent began attracting well-heeled New Yorkers looking for a weekend escape, and today's combination of art enthusiasts and Manhattanites lends the town an air of sophistication. Nonetheless, Kent remains low-key, with a main street just a half-mile long, and since it lies on the Appalachian Trail it's common to see backpackers strolling the sidewalks alongside the art buffs and antiquers.

The Town and around

Chief among the town's sights is the **Sloane-Stanley Museum**, Rte-7, one mile north of downtown (mid-May to Oct Wed–Sun 10am–4pm; $4; ☎860/927-3849), which houses a unique assortment of hand tools and implements made by early settlers and collected by noted Connecticut writer and artist Eric Sloane. One of the items on display, the leather-bound 1805 diary of one Noah Blake, was discovered by Sloane in a nearby house; Blake describes his austere house in great detail, parameters Sloane used to build a replica small wooden cabin next to the museum. The museum stands on the site of the once-thriving **Kent Iron Furnace**, which began production of pig iron in 1826 – ceasing seventy years later – and whose ruins can be seen adjacent to the museum.

Along with gallery-browsing and bookstore-perusing, Kent also provides various opportunities to explore the countryside, from camping and biking in the summer to snowshoeing and skiing in the winter. **Backcountry Outfitters**, 8 Old Barn Rd (☎860/927-3377), is a good stop for maps of local hikes and for any gear you may need. About four miles north of downtown on Rte-7, **Kent Falls State Park** is known for its namesake 250-foot falls (daily 8am–sunset; weekdays free parking, weekends $10; ☎860/927-3238). The most dramatic drop is a seventy-foot cascade that's visible from the road and not far from the parking lot, which detracts somewhat from the appeal; nonetheless, picnics are popular here, and a grassy lawn at the park entrance offers tables and pedestal grills.

Four miles northwest of downtown, **Macedonia Brook State Park** holds deep gorges, falls, and the 1350-foot summit of Cobble Mountain, which commands views as far as the Catskills in New York State. In the opposite direction, four miles south of town on Rte-7, a right turn at Bulls Bridge Road leads to **Bulls Bridge**, one of only two original covered bridges in the state which is open to vehicular traffic. Rebuilt, repaired, and restored over the years, it's certainly in better condition today than when George Washington crossed it on horseback. His horse stumbled on a broken plank and fell into the river, so the story goes: his expense reports for March 3, 1781 read: "getting a horse out of Bull's Bridge Falls, $215.00." White blazes at the parking area mark an entrance to the Appalachian Trail.

Practicalities

There are several nice **places to stay** in Kent. Most up-market is *The Inn at Kent Falls*, 107 Kent Cornwall Rd (860/927-3197, www.theinnatkentfalls.com; 7) – but don't be fooled: the falls are more than two miles up the road. The six rooms are elegant, with unique extras like a bathroom fireplace or a private library, and there's also a garden pool. Located at the top end of Kent's shopping district is the *Starbuck Inn*, 88 N Main St (860/927-1788, www.starbuckinn.com; 7), where highlights include a hearty breakfast and high tea and sherry served daily at 4pm. Macedonia Brook State Park has **camping** (mid-April to Sept; 860/927-3238; $11), but it's fairly primitive and alcohol is not allowed.

Kent makes for a great rest-stop for anyone with a **sweet tooth**. The classy patisserie *Belgique*, 1 Bridge St (860/927-3681; open Thurs–Sun), attracts wealthy weekenders with its handmade Belgian truffles, while up the street at the *Kent Coffee and Chocolate Company*, 8 Main (860/927-1445), the chocolates are delicious, and the prices much easier to digest. For some decent pizza and a drink, head to the no-frills *Kent Pizza Garden*, 17 Railroad Square (860/927-3733), where the taproom and patio draw a boisterous crowd on summer weekends. More staid, the *Fife 'N Drum Restaurant & Inn*, 53 N Main St (860/927-3509; closed Tues) offers heftier meals like roast duck flambeed tableside; its busy pub-style bar features nightly piano-playing by the longtime proprietor, Dolph Traymon, who has played with the likes of Peggy Lee and Frank Sinatra.

West Cornwall and Cornwall

Northeast of Kent on Rte-7, the minuscule village of **WEST CORNWALL** has a number of craft shops and restaurants, but is mainly known for its 172-foot bright-red, much-photographed **covered bridge**, built in 1864 of native oak and restored in recent years. **CORNWALL**, a quite separate village three miles east on Rte-4, is where the **Cornwall Foreign Mission School** was located from 1817 to 1827. Henry Obookiah, a young Hawaiian who managed to stow away on a New Haven-bound ship after his family was killed in a tribal war, converted to the Christian faith and spent several years preaching in and around the Litchfield Hills until dying of typhoid at the age of 26. His enthusiasm for the faith inspired the American Missionary Board to send a group of missionaries to Hawaii, a story fictionalized in James Michener's *Hawaii*.

A mile north of the town of **Cornwall Bridge** (not, in fact, where the bridge is located) on Rte-7 is the **Housatonic Meadows State Park**, a densely forested area which stretches for two miles along the Housatonic River and is popular with hikers and picnickers. **Clarke Outdoors**, 163 Rte-7 (860/672-

6365, Ⓦwww.clarkeoutdoors.com), rents kayaks, canoes, and rafts, and also offers guided river trips. In the winter, though, a better bet is the **Mohawk Mountain Ski Area**, Great Hollow Road (Ⓣ860/672-6100 or 1-800/895-5222, Ⓦwww.mohawkmtn.com), the largest in the state with five lifts and 24 trails good for all levels; a full day-pass costs $42.

Practicalities

There's very little in the way of **lodging** in the immediate vicinity, but you could try the *Housatonic Meadows Lodge*, 13 Rte-7, Cornwall Bridge (Ⓣ860/672-6064, Ⓦwww.housatonicmeadowslodge.com; ❻), where country quilts adorn five rooms, some with shared bath, in an attractive red lodge. The *Hilltop Haven B&B*, Dibble Hill Road, West Cornwall (Ⓣ860/672-6871; ❼) has two lace-trimmed rooms in a quiet hillside retreat. For **food**, there's hearty American fare at the *Cornwall Inn*, Rte-7, Cornwall Bridge (Ⓣ860/672-6884; closed Mon–Wed), where the juicy ribeye ($29) is the most expensive of the entrees; rooms are also available (❻). For a special night out, reserve a table well in advance at *RSVP for Dinner*, 8 Railroad Square (Ⓣ860/672-RSVP; open April–Dec): seating is limited to 25 per evening, and you can watch the chef as he prepares the impeccable French cuisine; bring your own wine.

Sharon, Lakeville, and Salisbury

Due west of West Cornwall on Rte-41, **SHARON** is yet another quintessential New England village with a long, narrow green, some pristine nineteenth-century homes, and a white-steepled church. At the **Sharon Audubon Center** on Rte-4, you can explore 1200 acres and eleven miles of nature trails where you may see beavers, muskrats, and even otters, and visit the interpretive center (trails daily dawn–dusk, center Tues–Sat 9am–5pm, Sun 1–5pm; $3; Ⓣ860/364-0520). The **Sharon Playhouse**, 49 Amenia Rd (Ⓣ860/364-SHOW, Ⓦwww.triarts.net) is known for its excellent summer theater and also offers readings of new works throughout the year.

Farther north, **LAKEVILLE** and neighboring **SALISBURY** are situated at the state's northwest border amid some of its most attractive scenery and an abundance of quaint guesthouses and inns. Lakeville's chief attraction, the **Holley Willams House**, rtes 41 and 44 (July & Aug Sat & Sun noon–5pm and by appointment; donation; Ⓣ860/435-0566), was the childhood home of Alexander Hamilton Holley, Connecticut governor from 1857 to 1858, whose "iron baron" father purchased the house in the late eighteenth century and expanded it to its current Classical Revival style in 1808. Today it has been recreated with original furnishings according to the diary of Maria Holley Williams, Alexander's half-sister, who inherited the house. Also part of the property, the **Salisbury Cannon Museum** (Ⓦwww.salisburycannonmuseum.org), in the adjacent Carriage House, uses hands-on exhibits to tell the story of the Revolutionary War cannon factory that provided ammunition for Washington's army.

Norfolk

Rte-44 leads east from Salisbury through dairy farming country to **NORFOLK**, a relatively undeveloped spot whose tall church steeple stands sentinel over a lush **village green**. Note the elaborate **Eldridge Fountain**, designed by Stanford White in 1889 as a drinking fountain for both people and their horses. Also on the green, the so-called Whitehouse was once part of the **Ellen Battell Stoeckel Estate**, owned until 1939 by a music-loving local resident who entertained such luminaries of the music world as Fritz Kreisler, Rachmaninov, and Sibelius. The estate was left to the **Yale Music School**, which organizes the Norfolk Chamber Music Festival each July and August. Concerts take place in the seven-hundred-seat "Music Shed" on the estate, at the intersection of rtes 44 and 272 (Ⓣ860/542-3000, Ⓦwww.yale.edu/norfolk). Norfolk began as a cultural center, however, with the opening of the **Norfolk Library** in 1889, a striking red-stone building with vaulted ceilings and stained-glass windows. In addition to housing books, the library also hosts monthly art exhibits and frequent concerts. Up the street and also on the green, the **Norfolk Historical Society Museum** (late May to early Oct Sat & Sun noon–4pm, other times by appointment; donation; Ⓣ860-542-5761), housed in the former Norfolk Academy, has on permanent display a traditional Norfolk country store as well as changing exhibits relating to town history.

Practicalities

Accommodation options in the Norfolk area include the *Blackberry River Inn*, 538 Greenwoods Rd, Rte-44 W (Ⓣ860/542-5100 or 1-800/414-3636, Ⓦwww.blackberryriverinn.com; ❺), which offers peace and quiet (and a pool) in an eighteenth-century Colonial, and the romantic *Manor House*, 69 Maple Ave (Ⓣ860/542-5690 or 1-866/542-5690, Ⓦwww.manorhouse-norfolk.com; ❼), a Victorian Tudor mansion that features Tiffany windows, with extensive gardens just outside them. Another nice choice is the *Mountain View Inn*, 67 Litchfield Rd (Ⓣ860/542-6991, Ⓦwww.mvinn.com; ❻), a beautifully restored 1875 house overlooking Norfolk that's particularly noted for its excellent breakfasts, which are included in the rates. For something to **eat**, the *Pub & Restaurant*, Rte-44 (Ⓣ860/542-5716; closed Mon), with English pub decor (if not atmosphere) offers good-value American fare, along with a remarkable selection of 150 excellent beers from around the world, like Aventinus from Germany and Pilsner Urquell from Czechoslovakia.

Torrington and around

It's no coincidence that **TORRINGTON**, the largest and least attractive town in northwest Connecticut, is also the area's business center. Even its main claim to fame – being the birthplace, in 1800, of abolitionist **John Brown** – fails to provide a reason for visiting, as the house in which he was born no longer stands. At the very least, Torrington does budget **accommodation**, like that at the *Super 8 Motel*, 492 E Main St (Ⓣ860/496-0811 or 1-800/800-8000; ❹). More expensive, but full of character, is the *Yankee Pedlar Inn*, opposite the Art Deco Warner Theatre at 93 Main St (Ⓣ860/489-9226, Ⓦwww.pedlarinn.com; ❺), with sixty rooms complete with Hitchcock furnishings, made in nearby Riverton and famous throughout the country for their elaborate stencil work. For something to **eat**, *Marino's*, 12 Pinewoods Rd (Ⓣ860/482-6864; closed Sun), serves Italian-American cuisine in a casual, laidback atmosphere, while *The Venetian Restaurant*, 52 E Main St (Ⓣ860/489-8592; closed Tues), is one of the best Italian restaurants around, and not overly expensive; try the homemade pastas or the veal.

Terryville and Bristol

An unusual opportunity is on offer in the village of **TERRYVILLE**, once an important lock and key manufacturing town, about twelve miles southeast of Torrington on Rte-6: the **Lock Museum of America**, 230 Main St (May–Oct Tues–Sun 1.30–4.30pm; $3; Ⓣ860/589-6359, Ⓦwww.lockmuseum.com), which stands on the site of the old Eagle Lock company factory and holds the largest collection of locks, keys, and ornate Victorian hardware in the US. Key items, so to speak, include a combination padlock dating to 1846, a 4000-year-old Egyptian-made pin tumbler lock, and the original patent model of the mortise cylinder pin lock designed by Linus Yale, Jr, in 1865.

In neighboring **BRISTOL**, part of the region once known as the "Switzerland of America," make time for the **American Clock & Watch Museum**, 100 Maple St (April–Nov daily 10am–5pm; $5; ⓣ860/583-6070), reputed to be the finest collection of American clocks in existence. There are more than 1500 of them, including "Dewey," one of a series of six clocks introduced in 1899 to commemorate the Spanish–American War, with a likeness of Admiral Dewey at the top. Be prepared to cover your ears on the hour, when hundreds of chimes resonate around the museum house. Equally unique, the **New England Carousel Museum**, 95 Riverside Ave (April–Nov Mon–Sat 10am–5pm, Sun noon–5pm; Dec–March Thurs–Sat 10am–5pm, Sun noon–5pm; $5; ⓣ860-585-5411, ⓦwww.thecarouselmuseum.org), houses a tremendous collection of antique carousel art and memorabilia, and its restoration department works to repair and create new carousel pieces.

Waterbury

At the very southern edge of the Litchfield Hills, and certainly no part of them in spirit, **WATERBURY** – known to the Indians as "the place where no trees will grow" because of persistent flooding – valiantly celebrates its glorious past of brass- and coppermaking. That's not necessarily a reason to come, though if you do, you'll find the requisite history in the **Mattatuck Museum**, 144 W Main St (Tues–Sat 10am–5pm, Sun noon–5pm except in July & Aug; $4; ⓣ203/753-0381, ⓦwww.mattatuckmuseum.org), which includes a permanent collection largely devoted to works of Connecticut artists, such as *Adirondack Landscape: Mount McIntire* by John Frederick Kensett and Frederic Edwin Church's *Icebergs*. The rest of downtown is pleasing enough, with red-brick and white marble municipal buildings, including the Chase Building and the former Waterbury National Bank, both designed by **Cass Gilbert**, architect of the Woolworth Building and the George Washington Bridge in New York. Look, too, at 389 Meadow St, for the current home of the *Waterbury Republican-American* newspaper. The building is the town's former main **railroad station**, and is modeled on City Hall in Siena, Italy, with a tall campanile-style tower that is the city's most notable landmark. Like nearby Bristol, Waterbury has a history of clock-making; the Waterbury Clock company was renamed Timex in the 1970s, and its progression through the years is recounted in the **Timex Museum**, 175 Union St (Tues–Sat 10am–5pm; $6; ⓣ203/755-TIME, ⓦwww.timexpo.com).

Practicalities

If you want to **stay** in Waterbury, the *Courtyard by Marriott*, 63 Grand St (ⓣ203/596-1000; ❻) is right downtown and has a fitness room and indoor pool. With a little more character, the *House on the Hill B&B*, 92 Woodlawn Terrace (ⓣ203/757-9901, ⓦwww.houseonthehill.biz; ❻), is a large 1888 home containing guestrooms and suites filled with antiques, and boasting fireplaces and an attractive wraparound porch. *Drescher's*, 25 Leavenworth St (ⓣ203/573-1743), a **restaurant** open since 1868, offers a variety of German and American dishes (most around $15) in a delightful antique-filled dining room.

Northeastern Connecticut

Once a prosperous textile-manufacturing region which spewed out cotton and silk, the predominantly rural **northeastern corner** of Connecticut, bordering Rhode Island and Massachusetts, has remained almost entirely devoid of major development and large-scale tourism. Its rolling hills and blossoming orchards are best viewed by driving (or, if you're up to it, biking) along the 32-mile stretch of scenic **Route 169**, from Canterbury to Woodstock. Along the way, you'll also spot some of the redundant old mills and warehouses, many of which have been carefully restored or converted into businesses. The best detours are in **Coventry**, home of Revolutionary War hero Nathan Hale; **Lebanon**, whose historic village green stretches a mile along Rte-87; and **Putnam**, named after the famous Revolutionary General Israel Putnam, alleged to have made the famous "whites of their eyes" command at the Battle of Bunker Hill.

Putnam is also a good stop for **information** about the area: The Last Green Valley office, 107 Providence St (ⓣ866/363-7226, ⓦwww.thelastgreenvalley.org) has brochures, free walking tour opportunities, and extensive local guides. Additional info centers are marked around the region with green flags and gold lettering reading "Info". The Mystic Country CVB (ⓣ1-800/TO-ENJOY, ⓦwww.mysticcountry.com) also publishes a guide to accommodation and attractions for the region. Bonanza **buses** (ⓣ888/751-8800), originating in Providence, RI, run through the region, with stops at Willimantic and Storrs; local transportation is virtually non-existent.

Scenic Route 169: Woodstock to Canterbury

Peaceful **WOODSTOCK** is notable as the site of the 1846 **Roseland Cottage** (June to mid-Oct Fri–Sun 11am–5pm; $8), the former summer retreat of Henry C. Bowen, publisher of abolitionist weekly paper *The Independent*. His striking salmon-colored Gothic Revival residence, designed by English architect Joseph Wells, is particularly interesting for its steep gables, profuse Gothic tracery, stained-glass windows, and opulent interior – a suitable setting for Bowen to entertain four US presidents (Grant, Hayes, Harrison, and McKinley) at his lavish Fourth of July parties. The house contains its original furnishings, and an adjacent barn includes an antique bowling alley.

Besides being named for the Revolutionary War general, **PUTNAM**, on Rte-44 southeast of Woodstock, was also an important stop on the Underground Railroad. After years in the economic doldrums, it's now one of the hottest antique-shopping areas in the Northeast. Most of the shops are on or around Main Street, where the highlight is a former Victorian department store that has been renovated to form the **Antiques Marketplace** (ⓣ860/928-0442, ⓦwww.antiquesmarketplace.com), with more than two hundred dealers plying their trade. East of town, on Town Farm Road, the 120-acre **Quaddick State Park** (daily 8am–sunset; weekdays free, summer weekends parking $10; ⓣ860/928-6121) is a good place to relax, with a vast, 466-acre reservoir and a separate swimming pond, with ample opportunities for hiking, boating, and fishing.

Canterbury

A small community at the junction of routes 14 and 169, **CANTERBURY** is home to the **Prudence Crandall Museum** (April to mid-Dec Wed–Sun 10am–4.30pm; $3; ⓣ860/546-9916), housed in an attractive 1805 home that became New England's first academy to admit black women. From 1834 to 1844 the academy was run by Baptist schoolmistress Crandall, who gained notoriety when she accepted a young African-American girl in her school. The residents' violent response – the building was stoned – led to the school's closure, and Crandall was taken to court, though later exonerated. There is a permanent display devoted to Crandall's life and work, and others on black history, abolitionism, and women's rights.

Practicalities

Places to stay in the area include the *King's Inn*, 5 Heritage Rd, Putnam (ⓣ860/928-7961 or 1-800/541-7304; ❹), a friendly hotel with well-appointed rooms plus its own steakhouse, and the *Inn at Woodstock Hill*, 94 Plaine Hill Rd, Woodstock (ⓣ860/928-0528, ⓦwww.woodstockhill.com; ❼), with spacious yet cozy rooms. *Woodstock Hill* also boasts an excellent **restaurant**, which features a sumptuous and pricey French-influenced American menu, with entrees like veal "cordon rouge." Back in Putnam, *Mrs. Bridges' Pantry*, 136 Main St (ⓣ860/963-7040; open 11am–5pm, closed Tues), is a British-style tearoom that serves Lapsang Soochong, Oolong, and everything in between. South toward Canterbury, in **BROOKLYN**, the *Golden Lamb Buttery*, 499 Wolf Den Rd (ⓣ860/774-4423; Tues–Sat lunch, Fri & Sat dinner), offers an unusual (and expensive) dining experience where diners meet at a set time in the barn, then are invited to take a hayride to view the pastoral setting. Dinner, accompanied by a singing guitarist, includes entrees like roast pork with apricots, garlic, and mushrooms.

Storrs and Coventry

West just off Rte-44, **STORRS** is home to the campus of the **University of Connecticut**, site of the **William Benton Museum of Art** (Tues–Fri 10am–4.30pm, Sat & Sun 1–4.30pm; free; ⓣ860/486-4520), with a program of changing exhibits, and a permanent collection of over four thousand items, which covers European and American paintings, among them works by Henry Ward Ranger, Ernest Lawson, Gustav Klimt, and Edward Burne-Jones; drawings, prints, and sculptures from the sixteenth century to the present day; and a large collection of theater drawings by Reginald Marsh. If you're green-thumbed, be sure not to miss the **University of Connecticut Greenhouses,** 75 N Eagleville Rd (Mon–Fri 8am–4pm; ⓣ860/486-4052), a complex containing more than three thousand plant species, including orchids, cacti, palm trees, a redwood, and even carnivorous aquatic plants.

COVENTRY, west of Storrs, is another quiet former mill community, though with a decent selection of restaurants and shops, plus the **Nathan Hale Homestead**, 2299 South St (mid-May to mid-Oct Wed–Sun 1–4pm; $4; ⓣ860/742-6917), a three-story farmhouse rebuilt in 1776 by his father, Deacon Richard Hale, just after Hale was hanged by the British as an American spy. More Hale memorabilia can be viewed close by at the **Strong-Porter House**, 2382 South St (mid-May to mid-Oct first and third weekend of each month

1–4pm; free; ⓣ860/742-1419), recently restored and the one-time home to Hale's maternal ancestors.

The area makes for a nice place to **stay**, with spots in Storrs like the *Fitch House B&B*, 563 Storrs Rd (ⓣ860/456-0922, ⓦwww.fitchhouse.com; ❻), an elegant Greek Revival mansion with three large, tastefully decorated rooms. Down the road, you can enjoy continental cuisine at the moderate to pricey *Altnaveigh Inn,* 957 Storrs Rd (ⓣ860/429-4490), an atmospheric country farmhouse. In Coventry, the *Bird-in-Hand*, 2011 Main St (ⓣ860/742-0032, ⓦwww.thebirdinhand.com; ❻), is an attractive antique-filled Colonial inn in scenic grounds, while the *Bidwell Tavern*, at no. 1260 (ⓣ860/742-6978), serves all-American food in a historic 1822 tavern.

Willimantic and Lebanon

South of Coventry, on the Willimantic River, lies **WILLIMANTIC** (in Native American language, "land of the swift running waters"), yet another mill village, once home to the Willimantic Linen Company. The company's former complex contains the **Windham Textile and History Museum**, 157 Union St (summer Thurs–Sun 1–4pm; rest of year by appointment; $5; ⓣ860/456-2178, ⓦwww.millmuseum.org), which preserves the thread-making machinery and workers' quarters typical of the late nineteenth and early twentieth centuries.

Straddling a village green that stretches more than a mile along Rte-87, **LEBANON** was home to one **Jonathan Trumbull**, ardent patriot and the only Crown-appointed governor to side with the Revolutionaries. It was his presence that encouraged a battalion of hussars under the leadership of the duc de Lauzun to camp here in 1780, awaiting Rochambeau and his men for the final push of the Revolutionary War. Two Trumbull homes are open to the public: the **Jonathan Trumbull House**, 169 W Town St (mid-May to mid-Oct Wed–Sun noon–4pm; $3; ⓣ860/642-7558), built in 1735 and furnished with period pieces; and the Georgian **Jonathan Trumbull Jr House**, 780 Trumbull Hwy (May–Oct Sat & Sun noon–4pm; free), built in 1769 by his son – a noted artist in his own right – and which contains intricate woodwork and a beautifully carved cherrywood banister in the main hall. Close by, at 149 West Town St, you can see Trumbull Sr's **War Office** (late May to Sept Sat & Sun noon–4pm; $2; ⓣ860/873-3399), a two-room office and store which became the headquarters of the Council of Safety, which plotted strategy and coordinated supplies during the war.

6

Vermont

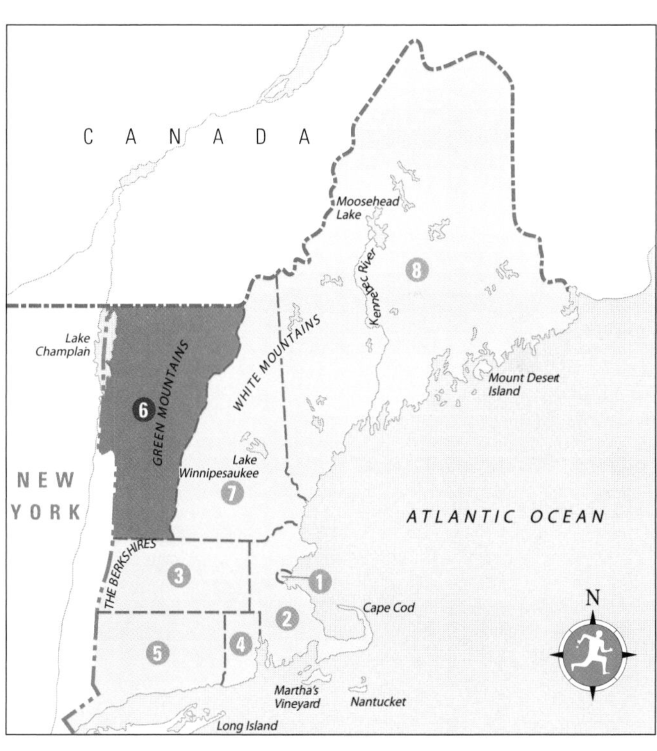

C A N A D A
Moosehead Lake
Kennebec River
8
Lake Champlain
GREEN MOUNTAINS
WHITE MOUNTAINS
Mount Desert Island
6
Lake Winnipesaukee
NEW YORK
7
ATLANTIC OCEAN
THE BERKSHIRES
3
1
Cape Cod
N
2
5
4
Martha's Vineyard
Nantucket
Long Island

CHAPTER SIX

Highlights

* **Long Trail** Walking the length of the entire state wins serious bragging rights for competitive hikers; for others, the magnificent vistas from Vermont's highest peaks will more than justify the effort. See p.402
* **Hildene** He may not have been president, but Robert Todd Lincoln's stately Manchester home is still a must-see. See p.408
* **Skiing** The state abounds with challenging mountains and excellent facilities. See pp.415 & 431
* **Montpelier** Relaxed, friendly, genuine, relatively tourist-free, the only state capital without a *McDonald's* is bounded by rivers and a forest of tall trees. See p.423
* **Ben and Jerry's Factory Tour** Who can resist a scoop of cold calories served in a cone? See p.428
* **Burlington** The perfect antidote for those charmed-out by Vermont's profusion of perfect villages: a real city, with a waterfront, a vibrant downtown, and the state's best restaurants and nightlife. See p.435
* **Shelburne Museum** Two centuries of American life stuffed into fifty acres of northern Vermont. See p.440

△ Long Trail cabin

Vermont

In many ways, **Vermont** comes closer than any other New England state to fulfilling the quintessential image of small-town Yankee America, with its white churches and red barns, covered bridges and clapboard houses, snowy woods and maple syrup. No city holds a population of even forty thousand (only Burlington comes close) and the chief tourist attraction is none other than Ben and Jerry's ice-cream factory in Waterbury. Though rural, the landscape is not all that agricultural, and much is covered by verdant, mountainous forests (the state's name supposedly comes from the French *vert mont*, or green mountain). True, in certain areas, the bucolic image proffered can seem a bit packaged, but you probably won't tire of trawling the state's many scenic byways and village greens.

The people who choose to live here represent a number of seemingly disparate groups – hippies, diehard conservatives, taciturn codgers who have never left the state – who tend to band together to preserve their environment and lament the advent of yet another ski resort. However, their political philosophies remain fiercely in contrast, which became all too clear when Governor **Howard Dean** signed Vermont's **civil union** bill into law in 1999, making Vermont the first state in the US to sanction same-sex marriage. While the governor and the action were widely praised, giving proof to those who proudly proclaimed Vermont "the most progressive state in the nation," another, more conservative, contingent condemned Dean as a "coward" giving in to pressure from "flatlanders" – a derogatory term for Vermont residents transplanted from other parts. Although Dean narrowly won re-election in 2000, the debate rages on, and in front of many a dilapidated farmhouse it's still possible to see signs reading "take back Vermont." Dean was catapulted onto the national stage in 2004 during his unsuccessful run as a Democratic presidential hopeful; like a comet, he burned brightly and too quickly, and by March 2004 he had already withdrawn from the race due to lack of support.

Vermont's liberal voice could be traced to it being the youngest of New England's states, settled last, early in the eighteenth century. As French explorers worked their way down from Canada, American colonists began to spread north; but even as that rivalry died down, a further antipathy developed between settlers from New Hampshire and those from New York. The wealthy New York merchants who built fine homes along the Connecticut River Valley thought of themselves as "River Gods," but the hardy settlers of the lakes and mountains to the west had little time for their patrician ways. The settlers' leader was the now-legendary Ethan Allen, who formed his Green Mountain Boys in 1770, proclaiming that "the gods of the hills are not the gods of the valley." When the Revolutionary War superseded such conflicts, this all-but-autono-

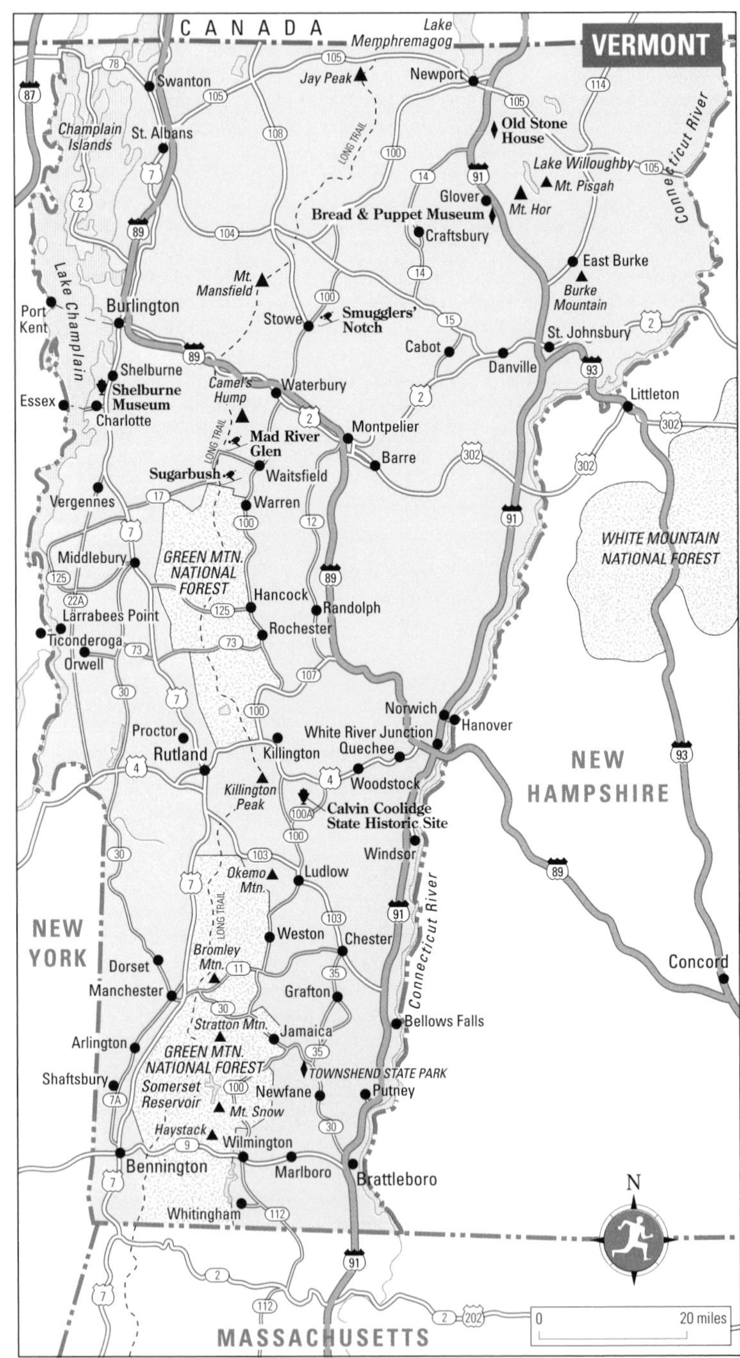
VERMONT
CANADA
Lake Memphremagog
Swanton
Jay Peak
Newport
Champlain Islands
St. Albans
LONG TRAIL
Old Stone House
Lake Willoughby
Mt. Pisgah
Connecticut River
Glover
Mt. Hor
Bread & Puppet Museum
Craftsbury
East Burke
Burke Mountain
Mt. Mansfield
Lake Champlain
Port Kent
Burlington
Stowe
Smugglers' Notch
St. Johnsbury
Cabot
Danville
Shelburne
Shelburne Museum
Charlotte
Essex
Camel's Hump
Waterbury
Littleton
Montpelier
Mad River Glen
Barre
Sugarbush
Waitsfield
Vergennes
Warren
WHITE MOUNTAIN NATIONAL FOREST
Middlebury
GREEN MTN. NATIONAL FOREST
Hancock
Randolph
Larrabees Point
Ticonderoga
Rochester
Orwell
Norwich
Hanover
Proctor
White River Junction
Rutland
Killington
Quechee
NEW HAMPSHIRE
Killington Peak
Woodstock
Calvin Coolidge State Historic Site
Windsor
Okemo Mtn.
Ludlow
NEW YORK
Weston
Chester
Bromley Mtn.
Dorset
Concord
Manchester
Grafton
Bellows Falls
Stratton Mtn.
Jamaica
Arlington
TOWNSHEND STATE PARK
Shaftsbury
Somerset Reservoir
Newfane
Putney
Mt. Snow
Haystack
Wilmington
Bennington
Marlboro
Brattleboro
Whitingham
N
MASSACHUSETTS
0
20 miles
87
78
105
108
114
100
14
91
2
7
89
104
15
93
302
17
12
125
22A
73
107
30
4
100A
103
11
35
7A
9
112
202

mous force captured Fort Ticonderoga from the British and helped to win the decisive Battle of Bennington. For fourteen years, Vermont was an independent republic (it was not one of the original thirteen states), with the first constitution in the world to explicitly forbid slavery and grant universal (male) suffrage. Once its boundaries with New York were agreed in 1791, it joined the Union. Incidentally, Brigham Young, the seminal figure of the Mormon religion, was born in Whitingham, Vermont shortly thereafter in 1801.

With the occasional exception, such as the extraordinary assortment of Americana at the **Shelburne Museum** near Burlington (a lively city worth visiting in any case), there are few specific sights as such to seek out; indeed, tourism here is more activity-oriented, with most visitors coming during two well-defined seasons: to see the **fall foliage** in the first two weeks of October, and to **ski** in the depths of winter, when resorts such as **Killington** and **Stowe** (home of *The Sound of Music*'s Von Trapp family) spring to life. For the rest of the year, you might just as well explore any of the state's minor roads that strike your fancy, confident that some captivating village will be around the corner, doubtless surrounded by lakes and mountains, and punctuated by lovely country inns in which to lodge overnight.

Southern Vermont

Of the two towns located at either end of Vermont's southern corridor – a mere forty miles from east to west linked by Hwy-9 – **Brattleboro** is probably your best bet. With three colleges in the area, it has the corresponding atmosphere of a college town. **Bennington** also has a college, but is sleepy in comparison. In between, the Green Mountain National Forest is dotted with traditional villages such as **Newfane** and a few worth a short investigation around **Mount Snow**. Closer to Bennington's side of the state, hikers can pick up the **Long Trail** near its southern terminus.

Brattleboro

If **BRATTLEBORO**, in the southeastern corner of the state, just off I-91, is your first taste of Vermont, it may come as a surprise that it's not a quaint, 1950s-throwback village. Its style is more that of central and northern Massachusetts college towns, with numerous little stores and coffeehouses, not to mention the liveliest nightlife scene in the state outside of Burlington, all catering to the youthful and vaguely "alternative" population that has moved into the surrounding hills during the past few decades. Sitting beside the Connecticut River, the city lies near the site of **Fort Dummer**, the first English settlement in the state, which was built to protect neighboring Massachusetts from Indian raids. Gradually businesses and farms sprang up alongside the river and the fort, and in the 1800s Brattleboro enjoyed a modest reputation as a railroad town and a mill town, even briefly as a health center, after pure springs were discovered along the Whetstone

Brook. Rudyard Kipling penned his two *Jungle Books* here, giving the town its lone claim to fame, though one you can't really experience fully – the only site related to him is his former home **Naulakha**, now used mainly as a rental property (though you still may be able to snag a tour).

Arrival, information, and city transit

If you're flying in, the closest major **airport** is in Hartford, Connecticut, approximately ninety minutes south of the Vermont border. Brattleboro is easily reached by **train**; two Amtrak coaches pass through daily, and the station is centrally located on Vernon Street. Meanwhile, Vermont Transit interlines with Greyhound **bus service** in these parts, and their terminal is located a couple of miles north of downtown near the junction of US-5 (Putney Road) and I-91 (Ⓣ802/254-6066). There are services from Brattleboro to Rutland, White River Junction, and destinations in Massachusetts such as Boston and Northampton. Brattleboro's **town bus**, The Brattleboro BeeLine (Ⓣ802/254-4541), can get you to the bus terminal, as well as various other points in and around town. The single fare is 75¢.

The **Chamber of Commerce**, 180 Main St (Mon–Fri 9am–noon and 1–5pm, Sat 10am–2pm; Ⓣ802/254-4565, Ⓦwww.brattleborochamber.org), has a standard selection of brochures on area attractions, and operates an information **kiosk** on the Brattleboro Town Common, just north of town on Putney Road. The **Southeast Vermont Welcome Center**, on I-91 south of Brattleboro in Guilford (daily 7am–11pm; Ⓣ802/254-4593), can lay claim to being the most elaborate visitors' center in the whole state, and has plenty of information about the various attractions in the Brattleboro area (the lobby is open 24 hours).

If you're interested in seeing the town from the **water** nearby, Connecticut River Safaris, north of town on Putney Road (Ⓣ802/257-5008), rents motorboats, canoes, and kayaks. The *Belle of Brattleboro*, also on Putney Road (June–Oct, plus special foliage cruises; $10; Ⓣ802/254-1263), seats about fifty people and runs cruises on the Connecticut, narrating its history, folklore, and wildlife. Sunset cruises are a bit lower-key, with cruise guides letting the view speak for itself.

Accommodation

A number of chain and independently owned **motels** line Putney Road (US-5) north of town, though the independent ones are cheaper and have a bit more character. There's a *Brattleboro North KOA* park for **camping** at 1238 Rte-5 in East Dummerston (Ⓣ802/254-5908), where sites go for $29.

Artist's Loft B&B and Gallery 103 Main St Ⓣ802/257-5181, Ⓦwww.theartistsloft.com. Tiny B&B above an art gallery offers only one suite, but it's a luxurious two-room overlooking the Connecticut River. Private entrance, video and book libraries available. ❹

Colonial Motel & Spa Putney Road, US-5 and Rte-9 Ⓣ802/257-7733 or 1-800/239-0032, Ⓦwww.colonialmotelspa.com. This family-owned and -operated lodge has quality rooms with indoor pool, sauna, health club, and Redwood hot tub. Their next-door restaurant serves fine dinners. ❸

Green River Bridge House 2435 Stage Rd Ⓣ802/257-5771 or Ⓣ1-800/528-1868, Ⓦwww.greenriverbridgehouse.com. This former 1830s post office was totally gutted and restored to high-end comfort. The three colorful rooms are tastefully decorated and overlook a quiet lawn with a view of a covered bridge and the gurgling river. Geared more toward couples than families. ❻

Forty Putney Road 192 Putney Rd Ⓣ802/254-6268 or 1-800/941-2413, Ⓦwww.putney.net/40putneyrd. Bed and breakfast in a French Baronial house decorated with antique furnishings. A manageable one-mile walk to the town center. ❻

Lamplighter Motel 1336 Putney Rd Ⓣ802/254-8025. One step up from a hostel, the basic rooms look like they haven't been redecorated since the 1960s, but they're clean and very cheap. ❷

Latchis Hotel 50 Main St Ⓣ802/254-6300, Ⓦwww.brattleboro.com/latchis. Small, thirty-room Art Deco hotel has a good location and has been nicely restored. The centrally controlled air-conditioning may leave you a bit chilly, though. The four-person suites are good value. ❹

The Town

Main Street spans the length of Brattleboro's diminutive downtown, lined with hip coffeehouses, art galleries, holistic apothecaries, and used-CD shops. You could spend time browsing in any of them, including **Vermont Artisan Designs**, 106 Main St, with its blown glass, intricate jewelry, and woodblock prints, or funky **Windham Art Gallery**, 69 Main St, an artists' cooperative exhibiting an eclectic array of fine arts (the featured artists can occasionally be seen prowling the halls). The town is rich in artistic tradition and sponsors a Gallery Walk every month, when local and regional artists are spotlighted in over forty of the town's galleries, inns, and cafés.

Just west off the southern end of Main Street is Brattleboro's concentration of **bookstores**. Brattleboro Books, 36 Elliot St, purveys a staggering array of used volumes at incredibly cheap prices. Across the street, at 25 Elliot, Everyone's Books is part leftist bookstore, with special sections for indie zines and anarchic political tracts, and part community center for the local counterculture. Book Cellar, at 120 Main St, is a more traditional independent option.

At the foot of Main Street, just before it intersects with Bridge Street, the 1930s Art Deco **Latchis Theatre** is worth a look for its sleek high Deco style and interior trimmings, including a series of faux-Greek friezes. Step in even if you have no intention of seeing a film. Across the bridge at 10 Vernon St, the **Brattleboro Museum and Art Center** (Jan and May–Dec, Wed–Mon 11am–5pm; $4; ☎802/257-0124) occupies the old railroad station building. It features changing – and sometimes rather nondescript – exhibits on contemporary art and regional history. From 1860 through the early twentieth century Estey organs were produced in Brattleboro and shipped to churches throughout the world. Several of them still reside at the **Estey Organ Museum,** 108 Birge St (June–Oct, Sat 10am–5pm, Sun 1–5pm; $2).

A couple of miles north of town, off I-91 in the village of Dummerston, is the home of Rudyard Kipling, called **Naulakha**. Kipling designed it and lived there from 1891 to 1896, writing some of his most celebrated works during the time, including *Captains Courageous* and *The First* and *Second Jungle Books*. Named after a temple in Janakpur, Nepal, the two-and-a-half-story, shingle-clad house is in great shape and contains some original furnishings. It also grants wonderful views of the Connecticut River Valley and Mount Monadnock across the border in New Hampshire. It's not regularly open for tours, but you may be able arrange one by calling ahead. If you're a Kipling diehard, rent the place and stay there for around $2000 a week, $250 a night in winter (call the Landmark Trust for information ☎802/254-6868).

Eating, drinking, and entertainment

Brattleboro's **restaurants** cater to the youthful counterculture with a variety of styles rarely duplicated in Vermont. Ranging from cosmopolitan and sophisticated to low-budget and health-conscious, most of the best options are on or just off Main Street, and the same goes for **bars** in the town. A good place to stock up for a camping trip is the Brattleboro Food Co-op, 2 Main St (☎802/257-0236), in the Brookside Plaza at the intersection of Canal and Main streets, which stocks a wide selection of organically produced foods. The local **music scene** bops with talented local acts on a near-nightly basis; pick up a Thursday edition of the *Brattleboro Reformer* for an exhaustive listing of the week's events. The Latchis Theatre's meticulously restored **cinema** shows both studio and indie flicks.

Amy's Bakery Arts Café 113 Main St ☎802/251-1071. Simple but tasty pastries, breads, and some basic sandwiches in a storefront on Main Stt. Good views from the outside tables out back, though. Open until 6pm.

Back Side Café 24 High St ☎802/257-5056. One of the town's older cafés, where most items on the menu are homemade. Good omelettes, burgers, soups, and desserts at bargain prices.

Dalem's Chalet 78 South St ☎802/254-4323. The German specialties (stuffed cabbage, bratwurst) are in line with the European Alpine lodge room, but there are also plenty of traditional steak and chicken selections too. Moderately priced.

Max's 1052 Western Ave ☎802/254-7747. Ambitious pasta and 'not pasta' dishes, with prices to match. You can choose from rabbit stew, Brazilian *feijoada*, or barbecue salmon, along with some seafood and interesting rigatonis and linguini. Closed Mon and Tues.

McNeill's Brewery 90 Elliot St ☎802/254-2553. Rough-hewn bar where you can sample eleven different varieties of their own microbrews, including Big Nose Blond, Old Ringworm, and Slopbucket Brown.

Mocha Joe's 82 Main St ☎802/257-7794. Good caffeine-filled beverages in a stylish basement below Main St. A dark and dingy alternative to the comfy chairs and soothing music found at *Starbucks* and the like.

Mole's Eye Café 4 High St ☎802/257-0771. Brattleboro's most happening nightspot, bar, and dance floor, with a wide range of live music most nights – blues, Latin, R&B, jazz, calypso – for about a $5 cover. Talented locals enjoy the open-mic night every Thursday. Closed Sun.

Riverview Café 3 Bridge St ☎802/254-9841. The good seafood and comfort food favorites make for an ample (and reasonably priced) meal, but the real treat is the outdoor dining on the deck, accompanied by great views of the Connecticut River.

Shin La Sushi Bar 57 Main St ☎802/257-5226. Pretty much your only sushi option for miles, Shin La has it in quantity. Chinese standards too.

North from Brattleboro: Newfane and Grafton

Slightly inland and north from Brattleboro, **NEWFANE** and **GRAFTON** are two beautifully restored villages offering the best of small-town Vermont with their white churches and romantic inns. There's nothing of real note to see in the former, but it boasts a town green flanked by no fewer than three white-steepled buildings: the union hall, the Congregational church, and the county court house – pretty enough if you're passing through. Just a few miles north of Newfane, **Townshend State Park** ($2.50; ⓣ802/365-7500) provides excellent opportunities for both casual and serious hikers. Its trails, open summer only, include the steep, rocky, 1680-foot climb to the summit of Bald Mountain; other trails are not quite as challenging. There's swimming, tubing, and canoeing at the nearby Townshend Dam. **Jamaica State Park** (end of April to mid-Oct; ⓣ802/874-4600), situated on a bend in the West River half a mile from the town of Jamaica, has a trail along the river which follows the old track of the Brattleboro Railroad and leads to the Ball Mountain Dam. On two weekends a year (in late April and late September) the dam is opened and water released into the river, an event which attracts numerous adrenalin-seeking canoeists and kayakers. **Extreme Adventures of Vermont**, in nearby Andover, (ⓣ802/875-4451, ⓦwww.extemeadventuresvt.com) offers a wide range of guided outdoor activities for a minimum of two people, from kayaking and hiking to whitewater rafting and winter caving.

If you're looking for a **place to stay** in Newfane, try the *West River Lodge & Stables*, 117 Hill Rd (ⓣ802/365-7745, ⓦwww.westriverlodge.com; ⑤), a nineteenth-century farmhouse where you can eat hearty breakfasts around an open fireplace before hitting the nearby hiking trails. In Newfane itself, smack on the green, the *Four Columns Inn*, 230 West St (ⓣ1-800/787-6633, ⓦwww.fourcolumnsinn.com; ⑥), has comfortable rooms, many with Jacuzzis, as well as a gourmet **restaurant** where the likes of Mick Jagger, Henry Kissinger, and Tom Cruise have sampled carefully prepared New American, Asian,

△ Newfane Village Green

and French cuisine. Also, on the Rte-30 edge of the green, the *Old Newfane Inn* (☎802/365-4427) – an old stagecoach stop – continues to serve up tasty capon and venison dinners to hungry travelers in the mood for hearty European-style preparations.

There's marginally more to do in Grafton than there is in Newfane, though still, the biggest draw here is a cheese shop, the **Grafton Village Cheese Company**, on Townshend Road, a half-mile south of the village (Mon–Fri 8am–4pm, Sat–Sun 10am–4pm; ☎802/843-2221 or 1-800/472-3866). Take some of their excellent cheddar with you on a picnic to nearby Townshend State Park. A little closer to town, the **Nature Museum**, 186 Townshend Rd (summer Sat–Sun 10am–4pm, other times call for appointment; $4; ☎802/843-2111), is a somewhat haphazard taxidermic and geological collection crammed into a former hall. If you've got time to kill and an abiding interest in local history, the Grafton Historical Society runs the **History Museum** at 147 Main St (late May to mid-Oct Sat–Sun 10am–noon & 2–4pm, daily during fall foliage; $3 donation; ☎802/843-1010), a collection of relics from Grafton homesteads, such as soapstones from the local quarries, textiles, and photos. They can also provide you with a helpful **walking tour** map. The *Old Tavern*, 92 Main St (☎1-800/843-1801, Ⓦwww.old-tavern.com; ❼), is an up-market **inn** and **restaurant** which sits in the heart of the tiny village and has been around since 1801, having accommodated such luminaries as Ulysses S. Grant, Nathaniel Hawthorne, and Henry David Thoreau. Continuing a few miles north on Rte-35, you will come to a junction and the pretty village of Chester.

West to Bennington: Mount Snow and around

Route 9 heads west from Brattleboro less than forty miles to Bennington; the first town of any size on the way is uninspiring **MARLBORO**, just 10.5 miles along. In midsummer, chamber music fanatics descend on the town, as it plays host to the **Marlboro Music Fest** (☎802/254-2394, Ⓦwww.marlboromusic.org). Barely ten miles farther you'll encounter **WILMINGTON**, a genial place with a country store full of the expected knickknacks, New England crafts, and more than enough maple syrup and cheese from the state's producers. The only real stop of note is the **Young & Constantin Gallery** at 10 South Main St (☎802/464-2515). Though they carry an assortment of expensive handcrafted items which can include ceramics and metal pieces, they specialize in glassworks, which look particularly radiant given that the gallery is housed in an 1830s restored church with stained-glass windows.

Wilmington is also home to the only traffic light between Brattleboro and Bennington. The only reason to turn left is to see the birthplace of Mormon prophet Brigham Young at **WHITINGHAM**, ten miles south on Hwy-100, marked by a granite monument on the town common. Traveling north, Hwy-100 ambles on to **Haystack Mountain** and **Mount Snow** in the town of **WEST DOVER**, both providing perfectly fine places to ski, and both officially part of the **Green Mountain National Forest** – though without the benefit of the press of other major snowbound havens such as Killington and Stowe. Still, that may be reason enough to opt for it, if you're looking to avoid the crowds while having your choice of types of run. *Mount Snow Resort* (☎802/464-2151, Ⓦwww.mountsnow.com) is the larger, and more popular, of the two, offering some 130 trails (lift tickets about $55); its sister mountain, Haystack (☎802/464-8301), has fewer than fifty but is usually less crowded and passes are approximately $10 less.

You'll also find plenty of outdoorsy stuff to occupy you here in the summer; Mount Snow has a sizeable **mountain-biking** fan base: the National Off-Road Bicycling Association has held championship events here since the late 1980s. It's $30 for lift and trail day passes, but note that all trails accessed by lift are for advanced-level bikers only. Mount Snow and the *Haystack Golf Club*, 70 Spyglass Drive, Wilmington (Ⓣ802/464-8301, Ⓦwww.haystockgolf.com) cater to the golfing crowd with championship courses.

The **Mount Snow Valley Chamber of Commerce**, West Main St, Wilmington (Ⓣ802/464-8092 or 1-877/VTSOUTH, Ⓦwww.visitvermont.com) can help with any questions you may have. If you wish to **stay** here, try the *Deer Hill Inn*, Valley View Road, West Dover (Ⓣ802/464-3100, Ⓦwww.deerhillinn.com; ❻) which has fourteen cozy and colorful rooms, or the *Snow Goose*, 259 Hwy-100 (Ⓣ802/464-3984, Ⓦwww.snowgooseinn.com; ❻), whose rooms have wood-burning fireplaces and Jacuzzis. If you wish to camp, Molly Stark State Park, 705 Rte-9 East (Ⓣ802/464-5460), has 23 tent sites ($14), but as this is on a popular travel route, you should reserve in advance.

There are several worthy (and expensive) **restaurants** here too, like the one at the *Deer Hill Inn*, and *The White House*, 178 Rte-9 East, Wilmington (Ⓣ802/464-2135), royally perched on a hilltop, where you can order Steak Diane or Veal Oscar. But even the ultra-casual *Dot's*, 3 Main St (Ⓣ802/464-7284), a lunch-counter diner in the center of town, has award-winning chili.

Bennington

Little has happened in **BENNINGTON** in the past two hundred years to match the excitement of the days when Ethan Allen's Green Mountain Boys were based here and known as the "Bennington Mob." Today, despite the presence of the exclusive, arts-oriented **Bennington College** – which has seen the likes of hot young authors Bret Easton Ellis and Donna Tartt pass through its halls – the city is a sleepy town most notable for its rich Revolutionary history and one fine museum of American folk art.

Settled in 1761 on a rise by the Walloomsac River, overlooking the valley between the Green and Taconic mountains, the town became a leading nineteenth-century industrial outpost for paper mills, potteries, gristmills, and the largest cotton-batting mill in the US. That heritage is preserved today in **Old Bennington**, just up the hill from the center of town, and the one obvious spot to explore.

Arrival and information

Bennington straddles the intersection of US-7 and Hwy-9, an intersection known locally as the "Four Corners." In town, Hwy-9 is referred to as Main Street, while the local stretches of US-7 above and below the Corners are called North and South streets. The nearest commercial **airport** is forty miles away in Albany, New York. The Vermont Transit **bus** terminal (Ⓣ802/442-4808) is in the center of town, one block from Main Street, with services to New York via Albany. A very convenient (and free) alternative if you're heading along Historic Route 7A is the Green Mountain Express (Ⓣ802/442-9458), which runs three times daily between Bennington and Manchester (with another free service connecting through to Rutland). The

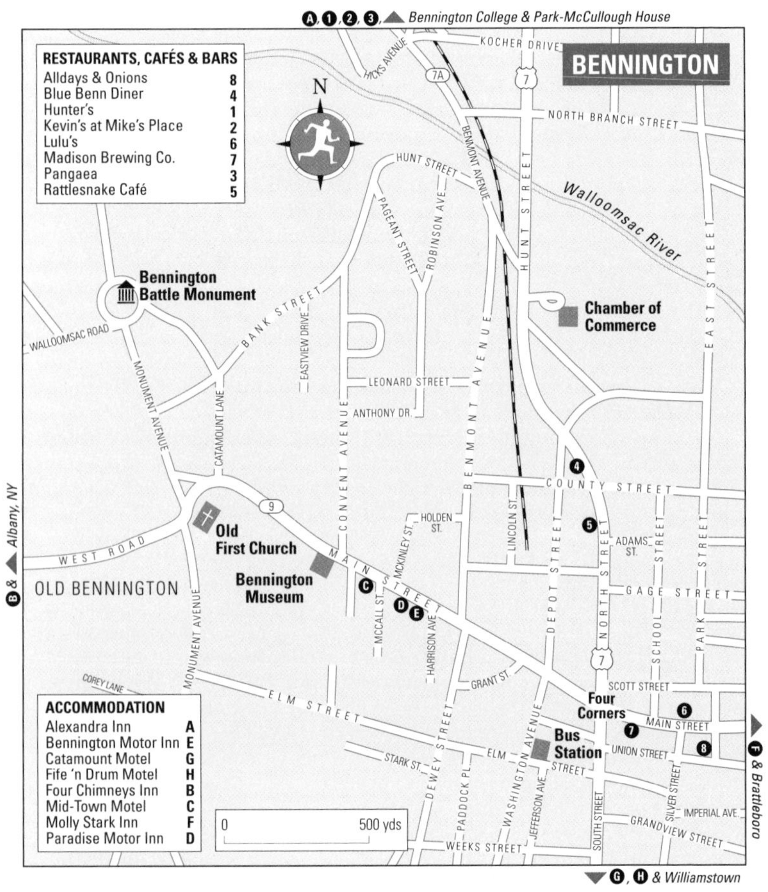

Bennington stop is at the Bank North parking lot, on Main Street one block east of Four Corners.

The **Bennington Area Chamber of Commerce**, north of Four Corners, Rte 7 (Mon–Fri 9am–5pm, Sat 10am–4pm, in summer also Sun 10am–4pm; ⓣ802/447-3311 or 1-800/229–0252, ⓦwww.bennington.com), should be your first stop for information on surrounding attractions; it has clean public restrooms to boot. There's also a **kiosk** with basic practical information at the Four Corners.

Accommodation

Cookie-cutter **budget motels** line South Street and West Main Street, and there are a few other options scattered about. Those who might prefer "name brand" chain motels will be disappointed in what the Bennington area has to offer (namely just a *Best Western* on Northside Drive), but its independent motels and hotels are generally clean and far less expensive than those found in other Vermont cities and towns. Several miles away in Woodford, the *Greenwood Lodge Hostel and Campsites*, Prospect Mountain off Rte-9, (ⓣ802/442-2547, ⓦwww.campvermont.com/greenwood), an HI/AYH-affiliated property, has dorm beds, with kitchen and recreation access, available for $26 ($23 for members) and wooded campsites for $20 (open mid-May to late Oct).

Alexandra Inn Rte-7A and Orchard Rd ⓣ802/442-5619 or 1-888/207-9386, ⓦwww.alexandrainn.com. Restored Colonial with twelve luxurious rooms featuring jet tubs and fireplaces, hearty gourmet breakfasts, and a garden and beautiful views from its two green acres. ❺

Bennington Motor Inn 143 Main St ⓣ802/442-5479 or 1-800/359-9900. Family-run inn, the smaller neighbor of the *Paradise Motor Inn*. Sixteen comfortable rooms with the standard conveniences, plus complimentary in-room movies. ❹

Catamount Motel 500 South St ⓣ802/442-5977. Immaculate quarters, featuring a pool and a picnic area in which to barbecue. Rural setting (plenty of greenspaces, in any case), yet within walking distance of downtown. ❸

Fife 'n' Drum Motel US-7 South, 1.5 miles south of Bennington ⓣ802/442-4074 or 442-4730, ⓦwww.sover.net/~toberua. Pleasant, large rooms with cable TV, coffeemakers, and air-conditioning. Pool, spa, and spacious lawn with grills. Closed Jan–April. ❷

Four Chimneys Inn 21 West Rd (Rte-9) ⓣ802/447-3500, ⓦwww.fourchimneys.com. Eleven comfortable, country rooms, most with a fireplace and sofa, in an elegant white manor on eleven acres of green. Full breakfast included. Restaurant is open for sumptuous dinners Wed–Sun. ❻

Mid-Town Motel 107 Main St ⓣ802/447-0189. Extremely basic efficiencies, somewhat less expensive and much less appealing than its numerous neighbors. Consider this one for its low rates and reasonably central location. ❸

Molly Stark Inn 1067 Main St ⓣ802/442-9631 or 1-800/356-3076, ⓦwww.mollystarkinn.com. Six double-occupancy guestrooms with quilts and claw-footed tubs in a cozy Queen Anne-style house, plus a self-contained cottage facing the woods. Full breakfast and friendly owners. ❹

Paradise Motor Inn 141 Main St ⓣ802/442-8351, ⓦwww.theparadisemotorinn.com. Perfectly satisfactory accommodation a few blocks from the Four Corners (some of the 76 rooms are even equipped with saunas). Heated outdoor pool and tennis courts. A relatively large hotel, so a good place to try if there are no vacancies elsewhere. ❹

The Town

There's nothing much doing in the center of Bennington, and the best place to begin your wanderings is around the western end of Main Street, in historic **Old Bennington**, an assortment of public and residential buildings done in all manner of architectural styles. The town's most prominent icon is the **Bennington Battle Monument**, 15 Monument Circle (daily: mid-April to late Oct 9am–5pm; $2), a 306-foot hilltop obelisk that commemorates the August 1777 Battle of Bennington. This pivotal conflict pitted the Continental Army against the superior forces of General Burgoyne, who had made it an objective to seize the arsenal depot at Bennington. The unexpected victory of the Revolutionaries bolstered their morale and debilitated Burgoyne's troops, contributing to their ultimate defeat at the subsequent Battle of Saratoga, the major turning point of the war. The hilltop the monument stands on was Burgoyne's objective (though the battle actually took place just over the Walloomsac River, in New York State). Just down Monument Avenue, **Old First Church**, erected in 1805, abuts a well-preserved cemetery holding the grave of poet and adoptive Vermonter Robert Frost. Signs point the way to his tombstone, which reads simply, "I had a lover's quarrel with the world," an epitaph that never ceases to amuse the church's many visitors.

△ Bennington Battle Monument

East of here, the **Bennington Museum and Grandma Moses Gallery**, 75 Main St (daily except Wed: 10am–5pm; $8; ⓣ802/447-1571, ⓦwww.benningtonmuseum.org), contains a fine array of Americana: several Tiffany lamps; a flag which may be the oldest American one in existence; tiny sewing machines; nineteenth-century furniture made by local craftsmen; and *The Wasp*, a 1925 luxury touring car, built in Bennington and the only surviving example of its kind. The highlight of the collection, however, is its exhibit on American folk artist Anna Mary Robertson Moses, known popularly as **Grandma Moses**. Moses, who first started painting her simple, pleasing representations of rural life at the age of 73, experienced a meteoric rise to fame in the worlds of high art and popular culture, and eventually lived to enjoy national adulation by the time she reached her hundredth birthday. In addition to the largest public collection of her work, the museum has a reconstruction of the schoolhouse she attended as a youngster, which displays many of her personal belongings, photographs, painting equipment, and awards.

Rte-7A splits off from US-7 and continues on to **NORTH BENNINGTON**, where three **covered bridges** – the Silk Road, Paper Mill Village, and the Burt Henry – span the Walloomsac River. This area is marked by reminders of late eighteenth-century industrial activity, notably the housing along Sage Street, which used to be inhabited by mill-workers; now they are regular apartments. The elaborate Greek Revival **Park-McCullough House**, Park and West streets (daily: late May to late Oct 10am–3pm, tours hourly; $8; ⓣ802/442-5441), a sumptuous 1864 mansion of 35 rooms, is filled with most of its original period furnishings, including children's toys; horse-drawn carriages reside in the carriage barn out back. The grounds and garden are open dawn to dusk.

In the nearby village of **SHAFTSBURY**, the **Robert Frost Stone House Museum**, 121 Rte-7A (May–Dec Tues–Sun 10am–5pm; $5; ⓣ802/447-6200), is yet another memorial to one of New England's favorite poets. The house should appeal to Frost enthusiasts who are dying to see the rooms in which poems such as *Stopping by Woods on a Snowy Evening* were crafted, and the surrounding scenery which no doubt provided valuable inspiration. For others, it will be just another pretty countryside dwelling in a part of the world where they're certainly not in short supply.

Eating, drinking, and entertainment

There's not an overwhelming variety when it comes to **restaurants** in Bennington, most seeming to serve the simple omelets-and-burgers-type fare found in most diners. Nights are fairly quiet, too, as the college population rarely gets too rowdy.

Alldays and Onions 519 Main St ⓣ802/447-0043. Creative meat and fish dishes at reasonable prices, served with bread from the in-house bakery. Essentially a breakfast and lunch place, though it's also open for dinner Thurs–Sat.
Blue Benn Diner 102 Hunt St ⓣ802/442-5140. Authentic, 1940s-era diner draws a diverse crowd of hard-boiled locals and artsy students. In a break with the unwritten code of diners, vegetarian dishes feature on the menu. Open from 6am daily.
Hunter's 782 Harwood Hill, near the intersection of US-7 and Rte-7A ⓣ802/442-7500. Remodeled barn turned gourmet restaurant, located on a hill with excellent views of New York, New Hampshire, and Massachusetts. Excellent – though moderately expensive – steaks and seafood. The adjacent *Lucky Labrador Tavern* has a more rustic feel (and drink specials some nights).
Kevin's at Mike's Place 27 Main St, N Bennington ⓣ802/442-0122. Local art and antiques line the walls of this comfort food restaurant (with prime rib specials, wings, burgers, and seafood on the menu) that doubles as a laidback casual venue for live bands or karaoke on the weekends.
Lulu's 520 Main St ⓣ802/442-9833. "Unusual meals from around the world," which nonetheless translates to meatloaf with mashed potatoes and shepherd's pie. You can't complain about the prices, though.
Madison Brewing Co 428 Main St ⓣ1-800/44BREWS. Fun, stylish brewpub with hearty burgers and six varieties of in-house beer. Live blues most nights of the week. Open daily until 2am.
Pangaea 1–3 Prospect St, N Bennington ⓣ802/442-7171. Very expensive menu (mains from $30) of shrimp, pheasant, and veal loin; the lounge food is simpler and much more economical. Almost forty beer and 75 wine options, from all over the world.
Rattlesnake Café 230 North St ⓣ802/447-7018. A popular Mexican joint – about the closest you'll come to exotic cuisine in Bennington.

The Green Mountains and Scenic Hwy-100

The **Green Mountains** that form the backbone of Vermont are not as harsh as New Hampshire's White Mountains, though the forests for which they are named are invariably buried in snow for most of the winter, and the higher roads are liable to be blocked for long periods. For the most part, the sides and the summits are covered with evergreens such as spruces, hemlocks, and firs, the inspiration to the French colonialists for the state's name (and, more obviously, the name of the range). Here and there, denuded patches mark where trees have been shaved away to create ski runs, but otherwise the usually peaceful Rte-100 and US-7, which run along the base of the mountains to the east and west respectively, offer unspoiled mountain views as well as a few charming towns along the way.

The bulk of the Green Mountain National Forest is concentrated in the southern part of the state, but its spine runs nearly up to the state capital, Montpelier, roughly parallel to the **Long Trail**, a hiking trail which cuts through the Green Mountains on its way from Massachusetts to the Canadian border.

North of Mount Snow, Hwy-100 snakes along the east of the Green Mountains and continues up to Killington and beyond. Along the way, the road passes through its share of predictably charming villages, of which **Weston** stands out as being one of the more attractive. A little farther north, the quaint town of **Ludlow** is at the base of **Okemo Mountain**, another of the state's fine ski resorts. A slight detour south along Rte-103 brings you to **Chester**, a pretty enough village in its own right and the departure point for scenic train rides. Back on Hwy-100, north of Ludlow, **Plymouth Notch** is the home of one of the finest presidential historic sites in the country, the **Calvin Coolidge State Historic Site**.

The Long Trail

Spanning the entirety of Vermont – 265 miles from the Massachusetts border to Québec – the **Long Trail** is one of America's premier **hiking trails**, popular with seasoned outdoorsmen but accessible for amateurs as well. It runs along the crest of the Green Mountains, affording fabulous views of small towns and vast stretches of countryside. The terrain is varied, to put it mildly, and becomes more rugged the farther north you go. If you've got your own transport, you'll find places to park at most trailheads along the way (note, however, that many access roads are closed during the winter months).

The presence of two-by-six-inch white blazes indicates that you're walking on the Long Trail. Intersections are usually marked with signs; double blazes signal important turns; and the almost one hundred side trails (totaling 175 miles) are blazed in blue and signposted. Those planning on hiking the entire length of the trail (hardy souls known within the local hiking community as "end-to-enders") should count on it taking between twenty-five and thirty days. The most conventional way of accomplishing this feat is to hike from shelter to shelter (see below), although with good preparation (and some transport assistance from others) you could complete the trail by taking only day-hikes. The southern part of the trail is actually also the Appalachian Trail. Both follow the same path for 97 miles before splitting near Rutland, the Appalachian veering east towards New Hampshire and Maine. From this junction, the Long Trail winds up to the Canadian border, 167 miles away. The two significant climbs on the southern part of the trail are to the summits of **Mount Stratton** (3936ft) and **Killington Peak** (4241ft). The northern section of the Long Trail is a more strenuous – and an ultimately more rewarding – hike, crossing some of the highest peaks in Vermont. **The Camel's Hump** (4083ft) and **Mount Mansfield** (4393ft) are both well-trod parts of the trail where you may get some fine views, but not the sense of splendid isolation that kicks in farther north across the Jay Peak Range, as the Long Trail nears its end.

Accommodation on the Long Trail consists of about seventy shelters, maintained during summer and usually no more than a gentle day's hike apart. A moderate fee is charged at sites with caretakers, and availability is on a first-come-first-served basis. All shelters are on the primitive side (no electricity or running water, for instance), and can be fully enclosed wood cabins, three-sided lean-tos, or tent sites. All sites have a water source, although this doesn't necessarily mean that the water is drinkable without first having been treated. The essential tome for those interested in doing some **further reading** is the *Long Trail Guide* ($16.95), published by the caretakers of the trail, the Green Mountain Club (Ⓣ802/244-7037, Ⓦwww.greenmountainclub.org).

Weston

One of the prettier villages along Hwy-100, **WESTON** spreads beside a little river on an idyllic green, where a stone slab commemorates the seventeen local soldiers who were killed on the same day during the Civil War, in Alexandria, Virginia. This is one of the few Vermont towns that tries to cater to a summer crowd, through various art-related and outdoor activities, but things never get so busy that you would mistake it for any sort of tourist haven.

In town, Hwy-100 turns into Main Street, and is lined with stores selling antiques, toys, and fudge. The spell is slightly broken when you realize that the **Vermont Country Store**, for all its seeming quaintness, is actually part of a corporate chain of superstores that relentlessly packages and markets the state's bucolic image. The **Weston Village Store** opposite contains a much more authentic – and cheaper – if not as vast, range of vaguely rural and domestic articles, such as gallon tins of real maple syrup and local cheeses.

Right on the town green, the 1797 **Farrar-Mansur House** (mid-June–Aug Wed, Sat & Sun 1–4pm; Sept to mid-Oct weekends 1–5pm; $3 donation requested), a former tavern that has been restored to depict lives of early Vermont settlers, presents an array of antique housewares and some decent American folk art. Next door, the **Old Mill Museum** (July–Aug Wed 1–5pm, Sat 10am–4pm, Sun 1–4pm; also Sept to mid-Oct weekends; $3 donation requested) occupies a converted sawmill and possesses an impressive historical assortment of tinsmith, woodworking, and farm and dairy tools. Also on the green, **Weston Playhouse** (Tues–Sun; ⓣ802/824-5288, ⓦwww.westonplayhouse.org) is a typical small-town Vermont theater, but spawned the career of the late Lloyd Bridges. It puts on a mixture of standard summer-stock musicals, occasionally with more daring offerings, such as works by Brian Friel and Molière.

Practicalities

The best **accommodation** in town is the lovely, centrally located *Inn at Weston* near the village green (ⓣ802/824-6789, ⓦwww.innweston.com; ❼), which also features a first-class restaurant serving divine steak au poivre, and a snug pub to boot. The *Darling Family Inn*, Rte-100 north of the green (ⓣ802/824-3223; ❹), is another nice bed-and-breakfast, set in a 170-year-old farmhouse. Decent alternatives away from the town center include the *Colonial House Inn & Motel*, south on Rte-100 (ⓣ802/824-6286 or 1-800/639-5033, ⓦwww.cohoinn.com; ❸), and the *Brandmeyer's Mountainside Lodge*, north on Rte-100 a little closer to town (ⓣ802/824-5851, ⓦwww.brandmeyerslodge.com; ❻). Both spots provide breakfast, though the *Colonial House* has the edge with its offer of fresh homemade cookies to all visitors.

If you're looking to **eat** more than just cookies, a magnificent soda fountain dominates the 1885 mahogany bar of the lunch-only *Bryant House* restaurant, Main Street (closed Sun; ⓣ802/824-6287), two doors down from the Vermont Country Store. The menu includes such classic New England fare as "johnny cakes" of cornbread with molasses.

Ludlow, Okemo Mountain, and around

About ten miles north of Weston, Hwy-100 gets slightly more built up as it nears **LUDLOW**, the access point for the family-owned **Okemo Mountain Resort** (lift tickets start at $63/day; ⓣ802/228-4041 or 1-800/786-5366 for reservations, ⓦwww.okemo.com). Intermediate skiers and snowboarders will find the 106 trails on Okemo Mountain and the seven trails on the neighboring mountain, Jackson Gore, challenging enough, although the expert will probably get bored after a while. One thing that Okemo can guarantee at all times is snow, no small thing this far south: its 95 percent snowmaking coverage is the largest of any resort in Vermont.

Eleven miles on, the village of **PLYMOUTH NOTCH,** just off Hwy-100 on Hwy-100A, is essentially a museum dedicated to the memory of the thirtieth president of the US – and one of the finest of its kind. The **Calvin Coolidge State Historic Site** (daily: late May to mid-Oct 9.30am–5pm; $7.50; ⓣ802/672-3773) goes one step farther than most other presidential historic sites by restoring not just a particular building connected in some way to the president, but an entire village. Coolidge was born in Plymouth Notch in 1872 and grew up here. He never lost ties to the town, taking the presidential oath of office here after the unexpected death of President Warren Harding (Coolidge was vice president at the time), and conducting "Summer White House" sessions in town as well. He was buried here in 1933. All of the buildings in which Coolidge's life – and a good part of his presidency

– played out have been kept more or less the way they were. Other structures such as a cheese factory, a Congregational church, and a general store (where Coolidge's father was storekeeper) help fill in the details of everyday life in the late nineteenth century.

Practicalities

The **Okemo Valley Regional Chamber of Commerce**, on Rte-103 in the Okemo Market Place (ⓣ802/228-5830, ⓦwww.okemovalleyvt.org), is an excellent source of information and advice, particularly if you've arrived in the area without pre-booked accommodation; they'll do their best to find something suitable, even during the busiest times of the year. A free **local bus** (ⓣ802/228-2841) connects Ludlow to Okemo Mountain all year, Monday through Friday.

Ludlow has no shortage of **places to stay**, although you should obviously plan ahead if you intend to arrive during the ski season or fall foliage. Luxurious lodgings within a mile of the lifts include the *Andrie Rose Inn*, 13 Pleasant St (ⓣ802/228-4846 or 1-800/223-4846, ⓦwww.andrieroseinn.com; ❻), and the *Governor's Inn*, 86 Main St (ⓣ802/228-8830 or 1-800/468-3766, ⓦwww.thegovernorsinn.com; ❻). Also close to the slopes, the *Best Western Ludlow Colonial Motel*, 93 Main St (ⓣ802/228-8188, ⓦwww.bestwesternludlow.com; ❹), has 48 comfortable rooms. The *Happy Trails Motel*, one mile south of town on Rte-103 (ⓣ802/228-8888 or 1-800/228-9984; ❹), has rooms with balconies and views of Okemo Mountain, as well as three self-catering suites and two cottages. There's nowhere to **camp** in town, but Coolidge State Park, a mile past the state historic site on Hwy-100A, does have facilities for tents and lean-tos (late May to mid-Oct; ⓣ802/672-3612).

Finding a reasonable place to **eat** after an exhausting day on the slopes won't be too difficult. *Wicked Good Pizza*, 117 Main St (ⓣ802/228-4131), sells New York-style pizza, calzone, sandwiches, and other stomach-fillers, which can be delivered free of charge if you can't be bothered to budge from your hotel room. Slightly more effort is required to eat at *Sam's Steakhouse*, Rte-103 (ⓣ802/228-2087), but the steaks and prime rib are worth it. For coffee, hot chocolate, soups, and the like, head for *Java Baba's*, Rte-103 in the Okemo Market Place (ⓣ802/228-2326), where the cozy atmosphere and comfy couches are welcome during the winter months.

Chester

It's easy enough to miss tiny **CHESTER**, at the junction of routes 103, 11, and 35, twelve miles south of Ludlow, though its prototypical Vermont charm may well draw you in. If so, drop by to see the chatty folks at the **Historical Society** on Main Street and Chester Green who can give you a walking-tour brochure to the historic houses scattered about town. Besides wandering through, you can jump aboard the **Green Mountain Flyer** (late June–Aug Tues–Sun, mid-Sept to mid-Oct daily; 1 departure 12.10pm; $14; ⓦwww.rails-vt.com), a sightseeing train that runs two-hour round-trips down to Bellows Falls, right at the New Hampshire border. The engine chugs along slowly, crossing rivers and passing covered bridges at a leisurely pace, leaving lots of time to take in the scenery, which is spectacular in the fall.

There is a good range of predictably quaint **accommodation** in Chester, much of it around the village green. The *Inn Victoria*, 321 Main St (ⓣ802/875-4288 or 1-800/732-4288, ⓦwww.innvictoria.com; ❻), goes to town on the Victorian theme with its ornate and comfortable rooms, and the friendly owners are proud of their British heritage. You could also try the *Chester House Inn*,

Chester's gentleman robber

The year 1886 ushered in a dark sixteen-year period of Chester's otherwise unremarkable history during which almost every store on Main Street was burgled at least once – the unfortunate Pollard's General Store being hit no fewer than six times. In the absence of an official police force in those days, the Board of Selectmen was charged with the responsibility for catching the thief, and First Selectman **Clarence Adams**, who was also a state legislator, library deacon, bank incorporator, and farm owner, took a particular interest in solving the mystery. He collaborated on precautionary measures with local businessmen, but all to no avail, as the rash of burglaries continued. Finally, one local proprietor devised an elaborate trap which involved rigging a shotgun to a window favored by the thief so that it would fire the gun when opened, a plan he was sure that Adams would approve of had the Selectman not been out of town when he thought of it. On July 29, 1902, news broke that Chester's most respected citizen, Clarence Adams, had been shot and wounded in the leg by highwaymen. It did not take long for the real truth to surface: Adams was Chester's notorious burglar. "What I have done I attribute to a spirit of adventure that was born in me," explained Adams in his confession. Sentenced to ten years in state prison for his multiple crimes, Adams died of pneumonia after two.

166 Main St (ⓣ1-888/875-2205, ⓦwww.chesterhouseinn.com; ❺), which has seven rooms with private baths, each decorated in a different style and color. Just off the green, *Rose Arbour* (ⓣ802/875-4766; ❺) is a pretty B&B with an attached tearoom; the top floor is a five-room suite, complete with kitchen. About one mile west of town, the *Motel-in-the-Meadow*, 936 Rte-11 (ⓣ802/875-2626, ⓦwww.motelinthemeadow.com; ❹), is a friendly "mom and pop" motel with perfectly comfortable, well-kept rooms and a small crafts shop featuring rag dolls made by Pat, the gregarious owner. The best place to **eat** in town is *Raspberries and Tyme*, on the green (Wed–Sun; ⓣ802/875-4486), serving large portions of creative salads, soups, and sandwiches.

Arlington and Historic 7A

US-7 and **Historic Route 7A** parallel each other as they run from Bennington north to Manchester, though the latter is the preferable road to take, not only a more picturesque drive but with a few notable stop-offs along the way. The great spine of the Green Mountains rises up to the east, with the Taconics somewhat more irregularly splayed out along the west, putting the route smack in the so-called "Valley of Vermont."

About halfway up Rte-7A, the small town of **ARLINGTON** is the former home of illustrator Norman Rockwell, who created some of his most memorable *Saturday Evening Post* covers while living here between 1939 and 1954. Though there is an **exhibit** in his honor at 3772 Rte-7A (daily: May–Oct 9am–5pm; $3; ⓣ802/375-6423), it only contains models of what he painted rather than actual paintings, and is easily missed. Four miles north, the **Equinox Sky Line Drive** (May–Oct; $7 toll per car and driver, $2 each additional passenger; ⓣ802/362-1114) branches off the highway, a six-mile stretch that winds and elbows its way around Mount Equinox, eventually reaching the 3816-foot summit, which offers views clear across to New Hampshire and Maine. Although the view is impressive, in a region so rich in scenery, it arguably doesn't justify the cost – unless you would enjoy the exhilarating driving experience.

Running alongside Rte-7A are the tracks of the old **Rutland Railway**, built in the 1850s and setting Vermont on its way toward prominence as a crossroads for north–south New York–Montréal and east–west Boston–Chicago rail traffic. "The Rutland" still traverses Bennington County, but its track bed is in need of such extensive repairs that a 10mph speed limit restricts the line to local freight use. Passenger traffic was mostly phased out by 1950.

Practicalities

There is a self-service **visitors' center** in Arlington on Rte-7A next to Stewart's convenience store, with all of the usual maps and brochures. The Green Mountain Express, a free **bus service** which runs between Bennington and Manchester four times daily, also leaves from Stewart's.

There is **accommodation** both in Arlington and along Rte-7A. The lovely landscaped grounds and two pet llamas at the *West Mountain Inn*, about half a mile west of Arlington on Rte-313 (Ⓣ802/375-6516, Ⓦwww.westmountaininn.com; ❼) are the trade-off for telephone- and TV-free rooms and a hefty price tag. The *Arlington Inn*, Rte-7A (Ⓣ802/375-6532 or 1-800/443-9442; ❺), is another very comfortable place to stay, this time in the middle of town. Cheaper lodgings can be found north of Arlington on Rte-7A at *Cut Leaf Maples Motel* (Ⓣ802/375-2725, Ⓔcutleaf@verizon.net; ❸) and the *Governor's Rock Motel* in Shaftsbury (closed Dec–May; Ⓣ802/442-4737, Ⓦwww.governorsrockmotel.com; ❹). You can **camp** at *Camping on the Battenkill*, Rte-7A, less than one mile west of Arlington (April–Oct; Ⓣ802/375-6663 or 1-800/830-6663), which has over a hundred sites starting at $20. The **restaurant** at the *West Mountain Inn* serves six-course dinners for $42. Otherwise, grab a soggy sandwich at Stewart's.

Manchester and around

The last town on Rte-7A before it merges with US-7 is **MANCHESTER**, which has been a summer resort hot spot for more than two hundred years, a fact evidenced by the town's ritzy accommodation and numerous shopping opportunities. Manchester and the surrounding area is also well situated for outdoor pursuits, especially skiing on nearby **Bromley** and **Stratton** mountains, and **fly-fishing** in its many trout streams, particularly the Batten Kill River. It's no small coincidence that **Charles Orvis**, founder of fly-rod manufacturer Orvis Company, is a Manchester native. A visit to the company's flagship store is a worthwhile excursion, even if you have no intention of making a purchase.

Arrival and information

The **Green Mountain Express** (Ⓣ802/442-9458), actually run by the local Red Cross, provides a local free service to Bennington, while Marble Valley Regional Transit runs **Commuter Connection**, a similar service north to Rutland (Ⓣ802/773-3244). You'll find plenty of information at the **Manchester and the Mountains Chamber of Commerce**, 5046 Main St, Suite 1, Manchester Center (Ⓣ802/362-2100 or 1-800/362-4144, Ⓦwww.manchestervermont.net), or the Visitors Information Center on the green nearby.

Accommodation

Manchester's resort status weighs heavily on the rates at the area's **inns and motels**. You'll find the most reasonably priced places outside Manchester Center.

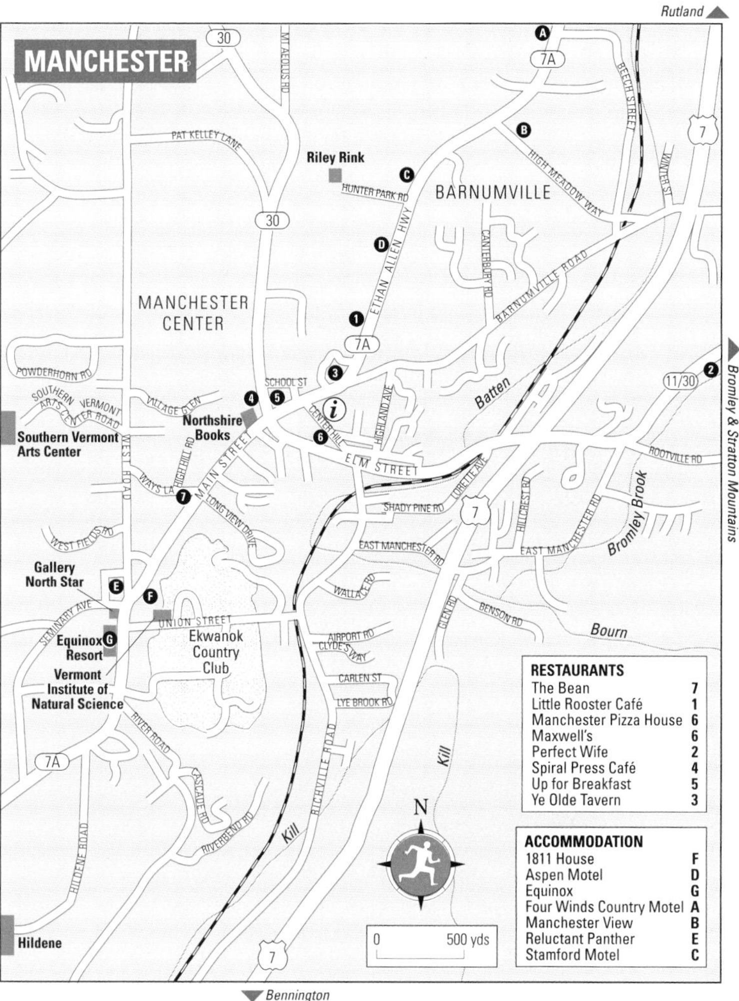

1811 House West Rd ⓣ802/362-1811 or 1-800/432–1811, ⓦwww.1811house.com. Thirteen immaculate Federal-period rooms, each with private bath, oriental rugs and antiques, await guests. Avail yourself of the private English pub with nearly a hundred single malt scotch whiskies, complementary sherry in the library, and full breakfast. One room at 6, the rest 8

Aspen Motel Rte-7A north of town ⓣ802/362-2450. Family-run motel that's been a fixture for years, with comfortable rooms, a pool, and a two-bedroom cottage available for larger groups. 5

Equinox Rte-7A ⓣ802/362-4700 or 1-800/362-4747, ⓦwww.equinoxresort.com. The swankiest digs in town, the sprawling *Equinox* is full of restored Victorian-era quarters, upscale amenities, and old-world New England charm. The spa is new, and there are hiking trails leading up the mountain. The *Charles Orvis Inn*, part of the complex, provides access to a billiards room, honor bar with cigars, and other luxuries, in the former home of Orvis himself. 9

Four Winds Country Motel 7379 Main St/Rte-7A ⓣ802/362-0905 or 1-877/456-7654, ⓦwww.fourwindscountrymotel.com. Ceramic-tiled baths and understated decor figure prominently at this simple country inn. Cable TV, microwaves, and front patio for every room. 4

Manchester View Rte-7A north of town ⓣ802/362-2739 or 1-800/548-4141, ⓦwww.manchesterview.com. Not much to look at from the road, the *View* has an unbeatable vista of the mountain in the morning. Each of the 35 relaxing, great-value rooms – including some spacious specialty rooms – comes with refrigerator and deck. Amenities include a heated pool, golf, and tennis. 5–6

Reluctant Panther Inn West Rd ⓣ802/362-2568 or 1-800/822-2331, ⓦwww.reluctantpanther.com. Modern furnishings line the splendid rooms here, with a full three-course Vermont breakfast included. Their excellent (and très expensive) gourmet restaurant is here too. 6

Stamford Motel Rte-7A ⓣ802/362-2342. Tastefully decorated budget motel, including a heated pool, with views from most rooms. 4

The Town

Route 7A heads right through the town center, known as **Manchester Village**; the first spot of interest is historic **Hildene** (tours June–Oct daily 9.30am–4.30pm, Nov–May Thurs–Mon 11am–3pm, grounds open daily 9.30am–5pm; $10 for tour ($4 youth), $5 for grounds only; ⓣ802/362-1788, ⓦwww.hildene.org), the 24-room Georgian Revival mansion belonging to longtime Manchester resident Robert Todd Lincoln, son of Abraham Lincoln and a prominent diplomat and businessman in his own right. It's a magnificent estate, set on more than four hundred acres, and made more intimate with many of the Lincoln family's personal effects, along with a working, gloriously resonant antique pipe organ. There are exhibits as well: in a new permanent one dedicated to President Abraham Lincoln, you can find one of his familiar black stovepipe hats – one of only three still in existence – along with presidential portraits, and other artifacts, and another gallery on changing locally flavored or political topics. More Vermont residents are celebrated at the **Gallery North Star**, Rte-7A a block north of the *Equinox* (Tues–Sun 11am–5pm, Mon 11am–3pm; ⓣ802/362-4541), which shows paintings, sculptures, and limited-edition prints of local artists. So, too, does the somewhat larger but less Vermont artist-centric **Southern Vermont Arts Center**, Rte-7A (Tues–Sat 10am–5pm, Sun noon–5pm; $6; ⓣ802/362-1405, ⓦwww.svac.org) on West Road, the oldest cultural institution in the state, which grew out of an association amongst local painters from nearby Dorset in 1929.

Farther up Rte-7A is **Manchester Center**, where **Northshire Bookstore** (ⓣ802/362-2200) ranks as one of the finest independent bookstores in New England. The flagship **Orvis Store**, a little farther north on Rte-7A (ⓣ802/362-3750), was opened in 2002, and doubles as a shrine to the company's locally born founder. As well as the extravagantly expensive fly-fishing rods, there's a trout-filled pond for casting demonstrations and beautiful handcrafted hunting rifles, yours for $10,000 and up. Go half a mile back down Rte-7A to the **Orvis Factory Outlet**, opposite the *Equinox* at 74 Union St (ⓣ802/362-6455), to pick up last year's models for around fifty percent less. Bargains are harder to find at the other designer **discount outlets** like Coach, Movado, and Baccarat, which are scattered around town (and best visited early or late in the day, to avoid the masses).

On a less commercialized note, the **Vermont Institute of Natural Science**, 109 Union St (ⓣ802/362-4374), offers natural history walks around the region, and maintains the trails in the **Equinox Preserve**, an 850-acre sprawl of land on the eastern side of Mount Equinox. **Riley Rink** at **Hunter Park**, on Rte-7A (ⓣ802/362-0150), functions as an Olympic-sized ice rink during winter and a performing arts center in summer; throughout July and August, the Vermont Symphony Orchestra (ⓣ802/864-5741 or 1-800/VSO-9293) also plays here.

Bromley and Stratton

The two **ski resorts** within striking distance of Manchester, both a short drive into the Green Mountains, offer quite different winter vacation experiences. The **Bromley Mountain Resort**, six miles east of Manchester on Rte-11 (one-day lift tickets $49 midweek, $57 weekend; ⓣ802/824-5522, ⓦwww.bromley.com), is the archetypal family resort – though whatever your level or age, you may want to avoid Bromley on Thursday afternoons, when Manchester's schoolchildren have time off to learn how to ski on many of the resort's 43 trails.

Larger and slightly higher than Bromley, the **Stratton Mountain Resort** (one-day lift tickets $59 midweek, $72 Sat or Sun; ⓣ802/297-4000 or 1-800/STRATTON, ⓦwww.stratton.com) ranks right up there with Killington and Stowe as one of Vermont's premier ski destinations. Although it's certainly a better choice for serious skiers than Bromley, you should also be aware that this far south you may be sliding on artificial snow the majority of the time. There is also good **cross-country skiing** on the twenty-plus miles of trails at the Stratton Nordic Center, some of the routes weaving through secluded forests and others cutting across open countryside.

In the summer, Bromley gets fairly raucous – it's transformed into an over-the-top family center called the **Thrill Zone**, complete with Alpine Slide, climbing wall, zipline, and go-carts (all-day package $49, half-day midweek and combo passes available; call for hours ⓣ802/824-5522). Over at Stratton, things are a bit more refined, with a focus on tennis and golf packages.

Eating, drinking, and entertainment

As with the town's accommodation, the **places to eat** in Manchester tend to be upscale and pricey – albeit rather good. The summer brings a variety of events to Hildene, including Shakespeare and craft fairs, and the **Manchester Music Festival** (ⓣ802/362-1956), a series of Thursday concerts, to the Southern Vermont Arts Center. In winter, the mountains often host events like the US Snowboarding Championships at Stratton, and Manchester's Winter Carnival is held every February.

The Bean 4201 Main St ⓣ802/362-0110. Decent and filling Mexican meals. Vegetarian-friendly.

The Little Rooster Café Rte-7A ⓣ802/362-3496. A small, chef-owned European-style café, serving omelets, waffles, baguettes, and cappuccinos for breakfast and lunch. Cash only.

Manchester Pizza House Rte-11/30 in Manchester Shopping Center ⓣ802/362-3338. It's plain as

Route 7: north to Rutland

Shortly after the end of Rte-7A, US-7 opens up into the "Valley of Vermont," between the Green and Taconic mountain ranges, making for a lovely drive. However, there are few convenient stopping places and a four-lane highway doesn't encourage a leisurely pace.

If you're looking to make the most of the scenery, you can **camp** at the **Emerald Lake State Park**, about nine miles north of Manchester on US-7 (mid-May to mid-Oct; ⓣ802/362-1655). It offers 105 campsites ($16), 36 lean-tos ($23), and easy access to the Long Trail, all on 430 acres that sit alongside Dorset Mountain. Unfortunately, the traffic noise from US-7 intrudes upon the tranquility. The 84-acre **Lake Shaftsbury State Park**, two miles south of Arlington on Rte-7A, has a furnished lakeside cottage available for $560 per week (mid-May to early Sept; reservations at ⓣ1-888/409-7579), which sleeps six, and has a full kitchen, too.

can be, but the pizza's good. All the usual toppings, plus calzone and pastas.

Maxwell's Flat Road Pub Rte-11/30 in Manchester Shopping Center ⓣ802/362-3721. Oldest tavern in town, with burgers and salads and pub grub. Live entertainment Wednesday and Friday, with karaoke on Saturday nights.

The Perfect Wife Rte-11/30 ⓣ802/362-2817. Cool creative fare (Peking duck with mandarin pancakes starter, pork with apricot-rum butter) on the expensive side, with a more traditional menu in the tavern room for the budget conscious.

Spiral Press Café 15 Bonnet St ⓣ802/362-9944. Your destination for the best in caffeinated drinks, alongside some muffins, bagels and sandwich specials. It's connected to Northshire Books (see p.408).

Up for Breakfast 4935 Main St ⓣ802/362-4204. If you crave interesting omelets, French toast, or blueberry pancakes, this is the obvious choice. Fun and friendly, with decent portions. Closes at noon weekdays, 1pm on weekends.

Ye Olde Tavern 5183 Main St ⓣ802/362-0611. The 1791 building is romantic and candle-lit, and the perfect place for American favorites ($15–25). Very extensive wine list.

Central Vermont

While **central Vermont**'s eastern edge is made up mainly of residences and small farms, the rest is a region of great diversity, home to a refined college town, **Middlebury**, picturesque small burgs like cultured but unstuffy **Woodstock** and sleepy **White River Junction**, and the tiny but appealing state capital, **Montpelier**. Two notable ski resorts are also here: rowdy **Killington**, the state's most popular, and **Stowe**, a highly regarded vacation spot with a long history both as a center of cross-country skiing and as the home of the Von Trapp family familiar from *The Sound of Music*. Central Vermont also holds the most visited attraction in the state: the **Ben and Jerry's Ice Cream Factory**, perhaps the purest embodiment ofVermont activism and "green" thinking, puts **Waterbury** on the map. All this stands in contrast to the greeting many travelers get upon their arrival in central Vermont: the gray of the major highways that intersect in lackluster **Rutland**.

Rutland and around

When Vermonters describe **RUTLAND**, halfway between Bennington and Burlington along US-7, as "a little bit of New Hampshire in Vermont," it is not meant as a compliment. Rather, the indictment is of a bland town dominated by a steady, though modest, industrial base and afflicted by a burgeoning strip-mall aesthetic. One of the few areas in the state where you can find actual "'traffic'", it is the state's second largest city after Burlington, with a population of about thirty thousand, most of whom are blue-collar laborers. Rutland's history as a marble-manufacturing center is still evident in its extensive use in the construction or embellishment of its downtown buildings. You may very well pass through, as Rutland is a key travel hub, and passing through is about all you'd need – or want – to do here.

Outside of town lies the most worthwhile **Norman Rockwell Museum**, east along US-4 (daily 8am–4pm; $4.50; ⓣ802/773-6095), which displays more than two thousand reproductions of Rockwell paintings, including early material and all of his *Saturday Evening Post* covers. It's a well-contextualized retrospective of his work, which is at times irritatingly wholesome but nevertheless an important contribution to American graphic art. The importance of marble to the development of the state is significant, but the **Vermont Marble Exhibit**, 62 Main St (daily: mid-May to Oct 9am–5.30pm; $7; ⓣ802/459-2300 or 1-800/427-1396), in the town of **PROCTOR**, northeast of Rutland, is mostly a treasure trove of kitsch. The "Hall of Presidents" features inexpertly carved marble busts of 41 chief execs; a vast warehouse is filled with marble kitchen and bathroom fixtures; and an exhibit titled "$CaCO_3$ – Mineral of Life!" helpfully demonstrates that calcium carbonate, one of the main compounds in marble and other stones, is used in other forms as a food additive – and displays some cereal boxes to prove it. A hilariously self-serious 1950s-documentary-style film on the history of Vermont marble, and an explanation of the extraction process, add a bit of education to the mix. If you're set on going, look for the free coupon for the site sometimes available at travel information centers. A short drive southwest from Proctor, on West Proctor Road, the **Wilson Castle** (daily: late May–Oct 9am–6pm; $8.50) is an intriguing relic of an aristocrat's past glory. The castle was built in 1867 by Dr John Johnson, who had married into English nobility and decided to take advantage of his wife's fortune by constructing a castle in a "blend of European styles." He spared no expense, recruiting the best craftsmen and materials from across Europe to fashion elements such as stained-glass ceilings. The Wilson family still owns it and has added to the already oversized manor. One of the strangest rooms that the Wilsons completed is the "art gallery," constructed before they realized that they had no *art*. Now it contains a small collection of works by local artists and designers. Upstairs in the bedrooms, the paint is peeling a bit, adding strangely to the air of faded grandeur.

Practicalities

Amtrak **trains** call in at the station in the Rutland Plaza, Merchant's Row; the bus terminal is in the center of town at 102 West St (ⓣ802/773-2774). Local **bus** company Marble Valley Regional Transit runs The Bus ($2; ⓣ802/773-3244), which can get you to Killington, if you want to base yourself here for ski season. They also run the free Rte-7 South Commuter Connection down to Manchester. The **Rutland Region Chamber of Commerce**, 256 N Main St (ⓣ802/773-2747 or 1-800/756-8880, ⓦwww.rutlandvermont.com), open year-round, is your best bet for information.

Aside from the standard hotel and motel chains, most of Rutland's **places to stay** are nondescript, independent motels, but they're generally cheap, clean, and close to major highways. Among the almost indistinguishable accommodations that line US-7 are the *Cold River Motel* (ⓣ802/747-6922; ❷), the *Red Roof Inn* (ⓣ1-800/733-7663 or 802/775-4303; ❸), and the *Roadway Inn* (ⓣ802/775-2575; ❸). *Iröquois Land* (May to mid-Oct; $20; ⓣ802/773-2832), three miles south of Rutland in Clarendon, is an adequate **campground**, though it tends to be dominated by the RV crowd.

Should you be waiting for a bus or train, there are, surprisingly, a couple of good **places to eat** interspersed among the fast-food joints, like *Three Tomatoes Trattoria*, 88 Merchant's Row (ⓣ802/747-7747), which has light, modern Italian dishes in a sleek setting. The *Coffee Exchange*, Merchant's Row at Center Street (ⓣ802/775-3337), is fine for a light snack and a beverage, with the added advantage of being near enough to the bus station to be able to see your bus arriving. *Jilly's Sports Bar*, 24 Merchant's Row (ⓣ802/775-6919), and *KD's Pub*, 31 Center St (ⓣ802/247-6868), are occasionally raucous **bar** and dance venues, featuring **live music**. For the pool-and-darts crowd, try *Magoo's*, 52 Strongs Ave (ⓣ802/773-9839) and hang with the locals.

Mount Independence

From Rutland, a forty-minute drive (US-7 to Rte 73) will bring you to this historic site outside **Orwell** on the very southeastern tip of Lake Champlain. **Mount Independence** was the scene of a major American defeat in the Revolutionary War. The fort was built in 1776, along with the more famous Fort Ticonderoga on the opposite shore, to repel a British attack from Canada. The two forts initially provided such an intimidating sight that British general Guy Carleton aborted his invasion in October 1776. However, the following winter was brutal, and most of the troops deserted, leaving 2500 American soldiers behind to fall ill or freeze to death. Springtime reinforcements were insufficient to withstand an attack from General Burgoyne, and the fort was abandoned on July 5, 1777. The British occupied the Mount until November of the same year, when they burned the fort in response to General Burgoyne's surrender across the water at Saratoga. Today, the **Mount Independence State Historic Site** (daily: late May to mid-Oct 9.30am–5pm; $5; ⓣ802/948-2000) is a pleasingly low-key affair, just a small museum with a few artifacts and some documentation of that dreadful winter, plus four hiking trails around the Mount, with a few spots marking relics of the fort (mostly piles of rocks that had been foundation). It's a relaxing place, with relatively few visitors and nice views of the lake by which to enjoy the solitude.

Middlebury

One of the most endowed (and expensive) colleges in the US and one of the prettiest and most diverse villages in the state is a 32-mile shot up US-7 from Rutland. In 1800, a small group of local citizens banded together to form a "town's college," primarily to train young men for the ministry. Middlebury College thrives today in the center of **MIDDLEBURY**, named for its central location between Salisbury and New Haven, two Vermont towns whose prominence has receded in the past two centuries. All roads converge at the **Middlebury Town Green**, an idyllic place with a pretty and ornate white **Congregational church** at its northern end, not to be confused with the more somber gray church on the green itself. Middlebury's small downtown has a fairly hip collection of shops, with a few bookstores, a record shop, and the **Vermont Craft Center at Frog Hollow**, 1 Mill St (ⓣ802/388-3177, ⓦwww.froghollow.org), a bright space showcasing high-quality crafts from all over the state. The **Henry Sheldon Museum of Vermont History**, 1 Park St (Mon–Sat 10am–5pm; $5; ⓣ802/388-2117), is an endearingly quirky collection of tools, household objects, and "one-of-a-kind oddities," such as the alleged remains of the "Petrified Indian Boy," actually a mid-nineteenth-century hoax bought into by, among others, the collector who established this museum.

Catch Rte-125 west to the **Middlebury College Museum of Art**, off Rte-30 (Tues–Fri 10am–5pm, Sat–Sun noon–5pm; free; ⓣ802/443-5007), for a look at the small permanent collection of nineteenth-century European and American sculpture and modern prints; the campus spreads out around it, with no other individually compelling sights, though it makes for a nice wander.

Farther down Rte-125, turn north on Rte-23 for the **UVM Morgan Horse Farm** (daily: May–Oct 9am–4pm; ⓣ802/388-2011) where you can tour the stables and admire the beautiful, world-famous descendants of Justin Morgan's stallion, the first native breed in North America.

Practicalities

The village green boasts two lovely **inns**, with others scattered along the way. Open since 1827, the *Middlebury Inn* (ⓣ802/388-4961 or 1-800/842-4666, ⓦwww.middleburyinn.com; ⑤), with 75 rooms, a porch with rocking chairs, an operational 1926 elevator, and a good restaurant, is possibly the pick of the two, while the aptly named *Inn on the Green* (ⓣ802/388-7512 or 1-888/244-7512, ⓦwww.innonthegreen.com; ⑤) has eleven rooms in a light blue Federal-style landmark building, with continental breakfast in bed included. Television junkies will want to make sure they check out the *Waybury Inn* (ⓣ802/388-4015 or 1-800/348-1810, ⓦwww.wayburyinn.com; ⑤), whose exterior was used on the TV show *Newhart*. The relationship with the show ends there, but there are fourteen comfortable, well-kept rooms inside the 1810 inn. There are a couple of **motels** two or three miles south of town along Rte-7; of these, the *Greystone Motel* (ⓣ802/388-4935; ④) and the *Blue Spruce Motel* (ⓣ802/388-4091 or 1-800/640-7671; ③) are clean and comfortable places to spend the night.

The **restaurant** scene in Middlebury is pretty good for a town of this size, owing largely to its collegiate associations; students, and their visiting parents, like variety. If you're in the mood for a hearty meal, check out the *Open Book Café* at the *Middlebury Inn*, where $17 buys you an entree of grilled chicken with blackberry relish and lemon beurre blanc, or most any item on the menu. The ostentatious *Fire and Ice*, 26 Seymour St (ⓣ802/388-7166), is a cavernous steak and seafood restaurant, with a massive salad bar and enough memorabilia to fill a museum, the centerpiece of which is a 22-foot motorboat from the Twenties. *Tully & Marie's*, 5 Bakery Lane (ⓣ802/388-4182), is more of a chic urban bistro, with sleek interior and views of Otter Creek. Also privy to views of the creek, *The Taste of India*, 1 Bakery Lane (ⓣ802/388-4856), has plenty of curry and rice dishes for a very reasonable $10 or so. Another ethnic eatery worth considering, if only for the slightly surreal experience of eating tacos in a dining room covered with frescoes of marlins and idyllic beaches whilst looking out on a Vermont village green, is the *Amigos Cantina*, 22 Merchant's Row (ⓣ802/388-3624). *The Dog Team Tavern*, Dog Team Road, off Rte-7 two miles north of town in New Haven (ⓣ802/388-7651), lets you have a proper Vermont feast, with local produce and specialties like maple oatmeal pie. Less expensive are *Rosie's*, south on Rte-7 (ⓣ802/388-7052), for hearty diner-style fare; *Green Peppers* at Shaw's Plaza (ⓣ802/388-3164), for the best pizza in town; and the *Blue Hen Deli*, 54 College St (ⓣ802/388-6408), with sandwich makings as well as wood-fired pizzas and the like.

Information on other Middlebury lodgings and activities can be found through the Addison County's visitor website (ⓦwww.midvermont.com), or by stopping by their offices at 2 Court St (ⓣ802/388-7951 or 1-800/SEE-VERMONT).

West on Hwy-125: Robert Frost country

Robert Frost spent 23 summers in Vermont on land that has since been overrun by Hwy-125 (also called the Robert Frost Memorial Highway), which cuts right across the Green Mountains from Rte-7 in East Middlebury to Hancock. The small cabin where he stayed, now a National Historic Landmark and owned by Middlebury College, stands a few miles down a dirt road from the **Robert Frost Wayside**, a small, peaceful picnic area right by the quiet two-lane highway (5.8 miles east of intersection with Rte-7). Across the street from the Wayside is the **Robert Frost Interpretative Trail**, a mile-long loop trail punctuated by placards quoting poems and excerpts of his work. Although it may not sound like much, it is actually quite evocative – an affecting environment in which to read his deceptively simple, old-fashioned works.

A few miles west along Hwy-125 is the small campus of **Bread Loaf**, the highly regarded summer writers' conference initiated at Frost's suggestion while he was a professor at Middlebury College. Though there's nothing much to see, just a few sturdily constructed beige wooden buildings, budding writers may want to stroll here and commune with the spirits of the notables, such as Frost, Willa Cather, and John Gardner, who have taught or studied here.

Killington

Twelve miles east of Rutland off US-4, Killington Resort has grown out of nothing since 1958 to become the most popular ski resort in the state. Killington's permanent population is roughly one thousand, but it's estimated that in season there are enough beds within twenty miles to accommodate some ten thousand people each and every night.

Arrival and information

You'll find the **Killington Chamber of Commerce** (Ⓣ802/773-4181 or 1-800/337-1928, Ⓦwww.killingtonchamber.com) easily enough on US-4 if you're driving east from Rutland. Your best bet via public transport during ski season is to travel on Amtrak to Rutland and take the Amtrak Connector to Killington, which meets trains upon arrival in the station ($10, call in advance for pick-up for weekday departures from Killington; Ⓣ802/773-3244).

Accommodation

You're spoiled for choice in terms of **accommodation** around these parts, though you may wind up paying a pretty penny, especially during prime skiing season. *Wise Vacations*, 405 Killington Access Rd (Ⓣ802/773-4202 or 1-800/639-4680, Ⓦwww.wisevacations.com), rents private homes and condos in and about Killington; prices vary, but they are only a bit higher than the average inn or B&B.

Cedarbrook Motor Inn US-4, near junction with Hwy-100 Ⓣ802/422-9666 or 1-800/446-1088. Good-value option outside the main ski area. ③

Cortina Inn 103 US-4 Ⓣ802/773-3333 or 1-800/451-6108, Ⓦwww.cortinainn.com. An excellent luxury inn, if not as close to the ski area as some. ⑥

Happy Bear Motel 1784 Killington Rd Ⓣ802/422-3305 or 1-800/518-4468. Very convenient though basic digs, with refrigerators and cable TV. "Cubs" (under 12) stay for free. ③

Inn at Long Trail Sherburne Pass Ⓣ802/775-7181 or 1-800/325-2540, Ⓦwww.innatlongtrail.com. After several nights spent in primitive shelters with no electricity or running water, hikers on the Long Trail will appreciate the comfort of this family-run B&B with tree-trunk beams and a stone fireplace. ④

Inn of the Six Mountains 2617 Killington Access Rd Ⓣ802/422-4302 or 1-800/228-4676, Ⓦwww.sixmountains.com. The name 'inn' is deceiving, as *Six Mountains* has almost 100 well-appointed quarters, with a spa, tennis court, and fitness and game rooms. Seasonal shuttle to Killington skiing. ⑥

Mountain Meadows Lodge 285 Thundering Brook Rd Ⓣ802/775-1010 or 1-800/370-4567,

Ⓦwww.mtmeadowslodge.com. To the side of Killington Access Road off US-4, about five minutes from Killington, you'll find an unspoiled lakeside farm set on the Appalachian Trail; it also has an above-average restaurant. ❺

Summit Lodge & Resort Killington Rd Ⓣ802/422-3535 or 1-800/635-6343, Ⓦwww.summitlodgevermont.com. Long-standing area favorite, with a casual lodge feel, enhanced by the owners' two friendly St Bernards guarding the lobby. Also runs coach tours to nearby attractions. ❹–❻

Val Roc Motel US-4, near junction with Hwy-100 Ⓣ802/422-3881 or 1-800/238-8762. Cheap spot, and quiet too. ❸

Skiing and other outdoor recreation

Sometimes called the "Beast of the East," on account of its size – its two hundred trails sprawl over seven mountains – and its notoriously rowdy nightlife, **Killington Resort** (Ⓣ802/422-6200 or 1-800/621-6867, Ⓦwww.killington.com) sports a freewheeling and wild attitude that can be fun. Indeed, Killington is often considered to be the eastern equivalent of Vail in the west, and the resort does provide the longest ski and snowboarding season in the eastern US. Lift tickets cost $67 per day or $1300 per season, with decent discounts for multi-day packages, early purchases, and purchases via the internet. A less boisterous option is nearby **Pico Mountain**, along US-4 (Ⓣ802/422-6200, Ⓦwww.picomountain.com), which is officially a part of Killington but much tamer and smaller in style and scale. Its 48 trails are best for skiers of mid-range ability, and there's not as much hotdogging as you'll find on the other peaks. Lift tickets are usually about $20 less per day than Killington; a season pass costs $399. (Killington lift tickets are also valid here.)

Like many other New England mountains, the area has opened itself up to **mountain-biking** and other sorts of antics in summer. Killington and Pico each have an Adventure Center, with a combination of climbing wall, and

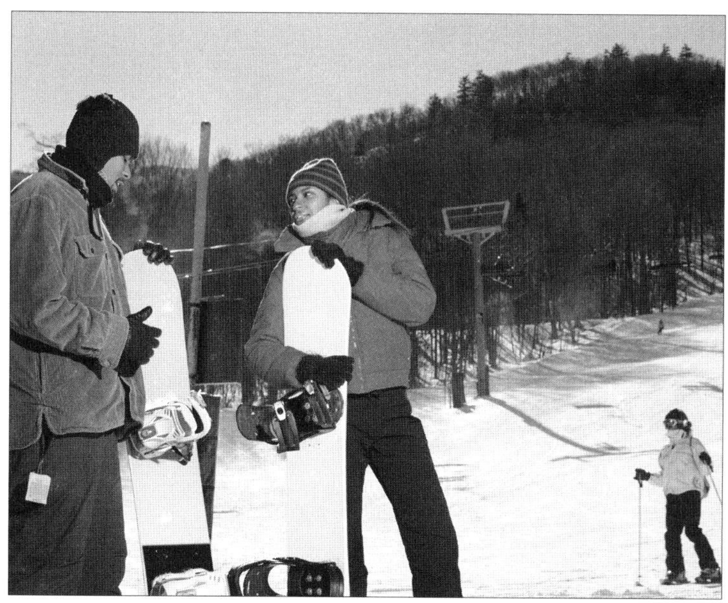

△ Snowboarding at Killington

alpine and water slides, with a skate park, mini-golf, and a "bungee thing" (weekends 10am–5pm, July to mid-Oct, call for schedule); you can buy single tickets, or an all-day pass for $30. Mountain-bikers at Killington can ride the Snowdon Single Track or Toughy Boy trails among 45 miles of other trails, all day for $8, but it's probably easier on the legs to opt for a half-day ($27) or full day ($32) of lift rides and trail access. Rentals are $45 a day.

The Long and Appalachian trails meet just north of here, so **hikers** can take the K-1 Gondola ($8 one-way, $13 round-trip) to the summit of Killington and hike down. Pick up trail maps and info beforehand at the Bike Shop at K-1 Lodge (☎802/422-6232).

Eating

There is a large variety of **dining** establishments – though many try to be ambitious, the greater number aim for simple satisfaction, and almost everything is to be found on Killington Road. Look to restaurants attached to inns or hotels for finer fare.

Birch Ridge Inn Killington Rd at Butler Rd ☎802/422-4293. The selections are frou-frou (risotto with duck confit, roasted apple and onion soup) and every bit as tasty. The Vermont maple crème brulee dessert is outstanding.

Casey's Caboose Killington Rd ☎802/422-3795. This favorite train-themed family restaurant offers free chicken wings at its daily happy hour.

The Garlic 1724 Killington Rd ☎802/422-5055. A not-very-Spanish version of tapas awaits in the Olive Bar, and in the restaurant, ravioli, chicken, and seafood are liberally spiked with the namesake seasoning.

Hemingway's US-4 ☎802/422-3886. You'll be served by a professional staff at one of Vermont's finest restaurants, with impeccable surroundings and presentation. The expensive and excellent nouvelle cuisine includes vegetarian-friendly options.

Panache at the *Woods Resort*, Killington Rd ☎802/422-8622. Grill fare with a spicy, modern twist. Adventurous offerings on the meaty menu include emu, wild boar, and yak.

Pizza Jerks 1307 Killington Rd ☎802/422-4111. Choose your camp: Tree Hugger (all veggie) or Carcass (all meat). You can have your "New York-style" pizza (or grinders, or calzone) with the local brew or wine at this ultra-casual stop.

Sushi Yoshi 1915 Killington Rd ☎802/422-4241. Chinese staples and Japanese sushi rolls - all affordable. Hibachi meals ($20+), too, for those looking for something a bit out of the ordinary.

Zola's Grille at the Cortina Inn, US-4 ☎802/773-3333. Fine diners enjoy veal roulade or grilled lamb chops in the snug and romantic dining room.

Drinking and entertainment

Killington does tend to attract a bit of a wild bunch, and accordingly, **drinking** is the most prevalent form of entertainment. A few places manage to scare up some live music or give crowds a place to dance.

McGrath's Irish Pub 709 US-4, at *Inn at Long Trail* ☎802/775-7181. Warm, inviting hangout, with traditional music on the weekends, and a tavern menu of American and Irish standards. Rumor has it they sell the most Guinness in the state.

Moguls Saloon Killington Rd ☎802/422-4777. Basic bar with cheap drafts and liquor and a large-screen TV.

Pickle Barrel Killington Rd ☎802/422-3035. A rowdy bar and a dance scene that gets crazy on winter weekends.

Skybox Grille in the Mountain Green Complex at the top of Killington Rd ☎802/422-7492. Sports-themed hangout, with 24 big-screen satellite TVs to park yourself in front of, with a draft, of course.

Wobbly Barn Steakhouse 2229 Killington Rd ☎802/422-6171. Some sort of lively entertainment every weekend, but a draw since 1963 is the beef and prime rib (broiled, mesquite-grilled and barbecued). Come for Wild Game Night on Tuesdays (elk, venison, buffalo) or Lynchburg Southern Barbecue Sundays for a bit of out-of-New-England amusement. Closed summer.

Woodstock and around

Since its settlement in the 1760s, **WOODSTOCK**, a few miles west of the Connecticut River on US-4, has been considered a bit more refined than its rural neighbors. In keeping with its reputation, the town has only submitted to the most cultured elements of the modern tourist industry. The artistic vibe here takes root from the town's status as the home of a few minor artists and writers, such as sculptor Hiram Powers, novelist Sinclair Lewis, and painter Paul Cadmus. Adding to its appeal are the distinguished houses that surround its oval green, most of which have been taken over by antiques stores and tearooms, and the art galleries and upscale eateries populating its tiny downtown area. However, it should most certainly not be confused with the Woodstock of festival fame, which is in New York. This Woodstock draws the well-heeled looking for a civilized getaway, and the closest it came to radical action during the Sixties was to build a new covered bridge, though it does have a Civil War-era history as a stop on the Underground Railroad, ushering southern slaves into the northernmost reaches of the Union.

Information

The **Woodstock Area Chamber of Commerce**, 18 Central St (ⓣ802/457-3555 or 1-888/4WOODSTOCK, ⓦwww.woodstockvt.com), has tons of visitor information, and also operates an information booth on the town green (June–Oct 9am–5pm; ⓣ802/457-1042).

Accommodation

Places to stay in Woodstock's center are plentiful and luxurious, but expensive. Sites farther from town get less expensive; there are relatively cheap cookie-cutter motor lodges along US-4 east of town. The information booth on the green can organize accommodation in private houses ("overflow homes") during very busy periods such as fall foliage.

1830 Shire Town Inn 31 South St, Rte-106 ⓣ802/457-1830 or 1-866/286-1830, ⓦwww.1830shiretowninn.com. In downtown Woodstock, this tiny (three distinct rooms), restored 1830 farmhouse offers mammoth beds, clawfoot tubs, and good breakfasts, across the street from Vail Field. ❺

Applebutter Inn US-4 in Taftsville ⓣ802/457-4158, ⓦwww.bbonline.com/vt/applebutterinn. Cozy B&B with comfortable beds, personable proprietors, and breakfasts featuring homemade granola. Four miles east of town. ❺

Ardmore Inn 23 Pleasant St ⓣ802/457-3887, ⓦwww.ardmoreinn.com. Charming Victorian/Greek Revival home with five airy, stylish rooms close to town. Daily breakfasts are huge and varied, and the friendly hosts provide guests with a treat or two to take home. ❻

Braeside Motel US-4 ⓣ802/457-1366, ⓦwww.braesidemotel.com. Not quite a mile east of the village, you'll find clean and basic family-owned motel digs with very few extra amenities, save for a swimming pool. ❹

Kedron Valley Inn Rte-106, South Woodstock ⓣ802/457-1473. A private lake and nearby stables, homemade quilts, fireplaces and Jacuzzis are extras at this ultra-comfortable spot with twenty-odd country-style rooms. ❻

Shire Riverview 46 Pleasant St ⓣ802/457-2211, ⓦwww.shiremotel.com. A good mid-range option on the eastern edge of town. Some rooms overlook the Ottauquechee River. ❹

Village Inn of Woodstock 41 Pleasant St ⓣ802/457-1255 or 1-800/722-4571, ⓦwww.villageinnofwoodstock.com. Quaint B&B, renovated in the Victorian style, with an inviting front porch and attractive gardens. The tavern room, for guests only, offers cocktails, beer, or espresso at the bar. ❺

Woodstock Inn and Resort 14 The Green ⓣ802/457-1100 or 1-800/448-7900, ⓦwww.woodstockinn.com. The largest, fanciest, and best around, with sumptuous rooms, beautiful grounds, an eighteen-hole golf course, and four gourmet restaurants. It's also got a winter sports facility, and a health and fitness center with a spa for the ultimate in pampering. ❽

The Town

Woodstock's center is an oval green at the convergence of Elm, Central, and Church streets, which are lined with architecturally diverse houses – New England clapboard is not nearly as prevalent here – that provide a genteel foreground to the landscape of rolling hills. The **Woodstock Historical Society**, 26 Elm St (May–Oct Mon–Sat 10am–4pm, Sun 12–4pm; $5; ⓣ802/457-1822, ⓦwww.woodstockhistsoc.org), is one of the best museums of its kind, with well-organized multimedia displays including tape recordings of older residents' reminiscences and an admirably complete town archive. Next door to the multimedia center, and included in the admission, is a slightly musty old house with a varied collection of artifacts. Don't miss the assemblage of children's toys and dolls, and the elegant drawing room with an antique harpsichord and gilt mirror from the 1790s. Another historical landmark, at 16 Elm Street, is **F.H. Gillingham's**, a country store where residents have bought their groceries since 1886. Among the wealth of national brands are locally produced items, like the yogurt and mozzarella from **Woodstock Water Buffalo**, off Rte-106 S (ⓣ802/457-4540, ⓦwww.woodstockwaterbuffalo.com), the only US farmstead creamery to use the milk from these animals, which are usually only found in South America, India, and Southeast Asia. They don't give tours, but the water buffalo enjoy meeting new people (hours are generally Mon–Fri 10am–2pm, but call for production schedule).

Also near the green are the town's many galleries, the most notable of which are **Woodstock Folk Art Prints and Antiquities**, 6 Elm St (ⓣ802/457-2012), which displays provocative local folk-art prints, and the **Steven Huneck Gallery**, 49 Central St (ⓣ802/457-3206), full of amusing, idiosyncratic sculptures and wood-block prints, mostly based on the artist's three very expressive dogs.

Three of the town's attractions located a little farther afield are devoted to the appreciation of forest and fauna, but two are still within walking distance. The museum section of **Billings Farm and Museum**, off Rte-12 north of town (May–Oct daily 10am–5pm; weekends late Nov–Dec 10am–4pm; $9.50; ⓣ802/457-2355), puts on demonstrations of antiquated skills, while the grounds are run as a modern dairy farm where you can pet cows and churn a bit of butter, if you're so inclined. Be sure not to miss the Academy Award-nominated documentary, *A Place in the Land*, which introduces the major players in the farm's – and the surrounding countryside's – history. Across the street from the Billings Farm, the **Marsh-Billings-Rockefeller National Historical Park** (daily: late May–Oct 10am–5pm; house and garden tours $6; ⓣ802/457-3368, ⓦwww.nps.gov/mabi) was originally the home of George Perkins Marsh, whose 1864 book *Man and Nature* is a seminal work of ecological thought, inspired by the author's distress at the deforestation of his native Vermont. The house was purchased in 1869 by Frederick Billings, who decided to put those principles into action on the property and the surrounding land, which he quickly snatched up. Billings, greatly influenced by Marsh's image of responsible farming and sustainable forestry, reseeded and replanted to bring back the carpet of greenery undone by logging during the early nineteenth century. Conservationist and philanthropist Laurence Rockefeller, who married Billings' daughter, Mary, took the ethos a step further by combining the ideals of preservation with the benefits of public access and enjoyment. The 553 acres of forest contain a network of carriage roads and **hiking trails**, some leading to splendid vistas with Mount Tom in the distance. The Woodstock Ski Touring Center grooms the carriage roads in winter for snowshoeing and cross-country skiing, and can provide you with passes and additional details (☎802/457-6674). Park rangers also periodically host similar events (contact the website or visitors center for information).

Perhaps the most visited attraction is **Sugarbush Farm**, 591 Sugarbush Farm Rd (Mon–Fri 8am–5pm, Sat & Sun 9am–5pm; ☎802/457-1757 or 1-800/281-1757), which somewhat dubiously claims to produce more "authentic" cheddar and maple syrup than other Vermont farms.

Eating and drinking

Woodstock's **restaurants**, expensive and undeniably good, cater for an upscale crowd. Many have somewhat cheaper tavern menus available for bar or outside dining. In any case, it's best to make reservations ahead of time. Restaurants attached to inns and B&Bs tend to be a little less expensive.

Bentley's 3 Elm St ☎802/457-3232. Upmarket versions of traditional bistro food (tequila and lime chicken, duck quesadillas, garlic and Guinness mussels, and the like) and a good range of microbrews. Casual and moderately priced.

East Ender US-4, a mile east of the village green ☎802/457-9800. Good for hearty breakfasts, and also evening dining on the wraparound porch.

Jackson House Inn and Restaurant US-4, 1.5 miles west of the village green ☎802/457-2065. Very upscale New American cuisine. Try to get a table with a view of the lovely four-acre garden. Extensive wine list and knowledgeable sommelier.

Kedron Valley Inn Rte-106, South Woodstock ☎802/457-1473. Eating in the tavern or on the formal front porch is more fun – and less expensive – than in the dining room, but the food, often from local sources, is superb throughout; the juicy tender steaks and local vegetables are uniformly praised. Reservations recommended. Closed Tues & Wed Nov–July.

Mangowood US-4, three miles west of village green at the *Lincoln Inn* ☎802/457-3312. New American cuisine with Asian accents such as ginger, shaoxing wine, and green curry. Expensive.

Mountain Creamery 33 Central St ☎802/457-1715. Filling country breakfasts and lunch fare served daily, as well as some fine homemade ice cream.

Pane Salute 61 Central St ☎802/457-4882. Italian fine dining, with wood-fired pizza options.

The Prince and the Pauper 24 Elm St ☎802/457-1818. Expensive Continental cuisine – braised veal, filet mignon – in an incongruously casual dining room. There's less expensive bistro fare as well.

Woodstock Coffee & Tea 43 Central St ☎802/457-9268. Get your morning fuel-up and muffin at this laidback eco-friendly shop, and lounge at the plain wooden tables and chairs for as long as you like.

Quechee

Six miles east of Woodstock, **QUECHEE** (pronounced quee-chee) is a peculiar mixed bag. The **town** proper is a combination of quaint Vermont village and expensive housing development, where you'll find several upmarket restaurants and B&Bs. Just down US-4 is **Quechee Gorge**, Vermont's greatest natural wonder, and a great place to camp. Adjacent **Quechee Gorge Village** is a mire of cheap tourist kitsch, hard not to notice but very easy to skip.

Even if you're just passing through, be sure to stop and ogle Quechee Gorge, the so-called "Grand Canyon" of Vermont. A delicate bridge spans the 165-foot chasm of the Ottauquechee River and hiking trails lead down through forests to the base of the gorge, where its scale seems even more impressive. If you have more time, hit the town of Quechee, where a waterfall on the river turns the turbines of **Simon Pearce Glass** on Main Street (daily 9am–9pm; ☎802/295-2711). Housed in a former wool mill, this is an unusual combination of glass-blowing center and restaurant. You can watch bowls and pots being made and then eat off them, overlooking the waterfall and a covered bridge. After that, visit the Raptor Center at the **Vermont Institute of Natural Science**

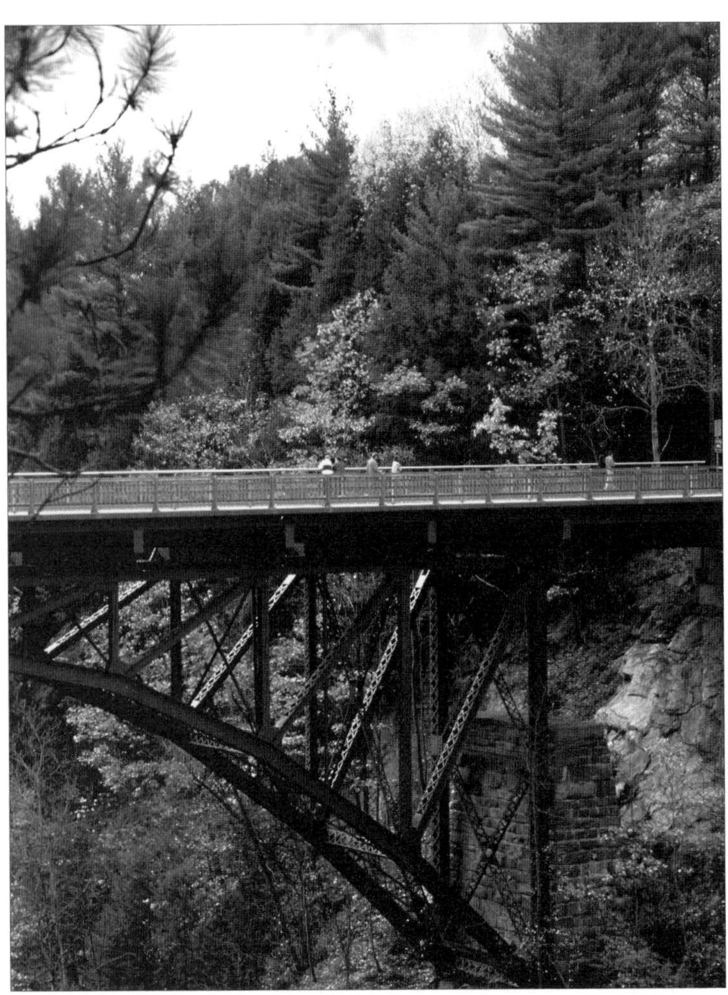

△ Quechee Gorge

on US-4 (May–Oct daily 10am–5pm; Nov–April Wed–Sun 10am–4pm; $8; ⓣ802/457-2779, ⓦwww.vinsweb.org). Tours reveal how it rescues and treats injured birds of prey. You can also view some of the recovering falcons, owls, and hawks (which are non-releasable to the wild due to injuries); some of these participate in thirty-minute programs (three times a day) where you can watch them in graceful, powerful action.

There is a good path for **biking**, known locally as the River Road, which starts in Main Street, Quechee Town, and leads west into Woodstock, following the Ottauquechee River and running parallel to US-4. Wilderness Trails, on Dewey's Mills Road next to the *Quechee Inn at Marshland Farm* (ⓣ802/295-7620), dispenses information on the challenging **hiking** and **cross-country skiing** trails behind Quechee Town, and also provides rentals (bikes $16/day, cross-country skis $13/day). For those more water-oriented, they also run river float trips ($35 kayak, $50 canoe), and offer a unique two-bike-plus-canoe rental package ($36).

Practicalities

If you're equipped to **camp**, the best place to stay is in the **Quechee Gorge State Park**, on Dewey Mills Road off US-4 (Ⓣ802/295-2990), which has 54 well-maintained sites ($14; no hook-ups) ensconced in a forest of fir trees. Foot trails lead to the gorge. The *Quality Inn*, on US-4 between the gorge and the village (Ⓣ802/295-7600 or 1-800/732-4376, Ⓦwww.qualityinnquechee.com; ❹), offers the area's least expensive accommodation. But if you're willing to shell out more, the town of Quechee has a few sumptuous **inns**. Just outside the town, the *Quechee Inn at Marshland Farm* on Quechee Main Street (Ⓣ802/295-3133 or 1-800/235-3133, Ⓦwww.quecheeinn.com; ❺). In addition to the inn's comfy 24 rooms with period furnishings and fabulous country setting, visitors can take advantage of its association with Wilderness Trails and the Vermont Fly-fishing School (Ⓣ802/295-7620). The *Parker House Inn*, located in a beautiful red-brick Victorian at 16 Main St (Ⓣ802/295-6077, Ⓦwww.theparkerhouseinn.com; ❻) has seven guestrooms and a restaurant cooking up sophisticated and diverse meals with local ingredients.

Most **restaurants** in the area are either chichi affairs or "family" establishments. The most notable exceptions are *Firestone's*, at Waterman Place along US-4 (Ⓣ802/295-1600), serving creative pasta dishes, flatbread pizzas, and traditional Vermont fare, such as game and fish and chips, which you can enjoy on their pleasant rooftop patio, and the *Quechee Village Deli*, 91 The Village Green (Ⓣ802/295-2786), which has tasty soups and sandwiches. The restaurant at *Simon Pearce Glass*, Main Street (Ⓣ802/295-1470), serves inventive New American-type entrees starting at around $20, as well as occasional no-nonsense Irish dishes such as beef and Guinness stew and shepherd's pie. If there's anything authentic at Quechee Gorge Village, it's probably the 1946 Worcester diner car which houses the *Farina Family Diner and Restaurant*, US-4 (Ⓣ802/295-8955), where the food is filling and inexpensive.

White River Junction and around

Perhaps the most exciting thing ever to happen in **WHITE RIVER JUNCTION** was the first use of nitrous oxide (laughing gas) as an anesthetic, in 1844. Still, it's an important travel hub – as far back as the mid-1860s five different railroads had terminal points in White River, and the community grew steadily until the rail transport industry went bust in the early 1900s. The town hosts an annual downtown street party celebrating its railroading history each September, and the train station even has a small, well-organized **Transportation Museum** (Tues, Fri 9am–1pm; free; Ⓣ802/291-9838).

The pride of White River Junction these days is the **Northern Stage**, at Briggs Opera House across from the train station (Ⓣ802/296-7000), an ambitious year-round stage company which performs, with the help of some top local and imported talent, a varied program of contemporary and classical pieces, musicals, and straight drama.

Fifteen miles north of White River Junction along I-91, in the town of **NORWICH**, is the **Montshire Museum of Science**, 1 Montshire Rd, exit 13 off I-91 (daily 10am–5pm; $7.50, children $6.50; Ⓣ802/649-2200, Ⓦwww

.montshire.net), intended for kids but well worth the detour even for adults. You'll see several aquariums with peculiar species of fish as well as machines illustrating the weirder side of physics, but the most engaging displays are the interactive brain-teasing puzzles. Also unique are its outdoor exhibits, one of which provides a "walking tour of the solar system." Admission includes access to its several easy hiking trails and picnic areas.

Practicalities

Amtrak *Vermonter* **trains** stop right by North Main Street, and buses come and go from the Vermont Transit Terminal right off I-91 exit 11 (Ⓣ802/295-3011). There is a very good **Welcome Center** at the train station (daily 9am–5pm; Ⓣ802/281-5050), where you can read brochures over free cups of coffee. If you're going to be here overnight, the best **place to stay** is the *Hotel Coolidge*, 39 Main St (Ⓣ802/295-3118 or 1-800/622-1124, Ⓦwww.hotelcoolidge.com; ❹), right in the town center, an old-fashioned railroad hotel with reasonable prices. The HI-affiliated **hostel** wing has clean dorm beds and kitchen access from $19 per night. On the outskirts of town, at I-91 exit 11, a number of hotel and motel chains offer similar accommodation at similar prices.

There's a nice variety of **places to eat.** Next door to the *Coolidge*, *Dan Wheeler's* in Main Street (Ⓣ802/280-1810), serves appetizers and hot and cold sandwiches in a darkish pub for lunch or dinner. The *Polka Dot Restaurant*, 1 N Main St (Ⓣ802/295-9722), is a shrine to camp, looking as if it were decorated largely by kids. It fixes up good milkshakes and patty melts. Unusually for a restaurant in a bus station, the *China Moon Buffet*, at the Vermont Transit Terminal (Ⓣ802/291-9088), gets rave reviews for its fresh and cheap buffet food. Far and away the most interesting culinary option in town is *Tip Top Café*, 85 N Main St (Ⓣ802/295-3312), where you can find sesame-crusted fish, an Asian wrap, or calypso-spiced pork shanks, along with pork and ginger meatloaf (as a sandwich or entree). It's casual, and not particularly expensive, either.

Windsor

About fifteen miles south of White River Junction, **WINDSOR** is just the Connecticut River's width away from the New Hampshire border. The original constitution of the Republic of Vermont was drawn up here in 1777, an event which made Windsor the "birthplace of Vermont." Today, the distinction is preserved in one of its two excellent museums, the **Old Constitution House**, Main Street (June to mid-Oct Wed–Sun 11am–5pm; $2.50; Ⓣ802/674-6628). Housed in the original tavern where the delegates met and constitutional debates took place, it contains a well-done re-creation of the tavern's interior plus a fascinating series of history-related displays, featuring rare artifacts such as coins and, more interestingly, newspapers from the brief republican period. Farther south along the banks

North to Montpelier: Route 12

If you're in no hurry on your way north, a worthwhile alternative to I-89 is little-traveled **Rte-12**, which passes through the towns of Bethel, Randolph, Northfield, and Riverton. You'll find very few B&Bs or country stores along this road; just thirty miles of rolling hills, farmland, and lakes. This is the real Vermont, and its lush beauty and traditional charm are as genuine as you'll find anywhere in the state. Be advised, though, that this is also a road with a fairly high concentration of "Take back Vermont" signs.

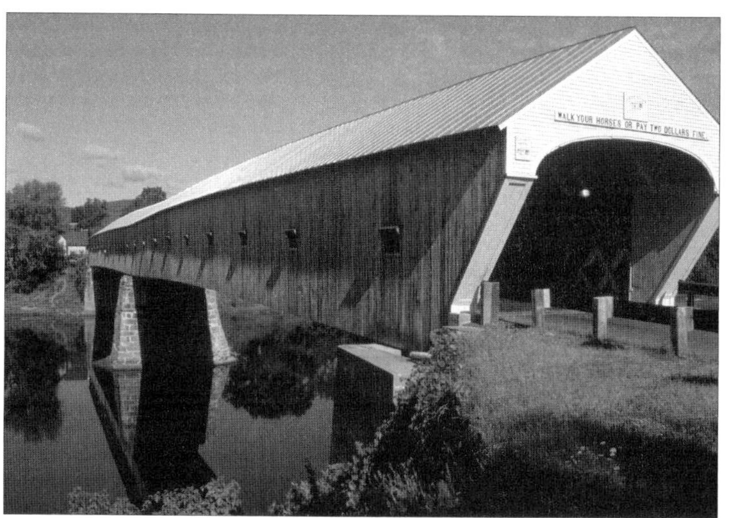

△ Cornish/Windsor covered bridge

of a Connecticut River tributary, the **American Precision Museum,** 196 Main St (daily: June–Oct 10am–5pm; $6; ⓣ802/674-5781, ⓦwww.americanprecision.org), focuses on mechanization – the construction, function, and historical significance of machinery, with a particular focus on the Industrial Revolution. The small but impressive displays of items (many still in working condition, such as "Mississippi" rifles and sewing machines) incorporate antique machine tools and interactivity to illustrate not only the importance of technology, but also the peculiar beauty of its precision. Close to the museum, Bridge Street branches off Main Street to the east; at its terminus, you'll find the **Cornish/Windsor covered bridge**, the longest such bridge in the US at nearly five hundred feet, which is open to traffic crossing over to New Hampshire.

For affordable **accommodation**, it's best to backtrack to White River Junction, or farther afield to Woodstock or Quechee. However, the *Juniper Hill Inn*, off US-5 on Pembroke Road (ⓣ802/674-5273 or 1-800/359-2541, ⓦwww.juniperhillinn.com; ❻), has thirty fastidiously kept rooms in a mansion overlooking the town. They also serve excellent, if rather formally presented, continental-style **food**. **Mount Ascutney State Park**, off Rte-44A, nine miles west of Windsor (May–Oct; ⓣ802/674-2060), maintains hiking trails and several **campsites** ($14) in a secluded setting with excellent views of the Green Mountains.

Montpelier

With fewer than ten thousand residents, **MONTPELIER** (mont-PEEL-yer), in a beautiful valley on the Winooski and North Branch rivers, is the smallest state capital in the country. Indeed, even when the legislature is not in session (May through December), you'll probably run into current Governor Jim Douglas, who's very visible (and is rumored to know the name and face of just about every citizen). Around the **Capitol** building – urban in style but not in scale – the vital downtown area is lined exclusively with nineteenth-century buildings – some with a slightly Southern antebellum flavor – and boasts a number of fine restaurants, museums, and theaters. Despite its considerable charms, the city still bears a low tourist profile, and it is this lack of commercialism that makes Montpelier a refreshing counterpoint to the cultivated rural quaintness that pervades the rest of the state.

Arrival, information, and city transit

Montpelier is fifty miles north of White River Junction. **Knapp Airport**, a postage stamp-sized airport about four miles from I-89 exit 7, serves Montpelier and surrounding communities. Montpelier shares a stop on Amtrak's *Vermonter* line with its neighbor Barre, the station lying two miles west of downtown near I-89. The **bus** terminal (Ⓣ802/229-9220) is next to the river a block from State Street, one of the town's main thoroughfares.

The **Vermont Division of Travel and Tourism**, 134 State St (daily 8am–8pm; Ⓣ802/828-5981 or 1-800/VERMONT, Ⓦwww.vermontvacation.com), offers plenty of information on local and statewide attractions. The nearby **kiosk**, just down State Street across from the Capitol, crams a large assortment of brochures and guides to area attractions into a small but well-kept space. Check out the daily *Times-Argus* for arts and entertainment schedules and listings. Students and locals take advantage of Green Mountain Transit Agency's **bus** service (Ⓣ802/223-7BUS), which can take them to Waterbury ($2) or Burlington ($4). The same company also makes runs to nearby Berlin and Barre.

Accommodation

There's a decent range of affordable **places to stay** in Montpelier, with some of the better options being, not surprisingly, bed-and-breakfasts. The riverside *Green Valley Campground*, northeast of town at the intersection of Rte-2 and Rte-302, four miles from exit 7 or 8 off I-89 (May–Nov; Ⓣ802/223-6217), offers 35 campsites from $25, with swimming, showers, convenience store, and a laundry room.

Betsy's Bed & Breakfast 74 E State St Ⓣ802/229-0466, Ⓦwww.betsysbnb.com. Relatively large, twelve-room B&B in two Victorian homes on a quiet, leafy street a few minutes' walk from downtown. Rooms are attractively (if busily) decorated; bathrooms in all rooms are a rarity for this type of accommodation. ❹

Capitol Plaza Hotel and Conference Center 100 State St Ⓣ802/274-5252 or 1-800/274-5252, Ⓦwww.capitolplaza.com. Luxurious digs across from the gorgeous Art Deco Capitol Theater. Friendly, family-run, and aimed at the business traveler. ❻

Gamble's Bed and Breakfast 16 Vine St Ⓣ802/229-4810. Three large and colorful rooms with shared baths show a little wear and tear, but you can't beat the price. No in-room phones or TV. ❸

Inn at Montpelier 147 Main St Ⓣ802/223-2727, Ⓦwww.innatmontpelier.com. Spacious, well-appointed rooms in a pair of Federal-style buildings. The continental breakfast is a bit skimpy, but access to common areas and a pleasant wrap-around porch are both welcome. ❺

Twin City Motel 1537 Barre–Montpelier Rd (US-302) just off I-89 exit 7 Ⓣ802/476-3104 or 1-877/476-3104, Ⓦwww.twincitymotel.com. Probably the pick of the several motels located a few miles southeast of town on the Barre–Montpelier Road. Rooms have usual motel amenities, like cable TV, fridge, and telephone. ❸

The Town

Diminutive **downtown Montpelier** is home to four college campuses – New England Culinary Institute, Woodbury College, Vermont College of Norwich

University, and Community College of Vermont – though it feels nothing like a college town. Its most visible landmark, the gilt-domed **State Capitol** rises high above the town center on State Street. Most visitors just stroll around the impeccably kept exterior gardens, particularly brilliant during fall, and photograph the statue of **Ethan Allen** guarding the front doors – though the statue of Vermont's first governor **Thomas Chittenden**, to the left of the main entrance, is more attractive. Feel free to pass through the Capitol's refurbished vaulted marble hallways to see the vast (10 by 20 foot) painting by Julian Scott, representing the Battle of Cedar Creek, a Civil War skirmish in which Vermonters played a pivotal role. Also here is a permanent exhibit of Vermont artists, and of course, the portraits of notable legislators, anchored by that of recent governor Howard Dean, rendered in contrast to all others, in his casual clothes and hiking boots. Informative and enthusiastic free **guided tours** of the Capitol are available every half-hour (Mon–Fri 10am–3.30pm; July to mid-Oct also Sat 11am–2.30pm; ⓣ802/828-2228).

The entirety of Vermont's history from the 1600s on is outlined in the **Vermont Historical Society Museum**, in the distinctive Pavilion Building at 109 State St (Tues–Sat 10am–4pm, also May–Oct Sun 12–4pm; $5; ⓣ802/828-2291, ⓦwww.vermonthistory.org). The evolution of Vermont's unique character, from early settlement to the present day, is illuminated with some thoughtful displays on the influence of Native Americans (evidenced here through a life-size Abenaki wigwam), the independence efforts of the Green Mountain Boys (there's a recreation of the Catamount Tavern, where they met to discuss current events), and state citizens' contributions (often of their lives) during more modern-day wartime.

East of the Capitol district, in College Hall on the campus of Norwich, lies the small but distinguished **T.W. Wood Gallery**, 36 College St (Tues–Sun noon–4pm, Thurs until 8pm; free; ⓣ802/828-8743), highlighted by a fascinating array of Vermont painter T.W. Wood's oil paintings of Civil War residents, plus experimental WPA American folk art and photos.

Montpelier's best spot for outdoor recreation is **Hubbard Park**, north of town on Hubbard Park Drive, 180 acres of grassy space, picnic areas, ponds, and trails. Ascend the fifty-foot stone **observation tower** in the park's center for spectacular views. Several hiking and mountain-biking trails wind through the hills, and in winter the trails are used for cross-country skiing and ice skaters take over the frozen ponds. *Onion River Sports*, 20 Langdon St (ⓣ802/229-9409), rents bikes in summer, snowshoes and skis in winter.

Eating

Students from the New England Culinary Institute (NECI) have lent their influence to Montpelier's cuisine, resulting in a number of less expensive, experimental **restaurants**. The area is blissfully resistant to fast-food and chain joints – it's the only US state capital without a *McDonald's*, though a *Subway* and a *Quizno's* have found their way onto Main Street. Organic gardeners and farmers bring their produce, herbs, flowers, and baked goods to the **Farmers Market** (May–Oct Sat 9am–2pm) in the parking lot next to *Julio's* (see overleaf).

Coffee Corner Main St at State ⓣ802/229-9060. A Montpelier standard for over sixty years. Scarf cheap diner food at Formica tables or rub elbows with Vermont's political potentates at the lunch counter. Daily 6am–3pm.

Capitol Grounds 45 State St ⓣ802/223-7800. The wooden interior of this former bank invites casual lounging over your morning coffee, which you can order from the genuinely friendly staff in four sizes: Conservative, Moderate, Liberal, and

Radical (20 oz). Good tea selection as well.

Julio's 54 State St ☎802/229-9348. Pretty good Tex-Mex for this area of New England. Cheap, filling burrito and enchilada dishes washed down with zippy margaritas. Don't blink or you'll miss the unobtrusive green door entrance.

La Brioche Bakery & Cafe 89 Main St ☎802/229-0443. Cheerful, well-designed bakery run by NECI. Good bread, espresso drinks, and the smell of the on-site bakery lure townies of all stripes. The 1/2 Bag Lunch, at $5, will get you half a sandwich, a small but interesting salad or soup, and a cookie (try the Vermont Crunchy: a peanut butter oatmeal cookie with chocolate chips and nuts). Closed Sun.

Main Street Grill and Bar 118 Main St ☎802/223-3188. The delectable, inventive specialties from NECI alums are sort of pricey, but worth it. American grill fare and shellfish are standouts. Also serves breakfast. The next-door *Chef's Table* (☎802/229-9202), run by the same folks, doesn't serve breakfast and is expensive, but also very good.

Mountain Café 7 Langdon St ☎802/223-0888. Huge, tofu- and tempeh-stuffed burritos, brought to life by zesty sauces. Certain "healthy" meats such as chicken and turkey also available. Closed Mon.

Rhapsody 28 Main St ☎802/229-6112. Hippy-friendly, multinational restaurant where you can wolf down curried tofu and vegan chocolate cake from the organic buffet. No meat here. Closed Sun.

Royal Orchid 38 Elm St ☎802/223-0436. Well-done Thai food (especially the pad thai) and amiable staff more than make up for the unspectacular decor.

Sarducci's 3 Main St ☎802/223-0229. Long-established, Tuscan-inspired trattoria next to the river. Pasta dishes will set you back around $10, or you could opt for a house specialty such as wood-roasted salmon in a white wine sauce.

Drinking and entertainment

The town's main drama venue is the **Lost Nation Theater** in the City Hall Arts Center on Main Street (☎802/229-0492), where the resident company performs everything from Shakespeare epics to popular musicals like *You're a Good Man, Charlie Brown* to experimental contemporary plays. Across the street, the **Savoy Theater** (☎802/229-0598) shows first-rate foreign, classic, and independent films. More current ones are screened at the **Capitol** (☎802/229-0343) on State Street. During the summer, the City Band holds well-attended evening concerts on the State House lawn, and the Vermont Philharmonic takes a turn in July. Other than that, there are a handful of decent **bars**; there are also all sorts of places that feature **live music** at least several nights a week.

Black Door Bar & Bistro 44 Main St ☎802/223-7070. Along with its trendy, moderately expensive bistro fare ($17 mains), live music (ranging from funky jazz to zydeco) is on offer Wed–Sat. Always $3 cover.

Charlie-O's 70 Main St ☎802/223-6820. Just a tad scruffy in this pleasant city, *Charlie-O's* is simple: a pool table, wood floors, and a bar. You can easily get your rock or blues fix here most weekends.

Langdon Street Café 4 Langdon St ☎802/223-8667. Music every night in a wood-paneled community space with the feel of a friend's living room. Mystery Fun Night, once a month – entailing anything from requiring all patrons and staff to speak Spanish, to Western-themed activities – can be great fun. And it's family-friendly, with beer, wine, and coffee drinks available, but no hard stuff. Closed Mon.

McGillicuddy's Irish Pub 14 Langdon St ☎802/223-2721. Standard bar fare, most notable for its really hot wings. Wide selection of microbrews. Draws a lively, younger crowd and gets loud and busy on weekends.

Positive Pi's 20 State St ☎802/229-0453. Live hip-hop or groove on weekends make the pizzas available here that much better. Sometimes a $3 cover.

Barre

Ten miles southeast of the state capitol along Rte-302, **BARRE** (pronounced "berry") is Vermont's immigrant center, having attracted Scots, Italians, and other ethnic groups almost a hundred years ago to work for the city's booming granite industry. Even today, a visitor to Barre may hear several languages spoken on the streets and in the stores. The main draw for tourists is the same thing that lured immigrants a century ago: granite, the rock on which this city was literally built.

Barre's main sight, while awaiting the opening of a new Granite Museum (ⓣ802/476-4605), is the **Rock of Ages Quarry**, I-89 exit 6 (May–Oct Mon–Sat 8.30am–5pm, Sun 10am–5pm; $4 for tours, otherwise free; ⓣ802/476-3119, ⓦwww.rockofages.com), which is actually southeast of town on Hwy-63 in the municipality of **Graniteville**. This is the world's largest deep-hole (600ft) granite quarry, as you'll almost certainly be told by the fleet of enthusiastic guides. You can check out one of the smaller but still connected quarries, grab a piece of granite, and watch the campy *You'll dig the Rock of Ages!* informational film all for free – ask for the self-guided tour map. If you've come all this way, though, it's just as well to shell out a few bucks for the narrated shuttle-bus tour that takes you to the far more impressive fifty-acre working quarries and through the manufacturing centers where artisans busy themselves making fleets of tombstones.

For anyone with more than a passing interest in the history of the region's residents (rather than its industry), the **Vermont History Center Library and Museum Store**, 60 Washington St (US-302) (Tues–Fri 9am–4.30pm; research fee $5; ⓣ802/479-8500), provides an engaging view of the state's past in its manuscripts, old family letters, maps, newspaper articles, genealogical trees, and transcribed oral histories detailing various immigrant fracases; even the naming of the town in 1793 spurred a fist-fight – won by Jonathan Sherman of Barre, Massachusetts.

Barre's cultural heritage is also evident in a pair of ostentatious granite monuments downtown. The 23-foot-tall **Italian-American Stonecutters' Monument**, at the intersection of North Main and Maple streets, captures a stoneworker in action and pays homage to the town's immigrant past. Similarly, the **Robert Burns Monument**, at Academy and Washington streets, celebrates the great Scottish poet. More interesting than either are the elaborate gravestones of **Hope Cemetery**, just north of town on Hwy-14. While the city's stonecutters lived modestly, they knew how to die in grand style, commemorating themselves and their families with massive, elaborately wrought granite tombstones up to ten feet in height and bearing impressively detailed artwork.

On a more contemporary cultural note, dance and musical performances take place at Main Street's **Barre City Hall and Opera House** (ⓣ802/476-8188), a fanciful building that has seen the likes of John Philip Sousa and Helen Keller on its stage. For the opposite of culture, you might opt for the surprisingly thrilling goings-on at the **Thunder Road Speedbowl,** 61 Fisher Rd ($9; ⓣ802/244-6963), which regularly offers stock-car racing on a short-track, high-banked motor speedway. It's loud, cheap, pulsating entertainment.

Practicalities

For **visitor information**, stop in at the kiosk in the Price Chopper parking lot along Main Street at the intersection with Hwy-14.

Low demand makes for cheap **accommodation** in Barre. The *Hollow Inn and Motel*, 278 S Main St (ⓣ802/479-9313 or 1-800/998-9444, ⓦwww.hollowinn.com; ❹), is on the fancy side, with a fitness center and complimentary continental breakfast. *Reynold's House B&B*, 102 S Main St (ⓣ802/479-5277; ❻), offers three well-lit, spacious guestrooms with detailed wood molding, bird's-eye maple, and well-chosen antiques. The *Days Inn*, 173–175 S Main St (☎802/476-6678 or 1-800/325-2525; ❸), has clean and reasonably priced rooms, along with an indoor pool.

Barre's Italian-American population may be deeply entrenched in the granite industry, but it hasn't created the profusion of authentic ethnic **restaurants** you might expect. The exception is *Del's*, 248 N Main St (☎802/476-6684), which serves up cheap, tasty pasta dinners and pizza on classic red-and-white-checked tablecloths. For a quick, light lunch, *Simply Delicious*, 160 N Main St (☎802/479-1498), vends a complement of homey soups and sandwiches, which you can enjoy while reading volumes donated by its next-door neighbor, Barre Books, an independent bookstore.

Waterbury

Few people gave much notice to **WATERBURY** before 1986; but ever since aging hippies Ben Cohen and Jerry Greenfield opened their headquarters and **Ben and Jerry's Ice Cream Factory** here, the city has been home to the number-one tourist destination in Vermont. The ice-cream empire, which began in 1978 as a homemade ice-cream stand at the front of a Burlington gas station is nestled one mile north of I-89 in the village of Waterbury Center, on the way up to Stowe. Its league of rabid fans includes not only sweet tooths, but believers in its earthy-crunchy philosophy. Indeed, the company is perhaps the only one existing with a three-part mission statement, which gives social, environmental, and financial benefits equal importance. Half-hour tours run by friendly, almost evangelical youths (daily tours: July to late Aug 9am–8pm; late Aug to Oct 9am–6pm; Nov–May 10am–5pm; June 9am–5pm; store and "scoop shop" closes one hour later; $3; ☎1-866/BJ-TOURS, ⓦwww.benjerry.com) feature a short film on the collaborators' early days, then head into the production factory where (weekdays) machines turn cream, sugar, and other natural ingredients into over fifty flavors and concoctions. Afterwards, you get a free mini-scoop of the stuff – you can buy more at the pricey gift shop and ice-cream stall outside. Every summer, free movie showings on Saturdays bring in tourists and locals alike to enjoy Ben and Jerry's mission of ice cream and entertainment.

There's not really much else to see in Waterbury; even the **culinary outlet shops** clustered along Hwy-100, each offering free samples of their wares in an attempt to seduce travelers, fail to glean much from the ice-cream rush. The pick of the bunch is probably the **Cabot Annex Store** (☎802/244-6334), where you can taste several varieties of the well-known Vermont cheddar cheese (see box on p.448 for more), though **Cold Hollow Cider Mill** (daily 8am–6pm; ☎802/244-8771), where you can see how cider is made, comes close, if only for the heavenly aroma of apples and cider donuts. However, if you're really looking for something to do, stop by the Waterbury Public Library at 28 N Main St and ask the librarians to let you into the **Waterbury Historical Society and Museum** (Mon–Wed 10am–8pm, Thurs–Fri 10am–5pm, Sat 9am–noon; ☎802/244-7036) upstairs, where they'll have to turn on the lights to let you into the small collection of musty Civil War and medical memorabilia. There are plenty of **craft** outlets, too, on Hwy-100, if you're so inclined.

Practicalities

Waterbury is 13 miles northwest of Montpelier via I-89. Amtrak's *Vermonter* **trains** pull into downtown Waterbury, either in the morning heading south or the evening heading north. For general tourist information, contact the **Waterbury Tourism Council** (Ⓦwww.waterbury.org) on Rte-100 near its intersection with Stowe Street.

There are several top-notch **accommodation** options in and around town. The Cape Cod-clapboard *Inn at Blush Hill*, 784 Blush Hill Rd just off Rte-100 (Ⓣ802/244-7529 or 1-800/736-7522, Ⓦwww.blushhill.com; ❺), sits atop a hill with fantastic views, and has Colonial antiques and canopy beds in each room. The Teutonic-themed *Grunberg Haus* on Rte-100 (Ⓣ802/244-7726 or 1-800/800-7760, Ⓦwww.grunberghaus.com; ❹) is a woodsy A-frame with great breakfasts and reasonable rates. Other quality establishments along Rte-100 near Waterbury Center include the *Birds Nest Inn* (two-night minimum, and closed Apr & Nov; Ⓣ802/244-7490 or 1-800/366-5592, Ⓦwww.birdsnestinn.com; ❻) and the *Old Stagecoach Inn* (Ⓣ802/244-5056 or 1-800/262-2206, Ⓦwww.oldstagecoach.com; ❹).

One of the better places to **eat** here is *The Alchemist*, 23 S Main St (Ⓣ802/244-4120), which serves its own brews along with panini, personal pizzas, and somewhat upscale pub food. *Arvad's*, 3 S Main St (Ⓣ802/244-8973), also serves up fresh grill fare with good pints of ale. *Coffee Bean Cafe*, in the *Best Western Hotel*, Rte-100 (Ⓣ802/244-1740), has satisfying diner fare, and also super desserts, coffee, and cocktails.

Stowe

Unlike most of Vermont's other ski towns, there is still a beautiful nineteenth-century village at the heart of **STOWE**, with a white-spired meeting house and a green to stroll around. Though Stowe was actually a popular summer destination even before the Civil War, what really put the town on the map as a ski resort was the arrival of the **Von Trapp family**, of *The Sound of Music* fame. After fleeing Austria during World War II, they settled here and established a lodge – since burned down – where Maria Von Trapp held her singing camps. A complex composed of a newly rebuilt lodge, restaurant, and mini-theme park devoted to the celebration of alpine culture has taken its place. Interfamily squabbling over the direction the lodge and its offshoots will take in the future doesn't seem to have interfered with its popularity. Regardless, a century's worth of experience catering to increasingly large crowds of skiers has rather swamped the approach road to the main ski area with malls, equipment stores, and sprawling condominium complexes – extremely at odds with the village below. Nonetheless, the setting remains spectacular, at the foot of Vermont's highest mountain, the 4393-foot **Mount Mansfield**.

Arrival and information

Green Mountain Transit Agency (Ⓣ802/223-7287 or 1-866/864-0211, Ⓦwww.gmtaride.org) provides **bus** service year-round to Waterbury, Montpelier, and Burlington. **Mountain Road** (Rte-108) is Stowe's primary thoroughfare, stretching from the main village up through the mountain gap known as "Smugglers' Notch," so named because forbidden trade with Canada passed through here during the War of 1812 at the time of Jefferson's Embargo Act. It also lived up to its nickname through its use by fugitive slaves on their way to Canada and, in the early part of last century, Prohibition-era bootleggers. The notch is generally closed during winter. The Mountain Road Shuttle runs up

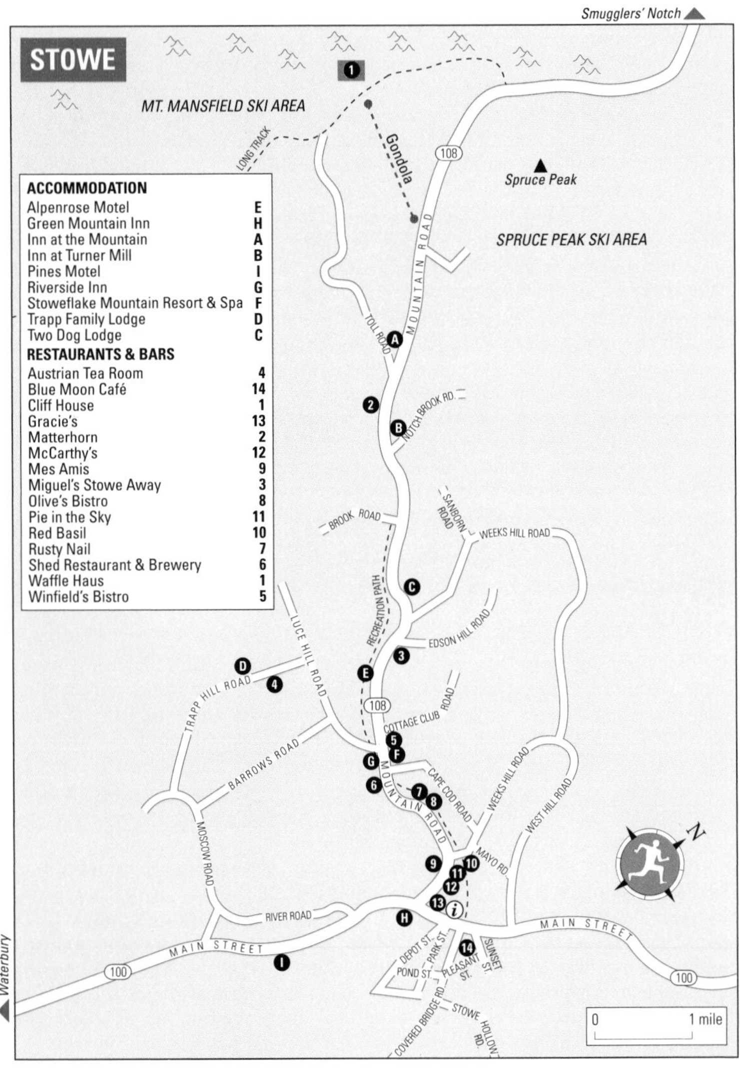

and down Mountain Road, stopping at the Town Hall in Stowe Village and the base of Mount Mansfield ($1). The staff at the **visitors' center**, 51 Main St, at Depot Road (summer: Mon–Sat 9am–8pm, Sun 9am–5pm, other months hours vary; Ⓣ802/253-7321 or 1-877/GOSTOWE, Ⓦwww.gostowe.com), are very helpful should you require further information or help in finding accommodation, and you can pick up coupons for discounts on local activities. Watch out, too, for the variety of **events** held throughout the year, like the ice carving and snow golf competitions at the amusing Winter Carnival (third week in January), and the Antique & Classic Car Show, which draws over 10,000 gawkers a day to the already busy summer scene (second weekend in August).

Accommodation

Multiple **accommodation** options line Mountain Road, and range from luxury resorts to modest B&Bs. During winter, reserve as far ahead as possible; otherwise, you'll probably be shut out. In summertime, many places close, but those that stay open can usually find a room for you – you might even be able to wrangle a discount if you're bold enough to ask the innkeeper. The closest **campground** is *Gold Brook Campground* (ⓣ802/253-7683), two miles south on Rte-100, with the usual amenities and sites from $22, but you can stake yourself out in Smugglers Notch State Park as well for $16 (ⓣ1-888/409-7579).

Alpenrose Motel 2619 Mountain Rd ⓣ802/253-7277 or 1-800/962-7002. Affordable small hotel located halfway between the ski slopes and Stowe Village, just off the Stowe Recreation Path. Rooms and efficiencies with private baths, cable TV, and refrigerators. German spoken. ❸

Green Mountain Inn 1 Main St ⓣ802/253-7301 or 1-800/253-7302, ⓦwww.greenmountaininn.com. Stately hotel built in 1833, centrally located (at a busy intersection) and amply outfitted. Offers not one, but two good restaurants, complimentary health club, and afternoon tea and cookies. ❻

Inn at the Mountain 5781 Mountain Rd ⓣ802/253-3656 or 1-800/253-4754. The slope-side accommodations are certainly comfortable, but the best thing about staying here is the "ski and stay special": two nights at the inn and a two-day ski pass only $198 per person. ❻

Inn at Turner Mill 56 Turner Mill Lane ⓣ802/253-2062 or 1-800/992-0016, ⓦwww.turnermill.com. Quaint streamside quarters with handcrafted yellow birch furnishings at the foot of Mount Mansfield. Swimming pool and excellent homemade breakfasts. ❹

The Pines Motel 1203 Waterbury Rd ⓣ802/253-4828. Cheap, fairly clean, basic motel rooms, one step above your average hostel. ❸

Riverside Inn 1965 Mountain Rd ⓣ802/253-4217 or 1-800/966-4217, ⓦwww.rivinn.com. Modest, basic hostelry with all the essentials including bed, bath, and phones, though not much more. ❸

Stoweflake Mountain Resort & Spa 1746 Mountain Rd ⓣ802/253-7355 or 1-800/253-2232, ⓦwww.stoweflake.com. Sumptuous rooms filled with tasteful antiques and homemade quilts, coffee and snacks throughout the day, well-informed and courteous staff, all set in sweeping grounds with pool, spa, and sports club. Definitely the best place to stay if you can afford it. ❼–❾

Trapp Family Lodge 42 Trapp Hill Rd ⓣ802/253-8511 or 1-800/826-7000, ⓦwww.trappfamily.com. Twenty-seven hundred acres of Austrian-themed ski resort (as fancy as it is expensive) on the site of the original Trapp family house, also the first cross-country ski center in America. Nightly entertainment can include concerts in the Trapp Meadow. Rates include cross-country ski passes and access to skiing and hiking trails. ❾

Two Dog Lodge 3576 Mountain Rd ⓣ802/253-8555 or 1-800/339-2364, ⓦwww.twodoglodge.com. Very close to Stowe Mountain (2 miles) and the Long Trail (3.5 miles), and on forty acres of woods and trails, *Two Dog* offers the best in pet- and people-friendly accommodation, with seventeen unique rooms, internet access, free breakfast, and Vermont artist Steven Huneck's carved animal accents all around. ❺

Skiing and other outdoor activities

Alpine experts hotly debate whether the **Stowe Mountain Resort** (ⓣ802/253-3000, ⓦwww.stowe.com) is still the "ski capital of the east," a distinction it clearly held until Killington and other eastern ski centers began to challenge its supremacy a decade or so ago. Regardless, it's an excellent mountain, refurbished to the tune of $20 million a few years back, and its popularity remains intact, as traffic through Stowe Village on winter weekends makes all too painfully clear. There are 48 well-kept trails spread over two ski areas, Mount Mansfield and Spruce Peak, with excellent options for skiers of every level (lift ticket $65 per day), and access to their cross-country trails is only $15 a day. A less crowded option is the family-oriented **Smugglers' Notch** (ⓣ802/664-8851 or 1-800/451-8752, ⓦwww.smuggs.com), on the other side of the mountain, a dramatic narrow pass with thousand-foot cliffs on either side that actually has more trails than Stowe (78, with about twenty "'expert'" runs), and is a little cheaper at $58 per day. Vouching for its suitability for parents and kids alike, the respected *Ski* magazine has consistently rated Smuggler's Notch as having the top ski-school program for families.

Stowe offers almost as much to do in the **summer**, when the crowds thin out considerably. Ascending to the peak of **Mount Mansfield** is a challenge no matter how you do it, and rewards with spectacular views all the way to Canada and the shores of Lake Champlain. Weather permitting, the easiest approach is the **Toll Road**, a winding ascent that begins seven miles up from the village (daily: late May to mid-Oct 9am–4pm; $18 per car), or by **gondola** (daily: mid-June to mid-Oct 10am–5pm; $16; ⓣ802/253-7311), which affords great views and drops off at **Cliff House**, a brief hike from the summit. If you've got the stamina, the most rewarding approach is to **hike** the full way to the Mansfield summit, a steep, steady, 4.7-mile climb up a section of the Long Trail with a trailhead on Rte-108 halfway through Smugglers' Notch. The notch is laced with miles of **hiking trails**; some of the best start out from Smugglers' Notch State Park, 6443 Mountain Rd (mid-May to mid–Oct; ⓣ802/253-4014).

Stowe's cross-country skiing trails double as **mountain-bike routes** during summer, and the Stowe Mountain Bike Club (ⓣ802/253-1947, ⓦwww.stowemtnbike.com), a kind of grassroots organization promoting responsible biking and trail accessibility, sponsors group rides twice a week. They also supply a list of rental outfits, including AJ's Ski & Sports, Mountain Road (from $27 a day; ⓣ802/253-4593 or 1-800/226-6257, ⓦwww.ajssports.com). For other speed demons, there's also an Alpine slide ($28 for three rides).

Nearby streams and small rivers offer ample opportunity for **canoeing** and **kayaking**: Umiak Outdoor Outfitters, 849 S Main St (ⓣ802/253-2317), gives tours on the gentle Lamoille River (from $30) and rents full sets of equipment, including watercraft, paddles, and life jackets, for $35 per day.

People who would rather keep to lower elevations would do well to use the **Stowe Recreation Path**, a 5.5-mile paved trail for bikers, runners, walkers, and rollerbladers which starts in the village behind the Community Church. It never feels too crowded and better still, it offers scenic views of the West Branch River and Mount Mansfield along the way. Be warned that the path does not make a full circuit, so plan ahead if you're going the entire length. If you get tired of activity, the huskies at Eden Mountain Dogsledding (in **Eden Mills**, 25 miles north of Stowe off Rte-100) will run on your behalf: sledding (in winter) or dog-carting (summer) provides for an expensive but exhilarating afternoon (call for details and to schedule ⓣ802/635-9070, ⓦwww.dogsledridesvermont.com).

Eating and drinking

There is a big choice of places to **eat** in and around Stowe, ranging from low-budget delis, bakeries, and pizza joints to rather expensive restaurants, frequently run by a nearby inn or resort. The **drinking** and **entertainment** scene draws together lounging après-skiers, hard-boiled locals, and well-heeled yuppies in various watering holes.

Restaurants

Austrian Tea Room 42 Trapp Hill Rd ⓣ802/253-5705. The high prices are more for the kitschy, Germanic atmosphere than the food, but the cuisine's still authentic enough and the setting fun (in season, try to get seated on the flower-lined balcony).

Blue Moon Cafe 35 School St ⓣ802/253-7006. Inventive, expensive New American fare featuring local game (braised venison and the like) and seafood; probably Stowe's best all-round dining choice. Good wine list.

Cliff House Gondola Summit, on the mountain ⓣ802/253-3665. Fine dining at the highest point in the state.

Gracie's Mountain Rd ⓣ802/253-8741. Dog-themed place good for lunchtime salads (Wolfhound Waldorff) and sandwiches (Pointer Roll-Up, Chihuahua burger). Also open well into the night for fuller dinners ($13–23) and a bit more variety.

McCarthy's Mountain Rd ⓣ802/253-8626. Irish-themed joint with great heaping breakfasts.

Mes Amis 311 Mountain Rd ⓣ802/253-8669. A local favorite serving rich French cuisine (homemade truffle pâté and the like) for dinner. Excellent service and affordable prices. Live jazz and blues Thurs and Sun. Closed Mon.

Olive's Bistro 1036 Mountain Rd ⓣ802/253-2033. Great tapas bar in addition to French-, Greek-, and North African-inspired Mediterranean specialties. Great selection of martinis, single malt scotches, and assorted cocktails. Closed Sun.

Pie in the Sky 492 Mountain Rd ⓣ802/253-5100. Casual joint offering wood-fired specialty pizzas you can design yourself, plus vegetarian entrees.

Red Basil 294 Mountain Rd ⓣ802/253-4478. The freshest herbs bring the Thai specialties (and your palate) to life. Sushi, too.

Waffle Haus Gondola Summit, on the mountain ⓣ802/253-3609. The perfect antidote to a morning of chilly winter activity: Belgian waffles and hot cider or cocoa for refueling. Wed–Sun 10am–3pm. It's just a regular snack bar in summer, though.

Winfield's Bistro 1746 Mountain Rd ⓣ802/253-7355. The liberal use of ingredients like "pecan dust," "tawny port syrup," and "lavender" on the menu tips this as a creative New American bistro (and also as "expensive"). Wed–Sun only, reservations recommended.

Bars

Matterhorn top of Mountain Rd ⓣ802/253-8198. The region's favorite bands have been coming here for years – you can enjoy the live music in the nightclub on weekends most of the year, or listen from the downstairs wood-paneled dining room.

Miguel's Stowe Away 3148 Mountain Rd ⓣ802/253-7574. Its lively margarita bar can get rowdy on weekends. Spicy, tangy Mexican and Tex-Mex treats, excellent by New England standards.

Rusty Nail 1190 Mountain Rd ⓣ802/253-6245, ⓦrustynailbar.com. Rotating blues, jazz, reggae and "British Invasion" nights fill the bill, but the Nail is also a sports bar with a twenty-foot screen TV. Check out the website for the entertaining story of the place's history, from its birth in 1969 through the disco era to today.

Shed Restaurant and Brewery Pub 1859 Mountain Rd ⓣ802/253-4364. Hearty American fare, specializing in the ample "Mighty Shed Burger." The attached bar has great daily specials on pints and bar chow – and surprisingly, has a number of vegetarian choices. Stowe's only brewpub. Open late.

Sugarbush and the Mad River Valley

An intriguingly named valley and a sweet-sounding mountain might lure you from I-89 to the route a bit less traveled: Hwy 100 south. Twelve miles off the interstate, is **WAITSFIELD**, bisected by the Mad River and a good base for the two popular ski resorts just west of it. The **Sugarbush Resort** (ⓣ802/583-6300 or 1-800/53-SUGAR, ⓦwww.sugarbush.com), actually closer to the town of **WARREN**, is about five miles south of Waitsfield on Hwy-100. The larger and more commercialized of the two area resorts, it consists of two hills, Lincoln Peak and Mount Ellen, with 115 trails (peak lift tickets about $65; for Mount Ellen only, $50) and year-round activities. Meanwhile, the cooperatively-owned **Mad River Glen** (ⓣ802/496-3551, ⓦwww.madriverglen.com), a short drive west of Waitsfield along Rte-17, is one of the most unadulterated resorts in North America, with narrow, unforgiving trails which look pretty much as they did when they were cut fifty years ago. In keeping with tradition, no snowboards are allowed here, although **Telemark skiing** is promoted aggressively. There are 44 trails (lift tickets $50), of which nearly half are considered to be suitable for the expert skier.

Horseback riding is a great summer or winter option in this area. From its deathly quiet and extremely lovely location on North Fayston Road off Rte-100, **Vermont Icelandic Horse Farm** (contact for schedule and pricing ⓣ802/496-7141, ⓦwww.icelandichorse.com) offers two- to five-day treks stopping at country inns from May through November, as well as shorter rides throughout the year starting at about $40. The easygoing personality of this breed, along with its smaller size, makes for a truly unique experience.

Practicalities

You'll really need a car to get to the Mad River Valley. A taxi from Waterbury to Waitsfield is a possibility, albeit an expensive one at $40 (try Mad Cab ⓣ802/793-2320). Once at Waitsfield, however, Mad River Valley Transit (ⓣ802/496-7433) has a **shuttle** service during ski season to Warren, the ski resorts, and to Montpelier. The **Sugarbush Chamber of Commerce**, Hwy-100 in Waitsfield (ⓣ802/496-3409 or 1-800/828-4748, ⓦwww.madrivervalley.com), can provide all sorts of information, and tell you about the annual Vermont Festival of the Arts (ⓦwww.vermontartfest.com), a three-week-long series of summer events that includes art showings, concerts, cheese-making, pottery and glass-blowing demos, and sometimes, sheepdog competitions.

Visitors will find ample **lodging** choices here, perhaps most notably the *1824 House* (ⓣ802/496-7555, ⓦwww.1824house.com; ❻) a country inn with three-course breakfasts in Waitsfield. Other comfortable places in Waitsfield and within easy reach of the slopes include the *Mountain View Inn* on Rte-17 (ⓣ802/496-2426; ❺) with seven guestrooms in a dark red restored farmhouse, and the sunny yellow *Mad River Inn* on Tremblay Road off Rte-100 (ⓣ802/496-7900; ❺). *Pepper's Lodge*, 3180 German Flats Rd in Warren (ⓣ802/583-2202; ❸), is geared to the no-frills set.

While the quiet community is not known for its **restaurants**, there are a few that are worth mentioning. At the junction of routes 17 and 100 in Waitsfield, *John Egan's Big World Pub & Grill* (ⓣ802/496-3033) has a random selection (rotisserie chicken, pad thai, lamb, Hungarian goulash), which is nonetheless well executed in a friendly ski-lodge atmosphere. Across the street, American favorites in a pub setting can be found at *The Den* (ⓣ802/496-8880). Somewhat more refined palates will be happier with *Chez Henri* in the Sugarbush Village in Warren (ⓣ802/583-2600), where French dishes like *filet au poivre* or *bouillabaisse* are served in a Parisian-style café. There is no **nightlife** to speak of, at least in summer, when you'll only have the crickets for entertainment.

Lake Champlain

Forming the boundary between Vermont and New York, the 150-mile-long **Lake Champlain** just nudges its way into Canada in the north and never exceeds twelve miles across at its widest point. Its area of about 490 square miles makes it the sixth largest body of freshwater in the US. Across the water from the flatlands of the Champlain Valley, the impassive Adirondack Mountains are always visible, looming up in the west. The first non-native to see the lake was French explorer **Samuel de Champlain** in 1609, who named it in his own honor. The life and soul of the valley is the French Canadian-influenced city of **Burlington**, whose longstanding trade links with Montréal have filled it with elegant nineteenth-century architecture. Within just a few miles of the center, US-2 leads north onto the supremely rural **Champlain Islands**, covered in meadows and farmlands.

Burlington

With a population of just around forty thousand, lakeside **BURLINGTON** is the closest Vermont gets to a city. It's also notable as one of New England's most purely enjoyable destinations – a hip, relaxed fusion of Montréal, eighty miles to the north, and Boston, over two hundred miles southeast. In fact, from its earliest days, Burlington looked as much to Canada as to the south. Shipping connections with the St Lawrence River were far easier than the land routes across the mountains, and the harbor became a major supply center. The city's founders included Ethan Allen and family. Far from being some impoverished Robin Hood figure, Ethan was a wealthy landowner, having purchased large tracts of Vermont land from New Hampshire royal governor Benning Wentworth; Allen's brother Ira set up the University of Vermont.

Burlington today is the definitive youthful university town. From its waterfront walkways to its lively brewpubs, the city is at once cosmopolitan and pleasantly manageable in scale. It's one of the few American cities to offer something approaching a café society, with a downtown – especially around the Church Street Marketplace – you can stroll around on foot, and plenty of open-air terraces. Politically, too, it's unusual: Bernard Sanders, the former "socialist" mayor of Burlington, was in 1990 elected to the House of Representatives from Vermont, the first political independent to go to Congress in forty years.

Arrival, information, and city transit

Burlington sits at the confluence of several major highways, US-7, US-2, and I-89. Amtrak *Vermonter* **trains** haul into the town of Essex Junction, an inconvenient five miles northeast of town (connecting buses $1.25). Note that the booking office is closed on weekends, at which time no tickets are sold. Vermont Transit **buses** stop in downtown Burlington at 345 Pine St, four blocks south of Main Street (Ⓣ802/864-6811). Vermont's only sizeable commercial **airport**, the Burlington International Airport (Ⓣ802/863-1889), is a few miles east of town along US-2 (buses to downtown run every half-hour 6.30am–10pm; $1); Continental Airlines and US Airways have services to and from Boston and New York City.

Practical information is available from the **Lake Champlain Regional Chamber of Commerce**, 60 Main St (July–Sept Mon–Fri 8.30am–5pm, Sat–Sun 11am–3pm; Oct–June Mon–Fri 8.30am–5pm; Ⓣ802/863-3489 or 1-877/686-5253, Ⓦwww.vermont.org). There are **information booths** at the airport and in the middle of Church Street (between Cherry and College streets, Ⓣ802/865-4636), which have a range of maps and brochures, as well as a courtesy phone for booking accommodation.

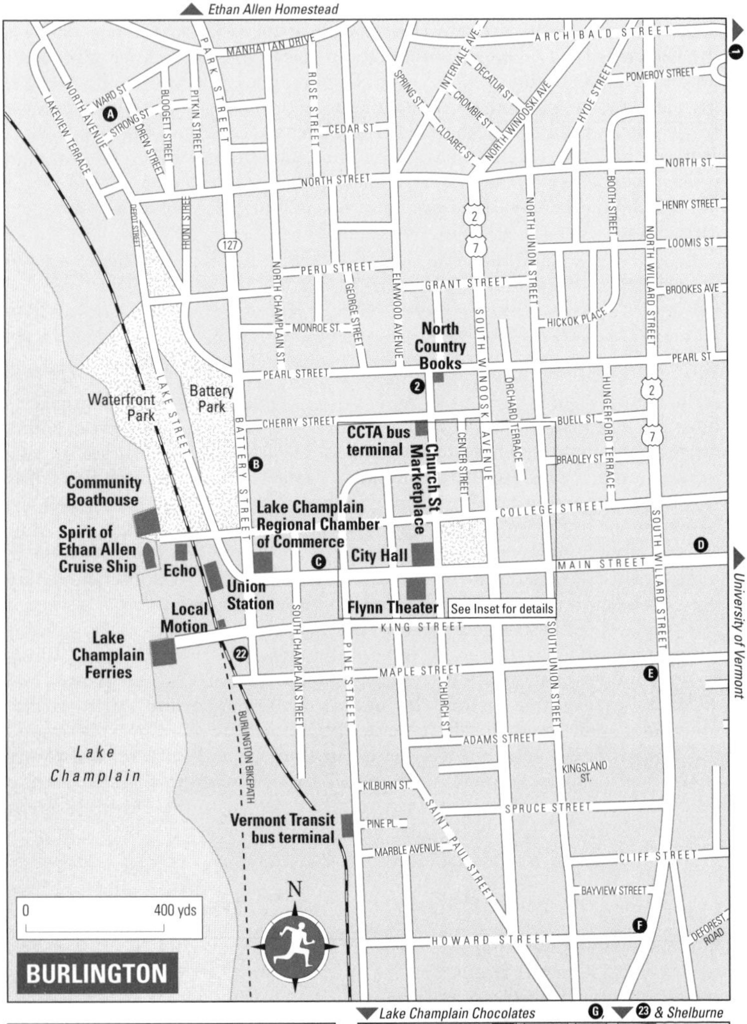

Ethan Allen Homestead
ARCHIBALD STREET
POMEROY STREET
MANHATTAN DRIVE
PARK STREET
ROSE STREET
SPRING ST.
INTERVALE AVE.
DECATUR ST
CROMBIE ST
CLOAREC ST
NORTH WINOOSKI AVE
HYDE STREET
WARD ST
NORTH AVENUE
LAKEVIEW TERRACE
STRONG ST
DREW STREET
BLODGETT STREET
PITKIN STREET
CEDAR ST
NORTH ST.
NORTH STREET
HENRY STREET
BOOTH STREET
NORTH UNION STREET
NORTH WILLARD STREET
LOOMIS ST
DEPOT STREET
FRONT STREET
127
2
7
PERU STREET
GRANT STREET
BROOKES AVE
NORTH CHAMPLAIN ST.
GEORGE STREET
ELMWOOD AVENUE
MONROE ST.
HICKOK PLACE
North Country Books
PEARL STREET
PEARL ST
SOUTH WINOOSKI AVENUE
ORCHARD TERRACE
HUNGERFORD TERRACE
Waterfront Park
Battery Park
LAKE STREET
CHERRY STREET
BUELL ST
CCTA bus terminal
Church St Marketplace
CENTER STREET
BRADLEY ST
BATTERY STREET
Community Boathouse
COLLEGE STREET
Spirit of Ethan Allen Cruise Ship
Lake Champlain Regional Chamber of Commerce
City Hall
SOUTH WILLARD STREET
MAIN STREET
Echo
Union Station
University of Vermont
Local Motion
Flynn Theater
See Inset for details
KING STREET
SOUTH UNION STREET
Lake Champlain Ferries
SOUTH CHAMPLAIN STREET
PINE STREET
MAPLE STREET
CHURCH ST
ADAMS STREET
BURLINGTON BIKEPATH
Lake Champlain
KILBURN ST.
KINGSLAND ST.
SAINT PAUL STREET
SPRUCE STREET
Vermont Transit bus terminal
PINE PL.
MARBLE AVENUE
CLIFF STREET
BAYVIEW STREET
N
0
400 yds
DEFOREST ROAD
HOWARD STREET
BURLINGTON
Lake Champlain Chocolates
G, 23 & Shelburne

CCTA bus terminal
Church St Marketplace
CENTER STREET
SOUTH WINOOSKI AVENUE
N
PINE STREET
COLLEGE STREET
SAINT PAUL STREET
CHURCH STREET
City Hall
MAIN STREET
Flynn Theater
0
200 yds

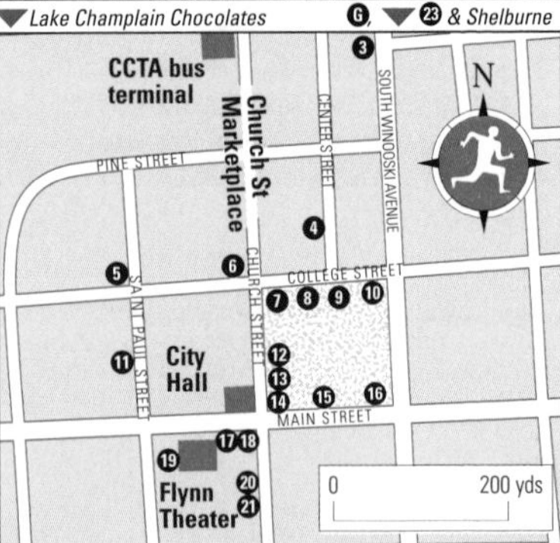

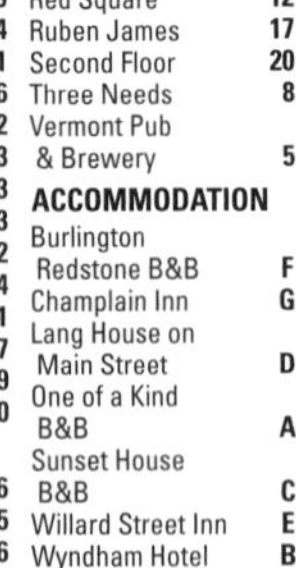

RESTAURANTS

American Flatbread	11
Augie's	9
Daily Planet	4
Five Spice Café	21
Leunig's Bistro	6
NECI Commons	2
Pauline's	23
Penny Cluse Café	3
Red Onion	13
Shanty on the Shore	22
Smokejack's	14
Sneakers	1
Sweetwaters	7
Trattoria Delia	19
Zabby & Elf's Stone Soup	10
Rasputin's	18
Red Square	12
Ruben James	17
Second Floor	20
Three Needs	8
Vermont Pub & Brewery	5

BARS & NIGHTLIFE

Club Metronome	16
Muddy Waters	15
Nectar's	16

ACCOMMODATION

Burlington Redstone B&B	F
Champlain Inn	G
Lang House on Main Street	D
One of a Kind B&B	A
Sunset House B&B	C
Willard Street Inn	E
Wyndham Hotel	B

Burlington is a great place for **walking**, as the main downtown shopping area is fairly compact. For those who choose to drive the town's streets, **parking** remains a bit of a problem: the numerous public garages are often full during the day, and most streetside meters only allow a maximum of two hours (a few let you linger only fifteen minutes). The local **CCTA** bus company (ⓣ802/864-0211, ⓦwww.cctaride.org) connects points all over the downtown area, and travels to the nearby cities of Winooski, Essex, and Shelburne ($1). You can get a route map and details of schedules at the main downtown terminal on the corner of Cherry and Church streets. CCTA also operates a very convenient – and free – shuttle, which runs along College Street between the University of Vermont and the waterfront with stops at the Fleming Museum and the Church Street Marketplace (every 15–30min: Mon–Fri 6.30am–7pm; late May to mid-Oct, also Sat–Sun 9am–9pm). The **Champlain Flyer** (ⓣ802/951-4010) is a commuter rail service which travels along the shoreline of Lake Champlain from Union Station at the end of Main Street to South Burlington, Shelburne, and Charlotte (mid-June to early Sept; $10).

Lake Champlain Ferries (ⓣ802/864-9804, ⓦwww.ferries.com) cross the lake to New York from **Burlington** (to Port Kent; hourly; $15), **Charlotte** (to Essex; every half-hour; $8.50), and **Grand Isle** (to Plattsburgh; every 20min; $8.50). All of these rates are one-way for a car and driver; for additional passengers as well as for cyclists and walk-ons the rate ranges from $3.25 to $4.25. You can rent **bikes** at **North Star Sports**, 100 Main St (ⓣ802/863-3832), and **Skirack**, 85 Main St (ⓣ802/658-3313), which also rents skis, snowboards, kayaks, and in-line skates.

Accommodation

The Burlington area has no shortage of moderately priced **accommodation**, though much of it is removed from the downtown area, along Williston Road (just west along US-2, off I-89 exit 14) and Shelburne Road (south of town along US-7). Downtown, there are several good places to stay within striking distance of the town's major attractions.

Downtown hotels, motels, and B&Bs

Burlington Redstone B&B 497 S Willard St ⓣ802/862-0508, ⓦwww.burlingtonredstone.com. Red-brick home, cluttered with antiques and work by local artists, convenient to downtown. Nice lake and mountain views from patios and porches. Reservations recommended. ❻

Champlain Inn 165 Shelburne St ⓣ802/862-4004. A classic roadside motel a couple of miles south of downtown, with 33 clean, basic, and affordable efficiencies including microwaves and refrigerators. ❸

Lang House on Main Street 360 Main St ⓣ802/652-2500 or 1-877/919-9799, ⓦwww.langhouse.com. Handsome 1881 Victorian conveniently located between UVM campus and downtown, offers nine rooms with blonde wood floors and fireplaces, many with views of Lake Champlain. ❻

One of a Kind B&B 53 Lakeview Terr ⓣ1-877/479-2736, ⓦwww.oneofakindbnb.com. Two cozy rooms, with extensive continental breakfast, right on the lake in a quiet area of town. ❹

Sunset House B&B 78 Main St ⓣ802/864-3790, ⓦwww.sunsethousebb.com. Good choice if you enjoy staying in family-run places with homey decor, "lived-in" rooms, and shared bathrooms. Prime location right in the center of downtown. ❹

Willard Street Inn 349 S Willard St ⓣ802/651-8710 or 1-800/577-8712, ⓦwww.willardstreetinn.com. Calling itself "Burlington's first historic inn," the large rooms at this distinctive home are brilliantly restored (but not frilly). You also get a 24hr pantry, excellent homemade breakfasts, and a lush, green, relaxing English garden. Ask about their voucher worth $5 off entry to the Shelburne Museum. ❻

Wyndham Hotel 60 Battery St ⓣ802/658-6500 or 1-800/996-3426, ⓦwww.wyndhamburlington.com. Recently renovated, upscale chain hotel (on the extravagant side) centrally located on a hillside fronting Lake Champlain. ❼

Hostels and camping

Lone Pine Campsite 52 Sunset View Rd, Colchester ⓣ802/878-5447, ⓦwww.lonepinecampsites.com. About eight miles north of town, with two hundred sites starting at $29 a night. No beach here, though two swimming pools should be adequate compensation. In any case, Lake Champlain is not too far away. May to mid-Oct.

Mrs Farrell's Home Hostel (HI-AYH) 27 Arlington Court ⓣ802/865-3730. Only six dorm beds at $23 for HI members and $25 non-members, so reservations are essential. Three miles out from the town center. Closed Nov–Apr.

North Beach Campground 60 Institute Rd ⓣ802/862-0942 or 1-800/571-1198. Less than two miles north of town on the shores of Lake Champlain. A total of 137 sites ranging from $22 to $31, various other facilities (including plenty for the kids), and access to a sandy beach. Open May to mid-Oct.

Out-of-town hotels and motels

Comfort Inn 1285 Williston Rd, South Burlington ⓣ802/865-3400. Chain motel with clean, basic, uniformly decorated rooms, pool and spa, coffee round the clock, and free continental breakfast and local calls. Most rooms are non-smoking. ❹

Heart of the Village Inn 5347 Shelburne Rd, Shelburne ⓣ802/985-2800 or 1-877/808-1834, ⓦwww.heartofthevillage.com. Nine beautifully decorated rooms in a pair of Victorian houses with period antiques and delectable breakfast. Cable TV available on request. ❻

Ho-Hum Motel 1660 Williston Rd, South Burlington ⓣ802/863-4551. This simple and reasonably priced motel, three miles east of downtown, almost lives up to its name. Four adjacent restaurants and a bike path nearby help liven it up. There is another motel of the same ilk south of the center at 1200 Shelburne Rd (ⓣ802/658-1314). ❸

Inn at Essex 70 Essex Way, Essex Junction ⓣ802/878-1100 or 1-800/727-4295, ⓦwww.innatessex.com. Country inn meets business hotel at this classy establishment about eight miles from Burlington, which has a golf course, a pool, comfortable rooms, and two excellent restaurants run by the New England Culinary Institute. Complimentary shuttle to nearby transportation. ❽

Inn at Shelburne Farms 1611 Harbor Rd, Shelburne ⓣ802/985-8498, ⓦwww.shelburnefarms.org/comevisitus/inn. Posh digs, perhaps the nicest around, in a mansion on the lovely Shelburne Farms. May–Oct. ❺

The City

Your natural inclination upon setting out to explore Burlington might be to head for the **waterfront**, one of the city's top destinations; indeed, kayaks seem to be strapped to the roof of every third car in Burlington. The aptly named **Waterfront Park** stretches a couple of miles along Lake Champlain, with ample green spaces, gorgeous swing benches that people tactfully compete for, and a popular dog run. At its northern end, **Battery Park** makes a particularly good place to watch the sun go down over the Adirondacks – especially when there's a band playing, as there usually is on summer weekends.

A good way to see the waterfront and some of the city beaches is the twelve-mile **Island Line bike path**, which follows a scruffy former railroad bed built by the Rutland Railway in 1900 to connect the Great Lakes with the New England seacoast. Starting a couple of miles south of Burlington's downtown, it winds on and about the shoreline, all the way north to Colchester, before ending abruptly past the end of Mills Point in Mallets Bay. **Local Motion** (ⓣ802/652-BIKE), the cycling advocacy group here, is pushing for the trail to connect to the Champlain Islands and on to Canada. It also rent bikes (mid-May to mid-Oct, $25 a day, $40 for two days) from its home on the path behind Union Station.

If you're looking to actually get on the water, convivial *Spirit of Ethan Allen III* (call for cruise options and pricing; ⓣ802/862-8300, ⓦwww.soea.com) sets out from the Community Boathouse at the end of College Street. You can rent motorboats and jet skis at **Winds of Ireland** (ⓣ802/863-5090), also in the Community Boathouse. At the end of College Street is **ECHO, the Leahy Center for Lake Champlain** (daily: 10am–5pm, Thurs until 8pm; $9, children

Ethan Allen and his Green Mountain Boys

"I am as resolutely determined to defend the independence of Vermont as Congress (are) that of the United States, and rather than fail, will retire with the hardy Green Mountain Boys into the desolate caverns of the mountains, and wage war with human nature at large."

Flamboyant and controversial, folk hero **Ethan Allen** (1738–89) typifies the independent ethos Vermont has long been known for, even if he did start out a Connecticut farmer. An early convert to the concept of republicanism, Allen gained renown as a statesman who united Vermonters in their cause for independence and their right to own land. He also helped establish the image of the rugged individualist, contemptuous of federal authority (be it the Crown or Congress), that is carried on by second-amendment fanatics and militiamen to this day.

In the 1760s, Benning Wentworth, the royal governor of New Hampshire, assumed his authority would naturally extend to the unclaimed territory to the north and west and began issuing New Hampshire Grants for the area now known as Vermont. After Wentworth had been distributing these grants for more than a decade, King George III decided that New York's governor wielded the rightful authority over the territory, and the original settlers and their townships were subjected to burdensome New York fees or, worse, had their lands confiscated.

The settlers responded by forming a citizens' militia, the **Green Mountain Boys**, to protect their rights, electing Ethan Allen as their colonel. Shortly thereafter, Allen and other family members formed the Onion River Land Company to speculate on the contested Wentworth land grants. This appears to have been a brilliant double strategy: as the Allens sold off the cheap grants to would-be settlers in Massachusetts and Connecticut, they increased the strength of their numbers opposing the Yorkers. And as the numbers increased to back up their claim to the land, the previously worthless grants increased in value accordingly. Eventually, the Allens were selling grants purchased at ten cents an acre for five dollars an acre, a pretty profit indeed. In the meantime, Allen and his fellow settlers were developing the area, building roads and establishing a population center on Burlington Bay.

Allen and (future traitor) Colonel Benedict Arnold were behind the assault on Fort Ticonderoga, the first British property taken by America. Allen eventually became commander of the armed forces of the Commonwealth of Vermont. While defending America's northern border from a renewed British assault from Canada, Allen and other Vermont representatives petitioned Congress to recognize Vermont and to admit her into the American Confederacy. When New York succeeded in blocking Vermont's attempts, the Allens began secret negotiations with the British to guarantee their sovereignty. These negotiations became considerably less attractive after the defeat of Cornwallis (1781) and the Treaty of Paris (1783).

With the coming of peace, Ethan Allen began to put together an impressive farm on the Winooski (Onion) River at Burlington, now known as the Ethan Allen Homestead (see overleaf), where he settled down to become a philosopher and writer. Allen died in 1789, only six years after peace with England, with Vermont yet to join the Union.

$6; ⓣ802/864-1848, ⓦwww.echovermont.org), which affords the opportunity to handle all sorts of slimy lake-dwelling creatures and peek in on intriguing exhibits on area marine life; it's more for the kids than their parents.

The **Church Street Marketplace**, a pedestrian mall a few blocks from the waterfront, holds Burlington's finest old buildings – including an attractive City Hall – and most of its modern cafés and boutiques. It's at its busiest at night and on weekend days, both good people-watching times. Although locals complain that the marketplace has become inundated with chain stores, it still supports a number of unique businesses. Avoid the huge Borders and instead leaf through the **Crow Bookshop**, 14 Church St (☎802/862-0848), or **North Country Books**, 2 Church St (☎802/862-6413), two of the better independent bookstores that pepper downtown. Another spot with local flavor is **Lake Champlain Chocolates**, 65 Church St (☎802/862-5185), a gourmet chocolate shop and café which tempts with hot chocolate and espresso, homemade ice cream, fudge, and, of course, chocolate. You can view the candy-making process at their **plant** nearby at 750 Pine St (Mon–Fri on the hour, 9am–2pm; free; ☎802/864-1807), learn how chocolate is produced, and of course, snag some free samples.

College Street leads east from the marketplace to the sleepy campus of the **University of Vermont** (better known as UVM, for Universitas Viridis Montis, a Latin rendering of the state's alleged, and grammatically dubious, French nomenclature). UVM, founded in 1791 by local hero Ethan Allen's brother Ira, is a comprehensive research university which houses Vermont's largest collection of art and anthropological pieces. The **Robert Hull Fleming Museum** (May to early Sept Tues–Fri noon–4pm, Sat–Sun 1–5pm; rest of Sept through April Tues–Fri 9am–4pm, Sat–Sun 1–5pm; $5; ☎802/656-2090, Ⓦwww.flemingmuseum.org), at 61 Colchester Ave, holds some good examples of European Baroque paintings and pre-Columbian artifacts. To catch more art, arrive on the first Friday of each month, when Burlington City Arts sponsors the free First Friday Artwalk, which traverses over fifteen downtown galleries from 5–8pm (April–Oct; ☎802/865-7166).

North of Burlington along Rte-127 in **WINOOSKI**, the **Ethan Allen Homestead** (June–Oct Mon–Sat 10am–4pm, Sun 1–4pm; rest of year call ☎802/865-4556 for hours; $5) is the 1787 farmhouse in which the Revolutionary War hero spent the last two years of his life. The attached museum is in a re-created eighteenth-century tavern. You can hear about colonial life and pastimes as you sit on uncomfortable, but true-to-period furniture. The 1400-acre farmland, which is owned by the Winooski Park District, is open to the public, meaning you can picnic on the grounds or even kayak your way here from Burlington.

More raucous fun can be had at the **Magic Hat Brewing Company**, five minutes south of downtown off Rte-7 at 5 Bartlett Bay Rd, South Burlington (store open Mon–Sat 10am–6pm, Sun noon–5pm; tours every hour Wed–Fri at 3–5pm, Sat 12–3pm; ☎802/658-BREW). Its free tours make the science of beer-making look fun, and free samples enhance the experience even further.

The Shelburne Museum

It takes a whole day, if not more, to fully appreciate the fabulous fifty-acre collection of unalloyed Americana gathered at the **Shelburne Museum**, seven miles south of Burlington on US-7 in Shelburne (daily: May–Oct 10am–5pm, guided tours at 1pm; $18, $9 children, grants two-day entry; ☎802/985-3346, Ⓦwww.shelburnemuseum.org). The brainchild of heiress Electra Havemeyer Webb (1888-1960), who aimed to create a distinctly American "collection of collections" is probably the nation's finest celebration of its own inventive past.

More than thirty buildings, some original and some newly constructed, dot the grounds. Besides seven fully furnished historic houses that were moved intact from elsewhere in the region, there's a smithy, a jail, and a general store, all of which aim to re-create aspects of everyday life over the past two centuries. Of the several buildings devoted to American high art, the most notable is the **Webb Gallery**, which focuses on nineteenth-century pieces. Much of this rotating collection consists of naturalist work, such as a fine range of James Audubon's bird prints; and there is also an intriguing portrait of Seneca Indian leader Sagayewatha and one of Anna Mary Robertson Moses' (aka Grandma Moses) few cityscapes, *Cambridge, ca. 1944.* The collection is most notable for its assemblage of folk art, including decoys, weather vanes, tools, quilts, carriages, and circus memorabilia. The carnivalesque theme continues at the horseshoe-shaped **Circus Museum**, a homage to spectacle, American-style, featuring Barnum & Bailey ads with harrowing representations of clowns and wild animals, as well as the Edgar Kirk Brothers Toy Circus, a tableau of the big top, carved over a fifty-year period and made up of over 35,000 wooden spectators, vendors, animal acts, and trapeze artists. Another must-see is the **Stagecoach Inn**, which holds a wonderfully nostalgic assemblage of trade and tavern signs, most notably cigar-store figures, and a giant copper tooth forged in 1900.

The collections go beyond Americana. One of the best buildings is the Greek Revival **Electra Havemeyer Webb Memorial Building**, constructed between 1960 and 1967, complete with towering Ionic columns. Within it, six rooms are a meticulous reconstruction of Webb's luxurious Manhattan apartment. The highlights are the works by Rembrandt and many French Impressionists, including Manet and Degas.

The grounds themselves are a joy to browse, and with the size of the place you'll rarely feel crowded; a stroll will bring you past lilac gardens in spring and stunning foliage in fall, over covered bridges, and to a working blacksmith's shop. The village includes a **Shaker barn** from Canterbury, a **schoolhouse**, a railroad station, even an enormous, 892-ton steam **paddlewheeler**, the *SS Ticonderoga*, that plied the lake waters between Burlington and Plattsburgh, NY before being retired in 1953. Its tiny quarters have been restored to its 1923 elegance, complete with concession stand and deck chairs. A lighthouse built in 1871 on Lake Champlain's Colchester Reef is now right next door.

Shelburne Farms

Next to the Shelburne Museum, **Shelburne Farms**, 1611 Harbor Rd (mid-May to mid-Oct 9am–5pm; $9 walking trails plus tour, $6 for just trails; ⓣ802/985-8686, ⓦwww.shelburnefarms.org) is a working farm reborn as a non-profit environmental education center. A guided tour of railroad mogul Dr Seward Webb's estate reveals his descendants' commitment to sustainable farming – though on an incongruously large scale. The undulating landscape is punctuated by three massive buildings: the main house, which overlooks Lake Champlain and the Adirondacks, a coach barn, and a horseshoe-shaped farm barn. You can get some scenic exercise in by walking the 4.5-mile Farm Trail that circles the property, or the half-mile Lone Tree Hill trail and numerous side paths diverging from the roadways. The farm's mansion is the *Inn at Shelburne Farms*, open mid-May to mid-October, with 26 deluxe guestrooms (see p.438). The dining room serves breakfast, dinner, and Sunday brunch. You can tour the grand inn and its gardens, and take tea there for $15 on Tuesdays and Thursdays.

Eating

Burlington's best **restaurants** are located along Main and Church streets. American cuisine dominates the menus but a few ethnic eateries provide alternatives. The presence of ten thousand students ensures that there are plenty of inexpensive spots, while the academic tone brings a certain sophistication to the café culture. Keep in mind that this is one of the most vehement anti-smoking towns in the state, and smoking is banned in most eateries.

American Flatbread 115 St Paul St ⓣ802/861-2999. Wildly popular, especially on weekends, with organically grown wheat for the dough and all natural toppings, including locally made cheeses and sausage. Closed between lunch and dinner.

Augie's 211 College St ⓣ802/865-2800. Dimly lit restaurant – indeed, at first glance it seems to be closed – serving spicy Cajun specials such as fried catfish, gumbo, and jambalaya.

Daily Planet 15 Center St, behind the Church Street Marketplace ⓣ802/862-9647. This brightly colored spot offers a creative menu melding Asian and Mediterranean cooking with old-fashioned American comfort food, à la *satay* burgers and *saag paneer* with mashed potatoes. Highly recommended.

Five Spice Café 175 Church St ⓣ802/864-4045. Excellent Southeast Asian fare, with vegetarian options, and elaborate, delightfully named dishes such as Evil Jungle Prince (chicken and veggies in a coconut milk curry). Inventive desserts (ginger tangerine cheesecake, for instance) and a popular dim sum brunch (for which reservations are essential) on Sundays.

Leunig's Bistro 115 Church St ⓣ802/863-3759 or 1-800/491-1281. Sleek, modern bistro (and priced accordingly) serving contemporary continental cuisine. Outdoor dining when weather permits and live jazz Tues–Thurs.

NECI Commons 25 Church St ⓣ802/862-6324. One of the seven Vermont restaurants operated by the New England Culinary Institute. It's a kick to take one of the high stools facing the open kitchen and watch the students churn out halibut in plum wine broth, vegan risotto, and "uncommon meatloaf," all under the watchful eye of the teacher chef. Very popular, so reservations are recommended. Closed Mon.

Pauline's Café and Restaurant 1834 Shelburne Rd, South Burlington ⓣ802/862-1081. Inventive American cuisine with a continental flavor, using local produce. Light meals in a casual setting downstairs, more formality and higher prices upstairs.

Penny Cluse Café 169 Cherry St ⓣ802/651-8834. Omelets made to order, pancakes, sandwiches, salads, and good vegetarian lunches for under $10. Only open for breakfast and lunch.

Red Onion 140 Church St ⓣ802/865-2563. The best sandwiches in town are made to order in this small shop with a mouth-watering menu, which includes some good vegetarian options. The "red onion" sandwich is a standout, and one can easily fill two people. Open daily, but closes 8pm.

Shanty on the Shore 181 Battery St ⓣ802/864-0238. Absolutely fresh seafood in a laidback setting with views of Lake Champlain. Burlington's best – if not only – raw bar.

Smokejack's 156 Church St ⓣ802/658-1119. Innovative American cuisine as well as standard steak and seafood, all smoked over an oak-wood grill. Their burgers are recognized as some of the best in the country. Liquid refreshment comes in the form of punchy Bloody Marys, intriguing cocktails, and a multitude of beer options. Choose from the many wines to help wash down the regional cheese plate.

Sneakers 36 Main St, Winooski ⓣ802/655-9081. This is the place for breakfast, and you ought to arrive early for it on weekends. Delicious waffles, homemade granola, eggs Benedict (try the smoked turkey eggs Benedict) and fresh squeezed juices served in a diner-like setting with Art Deco mirrors lining the walls. Good weekday lunches too.

Sweetwaters 120 Church St ⓣ802/864-9800. American grill standards in a converted bank with sidewalk dining, most notable for its bison burgers and extensive Sunday brunch. Attractive raised street terrace – open in good weather.

Trattoria Delia 152 St Paul St ⓣ802/864-5253. Traditional regional Italian fare that goes beyond the usual pasta dishes – try the wild boar served over soft polenta – and a great wine list, at reasonable prices.

Zabby and Elf's Stone Soup 211 College St ⓣ802/862-7616. Excellent "mostly vegetarian" café, featuring a wide variety of sandwiches, homemade soups, cakes, and the like.

Nightlife and entertainment

The **drinking** scene here is at its most active when school is in session, but Burlington's cafés and bars come to life during the summer as well. Though there are a handful of dance clubs, **nightlife** revolves mostly around live music. Pick up a copy of the free newspaper, *Seven Days*, which has listings of music and stage shows. Several of Burlington's concert venues are big enough to draw indie bands from New York and around New England, but the local band scene is a formidable presence in its own right. Downtown's Art Deco-style **Flynn Theater**, 153 Main St, across from City Hall and the Church Street Marketplace (Ⓣ802/863-5966), plays host to a wide array of talent; previous acts include local hippie heroes Phish and works by Broadway touring companies. Also, during the school year, UVM presents the **Lane Series** (Ⓣ802/656-4455), a collection of musical performances. You can hear everything from folk-pop, to jazz quartets, to the occasional opera. Beware that bars and clubs are quite strict about checking IDs, as this is a college town. Make sure to have proper proof of age when venturing out for the evening or you are guaranteed to be turned away.

Club Metronome 188 Main St Ⓣ802/865-4563. This very hip club above *Nectar's* (see below) hosts some live acts, but is mainly a funked-out dance venue featuring house and techno music. Saturday night's "Retronome" is when Eighties music dominates the dance floor.

Muddy Waters 184 Main St Ⓣ802/658-0466. Colorful, crunchy clientele adorn this popular coffeehouse with a crazy interior lined with used furniture, thrift-store rejects, plants, and rough-hewn paneled walls. Extremely potent caffeine beverages. Open late.

Nectar's 188 Main St Ⓣ802/658-4771. Follow the rotating neon sign to this retro lounge lined with vinyl booths and Formica tables. Sip a stylish cocktail, smoke a Lucky Strike, and tap your feet to lounge acts. This was the inspiration for Phish's 1992 album title *A Picture of Nectar*, as the club hosted many of their earliest shows. Cover charge on weekends or for bigger local acts.

Rasputin's 163 Church St Ⓣ802/864-9324. Popular UVM hangout with a raucous drinking scene that carries on until late in the evening. Good DJs pump up the energy level to new heights on weekends.

Red Square 136 Church St Ⓣ802/859-8909. For those in the mood for a cosmopolitan experience in the depths of the Green Mountains, *Red Square* is the place to sip cocktails amidst a highbrow clientele. The food menu is also quite inviting and worth further investigation. Live music every night, often jazz, played outside when the weather permits. Cover on weekends.

Ruben James 153 Main St Ⓣ802/864-0744. This joint brings in a slightly older crowd for mouth-watering microbrews, loud live bar music, pool tournaments, and football on the TV.

Second Floor 165 Church St Ⓣ802/660-2088. *Second Floor* serves as the site for some serious dancing, usually to hip-hop and techno, with the occasional theme night thrown in for variety.

Three Needs 207 College St Ⓣ802/658-0889. This bar does a fine job of taking care of its customers' three most important needs: great beer, cheap pool, and Sunday night *Simpsons* parties with excellent drink specials. Like a small private taproom; all microbrews, their own as well as "'guest"' beers.

Vermont Pub and Brewery 144 College St Ⓣ802/865-0500. Roomy and convivial brewpub, offering free tastes of its various beers – Dogbite Bitter is the best – plus a good inexpensive menu (until midnight) with live music on some weekends.

South of Burlington

Vermont is one of the few states with designated **Underwater Historic Preserves** (details on Ⓣ802/828-3226), where divers can see wrecks on the lake floor. There are several of these underwater "state parks" close to Burlington, and the best place to find out about them is at the **Lake Champlain Maritime Museum** in Basin Harbor, seven miles west of **VERGENNES** (daily: May to mid-Oct 10am–5pm; $9; Ⓣ802/475-2022, Ⓦwww.lcmm.org). The museum boasts a life-sized replica of the 1776 gunboat *Philadelphia II*, displays about Lake Champlain shipwrecks and the technology used to research them, and details of the horse-powered ferry that plied the lake a century ago. The museum is on the grounds of the Basin Harbor Club, where the *Red Mill Restaurant* serves three meals a day in summer, breakfast-only at other times.

Champlain Islands

Curling southward into Lake Champlain from Canada, the sparsely populated **Champlain Islands** comprise four narrow, oblong land masses – **NORTH HERO**, **GRAND ISLE**, **ALBURG**, and **ISLE LA MOTTE** – that never really caught on development-wise, despite being the site of the first settlement in Vermont, way back in 1666. After the Revolutionary War, Vermonters Ira and Ethan Allen staked claims to much of the islands' area, modestly naming them North and South Hero (the latter was later changed to Grand Isle). Today, though, the islands' only real industry is farming, evidenced by the silo-dotted hayfields and ubiquitous bovine odor.

French explorer Pierre de St-Paul's short-lived encampment is now occupied by **St Anne's Shrine**, on West Shore Road, Isle La Motte. Groups of devoted Catholics and amateur miracle purveyors surround a statue of a prayerful St Anne during the summer; the shrine is right near a popular beach. Also on the island is a massive granite statue of **Samuel de Champlain**, who first landed here in 1609. Grand Isle's claim to historical fame is the **Hyde Log Cabin**, US-2 (July to early Sept Thurs–Mon 11am–5pm; $1; ⓣ802/828-3051), built in 1783. Its modest museum is notable for its collection of household artifacts such as churns, rusty bedpans, and makeshift ovens from Vermont's earliest frontier days.

There is surprisingly little outdoor activity in these parts save for hunting and fishing, though some good opportunities exist for swimming during the summer. The area's best beach is the nearly half-mile strand at **Sand Bar State Park** (ⓣ802/893-2825), actually on the mainland just below the US-2 bridge to Grand Isle. If that one's too crowded (as it often is in summer), head to **Knight Point State Park**, North Hero (ⓣ802/372-8389), a placid, sandy shoreline enclosing a bay.

Practicalities

The Champlain Islands are accessible by road along US-2, which is linked to Grand Isle, North Hero, and Alburg by a network of bridges. Isle La Motte lies at the end of Rte-129. For a **place to stay** on the islands, the *Thomas Mott Homestead*, Blue Rock Road off Rte-78, Alburg (ⓣ802/796-4402 or 1-800/348-0843, ⓦwww.thomas-mott-bb.com; ❺), is the superior B&B choice, with large rooms, fantastic breakfasts, comfortable beds, modern furniture, and canoes, bicycles, and paddleboats ready for your use. Less expensive is *Charlie's Northland Lodge*, along US-2 in North Hero (ⓣ802/372-8822, ⓔdorclrk@aol.com; ❹), a cozy hostelry with shared baths. The Champlain Islands do offer some of Vermont's best **camping**. Knight Island State Park (ⓣ802/524-6353) is enormously secluded, with a multitude of unspoiled nature trails, though you should reserve early to get one of the seven primitive campsites ($14). Grand Isle State Park, 36 E Shore Rd S, Grand Isle (ⓣ802/372-4300), provides a suitable alternative, with 156 highly developed campsites ($16), complete with restrooms, hot showers, and RVs galore.

The islands offer nothing special in the way of **eating**, though carnivores will enjoy the *Sand Bar Inn*, US-2, South Hero (ⓣ802/372-6911), an all-American steakhouse with sweeping lake views. The *Ruthcliffe Lodge and Restaurant*, Old Quarry Road, Isle La Motte (ⓣ802/928-3200 or 1-800/769-8162), serves decent steak-and-potatoes type fare for daily dinner, though lodgers get breakfast too.

For information on attractions and accommodation, contact the **Lake Champlain Islands Chamber of Commerce**, US-2, North Hero (Mon–Fri 9am–4pm; ⓣ802/372-8400 or 1-800/262-5226, ⓦwww.champlainislands.com).

St Albans and around

Sleepy **ST ALBANS**, about halfway between Burlington and the Canadian border along I-89, is a town only by Vermont's standards, which means you can cover it by foot in less than an hour. Although there's some ugly mall sprawl to the north, St Albans' center has a large town green, landscaped on the slope of a hill, lined with churches at the top and small, mostly local, shops at the bottom. The town has the curious distinction as the site of the northernmost engagement of the Civil War. The "St Albans Raid" took place on October 22, 1864, when disguised Confederate soldiers entered the town from Canada, robbed its three banks of over $200,000, took some hostages, killed one citizen, and decamped to Québec, where they were arrested and tried but never extradited back to the US. The town makes much of this event, particularly during the Civil War Days festival in late October, when history buffs descend here to re-create the event. Meanwhile, the **St Albans Historical Museum**, Church Street, at Bishop (June–Oct Mon–Fri 1–4pm; $4; ⓣ802/527-7933), also has displays on the raid, as well as a range of exhibits that vary greatly in quality. The best of these are artifacts from the town's earliest days, including military memorabilia, a re-created railroad station, and arcane remedies and antique medical devices recovered from local physicians and apothecaries. St Albans is also, as seat of the largest maple-producing county in the US, home to Vermont's Annual Maple Festival, held in April, locally known as the "Sugarin' Off" party.

Practicalities

The **St Albans Area Chamber of Commerce**, 2 N Main St (ⓣ802/524-2444, ⓦwww.stalbanschamber.com), is your best bet for tourist information. The town is the last stop on Amtrak's *Vermonter* service. **Accommodation** in and around the town is reasonable compared to the rest of the state. Least expensive is the *Cadillac Motel*, 213 S Main St (ⓣ802/524-2191, ⓦwww.motel-cadillac.com; ❸), which is low on amenities, but very clean and surrounded by pleasant grounds with a waterfall. The area's best B&B is *Back Inn Time*, 68 Fairfield St (ⓣ802/527-5116; ❹), featuring antique-filled rooms in a restored Victorian. Special events include Murder Mystery Weekends and cooking lessons.

Eating options won't dazzle or disappoint. Hearty meat-and-potatoes fare can be had at *Diamond Jim's Grille*, north of town along US-7 (N Main Street), in the Highgate Mall Shopping Center (ⓣ802/524-9280). *Old Foundry*, 1-3 Federal St (ⓣ802/524-9665), serves steaks and broiled chicken in a fine-dining establishment (mains $12–20), while the more entertaining, ethnically confused bar/restaurant *McGuel's Irish Burro Café*, 18 Lake St (ⓣ802/527-1276; closed Sun), has south-of-the-border fare and a dizzying array of beers.

Around St Albans

The coast of Lake Champlain beckons a mere three miles west of St Albans along Rte-36, where the **Kill Kare State Park** (ⓣ802/524-6021; summer only) has some decent swimming and boating facilities, though it tends to be crowded. Better to take the $3 ferry to the state park on nearby **Burton Island** (ⓣ802/524-6353; summer only), much more secluded, with three miles of shoreline, hiking trails, and boat and canoe rentals, as well as 42 **campsites**. North of St Albans along I-89, just below the Canadian border, Rte-78 veers west to the **Missisquoi National Wildlife Refuge** in **SWANTON**

(Ⓣ802/868-4781; free), a remote lakeside nature preserve where you can meet Vermont's native beasts face-to-face. The fauna range from the mundane (waterfowl, deer, and turtles) to the borderline scary (vampire bats). Best to bring along bug repellent, especially during summer.

Northeast Kingdom

Remote and relentlessly rural, Vermont's **Northeast Kingdom** takes its name from a remark made by Vermont senator George Aiken in 1949, referring to the several counties that bulge out eastward to form the state's uppermost corner. The only locales approaching town status are **St Johnsbury** and **Newport**, at the region's southern and northern boundaries, each of which still has less than nine thousand inhabitants. I-91 slices through the kingdom, but you can't really appreciate the area's intense quiet and natural beauty without traveling along its innumerable back roads. Here you can drive for hours, passing through vast expanses of green, garnished by cows, barns, and other bucolic accessories. Aside from its idyllic character, the region offers little in the way of formal sights, with a few notable exceptions such as Glover's **Bread and Puppet Museum**, though opportunities for recreation abound; indeed two of the state's least crowded and most challenging ski areas, **Jay Peak** and **Burke Mountain**, are in this region.

St Johnsbury and around

The town of **ST JOHNSBURY**, estimated population 7560, imagines itself a thriving center in the midst of Vermont's sparsely populated northeast corner; however, its abundance of elaborate architecture, all turrets and marble and stained glass, seems terribly out of proportion to its size. Still, it's the biggest municipality around (the nearest town is Barre, 35 miles away on US-2), and an important travel hub if you happen to be heading this far up.

St J, as it's referred to by locals, grew from a frontier outpost to its current size thanks to the ingenuity of resident **Thaddeus Fairbanks**, the "scale king," who earned his fortune and a minor place in history by inventing the platform scale in the 1830s. Much of his wealth was showered on the city in the form of funding for new municipal buildings and elaborate churches. One place that celebrates his legacy, the Romanesque **Fairbanks Museum and Planetarium**, 1302 Main St, at Prospect (Mon–Sat 9am–5pm, Sun 1–5pm, planetarium shows Sat & Sun 1.30pm; museum $5, planetarium $3; Ⓣ802/748-2372, Ⓦwww.fairbanksmuseum.org), has the predictable range of platform scales, but also contains a collection of historical artifacts, from Civil War pieces to Zulu war shields, various Japanese handicrafts (an excellent collection of tiny *netsuke* figurines), antique dolls, and in the first floor's natural science exhibit, over one hundred tiny stuffed hummingbirds from all over the globe. It also serves as an official US **weather station**, though some of this is off limits to the public. Just down Main Street, the **St Johnsbury Athenaeum** (Mon & Wed 10am–8pm, Tues, Thurs & Fri 10am–5.30pm, Sat 9.30am–4pm, closed Sun; free; ⓣ802/748-8291) houses a number of excellent paintings from the Hudson River school, including Andrew Bierstadt's gargantuan *Domes of the Yosemite*. The Athenaeum and Museum are two of the fifteen or so architecturally significant buildings on Main Street, which also include several churches and private homes. These are all detailed in a sheet published by the Chamber of Commerce (see below), and a walk past them should while away a pleasant hour or so.

If you're caught in this part of the world with a yearning for something to do besides stroll, you may find your needs fulfilled by the surprisingly eclectic offerings at the **Catamount Arts Center**, 139 East Ave (ⓣ802/748-2600 or 1-888/757-5559). The small brick building houses a movie theater showing foreign and art films, a concert hall where the offerings focus on jazz, New Age, and world music, a café, and an excellent video store, specializing in foreign films.

△ Fairbanks Museum and Planetarium

Practicalities

The Northeast Kingdom Chamber of Commerce has a **Welcome Center** at 51 Depot Square (May–Oct: Mon–Sat 9am–8pm, Sun 11am–4pm; Nov–April: Mon–Fri 8.30am–5pm, Sat 10am–5pm; ⓣ802/748-3678 or 1-800/639-6379, ⓦwww.nekchamber.com), which dispenses information on the whole region. **Cyclists** should contact the Northeastern Vermont Development Association (ⓣ802/748-5181, ⓦwww.nvda.net) for their brochure which lists over twenty routes in the Kingdom.

Accommodation is limited mostly to relatively cheap, independent motels packed with travelers taking respite from their journeys along I-91. One of the better-equipped ones is the *Fairbanks Inn*, 401 Western Ave (ⓣ802/748-5666, ⓦwww.stjay.com; ⑥), which has a heated pool, putting green, and cable TV. There's also the *Yankee Traveler Motel*, 342 Portland St (ⓣ802/748-3156; ③), a 42-room hotel with a pool, cable TV, and cheerful staff. Cheaper and closer to the town center, the *Holiday Motel*, 222 Hastings Hill (ⓣ802/748-2393 or 742-8192; ④), has comfortable rooms with all the basics.

There is not as much choice as far as **eating** goes. Try *Elements*, 98 Mill St (ⓣ802/748-8400; closed Sun & Mon), which serves what they call "creative comfort food" in a familiar, brick-walled space. *Anthony's Diner*, at 321 Railroad St (ⓣ802/748-3613) is good for a quick grilled-cheese sandwich or meatloaf platter. A simple wrap or pastry with some strong coffee can be found at the *Boxcar Bookshop & Caboose Café*, 394 Railroad St (ⓣ802/748-3551), which also carries a quirky collection of books.

Vermont's cheeses

An economic lightweight at a national – and even a regional – level, Vermont does have a habit of doing a few things very well: ice cream, maple syrup, and, perhaps most notably, **cheese**. Of course, nostalgic cheese historians will look back to the heady days at the turn of last century when eighty percent of Vermont's milk was being churned into butter and cheese, and lament that things aren't what they once were. Still, the state produces a very respectable seventy million pounds of cheese a year, with a significant amount coming from family farms using traditional methods: the type of product good enough to scoop twelve awards at the 18th American Cheese Society Annual Conference & Judging in 2001. Predictably, the tourist industry has cashed in on the reputation of Vermont cheese, and refrigerators containing the most sought-after brands hum and rattle in gift shops statewide. If it's cheddar you're after, the best known is probably Cabot Cheddar, which comes in a variety of sharp flavors. Crowley Cheddar (made in Healdville) is less acidic and moister than the English-style cheeses made elsewhere in Vermont; Grafton Village Cheese is known for its older cheddars with an earthy, creamy taste; and Neighborly Farms (Randolph Center) carries the flag of organic cheddar. Cheeses made with sheep's milk, such as feta, camembert, and brie, are produced by Peaked Mountain Farm (Townsend) and Vermont Shepherd (Putney), among others. Lazy Lady Farm and Vermont Butter and Cheese Company are the top names in goat's-milk cheese. Such is the pull of cheese in this state, that several of the above-mentioned producers – and others not mentioned here – have formed the **Vermont Cheese Trail**, opening their doors to the paying public to reveal cheese-making methods and give away pound upon pound of free samples. For more information, contact the Vermont Cheese Council (Ⓣ802/985-8686 ext 46, Ⓦwww.vtcheese.com).

West of St Johnsbury

DANVILLE, a nondescript town that lies about ten miles west of St Johnsbury at the intersection of US-2 and Rte-15, stakes its limited claim to fame as the headquarters of the American Society of Dowsers, based in **Dowser's Hall**, on Danville Green (Ⓣ802/684-3417). Revealing what dowsers do are displays and literature on the practice of intuitively identifying underground water sources using a forked branch or pendulum.

Vermont is justifiably proud of its cheese (see box above), and the small town of **CABOT**, a few miles further west from Danville, is the epicenter of the state's cheese production. The **Cabot Creamery** (visitors' center: daily June–Oct 9am–5pm; Nov–Dec & Feb–May Mon–Sat 9am–4pm; Jan Mon–Sat 10am–4pm; Ⓣ1-800/837-4261) churns out around fifteen million pounds of cheese a year, or approximately twenty percent of the total state production. Tours leave every thirty minutes ($2), starting with a twelve-minute video explaining how Cabot got to where it is today, a walk through the plant itself, and ending with an opportunity to gorge yourself on the several different varieties of cheddar for which the company has become known.

CRAFTSBURY, farther north on slow, bumpy Rte-14, is just about in the middle of nowhere – which is exactly its appeal. This is as lovely a tiny Vermont town as you're likely to see, with a history that stretches back to the mid-eighteenth century and includes one native son who served as Vermont's governor. It has seen virtually no growth in the two-hundred-plus years since its inception; the town center, **Craftsbury Common**, consists of little more than a post office and some quaint inns, best of which are the very upmarket *Inn on the Common* (Ⓣ802/586-9619 or 1-800/521-2233, Ⓦwww.innonthecommon.

com; ❼), whose dining room, *Trellis*, serves excellent traditional American fare, and the homey *Whetstone Brook B&B*, 1037 S Craftsbury Rd (℡802/586-6916; ❹). While the main recreation here is getting away from activity, the surrounding hills are crisscrossed with a web of **trails** popular for mountain-biking and skiing. The Craftsbury Outdoor Center (℡1-800/729-7751) provides service for all your needs in these activities.

North to Canada

From St Johnsbury, I-91 runs north up to Canada; everything east of the highway is fairly mountainous, and there are a few good diversions not too far off the main road – though if you wander too far off you could easily get lost, as much of the region is undeveloped. This part of the Kingdom is home to pristine lakes and abundant wildlife, including some ten thousand moose.

Burke Mountain and Lake Willoughby

The cream of the United States' crop of young downhill skiers trains at the **Burke Mountain Resort**, Mountain Road, East Burke (℡802/626-3322, ⓦwww.skiburke.com), best approached from I-91 exit 23 onto US-5, then north on Rte-114. Because of the mountain's isolation, Burke's 43 trails are virtually deserted compared to places such as Killington and Stowe, but they're all tough; three-quarters of the trails are intermediate and higher (lift tickets $42 Mon–Fri, $52 Sat–Sun). The Cross Country Center has about fifty miles of groomed and back-country trails, and you can also take a lesson (℡802/535-7722, ⓦwww.burkexc.com). East Burke is also one of the access points to the **Kingdom Trails** (℡802/626-0737 or 802/535-5662, ⓦwww.kingdomtrails.org), a hundred miles of publicly and privately owned land where you can go **mountain-biking**, **hiking**, or **cross-country skiing** (trail passes $7 a day). You can get information on trail routes and access points at **East Burke Sports**, Rte-114, East Burke Village (℡802/626-3215, ⓦwww.eastburkesports.com), or, for $20 per hour, hire a guide for just about any activity possible here. Venture up US-5 to its intersection with Rte-5A and continue north for several miles to be rewarded with views of spectacular **Lake Willoughby**, which is flanked on either side by **mounts Hor** and **Pisgah**. Recreational opportunities abound, from jet-skiing to swimming (there are sand beaches at the lake's north and south ends). Be sure to take note of the waterfalls that line the mountainsides along Rte-5A. Few people **stay** in areas this remote, but the *Willough Vale Inn* (℡802/525-4123 or 1-800/594-9102, ⓦwww.willoughvale.com; ❺), just off Rte-5A, offers both rooms and lakefront cottages in a wonderfully secluded setting; there's also a first-rate restaurant. Incidentally, Robert Frost stayed here when it was Conley Farm in 1909, and composed *A Servant to Servants* after meeting the farm's proprietress. In season, you can also **camp** at Burke Mountain (May–Oct, $14 tent site or $18.50 for a lean-to).

Glover and Newport

The only reason to hit **GLOVER**, fifteen miles north of St Johnsbury (take Rte-122 north and turn right on Rte-16) is to stop by the **Bread and Puppet Museum** (daily 10am–6pm; free; ℡802/525-3031). The museum got its start in the 1960s from a traveling dramatic troupe that performed anti-Vietnam War puppet shows. The remarkably oversized puppets – they can be as big as five feet and require up to four people to operate – are on view in this peaceful barn setting, a far cry from the group's more volatile protest days. There are free performances every Sunday.

The obscurely located **Old Stone House**, about ten miles south of Newport, just off Rte-58 in Brownington (mid-May to mid-Oct Wed–Sun 11am–5pm; $5; ⓣ802/754-2022), is tricky to find but worth the trouble. Originally a schoolhouse built by the **Reverend Alexander Twilight**, said to be the country's first African-American college graduate and legislator (a point contested by some historians, due to Twilight's mixed-race background), today the building is home to an array of Vermont artifacts, including schoolroom supplies from the period.

The final stop on I-91 before the Québec border, unassuming **NEWPORT** seems more French-Canadian than New England in character. Its main draw is **Lake Memphremagog**, which spans the international border and was once a choice resort area surrounded by grand homes. The lake area is no longer quite so upscale, but still popular enough with vacationing Québecois, who flock here to boat, jet-ski, and swim. The town's drag, Main Street, is lined with quaint brick buildings, many of which are restored relics from the Victorian era. The best **dining** here is the *Eastside Restaurant*, Lake Road (ⓣ802/334-2340), with grilled steaks and chicken and a wonderful view of the lake, but running a close second is *Lago Trattoria*, 95 Main St (ⓣ802/334-8222), with a renowned menu of Italian favorites and hand-crafted pizzas. Serving a breakfast and lunch menu, *Brown Cow*, 350 E Main St (ⓣ802/334-7887), serves omelets and excellent soup, but closes by early afternoon. Should you need to **stay** in Newport, the *Newport City Motel*, 444 E Main St (ⓣ802/334-6558 or 1-800/338-6558; ❸), is a decent, if bland, option.

Jay Peak

The four-thousand-foot summit of the **Jay Peak Resort**, on Rte-242 (ⓣ802/988-2611 or 1-800/451-4449, ⓦwww.jaypeakresort.com), looms just south of the Canadian border, about fifteen miles west of I-91. Jay's 75 trails are some of New England's toughest, and typically only serious skiers venture this far out – unless coming down from Québec. Indeed, those visitors who can prove Canadian residency are allowed to buy the $58 lift tickets with the same amount of Canadian dollars, a concession which results in a considerable saving. Jay Peak consistently receives more snow than any other New England resort, an average of 351 inches a year, something which makes deep-powder skiing a distinct possibility through late April. It has also given the resort a name as the most exciting glade (or tree) skiing in North America. The most popular **accommodation** is *Hotel Jay* (make reservations through the resort at ⓣ1-800/451-4449; ❹), a snazzy ski lodge at the base of the peak; the hotel has deals on lift tickets, a hot tub, and the *Golden Eagle Lounge*, which hosts the area's best après-ski scene. In the summer, rates are lower, and there's an outdoor pool, golf course, and country club. The nearby *Jay Village Inn*, Jay Village (ⓣ802/988-2306; ❹), offers good-sized rooms overlooking the slopes, with billiards, hot tub, and a huge stone fireplace in the lobby. For a good meal, venture a few miles from Jay, where *The Belfry*, on Rte-242 in Montgomery Center (ⓣ802/326-4400), has a relaxed pub atmosphere and meaty specials.

New Hampshire

CANADA
Moosehead Lake
Kennebec River
8
WHITE MOUNTAINS
Lake Champlain
GREEN MOUNTAINS
6
Mount Desert Island
Lake Winnipesaukee
NEW YORK
7
ATLANTIC OCEAN
THE BERKSHIRES
3
1
Cape Cod
2
4
5
N
Martha's Vineyard
Nantucket
Long Island

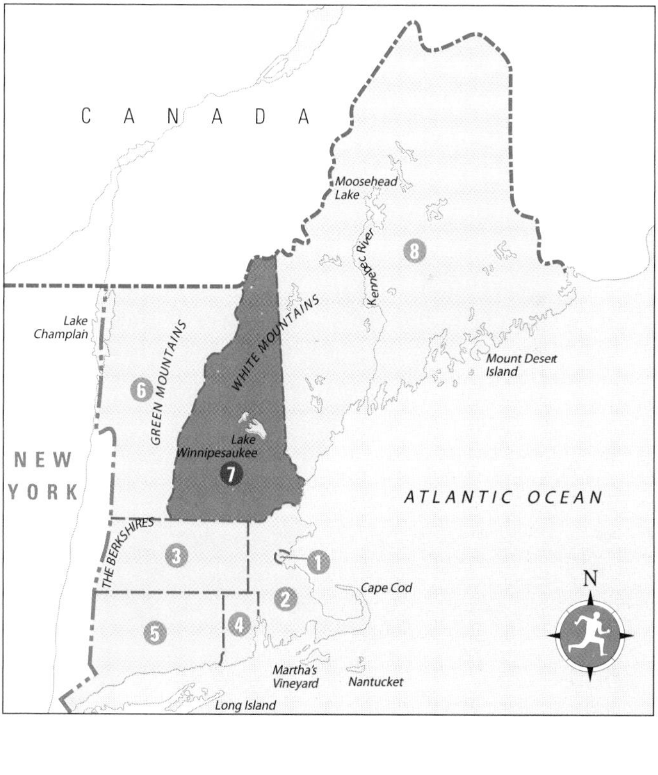

CHAPTER SEVEN
Highlights

* **Portsmouth** That rare commodity: a seaside town with culture and class, displayed in its historic buildings, gourmet restaurants, and highbrow shows. See p.459

* **Canterbury Shaker Village** Tours reveal the crafts and gadgets of an eighteenth-century religious community that died out only in 1992. See p.475

* **Lake Winnipesaukee** Whether from its eastern or western shores, this grand expanse of blue offers a multitude of watery activities. See p.490

* **Grand resort hotels** If you can afford it, hit the luxury of the *Mount Washington* or *Balsams* up in the White Mountains – a far cry from a spartan campground. See pp.512 & 520

* **Cross-country skiing, Jackson** For all its mountainous terrain, New Hampshire still has some excellent places for cross-country skiing, none finer than the pristine and varied trails at Jackson. See p.516

* **Mount Washington** So what if there's a road leading up to the summit of the highest mountain in the northeastern US – it's still one of the most remote, awe-inspiring, and unpredictably exciting places in New England. See p.518

△ A common loon

7

New Hampshire

Similar to Rhode Island, **New Hampshire** is a thin wedge of a state, the sixth smallest in the US, but with surprisingly diverse terrain. The short coastline is strewn with mellow, sun-drenched beaches and capped by **Portsmouth**, a well-preserved colonial town with a crop of excellent restaurants and stylish inns. Farther inland, there are over 1300 lakes to explore; the largest, **Lake Winnipesaukee**, is ringed with both tourist resorts and quiet villages. To the north, the splendor of the **White Mountains** spreads across the state, culminating in the highest peak in New England, the formidable **Mount Washington**. Quaint and relaxing communities are scattered across the southern part of the state, connected by shaded, winding country roads and the enduring small-town pride of their residents.

These days most visitors come to New Hampshire for its outdoor activities. In the warm summer months you can kayak, canoe, swim, fish, hike, climb, or bike, while during winter you can cross-country ski at tiny **Jackson** or downhill ski in the **Franconia Notch** area or at a dozen other ski resorts. As with much of the rest of New England, fall is a popular time to come, when the trees turn vibrant shades and the air temperature drops refreshingly.

All of this makes New Hampshire a busy place, even by New England standards. Much of the state is blanketed with bucolic rural scenery – around **Canterbury Shaker Village** near Concord, for example – but the current tourist authority's motto, "The Road Less Traveled," is not entirely accurate. Some of the major destinations, such as **Weirs Beach**, **North Conway**, and **Hampton Beach**, are extremely well traveled. But if you steer clear of these main draws, the lakes, islands, and snowcapped peaks that define New Hampshire remain both resoundingly spectacular and remote.

Some history

The people of New Hampshire have been an independent and individualistic lot ever since the first settlers survived out of sheer persistence. It was originally explored by Martin Pring in 1603, but the first European settlement was not established until 1623, when Englishman David Thomson brought a small group to **Odiorne Point**, at the mouth of the Piscataqua River.

Soon after, the Royal Council of New England issued land grants to Sir Ferdinando Gorges and John Mason, who founded the Laconia Company with the intention of turning a profit in the fur trade. Without ever having laid eyes on the land, Mason named the region New Hampshire, after his home county in England. Their colony struggled, and after Mason died in 1635, the company was dissolved. A small group of settlers, however, persisted at **Strawbery Banke**, now Portsmouth, ignoring land ownership laws and taking large plots for themselves.

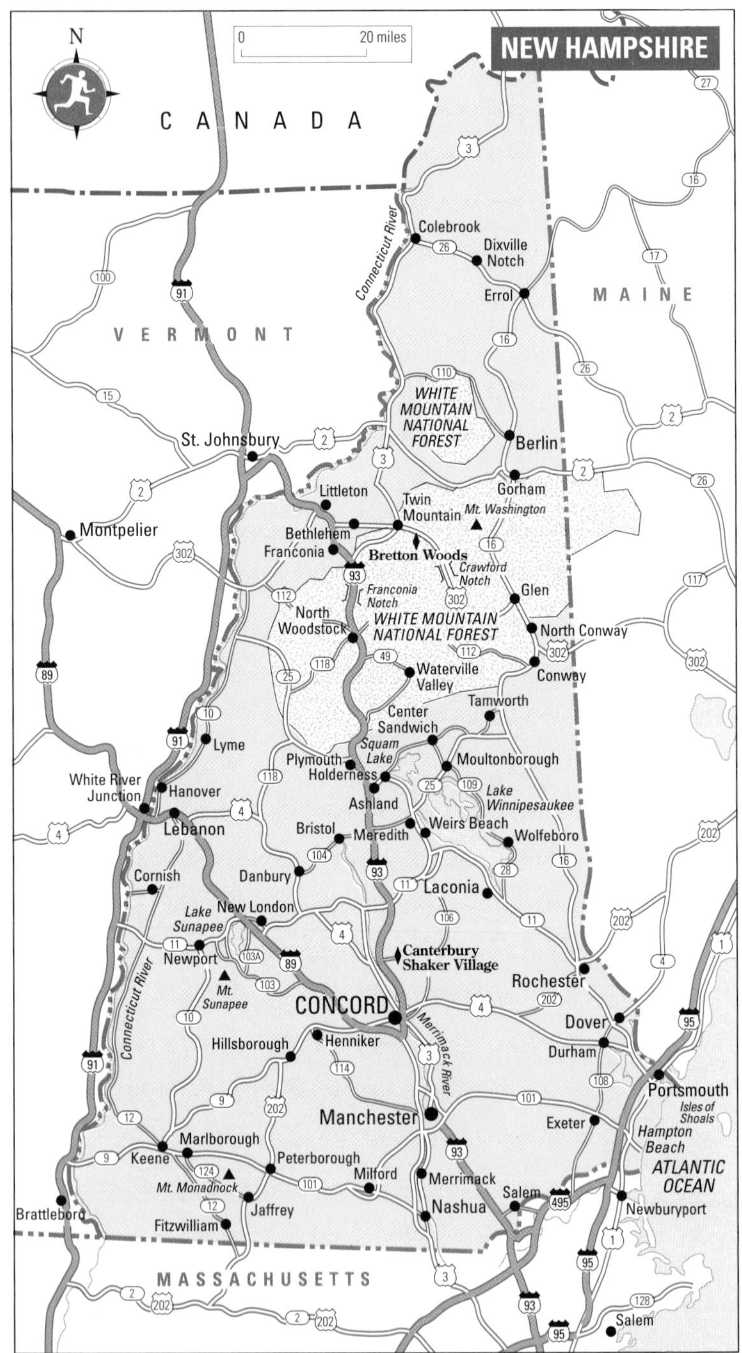
NEW HAMPSHIRE
N
0
20 miles
CANADA
VERMONT
MAINE
MASSACHUSETTS
ATLANTIC OCEAN
Connecticut River
Merrimack River
WHITE MOUNTAIN NATIONAL FOREST
Colebrook
Dixville Notch
Errol
Berlin
Gorham
St. Johnsbury
Montpelier
Littleton
Twin Mountain
Mt. Washington
Bethlehem
Franconia
Bretton Woods
Crawford Notch
Franconia Notch
Glen
North Woodstock
North Conway
Conway
Waterville Valley
Tamworth
Center Sandwich
Squam Lake
Lyme
Plymouth
Holderness
Moultonborough
Lake Winnipesaukee
White River Junction
Hanover
Ashland
Lebanon
Bristol
Meredith
Weirs Beach
Wolfeboro
Cornish
Danbury
Laconia
Lake Sunapee
New London
Newport
Mt. Sunapee
Canterbury Shaker Village
Rochester
CONCORD
Dover
Durham
Hillsborough
Henniker
Portsmouth
Isles of Shoals
Manchester
Exeter
Hampton Beach
Keene
Marlborough
Peterborough
Mt. Monadnock
Milford
Merrimack
Salem
Newburyport
Brattleboro
Jaffrey
Nashua
Fitzwilliam
Salem
3
27
16
26
17
100
91
110
15
2
26
117
302
89
112
93
118
25
49
10
109
4
202
104
28
11
106
103A
103
114
108
101
9
12
124
495
1
95
128

While only the few miles of seashore held sizeable seventeenth-century European communities, the harsh, glacier-scarred interior of New Hampshire, with its dense forests and forbidding mountains, remained the exclusive preserve of the Abenaki and Pennacook tribes of the **Algonquin Indians**. Relations with the Indians turned sour as settlers became more ambitious, damming rivers, logging the forests, and introducing livestock. Fearing they would lose their natural resources forever, the Indians attacked European settlements throughout New Hampshire in 1675. The conflict, known as King Philip's War, continued for several decades, but by the turn of the century the Indian population had been reduced from tens of thousands to less than a thousand – and by 1730, had just about vanished from the state.

By this time, **Portsmouth** was a thriving port, and the financial backbone of the colony. Timber companies and shipbuilding businesses flourished as loggers pushed farther inland from Portsmouth and up the Connecticut River from the south. By the mid-eighteenth century, an extremely profitable mast trade had been established, fueled by the region's dense supply of pine trees and the expansion of England's merchant marine fleet. Just before the Revolutionary War, upon hearing that the king had issued an edict forbidding shipment of gunpowder to the colonies, some four hundred New Hampshire residents invaded **Fort William and Mary**, one of the first overt acts in defiance of England. In January 1776, New Hampshire became the first American state to declare its independence.

Life remained a struggle for many of the settlers. When it became clear that farmers could make little agricultural impact on the rocky terrain of the "granite state," many laborers departed for more fertile lands to the west. With the coming of the Industrial Revolution, however, towns in the Merrimack Valley, such as Nashua, Concord, and Manchester, became major manufacturing centers. Water-powered textile mills were set up along the Merrimack River, and at one point the enormous brick **Amoskeag Mills** in Manchester produced more cloth than any other textile facility in the world.

For a while, the ruthless timber companies looked set to strip all northern New Hampshire bare, but the pristine landscape of the White Mountains turned out to be the state's greatest asset. Large-scale summer tourism began in the latter half of the nineteenth century, when city folk checked into the several dozen grand resort hotels (the *Mount Washington* in Bretton Woods and the *Balsams* in Dixville Notch are the only two that remain), which stood majestically at the foot of the mountains. At one time, fifty trains brought travelers to the mountains daily to see such increasingly famous sites as the now collapsed **Old Man of the Mountain**; many also rode the rickety **Cog Railway** (still operational) to the harsh and unpredictable summit of Mount Washington.

New Hampshire transport

Several major airlines fly in and out of the state's main **airport**, Manchester International (☎603/624-6539), which is conveniently located just off I-93. That's about all that is convenient as far as public transport in New Hampshire is concerned. **Train** services are limited to the tourist trains which run in the mountain areas and Amtrak's new *Downeaster*, which only stops in at the sleepy towns of Exeter, Durham, and Dover. You can get to a few more places by **bus**, but don't bank on seeing much of the northern part of the state if you don't have your own car. Companies which serve New Hampshire include Concord Trailways (☎1-800/639-3317), C&J Trailways (☎603/430-1100 or 1-800/258-7111), and Vermont Transit Lines (☎1-800/552-8737).

Tourism is now the state's top money earner, but outside of tourism centers long-time New Hampshire residents are often suspicious and unaccepting of outsiders. Like frontier people, they've opted for a less intrusive government with fewer laws and regulations. There is no sales or even personal income tax here – in fulfillment of the state motto, "Live Free or Die."

New Hampshire has also earned a degree of political clout as the venue of the **first primary election of each presidential campaign**, with its villages used to playing host to would-be presidents on the stump. The New Hampshire presidential primary is viewed by many as a make-or-break event, and since the first one in 1952 the state has picked the candidates eventually nominated by both the Democrats and the Republicans about 85 percent of the time.

The seacoast region

New Hampshire's **coastline** stretches for just eighteen miles, the shortest of any US state with ocean access. Its sandy length, filling up the area between Hampton Beach on the south end and Portsmouth on the north, is well developed, but it's not difficult to find sparsely populated beaches.

Though separated by such a short distance, the two main coastal towns couldn't be less similar. **Portsmouth**, New Hampshire's resurgent cultural center, is bursting with well-preserved Colonial architecture, gourmet restaurants, and historic attractions; **Hampton Beach** is a sprawling arc of sand packed in summer with giggling teenagers and lined with a corresponding collection of video arcades, ice-cream parlors, and waterslides. In between, sleepy towns – small collections of a few elegant white-clapboard buildings and some ill-placed strip malls, really – blend into each other, spilling into laidback beaches, such as **Jenness State Beach** and **Wallis Sands State Beach**.

West of busy I-95 – the main thoroughfare up from Massachusetts – the density of attractions (and people) drops off sharply. The handsome and historically significant town of **Exeter**, with its shady streets lined with stately mansions, is home to the country's premier college preparatory school, Phillips Exeter Academy; to the north, **Durham** is centered around the University of New Hampshire's flagship campus.

Hampton Beach and around

It's difficult to understand why **HAMPTON BEACH** is so popular. The favorite vacation spot of many thousands of East Coasters – who gorge happily in the town's bad restaurants and pack themselves onto the crowded band of white sandy beach that stretches along the tacky strip – the town's ugly sprawl of cheaply constructed condominiums spreads across the flat, narrow peninsula that juts into the mouth of the Hampton River. It's a decidedly family-friendly resort, with enough arcades and waterparks to keep youngsters happy for days, but that aside there aren't many good reasons to stop here, unless you enjoy

Literary New England

Ticknor & Fields publishing house, Boston c. 1857

Perhaps fitting for a region dominated by institutions of higher learning, New England has an undeniably strong **literary heritage**. In some ways this is where American literature began, spurred by the religious sermons of Cotton Mather and the Puritan histories of William Bradford in the seventeenth century but truly coming into its own and asserting a dominant influence throughout the nineteenth century and well into the next. During that period Boston was the publishing center of the US, and the regional writers that now figure most prominently in the American literary canon were hard at work, often in close proximity to one another: the nature writers, Thoreau and Emerson; poets Emily Dickinson, Henry Wadsworth Longfellow, Robert Frost, and Wallace Stevens; and novelists Nathaniel Hawthorne, Henry James, William Dean Howells, Mark Twain, and Edith Wharton. More contemporary authors such as John Updike, John Cheever, and even Stephen King have kept the tradition very much alive.

Nature and transcendentalism

A rather logical progression from literature that extolled faith and the Puritan way of life, the **transcendentalist movement** of the 1830s and 1840s, spearheaded by **Ralph Waldo Emerson**, was born of a passion for rural life, intellectual freedom, and belief in intuitive knowledge and experience as a way to enhance the relationship between man, nature, and the "over-soul." Much of the rhetoric came from what is essentially the movement's founding document, Emerson's 1836 essay *Nature*, written not long after he moved to Concord, Massachusetts. The freethinking the movement unleashed put local writers at the vanguard of American literary expression; articles by **Henry David Thoreau**, **Louisa May Alcott**, **Bronson Alcott** (Louisa's father), and other members of the Concord coterie filled the pages of *The Dial*, the transcendentalist journal founded by Emerson and edited by **Margaret Fuller**. An early feminist, Fuller also wrote essays prodigiously, while Alcott penned the classic *Little Women*.

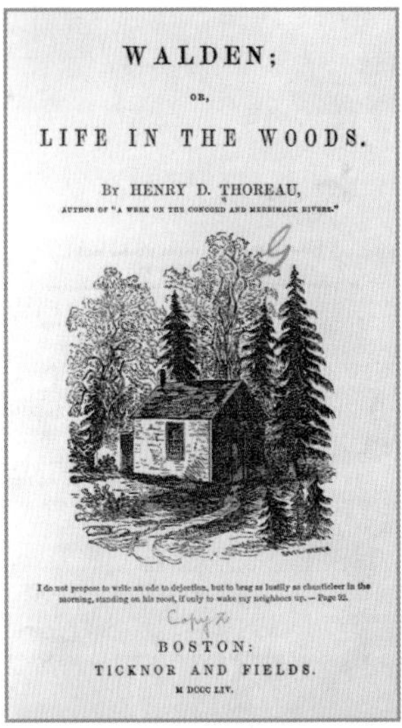
WALDEN;

OR,

LIFE IN THE WOODS.

BY HENRY D. THOREAU,

AUTHOR OF "A WEEK ON THE CONCORD AND MERRIMACK RIVERS."

I do not propose to write an ode to dejection, but to brag as lustily as chanticleer in the morning, standing on his roost, if only to wake my neighbors up. — Page 92.

BOSTON:

TICKNOR AND FIELDS.

M DCCC LIV.

The most famous work from that time remains *Walden*, Thoreau's searching and introspective study in solitude, covering the two years he spent living in a home-made hut near Walden Pond. The pond today attracts droves of visitors, so solitude may be harder to find. In any case, it was actually one of only two books he published during his lifetime, the other being *A Week on the Concord and Merrimack Rivers* in 1849. Indeed, he was thought of as something of an eccentric, both locally and by the literary establishment. "If I seem out of step with the world," he said, "it is because I hear another drummer."

The Gothic tradition

While some New England authors drew on nature as a freeing and benevolent force, others saw it less benignly. Salem (Massachusetts) resident **Nathaniel Hawthorne** wrote moralistic stories that occasionally approximated **Gothic horror** and often cast a suspicious eye on nature and society. In the creepy *Young Goodman Brown*, set during the time of the Salem Witch Trials, a man goes to meet an evil figure – who may well be the devil – in the Massachusetts woods, while *The House of the Seven Gables*, another story alluding to the witch trials (Hawthorne was actually a descendant of one of the judges), treats the disintegrating house itself as a force of nature, capable of destroying those within it.

Nathaniel Hawthorne

These were just the kind of themes taken up by future New England horror writers, most notably Rhode Island's

A literary tour of New England

You can do much more than just soak in the highbrow atmosphere at the region's universities or linger with a book in one of the many coffeehouses and cafés that inevitably surround them; you can go straight to the literary sources themselves. Visit the homes where Longfellow (Cambridge), Alcott (Orchard House in Concord), Dickinson (Amherst), Twain (New Haven), Wharton (The Mount, near Lenox, Massachusetts) and many more notables were either born, reared, or spent their time toiling away on the classics so familiar to all. Or visit sites made famous by the works themselves, like the House of the Seven Gables in Salem, or the Seamen's Bethel in New Bedford (*Moby Dick*). Whether meditating by Walden Pond or stopping in the snowy woods one evening near Robert Frost's farm in Derry, New Hampshire (or the one in southern Vermont), you're sure to feel some spirit move you.

House of the Seven Gables

Emily Dickinson Homestead

H.P. Lovecraft and Maine's **Stephen King**. A literary outsider, Lovecraft was born in Providence, Rhode Island, in 1890 and spent nearly all his life in New England until his death in 1937. He's best known for his creation of the so-called *Cthulhu Mythos*, a pantheon of ancient gods that lurk beneath the surface of our everyday lives, influencing terrible events and destined one day to rise again. Lovecraft's stories have all the classic motifs of horror fiction, but mix with this a local sensibility and evocations of ancient and sinister New England landscapes.

King on the other hand needs little introduction – one of the most popular writers of his day and still a reliable bestseller, he is the creator of nearly fifty horror novels and plenty more short stories, most of them set in small, unsuspecting New England towns not unlike Bangor, Maine, where he was born. Favorites include *Salem's Lot*, *The Stand*, and *The Dead Zone*, though perhaps the most appropriate convergence of local landscape and New England pride comes in *The Girl Who Loved Tom Gordon*, in which a young girl gets lost in the woods and keeps herself sane by imagining she's talking to (then) Boston Red Sox pitcher Tom Gordon.

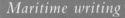

Robert Frost Farm

New England poetry

"Listen my children and you shall hear/ Of the midnight ride of Paul Revere." Schoolchildren have indeed been hearing those words – the opening couplet of "The Midnight Ride of Paul Revere" – for decades. They were written by **Henry Wadsworth Longfellow**, who besides becoming America's most popular poet for a long spell was also a regular at the literary salons in Boston that became the *Atlantic Monthly*.

While Longfellow celebrated both everyday and heroic Americans in his verse, **Emily Dickinson** wrote much more personal and ultimately much more affecting poetry, albeit works that didn't see the light of day until after her death. Her anxieties and preoccupations could be glimpsed in the powerful "My life had stood – a loaded gun" and "Because I could not stop for Death." **Robert Frost**, who owned a number of farms throughout the region, might be considered the prototypical New England poet, not least for his pastoral evocations and philosophical musings ("Stopping by Woods on a Snowy Evening," "The Road Less Traveled").

Maritime writing

The imagery of **maritime writing**, a New England literary tradition that flowered in the nineteenth century, often stands in stark contrast to the twee clapboard cottages and bucolic village squares often associated with the region. The genre's classic narrative is 1840's *Two Years Before the Mast*, written by a young seaman, Richard Dana, though the book best known to most is **Herman Melville**'s *Moby Dick*, a heroic allegory which also works as an almost encyclopedia-like introduction to whaling. Every year on January 3, the anniversary of Melville's first trip aboard the whaling ship *Acushnet*, fans gather at the **New Bedford Whaling Museum** for a marathon reading of the American classic. "Call me Ishmael," the first reader intones, kicking off a multi-lingual account of Captain Ahab's pursuit of the white whale. The event is free to all and includes hearty whaleship fare and drinks, such as grog and cider. When it's finished, around 25 hours later, you may well be hooked on tales of the high seas for life.

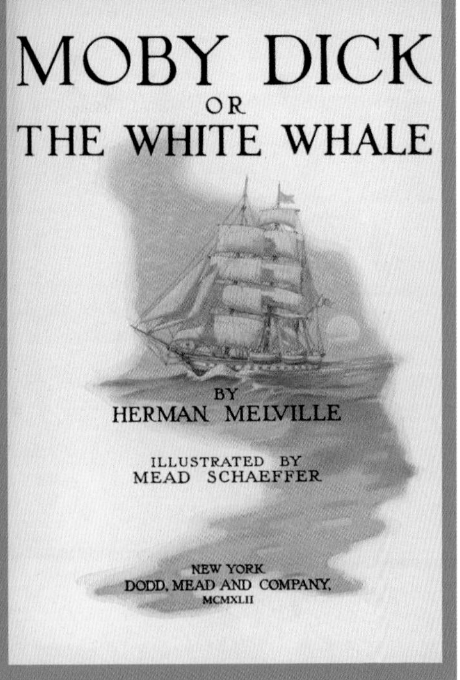

MOBY DICK
OR
THE WHITE WHALE
BY
HERMAN MELVILLE
ILLUSTRATED BY
MEAD SCHAEFFER
NEW YORK
DODD, MEAD AND COMPANY,
MCMXLII

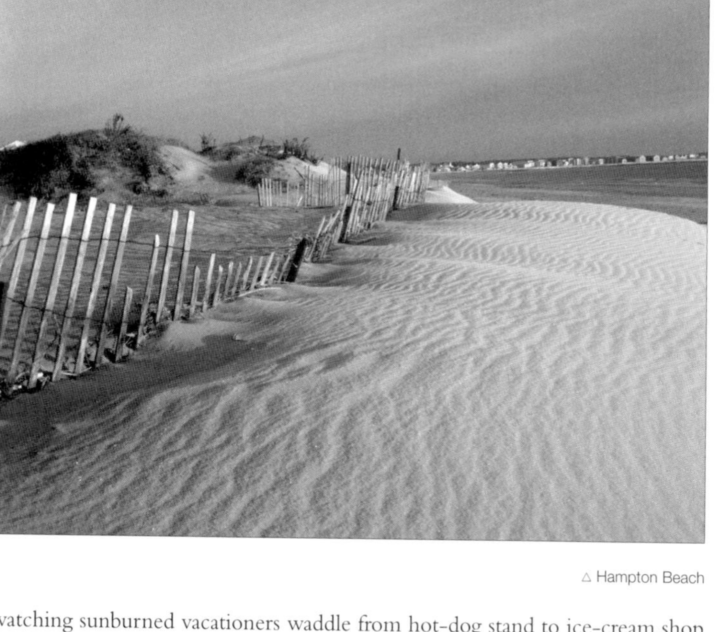

△ Hampton Beach

watching sunburned vacationers waddle from hot-dog stand to ice-cream shop to the beach and back again. One bright spot is the well-known *Hampton Beach Casino Ballroom*, a large performance venue right along the strip at 169 Ocean Blvd (call ⓣ603/929-4100 for information; tickets $15–30). This is the top choice for touring performers in the state, hosting nationally known rock bands and comedians. If you absolutely must **stay** here, the **Hampton Beach Chamber of Commerce** (ⓣ1-800/GET-A-TAN, ⓦwww.hamptonbeach.org) will help with room reservations. If you're **hungry**, you could stop at *Little Jack's Seafood*, 539 Ocean Blvd (ⓣ603/926-8053), for lobster "in the rough" and other seacoast specialties, but don't come with high expectations.

The beach is more pleasant a few miles north along Rte-1A at **NORTH HAMPTON BEACH**, a more peaceful stretch of sand with abundant metered parking – though it still catches a bit of the slough from Hampton Beach. If you're in the area, you might also stop by the colorful **Fuller Gardens** (daily mid-May to mid-Oct 10am–5.30pm; $6.50; ⓣ603/964-5414), at the junction of Rte-1A and Rte-111. Designed in 1939 for Massachusetts governor Alvin Fuller, the gardens include over two thousand rose bushes and a Japanese section complete with bonsai trees.

Continuing north, Rte-1A winds along a picturesque strip of rocky coastline that includes "millionaires' row," where a collection of stately homes greets the ocean from enormous bay windows. There's a paved **walking path** along the water if you decide you'd like to take in the finely restored private oceanfront mansions at a more leisurely pace. In **RYE HARBOR**, at the State Marina, you can go **whale-watching** with Atlantic Fleet (late May to mid-Oct; $32,

Seabrook Nuclear Power Station

Talk of a New England nuclear power plant began as early as the 1950s, but it wasn't until the energy crisis of the mid-1970s that legislators got serious. Construction of the **Seabrook Nuclear Power Station**, located about five miles south of Hampton on Rte-1, began in 1976, and vocal **protest** followed soon after. What started as a grassroots campaign, however, exploded into a national debate about the safety and feasibility of nuclear power. The construction spawned an outburst of vocal environmental groups, most notably the so-called **Clamshell Alliance**, which staged a sit-in by two thousand of its members in April 1977. However, New Hampshire residents and politicians – including then-governor John Sununu – generally supported the construction, seeing it as a long-term energy saver, while residents of neighboring Massachusetts, fearing negative environmental impacts, remained staunchly opposed. Even Vermont ice-cream maker **Ben and Jerry's** got involved in the fray, erecting a billboard in Boston that read "Stop Seabrook. Keep our customers alive and licking." Nevertheless, construction continued, and in 1990, after four years of testing and safety inspections, the nuclear plant began producing power.

In the process, expenses ballooned a staggering $4 billion over budget, and forced New Hampshire's largest utility, the Public Service Company of New Hampshire, which owned 36 percent of the facility, to file for bankruptcy. The station, now owned mostly by Florida Power & Light, provides power for about one million New England homes, and spews out more than nine million megawatt hours of electricity per year. For their troubles, New Hampshire residents currently pay the highest electric rates in the country, roughly twice the national average.

One small consolation that accompanied Seabrook's construction was the opening of the **Science and Nature Center at Seabrook Station**, on US-1 in Seabrook (by appointment only, call for reservations ⓣ603/773-7219 or 1-800/338-7482), where you can explore various exhibits about nuclear energy, electricity, and the environment, including displays of flora and fauna that populate the salt marshes nearby.

$22 children; ⓣ603/964-5220 or 1-800/WHALE-NH). Popular with surfers and families alike, **Jenness State Beach**, a little farther north along Rte-1A, is even more serene, with few buildings and a protected stretch of white sand. Nearby **Wallis Sands State Beach** ($10 per car) is also a good bet for swimming and sunning.

North towards Portsmouth

At the mouth of the Piscataqua River along Rte-1A, **Odiorne Point State Park** ($3; ⓣ603/436-7406) marks the site of New Hampshire's first settlement, established in 1623 but vacated shortly after in favor of what is now Portsmouth. The park consists of some three hundred acres of protected coastline with a well-maintained network of trails that includes a beautiful seaside bike path and picnic benches. It's also home to the **Seacoast Science Center**, 570 Ocean Blvd (daily 10am–5pm; $3; ⓣ603/436-8043, ⓦwww.seacentr.org), which presents a vaguely diverting array of science and natural history exhibits and has an indoor tide-pool touch-tank and a thousand-gallon aquarium.

Along the eastern shore, on the island of **New Castle**, a wealthy suburb of Portsmouth, there are a couple of historically relevant forts. **Fort Constitution** (formerly Fort William and Mary), along Rte-1B at the mouth of Portsmouth Harbor, was the site of one of the first overt acts of rebellion against the British, when, at the urging of Paul Revere, angry colonists attacked, pilfering gunpowder and cannons from unsuspecting British soldiers. Only the base of the walls remains, however. Just south stands **Fort Stark,** active in every war from the Revolutionary War through World War II. You can make a self-guided tour of the ten-acre site, including parts of the remodeled fort, but the ocean views are more eye-catching.

Portsmouth

Surprisingly attractive **PORTSMOUTH**, off of I-95 at the mouth of the Piscataqua River, blends small-town accessibility with the enthusiasm of a rejuvenated city. Having endured the many cycles of prosperity and hardship typical of many New England colonial towns – including, most devastatingly, several major fires and the inevitable loss of its prominence as a port – Portsmouth has found its most recent triumphs in the cultural arena. Artists, musicians, writers, tourists, and, notably, gourmet chefs, attracted by Portsmouth's affordability, authentic colonial flavor, and youthful exuberance, have converged on the quaint seaside town in recent years. This has made the town exceptionally young (the average age is 24), if a bit racially homogenous; still, with an attractive town center, a wealth of good restaurants, clean, uncongested streets, an inviting riverside park, and an unusual abundance of well-preserved Colonial buildings, it certainly makes for pleasant exploration.

Some history

Founded in the 1620s by English merchants hoping to turn a quick profit in the fur and fish trade, Portsmouth was, after Jamestown, the second New World commercial settlement of any size. Though initial efforts faltered with the death of leader John Mason in 1635, the immigrants soon established Portsmouth as a premier **seaport**, with thriving **shipbuilding** and commercial **fishing** industries. Demand for manual labor at the busy port was high, and religious dissenters and common criminals from Puritan Massachusetts fled to Portsmouth during its early years, prompting complaints that the settlement attracted, and even welcomed, "desperately wicked" characters. With an abundance of timber in the surrounding regions, the prosperous shipyards produced enormous masts, trading vessels, and warships more cheaply than their British counterparts, and Portsmouth's ships were soon carrying goods – and fighting wars – all over the world.

As industry flourished, so did a well-heeled aristocratic class of merchants and ship captains, who constructed many of the fine eighteenth-century mansions and commercial buildings that remain prominent in the town today. However, the city's golden age peaked in 1800, after which the combination of the 1807 Embargo Act, the War of 1812, and three devastating **fires** plunged the city into decline.

Portsmouth went on to become a major center for **beer and ale** production after the Civil War, when the brick buildings along Market Street all housed breweries, though this industry, too, was to practically disappear with the onset of Prohibition. By the turn of the twentieth century, the **Portsmouth Naval Shipyard**, founded in 1800 by John Paul Jones as the US government's first shipyard had become the area's largest employer. (Though still active today, just across the Piscataqua River, the shipyard is in danger of being closed.) As a result, Portsmouth became notorious as a seedy port of call, complete with a busy **red-light district**, a skyrocketing crime rate, and a raucous assortment of grungy taverns.

After angry citizens drove the revelers and prostitutes from their city in the early 1900s, Portsmouth settled into a long period of stagnation, still heavily dependent on the government-sponsored shipyard for its well-being. It wasn't until the 1950s that the city began to actively preserve and restore its colorful Colonial past, as citizens organized to save the area now known as the "Strawbery Banke Museum" from demolition. Today Portsmouth remains one of the best-preserved Colonial towns in New England.

Arrival and information

Portsmouth's city center is huddled along the southern bank of the **Piscataqua River**, at the mouth of one of the finest natural harbors on the East Coast, just across from Kittery, Maine. Surrounded by water on three sides, the town is compact and easily manageable on foot. At its heart, **Market Square** is flanked by the towering North Church.

Portsmouth is most easily accessible via **public transport** from Boston, either on C&J Trailways (Ⓣ1-800/258-7111), with frequent daily services from Boston, Newburyport (MA), and Durham (NH), or Vermont Transit Lines (Ⓣ603/436-0163), which runs buses five times daily along the coast between Boston and Portsmouth, stopping in Market Square opposite North Church. By **car**, the easiest way to reach downtown Portsmouth is via exit 7 (Market

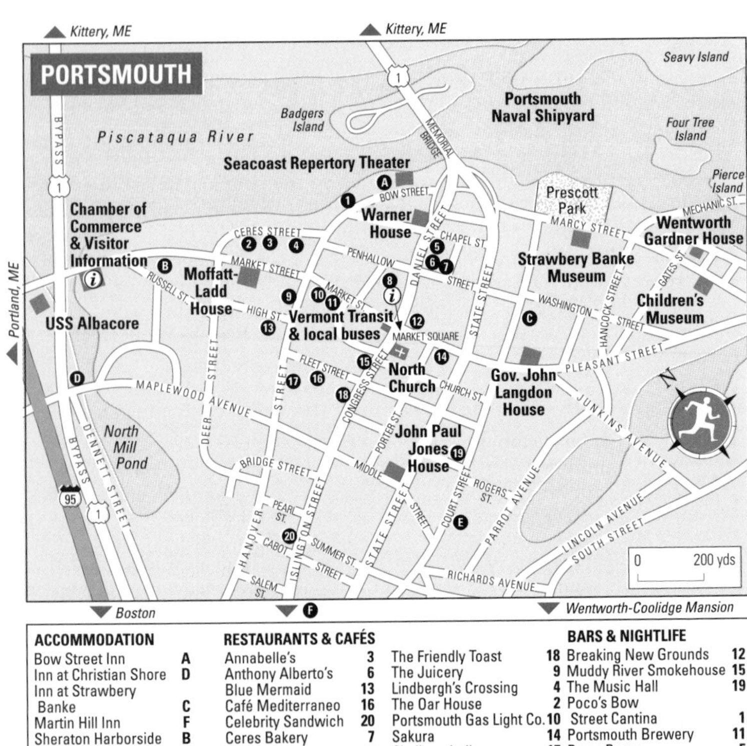

△ The Piscataqua River

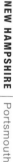

Street) off of **I-95**. **Rte-1A**, which becomes Miller Avenue, and **US-1**, which becomes Middle Street, both pass directly through the city center and continue into Maine, across the Memorial Bridge. **Parking** near the waterfront is scarce in the summer; there's a public garage at the intersection of Hanover and High streets. You can usually find non-metered parking next to South Mill Pond, along Parrot Avenue, a short walk from Market Square.

The **Greater Portsmouth Chamber of Commerce**, 500 Market St (late May to mid-Oct Mon–Fri 8.30am–5pm, plus Sat & Sun 10am–5pm in summer; Ⓣ603/436-1118, Ⓦwww.portsmouthchamber.org), a fifteen-minute walk from Market Square, houses an ample collection of brochures and can help you find a room, although your choices will be limited to chamber members. They also operate an information **kiosk** in Market Square during the summer (daily 9am–5pm). For travel books, guides, and maps, you can't do much better than Gulliver's, downstairs at 7 Commercial Alley, off Market Street (Ⓣ603/431-5556, Ⓦwww.gulliversbooks.com).

City transit

The **Coast Trolley** (Mon–Sun 10.30am–5.30pm; Ⓣ603/743-5777; $1) runs in a small loop around the city, stopping at most attractions. The **Seacoast Trolley** (mid-June to early Sept; $6 per day; Ⓣ603/431-6975) links historic Portsmouth with several beaches, shopping malls, and local sights, and stops at Market Square hourly. You can rent **bikes** from Portsmouth Rent & Ride, 37 Hanover St (Ⓣ603/433-6777) for $29 a day, $19 for a half-day, which also rents kayaks ($49) and offers tours ($65) and lessons ($100). In the winter you can rent cross-country skis here ($19 half day, $29 full).

Several companies run **cruises** in Portsmouth Harbor and beyond. Portsmouth Harbor Cruises, at the Ceres Street Dock, features several trips, and has a full bar aboard every boat (90min harbor cruise $15; 60min evening cruise $12; call Ⓣ603/436-8084 or 1-800/776-0915 for departure times, Ⓦwww.portsmouthharbor.com). The Isles of Shoals Steamship Company, nearby at

315 Market St (ⓣ603/431-5500 or 1-800/441-4620, ⓦwww.islesofshoals.com), offers similar trips, including a $24 journey to the Isles of Shoals. With both companies, you need to buy your tickets in advance to guarantee a spot. If you'd rather see the coastline up close, daily kayaking tours are offered by Portsmouth Kayak Adventures, 185 Wentworth St (ⓣ603/559-1000; $55), which originate at their store in Witch Cove Marina, south of the town center.

Accommodation

Accommodation in and around Portsmouth's historic district can be expensive – in high season on weekends you'll likely pay $100 or more for a good room in a bed-and-breakfast. A collection of slightly cheaper – and less pleasant – **motels** can be found at the traffic circle where I-95, the Rte-1 bypass, and routes 4 and 16 intersect. Staying in a restored old inn is well worth the extra cash. Call ahead to reserve a room on summer weekends or holidays and be aware that prices can go up by as much as forty percent during high season; midweek accommodations are usually cheaper. **Camping** in the area is limited to crowded RV-type parks, such as the *Shel-Al Campground*, US-1, North Hampton (ⓣ603/964-5730, ⓦwww.shel-al.com; $20), and the *Wakeda Campground*, Rte-88, Hampton Falls (ⓣ603/772-5274, ⓦwww.wakedacampground.com; $25).

In town

Bow Street Inn 121 Bow St ⓣ603/431-7760, ⓦwww.bowstreetinn.com. Portsmouth's only waterfront inn is centrally located and comfortable. The ten cozy rooms occupy a remodeled brick brewery; two rooms offer full harbor views. Continental breakfast included. 6

Inn at Christian Shore 335 Maplewood Ave ⓣ603/431-6770. Early nineteenth-century Federal-style house with six rooms full of tasteful antique furnishings, and big, tasty gourmet breakfasts. 5

Inn at Strawbery Banke 314 Court St ⓣ603/436-7242 or 1-800/428-3933, ⓦwww.innatstrawberybanke.com. Seven bright, relaxing rooms, in a sumptuous old Colonial home near the waterfront. Reservations strongly recommended. 6

Martin Hill Inn 404 Islington St ⓣ603/436-2287. Meticulously furnished house with seven guestrooms and a shaded garden within walking distance of the city center. Excellent full breakfast and helpful innkeepers. 5

Sheraton Harborside 250 Market St ⓣ603/431-2300 or 1-877/248-3794, ⓦwww.sheratonportsmouth.com. Large hotel with conference facilities and a predominantly business clientele. Predictably comfortable and expensive, but enjoys a central location on Market Street. 7

Sise Inn 40 Court St ⓣ603/433-1200, ⓦwww.siseinn.com. One of the larger inns in Portsmouth, this Queen Anne-style home of 1880s shipping magnate John Sise has 34 elegantly appointed, luxurious rooms with phones and TVs. The breakfast is a delicious self-serve buffet. 7

Near the traffic circle

Anchorage Inn 417 Woodbury Ave ⓣ1-800/370-8111, ⓦwww.anchorageinns.com. A large and comfortable modern hotel with 93 rooms, an indoor pool, sauna, and whirlpool. 5

Holiday Inn Portsmouth 300 Woodbury Ave ⓣ603/431-8000. Standard – yet comfortable and clean – rooms, outdoor pool, and game and exercise rooms at this business hotel. 5

Port Inn Rte-1 Bypass South ⓣ603/436-4378 or 1-800/282-PORT, ⓦwww.theportinn.com. These good-value, comfortable rooms, some with microwaves and refrigerators, are (depending on the season and day) among the cheapest in Portsmouth. 4

The Town

Market Square, where Daniel, Pleasant, Congress, and Market streets all converge, has been Portsmouth's commercial center since the mid-eighteenth century. Once a military training site, the brick-dominated square is now surrounded by a bustling assortment of cafés and gift shops. Despite the upscale shopping, the square maintains an unpretentious, lived-in feel – almost everywhere you turn, evidence of the town's history reveals itself. It's the best spot to get oriented and begin your wanderings; in fact, this is where you pick up the informative **Portsmouth Harbor Trail** walking-tour guide and map (32-page color guide and map $2; guided tours $8; ⓣ603/436-3988), detailing a series of three walks tracing the city's history that originate in the square.

You can start by admiring the architecture of old brick buildings such as the **Athenaeum**, 9 Market Square (open to the public Tues & Thurs 1–4pm, Sat 10am–4pm; ⓣ603/431-2538), one of the oldest private libraries in the country. The 1854 **North Church**, also constructed with bricks, flanks the southwest side of the square, and its towering spire makes it the tallest building you'll see in town.

Market Street

Scanning the chic boutiques and fashionable restaurants that line **Market Street**, it's hard to believe the brick buildings that house them were once occupied by breweries. In the late nineteenth century, when Portsmouth's **beer and ale industry** was booming, Frank Jones, its most famous brewer and founder of the Portsmouth Brewery Company, created what was once considered to be the best beer in the nation– aptly named "Frank Jones Ale." Jones and his competitors were shut down during Prohibition and never recovered. The company's old brick warehouse, at 125 Bow St, was transformed in 1979 into a theater, presenting mostly mainstream plays and musicals. The closest you can get to Portsmouth's storied brewing history today is a trip to the **Redhook Brewery**, 35 Corporate Drive (call for tour schedule; $1; ⓣ603/430-8600), though even they aren't native, as the company was founded in Seattle, Washington.

Of the striking selection of grand old timber mansions in Portsmouth, the **Moffatt-Ladd House**, 154 Market St (mid-June to Oct Mon–Sat 11am–5pm, Sun 1–5pm; $6), is one of the most impressive. Completed in 1763, after no fewer than 467 days of construction, the house is particularly notable for its Great Hall, which occupies more than a quarter of the first floor. Using inventories left by Captain John Moffatt, who designed the home and later monitored his lucrative shipping business from an office on the second floor, historians have transformed the Yellow Chamber (also on the second floor) into one of the best-documented eighteenth-century American rooms. Portraits of past occupants by artists such as Gilbert Stuart hang throughout the home and include a painting of William Whipple, who signed the Declaration of Independence and lived here in the late eighteenth century. For information on other historic homes which are open to the public, see box on p.465.

Farther up Market Street, next to the salt piles along the river, is the departure point for harbor cruises and for boats (see "City transit," p.461) that take you ten miles off the coast to the Isles of Shoals, a summer meeting-place for many well-known writers of the nineteenth century, including Nathaniel Hawthorne and Annie Fields.

Still farther along Market Street, at no. 600, you'll find the **USS Albacore Park and Port of Portsmouth Maritime Museum** (daily: late May to mid-Oct 9.30am–5pm; rest of year 9.30am–4.30pm; $5; ⓣ603/436-3680), a worthwhile diversion highlighted by a 205-foot, 1200-ton **submarine**. Built in 1952, it was then the fastest electric/diesel submarine in the world. Tours of the underwater vessel offer glimpses of the cockpit, cramped living quarters, and the engine room.

Prescott Park and the Children's Museum

At the other end of the historic district, along the river and adjacent to the Strawbery Banke Museum, is beautiful **Prescott Park**, Marcy Street

(Ⓣ603/431-8748), a welcoming expanse of grass and shrubbery that slopes gently toward the water's edge. Featuring free music and entertainment throughout the summer, the park is immaculately maintained – especially the colorful All-American Show Garden – and is a great spot for a picnic or afternoon nap. You could also check out the **Sheafe Warehouse Museum**, in Prescott Park on the waterfront (summer only; Ⓣ603/436-2848), which houses a mildly engaging free collection of mostly nautical paraphernalia. The **Point of Graves cemetery**, a creepy plot of crumbling headstones across from Prescott Park on the southeast corner of Mechanic Street near the bridge to Pierce Island, is the oldest in the city – the oldest headstone dates from 1682.

Though you'd never suspect it now, Marcy Street, which borders Prescott Park on its west side, was once a source of town shame, home to a strip of internationally notorious brothels patronized by sailors from across the river. Prostitution had subsided by the early twentieth century, and few reminders of those days are left, but the otherwise undistinguished home of one of Portsmouth's most prominent madames, Alta Roberts, who greeted her customers with a mouthful of gold teeth, still stands at 57 Marcy St. The Children's Museum of Portsmouth, with hands-on exhibits that investigate a range of diverse topics, such as anatomy, lobstering, sound, and earthquakes, is close by at 280 Marcy St (summer Mon–Sat 10am–5pm, Sun 1–5pm; closed Mon rest of year; $6; Ⓣ603/436-3853).

The Strawbery Banke Museum

Although historic buildings can be found all over Portsmouth, for a more concentrated look at American architecture over the last three centuries, pay a visit to the **Strawbery Banke Museum**, 64 Marcy St (May–Oct Mon–Sat 10am–5pm, Sun noon–5pm, Nov–Dec and Feb–Apr guided walking tours offered on the hour Thurs–Sat 10am–2pm, Sun noon–2pm; $15, winter $10; tickets good for two consecutive days; Ⓣ603/433-1100, Ⓦwww.strawberybanke.org), a fenced-off ten-acre neighborhood that takes in a collection of twenty-nine meticulously restored and maintained old wooden buildings (though some can only be viewed from the outside). This area began life as the home of wealthy shipbuilders and was successively the lair of privateers and a red-light district before turning into respectable – and, in the 1950s, decaying – suburbia. It was decided to recreate its former appearance, mainly by clearing away the newer buildings (only two of the houses on display were moved here). A few people still live here, tucked away on the upper floors, but the complex really serves as a living museum that you can explore either on a guided tour or at your own whim; in either case, several of the houses have well-informed attendants.

Each building is shown in its most interesting former incarnation, whether that be 1695 or 1955, and in the **Drisco House**, the first you come to, two eras collide: half of the house is outfitted as from the 1790s, the other half, the 1950s. The 1766 **Pitt Tavern** holds the most historic significance, having acted as a meeting-place during the Revolution for patriots and loyalists (it still functions as a Masonic lodge, which explains why you can't go upstairs). Tiny glasses remind you that its clientele drank gin rather than beer. The museum also contains the boyhood home of novelist **Thomas Bailey Aldrich** (1836–1907), which he depicted in his semi-autobiographical novel, *The Story of a Bad Boy*. Even the gardens here are historically accurate, recreated from surviving plans from different time periods.

Traditional crafts are studied and practiced here; the **Lowd House** contains a display on New England craftsmen and the implements they used, and in the

Portsmouth's historic homes

Beyond the walls of Strawbery Banke, Portsmouth is home to an uncharacteristically large number of painstakingly restored **Colonial homes**, which, during the summer, are open to the public. Almost as impressive as the buildings themselves is the unrelenting resolve of the people who devote their lives to the structures' impossibly finicky restoration, with attention even given down to the exact pattern and dye-type used in eighteenth-century wallpapers. The hourly tours, led by scholars full of arcane knowledge and stories, can be fascinating, although after one or two, you will have probably had your fill. Most cost $6, but after your first one the rest are $5 (exceptions are noted below). The presence of a blue flag outside a building indicates its status as a historic home which welcomes visitors.

Governor John Langdon House 143 Pleasant St (June to mid-Oct Fri–Sun tours on the hour 11am–4pm; ⓣ603/436-3205). Three-term governor, New Hampshire Senate president, and delegate to the 1787 Constitutional Convention, John Langdon and his wife, Elizabeth, hosted many big-name visitors here, including George Washington. The home, constructed in 1784 with particular attention to interior detailing and woodwork, is in every way a tribute to his affluence and influence.

John Paul Jones House 43 Middle St (daily late May to mid-Oct 11am–5pm; $10; ⓣ603/436-8420). Home to the Portsmouth Historical Society's museum, this 1761 Georgian structure was where John Paul Jones, the US's first great naval commander, stayed while his ships, the *Ranger* and the *America,* were being outfitted in the Langdon shipyards. Inside the boxy yellow structure you can view some of his naval memorabilia and period-furnished rooms. The museum mounts changing exhibits, such as that on the Portsmouth Peace Treaty (1905) that ended the Russo-Japanese War. The US hosted its first international treaty signing in Portsmouth.

Warner House 150 Daniel St (early June to late Oct Mon–Sat 11am–4pm, Sun noon–4pm; ⓣ603/436-5909). Built for local merchant and shipowner Captain Archibald MacPhaedris in 1716, the Warner House was one of the first buildings in America to be designated a national historic landmark – and examining its laundry list of other "firsts," it's not hard to see why: it was the first brick house constructed in the state; it contains New Hampshire's oldest murals, painted on the staircase wall; and the murals contain some of the earliest known images of Native Americans. Additionally, Benjamin Franklin is said to have installed the lightning rod on the west wall.

Wentworth-Coolidge Mansion 375 Little Harbor Rd, off of Rte-1A (mid-May to mid-Oct, call for tour schedule; $7; ⓣ603/436-6607). Home to royal governor Benning Wentworth, who was in office from 1741 to 1766, this massive 42-room, mustard-yellow mansion hosted the Royal Council meetings of the earliest New Hampshire state government. The rambling building, which is beautifully situated on an isolated plot overlooking Little Harbor, hosts occasional concerts and classes during the summer. It's not furnished, but the wallpaper in several of the rooms is original (though faded), and there are several original Wentworth items on display – among them some fancy imported Chinese porcelain.

Wentworth-Gardner House 50 Mechanic St (mid-June to mid-Oct Tues–Sun 1–4pm; ⓣ603/436-4406). Painstakingly restored, and complete with a gray blocked facade, this 1760 home is considered one of the finest examples of Georgian architecture in America.

Dinsmore Shop, an infinitely patient cooper manufactures barrels with the tools and methods of 1800. The **Mills Zoldak pottery shop** (ⓣ603/431-5746), open year-round, produces attractive low-priced ceramics. After 5pm, the museum opens its gates, and you can wander around for free and observe the building's exteriors in the waning hours of the day (though it's hardly the same experience).

Eating

Portsmouth likes to bill itself as the "food capital of New England," and while this may be an exaggeration, there are undoubtedly plenty of good spots in town to grab an excellent – even gourmet – meal. Portsmouth's **restaurants** include both expensive highbrow **bistros** and cheap, down-to-earth **cafés**. You can still stretch your culinary dollar quite a long way in this town, although the recent surge in tourism is already affecting menu prices at the best-known spots. There is a particularly high concentration of places to eat along Ceres Street and Bow Street, and you should treat yourself to at least one waterfront meal at one of the outdoor patios or decks that line the Piscataqua River.

Annabelle's 49 Ceres St ☎603/436-3400. Highly caloric homemade ice cream, in ultra-delicious flavors like raspberry chocolate chip and Yellow Brick Road (golden vanilla with roasted pecans and caramel). A city favorite since 1982.

Anthony Alberto's 59 Penhallow St ☎603/436-4000. Excellent, cozy Italian restaurant, frequent recipient of *Yankee Travel* and *Wine Spectator* awards. Try the homemade ravioli of the day.

Blue Mermaid 409 The Hill, Hanover and High streets ☎603/427-2583. A carefully selected, though not particularly large, selection of mid- to high-priced grill food with Caribbean and Pacific Rim influences. Meals come with homemade fire-roasted "sunsplash" salsa.

Café Mediterraneo 152 Fleet St ☎603/427-5563. Reasonably priced (entrees are $15–18), authentic, fresh, and delicious southern Italian meals near Market Square.

Celebrity Sandwich 171 Islington St ☎603/433-2277. Great, enormous deli sandwiches (all named after celebrities, though only a few, such as the "David Letterman ham sandwich," make much sense) with cheap daily specials and a handful of tables.

Ceres Bakery 51 Penhallow St ☎603/436-6518. Excellent fresh breads, good soups, and an assortment of fine pastries in this down-to-earth café with a bright blue exterior. Open until 5pm, closed Sun.

The Den 10 Commercial Alley. No phone. This is the place for lovers of strong brews (from Black Bear Micro-Roastery). There are a few quiet tables outside in the low-traffic alleyway.

The Friendly Toast 121 Congress St ☎603/430-2154. Kitschy thrift-store decor with an interesting selection of cheap sandwiches and omelets, a huge drink menu of mixed drinks, shakes, and coffees, and an equally eclectic crowd. The portions are enormous – try Matt's Sandwich, with black beans, avocado, and cheese. Open 24hr on weekends, 7am–11pm during the week.

The Juicery 51 Hanover St ☎603/431-0693. The healthiest hole-in-the-wall in Portsmouth – if not the state. Order something fruity from the organic juice bar, or try one of several vegan wraps. Take-out only.

Lindbergh's Crossing Bistro and Wine Bar 29 Ceres St ☎603/431-0887. One of Portsmouth's newer eateries is fast becoming one of its most popular. The creative French cuisine, which ranges from seared tuna to crispy duck, is expensive (around $20 per entree) but worth it.

The Oar House 55 Ceres St ☎603/436-4025. One of Portsmouth's several slightly old-fashioned gourmet standbys serves standard seafood and grilled meat entrees for $20 and up. You can do just as well with an appetizer and a salad for the same price. There's an outdoor patio right on the harbor.

Portsmouth Gas Light Co 64 Market St ☎603/430-8582. Portsmouth's favorite pizza joint, with a wide selection of brick-oven pizzas, and do-it-yourself tasty toppings. All-you-can-eat pizza special for $6.50, weekdays 11.30am–2pm.

Sakura 40 Pleasant St ☎603/431-2721. The best Japanese restaurant in the area, with fresh sushi, sashimi, tempura, and teriyaki. The combination sushi platter ($28) is enough for four or five; the raw lobster is arguably too much, even for one.

Shalimar India 80 Hanover St ☎603/427-2959. For those looking for a little spice, the North Indian choices are the best around. Vegetarian options, too.

Nightlife and entertainment

Despite its size, Portsmouth's **social scene** can be pretty stimulating. Although the place tends to shut down well before midnight, on summer weekends the streets – particularly around **Market Square** and along **Bow Street** and **Ceres Street** – are full of well-dressed couples, noisy high-school kids, tattooed slackers, and fun-seeking tourists. The city is home to several vibrant **cafés**, a host of well-attended **bars**, and its several **live music** venues present a diverse range of bands – from punk to folk to jazz. If theater is your thing, the **Seacoast Repertory Theatre**, 125 Bow St (Ⓣ603/433-4472 or 1-800/639-7650, Ⓦwww.seacoastrep.org), housed in a converted brewery, is Portsmouth's major performing arts theater, presenting mainstream professional stage productions. For complete up-to-date listings, the *Portsmouth Herald* prints an exhaustive **entertainment** supplement (*Spotlight*) every Thursday.

Breaking New Grounds 14 Market St Ⓣ603/436-9555. This friendly coffeeshop is always bustling, from 6.30am to 11pm (midnight on weekends). Grab an excellent cup of freshly ground coffee and relax with a book at one of several indoor tables, or take it outside to watch the Market Square goings-on.

Muddy River Smokehouse 21 Congress St Ⓣ603/430-9582. Eclectic mix of DJs, reggae, acoustic and rock Thurs–Sat. Decent bbq upstairs.

The Music Hall 28 Chestnut St Ⓣ603/436-2400. Boasting some nine hundred seats, Portsmouth's largest performance space hosts well-known nationally touring folk, rock, jazz, and blues bands, classical concerts, plus dance, theater, and other performances throughout the year.

Poco's Bow Street Cantina 37 Bow St Ⓣ603/431-5967. The okay food is typical Mexican fare, but the best reason to come is great margaritas on the riverfront patio.

Portsmouth Brewery 56 Market St Ⓣ603/431-1115. Typical microbrew pub, with attractive wood paneling, extensive pizza and burger menu, visible beer tanks, towering ceilings, and a rowdy young crowd. The beer here is exceptional; don't miss the Old Brown Dog. Open until 1am nightly, with occasional live music.

Press Room 77 Daniel St Ⓣ603/431-5186. Popular for its nightly live jazz, blues, folk, and bluegrass performances, which feature local and national talents. Also serves inexpensive salads, sandwiches, and soups in a casual pub-style setting.

Around Portsmouth

Inland from Portsmouth, the area between I-95 and Rte-125 has a few historically notable cities, namely **Exeter**, **Durham**, and **Dover**, although aside from Exeter's colonial charm and historic architecture, there's really not much in the way of sightseeing. Perhaps the simplest way of **arriving here** if you haven't got your own transport is by hopping on Amtrak's *Downeaster* service between Boston and Portland, Maine, which stops four times a day in either direction at Exeter, Durham, and Dover.

Exeter

Eight miles west of the Atlantic down Rte-101 from Portsmouth, friendly **EXETER** was settled in 1638 by a rebellious Bostonian preacher, the Reverend John Wheelwright. Sitting on the Squamscott River and an abundance of timber, Exeter thrived in the eighteenth century, selling masts and lumber to both local and English shipbuilders. It became the state capital in 1775 (Portsmouth, the previous capital, was too Loyalist), and by early 1776, the provincial congress had signed a state constitution, making New Hampshire the first state to formally declare its independence from England. Exeter's tree-shaded avenues and stately old neighborhoods make the charming town worth a stop.

The Town

Phillips Exeter Academy, one of the top college preparatory schools in the United States, occupies a large portion of the attractive town center, its heavy-set regal brick buildings sprawling over acres of well-manicured lawns. Founded in 1781 by Dr John Phillips, the school counts among its long list of prominent alumni the great orator Daniel Webster (see p.486). Along Front Street (Rte-111), near Elm Street south of the center of town, is the school's boxy brick **library**, designed by architect Louis Kahn in 1971, and featured in many architecture textbooks. Begin your self-guided walking tour of the campus at the admissions office (Ⓣ603/777-3433) on Front Street across from the Phillips Church.

The well-preserved Art Deco Ioka Theater (Ⓣ603/772-2222), right in the center of town at 55 Water St, has been in continuous operation since it opened with a screening of *The Birth of a Nation* in 1915. You can usually take a peek inside during off-hours. A hundred yards down the street, in the center of the traffic circle, the Swasey Pavilion, a prominent circular bandstand, was designed by Henry Bacon, the architect of the Lincoln Memorial. The Exeter Brass Band, founded in 1847, still gives summer concerts here. Exeter native Daniel Chester French, who sculpted the sternly seated Abe Lincoln inside the Lincoln Memorial, also created Exeter's World War I Memorial, in Gale Park on Front Street.

The **American Independence Museum**, in the Ladd-Gilman House at 1 Governors Lane, just north on Water Street (tours hourly May–Oct Wed–Sat 10am–4pm; $5; Ⓣ603/772-2622), houses an important, if slightly dull, collection of documents and artifacts investigating New Hampshire's role in the American Revolution, including the copy of the Declaration of Independence, annotated draft copies of the US Constitution, and a few oddities, including a ring containing a piece of George Washington's hair in a tiny glass case. Exeter stages the elaborate **Revolutionary War Festival** (call the American Independence Museum for details) the third weekend in July, when the grounds of the museum are transformed into a militia encampment, with some residents in full colonial militia garb, and the vigor with which the battles and costumes are re-created is both frightening and fascinating. Lastly, the **Moses-Kent House Museum**, 1 Pine St (summer Thurs & Sat 1–4pm; $5; Ⓣ603/772-2044), built in 1868 for Henry Moses, a local wool merchant, retains its original furnishings. Its grounds were laid out by Frederick Law Olmsted, best known for designing New York City's Central Park.

Practicalities

For local information, contact the **Exeter Area Chamber of Commerce**, 120 Water St (Ⓣ603/772-2411, Ⓦwww.exeterarea.org). There are several upscale **places to stay**, although the rates are relatively expensive. The *Inn by the Bandstand*, in the center of town at 4 Front St (Ⓣ603/772-6352, Ⓦwww.innbythebandstand.com; ❻), is a lovingly restored Federal-style inn, constructed in 1809; many rooms have brick fireplaces. The *Inn of Exeter*, 90 Front St (Ⓣ603/772-5901 or 1-800/782-8444, Ⓦwww.someplacesdifferent.com; ❻), offers easygoing elegance and superior service in a three-story brick Georgian-style building. You can **camp** at the wooded *Exeter Elms Family Campground*, 188 Court St, two miles south on Rte-108 (Ⓣ603/778-7631 or 1-866/778-7631, Ⓦwww.exeterelms.com), for $25 per site.

While Exeter does not have any great wealth of good places to eat, there are a few affordable options worth noting. The *Green Bean on Water*, 33 Water St (Ⓣ603/778-7585; closed Sun), serves fresh sandwiches on homemade bread in a casual café with outdoor seating. The *Tavern at River's Edge*, 163 Water St (Ⓣ603/772-7393; closed Sun), has a good range of international cuisine in a cozy, more formal Victorian dining room along the river. As its name suggests, *Penang and Tokyo*, 97 Water St (Ⓣ603/778-8388), offers well-prepared Malaysian and Japanese cuisine, something of a rarity in these parts. For pastries, fresh breads, light salads, coffee, and espresso, head to the *Baker's Peel*, at 231 Water St (Ⓣ603/778-0910).

Durham and Dover

Along US-4 northwest of Portsmouth, the University of New Hampshire's flagship campus dominates **DURHAM**, which was originally settled in 1635, and the university maintains the youthful exuberance of a typical college town during the school year. Between 1675 and the early eighteenth century, the town was the site of some of the worst Indian massacres in America. Commanded by the French, the natives attacked repeatedly and often, destroying homes and killing British settlers. There's little reminder of this past today: Durham's **Main Street** is a collection of used bookstores. For breakfast or lunch (Mon–Fri) or an ice-cream snack (Sat), visit the UNH Dairy Bar, Depot St (Ⓣ603/862-1006; closed Sun), which is actually a training ground for the university's restaurant management students. The campus's main **theater**, in the Paul Creative Arts Center (Ⓣ603/862-2290), puts on several respectable productions each year.

DOVER, a former mill town just off the Spaulding Turnpike (Rte-16) near the Maine border, was one of the first four cities to be established in the state. You might stop off for a meal at one of the several affordable eateries along its pleasant downtown strip – try *Crescent City Bistro*, 83 Washington St (Ⓣ603/742-1611), which serves New Orleans Creole dishes and has a wide selection of rums at the bar. Otherwise, there's nothing to see here.

The Merrimack Valley

The financial and political heartland of New Hampshire is the **Merrimack Valley**, which – first by water along the Merrimack River and now by road via I-93 – has always been the main thoroughfare north to the lakes, the White Mountains, and Québec. It was first settled by the Penacook Indians, but early pioneers had established a trading post near Concord by 1660, and by the 1720s large groups of Protestant Anglo-Saxons were calling the area home. In the nineteenth century, the valley was booming with industrialization, and Nashua, Manchester, and Concord were all major manufacturing centers. **Concord** became the state's capital in 1784 and it remains the center of New Hampshire's political life – particularly evident during the quadrennial presidential primaries – while **Manchester** is the most populous city in the state, with ample evidence of its gritty industrial past.

Manchester

Although **MANCHESTER** is New Hampshire's largest city (population 107,000) and a major business hub, it does not hold much interest for visitors, aside from an excellent art museum. Indeed, the Chamber of Commerce's tourist guide lists the city's proximity to everywhere else in the state as its major attraction. The place is rather rough around the edges and unmistakably urban, and, although town officials are constantly dreaming up new ways to revitalize the downtown and riverfront areas, most of these efforts reek more of desperation than genuine civic improvement.

Once a prosperous mill town, Manchester has been in a perpetual state of recovery ever since the **Amoskeag Manufacturing Company** went belly-up in 1935. From 1838 to 1920, the company was the world's largest textile manufacturer, and in fact provided all the denim for Levi Strauss & Co's riveted blue jeans in the late 1800s. At its peak the company employed 17,000 people and spewed out over four million yards of cloth per week. The textile company – and the entire town of Manchester, for that matter – was the brainchild of a group of Boston entrepreneurs, who purchased 15,000 acres of land around the Amoskeag Falls, acquired the rights to water power along the entire length of the Merrimack River, built a dam, and constructed the enormous brick Amoskeag Mills in the early 1830s. Once cutting-edge examples of manufacturing efficiency, the mills, which stretch for over a mile along the eastern side of the river, are now run down and largely deserted – depressing reminders of lost prosperity.

That's not to say that the entire grouping of buildings remains dormant; a group of local businessmen bought the crumbling structures for $5 million and the slow process of converting the mills into apartments, offices, and retail space is well under way. Optimistic residents claim Manchester is going through a "renaissance" of sorts, but there's still a long way to go.

Arrival, information, and city transit

Manchester is one of New Hampshire's few transportation hubs, and getting to the city is not particularly difficult. **Manchester International Airport**, off of Rte-3A, is served by several major carriers. From downtown's **Manchester Transportation Center**, 119 Canal St, at Granite (Ⓣ603/668-6133), you can get to just about anywhere that buses run to in the state, and beyond. The **Manchester Area Convention & Visitors Bureau**, 889 Elm St (Ⓣ603/666-6600, Ⓦwww.manchester-chamber.org), has brochures and the like, and there is also an **information kiosk** in the city center on Elm Street next to Veteran's Park and at the airport. The **Manchester Transit Authority** (Ⓣ603/623-8801) runs an extensive network of buses all over town ($1), although apart from the service to the airport (Mon–Fri 5.25am–5.25pm, Sat 8.25am–4.25pm, limited service Sun from the Manchester Transportation Center), tourists will not have much cause to use it; most of the city's limited attractions are concentrated in the downtown area and easily accessible by foot.

Accommodation

With little tourism to speak of, the city's few **hotels** count the infrequent presidential primary as their major source of business. Most of the politicos stay at the *Radisson Manchester*, 700 Elm St (Ⓣ603/625-1000 or 1-800/333-3333; ❻), which becomes a media circus during the primary. At other times it's as comfortable a hotel as you'll find in these parts, with a downtown location second to none. Elsewhere, you might try the *Rice Hamilton*, 123 Pleasant St (Ⓣ603/627-7281; ❹), which has surprisingly well-kept, spacious rooms with kitchens in a run-down brick boarding house, or the *Fairfield Inn*, 860 S Porter St (Ⓣ603/625-2020; ❹), a fairly standard but quite clean and adequate place for a night's sleep. The *Derryfield Bed and Breakfast*, 1081 Bridge St (Ⓣ603/627-2082; ❹), has three quiet, affordable rooms and great breakfasts.

The City

Manchester's main commercial drag, **Elm Street**, runs north to south along the Merrimack River and doubles as US-3. The **Amoskeag Mills** are several

△ The Zimmerman House

blocks west along the banks of the river between Bridge and Granite streets. You can get a good look at the mills, the **Amoskeag Dam**, and the city skyline from the **Amoskeag Falls Scenic Overlook** (daily: mid-April–Oct 8am–6.30pm; free), along the river north of Bridge Street. Alternatively, take a stroll along the **Riverwalk**, a pedestrian path on the river's east bank, or visit the Manchester Historic Association's recently opened **Millyard Museum**, Commercial Street, at Pleasant (Tues–Sat 10am–4pm, Sun noon–4pm; $6), which has exhibits chronicling the town's history, including looms from the mills and a re-creation of what Elm Street looked like back in the days when Manchester was an economic player to be reckoned with.

As New Hampshire's best fine arts museum, the **Currier Museum of Art**, just north of Bridge Street between Union and Beech streets at 201 Myrtle Way (Sun, Mon, Wed, & Fri 11am–5pm, Thurs 11am–8pm, Sat 10am–5pm; $5, free Sat 10am–1pm; ⓣ603/669-6144, ⓦwww.currier.org), featuring works by such well-known European and American painters as Monet, O'Keeffe, Hopper, Matisse, and Wyeth, is well worth the stop. Notable paintings include Picasso's colorful *Spanish Woman Seated in a Chair*, from 1941, and Winslow Homer's straightforward watercolor *American in the Woods*. There's also a fair number of local paintings, such as Jasper Francis Cropsey's glowing *American Indian Summer Morning in the White Mountains,* from 1857. The museum also maintains the nearby **Zimmerman House** (Thurs–Mon; tours by reservation $9), designed in 1950 by Frank Lloyd Wright, a one-story wooden structure epitomizing Wright's vision of form in harmony with landscape. For more lively entertainment, ice hockey fans might want to see who's playing at the brand new

Verizon Wireless Arena, 555 Elm St (Ⓣ603/644-5000), which also presents rock concerts, sporting events, and other spectacles.

Eating and drinking

Manchester does not boast any great wealth of **restaurants** either, although there are a few of note. Local institution *Chateau Restaurant*, 201 Hanover St (Ⓣ603/627-2677), is an old-fashioned upscale eatery with a private club atmosphere, where most plates are still under $20. For good Italian food, head to the bustling *Fratello's*, 155 Dow St (Ⓣ603/624-2022). The *Venetian Canal Espresso Caffe*, 805 Canal St (Ⓣ603/627-9200), is good for gourmet **coffee** and snacks. The city's younger crowd **drinks** beer and listens to live music at *Jillian's*, right along the river at 50 Phillippe Cote (Ⓣ603/626-7636).

South of Manchester

South of Manchester along US-3 near the Massachusetts border, **NASHUA**, New Hampshire's second largest city (population 86,000), does not hold much interest for tourists either, its suburban sprawl dominated by strip malls and car dealerships. Plenty of its citizens still choose to work in Boston, though Massachusetts no longer allows employees to escape state taxes by living across the border in New Hampshire. The **downtown** area, along Main Street, is pleasant enough, with a short strip of shops and *Michael Timothy's*, 212 Main St (Ⓣ603/595-9334), one of the state's top restaurants, which serves creative wood-grilled fare, such as sea bass, duck, and pizza alongside an excellent wine list.

Alongside the Daniel Webster Highway (Rte-3) in **MERRIMACK**, the massive **Anheuser Busch Brewery** (daily: May & Sept–Dec 10am–4pm; June–Aug 9.30am–5pm; Jan–April Thurs–Mon 10am–4pm; Ⓣ603/595-1202, Ⓦwww.budweisertours.com), the largest beer brewer in the world, offers free tours of its beer-making facility – one of thirteen it operates nationwide. Afterwards, you're treated to complimentary tastings of several of its well-known (and lesser-known) products. Outside, you can wander over to see the **Clydesdale stables**, where the enormous horses associated with the brewery are groomed, trained, and usually on display.

The **Robert Frost Farm** (mid-June to early Sept Wed–Sun 10am–5pm; rest of year Sat & Sun 10am–5pm; $7; Ⓣ603/432-3091), just off of Rte-28 (take exit 4 from I-93), north of Salem and south of Derry, is slightly difficult to find, but worth visiting for its small exhibit of Frost's handwritten poems and photos, an hour-long guided house tour filled with peeks into Frost's character, and a nature trail. Frost lived at the farm between 1900 and 1911, and composed or drew inspiration for many of his most famous poems here, including *Mending Wall* (you can still see part of the wall in question running the edge of the property). Though looked upon locally as a failed farmer and a bit of an eccentric, he gave such a moving reading of his poem *Tuft of Flowers* to the local Derry Village Men's Club that the teachers in the group convinced him to take a position teaching English at the nearby Pinkerton Academy, where he worked for two years before turning to writing full time. Another of the poet's homes can be found in Franconia (see p.508).

A rather unusual attraction, **America's Stonehenge**, is off of Rte-111 in North Salem (daily: Jan–Oct 9am–5pm; Nov–Dec 9am–4.30pm; $9; Ⓣ603/893-8300, Ⓦwww.stonehengeusa.com). This grouping of stone slabs and tunnels purports to be a site of ancient and mysterious origins – perhaps some sort of sacrificial altar. There is undoubtedly an atmosphere to the place, but note that all the experts featured in the portentous documentary shown to visitors are employed by the site.

If you're looking for a **place to stay** in the Merrimack area, the best choice is the *Merrimack Hotel and Conference Center*, on the Daniel Webster Highway close to the Anheuser Busch Brewery (Ⓣ603/424-8000; ⑤), a business hotel (like many this close to Manchester Airport) with pool, fitness center, and comfortable rooms. They also have a free shuttle to and from the airport and Manchester's downtown bus terminal. *Maryann's*, 29 E Broadway (daily until 2pm; Ⓣ603/434-5785) in Derry, a popular 50s-themed diner with a huge menu, makes a good stop for something to **eat** on the way to the Frost farm.

Concord and around

Just twenty minutes north by car from Manchester along I-93, New Hampshire's state capital, **CONCORD** (pronounced "conquered"), like its larger neighbor, does not hold much fascination for travelers. Much of its population lies in the rather spread-out suburbia that surrounds the town. Downtown, the highlights are the State House and the Museum of New Hampshire History, both easily seen in a morning or an afternoon. The Christa McAuliffe Planetarium is a good option for the other half of the day, while the nearby Canterbury Shaker Village, the area's outstanding attraction and the best reason for coming to Concord, has enough to keep you busy for at least a day.

Arrival and information

Concord is readily accessible via **public transportation** and easily reached by **car** from I-93, which passes through the eastern side of the town. Concord Trailways and Vermont Transit Lines stop at the **Concord Trailways Terminal**, 30 Stickney Ave, and provide service to other parts of New Hampshire and New England. Concord Area Transit (CAT) provides a decent **local transportation** service (Ⓣ603/225-1989); note, however, that it does not go to the nearby Canterbury Shaker Village.

The **Greater Concord Chamber of Commerce** (Mon–Fri 8am–5pm, Sat 9am–3pm; Ⓣ603/224-2508, Ⓦwww.concordnhchamber.com) is located in plush offices about a mile north of the town center at 40 Commercial Street. It also maintains an **information kiosk** in front of the State House (Fri noon–3pm, Sat 1–4pm), which distributes historical walking-tour brochures. The local newspaper, the *Concord Monitor*, is widely available and offers **entertainment listings**.

Accommodation

Concord is short on remarkable **accommodation**, although a minimum of basic, cheap lodging is available on the outskirts of town near the interstate. Smaller towns in the surrounding countryside, such as Henniker, feature some first-rate bed-and-breakfasts.

Centennial Inn 96 Pleasant St Ⓣ603/225-7102. Probably the most upscale choice of Concord's lodging options, with spacious rooms, grand Victorian touches, and amenities such as in-room phones and cable TV. Also has live music on Sunday evenings. ⑥

Comfort Inn 71 Hall St Ⓣ603/226-4100. Comfortable rooms, a tad more stylish than the chain's

Concord coaches

Carriage manufacturing became one of Concord's best-known industries in the mid-nineteenth century, when Abbot, Downing & Co became the major supplier for Ben Holladay's Overland Trail Stage Route. Locals Lewis Downing and Stephen Abbot had constructed the first Concord coach in 1827, and their beautifully painted stagecoaches were soon known throughout the developing West as the best mode of transportation available. In addition to durable construction and dependable quality, Concord coaches earned a good reputation for their wheels, which were made with seasoned white oak and fitted with handmade spokes, making them more likely to maintain a round shape. The coaches used three-inch-thick leather bands rather than springs to support the passenger compartment, prompting Mark Twain to describe a Concord coach as a "cradle on wheels" in his novel *Roughing It*. Weighing over a ton and costing roughly $1000 at the time, Concord coaches carried up to twelve passengers, and, with four to six horses out front, could travel fifteen miles an hour. Used by Wells Fargo Bank, they soon became familiar sights in such far-off places as South America and Australia. You can see a real one at the Museum of New Hampshire History (see below).

usual offerings, largely for the business set. Most with microwaves and refrigerators. ③

Holiday Inn 172 N Main St ⓣ603/224-9534, ⓦwww.concordhi.com. Popular with visiting politicians and business people due to its proximity to the State House and other public buildings. Predictably comfortable rooms and good facilities, including pool, sauna, and fitness center. ⑤

The Town

Government is the main focus in Concord, employing almost a third of its residents, and the town consequently seems to revolve, both physically and spiritually, around the gold-domed **State House** on Main Street (Mon–Fri 8am–4.30pm; ⓣ603/271-2154). The building's handsome stone facade was quarried from local granite using convict labor. Designed by Stuart J. Park, the original structure was completed in 1819, to be expanded and twice remodeled later. The state legislature – the largest in the country, with some four hundred members – has met continuously in the same chambers since June 2, 1819, the longest such tenure in the US. Inside, haunting portraits of over 150 legislators hang on all three floors. Both self-guided and guided tours are available from the visitors' center on the first floor. Outside, bronze statues of New Hampshire political notables, including Daniel Webster and President Franklin Pierce, strike dignified poses.

The small **Museum of New Hampshire History** (Tues–Sat 9.30am–5pm, Sun noon–5pm; July–Oct 15 & Dec also open Mon 9.30am–5pm; $5.50, $3 children; ⓣ603/228-6688, ⓦwww.nhhistory.org) is tucked behind the brick buildings on Main Street across from the State House, in **Eagle Square**. In the gallery on the first floor, you can browse the well-presented collection of paintings, photographs, maps, and artifacts, including a restored Concord coach (see box above) and a Native American canoe, which chronologically trace the state's history. Upstairs are rotating displays, a replica forest fire watch tower, and various hands-on exhibits for the kids.

At the north end of Main Street, at 14 Penacook St, is the **Pierce Manse** (mid-June to early Sept Mon–Fri 11am–3pm; $3), where Franklin Pierce lived with his family between 1842 and 1848. Notable mainly as one of the United States' least successful presidents (see box, p.480), Pierce set up a successful private law practice while in residence here. The restored white two-story 1838 home is now a museum filled with the former president's personal effects, such as his top hat and some period furniture, including the family's writing table. It's open for tours during the summer. Pierce is buried in the **Old North Cemetery**, near the intersection of North State Street and Keane Avenue, in the northern end of the downtown area.

Across the river, the **Christa McAuliffe Planetarium**, 3 Institute Drive (Mon–Sat 10am–5pm, Sun noon–5pm; free entry, $8 per show; ⓣ603/271-7827, ⓦwww.starhop.com), named for the Concord High School teacher who perished in the Space Shuttle *Challenger* disaster in 1986, stages impressive public astronomy shows in its 92-seat theater and hosts free Skywatch events the first Friday of every month. The planetarium also has interactive exhibits, such as the Pathfinder, where you rescue a team of three astronauts lost in space in the year 2058. McAuliffe was selected from a pool of 11,500 applicants to participate in the tragic space trip that ended her life just 73 seconds after lift-off.

Canterbury Shaker Village

About twenty minutes north of Concord, in Canterbury Center, **Canterbury Shaker Village**, exit 18 off I-93, 288 Shaker Rd (daily: mid-May to Oct 10am–5pm; Nov, Fri–Sun 10am–5pm; $15, good for two consecutive days; ⓣ603/783-9511, ⓦwww.shakers.org), is New England's premier museum of Shaker life, and perhaps the most fascinating tourist destination in New Hampshire. The tranquil village, a collection of simple, box-like buildings, is beautifully spread out over a set of rolling hills, overlooking the greenery of the countryside, and the site's quiet isolation is soothing. Founded by Mother Ann Lee in 1774, the Shakers, after breaking off from the Quakers, were one of the religious sects that sought refuge in the New World. In 1792, Canterbury became the sixth of nineteen Shaker communities, and, at its zenith in the mid-nineteenth century, there were some three hundred people living on the grounds. The last Shaker living in Canterbury died in 1992 at age 96; today, only a handful of Shakers remain in the world – all live in New Gloucester, Maine.

So named because of their tendency to dance in church (thereby shaking off sins and evil), the Shakers lived apart from the world in communities devoted to efficiency, equality, pacifism, a strong work ethic, cooperative living, and celibacy. Shakers relied upon conversion and adoption to expand their influence; orphans were readily accepted into the community, and at one point the state of New Hampshire opened a foster home in Canterbury Village. However, the Shakers' decline in the early twentieth century was ultimately exacerbated by their self-imposed sexual chastity.

Believing that technology would create more time for worship, the Shakers were creative and industrious inventors. Several of these inventions, such as a seed spreader used in agriculture, as well as some fine examples of Shaker furniture craftsmanship, are presented during several different thirty-minute **tours** of the village. Led by Shaker experts, the engrossing tours also introduce the ideals, day-to-day life, and architecture (there are 25 perfectly restored buildings on the site) of these people as you wander from building to building – including the church, the schoolhouse, and the laundry room – and around the property. There is also an acclaimed restaurant on the property, the *Shaker Table*, serving Shaker specialties (see review overleaf).

Eating, drinking, and entertainment

Concord's **restaurants** can seem uninspired when compared with those of Portsmouth. However, you can find some good-value lunches around the State

House, and Loudon Road, east of the Merrimack River, is lined with fast-food and national chain restaurants. Note that many of the town's eateries are closed on Sundays, if not the whole weekend. Other than a couple of basic, typical bars, some with **live music**, there is really no nightlife to speak of here.

Barley House 132 N Main St ⓣ603/228-6363. Watering hole for state legislators on lunch breaks from the State House opposite. Good, mostly inexpensive pub-style food and live music, especially jazz, Thurs, Fri & Sat. Closed Sun.

Capitol Grille 1 Eagle Square ⓣ603/228-6608. The restaurant serves sandwiches, steaks, pasta, and seafood dishes, but patrons come as much for the karaoke on Sun & Thurs, and the live music or DJs on Fri & Sat.

Eagle Square Deli 5 Eagle Square ⓣ603/228-4795. Excellent deli sandwiches-to-go across from the History Museum. Open Mon–Fri, until 2pm.

Margaritas 1 Bicentennial Square ⓣ603/224-2821. Housed in a former police station, this popular chain serves some of the biggest Mexican dishes around. You can sit in a former jail cell downstairs while you sip your margarita and carouse with local singles – very atmospheric. Free appetizers 4–7pm.

Shaker Table 288 Shaker Rd, Canterbury ⓣ603/783-4238. Imaginative Shaker-inspired specialties, with largely local, organically grown ingredients, such as ginger carrot puree with flower petals, Canterbury pot roast, sarsaparilla barbecued hen, lavender crème brûlée. Lunches and four-course candlelit dinners are served. Closed Jan through mid-April.

West of Concord: Henniker

The pleasant, relatively tourist-free residential town of **HENNIKER** ("The only Henniker on Earth!"), west of Concord on Rte-114 along the border of the Merrimack Valley, was settled by families from the *Mayflower*, many of whose descendants still live in the area. Residents enjoy the peaceful seclusion, so much that they raised $100,000 in a successful campaign to keep retail giant Rite Aid Pharmacy from building a store in the quaint downtown area.

In Henniker's center, along the Contoocook River ("Tooky"), **Main Street** is home to an agreeable group of shops, including the nostalgic Henniker Pharmacy, where you can order ice cream and sandwiches at an old-fashioned soda counter in back. The Old Number Six Book Depot, 26 Depot Hill Rd (up the hill from the Town Hall), with an enormous stock of new and used **books** on all subjects, is worth a browse.

There are a couple of good **hikes** in the area: try the Mount Liberty Extension trail, which winds up a gentle slope to the top of Mount Liberty, one mile west of the center of town off of Western Avenue at the end of Liberty Hill Road. Baseball great Ted Williams regularly went **fly-fishing** along the Contoocook River between Henniker and Hillsborough, and it's still a popular spot between May and October. During the winter, you can **ski** at the family-oriented **Pats Peak Ski Area** (ⓣ603/428-3245, ⓦwww.patspeak.com), although with only seven hundred vertical feet of trails the terrain is rather limited.

Practicalities

Henniker has several excellent **accommodation** options, none better than the *Colby Hill Inn*, half a mile from the center of town off of Western Avenue (ⓣ603/428-3281 or 1-800/531-0330, ⓦwww.colbyhillinn.com; ❻), a romantic 1795 country farmhouse with friendly owners, delicious breakfasts, and a gourmet restaurant. Closer to town, the *Henniker House*, 2 Ramsdell Rd (ⓣ603/428-3198, ⓦwww.hennikerhouse.com; ❹), offers unpretentious lodging along the river in a converted hospital. You can **camp** at the family-oriented *Keyser Pond Campground*, 47 Old Concord Rd (mid-May to mid-Oct; ⓣ1-800/272-5221, ⓦwww.keyserpond.com; $30 per site with water and electricity), or *Mile-Away Campground*, 41 Old West Hopkinton Rd (ⓣ603/428-7616; $27 per tent site, $34 RV site).

There are also a few good places to eat in Henniker. The *Colby Hill Inn* (see above) features expertly prepared upscale food (entrees are $26–31), including pan-seared duck breast and lobster-stuffed chicken breast, in a relaxed but elegant setting overlooking a garden. Along the river, *Daniel's Restaurant and Pub*, Main Street (Ⓣ603/428-7621), serves reasonably priced soups, pastas, and meat entrees on a riverside dock.

The Monadnock region

Known as the "quiet corner," the **Monadnock region**, which occupies the southwestern portion of New Hampshire, encompassed deserted country roads and typically quaint church-spire-filled New England towns that center around the lonely 3165-foot peak of **Mount Monadnock**. Aside from the gentle slopes of the mountain itself, which attract plenty of outdoor enthusiasts, the region boasts no real stand-out tourist attractions, and, although the slow pace and rolling hills can be addictive, you may very well find yourself restless with the desire to move on after a day or so of exploring.

You can get a good feel for small-town New England living at any of the region's many picturesque villages, but several are worth highlighting. **Keene**, an amiable place with a provincial disposition, is the area's most populous community; **Peterborough**, along US-202, is the region's – perhaps the state's – artistic center; **Hillsborough** was the birthplace of New Hampshire's only US president, Franklin Pierce; **Jaffrey** rests quietly at the base of Mount Monadnock next to the state park; and **Fitzwilliam** is a classic New England community, incorporated in 1773. Attractive places to stay, mainly of the bed-and-breakfast and country-inn variety, can also be found just about anywhere; Keene, the region's main commercial center, also has a smattering of chain hotels. Those who have come to climb Mount Monadnock will find reasonable places to camp nearby.

Arrival, information, and getting around

Vermont Transit **buses** going to Boston, Montréal, and various points in Vermont stop at a terminal in downtown Keene (Ⓣ603/352-1331), where you can also catch various local buses. Along with Keene, Fitzwilliam is the only town in the Monadnock region which is somewhat accessible by public transport. A Vermont Transit (Ⓣ603/522-8737) bus stops at the Fitzwilliam Inn, 526 Main St, but only once a day, traveling from Brattleboro, Vermont to Boston.

By far the best way to get around is by **car**, which will allow easy access to the region's many quiet backcountry roads. You can **rent** a vehicle from **Enterprise**, 535A Main St, in Keene (Ⓣ603/358-3345) or in Peterborough at 1 Jaffrey Rd (Ⓣ603/924-9058). **Biking** is also a good way to explore the pleasant countryside of the Monadnock region, although the terrain can at times be a bit hilly. For mountain-bike rentals, the only place for miles is **Summers Backcountry Outfitters**, 16 Ashuelot St, Keene (Ⓣ603/357-5107); they'll also give you plenty of advice on routes.

For tourist **information** and accommodation bookings, try the **Greater Keene Chamber of Commerce**, 48 Central Square in Keene (Ⓣ603/352-1303, Ⓦwww.keenechamber.com), the **Peterborough Chamber of Commerce**, at the junction of Rte-101 and US-202 (Ⓣ603/924-7234, Ⓦwww.peterboroughchamber.com), or the **Hillsborough Chamber of Commerce**, 25 School St (Ⓣ603/464-5858, Ⓦwww.hillsboroughnhchamber.com), for more information on the town and its five stone arch bridges. Meanwhile, the *Monadnock Magazine*, published in Peterborough and distributed throughout the region, has entertainment listings and local-interest stories.

Keene

KEENE, with 23,000 residents, is the most populous of the cities in the Monadnock region, though in truth it has little competition, and you would hardly call it cosmopolitan. The architecture here is noticeably more modern, and, although the town manages to maintain a friendly, if somewhat dull charm, there's not much to do other than shop and eat in the downtown area, along the unusually wide **Main Street**, allegedly the "widest Main Street in the US," which culminates in the lovely **Keene Common**. For what it's worth, the town was a well-known crafts center in the early nineteenth century, when **glass** and **pottery** production was at its peak; a marker along Main Street denotes the site of the **Hampshire Pottery Works**, the most successful of the local manufacturers. Still standing at 399 Main St, the **Wyman Tavern** (June to early Sept Thurs–Sat 11am–4pm; $2; Ⓣ603/352-5161) was built in 1762 by Isaac Wyman, a staunch patriot who later led a group of Minute Men from the tavern south to fight in the Revolutionary War. The tavern was also the site of the first official meeting of the trustees of Dartmouth College, which was founded in 1769. The restored taproom, living quarters, and ballroom are open to the public. While you're down in that part of town, it's worth stopping in at the **Thorne-Sagendorph Art Gallery** (Sat–Wed noon–4pm, Thurs–Fri noon–7pm; July & Aug closed Mon–Tues; free; Ⓣ603/358-2720) on the attractive campus of Keene State College. It's pretty tiny (one room for the permanent collection and one for temporary exhibits), but the eclectic permanent collection ranges from African statues to Robert Mapplethorpe photographs to a Goya print. Take some time to peruse Peter Milton's print, *20th Century Limited*, which depicts last century's cultural achievements as a train wreck, from which only a few things have been rescued.

Burdick Chocolates

Northwest of Keene, off of Rte-12, in the tiny white-clapboard town of **Walpole**, where Louisa May Alcott summered, and where documentary filmmaker Ken Burns currently lives, you can find one of New Hampshire's most delectable stores, **Burdick Chocolates** (Ⓣ603/756-3701 or 1-800/229-2419, Ⓦwww.burdickchocolate.com). Situated in an unassuming storefront along Main Street, the chocolate here has been rated the best in the country by *Consumer Reports* magazine – and deservedly so. Swiss-trained Larry Burdick makes his homemade treats from French Valrhona chocolate before shipping them to the nation's finest restaurants and shops, such as *Bouley* in New York City. If the chocolate isn't enough, you can get coffee and pastries in the adjoining café.

Practicalities

Apart from a few chain hotels on the outskirts of town, Keene plays host to a couple of **places to stay**. The *Carriage Barn Bed and Breakfast*, 358 Main St (Ⓣ603/357-3812, Ⓦwww.carriagebarn.com; ❹), has four guestrooms with private bath in a cozy house just a few minutes' walk from the shops, restaurants, and entertainment of downtown Keene. A little farther from the town center, next to the pond which shares its name, the *Goose Pond Guest House*, East Surrey Road (Ⓣ603/357-4787, Ⓦwww.goosepondguesthouse.com; ❺), enjoys an idyllic location among orchards and berry patches, with cozy rooms packed with antique furnishings.

If you're looking for a bite to **eat**, there are a few places worth noting. The popular *176 Main*, at that location (Ⓣ603/357-3100), has a huge and varied menu of excellent-value salads, soups, sandwiches, and main meals, served in a rustic and intimate dining room, as well as a large selection of tap and bottled beers. For authentic Italian food in a warm setting full of plants, head to *Nicola's Trattoria*, 39 Central Square (Ⓣ603/355-5242), which serves traditional pasta and meat entrees. *Brewbakers*, 97 Main St (Ⓣ603/355-4844), is a hip coffee joint with comfy couches that also serves cheap soups, sandwiches, and salads. One of the top spots for **shopping** is the Colony Mill Marketplace, 222 West St, a converted brick wool mill with an interesting grouping of relatively upscale shops. The Marketplace also houses the best **place to drink** in town, the *Elm City Brewery and Pub* (Ⓣ603/355-3335), which serves hearty American meals in addition to its own microbrews.

Hillsborough

About 25 miles northeast of Keene on Rte-9, the tiny town of **HILLSBOROUGH** – actually a grouping of four small villages (Hillsborough Bridge Village, Center Village, Lower Village, and Upper Village) – is the birthplace of Franklin Pierce (see box overleaf), fourteenth president of the United States and the only New Hampshire native to have attained the position. You can tour his brightly restored boyhood home, the **Franklin Pierce Homestead**, at the intersection of Rte-9 and Rte-31 (July & Aug Mon–Sat 10am–4pm, Sun 1–4pm; June & Sept Sat 10am–4pm, Sun 1–4pm; $5; Ⓣ603/478-3165), where the docents downplay Pierce's shortcomings – alcoholism, ineffective leadership – to portray him as a misunderstood hero. The building is a fine (if slightly larger) example of the Federal-style homes that were common in the region, and Franklin lived here on and off until he was 30. The rooms inside are relatively bare, though there are a few nicely painted wallpapers, including one that depicts the harbor at Naples.

The house was built by Franklin's father, **Benjamin Pierce**, who first came to Hillsborough in 1786, after having served as a general in the Revolutionary War under George Washington. He was elected a representative to the legislature for the towns of Hillsborough and Henniker in 1789 and went on to a fifty-seven-year career in public office, including two terms as governor of New Hampshire.

One of Hillsborough's four municipalities, **Hillsborough Bridge Village**, at the intersection of Rte-9 and Rte-149, is home to the area's one-street downtown area. You can still see the structural remnains of the nineteenth-century **Contoocook Mills**, abandoned in the early 1900s, along the banks of the river, reminders of the town's once successful textile-manufacturing industry. Also worth a quick look, the **Kemps Truck Museum**, along the river on

Franklin Pierce

Not highly rated in history's annals, **Franklin Pierce** was born in Hillsborough, New Hampshire, on November 23, 1804. Though Ralph Waldo Emerson wrote that Pierce was "either the worst, or one of the weakest of all our Presidents," modern New Hampshire residents overlook his shortcomings in the White House and have in fact transformed him into something of a local hero.

Handsome, charming, and amiable in his younger years, Pierce studied law at Bowdoin College in Maine before returning to New Hampshire to win his first election to public office. Only 25 at the time, he served in the state legislature, and later became speaker of the New Hampshire House. Pierce served five terms in the House of Representatives before being elected to the United States Senate. But his love of the law ultimately led him to return to Concord and set up a successful law practice. After serving in the Mexican War, he unexpectedly received the nomination for president at the Democratic National Convention in 1852, when his party could not make a decision on any of the other four candidates. Even more surprisingly perhaps, Pierce edged out Whig candidate Whitfield Scott in the general election.

Pierce's presidency began on a particularly black note, when his only remaining son, Bennie, was killed in a train accident just before the inauguration. Pierce's wife, Jane, was rarely seen in public afterwards, and it was said that Pierce himself never recovered. At a time when the nation was severely divided over slavery, Pierce remained staunchly opposed to antislavery legislation, wrongly believing that his status as a Northerner with Southern values would strike an acceptable compromise with the nation. With his signing of the 1854 Kansas–Nebraska Act, which allowed settlers to choose whether to allow slavery, conflict erupted in Kansas, and Pierce effectively lost his authority over the American people. By then he'd become a problem alcoholic, and it is said that Pierce's parting words from the White House were, "Well, I guess there's nothing left to do but go get drunk." To this day, Pierce is the only US president not to have been nominated by his party for a second term.

River Street off of Rte-149, is really more like a free parking lot full of rusting old trucks, though it supposedly holds the biggest collection of Mack trucks in the world.

Once you've tired of the **antique shops** in the center of town, head for the **Fox State Forest**, a state-maintained nature preserve south of town, which has over twenty miles of good hiking and cross-country skiing trails, as well as some interesting wetland areas. You can get a trail map and advice at the Fox Forest Headquarters (Ⓣ603/464-3453), along Center Road south of town.

The quiet country roads of Hillsborough cross some well-constructed old **stone arch bridges**. Built by skilled Scotch-Irish stonemasons in the mid-nineteenth century, the bridges, some built without mortar, are still in use. The finest bridge can be seen near the Pierce House, at the junction of Rte-9 and US-202, where there is also a small park with picnic benches.

While Hillsborough has a number of things to keep you busy, you're better off heading to either Keene or Peterborough for places to stay or eat.

Peterborough

The proud riverfront town of **PETERBOROUGH**, south of Hillsborough along Rte-202, has a youthful artistic focus these days. Immortalized by Thornton Wilder in the play *Our Town* and now boldly claiming to be "an entire community devoted to the arts," Peterborough is home to a wide range of cultural activities, but really centers on the **MacDowell Colony**, 100 High St (Ⓣ603/924-3886, Ⓦwww.macdowellcolony.org), which hosts over two hundred artists – including musicians, painters, filmmakers, and photographers – in its 32 private studios each year. Dedicated to providing an environment free of distraction since its founding in 1907, the privately funded colony has hosted such notables as Alice Walker, Studs Terkel, Milton Avery, Thornton Wilder, Oscar Hijuelos, and Willa Cather. Artists open their studios to the public only once a year on Medal Day, usually in mid-August (call the Colony for exact date), when the Edward MacDowell Medal is awarded to "an American creative artist whose body of work has made an outstanding contribution to the national culture."

The tiny, brick-dominated downtown, centered around **Grove Street**, was largely the inspiration of architect Benjamin Russell, who designed the Town House, where the city still holds town meetings, as well as the Historical Society and the Guernsey Building office complex. Inside the Historical Society building, 19 Grove St (Mon–Fri 10am–4pm; Ⓣ603/924-3235), a dusty hodgepodge of old artifacts, including photographs and farming tools, describes the "story of a typical New Hampshire town." One of the finest bookstores in the state, the Toadstool Bookshop, 12 Depot Square (Ⓣ603/924-3543), has a huge selection of fiction, nonfiction, and travel books.

Three miles east of Peterborough along Rte-101, **Miller State Park** (Ⓣ603/924-3672; $3) has a few excellent hikes. Try the Wapack Trail, which takes you to the 2290-foot summit of Pack Monadnock Mountain (2.8 miles round-trip), from which you can sometimes see the Boston skyline to the southeast and Mount Washington to the north.

Practicalities

The most convenient **place to stay** is the *Peterborough Manor Bed and Breakfast*, 50 Summer St (Ⓣ603/924-9832, Ⓦwww.peterboroughmanor.com; ④), which has six sunny rooms with private bath in an 1890s Victorian mansion. Otherwise, the *Apple Gate Bed and Breakfast*, 199 Upland Farm Rd, two miles from downtown (Ⓣ603/924-6543; ④), offers pretty much the same level of comfort at similar prices. Of several **places to eat** in Peterborough, *Aqua Bistro*, Depot Square (closed Mon; Ⓣ603/924-9905), is the most interesting, serving delicious and creative American bistro dinners and a wonderful weekend brunch. *Harlow's Deli and Café*, 3 School St (Ⓣ603/924-6365), serves up good sandwiches and pizza as well as a healthy dose of town gossip in a friendly, relaxed pub where the bartender knows the customers by name. For fancy sandwiches, head to *Twelve Pine*, Depot Square (Ⓣ603/924-6140), which also serves espresso and fresh juice and has café seating.

Each year in mid-July, Peterborough hosts the **Monadnock Festival for the Arts** (Ⓣ603/924-7234), a weekend of dance, art, theater, and music. From late June through mid-September, the **Peterborough Players** (Ⓣ603/924-7585, Ⓦwww.peterboroughplayers.com) stage acclaimed traditional and experimental theater performances in a renovated eighteenth-century barn on Hadley Road off of Hancock Middle Road, a few miles outside of town.

Jaffrey and Monadnock State Park

The area commonly referred to as **JAFFREY** actually takes in the towns of Jaffrey and Jaffrey Center. Not much goes on in the former, and you're better off concentrating on picturesque Jaffrey Center, long the domain of novelist Willa Cather, who came to Jaffrey Center every fall during the early twentieth century to work and enjoy the quiet countryside. In a studio in the woods, Cather wrote parts of the novels *My Ántonia* (1918) and *One of Ours* (1922). Cather is buried beside her lover, Edith Lewis, in the **Old Town Burial Ground**, along Rte-124 in Jaffrey Center.

Beyond that, you really visit Jaffrey for **Mount Monadnock**, reputedly the second most-climbed mountain in North America and the centerpiece of **MONADNOCK STATE PARK** (year-round; ⓣ603/532-8862; $3), just outside town heading west on Rte-124. The park is the most striking natural feature of the Monadnock region, a rolling countryside carpeted with dense stands of birch and pine trees. Although the mountain is only 3165ft high, its gently sloping peak seems dominant because it is so isolated. The peak was a popular spot with nineteenth-century writers and artists; indeed, Henry David Thoreau hiked and camped around the top of the mountain many times, writing of the experience, "It is a very unique walk . . . it often reminded me of my walks on the beach, and suggested how much both depend for their sublimity on solitude and dreariness. In both cases we feel the presence of some vast, titanic power." You can read more from Thoreau's journals and learn about the history of the park at the **visitors' center**, near the parking lot. They also have information about the park's forty miles of scenic hiking trails; the White Dot Trail is the most popular and direct route to the summit, taking about three and a half hours round-trip. If you reach the peak (which will likely be crowded) on a clear day, you'll be able to see all six New England states.

Practicalities

You can **camp** in the park at the base of Mount Monadnock all year round, with the 21 basic tent sites costing $18 (ⓣ603/271-3628 for reservations). Closer to Jaffrey, the *Emerald Acres Campground*, 39 Ridgecrest Rd (May to mid-Oct; ⓣ603/532-8838), has 52 pleasant sites in a pine forest bordering a small pond for $20.

The *Inn at Jaffrey Center*, 379 Main St (ⓣ603/532-7800, ⓦwww.theinnatjaffreycenter.com; ❺), enjoys, as its name suggests, a central location in Jaffrey Center, with eleven individually decorated rooms in a house with a nice shady garden. Meanwhile, *The Currier's House*, 5 Harkness Rd (ⓣ603-532-7670, ⓦwww.thecurriershouse.com; ❹), also in town, has views of Mount Monadnock and a back porch from which to enjoy them. Just outside of town, the antique-filled *Benjamin Prescott Inn*, 433 Turnpike Rd, off of Rte-124E (ⓣ603/532-6637 or 1-888/950-6637, ⓦwww.benjaminprescottinn.com; ❹), offers ten quiet rooms and gourmet New England breakfasts which, on Saturdays at least, include sweet strada (a sort of soufflé) with raspberry syrup and toffee-pecan coffee cake.

Fitzwilliam

Apart from being one of the more eye-pleasing towns in an undeniably picturesque region, the main reason for visiting **FITZWILLIAM**, south of Keene on Rte-12, is for its concentration of good accommodation. Otherwise, once you have absorbed the village's simple charms, consider making a trip to the nearby **Rhododendron State Park**, on Rte-119 five miles west of town (year-round; ⓣ603/239-8862), particularly in mid-July when the park's sixteen acres of wild rhododendrons are in full bloom.

The longstanding *Fitzwilliam Inn*, Rte-119 (Ⓣ603/585-9000), is closed for renovation at the time of writing, but there are other **places to stay**. The *Amos A. Parker House*, 149 Rte-119 (Ⓣ603/585-6540; ❺), is a small, homey bed-and-breakfast surrounded by beautifully manicured gardens; the *Hannah Davis House*, 106 Rte-119 (Ⓣ603/585-3344; ❹), another fine B&B, occupies an elegantly restored and furnished 1820s Federal-style home. The five suites and two cottages at *Unique Yankee Water B&B*, 354 Upper Troy Rd (Ⓣ603/242-6706; ❺), all have romantic open fireplaces and good views of Mount Monadnock.

Dartmouth – Lake Sunapee Region

The **Connecticut River** forms the entire western border of New Hampshire. Along its banks, a smattering of typically quaint New England villages, connected by empty, winding country roads, are spread between serene stretches of misty, rolling, green farmland. At the region's heart, **Hanover** is New Hampshire's intellectual center, the home of arch-conservative **Dartmouth College**, which attracts some of the country's best students and maintains an active arts scene. To the south, tiny **Cornish** was once a popular artists' colony, while **Lyme**, north of Hanover, is centered around a particularly attractive town green. As I-89 runs south from Hanover towards Concord, it grazes the northern tip of **Lake Sunapee**, a quieter alternative to more developed lake areas further east.

Hanover

Almost everyone in **HANOVER** has some connection to **Dartmouth College**. Indeed, the city and college are pretty much one and the same thing. Hanover received its official charter in 1761, just eight years before Dartmouth was founded. The college's reputation as one of the more conservative Ivy League schools is not unfounded; in fact, as you walk around, you'll notice that many of the students look strikingly alike: clean-cut preppy-types, most of them white. Stereotypes aside, though, it's an active place, with all the cultural and other benefits you expect from a college town: a good museum; regular performances by international musicians, dancers, and actors; good bookstores; and decent places to eat and drink.

Arrival, information, and city transit

Amtrak's *Vermonter* **train** stops across the river in White River Junction, less than five miles from Hanover, once a day; local buses (see below) will get you into town from there. Vermont Transit **buses** between Boston and Montréal

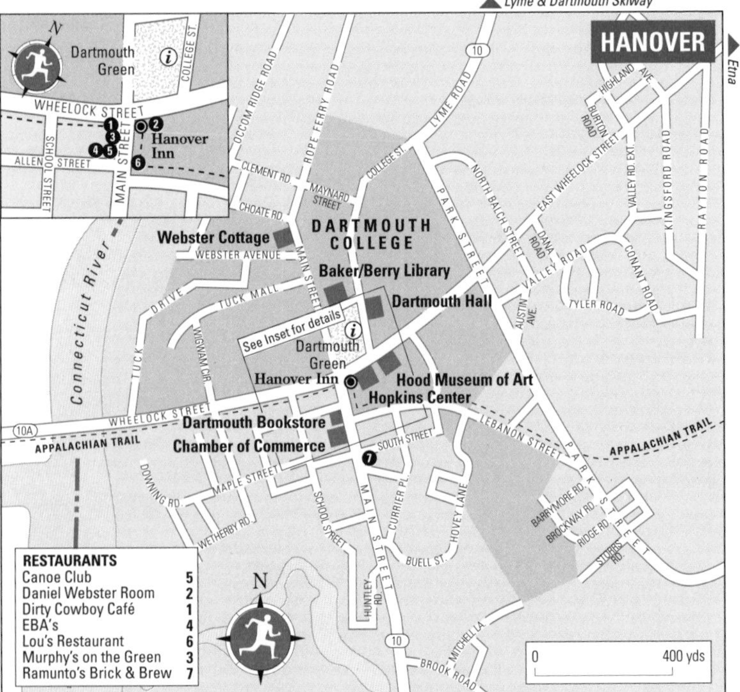

stop in Hanover at the *Hanover Inn*. There is a major terminal in White River Junction (ⓣ802/295-3011), with buses south to Boston via Manchester (NH), and as far north as Montréal, via Burlington (VT). The Concord Trailways-affiliated Dartmouth Coach (ⓣ1-800/637-0123) also has services to and from Boston and its airport, although fares are steeper than on Vermont Transit. Like the rest of New Hampshire, the upper Connecticut River Valley is most easily accessible by **car**. From the south, **I-91** blasts up the western side of the Connecticut River in Vermont, while **Rte-12A** and **Rte-10**, the slower, more scenic choices, trace the riverbank on the New Hampshire side. From Concord, I-89 passes through Lebanon and West Lebanon before crossing into Vermont; to get to Hanover, take Rte-120 north from Lebanon or Rte-10 north from West Lebanon.

The **Hanover Area Chamber of Commerce**, Nugget Building, 48 South Main Street (Mon–Fri 9am–noon and 1–4pm; ⓣ603/643-3115, ⓦwww.hanoverchamber.org), has only a moderate selection of brochures and tourist information. Probably your best bet during summer is the **information booth** on the green (ⓣ603/643-3512), jointly maintained by Hanover and Dartmouth College, and usually attended by enthusiastic students and retired alumni eager to spread the word about their old stomping grounds.

In and around Hanover, Advance Transit (ⓣ802/295-1824, ⓦwww.advance-transit.com) provides a comprehensive free local bus service, stopping in front of the *Hanover Inn* and at the Dartmouth Bookstore (among other stops in town) and connecting Hanover with Lebanon and West Lebanon, as well the nearby

Vermont towns of Norwich, Wilder, Hartford Village, and White River Junction. You can get a schedule and route map at the Chamber of Commerce.

Accommodation

Accommodation in Hanover tends to be tidy, expensive, and luxurious. Things are mellower (though usually just as expensive) in the surrounding countryside.

Chieftain Motor Inn 84 Lyme Rd ⓣ603/643-2550, ⓦwww.chieftaininn.com. About two and a half miles north of Hanover, the best of the few budget places in the area has access to a guest kitchen, and complimentary canoes for use in the nearby river. ❺

Hanover Inn corner of Main and Wheelock streets ⓣ603/643-4300 or 1-800/443-7024, ⓦwww.hanoverinn.com. The top end of Hanover's accommodation options, with dozens of spacious, elegantly furnished rooms, overlooking Dartmouth Green. See also below. ❾

Moose Mountain Lodge end of Moose Mountain Road, Etna ⓣ603/643-3529, ⓦwww.themoose-mountainlodge.com. Just east of Hanover, in Etna, the *Lodge* is a marvelously remote option year-round, but is best as a base in winter for cross-country skiing. Meals available; no credit cards. Open late Dec–Feb and mid-June to mid-Oct. ❼

Sunset Motor Inn Rte-10, 2 miles south of Hanover ⓣ603/298-8721. This mom-and-pop run place has eighteen clean rooms overlooking the Connecticut River, and offers a decent continental breakfast. ❸

Trumbull House Bed and Breakfast 40 Etna Rd ⓣ603/643-2370 or 1-800/651-5141, ⓦwww.trumbullhouse.com. Four miles east of Dartmouth Green, *Trumbull House* provides luxury accommodation in a quiet country setting. ❻

The Town

The town's focal point is grassy **Dartmouth Green**, bounded by Main, Wheelock, Wentworth, and College streets. The Dartmouth-owned **Hood Museum of Art**, on Wheelock Street at the green, is Hanover's main draw off the central campus (Tues & Thurs–Sat 10am–5pm, Wed 10am–9pm, Sun noon–5pm; free; ⓣ603/646-2808, ⓦhoodmuseum.dartmouth.edu), with paintings by Picasso and Monet as well as outstanding works by several American artists – Gilbert Stuart, Thomas Eakins, and John Sloan. The standouts include Frederick Remington's hauntingly realistic painting of three Native Americans and a settler, *Shotgun Hospitality*; a fine collection of portraits, including Joseph Steward's *Portrait of Eleazar Wheelock*, the founder of Dartmouth College; John Singleton Copley's bloody *A Youth Rescued from a Shark*; and detailed etchings by Rembrandt. In addition, the museum also has a comprehensive collection of Greek, Assyrian, and African objects. The adjacent cultural complex, the **Hopkins Center for the Arts** (ⓣ603/646-2422, ⓦhop.dartmouth.edu), screens international art and classic movies year-round (tickets $7). It also presents globally acclaimed musicians, acting companies, and dance troupes, as well as student performances.

Next door, the venerable **Hanover Inn**, founded by General Ebenezer Brewster in 1780, is a local landmark, standing five stories high with a classic-looking brick facade. Although devastating fires and extensive renovations have obscured the inn's Colonial charm, its lobby is still bustling with visiting parents, scholars, and performers. Previous guests at the inn, owned and operated by the college, include then-President Clinton, dancer Mikhail Baryshnikov, and the rock band Kiss. **South Main Street**, which runs along the west side of the inn, holds most of the town's eateries, bars, and shops, and is pleasant enough to wander around.

Dartmouth College

Majestic **Dartmouth College** (Ⓦwww.dartmouth.edu), founded by Reverend Eleazar Wheelock in 1769, is the ninth oldest college in the United States. The school was initially an outgrowth of a school for Native Americans that Wheelock had established in Connecticut, but in reality few Native Americans ever studied here. Named for its financial backer, the Earl of Dartmouth, the Ivy League institution attracts some of the top students in the world today, with particularly strong programs in medicine, engineering, and business.

The stately two-hundred-acre campus is spread out around Dartmouth Green, a good starting point for a look at the grounds. Flanking the north end of the green, along Wentworth Street, the looming **Baker/Berry Library**, with its 207-foot bell tower, is an imposing landmark. Inside, on the lower level, it holds the most arresting attraction on the campus, José Clemente Orozco's series of enormous **frescoes**. The Mexican artist painted these politically rousing murals, commissioned by the trustees of the college, between 1932 and 1934, while he was an artist-in-residence and visiting professor at Dartmouth. It's easy to see why conservative college officials and alumni viewed the violent depiction of the artist's stated theme, *An Epic of American Civilization*, as a direct insult. On one of the detailed, realistic panels, for example, a skeleton gives birth while lying upon a bed of dusty books, as a group of arrogant, robed scholars look on. In another panel, a large Jesus-like figure stands angrily next to a felled cross with an axe in his hand. Though college officials initially threatened to paint over the murals, they soon backed down, careful to avoid living up to Orozco's vision. Upstairs on the ground floor, check out the library's map room, which holds 150,000 sheet maps and seven thousand atlases.

On the east side of the green stands **Dartmouth Row**, a collection of four impressive old buildings that look out over the grass from a slight hill. **Dartmouth Hall**, an imposing white building with a large "1784" on its hulking pediment, was the college's first permanent structure and remains a symbol of Dartmouth's academic prowess. Although it burned to the ground in 1904, the restored structure, which today houses Dartmouth's language and literature departments, remains on its original foundation. The other three halls in the row, **Reed**, **Thornton**, and **Wentworth**, house Dartmouth's history and philosophy departments, and the Dean's office, respectively.

Birthplace of Daniel Webster

New Hampshire's best-known statesman, orator, and public figure, **Daniel Webster**, was born in 1782 in the tiny two-room farmhouse on Flaghold Road off of Rte-127 in **FRANKLIN**, twelve miles west of Laconia (see p.493). Now known simply as the **Daniel Webster Birthplace** (late May to early Sept, weekends 10.30am–5.30pm; $3; Ⓣ603/934-5057), the restored home contains period furniture, antiques, and some Webster memorabilia, including books he read as a child. Webster attended Phillips Exeter Academy, graduated from Dartmouth College in 1801, and went on to build a successful law practice before serving in Congress from 1813 to 1817 and in the US Senate from 1827 to 1841. He loomed large on the political scene in his day, delivering persuasive speeches on topics as far-ranging as states' rights, slavery, the Union, the US–Canadian border, and Dartmouth College. As secretary of state under presidents William Henry Harrison, Tyler, and Fillmore, Webster remained a staunch defender of the Union. During a particularly heated discussion in 1850, in which Webster debunked the idea of states' rights, he coined the memorable phrase "Liberty and Union, now and forever, one and inseparable." In perhaps his most famous debate, the Dartmouth College Case of 1817, Webster defended his alma mater before the Supreme Court, which decided that states could not interfere with royal charters.

Farther north along Main Street, the memory of the school's most celebrated graduate, Daniel Webster, the brilliant lawyer, senator, and orator, is preserved in **Webster Cottage**, 32 N Main St (late May to mid-Oct Wed, Sat & Sun 2.30–4.30pm; free; ⓣ603/643-6529), where he supposedly lived during his senior year. Webster later succeeded in defending the college before the Supreme Court in the landmark Dartmouth College Case of 1817, which determined that the power to make an institution public rests with those who control it, rather than with those who have funded it.

Eating and drinking

Canoe Club 27 S Main St ⓣ603/643-9660. The vibe is more easygoing than the prices on this satisfying menu. But it's a spirited place, with live music – whether jazz guitar, blues piano, or acoustic folk – 363 days a year.

Daniel Webster Room inside the *Hanover Inn*, corner of Main and Wheelock streets ⓣ603/643-4300. The most elegant (and most expensive) restaurant in town, boasting a traditional menu of finely grilled meats at $23–30 per entree.

Dirty Cowboy Café 7 S Main St ⓣ603/643-1323. Get your usual coffee drinks, as well as smoothies and fresh-squeezed juices here.

EBA's (Everything But Anchovies) 5 Allen St ⓣ603/643-6135. Families dine on salads and burgers here, but the real deal is the pizza (28 toppings and eighteen specialty pies). And yes, you can get anchovies if you want.

Lou's Restaurant 30 S Main St ⓣ603/643-3321. Filling breakfasts of tasty hashbrowns, eggs, and sausage for under $10. Serves lunch also, but it's not as good. Closes at 5pm.

Murphy's on the Green 11 S Main St ⓣ603/643-4075. The best spot in town for a drink is also a popular restaurant serving an eclectic array of healthy American cuisine. The good draft selection includes regional favorites Smuttynose and Magic Hat, along with Bass, Guinness, and Harp.

Ramunto's Brick and Brew 68 S Main St ⓣ603/643-9500. Serves delicious and affordable pizzas and has several beers on tap; open every night until at least midnight.

Around Hanover: Lyme and Cornish

Time stands still in tiny **LYME**, ten miles north of Hanover along Rte-10. The grassy town center is perfect for an evening stroll, which will take you past the attractive 1811 white-clapboard **Lyme Congregational Church**, featuring a bell supposedly cast by Paul Revere. After checking out the church's beautiful interior woodwork, have a look at the spooky old cemetery out back.

Other than a collection of scenic pastures and a few covered bridges, there's not much left in the town of **CORNISH**, 25 miles south of Hanover along Rte-120, which was a well-known artistic center in the late nineteenth century. The thing to see here is the **Saint-Gaudens National Historic Site**, off Rte-12A (daily: late May to late Oct 9am–4.30pm; $5; ⓣ603/675-2175, ⓦwww.sgnhs.org), where sculptor Augustus Saint-Gaudens lived and worked from 1885 until his death in 1907. Saint-Gaudens was best known for his life-like heroic bronze sculptures, including the Shaw Memorial in Boston and the General William T. Sherman Monument in New York City. Many well-known artists, writers, poets, and musicians, including Maxfield Parrish, Kenyon Cox, and Charles Platt, followed Saint-Gaudens to Cornish, establishing the **Cornish Colony**. Saint-Gaudens' house and studio and several galleries are open to the public. Take the time to wander around the beautiful grounds, which feature well-cared-for gardens, two wooded nature trails, and a relaxing expanse of green grass. You can also check out works in progress by the artist-in-residence at the **Ravine Studio**, in the woods along the northern edge of the property. Just north along Rte-12A, works by many of the area's famed artists are on display at the small **Cornish Colony Gallery and Museum** (late May–Oct 9am–5pm; $5; ⓣ603/675-6000), whose gardens were designed by Rose Standish Nichols, the first female landscape architect in America.

Outdoor activities in the Dartmouth area

Quick to take advantage of their rather isolated location, Dartmouth students and Hanover residents take their **outdoor** time seriously. Hiking, biking, rowing, and swimming are all popular, as are skiing (both cross-country and downhill) and skating. The town's residents include best-selling travel author Bill Bryson, one of whose books, *A Walk in the Woods*, chronicles his adventures along the three-thousand-mile Appalachian Trail, which runs right through Hanover along Rte-10A – during the summer, grizzled hikers trudge into town with some regularity. The Dartmouth Outing Club, in Robinson Hall (ⓣ603/646-2428), maintains hundreds of additional miles of **hiking trails** in the area and also leads group **bike rides**.

You can **rent mountain bikes** (and snowshoes in the winter) for $20 per day from Omer and Bob's Sportshop, 7 Allen St (ⓣ603/643-3525). **Rowing** on the Connecticut River remains an extremely popular way to take in the scenery while getting some exercise; the Ledyard Canoe Club (ⓣ603/643-6709) rent **canoes** and **kayaks** ($15–25 per day) and can suggest routes. In the winter, Dartmouth's very own **alpine ski** area, the Dartmouth Skiway, ten miles north in Lyme (ⓣ603/795-2143; $20–26 weekdays, $38 weekends), rents skis and snowboards. Dartmouth Outdoor Rentals (ⓣ603/643-6534) rents skiing and **ice-skating** equipment, snowshoes and snowboards, as well as mountaineering gear and tents.

If you're in the mood for an Ivy League-flavored **workout**, Dartmouth's enormous athletic facility (ⓣ603/646-3074, ⓦathletics.dartmouth.edu), centered around the **Alumni Gymnasium**, along East Wheelock Street, has a modern fitness center, two pools, tennis courts, racquetball and squash courts, and a basketball court. Non-students can buy an all-day guest pass for $8.

A few minutes south of town off of Rte-12A, the nearly five-hundred-foot-long **Cornish-Windsor covered bridge**, connecting New Hampshire with Vermont, is the longest one in the US, though unless you're an enthusiast, it may not be worth seeking out. It was constructed in 1866 and restored in 1989. A little farther south, on Springfield Road just off of Rte-11 in **Charlestown**, the **Fort at No. 4** (June–Oct Wed–Sun 10am–4.30pm; $8; ⓣ603/826-5700) hokily re-enacts colonial life in the 1740s and 1750s. Costumed interpreters roam the grounds, acting out the chores and activities of the day in various re-created living quarters and work areas, including an old blacksmith's workshop and a candle-making shop.

If you're looking for a comfortable **place to stay**, the best is the luxurious *Chase House Bed and Breakfast*, on Rte-12A (ⓣ603/675-5391, ⓦwww.chase-house.com; ⑥). The well-decorated nineteenth-century mansion is also the birthplace and one-time residence of Salmon Portland Chase, Chief Justice of the US Supreme Court in the 1860s, in whose honor the former Chase Manhattan Bank was posthumously named. Today the inn features seven exquisitely furnished rooms and delicious breakfasts (included).

Lake Sunapee and around

LAKE SUNAPEE, the northern tip of which just brushes I-89, lies about twenty-five miles south of Hanover. The lake had been popular as a summer escape since the beginning of the nineteenth century, but with the arrival of train connections to **Newbury** at the lake's southern tip, the area exploded with a booming tourist trade. Steamboats full of vacationing Bostonians and New Yorkers plied the waters, while mansions and luxury hotels began appearing on the shore. Among the notables who made their homes here were the Colgates (of Colgate-Palmolive fame) and Secretary of State John Milton Hay, whose mansion The Fells still stands. The advent of the automobile effectively ended Sunapee's boom time and saved it from development on the atrocious scale of its huge northeastern neighbor, Lake Winnipesaukee. Today, the Sunapee region is a very low-key place, although recent heavy investment, especially in Mount Sunapee (see below), while no doubt providing a new boom, may also sound the death knell for its secluded charm. Enjoy it while it lasts, and know that you're still in rockin' good company – Aerosmith's Steven Tyler has a house on the lake.

Sunapee Harbor and around

The action, such as it is, is all on **Sunapee Harbor**. A far cry from the lake's heyday, the only boats on the clear, clean waters (Sunapee is a spring-fed lake) now are the occasional mail boat and regular **boat tours**, such as those run by Sunapee Cruises (daily: July to early Sept 2pm; late May–June & early Sept to mid-Oct weekends 2pm; $16; Ⓣ603/763-4030, Ⓦwww.sunapeecruises.com). The knowledgeable captain will share Sunapee lore and point out the sights, such as the former Colgate estate and the lake's three lighthouses. True boat aficionados won't want to miss the annual **Antique and Classic Boat Parade** in August (contact the Lake Sunapee Protective Association in Sunapee Harbor for details; Ⓣ603/763-2210).

On the opposite shore, in Newbury, stands the Hay family estate, **The Fells**, off Rte-103A (grounds open year-round, dawn to dusk; house tours, late May to mid-Oct weekends and holidays 11am–5pm; $6, including grounds admission; Ⓣ603/763-4789). John Milton Hay was an adviser and friend of Abraham Lincoln, who later became secretary of state under Teddy Roosevelt. He built his mansion here in the 1870s, and it was passed on to his son, Cecil, who just happened to be a talented landscape artist and designed the grounds of the mansion in a pleasing mix of Asian and European styles. Cecil was also a concerned preservationist, and his distress at the rapid deforestation of the area led him to donate 675 acres of **forest** to the Society for the Protection of New Hampshire Forests. These days, the mansion itself is empty, and the guided tours, while enjoyable, tend to make visitors feel as if they are being shown the house for prospective purchase. Far more interesting are the **gardens** that surround the house, with the borrowed scenery of the lake and forests adding to their charm. There are also **nature trails** through those 675 acres, which provide good opportunities for bird-watching.

Winter activities in the area take place at **Mount Sunapee** (Ⓣ603/763-2356, Ⓦwww.mountsunapee.com; lift passes from $54), a family-oriented resort at the northern end of the lake. Fifteen million dollars' worth of investment over the past eight seasons has led to improvements to lifts, snowmaking facilities, and transportation to the mountain, as well as the opening of two new teaching trails. Indeed, the gentle slopes of Mount Sunapee will suit learners and the mildly proficient more than expert skiers.

Practicalities

About three miles from Lake Sunapee's eastern shore, one of the larger towns in the area, **New London**, is the home of the **Lake Sunapee Chamber of Commerce** (Ⓣ1-877/526-6575, Ⓦwww.lakesunapeenh.org), which should be able to orient you to the area and will happily help you find **accommodation**. In Newbury, the *Best Western Sunapee Lake Lodge*, 1403 Rte-103 (Ⓣ603/763-

2010 or 1-800/606-5253, Ⓦwww.sunapeelakelodge.com; ❺), is within walking distance of the ski resort, and while the rooms are much like any other hotel of this genre (comfortable and impersonal), there are plenty of them. More picturesque rooms with mountain views can be found in Sunapee at the *Blue Acorn Inn* (Ⓣ603/863-1144, Ⓦwww.blueacorninn.com; ❹) or at the *Inn at Sunapee*, 125 Burkehaven Hill Rd (Ⓣ603/763-4444 or 1-800/327-2466, Ⓦwww.innatsunapee.com; ❺), a converted 1875 farmhouse which overlooks the lake. There's also an attached **restaurant**, specializing in creative, fresh American food with an Asian flair. A better selection of dining choices can be found in New London, where *Flying Goose Brew Pub and Grille*, at 40 Andover Rd (Ⓣ603/526-6899), or *Peter Christian's Tavern* on Main St (Ⓣ603/526-4042), will present you with an atypical pub menu and a choice of ice-cold local drafts.

The Lakes Region

The vacation-oriented **LAKES REGION**, occupying the state's central corridor, east of I-93, almost doubles its population between May and September, when visitors throng the area's restaurants, hotels, lakefront cottages, beaches, and crystal-clear waters. On warm summer weekends the lakes can seem overrun with pleasure craft, all of which are available for rent at the many town marinas. Fishing, swimming, camping, and relaxing on the beach are also popular, and you can enjoy a view of the lakes from afar after hiking to the top of one of the peaks that wrinkle the countryside.

There are literally hundreds of lakes here, created by the snowmelt flowing south from the White Mountains. The biggest by far is **Lake Winnipesaukee**, at some 72 square miles the definitive center of the region. Long segments of the shoreline, especially in the east, are carpeted with thick forests that sweep down from surrounding hills. The lake is dotted with 274 islands – most of which are privately owned – and its irregular shape, a seemingly endless continuum of inlets and peninsulas, resembles a giant paint splatter. The eastern and western shores of Lake Winnipesaukee are quite distinct: sophisticated **Wolfeboro** is the center of the sparsely populated and more upscale region to the east, while **Weirs Beach** is the most developed stretch of the crowded western shore. Farther north, the down-to-earth nineteenth-century towns around beautiful **Squam Lake** are some of the most inviting in the region.

The western Winnipesaukee shore

The western Winnipesaukee shore, the most visited part of the Lakes Region, can be a relaxing or lively spot to spend a day or two depending on where you chose to go. Once inhabited by the Abenaki Indians, its position on the major north–south stagecoach route in the early nineteenth century, and, later, the railroad route north to the increasingly popular White Mountains, made it a major stopover. Nowadays, gas stations, cheap hotels, and convenience stores line the major roadways, such as US-3 and Rte-11, although nearly every

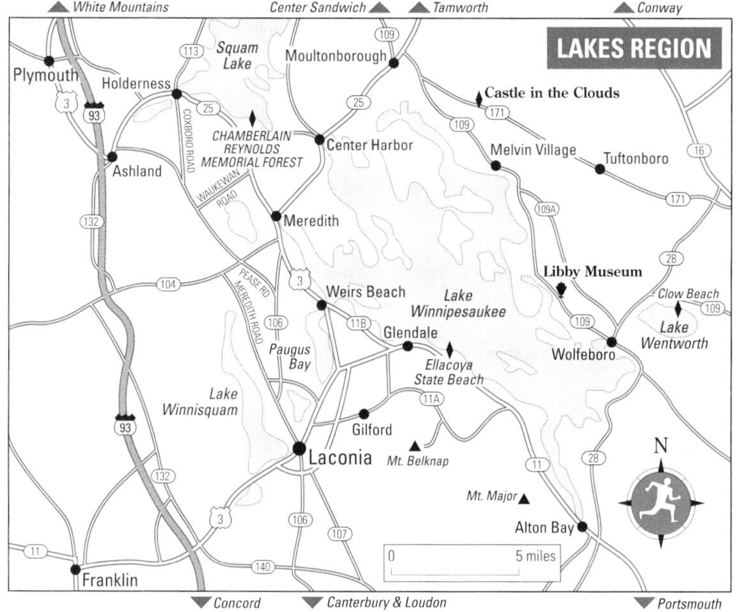

town in the area boasts sweeping views of some body of water. Downtown **Meredith**, squeezed between Lake Waukewan and Lake Winnipesaukee, is an appealing collection of shops, restaurants, and sumptuous lodgings, while **Weirs Beach**, south along US-3, is the epitome of summertime overkill, with enough arcades, ice-cream parlors, and roadside fun-parks to keep the kids happy for weeks. Undistinguished **Laconia** is the biggest town in the area, while the resort town of **Gilford** maintains a more relaxed disposition.

Arrival, information, and getting around

You'll really need a car to get around the lakes area, as **public transport** is extremely limited around Lake Winnipesaukee, although Concord Trailways (ⓣ1-800/639-3317) calls in at Meredith (at Mobil Mart, close to the center on Rte-25), at Center Harbor (at Fred Fuller's Oil on Rte-25), and at Moultonborough on the eastern side all year. Once in Meredith, you can **rent a car** from Meredith Ford (ⓣ603/279-4521), at the intersection of US-3 and Rte-25. Your best source for **information** on the western shore (they also have info on Squam Lake) is the **Meredith Area Chamber of Commerce** (daily 9am–5pm; ⓣ603/279-6121, ⓦwww.meredithcc.org), on US-3 just south of downtown Meredith. They distribute loads of brochures about local attractions and restaurants, and can provide details on lodging availability. You may also want to pick up a copy of *Weirs Times* or *The Laker*, free entertainment and local events guides widely available.

Weirs Beach

The short boardwalk at **WEIRS BEACH**, the very essence of seaside tackiness – despite being fifty miles inland – is the summer social center of the Lakes Region. Its wooden jetty overflows with vacationers from all over New England, and its amusement arcades jingle with cash; there's even a little crescent of

△ Weirs Beach neon sign

sandy beach, suitable for family swimming. The roads are lined with neon signs, mini-golf courses, waterslide playland extravaganzas, and motels clogged with family-filled minivans.

You'd best head elsewhere if you're looking for a relaxing lakeside afternoon. If you're up for a few hours of slippery diversion in the sun, however, you might try the better of the two competing **water parks**, Surf Coaster USA (daily: late June to early Sept 10am–6pm; $27; ⓣ603/366-5600), which offers dramatic rides and a wave machine on Rte-11B just south of town. Failing that, a great way to take in Winnipesaukee's beautiful expanse of inlets and peninsulas and get away from the ugliness of Weirs Beach is to board the **MS Mount Washington** (mid-May to Oct; ⓣ603/366-5531 or 1-888/843-6686, ⓦwww.cruisenh.com; $20, 150min), a 230-foot monster of a boat which departs from the dock in the center of town several times a day to cruise to Wolfeboro on the lake's western side. Dinner cruises depart several times per week (around $30). Other day cruises are available on the smaller *MV Doris E* ($10, one hour) and the real US mail boat, *MV Sophie C* ($16, two hours), which gives you a better opportunity to see some of the lake's many islands as *Sophie C* makes its deliveries.

Practicalities

If you want to find a **place to stay** within earshot of the amusement arcades and close enough to smell the hot dogs, there are plenty of choices on Tower Street, up the hill behind the jetty. There is a real army barracks feel to the *Half Moon Motel & Cottages*, 12 Tower St (ⓣ603/366-4494, ⓔhalfmoonmotel@weirsbeach.com; ❹), where a block of motel rooms and individual cottages (some with kitchens) are laid out around the austere pool with military precision. Slightly cozier is the *Bear Tree Lodge*, 2.5 miles up Rte-3 toward Meredith (ⓣ603/279-9013, ⓦwww.beartreelodge.com; ❸), whose rooms include efficiency kitchens, and where off-season room rates are among the cheapest you'll find anywhere in New Hampshire. For something to eat, you're better off heading to nearby Meredith. If, however, you simply need a quick fill-up, the hot-dog stands and burger bars by the jetty will do the trick.

Meredith

MEREDITH, four miles north of Weirs Beach, is more upscale than its neighbor. The friendly town center, up the hill behind the Mill Falls Shopping Center development, spills into the pleasant **Meredith Marina**, 2 Bayshore Drive (ⓣ603/279-7921), where you can rent a motorboat for a mere $275 per day, $195 per half-day. The **Winnipesaukee Scenic Railroad** (late May to early June & early Sept to mid-Oct weekends only; daily mid-June to early Sept; $10 for 1hr, $11 for 2hr; ⓣ603/279-5253, ⓦwww.hoborr.com) operates scenic trips along the lakeshore between Meredith and Weirs Beach. The sandy town **beach**, with mountain views, is located on Waukewan Street along the shores of tiny **Lake Waukewan**. Right outside the center of town, a pretty little **lakeside park** makes for a pleasant stroll; while you're there, you can ponder who decided to mount the anti-aircraft gun from a World War II battle cruiser on the grass.

Just outside Meredith, off of US-3, **Annalee's Doll Museum** (daily 9am–5pm; ⓣ603/279-6542 or 1-800/433-6557) is actually a hard-sell toy shop, specializing in painted-felt dolls. Those items onto which they've managed to stitch the heads backwards are offered at a 25-percent reduction.

Practicalities

The **Meredith Area Chamber of Commerce** (daily 9am–5pm; ⓣ603/279-6121, ⓦwww.meredithcc.org), on US-3 can answer any questions on local accommodation or restaurants. For those who wish to **camp** in the area, try *Harbor Hill* (ⓣ603/279-6910), 1.5 miles up Rte-25, with tent sites ($24) and camper cabins ($60), and a swimming pool and camp store on the premises. Certainly the **place to stay** in town is *The Inns at Mill Falls*, 312 Daniel Webster Hwy (ⓣ603/279-7006 or 1-800/622-6455, ⓦwww.millfalls.com; ❼–❾), actually a set of four notable accommodations: the *Inn* and *Chase House* feature large plush rooms that overlook the lake, while the waterside *Inn at Bay Point* and *Church Landing,* with its polished rustic lakehouse interior, up the style level considerably. Some cozy B&Bs are also strewn around: at Main and Waukewan streets, the *Meredith Inn*, a rose-colored Victorian (ⓣ603/279-0000, ⓦwww.meredithinn.com; ❺), and *Tuckernuck Inn*, 25 Red Gate Lane (ⓣ603/279-5521, ⓦwww.thetuckernuckinn.com; ❺), are both good value choices.

As for **eating**, you could do worse than end up in Meredith. For a quick bite of authentic Chinese, *Phu Jee*, 55 Main St (ⓣ603/279-1129), will do the trick for less than $15, and *Camp* (ⓣ603/279-3003) is an entertaining trip back to summer camp, complete with log-cabin walls, a screen-door, and casual comfort food like fried chicken, pan-fried trout, and s'mores. *Town Docks* (ⓣ603/279-3445) will give you a seafood fix, and *Lago* (ⓣ603/279-2253), 1 Bay Point at routes 3 and 25, has the best Italian in town, with a busy terrace on the water. Perhaps the best dinner option in town is *Lakehouse Grill* at the *Church Landing* inn, 312 Daniel Webster Hwy (ⓣ603/279-5221). Creative starters, heaping main plates of pork, steak, or salmon ($17–23),' and a fairly happening bar scene await you just about every night.

Laconia and Gilford

LACONIA, southwest from Lake Winnipesaukee on the shores of **Winnisquam Lake**, has long been the most populated town in the Lakes Region, established as a trading and manufacturing center after the railroad reached the city in 1848. Some of the factories in use back then – when they produced such things as nails and hosiery – continue as office space. Today Laconia is mostly just convenient as a place to pick up supplies. Beyond the commercial strip of malls and fast-food joints is the downtown's short, depressed stretch of empty storefronts.

The pleasant village of **GILFORD** (east of Laconia along Rte-11A) is worth a quick detour, though there is not a whole lot to actually see or do there. For excellent vistas of the lake and surrounding region, head for the top of **Mount Belknap**, which at 2384 feet is the highest peak in the Belknap Range, along the west side of the lake. The easiest and shortest route up the mountain begins along Belknap Mountain Carriage Road; turn off Rte-11A at the lights in the center of Gilford, drive through the village on Cherry Valley Road and follow the signs for the Fire Tower on Belknap. If you're feeling more sedentary, **Ellacoya State Beach**, along Rte-11 (mid-May to mid-Oct; $3; ⓣ603/293-7821), is one of the finer sandy beaches – and the only one that's state-maintained – on Lake Winnipesaukee, with six hundred feet of sand, and a **campground** that affords some great views of the lake from many of its 38 sites ($42).

Practicalities

If you prefer the more laidback atmosphere here than at Meredith and certainly Weirs Beach, you will find some reasonable **places to stay** in Gilford. The *Belknap Point Motel*, 107 Belknap Point Rd (ⓣ1-888/454-2537, ⓦwww.bpmotel.com; ❺), offers somewhat modern lakeside accommodations in a boxy, white building with a good view of the lake and mountains. Some rooms have full kitchens and can be rented by the week. Slightly more upscale, *B Mae's Inn & Suites*, 17 Harris Shore Rd (ⓣ603/293-7526 or 1-800/458-3877, ⓦwww.bmaesresort.com; ❻), has two pools, a Jacuzzi, and an exercise room – all within walking distance of the beach. Just past Gilford on Rte-11A, *Gunstock* (ⓣ603/293-4341 or 1-800/486-7862, ⓦwww.gunstock.com) doubles as an alpine ski area during the winter and a recreation area during the summer, and offers lodging. Summer activities include mountain-bike riding, horseback riding, and hiking (visit the store for rentals, trail maps, and advice). **Campsites** are available for $25 a night, while camping cabins, with electricity and water, can be had for $60 per night.

For a drink or hearty snack in Gilford, try *Patrick's Pub*, at the intersection of Rte-11 and Rte-11B (ⓣ603/293-0841). If you're looking for **entertainment**, head to the largest musical venue in the Lakes Region, the Meadowbrook Musical Arts Center, also in Gilford (ⓣ603/293-4700, ⓦwww.meadowbrookfarm.net), with room for almost six thousand concertgoers.

The eastern Winnipesaukee shore

The eastern shore of Lake Winnipesaukee is a lot less developed than the western shore, with a more polished and elegant air about it, and the refined quality of the food, lodging, and atmosphere is reflected in steeper prices. First established as a popular summer destination in the late eighteenth century by Governor John Wentworth, still rates tourism as its major industry, but in a much more relaxed fashion: there are no mini-golf courses or waterslides, and fewer children. Wealthy families vacation year after year at the many splendid privately owned homes along Lake Winnipesaukee's shore, and couples flock to the many secluded country B&Bs of the region. This side of the lake is also better for walking and outdoor activities, although most visitors in search of rugged adventure head farther north for the popular peaks of the White Mountains. There are several good public beaches around **Wolfeboro**, the most populated and interesting town in the area. North of Lake Winnipesaukee is the quiet town of **Moultonborough**, home to one of the oldest country stores in the US. Nearby, architecturally eclectic **Castle in the Clouds** makes for an interesting diversion, as does the **Loon Center**.

Many hotels, inns, and B&Bs are only available seasonally, so call ahead, especially in winter months. Camping in the quiet birch forests that crowd the lake's shore is also a pleasant summer option, although insect repellent is an absolute must.

Arrival, information, and getting around

If you're traveling by **car**, the drive along Rte-25 and Rte-109 from the eastern to western side of the lake is the easiest and most scenic route; using Rte-11 and Rte-28 through Alton Bay around the south end of the lake is slightly faster. **Local transportation** is scarce, although the **Wolfeboro Trolley Company** operates "Molly the Trolley" during the summer, which makes a short, narrated loop around Wolfeboro (Ⓣ603/569-1080; $5). Tickets are good for an entire day. Concord Trailways stops in Moultonborough (at the Moultonborough Emporium on Rte-25) year round. You can also cross the lake from west to east by **boat**. The *MS Mount Washington* (see p.492) runs at least two round-trips a day from Weirs Beach to Wolfeboro; skip the return portion of the cruise if you want to stay on the eastern shore overnight. The best source for **information** on the eastern shore is the **Wolfeboro Chamber of Commerce**, in the old red railroad building on Railroad Street in the center of town (Ⓣ603/569-2200 or 1-800/516-5324, Ⓦwww.wolfeborochamber.com), which stocks the usual dizzying array of brochures and will give the lowdown on local lodging.

Wolfeboro

Because Governor John Wentworth built his summer home nearby in 1768, upscale **WOLFEBORO** claims to be "the oldest summer resort in America." Sandwiched between lakes Winnipesaukee and Wentworth, at the intersection of Rte-109 and Rte-28, it has little to show for that history, but it's a relaxing place to spend a bit of time. The short, bustling Main Street (Rte-109) can be fun if you want to while away a few hours strolling from boutique to boutique, with fine views of the lake never too far away. The 4300-square-foot summer mansion of Governor John Wentworth, known as the Wentworth House Plantation, with its own saw mill, orchards, workers' village, and six-hundred-acre deer park, was, at the time, a sort of Hearst Castle of New Hampshire. It burned to the ground in 1820 and was never rebuilt, but the area once occupied by the plantation, on Rte-109 three miles southeast of Rte-28, is now the **Governor John Wentworth State Historic Site** (summer only; $3), an undeveloped park and archeological site.

Another worthwhile stop, a few miles north of downtown Wolfeboro on Rte-109, is the eclectic **Libby Museum** (June to mid-Sept Tues–Sat 10am–4pm, Sun noon–4pm; $2; Ⓣ603/569-1035), where an early twentieth-century dentist's obsession with evolution is manifested by ineptly stuffed animals (one can only hope he was a better dentist than taxidermist) and the skeletons of bears, orangutans, and humans. There's also a mastodon's tooth, a random collection of fossils and insects, Native American artifacts, and a fingernail supposedly pulled out by its Chinese owner to demonstrate his newfound Christian faith. The setting of the museum, in a 1912 Historic Landmark house with a superb view of the lake and a grassy lakefront park, makes the detour even more rewarding.

A great way to take in Lake Winnipesaukee's grandeur is aboard the famous **MS Mount Washington** (see p.492), a 230-foot cruiser that departs from the dock in the center of town and connects with Weirs Beach across the lake.

Accommodation

Lake Motel 280 S Main St ⓣ603/569-1100 or 1-888/569-1100. Modern accommodation, with tennis courts and private sandy beach; some rooms with kitchen. Open May to Oct. ⑤

Lakeview Inn and Motorlodge 200 N Main St ⓣ603/569-1335, ⓦwww.lakeviewinn.net. Nicely decorated rooms with modern amenities, in a restored inn and two-story hotel overlooking Wolfeboro. ④

Tuc' Me Inn B&B 118 N Main St (Rte-109N) ⓣ603/569-5702, ⓦwww.tucmeinn.com. Cozy, 1850 Federal/Colonial inn close to the lake and town. Rooms are tastefully furnished and full breakfast is included. ⑤

Willey Brook Campground Rte-28 ⓣ603/569-9493, ⓦwww.willeybrookcampground.com. Three miles north of Wolfeboro and only one mile from Wentworth State Beach. Open mid-May to mid-Oct; sites $20.

Wolfeboro Inn 90 N Main St ⓣ603/569-3016 or 1-800/451-2389, ⓦwww.wolfeboroinn.com. Built in 1812, this historic inn is on the waterfront (with its own beach), and is the only full-service lodging on this side of the lake. It has 44 elegant, modern-country style rooms, some with private balconies. ⑦

Eating and drinking

The Cider Press 30 Middleton Road ⓣ603/569-2028. Hearty American food – ribs, steak, grilled salmon – in a rustic, candlelit dining room.

Lydia's Café 33 N Main Street ⓣ603/569-3991. Fruit smoothies, espresso drinks, bagels, and excellent sandwiches are served in this cute café in the town center.

The Strawberry Patch 50 N Main St ⓣ603/569-5523. Excellent, freshly prepared breakfasts and lunches in a cozy and unpretentious dining room. Daily, 7.30am–2pm.

Wolfeboro House of Pizza 37 N Main Street ⓣ603/569-8408. Good Greek-owned place, serving tasty pizzas, pastas, and subs – but not a *souvlaki* or *baklava* in sight.

The Wolfeboro Inn 90 N Main St ⓣ603/569-3016. Of the inn's restaurants, the fancy *1812 Room* serves fine, expensive, New England-style cuisine, but *Wolfe's Tavern*, a dark pub-like eatery, is the better value of the two. Enjoy one of their 72 beers on tap (and ask about the 1900 pewter beer mugs on the ceiling).

Wolfetrap Grill and Rawbar 17 Bay St ⓣ603/569-1047. Unpretentious and basic restaurant just outside of town. The range of seafood plates includes lobster, clams, and softshell crab dinners. Open May to early Sept.

Moultonborough and around

Other than some remote B&Bs and quiet country roads, there's not much to the sprawling town of **MOULTONBOROUGH**, north of Lake Winnipesaukee on Rte-25. If you're passing through, however, you might take a break in the **Old Country Store**, at the intersection of routes 25 and 109. One of the oldest of its kind, it sells everything from homemade dill pickles to penny candy to brass door knockers and carved wooden ducks. The bizarre "museum" upstairs houses a dusty collection of artifacts, including axes, saws, and carved Indian sculptures. For some time in the sun, the **town beach** (make a right off of Rte-25 onto Moultonboro Neck Road, follow to near the end of Long Island Road), is a particularly good spot for picnicking and swimming. There's also a popular beach at the intersection of routes 25 and 25B.

Two miles east of town on Rte-171, **Castle in the Clouds** (daily: mid-May to mid-Oct, 10am–4pm; $10; ⓣ603/476-2352 or 1-800/729-2468) stops just short of being a complete tourist trap. The 5200-acre mountain estate of

Eastern shore outdoor activities

The eastern shore has enough **outdoor activities** to keep even the most avid enthusiast busy. Hiking, boating, sailing, fishing, swimming, mountain-biking, and kayaking are all big in summer, while cross-country skiing and snowmobiling should sate any outdoor urges during the winter.

The best public **beach** for swimming and picnicking in the Wolfeboro area is **Clow Beach** (mid-June to early Sept; $3; ⓣ603/569-3699) in Wentworth State Park on Lake Wentworth. **Brewster Beach** (mid-June to early Sept; ⓣ603/569-1532) on Lake Winnipesaukee at the end of Clark Road south of town is also good for sunbathing and swimming. Once you're done sunning yourself, there are a couple of decent, if gentle, local **hiking routes**. The **Mount Major Trail**, north of Alton on Rte-11, offers excellent lake views and takes about an hour and a half to cover 1.75 miles. The scenic trail to the top of **Bald Peak**, at the Moultonborough–Tuftonboro town line on Rte-171, is a mile long. The Mount Flag Trail in Tuftonboro is a strenuous seven-mile loop. For a shorter jaunt (half a mile), with rewarding panoramic views of the lake and surrounding forests, try the **Abenaki Tower Trail**, off of Rte-109 in Tuftonboro across from Wawbeek Road, featuring an eighty-foot tower overlooking Lake Winnipesaukee and the Ossipee Mountains. **Snowmobiles** and **cross-country skiers** fill the trails during winter months; call the Cross Country Ski Association (ⓣ603/569-3151) or the New Hampshire Snowmobile Association (ⓣ603/224-8906, ⓦwww.nhsa.com) for information and guidance.

As for **watersports**, Wet Wolfe Rentals, 17 Bay St, Wolfeboro (ⓣ603/569-3200), rents waverunners for a minimum of two hours ($100) or a sixteen-foot aluminum hull with 25hp motor for $200 a day. Goodhue Hawkins Navy Yard, at 244 Sewall Rd in Wolfeboro (ⓣ603/569-2371), rents **boats for** $295 a day. You can take an all-inclusive light-tackle guided **fishing** trip with Angling Adventures, 79 Middleton Rd, Wolfeboro (ⓣ603/569-6426), for $240 per person ($280 for two). The Winnipesaukee Kayak Company, 17 Bay St in Wolfeboro (ⓣ603/569-9926), rents **kayaks** for $40 per day and canoes for $50 per day and also leads various tours and multi-day excursions.

eccentric millionaire Thomas Plant is saved by the uniqueness of the house itself, an interesting amalgamation of architectural styles from around the world, betraying Spanish, Japanese, and Swiss influences. The roof, for example, is covered with red tiles, while the facade recalls a ski chalet. Built in 1913 and designed by Plant, the massive hilltop mansion was somewhat advanced for its time, with a centralized vacuum system, intercom, and a self-cleaning oven. A brewery (whose Lucknow Beer can be found at local stores) has been added, and it and bottling plant for mountain-spring water are included in the tour.

The Loon Preservation Committee maintains the small **Loon Center**, along quiet Lee's Mills Road off of Blake Road (Mon–Fri 9am–5pm; July to mid-Oct also weekends 9am–5pm; free; ⓣ603/476-5666), which houses a collection of exhibits about the endangered and much-loved birds, focusing on environmental awareness and the negative impact of pollution. You can view Lake Winnipesaukee from several points along the **Loon Nest Trail**, which begins at the center and winds through upland forests and marshes, and maybe even catch a glimpse (or at least hear the distinguished sounds) of one of the speckled birds.

A good place to **stay** is the *Olde Orchard Inn*, Lee Road (ⓣ603/476-5004 or 1-800/598-5845; ❹), a relaxing bed-and-breakfast in the middle of an apple orchard. Some of the nine rooms feature fireplaces and Jacuzzis. Meanwhile, the best place to **eat** in town (dinner only) is *The Woodshed*, Lee Road (closed Mon; ⓣ603/476-2311), an old barn-turned-restaurant where prime rib is the specialty, and moderately priced lamb chops, lobster, and grilled fish are also on the menu. Ask for a table in the screened-in patio on warm summer evenings.

Squam Lake

Much smaller than its sprawling neighbor, but still the second largest body of water in the state, beautiful **Squam Lake** can actually hold more appeal than Lake Winnipesaukee. The pace is slower, the roads less crowded, and, thanks to a conscientious group of old-money landowners, the land has been less developed.

As expected, most of the activities here revolve around the **outdoors**; hiking, boating, swimming, or simply relaxing on the beach are all popular during the summer months. It's easy to see why producers chose this lake as the setting for the 1981 film *On Golden Pond*, starring Jane and Henry Fonda – the lake is pristine and glassy, and the setting sun brings a quiet calm over the water and surrounding forests. With a population of 1700, **Holderness** is the largest town on the lake, although it's really nothing more than a gas station, a few stately old inns, a couple of restaurants, and a dock, though there's a great beach and some enjoyable hikes here. **Center Sandwich**, to the north of Squam Lake, and **Center Harbor**, to the south of Squam Lake on the Lake Winnipesaukee shore, also maintain their nineteenth-century quaintness, while **Ashland**, closer to I-93, near Little Squam Lake, has several good restaurants.

Holderness

Named for the Earl of Holderness, a friend of Governor Wentworth's, **HOLDERNESS**, at the intersection of US-3 and Rte-113, was granted its original town charter in 1751. The popular statesman Samuel Livermore had acquired half of the town's land by the late eighteenth century, building a church and housing. Although nothing of much historical significance ever happened here, the Holderness School has remained a prestigious college preparatory school since its founding in 1879. The unpretentious village brings together a loosely defined grouping of buildings along the lakeshore next to a well-used public dock.

The general store in town is the place to come for supplies and provisions before you head out for a day on the lake, and the best local **beach** is accessible along a short trail through the **Chamberlain-Reynolds Memorial Forest**, off of College Road. To get there from Holderness, follow US-3 south, take a left on Rte-25B, and a left on College Road. Park in the small lot and follow the Ant Hill Trail for about twenty minutes – be sure to bring some insect repellent. The most popular **hike** in the area begins at the Rattlesnake Trailhead along Rte-113 and follows the **Old Bridle Path** to the top of **Rattlesnake Mountain**, providing spectacular views of Squam Lake and the surrounding hills, with only half an hour of effort. Other trails to the top of Rattlesnake Mountain, such as the **Ramsey Trail**, begin along Pinehurst Road, also off Rte-113. The **Mount Morgan Trail** begins at the trailhead along Rte-113, 5.4 miles northeast of US-3, and ascends 1400 feet along a 2.1-mile trail. Additional hiking suggestions are available at the Squam Lakes Association headquarters (see opposite).

A delicate glimpse of the area's natural habitat and inhabitants is afforded by the **Squam Lake Natural Science Center**, near the intersection of Rte-113 and Rte-25 in the center of town (daily: May–Oct 9.30am–4.30pm; $12;

The Barnstormers

Founded in 1931 by Francis Cleveland (son of 22nd US president Grover Cleveland), his wife Alice, and Edward Goodnow, the **Barnstormers** (Ⓣ603/323-8661, Ⓦwww.barnstormerstheatre.com) is the oldest professional summer theater group in the state. It is also perhaps the only theater company in the country in which the same actors perform a different play each week, rehearsing the following week's play during the day while acting in the current production at night. Presenting a wide range of productions, the theater company plays to consistently large crowds. Housed in a refurbished old store in the center of **Tamworth Village** since 1935, the company typically produces eight plays per summer. Call Ⓣ603/323-8500 from late May until the end of the season for schedule and ticket information.

Ⓣ603/968-7194, Ⓦwww.nhnature.org), which features live animals – including bears, bobcats, owls, and otters – housed in settings that resemble their natural habitats along a quarter-mile nature walk. Compared to a typical zoo, it's refreshingly spacious, though numerous hands-on exhibits and educational presentations tend to attract large groups of schoolchildren.

Watersports and activities

Squam Lakes Tours (Ⓣ603/968-7577) is one of several companies offering **boat rides** in and out of the picturesque lake's many coves and inlets. Its two-hour jaunts ($18), which depart from the dock a half-mile south of town at 10am, 2pm, and 4pm, include a look at the **Thayer Cottage**, where the bulk of *On Golden Pond* was filmed. The ninety-minute trips offered by Science Center Lake Cruises (depart from beside *Walter's Basin* restaurant on Rte-3; $18, $14 youth; Ⓣ603/968-7194) at 11am, 1pm, and 3pm are more focused on observing the endangered loons which inhabit the lake; and the final cruise of the day is led by a qualified naturalist. If you'd rather steer your own boat, rent a five-person motorboat for $119 per day or a three-person canoe for $39 per day from Squam Lakeside Farm, on US-3 (Ⓣ603/968-7227). The **Squam Lakes Association** (SLA), with a helpful office on US-3 (Ⓣ603/968-7336, Ⓦwww.squamlakes.org; June to Aug daily 9am–4.30pm; May & Sept to mid-Oct Sat–Sun only, 9am–4pm), rents **canoes** and **kayaks** ($45/day), and **sailboats** ($55/day), and sells trail guides to the region ($5). They also run half-day kayak tours and give lessons ($50). The nearest place to rent a **bicycle**, is seven miles away, off I-93 exit 25 in Plymouth, at Rhino Bike Works, 1 Foster St (Ⓣ603/536-3919), where you can also get advice on local trails and routes.

Practicalities

By far the ritziest and most expensive **place to stay** in Holderness is the *Manor on Golden Pond*, on US-3 overlooking the lake (Ⓣ603/968-3348 or 1-800/545-2141, Ⓦwww.manorongoldenpond.com; ❽), an elegant mansion complete with crystal chandeliers, sweeping vistas, and roaring stone fireplaces. Their *Wine Spectator* Award-winning dining room offers gourmet New American cuisine. Less expensive and more down-to-earth, the welcoming *Inn on Golden Pond*, on US-3 along Little Squam (Ⓣ603/968-7269, Ⓦwww.innongoldenpond.com; ❻), has eight large rooms, friendly hosts, full breakfasts, and table tennis in the game room. Though its rooms are nothing special, the well-situated *White Oak Motel*, at the intersection of Rte-25 and US-3 (Ⓣ603/968-3673 or 1-888/965-1850, Ⓦwww.whiteoakmotel.com; ❹), is the cheapest place around. They also rent cottages for $595–899 per week, as does *Cottage Place on Squam Lake* (Ⓣ603/968-7116, Ⓦwww.cottageplaceonsquam.com; ❺ per night). The

Squam Lakes Association maintains primitive **camping sites** on Moon Island, Bowman Island, and in the Chamberlain-Reynolds Memorial Forest, costing $45 per site (up to six people) on weekends, $40 per site weekdays (reservations required; call ⓣ603/968-7336; May–Oct).

The only waterfront **restaurant** in town, *Walter's Basin*, on US-3 (ⓣ603/968-4412), serves decent rainbow trout and other fish dishes in a pleasant setting. The Golden Pond Country Store (daily 6am–10pm; ⓣ603/968-3434), at the intersection of US-3 and Rte-113, sells pizza, deli sandwiches, fishing supplies, groceries, beer, newspapers, gas, and just about anything else you might need.

Center Harbor and Center Sandwich

The relaxing village of **CENTER HARBOR**, nicely situated close to Squam's eastern shore, is a good base from which to explore the Lakes Region, especially if you have a car. There isn't much here except for the usual lake-based diversions of canoeing, kayaking, and boat cruises (the *MS Mount Washington* stops here on Mondays – see p.492 for more details), but it's close to the larger settlements of Lake Winnipesaukee if you're looking for some action. You can also get to Center Harbor by **bus**; Concord Trailways stops at Fred Fuller's Oil on Rte-25 four times a day. If you're looking for a **place to stay**, the *Kona Mansion Inn,* Moultonboro Neck Road (ⓣ603/253-4900; ❺), has tennis, golf, and swimming in a tranquil lakeside setting with a country club atmosphere. For a more rugged experience, at the south end of town on the shore of Lake Winnipesaukee, the enormous (151-site) family-oriented *Arcadia Campground* (ⓣ603/253-6759) offers such amenities as a grocery store and video room.

Nine miles northeast along Rte-113, at the base of the Sandwich Range, **CENTER SANDWICH** groups a string of white-clapboard buildings, including a general store and steepled church, in a quaint version of a New England town. Though it's right next to Squam Lake, you'd never know it; the dense forest along the shoreline, which is largely privately owned, obscures the view. The best **place to eat** in town is the *Corner House Inn*, 22 Main St (ⓣ603/284-6219), an informal, historic (the structure's been around since 1849), and popular joint with both casual and upscale food. To **stay** overnight, you could try the blue-shuttered *Strathaven Inn*, 576 North Sandwich Rd (no credit cards; ⓣ603/284-7785; ❹), with four cozy rooms (two with shared bath) in a quiet setting.

Ashland

Though tiny **ASHLAND** was a thriving manufacturing town in the nineteenth century, producing lumber, wool, gloves, and paper, it's now little more than a sleepy village. There's not much to stop for, unless you need a quick bite to eat or a place to sleep without straying too far from I-93. If you decide to **stay the night**, the *Glynn House Inn*, 59 Highland St (ⓣ603/968-3775 or 1-800/637-9599, ⓦwww.glynnhouse.com; ❻), with ornate woodwork, a wraparound porch, fireplaces in most rooms, hearty breakfasts, and afternoon tea and sherry is one of the better-looking and more comfortable B&Bs in the state. Much cheaper, and right off I-93, is the *Comfort Inn*, 53 West St (ⓣ603/968-7668, ⓦwww.lakesregioncomfortinn.com; ❸), which has the usual hotel amenities and a heated pool. For a bite to **eat**, hit the *Common Man*, in a rustic brick building at 60 Main St (ⓣ603/968-7030); it serves great lunches and gourmet dinners, specializing in lobster bisque and roast prime rib. Less formal is the *Ashland House of Pizza*, also on Main Street (ⓣ603/968-3686), which has good pizzas and sandwiches.

North to the White Mountains

US-3 west from Ashland intersects with I-93, which heads north to Lincoln and North Woodstock in the White Mountains. At the foot of the mountains, in **Plymouth**, you can either continue north along the interstate or head another five miles west to the **Polar Caves** (daily: early May to late Oct 9am–5pm; $11) – though these are not so much caves as a cascade of clammy granite boulders tumbled against a hillside, between which visitors find pleasure in squeezing themselves – while paying handsomely for the privilege. For inexpensive food in town, *Biederman's Deli* (ⓣ603/536-DELI) for lunch, or *Kel C's Kitchen* (Tues–Fri 6am–2pm, Sat & Sun 7am–1pm, closed Mon, ⓣ603/536-9681) for breakfast, both on Main Street, should do the trick. On your way out of town, pick up a Swedish coffee ring at *Anderson's Bakery*, 61 Main St (ⓣ603/536-2669) to eat in the car on the way back to civilization.

The White Mountains

Thanks to their accessibility from both Montréal and Boston, the **WHITE MOUNTAINS** have become a year-round tourist destination, popular with summer hikers and winter skiers alike, and attracting over six million annual visitors. It's a commercialized region, with quite a lot of tourist development flanking the main highways, but the great granite massifs retain much of their majesty and power. **Mount Washington**, the highest peak not only in the range, but in the entire Northeast, can claim some of the severest weather in the world – conditions harsh enough to produce a timberline at four thousand feet, as compared to around ten thousand feet in the Rockies.

Vacationing in these mountains is not a new trend – this area has long been appreciated for its exquisite beauty. After railroads were built through here during the mid-nineteenth century, lumber companies bought up much of the land and began to log the forest. However, quick to recognize the value of the mountains' beauty, local residents formed influential conservationist groups, such as the **Appalachian Mountain Club** (AMC), and eventually ensured the passage of the Weeks Act in 1911, which allowed the federal government to purchase the land to preserve it. The national forest area now encompasses almost 800,000 acres, covering much of the northern part of the state and even spilling over into Maine.

White Mountains parking fees

You will need a **parking pass** for your vehicle when you park and leave it unattended in the White Mountains National Forest, though not if you're just stopping briefly to take pictures or use restrooms, nor if you're staying in a National Forest campground. Passes cost $5 for seven consecutive days, and you can buy them from many local stores and at all Forest Service offices. If you have not had time to buy a seven-day or annual pass, or you decide on the spur of the moment to hike to the top of a mountain or spend the afternoon at a swimming hole, you can purchase a day-pass for $3 at selected sites across the forest; however, you will have to call the Forest Service to find them (ⓣ603/745-3816).

Piercing the range are only a few high passes – here called "**notches**" – discovered by early pioneers during arduous crossings. The roads through these gaps, such as the **Kancamagus Highway** between **Lincoln** and **Conway**, make for predictably scenic routes. However, you won't really have made the most of the White Mountains unless you also set off, on foot, bike, or skis, across the long expanses of thick evergreen forest that separate them, with mountain peaks poking out in all directions. Some of the best hiking trails are in the state parks of **Franconia Notch**, straddling I-93, **Crawford Notch**, straddling US-302, and **Pinkham Notch**, along the eastern base of Mount Washington. Downhill skiing is popular at resorts such as **Waterville Valley** and **Loon Mountain**, both a few miles east of I-93, while cross-country skiing is

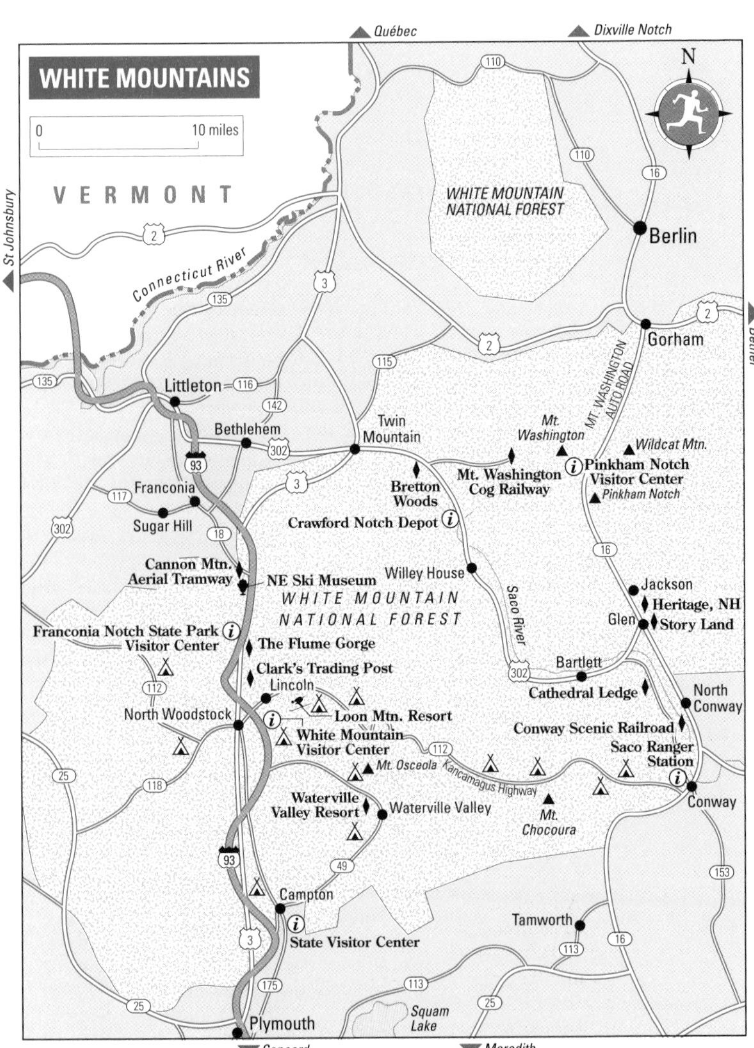

particularly good at **Jackson** in the eastern part of the White Mountains, which, along with **North Conway** and **Glen**, makes up the region's most built-up area, the **Mount Washington Valley**. Even if you don't intend to stay, check out the grand resort hotels in **Bretton Woods** and **Dixville Notch** (the first town in New Hampshire – and therefore the nation – to announce the results of its primary elections).

It's best to have your own transport, as ever, but somewhat regular **bus services** to the White Mountains from the southern part of the state are provided by Concord Trailways, stopping at Berlin, North Conway, Conway, Franconia, Gorham, Jackson, Lincoln, Littleton, and at the Pinkham Notch AMC Camp.

Waterville Valley

East of I-93 along Rte-49, the sparkling **Waterville Valley Resort** (ⓣ1-800/468-2553, ⓦwww.waterville.com) was the brainchild of shrewd developer Tom Corcoran, who bought the *Waterville Valley Inn* and its surrounding land in 1965 with the intent of creating a family-oriented outdoor center. The many resort-goers enjoying all manner of summer and winter activities are evidence enough that he succeeded – not altogether surprising considering the stunning tree-covered setting.

At the center of the resort is the creatively named **Town Square**, a contrived development of shops and restaurants alongside the smallish **Corcoran's Pond**, where you can lounge on a short strip of sand or rent a kayak ($9/hr), canoe ($11/hr), or paddleboat ($13/hr). Nearby, the Adventure Center (ⓣ603/236-4666) rents **mountain bikes** for $30 per day and sells trail maps for $2.50. You can also rent bikes and ride the lift to the top of the hill at **Snow's Mountain** ($40 per day).

Though relatively active in summer, Waterville Valley really comes to life in the winter months, and the intermediate slopes of the **ski** area (lift tickets $44, equipment rental $32), a network of chairlifts covering 2020 vertical feet on Mount Tecumseh and Snow's Mountain is usually packed. The Nordic Center at Waterville Valley has over forty miles of **cross-country trails** (ⓣ603/236-4666; $16 trail fee, $18 equipment rental).

The rugged area surrounding Waterville Valley makes for excellent **hiking** and **camping**. Of several notable hikes that originate along Tripoli Road, the **Mount Osceola Trail** is the best. The partially unpaved alternate route between I-93 and Waterville Valley is a strenuous seven-mile trek to a ridge at 4326ft.

Practicalities

The **Waterville Valley Region Chamber of Commerce**, 12 Vintner Rd in neighboring Campton (daily 9am–5pm; ⓣ603/726-3804 or 1-800/237-2307, ⓦwww.watervillevalleyregion.com), is your best bet for information on hiking, camping, and lodging in the area; it stocks the usual range of brochures and has helpful attendants and good maps. The **Pemigewasset Ranger District** office on Rte-175 in Plymouth (ⓣ603/536-1310) is also a good source of information on hiking and camping in the region. The **Waterville Valley Recreation Department** (ⓣ603/236-4695) sells trail maps, parking passes for the White Mountains National Forest, and fishing licenses.

Accommodation options in the immediate Waterville Valley area are geared to families and all-inclusive vacationers. During the summer, prices are surprisingly reasonable, and rates at all nine of the resort's lodges, inns, and condos include use of the athletic club, mountain-bike rental, golf, tennis courts, and kayak rental. The *Best Western Silver Fox Inn* (Ⓣ1-888/236-3699, Ⓦwww.silverfoxinn.com; ❺) is not your usual chain hotel: it's got attractive common areas, and the price includes unlimited tennis-court time and two hours' bike rental. At the *Black Bear Lodge*, 3 Village Rd (Ⓣ603/236-4501 or 1-800/349-2327, Ⓦwww.black-bear-lodge.com; ❻), the units can sleep up to six people, and the *Snowy Owl Inn*, 4 Village Rd (Ⓣ603/236-8383 or 1-800/766-9969, Ⓦwww.snowyowlinn.com; ❹), has 85 rooms with cozy fireplaces and attractive furnishings. Be aware, though, that prices go up by as much as fifty percent in winter. In Campton, which has a number of pleasant B&Bs, the *Osgood Inn*, 14 Osgood Rd (Ⓣ603/726-3543; no credit cards; ❹), housed in a stately old home with a sun-drenched back porch, is one of the better ones.

You can camp at the *Waterville Campground*, with 25 wooded sites off of Tripoli Road, ten miles east of I-93 (open all year; Ⓣ1-877/444-6777; $16), or the privately owned *Branch Brook Campground*, Rte-49, Campton (Ⓣ603/726-7001; $20). There are thirteen tent sites at the *Osceola Vista Campground* (Ⓣ1-877/444-6777; $16), just outside of Waterville Valley on Tripoli Road, and undeveloped wilderness sites with no facilities between Waterville Valley and I-93 along Tripoli Road (get a parking/camping permit at the Fee Station, I-93 exit 31).

Most of the places to eat in the Waterville Valley are just the sort you'd expect in a heavily marketed resort community: slightly monotonous and not great value for money. There's a no-nonsense pizza joint, the *Waterville Pizza Company* (Ⓣ603/236-FOOD), in the lower level of the Town Square, and a more upscale restaurant serving creative American cuisine with a seasonally changing menu, the *Wild Coyote Grill*, above the White Mountain Athletic Club on Rte-49 (Ⓣ603/236-4919). For better value, you're better off in nearby Campton, where you can stuff yourself with large portions of well-prepared pasta, seafood, chicken, steak, or, on Wednesday evenings, Mexican food at the *Mad River Tavern*, Rte-49 just off of I-93 exit 28 (closed Tues; Ⓣ603/726-4290). The *William Tell*, Rte-49 (Ⓣ603/726-3618), is a bit more expensive and less relaxed, but nonetheless serves good Swiss and German specialties. The Jugtown Country Store, in Town Square (Ⓣ603/236-3669), with a full-service deli and wide selection of cheeses and breads, is good for picnic supplies.

Lincoln and North Woodstock

Straddling opposite sides of I-93 at the entrance to the Kancamagus Highway, the twin towns of Lincoln and North Woodstock maintain relatively distinctive personalities while catering to both skiers and hikers. **NORTH WOODSTOCK**, a small-town mountain retreat at the intersection of Rte-3 and Rte-112, is the nicer and more low-key of the two, with a short, attractive row of restaurants and shops and a couple of good places to stay. On the other hand, **LINCOLN**, a continuous strand of strip malls and condominium-style lodgings, is less appealing, though it makes a good base from which to explore the western White Mountains. Neither town offers much in the way of things to see – the real attraction lies in getting out of town and into the forest or onto the slopes.

The area was sparsely peopled until 1892, when lumber baron James Henry transformed it into a bustling logging center, complete with a school, hospital, and housing for his hundreds of workers. By the mid-twentieth century, logging had faded and tourism became the town's livelihood. Today, it's difficult to recognize that Lincoln's **Millfront Market Place**, surrounded by enormous parking lots along Main Street, was once a timber mill, though logging trucks from points farther north still occasionally rumble past town along I-93.

Information and accommodation

The enormous **White Mountains Visitor Center**, in North Woodstock near I-93 (daily 9am–5pm; ⓣ603/745-8720 or 1-800/FIND-MTS, ⓦwww.visitwhitemountains.com), gives lodging advice and sells maps of the region, including the excellent *Trail Map & Guide to the White Mountain National Forest* ($4.95), which gives 250 trail descriptions and is essential if you plan on embarking on any extended hiking expeditions. The **Lincoln-Woodstock Chamber of Commerce**, in the Depot Mall on the east side of Lincoln along Main Street (daily 9am–5pm, winter until 7pm; ⓣ603/745-6621, ⓦwww.lincolnwoodstock.com), has more brochures and serves as a room reservation center for the region.

There are many solid opportunities for **camping**, the closest being *Russell Pond Campground*, off Tripoli Road, 3.7 miles east off I-93 exit 31 ($20; ⓣ603/726-7737, ⓦwww.campsnh.com). It's near a pond and has 86 well-maintained spots and hot showers. A bit farther away, *Lost River Valley Campground,* on Rte-112 four miles west of I-93 (ⓣ1-800/370-5678), has over a hundred sites (from $23.50) and a playground. Five miles farther down Rte 112, *Wildwood Campground* ($16; no reservations, see *Russell Pond* contacts for info) offers 26 wooded sites with picnic tables.

Econolodge Inn & Suites just off I-93 exit 33, Lincoln ⓣ603/745-3661 or 1-800/762-7275, ⓦwww.econolodgeloon.com. Slightly more luxurious than the *Franconia Notch Motel*, this is super value, with a pool, sauna, Jacuzzi, and exercise room. ❹

Franconia Notch Motel US-3, 1 mile from I-93 exit 33, Lincoln ⓣ1-800/323-7829, ⓦwww.franconianotch.com. Standard, clean lodging along an alarmingly tacky strip. ❹

Indian Head Resort US-3, Lincoln ⓣ1-800/343-8000, ⓦwww.indianheadresort.com. An unpretentious resort motel with plenty of facilities and outdoor activities. Its restaurant serves fairly good comfort food, with some veggie selections available. ❻

Wilderness Inn intersection of US-3 and Courtney Street, just south of Rte-112, North Woodstock ⓣ603/745-3890 or 1-888/777-7813, ⓦwww.thewildernessinn.com. Guests in the seven antique-furnished rooms enjoy sumptuous breakfasts. ❹

Woodstock Inn US-3, Main St, North Woodstock ⓣ603/745-3951 or 1-800/321-3985, ⓦwww.woodstockinnnh.com. In the center of town, comfortable carpeted rooms, an outdoor Jacuzzi, and reasonable ski/lodging packages. ❺

Loon Mountain Resort

Though Lincoln and North Woodstock are relatively busy in summer months, they really come to life in the winter with enthusiastic skiers and snowboarders who hit the slopes at the nearby **Loon Mountain Resort** (ⓣ603/745-8111 or 1-800/229-LOON, ⓦwww.loonmtn.com), two miles east of I-93 on the Kancamagus Highway. Lift tickets for adults cost $52 at Loon ($59 on weekends), and equipment rental is available at the base of the mountain. The trails, while interesting for intermediate skiers, might not be challenging enough for the expert. During the summer, Loon offers many of the activities you'd expect from a large full-service mountain resort – swimming, tennis, aerobics, horseback riding, mountain-biking – and if you'd like a nice view of the surrounding terrain without going through the trouble of hiking or biking up the mountain, you can ride the **gondola** to the top for $10.50. You can rent a **mountain bike** for $33 per day at the base of the mountain. There's also a stable offering **horseback** trail rides for $39–59 per hour. In Lincoln, you can rent bikes at All Seasons Adventures, 78 Main St (ⓣ603/745-6466) or Roger's Ski Outlet, also on Main Street (ⓣ603/745-8347); true to their names, you can rent winter equipment at either as well.

Clark's Trading Post

A mile north of town along Rte-3, local landmark **Clark's Trading Post** (daily mid-June–Aug 9.30am–6pm; weekends only May to mid-June & Sept to mid-Oct 10am–5pm; $12; ⓣ603/745-8913, ⓦwww.clarkstradingpost.com) is a much-touted, family-friendly collection of tourist attractions, including a haunted house, an 1890s fire station, bumper boats, the "Old Man" climbing tower, and a thirty-minute black bear show, in which a group of bears do tricks for their longtime trainer – just the ticket if you're in the mood for some hokey tourist fodder, or have kids in tow.

Eating, drinking, and entertainment

There's ample selection in both Lincoln and North Woodstock for food and drink. The **Papermill Theatre Company**, in the Mill at Loon Mountain on Main Street, Lincoln (ⓣ603/745-2141), presents "Broadway blockbusters" and children's plays during the summer.

Clement Room Grille in the *Woodstock Inn*, Rte-3, Main St, North Woodstock ⓣ603/745-3951. Feast on duck, veal, seafood, or steak; it's definitely North Woodstock's most elegant dining experience.

GH Pizza Main St, Lincoln ⓣ603/745-6885. *GH* has the best pizza in town – though the dining room's not particularly interesting.

Gordi's Main St, Lincoln ⓣ603/745-6635. Catering to the jovial after-ski crowd, *Gordi's* is more upscale than other Lincoln restaurants, specializing in seafood and straightforward meat dishes.

Kimber Lee's Deli in the Lincoln Depot, eastern edge of town ⓣ603/745-3354. Good sandwiches and deli salads.

Truant's Taverne 98 Main St, North Woodstock ⓣ603/745-2239. A cozy, affordable restaurant serving well-cooked American grill fare.

Woodstock Station in the *Woodstock Inn*, Rte-3, Main St, North Woodstock ⓣ603/745-3951. A great place to go for drinks – the beer is brewed on the premises – and nearly every night there's live entertainment. The range of hearty food includes pizza, pasta, steak, seafood, and burritos.

The Kancamagus Highway

Affording plenty of panoramic glimpses of the tree-coated peaks and valleys that fade into a sunny horizon to the south, the **KANCAMAGUS HIGHWAY**, running 34 miles between Lincoln and Conway, is one of only two National Scenic Byways in northern New England. The road is named for **Chief Kancamagus** ("Fearless One"), whose grandfather united seventeen Indian tribes into the Panacook Confederacy in 1627. Chief Kancamagus struggled to maintain peace between the Indians and pioneering whites, but bloodshed eventually forced the tribes to scatter to the north.

You can easily pass a pleasant afternoon driving the length of "the Kank" and parking briefly at a couple of the designated lookouts, but you'll gain a better appreciation of the area if you take a hike or have a swim in the Swift River, which runs parallel to the highway for twenty miles. Better still, plan to camp at one of the many well-maintained campgrounds along the road (see p.508).

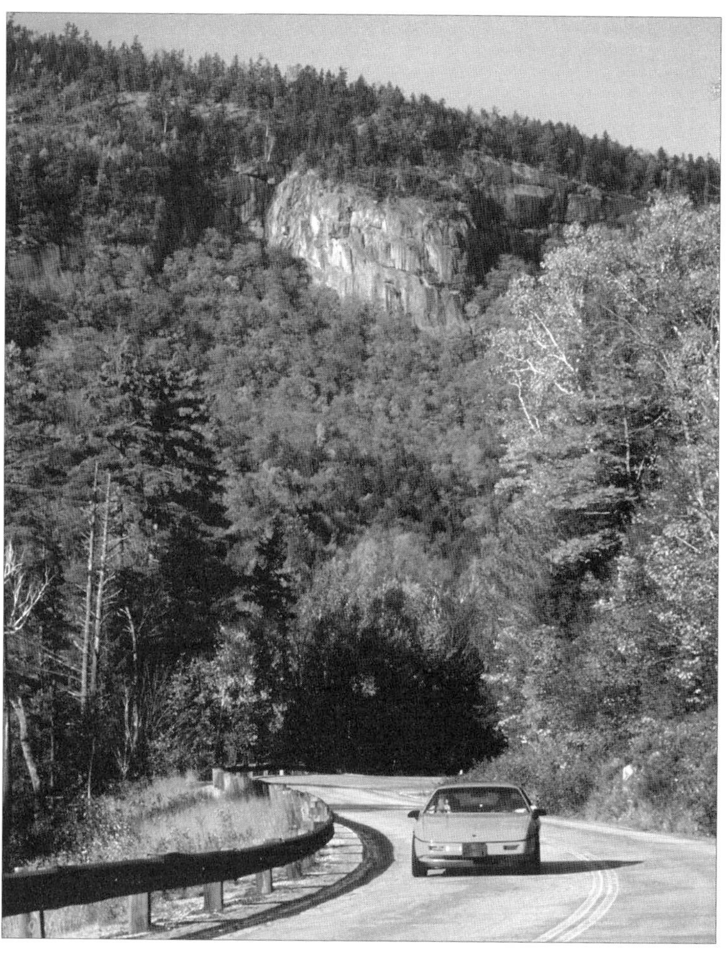

△ The Kancamagus Highway

No motorist services are available, so don't forget to pick up your supplies and gas in Lincoln or Conway.

Hiking and camping along the Kancamagus

The **Saco Ranger Station**, on the Kancamagus Highway near Rte-16 in Conway (☎603/447-5448), is staffed with friendly rangers who can give advice on hiking and camping along the road. They sell trail maps, which you are well advised to pick up. Among the particularly good **hikes** along the Kancamagus are the **Lincoln Woods Trail** (five miles east of I-93), an easy 2.9-mile walk to the Franconia Falls, which are good for swimming and sunbathing; the **Greeley Ponds Trail** (nine miles east of I-93), a five-mile round-trip to a dark aqua body of water; the **Mount Potash Hike** (thirteen miles west of the Saco Ranger Station), a more difficult four-mile round-trip to the summit of Mount

Potash (2660ft); and the **Sabbaday Falls Hike** (fifteen miles west of the Saco Station), a half-mile walk to the waterfalls, which, although stunning, are not suitable for swimming.

About ten miles outside of Conway lies **Mount Chocorua**. Although just 3475ft high, the little curved granite notch on the top, looking like a perched cap, makes it one of the most distinctive mountains visible from this area. It's a strenuous climb, and if you're in good shape, it should take several hours to reach the summit via the Champney Falls Trail (7.6 miles return). The top – that notch you can see – is particularly beautiful, as you emerge from the forest to a stretch of pure rock. The views, including the "Presidential Range," are, of course, stunning.

The six **campgrounds** along the well-traveled Kancamagus Highway are usually populated with vacationing families, and most crowded in July and August. Traveling from west to east, you'll hit *Hancock* (five miles east of Lincoln; ⓣ603/447-5448 for information) and *Big Rock* (two miles farther; same phone), which are the only ones open year round. Twelve miles east is *Jigger Johnson*, near the historic Russell Colbath House, and another 2.5 miles on, *Passaconway* (both same phone as above). A stretch of 6.5 miles brings another pair of campgrounds (ⓣ603/745-3816 for both): *Covered Bridge* and *Blackberry Crossing*, on opposite sides of the road near the Lower Falls, a jumble of boulders abutting a set of small waterfalls, usually beset by groups picnicking or sunbathing. Just six miles from here is the terminus of the Highway at Conway.

The campgrounds are often rather primitive affairs (many have vault toilets, for instance), and sites are allocated on a first-come-first-served basis. Fees are $16–18 per site, and aside from the noted exceptions, are open mid-May to mid-October. Call ⓣ1-877/444-6777 to reserve at *Covered Bridge*, the only campground that accepts reservations.

Franconia and around

North on I-93, past Lincoln and North Woodstock, the White Mountains continue to rise dramatically above either side of the freeway, boldly announcing their presence with enormous tree-covered peaks. **Franconia Notch State Park** is the highlight of the area, with miles of hiking trails and several natural wonders. Past the White Mountains, farther north along I-93, the landscape flattens into an inviting valley dotted with former resort towns turned quiet mountainside retreats, such as pleasant **Franconia**, secluded **Sugar Hill**, sleepy **Bethlehem**, and the largest town in the area, **Littleton**.

Franconia

FRANCONIA, a friendly village along I-93 in the rolling grassy hills just north of Franconia Notch State Park and the White Mountains, began attracting summer vacationers, such as the literary notables Nathaniel Hawthorne and Henry Wadsworth Longfellow, soon after railroad tracks made the town accessible in the mid-nineteenth century; today, skiers and leaf-peepers come in droves to check out the area's fall foliage and snow-covered slopes. The town is best known as the one-time home of poet **Robert Frost**. After owning a small farm in Derry, and living for a stint in England, Frost settled here in 1915 at age 40. You can visit his old home, now known as the **Frost Place**, Ridge Road off of Bickford Hill Road one mile south on Rte-116 (July to mid-Oct Wed–Mon 1–5pm; June weekends only; $4; ⓣ603/823-5510), where he lived with his wife and children for five years and wrote many of his best-known poems, including *The Road Not Taken*. Memorable largely for the inspiring panorama of mountains in its backdrop, the poet's former home is now a Center for Poetry and the Arts, with a poet-in-residence, readings, workshops, and a small display of Frost memorabilia, such as signed first editions and photographs. There's a short **nature trail** complete with placards displaying Frost's poetry and signs that supposedly mark the exact spot certain poems were composed. A longer and more rewarding hike begins 3.4 miles south of Franconia on Coppermine Road off of Rte-116, following the **Coppermine Trail** to the beautiful **Bridalveil Falls** cascading eighty feet. The wooden Coppermine Shelter, near the end of the 2.5-mile excursion, is a good spot to camp, although there are no facilities. For advice on **bike routes** in the area and to rent bikes ($19 per day), stop in at the Franconia Sport Shop, Main St, Franconia (ⓣ603/823-5241).

Accommodation

Bungay Jar 791 Easton Valley Rd, Franconia ⓣ603/823-7775 or 1-800/421-0701, ⓦwww.bungayjar.com. Eight cozy rooms and suites, with the best linens, CD library and complimentary beverages. Good mountain views, and a popular place with skiers in winter. ❻

Foxglove, A Country Inn Rte-117, Sugar Hill ⓣ603/823-8840, ⓦwww.foxgloveinn.com. This secluded inn is ideal for romantic getaways, with private porches, fountains, and fireplaces. ❺

Franconia Inn Easton Valley Rd/Rte-116 ⓣ603/823-5542 or 1-800/473-5299, ⓦwww.franconiainn.com. A 31-bed inn two miles south of Franconia, with great views, a relaxing porch, and an excellent restaurant; it's a good cross-country ski base, too. ❺

Fransted Campground Rte-18, Franconia ⓣ603/823-5675, ⓦwww.fransteadcampground.com. This family-oriented campground is a developed site with private streamside tent sites. Open mid-May to mid-Oct; $22/site.

Gale River Motel 1 Main St, Franconia ⓣ603/823-5655 or 1-800/255-7989, ⓦwww.galerivermotel.com. Slightly cheaper lodgings than others nearby, this sweet little ten-room motel has a heated outdoor pool, hot tub, and homemade chocolate chip cookies. Two cottages sleep four to six people. ❹

Lovetts Inn Rte-18, Sugar Hill ⓣ603/823-7761 or 1-800/356-3802, ⓦwww.lovettsinn.com. *Lovett's*, peacefully set at the foot of Cannon Mountain, is a 1794 Cape Cod-style home complete with swimming pool, a comfortable common area, cozy rooms, an excellent restaurant, and charming staff. ❺

Sunset Hill House 231 Sunset Hill Rd, Sugar Hill ⓣ603/823-5522 or 1-800/786-4455, ⓦwww.sunsethillhouse.com. This country inn is in a fine location on a quiet hill (with great sunsets), and all the uniquely decorated rooms have a view of the mountains. The romantic dining room features gourmet meals like maple-glazed salmon with caviar. ❻

Eating

The Franconia region is not known for fine **dining**, although many of the inns and B&Bs in Franconia and neighboring Sugar Hill serve excellent (if expensive) food in dining rooms that welcome non-guests.

Franconia Inn Easton Valley Rd/Rte-116 ⓣ603/823-5542. The inn offers elegant first-class service in its candlelit dining room, and features well-prepared steak and seafood dishes. See also accommodation review above.

Grateful Bread Main St, Franconia ⓣ603/823-5228. Purveyors of nutritious homemade organic breads, muffins, and croissants.

Lovetts Inn Rte-18, Sugar Hill ⓣ603/823-7761. Some of the best gourmet food in the area, including well-prepared classics such as grilled salmon and stuffed chicken breast. Entrees go for about $20, and reservations are a good idea. See also accommodation review above.

Polly's Pancake Parlor I-93 exit 38, Rte-117, Sugar Hill ⓣ603/823-5575. *Polly's* might be in the middle of nowhere, but it's well worth the trip if you love pancakes. The original menu – around since the opening 65 years ago – has since been supplemented by healthier options. Open early May–Oct.

Franconia Notch State Park

I-93, speeding up towards Canada, and the more leisurely US-3 merge briefly as they pass through **Franconia Notch State Park** (ⓣ603/823-8391). Though it's dwarfed by the surrounding national forest, and split in two by the noisy interstate, the park, which features excellent hiking and camping, has several sights that are well worth a visit.

From the **Flume Gorge Visitor Center**, I-93 exit 33 (daily: May to late Oct 9am–5pm; ⓣ603/745-8391), where there is a helpful information desk, a cafeteria, and a gift shop, you can walk or ride the shuttle bus to the short trail that leads through the narrow riverbed gorge, otherwise known as the **Flume** (entry $8). Formed nearly 200 million years ago and discovered in 1808 by 93-year-old "Aunt" Jess Guernsey, the 800-foot gorge has been fitted with a wooden walkway that weaves back and forth across cascading falls and between towering sheer granite walls. With the sound of rumbling water echoing through the damp and misty crevice, it's more impressive than you might expect, though during high season the tourist crush can be overwhelming. From the visitor center parking lot, the 1.4-mile **Mount Pemigewasset Trail** leads up a moderate incline to the 2557-foot summit of Mount Pemigewasset, affording views of the Franconia Range.

The Old Man of the Mountain and Cannon Mountain

A mile or so north, you can admire the **Basin**, a curious 25,000-year-old 20-foot-wide granite pothole that catches the surging waters of a cascading waterfall. From the Basin, a marked trail links with the **Cascade Brook Trail**, traversing three miles to **Lonesome Pond**. Up until May 2003, a natural rock formation known as **Old Man of the Mountain** for its semblance to an old man's profile could be viewed from a lookout on I-93. Held together with wires for years, it finally succumbed to the forces of gravity and slid off the mountain. Created by ages of glacial recession and granite-cracking ice, it had inspired scores of powerfully magnified photographs and New Hampshire's license plates, and generated a sort of affection among the locals. You can still see it on the 2002 New Hampshire state quarter, and in pictures at various area visitor centers (a small commemorative museum is also in the works).

Just north of the lookout, state-owned **Cannon Mountain** offers rides to the top of its 4180-foot peak in an **aerial tramway** (daily: late May to mid-Oct 9am–5pm; $10 round-trip, $8 one-way), displaying panoramic views of the mountains that are especially impressive – and popular – during the early fall foliage season. During the winter, Cannon Mountain (ⓣ603/823-8800, ⓦwww.cannonmt.com; adult full-day lift ticket $38) offers some of the more challenging **alpine skiing** terrain in the state. You can browse through a collection of old ski equipment and photos or watch a vintage ski flick at the **New England Ski Museum**, next to the tramway (late May to mid-Oct & Dec–March noon–5pm; free; ⓣ603/823-7177). If you'd rather hike to the top of the mountain, take the slightly difficult, roughly two-mile **Kinsman Ridge Trail** from the southwest corner of the tramway parking lot. An equally rewarding, but shorter and less strenuous half-mile hike leads to **Artists Bluff** overlooking Echo Lake; the trail begins in the parking area on the north side of Rte-18, across from the Peabody Base Lodge. At **Echo Lake** you can swim, rent a canoe ($10/hr), or just enjoy the short stretch of sand (daily: mid-June to early Sept 10am–5.30pm; $3).

Practicalities

As well as the Flume Gorge Visitor Center (see opposite), you can get advice about the outdoor activities available in the park from the *Lafayette Place Campground* off of I-93 (mid-May to mid-Oct; ⓣ603/271-3628; $16), which, despite being a bit close to the interstate, is a good place to **camp**. The quieter sites are along the western edge of the grounds where car noise is minimal.

Bethlehem and Littleton

Northeast of Franconia along US-302, **BETHLEHEM**, an attractive community composed mostly of old resorts and counting among its regular summer visitors a large group of Hasidic Jews, boasts one of the more remarkable sights in the area at the **Crossroads of America**, corner of US-302 and Trudeau Road (June to mid-Oct Tues–Sun 9am–5pm; $4; ⓣ603/869-3919), where an obsessively detailed model railroad set – one of the largest in the world – is on display. Lights are controlled to reflect the passage of day and night, and the display is punctuated by some amusing attention to detail, such as a wandering cow scared off the tracks by an oncoming train.

A few miles northwest along US-302, **LITTLETON**, straddling the Ammonoosuc River, has a compact Main Street that's lined with attractive old brick buildings and the largest population in the area at six thousand. Though there's really not much to see, the town is a good place to find reasonably priced accommodations, and strolling the pleasant Main Street will while away an hour or so. A stop in at Chutter's, 43 Main St (ⓣ603/444-5787), which holds the Guinness Book World Record for Longest Candy Counter (at 111ft), is good for some goofy fun: grab a paper bag and start filling from the 600-odd jars of gummy chicken feet, malted milk balls, fruit sours, and bubble gum.

Practicalities

The **Bethlehem Visitors Center** is at 2182 Main St (Jan–Feb, Tue & Thurs noon–2pm, Sat 10am–2pm; June Sat 11am–4pm; July–Aug and late Sept to mid-Oct: daily 11am–4pm; ⓣ1-888/845-1957, ⓦwww.bethlehemwhitemtns .com), while the **Littleton Area Chamber of Commerce** (ⓣ603/444-6561, ⓦwww.littletonareachamber.com) has an information booth (late May to mid-Oct, Mon–Fri 9am–5pm) downtown across from *Thayer's Inn*, and is a good bet for information on lodging and area activities. The **Ammonoosuc Ranger Station**, Trudeau Road, Bethlehem (ⓣ603/869-2626), is particularly good for backcountry wilderness help.

As a general rule, Bethlehem is the place to go for superior **accommodations**, while Littleton has a number of reasonably priced places to stay. *Thayer's Inn*, 111 Main St, Littleton (ⓣ603/444-6469 or 1-800/634-8179; ❸) is the creaky but comfortable local landmark, having hosted the likes of Richard Nixon and Ulysses S. Grant, while down the street at 2 West Main, *Beal House Inn* (ⓣ603/444-2661 or 1-888/616-2325, ⓦwww. bealhouseinn.com; ❺), housed in a charming 1833 farmhouse, is a bit more expensive. In Bethlehem, rich wood floors and furnishings reflect the elegance of relaxing *Mulburn Inn*, an English Tudor at 2370 Main St (ⓣ603/869-3389 or 1-800/457-9440, ⓦwww.mulburninn.com; ❺), and the *Adair Country Inn*, 80 Guider Lane (ⓣ603/444-4823 or 1-888/444-2600, ⓦwww. adairinn.com; ❼) features deluxe antique-furnished rooms, sweeping views, and an impeccable staff.

Dining is usually a fairly casual affair in these parts, like at the *Littleton Diner*, 145 Main St (ⓣ603/444-3994), or at *Rosa Flamingoes*, 2312 Main St in Bethlehem (ⓣ603/869-3111), which has some decent Italian dishes to its credit and also serves as a lively place to grab a cocktail. The restaurant at the *Beal House Inn*, 2 West Main (☎603/444-2661), has a menu that spans the globe and features wood-grilled items in an intimate bistro setting (Wed–Sun).

Bretton Woods and around

The ease with which US-302 now crosses the middle of the mountains belies the effort that went into cutting a road through **Crawford Notch**, a twisty and beautiful pass halfway between the Franconia area near Vermont and Conway, near Maine. The main man-made attraction on the route is the magnificent **Mount Washington Hotel**, which stands in splendid isolation in the wide mountain valley of **BRETTON WOODS**. A few miles east of the town of Bretton Woods is the **Mount Washington Cog Railway,** probably the most romantic way of getting to the summit of Mount Washington. West of Bretton Woods lies **TWIN MOUNTAIN**, a depressed down with no-frills motels. South of the town is the **Zealand Trail**, which begins at the end of Zealand Road and ends, 2.7 miles and ninety minutes later, at the Zealand Pond, Zealand Falls, and the AMC *Zealand Falls* hut (see box on p.518).

The Mount Washington Hotel

At the grand opening of the **Mount Washington Hotel**, US-302, Bretton Woods (☎603/278-1000 or 1-800/258-0330, Ⓦwww.mtwashington.com; ❽) in the summer of 1902, developer Joseph Stickney reputedly exclaimed, "Look at me gentlemen … for I am the poor fool who built all this!" Its glistening white facade, capped by red cupolas and framed by the western slopes of Mount Washington rising behind it, has barely changed since then. In its heyday, a stream of horse-drawn carriages brought families (and servants) up from the train station, deliberately located at a distance to increase the sense of grandeur. Displays in the lobby commemorate the **Bretton Woods Conference** of 1944, which laid the groundwork for the postwar financial structure of the capitalist world, by setting the gold standard at $35 an ounce (it's now about $310), and creating the International Monetary Fund and the World Bank.

Restoration by a group of investors who purchased the decaying building and surrounding property in 1991 for a mere $3.1 million has ensured that the cruise-ship-sized hotel remains marvelously – if somewhat eerily – evocative of past splendor, with its quarter-mile terrace, white wicker furniture, grand dining room, and 24-carat views. The hotel is not the one featured in the movie *The Shining*, but it's said to have inspired the story and is worth checking out even if you're not staying. None other than Babe Ruth reputedly got sauced in the former speakeasy downstairs – fittingly known as the "Cave" because of its faux-rocky walls – before sauntering to the indoor pool down the hall and taking a fully clothed dip; these days, the bar hosts more mellow live entertainment nightly, though the rock walls are still there. In the 1990s the resort opened its doors to the winter ski crowd for the first time, and in the summer there are weekend golfing, tennis and spa packages, along with an equestrian center and miles of hiking trails. Also on the property, the 33-room *Bretton Arms Country Inn* (☎603/278-1000; ❺), has more affordable rooms, while the *Lodge at Bretton Woods*, across US-302 from the *Mount Washington* (same phone; ❹), has modern rooms even cheaper.

△ Mount Washington Cog Railway

Mount Washington Cog Railway

It took a hundred men three years to build the **Mount Washington Cog Railway**, off of Mount Clinton Road at the base of Mount Washington. Completed in 1869, its rickety trains lumber up gradients as steep as 38 per cent – the second steepest railway in the world – while consuming a ton of coal and a thousand gallons of water and spewing out thick gray clouds of heavy smoke. It's a truly momentous experience, inching up the steep wooden trestles while avoiding descending showers of coal smut, though anyone who's not an antique train aficionado might find it not really worth the money. The three-hour round-trip (with a scant twenty minutes at the summit) costs $49, and trains leave hourly (late May to late Oct; call for other dates and times; ⓣ603/278-5404 or 1-800/922-8825). These also run in the winter, so you can ride partway up the mountain, and ski down on groomed trails parallel to the tracks.

If you'd rather **hike** up Mount Washington, the **Ammonoosuc Ravine Trail** starts in the Cog parking lot, hooking up with the Crawford Path at the AMC's *Lakes of the Clouds* hut (see box on p.518). If you're in good physical shape, the 4.5-mile trip takes roughly four and a half hours one-way. This hike is not for the faint-hearted, however, due to the extremely unpredictable weather once you near the peak (for more, see "Driving and hiking to the summit", p.518). Take warm clothing (temperatures above the tree line can be fifty degrees colder than at the base), plenty of water and food, and do not hesitate to turn back if the weather turns foul; several hikers die of exposure to the harsh weather atop the mountain every year. Another option, the **Jewell Trail**, also originating in the parking lot, zigzags up the north shoulder to the summit in 4.6 miles (roughly four hours).

Crawford Notch State Park

Within White Mountain National Forest, **Crawford Notch State Park** is split in two by US-302, which winds through the dramatic gap formed by the steep slopes of Mount Field to the west and Mount Jackson to the east. Discovered in 1771 when hunter Timothy Nash was tracking a moose through the woods, the notch was soon recognized as a viable route through the White Mountains to points farther north. A railroad was completed at great expense in 1857. The old **Crawford Notch Depot** along US-302 south of Bretton Woods and across from tiny Saco Lake is now a helpful AMC-maintained **information center** and retail store selling backcountry necessities (daily May–Oct 9am–5pm; ⓣ603/278-5170). Recommended **hikes** in the area include the **Mount Willard Trail**, a 1.4-mile (1hr) jaunt up to amazing views of Crawford Notch starting at the Crawford Notch Depot. In the shadow of Mount Crawford, the **Willey House**, named for a family who lived on the site and died in a terrible landslide in 1826, now serves as the **park headquarters** (ⓣ603/374-2272), selling maps and trail guides and offering advice on camping; they also maintain a small café. Half a mile south on U.S. 302, the **Arethusa Falls Trail** is a short but steep walk to the highest falls in the state. Just across US-302, the *Dry River Campground* (May to mid-Dec; ⓣ603/271-3628; $18) has 36 wooded sites, thirty of which are by reservation only; note that there is no water after mid-October. AMC's *Highland Center at Crawford Notch* (ⓣ603/278-4453), only 2 years old, is a great choice year-round: an environmental education center which also offers lodging in private rooms ($105–135 per person, double occupancy, $68–77 with shared bath). Hearty alpine breakfasts and family-style dinners are included, as are a full roster of activities like guided hikes and game nights, and free L.L. Bean gear for use in AMC programs (at a small fee for your private use). The *Shapleigh Bunkhouse* dorm gets you a bed and breakfast, plus access to the same amenities, for $35.

The Mount Washington Valley

There are no clear boundaries to the **Mount Washington Valley**, though it is generally thought to center around the crowded town of **North Conway**, a once-beautiful mountainside hamlet now overwhelmed by outlet malls and other modern encroachments. In general, the region is more congested than the western White Mountains, but if you can avoid the crowds that cram their cars onto the mile-long strip of Rte-16/US-302 south of downtown North Conway, you'll find there's plenty to do around here. In the winter, there are numerous trails for **cross-country skiers**, while in the summer **rock climbers** test their skills on the highly popular **Cathedral Ledge**. North of North Conway, the pace slows and opportunities for solitary hiking and camping increase. The low-key town of **Glen** is home to **Story Land,** a children's fantasy park, while peaceful **Jackson** has excellent cross-country skiing trails and an unusual concentration of first-class lodging and eating, presenting a good opportunity to spoil yourself amid the quiet splendor of the greenery.

Hiker shuttle service

The AMC runs a hiker **shuttle service** daily from June through mid-October with vans that make stops at many of the trailheads and AMC lodges throughout the Mount Washington region (call ⓣ603/466-2727 for information, reservations strongly recommended). Stops include the Crawford Notch Depot (see above) and the Pinkham Notch Visitor Center (see p.517). Drivers will stop anywhere along the route if requested, and the trips cost $12, no matter how long you ride.

North Conway

Whichever way you approach **NORTH CONWAY**, you're in for a depressing time. From the north, the joining of Rte-16 and US-302 at Glen eventually becomes a veritable turmoil of shopping malls and theme parks, while from the south, the strip between Conway and North Conway is an orgy of factory outlets, fast-food places, and the over-eager shoppers who have sought them out. Fortunately, there is some relief in the town itself, a village that manages to maintain a hint of rustic backcountry appeal. The centerpiece of downtown is the **North Conway Railroad Station**, a hulking brown and yellow 1874 Victorian structure that you can't miss along Main Street. From here, the **Conway Scenic Railroad** (mid-April to late Dec, call for reservations and schedule; ⓣ603/356-5251 or 1-800/232-5251, ⓦwww.conwayscenic.com) runs antique steam trains to Bartlett ($18.50 round-trip, 105min), Conway ($11.50 round-trip, 55min), the Crawford Notch Depot ($38 round-trip, 5hr), and the Fabyan Station in Bretton Woods ($43 round-trip, 5.5hr). The trains are especially worth the money in early fall, when the trees are at their peak– reservations are a must.

West of town along River Road, you can go for a swim at refreshing **Echo Lake** (not to be confused with the Echo Lake in Franconia Notch State Park) beneath the towering granite face of the White Horse Ledge. Just north off of West Side Road, scores of rock climbers test their skills on the wall of the steep, sheer faces of towering **Cathedral Ledge**, the most popular spot for the sport in the state. Chauvin Guides in North Conway (ⓣ603/356-8919, ⓦwww.chauvinguides.com) offer various **guided climbs** and lessons starting at $115. You might also check with **Eastern Mountain Sports** on Main Street in North Conway for guidance (ⓣ603/356-5433). If you'd rather not spend hours (and lots of money) tethered to the cliff's sheer face, you can simply drive to the top, where you're presented with views of the entire area. You can also hike to the ledge, along the **Bryce Path**, a steep trail that originates at the base of the Mount Washington Auto Road and takes about an hour each way. North of the entry to **Cathedral Ledge State Park** on North River Road, you can hike to **Diana's Bath**, an easy half-mile walk to a cool running mountain stream along the Moat Mountain Trail. For a longer trek, head to the top of **Mount Kearsarge** from the north side of Hurricane Mountain Road, one and a half miles west of Rte-16; it's a three- to four-hour round-trip that is rewarded with panoramic views.

Practicalities

The **Mount Washington Valley Chamber of Commerce** in North Conway (ⓣ603/356-3171 or 1-800/367-3364, ⓦwww.mtwashingtonvalley.org) has a reservation service and information on local attractions, while the **Conway Village Chamber of Commerce**, south of town along Rte-16 (ⓣ603/447-2639, ⓦwww.conwaychamber.com), will also help with places to stay and has hiking maps.

There is an HI/AYH **hostel** in Conway called the *Albert B. Lester Memorial Hostel*, 36 Washington St (ⓣ603/447-1001), which has particularly clean dorm lodging for $21 per night and private rooms for $52. **Camping** in the area is available at the *Saco River Camping Area*, in North Conway off of Rte-16 (early May to mid-Oct; ⓣ603/356-3360; from $21), whose wooded and open sites are nicely located along the Saco River, well enough away from the highway. Otherwise, there are plenty of **places to stay** in North Conway. Though it's right on the busy main road, the spacious rooms, gracious hosts, delicious food, and mountain view at the ✪ *1785 Inn*, Rte-16 (☎603/356-9025 or 1-800/421-1785, ⓦwww.the1785inn.com; ❹), make this a good base from which to explore (or to shop). Another good base, this time for rock climbers and other outdoors types, is the *Spruce Moose Lodge*, 207 Seavey St (☎1-800/600-6239, ⓦwww.sunnyside-inn.com; ❹), which occupies a quiet spot well off the main drag, and has nine conservatively decorated rooms and five cottages. The *Nereledge Inn*, River Road (☎603/356-2831 or 1-888/356-2831, ⓦwww.nereledgeinn.com; ❹), is a friendly and informal Colonial inn with wood stoves and fireplaces near skiing, the Saco River, and rock climbing. The *School House Motel*, on Rte-16 near the shopping outlets (☎603/356-6829 or 1-800/638-6050, ⓦwww.schoolhousemotel.com; ❸), is probably the cheapest in town.

Probably the best **place to eat** in North Conway is the *1785 Inn* (see above), with its highly praised, expensive gourmet food, such as venison with rosemary cherry bourbon glaze ($29), served in a dark, romantic dining room. You can get big portions of freshly prepared Italian dishes at ✪ *Bellini's*, 33 Seavey St (closed Mon & Tues; ☎603/356-7000), all served in an attractively decorated dining room. If you're after something a little spicier, *Shalimar*, 27 Seavey St (☎603/356-0123), has a huge menu of reasonably priced authentic Indian dishes, with a good selection of vegetarian specialties. *Chef's Market*, 2724 Main St (☎603/356-4747), has great fussy sandwiches, pasta salads and smoothies for lunch. For **entertainment**, you may find rock & roll, or Irish music, at ✪ *Horsefeather's*, Main Street (Rte-16) (☎603/356-6862), on the weekends, in addition to what many consider to be the best burgers in town.

Jackson and Glen

With a high concentration of first-class lodgings and restaurants, a close-knit population, and hundreds of miles of trails within easy reach, **JACKSON** is one of the premier **cross-country ski** centers in the country. Indeed, the **Jackson Ski Touring Foundation**, 153 Main St(☎603/383-9355 or 1-800/927-6697, ⓦwww.jacksonxc.org), with 158km of trails, has frequently been rated the number one cross-country ski area in the East by various big-name industry magazines. The trails run over rolling countryside, woodland terrain, mountain descents, and race-course areas, and are all perfectly maintained. In order to use them, you have to be a member of the Ski Touring Foundation. Day memberships cost $15, and you can rent equipment for $16 a day (snowshoes for $12). On hot summer days, a great place to cool off is at **Jackson Falls**, which tumble down a stretch of boulders and rocks in the riverbed along Rte-16B.

If you're traveling with children, don't miss New Hampshire landmark **Story Land**, on Rte-16 in **GLEN** (mid-June to early Sept daily 9am–5pm; early June & early Sept to mid-Oct Sat & Sun only 9am–5pm; $22; ☎603/383-9776), a colorful children's theme park, akin to a miniature Disneyland, with immaculately maintained grounds, rides such as the "Turtle Twirl" and "Bamboo Chutes," and lots of places for climbing and exploring. Next door, **Heritage New Hampshire** (same schedule as Story Land; $11; ☎603/383-4186) takes a somewhat hokey and outdated Anglocentric look at New Hampshire history through interactive exhibits and badly animated mannequins. You start with a simulated ride aboard a creaky ship bound for the New World and end with a rickety "train ride" through the White Mountains.

For any further information, contact the **Jackson Area Chamber of Commerce** (☎603/383-9356 or 1-800/866-3334, ⓦwww.jacksonnh.com).

Accommodation

Bernerhof Inn US-302, Glen ⓣ603/383-9132 or 1-800/548-8007, ⓦwww.bernerhofinn.com. Nine comfortable and elegant guestrooms, with conscientious service. There's also a pub and a gourmet restaurant on the first floor. ❺

Inn at Thorn Hill Thorn Hill Rd, Jackson ⓣ603/383-4242 or 1-800/289-8990, ⓦwww.innatthornhill.com. A luxurious hillside inn with wraparound porch, complete with designer furnishings, whirlpool tubs, and private cottages out back. Rates include a three-course dinner at the inn's gourmet restaurant. ❽

Village House Rte-16A, Jackson ⓣ603/383-6666 or 1-800/972-8343. A pleasant B&B just beyond the covered bridge, with private baths and a great big porch. ❹

Wildcat Inn & Tavern Rte-16A, Jackson ⓣ603/383-4245 or 1-800/228-4245, ⓦwww.wildcattavern.com. Cozy and unpretentious, the *Wildcat* is right in the center of town and has a comfortable ski-cabin feel. Especially popular in winter (as is the tavern). ❻

Will's Inn US-302, Glen ⓣ603/383-6757 or 1-800/233-6780, ⓦwww.willsinn.com. Family-friendly, cheap, and perfectly satisfactory. Plus, there's a heated pool. ❸

Eating, drinking, and nightlife

As You Like It Jackson Falls Marketplace, Jackson ⓣ603/383-6425. Great homemade coffee cake, cookies, pies, and bread, also deli sandwiches and panini. Closed Mon & Tues.

Christmas Farm Inn Rte-16B, Jackson ⓣ603/383-4313. A romantic, chichi restaurant, centrally located and good for special occasions. Dishes include balsamic roasted salmon and herb-crusted rack of lamb.

Red Parka Pub US-302, Glen ⓣ603/383-4949. A favorite place in Glen for a few drinks and some sports on the TV. The place hops especially during ski season and at weekends, when there's live music. Monday is open-mic night.

Shannon Door Rte-16, Jackson ⓣ603/383-4211. The town's longstanding Irish pub, with a suitably dark bar, plenty of Guinness, and live entertainment Thurs–Sun.

Wildcat Inn & Tavern Rte-16A, Jackson ⓣ603/383-4245. Gourmet country cuisine in the dining room and garden, while cheaper sandwiches and appetizers are served in the less-formal couch-filled tavern, which often hosts a lively après-ski scene.

Yesterday's Rte-16A, Jackson ⓣ603/383-4457. Big, cheap American breakfasts are the order of the day here.

Pinkham Notch and Mount Washington

Roughly ten miles north of Jackson along Rte-16, **PINKHAM NOTCH**, along the eastern base of towering **MOUNT WASHINGTON**, is as beautiful a mountain pass as there is in the National Forest, with a reputation for serious outdoor activity. The Appalachian Trail and a number of other remote wilderness trails converge here, making the Notch overrun with adventurers during the summer. Luckily, the crowds don't detract too much, and they're easy to forget once you've made your way into the forest.

The best place to get information on hiking, camping, and a whole range of other outdoor activities is at the AMC's **Pinkham Notch Visitor Center**, Rte-16 (daily 6.30am–10pm), where you can buy the indispensable and exhaustive *AMC White Mountain Guide* ($22.95), good hiking maps, supplies, and basic camping/mountaineering equipment. The center organizes workshops, guided trips, and programs that cost anywhere from a couple of dollars to a couple hundred dollars. They serve three hearty family-style **meals** per day at long picnic tables in a huge, noisy dining room at the visitor center; the fixed-price dinner ($17) includes salad, soup, vegetables, homemade breads and dessert, an entree, and plenty of conversation about the day's hike. As if that weren't enough, the club maintains the *Joe Dodge Lodge* (ⓣ603/466-2727), where you can get a bunk, dinner and breakfast for $62; for an additional $9 you can have a family room with a double bed. The *Dolly Copp Campground*

AMC mountain huts

The Appalachian Mountain Club (AMC) operates eight delightfully remote mountain huts in New Hampshire along a 56-mile stretch of the famed Appalachian Trail, each about a day's hike apart. Generally open from June through mid-October (exceptions are noted below), these spots offer full-service lodging in season, and two hot meals per day, for $79 per night, making them a fairly popular choice – reservations are required (Ⓣ603/466-2727). At some of the huts, self-service lodging is available (without sheets, heat, or food) for $28. For additional information, contact the Appalachian Mountain Club, 5 Joy St, Boston, MA 02108 (Ⓣ617/523-0655, Ⓦwww.outdoors.org).

Carter Notch (self-service all year). Accessible via the Nineteen Mile Brook Trail and the Wildcat Ridge Trail, both originating along Rte-16 north of Jackson.
Galehead. On the Garfield Range, this is the most remote hut in the chain. Accessible via the Gale River Trail and the Garfield Ridge Trail, both originating off of US-3 south of Bethlehem.
Greenleaf. Accessible via the Greenleaf Trail and the Old Bridle Path Trail, off of I-93 in Franconia Notch State Park (see p.510).
Lakes of the Clouds (full service in season: June to mid-Sept). On the southern shoulder of Mount Washington, this is the highest and most popular of the huts. Accessible via the Ammonoosuc Ravine Trail and Crawford Path, off of Mount Clinton Road, just south of Bretton Woods.
Lonesome Lake. Good family destination, with daily hikes and activities. Accessible via the Cascade Brook Trail, Dodge Cutoff Trail, Fishin' Jimmy Trail, Lonesome Lake Trail, and the Whitehouse Trail, west of I-93 in Franconia Notch State Park.
Madison Spring (full service in season: June to mid-Sept). Great sunsets from a perch above the Madison Gulf. Accessible via the Crawford Path, Gulfside Trail, Westside Trail, and the Valley Way Trail, southwest of Gorham off of US-2.
Mizpah Spring. On Mount Clinton above Crawford Notch. Accessible via the Mount Clinton Trail and the Webster Cliff Trail near Crawford Notch State Park along US-302.
Zealand Falls. Open all year, near waterfalls and good backcountry skiing. Accessible via the Zealand Trail, off of Zealand Road south of Twin Mountain.

(Ⓣ603/466-2713; $18) has 177 **campsites** and is open from mid-April through mid-October.

On the east side of Rte-16 across from the visitor center, local favorite **Wildcat Mountain** (Ⓣ603/466-3326 or 1-800/255-6439, Ⓦwww.skiwildcat.com) offers some of the best and most challenging **skiing** ($55, with additional days $25 each) in the state during the winter, as well as **mountain-biking** and **gondola rides** to the 4062-foot summit of Wildcat Mountain (daily: mid-June to mid-Oct 10am–5pm; late May to mid-June weekends only; $10).

Mount Washington

The 6288-foot **MOUNT WASHINGTON**, the highest peak in the northeastern US, was named for George Washington before he even became president. Over the years, other mountains in this "Presidential Range" have taken the names of Madison, Jefferson, and even Eisenhower – though it should be noted that Mount Nancy was called that long before the Reagans were in the White House, and Mount Deception just happens to be close by.

Driving and hiking to the summit

On a clear day, you can see all the way to the Atlantic and into Canada from the top of Mount Washington, once called the "second greatest show on earth" by

P.T. Barnum, but the real interest in making the ascent lies in the extraordinary severity of the weather up here. The wind exceeds hurricane strength on over a hundred days of the year, and in 1934 it reached the highest speed ever recorded anywhere in the world – 231mph.

On the way to the top, you pass through four distinct climate zones, with century-old fir and ash trees so stunted as to be below waist height, before emerging amid Arctic tundra. The drive up the **Mount Washington Auto Road**, ascending eight miles up the east side of the mountain from Rte-16 south of Gorham (early May to late Oct – weather permitting – 7.30am–6pm in peak season; call ⓣ603/356-0300 to check weather conditions), is not quite as hair-raising as you may expect, although the hairpin bends and lack of guard-rails certainly keep you alert. There's a $18 toll for private cars and driver (plus $7 for each additional adult and $4 for kids), which includes a "This car climbed Mt. Washington" bumper sticker and a short audio-tour cassette. Specially adapted minibuses, still known as "stages" in honor of the twelve-person horse-drawn carriages that first used the road, give narrated **tours** (daily 8.30am–5pm; $24, 90min round-trip; ⓣ603/466-3988, ⓦwww.mtwashingtonautoroad.com) as they carry groups of tourists up the mountain. Driving takes thirty or forty minutes under normal conditions. The record for the annual running race up the mountain, held each June, currently stands at an incredible 58 minutes 20 seconds.

Some fifteen **hiking trails** – in addition to the Appalachian Trail itself – lead to the summit of Mount Washington. Unequaled vistas, beautiful flora, and the satisfaction of reaching the top make this hike a particularly thrilling experience. The most direct route on the eastern side of the mountain is the **Tuckerman Ravine Trail**, which originates at the AMC Pinkham Notch Visitor Center (see p.517) and traverses the often snow-filled Tuckerman Ravine, a popular place for backcountry skiing. If you're in good condition, the 4.1-mile trail can be completed in about four and a half hours, and it is possible to hike up and back in one day, but don't forget that the weather at the top of the mountain is very unpredictable, and potentially very dangerous: even when it's seventy degrees and sunny at the base, the summit, some 4000 feet above, can be below freezing. The weather can change very quickly, and you should not hesitate to turn back should any signs of a storm become apparent; indeed, each year the conditions claim several lives –the roll-call of the 124 victims to die on the mountain does include the duo that attempted to slide down on "improvised boards." Anyone who can manage to make it to the summit from mid-October through mid-May won't find a hospitable environment: besides the erratic weather, there is no shelter, restrooms, food, or water. In New Hampshire parlance, this translates to "no nothin'."

For hikes to the summit that originate on the west side of the mountain, see p.507. You can also ride to the top on the coal-fired steam train of the **Mount Washington Cog Railway**, originating in Bretton Woods – also detailed on p.507. Incidentally, unless otherwise posted, you can **camp** anywhere on Mount Washington below the tree line two hundred feet from the trail and water sources, and a quarter-mile from any road or facility.

The summit

On the summit, you'll see the remarkable spectacle of buildings actually held down with great chains; many have been blown away over the years, including the old observatory, said to have been the strongest wooden building ever constructed. At the newer (and hopefully stronger) **weather observatory** (ⓣ603/356-2137, ⓦwww.mountwashington.org), scientists research the effects of wind, ice, and fog; their various findings are displayed at a small museum downstairs (daily 10am–5pm; free). You can climb the few remaining feet to the actual summit point, sadly surrounded with cement structures – including a large viewing platform – and smothered by photo-snapping tourists balancing themselves on lichen-covered rocks. The **Tip Top House**, once a hotel for wealthy travelers, has been turned into an unremarkable historic museum (free entry), providing "a link between the mountain's past and present" through antique furniture and a restored interior.

Gorham and beyond

Spread out along the northern reaches of the White Mountain National Forest, working-class **GORHAM** can be used as an inexpensive base from which to visit Mount Washington and other nearby peaks. Basic, affordable **accommodation** can be found at the *Hikers Paradise Hostel*, 370 Main St (Ⓣ603/466-2732 or 1-800/470-4224, Ⓦwww.hikersparadise.com), where you can get a bed, sheets, full kitchen, and full (shared) bath for $17. For **camping**, the *Moose Brook State Park*, Jimtown Road, off Rte-2 in Gorham (late May to mid-Oct; Ⓣ603/466-3860; $18 per site), has 62 secluded tent sites. Reasonably priced homemade Italian **food** can be had at *La Bottega Saladino* on Main Street (Ⓣ603/466-2520), while *Yokohama*, at 288 Main St (Ⓣ603/466-2501), is good for reasonably priced Asian (and American) specialties.

Up north on Rte-16, **DIXVILLE NOTCH** is a quiet hideaway centered on the sprawling turn-of-the-century *Balsams Hotel* (Ⓣ603/255-3400 or 1-800/255-0800 in NH or 1-800/255-0600 outside NH, Ⓦwww.thebalsams.com; ⑧), another of the last grand White Mountains resort hotels. Built in the 1860s, the enormous red-capped palace has 202 guestrooms, its own lake,

First-in-the-nation presidential primary

The mountains of the "Presidential Range" might have made the state's name in tourist guides, but New Hampshire and the tiny mountain village of **DIXVILLE NOTCH** are really famous for a quite different presidential connection: the primary election. Since 1952, New Hampshire has been the first state in the US to hold its presidential primary, which more or less marks the start of the winnowing process to see who each party's presidential candidates will be, and Dixville Notch has had the privilege of being the first town in the state – and therefore the nation – to report its results. Every four years, the tiny electorate of Dixville Notch (year-round population: 32) files into the ballroom at the *Balsams Hotel* (guestrooms: 202) just before midnight on election day, to cast votes at the stroke of midnight. Since 1968, Dixville Notch has never failed to predict the Republican nominee, and the state as a whole has a good record for picking the candidates eventually nominated by both Democrats and Republicans to run for president. Due to the high media profile of the primary, as well as the state's compact size, campaigning is based very much on knocking on doors and actually meeting the people. Indeed, the primary's popularity and easy access have encouraged a number of lesser-known candidates to participate. New Hampshire voters have been wooed by visionary candidates such as Russell Fomwalt, who recommended that the military occupy high schools to prevent violence; the innovative Austin Burton (alias Chief Burning Wood), who once tried to pay his $1000 filing fee by mailing a snakeskin to the secretary of state; and the environmentally friendly Caroline Killeen, who argued that "America needs trees, not Bushes."

15,000 acres of land, a golf course, and a ski area. Rates include all meals and use of facilities.

For detailed information on other lodging and eating options in these farthest reaches of the state, contact the **Northern White Mountain Chamber of Commerce**, 164 Main St in Berlin (Ⓣ603/752-6060 or 1-800/992-7480, Ⓦwww.northernwhitemtnchamber.org), or **North Country Chamber of Commerce**, in Colebrook (Ⓣ603/237-8939 or 1-800/698-8939, Ⓦwww.northcountrychamber.org), just across the Connecticut River from Vermont, at the end of Highway 26.

8

Maine

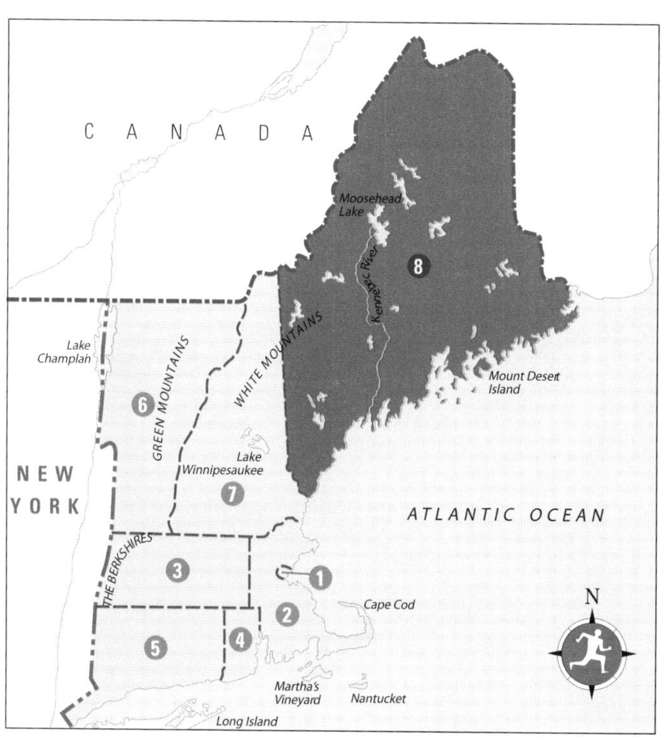
CANADA
Moosehead Lake
Kennebec River
8
WHITE MOUNTAINS
GREEN MOUNTAINS
Lake Champlain
6
Mount Desert Island
Lake Winnipesaukee
7
NEW YORK
ATLANTIC OCEAN
THE BERKSHIRES
3
1
Cape Cod
2
4
5
N
Martha's Vineyard
Nantucket
Long Island

CHAPTER EIGHT **Highlights**

* **Southern coast beaches** Although the water can be chilly, Maine's popular southern beaches are uniformly picturesque. See p.529

* **Portland** As cosmopolitan as the state gets, coastal Portland has everything to offer, save big-city aggravation and high prices. See p.535

* **Camden** Among Maine's most beautiful, Camden's harbor is filled with windjammers and protected by verdant forest. See p.562

* **Castine** Nearly surrounded by the waters of Penobscot Bay, this tiny town of gardens and hilly streets is one of New England's most picturesque. See p.570

* **Acadia National Park** Bike, boat, hike, climb, or simply commune with nature in the state's recreational mecca. See p.578

* **Bethel** Close to the White Mountains, remote Bethel is the quintessential New England small town and a hub for winter and summer outdoor adventures. See p.588

* **Mount Katahdin** In the deepest heart of Maine, the beginning of the Appalachian Trail sits atop this 5300-foot peak. See p.597

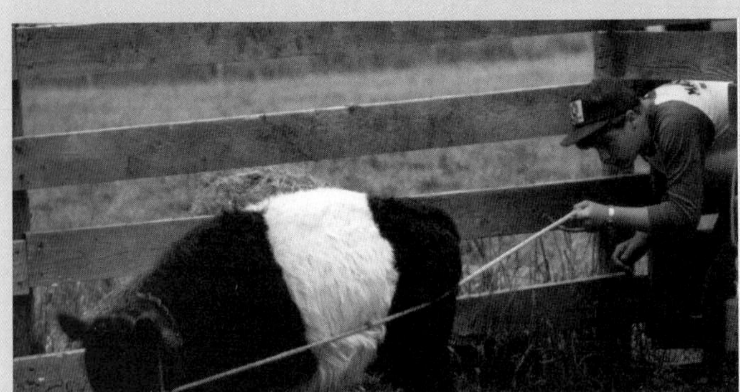

△ Belted Galloway cow

Maine

As big as the other five New England states combined, **MAINE** has barely the population of Rhode Island. In theory, therefore, there's plenty of room for its massive summer influx of visitors; in practice, the majority of these head for the extravagantly corrugated **coast**. In the shoreline's southern reaches, the beach resort towns of **Ogunquit** and **Old Orchard Beach** quickly lead up to Maine's most cosmopolitan city, **Portland**. The **Mid-Coast**, between the quiet college town of Brunswick and blue-collar Bucksport, is characterized by a craggy, irregular seashore, with plenty of dramatic, windswept peninsulas and sheltered inlets to explore, though in the well-touristed towns of **Boothbay Harbor** and **Camden**, you'll certainly have company on your wanderings. **Down East**, beyond the moneyed Blue Hill Peninsula, **Mount Desert Island** holds Maine's most popular outdoor escape, **Acadia National Park**, in addition to the bustling summer retreat of **Bar Harbor**. Farther still up the coastline, you'll find less cooperative weather and increasingly uninhabited scenery, capped by the candy-striped lighthouse at **Quoddy Head,** the easternmost part of the country.

You only really begin to appreciate the size and space of the state, however, farther north or inland, where vast tracts of mountainous forest are dotted with lakes and barely pierced by roads – more like the Alaskan interior than the RV-cluttered roads of the Vermont and New Hampshire mountains. This region is ideal territory for hiking and canoeing (and spotting moose), particularly in **Baxter State Park**. In the northwestern part of the state, closer to the New Hampshire border, a cluster of ski resorts lie scattered about the mountains, highlighted by **Sugarloaf USA**, perhaps the finest place to ski in all New England.

Although Maine is in many ways inhospitable – the **Algonquin** called it the "Land of the Frozen Ground" – it has been in contact with Europe ever since the **Vikings** explored it, around 1000 AD. For the navigator Verrazano, in 1524, the "crudity and evil manners" of the Indians made this the "Land of Bad People," but before long European fishermen were setting up camps each summer to dry their catch. Francis Bacon in turn said that the English settlers were "worse than the very Savages, impudently lying with their Women, teaching their men to drink drunke, and … to fall together by the eares."

North America's first agricultural **colonies** were in Maine: de Champlain's **French** Protestants near Mount Desert Island in 1604, and an **English** group that survived one winter at the mouth of the Kennebec River three years later. In the face of the unwillingness of subsequent English settlers to let them farm in peace, local Indians formed long-term alliances with the French and, until as late as 1700, regularly drove out streams of impoverished English refugees. By 1764, however, the official census could claim that even Maine's black population was more numerous than its Native Americans.

Finding your way in Maine

With public transport falling a long way short of meeting travelers' needs, the vast majority of visitors to Maine **drive**. The most enjoyable route to follow is **US-1**, which runs within a few miles of the coast all the way to Canada. Many hotels, restaurants, and attractions can be found along US-1 – but their addresses may or may not reflect that. In each coastal town, US-1 usually becomes a named street; sometimes several names are used. All this may make your destination deceptively difficult to locate, but the locals will inevitably provide cheerful assistance, so just relax and allow a few extra minutes. You should be prepared for backups at the height of the summer season, however. If you're in a hurry, **I-95** offers speedy (though tolled in parts) access to Portland and beyond. In the interior, the roads are quiet and the views spectacular; many routes belong to the lumber companies, who keep careful track of who you are and where you're going (and charge you for the privilege). At any time of year, bad weather can render these roads suddenly impassable; be sure to check before setting off.

At first considered part of Massachusetts, Maine became a separate entity only in 1820, when the Missouri Compromise made Maine a free, and Missouri a slave, state. In the nineteenth century, its people had a reputation for conservatism and resistance to immigration, manifested in anti-Irish riots. Today, the **economy** remains heavily based on the sea, although many of those who fish also farm. Lobster fishing in particular has defied gloomy predictions and boomed again, as evidenced by the many thriving **lobster pounds**.

Maine's climate is famously harsh. In winter, most of the state is under ice; in early 1998, a severe ice storm left many residents huddled in their homes without power or running water for several weeks. Summer is short and usually heralded in early June by an infestation of tiny black flies, though the tourist season doesn't come into full swing until July. **Fall colors** begin to spread from the north in late September – when, unlike elsewhere in New England, off-season prices apply – but temperatures drop sharply, usually becoming quite frosty by mid-October.

The southern coast

Stretching between the two shopping hubs of **Kittery** and **Freeport**, Maine's **southern coast** is its most settled part. Blessed with the state's best **beaches** – indeed, most of its beaches – the southern coastline was already a popular summer vacation spot by the mid-nineteenth century, when frequent trains brought city-dwellers up from Boston and New York or down from Canada. The eleven-mile strip of sand at **Old Orchard Beach** is still one of the finest in the country, attracting correspondingly huge crowds in July and August. The other popular beach resort town in the area, **Ogunquit**, only slightly less overrun in summer, is more attractive, with a long-established artist community and a collection of excellent restaurants to boot. Though commercial develop-

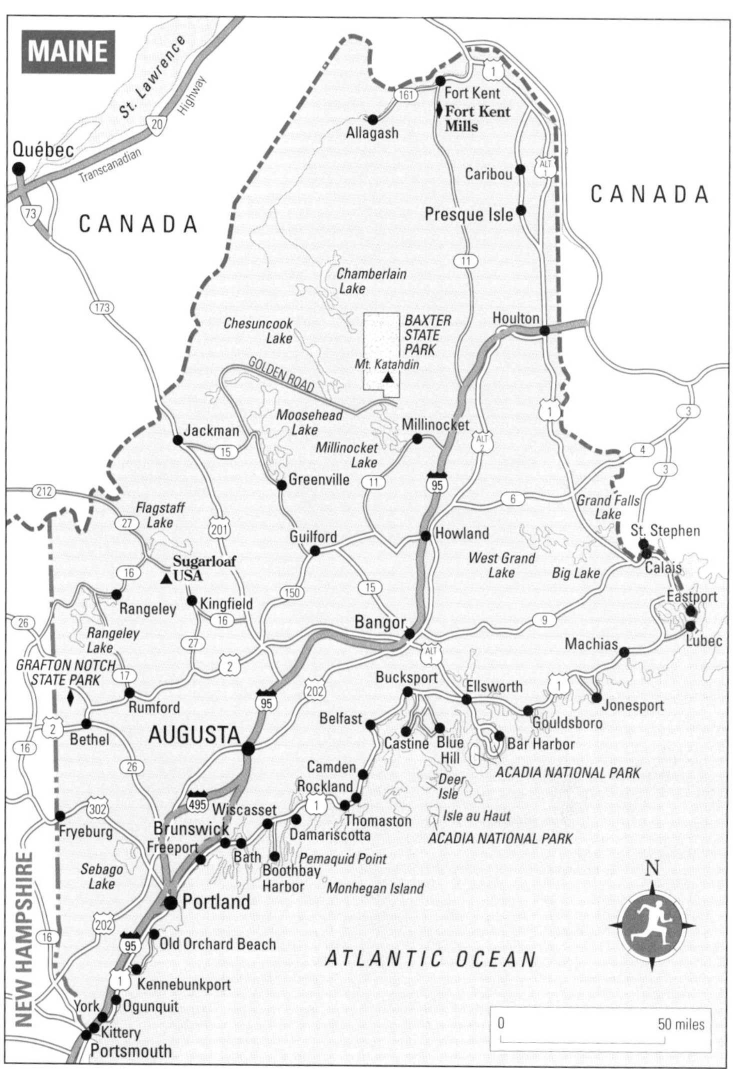

ment has scarred some of the area's landscape with malls and fast food, you can still find attractive old towns with plenty of historical interest, such as **York**, the first chartered city in America, and beautiful **Kennebunkport**, best known as the site of ex-president George Bush's summer home. In the northern part of the region, the coastline becomes more varied and prone to peninsulas, harbors, inlets, and islands. At the mouth of the Fore River, Maine's largest city, **Portland**, has experienced a cultural resurgence over the past few years, with a hip, twenty-something population, newly opened inventive restaurants, and a lively music scene.

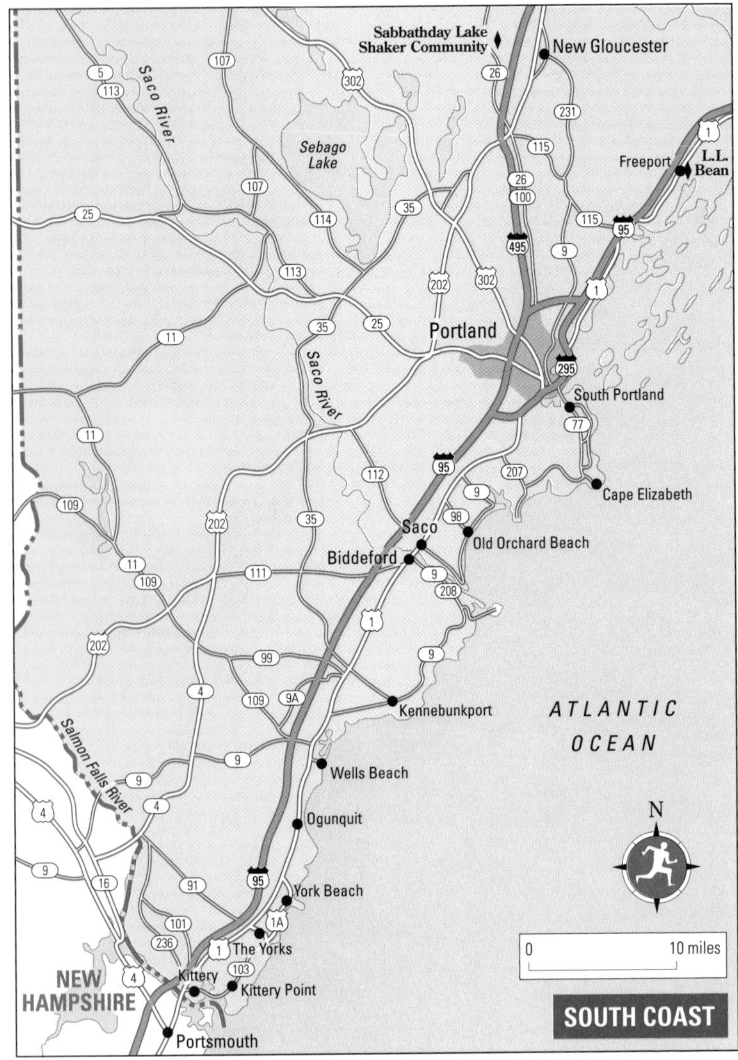

Kittery and the Yorks

KITTERY is only just in Maine, right across the Piscataqua from Portsmouth, NH (see p.459), and it makes for an excellent place to get oriented, namely at its very complete **information center** at the intersection of I-95 and US-1 (daily: summer 8am–6pm; rest of year 9am–5.30pm; ☎207/439-1319), which has scads of brochures, weather information services, and volunteers who can give insiders' tips and help make reservations. If you follow US-1 through Kittery, you'll pass a nearly endless string of **outlet shops** (Ⓣ1-888/KITTERY, Ⓦwww.thekitteryoutlets.com), though these lag behind the quality of those in Freeport, about 75 minutes up the road. In the Maine Outlet mall, the Greater York Region Chamber of Commerce runs a tourist information center (Mon–Fri 9am–5pm; Ⓣ207/439-2576).

The small bit of land south along Rte-103 called Kittery Point makes for a pleasant drive, taking you a few miles and a thousand cultural light years from the outlet-shopping hordes. It also takes you past the 1714 First Congregational Church, Maine's oldest house of worship, to a rocky cliff overlooking the Portsmouth Naval Shipyard (also called the Kittery Naval Yard) on Seavey Island, where the treaty ending the Russo–Japanese War of 1905 was signed. Kittery was a major shipbuilding center by the mid-eighteenth century, when the *Ranger* sailed out of a Kittery shipyard under the command of Revolutionary War hero John Paul Jones. For a detailed look at the city's naval, shipbuilding, and cultural history, including a fourteen-foot model of the *Ranger*, stop off at the Kittery Historical and Naval Museum, on Rogers Road near the intersection of US-1 and Rte-236 (June to mid-Oct Tues–Sat 10am–4pm; $3; Ⓣ207/439-3080).

Close by is one of Kittery Point's best places to eat, *Cap'n Simeon's Galley*, 90 Pepperrell Rd (May to mid-Oct daily; mid-Oct through April closed Tues; Ⓣ207/439-3655), with a well-priced menu specializing in seafood and an outdoor deck overlooking picturesque Pepperrell Cove. Back on US-1 in Kittery is longtime local favorite *Bob's Clam Hut* (Ⓣ207/439-4233), a campy fish eatery open since 1956. Some of the best places to stay in town are the inviting *Portsmouth Harbor Inn & Spa*, 6 Water St (Ⓣ207/439-4040, Ⓦwww.innatportsmouth.com; ⑦–⑧), the clean, adequate *Coachman Motor Inn*, right near the outlets at 380 US-1 (Ⓣ207/439-4434, Ⓦwww.coachmaninn.net; ⑥–⑦), and *Enchanted Nights B&B*, 29 Wentworth St (Ⓣ207/439-1489, Ⓦwww.enchantednights.org; ④).

The Yorks

The pleasant **YORKS,** a few miles north of Kittery on US-1, comprise four separate entities: York Village, Cape Neddick, scenic York Harbor, and lounge-worthy York Beach. This cumulative network of towns is sometimes vaguely referred to as "York." At any rate, it bears the distinction of being America's first chartered city, incorporated as Georgeana in 1642 – though it was subsequently demoted to the status of "town" in 1670. Its past is well preserved

Surfing Maine's southern coast

A small number of hardy souls brave the cold tumult of the North Atlantic to pursue the unlikely pastime of **surfing** off Maine's coast; indeed, it's said that there are only a hundred or so Maine residents who surf regularly year-round (twenty of those in Portland), no matter the weather. While 50°F waters in northern California are considered cold, the water here in January can dip below 40°F, daunting even with the newest developments in wet-suit technology. Though wave and tide conditions are usually best in fall and winter, on certain warm summer days the waves come up and the crowds swell with the tides. The best spots are at **Higgins Beach**, south of Portland in Scarborough, **Fortune Rocks** in Biddeford, **Gooch's Beach** in Kennebunk, **Old Orchard Beach**, **York Beach**, and **Wells Beach**. For equipment **rentals** and **information** on conditions, contact Liquid Dreams Surf, 365 Main St (US-1), Ogunquit (Ⓣ207/641-2545), or Wheels and Waves, 579 Post Rd (US-1) in Wells (Ⓣ207/646-5774).

in the series of seven buildings that comprise the Old York Historical Society. **Jefferd's Tavern**, 5 Lindsay St, offers a starting point for the tour of the old buildings (mid-June to early Sept Mon–Sat 10am–5pm; ⓣ207/363-4974; $10), with a visitors' center where tickets are sold. Foremost among the structures is the **Old Jail**, 207 York St, which really is old – it's the earliest British colonial public structure still standing on its original site, dating from 1653. It was used as Maine's primary prison until the Revolution and continued to confine York County prisoners until the Civil War. Inside, a museum reconstructs the surprisingly plush jailer's quarters and has displays on some of the more colorful criminals to do time here. Old York also includes the **Old Schoolhouse**, which houses exhibits on education in the eighteenth century; the **John Hancock Warehouse and Wharf**, which has maritime exhibits in the original Customs House; and the **Old Burying Yard**, where it's rumored that a grave covered with a stone slab was thus protected to prevent its occupant, reputedly a witch, from escaping. In fact, the slab was actually placed there by her husband to prevent cattle from grazing on her grave. If you'd like to talk to her (or one of her friends) yourself, you may want to attend one of Ghostly Tours' candle-lit strolls through the town (ⓣ207/363-0000).

As well as its historical attractions, York boasts several fine beaches and invigorating cliff walks. Head beyond Old York, for example, towards Nubble Light, at the end of Shore Road, off Rte-103, at York Beach, where you'll find one of Maine's most striking lighthouses, situated on an island of its own and observable from a rocky promontory. If you have little ones in tow, or if you're even remotely interested in jumping up and down, be sure to visit the **Wiggly Bridge**, a local landmark just off Rte-1A on Lilac Lane (Rte-103). This flexible mini-bridge enables you to jump wildly while watching the tide go in or out beneath your feet.

Practicalities

York boasts some fine **accommodation**, best of which is the 47-room *York Harbor Inn*, on Rte-1A in York Harbor (ⓣ207/363-5119 or 1-800/343-3869, ⓦwww.yorkharborinn.com; ❼), a beautifully appointed inn on the shore with several inviting common areas. It also has a sunlit, scenic fine-dining restaurant, as well as the *Ship's Cellar Pub*, for burger-and-beer cuisine. Just around the bend (still on Rte-1A) is the very swish *Stage Neck Inn* (ⓣ207/363-3850 or 1-800/222-3238, ⓦwww.stageneck.com; ❽), which has incredible ocean views and luxurious amenities, while right by York beach is the brightly colored, cheerful *Katahdin Inn*, 11 Ocean Ave Extension (ⓣ207/363-1824, ⓦwww.thekatahdin.com; ❺–❻). A number of cheaper motels and B&Bs can be found along Long Beach Avenue.

As for **food**, the *Lobster Barn*, on US-1 in York Village (ⓣ207/363-4721), has a relaxed atmosphere and well-priced lobster dinners that are served outdoors when weather permits. If you prefer your seafood in a more maritime setting, try the informal *Cape Neddick Lobster Pound* right on the water on Shore Road, Cape Neddick Harbor (ⓣ207/363-5471). In York Village's main square, *Carla's Pastries & Café*, 241 York St (ⓣ207/363-4637; breakfast and lunch only), will entice you with its bold, aquamarine interior, fresh salads, and delectable pastries. Nearby *Rick's*, 240R York St, York Village (ⓣ207/363-5584; closed Mon) opens early for big breakfasts and laidback lunches. Out at York Beach, local institution *The Goldenrod*, 2 Railroad Ave (ⓣ207/363-2621), has been churning out saltwater taffy for more than a hundred years. It currently resembles the New York Stock Exchange of candy, replete with crying children and frenzied customers trying to get their order heard. The view is safer from the sidewalk, where you can quietly watch its hypnotizing taffy machine pull and wrap the "Goldenrod Kisses."

Ogunquit

Approaching the small oceanside town just north of York, it's not difficult to imagine why Maine's Native Americans named the place **OGUNQUIT**, meaning "beautiful place by the sea." Though the area was more attractive before it was developed into a summertime resort, its most prominent and stunning feature – the beach – still makes it a worthwhile spot for a visit. In the nineteenth and twentieth centuries, Ogunquit enjoyed fame as the vacation spot of choice for such rich and famous folks as Bette Davis and Tommy Dorsey, and its beachfront was lined with wooden luxury hotels, most of which are gone today. Also gone is the town's reputation as an artists' colony, though a few galleries remain to illustrate that chapter of its history. The town has a little bit of a privileged attitude, but streets named Whistling Oyster Lane and Ho Hum Hill point to the playful character underneath.

Information and getting around

The **Ogunquit Chamber of Commerce**, just south of Ogunquit Village on US-1 (daily 9am–5pm; ⓣ207/646-2939 or 1-800/639-2442, ⓦwww.ogunquit.org), has brochures year-round and operates as a fully staffed **information center** from May to October (daily 9am–5pm; ⓣ207/646-5533). The town is small and traffic can be terrible, so it may be a good idea to use the **trolley** ($1.50), which connects Perkins Cove, Ogunquit Square, the beach, and the strip of motels along US-1 to the north. Wheels and Waves, in Wells, two miles north of Ogunquit Square on US-1 (ⓣ207/646-5774), rents **mountain bikes** and has maps of local cycling trails.

If you're looking to get out on the water, a number of **sailing cruises** depart from Perkins Cove. Both Finestkind (ⓣ207/646-5227) and The Silverlining (ⓣ207/646-9800) run several cruises daily from May to October; the *Bunny Clark* caters to deep-sea fishing enthusiasts (ⓣ207/646-2214; $45 half-day, $65 full day); and the *Deborah Ann* charters whale-watching expeditions from mid-June to August (ⓣ207/361-9501).

Accommodation

The pier at the beach has some decent **hotels** that tend to be high-priced due to their proximity to the ocean. Shore Road has a number of good-quality **B&Bs** within walking distance of the beach, town square, and Marginal Way. The stretch above Ogunquit Square along US-1 North has cheap **motels**, and once you get to the town of **Moody**, a mile out, prices drop precipitously. The best **camping** in the area is at *Pinederosa Campground*, 128 North Village Rd in Wells (ⓣ207/646-2492; $23), or *Dixon's Coastal Maine Campground* (ⓣ207/363-3626; $26), 1740 US-1 in Cape Neddick.

Beachmere Inn Shore Rd ⓣ207/646-2021 or 1-800/336-3983, ⓦwww.beachmereinn.com. Beautiful rooms in a quirky, turreted old wooden hotel that overlooks the ocean. The restored inn also operates a few more modern, motel-style buildings nearby. ❽

Juniper Hill Inn 336 US-1 N ⓣ207/646-4501 or 1-800/646-4544. Luxury beachside accommodation with indoor pool, fitness center, and spacious, if somewhat plain, rooms. ❻

Meadowmere Resort 74 S Main St (Rte-1) ⓣ207/646-3787, ⓦwww.meadowmere.com. This spacious resort inn has appealing rooms, a fitness center, day spa, restaurant, and happy guests. ❼

The Nellie Littlefield House 27 Shore Rd ⓣ207/646-1692. Individually designed, well-appointed B&B rooms in a pretty house just outside the square. ❼

Pine Hill Inn 13 Pine Hill Rd ⓣ207/361-1004. Quiet, secluded B&B in a Victorian cottage off of

Shore Rd within walking distance of Perkins Cove. Great breakfasts. ❻

Seacoast Motel US-1 N ⓣ207/646-2187. Basic, clean motel north of the square. ❻

Terrace by the Sea 11 Wharf Lane ⓣ207/646-3232, ⓦwww.terracebythesea.com. Their gorgeous garden will lure you into this plush motel. Located on the water's edge with spectacular views from many of its rooms. Closed Nov–March. ❺

Wells-Ogunquit Resort Motel 203 US-1 N ⓣ207/646-8588 or 1-800/556-4402. Impeccably kept modern motel rooms with cable and refrigerators, plus barbecue set-ups outdoors. Open May–Oct only. ❹

The Town

Ogunquit Square, along Main Street (US-1), is the center of town, home to most of Ogunquit's best restaurants, coffeehouses, and quirky shops. East of the square, Beach Street leads over the Ogunquit River to one of Maine's finest **beaches**, three miles of sugary white sand. The water is always freezing, but the sun is mellow and the sand great for sunbathing. Parking near the pier costs $5, but there's a better way to access the beach: take US-1 north of Ogunquit Square and go right on Ocean Street, which leads to a less populated area of the beach – and cheaper parking.

Perkins Cove, a pleasant knot of restaurants and shops a few miles south of Ogunquit Square, is best reached by walking along **Marginal Way**, a windy path that traces the crescent shoreline from Ogunquit Beach. The two-mile trail offers unspoiled views of the Atlantic's rocky coast, particularly stunning in fall when the ocean undulates alongside the fiery foliage. The folk art, pottery, and jewelry shops in and around the cove warrant maybe an hour's browse, and there are a few places to indulge in an ice-cream cone or some saltwater taffy. A half-mile south of Perkins Cove at 543 Shore Rd is the **Ogunquit Museum of American Art** (July to mid-Oct Mon–Sat 10.30am–5pm, Sun 2–5pm; $5; ⓣ207/646-4909), which the late director of the Met in New York, Henry Taylor, called "the most beautiful little museum in the world." Its tiny space is blessed with a strong collection of nineteenth- and twentieth-century American art, including sumptuous seascapes by Marsden Hartley and Rockwell Kent, enhanced by the museum's sweeping ocean views. The grounds feature

△ Ogunquit Beach

a diverse sculpture garden, where grinning animal sculptures intermingle with serene marble women.

Eating, drinking, and entertainment

You'll find the standard profusion of **lobster shacks** and touristy seafood restaurants all over Ogunquit, but the best eateries are in the town square and around Perkins Cove. There are also a couple of decent pubs and **bars** in town, offering occasional live musical acts and friendly piano-bar sing-alongs.

For more serious entertainment, the **Ogunquit Playhouse** along US-1 south of town (mid-June to Aug; tickets ⓣ207/646-5511) has been called "America's foremost summer theater" for most of its seventy years, and usually attracts a few big-name performers each season.

Arrows Restaurant Berwick Rd, just outside Ogunquit Square ⓣ207/361-1100. Excellent, though frightfully expensive (mains at $40) New American cuisine in a Victorian house surrounded by gardens. Reservations recommended. Weekends only Oct–Nov, closed Dec–April.

Barnacle Billy's Perkins Cove ⓣ207/646-5575. An Ogunquit standby, with a casual café next door. The lobster and fried fish are a bit overpriced (particularly when you factor in the parking fees), but it's still a good spot.

Blue Water Inn 111 Beach St ⓣ207/646-5559. Right on the river and a stone's throw from the beach, the *Blue Water Inn* serves up fresh seafood at amazing prices.

Five-O 50 Shore Rd ⓣ207/646-5001. With its buttery interior, creative New American cuisine, and adjacent first-rate lounge, *Five-O* makes for a good evening splurge.

Jonathan's 2 Bourne Lane ⓣ207/646-4777. Live entertainment – musical and otherwise – nightly from April to Oct, with a decent restaurant serving seafood, pasta, and creatively prepared meats. Reservations recommended.

Joshua's Restaurant 1637 US-1, Wells ⓣ207/646-3500. Inside this unassuming chocolate-colored house chef Joshua Mather grills, sears, and sautés some of Maine's best cuisine. Many of the dishes use ingredients from his own local farm. Dinner only, reservations recommended.

La Pizzeria 239 Main St, Ogunquit Square ⓣ207/646-1143. Good pizza joint right in the center of town. They also have sub sandwiches and basic salads.

Mekhong Thai II 657 US-1 ⓣ207/641-8805. Softly lit interior amidst intricate Thai decor. Those in the know order the *tom kha gai* soup (spicy coconut-milk soup with chicken, lemongrass, mushrooms, and fresh lime juice).

Native Grounds 230 Main St, Ogunquit Square ⓣ207/646-0955. Funky joint for light lunch fare. Create-your-own sandwiches and good soups of the day, to be enjoyed in pleasant outdoor seating area.

The Old Village Inn 240 Main St ⓣ207/646-7088. Upmarket seafood with a New American twist. Try the tequila lime shrimp or *osso buco*; the lobster bisque, too, is locally famous. There's also a cheaper pub menu if you're strapped for cash.

Poor Richard's Tavern 2 Pine Hill Rd ⓣ207/646-4722. Authentic old-time New England pub grub in a 1780 Colonial building that was once a coach stop on the road between Boston and Portland.

Vinny's East Coast Grill US-1 one mile north of the town center ⓣ207/646-5115. Another lower-cost option, it's essentially a sports bar with casual dinners, featuring sandwiches and salads.

North to Portland

After Ogunquit, the coastal route meanders on a bit, with distances between towns beginning to stretch. In this thirty-or-so-mile stretch up to Portland, the main points of interest are in **Kennebunkport** and **Old Orchard Beach**.

Kennebunkport

The recent history of **KENNEBUNKPORT** illustrates the truth of Oscar Wilde's aphorism, "There is only one thing in the world worse than being talked about, and that is not being talked about." Kennebunkport was perfectly happy as a self-contained and exclusive residential district before its worldwide exposure as the home of (the senior) **George Bush**'s "summer White House." If anything, locals seemed to feel that George lowered the tone of the place by becoming president. There were complaints at having to bear the extra cost of policing, and talk of a "lower class" of gawking visitors clogging the streets and driving the old money away. However, interest subsided after Bush lost the presidency to Bill Clinton in 1992, and now it's quite apparent that Kennebunkport isn't that different from any other place along the coast – which bothers the locals even more.

Fortunately, Kennebunkport has been blessed with beaches as well as bluebloods. The best is **Goose Rocks Beach**, about three miles north of town on King's Hwy (off Dyke Road via Rte-9). It's a premium stretch of expansive sand, though you will need a parking permit to park here; call the Kennebunkport police ($5 daily; ⓣ207/934-2001). Neighboring Kennebunk is home to a trio of lovely beaches: Kennebunk, Mother's, and Gooch's, all of which are located on Beach Street off Rte-9 South. Once again, you will need a permit to park here (same price as above; ⓣ207/967-4243), although if you're staying in town you can walk.

The **Seashore Trolley Museum**, 195 Log Cabin Rd off Rte-9 or US-1 (daily May to mid-Oct 10am–5pm; $7.50; ⓣ207/967-2712, ⓦwww.trolleymuseum.org), holds a surprisingly engaging display on the history of the trolley car (of all things) in northern New England. You can take a twenty-minute ride on a vintage trolley car through the Maine woods, along a stretch of track that used to be part of a line that allowed travelers to go from Bangor to Washington, DC, entirely by trolley. Best is the collection of old trolleys from around the world, including the original New Orleans trolley that ran along Desire Street, made famous in the Tennessee Williams play *A Streetcar Named Desire*.

Practicalities

Eating in Kennebunkport doesn't necessarily require a second mortgage. *Alisson's*, 11 Dock Square (ⓣ207/967-4841), is a fun, relaxed place to hang out and chow on seafood. They have a late-night menu, for this area at least (food is served in the pub until 11pm Fri & Sat, until 10pm the rest of the week), as well as a lively bar. *Federal Jack's*, off Rte-9 (ⓣ207/967-2211), makes great appetizers – try the Goat Island mussels or Maine steamers – and features an on-site **microbrewery** that produces an excellent Shipyard Ale. In Lower Village Kennebunk, *Grissini Trattoria and Panificio*, 27 Western Ave (ⓣ207/967-4322), has pricey but tasty Italian food you can eat on an outdoor patio.

Old Orchard Beach

During the late nineteenth and early twentieth centuries, **OLD ORCHARD BEACH** (OOB, in local parlance) stood alongside Ogunquit as a classic New England resort town, drawing upper-crust citizens from all over the eastern seaboard to stay in its massive wooden seafront hotels. After World War II, its popularity and property values declined steadily, and in 1980 the town attempted to rectify the situation by refurbishing its decaying, carnivalesque pier. Almost overnight, OOB regained its status as a major hotspot, though it resembled the spring break town of Fort Lauderdale more than the posh resort of old. Things have calmed down a bit, even if a slightly corny party atmosphere remains, especially along the waterfront.

The main draw here is the **beach**, a fantastic seven-mile strip of white sand that competes with any in New England. It can get intolerably crowded during summer and holiday weekends, in which case you'd do better to find another stretch of shore. It's free, but **parking** can be pricey; lots that charge $5–7 per day are reasonable. Just off the beach is the **pier** and Palace Playland (ⓣ207/934-2001), with classic amusement-park attractions such as a Ferris wheel, bumper cars, and a vintage carousel dating from 1906. The entirety of **Old Orchard Street** (which leads down to the pier and beach) and **Grand Avenue** (which runs parallel to the ocean), are dotted with attractions, including instant-photo booths, cotton-candy vendors, and stores where you can design your own souvenir T-shirt. It's hopelessly tacky, but at least with its campy carnival vibe it's an alternative to its sedate neighbors.

Practicalities

The **Old Orchard Beach Chamber of Commerce**, on First Street (Sept–June Mon–Fri 8am–4pm, July & Aug daily 9am–5pm; ⓣ207/934-2500, ⓦwww.oldorchardbeachmaine.com), operates an information center and can help arrange accommodation. Although the town is packed with **places to stay**, it can fill to capacity; definitely call ahead for reservations. The seafront is dotted with pricey motels, though they sometimes have the advantage of owning a small strip of private beach – an invaluable respite from the maddening crowds. *White Lamb Cottages* (ⓣ207/934-2221 or 1-800/203-2034, ⓦwww.janelle.com; ❼) is a series of stand-alone beach cottages done up in 1940s-era style; the same people also run the well-appointed *Edgewater Inn*, right on the water at 57 W Grand Ave (ⓣ207/934-3731 or 1-800/203-2034, ⓦwww.janelle.com; ❼). More downmarket options include the *Americana Motel*, 1 Heath St (ⓣ1-800/NJOYOOB, ⓦwww.americanaoldorchard.com; ❺), and the *Green Dolphin*, 62 E Grand Ave (ⓣ207/934-4764, ⓦwww.greendolphinmotel.com; ❺), both of which offer unremarkable motel digs, but are nonetheless conveniently located near the pier.

Eating in OOB is not such a treat. You'll find an overabundance of pizza and burger joints crowding the main thoroughfares, although there are a few nearby exceptions, most notably *Joseph's by the Sea*, 55 W Grand Ave (ⓣ207/934-5044), whose deservedly expensive menu includes – but, thankfully, does not focus exclusively on – seafood, and the great ocean views are a bonus. *Denny Mike's Smokehouse BBQ & Deli*, 27 W Grand Ave, (ⓣ207/934-2207), serves surprisingly good barbecue and onion rings, while *The Landmark Restaurant*, 28 E Grand Ave (ⓣ207/934-0156), does simple Maine fare like haddock with crumb topping.

Portland

The largest city in Maine, with a population hovering around 65,000, **PORTLAND** was founded in 1632, at a superb point on the Casco Bay Peninsula, and quickly prospered, building ships and exporting its great supply of inland pines for use as masts. A long line of wooden **wharves** stretched along the seafront, with the merchants' houses on the hillside above. From the earliest days it was a cosmopolitan city, with a large free black population who traditionally worked as longshoremen; there was great bitterness when Irish immigrants began to muscle in on the scene in the 1830s. When the **railroads** came, the Canada Trunk Line had its terminus right on Portland's quayside, bringing the produce of Canada and the Great Plains one hundred miles closer to Europe than it would have been at any other major US port. Some of the wharves are now

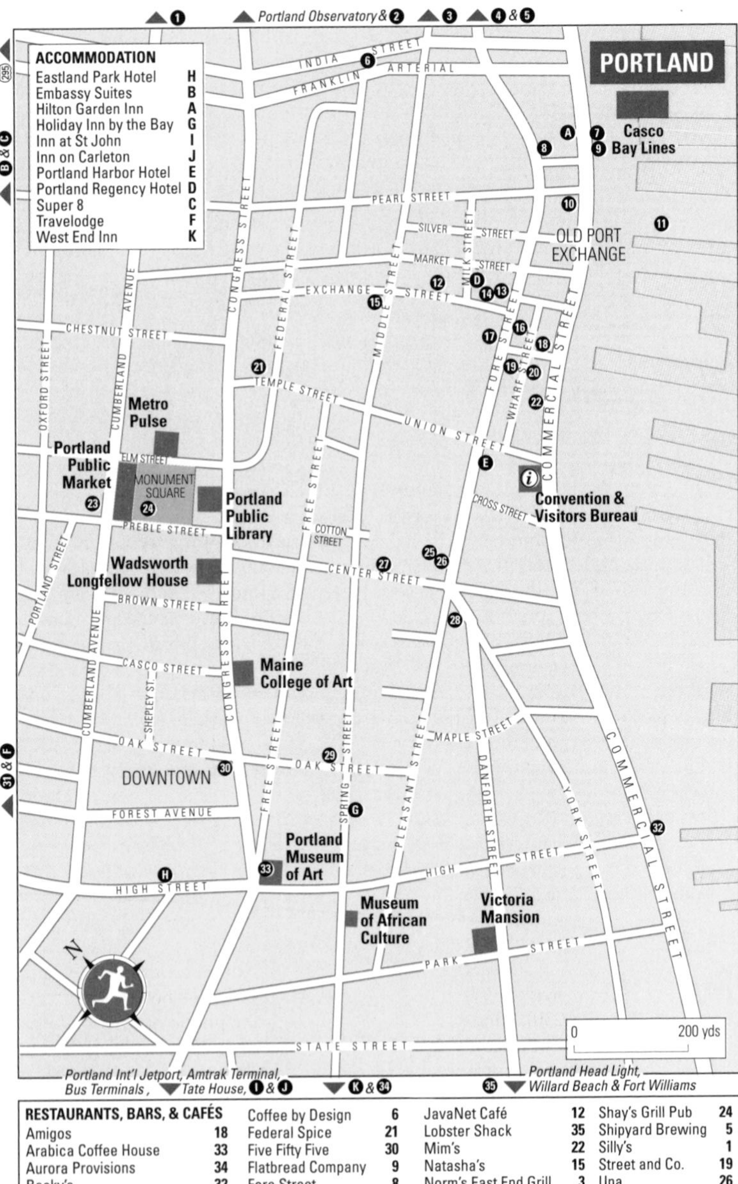

RESTAURANTS, BARS, & CAFÉS							
Amigos	18	Coffee by Design	6	JavaNet Café	12	Shay's Grill Pub	24
Arabica Coffee House	33	Federal Spice	21	Lobster Shack	35	Shipyard Brewing	5
Aurora Provisions	34	Five Fifty Five	30	Mim's	22	Silly's	1
Becky's	32	Flatbread Company	9	Natasha's	15	Street and Co.	19
Blue Spoon	2	Fore Street	8	Norm's East End Grill	3	Una	26
Breaking New Grounds	13 & 23	Great Lost Bear	31	Portland Roasting Co	10	Walter's Café	14
Brian Boru Public House	27	Gritty McDuff's	16	Ribollita	4	Wine Bar	20
Bull Feeney's	17	Herb's Gully	29	RiRa	7	Yosaku	28
		J's Oyster	11	Rivalries	25		

taken up by new condo developments, though **Custom House Wharf** remains much as it must have looked when novelist Anthony Trollope passed through in 1861 and said, "I doubt whether I ever saw a town with more evident signs of prosperity." Most of the town he saw, including half the churches, nearly all of the public buildings, and hundreds of houses, was destroyed by an accidental fire in 1866 that was started during a Fourth of July celebration (Indians in 1675, and the British in 1775, had previously burned Portland deliberately).

Grand Trunk Station was torn down in 1966, and downtown Portland appeared to be in terminal decline until a group of committed residents undertook the energetic redevelopment of the area now known as **Old Port Exchange**. In more recent years, downtown Portland, particularly along **Congress Street**, has also undergone a renaissance of sorts, spurred by a high concentration of artists, some wise city-planning, and the opening of a new L.L. Bean outlet in the late 1990s. These successes, and a small but unexpected wave of immigration in the mid-1990s, have revitalized the city, keeping it at the heart of Maine life – but you shouldn't expect a constant hive of energy. Portland is simply a quite pleasant, sophisticated, and, in places, very attractive town, where one can experience the benefits of a large city at a lesser cost and without the hassle.

Arrival and information

Both I-95 and US-1 skirt the peninsula of Portland, quite near to the city center, while I-295 goes through it; **Portland International Jetport** (ⓣ207/774-7301) abuts I-95. Most major carriers serve the airport, which is connected with downtown by the city **bus** (#5; no service Sun; $1; ⓣ207/774-0351, ⓦwww.transportme.org) and the less frequent **Portland Explorer** (buses hourly until 6pm; $2; ⓣ207/774-0351, ⓦwww.transportme.org).

Amtrak's *Downeaster* pulls into Portland four times daily from Boston's North Station (one-way $22; ⓣ1-800/USA-RAIL, ⓦwww.amtrakdowneaster.com), arriving at the Portland Transportation Center (ⓣ207/828-3939). From the terminal, located three miles from the city center at 100 Thompson's Point Rd just off Congress Street and adjacent to I-295, shuttles, city buses, and taxis can ferry you downtown.

Also arriving here, Concord Trailways (ⓣ207/828-1151 or 1-800/639-3317) is the principal **bus** operator along the coast, with frequent service from Boston and Bangor. Vermont Transit Lines (ⓣ207/772-6587 or 1-800/451-3292) has a direct connection service with Greyhound and runs to Montréal, New Hampshire, and Vermont as well as to points throughout Maine from its station at 950 Congress St, on the eastern edge of downtown.

Car rentals are available from the local offices of National and Alamo (ⓣ207/775-0855), Avis (ⓣ207/874-7500), Budget (ⓣ207/774-8663), and Enterprise (ⓣ207/772-0030); consult Basics (p.43) for toll-free phone numbers. **Parking** can be a hassle in Portland. The parking meters charge 25¢ per half-hour, but finding a parking place can sometimes seem well-nigh impossible. The city makes up for this to some degree with a glut of parking garages, including the Fore Street Garage at no. 427, and the Casco Bay Parking Garage at 54 Commercial St.

The **CVB of Greater Portland** is at 245 Commercial St (Mon–Fri 8am–5pm, Sat 10am–3pm; ⓣ207/772-5800, ⓦwww.visitportland.com), and there's a less harried information office at the Jetport (ⓣ207/775-5809). Furthermore, all manner of details concerning transportation within the area, whether by bus, boat, or train, can be found at ⓦwww.transportme.org. The Portland Public Library, 5 Monument Square, at the corner of Congress and Elm (ⓣ207/871-1700, ⓦwww.portlandlibrary.com), has free **Internet access**.

City transit and tours

Downtown Portland and the Old Port are each compact enough to stroll around, though they're served by a comprehensive **bus** system ($1; ⓣ207/774-0351); stop by the Metro Pulse, the hub of the bus system, at the Elm Street Garage near Congress Street for a detailed route map. CycleMania, 59 Federal St (ⓣ207/774-2933), rents **bicycles** for $20 a day, which you can ride around the city's hundreds of acres of undeveloped land. Call Portland Trails (ⓣ207/775-2411, ⓦwww.trails.org) for more information on bike or walking trails all over the city. **Tour companies** abound: two of the most entertaining are Mainely Tours, 163 Commercial St (May–Oct; $15; ⓣ207/774-0808), which gives an overview of town history and allows you to hop on and off its jaunty trolley, and the amphibious Downeast Duck Adventures, at the same address (May–Oct; $22; ⓣ207/774-DUCK), which whisks you through historical Old Port and then takes you into Casco Bay to view the Calendar Islands. For $10 tours of Portland's historic homes, contact Greater Portland Landmarks, 165 State St (ⓣ207/774-5561).

Accommodation

Finding a room in Portland is no great problem if you book in advance for the summer and fall, but you'll generally pay more for **accommodation** in town than for space in one of several **budget motels** that cluster around exit 48 off I-95. The extra cost can be worth it, however; Portland has some great old renovated hotels and you'll save in transportation costs by staying closer to downtown or the Old Port. The closest **campground** is *Wassamki Springs*, 56 Saco St in Scarborough, off Rte-22 towards Westbrook (ⓣ207/839-4276; May to mid-Oct only; $39).

Eastland Park Hotel 157 High St ⓣ207/775-5411 or 1-888/671-8008, ⓦwww.eastlandparkhotel.com. Luxury, centrally located accommodation that has a business center as well as a cocktail lounge with sweeping views of the city. 8

Embassy Suites 1050 Westbrook St ⓣ207/775-2200 or 1-800/EMBASSY. Spacious suites for the price of a hotel room, overlooking Portland's tiny Jetport. Rates include full breakfast and afternoon cocktails. 7

Hilton Garden Inn 65 Commercial St ⓣ207/780-0780, ⓦwww.hiltongardeninn.com. Fitness center, whirlpool, and wireless Internet, all in a snappy location that overlooks the harbor. Still, the rooms are bland, considering the price. 8

Holiday Inn by the Bay 88 Spring St ⓣ207/775-2311 or 1-800/345-5050, ⓦwww.innbythebay.com. Fairly standard link in the *Holiday Inn* chain, with 239 rooms, many of which overlook Casco Bay. 7

Inn on Carleton 46 Carleton St ⓣ207/775-1910 or 1-800/639-1779, ⓦwww.innoncarleton.com. A nicely restored, clean Victorian brownstone on a quiet street in Portland's historic district. Breakfast included. 6

Inn at St John 939 Congress St ⓣ207/773-6481 or 1-800/636-9127, ⓦwww.innatstjohn.com. Elegant but comfy rooms in a renovated old hotel located a short drive from the museums. No elevator. Breakfast included. 6

Portland Harbor Hotel 468 Fore St ⓣ207/775-9090 or 1-888/798-9090, ⓦwww.theportlandharborhotel.com. One of the city's newer hotels, in a great location near the waterfront; many rooms overlook the English garden. 8

Portland Regency Hotel 20 Milk St ⓣ207/774-4200 or 1-800/727-3436, ⓦwww.theregency.com. Fancy rooms – some with bay views – in a beautifully renovated brick armory building not far from the Old Port. 7–8

Super 8 108 Larrabee Rd ⓣ207/854-1881 or 1-800/800-8000, ⓦwww.super8.com. Budget suites near I-95 with microwaves, fridges, and a free continental breakfast. 6

Travelodge 1200 Brighton Ave ⓣ207/774-6106, ⓦwww.travelodge.com. Good-value chain offers affordable doubles on the western edge of the peninsula near the Maine Medical Center. 5

West End Inn 146 Pine St ⓣ1-800/338-1377, ⓦwww.westendbb.com. Charming 1871 brick townhouse in the historic district. Full breakfast included. 7

The City

Central Portland consists of two main districts. **Downtown** refers to the city's business district, bisected by Congress Street, where you'll also find several museums, the Civic Center, and a smattering of good restaurants. The **Old Port**, to the southeast, bustles with lively shops, bars, and eateries. Commercial Street runs along the water's edge, but Fore Street, just inland, has most of the area's attractions.

Downtown Portland

Portland's single best destination, the **Portland Museum of Art** (PMA), in the heart of downtown at 7 Congress Square (Tues–Thurs, Sat & Sun 10am–5pm, Fri 10am–9pm; June to mid-Oct also Mon 10am–5pm; $8; ⓣ207/775-6148, ⓦwww.portlandmuseum.org), was designed in 1988 by the renowned I.M. Pei and Partners, and many parts of the museum afford superb views of the bay – on a clear day you can see all the way to Mount Washington in New Hampshire. One of the museum's highlights is its stunning collection of glass: encompassing the 1840s to the present, the European and American lamps and vases glow in a riot of color as if naturally fluorescent. Elsewhere, ships and images of the sea are prevalent, as reflected by Winslow Homer's sentimental seascapes. An earthy alternative to the maritime pieces is *Woodsmen in the Woods of Maine* by Waldo Peirce. Rich and dark, it was commissioned by the Westbrook Post Office in 1937 and is displayed here with the clouded-glass mailroom door still intact. There's also a strong collection of modernist works by the likes of Nevelson, Indiana, and Hartley. Adjoining the main building is the impressive Federal-style **McLellan House**, built for a city shipping magnate in 1801, and the **L.D.M. Sweat Memorial Galleries** (1911), both recently opened after twenty years of closure thanks to an $8 million restoration. The Sweat Galleries focus on American art (especially landscapes) through 1900, incorporating both decorative and fine-art pieces. Scenes specific to Maine are well displayed here in works by naturalist Frederic Church (see the romantic *Mount Katahdin from Millinocket Camp*) and in the evocative Wyeth pieces.

Several excellent art galleries have recently taken hold in the newly resurgent downtown, including the well-tailored **Institute of Contemporary Art** at the Maine College of Art, 522 Congress St (Wed & Fri–Sun 11am–5pm, Thurs 11am–7pm; free; ⓣ207/879-5742), which showcases works that demonstrate new perspectives and trends in contemporary art, such as William Pope.L's *eRacism*, best known for *Eating the Wall Street Journal*, wherein the artist chews and regurgitates pages from the corporate-minded newspaper. Also worth a look, **The Museum of African Culture**, 122 Spring St (Tues–Fri 10.30am–5pm, Sat 12.30–5pm; free; ⓣ207/871-7188), is the only museum in New England devoted exclusively to African art and culture. It houses an eye-catching collection of sub-Saharan masks with complete ceremonial regalia.

Not all that much of old Portland survives thanks to the fires over the years, though various grand mansions can be seen along Congress and Danforth streets in the downtown area. A few of the oldest houses are open to the public, most notably the **Wadsworth-Longfellow House** at 485 Congress St (June–Oct Tues–Sun 10am–4pm; Nov–May Wed–Sat noon–4pm; $7), Portland's first brick house, built in 1785 by Revolutionary War hero Peleg Wadsworth, grandfather of poet Henry Wadsworth Longfellow. Longfellow spent his boyhood here, and at age 13 published his first poem in the *Portland Evening Gazette*. The house is furnished with a hodgepodge of Federalist furniture, all original to the Longfellow family. Next door, at 489 Congress St, the **Maine Historical Society**

(June–Oct daily 10am–4pm; free with admission to Wadsworth-Longfellow House, otherwise $4; Ⓦwww.mainehistory.org) has rotating displays of art and Maine-related historical artifacts, as well as an extensive library.

Another building that survived the fires, slightly west of downtown, is the Georgian **Tate House**, 1270 Westbrook St (mid-June to Sept Tues–Sat 10am–4pm, Sun 1–4pm; Oct Fri–Sun same times; $7; Ⓣ207/774-6177, Ⓦwww.tatehouse.org). As mast agent for the British Royal Navy, Tate found financial success marking the tallest, broadest, straightest pines as property of the king – no matter whose land they were on – and using them for ship masts. The exterior of the building merits attention for its clerestory, an indented wall rising above the gambrel roof on the second story, while the furnishings and decorations inside reflect a style typical of a wealthy eighteenth-century official. Closer to the Old Port, the **Victoria Mansion**, 109 Danforth St (May & June Tues–Sat 10am–4pm, Sun 1pm–5pm; July–Oct daily 10am–4pm, Sun 10am–5pm; $10; Ⓣ207/772-4841, Ⓦwww.victoriamansion.org), is an Italianate brownstone constructed in 1859 as a summer home for luxury hotelier Ruggles S. Morse. The exquisite interior includes fresco-ornamented walls and ceilings, a freestanding staircase made of Santo Domingo mahogany, and floor-to-ceiling gold-leaf mirrors.

Old Port district

For relaxed wandering, the restored **Old Port Exchange** near the quayside, between Exchange and Pearl streets, is quite entertaining, with all sorts of red-brick antiquarian shops, specialist book and music stores (especially on Exchange Street), and other esoterica. Several companies operate **boat trips** from the nearby wharves. The *Palawan*, a vintage 58-foot ocean racer, sails

Portland's festivals

As with many larger New England cities, Portland hosts its share of **festivals** outside of the typical holiday celebrations. Craft booths, plenty of food, and opportunities for people-watching are standard. In some cases, you should call ahead to double-check dates.

Old Port Festival, first Sun in June. Old Port Exchange. Crafts, food booths, music, and other live entertainment (Ⓣ207/772-6828).

Greek Heritage Festival, last weekend in June. 133 Pleasant St. Greek food (especially good fresh-baked pastries), traditional music, and folk-dancing demonstrations (Ⓣ207/774-0281).

Portland Symphony Orchestra Independence Pops Concert, around July 4. Free outdoor concert by the PSO followed by fireworks (Ⓣ207/773-6128).

Italian Street Festival, weekend before Aug 15, Feast of Assumption. 72 Federal St. Ethnic celebration featuring live bands, kids' games, and indulgent Italian food (Ⓣ207/773-0748).

MS Regatta Harborfest, mid-Aug. Sailboats and tugboats strut their stuff in the harbor while a cocktail party and shoreside festival carry on at the pier (Ⓣ207/781-7961).

Sidewalk Art Festival, late Aug. Congress St. The downtown area is blocked off for the largest art show in northern New England (Ⓣ207/772-5800).

Maine Brewer's Festival, first Sat in Nov. Maine's finest microbrewers serve up their best beers alongside food, games, and tunes ($22; Ⓣ207/772-2739, Ⓦwww.mainebrew.com).

Holiday Gala, mid-Dec. The Victorian Mansion is bedecked in its Christmas finery and guests enjoy holiday foods and tunes.

around the harbor and to the Casco Bay islands and lighthouses from DiMillo's Marina off Commercial Street (daily in summer; 2hr trip morning $20, 3hr afternoon $40; ⓣ207/773-2163 or 1-800/284-PAL1), while Bay View Cruises, 184 Commercial St, offers seal-watching excursions all year (May weekends, June–Sept daily, fewer in winter; $8; ⓣ207/761-0496). Casco Bay Lines runs a twice-daily **mailboat** all year, and additional **cruises** in summer, to six of the scenic Calendar Islands in Casco Bay, from its terminal at Commercial and Franklin streets ($10–18.50; ⓣ207/774-7871, ⓦwww.cascobaylines.com). Long, Peaks, and Cliff islands all have accommodation or camping facilities.

If you follow Portland's waterfront to the end of the peninsula, you'll come to the **Eastern Promenade**. Once the bastion of the town's wealthy families, (who've since moved on to the **Western Promenade**), it became almost exclusively residential after the last fire and is remarkably peaceful for being so close to downtown. A big beach lies below the headland, while above, at the top of Munjoy Hill at 138 Congress St, is the shingled, eight-sided 1807 **Portland Observatory** (June to mid-Oct 10am–5pm; $5), the oldest remaining signal tower in the country; you can climb its 103 steps for an exhilarating view of the bay and the city.

Cape Elizabeth

Across the harbor, in Cape Elizabeth at Fort Williams State Park, lies the **Portland Head Lighthouse**, the oldest in Maine, commissioned in 1790 by George Washington. An active light still in use by the coast guard, it also houses an excellent **museum** on the history of Maine's lighthouses (June–Oct daily 10am–4pm; April–May & Nov weekends only 10am–4pm; $2). The small but intelligent collection traces lighthouse history back to 300BC when Ptolemy II of Egypt built a lighthouse on the island of Pharos in Alexandria harbor. Best are the displays combining lighthouse literature and art, such as Longfellow's paean *The Lighthouse* and reproductions of Edward Hopper's forlorn watercolors, both

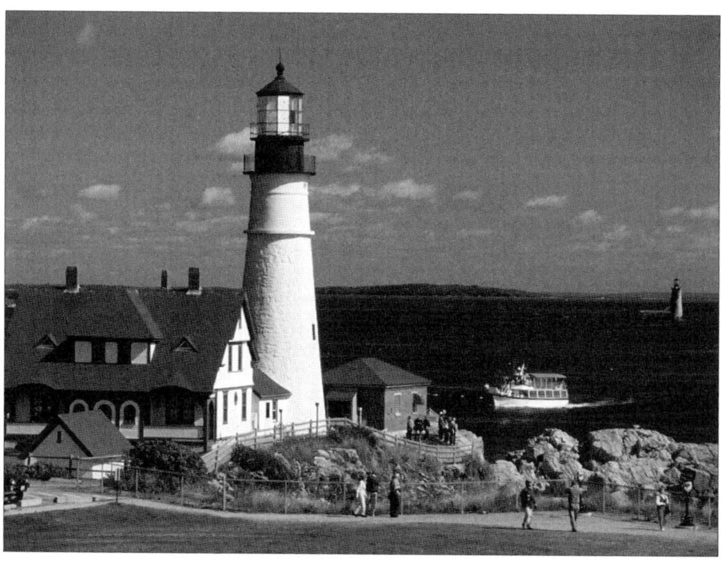

△ Portland Head Lighthouse

of which were inspired by Portland Head. A few miles south is another lighthouse commissioned by George Washington, **Cape Elizabeth Lighthouse**, one of the more recognizable landmarks of the state, and captured on countless postcards and posters. This lighthouse is also still active, and the unpredictable, ear-splitting blasts from its horn jolt anyone in the vicinity. A short drive through the neighborhoods of Cape Elizabeth, with its stately homes and comfortable spaces, is also pleasant. Nearby, **Two Lights State Park** has easy shoreside trails and picnic areas (day-use fee $1.50).

Eating

Portland's relatively low rents and young, hip population have given rise to a concentration of experimental, though still quite affordable, **restaurants**. Throw a rock in the Old Port district and you'll hit one; check around the downtown area near the Portland Museum of Art, too. Also in the downtown area, you'll find the **Portland Public Market**, at Monument Square between Elm and Preble streets (Mon–Sat 7am–7pm, Sun 10am–5pm; ⓣ207/228-2000, ⓦwww.portlandmarket.com), an indoor food bazaar where you can buy fresh breads, organically grown vegetables, a variety of local beers, specialty cheeses, and a whole host of other yuppyish eats. Be wary of the larger, more touristed restaurants along the waterfront, where the ambience may be grand, but the food is probably bland. People eat out a lot here, so at least inquire about reservations Thursday through Sunday.

Restaurants

Aurora Provisions 64 Pine St ⓣ207/871-9060. Upscale market/deli with mouth-watering sandwiches, a full selection of coffee, drinks, pastries, salads, desserts, and a small seating area. Perfect for picnic fare. Closed Sun.

Becky's 390 Commercial St ⓣ207/773-7070. The best breakfast spot in Portland, serving hearty American portions, including homemade muffins, from 4am (for the fishermen) until 9pm. Vintage Maine.

Blue Spoon 89 Congress St ⓣ207/773-1116. Over the hill in location only, beloved *Blue Spoon* features modern fare like the locally famous chicken under a brick, or the open-faced prosciutto and poached egg. Open for lunch and dinner.

Federal Spice 225 Federal St ⓣ207/774-6404. Eclectic international wraps and quesadillas influenced by Southeast Asian and Caribbean cuisine, all very hot, spicy, and cheap.

Five Fifty Five 555 Congress St ⓣ207/761-0555. Upscale, organic dinner spot with garlicky mussels and line-caught Atlantic swordfish, served in an airy dining room.

Flatbread Company 72 Commercial St ⓣ207/772-8777. Tasty pizza, made with flatbread dough, their own sauce, and all-natural ingredients, in a hip waterfront location.

Fore Street 288 Fore St ⓣ207/775-2717. One of Portland's foremost restaurants, in a huge old warehouse space, serving the likes of white carrot bisque and *panzanella* with fresh mozzarella. Reservations recommended.

Herb's Gully 55 Oak St ⓣ207/780-8080. Tasty, creatively constructed burritos ("hand-rolled fatties"), quesadillas, and side dishes. They also mix drinks like the "kind buzz" (banana, honey, vanilla, and bee pollen).

J's Oyster 5 Portland Pier ⓣ207/772-4828. Classic old-school raw bar serving oysters and steamers right on the waterfront.

Lobster Shack 225 Two Lights Rd, five miles south of Portland in Cape Elizabeth ⓣ207/799-1677. Perhaps the best seafood-eating scenery in all of Maine – lighthouse to the left, unruly ocean to the right. Plus, the seafood is fabulous.

Mim's 205 Commercial St ⓣ207/347-7478. Contemporary fare served in a sleek, modern setting, replete with faux suede and Ikea-esque seating. Reservations recommended.

Natasha's 82 Exchange St ⓣ207/774-4004. Upscale, intimate restaurant serving composed New American cuisine like crispy peanut tofu and merlot-braised apple medallions.

Norm's East End Grill 47 Middle St ⓣ207/253-1710. Crave-worthy barbecue joint satisfying a nice mix of customers. The classics (pulled pork, corn bread, barbecued chicken) are all well represented here, with some good veggie options too.

Ribollita 41 Middle St ⓣ207/774-2972. Reasonably priced, fresh handmade pasta and other Italian fare in a cozy, narrow, brick-walled dining room. Closed Sun and Mon.

RiRa 72 Commercial St ⓣ207/774-4446. A more creative choice for dinner than one would expect from an authentic Irish bar (albeit, one with cupboards full of antique china in the dining room). Lunch, featuring some more traditional Irish favorites, can be had for under $10.
Shays Grill Pub 18 Monument Square ⓣ207/773-2626. Home to what is possibly Portland's best burger and onion strings; atmospheric drinking ambience.
Silly's 40 Washington St ⓣ207/772-0360. Burgers, pies, and particularly fine milkshakes in a space adorned with wacky Americana.
Street and Co. 33 Wharf St ⓣ207/775-0887. A great special-occasion seafood spot where the cuts are grilled, blackened, or broiled to perfection. There are a few good non-fish items as well. Reservations recommended.
Walter's Café 15 Exchange St ⓣ207/871-9258. New American cuisine in a hip, high-ceilinged dining room with an open kitchen. Most entrees go for $13–20.
Wine Bar 38 Wharf St ⓣ207/773-6667. Really more a restaurant than either a café or wine bar. They do serve good vino by the glass and bottle, and have inventive French/New American fusion fare, such as lobster and brie ravioli, and chicken and apple burritos. Very casual.
Yosaku 1 Danforth St ⓣ207/780-0880. Fantastic, extensive sushi and sashimi menu. Patrons content themselves by sitting at the outdoor deck with its mini-Japanese garden.

Drinking and nightlife

The bar–restaurant distinction is blurry in Portland; most watering holes serve food, and many eateries have good selections of microbrews and wine. There are a good many **bars** scattered throughout the Old Port district, of which a number feature live rock music. ID policies are strict and bars aren't allowed to serve after 1am. **Cafés** are becoming increasingly popular with Portland's youthful population and frequently offer Internet access. On the weekends they're generally as crowded and lively as bars. Portland's **club scene** is somewhat tamer, but there are a few raucous dance and music venues.

Cafés

Arabica Coffee House 16 Free St ⓣ207/879-0792. Mellow café with numerous types of imported java. Comfortable but limited seating.
Breaking New Grounds 13 Exchange St ⓣ207/761-5637. Sleek but warm two-story interior, packed with young hipsters. Particularly strong caffeine beverages.
Coffee by Design 67 India St ⓣ207/879-2233. They roast their own beans at this small local chain. There is also a wide assortment of teas and some tasty pastries.
JavaNet Café 37 Exchange St ⓣ1-800/JAVA-NET. It's part of a burgeoning chain, but the coffee's good, the couches are comfy, and there's Internet access for $9 an hour.
Portland Roasting Co 111 Commercial St ⓣ207/761-9525. Euro-style coffeehouse with in-store roasted beans and the standard cappuccinos and lattes.

Bars and microbreweries

Amigos 9 Dana St, off Commercial St ⓣ207/772-0772. In summer it's a bit of a lust magnet, but that's not necessarily a bad thing. All stripes of Portlanders squish into this low-key, centrally located bar.
Brian Boru Public House 57 Center St ⓣ207/780-1506. Traditional Irish pub serving Guinness, with a big, if typical, menu and great outdoor deck.
Bull Feeney's 375 Fore St ⓣ207/773-7201. They go the extra mile here, matching up your beer with a glass displaying the corresponding brand name – it's thought to bring out the flavor. Another Irish option, with live music on the weekends.
Great Lost Bear 540 Forest Ave ⓣ207/772-0300, ⓦwww.greatlostbear.com. According to *The Malt Advocate*, one of the top ten beer bars in the US. Try one from their 53 taps, including fifteen state microbrews. Decent pub grub, too.
Gritty McDuff's 396 Fore St ⓣ207/772-2739, ⓦwww.grittys.com. Portland's first brewpub, making Portland Head Pale Ale and Black Fly Stout. Food, folk music, long wooden benches, and a friendly (if a little self-consciously British) atmosphere, which can get rowdy on Saturday nights.
Rivalries 10 Cotton St ⓣ207/774-6604. Packed with energetic fans, this recent addition to Portland's scene is a clean, hip, two-story sports bar.
Una 505 Fore St ⓣ207/828-0300. Rare for this neck of the woods: a sophisticated martini bar with chi-chi decor, all to the tune of a local DJ.

Dance clubs and music venues

Asylum 121 Center St ⓣ207/772-8274. Loud, somewhat stylish dance club/bar popular with Portland's twenty-something singles set. DJ and dancing on weekends as well as occasional up-and-coming bands. Cover $5–14. They also have a sports bar, so you can check the score between tunes.

Big Easy Blues Club 55 Market St ⓣ207/871-8817. Mellow blues joint with local acts, mostly blues with some jazz and rockabilly shows, rather tame on weekdays; more active on weekends.

Geno's 625 Congress St Rock (no phone). Venue featuring mostly local indie acts.

Port Hole 20 Custom House Wharf ⓣ207/780-6533. Their summertime Sunday reggae shows, held on a sunny deck in the harbor, are seriously bumping.

Space Gallery 518 Congress St ⓣ207/828-5600, ⓦwww.space538.org. Cool, artsy space which displays contemporary works and books some moderately rocking bands.

Performing arts and film

There are several options for the **performing arts** in Portland. Chamber music, opera, dance, and touring theater productions are often featured as part of PCA Great Performances series held at Merrill Auditorium (tickets ⓣ207/842-0800, ⓦwww.pcagreatperformances.org), while the Portland Stage Company puts on larger-scale productions at the Portland Performing Arts Center, 25A Forest Ave (ⓣ207/774-0465). Portland Parks and Recreation (ⓣ207/756-8130, ⓦwww.ci.portland.me.us) sponsors free outdoor noontime and evening jazz and blues concerts at various locations throughout the city during the summer. You can find indie-type films at The Movies, 10 Exchange St (ⓣ207/772-9600). The free *Portland Phoenix* (ⓦwww.portlandphoenix.com) has listings of all local events. Maine's biggest gigs take place each summer at Old Orchard Beach, roughly ten miles south of Portland, but some mid-level shows come to town at the Merrill Auditorium, 20 Myrtle St. Call PorTix (ⓣ207/842-0800) for all area ticketing sales and information.

Sports

Sports fans should take a trip to Hadlock Field, an intimate baseball stadium on Park Avenue where the minor-league **Portland Sea Dogs** (ⓦwww.portlandseadogs.com; now affiliated with the Red Sox) play from May to October. Tickets are wildly inexpensive (the prices top out at about $8). Call ⓣ207/879-9500 for ticket and schedule information. Other sporting choices: Portland Pirates hockey (ⓣ207/828-4665) and harness racing in nearby Scarborough Downs (ⓣ207/883-4331).

Freeport

Sixteen miles north of Portland along the coast, **FREEPORT** is simply one long outlet shopping mall, though the town was once one of Maine's primary shipbuilding centers. Huge logs were brought here that would ultimately be used for ship masts; this is still evident in the wide shape of the town square at Main and Bow streets, which was fashioned to give the gigantic logs plenty of room to swing as the carts turned on the way to the mast landing. Freeport's prominence was such that the town's **Jameson Tavern** is believed (though not without dispute) to have been the place where the treaty separating Maine from Massachusetts was signed in 1820.

The shipping industry fell into disrepair following the Civil War, but Freeport managed a big comeback fifty years later when a fishing-boot maker by the

Sabbathday Lake Shaker Community

North of Portland off of Rte-26, at 707 Shaker Rd in **NEW GLOUCESTER**, is the Sabbathday Lake Shaker Community, the last remaining active Shaker community. Founded in 1783, the village is made up of eighteen buildings, all constructed in the beautifully functional fashion typical of the Shakers. Though their numbers have dwindled to a mere seven, the remaining Shaker members remain true to their simple, celibate, religious lives, and they welcome visitors to their 10am Sunday worship service. Tours of the grounds (every hour on the half, starting at 10.30am, last tour at 3.15pm; $6.50 introductory tour, $8 extended tour) take in several of the buildings, including the meeting house, where the Shaker Museum has many of the religious community's innovative furniture, textile, and farm-tool designs on display (end of May to mid-Oct Mon–Sat 10am–4.30pm; ⓣ207/926-4597, ⓦwww.shaker.lib.me.us). It's all well worth the detour, though the Canterbury Shaker Village in New Hampshire (see p.475) is more impressive.

name of **Leon L. Bean** planted the seeds of what has become an unbelievably successful outdoors-wear manufacturer – it's now Maine's number-one tourist destination. L.L. Bean's store stood alone along Freeport's Main Street for decades until the 1980s, when it was joined by countless factory outlets and the town developed its current character.

Arrival and information

The best way to get to Freeport is by **car** – there's no public transport, and the closest a bus comes is to Portland, from where you'll need to take a **taxi** or van the rest of the way. Try Classy Taxi (ⓣ1-800/499-0663) or Freeport Taxi (ⓣ207/865-9494). Mermaid Transportation (ⓣ1-800/696-2463, ⓦwww.gomermaid.com) also offers **van** service to Freeport from Portland for $100 round-trip. Drop by the incredibly complete Freeport Merchants' Association, in a restored old tower at 23 Depot St (ⓣ207/865-1212 or 1-800/865-1994), for reams of area **information** as well as public restrooms, an ATM, and a staff of senior citizens who will provide far more assistance than you'll ever need.

Accommodation

There's no shortage of quality **B&Bs** in town, but if you're low on cash, some cheap motels line US-1 south of Freeport. (Better still, stay in Portland and make a quick trip through Freeport.) The best nearby **camping** is at the oceanside *Recompense Shores*, 134 Burnett Rd (ⓣ207/865-9307; $16–30), near Casco Bay, which has one hundred well-kept and -spaced sites. You can also camp along the shores of the bay at the *Flying Point Campground*, 10 Lower Flying Point Rd (ⓣ207/865-4569; $25), which is near nature trails and the town beach.

Best Western Freeport Inn 32 US-1 S ⓣ207/865-3106. Clean, comfortable rooms. They also have a café that serves homespun breakfasts good enough to attract the locals. ❼

Brewster House 180 Main St ⓣ207/865-4121. B&B set in a beautifully restored Queen Anne cottage with antique furnishings. ❻

Clipper Inn 181 Main St ⓣ207/865-9623 or 1-866/866-4002. Seven pleasant rooms in a vintage sea captain's home. There is also an enclosed hot springs spa, bike access, and fabulous breakfasts. ❼

Harraseeket Inn 162 Main St ⓣ207/865-9377 or 1-800/342-6423. Wonderful, albeit pricey, clapboard B&B inn with some eighty rooms and an indoor pool. ❽

Maine Idyll Motor Court 1411 US-1 N ⓣ207/865-4201. Basic but romantic cottage quarters in woodsy area a few miles north of town. Blueberry muffins in the morning. ❹

Village Inn 186 Main St ⓣ207/865-3236 or 1-800/998-3649. Motel-style units in the rear building, breakfast in the dining room of the proprietors' home. ❺

The Town

Freeport owes virtually all of its current prosperity to the invention by Leon Leonwood Bean, in 1912, of a particularly ugly rubber-soled fishing boot. The boot is still available, and **L.L. Bean's** has grown into a multi-national clothing conglomerate, housed in an enormous 90,000-square-foot factory outlet building on Main Street (ⓣ1-800/441-5713 or 207/552-6879, ⓦwww.llbean.com) that literally never closes. In theory, this is so pre-dawn hunting expeditions can stock up; all the relevant equipment is available for rent or sale, and the store runs regular workshops to teach backcountry lore. In practice, though, the late-night hours seem more geared toward local high school students, who attempt to fall asleep in the tents without being noticed by store personnel. It's worth a spin just to gawk at the four stories packed with more camping supplies and dense plaid outerwear than the eye can see; there's also a full café, a trout pond with a waterfall, and a self-congratulatory chronicle of the chain's history located just inside the main entrance. There are plenty of other **outlet stores** nearby, with chic fashion stops like Donna Karan, Brooks Brothers, and Burberry, alongside the ones geared toward rugged outdoorsmen (Patagonia, Timberland, and North Face). The **Frost Gully Gallery**, 1159 US-1 N (Mon–Fri noon–5pm; ⓣ207/865-2555), usually has a fine display of oil paintings by both local and nationally known artists, and will provide a respite from the blatant commercialism found elsewhere in town.

Now a lone reference to the city's life before Bean, the **Soldiers and Sailors Monument**, on Bow Street, was dedicated by Civil War general Joshua Chamberlain, and boasts cannons that were used at the Battle of Bull Run as well as Sherman's march to the sea. To get even farther away from the shops, however, head a mile south of Freeport to the sea, where the very green cape visible just across the water is **Wolfe's Neck State Park**. In summer, for just $1.50, you can follow hiking and nature trails along the unspoiled fringes of the headland. For a more bizarre change of pace, check out the **Desert of Maine**, 95 Desert Rd, exit 20 off I-295 (May to mid-Oct; $7.75; ⓣ207/865-6962, ⓦwww.desertofmaine.com), a vast expanse of privately owned sand deposited just inland from Freeport by a glacier that slid through eleven thousand years ago. This tiny, self-contained desert ecosystem spread and ultimately engulfed the surrounding homes and trees; you can still see them today, half-buried in the sand. There's a kitschy gift shop for souvenirs, a display of little test tubes of sand from locations all over the world, and a small museum housed in a 1783 barn.

Eating and drinking

Restaurants in the area cater to the upscale crowd that seeks out the outlets. They're all done up to match the town's strict aesthetic zoning laws; even the *McDonald's* is disguised by a weathered-clapboard motif.

Broad Arrow Tavern 162 Main St, in the *Harraseeket Inn* ⓣ207/865-9377. Gourmet pizzas, pulled-pork sandwiches, and a great lunch buffet.

China Rose 23 Main St ⓣ207/865-6886. Reputed to be some of Maine's best Szechuan and Hunan cuisine. Also has a surprisingly good sushi bar upstairs.

Conundrum Wine Bistro 117 Rte-1 S ⓣ207/865-4321. The best food in Freeport. Most people come for the swanky martinis – then they get hooked on the fresh, eclectic entrees.

Harraseeket Lunch & Lobster Co off Rte-1, South Freeport ⓣ207/865-4888. Extending on its wooden jetty into the peaceful bay, this makes a great outdoor lunch spot.

Isabella's Sticky Buns Bakery Café 2 School St ⓣ207/865-6635. Breakfast, coffee, and sandwiches; open from 6am.

Jameson Tavern 115 Main St ⓣ207/865-4196. It's a tourist trap – this is allegedly where the papers were signed that separated Maine from Massachusetts. Meat-oriented menu highlighted by steak *au poivre*. Wash it down with the house brew, Jameson's Black and Tan. The taproom menu has lighter, less expensive fare.

Lobster Cooker 39 Main St ⓣ207/865-4349. A particularly good seafood restaurant specializing in lobster and crabmeat rolls.

The Mid-Coast

Stretching roughly from the quiet college town of **Brunswick** up to blue-collar **Bucksport**, Maine's central coast is a study in geographic, economic, and cultural contrasts. The shore here is physically different from the southern coast, with engaging peninsulas such as the **Harpswells** and **Pemaquid Point**, which provide divergent alternatives to well-traveled US-1. Much of this region prospered in the late nineteenth century as a major shipbuilding and trading center, as evidenced by its wealth of attractive old captains' homes; today, only **Bath** remains as a ship manufacturer. Throughout, the focus is still unquestionably the sea, be it for livelihood, sustenance, or entertainment. Consequently, one of the best ways to see the area is by boat; from most coastal towns, you can catch a scenic maritime tour. Remote **Monhegan Island**, a lobstermen's hub and artists' retreat eleven miles offshore, is accessible only by boat.

Lobsters are a way of life in Maine, and the alien-looking crustaceans are especially important to **Rockland**, home to the most active lobster industry in the state. Busy **Camden**, just beyond Rockland, is known for its fleet of recreational **windjammers**, while picturesque fishing villages such as **Round Pond** and **Tenants Harbor** – tiny windows into the real Maine – can be found throughout, somehow managing to coexist with overrun summer tourist resorts like **Boothbay Harbor**, which is all but deserted in the winter. In the face of dwindling industry, it's hard to say what will happen to these smaller settlements; some have reluctantly begun to promote tourism.

Brunswick and the Harpswells

A few miles from Freeport is **BRUNSWICK**, home since 1794 to the private, well-respected Bowdoin College (ⓦwww.bowdoin.edu). The town is attractive enough, with a concentration of old brick and clapboard homes and buildings, but apart from the small campus itself – at the south end of Maine Street – and a couple of unobtrusive cafés, there's little evidence of student life here.

Information and getting around

The **Southern Midcoast Maine Chamber of Commerce** at 59 Pleasant St, Brunswick (ⓣ207/725-8797, ⓦwww.midcoastmaine.com) is particularly helpful, with a typical array of brochures and a knowledgeable staff. **Public transporta-**

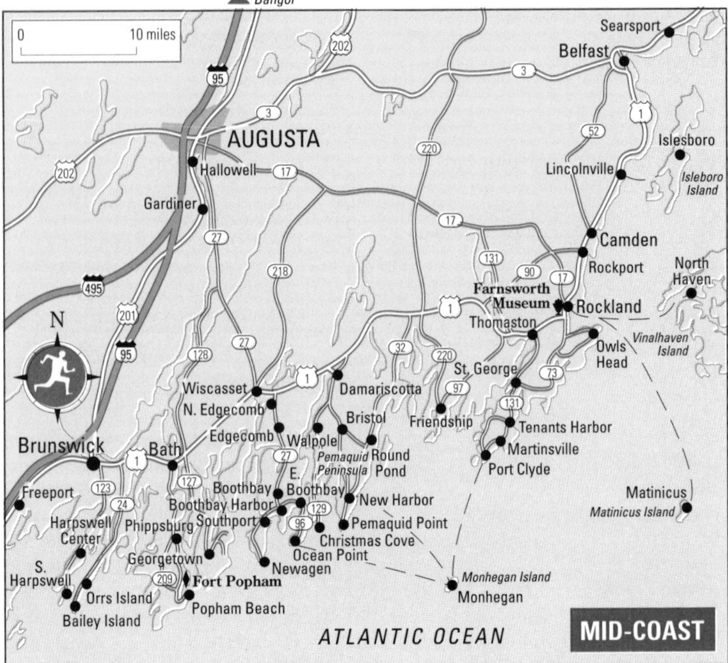

tion to and from Brunswick is fairly frequent: Vermont Transit/Greyhound stops at the depot at 206 Maine St (☎1-800/231-2222), from where you can catch **buses** to most other parts of New England. Concord Trailways (☎1-800/639-3317) stops at 162 Pleasant St before continuing north to Bangor or south to Boston.

If you're moving on from Brunswick to Rockland, consider the **Maine Coastal Rail Excursions** (July to late Aug Thurs–Sat 10am, Sun 10am & 8pm; Sept to late Oct Sat 10am, Sun 10am & 8pm; $30 round-trip ☎1-866/637-2457, www.maineeasternrailroad.com), which provides scenic two-hour coastal trips between the two towns (with stops in Bath and Wiscasset) in its restored Art Deco railcars. The train is equipped with a lounge and dining area; in the latter you can sip wine and watch the coastline go by – particularly stunning during the fall.

Accommodation

There are many **places to stay** in Brunswick, and most of the time you shouldn't have trouble finding a good-value room. The best place to **camp** is at the *Orrs Island Campground*, on the island of the same name in the **Harpswells** along Rte-24 (☎207/833-5595; end May to mid-Sept; $33–37).

Brunswick B&B 165 Park Row ☎207/729-4914 or 1-800/299-7914. A gracious old inn decorated with antiques and quilts. Located in the town center within walking distance of the college. 6

Captain Daniel Stone Inn 10 Water St ☎207/725-9898 or 1-877/573-5151. Elegant, Federal-style rooms and suites supplied with modern amenities. There is also a good restaurant with dining on the verandah in the summertime. 7

Harpswell Inn 108 Lookout Point, Harpswell ☎207/833-5509 or reserve at 1-800/843-5509.

An exceedingly comfortable place with nine rooms and three suites. It's centered on a pleasant green, overlooking lobster boats in the cove. ❻

Travelers Inn 130 Pleasant St ☎207/729-3364. A quiet and clean no-frills hotel half a mile from the town center. ❹

The Town

Free tours of **Bowdoin College**, which counts among its alumni Henry Wadsworth Longfellow, Nathaniel Hawthorne, and Franklin Pierce, begin at the Admissions Office (tours Mon–Fri 11.30am, 1.30pm & 3.30pm, Sat 11.30am only; ☎207/725-3958). After decades of disagreement, experts now generally conclude that former student Admiral Robert Peary was the first man to reach the North Pole in 1909; whatever the truth, his caribou fur parka, sled, and notebooks, to be found at the **Peary-MacMillan Arctic Museum** (Tues–Sat 10am–5pm, Sun 2–5pm; free; ☎207/725-3416), will be captivating to anyone who longs to experience ice floes and blizzards.

Another distinguished alum of the college, Civil War hero General Joshua Chamberlain graduated in 1852 and became a professor at the school in 1855. At the onset of the Civil War, and with no military training, he volunteered to serve, going on to fight in 24 battles and being awarded the Congressional Medal of Honor. Perhaps most notably, at the end of the war he was selected by Ulysses S. Grant to accept the formal surrender of the Confederate troops. He later became governor of Maine and, in 1871, president of Bowdoin College. The general's varied career is documented at the **General Joshua L. Chamberlain Museum**, 226 Maine St (May–Oct Tues–Sun 10am–4pm; $5; ☎207/729-6606). Tours of his restored home begin twice each hour.

The ideal time to visit Brunswick is Labor Day weekend, in early September, when the town hosts a **Bluegrass Festival** (☎207/725-6009) out on Thomas Point Beach, reached by following Rte-24 from Cook's Corner.

The Harpswells

South of Brunswick, the narrow, forested peninsulas collectively known as the **Harpswells** make for a welcome escape from the bustle of US-1. The only problem is that once you get to the end of one of the thrusts of land, you have to turn right back around and retrace your tracks. Rte-123 weaves down the Harpswell Neck past Maine's **oldest meeting house** (1757) in Harpswell

Harriet Beecher Stowe

Harriet Beecher Stowe (1811–96), a native of Litchfield, Connecticut, moved to Brunswick with her family from Ohio in the spring of 1850 when her husband, Calvin, took a position as a professor of religion at Bowdoin College. While her family struggled financially, it was here that Stowe formulated and wrote *Uncle Tom's Cabin*, the emotional anti-slavery novel that would go on to become the bestseller of the century. The book is credited with bringing morality and respectability to the abolitionist cause, and when Abraham Lincoln met Stowe years later he reportedly remarked, "So you're the little lady who wrote the book that started the war."

The passage of the 1850 **Fugitive Slave Act**, which stipulated that it was illegal for any citizen to assist an escaped slave and demanded that escaped slaves be apprehended and deported back to the "rightful" owner, outraged Stowe, who conceived of the death of Uncle Tom while sitting at worship in Brunswick's historic **First Parish Church**, 223 Maine St (☎207/729-7331). Encouraged by her husband, she published her violent story serially in the *National Era*, an abolitionist weekly. The **Harriet Beecher Stowe House** at 63 Federal St is now privately owned.

Center, and clear down to South Harpswell, where the Basin Cove Falls, created by the tidal flows, are popular with canoeists and kayakers. Rte-24 heads down another long, finger-like strip to **Bailey Island** (one of Casco Bay Cruise Line's stops), first crossing Orr's Island and then the **Cribstone Bridge**, which allows tides to flow right through it. Bailey Island's highlight is the **Giant Staircase**, off of Rte-24 on the eastern shore of the island, a massive waterfront stone stairway that's good for exploring. On Orr's Island, you can rent **kayaks** from H2Outfitters (Ⓣ207/833-5257 or 1-800/20-KAYAK); they also provide instruction and lead day and multi-day trips.

Eating and drinking

Back Street Bistro 11 Town Hall Place Ⓣ207/725-4060. Easily one of Brunswick's best restaurants, with the likes of bleu cheese-crusted steak and creative seasonal salads. Fine dining as well as inexpensive options in a side street off the square.

Bombay Mahal 99 Maine St Ⓣ207/729-5260. Inexpensive Indian specialties, such as a good chicken curry for $10. There is also a very affordable buffet on Sat & Sun.

Dolphin Marina 515 Basin Point Rd, South Harpswell Ⓣ207/833-6000. A tiny, almost hidden restaurant that serves up reasonably priced and simple yet robust seafood meals overlooking the working harbor – don't miss the fish chowder.

Little Dog Coffee Shop 87 Maine St Ⓣ207/721-9500. A cool little spot for hanging out. Lounge on one of their burgundy couches while sipping a *breve* and noshing on locally made ginger cookies.

Richard's 115 Maine St Ⓣ207/729-9673. Tasty, good-value German and American cuisine. The German entrees are available in two sizes, the larger of which is huge; you can also get your favorite wursts by the pound. Excellent beer selection, too.

Scarlet Begonias 212B Maine St Ⓣ207/721-0403. Creative home-cooking – soups, salads, pizza, and pasta – amidst plants bedecked with lobster lights. Great local eatery. Closed Sun.

Star Fish Grill 100B Pleasant St Ⓣ207/725-7828. A variety of fresh local seafood and vegetarian dishes served in an informal yet sophisticated atmosphere. Closed Mon.

Bath

Crossing the bridge into the small, community-minded town of **BATH** on US-1, it's hard to miss the enormous industrial supply cranes, tools of the massive **Bath Iron Works** shipyard, that jut rigidly into the skyline. The town of Bath has an exceptionally long history of **shipbuilding**; the first vessel to be constructed and launched here was the *Virginia* in 1607. Shipbuilding continued to be a major industry in the region throughout the eighteenth century, and between 1800 and 1830, nearly 288 ships set sail out of Bath's port. Bath Iron Works, founded in 1833, attracted job-seeking Irishmen in such numbers as to provoke a mob of anti-immigrant "Know Nothings" to burn down the local Catholic church in July 1854. Smaller trading vessels gave way to larger ships and in 1841, Clark & Sewall, one of the major builders at the time, launched the 1133-ton *Rappahannock*, at the time the world's largest ship. Despite changes in the shipbuilding market, Bath's military contracts were never in short supply, and during World War II more destroyers were built here than in all Japan.

Accommodation

Bath is not short on good-value **accommodations**, mostly of the inexpensive bed-and-breakfast variety. There's **camping** south of town along the water in Perry Cove at the *Meadowbrook Camping Area*, Meadowbrook Road (May–Sept; Ⓣ1-800/370-2267; $25). Two more campgrounds lurk farther south along the Phippsburg Peninsula: *Hermit Island* at the end of Rte-216 (late June to mid-

Oct; ⓣ207/443-2101; $35–40), where you can rent small boats and camp near a white-sand beach, and *Ocean View Park*, near Popham Beach (mid-May to Sept; ⓣ207/389-2564; $38).

Benjamin F. Packard House 45 Pearl St ⓣ207/443-6004 or 1-866/361-6004. Simple, period-furnished rooms in a 1790 Georgian house; full breakfast included. ❼

Fairhaven Inn 118 North Bath Rd ⓣ207/443-4391 or 1-888/443-4391. You'll find a bit of rural flavor here – hiking and cross-country skiing trails are right nearby – plus a fine breakfast. ❺

Galen C Moses House 1009 Washington St ⓣ207/442-8771. A colorful restored mansion whose proprietors are almost as eccentric as the fabulous decorations; a delicious gourmet breakfast is included. ❻

Inn at Bath 969 Washington St ⓣ207/443-4294, ⓦwww.innatbath.com. An 1810 Greek Revival house with friendly service and tastefully decorated rooms, some with wood-burning fireplaces. ❼

Small Point B&B 312 Small Point Rd, Rte-216, Phippsburg ⓣ207/389-1716. A restored 1890s farmhouse in an isolated coastal location, this B&B offers good value and wonderful morning repasts. ❺

The Town

With more than seven thousand employees, **Bath Iron Works**, two miles south of the town center, is the largest private employer in the state – and, thanks to a continuous stream of government contracts, the only shipbuilder remaining in Bath. As the place churns out massive destroyers and cruisers, shift workers keep the factory running around the clock; you should aim to avoid driving anywhere in Bath around 3.30pm, when shifts change and traffic slows. The Works are only open to visitors for special occasions such as ceremonial launchings – grand affairs that take place twice yearly and feature speeches by senators and the like. However, at the **Maine Maritime Museum**, 243 Washington St, next to the Iron Works (daily 9.30am–5pm; $9.75 for two days; ⓣ207/443-1316, ⓦwww.bathmaine.com), you can tour the old Percy & Small shipyard, explore several visiting historic vessels, or browse the Maritime History Building, where galleries house an interesting range of ship-related paintings, photographs, and

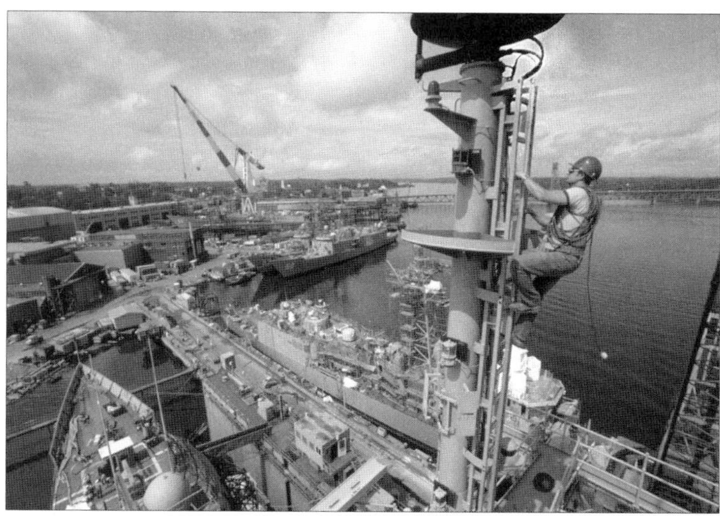

△ Bath Iron Works

AMC huts on Georgetown Peninsula

The **Appalachian Mountain Club** (general info ⓣ603/466-2727, for reservations call Loretta at 781/784-6971, ⓦwww.outdoors.org) maintains a couple of excellent low-budget **accommodations** on Georgetown Peninsula. At the *Knubble Bay Camp*, a friendly riverfront cabin with a nice porch and kitchen ($75 per day for three people, $11 each additional person; cabin rented exclusively to one party), there's bunk space for fifteen as well as tent sites. The site is accessible by car and parking is available ($1 per day). You can also rent canoes for $20 per day. A much more primitive option is the secluded wilderness campground at Beal Island (closed in winter; $12 per night), which is accessible only by canoe or kayak from the cabin.

artifacts. The museum also runs **boat trips** along the Kennebec River (an extra $10; call for schedule).

A pretty fourteen-mile drive south along Rte-209 leads to gorgeous **Popham Beach** ($4; ⓣ207/389-1335), at the end of the Phippsburg Peninsula, and part of a 529-acre state park. Outside of its scenic sands, you can explore **Fort Popham**, a nineteenth-century granite fort; it also has some nicely situated picnic benches that face the ocean. The **Georgetown Peninsula**, just east from Bath and down Rte-127, contains another superior beach at **Reid State Park** (ⓣ207/371-2303), where the dunes flatten out into three miles of beautiful sandy seashore.

Eating and drinking

The majority of Bath's **restaurants** are hearty no-nonsense grub-holes that cater to off-duty BIW employees.

Beale Street Barbeque and Grill 215 Water St ⓣ207/442-9514. Hickory-smoked Memphis barbecue plates in an airy, modern dining room. Takeout available.

The Cabin 552 Washington St ⓣ207/443-6224. Near the museum, the *Cabin* dishes out some of Maine's best pizza in dark, wooden booths.

Mae's Café 160 Centre St ⓣ207/442-8577. Brunch is particularly good, with inventive eggs benedict and French toast with homemade cinnamon-swirl bread. The desserts are also delicious.

Robinhood Free Meetinghouse Robinhood Rd, Georgetown, north of Bath along Rte-127 S ⓣ207/371-2188. This is one of Maine's premier restaurants, and worth the detour. Housed in Georgetown's former town hall, the creative American bistro integrates interesting touches of Cajun, Italian, and Szechuan cuisine into its $25-and-up entrees. Reservations recommended.

Solo Bistro Bistro 128 Front St ⓣ207/443-9815. Very hip bistro with bright, modern seating. Dinner is a tasty, upscale affair with the likes of spiced pork tenderloin and gorgonzola polenta.

Wiscasset

Pretty **WISCASSET**, ten miles on from Bath, is dominated by the bridge which carries US-1 over the Sheepscot River – and in the summer, the gently arching span is itself dominated by slow-moving cars usually headed to or from the coast farther north. Tourism has caught on here, perhaps partially on account of Wiscasset's easily accessible town center, right where the bridge meets the river's west bank. In recent years, the town lumberyard, grocery, and newsstand have all been replaced by antique shops and art galleries. Further erosion of the town's character occurred in 1997, when two famous **shipwrecks**, the four-masted schooners *Luther Little* and the *Hesper*, which had sat in the bay shallows for more than sixty years, were carted away, rotted beyond recognition.

The Town

Like many of Maine's coastal towns, Wiscasset prospered in the late eighteenth century as a shipbuilding and lumbering center. The large homes and mansions of wealthy shipping merchants and lumber barons still stand in the town's **historic district**, situated near US-1 and the waterfront, the best example of which is the towering white Federal-style **Nickels-Sortwell House** on 121 Main St (US-1) in the center of town (June to mid-Oct Wed–Sun 11am–4pm; $5; ⓣ207/882-6218). Commissioned by shipmaster William Nickels in 1807 (he lost his fortune only a few years later due to the devastating effect of the Embargo Act of 1807 and the War of 1812), the house features fine woodwork throughout and pretty surrounding grounds. Hourly tours lead through the period-furnished rooms and up the handsomely curved three-story stairway.

The **Musical Wonder House**, 18 High St (June–Oct daily 10am–5pm; tours 11am, 1pm & 3pm; $2; ⓣ207/882-7163 ⓦwww.musicalwonderhouse.com), is proof that if you amass enough of an obsolete technology, the collection will someday be remarkably fascinating. This 1852 sea captain's mansion is stuffed with player pianos, phonographs, and antique music boxes, most still in working order, and the eccentric owner of the place takes particular delight in showing off his bizarre treasures. Daily listening tours are separated into two parts following a roughly chronological order ($15 for one half or $20 for both); one half is enough.

A couple of blocks off the main drag, the **Maine Art Gallery**, housed in an old schoolhouse building on Warren Street (mid-May to Oct Tues–Sat 10am–4pm, Sun 1–4pm; free; ⓣ207/882-7511), exhibits – and sells – the works of up-and-coming Maine artists.

Practicalities

Area **accommodations** include the comfortable *Wiscasset Motor Lodge*, three miles south of town at 596 Bath Rd, aka US-1 (ⓣ1-800/732-8168; ❸; April–Nov), and the *Sheepscot River Inn* (ⓣ207/882-6343 or 1-800/437-5503; ❻), which offers rooms and cottages on Wiscasset Harbor in Edgecomb, north of town. The *Cod Cove Inn* on Rte-1 (ⓣ1-800/882-9586; ❼) is a bit more upscale, with balconies, views of the sea, cable TV, and phones, while the good-value *Marston House*, on Main Street at Middle (ⓣ207/882-6010; ❺; May–Oct), offers pretty rooms, a garden, and a tasty light breakfast. The lakeside *Chewonki* **campground**, 235 Chewonki Neck Rd, off Rte-144 via US-1 (ⓣ207/882-7426; $28–45), has tremendous river views as well as a friendly staff.

For **food**, head to *Sarah's Café* on US-1 (Water St) in the center of town (ⓣ207/882-7504), where you can get pizzas, salads, pasta, and even some Mexican dishes at the right price. Eating at *Red's Eats* (ⓣ207/882-6128), across the street from *Sarah's*, is bit of a gastronomic rite of passage. People line up and down the block to get their hands on his justly famous lobster rolls. Just down the street is *Treats* (ⓣ207/882-6192), with a great selection of gourmet baked and picnic goods, including sandwiches, fresh breads, imported cheeses, pastries, a huge wine selection, and good fresh coffee.

Boothbay Harbor

Due south from Wiscasset on Rte-27, the seaside town of **BOOTHBAY HARBOR** is for no obvious reason one of Maine's most crowded resorts.

Much of the town's history as a prosperous fishing and shipbuilding center has been obscured by tourism, which has been an active pursuit here since the late nineteenth century, resulting in a wealth of predictable shops and restaurants. Nevertheless, the village is beautifully situated on a well-protected harbor, and has a lively town center, some good inns, and ample opportunities to explore the sea and surrounding coast. For a more genuine Maine experience, however, you might try the less popular neighboring Pemaquid Peninsula or even the Blue Hill Peninsula, closer to Bar Harbor.

Arrival, information, and getting around

Less than fifteen miles south of US-1 along Rte-27, several towns near the end of the Boothbay Peninsula share similar names, the most active of which, Boothbay Harbor, is crowded into a tiny strip of land on the western edge, along **Commercial Street** and **Townsend Avenue**. The rest of the settlement spreads out around a tiny cove, thinning into quaint residential neighborhoods southwest on Southport Island and southeast towards Ocean Point. Oak and Commercial streets are one-way headed west, while Townsend is one-way east, heading back to Rte-27.

The town is not easily reached via **public transport**; Concord Trailways (ⓣ1-800/639-3317) stops in Wiscasset twice daily, from where you can catch a taxi on to Boothbay; call Platinum Plus (ⓣ207/380-5148). Courtesy **trolleys** run frequently from the Meadow Mall, on Rte-27 across the street from the Chamber of Commerce (10am–5pm in summer), to various points in town. The Chamber itself (ⓣ207/633-2353), is a very good source of **information**, with binders on local accommodations and a reservation service. The Boothbay Harbor Memorial Library, 4 Oak St (ⓣ207/633-3112), has free **Internet access**.

Though it's quite likely you'll have arrived by car, Boothbay Harbor is definitely not well designed for auto travel and is best explored **on foot**. The town's windy, narrow, and confusing streets are packed with cars all summer long and **parking** can be a nightmare. It's a good idea to park farther out – say along West, Howard, or Sea streets – or take the shuttle into town from the Meadow Mall.

Accommodation

You can always find some sort of **place to stay** in Boothbay Harbor, but if you want a shorefront room in the summer, plan to book at least a month in advance. In addition to several large, undistinguished resort-style motels there are lots of smaller bed-and-breakfasts in the town center and on the eastern shore of the harbor. Prices are considerably lower at the beginning and end of the tourist season – early June and Sept – and many places close down completely by mid-Oct.

Anchor Watch B&B 9 Eames Rd ⓣ207/633-7565, ⓦwww.anchorwatch.com. Pamper yourself in this beautiful little B&B with an ocean view, just outside the town center. ❼

Captain Sawyer's Place 55 Commercial St ⓣ207/633-2290. The rooms are not huge, but the staff is very friendly and the price is cheaper than most of the other places on the strip. Continental breakfast included. ❺

Fisherman's Wharf Inn 22 Commercial St ⓣ1-800/628-6872. Very centrally located (it's right on the wharf) with large, clean rooms, many with porches facing the working harbor. ❻

The Thistle Inn 55 Oak St ⓣ207/633-3541. If you're willing to forego a water view, this vintage sea captain's home has beautiful rooms, unbelievable food, and fantastic innkeepers – it's maybe the best accommodation in town. Open all year. ❺

Topside Inn 60 McKown St ⓣ207/633-5404. Pleasant rooms in an old sea captain's house on the top of a hill; great view of the harbor. Open May to mid-Oct. ❻

Welch House 56 McKown St ⓣ1-800/279-7313, ⓦwww.welchhouse.com. This gabled white-clapboard house perched on a hill affords excellent views from its rooftop deck. Light and airy guest rooms are tastefully furnished and a buffet breakfast is included. ❻

The Town

Aside from taking a quick stroll around the town's hilly, shop-lined streets, Boothbay Harbor's main attraction lies in the inordinate number of **boat trips** on offer from the harbor behind Commercial Street. Some depart for Monhegan Island, while others circle along the rocky coast, taking in the dramatic scenery from the water. Balmy Days Cruises (ⓣ207/633-2284 or 1-800/298-2284) is as good as any of the outfits on the waterfront, with all-day trips to Monhegan Island costing $32 and harbor tours for $12. A cruise aboard the traditional windjammer *Eastwind*, departing from the wharf three times daily (May–Oct; 2.5hr round-trip; ⓣ207/633-6598), costs $24. In general, smaller boats depart from Ocean Point; try Windborne Cruises forty-foot sailboat (ⓣ207/882-1020). If you'd rather explore the coast under your own power, contact the Tidal Transit Company (ⓣ207/633-7140), which offers **kayak** rentals ($15/hr) and tours ($35) and also rents **bikes** ($25/day).

On foot, the most immediate view of the harbor is from the thousand-foot-long wooden **footbridge** that connects downtown to the east side of town. If you venture all the way across, head south along Atlantic Avenue to the pretty **Our Lady Queen of Peace** church, which holds its holy water in clam shells and has some fine architectural details. Unless you're on the move with small children, skip the rather unimpressive state-run **Marine Resources Aquarium** on McKown Point Road in West Boothbay Harbor (June–Sept daily 10am–5pm; $5; ⓣ207/633-9559), which houses a touch tank in addition to a small number of other displays.

Ocean Point and Southport Island

There's plenty of less crowded land to explore in the area surrounding the busy town. At the end of the pretty fifteen-minute drive south along Rte-96 to desolate **Ocean Point**, you are rewarded with views of the horizon across the open ocean, interrupted only by Squirrel Island, a sparsely populated fishing village, Fisherman Island to the south, and Ram Island, with its prominent lighthouse. A few miles north on the same peninsula, the **Linekin Preserve** maintains extensive **hiking trails** on nearly a hundred acres of wilderness between Rte-96 and the coast.

On relatively deserted **Southport Island**, south on Rte-27, you can drive all the way down to Newagen, with its views of the Cuckolds Lighthouse, a half-mile out to sea. Along the western side of the island, you will find **Hendrick's Head Light** (now privately owned and visible only from the water). Popular lore has it that its keepers once adopted the only survivor of a terrible shipwreck – a tiny baby girl that they found inside a feather-lined box.

Eating and drinking

For all the big tourist money that comes into Boothbay Harbor every summer, the **culinary scene** is surprisingly drab. While standard gourmet meals are available at several of the smaller inns, prices can be prohibitively high. Still, there are a number of good eats to be had. Many restaurants close between October and May.

Blue Moon Café 54 Commercial St ☎207/633-2349. Of the places right on the water, this is probably the least expensive; better still, it serves a variety of delicious hot and cold sandwiches, including veggie specials. There's indoor and outdoor seating, and it's open for breakfast and lunch.
Daily Catch 93 Townsend Ave ☎207/633-0777. Respectable seafood spot with a wine bar and occasional live jazz. Open late by Boothbay standards; May–Oct only.
Ebb Tide 43 Commercial St ☎207/633-5692. Cheap, utilitarian breakfasts and dinners are served all day at this plain blue-collar joint right in the center of town. If you're here in the summer, don't miss the fresh peach shortcake.
Lobsterman's Co-op 97 Atlantic Ave ☎207/633-4900. Working lobster pound that dishes up ultra-fresh lobsters at minimal prices, as well as a range of sandwiches.
MacNab's Tea Room 5 Yu Lane, off Back River Rd ☎1-800/884-7222. A nice alternative in these parts: scones, English muffin sandwiches, salads, and a wide assortment of teas (formal tea by reservation). Closed Sun & Mon.
Robinson's Wharf Rte-27, Southport Island ☎207/633-3830. Lots of indoor and outdoor seating at this lobster pound where you can pick out your very own lobster. In addition to fresh seafood, they serve burgers, sandwiches, and blueberry pie.
Spruce Point Inn 88 Grandview Ave, off Atlantic Ave ☎207/633-4152 ext 605. Boothbay's swankiest dinner spot, with New American fare such as candied duck breast, shrimp amaretto, and lobster spring rolls. There's a great view of the water, too, but it all comes with a price: entrees go for $15–25. Reservations recommended.
The Thistle Inn 55 Oak St ☎207/633-3541. Easily the best restaurant in Boothbay, serving creative dishes like tempura banana and bleu cheese salad, as well as perfectly seared tuna, fruit-infused martinis, and great key lime pie. Reservations recommended.

Damariscotta and the Pemaquid Peninsula

The compact town of **DAMARISCOTTA**, just off US-1 across the Damariscotta River from neighboring Newcastle, does not have any real sights, per se, although its Main Street is a good place to stop for lunch or a stroll.

From town, River Road leads south to **Dodge Point**, where you can **hike** along several miles of trails or hang out on the sandy **beach** along the Damariscotta River in summer. It's also a popular spot for **fishing**, where anglers fish for striped bass, bluefish, and mackerel. You can dig for clams in the offshore tidal flats – contact the Newcastle Town Office (☎207/563-3441) for rules and regulations.

Damariscotta is a pleasant place to stay while exploring the rest of the Pemaquid Peninsula. The best **accommodation** in the area, however, is at *Blue Skye Farm* in Waldoboro, just north of town at 1708 Friendship Rd (follow the signs from US-1; ☎207/832-0300; ❺). This B&B is favored year-round for its surrounding one hundred acres of woodland and its well-priced, appealing accommodations. The best part, however, is its fantastic proprietors. The *Newcastle Inn*, at 60 River Rd in Newcastle (☎1-800/832-8669; ❽–❾), is another great spot with lots of character as well as fifteen unique rooms named for lighthouses, while the *Flying Cloud B&B*, 45 River Rd (☎207/563-2484; ❺), is an immaculately restored 1840s sea captain's home with five guestrooms and an elegant yet cozy atmosphere.

On US-1 east of town in **Waldoboro** is the legendary *Moody's Diner* (☎207/832-7785) a Maine institution for more than fifty years. *Moody's* is the real deal, open late and oozing nostalgia, with inexpensive daily specials, soups, and fourteen types of freshly made pies. The *Salt Bay Café*, 88 Main St (☎207/563-3302), is another local favorite, with simple but fresh seafood, soups, sandwiches, and steaks.

The Pemaquid Peninsula

Meaning "long finger" in the native language, the **Pemaquid Peninsula** points some fifteen miles south of US-1 along routes 129 and 130, culminating in the rocky **Pemaquid Point**. Archeological studies have recently concluded that this was the site of English settlers in 1626 – making it the northernmost British colonial settlement. **Colonial Pemaquid**, a small state-run museum on the site of the settlement, just west of New Harbor off of Rte-130 (late May to early Sept daily 10am–7pm; $3; ⓣ207/677-2423), houses ancient pottery, farming tools, and other household items. Over the years, ongoing excavation has also unearthed stone walls and foundations dating back to the seventeenth century. Within the nineteen-acre historical site stands a 1908 replica of **Fort William Henry**, the original built in 1677 by English settlers to ward off pirates, the French, and Native Americans, who are believed to have inhabited the peninsula as early as two thousand years ago. Though the robust fortress was thought to be rather impenetrable, it was overrun three times in the seventeenth century. There are good **ocean views** from the top of the massive stone citadel.

Nearby, the sands of **Pemaquid Beach**, just off Snowball Hill Road, are some of the most inviting in the state, and are correspondingly crowded on sunny summer weekends. Nevertheless, it's a great place to catch some rays, and even though the water can be cold, swimming is not impossible (parking $2). There's another, smaller **beach** all the way around the bend near the end of Rte-129 on Rutherford Island at **Christmas Cove**, so named by Captain John Smith after the day on which he discovered it.

Just north of Pemaquid Beach, from Shaw's Fish and Lobster Wharf in quaint **New Harbor**, Hardy Boat Cruises (ⓣ207/677-2026) runs daily **boat trips** (9am & 2pm) out to Monhegan Island for $28 round-trip, in addition to seal watches ($10), puffin watches ($20), and shorter scenic cruises ($10 and up).

South along Rte-130, at the tip of Pemaquid Point, the **Pemaquid Point Lighthouse** ($2) sits on a dramatic granite outcrop constantly battered by the violent Atlantic surf. You can wander around the small park for a good view

△ Pemaquid Point Lighthouse

Maine lighthouses

There is probably no better place to observe **lighthouses** than on the Maine coast, where some 68 of the structures direct ships of all sizes through the varied rocky inlets and along the jutting peninsulas from Kittery up to Quoddy Head. For centuries much of Maine's economy has centered on the sea, and the lighthouses here have become symbols of this dependence (not to mention the saving grace of many a passing ship). Consequently a series of museums serves to illustrate their history and importance, none more prominent than the **Maine Lighthouse Museum** in Rockland (see p.561). There's even a quarterly publication, *Lighthouse Digest*, devoted to the curious structures. Some of Maine's most dramatic lighthouses include the lonely **West Quoddy Head Light** (p.582), a candy-striped beauty in Lubec; the scenic **Pemaquid Point Light** (see overleaf), south of Damariscotta; and the **Cape Elizabeth Lighthouse** (p.541), near Portland, which was commissioned by none other than George Washington. The *Elms B&B* in Camden runs structured **lighthouse tours** of varying lengths on a restored lobster fishing boat – call ⓣ207/236-6060 or 1-800/388-6000 for more information.

of the salt-stained lighthouse, built in 1827 and still operational, but be careful not to get too close to the slippery rocks at the water's edge. The adjoining keeper's quarters have been transformed into the small **Fishermen's Museum** (May–Oct 10am–5pm; donation requested), containing uninspired exhibits related to the local fishing trade and, more interestingly, a map of Maine with a photo and description of each of the state's 68 lighthouses.

Another potential diversion on the Pemaquid Peninsula is the **Thompson Ice House**, Rte-129 north of South Bristol (July & Aug Mon, Fri & Sat 1–4pm; free; ⓣ207/644-8551). Although modern refrigeration has eliminated the ice industry, this ice house was in operation for 150 years, harvesting ice from a nearby pond and shipping it to points as far away as South America. Business mostly halted here in 1986, but the building, which sports ten-inch-thick sawdust-insulated walls, has been restored into a museum and working ice-harvesting facility. In the summer, you can check out a display of the defunct trade's tools and gaze at photos depicting ice harvesters in action. In February, townspeople still gather to collect ice from a pond using old-fashioned tools before burying the blocks in hay until summer, when they are sold to local fishermen.

Practicalities

Just back from the Pemaquid Lighthouse, you can enjoy reasonably priced American **food** with a fine view of the water at the small café that adjoins the Sea Gull Gift Shop (ⓣ207/677-2374). The *Anchor Inn* on Harbor Road in Round Pond (ⓣ207/529-5584) is another good bet, with crab cakes, stuffed lobster, pastas, and succulent steaks in a rustic dining room overlooking the harbor. There are also a number of traditional **lobster pounds** on the peninsula in New Harbor and Round Pond.

If you'd like to stay close to the lighthouse, the *Hotel Pemaquid*, only 100yds away at 3098 Bristol Rd, Rte-130 (ⓣ207/677-2312; ❹; June–Oct, no credit cards), offers Victorian furnishings in casual surroundings – some rooms share baths. Another option is the *Gosnold Arms* on Rte-32 in New Harbor (ⓣ207/677-3727; ❺), with country furnishings and superb harbor views. Basic **campsites** are available up the road near Pemaquid Beach at the *Sherwood Forest Campsite*, on Pemaquid Trail in New Harbor (ⓣ207/677-3642 or 1-800/274-1593; $25–29), which has multiple aquatic options: the ocean is only 800ft away, plus they have their own swimming pool.

Monhegan Island

Deliberately low-tech **MONHEGAN ISLAND**, eleven miles from the mainland, has long attracted a hardy mix of artists and fishermen. It also attracts its fair share of tourists, but for good reason: it's the most worthwhile jaunt away from the mainland along the entirety of the Maine coast. Sailor David Ingram recorded the first description of the place in 1569, calling it "a great island that was backed like a whale." Not much has changed since artist Robert Henri first came here in the early 1900s looking for tranquility and solitude – credit cards are not readily accepted, very few public phones are available, and there's only one public restroom. Though there were already a few artists residing on the island at the time, Henri introduced the place to his students George Bellows and Rockwell Kent, which established the place as a genuine artist's colony. Edward Hopper also spent time painting here, and the youngest of the Wyeth family, Jamie, currently calls Monhegan his summertime home.

The small village – occupying only twenty percent of the island – huddles around the tiny harbor, protected by Manana and Smutty Nose islands. Other than a few old hotels and some good restaurants, there's not much here – even automobiles are seldom heard; just as well, because there are some seventeen miles of **hiking trails** that crisscross the eastern half of the island, leading through dense stands of fir and spruce to the headlands, 160ft above the island's eastern shore. Monhegan Associates publishes a reliable **trail map**, available at most island stores, which is quite handy since trails are not always clearly marked.

The **Monhegan Island Lighthouse**, on a hill overlooking the village (and a great place to watch the sunset), was erected in 1824 and automated in 1959. You can check out the **Monhegan Historical and Cultural Museum** inside the former keeper's house (July–Sept daily 11.30am–3.30pm; donation), which recently opened a new building to house the work of Monhegan artists, including a few paintings by Rockwell Kent and Jamie Wyeth. Other rooms display artifacts, photographs, and documents relating to island history and natural features.

In summer, some of the artists in residence on the island open their **studios** to visitors. For times and locations, check the bulletin boards around town. You can also see works by local artists at one of several **galleries** – the Lupine Gallery (ⓣ207/594-8131) at the end of Wharf Hill Road has a consistently good grouping of local works on display.

Getting to Monhegan Island

You can access Monhegan from three different towns: Port Clyde, Boothbay Harbor, and New Harbor. To ensure a spot with one of the three boat carriers that connect the mainland with Monhegan, you should call in advance. The boats depart from Port Clyde for Monhegan three times daily during the summer and less often during the winter, arriving about an hour later, depending on which boat is in service ($16 one-way, $27 round-trip; ⓣ207/372-8848, ⓦwww.monheganboat.com). From Boothbay Harbor you can take the *Balmy Days III* (end of May to mid-Oct; $32 round-trip; ⓣ207/633-2284 or 1-800/298-2284, ⓦwww.balmydayscruises.com), which departs once daily at 9.30am and takes ninety minutes. The *Hardy Boat* takes seventy minutes to get from Shaw's Wharf in New Harbor (see p.557) to Monhegan (late May & early Oct departs Wed, Sat & Sun at 9am; June–Oct daily at 9am and 2pm; $28 round-trip; ⓣ207/677-2026 or 1-800/278-3346, ⓦwww.hardyboat.com).

Practicalities

There's not a great deal of **accommodation** choice on the island, so you should plan on reserving your room well in advance of your visit. The largest place to stay is the *Island Inn* (ⓣ207/596-0371; May–Oct; ❼), an attractive 1807 structure overlooking the harbor. Many of the rooms at the funky *Trailing Yew* (ⓣ207/596-0440; May–Oct; ❹), spread out among several buildings, do not have heat or electricity, while the guest accommodation at *Shining Sails B&B* (ⓣ207/596-0041, ⓦwww.shiningsails.com; ❺) is modern, with private baths; some even have small decks with ocean views. The *Hitchcock House*, at the top of Horn's Hill (ⓣ207/594-8137; ❹), has two simple efficiencies with living and kitchen area and deck; they also have several private rooms.

The island's selection of sit-down **restaurants** are all good, hearty, and surprisingly affordable affairs. At the *Trailing Yew* (see above), big family-style seafood dinners cost just $18 per person. The *Monhegan House Café* (ⓣ207/594-7983) is a little more formal, with a menu featuring simple meat, fish, and vegetarian dishes. You can get soups and sandwiches as well as groceries at *North End Market*, up the hill and to the right from the wharf (ⓣ207/594-5546). For light **snacks and coffee**, head to the *Barnacle* (late May to mid-Oct) overlooking the wharf; it houses the only ATM on the island and serves salads, sandwiches, espresso drinks, and baked goodies.

Rockland

Driving down Main Street in seaside **ROCKLAND**, you might observe a rusty old truck to your left and, a minute later, a shiny BMW to your right. Such is the mix of communities that make up Rockland, one of the more hip settlements in Maine. The town has historically been Maine's largest lobster distributor, and boasts the busiest working harbor in the state. This blue-collar vibe is anchored by a strong arts and cultural scene: on top of the more standard signs of tourism, Rockland is home to some remarkable museums and a newly reopened Art Deco movie theater.

The Town and around

The town's centerpiece is the outstanding **Farnsworth Museum**, 16 Museum St (late May to mid-Oct daily 10am–5pm; rest of year Tues–Sat 10am–5pm, Sun 1–5pm; $10; ⓣ207/596-6457), established in 1935 through the bequest of the reclusive Lucy Farnsworth, who rather surprised the town when her will left $1.3 million to build a museum in her father's honor. The museum is spread over several buildings, including the **Wyeth Center**, a beautiful gallery space in a converted old church that holds two floors' worth of works by Jamie and N.C. Wyeth. Across the street (at the museum proper), the impressive collection spans two centuries of American art – much of it Maine-related. The focal point is the permanent "Made in Maine" exhibit, which features landscapes and seascapes by Fitz Hugh Lane, portraits by American Impressionist Frank Benson, watercolors by Winslow Homer, and, of course, dramatic canvases from the Wyeths, like *Adrift* and *Airborne*. The museum does not own *Christina's World*, Andrew Wyeth's most famous work (it's at the MoMA in New York), but you can visit the field and home depicted in the painting at the **Olson House**, Hathorn Point Road, just outside of town in Cushing (late May to mid-Oct daily 11am–4pm; $4 or free with museum admission). Admission to the museum also gets you into the **Farnsworth Homestead**, tucked between museum buildings on Elm Street (late May to mid-Oct Mon–Sun 10am–5pm), a fine example of Victorian opulence.

Rockland's other star attraction is the newly reopened **Strand Theater**, 345 Main St (tickets $8; ⓣ207/594-0060), showing classic films like *North by Northwest*, as well as contemporary indie fare. The lush theater was originally opened in 1923, closed rather mysteriously in 2000, and then reopened in 2005 after an extensive restoration. Another worthwhile museum, the **Maine Lighthouse Museum**, in the same building as the Chamber of Commerce, 1 Park Drive (Mon–Fri May–Oct 9am–4.30pm, Sat & Sun 10am–4pm; rest of year closed Sun; donation; ⓣ207/594-3301), allows you to peruse one of the largest collections of lighthouse memorabilia and artifacts in the country. It's fun to press the buttons that trigger various foghorns and bells, but the real attraction is the curator, who probably knows more about lighthouses than anyone in existence. The **Owls Head Transportation Museum**, three miles south of Rockland on Rte-73 at Owls Head (April–Oct daily 10am–5pm, rest of year daily 10am–4pm; $7; ⓦwww.owlshead.org), is a similarly niche-oriented spot, with a vintage (mostly working) collection of cars, motorcycles, and planes from a bygone era, including a full-scale replica of the Wright Brothers' 1903 *Flyer*. During the summer they also do great airplane shows.

The harbor

From Rockland's enormous **harbor**, a number of powerboats and **windjammers** compete for your business with offers of everything from leisurely morning breakfast cruises to week-long island-hopping charters. The majority set sail for three to six days at a time, costing a little more than $125 per night, including all meals. If you've got the time and money, do it. You really can't go wrong with any of the options, but a few boats to try include the luxurious 68-foot *Stephen Taber* (ⓣ1-800/999-7352), the three-masted *Victory Chimes*, featured on the Maine state quarter (ⓣ1-800/745-5651), or the 95-foot *Schooner Heritage* (ⓣ1-800/648-4544). If you're having trouble finding what you want, stop by the Chamber of Commerce at 1 Park Drive, or call the Maine Windjammer Association (ⓣ1-800/807-9463) or the North End Shipyard (ⓣ1-800/648-4544).

Down the road at 517A Main St, the **Maine State Ferry Service** (ⓣ207/596-2202 or 1-800/491-4883) runs modern vessels at frequent intervals out to the summer retreats of Vinalhaven (75min; $12) and North Haven (1hr; $12), both of which make for relaxing day-trips from the mainland. For views of the water without actually boarding a boat, head to the **Rockland Breakwater**, a man-made granite structure jutting not quite a mile into the water and providing additional protection for the harbor. At its terminus lies the picturesque Rockland Breakwater lighthouse. To get there, take Waldo Avenue south from US-1 to Samoset Road. Go right on Samoset and the road will dead-end into Marie Reed Park, at the base of the breakwater.

St George Peninsula

South of Rockland, the lovely **St George Peninsula**, in particular the village of Tenants Harbor, inspired writer Sarah Orne Jewett's classic Maine novel *Country of the Pointed Firs*. Jewett describes the landscape so deftly that you can still pick out many of the sites depicted in the book, much of which was written in a tiny schoolhouse in Martinsville, since rebuilt. Boats sail from the hamlet of Port Clyde, at the tip of the peninsula, to **Monhegan Island**. You may recognize Port Clyde's picturesque 1857 Marshall Point Lighthouse from the Tom Hanks movie *Forrest Gump*; there's a small historical museum in the old keeper's house.

Practicalities

Thanks to Colgan Air, you can **fly** to Rockland's Knox County Regional Airport direct from Boston, though the cost is a steep $350 round-trip. The **bus station** is at the Maine State Ferry building, 517A Main St, just a short walk away from the **Chamber of Commerce** (same hours as Lighthouse Museum, see overleaf; ⓣ207/596-0376), which has comprehensive listings and information.

A good **place to stay** in the town center is the *Captain Lindsey House Inn*, 5 Lindsey St just off Main (ⓣ207/596-7950 or 1-800/523-2145; ❻–❼), snugly decorated with down comforters and puffy pillows. In a turreted Victorian mansion, the *LimeRock Inn*, 96 LimeRock St (ⓣ207/594-2257 or 1-800/LIME-ROCK, ⓦwww.limerockinn.com; ❻) has elegant yet comfortable rooms, sweet and savory breakfasts, and great proprietors. South of town, along the water in Tenants Harbor, the *East Wind Inn* (ⓣ207/372-6366, ⓦwww.eastwindinn.com; ❼) is a cozy old building with a huge porch and a formal dining area.

You won't go hungry in Rockland. Some of the best **food** in town can be had at funky and perennially crowded *Café Miranda*, tucked away at 15 Oak St just off Main (ⓣ207/594-2034); the appetizing array of international entrees ranges from saffron risotto with roasted mussels ($16.50) to Armenian lamb ($18.50). Situated at 421 Main St right in the center of town, *Amalfi* (ⓣ207/596-0012; closed Sun & Mon; reservations recommended) features Mediterranean fare with a seafood twist – this translates into goat milk's cheese flamed with ouzo as well as Moroccan spice-rubbed haddock fillet. The *Waterworks Pub and Restaurant*, 7 Lindsey St just off Main (ⓣ207/596-2753), has good pub grub and is deservedly popular. Another popular spot is the atmospheric *Kate's Seafood*, just south on US-1 (ⓣ207/594-2626; closed Mon), with simple, standout seafood. *Second Read*, 328 Main St (ⓣ207/594-4123), is a friendly place to drink locally roasted **coffee**; they also have light lunch options, pastries, a good selection of used books, and occasional live music.

Camden

The adjacent communities of Rockport and **CAMDEN** split into two separate towns in 1891 over a dispute as to who should pay for a new bridge over the Goose River between them. Since then Camden has clearly won the competition for tourists; indeed, it's one of the few towns in Maine that attracts visitors year-round. It's a good thing, too, considering the town's recent economic woes: in 2004, Camden lost nine hundred jobs when the MBNA banking firm moved its New England HQ to Belfast. Today the essential stop in town is **Camden Hills State Park**, which affords beautiful coastal views and has good camping. Camden's other highlight is its huge fleet of wind-powered schooners known as **windjammers**, many of which date back to the late nineteenth century, when the town was successful in the now-defunct shipbuilding trade.

Arrival and information

Concord Trailways' closest **bus** stop is in Rockport at the Gulf Service station on US-1. Once here, downtown is actually compact enough to be explored **on foot**. If you've got your car, know that **parking** can be a problem, but with patience you can usually find something on Chestnut Street or by the police station on Washington Street.

Camden's **information office**, down at 2 Public Landing (Ⓣ207/236-4404, Ⓦwww.camdenme.org), is usually a big help with finding a place to stay; they also stock a typically dizzying array of brochures. You can get free **Internet access** at the Camden Public Library, located partially underground on Atlantic Avenue, across from Harbor Park. Published every Wednesday and available at many shops, *Steppin' Out* has comprehensive **listings** of all the goings-on in the area.

Accommodation

While **accommodations** in Camden are plentiful, they are not cheap; it's very difficult to find a room for less than $100. The budget spots congregate along US-1 farther north in Lincolnville. There are over a dozen B&Bs in the immediate area, but you'd still be well advised to call in advance if you plan on staying here, especially on summer weekends; Camden Accommodations runs a **reservation service** (Ⓣ207/236-6090) for longer-term accommodations such as house rentals. Most of the hotels and B&Bs stay open all year here. Camden Hills State Park (see overleaf) is one of the best places to **camp** along the coast (Ⓣ207/236-3109), though it's often full.

The Belmont 6 Belmont Ave Ⓣ207/236-8053 or 1-800/238-8053, Ⓦwww.thebelmontinn.com. Decorated with conservative elegance, this stately inn sits on a residential street just beyond the commercial district. The dining room is open to the public, serving gourmet meals in a formal atmosphere. 6

Camden Maine Stay Inn 22 High St Ⓣ207/236-9636, Ⓦwww.camdenmainestay.com. Beautiful, three-story white-clapboard 1813 inn, with eight inviting rooms, of which two share a bathroom. 7–8

Captain Swift Inn 72 Elm St Ⓣ207/236-8113 or 1-800/251-0865, Ⓦwww.swiftinn.com. Four rooms in a restored Federalist-period house – ask for one in the rear if possible, as the traffic on US-1 (Elm St) can be bothersome. 6

Ducktrap Motel US-1, Lincolnville Ⓣ207/789-5400 or 1-877/977-5400. Cute basic budget option north of town. 3

The Elms B&B 84 Elm St Ⓣ207/236-6060 or 1-800/388-6060, Ⓦwww.elmsinn.net. A Colonial home on the southern end of a long strip of B&Bs along Elm St. The rooms are cozy (you can choose and reserve your room directly from the user-friendly website), and the bubbly owners – lighthouse enthusiasts – offer a range of lighthouse tours. 7

Good Guest House 50 Elm St Ⓣ207/236-2139. There are only two guest rooms in this pleasant home, which happens to be one of the best-value options in the center of town, with a couple of large, clean, beautifully decorated rooms. 4

Inn at Sunrise Point Fire Rd 9, off US-1, Lincolnville Ⓣ207/236-7716 Ⓦwww.sunrisepoint.com. This secluded, luxurious B&B frequently graces the pages of travel magazines, and with good reason – its indulgent rooms and stunning views continue to lure back guests. 8

The Town and around

As in Rockland, Camden's specialty is organizing sailing expeditions of up to six days in the large schooners known as **windjammers**. Daysailers, which tour the seas just beyond the harbor for trips that range from two hours to all day, include the *Appledore* (Ⓣ207/236-8353), the *Surprise* (Ⓣ207/236-4687), and the *Olad* (Ⓣ207/236-2323). Sails on these boats cost anywhere from $25 to $80 and can often be booked on the same day – each vessel usually has an information table set up along the public landing. Longer **overnight trips**, including all meals, can cost from $550 to $1200 (for six days) and should be booked in advance; the boats stop at various points of interest along the coast, such as Castine, Stonington, and Mount Desert Island. Contact the Maine Windjammer Association (Ⓣ1-800/807-9463) or the North End Shipyard (Ⓣ207/594-8007 or 1-800/648-4544) for information and schedules.

In the center of town, immaculately maintained **Harbor Park**, right where the whitewater of the Megunticook River spills into the sea, is a good spot to relax or have a picnic after wandering the town's small shopping district, which runs south from Main Street along the water. Farther down Bayview Street, which holds many of the shops, tiny **Laite Beach** looks out onto the Penobscot Bay.

Camden Hills State Park and Aldermere Farm

Just north of town, US-1 leads towards **Camden Hills State Park** ($3 entrance fee), the best spot around for **hiking** and camping. Rather than drive, pick up the **Mount Battie Trail** (45min) that begins at the intersection of Spring Street and Harden Avenue, a short walk from the town center. The panoramic views of the harbor and Maine coastline from the top of 790-foot Mount Battie are hard to beat; on the summit, you can climb to the top of the circular World War I memorial for the best vantage point. It was here that poet Edna St Vincent Millay (see box below) penned part of her most recognized poem, *Renascence*, which is commemorated with a small plaque. There's a variety of other trails in the area, including ones that head to the summits of **Ocean Lookout** and **Zeke's Lookout**; you can get a decent free hiking map at the ranger station in the parking lot at the park entrance just off of US-1.

Don't underestimate the magnetism of the Belted Galloway cows at **Aldermere Farm**, on Russell Avenue in Rockport (Ⓣ207/236-2739, Ⓦwww.aldermere.org). These quirky, endearing "Oreo cookie cows" (so named for the

Edna St Vincent Millay

Edna St Vincent Millay came to Camden with her divorced mother, Cora, and two sisters in 1900, when she was 8 years old. Her mother encouraged all the sisters in the arts, and Edna (she insisted on being called "Vincent") excelled in writing. As a young child, she had poems published in *St Nicholas*, a children's magazine, and by age 20 she had won international recognition with her poem, *Renascence*, which she first recited at the *Whitehall Inn*, 52 High St (Ⓣ207/236-3391 or 1-800/789-6565). Today, the inn maintains a small collection of writings, photos, and scrapbooks depicting her playful Camden childhood. Millay reputedly had a rather carefree adulthood, too: an acknowledged bisexual, she had many affairs with women, and when she finally did marry a man, it was on open terms. A lifelong smoker, she died of heart failure in 1950. Published in 1917, her locally famous poem *Afternoon on a Hill* supposedly describes her wanderings in the Camden Hills:

I will be the gladdest thing
  Under the sun!
I will touch a hundred flowers
  And not pick one.

I will look at cliffs and clouds
  With quiet eyes,
Watch the wind bow down the grass,
  And the grass rise.

And when lights begin to show
  Up from the town,
I will mark which must be mine,
  And then start down!

funny white stripe of hair that's sandwiched between their black front and back) have been amusing passersby for ages. The farm doesn't currently have any public programming, per se, but the cows are nearly always in plain view of their camera-snapping fans.

Eating and drinking

Camden has a good array of **eating and drinking** spots – from gourmet restaurants to casual seafood joints to busy bars. One thing is for sure: on summer weekends, they're all going to be packed, so plan on waiting for a table. There's also a somewhat active **nightlife** – for Maine at least.

Camden Bagel Café 26 Mechanic St ⓣ207/236-2661. Popular morning spot with tables in a sunny dining area; lots of fresh bagels, coffee, sandwiches, and salads.

Camden Deli 37 Main St ⓣ207/236-8343. Great variety of bulging, gourmet sandwiches and deli salads, right in the center of town, overlooking the harbor. They also serve beer and wine.

Cappy's Chowder House 1 Main St ⓣ207/236-2254. This cramped, child-friendly bar and restaurant is the place to go in town for a casual drink or meal.

Francine 55 Chestnut St ⓣ207/230-0083. Elegant French bistro amidst tealights and aubergine walls. The menu changes daily, and features fresh fare such as haddock with mint and tomato chutney ($23) or Charentaise melon salad with goat cheese, cucumbers, and crispy prosciutto ($8).

Frogwater Café 31 Elm St ⓣ207/236-8998. A lively, informal joint with tasty renditions of steak, seafood, pasta, chicken standbys, and plenty of veggie options.

Gilbert's Publick House under *Peter Ott's Steakhouse*, Bayview St ⓣ207/236-4320. With lots of beer signs and a big-screen TV, the *Publick House* looks a little like a fraternity basement, but that doesn't stop people from filling up the dance floor to the tune of cheesy Top-40 hits and alternative rock, sometimes live (Thurs–Sat).

Lobster Pound Restaurant US-1, Lincolnville Beach ⓣ207/789-5550. Casual and wildly popular seaside restaurant serving heaps of the bright-red crustaceans.

Natalie's on the Mill 43 Mechanic St ⓣ207/236-7008. A good place to splurge – scenic views, pretty interior, and well-composed, good-looking New American cuisine (entrees $30 and up).

South by Southwest 31 Elm St ⓣ207/236-7025. Good Southwestern and traditional Mexican fare – enchiladas, quesadillas, and salads. Open daily 7am–2pm.

Waterfront Restaurant Bayview St ⓣ207/236-3747. The delicious clam chowder, fisherman's stew, and fresh seafood pastas are a bit expensive, but you can't beat the dockside seating.

Whalestooth Pub & Restaurant US-1, Lincolnville Beach ⓣ207/789-5200. A few miles north of Camden, this year-round local favorite has a chatty ambience and enjoyable steak and fish fare.

Rockport

Just south of Camden, a bit of **ROCKPORT's** lime-producing past can be viewed via the decaying **lime kilns** in pleasant Marine Park, next to the harbor just off US-1. The park also houses a statue of Rockport's most famous former citizen: André the seal. André was adopted in 1961 after Harry Goodbridge found the little seal pup abandoned out in the water. Goodbridge brought him home, taught him some fabulous tricks, and made him a part of the family. In his lifetime, André spent his winters at the Boston aquarium, and come fall, would miraculously find his way back home to the Goodbridge residence in Rockport (a distance of 150 miles). At one point he was created honorary harbor-master, and in 1978, helped to unveil this statue, done in his likeness.

The tiny town center holds a couple of decent galleries, such as the **Center for Maine Contemporary Art**, 162 Russell Ave (Tues–Sat 10am–5pm, in summer also Sun noon–5pm; $5; ⓣ207/236-2875), where local artists display their works, and the **Maine Photographic Workshops**, nearby at 2 Central St (Ⓣ207/236-8581), which is somewhat well known for its school of photography. Right across the street, the friendly *Corner Shop* (Ⓣ207/236-8361; closes 2pm) serves up one of the best **breakfasts** in the area, with big and cheap omelets in a sunny room.

Belfast

Cozy **BELFAST** feels like the most lived-in and liveable of the towns along the Maine coast. Here the shipbuilding boom is long since over (and the chicken-processing plant that regularly turned the bay blood-red has also gone), but the inhabitants have had the waterfront declared a historic district, sparing it from over-commercialization and major condo development. As you stroll around, look out for any number of whitewashed Greek Revival houses, particularly prevalent along the wide avenues in the southern half of town between Church and Congress streets. At 70 Church St, in an unbelievable stroke of excessive historic puns, there once lived Mrs Wealthy Poor and her husband, who ran a drugstore on High Street. You can pick up a copy of the *Belfast Historic Walking Tour* at the convivial **information office** (Ⓣ207/338-5900), at the foot of Main Street by the bay. Belfast was a lively center in the 1960s and its stores, community theater groups, and festivals attest to its continued vibrance.

Practicalities

Up from the bay at 96 Main St, spacious *Chase's Daily* (Ⓣ207/338-0555; closed Mon) is a great spot for **food**, with fresh eats like breakfast burritos and peach smoothies with ginger and lime. At 2 Fairview St, *Young's Lobster Pound* (Ⓣ207/338-1160) serves up $11 fresh-boiled lobster dinners, among the best in the state, with sunset views. *Darby's*, at 155 High St (Ⓣ207/338-2339), is a bit overpriced but nevertheless serves up delicious food such as pecan haddock, pad thai, and filet mignon; the adjoining **pub** specializes in Scotch whiskies. *Rollie's Bar and Grill*, back on the hill at 37 Main St (Ⓣ207/338-4502), is a rough-and-ready bar open until 1am every day of the year, that is (surprisingly) also pretty popular for breakfast.

For **accommodation**, try the *Alden House*, 63 Church St (Ⓣ207/338-2151, Ⓦwww.thealdenhouse.com; ❺–❻), a beautiful 1840 Greek Revival house run as a B&B by two genial hostesses; the comfortable *Harbor View House*, 213 High St (Ⓣ207/338-3811 or 1-877/393-3811; ❻); or the pretty Victorian *Jeweled Turret Inn* with friendly hosts and good breakfasts, 40 Pearl St (Ⓣ207/338-2304 or 1-800/696-2304; ❻–❼). Along US-1, across the Passagassawakeag River in East Belfast, are several inexpensive motels, including the decent *Gull* (Ⓣ207/338-4030; ❹).

Bucksport

Named after founder Colonel Jonathan Buck, who's buried at the Bucksport Cemetery near the Verona Bridge, quiet **BUCKSPORT** was first settled as a trading post in 1762. Today, the International Paper Company's enormous riverside factory dominates the town's skyline and employs a high percentage of its 4908 inhabitants. The town is trying hard to shed its workaday image to attract more visitors, but the problem is that there's not a whole lot to do here.

One place worth checking out is **Northeast Historic Film**, in the restored 1916 Alamo Theater building at 85 Main St (Mon–Fri 9am–4pm; ⓣ207/469-0924, ⓦwww.oldfilm.org). NHF collects and screens film and video related to the history and heritage of northern New England; this even includes your old family films, which they'll edit and store for free. Call in advance and ask about tours – they'll take you into their amazing (and freezing) climate-controlled film storage room, and show you the ins and outs of their film equipment set-up. The real treat, however, is the chance to watch one of the Sunday matinees, or to catch their annual Northeast silent film festival.

Even if you have no particular interest in the military, the hulking **Fort Knox**, just across the Penobscot River from Bucksport (May–Oct daily 9am–sunset; $3; ⓣ207/469-7719), still merits a wander round its castle-like structure. You can climb up and down circular stairways, stagger through countless tunnels that disappear into total darkness, investigate officers' quarters, and clamber to the top of the fort's thick granite structure, from which you can admire Bucksport's factory skyline. With all the cannon mounts – there are over 130 in all – it's hard to believe this place never saw any action, though it was manned from 1863 to 1865 during the Civil War.

Down East Maine

So called because sailors heading east along the coast were also usually heading downwind, **Down East** Maine has engendered plenty of debate over its boundaries – some wishing to draw its western line at Ellsworth, or Belfast, or even include the entire state in their definition. It's all a matter of pride, of course; to be a downeaster means to be tough and fiercely independent – though it would be unfair to say unfriendly. For the purposes of this book at least, we've defined "Down East" as the Maine coast east of Bucksport, including the **Blue Hill Peninsula**, home to several wealthy summer towns, extremely popular **Mount Desert Island**, the second most visited place in the state, and the nearly deserted shoreline that stretches a hundred lonely miles between the strip mall town of Ellsworth and the point farthest east in the United States at **West Quoddy Head**.

As you make your way up the coast – particularly once you pass Mount Desert Island and **Acadia National Park** – the terrain and the population become more rugged and less prone to tourism. The weather here is also less forgiving, and the coast near the Canadian border is normally foggy for half the year.

The Blue Hill Peninsula

It used to be that the **Blue Hill Peninsula**, reaching south from Bucksport, was a sleepy expanse of land, too far off the primary roads to attract much attention. But word is slowly getting out about this beautiful area, blanketed with fields of wild blueberries and their pinkish-white flowers, and dotted with both dignified old-money towns like **Castine** and **Blue Hill** and hardcore fishing villages

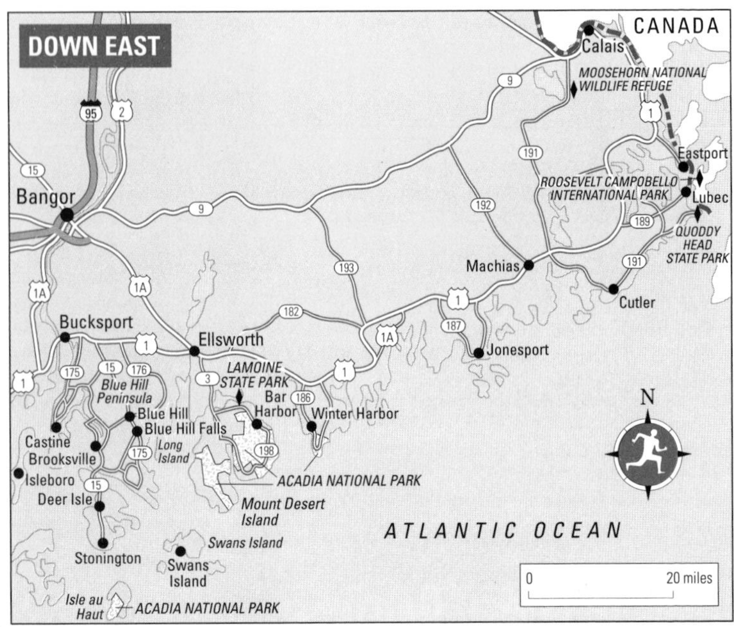

like **Stonington** and **Deer Isle**. Even farther off the established tourist trail, **Isle au Haut** is a remote outpost accessible only by mail boat. In the smaller towns between, you'll find close-knit communities of people who can trace their ties to the peninsula back for several generations. Year-round residents are friendly folk, but they are also understandably protective of the privacy they have come to cherish. As you might expect, the main draw down here is the tranquility that comes with isolation, and while the area presents ample opportunities for exploration, you might find yourself content with a good book, an afternoon nap, a gourmet meal, and a night in a posh B&B.

Arrival, information, and getting around

The Blue Hill Peninsula is deceptively large, and, with somewhat indirect roads, it can take well over an hour to reach its southernmost point. It's a good idea to pick up a detailed DeLorme map before you set out to explore the area – even some of the locally produced plans can't seem to keep all the different numbered roads straight. **Cycling** is a good way to get around; your best bet for renting is probably at the Rocky Coast Outfitters, on Grindleville Road (ⓣ207/374-8866), and they also do kayak and canoe rentals. Public transport is not available, though if you're really in a bind, you can grab a **taxi** by calling Airport & Harbor Taxi (ⓣ207/667-5995).

The Blue Hill Peninsula Chamber of Commerce is at 28 Water St, in Blue Hill proper (ⓣ207/374-3242). Most inns and shopkeepers are also well equipped to provide just about all the information you need, including regional maps. The local chambers of commerce maintain **websites** at ⓦwww.bluehillme.com and ⓦwww.deerislemaine.com.

Accommodation

Cheap **accommodations** on the Blue Hill Peninsula are pretty much non-existent. If you're not traveling in the off season, plan to spend $100 or more per night; for a comparable amount, you may be able to rent a small house or cottage. There are two places to **camp** here, both on Deer Isle: *Sunshine Campground*, way out near the end of Sunshine Road (Ⓣ207/348-2663), has 22 sites from the end of May through mid-October, while *Greenlaws*, in Stonington (Ⓣ207/367-5049), is more RV-oriented.

Blue Hill and around

Blue Hill Inn Union St Ⓣ207/374-2844 or 1-800/826-7415, Ⓦwww.bluehillinn.com. Romantic 1830 inn with inviting rooms and decor. Guests are treated to outstanding gourmet meals. (A small apartment, Cape House, is available in winter for $165 per night, two-night minimum.) May–Nov only. ❼

Captain Isaac Merrill Inn One Union St Ⓣ207/374-2555. White-clapboard house in the center of town with fireplaces throughout and a decent restaurant downstairs. ❼

Heritage Motor Inn Rte-172 Ⓣ207/374-5646. Pleasingly located and moderately priced motor inn with good-sized rooms, all with views. They also have a number of brand-new townhouse efficiencies – minimum one-week stay in summer. ❺

Oakland House 435 Herrick Rd, Brooksville Ⓣ207/359-8521 or 1-800/359-7352, Ⓦwww.oaklandhouse.com. Stay in the immaculately refurbished old stone inn or one of the well-maintained cabins strewn about the property, which is situated in a remote area along the Eggemoggin Reach. Follow the signs down Rte-15 to get here. ❼–❽

Castine

Castine Inn 1 Main St Ⓣ207/326-4365, Ⓦwww.castineinn.com. One of the few old inns (1898) in the state that was actually built as an inn, this Castine fixture now offers updated amenities and has friendly, helpful hosts. Open May–Sept. ❻–❽

Manor Inn Battle Ave Ⓣ207/326-4861, Ⓦwww.manor-inn.com. Constructed as a summer home for a yachting commodore, the *Manor* looks a little incongruously like a sort of New England castle. The inn offers fourteen rooms beautifully decorated in eclectic lodge style, plus immediate access to hiking and cross-country skiing trails. They specialize in weddings. ❻–❽

Pentagoet Inn 26 Main St Ⓣ207/326-8616 or 1-800/845-1701, Ⓦwww.pentagoet.com. A welcoming old 1894 inn with sixteen rooms restored to reflect an earlier era with the help of the antique-buff owners and period steamboat lithos. The inn also has a quiet and sophisticated pub, *Passports*, a huge porch, and great fine dining. May–Oct only. ❻–❼

Stonington

Boyce's Motel 44 Main St Ⓣ207/367-2421 or 1-800/224-2421. Centrally located, basic, clean rooms at the right prices. They also have full apartments, with kitchens and living rooms, for $600 per week. Open all year. ❹

Inn on the Harbor Main St Ⓣ207/367-2420. Stonington's fanciest (and priciest) accommodations – there are even spa services. It also has the best location, with a fine view of the harbor. Open all year; breakfast included. ❻

Pres du Port B&B W Main St at Highland Ave Ⓣ207/367-5007. Brightly wallpapered, whimsically furnished B&B with a great view from the upstairs deck. Also has one endearing little room for only $40. No credit cards. June–Oct only. ❼

Blue Hill

Though wealthy **BLUE HILL**, at the intersection of routes 172, 176, and 15 adjacent to the Blue Hill Harbor, makes a fairly good portion of its living from tourism, you'd be hard pressed to find a Maine T-shirt or even a lighthouse figurine around town. There isn't so much to do here, but plenty come for the opportunity to lounge in its quietude.

Several well-known writers, among them E.B. White, have made their homes in the Blue Hill Peninsula. Blue Hill proper boasts two excellent bookstores. North Light Books, 58 Main St (Ⓣ207/374-5422), is a great source for **travel books** and maps as well as fiction, specialty titles, and art supplies. It's also home to one very fat and famous cat. The larger Blue Hill Books, 26 Pleasant St (Ⓣ207/374-5632), is a more comprehensive independent bookseller.

It's a relatively short walk (30–45min) up to the top of **Blue Hill Mountain**, from which you can see across the Blue Hill Bay to the dramatic ridges of Mount Desert Island. The trailhead is not difficult to find, halfway down Mountain Road between Rte-15 and Rte-172. South on Rte-175, **Blue Hill Falls** is a good spot to give kayaking a try: the Activity Shop in Blue Hill at 61 Rte-172 (Ⓣ207/374-3600, Ⓦwww.theactivityshop.com), has canoe and kayak rentals that they'll even deliver to your door ($25 a day and up; reservations recommended).

Castine

CASTINE, nearly surrounded by water on the northern edge of the Penobscot Bay, is one of New England's most quietly beautiful towns, with nicely kept gardens, enormous elm trees arching over many of the hilly streets, and a peaceful, subdued sophistication. Named for Jean Vincent d'Abbadie de St Castin, a Frenchman who was deeded the land in 1667, the historically disputed peninsula has been occupied at various times by the French, British, Dutch, and, obviously, Americans. The British assumed control in 1779 when General Francis McLean stormed ashore with seven hundred men and built **Fort George**, now little more than a few mounds along Wadsworth Cove Road. The Americans responded by sending 32 vessels carrying some 1400 men, and what followed was arguably the worst American naval defeat in history. Unable to agree on a plan of attack against the weaker British forces on land, the Americans sat in the bay until a larger British fleet arrived, forcing them to retreat up the Penobscot, abandon their ships, and walk back to Boston. Among the officers court-martialed upon their return was Paul Revere, whose military career never really recovered. The military battles that occurred here are noted throughout town with various plaques and signs; a brochure and **map** entitled *Welcome to Castine* is available at any local shop for a full listing of all the historic sites.

Castine's small population is a mix of summer residents, a number of well-known poets and writers (Elizabeth Hardwick, founder of *The New York Review of Books* among them) and year-round people, many of whom are employed by the **Maine Maritime Academy**, with buildings both along the water and back on Pleasant Street. It's pretty tough to miss the *State of Maine*, the huge ship that's usually docked at the landing (except in May and June) and used to train the academy's students, who give tours in the summer (call Ⓣ207/326-4311 for schedules, or walk up the plank and ask). Take a stroll down **Perkins Street** to check out the string of enormous mansions looking out over the water. Between these ostentatious summer retreats are a number of old historic buildings, such as the 1665 **John Perkins House**, the town's earliest, which is occasionally open to the public. There is also the *Compass Rose Bookstore and Café*, 3 Main St (Ⓣ207/326-9366), a welcoming book-browsing space. When you tire of wandering around the town, Castine Kayak Adventures (Ⓣ207/326-9045) runs various **sea-kayaking** tours ($55–105, includes equipment and instruction), as well as bike rentals ($24/day) from Dennett's Wharf next to the public boat landing.

Stonington and Isle au Haut

Deer Isle is an eclectic mix of seclusion and sophistication. In recent years, a serenity-seeking tourist crowd has paved the way for things like espresso machines and spa treatments in what have historically been fishing villages.

Ultimately, though, that's not such a bad thing, as tourism does not overwhelm the community, and visitors get to drink cappuccinos amidst incredible harbor views. Clear down at the end of Rte-15, it doesn't get much more remote than beautiful **STONINGTON**, a working fishing village whose residents have long had a reputation for superior seamanship; many pirates and smugglers reputedly made port here in the late nineteenth century – no doubt due to its exceptional isolation. Over the past hundred years, the place has found hard-earned prosperity in the sardine-canning and granite-quarrying businesses; now it has turned to lobstering. The history of the granite quarries is brought to life at the **Deer Isle Granite Museum**, 51 Main St (June–Aug Mon–Sat 10am–5pm, Sun 1–4.30pm, closed Wed; ⓣ207/367-6331; donation), which counts as its centerpiece a working model of the quarry as it stood in 1900.

Mail boats headed for **ISLE AU HAUT** (pronounced "I'll ah hoe") depart from the Stonington landing several times daily (ⓣ207/367-5193, ⓣ207/367-6516; $16 one-way). On this lonely island, you can explore the trails of the less-visited part of **Acadia National Park** – highlighted by the rocky shoreline, bogs, and dense stands of spruce trees. Alternatively, you can charter your own boat for a reasonable price from Captain Bill at Old Quarry Charters, in Stonington (ⓣ207/367-8977, ⓦwww.oldquarry.com), who, in addition to Isle au Haut, will take you anywhere on the Maine coast.

Eating and drinking

Most of the **eateries** on the peninsula cater to the expensive tastes (and fat wallets) of wealthy summer residents; **Castine** and **Blue Hill** have the best concentration of places, though even on the remote **Deer Isle** there are a couple of prix-fixe gourmet spots.

Blue Hill and around

Arborvine Main St ⓣ207/374-2119. Tasty, contemporary fare like mushroom and leek risotto and local Damariscotta River oysters, served in an 1800s-style home. Try the plum napolean with whipped cream for dessert. Reservations recommended; closed Mon.

Café Velouria Water St ⓣ207/374-5775. Eclectic, tasty little sandwich shop, just off of Main St.

Morning Moon Café 1 Bay Rd, at intersection of Rte-175 and Naskeag Point Rd, Brooklin ⓣ207/359-2373. South of Blue Hill and known as "The Moon," this is a popular gathering spot for breakfast and lunch. Closes 2pm; closed Mon.

Pain de Famille 9 Main St (no phone). The aromas will lure you in to this low-key local bakery. Artisan breads, veggie and vegan sandwiches, cookies, and good pizza on Friday nights.

The Wescott Forge 66 Main St ⓣ207/374-9909. The best of both worlds: fabulous fine dining on a sunny deck and a plush lounge that's open late. Lunch is less expensive and just as good. Closed Sun.

Castine

Castine Variety 1 Main St ⓣ207/326-8625. The real draw here is not the food – though it was recently voted "best lobster roll" by Maine residents – but rather the opportunity to sit at the tiny counter and chat with the well-connected proprietor.

Dennett's Wharf 15 Sea St ⓣ207/326-9045. Dine on typical sea fare and then wash it down with one of several Maine microbrews on tap, all while enjoying a fine view.

The Pentagoet Inn Main St ⓣ207/326-8616. Lobster *bouillabaisse*, warm asparagus salad with prosciutto crisps, and pistachio-dusted diver scallops, served in an atmospheric, elegant dining room.

Stonington

Maritime Café 27 Main St ⓣ207/367-2600. Pristine café featuring seafood victuals, crepes, and espresso. Ridiculously good views of the harbor.

Harbor Café Main St ⓣ207/367-5099. A salty ambience – it's where the fishermen come in the morning – with sandwiches, coffee, and muffins; right in the center of town.

East to Mount Desert Island

Aside from a short strip of quaint brick gift shops and a couple of cafés along the old part of Main Street (US-1), most of **ELLSWORTH** has been overdeveloped into a disastrous sprawl of parking lots and chain stores. There's predictably little to see, although you might check out the **Woodlawn Museum**, on Rte-172 just south of US-1 (June–Sept Tues–Sat 10am–5pm, Sun 1–4pm; May and Oct Tues–Sun 1–4pm; $7.50; ⓣ207/667-8671), a huge and splendid Federal period house with original furnishings amidst a pleasant park and two miles of trails. Otherwise, stop here only for provisions or a quick bite to eat before you head south to Mount Desert Island. The beloved *Riverside Café*, at 151 Main St (ⓣ207/667-7220), is a friendly local haunt for **breakfast** or **lunch**.

If you're arriving in the Acadia region in high season (July & Aug) and the traffic is unbearable along busy Rte-3, head off down Rte-184 to **Lamoine State Park** ($2), just north of Mount Desert Island along the shores of Frenchman Bay. There are no hiking trails, but there are plenty of beautiful spots to have a picnic or wander the coast. The 61-site **campground** (mid-May to mid-Oct; park info ⓣ207/667-4778, reservations ⓣ207/287-3824; $20/night) here is rarely full – maybe because it offers no hookups or hot showers – and has some well-situated tent sites that offer views of the island. Nearby, Lamoine Beach is the best **swimming** beach in the area.

Mount Desert Island

Considering that several million visitors come to **Mount Desert Island** each year, that it contains most of New England's only national park, and that it boasts not only a genuine fjord but also the highest headland on the entire Atlantic coast north of Rio de Janeiro, it is quite an astonishingly small place, measuring just fifteen by twelve miles. It is, of course, simply one of three hundred rugged granite islands along the Maine coast; the reasons to select this one, however, are plentiful. Aside from its obvious charms, Mount Desert is the most accessible of the islands (it's been linked to the mainland by bridge since 1836), possesses the best facilities, and offers water- and land-based activities galore.

The island was named *Monts Deserts* (bare mountains) by Samuel de Champlain in 1604 and fought over by the French and English for the rest of the century. Although all existing settlements date from long after the final defeat of the French, the name remains, still pronounced in French (more like *dessert*, actually). After landscape painters Thomas Cole and Frederic Church depicted the island in mid-nineteenth-century works, word spread about its barren beauty, and by the end of the century, tourism was a fixture here. America's wealthiest families – among them the Rockefellers, Pulitzers, and Fords – erected palatial estates in **Bar Harbor**, and later (under the leadership of Harvard University president Charles Eliot) established the organization that would later work to create Acadia National Park, the first national park donated entirely by private citizens. In 1947, a fire destroyed many of the grand cottages, including Bar Harbor's "Millionaires' Row," putting an end to the island's grand resort era. The fire didn't entirely tarnish the island's luster, however, and the place now attracts vacationing middle-class families and outdoor enthusiasts in addition to the frighteningly rich.

Somes Sound roughly divides the island in half; the east side is more developed and ritzy, holding the island's social center and travel hub Bar Harbor as

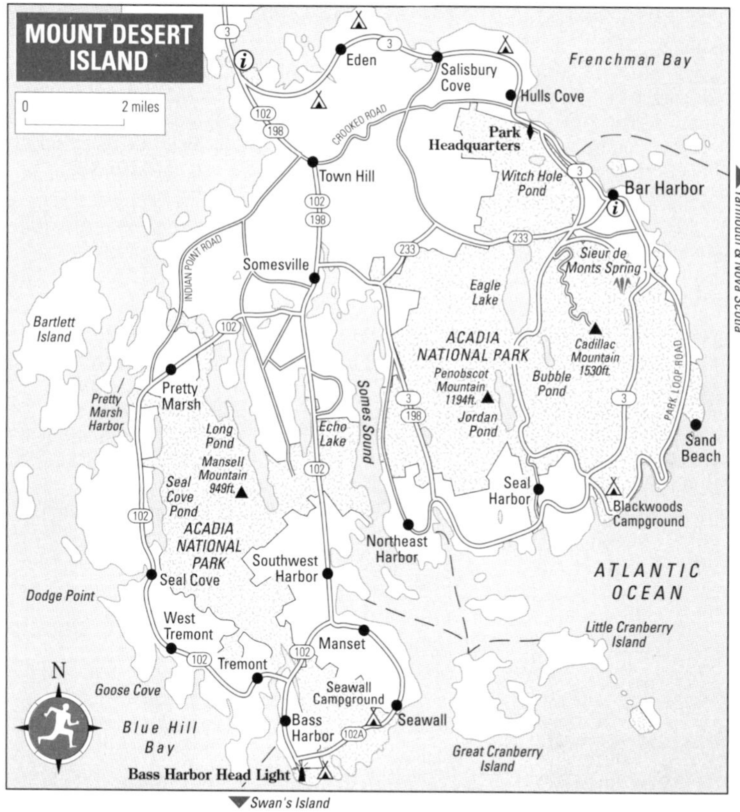

well as **Northeast Harbor**, the site of huge summer homes for many a CEO. The west side, known to some as the "quiet side," is rather sedate, with a few genuine fishing villages and year-round settlements like low-key **Southwest Harbor**, actually fast catching on as a popular destination in its own right. **Acadia National Park**, which covers much of the island, has great opportunities for camping, cycling, canoeing, kayaking, hiking, and bird-watching, though you're hardly ever very far from civilization.

Arrival, information, and getting around

If you're **driving**, Mount Desert is easy enough to get to along Rte-3 off US-1, although in high summer roads on the island itself get congested (and the horse-drawn tours don't help). **Public transport** is minimal outside of Bar Harbor, though once you get there, take advantage of the free Island Explorer **shuttle buses** (ⓦwww.exploreacadia.com), which travel through Acadia to Bar Harbor, and even out to the airport.

Vermont Transit Lines **buses** (ⓣ1-800/552-8737) run to Bar Harbor from Boston, Bangor, and Portland from mid-June to early Sept. West's Coastal Connections (ⓣ207/546-2823 or 1-800/596-2823) travels between Bangor and the border town of Calais via Ellsworth.

Mount Desert is also accessible via airplane. **Flights** into Bar Harbor are relatively infrequent and expensive – Bar Harbor/Hancock County Airport (☎207/667-7432), on Rte-3 in Trenton, has a limited service run by Colgan Air. Flights are more feasible via Bangor International Airport, 45 miles away, which is served by Continental, Delta, and Northwest. If you're coming from (or have a desire to visit) Yarmouth, Nova Scotia, the speedy "Cat" **ferry** takes two and three-quarter hours to reach Bar Harbor (one-way fares: mid-June to mid-Sept cars $99 plus fuel surcharge, people $58; mid-May to mid-June and mid-Sept to mid-Oct cars $89 plus fuel surcharge, people $48; ferries leave Bar Harbor daily at 8am; ☎1-888/249-7245, Ⓦwww.catferry.com).

Information

The **Acadia Information Center**, on Rte-3 just before you cross the bridge to Mount Desert Island (daily: May & June 9am–6pm, July & Aug 9am-8pm; Sept to mid-Oct 9am–6pm; ☎207/667-8550 or 1-800/358-8550), is an advisable stop for lodging and camping information if you don't already have a reservation, and they have decent free maps of the island. There's also a tourist information office in Bar Harbor in the municipal building on 93 Cottage St (☎207/288-5103), as well as a seasonal office at 1 West St.

There are numerous **information** outlets at Acadia during the summer, the best of which is the Hulls Cove Visitor Center, just off of Rte-3 at the entrance to the Park Loop Road (mid-April–June 8am–4.30pm, July & Aug 8am–6pm; Sept & Oct daily 8am–5pm; ☎207/288-3338). Here you can inquire about hiking routes and purchase maps. You can also obtain more information about the park by writing or calling the National Park Service at **Park Headquarters**, PO Box 177, Bar Harbor, ME 04609 (☎207/288-3338, Ⓦwww.nps.gov/acad).

Accommodation

Rte-3 into and out of Bar Harbor is lined with budget motels, which do little to improve the look of the place but satisfy an enormous demand for **accommodation**. Rates increase drastically in July and August, and anywhere offering sea views will cost a whole lot more. In season, it's difficult to find a room for less than $100 in Bar Harbor; elsewhere, prices are a little less exorbitant. Despite the island's 4500 rooms, everywhere tends to be booked up early, so call ahead to check for availability. For help with **reservations**, call or stop in at the Acadia Information Center (see "Information" above). If you're really pressed for cash, or if the island is full, it may be cheaper to stay in **Ellsworth** and drive onto the island each day, though the drive to the far south end can be quite time-consuming, with all the auto congestion. **Camping** in Acadia itself is a better (and prettier) budget option but spaces are in short supply; here too you will need to call well in advance for July and August.

Bar Harbor

Acadia Hotel 20 Mount Desert St ☎207/288-5721 or 1-888/876-2463, Ⓦwww.acadiahotel.com. One of the more affordable spots in town. The rooms in this old hotel are newly renovated but a bit overdone. You get a discount if you reserve through the website. ❻

Aysgarth Station 20 Roberts Ave ☎207/288-9655, Ⓦwww.aysgarth.com. On a quiet side street a short walk from the center of town, this small, country-style B&B offers friendly service and a laidback atmosphere. ❻

Bar Harbor Hostel 321 Main St ☎207/288-5587 Ⓦwww.barharborhostel.com. Clean, safe, friendly, brand-new hostel right near the center of town. Dorm bed $25 a night (plus linens), private room $80.

Bar Harbor Inn Newport Drive ☎207/288-3351 or 1-800/248-3351, Ⓦwww.barharborinn.com. Perhaps the grandest hotel in town, the inn has 153

Camping on Mount Desert Island

There are three **campgrounds** in Acadia National Park, two public and one private. **Blackwoods**, near Seal Harbor (ⓣ207/288-3274), is open all year, with reservations taken starting in February (through the National Park Service, ⓣ1-800/365-2267, or through ⓦreservations.nps.gov; $20). At **Seawall**, off Rte-102A near Bass Harbor (ⓣ207/288-3338; $50 per site, which accommodates fifteen people), campsites are available on a first-come, first-served basis (closed Oct to mid-May). The Appalachian Mountain Club maintains the private **Echo Lake Camp** (July to early Sept; ⓣ603/466-2727; $440 per week), an extremely popular lakefront camp in Acadia National Park between Somesville and Southwest Harbor, with tent sites, beds, a dining room, kitchens, shared bathhouses with hot showers, canoes, and kayaks; rates here include three family-style meals a day. The following list of privately owned campgrounds on the island is not exhaustive but it should be sufficient; for a more complete guide, contact the information center. Most charge about $30 per night, or more for a waterfront location. Also, the months they are open vary – it is advisable to call before setting out.

Bar Harbor 409 Rte-3, Bar Harbor ⓣ207/288-5185
Bar Harbor KOA 136 County Rd, Bar Harbor ⓣ207/288-3520
Bar Harbor Woodlands KOA 1453 Rte-3, Bar Harbor ⓣ207/288-3520
Bass Harbor Bass Harbor ⓣ207/244-5857
Mt. Desert Rte-198, Somesville ⓣ207/244-3710
Mt. Desert Narrows 1219 Rte-3, Bar Harbor ⓣ207/288-4782
White Birches 195 Seal Cove Rd, Southwest Harbor ⓣ207/244-3797

rooms in three buildings with modern amenities decorated attractively, yet unfussily. The eight-acre property is right on Frenchman Bay, and the views from many of the rooms can't be beat. ❼–❽

Mount Desert YWCA 36 Mount Desert St ⓣ207/288-5008. Centrally located women-only accommodation. Beds in dorm-style rooms start at $25, and are $70 for the week. Beds also available from $95 per week (single) or $80 (double).

The Ridgeway Inn 11 High St ⓣ1-800/360-5226, ⓦwww.theridgewayinn.com. You'll be well cared for at this low-key little B&B on a quiet street just around the corner from the town center. ❻–❼

The Tides 119 West St ⓣ207/288-4968. On a fairly residential street but still within a few minutes of the center of town, this elegant, somewhat formal pale-yellow mansion affords ocean views from all of its luxurious rooms. ❽–❾

Ullikana B&B 16 The Field ⓣ207/288-9552. The place to go in town for a romantic splurge; nicely decorated rooms and unbelievably sumptuous breakfasts. ❼–❾

Southwest Harbor and the west side

The Claremont 22 Claremont Rd, off Clark Point Rd, Southwest Harbor ⓣ207/244-5036 or 1-800/244-5036, ⓦwww.claremonthotel.com. Classic old-fashioned hotel with tennis and croquet, an excellent shorefront, and boating. On Friday nights the fine dining is accompanied by live piano-playing. They also have a number of cottages. Mid-May to mid-Oct. ❽–❾

The Inn at Southwest 371 Main St, Southwest Harbor ⓣ207/244-3835, ⓦwww.innatsouthwest.com. Brilliant old Victorian inn in the center of town with a cozy living room, cheery bedrooms, hearty breakfasts, and attentive innkeepers. Inexpensive off-season rates. ❻–❼

Lindenwood Inn 118 Clark Point Rd, Southwest Harbor ⓣ207/244-5335 or 1-800/307-5335, ⓦwww.lindenwoodinn.com. This first-class inn offers tastefully redecorated rooms and African accents in a stylish turn-of-the-century captain's home. Breakfast included. ❻–❾

The Yellow Aster 53 Clark Point Rd, Southwest Harbor ⓣ207/244-4422 or 1-800/724-7228, ⓦwww.yellowaster.com. Spotless and bright four-room B&B decorated with local artwork, with wholesome organic breakfasts and a bit of a new-agey feel. ❻

Bar Harbor

The town of **BAR HARBOR** began life as an exclusive resort, summer home to the Vanderbilts and the Astors, but the great fire of October 1947 that destroyed their opulent "cottages" changed the direction of the town's growth. Many of the old-money families rebuilt their summer estates in hyper-rich **Northeast Harbor**, southwest along Rte-3, and Bar Harbor is now firmly geared towards tourists – though it's by no means downmarket. There's not all that much to do in town, even in high summer. However, the ambience is sufficient for it to take a while to realize that once you've strolled around the village green, and walked along the **Shore Path** past the headland of the *Bar Harbor Inn* and along the coast for views of the ocean and Frenchman Bay, you've seen most of what Bar Harbor has to offer.

In high season up to 21 different **sea trips** set off each day, for purposes ranging from deep-sea fishing to cocktail cruises. Among the most popular are the **whale-watching,** puffin, and seal trips run by Bar Harbor Whale Watch Company, 1 West St (☎207/288-2386 or 1-800/WHALES-4). Cruises, which depart adjacent to the Town Pier, take about three hours and cost around $45. With Downeast Windjammer Cruises, you can also enjoy a two-hour trip on the impressive **schooner** *Margaret Todd* or a deep-sea fishing experience on

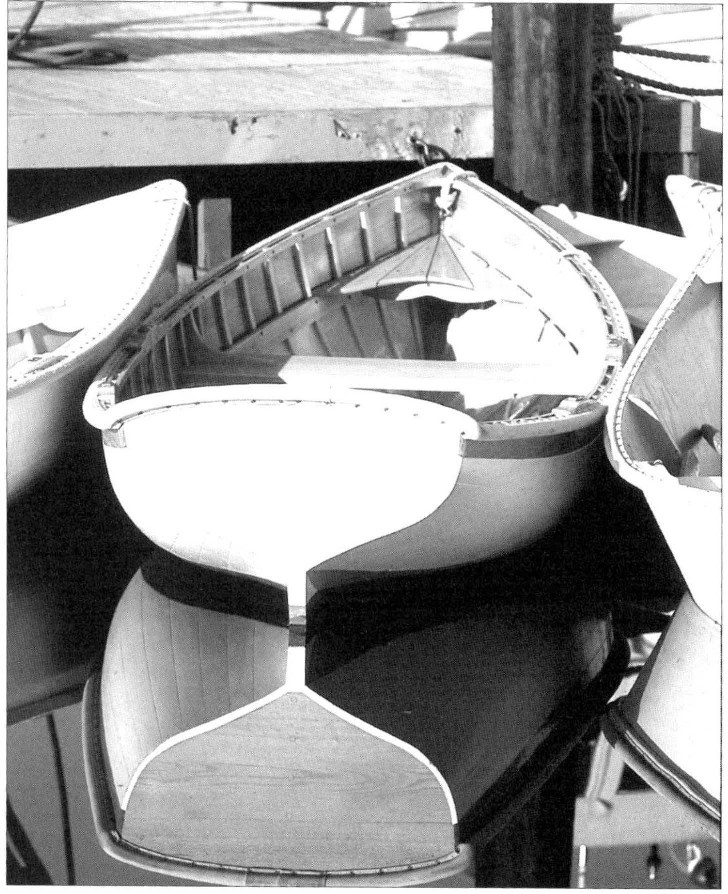

△ Mount Desert Island rowboats

the *Katherine* (leaving from the *Bar Harbor Inn* pier daily June–Oct; $29.50 and $39.50 ⓣ207/288-4585).

One of the town sights in its heyday was the "Indian Village," a summer encampment where Native Americans came to sell pottery, necklaces, and trinkets to tourists; it was cleared away in the 1930s to make room for a new ballpark. Nowadays, Wapanahki heritage is preserved in a far more inspiring space – the Robert **Abbe Museum**, 26 Mount Desert St (mid-May to mid-Oct daily 9am–5pm, Thurs–Sat until 9pm; rest of year Thurs–Sun 10am–5pm; $6, children $2, admission includes Sieur de Monts location; ⓣ207/288-3519, ⓦwww.abbemuseum.org), which has a number of gorgeously constructed exhibit spaces full of light and pale wood paneling. Although the opening displays on Wapanahki culture are well put together, the Abbe's knockout piece is the "Circle of the Four Directions," a contemplative, circular space built of cedar panels that span upward into an arced skylight. If that's not enough to wow you, they even have an original piece from glass wizard Dale Chihuly, his personal gift to the museum. The museum's original building, which shows Maine archeological findings and relates the history of the institution, is included in the admission price, and is just a couple of miles south of Bar Harbor at Sieur de Monts Spring, just off the Park Loop Road (daily mid-May to mid-Oct 9am–4pm).

Acadia National Park

ACADIA NATIONAL PARK, sprawled out over most of Mount Desert Island, the Schoodic Peninsula to the east, and Isle au Haut to the south, is the most visited natural place in Maine. It's visually stunning, with dramatic rolling hills carving smooth rocky silhouettes into the misty horizon. Dense stands of fir and birch trees hide over 120 miles of **hiking trails** (see box opposite) that pop into view on the island's 26 boulder-like summits. In fact, there's all you could want here in terms of mountains and lakes for secluded rambling, and such **wildlife** as seals, beavers, and bald eagles is not scarce. The two main geographical features are the narrow fjord of **Somes Sound**, which almost splits the island in two, and **Cadillac Mountain**, an unbelievable place to watch the sunrise, though the summit of the 1530-foot mound offers tremendous ocean views at any time of the day (assuming clear weather). It can be reached either by a moderately strenuous climb – more than you'd want to do before breakfast – or by a very leisurely drive, winding up a low-gradient road.

The most enjoyable way to explore is to ride a rented **bicycle** around the 45 miles of one-lane gravel-surfaced "**carriage roads**," built by John D. Rockefeller Jr as a protest against the 1913 vote that allowed "infernal combustion engines" onto the island. Keep your eye out for several ornate **granite bridges**, commissioned by Rockefeller and built by architects William Welles Bosworth and Charles Stonington. Three companies rent mountain bikes for less than $20 per day. There's Bar Harbor Bicycle Shop, at 141 Cottage St on the edge of town (Ⓣ207/288-3886), and Acadia Bike & Canoe, across from the post office at 48 Cottage St (Ⓣ207/288-9605); Southwest Cycle does the same on Main Street in Southwest Harbor (Ⓣ207/244-5856 or 1-800/649-5856). All provide excellent maps and are good at suggesting routes. Be sure to carry water, as there are very few refreshment stops inside the park.

If you'd prefer to get out on the water, you can take a four-hour guided **kayak tour** ($45) from May to October with National Park Sea Kayak Tours, 39 Cottage St (Ⓣ207/288-0342 or 1-800/347-0940, Ⓦwww.acadiakayak.com), which also leads overnight sea-kayaking trips. (They also offer downhill bike rides from the top of Cadillac Mountain.) Just up the street at no. 48, Coastal Kayaking Tours offers similar kayaking trips, including overnight island camping packages (Ⓣ207/288-9605 or 1-800/526-8615). With an abundance of rocky cliffs and overhangs, **rock climbing** is also popular here, and Acadia Mountain Guides (Ⓣ207/866-7562 or 1-888/232-9559) conducts half-day and full-day climbs, with prices at $50–100 a head, depending on the number of people in your group.

The park is open all year, with a summer-only **visitors' center** in Hulls Cove (May–Oct) at the entrance to the Loop Road north of Bar Harbor (see "Information," p.574), and one on the village green in Bar Harbor. The entrance fee is $20 per car for a seven-day pass, or $5 if you enter on bike or cycle. Many visitors do nothing more than drive the length of the 27-mile Park Loop Road, which admittedly winds through some of the park's most arresting areas, but you should also make the effort to get onto the trails. The only fee collection station is on Park Loop Road near **Sand Beach**, five miles south of Bar Harbor, but there are several other spots (including the aforementioned visitor center in Bar Harbor) where you can purchase a pass.

Hiking on Mount Desert Island

It's no secret that Mount Desert Island offers some of the most exhilarating **hiking** in New England – most of its hundred miles of trails are deserted only in the dead of winter. Though by no means exhaustive, the following list highlights some of the best hikes. If you plan on exploring the island's trails extensively, get your hands on a copy of the detailed guidebook *A Walk in the Park*, published locally ($15) and available at the park visitors' center. The Southwest Harbor Chamber of Commerce (☎207/244-9264 or 1-800/423-9264) prints a decent map (free) of the west side of the park, detailing some two dozen hikes.

Easy

Flying Mountain Trail, five minutes north of Southwest Harbor, just off of Rte-103 on Fernald Point Road. This short (0.7-mile) hike affords beautiful views at the top of 284-foot Flying Mountain. (1hr)

Jordan Pond Shore Trail, from the Jordan Pond parking area. A 3.3-mile loop that roughly follows the water's edge. (2hr)

Ship Harbor Nature Trail, at the southern end of the park off of Rte-102A near the Bass Harbor Head Light. An easy 1.3-mile trail that loops out along the coast and back. (45min)

Moderate

Bubble Rock Trail, starting at Bubble Rock parking area. Two one-mile forest loop trails, with some vistas of Jordan Pond. (1hr)

Great Head Loop, beginning at Sand Beach on the Park Loop Road. Scenic 1.5-mile trail leads along towering cliffs right above the sea. (45min)

South Ridge Trail, departing from Rte-3, near the Blackwoods Campground. This trail is the best way to get to the top of Cadillac Mountain, the highest point on the island at 1530ft. The 7.4-mile round-trip is not particularly strenuous but very rewarding. (5hr)

Strenuous

Acadia Mountain Trail, a few miles south of Somesville, on the east side of Rte-102. A relatively steep ascent to the top of the 700-foot mountain, with fine views of the Somes Sound. 2.5 miles round-trip. (1.5hr)

The Beehive, just north of the Sand Beach parking area. A short one-mile trip up iron rungs on exposed ledges. There's a swimming pond near the top called the Bowl. (45min).

Mansell Mountain, at the south end of Long Pond, near Southwest Harbor. Trees impair the views from the 950-foot summit, but the two-mile hike along the Perpendicular Trail features stairways carved into the rock and unparalleled seclusion. (2hr)

Penobscot Mountain, departs near the Jordan Pond House. This 2.6-mile trail (round-trip) affords panoramic views, second only perhaps to those from Cadillac Mountain. (3hr)

Southwest Harbor and Bass Harbor

The western half of Mount Desert Island was for many years unflatteringly called the "Backside" by well-heeled and snooty residents of Bar Harbor. But while its quiet hamlets still maintain a much slower pace than Bar Harbor proper, the area is not without appeal, especially if you're seeking refuge from the crowds.

SOUTHWEST HARBOR, along Rte-102 across from Northeast Harbor, is the center of this side's action, so to speak. The small "downtown" is graced

The Schoodic Peninsula

A small section of Acadia National Park lies isolated at the end of the **Schoodic Peninsula**, some eight miles south of US-1 along Rte-186, where Schoodic Point overlooks a rocky shoreline that spills out into the crashing surf, creating many natural picnic benches. Watch out for the menacing gulls, who easily quell their fear of humans in search of sandwiches to grab.

The Point is the most scenic of stops on the peninsula, though there are plenty of places to pull off Rte-186 and explore a bit of the coast on foot. The pleasant little village of **WINTER HARBOR**, northwest of the park along Rte-186, is a worthwhile stop, if for no other reason than to grab a fresh smoothie at local hangout *JM Gerrish*, 352 Main St (Ⓣ207/963-2727), or to pick up some of their sumptuous picnic fare. If you prefer, you can take the ferry over from Bar Harbor – there are five round-trips a day ($29; Ⓣ207/288-2984).

If you are in the area, don't miss the yearly **lobster festival** in Winter Harbor, held the second Saturday in August, when lobster lovers converge on the tiny town to down heaps of the tender meat, shop for crafts, listen to live music, and watch a parade.

with a couple of top-notch restaurants and the surrounding area has a smattering of cozy, out-of-the-way accommodations. The streets here are quiet at 8pm on Saturday nights in high summer – though how long it will remain that way in the face of increased tourist traffic is doubtful. Regardless, Southwest Harbor makes for a good base from which to explore the western half of Acadia, and, if you plan on visiting the neighboring Swans Island or Long Island, the state ferry is only a couple of miles away in Bass Harbor.

South along Rte-102, **BASS HARBOR** is even further removed, the simple homes that line its streets reflecting the modest middle-class lifestyle of its residents. At the southernmost tip of the island, just off of Rte-102A, you'll find the much-photographed **Bass Harbor Head Light**, perched on the rocks and tucked behind the trees. Though the 1858 structure is not open to visitors, you can walk down a short seaside path for a good view of the lighthouse and the ocean beyond. If you prefer to explore the water itself, take a three-and-a-half-hour lunch **cruise** from Island Cruises ($25, lunch not included), to the fishing village of Frenchboro on Long Island, or a two-hour nature cruise aboard the forty-foot *R.L.Gott* (mid-June to mid-Oct; $20; Ⓣ207/244-5785). The Maine State Ferry also runs **boats** between Bass Harbor, Swans Island, and Frenchboro several days per week (Ⓣ207/244-3254).

Eating and drinking

Mount Desert's most memorable **eating** experiences are to be found in the many **lobster pounds** all over the island, but for nightlife Bar Harbor is where the people are. Cottage Street is a much more promising area to look for food and evening atmosphere than the surprisingly subdued waterfront. As usual, **seafood** is everywhere, although, thankfully, there are some more creative options available.

As for other diversions, the Art Deco Criterion cinema at 35 Cottage St (Ⓣ207/288-3441) looks exactly as it did when it was built in 1932 and shows current favorites. But perhaps the most unusual of choices is the Great Maine Lumberjack Show (on Rte-3 in Trenton; mid-June to Aug every night at 7pm; Ⓣ207/667-0067, Ⓦwww.mainelumberjack.com). Hosted by Timber Tina, a logging sports champion who has competed around the world, it's campy family fun, with bits of history, humor, axes, and sawdust flying through the air.

Bar Harbor

The Alternative Market 16 Mt Desert St ☎207/288-8225. Bag lunches, big sandwiches, soups, smoothies, and fresh-squeezed juices.

The Burning Tree Rte-3, Otter Creek ☎207/288-9331. A few miles south of Bar Harbor, this outwardly unimpressive seafood restaurant spices up its brilliant entrees ($15–20) with tasty Southwestern and Caribbean touches. Reservations a must in July and Aug; closed Mon and Tues starting in Sept. Closed mid-Oct to mid-June.

Café Bluefish 122 Cottage St ☎207/288-3696. Charming, eclectically decorated little restaurant specializing in exceptional seafood and poultry dishes with a twist, such as the intensely flavored pecan-crusted halibut ($20) and award-winning lobster strudel ($27).

Café This Way 14 Mt Desert St ☎207/288-4483. Fresh, creative breakfast options like the café monte cristo (a French toast sandwich with eggs, ham, cheddar cheese, and syrup on the side), good orange juice, and eight omelet varieties. Very busy in summer. They also serve dinner.

Geddy's 76 Main St ☎207/288-5077. You can't miss the glam-rock lobster claws jutting out from Geddy's exterior. The interior is better-looking, plus they serve up good family fare (steak, seafood, pasta).

George's Restaurant 7 Stephens Lane (off Main St) ☎207/288-4505. Where the hoi polloi take guests they want to impress. Though upscale, it's still approachable, and the food – grilled lobster tail with ricotta and tarragon gnocchi – is impressive.

Havana 318 Main St ☎207/288-CUBA. American dining with a Latin sensibility, which translates into lemon and cilantro cured local salmon. Cool modern ambience, sometimes with low-key live music.

Jordan Pond Park Loop Rd, Acadia National Park ☎207/276-3316. In the heart of Acadia National Park between Bar Harbor and Northeast Harbor. Serves light meals, ice cream, and popovers (light, puffy egg muffins). Afternoon tea, a longtime Acadia tradition, is served in the beautiful lakeside garden 11.30am–5.30pm.

McKay's 231 Main St ☎207/288-2202. The interior feels like your grandfather's den (assuming your grandfather has a good sense of modern aesthetics). Slightly upscale, creatively prepared meats and fishes for lunch and dinner.

Morning Glory Bakery 39 Rodick St ☎207/288-3041. Fabulous fresh-baked breads, coffee, and pastries served at a purple-trimmed cottage. Closed Sun.

Reel Pizza Cinerama 35 Kennebec Place, directly next to the Village Green ☎207/288-3828 takeout, 207/288-3811 movie info. Eat pizza and watch artsy or blockbuster films on the big screen. It's a great concept, and it works. Movie tickets are $6.

Rupununi 119 Main St ☎207/288-2886. Overpriced pub grub served until late – stick to the burgers. The bar stays open until 1am.

Siam Orchid 30 Rodick St ☎207/288-9669. Large selection of tasty, authentic Thai food with polite service; most entrees cost under $11.

Thirsty Whale 40 Cottage St ☎207/288-9335. As rowdy as Bar Harbor gets. Live music every night of the week in season. Plus they have the best fish sandwiches in town.

Southwest Harbor and Bass Harbor

Beal's Lobster Pier 182 Clark Point Rd, Southwest Harbor ☎207/244-7178. Fresh seafood for under $10, on a rickety wooden pier. You can pick out your own lobster from a tank, or choose from a small menu of other seafood choices. Closed Nov–April.

Deck House Restaurant & Cabaret Theater Great Harbor Marina, at end of Apple Lane, Southwest Harbor ☎207/244-5044. Full dinner plus more than a dozen songs performed in the round nightly, June–Sept.

Eat a Pita & Café 2 326 Main St, Southwest Harbor ☎207/244-4344. A great casual, cozy, and affordable spot with delicious, healthy gourmet food (pastas, salads, pita sandwiches, seafood), candlelit tables, and friendly service. Lunch and dinner served.

Red Sky 14 Clark Point Rd, Southwest Harbor ☎207/244-0476. Seasonal, new American cuisine served in a popular, fairly upscale eatery.

Seafood Ketch McMullen Ave, Bass Harbor ☎207/244-0476. Great super-fresh seafood overlooking Bass Harbor. Reservations recommended.

Thurston's Lobster Pound Steamboat Wharf Rd, Bernard ☎207/244-3320 or 1-800/235-3320. Dine on your lobster of choice amidst a casual cafeteria-style layout overlooking Bass Harbor. Open end of May to Oct.

East to Canada

Looking at a typical map of the United States, you'd never dream that Canada stretches eastward for five hundred miles beyond Maine. Indeed, few travelers venture into the hundred miles of Maine lying east of Acadia National Park, mainly because it is unpopulated, windswept, and remote. In summer, though, the weather here is usually no worse than the rest of Maine, and the coastal drive is exhilarating – it runs next to the Bay of Fundy, which has the highest tides in the nation. Tourism is not big business in these parts, but each village has one or two B&Bs and low-priced restaurants (and plenty of space in which to enjoy it). Outside of the rugged scenery, highlights include picturesque **West Quoddy Head**, the easternmost point in the United States, the quiet seaside town of **Lubec,** and wild **blueberries** – ninety percent of the nation's crop comes from this part of Maine.

Machias

MACHIAS, on US-1, sports a little waterfall right in the middle of town, and was the unlikely location of the first naval encounter of the Revolutionary War, in 1775, when the townsfolk, brandishing pitchforks, swords, and firearms, commandeered the British schooner *Margaretta* after refusing to provide it with provisions. The attack was planned in the still-standing gambrel-roofed **Burnham Tavern**, Rte-192 just off of US-1 (mid-June to Aug, Mon–Fri 9am–5pm; $2; ⓣ207/255-4432), which has been restored to approximate the tavern's original colonial set-up, and to commemorate its place in history.

The best place to **eat** here is the *Artist's Café*, 3 Hill St (ⓣ207/255-8900), with its slightly upscale, frequently changing menu; chicken parmesan and lobster linguini are typical offerings. Meals are also good value at the bluesy and fresh *Fat Cat Deli*, 28 Main St (ⓣ207/255-6777). Nearby is the *Machias Motor Inn* (ⓣ207/255-4861; ❹), which has sundecks and superb views. The restored *Riverside Inn and Restaurant*, on US-1 in East Machias (ⓣ207/255-4134; ❺), overlooks the Machias River and has a tasty prix-fixe menu six days a week. Cheaper and less romantic, but still comfortable, is the *Bluebird Motel*, a mile south of town on US-1 (ⓣ207/255-3332; ❹).

East of town, Rte-191 heads along a regal and desolate portion of shoreline known as the **Bold Coast**. From the parking lot along Rte-191, four miles east of **CUTLER**, two **hiking loops** head out to the windswept coast and back. There's a small beach at Long Point Cove and you can sometimes catch a glimpse of humpback whales from the cliffs. The Cobscook Trails Coalition (ⓣ207/827-1818) has information on the trails and campsites along the way.

Aim to visit Machias the second week of August, when they have their annual blueberry festival (ⓦwww.machiasblueberry.com), featuring craft fairs, fireworks, and general blueberry feasting.

West Quoddy Head, Lubec, and Campobello Island

With a distinctive red-and-white striped lighthouse dramatically signaling its endpoint, **WEST QUODDY HEAD** is the easternmost part of the United States, jutting defiantly into the stormy Atlantic. You can see Canada just across the Bay of Fundy, though for a better view, take the three-mile east trail in **Quoddy Head State Park** that traces a winding line along precipitous cliffs and also diverges onto a fantastic bog trail.

Just beyond the turnoff for Quoddy Head, tiny **LUBEC** was once home to more than twenty sardine-packing plants. They're all gone now, but the remnants of **McCurdy's** fish company, on Water Street, are enough to evoke visions (and maybe even smells) of more prosperous times. Of several decent B&Bs

in town, try the friendly *Peacock House*, 27 Summer St (ⓣ207/733-2403, ⓦwww.peacockhouse.com; ⑤–⑥), which has an atmosphere of casual elegance, or the *Home Port Inn*, 45 Main St (ⓣ207/733-2077 or 1-800/457-2077; mid-June to mid-Oct; ⑤), an old 1880 house with seven guestrooms. The *Sunset Point Trailer Park*, on the west end of town, has scenic **campsites** overlooking the water (ⓣ207/733-2272).

Campobello Island

Lubec is the gateway to **CAMPOBELLO ISLAND**, in New Brunswick, Canada where President Franklin D. Roosevelt summered from 1909 to 1921, before he became president, and to which he occasionally returned while in office. The barn-red cottage is now open to the public, furnished just as the Roosevelts left it. There is also a sleek and informative visitors' center, with additional exhibits relating to the Roosevelts. The rest of **Roosevelt Campobello International Park** (mid-May to mid-Oct daily 9am–5pm; free; ⓦwww.fdr.net), located on Canadian soil but held jointly with the United States, is good for a couple of hours' wandering. There are several coastal trails and picnic areas, and the drive out to **Liberty Point** is worth the effort. (Note: although Americans do not currently need a passport to cross into Canada, US border crossings continue to get more rigorous, and it would behoove you to bring one along).

Eastport

The attractive seaside town of **EASTPORT**, afloat on Moose Island between Cobscook and Passamaquoddy bays at the end of Rte-190, is quite a way off the beaten track. Canada is only several miles away, but the closest border crossing is twenty-eight miles north in Calais, and the bridge to Campobello Island in Lubec is forty miles from here by car – you have to drive all the way around Cobscook Bay to get there. The quiet town maintains the lonely air of a remote outpost, with spotty weather, hills that slope gently toward a collection of Canadian islands just across the bay, and lots of old brick and clapboard buildings. Eastport's major claim to fame is that it is home to the largest whirlpool in the western hemisphere, ignobly dubbed the "Old Sow." At least ten people have met their end in Old Sow, but you can view it safely at the terminus of Clark Street.

A result of the somewhat active local arts community, the Eastport Gallery, 52 Water St (ⓣ207/853-4166), is worth a spin, usually housing an interesting collection of works by Maine artists in its two-story exhibit space. If you're looking to get out on the water, the romantic windjammer *Sylvina W. Beal* (used as a setting in the *Age of Innocence*, no less) offers whale-watching and sunset cruises (ⓣ207/853-2500).

Practicalities

There are several good **restaurants** in town, two culinary landmarks, and some good-value **accommodation**. *La Sardina Loca*, 28 Water St (ⓣ207/853-2739), serves a host of Mexican entrees for less than $10 a piece in a wonderfully eclectic interior. The *Eastport Chowderhouse*, 167 Water St (ⓣ207/853-4700), dishes up wicked good fresh seafood, some caught that day from their backyard. *Raye's Mustard*, 83 Washington St (ⓣ207/853-4451), has been producing its "liquid gold" for over one hundred years – it's the country's last surviving stone mustard mill, while another local landmark, *Katie's on the Cove,* north of town on Rte-1, doles out unbelievably good confections from a little canary-yellow house

(Ⓣ207/853-4172 Ⓦkatiesonthecove.com). The recently renovated *Chadbourne House*, an elegant Federalist home at 19 Shackford St (Ⓣ207/853-2727 or 1-888/853-2728; ❻), has spacious rooms, many with fireplaces, while the *Motel East*, 23A Water St (Ⓣ207/853-4747; ❺), has scenic porches overlooking the bay. Halfway between Eastport and Lubec off of US-1, **Cobscook Bay State Park** has the best **camping** around (mid-May to mid-Oct; Ⓣ207/726-4412), with over a hundred beautifully situated campsites and good facilities.

Calais

The border between the United States and Canada weaves through the center of **Passamaquoddy Bay**; the towns to either side get on so well that they refused to fight in the US–UK War of 1812, and promote themselves jointly to tourists as the **Quoddy Loop**. It's perfectly feasible to take a two-nation vacation, but each passage through customs and immigration between **CALAIS** (pronounced "callous") in the States and **St Stephen** in Canada does take a little while – and watch out for the confusion stemming from the fact that they're in different time zones. No trace now remains of Samuel de Champlain's 1604 attempt to found a colony on the diminutive St Croix Island, which you can view via an International Historic site commemorating de Champlain on US-1. In town, the *Wickachee Dining Room*, 638 Main St (Ⓣ207/454-3400), serves big plates of seafood and steak. West's Coastal Connections (Ⓣ207/546-2823 or 1-800/596-2823) runs a once-daily bus from Calais to Ellsworth and Bangor. The **visitors' center**, in rather hokey Downeast Heritage Museum at 39 Union St (Ⓣ207/454-2211), has loads of information on activities and accommodations and a helpful staff.

Nearby, the Baring division of the **Moosehorn National Wildlife Refuge**, between Rte-191 and Charlotte Road (Ⓣ207/454-7161), is a good place to catch a glimpse of a bald eagle or woodcock; they maintain some sixty miles of hiking trails – also good for cross-country skiing in winter.

Inland Maine

The vast expanses of the **Maine interior**, stretching up into the cold far north, consist mostly of evergreen forests of pine, spruce, and fir, interspersed by the white birches and maples responsible for the spectacular fall colors. Only in the remote north is much of it genuine wilderness, however; elsewhere what you see is more likely to be woodlands cultivated by the timber companies.

Distances are large. Once you get away from the two largest cities nearer the sea – **Augusta**, the capital, and **Bangor** – it's roughly two hundred miles by road to the northern border at **Fort Kent**, while to drive between the two most likely inland bases, **Greenville** and **Rangeley** (where exiled psychologist Wilhelm Reich lived and is buried), takes three hours or more. Driving (there's no public transport) through this mountainous scenery can be a great pleasure, but you do need to know where you're going. There are few places to stay, even fewer gas stations, and beyond Bangor many roads are tolled access routes belonging to the lumber companies: gravel-surfaced, vulnerable to bad weather, and in any case often not heading anywhere in particular.

This landscape has evolved in a very unusual way. Many communities grew up without roads to serve them, back in the days when the timber harvest was floated downriver to the sea; other more recent settlements have only ever been accessible by seaplane. Now that mighty trucks carry the tree trunks instead, roads are finally being pushed through, amid complaints that they are ruining the whole feel of the place.

If you have the time, this is great territory in which to **hike** – the **Appalachian Trail** starts its two-thousand-mile course down to Georgia at the top of Mount Katahdin – or **raft** on the swift **Penobscot** or **Kennebec** rivers. **Skiing**, too, is a popular activity, particularly at **Sugarloaf** or in the area around **Bethel** near the New Hampshire border, where the White Mountain National Forest extends into Maine.

Especially around the beautiful **Baxter State Park** and enormous **Moosehead Lake**, the forests are home to deer, beaver, a few bears, some recently introduced caribou, and plenty of **moose**. These endearingly gawky creatures (they look like badly drawn horses and are virtually blind) tend to be seen at early morning or dusk; in spring they come to lick the winter's salt off the roads, while in summer you may spot them feeding in shallow water. They do, however, cause major havoc on the roads, particularly at night, and each year significant numbers of drivers are killed in collisions with these hefty creatures.

Augusta and Hallowell

The capital of Maine since 1831, **AUGUSTA**, thirty miles north of Brunswick, is much quieter and less visited now than it was a hundred years ago. The lumber industry here really took off after the technique of making paper from wood was rediscovered in 1844, and Augusta also had a lucrative sideline at the time: each winter hundreds of thousands of tons of **ice**, cut from the Kennebec River, were shipped out as far as the Caribbean, in a trade now all but forgotten by history. There are informative displays on that past in the **Maine State Museum** (Mon–Fri 9am–5pm, Sat 10am–4pm, Sun 1–4pm; $2; ⓣ207/287-2301, ⓦwww.state.me.us/museum), housed inside the ugly governmental complex that's shared by the Maine State Library and Archives just south of the capitol on State Street. Walking through dimly lit hallways past the well-designed and intriguing (if slightly outdated) "Twelve Thousand Years in Maine" exhibit, you actually get quite a good sense of how the state has developed over the centuries. Also of note is "Made in Maine," centered on a functional three-story water-powered mill and including a fantastic collection of old looms and antique forms of transport.

Next door, the 180-foot dome of the imposing **Maine State House** (Mon–Fri 8am–5pm), a Charles Bulfinch design, is visible from nearly anywhere in Augusta. The rather impressive granite structure, completed in 1832, has been subject to several renovations that have nearly doubled its size. You can take a self-guided **tour**, though unless you have a particular interest in politics or architecture, this should kill no more than twenty minutes of your time. If you're so inclined, free guided tours can be arranged by calling the museum at ⓣ207/287-2301.

Hallowell

Just two short miles south of Augusta beside the gently sloping banks of the Kennebec River, the quaint haven of **HALLOWELL** is far more pleasant than its governmentally focused neighbor, especially along its main drag, **Water Street**, lined with some excellent **restaurants** and a couple of diverting bookstores and antique shops. Once a major port for lumber and granite, as well as a shipbuilding center, the place boasts a number of stately historic homes left over from those prosperous times, mostly perched in the picturesque hills above town. A small population of artists and craftsmen has arrived in recent years; for **information** on visiting one of the many studios in the area, contact the Kennebec Valley Chamber of Commerce (Ⓣ207/623-4559).

Practicalities

If you plan to stay in the Augusta area, the best-value **accommodation** is *America's Best Inn*, 65 Whitten Rd at the Maine Turnpike's Augusta Winthrop exit (Ⓣ207/622-3776; ❺). The sole **B&B** is over in Hallowell, the *Maple Hill Farm*, set on 62 acres on Outlet Road, off of Shady Lane (Ⓣ207/622-2708 or 1-800/622-2708, Ⓦwww.maplebb.com; ❻); you can feed the farm animals in the morning before enjoying a delicious breakfast. Decent family **camping** is available in Winthrop at the *Augusta West Lakeside Resort* (May 15 to Oct 15; Ⓣ207/377-9993).

For **food**, the *Thai Star*, 611 Civic Center Drive (Ⓣ207/621-2808), has an authentic menu featuring spicy crispy duck, yellow curry, and jasmine rice. Along the short main drag of Hallowell, *Slates*, 167 Water St (Ⓣ207/622-9575), is one of the best restaurants in the state, with a friendly atmosphere, fair prices, and original entrees like shrimp and scallops with coconut pie sauce over jasmine rice. Nearby, *Hattie's Chowder House*, 103 Water St (Ⓣ207/621-4114), has lobster stew so good it is mail-ordered across the country. The *Liberal Cup*, 115 Water St (Ⓣ207/621-2739), has great pub grub and six beers on tap that are brewed on the premises.

Bangor

BANGOR, 120 miles northeast of Portland at the intersection of Rte-1A and I-95, is not a place to spend much time, although its plentiful motels and the big new Bangor Mall on Hogan Road north of town make it a good last stop before the interior. As Maine's third largest city (32,000 people), the place is noticeably more urban and rough around the edges (for Maine, at least) than the state's smaller towns, serving as a major source of goods and services for the stretch of coast twenty miles south.

In its prime, Bangor was the undisputed "Lumber Capital of the World." Every winter its raucous population of "River Drivers" went upstream to brand the felled logs, which they then maneuvered down the swiftly flowing Penobscot River as the thaw came in April, reaching Bangor in time to carouse the summer away in the grog shops of Peppermint Row. Bangor also exported ice to the West Indies – and got rum in return. The forests were thinning and the prosperous days were coming to an end, however, when in October 1882, Oscar Wilde addressed a large crowd at the new Opera House and spoke diplomatically of "such advancement... in so small a city." A devastating fire in 1911 leveled much of the city, although a fair number of the lumber barons' lavish mansions survived.

Arrival, information, and accommodation

Many of the major airlines service the newly renovated **Bangor International Airport** (Ⓣ207/992-4600) on the western edge of town. Frequent **bus service** is available from Bangor to most other parts of the state. Concord Trailways, which docks at the Transportation Center at 1039 Union St (Ⓣ207/942-0807), can take you to Portland, Camden, and a number of smaller coastal cities. The CYR Bus Line (Ⓣ1-800/244-2335) heads north from both the Trailways and the Transit center and then heads north to Caribou, stopping in several small towns along the way. Vermont Transit Lines/Greyhound has a terminal at 158 Main St (Ⓣ207/945-3000), from which you can travel to Boston via Portland and Portsmouth or connect with Greyhound routes to other destinations. If you're spending any time at all in Bangor, you will find **BAT Community Connector** (Ⓣ207/992-4670; 85¢, carnet of five tickets $3) to be a handy means of getting around – look for the red bus with the black and gray bat outline on the side. Pick up a route map from any bus driver.

There's a helpful **information** center at the Bangor Region Chamber of Commerce, 519 Main St (Ⓣ207/947-0307, Ⓦwww.bangorregion.com), which has the typical collection of brochures and hotel information. Right in the center of town is Bangor's best **place to stay**, the *Charles Inn*, 20 Broad St (Ⓣ207/992-2820; ❺), an old green-brick building with 33 comfortably furnished rooms and a great art collection. Cheaper are the *Motel 6*, 1100 Hammond St (Ⓣ207/947-6921 or 1-800/466-8356; ❸), and the *Main Street Inn*, opposite the Paul Bunyan statue at 480 Main St (Ⓣ207/942-5282; ❹). For a somewhat grander experience, the *Lucerne Inn* in nearby Holden combines accommodation, access to golf facilities, a lakeside setting, three-course dinner, and continental breakfast (Ⓣ1-800/325-5123; ❻–❽).

The Town

One of the mansions that survives along West Broadway, complete with a spider-web-shaped iron gate, is now the suitably Gothic residence of horror author **Stephen King**, a Maine native who relocated here in 1980. You can browse the full collection of King's works, including some limited editions and collectibles, at Bett's Bookstore, 584 Hammond St (Ⓣ207/947-7052).

Bangor's other claim to fame, the 31-foot **Paul Bunyan** statue along Main Street south of downtown, is perhaps the largest such statue in the world – excepting one or two in Minnesota – though it looks more like a brightly painted model airplane kit than a statue. Bunyan was allegedly born here in 1834, though several other prominent logging towns across the US would probably dispute that claim. From mid-May until the end of July there's **harness racing** at Bass Park on Main Street (Ⓣ207/947-6744), just behind the statue; admission is free but the potential to lose money is unlimited.

Downtown, the **Bangor Museum and Center for History**, 6 State St (Tues–Fri 10am–4pm, Sat noon–4pm; free; Ⓣ207/942-1900), has an extensive collection of antique photographs and daguerrotypes, as well as some very cool "historic" clothing. Another museum sporting vintage artifacts is the **Cole Land Transportation Museum**, 405 Perry Rd (from I-95 follow signs to War Memorials; May to mid-Nov daily 9am–5pm; adults $6, children free; Ⓣ207/990-3600). The museum is packed with a fantastic collection of antique fire trucks, trains, and frighteningly large snowplows; the latter look like they could plow your house up along with the snow.

If you've got the time, drive up to the **Thomas Hill Standpipe**, off of Union Street on Thomas Hill Road. The massive cylindrical water tank was constructed in 1897 and still provides 1.75 million gallons of water to the residents of Bangor. Though there's really not much to it, the strange shingled structure is set on a hilltop with a partial view of the landscape. A couple of times a year, and usually in the first week of October, the standpipe's observatory is opened to the public, providing panoramic views of the surrounding countryside. Call the Chamber of Commerce (Ⓣ207/947-0307) for details.

A few miles north of Bangor, the Maine Center for the Arts (Ⓣ207/581-1755), at the University of Maine in **Orono**, runs a series of big-name concerts each summer.

Eating and drinking

Though Bangor does not have any great wealth of good **places to eat**, there are a number of pleasant spots. The family-owned *Thistles Restaurant,* 175 Exchange St (Ⓣ207/945-5480), serves up tasty, fairly upscale foods – grilled swordfish, Maine crab cakes, paella – for lunch and dinner. *Bagel Central*, 33 Central St (Ⓣ207/947-1654), has fresh bagels and a huge selection of other kosher foods. Beloved *Dysart's* (Ⓣ207/942-9878), a few miles south in Hermon (off I-95) has been a Maine institution for over 35 years. Essentially a 24-hour truck stop, they have a roomy diner with great trucker food, showers, and a barber shop.

The place to **drink** in town is *The Whig and Courier*, 18 Broad St (Ⓣ207/947-4095), a straightahead pub, with burgers, cheesesteaks, and a wide variety of beers on tap. The *New Moon Café*, 49 Park St (Ⓣ207/990-2233), has snacks, coffee, and espresso, and occasional live music.

Bethel and around

The remote, quintessentially New England town of **BETHEL**, nestled in the western Maine mountains about seventy miles north of Portland, may appear rather sleepy, but it's an excellent year-round base from which to explore the outdoors, most notably in the **White Mountains** and **Grafton Notch State Park**. Bethel has long attracted a rather academic and prosperous population; the prestigious Gould Academy is here, and the town was once home to the clinic of the famous neurobiologist Dr John Gehring for people with neurological disorders.

Arrival and accommodation

Bethel is not accessible via public transit, though the Airport Car Service runs from Portland (Ⓣ1-800/649-5071) for about $90 (it works out considerably less the more passengers there are); call at least 24 hours in advance. A similar service is operated by Airport Limo & Taxi (Ⓣ207/773-3433 or 1-800/517-9442). Bethel does, however, have a good concentration of **places to stay** once you do get there. The local Chamber of Commerce, on Cross Street (Mon–Fri 8am–5pm, Sat 10am–6pm, Sun noon–5pm; Ⓣ207/824-2282 or 1-800/442-5826, Ⓦwww.bethelmaine.com), can help you out if you need. For **camping**, *Crocker Pond Campground* off of Songo Pond Rd (Rte-5) just south of town (Ⓣ207/824-2134; $14; mid-May to mid-Oct), has eight secluded and rather primitive campsites that are maintained by the US Forest Service, while the more family-oriented *Bethel Outdoor Adventures*, 121 Mayville Rd (Rte-2; Ⓣ207/824-4224 or 1-800/553-3607), has both RV and tent sites on the banks of the Androscoggin River.

Bethel Inn Resort and Country Club on the Common ⓣ207/824-2175 or 1-800/654-0125. A full-service four-season resort, complete with golf course, tennis courts, a health club, fine dining, and pub. In the winter, they have 25 miles of groomed cross-country ski trails. ❼–❽

Briar Lea B&B Rte-2 east of Bethel Village ⓣ207/824-7277 or 1-877/311-1299, ⓦwww.briarleainn.com. Renovated 150-year-old Georgian farmhouse with a full-service English pub, and quite affordable too. ❹–❼

Chapman Inn on the Common ⓣ207/824-2657, ⓦwww.chapmaninn.com. Another fine B&B-like option, also with dorm beds ($33, including breakfast). ❷–❺

The Town

The **Bethel Common**, at the south end of Main Street along Broad, is flanked by a number of stately white-clapboard nineteenth-century homes and dominated by the sprawling **Bethel Inn and Country Club** (see above), whose yellow Victorian buildings and first-rate golf course spread out over several acres of grassy terrain. The 1813 Federal-style Dr Moses Mason House, part of the **Bethel Historical Society's Regional History Center**, is also on the Common (July & Aug Tues–Sun 1–4pm; other months by appointment; $3; ⓣ207/824-2908), holds an engaging and worthwhile museum that includes murals by painter Rufus Porter, period furnishings, and special exhibits relating to regional history. You might also cross the street to check out the **John Hastings Homestead**, which was built in 1820 for a founder of the Gould Academy, and has been preserved as it stood a century ago. For a more detailed look at the town's architectural highlights, pick up the **walking tour** brochure at the Historical Society or the Chamber of Commerce.

Skiing and other activities

Just a few miles north of Bethel off of Rte-2 on Sunday River Road, the **Sunday River Ski Resort** ($59 for a full-day lift ticket; ⓣ207/824-3000 or 1-800/543-2754, ⓦwww.sundayriver.com), is fast becoming one of the major alpine ski areas in New England. Their snowmaking system (copied by other resorts) guarantees "the most dependable snow in the Northeast" for skiing between November and May, with eighteen lifts servicing eight mountain peaks.

Bethel is also known for its **cross-country skiing**, and there are several privately owned centers in addition to the trails maintained in the White Mountain National Forest and Grafton Notch State Park. Some 25 miles of cross-country ski trails penetrate the wilderness at the beginner-oriented *Sunday River Inn & Cross Country Ski Center*, on Sunday River Road (ⓣ207/824-2410). Don't miss the trail that leads to the 1872 Artist's Covered Bridge, off of Sunday River Road, which is a good spot for swimming during the summer. You can also cross-country ski at Carter's Cross Country Farm & Ski Shop, with eighteen miles of trails at its location off of Rte-26 in Oxford, and forty miles of groomed trails in Bethel on Intervale Road (ⓣ207/539-4848).

For warm-weather activities, stop by *Bethel Outdoor Adventures,* on Rte-2 just east of Bethel Village (ⓣ207/824-4224 or 1-800/533-3607). They have **bike rentals** ($25/day) and route advice; they also rent **canoes** and **kayaks** and do guided trips.

Eating, drinking, and entertainment

Bethel's Best Rte-2, one mile west of Bethel Village ⓣ207/824-3192. Casual place for excellent pizza that also serves ice cream, clam chowder, lobster rolls, and hearty breakfasts.

Café Di Cocoa 119–125 Main St ⓣ207/824-5282. Bold vegetarian and ethnic specialties, sandwiches, soups, and espresso in a funky dining room. Their hours can be spotty – give them a call first.

Cho Sun 141 Main St ☎207/824-7370. Really good sushi and sashimi spot right in the center of town. Dinner only.

L'Auberge Country Inn and Bistro Mill Hill Rd off the Common ☎207/824-2774 or 1-800/760-2774. Gourmet meals (rack of New Zealand lamb, veal saltimbocca, and seafood *bouillabaisse*) are unfussily served in a beautifully converted country barn (the seven guestrooms there start at $149).

Matterhorn Ski Bar on Sunday River Rd in Newry ☎207/824-6271. This après-ski spot absolutely smokes in the wintertime: filled with winter revelers getting their grub on before hitting the slopes.

S.S. Milton 43 Main St ☎207/824-2589. Fairly casual spot with simple fare like tortellini alfredo and pan-seared sea bass. Open for lunch and dinner. In the summer, there's a sunny patio.

Sudbury Inn & Suds Pub 151 Main St ☎207/824-6558. The best of both worlds: incredible fine dining upstairs, hot spot for drinking downstairs, with live entertainment five nights per week and a good selection of microbrews until 1am.

Sunday River Brewing Co. north of town along Rte-2 at Sunday River Rd ☎207/824-4253. Particularly popular with skiers, serving freshly brewed ales and hearty pub fare, with occasional live music. Open year round.

Maine's White Mountains

Bethel sits just on the edge of the fifty thousand acres of the **White Mountain National Forest** that fall within Maine's borders, the center of which is **Evans Notch**, just as spectacular as any found in New Hampshire. Stop by their helpful **visitors' center**, at the intersection of Rte-2 and the Parkway, Bethel (☎207/824-2134), for maps, hiking suggestions, and information on campsite and shelter availability. There are a number of **backcountry shelters** in the forest, some nothing more than a sleeping platform with a pit toilet, but providing a unique experience in the middle of nowhere. All are accessible only on foot (located at least a couple of miles away from the trailhead) and are free on a first-come, first-served basis. Particularly good **hikes** through the sections of birch, maple, and pine include the moderately difficult 6.3-mile (about 5hr) **Caribou Mountain Loop**, starting at the trailhead on Rte-113, following the Mud Brook Trail, and ending at the summit of Caribou Mountain, and the easier 1.8-mile (about 1.5hr) loop that begins on Rte-113, across the bridge just north of *Hastings Campground* and leads up to the **Roost**, a granite overlook providing views of the Wild River Valley and Evans Notch.

North from Bethel: Grafton Notch State Park

North of Bethel, Rte-26 bisects beautiful **Grafton Notch State Park** (mid-May to mid-Oct; $2; ☎207/824-2912), a patch of rugged mountains, gurgling streams, cascading waterfalls, and bizarre geological formations. Among these, **Screw Auger Falls**, where the Bear River has carved out a twisting gorge through the solid granite, is good for wading. Just north, easy trails lead to **Moose Cave Gorge** and through the 45-foot-deep **Mother Walker Falls Gorge**, which features several natural stone bridges. More difficult trails head up **Old Speck Mountain**, Maine's third highest. Follow the 3.9-mile (one-way) **Old Speck Trail**, which traces the Appalachian Trail, from the Grafton Notch trailhead parking area up numerous switchbacks, past the Cascade Brook Falls to the Mahoosuc Trail, which eventually affords sweeping views at the summit. A somewhat shorter option is the **Table Rock Loop** (a two-hour jaunt with some very steep sections) that also departs from the main trailhead parking area up **Baldpate Mountain** to Table Rock, where you are treated for your efforts with mountain views. The State Park Office, or the Bethel Area Chamber of Commerce (see p.588) can provide you with maps and other necessary info. There are no campgrounds in Grafton Notch State Park.

Rangeley

RANGELEY is only just in Maine, a little way east of New Hampshire and fewer than fifty miles from the Canadian border, at the intersection of routes 4 and 16. Furthermore, as the sign on Main Street boldly declares, it is equidistant from the North Pole and the Equator (3107.5 miles), though that doesn't mean it's on the main road to anywhere. It has always been a resort, served in 1900 by two train lines and several steamships, with the real attraction then being the fishing in the spectacularly named Mooselookmeguntic Lake.

Today there's still one primary, albeit unorthodox, attraction, the remote **Wilhelm Reich Museum**, on Dodge Pond Road, about halfway along the north side of Rangeley Lake, a mile up on a side track off Rte-16 (July & Aug Wed–Sun 1–5pm; Sept Sun 1–5pm; $6; ⓣ207/864-3443, ⓦwww.wilhelmreichmuseum.org), where Wilhelm Reich eventually made his American home after fleeing Germany in 1933. Although he was an associate of Freud in Vienna and wrote the acclaimed *Mass Psychology of Fascism*, Reich is best remembered for developing the orgone energy accumulator. He claimed it could concentrate atmospheric energy; skeptical authorities focused on the not very specific way in which it was said to collect and harness human sexual energy. In a tragic end to his career, Reich was imprisoned after a wayward student broke an injunction forbidding the transportation of his accumulators across state lines, and he died in the federal penitentiary in Lewisberg, PA, in November 1957. He is buried here, amid the neat lawns and darting hummingbirds, and his house remains a museum for the reflection of his work.

South of town along Rte-17, it's worth seeking out **Angel Falls**, which, at ninety feet, are the highest in Maine. There's a good **swimming** spot at the base. Getting there is a bit complicated: take Rte-17 17.6 miles south of Oquossoc, turn west off Rte-17, cross the bridge, at highway mile marker 6102, turn right onto the old railroad line, after 3.5 miles, turn left on the gravel road, stay left through small gravel pits. Follow the marked trail, approximately one mile from this point. Nearby, in the old mining town of Byron, you can also swim in the crystal-clear waters of **Coos Canyon**, just off of Rte-17.

Practicalities

The *Rangeley Inn* at 2443 Main St (ⓣ207/864-3341, ⓦwww.rangeleyinn.com; ⑤) stands between Rangeley Lake and the smaller bird sanctuary of Haley Pond, so you can stay right in town and have a room that backs onto a scene of utter tranquility; there's also a gorgeous old wooden dining room. *North Country Inn B&B* at 2544 Main St (ⓣ207/864-2440, ⓦwww.northcountrybb.com; ⑥) is a good second choice. Otherwise, the Chamber of Commerce (see below) can provide lists of private home/condo rentals and "remote campsites" around the lake – which really are remote, several of them inaccessible by road. The *Red Onion*, 2511 Main St (ⓣ207/864-5022), is good for an array of inexpensive **food** including pizza, steak, and pasta. The best food in the area is at the *Porterhouse Restaurant*, in Eustis (take Rte-16E to Rte-27N and it's four miles up on Rte-27N; ⓣ207/246-7932). Set in a 1908 farmhouse, it offers exquisitely prepared entrees and an award-winning wine list.

Just south of the *Porterhouse* is the pretty *Cathedral Pines* **campground** (ⓣ207/246-3491). Twenty miles north of Rangeley, the peaceful *Grants Camps* beside Kennebago Lake (ⓣ1-800/633-4815) arranges fishing, canoeing, and windsurfing, with accommodation in comfortable cabins overlooking the lake, including all meals, costing around $145 per person per day; there are lower weekly rates. Rangeley Lakes' **Chamber of Commerce**, at 6 Park

AMC mountain huts in western Maine

The Appalachian Mountain Club (Ⓦwww.outdoors.org). maintains a host of remote **mountain huts** and **camps**, and there's a concentration in western Maine near the White Mountains. If you have your own tent and cookstove, these well-kept facilities offer endless outdoor options, especially if you're kayaking or canoeing. If you have questions or to make reservations, call or write the Pinkham Notch Visitor Center, PO Box 298, Gorham, NH 03581 (Ⓣ603/466-2727). Other AMC mountain huts in Maine are located on Mount Desert Island and near Georgetown Island, south of Bath.

Cold River Camp, North Chatham, NH (early July to mid-July, weekly rate $420; mid-July to early Sept weekly rate $490; early Sept to mid-Sept $50/day. Situated in the beautiful and undeveloped Evans Notch area of the White Mountain National Forest near the Maine border, this hundred-plus-acre site offers a full range of facilities such as cabins, electricity, hot showers, linens, a recreation hall, and a screened tea house. Rates include meals and firewood. Three nights' minimum stay in summer; cash only.

Swan's Falls Campground, Fryeburg (mid-May to mid-Oct; Ⓣ207/935-3395; $6 per night nonmembers, $5 members). Eighteen tent sites, several shelters, canoe access, toilets, and hand-pumped water in a pine forest along the Saco River near the White Mountains. Some campsites are accessible by car and all are quiet during the week. Parking costs an additional $5 per day.

Rd (Ⓣ207/864-5364 or 1-800/MT-LAKES, Ⓦwww.rangeleymaine.com), has details of various activities, including snowmobiling and moose-watching **canoeing** expeditions. One fun thing to do is take a **seaplane** trip with the Lake Region Air (Ⓣ207/864-5307), a fifteen-minute tour, flying low over vast forests and tiny lakes; it costs $35 per person.

Sugarloaf USA and Kingfield

The road east of Rangeley cuts through prime moose-watching territory – in fact, locals call Rte-16 "Moose Alley." After about fifty miles, in the Carrabassett Valley, looms the huge mountain of **SUGARLOAF USA**, Maine's biggest ski resort (lift tickets $61; Ⓣ207/237-2000 or 1-800/843-5623, Ⓦwww.sugarloaf.com). A spectacular place for skiers of all abilities (with over 120 trails), this condo-studded center would be a more popular destination if it weren't for the fact that the nearest airport is a two-hour drive away in Portland. Summer activities include guided **mountain-bike tours** over the extensive trail system on the ski mountain; you can set one up, or just rent a bike, courtesy of the Sugarloafer Shop (Ⓣ207/237-6718). There's also a full complement of hiking, canoe trips, and cookouts, plus a **golf** course designed by Robert Trent Jones Jr.

Kingfield

The best base for Sugarloaf is fifteen miles south in the tiny town of **KINGFIELD**. The *Mountain Village Inn*, 164 Main St (Ⓣ1-866/577-0741; ❻–❼) has welcoming, recently-remodeled rooms and terrific views of Sugarloaf mountain from its sunny dining room; breakfast is included. In the center of town, at 246 Main St, the *Herbert Grand Hotel* (Ⓣ1-888/656-9922; ❺) has less attractive but functional rooms and a good restaurant. On Rte-142 in Weld, southwest of Kingfield, the *Lake Webb House* (Ⓣ207/585-2479; ❹) offers very affordable accommodation in an old farmhouse with a huge porch; breakfast is included. For **food**, the groovy *Orange Cat Café* at 329 Main St (Ⓣ207/265-2860) has fresh wraps, salads, and espresso, while *The Village Inn Restaurant*, Rte-27, Belgrade Lakes (Thurs–Sat 5–9 pm; Ⓣ207/581-1154), is the place to get award-winning roast duckling.

Kingfield was the birthplace of twins Francis and Freelan Stanley, who invented, among other things, the famous Stanley Steamer car, and the dry-plate photographic process (which they sold to Kodak, amassing a considerable fortune). The **Stanley Museum** at 40 School St (June–Oct Tues–Sun 1–4pm; Nov–May Mon–Fri 9am–4pm; $4; Ⓣ207/265-2729, Ⓦwww.stanleymuseum.org) celebrates their story. Part of the main room is given over to their sister Chansonetta, a remarkable photographer whose studies of rural and urban workers have been widely published. Other exhibits include working steam cars from the early 1900s – if you're lucky, they might have one fired up when you arrive.

Moosehead Lake and around

Serene waters lap gently at the miles of deserted, thickly wooded shores around desolate **Moosehead Lake**, which at 117 square miles is the largest lake in Maine. As part of Maine's remote interior, the region was once relatively unknown, visited by Maine families, snowmobile fanatics, and serious hunters and fishermen; it's only now that more widespread discovery is taking place. **Greenville** is the sole settlement of any size on the lake, and it makes a good base from which to explore the area, especially if you're after moose sightings or intend to go whitewater rafting, though **The Forks**, a sporty settlement along the **Kennebec River** and US-201, has emerged as the center of the whitewater industry. West of the lake along Rte-15, gritty **Jackman**, big with the **snowmobile** crowd in winter, is the last stop before the Canadian border on the way to Québec.

Getting to Moosehead Lake

Moosehead Lake is roughly two and a half hours from Portland by car; the best way is via I-95 as far as Newport to Rte-11, Rte-23, and then Rte-6 N. While

△ Moosehead Lake

the majority of the **roads** in northern Maine are owned and maintained by huge logging and paper conglomerates, the public is often permitted access. On the **Golden Road**, for example, which connects Millinocket with the Québec border, travelers can pay a $4 fee at one of several gates for the privilege of driving its 96-mile length. Keep in mind, however, that the often unpaved roads are used primarily by logging trucks and that services are few and far between. Use caution and always yield to passing logging trucks. Distances are great and poor road conditions dictate slow travel speeds; be sure you have a good map and plenty of gas before you set out. In the towns especially, pay attention to the posted **speed limits** – local police are not shy about giving tickets if you're going only a few miles per hour too fast. For **information** on road availability and fees, call the Katahdin Paper Company at ⓣ207/723-2225.

Greenville and around

With a population of 1800, the rugged outpost of **GREENVILLE**, at the southern end of Moosehead Lake, is another nineteenth-century lumber town that now makes its living primarily from tourism. People come from all over to see wild **moose**, indigenous to the area, and which the town has been quick to exploit; there is nary a business around here that doesn't somehow incorporate the animal into its name. For several weeks in May and in June, there's even an annual celebration, creatively named **Moosemainea** (ⓣ207/695-2702 ⓦwww.mooseheadlake.org). The *Birches Resort* (see below) offers, for $28, moose-spotting cruises, where you're also likely to see eagles, bears, and peregrine falcons.

The town is quite pretty, and quite small, although it is well positioned for explorations throughout the Maine woods. Greenville's main attraction is the restored **steamboat**, *Katahdin*, which tours the lake and serves as the floating Moosehead Marine Museum – but watch out, ladies, no high heels or smoking on the ship (cruises: June to early Oct; Tues, Thurs, Sat & Sun 12.30pm, Wed 10am; 3hr cruise $30, 5hr cruise Wed $35; ⓣ207/695-2716). Near the dock, tiny **Thoreau Park** has a couple of picnic tables and a sign commemorating and describing the writer's 1857 visit to Moosehead Lake.

You'll soon want to get out of town, however, and a good way to explore is on a **mountain bike**; you can rent them ($25/day), along with canoes, kayaks, and camping equipment at Northwoods Outfitters, on Main Street (ⓣ207/695-3288 or 1-866/223-1380, ⓦwww.maineoutfitter.com). Greenville is also the largest **seaplane** base in New England; contact Currier's Flying Service (ⓣ207/695-2778) or Folsom's (ⓣ207/695-2821) for flight times and prices.

If you do choose to wander, one spot worth a visit is **Kineo**, an isolated nature preserve in the middle of the lake. Island trails lead to the top of dramatic **Mount Kineo**, whose flint-like cliff face rises some 800ft above the lake's surface. Shuttle boats to Kineo leave from Rockwood (daily 8am–5pm; $10).

Other good **hikes** in the area include the trip to **Gulf Hagas**, a 300-foot gorge fifteen miles east of town off of Greenville Road; the walk to an old B-52 crash site on nearby Elephant Mountain; and difficult climbs to the summits of 3196-foot **Big Moose Mountain** and 3230-foot **Big Spencer Mountain**. Contact the Chamber of Commerce for more information.

Practicalities

The **Chamber of Commerce**, just south of town on Rte-6/15 (summer daily 9am–5pm; rest of year Mon–Sat 10am–4pm; ⓣ207/695-2702), has lots of information about area activities and accommodation. As an alternative, the **Maine Forest Service** (ⓣ207/695-3721) can provide information on their many free campsites in the area. There's not too much in the way of **food** options here; one of the local favorites is *The Rod & Reel*, on Pritham Avenue (ⓣ207/695-0388), which serves fresh fish entrees on its outdoor patio. Also on Pritham Avenue, the *Stress Free Moose Pub & Café* (ⓣ207/695-3100) has tasty pub grub and a good selection of beers on tap (plus they're open late). *Kelly's Landing* (ⓣ207/695-4438) is good for lunches and big weekend breakfasts.

Accommodations are generally upscale wilderness retreats that were built for rugged hunters, though there are exceptions. The *Birches Resort*, north of Greenville near the small village of Rockwood (ⓣ207/534-7305 or 1-800/825-9453, ⓦwww.birches.com; ❶–❽), for example, offers both rustic (tents, yurts) and first-class accommodations along with a host of outdoor activities. There's also a fairly gourmet dining room overlooking the lake. More traditional choices back in Greenville include the *Pleasant Street Inn*, on Pleasant Street (ⓣ207/695-3400; ❻), and the unbelievably well-appointed *Blair Hill Inn* – lavish rooms, fabulous views of the lake, incredible fine dining (lit with original Tiffany lamps), and even an excellent summer concert series (ⓣ207/695-2229; ❾). Another luxurious spot is the *Lodge at Moosehead Lake* (ⓣ207/695-4400; ❽), on Lily Bay Road, with a beautiful hillside location.

North of Greenville, the *Oak Lodge*, an old cottage with five guestrooms (ⓣ407/889-7971, ⓣ207/534-7415; ❺), is the only place to stay on Kineo; breakfast is included.

Jackman

Fifty miles west of Greenville, there's not much to **JACKMAN**, another old logging town that's somewhat reluctantly attempting to make the transition into a tourist destination. Situated next to deserted Wood Pond, less than twenty miles from the Canadian border (many of the radio stations here are in French), its main attraction is as a haven for **snowmobiles**, which take over the parking lots and surrounding lumber roads in winter. You can rent one of the noisy craft at Dana's Rentals on Main Street (ⓣ207/668-7828) from about $160–240, depending on the day of the week and how much power you want. **Ice fishing** is also popular in winter and several local businesses sell non-resident licenses, bait, and tackle. In summer, a forty-mile circuit known as the Moose River **Bow Trip** is one of the better flat-water **canoe trips** in the state, with good fishing and several **campsites** scattered along the way. The Jackman Moose River Chamber of Commerce, Main Street (ⓣ207/668-4171, ⓦwww.jackmanmaine.org), can help you locate a guide, if you so desire.

The newly refurbished *Bishops Motel*, right in the center of town at 461 Main St (ⓣ1-888/991-7669, ⓦwww.bishopsmotel.com; ❹–❺), provides basic, clean **rooms** at reasonable rates. *Sally Mountain Cabins*, 9 Elm St (ⓣ207/668-5621 or 1-800/644-5621; $28 per person), has rustic cabins along the lake with full kitchens and private baths. The *Moose Point Tavern*, 16 Henderson Rd (ⓣ207/668-4012), is the best place to **eat** in town, not just for its lake views, but its hearty selection of meat dishes, including venison steak with cranberry-chipotle sauce ($26); there's also a pleasant bar on the premises.

Baxter State Park and the far north

Driving through northern Maine can feel as though you're trespassing on the private fiefdoms of the logging companies; only **Baxter State Park** is public land. However, you're pretty much free to hike, camp, and explore anywhere you like, so long as you let people know what you're doing (only a sensible precaution, after all). The scenery is pretty much the same everywhere, although of course to get the best of it you need to leave your car at some point and set off into the backwoods.

Whitewater rafting

The **Penobscot** and the **Kennebec** are the two most popular rivers in Maine for the exhilarating sport of **whitewater rafting**, which has caught on in the past decade as a major recreational activity here. **The Forks** (population: 35), along Hwy-201 between Kingfield and Greenville, is the undisputed rafting center, and the majority of the outfitters are based there, along with the deluxe lodges and camps they've built to house the eager outdoors enthusiasts. Run from mid-May to mid-October, most trips depart in the early morning and return by mid-afternoon and require advance reservations. Levels of difficulty vary, but the rafting companies insist that people of all athletic abilities are welcome on most trips, which, as dictated by state law, are all led by certified "Maine guides." However, many companies do have age requirements, of which you must be aware if there are children with you. Raft Maine (Ⓣ1-800/723-8633, Ⓦwww.raftmaine.com) is an association comprised of several outfitters that can answer your questions. The following is but a partial list of potential – and reliable – options.

Magic Falls The Forks Ⓣ207/663-2220 or 1-800/207-RAFT(7238), Ⓦwww.magic-falls.com. One of the smaller, more personal rafting companies. Runs the Kennebec, and Dead rivers. One-day trips cost $70–99, with several special events planned. There's a new lodge with a bar and riverside cabins.

New England Outdoor Center Hwy-201, thirteen miles past Bingham in Caratunk Ⓣ207/723-5438 or 1-800/766-7238, Ⓦwww.neoc.com. A family-oriented outfit that puts on day-trips on the Kennebec, Penobscot, and Dead rivers, as well as two-day combination packages at a variety of accommodation types. They operate facilities both in Caratunk, south of The Forks, and at the Rice Farm, near Millinocket; there are also lakeside cabins on Millinocket Lake. Rafting trips cost $79–119 and include a guide, equipment, and a nourishing grilled lunch.

Northern Outdoors Hwy-201, The Forks Ⓣ1-800/765-7238, Ⓦwww.northernout-doors.com. The oldest (since 1976) and largest of Maine's whitewater outfitters, running both the Kennebec and the Penobscot and offering longer overnight trips with lobster-bake dinners. One-day trips cost $89–125, including lunch. The outfit operates relatively upscale facilities at the *Forks Resort Center* and the *Penobscot Outdoor Center*, near Baxter State Park, but they also have inexpensive cabin and tent accommodations.

Professional River Runners Hwy-201, West Forks Ⓣ207/663-2229 or 1-800/325-3911, Ⓦwww.proriverrunners.com. Smaller outfit, family-owned and -operated, that runs both single-day and overnight trips; their guides are particularly good. They run *Grand View Lodging*, which has B&B and furnished cottage and condo facilities; there are also campgrounds by the Kennebec River. Full-day trip on the Penobscot or Kennebec costs $55–100.

Wilderness Expeditions *Birches Resort*, off of Rte-15, Rockwood Ⓣ1-800/825-9453, Ⓦwww.birches.com. Another of the large, full-scale resorts, with a base off of Rte-157 near Baxter State Park, along Hwy-201 just north of The Forks, and on Moosehead Lake near Rockwood. In addition to whitewater rafting, they offer many other activities, including kayaking, moose cruises, eco-tours, and, in winter, cross-country skiing and snowmobiling. The facilities are top-notch. One-day rafting trips cost between $79 and $115, depending on the month, day, and river. Half-day trips are also available.

Katahdin Iron Works and Millinocket

Five miles north of Brownsville Junction on Rte-11, an inconspicuous left turn leads to the **Katahdin Iron Works** (summer daily 9am–5pm), built in 1843. It's quite remarkable how little remains of what one hundred years ago was a thriving industrial community: one solitary brick oven and the tower of the blast furnace, stark and forlorn at the end of a few miles of gravel track. In good summer weather, it's possible to continue along the track across the hills to Greenville.

Farther north, **Millinocket** is a genuine company town, built on a wilderness site by the Great Northern Paper Company in 1899–1900 as the "magic city of the North." Public curiosity was so great that three hundred people came on a special train from Bangor to see what was happening. In 1990 the company was taken over by multinational Bowater Incorporated, and although the townspeople made a killing from cashing in their stock, their homes were almost unsellable, and their jobs became tentative at best. The company is currently dubbed Katahdin Paper, and is owned by Brascan Corporation. The hundred-year-old manufacturing facilities still churn out nearly twenty percent of the newsprint produced in the United States. There's nothing to see or do here, but you might consider stopping off to pick up some supplies or grab a hot meal at the *Appalachian Trail Café*, 210 Penobscot Ave (Ⓣ207/723-6720).

It's also not a bad place to **stay** if the weather's bad; try the newly opened *Gateway Inn*, Rte-157 just off I-95 at the Medway exit (Ⓣ207/746-3193; ❹), many rooms have decks with views of Katahdin. Next to Millinocket Lake, ten miles northwest, several whitewater rafting companies have set up lodgings and **campsites** as bases for their trips down the Penobscot River (see box opposite for details).

The park

By now you're approaching the southern end of sprawling and unspoiled **BAXTER STATE PARK** itself, with (on a clear day) the 5268-foot peak of imposing and beautiful **Mount Katahdin** visible from afar. Entrance to the park, collected at the Togue Pond Gate on Park Tote Road, costs $12 per car, and you should plan to arrive early in the day, as only a limited number of visitors are permitted access to Katahdin trailheads (though this limit rarely comes into effect outside of July and August). The enormous park – covering over 200,000 acres – was the single-handed creation of former Maine governor Percival P. Baxter, who, having failed to persuade the state to buy the imposing Katahdin and the land around it, bought it himself between the 1930s and 1960s and deeded it bit by bit to the state on condition that it remain "forever wild." A 2600-acre parcel was recently added and, amid some controversy, the State Park Authority refused to prohibit hunting and trapping on the newly acquired land. Nevertheless, the park's majestic green peaks (48 in all) and deserted ponds remain tremendously remote and pristine, and sightings of bears, bald eagles, and (of course) moose are not uncommon.

Hiking and camping

Hiking is the major pursuit here; indeed, the northern terminus of the **Appalachian Trail** is at the top of Mount Katahdin. Among the park's 186 miles of trails, don't miss **Knife's Edge**, a thrilling walk across a narrow path that connects Katahdin's two peaks. The higher and typically more crowded of these, **Baxter Peak**, can also be reached via the **Hunt Trail** (5.2 miles, from Katahdin Stream), the **Cathedral Trail**, and the **Saddle Trail** (both around two

△ Moose, Baxter State Park

miles, originating at Chimney Pond). For a less crowded but equally rewarding jaunt, head to the top of Hamlin Peak on the two-mile **Hamlin Ridge Trail**, which starts at Chimney Pond. Wherever you plan to hike, stop beforehand at either the headquarters in Millinocket, 64 Balsam Drive next to *McDonald's* (Ⓣ207/723-5140, Ⓦwww.baxterstateparkauthority.com), the visitors' center at Togue Pond (at the south entrance to the park – also a good place to **swim**), or at any of the park's campgrounds for a detailed **hiking map**. Water in the park is not treated and you should take care to carry as much as you'll need.

There are ten designated places to **camp** in Baxter, providing an array of options from basic tent sites to cabins equipped with beds, heating stoves, and gas lighting. Prices range from $9 to $25 per person per night and most sites are open from mid-May to mid-October. Reservations are accepted only via regular mail, although you can check by phone for cancellations or last-minute openings and pay by credit card over the phone (contact park headquarters).

North to Canada

The northernmost tip of Maine is taken up by **Aroostook County**, which covers an area larger than several small states. Although its main activity is the large-scale cultivation of potatoes, it is also the location of the **Allagash Wilderness Waterway**, where several whitewater rafting companies put their boats in (see box on p.596).

Britain and the United States all but went to war over Aroostook in 1839; at **Fort Kent**, the northern terminus of US-1 (which starts way down south in Key West, Florida), the main sight is the solid cedar **Fort Kent Blockhouse**, which was built to defend American integrity and looks like a throwback to early pioneer days. People come from all around to eat at *Eureka Hall* (33 miles south, off Rte-161 in Stockholm, Ⓣ207/896-3196), an institution of Aroostook County that serves up homestyle meals and incredible desserts. Reservations are recommended for weekend meals.

Contexts

Contexts

A brief history of New England

It's generally accepted that people of mixed Mongolian descent, from northeast Asia, crossed the frozen Bering Straits and established settlements on the American continent sometime between 12,000 and 25,000 years ago, gradually spreading eastwards over the next several millennia, and arriving in what would come to be known as New England between 9000 and 3000 BC. It's unclear whether or not these peoples were the ancestors of the Algonquins, who greeted the Europeans when they arrived in the sixteenth and seventeenth centuries, or whether they had died off before the tribes we consider "Native American" came here.

Native peoples and early Europeans

The first documented **Europeans** to visit these shores were not English, but Norse. In about 1000 AD, King Olaf of Norway commissioned Leif Eriksson to bring Christianity to a new Viking settlement in Greenland. Like the pilgrims who were to follow six centuries later, Eriksson was blown off course, and came ashore somewhere between Newfoundland and Massachusetts. Discovering a new land where wild grapes grew in abundance, he dubbed it Vinland the Good.

Early European settlers applied the name **Algonquin** to the various groups of hunting peoples they encountered on the east coast of North America. Fiercely independent of each other, yet linked by the various dialects of the Algonquin tongue and by common cultural ties and organizational structures, it's unlikely that they arrived in New England much before the fourteenth or fifteenth centuries – not long before the first European settlers. By 1600, there were only about 25,000 of them, broken into a dozen or so tribal nations, among them the **Narragansetts** of Rhode Island, the **Abnaki** of Maine, and smaller groups such as the **Niantics** and **Pequot** in Connecticut, all of whom used the land to hunt, fish, and grow crops such as beans, squash, tobacco, and corn.

European explorations

In the sixteenth century, Spanish conquistadors had focused almost exclusively on the southern regions of what is now North America, leaving the Dutch, English, Portuguese, and French to explore the cooler and less hospitable shores of New England – motivated not so much by the spirit of adventure as by the determination to find an easy passage to the Orient and its treasures. Six years after Columbus's first voyage, in 1492, **John Cabot** nosed by the shores of New England, in search of the elusive Northwest Passage. Cabot, who came ashore somewhere in Labrador, claimed all America east of the Rockies and north of

Florida for England, and was awarded a generous £30-a-year pension by King Henry VII on his return. Meanwhile, **Giovanni de Verrazano**, for Francis I of France, traveled as far north as Rhode Island's Narragansett Bay, though the thought of establishing a settlement scarcely crossed his mind.

In 1583, **Sir Humphrey Gilbert** became the first Englishman to attempt the settlement of North America. Sailing from Plymouth, in the English county of Devon, he aspired to set up a trading post at the mouth of the Penobscot River, but he lost his life in a violent storm on the crossing over. More Englishmen followed him. Between 1602 and 1606, Bartholomew Gosnold, Martin Pring, and George Weymouth set out to tap New England's lucrative sassafras bark, used by the Indians to cure many ailments, and regarded in Europe as an effective panacea for all ills. Meanwhile, farther north, the French were making inroads: Samuel de Champlain had traversed the lake that today bears his name as early as 1609.

In 1606, King James I granted a charter to the **Virginia Company of Plymouth**, with permission to establish a colony between North Carolina and Nova Scotia. A year later, a hundred adventurous souls led by Pring, Raleigh, and Sir Fernando Gorges set out from Plymouth, their ships laden with food, livestock, and trinkets to barter. Arriving on Parker's Island off the coast of Maine, they made a short go of it, but were soon repelled by the hostile winter weather.

Despite their lack of success, they took home with them stories of a land of fast-flowing streams and rivers, verdant forests, and friendly native peoples – so positive a picture, in fact, that the Plymouth Company commissioned distinguished surveyor **John Smith** to research the region's potential for development. Sailing along the Massachusetts coast in 1614, he named the region "**New England**." It was his book, *A Description of New England*, which persuaded the Pilgrims to migrate to these shores.

The Pilgrim Fathers

By the early seventeenth century, Europe was in religious turmoil: on mainland Europe, Luther, Calvin, and the other Protestant reformers had begun a religious revolution against Roman Catholicism. The new **Church of England** that was created as a result of this revolution claimed to be both Catholic and reformed in an attempt to appease the varying factions within its ranks. The religious zealots who opposed all aspects of Catholicism, called **Puritans**, enjoyed a degree of respectability during the reign of Elizabeth I, with growing numbers of followers in all walks of life. However, after the accession of the pro-Catholic king, James I, in 1603, the Puritans found themselves increasingly harassed by the authorities.

Therefore, 66 of the Puritans negotiated a deal with the Plymouth Company to finance a permanent settlement in North America, where they would be free to practice their own religion. Chartered by separatist leader John Carver, the *Mayflower* had a passenger list that included the English separatists plus hired help, including Myles Standish, professional soldier, and John Alden, a cooper. In all, just over one hundred passengers set sail aboard the *Mayflower* from Southampton, England, on September 16, 1620.

After two months at sea, they reached the North American coast at **Provincetown, Cape Cod**, on November 19. The same day, 41 men signed the so-called **Mayflower Compact**, in which they agreed to establish a "Civic Body Politic" (temporary government) and to be bound by its laws:

In the name of God, Amen. We, whose names are underwritten, the loyal subjects of our dread sovereigne Lord, King James, by the grace of God, of Great Britaine, France, and Ireland king, defender of the faith etc., having undertaken, for the glory of God, and advancement of the Christian faith, and honour of our king and country, a voyage to plant the first colony in the Northerne parts of Virginia, doe, by these presents, solemnly and mutually in the presence of God, and one of another, covenannt and combine ourselves together into a civill body politick, for our better ordering and preservation and furtherance of the ends aforesaid; and by virtue hereof to enacte, constitute, and frame such just and equall laws, ordinances, acts, constitutions, and offices, from time to time, as shall be thought most meete and convenient for the generall good of the Colonie unto which we promise all due submission and obedience. In witness whereof we have hereunder subscribed our names at Cape-Codd the 11, of November, in the year of the raigne of our sovereigne lord, King James, of England, France, and Ireland, the eighteenth, and of Scotland the fiftie-fourth. Anno. Dom. 1620.

The Compact became the basis of government in the Plymouth Colony and **John Carver** was elected their first governor. The new arrivals had landed on a virtually barren stretch of the coast, and soon resettled across the bay, arriving at what is now Plymouth, Massachusetts, on December 26, 1620.

The early colonists

Only half the colonists survived their first **winter** on American soil. Unaccustomed to the extreme cold, and living in shelters built of tree bark, many died from pneumonia; scurvy and other infections killed many more. It would have been even worse but for **Squanto**, a Native American who had spent time in England. He managed to enlist the support of Massassoit, the local Wampanoag sachem, who signed a Treaty of Friendship, and plied the visitors with food. Exactly a year after their arrival in Plymouth, the surviving separatists would sit down with the Indians to enjoy a feast of roast game, eel, fruits, vegetables, and cornbread – an occasion still celebrated today as Thanksgiving.

Weeks later, these first settlers were joined by 35 more, laden with provisions, and by 1624 Plymouth had become a thriving village of thirty cottages. News of the community's success reached England, and in 1629 another group, led by London lawyer John Winthrop, obtained a royal charter as the "Company of the Massachusetts Bay in New England." Winthrop had lofty goals for the town he was to settle in New England, saying that it should be a "city upon a hill" – meaning a model Christian town that others would look to as an example. That summer Winthrop and more than three hundred settlers arrived at Salem; thousands more followed in the 1630s, as persecution of Puritans, led by Charles I's sidekick, Archbishop William Laud, intensified. Dozens of new communities were formed; many, such as Dorchester, Ipswich, and Taunton, were named after the towns and villages the settlers had left behind. By 1640, the **Massachusetts Bay Company** comprised around 10,000 colonists.

As the European population grew, so did the perceived need for clergy, preferably trained in New England. As a result, in 1636, **Harvard College** was established for that specific purpose, while a General Court was formed to administer the colony's affairs, including justice.

At this stage, new arrivals in the colonies were not limited to Massachusetts. In **Connecticut**, the Revd Thomas Hooker established the community that became Hartford, while Theophilus Eaton and John Davenport founded New Haven. But frictions were already developing among the more zealous settlers, who were rapidly showing themselves to be even less tolerant than their oppressors back in England. The **Revd Roger Williams**, hounded out of the Massachusetts Bay Colony in 1636 for his liberal views, established a new settlement of twenty families at Providence, in 1638, on land made available by two Indian sachems he'd befriended. The new **State of Rhode Island and Providence Plantations**, in its 1663 charter, guaranteed religious freedom for all: Jews, Huguenots, even the despised Quakers. Communities were also established in New Hampshire in 1638, and Maine in 1652.

Meanwhile, zealous Puritans worked at **converting** the Indians to their faith, translating the Bible into Algonquin and setting up special communities for Christian Indians along the Connecticut River and on Cape Cod, which became known as "praying towns." Several Algonquins were sent to Harvard to train as Christian clergy – although only one completed the training successfully – and by the 1660s, the Christian faith accounted for one-fifth of all Indians. However, the settlers' arrogant attempt to persuade the Indians to give up their native culture and traditions led to profound unhappiness, and eventually to bloodshed.

At first, the new settlers and the Native Americans were able to coexist peacefully, though **diseases** introduced by the colonists may have been directly responsible for a plague which killed more than a third of all the Algonquins. As the colonists ventured south, they began to meet growing resistance from the Indians, particularly the proud Pequot tribe, with whom war erupted in 1636, at Fort Mystic and Fairfield; many lives were lost on both sides. Then, in 1675, Narragansett leader Metacom, also known as Philip, persuaded feuding groups of Indians, principally the Nipmucks, Narragansetts, and Wampanoags, to bury their differences and join in a concerted campaign against the settlers. Known as **King Philip's War**, hostilities culminated in the **Great Swamp Fight** in Kingston, Rhode Island. More than 2000 Indians were slain, including Metacom himself. Even more significantly, it signaled the breaking of the Indian will in New England.

The road to revolution

Up until the middle of the seventeenth century, the colonies had largely been left to take care of their own political structures. England, after all, was preoccupied with its own domestic concerns – a bloody civil war, the beheading of Charles I, and the establishment of Oliver Cromwell's parliamentary republic – and was scarcely interested in events happening three thousand miles away. The resulting vacuum was a breeding ground for the seeds of separatism, sentiment fueled by speculation that the Crown would soon seek to appoint its own governor to take charge of colonial affairs.

In 1686, King James II revoked the northern colonies' charters and attempted to create a **Dominion of New England** stretching from Maine to New Jersey. Spun as a security measure to protect the English communities from the French and the Indians, it was in reality an attempt to keep tabs on an increasingly defiant and potentially troublesome populace. The king's first gubernatorial appointees were staunch Anglicans, the second of whom imposed taxes as the disenfranchised populace grew increasingly frustrated.

A new respect between the Crown and colonies was temporarily forged in 1689, when the "Glorious Revolution" brought Protestants William and Mary to the British throne. The despised governor Edmund Andros was removed and put in jail, and the old powers of self-government restored. When King George III came to the throne in 1760, however, things went back to the way they had been heading; George demanded obedience from America and soon demonstrated that he would go to any lengths to get it. In a move designed not so much to raise revenue as to remind the colonists who was boss, he was responsible for the **Revenue Act of 1764**, imposing taxes on sugar, silk, and wine, which resulted in a boycott of British goods and supplies.

The situation deteriorated further in 1765, with London's introduction of the **Stamp Act** and the imposition of taxes on commercial and legal documents, newspapers, and even playing cards. Throughout New England, protests erupted. Tax officials were the defendants in mock trials, and their effigies hanged. The bulk of the demonstrations were peaceful, but in Boston, the houses of stampman Andrew Oliver and Governor Thomas Hutchinson were plundered. The British prime minister, William Pitt, **repealed** the Act in March 1766.

Then, in the summer of 1767, the new British prime minister Charles Townshend arrogantly taunted the colonies with his famous remark, "I dare tax America." The subsequent **Townshend Acts**, which introduced harsh levies on imports such as paper, glass, and, most provocatively, tea, prompted the dispatch to Boston of two regiments of redcoats. On March 5, 1770, a crowd of several hundred Bostonians gathered to ridicule a solitary "lobster-back" standing sentinel outside the customs house. Initially peaceful, the scene turned ugly as stones and rocks were thrown, and seven nervous reinforcements arrived, one firing on the crowd without orders. In the panic, more shots followed. Three colonists were pronounced dead and two were mortally wounded, the first martyrs in an event that was to become known as the **Boston Massacre**.

Things would have gone downhill more quickly but for the **economic prosperity** that New England, and particularly Boston, was beginning to enjoy. Eventually the Townshend Acts were repealed, though not the tax on East Indian tea, which was boycotted by the colonists. Dutch blends were smuggled in, and a special brew called Liberty Tea was concocted from sage, currant, or plantain leaves. Britain responded in September 1773 by flooding the market with its own, subsidized blend – half a million pounds of the stuff.

Resistance focused on Boston, where the **Massachusetts Committee of Correspondence**, an unofficial legislature, and the local chapter of the **Sons of Liberty**, a fast-growing pseudo-secret society, organized the barricading of the piers and wharves and demanded Governor Hutchinson send home the tea-filled clipper *Dartmouth*. When he refused, sixty men disguised as Mohawk Indians, Samuel Adams and John Hancock among them, surreptitiously climbed aboard and dumped 350 crates of the tea into Boston Harbor. The date was December 16, 1773, and the event captured the world's imagination as the **Boston Tea Party**.

This blatant act of defiance rattled Parliament, which introduced the so-called "**Coercive Acts**": among them, the Boston Port Act sealed off the city with a massive naval blockade. Meanwhile, American patriots from Massachusetts, Rhode Island, and other states gathered in Philadelphia for the **First Continental Congress**, convened on September 5, 1774. Though British garrisons still controlled the major towns, such was the antagonism in rural areas that policing them was becoming virtually impossible for the British. All the while locals continued to stockpile arms and munitions.

In April 1775, London instructed its Boston commander General Thomas Gage to put down rebellion in rural Massachusetts, where the provincial congress had assumed de facto political control. On the night of April 18, Gage dispatched seven hundred soldiers to destroy the arms depot in Concord, while at nearby Lexington seventy colonial soldiers, known as **Minute Men** (because they were prepared to fight at a moment's notice), lay in wait, having been warned of the plan by Paul Revere and William Dawes.

On Concord's Town Common, British musket fire resulted in the deaths of eight Americans. The British moved on to Concord, oblivious of the ambush that resulted in the deaths of 273 British soldiers, British retreat, and American jubilation. As news of the victory spread, rumors of plunder and pillage by British troops further fueled American resentment.

A couple of months later, the war intensified with the **Battle of Bunker Hill**, on Boston's Charlestown peninsula, which General Artemus Ward of the Continental Army had ordered to be fortified – though it was actually on nearby Breed's Hill, not Bunker, where the American forces were stationed. On June 17, the redcoats attacked twice, but were twice rebuffed. The third attempt succeeded, because the Americans ran out of ammunition. For this reason alone, the much-celebrated order "don't fire until you see the whites of their eyes" was given – some say by Colonel William Prescott, others General Isaac Putnam – specifically to save on ammunition. Bunker Hill, with a thousand British casualties, was an expensive triumph for the Crown. Worn down by lack of manpower, low morale, and growing American resistance, less than a year later an embattled General Gage ordered a **British withdrawal** to Halifax, Nova Scotia.

The **Declaration of Independence** – with fifty-six signatories, fourteen of whom were from the New England states of **Massachusetts**, **Connecticut**, **New Hampshire**, and **Rhode Island** – was adopted by the Continental Congress on July 4, 1776.

△ The signing of the Declaration of Independence

Even after victory, all was not plain sailing. In a move designed to protect the states' newly independent status, the thirteen independent colonies hammered out an integrated union in 1781, though not without the concern that a centralized federal system would be just as bad as British rule. For that reason, heroes Sam Adams and John Hancock gave only grudging support to the Constitution, and representatives from Rhode Island consistently voted against it, relenting only after the Bill of Rights was added.

With the Declaration of Independence, the families who had settled **Vermont** pondered their future. In January 1777, the state proclaimed itself independent, and at Windsor in July, seventy delegates unanimously adopted a constitution that was almost an exact replica of Pennsylvania's. Vermont remained an independent state until 1791, when it was admitted to the Union as the **fourteenth state**.

Maine's statehood was not gained until 1820, after the eastern part of the state had been occupied by the British during the War of 1812. According to the Missouri Compromise of 1820, Maine was admitted to the Union as a free (anti-slavery) state, balanced by Missouri, a slave state.

Nineteenth-century development

New England began as a predominantly **agricultural region**, particularly the areas away from the coast, where maritime trading and commerce was found. Maine and New Hampshire developed important trades in timber, agriculture, and fishing, with some shipbuilding on the coast at Bath, Maine, and Portsmouth, New Hampshire. The opening of the **Champlain Canal**, connecting Lake Champlain to the Hudson River, made it possible for Vermont farmers to ship goods to New York City, stimulating agriculture and wool production, at least until the 1860s when dairy farming began to take hold. But, apart from some lush pockets of Vermont, the soil was generally poor; plowing was difficult, and the long, cold New England winters meant that for a large part of the year the ground was frozen solid. The land lent itself to little more than subsistence farming – with small farms, wheat, corn, pigs, and cattle – and New England could never compete with the vast wheat- and dairy-producing areas of the growing Midwest.

But New England's true prosperity came first as a result of its **connection with the sea**; fishing, especially for cod, was important, as was the production of whale derivatives, especially oil, used for heating and lighting. More adventurous sea captains, many of them based in Boston or Salem, Massachusetts, ventured farther afield, and brought back great treasures from India and China, including tea, spices, silk, and opium.

Several communities, such as Newport and Providence, Rhode Island, flourished on the back of the so-called **Triangular Trade**; ships unloaded West Indian molasses, reloaded with rum, then sailed to Africa, where the rum was exchanged for slaves, in turn shipped to the West Indies and traded for molasses. **Shipbuilding** industries flourished, particularly in places such as Essex, Massachusetts, which earned a reputation for manufacturing swift, easily maneuverable vessels. But the first two decades of the nineteenth century showed how volatile maritime trade was, especially with so many political uncertainties, notably the Napoleonic Wars, Thomas Jefferson's Embargo Acts (which prohibited all exports to Europe and restricted imports from Great Britain – a response to British and French interference with American ships), and the War of 1812. There was a clear need for New England to diversify its economy if its prosperity were to grow.

The Industrial Revolution

In 1789, **Samuel Slater**, a skilled mechanic from England, sailed to New York disguised as a laborer. The emigration of skilled mechanics was forbidden by the British government, and there were serious penalties for those found smuggling the specifications and drawings for the pioneering industrial machinery that had earned Britain her nickname as the "workshop of the world." Slater, though, had been able to memorize the specifications for his boss Richard Arkwright's factory-sized cotton-spinning machine, which was set to revolutionize the highly inefficient existing system of individual looms. Financed by Moses Brown, a Providence Quaker, he set up the nation's first successful **cotton mill** at Pawtucket, Rhode Island. Though an important milestone in the Industrial Revolution, working conditions at the mill were hellish, and these, together with poor pay, inspired the nation's first industrial strike in 1800.

Another entrepreneur determined to duplicate British weaving feats was Bostonian **Francis Cabot Lowell**, a self-styled "industrial tourist" who spent $10,000 of his own money plus $90,000 from his "Boston Associates" to set up a small mill with a power loom and 1700 spindles at Waltham, west of Boston. Lowell's **Merrimack Manufacturing Company** proved extremely profitable, with sales at $3000 in 1815 and reaching $345,000 in 1822. In 1826, having already uprooted to Chelmsford, the business moved again, to a purpose-built community named "Lowell" after its founder. Lowell's enlightened, anthropological approach was continued by his associates after his death: young female workers lived in dorms to protect their honor, received education, and were given sufficient time off to engage in a variety of leisure pursuits.

New England was fast becoming the **industrial center** of the US, home to some two-thirds of the nation's cotton mills, half of which were in Massachusetts. Tiny Rhode Island processed twenty percent of the nation's wool, and in Connecticut **Sam Colt** and **Eli Whitney**, known for his invention of the cotton gin, manufactured the first firearms with interchangeable parts. Connecticut also became home to a thriving watch- and clock-making industry. In the fields of paper and shoe manufacture and metalworking New England, in particular New Hampshire, was unsurpassed.

Culture and education

New England, particularly Boston, had always set a strong standard as far as **education** and **literature** were concerned. The nation's first secondary school, Boston Latin, opened in 1635, closely followed by Harvard in 1636. In Connecticut, Yale University was established in 1701, while Rhode Island's Brown University, originally Rhode Island College, came into being in 1764. Farther north, New Hampshire's Dartmouth College dates from 1769, and Bowdoin College in Maine from 1796.

In 1639, America's first **printing press** was set up in Cambridge, where the *Bay Psalm Book*, *New England Primer*, and freeman's oath of loyalty to Massachusetts were among the first published works. The colonies' first newspaper, *Publick Occurrences, Both Foreign & Domestick*, came into being in 1690, and was succeeded by the more popular *Boston News-Letter* in 1704. By the 1850s, more than four hundred periodicals were in print. Libraries such as Hartford's famous Wadsworth Atheneum and the Providence Atheneum both came into existence in the mid-nineteenth century, while in 1854 the Boston Public Library, with 750,000 volumes, became the world's first free municipal library.

At the same time, the region became home to some of the nation's greatest thinkers, philosophers, essayists, artists, and architects. Among them were Henry David Thoreau, the **transcendentalist** philosopher and essayist; Louisa May Alcott, author of *Little Women*; Winslow Homer, noted for his marine watercolors; poet Emily Dickinson; and novelists such as Nathaniel Hawthorne, whose most famous book, *The Scarlet Letter*, is set in Salem and Concord, Massachusetts. In Connecticut, Mark Twain had set up home at Nook Farm, near Hartford, as had Harriet Beecher Stowe, the author of *Uncle Tom's Cabin*.

Not coincidentally, a strong cultural identity developed, focusing again on Boston, where the 1871 founding of the **Museum of Fine Arts** was followed a decade later by the Boston Symphony Orchestra and the Boston Pops. New Haven became an important focus for theater in Connecticut, with the establishment of the Long Wharf, Shubert, and Yale Repertory theaters.

The Civil War

The type of **anti-slavery sentiment** Stowe had advocated in *Uncle Tom's Cabin* was echoed by a number of Northerners, though in general, when it came to slavery New Englanders held ambivalent views, even though all of the region's states had outlawed the practice. Still, it would prove to be the catalyst for the bloodiest conflict ever seen on American soil, the **Civil War**.

From the moment of its inception, the unity of the nation had been based on shaky foundations. Great care had gone into devising a Constitution that balanced the need for a strong federal government with the aspirations for autonomy of its component states. That was achieved by giving Congress two separated chambers – the House of Representatives, in which the number of representatives from each state depended on its population, and the Senate, where each state elected two members, regardless of size. Thus, although in theory the Constitution remained silent on the issue of slavery, it allayed the fears of the less populated Southern states, that the voters of the North might destroy their economy by forcing them to abandon their "peculiar institution." However, it soon became apparent that the system only worked so long as there were roughly equal numbers of "free" and slave-owning states.

At first, it seemed possible that the balance could be maintained – in 1820, under the Missouri Compromise, Missouri was admitted to the Union as a slave-owning state at the same time as Maine was admitted as a "free" one. In 1854, the **Kansas–Nebraska Act** forced the issue to a head, allowing both prospective states self-determination on the issue. John Brown's raid on the Armory at Harpers Ferry, West Virginia, in which he intended to seize arms for a slave rebellion, was quashed, and Brown hanged. The Civil War began. Though **no battles** were fought in New England, the region sent thousands of men to bolster the Union cause, many of whom would never return. In the end, it was not so much the brilliance of the generals as sheer economic power that won the war for the Union. It was the North, with New England leading the way, that could maintain full trading with the rest of the world while diverting spare resources to the production of munitions.

Into the twentieth century

The Industrial Revolution and the Civil War were two factors that combined to create a vast sea change for New England in the latter half of the nineteenth century. Perhaps the most important factor was that the frontiers of the US moved west, and other regions began to play their part in the development of the nation. Despite its **diminishing influence** on the national stage, New England continued the strong tradition of social reform exemplified by William Lloyd Garrison and others long before the Civil War erupted, paving the way in the fields of prison reform and health and mental health provision.

Meanwhile, the ethnic and religious make-up of New England was changing rapidly. No longer was it the preserve of white Anglo-Saxon Protestants; following the potato famine, **Irish immigrants** began pouring over in the 1840s. Soon more than a thousand Irish immigrants a month were arriving in Boston, while Catholics from Italy, French Canada, Portugal, and Eastern Europe accounted for two-thirds of the total population growth during the nineteenth century. Indeed, by 1907, seventy percent of Massachusetts' population could claim to be of non-Anglo-Saxon descent. Even in less developed New Hampshire, one out of every five had adopted, not inherited, the US flag.

Such waves of immigration provoked some backlash, with the openly racist **Know-Nothing** party gaining governorships in Massachusetts, Rhode Island, Connecticut, and New Hampshire; membership of the American Protective Association and Immigrant Restriction League increased dramatically; and signs such as "No Irish Need Apply" were found on the doorsteps of many a business.

Still, immigrants found ways of working the political system, especially the Irish, and, in 1881, John Breen from Tipperary became the first Irishman to take up an establishment position, as mayor of Lawrence, Massachusetts. This had a profound motivating effect on his fellow countrymen, and three years later, Hugh O'Brien won the Boston mayorship, while Patrick Andrew Collin represented Suffolk County with a congressional seat in the nation's capital. By the turn of the twentieth century, immigrants were represented at all levels of government.

But political scandal and **corruption** were never far away. "Boss" Charlie Brayton and the *Providence Journal* ring bought their way to office in Rhode Island, with individual votes costing $2 to $5, and up to $30 in hotly contested elections. Others abused the privileges of the solid ethnic support they enjoyed: **James Michael Curley**, elected Boston mayor four times, and voted governor of Massachusetts 1934–38, did much to improve the welfare of the poor, but also doled out jobs and money to community leaders who carefully manipulated the electorate and its votes.

With the huge influx of mainly poor immigrants, especially from Catholic countries, a "**New Puritanism**" began to take hold. Encouraged by Catholic leader William Cardinal O'Connell and the closely associated **Watch and Ward Society**, moralists lobbied for the prohibition of, among other things, Hemingway's *The Sun also Rises* and a variety of plays and books.

The southern exodus

As time passed, other regions began to challenge New England's claim to be the manufacturing capital of the US. Many companies **moved south**, where costs were much lower, and by 1923 more than half of the nation's cotton goods were being woven there. Industrial production in Massachusetts alone fell by more than $1 billion during the 1920s, while unemployment skyrocketed in some towns to 25 percent, and up to 40 percent after the Wall Street crash of 1929. The **Great Depression** hit New England particularly hard and, with few natural resources to draw upon and human resources moving to the South, industry here never really recovered. From the boom days of the late nineteenth century, when hundreds of thousands of New Englanders were engaged in textiles, the figure had dropped to fewer than 70,000 by the 1970s. By 1980, the region which had given birth to America's Industrial Revolution was headquarters to only fourteen of the nation's top five hundred companies.

Recent history

Political collaboration, instead of confrontation, between New England's "Brahmin" political set, and the second- and- third-generation sons and daughters of immigrants, began to pay off in a common quest to find an answer to New England's economic and social problems, and by the 1980s the region was beginning to experience something of an **industrial resurgence**. New industries, such as the production of biomedical machinery, electronics, computer hardware and software, and photographic materials sprang up throughout the region, but especially along Route 128 west of Boston, which has become New England's so-called Silicon Valley. During this period, Boston became the country's mutual fund capital, Hartford's insurance industry continued to flourish, and tourism asserted itself as the region's second largest source of income. New England became known for its political stability and, at the same time, for leading the way with anti-pollution laws, consumer rights, handgun controls, and civil rights legislation.

Though the nationwide **economic slump** in the late 1980s and early 1990s caused problems in those larger urban centers which had failed to address the social consequences of the demise of traditional manufacturing industries, the area managed to rebound again. Almost unparalleled prosperity accompanied by low unemployment, especially in the latter half of the 1990s, meant that more money was freed up for the benefit of long-neglected areas that needed attention: roads and infrastructure, crime prevention, schools, and social provision. At the same time **urban regeneration**, sometimes on a spectacular scale (in Providence, Rhode Island, for example), and the continued development of new, mostly computer-related and service industries have put the region more or less back on track. The area now lays claim to thirty of the top five hundred companies in the US, more than double its share a quarter-century ago.

The present and the future

Like most of the country, the region took another hit with the slowdown of the economy in the wake of the bursting of the dot-com bubble and September 11, 2001. On the whole, however, positive factors remain in place. Ethnic tensions are less of a problem here than they have ever been; significant measures to protect the environment have been enacted in several states; and improvement in the frequency and duration of rail services along the northeast corridor – and in commuter services generally – will lead, planners hope, to fewer cars on the road. Politically, liberalism and, to an extent, libertarian values, remain prominent. Most senators and representatives that hail from New England are Democrats or notably liberal Republicans in a US congress with a far-right majority. Democrat **John F. Kerry**, the junior senator from Massachusetts, lost his bid for the presidency in 2004 against George W. Bush, though by a very narrow margin. Though many argued that Kerry's loss could be attributed to the fact that New Englanders, and New England liberals in particular, are seen as being out of step with conservative Middle American values, it's important to note that the current governors of Rhode Island, Massachusetts, Connecticut, and Vermont are Republican.

Nevertheless, in January of 2002 the Vermont Supreme Court rejected challenges to the state's **civil union laws**, reconfirming it as the most gay- and lesbian-friendly state in New England – if not the nation; Massachusetts followed suit with similar laws in 2004. In a similar vein, Maine and Rhode Island have recently flouted federal statutes by making **medical marijuana** legal, even in the face of a Supreme Court ruling stating that ailing users can be federally prosecuted. Though New England is not as liberal as the national press often makes it out to be (as evidenced by the Republican governors mentioned above), a streak of independent thought and self-determination still runs strong in the region – a streak which can in many ways be traced all the way back to the first settlers who came undaunted to these wild shores.

New England on film

As picturesque and as rich in narrative as New England is, the region has always seemed inhospitable to the young turks of Hollywood. For one thing it is as far from Los Angeles, both geographically and psychologically, as you can get in the continental United States; for another, the weather, though undeniably cinematic, is famously unpredictable. Nevertheless, there are plenty of films set in New England.

Films drawing their inspiration from the region often have a particularly local subject matter – academia or witchcraft, for example – or sometimes literary adaptations. Indeed, Hollywood has gamely hacked away at whole schools of unfilmable New England novels, usually failing more spectacularly with each attempt (see, for example Demi Moore's take on Hester Prynne in *The Scarlet Letter*).

The following films are all set in one of New England's six states (though Massachusetts, and especially Boston, predominates). They weren't, however, necessarily filmed in New England: many were shot in California, some in England, and quite a number conveniently across the border in Canada. The entries preceded by ⭑ are **highly recommended** films.

The Actress George Cukor, 1953. A unique portrait of Boston in the early 1910s, *The Actress* is based on a play by Ruth Gordon about her early life in nearby Wollaston. Though the film, which stars Jean Simmons as Gordon and a deliciously cantankerous Spencer Tracy as her father, is largely studio-bound, it is full of historical tidbits.

⭑ **Affliction** Paul Schrader, 1998. One of the best New England movies of recent years, this brooding tale of violence shattering the placid surface of a snowbound New Hampshire town hardly does wonders for the tourist trade. Nick Nolte is superb as the divorced small-town cop stumbling through middle age, whose father's legacy of abuse is too heavy a load to bear.

Alice's Restaurant Arthur Penn, 1969. Built around Arlo Guthrie's hit song of the same name, this quizzical elegy for counterculture brought the hippie nation to the Berkshire town of Stockbridge in western Massachusetts.

⭑ **All That Heaven Allows** Douglas Sirk, 1955. Sirk's splendid technicolor masterpiece recounts the forbidden romance of a middle-aged widow (Jane Wyman) and her strapping, Thoreau-quoting gardener (Rock Hudson). This devastating portrait of the small minds of the local country-club set served to show that the Puritanism of the seventeenth century was alive and well in postwar New England.

⭑ **Beetlejuice** Tim Burton, 1988. In this early Burton comedy, a recently deceased couple played by Geena Davis and Alec Baldwin decide to haunt their historic New England home until its new tenants – an abrasive New York family – decide to leave. The couple gets some unwanted "help" from Beetlejuice (Michael Keaton), and a very young Winona Ryder contributes a great performance as the city couple's goth daughter. Though the action takes place in Connecticut, the film was made in Vermont.

Between the Lines Joan Micklin Silver, 1977. Shot on location, this multi-character comedy-drama documents the dying throes of counterculture in late 1970s Boston by focusing on the ragtag staff of underground newspaper *The Back*

Bay Mainline (based on the real-life *Real Paper*).

The Boston Strangler Richard Fleischer, 1968. Boston is set on edge by a series of brutal murders. Shot like a documentary, with a panoply of split-screen effects, this true-life crime story, starring a jittery Tony Curtis as the titular handyman, starts out well but soon gets bogged down in psychobabble.

The Bostonians James Ivory, 1984. Merchant-Ivory's high-minded Henry James adaptation is set in 1875 Boston. New England women's libbers and a Southern male chauvinist battle for the soul of one very pliable young woman in the drawing rooms of Cambridge, on the lawns of Harvard, and on the beaches of Martha's Vineyard. Vanessa Redgrave and Christopher Reeve, as the opposing armies, are superb.

Carousel Henry King, 1956. Loutish Maine carnival barker Billy Bigelow (Gordon MacRae), who resorts to crime to support his wife (Shirley Jones) and unborn child, is killed in a robbery attempt. Years later, heaven's Starkeeper allows him to return to earth to see his daughter graduate from high school. The film's bizarre treatment of spousal abuse – Billy hits his wife "hard" and to her it feels like a kiss – makes this the hardest of Rogers and Hammerstein musicals to love.

Christmas in Connecticut Peter Godfrey, 1945. Barbara Stanwyck plays a Manhattan magazine writer who has faked her way to being the Martha Stewart of her day. When her publisher asks her to invite a war hero to her Connecticut farm for Christmas, Stanwyck has to conjure up the idyllic New England existence she'd only written about. Unfortunately the results are convoluted, and the studio-built Connecticut is – ironically – clearly a fake.

Cider House Rules Lasse Hallstrom, 1999. Surprisingly well-received adaptation of John Irving's novel (see "Books"), in which a shifting Maine backdrop sets the stage for a somewhat didactic, if winning, meditation on love, suffering, and the thorny issue of abortion.

A Civil Action Steve Zaillian, 1998. John Travolta struts his stuff as a cocky ambulance-chasing Boston lawyer who loses everything but regains his soul when he takes up the case of a group of families in a nearby town who believe their children developed leukemia after drinking contaminated local water. A rainy, wintry vision of New England enlivened by Robert Duvall as a devilish old pro who'd rather be at Fenway Park than in court.

The Crucible Nicholas Hytner, 1996. A riveting adaptation of Arthur Miller's classic allegory of McCarthyism, set during the Salem witch trials of 1692. Winona Ryder and her friends are spied dancing by firelight and accused of witchcraft; to save themselves they start naming names. Daniel Day-Lewis is suitably tortured as Ryder's Puritan lover caught between Plymouth Rock and a hard place.

Dolores Claiborne Taylor Hackford, 1995. On a dreary island off the coast of Maine, a housekeeper (Kathy Bates) is suspected of murdering her wealthy employer, and even her neurotic journo daughter from New York (Jennifer Jason Leigh) thinks she's guilty. This lovingly crafted Gothic sleeper was adapted from a Stephen King novel, and, although it succeeds admirably in conveying the weather-beaten charms of the Maine coast, it was actually shot in Nova Scotia.

The Europeans James Ivory, 1979. Shot against the gorgeous fall foliage of New Hampshire and Massachusetts, Merchant-Ivory's genial adaptation of Henry James's novella pits New England sobriety ("There must be a thousand ways to be dreary and sometimes I think we make use of them all," pines Lisa Eichhorn) against the dizzy charms of a couple of European visitors to the suburban countryside of nineteenth-century Boston.

Far From Heaven Todd Haynes, 2002. Haynes's ode to Douglas Sirk (see *All That Heaven Allows* on p.613) stars Julianne Moore as a perfect 1950s Connecticut housewife, confronted first with sexual anxiety as a result of her husband's activities, then with racial pressures when she takes up with their gardener (Dennis Haysbert).

Good Will Hunting Gus Van Sant, 1997. When money-minded producers suggested shooting their script up in Canada, Beantown buddies Ben Affleck and Matt Damon insisted that the verisimilitude of Boston locations was essential to their script about a South Boston townie tough who is a closet math wizard. They got their way and won a "Best Screenplay" Oscar, along with a one-way ticket to stardom.

The House of the Seven Gables Joe May, 1940. Fusty superstition battles liberal enlightenment in eighteenth-century Massachusetts in this histrionic adaptation of Nathaniel Hawthorne's Gothic family saga. George Sanders and Vincent Price play yin-yang siblings fighting for control of their accursed family mansion, against a background of abolitionism and the birth of photography.

The Ice Storm Ang Lee, 1997. Suburban living in 1970s Connecticut – bellbottoms, key parties, etc – is laid bare in all its formica-covered splendor in this disturbing adaptation of Rick Moody's novel, starring Kevin Kline, Sigourney Weaver, and Joan Allen. The production design is priceless, and the titular squall that climaxes the film is a magnificent cinematic specimen of New England weather.

In the Bedroom Todd Field, 2001. Against the backdrop of Maine's small harbor-town lobster docks, a college-age boy begins seeing a local divorcee with an angry ex-husband. After an unexpected tragedy, his parents (Sissy Spacek and Tom Wilkinson) dissect the affair and their pivotal roles in this emotionally draining drama. Wilkinson wins the best-Maine-accent-by-a-foreigner award.

Jaws Steven Spielberg, 1975. Spielberg's toothsome blockbuster took the well-worn New England trope of the destructive outsider disrupting the well-ordered life of the community and gave it its ultimate id-like expression in the form of a killer shark who wreaks havoc on the shores of Martha's Vineyard (known here as Amity Island).

The Last Hurrah John Ford, 1958. The great John Ford was born and raised in Maine, but this is one of his few depictions of the Northeast. Spencer Tracy plays the no-nonsense Irish-American mayor of a New England town (a thinly veiled Boston) whose career is on the wane. It's talky and sentimental, but pulls no punches in its depiction of the snobbery of the local bluebloods towards the Boston Irish.

Leave Her to Heaven John M. Stahl, 1945. A stunning, too-little-known gem, in which Gene Tierney plays a woman who loves too much. Half of this gorgeously colorful movie takes place in New Mexico, but the scenes in Maine – especially a devastating scene involving a rowboat, a lake, and a pair of sunglasses – are indelible.

Legally Blonde Robert Luketic, 2001. In this fluff but fun movie, the ditzy but charming Reese Witherspoon, a sorority girl from California, follows her boyfriend to Harvard Law School, where she charms the cold town friendly and clinches a murder trial defense on which she's assisting.

Little Women George Cukor, 1933; Gillian Armstrong, 1994. Despite the reams of New England literature massacred by Hollywood, Louisa May Alcott's timeless classic, set in Concord, has fared remarkably well, with not one but two wonderful adaptations. The first, Cukor's in 1933, stars a rambunctious Katherine Hepburn as Jo; the second, made some sixty years later by Gillian Armstrong, has Winona Ryder in the lead role and Susan Sarandon as the ever-wise Marmee.

Love Story Arthur Hiller, 1970. The Harvard preppie (Ryan O'Neal) and the working-class Radcliffe wiseacre (Ali McGraw) fall head over heels against a backdrop of library stacks, falling leaves, tinkling pianos, and low-rent Cambridge digs. The tragedy in this four-hankie blockbuster only kicks in when the lovebirds relocate to New York.

Malice Harold Becker, 1993. In a small college town in Massachusetts (the film was shot at Smith College in Northampton) the blissful life of newlyweds Bill Pullman and Nicole Kidman is rocked by the arrival of diabolically charismatic Harvard doctor Alec Baldwin – a surgeon with a "God complex." A devilish little thriller.

Mermaids Richard Benjamin, 1990. Single mom Cher relocates her two daughters (Winona Ryder and Christina Ricci) to a small Massachusetts town. Elder daughter Winona, though Jewish, decides she wants to become a nun, and suffers various other growing pains, while Cher finds love with Bob Hoskins and becomes a better mother. Both Cher and the Massachusetts setting are fabulous.

Misery Rob Reiner, 1990. Adaptation of popular Stephen King novel, and certainly one of the more successful screen transformations, with a chilling Kathy Bates as novelist James Caan's biggest fan. The dreary and ominous New England backdrop is perfect – though most action takes place inside a house.

Moby Dick Lloyd Bacon, 1930; John Huston, 1956. Melville's classic, which begins in New Bedford, Massachusetts, has been given at least two very different treatments by Hollywood. Bacon's early version, starring John Barrymore, runs a skimpy 75 minutes and turns Captain Ahab's monomaniacal quest into a love story with a happy ending. Huston's reverential 1956 version, with Gregory Peck as Ahab, is visually striking, but still unequal to the task.

Mystic Pizza Donald Petrie, 1988. The film that put both Julia Roberts and Mystic, Connecticut, on the national map. Shot on location in Mystic and nearby Rhode Island, this mildly entertaining tale of the romantic travails of three young waitresses at the local pizza joint is set in the town's Portuguese lobster-fishing community.

Next Stop Wonderland Brad Anderson, 1998. The title of this thinking woman's indie romance actually refers to the final stop of Boston's blue line subway, where luckless nurse Hope Davis finally crosses paths, after many a false start, with the man of her dreams. The Boston Aquarium has a major supporting role.

On Golden Pond Mark Rydell, 1981. The pond of the title is really Squam Lake in New Hampshire's Lakes Region, where, one summer, a crabby Boston professor (Henry Fonda in his final film) and his wife (Katherine Hepburn) get in touch with their inner child. A breathtakingly picturesque but schmaltzy tear-jerker that probably did more for New England tourism than all the other films listed here combined.

The Perfect Storm Wolfgang Petersen, 2000. George Clooney, Diane Lane, and Mark Wahlberg star in this adaptation of Sebastian Junger's bestseller about a swordfishing boat's doomed journey into the heart of the "storm of the century." The film's best moments are on shore, in its rich portrait of the fishing community of Gloucester, Massachusetts; once at sea, it's an empty special-effects extravaganza.

The Raid Hugo Fregonese, 1954. A brutal Civil War tale of a band of escaped Confederate prisoners, who, in 1864, infiltrated the picturesque Vermont town of St Albans intending to raze it to the ground. Based on a true story, this little-known gem stars Van Heflin, Lee Marvin, and Anne Bancroft, who plays the beautiful Yankee widow whose hospitality puts a spanner in the Rebs' plan of action.

Reversal of Fortune Barbet Schroeder, 1990. Opening with a jaw-dropping aerial sequence of the mansions of Newport strung along the Rhode Island coastline, this witty film dramatizes the case of Claus von Bülow, who was convicted of attempting to murder his heiress wife Sunny, and then acquitted in the Rhode Island Supreme Court with the help of Harvard lawyer Alan Dershowitz.

The Russians Are Coming! The Russians Are Coming! Norman Jewison, 1966. A comic vision of Cold War paranoia in which a Russian submarine runs aground off fictional "Gloucester Island" somewhere on the New England coast, causing panic in this archetypally dozy community. A precursor, of sorts, to *Jaws,* this blockbuster farce was actually shot on the coast of Northern California.

The Scarlet Letter Victor Seastrom, 1926; Wim Wenders, 1973; Roland Joffe, 1995. Hawthorne's masterpiece has been treated about as woefully by Hollywood as Hester Prynne was treated by the good people of Salem. The first, silent, adaptation of the book, starring Lillian Gish, is the best, though it reduces Hawthorne's symbol-laden complexities to a tragic pastoral romance. Wenders' 1973 version – filmed in Spain with German actors – is about as much fun as Salem on the Sabbath, while the 1995 Demi Moore vehicle supplies the story with some racy sex scenes and a new happy ending.

Splendor in the Grass Eli Kazan, 1961. Though its handful of scenes set at Yale University are confined to studio sets, Kazan's Kansas melodrama bears mention for the pivotal role that New Haven's legendary pizza pie plays in the proceedings. To wit, Warren Beatty reneges on his promise to return to high-school sweetheart Nathalie Wood when he is seduced by a pizza and marries the pizza-maker's daughter.

Starting Over Alan J. Pakula, 1979. Burt Reynolds leaves his unfaithful, song-writing wife in their swanky Manhattan pad and moves to a cold-water Boston flat to start over. A wonderful and little-known comedy romance, co-starring Jill Clayburgh, written by James L. Brooks, and shot by Bergman's cinematographer Sven Nykvist.

State and Main David Mamet, 2000. A slick Hollywood film crew lands in uptight small-town Vermont after having been run out of New Hampshire for unknown, but undoubtedly lurid, reasons. Mamet uses all his trademarks to take on sometimes obvious targets, but this screwball comedy, by virtue of its winning performances and often hilarious dialogue, still feels fresh.

The Swimmer Frank Perry, 1968. A splendid curio adapted from John Cheever's brilliant short story of the same name, in which upscale rural Connecticut is imagined as a lush Garden of Eden through which broad-chested, swimsuited Burt Lancaster makes his allegorical way home one summer afternoon, going from swimming pool to swimming pool.

There's Something About Mary Farrelly Brothers, 1998. If Rhode Island is to go down in the annals of cinema history it would have to be as the site of Ben Stiller's notorious pre-prom mishap with a zipper in this gross-out masterpiece. There are some nice views of the Providence waterfront before the film relocates to Miami in pursuit of the eponymous object of desire.

Tough Guys Don't Dance Norman Mailer, 1987. Set in Provincetown, on the beckoning fingertip of Cape Cod, Mailer's bizarre retelling of his own novel is a convoluted affair involving an over-intoxicated writer (Ryan O'Neal), a gay-bashing sheriff, a Southern millionaire, a buxom Bible-bashing gold digger, drug-dealing lobster men, and a severed head.

The Trouble with Harry Alfred Hitchcock, 1955. A black comedy painted in the reds and golds of a perfect Vermont fall. The trouble with Harry is that he keeps turning up dead and everybody, including his young wife (Shirley MacLaine in her debut), thinks they may have killed him. The trouble, meanwhile, with fall in Vermont is the weather, and, though shooting began on location, Hitchcock's crew eventually had to retreat to Hollywood with truckloads of leaves to finish the film.

The Verdict Sidney Lumet, 1982. Gripping courtroom thriller, with Paul Newman as an alcoholic has-been lawyer given one last lease on life – trying a medical malpractice suit against a big Massachusetts hospital.

Vermont is for Lovers John O'Brien, 1993. A charming, semi-documentary, indie comedy about a New York couple who travel to Vermont to get married, come down with a bad case of cold feet, and turn to the locals – all real Vermonters and neighbors of O'Brien – for advice. Scene-stealing septuagenarian sheep farmer Fred Tuttle then had a spin-off in O'Brien's spoof of Vermont politics, *Man with a Plan* (1995).

Walk East on Beacon Alfred L. Werker, 1952. A very matter-of-fact thriller about FBI agents ferreting out communists in Cold War Boston. Shot documentary-style, the film tempers its pinko-bashing paean to Hoover's boys with the more engaging nuts and bolts of their activities and plenty of vivid location footage.

White Christmas Michael Curtiz, 1954. Singing and dancing army buddies Bing Crosby and Danny Kaye take a break from hoofing in Manhattan and take the train up to Vermont for a skiing holiday, only to find there hasn't been snow all year. One of the very few musicals to be set in New England, beloved for its Irving Berlin score, and that magical snowy finale.

The Witches of Eastwick George Miller, 1987. An arch, handsome, but ultimately hollow adaptation of John Updike's novel about three love-starved women who conjure up a rather unwelcome visitor to their sleepy Massachusetts town. The film was shot in Cohasset, just south of Boston – as picture-perfect a New England town as you, or the Warner Bros. production designers, could hope to find.

With Honors Alek Keshishian, 1994. Brendan Frasier plays a hard-working Harvard senior who is left with only one copy of his thesis when his computer crashes. It inevitably falls into the hands of a clever homeless man (Joe Pesci), who soon inserts himself into Frasier's home and group of friends – comedy ensues and life lessons are learned in this fun, college-based film.

Books

Below are some of the best books to employ New England as a backdrop for storytelling and otherwise; publishers are listed after the title. As with film, entries preceded by ★ are highly recommended.

Travel, impressions, poetry, and drama

James Chenoweth *Oddity Odyssey* (Henry Holt US). Fun little book that tries to point out some of the more intriguing and humorous episodes and myths surrounding the sights and major players in New England's history.

Emily Dickinson *The Complete Poems* (Little, Brown). The ultimate New England poet, who spent all her life in the same town – indeed the same house – and quietly recorded the seasons, local incidents, and her own thoughts on life in a series of insightful poems.

T. S. Eliot *The Complete Poems and Plays* (Harcourt). Eliot is considered to be a British poet as often as he is an American one, and we can hardly take sides in that argument. However, he did spend time at Milton Academy in Milton, MA; enjoyed summers in Gloucester; and attended Harvard College. Nowhere is the New England influence more obvious in than in his *Four Quartets*.

Robert Frost *The Collected Poems* (Henry Holt). Frost's poems skillfully evoke the New England landscape, especially the collection *North of Boston*. They remain classics, despite their sometimes too-familiar feel.

Donald Hall *Old and New Poems*; *Life Work*; *The Ox-Cart Man* (Mariner Books, Beacon Press, Puffin). Hall is a New England poet's poet; he lives in rural New Hampshire and was married to Jane Kenyon (see below) until her death in 1995. He has also written non-fiction about New England, and even a few children's books, including the much-loved *Ox-Cart Man*.

Jane Kenyon *Collected Poems* (Graywolf). Kenyon was New Hampshire's poet laureate when she died of leukemia in 1995. Her poems have New England themes, but also deal wisely with depression, a disease she had fought since childhood.

Maxine Kumin *Selected Poems; The Long Marriage* (W.W. Norton). Kumin is not as well known as her best friend Anne Sexton, but her poetry is deeply rooted in the New England landscape, Massachusetts and New Hampshire mostly. She is also the author of twenty children's books and a mystery novel.

Henry Wadsworth Longfellow *Poems and Other Writings* (Library of America). Longfellow celebrated both common and heroic New Englanders in his sometimes whimsical verse; perhaps a bit light for some, but very much central to New England society over the mid-nineteenth century.

Robert Lowell *Life Studies*; *For the Union Dead* (Noonday Press). Unbelievably affecting stuff from arguably New England's greatest twentieth-century poet, tackling family and social issues with striking precision.

Arthur Miller *The Crucible* (Penguin). This compelling play about the 1692 Salem witch trials is peppered with quotes from actual transcripts and loaded with appropriate levels of hysteria and fervor – a must for witch fanatics everywhere.

Eugene O'Neill *The Complete Plays* (Library of America). One of America's best-known playrights, O'Neill received the 1936 Nobel Prize for literature. His most famous play, *Long Day's Journey into Night,* is a semi-autobiographical portrait of his family, focusing on his mother's morphine addiction, which takes place in a seaside Connecticut home, much like the one he grew up in.

Wallace Stevens *The Palm at the End of the Mind* (Vintage). Stevens never quit his job as a lawyer for an insurance firm in Connecticut, even as his success as a poet grew. Though he used simple, straightforward language – Stevens wanted to create a distinctly American idiom for poetry – his work is still considered difficult. He is best known for his exquisite reverie *Thirteen Ways of Looking at a Blackbird.*

Henry David Thoreau *Cape Cod; The Maine Woods; Walden* (Penguin US). *Walden* is basically a transcript of Thoreau's attempt to put his transcendentalist philosophy into practice, by constructing a cabin on the banks of Walden Pond, near Concord, Massachusetts, and living the simplest of lives based on self-reliance, individualism, spiritual enlightenment, and material frugality. Nature also plays a part in *Cape Cod* and *The Maine Woods*, accounts of the writer's walking trips published after his death.

History, culture, and society

William Corbett *Literary New England: a History and Guide* (Faber). A guide to the literary haunts of New England – full of trivia, basically, but entertainingly so.

Malcolm Cowley *New England Writers and Writing* (University Press of New England). A compilation of previously published essays on nineteenth- and twentieth-century New England writers (some of whom Cowley knew personally), and including discussion of the work of Hawthorne, Whitman, and John Cheever, among others. Also included are writings by Cowley himself on aspects of New England life.

Children's literature

Perhaps because its rich history is taught in schools across the country, or maybe for more romantic reasons, New England has served as a sort of muse for **children's book authors** throughout the years.

Some of the best are by **Robert McCloskey**, who wrote and illustrated the timeless *Make Way for Ducklings*, *Blueberries for Sal*, *One Morning in Maine*, and *Time of Wonder*, all of which employ, to great effect, New England's landscape and wildlife. The poet **Donald Hall** has written several New England-based children's books, each beautifully rendered by a different illustrator: *The Ox-Cart Man* has illustrations by Barbara Cooney; *Lucy's Summer* and *Lucy's Christmas* by Michael McCurdy; and *The Man Who Lived Alone* by Mary Azarian.

For slightly older readers, Vermonter **Robert Newton Peck** has written over eighty children's books, the best-known being his *Soup* series, published in the 1970s about a small-town Vermont boy named Soup and his buddy, who can't keep out of trouble. One-word author **Avi** lived in the historic part of Providence for many years, a locale that inspired *Something Upstairs*, in which a 13-year-old boy befriends the ghost of a slave who lived in his attic hundreds of years ago. Lastly, **Lois Lowry** wrote the much-loved series of books about Anastasia Krupnik, a spirited pre-teen who lives in Boston with her very realistically rendered family.

David Hackett Fischer *Paul Revere's Ride* (University of Massachusetts Press/Oxford University Press). An exhaustive account of the patriot's legendary ride to Lexington, related as a historical narrative.

Sean Flynn *3000 Degrees* (Warner). Gripping retelling of the 1999 four-alarm fire in Worcester, MA, that resulted in the deaths of six firefighters.

Sebastian Junger *The Perfect Storm* (Fourth Estate UK; HarperCollins US). A dramatized account of a storm off the New England coast in 1993, and a rip-roaring read of a book.

Mark Kurlansky *Cod* (Penguin). Does a fish merit this much obsessive attention? Only in New England. Kurlansky makes a good case for viewing the cod as one of the more integral parts of the region's fabric.

J. Anthony Lukas *Common Ground: a Turbulent Decade in the Lives of Three American Families* (Vintage US). A Pulitzer Prize-winning account of three Boston families – one Irish-American, one black, one white middle-class – against the backdrop of the 1974 race riots sparked by court-ordered busing to desegregate public schools.

David McCullough *John Adams* (Simon & Schuster) This 2002 life of the country's second president, by America's preeminent popular (and, coincidentally, New England-based) biographer became an instant bestseller. Adams spent much of his life in Massachusetts, and McCullough manages through skilled storytelling to make the history of this lesser-known founding father eminently engaging.

Louis Menand *Metaphysical Club* (Farrar, Straus and Giroux USA). Arguably the most engaging study of Boston heavyweights Oliver Wendell Holmes, William James, Charles Sanders Pierce, and John Dewey ever written, this Pulitzer Prize-winning biography links the foursome through a short-lived 1872 Cambridge salon and extols the effect of their pragmatic idealism on American intellectual thought.

Nat Philbrick *In the Heart of the Sea: the Tragedy of the Whaleship Essex* (Penguin). Basically the story behind *Moby Dick*, and a true one at that, exploring the Nantucket whaling industry through the *Essex*'s saga. Gripping, if a bit too straightforward.

Dan Shaughnessy *The Curse of the Bambino*; *Reversing the Curse* (Penguin, Houghton Mifflin). Shaughnessy, a Boston sportswriter, strikes a chord with every long-suffering Red Sox fan by examining the team's "curse" – no championships since 1918, until their triumphant 2004 win (hence, *Reversing the Curse*) – that began just after they sold Babe Ruth to the Yankees.

Scott Turow *One L: the Turbulent True Story of a First Year at Law School* (Warner Books). Turow, author of the thriller *Presumed Innocent*, recounts his first year at Harvard Law, and all the trials, tribulations, and tension that it entailed. It's quite a well-written, evocative book, but mainly of interest to law students and lawyers.

Hiller B. Zobel *The Boston Massacre* (W.W. Norton). A painstaking account of the circumstances that precipitated one of the most highly propagandized pre-Revolution events – the slaying of five Bostonians outside the Old State House.

Architecture and design

Mona Domosh *Invented Cities: the Creation of Landscape in Nineteenth-Century New York and Boston* (Yale University Press US). Fascinating historical account of how these very different cities were shaped according to the values, beliefs, and fears of their respective societies.

Elaine Louie and Solvi dos Santos *Living in New England* (Simon & Schuster). Well-illustrated coffee-table book about the interiors, rather than architectural styles, of New England homes.

Naomi Miller and Keith Morgan *Boston Architecture 1975–1990* (Prestel). Contextualizes Boston's transformation into a modern city, with emphasis on the building boom of the 1980s, but also detailing the early development and architectural trends of centuries before. Plenty of photographs, too.

Susan and Michael Southworth *AIA Guide to Boston* (Globe Pequot US). The definitive guide to Boston architecture, organized by neighborhood. City landmarks and dozens of notable buildings are given exhaustive but readable coverage.

Nature and specific guides

Appalachian Mountain Club *Maine Mountain Guide: The Hiking Trails of Maine* (Appalachian Mountain Club). Meticulous hiking guide, with detailed color maps, that should get you through both the popular and more backwoods sections of the state.

Marilyn Dwelley and Fay Hyland *Trees and Shrubs of New England* (Down East Books). Accessible field handbook to outdoor New England, useful if you'll be doing some hiking and camping in the various parks and mountains.

Tom Wessels *Reading the Forested Landscape: Natural History of New England* (Countryman Press). Less an outdoors guide than a deconstruction of why the land and trees are like they are today. Uniquely informative.

Fiction

Louisa May Alcott *Little Women* (Puffin). A semi-autobiographical novel, drawing on family experiences, Alcott's novel remains a classic to this day.

Judy Blume *Summer Sisters* (Dell). Blume is most famous for her young adult books, though this slightly trashy novel about the exploits of two women who summer on Martha's Vineyard is nevertheless an enjoyable read.

Gerry Boyle *Lifeline* (Berkley). Hard-hitting suspense novel about an ex-big-city reporter looking for solace in small-town Maine, only to find that crime exists there, too. Others in the series include *Bloodline* and *Deadline*.

James Casey *Spartina* (Vintage). Set in the fishing world of Narragansett Bay, Rhode Island, this memorable, spare work about a man struggling with pretty much every imaginable aspect of his life captured the National Book Award in 1989.

John Cheever *The Wapshot Chronicle* (Vintage). This was Cheever's first novel, and documents the weird doings of the Wapshot family, of St Botolph's, Massachusetts. The sequel, *The Wapshot Scandal*, continues the family saga. Cheever is also famous for his short stories, many of which take place in New England.

Michael Crichton *A Case of Need* (Signet USA). Winner of the 1969 Edgar Award for best mystery novel, this gripping medical thriller, which opens with a woman bleeding to death in a Boston hospital, was written long before Crichton conceived of the hit television drama *ER*, and under a pseudonym to boot.

Bret Easton Ellis *The Rules of Attraction* (Picador UK; Vintage US). Another of Ellis's sex, drug, and booze-driven narratives, this time charting the romantic progress of a few students through Vermont's fictional Camden College. Still, strangely compelling.

Mary Eleanor Freeman *A New England Nun and Other Stories* (Penguin Books). Relatively unknown these days, Freeman enjoyed quite a fashion about a century ago for her tales of rural New England life. Worth seeking out.

Elizabeth Graver *Unravelling* (Hyperion). In distinct and compelling fashion, Graver charts a young woman's progress on the bleaker edges of New England life: its farms and factory mills.

Nathaniel Hawthorne *The House of the Seven Gables*; *The Scarlet Letter*. Born in Salem, Massachusetts, in 1804, Hawthorne was descended from a judge at the famous witch trials, and this (and the curse that ensued) provides the story for *The House of the Seven Gables*. *The Scarlet Letter* is a moral tale of guilt, judgment, and redemption. Both Penguin and Bantam do low-priced paperback editions.

George V. Higgins *Penance for Jerry Higgins* (Abacus UK). Ace crime writer and former district attorney who portrays the seamier side of Boston life in this and most of his other novels.

John Irving *The Cider House Rules* (Black Swan UK; Vintage US). Irving writes huge, sprawling novels set all over New England. This one, suitably Dickensian in scope, is neither his most popular (*The World According to Garp*) or beloved (probably *A Prayer for Owen Meany*). But it is perhaps his best – a fascinating meditation on, of all things, abortion.

Henry James *The Bostonians*; *The Europeans* (Penguin). The first is James's soporific satire tracing the relationship of Olive Chancellor and Verena Tarrant, two fictional feminists, in the 1870s; the second is much more fun: an early James novella about Europeans who travel to New England and find love, yet are astounded by the area's puritanical culture.

Sarah Orne Jewett *A Country Doctor* (Bantam US). One of the lesser-known late nineteenth-century New England novelists, but one of the most locally evocative. Packed full of period detail, this novel, about a Maine woman who refuses marriage so she can pursue her ambition to become a doctor, is a marvelous account of life in rural Maine.

Denis Johnson *The Resuscitation of a Hanged Man* (Penguin). Not Johnson's best work, but still a diverting, suspenseful read, in which a Provincetown disc jockey starts tracking the life of a lesbian with whom he becomes enamored.

Jack Kerouac *Maggie Cassidy* (Penguin). The protobeatnik grew up in New England; here, he traces the arc of a youthful romance, to fine effect, with an equally fine setting in a small Massachusetts mill town.

Stephen King *Different Seasons*; *Dolores Claiborne* (Penguin). Born in Maine, King is incredibly prolific, and doesn't always hit the mark; some of his writings do manage, though, quite well to evoke his home state and region; these are two of the better ones.

Wally Lamb *She's Come Undone* (Simon & Schuster). This debut novel is a harrowing and brutal story of a young girl in harsh circumstances, which is lightened by hopeful humor. Its first-person female narrative, despite being written by a man, is credible and moving.

Dennis Lehane *Darkness, Take My Hand* (Avon). Lehane sets his mysteries on the working-class streets of south Boston; they are all excellent and evocative, but this is probably the cream of the crop. His most recent, *Mystic River* (William Morrow), is highly recommended, too.

H.P. Lovecraft *The Best of H.P. Lovecraft: Bloodcurdling Tales of Horror and the Macabre* (Ballantine). The best stories from the author whom Stephen King called "the twentieth century's greatest practitioner of the classic horror tale."

Herman Melville *Moby Dick* (Penguin). The incomparable story of a man's obsession with a great white whale. Plenty of descriptive prose on the whaling industry and its effect on places like New Bedford and Nantucket.

Grace Metalious *Peyton Place* (Northeastern University Press US). A saucy and sexy, if not particularly well-written, romp through a small New England town's existence. The book that inspired the TV show and movie of the same name.

John Miller and Tim Smith (eds) *Cape Cod Stories* (Chronicle US). Well-selected stories, essays, and excerpts from a mostly predictable crop of writers – Thoreau, Updike, and so on.

Susan Minot *Folly*; *Monkeys* (Washington Square Press, Vintage). This obvious nod to Edith Wharton's *Age of Innocence* is set in 1917 Boston instead of New York, and details the proclivities of the Brahmin era, in which women were expected to marry well, and the heartbreak that ensues from making the wrong choice. *Monkeys* tackles the life of a more recent but no less tragic family.

Rick Moody *The Ice Storm* (Warner). Two neighboring families from Connecticut whose process of collapse is a tawdry Seventies tale of alcoholic excess, wife-swapping, adultery, and alienation – all brought to a shuddering and tragic climax by the storm of the book's title. Made into a stylish and affecting movie.

Robert B. Parker *A Triple Shot of Spenser* (Berkley Trade). Parker, a prolific mystery author with more than forty novels behind him, is best known for his Spenser series, about a Boston private eye whose name is spelled, as he enjoys saying, "like the poet."

Sylvia Plath *The Bell Jar* (Harper Perennial US). Angst-ridden, dark, cynical – everything a teenaged girl wants out of a book. The second half of this brilliant (if disturbing) autobiographical novel about Esther Greenwood's mental breakdown after a summer spent working at a New York fashion magazine, is set in Boston suburbs, where she winds up institutionalized in a mental hospital.

Annie Proulx *Heartsongs* (Fourth Estate UK; Macmillan US). Gritty stories of life in rural and blue-collar New England – beautifully crafted tales that evoke elemental themes. Also worth your while, Proulx's novel *The Shipping News* won the National Book Award and the Pulitzer Prize for fiction.

Philip Roth *The Human Stain* (Vintage International). A fair portrait of life in a small New England college town, in which Colman Silk, a man who carries a secret, is fired from his job as an English professor for racism and subsequently has an affair with a much younger woman.

Richard Russo *Empire Falls* (Vintage). This Pulitzer Prize-winner takes place in Empire Falls, Maine, a small, failing blue-collar town. Miles Roby runs the town's most popular diner, which he hopes someday to inherit from its sadistic, controlling owner. While the plot may be familiar, the relationships between the characters in the town make this a compelling read; it's also an excellent look at class issues in New England.

George Santayana *The Last Puritan* (MIT Press). The philosopher's brilliant "memoir in the form of a novel," set around Boston, chronicles the short life and education of protagonist Oliver Alden coming to grips with Puritanism.

Zadie Smith *On Beauty* (Penguin). The young novelist famous for her debut *White Teeth* re-writes *Howard's End* with interracial and cross-continental couples in her third novel, set on the campus of a fictional New England college. The book's setting is based closely on Smith's two years' teaching at Harvard.

Wallace Stegner *Crossing to Safety* (Penguin). The saga of two couples who form a lifelong bond, set partly in Vermont. It might seem a bit slow and sentimental at first glance, but Stegner's strong writing should win you over.

John Steinbeck *The Winter of Our Discontent* (Penguin). A late work by Steinbeck, published in 1961, and examining the collapse of an old New England family under pressure from the modern world.

Eleanor Sullivan *Murder in New England* (Castle). A collection of pulpy murder mystery stories by Isaac Asimov, Ed Hoch, and Brendan DuBois, among others, fixating on the death of a Harvard man, eerie happenings off I-95, and Rhode Island lights.

Donna Tartt *The Secret History* (Penguin UK; Ballantine US). An "It" book from the early 1990s, and one that actually resonates, this centers on a small group of students at a fictional Vermont college, modeled after Bennington, and the murderous turns their elite cadre takes. Short on landscape, but a surprisingly diverting tale.

Mark Twain *A Connecticut Yankee in King Arthur's Court* (Bantam Classics). Twain is not often thought of as a New Englander, but he spent many years in Hartford, Connecticut, which gave him time to conjure up his hilarious protagonist for this 1889 book: Hank Morgan, a contemporary newspaperman, is somehow transported to medieval England, where he uses his Yankee ingenuity to make himself powerful.

John Updike *The Witches of Eastwick* (Ballantine). Satirical witchy tale set in rural 1960s Rhode Island and chock-full of hypocrisy, adultery, and wickedness; in short, a fun read.

David Foster Wallace *Infinite Jest* (Little, Brown US). Not the kind of book you want to pack for your travels (it's a whopping 1088 pages), some of this sprawling and often hilarious opus's best passages take place at Enfield, a tennis academy outside Boston, while other nuggets involve a Cambridge store owner in a Canadian separatist terrorist plot.

Dorothy West *The Wedding* (Anchor). West is best known as an author of the Harlem Renaissance, publishing most of her works in the 1940s, though in 1995, fifty years later, she came out with this touching family novel that takes place among the wealthy black community that vacations on Martha's Vineyard.

Edith Wharton *Ethan Frome* (Penguin). A distilled portrait of stark, icy New England that belies the fiery emotions blazing underneath. The title character's perverse, tragic odyssey is riveting; the writing simple and superb, especially evocative of the Massachusetts farmscape in which the story is set.

Travel store

UK & Ireland
Britain
Devon & Cornwall
Dublin DIRECTIONS
Edinburgh DIRECTIONS
England
Ireland
The Lake District
London
London DIRECTIONS
London Mini Guide
Scotland
Scottish Highlands & Islands
Wales

Europe
Algarve DIRECTIONS
Amsterdam
Amsterdam DIRECTIONS
Andalucía
Athens DIRECTIONS
Austria
Baltic States
Barcelona
Barcelona DIRECTIONS
Belgium & Luxembourg
Berlin
Brittany & Normandy
Bruges DIRECTIONS
Brussels
Budapest
Bulgaria
Copenhagen
Corfu
Corsica
Costa Brava DIRECTIONS
Crete
Croatia
Cyprus
Czech & Slovak Republics
Dodecanese & East Aegean
Dordogne & The Lot
Europe
Florence & Siena
Florence DIRECTIONS
France
French Hotels & Restaurants
Germany
Greece
Greek Islands
Hungary
Ibiza & Formentera DIRECTIONS
Iceland
Ionian Islands
Italy
The Italian Lakes
Languedoc & Roussillon
Lisbon
Lisbon DIRECTIONS
The Loire
Madeira DIRECTIONS
Madrid DIRECTIONS
Mallorca DIRECTIONS
Mallorca & Menorca
Malta & Gozo DIRECTIONS
Menorca
Moscow
The Netherlands
Norway
Paris
Paris DIRECTIONS
Paris Mini Guide
Poland
Portugal
Prague
Prague DIRECTIONS
Provence & the Côte d'Azur
Pyrenees
Romania
Rome
Rome DIRECTIONS
Sardinia
Scandinavia
Sicily
Slovenia
Spain
St Petersburg
Sweden
Switzerland
Tenerife & La Gomera DIRECTIONS
Turkey
Tuscany & Umbria
Venice & The Veneto
Venice DIRECTIONS
Vienna

Asia
Bali & Lombok
Bangkok
Beijing
Cambodia
China
Goa
Hong Kong & Macau
India
Indonesia
Japan
Laos
Malaysia, Singapore & Brunei
Nepal
The Philippines
Singapore
South India
Southeast Asia
Sri Lanka
Taiwan
Thailand
Thailand's Beaches & Islands
Tokyo
Vietnam

Australasia
Australia
Melbourne
New Zealand
Sydney

North America
Alaska
Boston
California
Canada
Chicago
Florida
The Grand Canyon
Hawaii
Honolulu
Las Vegas DIRECTIONS
Los Angeles
Maui DIRECTIONS
Miami & South Florida
Montréal
New England
New Orleans DIRECTIONS
New York City
New York City DIRECTIONS
New York City Mini Guide
Orlando & Walt Disney World DIRECTIONS
Pacific Northwest
The Rocky Mountains
San Francisco
San Francisco DIRECTIONS
Seattle
Southwest USA
Toronto
USA
Vancouver
Washington DC
Washington DC DIRECTIONS
Yosemite

Caribbean & Latin America
Antigua & Barbuda DIRECTIONS
Argentina
Bahamas
Barbados DIRECTIONS
Belize
Bolivia
Brazil
Cancùn & Cozumel DIRECTIONS
Caribbean
Central America
Chile
Costa Rica
Cuba
Dominican Republic
Dominican Republic DIRECTIONS
Ecuador
Guatemala
Jamaica
Mexico
Peru
St Lucia
South America
Trinidad & Tobago
Yúcatan

TRAVEL

Africa & Middle East
Cape Town & the Garden Route
Egypt
The Gambia
Jordan
Kenya
Marrakesh DIRECTIONS
Morocco
South Africa, Lesotho & Swaziland
Syria
Tanzania
Tunisia
West Africa
Zanzibar

Travel Theme guides
First-Time Around the World
First-Time Asia
First-Time Europe
First-Time Latin America
Travel Online
Travel Health
Travel Survival
Walks in London & SE England
Women Travel

Maps
Algarve
Amsterdam
Andalucia & Costa del Sol
Argentina
Athens
Australia
Baja California
Barcelona
Berlin
Boston
Brittany
Brussels
California
Chicago
Corsica
Costa Rica & Panama
Crete
Croatia
Cuba
Cyprus
Czech Republic
Dominican Republic
Dubai & UAE
Dublin
Egypt
Florence & Siena
Florida
France
Frankfurt
Germany
Greece
Guatemala & Belize
Hong Kong
Iceland
Ireland
Kenya
Lisbon
London
Los Angeles
Madrid
Mallorca
Marrakesh
Mexico
Miami & Key West
Morocco
New England
New York City
New Zealand
Northern Spain
Paris
Peru
Portugal
Prague
Rome
San Francisco
Sicily
South Africa
South India
Spain & Portugal
Sri Lanka
Tenerife
Thailand
Toronto
Trinidad & Tobago
Tuscany
Venice
Washington DC
Yucatán Peninsula

Dictionary Phrasebooks
Croatian
Czech
Dutch
Egyptian Arabic
French
German
Greek
Hindi & Urdu
Italian
Japanese
Latin American Spanish
Mandarin Chinese
Mexican Spanish
Polish
Portuguese
Russian
Spanish
Swahili
Thai
Turkish
Vietnamese

Computers
Blogging
iPods, iTunes & Music Online
The Internet
Macs & OS X
Music Playlists
PCs and Windows
Website Directory

Film & TV
Comedy Movies
Cult Movies
Cult TV
Gangster Movies
Horror Movies
James Bond
Kids' Movies
Sci–Fi Movies

Lifestyle
Ethical Shopping
Babies
Pregnancy & Birth

Music Guides
The Beatles
Bob Dylan
Cult Pop
Classical Music
Elvis
Frank Sinatra
Heavy Metal
Hip-Hop
Jazz
Opera
Reggae
Rock
World Music (2 vols)

Popular Culture
Books for Teenagers
Children's Books, 0-5
Children's Books, 5-11
Conspiracy Theories
Cult Fiction
The Da Vinci Code
Lord of the Rings
Shakespeare
Superheroes
Unexplained Phenomena

Sport
Arsenal 11s
Celtic 11s
Chelsea 11s
Liverpool 11s
Man United 11s
Newcastle 11s
Rangers 11s
Tottenham 11s
Cult Football
Muhammad Ali
Poker

Science
The Universe
Weather

★ waterproof

★ rip-proof

★ amazing value

CITY MAPS

Amsterdam ·Athens · Barcelona · Berlin · Boston · Brussels · Chicago · Dublin Florence & Siena · Frankfurt · Hong Kong · Lisbon · London · Los Angeles Madrid · Marrakesh · Miami · New York · Paris · Prague · Rome · San Francisco Toronto · Venice · Washington DC and more...

US$8.99 Can$13.99 £4.99

COUNTRY & REGIONAL MAPS

Algarve · Andalucía · Argentina · Australia · Baja California · Brittany · Crete Croatia · Cuba · Cyprus · Czech Republic · Dominican Republic · Dubai · Egypt Greece · Guatemala & Belize · Iceland · Ireland · Kenya · Mexico · Morocco New Zealand · Northern Spain · Peru · Portugal · Sicily · South Africa · South India · Sri Lanka · Tenerife · Thailand · Trinidad & Tobago · Tuscany · Yucatán Peninsula · and more...

US$9.99 Can$13.99 £5.99

MAPS

Small print and

Index

A Rough Guide to Rough Guides

Published in 1982, the first Rough Guide – to Greece – was a student scheme that became a publishing phenomenon. Mark Ellingham, a recent graduate of English from Bristol University, had been traveling in Greece the previous summer and couldn't find the right guidebook. With a small group of friends he wrote his own guide, combining a highly contemporary, journalistic style with a thoroughly practical approach to travelers' needs.

The immediate success of the book spawned a series that rapidly covered dozens of destinations. And, in addition to impecunious backpackers, Rough Guides soon acquired a much broader and older readership that relished the guides' wit and inquisitiveness as much as their enthusiastic, critical approach and value-for-money ethos.

These days, Rough Guides include recommendations from shoestring to luxury and cover more than 200 destinations around the globe, including almost every country in the Americas and Europe, more than half of Africa and most of Asia and Australasia. Our ever-growing team of authors and photographers is spread all over the world, particularly in Europe, the USA, and Australia.

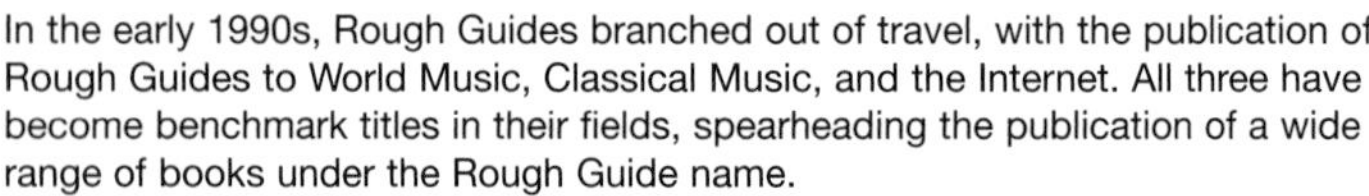

In the early 1990s, Rough Guides branched out of travel, with the publication of Rough Guides to World Music, Classical Music, and the Internet. All three have become benchmark titles in their fields, spearheading the publication of a wide range of books under the Rough Guide name.

Including the travel series, Rough Guides now number more than 350 titles, covering: phrasebooks, waterproof maps, music guides from Opera to Heavy Metal, reference works as diverse as Conspiracy Theories and Shakespeare, and popular culture books from iPods to Poker. Rough Guides also produce a series of more than 120 World Music CDs in partnership with World Music Network.

Visit ⓦ www.roughguides.com to see our latest publications.

Many Rough Guide travel images are available for commercial licensing at ⓦ www.roughguidespictures.com

Rough Guide credits

Text editor: Hunter Slaton
Layout: Dan May
Cartography: Jai Prakash Mishra
Picture editor: Sarah Smithies
Production: Katherine Owers
Proofreader: Jennifer Speake
Cover design: Chloë Roberts

....

Editorial: **London** Kate Berens, Claire Saunders, Geoff Howard, Ruth Blackmore, Polly Thomas, Richard Lim, Clifton Wilkinson, Alison Murchie, Karoline Densley, Andy Turner, Keith Drew, Edward Aves, Nikki Birrell, Helen Marsden, Alice Park, Sarah Eno, Joe Staines, Duncan Clark, Peter Buckley, Matthew Milton, Tracy Hopkins, David Paul, Lucy White, Ruth Tidball; **New York** Andrew Rosenberg, Steven Horak, AnneLise Sorensen, Amy Hegarty, Hunter Slaton, April Isaacs, Sean Mahoney
Design & Pictures: **London** Simon Bracken, Dan May, Diana Jarvis, Mark Thomas, Jj Luck, Harriet Mills, Chloë Roberts; **Delhi** Madhulita Mohapatra, Umesh Aggarwal, Ajay Verma, Jessica Subramanian, Amit Verma, Ankur Guha, Pradeep Thapliyal
Production: Sophie Hewat, Katherine Owers, Aimee Hampson
Cartography: **London** Maxine Repath, Ed Wright, Katie Lloyd-Jones; **Delhi** Manish Chandra, Rajesh Chhibber, Jai Prakash Mishra, Ashutosh Bharti, Rajesh Mishra, Animesh Pathak, Jasbir Sandhu, Karobi Gogoi, Pradeep Thapliyal
Online: **New York** Jennifer Gold, Suzanne Welles, Kristin Mingrone; **Delhi** Manik Chauhan, Narender Kumar, Shekhar Jha, Rakesh Kumar, Chhandita Chakravarty
Marketing & Publicity: **London** Richard Trillo, Niki Hanmer, David Wearn, Demelza Dallow, Louise Maher, Jess Carter; **New York** Geoff Colquitt, Megan Kennedy, Katy Ball; **Delhi** Reem Khokhar
Custom publishing and foreign rights: Philippa Hopkins
Manager India: Punita Singh
Series editor: Mark Ellingham
Reference Director: Andrew Lockett
PA to Managing and Publishing Directors: Megan McIntyre
Publishing Director: Martin Dunford
Managing Director: Kevin Fitzgerald

Publishing information

This 4th edition published May 2006 by **Rough Guides Ltd**,
80 Strand, London WC2R 0RL
345 Hudson St, 4th Floor,
New York, NY 10014, USA
14 Local Shopping Centre, Panchsheel Park,
New Delhi 110017, India
Distributed by the Penguin Group
Penguin Books Ltd,
80 Strand, London WC2R 0RL
Penguin Putnam, Inc.
375 Hudson Street, NY 10014, USA
Penguin Group (Australia)
250 Camberwell Road, Camberwell,
Victoria 3124, Australia
Penguin Books Canada Ltd,
10 Alcorn Avenue, Toronto, Ontario,
Canada M4V 1E4
Penguin Group (New Zealand)
Cnr Rosedale and Airborne Roads
Albany, Auckland, New Zealand
Cover concept by Peter Dyer.

Typeset in Bembo and Helvetica to an original design by Henry Iles.

Printed and bound in Italy by Legoprint SpA

656pp includes index

A catalog record for this book is available from the British Library

ISBN 1-84353-640-4

ISBN 13: 9781843536406

1 3 5 7 9 8 6 4 2

Help us update

We've gone to a lot of effort to ensure that the 4th edition of **The Rough Guide to New England** is accurate and up to date. However, things change – places get "discovered," opening hours are notoriously fickle, restaurants and rooms raise prices or lower standards. If you feel we've got it wrong or left something out, we'd like to know, and if you can remember the address, the price, the time, the phone number, so much the better. We'll credit all contributions, and send a copy of the next edition (or any other Rough Guide if you prefer) for the best letters. Everyone who writes to us and isn't already a subscriber will receive a copy of our full-color thrice-yearly newsletter. Please mark letters: "**Rough Guide New England Update**" and send to: Rough Guides, 80 Strand, London WC2R 0RL, or Rough Guides, 345 Hudson St, 4th Floor, New York, NY 10014. Or send an email to Ⓔ **mail@roughguides.com**
Have your questions answered and tell others about your trip at
Ⓦ **www.roughguides.atinfopop.com**

Acknowledgements

Ken Derry thanks Jeannie Herbert and Julie Zomar at the Central Massachusetts Convention and Visitors Bureau and Cheri McBride at the Greater Springfield Convention and Visitors Bureau for dropping everything in making arrangements at all the great places along the way. Thanks also to Hunter Slaton and Douglass and Martha Derry.

Sarah Hull would like to thank her family, who rallied spectacularly for the cause; the Boston NHPS – particularly the fantastic John Manson, historical savior; her Stuart Smalleys: Rachel H., Davey B., Ali Astro, and Ben Bagocius; the Aussies; 3750 et al; Chicken Corner; Len Podis; Veronika V.; Eric at the Weekly Dig; Dan Shaughnessy at the Globe; Carter Long at the MFA; and David Ortiz.

S.E. Kramer thanks Jacob Kramer and Liz Gately for their contributions. Thanks as well to Jay Gabler, Matt Hudson, Lucy Baker, Nancy Cole, Nico Muhly, Dan Epstein, and Ben Rahn for finding me new films, mystery authors, children's books, and other cultural paraphernalia from our home states. Thanks to Hunter Slaton for infinite patience. Robbie, I should probably just give you every cent the Rough Guide has paid me and all my money as well in thanks for your help, but since that would be an insultingly small amount, I hope you'll accept this humble dedication instead.

Emma Lozman For help along the way, many thanks to Steven Granato, Paul Kalanithi, Megan Tepper-Rasmussen, Carey Jones and Ethan Klein, Birch Stoner, Anne Marie McLaughlin, Merrilee Zellner, Kathy Szabo, Teri McCombe, and Island Moped & Bike. Special thanks to Charlotte Tiffany and Jon Stephenson for their hospitality, and to Hunter for being a great editor and an all-around nice guy. Love and huge thanks always to mum and Jay, especially for a fabulous summer in CT.

The editor would like to thank his authors for all their hard work, Christina Knight for editing Vermont and New Hampshire, Dan May for his tirelessness and good cheer, cartography in London and Delhi, Sarah Smithies for her fine photo research, and Andrew Rosenberg for editorial guidance.

Readers' letters

Thanks to all the readers who have taken the time to write in with comments and suggestions (and apologies if we've inadvertently omitted or misspelt anyone's name):

Lauren Nicholson

Photo credits

Cover

Front picture: Church and autumnal foliage, NH © Getty
Back picture: Lobster traps © Alamy
Inside back picture: Nubble Lighthouse, York Harbor, ME © Andre Jenny/Alamy

Title page

Cranberry harvest, Carver, MA © Lee Snider/Photo Images/Corbis

Full page

Annisquam Lighthouse at Cape Ann, Boston, MA © Richard Cummins/Corbis

Introduction

Sap bucket on a sugar maple, NH © Jerry and Marcy Monkman/Ⓦ ecophotography.com/Alamy
Boston's Trinity Church reflected in John Hancock Building © Ralph Morang/Ⓦ www.newenglandphoto.com
West Arlington, VT, red covered bridge © Dennis Hallinan/Alamy
Two lobstermen on boat lifting lobster trap © Tom Stewart/Corbis
Historic Plymouth Rock, Plymouth, MA © Mark E. Gibson/Corbis
Vermont's Green Mountains © Sandy Macys
NE Forest in autumn, Acadia National Park, ME © Darrell Gulin/Corbis
Jack-o'-lanterns, Salem, MA © Richard T. Nowitz/Corbis

Things not to miss

01 Burlington, VT © Gary Neil Corbett/Superstock
02 Acorn Street, Beacon Hill, Boston, MA © Amanda Hall/Robert Harding/Getty Images
03 Mansion interior in Newport © Nicholas DeVore III/Network Aspen
04 Freedom Trail signage © Rough Guides
05 Provincetown beaches © Brooks Kraft/ Corbis
06 Mount Mansfield, Stowe © Phil Schermeister/ Network Aspen
07 Shaker Craftsman, Canterbury Shaker Village © David G. Houser/Houserstock
08 Performance at Tanglewood © Nicholas DeVore III/ Network Aspen
09 Kitchen Exhibit, Shelburne Museum © Courtesy of Shelburne Museum
10 Naumkeag mansion and gardens © A. Merullo/ The Trustees of Reservations
11 Verandah overlooking the sea, Block Island, RI © Bob Krist/Corbis
12 Aerial of Fanueil Hall and Quincy Market © Nicholas DeVore III/Network Aspen
13 Worcester Art Museum © Robert Arnold/ Worcester Art Museum
14 Whale-watching © Clineff Kindra/Index Stock Imagery/Ⓦ photolibrary.com

15 Oar House Restaurant, Portsmouth © Ralph Morang/Ⓦ www.newenglandphoto.com
16 College Hill, Providence © Nicholas DeVore III/Network Aspen
17 Boat in Mystic Seaport © Christie Parker/Houserstock
18 Harvard Square © Angus Oborn/Rough Guides
19 Sterling Library, Yale University © Michael Marsland/Yale University
20 Blueberry buckets © Ben R. Frakes/Houserstock
21 Mass MoCA, North Adams © Swerve/Alamy
22 Mount Abraham, on the Long Trail © Sandy Macys
23 Battle re-enactment at Exeter © Ralph Morang/Ⓦ www.newenglandphoto.com
24 Acadia National Park © Ben R. Frakes/Houserstock
25 Beach cottage on Nantucket © Dave G. Houser/Houserstock
26 Ben & Jerry's Factory Tour © Courtesy of Ben and Jerry's
27 Monhegan Island © Ralph Morang/Ⓦ www.newenglandphoto.com
28 The State House in Montpelier, VT, in the autumn © Andre Jenny/Alamy
29 Autumn leaf color Litchfield Hills, CT © Don Gray/Photofusion Picture Library/Alamy
30 Mount Washington Hotel © Phil Schermeister/Network Aspen

Black and whites

p.76 Fenway Park in Boston © Jeff Zelevansky/Icon SMI/Corbis
p.91 Boston Common © Rough Guides
p.97 Faneuil Hall © Rough Guides
p.107 Statue of Paul Revere © Rough Guides
p.110 USS Constitution © Rough Guides
p.121 The Public Garden © Mel Longhurst/Travel Ink
p.135 Arnold Arboretum © Rough Guides
p.139 Aerial of Harvard University © Nicholas DeVore III/Network Aspen
p.166 Lobster restaurant on Cape Cod © Swerve/Alamy
p.170 Minute Man statue © Rough Guides
p.179 Witch Trials Memorial © Bill Bachmann/Network Aspen
p.182 The Dry Salvages, off the coast of Cape Ann © Philip Scalia/Alamy
p.193 New Bedford fishing boats © Swerve/Alamy
p.202 Cape Cod potato chips © Ed Quinn/Corbis
p.221 Jetty, Provincetown © Gary Faye/ Getty Images
p.224 Oak Bluffs, Martha's Vineyard © Enigma/Alamy
p.246 Round stone barn, Hancock Shaker Village © Andre Jenny/Alamy
p.254 Basketball Hall of Fame interior © Andre Jenny/Alamy
p.263 Emily Dickinson's grave © Ken Derry
p.277 The Mount © Ken Derry
p.282 War Memorial Tower © Andre Jenny/Alamy
p.288 WaterFire, Providence, RI © Andre Jenny/Alamy
p.296 Union Station, Providence, RI © Andre Jenny/Alamy
p.308 Interior view of the Touro Synagogue © Bettmann/Corbis
p.312 Green Animals Topiary Garden © Bob Krist/Corbis
p.324 Block Island lighthouse © Peter Casolino/Alamy
p.328 Covered bridge, Cornwall, CT © Dale C. Spartas/Corbis
p.335 Mystic Pizza sign © Kit Kettle/Corbis
p.344 Thimble Islands sailboats and grasses © Peter Casolino/Alamy
p.350 Nathan Hale statue © James Marshall/Corbis
p.367 Mark Twain House © Andre Jenny/Alamy
p.372 Dinosaur State Park © Richard Cummins/Corbis
p.388 Long Trail cabin near Mt Mansfield © Andre Jenny/Alamy
p.395 Windham County Courthouse, Newfane, VT © Andre Jenny/Alamy
p.400 Bennington Battle Monument © Lee Snider/Photo Images/Corbis
p.415 Slopes near Killington, VT © Chris Clinton/Getty
p.420 Bridge across Quechee Gorge © Phil Schermeister/Corbis
p.423 Cornish/Windsor covered bridge © Lee Snider/Photo Images/Corbis
p.447 Grizzly bear at Fairbanks Museum © Ashley Cooper/Corbis
p.452 Common loon on nest © Lynn M. Stone/Nature Picture Library
p.457 Hampton Beach © Erin Paul Donovan/Alamy
p.461 Bridge over the Piscataqua River © Andre Jenny/Alamy
p.471 Exterior view of Zimmerman House © Thomas A. Heinz/Corbis
p.492 Weirs Beach sign, Lake Winnipesaukee © Swerve/Alamy
p.507 Rte-112 on Kancamagus Pass © Joe Sohm/Visions of America/Alamy
p.513 Mount Washington Cog Railway © Andre Jenny/Alamy
p.524 Belted Galloway Calf © Kevin Fleming/Corbis
p.532 Ogunquit Beach © Judy Griesedieck/Corbis
p.541 Portland Head Lighthouse © Stephen Saks Photography/Alamy
p.551 Bath Iron Works Shipyard © Kevin Fleming/Corbis
p.557 Pemaquid Point © Andre Jenny/ Alamy
p.577 Rowboats, Mount Desert Island © Ralph Morang/Ⓦ www.newenglandphoto.com
p.593 Island and cabin on Moosehead Lake © Wolfgang Kaehler/Corbis
p.598 Moose, Baxter State Park © Blickwinkel/Alamy
p.606 Signing of the Declaration of Independence © Popperfoto/Alamy

Food and drink insert

Boston baked beans, Durgin Park restaurant © Dave Bartruff/Corbis
Maine lobsters © Ralph Morang/Ⓦ www.newenglandphoto.com

Fourth of July Clambake, Edgartown, Martha's Vineyard © Kelly-Mooney Photography/Corbis
Boston Union Oyster House interior © Rough Guides/Angus Oborn
Chowder with whole clams © David Trozzo/Alamy
Vermont maple syrups and sugars © Phil Schermeister/Corbis
Close-up of ripe blueberries growing in Calais, ME © Alan Briere/DK Images
Autumn cranberry harvest, Carver, MA © Swerve/Corbis
Glass of John Harvard microbrewery beer © Clive Streeter/DK Images

Literary insert
Wm. D. Ticknor & Co. Books & Stationary, Boston © American Stock/Getty
Title page from the 1st edition of Thoreau's Walden © Corbis
Portrait of Nathaniel Hawthorne © Mathew B. Brady/Bettmann/Corbis
House of the Seven Gables, Salem, MA © Lee Snider/Photo Images/Corbis
Dickinson Homestead, MA © James Marshall/Corbis
Robert Frost's mailbox © Richard T. Nowitz/Corbis
Frontispiece to Moby Dick © Mary Evans Picture Library/Alamy

Index

Map entries are in color.

C

D

L

M

N

O

P

Q

R

S

T

Map symbols

maps are listed in the full index using colored text

International boundary	Accommodation
State boundary	Skiing
Chapter division boundary	Camp
55 Interstate	Mountain peak
2 U.S. Highway	Waterfall
114 State Highway	Spring/spa
15 Canadian Autoroute	Lighthouse
Railway	Museum
Tunnel	Monument
4WD track	Stately home
Pedestrianized road	Statue
Path / bicycle trail	Tourist office
Ferry route	Post office
River	Hospital
Cable car	Building
General point of interest	Church
Airport	Cemetery
Ⓣ station	Park
Gate	National park
Garden	Marsh